Patricia D. Corner

Measurement, Design, and Analysis

An Integrated Approach

Measurement, Design, and Analysis

An Integrated Approach

Elazar J. Pedhazur

Liora Pedhazur Schmelkin
Hofstra University

LEA

LAWRENCE ERLBAUM ASSOCIATES, PUBLISHERS

1991   Hillsdale, New Jersey   Hove and London

Lawrence Erlbaum Associates Inc., Publishers
365 Broadway
Hillsdale, New Jersey 07642

Library of Congress Cataloging-in-Publication Data

Pedhazur, Elazar J.
    Measurement, design, and analysis : an integrated approach /
  Elazar J. Pedhazur, Liora Pedhazur Schmelkin.
       p.   cm.
    Includes bibliographical references and index.
    ISBN 0-8058-1063-3
    1. Social sciences—Research—Methodology.   2. Social sciences—
  Statistical methods.   3. Psychology—Research—Methodology.
  I. Schmelkin, Liora Pedhazur.   II. Title.
  H62.P325 1991
  300'.1—dc20   91-7184
                                                     CIP

Printed in the United States of America
10 9 8

To Geula
Alan, Danielle, Alex, and Ben   Hadar, Lois, and Pearl

Contents

PART 3: ANALYSIS

Preface

As we begin the writing of this preface, we are reminded of Richards's (1926) observation about his book on the principles of literary criticism: "Few of the separate items are original. One does not expect novel cards when playing so traditional a game; it is the hand which matters" (p. 1). Much has been written on one aspect or another of the topics we address. We hope that we succeeded in dealing a distinctive hand—more important, that the hand we dealt will matter to you.

As indicated by the title of the book, we attempted to present an integrated approach to research in sociobehavioral sciences.[1] An overview of the content, organization, and orientation of the book is given in Chapter 1. Here, we will explain briefly what we hoped to accomplish in the writing of this book.

Generally, the topics we address are dealt with disjointly in textbooks and courses. For example, in books and courses devoted to statistics, substantive and measurement issues tend to be disregarded, unwittingly creating the impression that they have no bearing on the analysis of the data and on the interpretation of the results. In books and courses on measurement, little or no attention is paid to design and analytic questions, and books and courses in research design tend to treat analytic and measurement issues superficially or to ignore them altogether.

This fragmentary approach inevitably fosters a lack of appreciation of the interrelations and interdependencies among the various aspects of the research endeavor. As a result, many students, especially those not planning to engage in research except for the obligatory dissertation or terminal project, view the expectation that they be conversant in "methodology" as inane, if not sadistic.

We are *not* suggesting that it is imperative for all professionals, regardless of their specialties and substantive interests, to be "expert" in measurement, design, and analysis. We do, however, contend that a basic understanding of these areas and how they bear on one

---

[1]Although some authors distinguish between social and behavioral sciences, most use these terms interchangeably. Yet it has become common practice to refer to "social and behavioral sciences" and "social and behavioral research." For convenience, we adopted Gergen's (1986) nomenclature and speak of sociobehavioral sciences and sociobehavioral research.

another is essential for becoming an intelligent consumer of research, not to mention a competent researcher.

Our aim, then, is to help you become not only proficient in various aspects of research but also to develop the perspective that takes into account their interrelations and interdependencies. Moreover, we hope to help you learn to appreciate the paramount role of theory in guiding the research enterprise.

Although we assume that you have a background in statistics on the level of an introductory course (e.g., variance, covariance, simple ANOVA, correlation), we review these topics before extending the presentation to more advanced ones. A perusal of the table of contents and of Chapter 1 will reveal that we present some advanced topics that until recently were accessible only to people versed in the mathematical language in which they are necessarily couched. However, the widespread availability of computers and software has made it possible even for people lacking in mathematical background to apply the most sophisticated of analytic approaches. The ease with which this can be done has, unfortunately, contributed to a dramatic increase in misapplications of analytic techniques and misinterpretations of results. In the hope of helping you learn to apply meaningfully the analytic approaches we present, we offer extensive commentaries on inputs and outputs of computer programs in the context of the topics being presented.

We doubt whether the wide array of topics we present can be covered, let alone mastered, in a two-semester course. Accordingly, we hope that ours will not be one of those books you rush to sell as soon as the semester is over. We hope that this book will become a companion to which you will keep returning as you broaden and deepen your understanding of research. It is primarily with this in mind that we have provided an extensive bibliography that, we believe, you will find invaluable in your pursuit of knowledge in the broad area of sociobehavioral research.

Finally, as is discussed in Chapter 1, the organization and the mode of presentation afford a great deal of flexibility in the choice and sequencing of topics as well as the level of sophistication with which they are dealt. We hope that this will enable instructors to tailor the book according to their emphases and the level of their students.

Acknowledgments

We are indebted to Jim Gibbons, Office of Epidemiologic Research, New York City Department of Health; Dr. Ellen Koenigsberg; Professor Robert L. Linn, University of Illinois; and Dr. Elizabeth Taleporos, New York City Board of Education, for reviewing portions of the manuscript and for their constructive suggestions for its improvement.

It is with great pride and pleasure that we acknowledge the assistance of Hadar Pedhazur—computer Maven par excellence—who came to our rescue whenever it was necessary to tame our computers, to upgrade them, or to tailor software to our needs.

Our deepest appreciation to Larry Erlbaum for the understanding and patience he exhibited in the face of repeated delays in the completion of the manuscript. His empathy toward authors is in the best tradition of book publishing. We are indebted to Art Lizza for guiding the production of the book with great skill, perspicacity, and responsiveness.

The second author wishes to thank Hofstra University for its support during the writing of this book.

Elazar J. Pedhazur
Liora Pedhazur Schmelkin
Brooklyn and Oceanside, New York

Chapter 1
Overview

Unfortunately, many students and professionals in sociobehavioral sciences lack the background necessary to be intelligent consumers of research literature in areas of their interest or employment. Further, in an era of specialization, students and professionals alike frequently resort to the "services" of a "methodologist-consultant" when doing research. Regrettably, expert advice, necessary and beneficial in many situations, is frequently confused with expert prescriptions. Many researchers and doctoral students deem it proper to delegate to the "consultant" the "tasks" of analyzing the data, interpreting the results, and drawing implications from them. Following blindly consultants' prescriptions or entrusting them with the analysis of the data and interpretation of the results is nothing short of bidding them do one's thinking.

A pernicious consequence of this state of affairs is the tendency to not exercise one's critical faculties altogether. Many professionals do not deem it their role to assess research reports but rather to become familiar with their findings, conclusions, and implications. Thus, acceptance or rejection of findings and implications is based not on informed judgment but on extraneous matters (e.g., conventional wisdom, status of the author of the study). We invite you to consider the potentially deleterious effects of this state of affairs on practice and policy decisions in the broad domain of sociobehavioral sciences.

ABOVE ALL: THINK!

The obvious bears, indeed requires, repeating: To be meaningful, any activity, including the reading of research reports, has to emanate, first and foremost, from sound critical thinking. If there is a message we would like to convey from the very beginning, it is that you exercise common sense, that you not let mumbo jumbo and technical jargon get the better of you. An adverse effect of inordinate reliance on methods and quantification is a diminution of critical thinking among researchers and consumers of research alike. There is such an allure, an almost magical quality, in specialized terminologies, in formulas and fancy analyses, particularly when performed by computer, that the likelihood of giving little or no thought to what they mean is high.

1

Needless to say, knowledge of the methods and analytic approaches employed is essential for a critical evaluation of a research report. Nevertheless, to underscore the importance of using common sense, we would like, at this early stage, to give some examples where exercising it would have sufficed to cast doubt about authors' assertions. Consider the following "justification" offered by Long (1986) for her use of an instrument in her study: "Although the BSRI [Bem Sex-Role Inventory] has been criticized . . . it continues to be widely used" (p. 324. For the same "justification," see Long, 1989, p. 85). Or consider Furnham's (1984) statement that the instruments used in her study "were chosen for their robustness, [and] psychometric satisfactoriness" (p. 283). Referring to one of the instruments, Furnham stated: "It has been found to be a reliable, valid, and economic instrument and used in many studies" (p. 284). Other instruments were characterized as having "a satisfactory psychometric structure" (p. 284) and/or as having "been used extensively" (p. 284).

The preceding quotations constitute *all* one is told about the properties of the measures used. We hope you see the vacuousness of such statements, even if you know little about measurement.

Here is a different kind of example. Reporting on experiments on the "consequences of schematic referencing for social behavior," Sandelands and Calder (1984, p. 755) stated:

We first tested the possibility that words in the self-referencing condition were more unusual or less common. All of the words given by subjects were coded for their occurrence in everyday language using word frequency norms (Thorndike & Lorge, 1941). (p. 761)

We submit that a modicum of thought would suffice to question, if not reject out of hand, the appropriateness of word frequency norms established in the late 1930's for research carried out in the 1980's. Yet the authors apparently felt that a criterion, no matter how irrelevant, was required lest they be criticized for making unsubstantiated claims. Indeed, so ingrained is the norm of following scientific protocol that the mere inclusion of a reference, no matter how irrelevant, seems to endow the presentation with an aura of scientific rigor and objectivity, even in the eyes of referees and editors.

To reiterate: In order to become an intelligent consumer of research, not to mention a competent researcher, it is essential that you develop knowledge and skills in various aspects of the research endeavor. However, *no amount of technical proficiency will do you any good if you do not think*.

We turn now to an overview of the content of the book, its organization, and orientation.

CONTENT

Presentations of measurement, design, and analysis—the major areas to which this book is devoted—have filled many books and myriad articles. Therefore, it goes without saying that our treatment is not exhaustive. In this section, we delineate the topics we have chosen to present and make some general observations about the reasons for our choices.

MEASUREMENT

Measurement is the Achilles' heel of sociobehavioral research. Although most programs in sociobehavioral sciences, especially doctoral programs, require a modicum of exposure to statistics and research design, few seem to require the same where measurement is concerned. Thus, many students get the impression that no special competencies are necessary for the development and use of measures, and it is, therefore, not surprising that little or no attention is given to properties of measures used in many research studies. Unfortunately, many readers and researchers fail to realize that no matter how profound the theoretical formulations, how sophisticated the design, and how elegant the analytic techniques, they cannot compensate for poor measures.

Many books and numerous articles, whose presentations vary in scope, depth, and sophistication, are available in the broad area of measurement. Some offer general introductory overviews, whereas others deal with more or less specific topics. For example, there are many books and papers on the measurement of achievement, mental abilities, attitudes, and personality, to name but a few areas. Furthermore, there are books and papers devoted to measurement theory, measurement models, psychometric theory, or some such characterization. Certain topics may be unique to a given area, whereas others may require more or less elaboration, depending on the specific context. For example, topics such as multiple-choice versus essay tests, guessing, grading practices, criterion-referenced versus norm-referenced tests, and test equating are dealt with primarily, if not exclusively, in presentations devoted to achievement testing. Projective techniques, response styles, response sets, and the like are generally discussed in presentations dealing with the measurement of personality, attitudes, and the like. Measurement theories also differ to a greater or lesser extent, depending on the specific substantive area addressed (e.g., achievement, abilities, attitudes, personality).

The foregoing remarks should suffice to indicate why choices of topics, scope of coverage, level of presentation, and the like must be made. Our choice of topics was determined primarily on the basis of their role in the research endeavor and in light of their generality or pervasiveness.

Chapter 2 is devoted to a general introduction to the role of measurement in scientific inquiry. Among topics included are definition of measurement, scales of measurement, and the relation between measurement and statistics.

Validity is the single most important topic in sociobehavioral measurement; therefore, we devote two chapters to it. Chapter 3 focuses on criterion-related validation, and Chapter 4 focuses on construct validation.

Among topics presented in Chapter 3 are definition of criterion, nature and types of criteria, prediction, predictive efficiency, and differential prediction.

Chapter 4 begins with a consideration of the meaning of construct and its relation to indicators. Construct validation approaches are then presented under three main headings: (a) logical analysis, in the context of which are discussed such aspects as construct definition, item content, measurement and scoring procedures; (b) internal-structure analysis, in the context of which intuitive introductions to exploratory and confirmatory factor analysis are given; and (c) cross-structure analysis, in the context of which notions of convergent and discriminant validation, and the use of the multitrait-multimethod matrix approach for assessing them, are presented. The chapter concludes with a comment on content validity.

Chapter 5 is devoted to theoretical and practical considerations in the estimation of reliability. Among topics presented are status of reliability in measurement and research, conceptions of reliability, classical test theory and some variations on and extensions of it, approaches to the estimation of reliability with an emphasis on internal consistency, relations between validity and reliability, and adverse effects of unreliability.

Chapter 6 provides an introduction to selected approaches to measurement in sociobehavioral research, organized under the following categories: (a) Rating Scales, (b) Semantic Differential, (c) Interviewing, and (d) Observation. Issues addressed in connection with each of the preceding include construction, application, analysis, interpretation, and sources of bias.

DESIGN

Part 2 begins with a general introduction to science and scientific inquiry (Chapter 7). Among topics addressed are basic versus applied research, differences and similarities between natural and sociobehavioral sciences, sociobehavioral research findings and policy advocacy, and substance and methods in sociobehavioral sciences.

Chapter 8 is addressed to definitions and variables. Under the former, we discuss the role of definitions in scientific inquiry, criteria for good definitions, theoretical definitions in general and in sociobehavioral research in particular, and empirical definitions. Variables are then defined and discussed from measurement and design perspectives.

The three interrelated topics of theory, problems, and hypotheses are the subject of Chapter 9. After some observations regarding definitions of theory, we concentrate on its paramount role in scientific research. Issues considered include theory and facts, theory as frame of reference, and the biasing effects of theory. This is followed by a consideration of confirmation and falsification in scientific inquiry, and the progress of science. The state of theory in sociobehavioral sciences is then examined. Observations about the volatility of sociobehavioral research conclude this section.

The section on problems begins with a discussion of what constitute problems in scientific research. This is followed by a presentation of different formats for problem statement. Relations of problem formats to given theoretical formulations and their implications for the type of design and analysis to be used are discussed and illustrated. We then take up the complex questions of the substantive meaningfulness of problems, researchable and nonresearchable problems, and the role of past research in problem formulation.

The section on hypotheses begins with a presentation and discussion of hypotheses whose formats parallel those of problem statements presented earlier. This is followed by a discussion of hypotheses as both guides and misguides—the role of disconfirmation and of testing alternative hypotheses derived from different theoretical perspectives. A special section is then devoted to statistical tests of hypotheses. Among topics dealt with are controversies surrounding such tests, interpretation and misinterpretation of P values, and distinction between statistical significance and substantive importance. The chapter concludes with a presentation of the components of a decision-based approach to statistical tests of hypotheses.

Chapter 10 is devoted to basic principles and concepts of research design. Two interrelated themes are presented: control and validity. Following a discussion of the critical role of control in scientific inquiry, different forms of control are presented and their relations to the type of research design considered.

The broad topic of validity is then taken up. After a brief overview, the remainder of this section is devoted to internal and external validity. Various threats to internal and external validity are discussed in varying detail, depending on their complexity.

Chapter 11 supplements Chapter 10 by focusing on pervasive artifacts and pitfalls in sociobehavioral research and the threats they pose to the validity of conclusions from such research. The chapter is organized around two major sources of artifacts and pitfalls: the subjects and the researcher. As in Chapter 10, topics are dealt with in greater or lesser detail, depending on their pervasiveness and/or complexity.

Each of the next three chapters is devoted to a different class of designs: Chapter 12 is addressed to experimental designs, Chapter 13 to quasi-experimental designs, and Chapter 14 to nonexperimental designs. Broadly, these chapters consist of definitions and elaborations of elements of the class of designs under consideration; their unique features, strengths, and weaknesses, with special emphasis on their implications for validity; and research examples.

There then follows a presentation of some elementary designs along with suggested analytic approaches described on an intuitive level. For each approach under consideration, references are made to specific chapters in Part 3 of the book where it is presented in detail (see section titled Organization, below).

Rounding out Part 2 is an introduction to sampling (Chapter 15). The chapter begins with some definitions concerning samples and sampling strategies. This is followed by a discussion of purposes and advantages of sampling. Pursuant to a distinction between non-probability and probability sampling, the presentation is limited to the latter. Among topics presented are properties of estimators, sampling distributions, selected sampling strategies, and effect size and its relation to power analysis and the determination of sample size.

ANALYSIS

Before describing the contents of Part 3, we make some preliminary remarks about analysis, following which we state our assumptions regarding your background in this area. The scope and method of our presentation of analytic techniques are then commented upon.

PRELIMINARY REMARKS

Speaking of *The Charms of Statistics*, Galton (1889) observed:

Some people hate the very name statistics, but I find them full of beauty and interest. *Whenever they are not brutalised, but delicately handled by the higher methods, and are warily interpreted* [italics added], their power of dealing with complicated phenomena is extraordinary. (p. 62)

As we noted in the preface, statistics are generally presented with little or no attention to substantive context, the characteristics of the design in which they are applied, or the properties of the measures used. Thus dismembered, it is not surprising that statistics are misinterpreted, hated, and brutalized.

Adverse effects of uncritical adherence to expert advice concerning data analysis and interpretation of results, and the failure to exercise common sense, were commented upon earlier. The problems are exacerbated by "experts" offering advice even when they are not familiar with or do not understand the substantive issues and processes involved. Some act as if substantive, design, and measurement issues are irrelevant; that all one needs to know is which are the X's and which are the Y's. Being concerned with such potential abuses, Sir Ronald Fisher (1966), who more than any other person was responsible for modern conceptions of research design and analysis, had this to say:

The statistician cannot evade the responsibility for understanding the processes he applies or recommends. My immediate point is that the questions involved can be dissociated from all that is strictly technical in the statistician's craft, and, *when so detached*, are questions only of the right use of human reasoning powers, with which all intelligent people, who hope to be intelligible, are equally concerned, and on which the statistician, as such, speaks with no special authority. *The statistician cannot excuse himself from the duty of getting his head clear on the principles of scientific inference, but equally no other thinking man can avoid a like obligation* [italics added]. (pp. 1–2)

From the foregoing, it should be clear, we hope, that the choice of an analytic approach is by no means a routine matter. All aspects of the study in question (e.g., theoretical formulation, design characteristics, properties of instruments) have to come into play in the course of deciding on the analytic approach to be used. It should, therefore, come as no surprise when experts disagree about the "correct" analysis, especially in relatively complex studies. The arduous process of deciding on the "correct" analytic approach is well illustrated by Milavsky, Kessler, Stipp, and Rubens (1984). Reporting on their experience in selecting an analytic approach for their large-scale study on television and aggression, they related that, during a period of about three years, they consulted with a number of scholars as to the "best" analytic approach. The consultants were in agreement that the approach Milavsky et al. "used was inadequate, but they did not agree on a preferred method. Indeed, they disagreed quite sharply on the latter" (p. 183). Milavsky et al. stated that the matter was resolved when they

decided that the structural equations approach is the best. From then on, it was a matter of obtaining the LISREL program, getting it to run on our computers, and learning how to use and interpret it. That's when the data analysis really began, *starting with redoing all the early tabular analyses* [italics added]. (p. 183)[1]

The reciprocal relations among various aspects of a study and the analytic approaches used in it are discussed in various chapters, where we also show how applications of different analytic approaches to the same data may lead to different conclusions. In the present context, we would only like to draw attention to Duncan's (1978) comment to the effect that when he and his students reanalyze data from published studies, using more "rigorous" (appropriate?) techniques, they

find almost invariably that (a) the original author claimed relationships that are not adequately substantiated by the data when rigorous tests are employed or (b) overlooked important relationships in those same data or, most likely, (c) both. (p. 404)

ASSUMPTIONS ABOUT YOUR BACKGROUND

We assume that you have had an exposure to statistics on the level of an introductory course; that is, you have some familiarity with basic concepts and approaches (e.g., sum of squares, standard deviation, standard error, t and F ratios, simple analysis of variance, correlation analysis). We hasten to add that we do not hold this assumption too seriously. As a result of teaching courses in research design for which a two-semester course in statistics is a prerequisite, we have come to believe that students would probably be better off if they were not exposed to a "traditional" statistics course. Probably because such courses tend to be taught in substantive and design vacuums, students fail to see "the point of it all." Further, we get the strong impression that many react as if the subject matter is presented in a foreign language with which they have no familiarity. Their technical meanings aside, we have the distinct impression that when reference is made to such terms as deviations of scores from the mean, variance, variables, or correlations, many students seem to react as if these terms are devoid of any meaning in the English language.

In view of all this, we deem it essential to review some basic statistical concepts. In the event you are in need of such a review, we urge you to give statistics a second chance. It is our hope that you will see them in a different light, perchance even get to like them! If, on the other hand, you are in no need of such a review, we hope you will understand our motives in presenting it and will simply skip sections addressing topics with which you are thoroughly familiar.

---

[1]For an introduction to structural equation modeling, an orientation to LISREL, and illustrative applications, see Chapters 23 and 24.

SCOPE AND MODE OF PRESENTATION

The range of concepts and analytic approaches we present is rather wide, from very elementary (e.g., variance, covariance) to very advanced (e.g., structural equation modeling). Some would probably be critical of this sort of packaging. Others, on the other hand, would probably question the omission of certain approaches (e.g., analysis of contingency tables, time series analysis). In what follows, we give an explanation for our choice of analytic approaches to be presented and the mode in which we present them.

We concentrate on analytic approaches corresponding to major topics and primary designs introduced in Parts 1 and 2. For example, factor analysis (Chapters 22 and 23) is explained and illustrated from the frame of reference of construct validation (Chapter 4). Similarly, we present variations on applications of regression analysis with continuous and/or categorical independent variables (Chapters 17 through 21) that are consistent with assorted designs introduced in Chapters 12 through 14.

Our concern throughout is with applications—with the fit between analysis and other aspects of the research endeavor. We believe this can be best accomplished by means of examples. In our view, methods come alive through examples, especially for people who are not mathematically inclined and whose primary, if not sole, concern is with applications and interpretations. It is in the course of applying a method that one can better appreciate its relevance to a given problem and set of circumstances, and it is thus that one learns how to interpret results. Indeed, "Methodology, like sex, is better demonstrated than discussed" (Leamer, 1983, p. 40).

Accordingly, all topics and approaches are presented in the context of simple numerical examples that are thoroughly analyzed and interpreted in some detail. In what follows, we make several points about our numerical examples.

Although we attempt to couch our numerical examples in some substantive context, this is necessarily done in a skeletal form, in the sense of giving a flavor of the variables and a broad depiction of an hypothetical model. Obviously, it is not possible in a book such as this one to go into detailed theoretical considerations. When deemed useful, we provide some references to the literature on a topic under consideration. Whatever the case, we keep reminding you in various places that the substantive examples we use are *illustrative*, that *no claims are made or implied as to their plausibility or validity*.

Inevitably, our choice of examples is influenced by our substantive interests in areas with which we are more or less conversant. These include research in psychology in general (and social psychology in particular) and educational research, especially large-scale studies concerned with school effects in the broadest sense. If you feel uncomfortable with our examples, we urge you to substitute examples from your field of interest.

We use small, hence unrealistic, numerical examples so as not to get sidetracked by the mechanics of the calculations. Such examples are used even when the analysis is carried out by computer, as this enables us to demonstrate how some of the results were arrived at, using some hand calculations and relating them to formulas and approaches presented in connection with the topic under consideration. We believe this approach to be helpful inasmuch as it also affords the use of concrete and manageable examples in the course of explaining various features of the output of a given computer program.

Following passively the presentation of a method or a technique generally lulls one into believing that one understands it and will know how to implement it when necessary. There is probably nothing more sobering than attempting to carry out an analysis one presumes familiarity with and discovering that one does not even know where to begin. To avoid this predicament, we strongly recommend that you replicate our analyses and do some others. It is for this reason that we also include study suggestions that would afford you an opportunity to exercise what you have learned of a given analytic approach. We suggest that at the initial learning stages you carry out the calculations by hand as well as by computer. When you feel relatively comfortable with the ideas behind a given analytic technique, you can, of course, relegate the drudgery of the calculations to the computer.

CONTENT

Computer analysis plays a central role in our presentation of the various analytic approaches. Accordingly, the first chapter in Part 3 (Chapter 16) is devoted to an introduction to computers and computer programs. The chapter begins with some general observations concerning computers, advantages of computer data analysis, misconceptions about computers, and the adverse effects of beliefs in the infallibility of computers and software. A discussion of basic components of statistical software and some suggestions on how to go about evaluating such software is then given. This is followed by an outline of our criteria for the selection of programs to be used in this book and a listing of the statistical packages we use. Some considerations in the use of statistical software are then discussed. The following are among topics addressed: the use of manuals, program defaults, creating and editing input files, and error messages. The next section outlines conventions followed in this book concerning input and output files and the nature and purpose of our commentaries on input and output. The final section is devoted to introductions to each of the statistical packages used in this book and to a description of the conventions we follow in using them.

Chapter 17, which is devoted to simple regression analysis, begins with a review of basic statistical concepts (e.g., variance, covariance). This is followed by presentations of elements of simple regression analysis (e.g., the regression equation, partitioning of sums of squares). Advantages of using graphs in regression analysis are then discussed, and examples of graphs generated by computer programs are given. The next section is devoted to statistical tests of significance in regression analysis. Assumptions underlying the regression model are then delineated and effects of departures from them reviewed. The next major section, devoted to diagnostics, is comprised of two subsections: analysis of residuals and influence analysis. In both subsections, discussions and illustrations of some of the major approaches are given in the context of numerical examples. The chapter concludes with a comment on the correlation model.

Multiple regression analysis in explanatory research is the topic of Chapter 18.[2] Virtually all aspects of the analysis and interpretation of results can be readily understood for the case of two independent variables, and hand calculations for this special case are fairly simple; therefore, much of the chapter is addressed to it. The case of more than two independent variables is then presented, and illustrative analyses by computer are given and commented upon.

Because of widespread misconceptions and misapplications of variance partitioning, especially in the form of hierarchical regression analysis, we devote a special section to it. Shrinkage and its relation to sample size are then discussed. This is followed by a discussion of multicollinearity, its adverse effects and some suggested remedies. The chapter concludes with a section on curvilinear regression analysis.

---

[2]The distinction between explanatory and predictive research is discussed in various chapters (e.g., Chapters 3, 8, 10).

Chapter 19 addresses the analysis of designs consisting of a categorical independent variable (e.g., different treatments, marital status, race). After introducing the notion of coding information contained in such a variable, it is shown how the coded information is used in regression analysis. Three coding schemes are presented, and unique features of each are discussed and illustrated through their applications in the analysis of the same numerical example.

The topic of multiple comparisons among means is then presented and illustrated for a priori and post hoc comparisons. It is shown how some such comparisons may be obtained directly from a regression analysis in which a relevant coding scheme is used.

The chapter concludes with a section on similarities between regression analysis and simple analysis of variance when applied in a design with a categorical independent variable. It is shown that differences in terminologies and mechanics of the analysis notwithstanding, essentially the same ends are accomplished by the two analytic approaches.

Extensions of ideas and approaches introduced in Chapter 19 are presented in Chapter 20 for the case of multiple independent categorical variables or factorial designs. It is shown how the coding schemes introduced in Chapter 19 can be used in designs with any number of categorical independent variables. Advantages of factorial designs, especially in affording detection of interactions among independent variables in their effects on the dependent variable, are reviewed and illustrated for a design consisting of two categorical independent variables or two factors. Among other things, the notion of focused comparisons pursuant to the finding of an interaction is explained. It is shown how the calculations may be carried out by hand, using results obtained from a regression analysis, or by computer through the use of relevant subcommands.

The formulation of hypotheses in the context of factorial designs is then discussed and illustrated for cases where an interaction is expected and for ones where it is not expected.

Analysis of designs with more than two factors is then reviewed. A research example of a design with three factors is used to elucidate some of the basic ideas.

We then turn to a presentation of nonorthogonal designs (i.e., designs with unequal cell frequencies). Pursuant to a discussion of the critical difference between experimental and nonexperimental designs with unequal cell frequencies, issues concerning analysis and interpretation of each are dealt with separately.

A section addressing similarities and differences between multiple regression analysis and analysis of variance concludes the chapter.

Chapter 21 is devoted to the analysis of designs with both categorical and continuous independent variables. Accordingly, approaches introduced separately in Chapters 17 through 20 are fused in this chapter. Two basic designs are presented and their analyses illustrated: Attribute-Treatment-Interaction (ATI) and Analysis of Covariance (ANCOVA). It is shown that the distinction between these designs is inherent *not* in the analytic approach but rather in the focus of the study. When the focus is on studying whether there is an interaction between attributes of individuals and treatments in their effects on the dependent variable, the design is conceived of as ATI. When, in contrast, the focus is on controlling for attributes of individuals while studying treatment effects, the design is conceived of as ANCOVA. In both instances, however, the analysis is applied to data obtained in experimental designs (see Chapter 12).

Use of ANCOVA in quasi-experimental designs (Chapter 13) for the purpose of adjusting for differences among nonequivalent groups is then taken up. In addition to very serious design and logical problems arising in connection with such use, biasing effects of errors of measurement of the covariate are discussed and illustrated. Alternatives to ANCOVA in quasi-experimental designs are then reviewed. Generalizations and extensions of the analytic approach under consideration to other designs (e.g., regression discontinuity, factorial) are then outlined.

Exploratory factor analysis is the topic of Chapter 22. The chapter begins with an introduction to factor analysis and its relation to theory. This is followed by some comments about properties of matrices used in factor analysis. Two numerical examples—one in which the factors are not correlated and one in which they are correlated—are then analyzed and commented upon. The focus throughout is on the use of factor analysis in the process of construct validation. Among topics discussed are the distinction between principal components and factor analysis, communality and uniqueness, orthogonal and oblique rotations, factor matrices, reproduced correlations, interpretation and naming of factors, sampling and sample size, factor scores, construction of factor-based scales, and reporting results of factor analysis.

Chapter 23 is devoted to confirmatory factor analysis (*CFA*). After a brief introduction, *CFA* is presented as a submodel of structural equation modeling (*SEM*), which is the topic of Chapter 24. There then follows an orientation to LISREL—a computer program used in Chapters 23 and 24. Among major topics addressed in the orientation are matrices in the LISREL submodel used for *CFA*, LISREL control statements and defaults, and model specification. The same numerical examples used in exploratory factor analysis (Chapter 22) are then subjected to *CFA*. Topics presented in the context of commentaries on the output include logic, method, and assumptions pertaining to model testing; and goodness-of-fit indices.

An orientation to EQS—another computer program used in Chapters 23 and 24—is the topic of the next section. Nomenclature, input, and control statements used in EQS are reviewed. One of the numerical examples analyzed earlier through LISREL is analyzed through EQS. Unique features of this program as well as similarities and differences between it and LISREL are considered in the course of commentaries on the output.

There then follow considerations of the analysis of multitrait-multimethod matrices in the context of confirmatory factor analysis. An example of a matrix consisting of three traits and three methods is analyzed. The following are among topics considered in connection with this analysis: tests of nested models; revision of models; use of some indices reported in the programs under consideration for the purpose of model revision; and partitioning of variance into components due to trait, method, and error.

The concluding section of the chapter is addressed to measurement models introduced in Chapter 5. Specifically, the parallel, tau-equivalent, and congeneric models are examined. A small numerical example is used to illustrate tests of such models.

Chapter 24 constitutes an introduction to the formulation, estimation, and interpretation of structural models. The controversial topic of causation is considered with respect to conception, definition, relation to theory, and type of design.

There then follows an orientation to the analysis of structural models through LISREL. In a manner similar to the orientation given in Chapter 23, matrices used in structural models are explained and illustrated. This is followed by an explanation of input and control statements. Analogously, an orientation to EQS is given and its application illustrated.

Several numerical examples are analyzed, using segments of the same illustrative data as well as the entire data set. The purpose of using first segments of the data is to discuss and illustrate the analysis and interpretation of different models. Some of the topics introduced in connection with the analysis of the various models are the use of single versus multiple indicators, direct and indirect effects, and standardized and unstandardized solutions. Brief introductory commentaries on selected topics conclude the chapter.

ORGANIZATION

The decision regarding the organization of the book was, to say the least, challenging. In our search for a structure that will afford an orderly presentation of the wide scope of topics without losing sight of their interrelations and interdependencies, we considered several different ones. Although we recognize that you may not deem the structure we have settled on as being the best, we hope that you will still find it useful. In the hope of increasing the likelihood of this being the case, we sketch some main aspects of the organization and also offer some recommendations on how you may proceed. In the final analysis, however, it is you who should organize the materials in a manner that best suits your needs and aims.

The overall structure of the book is, we believe, evident from our description of its content in the preceding section. In what follows, we comment on some specific aspects of the organization.

RECURRING THEMES

The organization can probably be best characterized as one of recurring themes presented on several levels and from different perspectives. For the most part, each theme is presented first on an intuitive level. Subsequently, it is dealt with more formally and rigorously. In many instances, the same theme is considered from more than one of the major perspectives of this book (i.e., measurement, design, and analysis).

An example will, we believe, help clarify what we have in mind. The notion of indicators is introduced on an intuitive level from a measurement perspective, focusing on construct validation (Chapter 4). Indicators are then discussed from the design perspective (e.g., Chapters 12 and 13). Issues concerning analysis are addressed in general terms only in the aforementioned contexts, and references are made to sections of Part 3 (e.g., Chapters 23 and 24) where presentations of relevant analytic approaches are given.

From the preceding, it may be discerned that, as one of the means of sustaining an integrated approach while keeping the presentation manageable, we resort to frequent cross referencing and recommendations that you peruse various sections of the book while studying a given topic. For example, references to presentations of relevant analytic approaches are given in measurement and/or design contexts. Similarly, references to discussions of relevant measurement and/or design issues are given in connection with presentations of different analytic approaches.

We attempt to accomplish the same ends also through repeated use of the same illustrative substantive examples in various contexts. Thus, a substantive example introduced in connection with a measurement issue (e.g., item content) may then be taken up again in connection with a design question (e.g., internal validity) and/or a given analytic approach (factor analysis).

Your decision if and when to peruse different sections of the book while studying a given topic would have to depend, among other things, on your background, needs, aims, and study habits. Thus, if all you wish is to get a general idea about a given topic (e.g., factor analysis), and if you can tolerate the inevitable ambiguity that is likely to ensue, then a reading of our general remarks about this topic in Chapter 4 may suffice. If you aim at a better grasp of factor analysis, perhaps because you wish to be better able to follow a paper in which it was applied, you would also have to read at least some sections of Chapter 22.

However, if you wish to develop a more thorough understanding of factor analysis as well as the ability to apply it, then you would probably find it essential to study not only Chapters 22 and 23 but also various references given therein for more detailed treatments and/or extensions.

REFERENCES

As you will soon discover, we provide abundant references in connection with almost every topic. The references are provided so that they are readily available to you when you need them. It is likely that you would ignore some or all the references when reading about a topic from one perspective (e.g., getting a general idea about it) but that you would find it necessary to peruse many of them when reading about the same topic from another perspective (e.g., attempting to deepen and extend your understanding of it).

STUDY SUGGESTIONS

Study suggestions are provided for selected chapters, in connection with analytic approaches. Earlier, we commented on the importance of carrying out analyses, not just reading about them. It is with this in mind that such study suggestions are included. Answers are provided so that you may check your work.

In some study suggestions, we recommend that you read cited research reports and reanalyze the data they report. We do this for several interrelated reasons when: (a) we feel it would enable you to better appreciate what the author(s) of the report in question has done and to be in a better position to evaluate the findings, conclusions, and implications; (b) it appears that a different analytic approach is more "appropriate" or that the practice of carrying out an alternative analysis would reinforce ideas presented in the body of the text; and (c) we believe it would enhance your ability to read and evaluate research perceptively.

ORIENTATION

We realize that certain aspects of our orientation will strike some, possibly you among them, as being harsh and perhaps unduly pessimistic. We would, therefore, like to explain those aspects of it that might be thus perceived. Impressions one may form to the contrary notwithstanding, our aim is not to sow despair but rather to apprise you of some serious problems and difficulties in the conduct of sociobehavioral research. We recognize that even among those who share our general views and intentions, some would question the wisdom of presenting them in an introductory text on the grounds that this would disillusion and discourage students. In our opinion, students are in no need of protection from harsh realities of the research scene. On the contrary, we believe students resent being thus treated, especially upon discovering little resemblance between research in the "real world" and its general portrayal in textbooks and classrooms.

It boils down to the question of when and by whom are students to be made aware of complexities attendant with doing research. The penchant to encourage, indeed expect, students to do research even when they are ill prepared to do so is probably motivated by the belief in learning by doing. We submit that what students tend to learn most under such circumstances is that doing scientific research requires little preparation and even less knowledge.

CRITIQUES OF STUDIES AND MEASURES

In line with the preceding, a major aspect of our original manuscript consisted of critical evaluations of research studies in which analytic and/or measurement approaches under discussion have been used. We felt this to be a valuable means of focusing upon specific misapplications and misinterpretations, thereby leading to a better appreciation of the specific method being considered as well as the overall research process. It was, therefore, with great reluctance that we deleted most of the research examples when time came for drastic cuts in the manuscript so as to render it of manageable size. Even the relatively few examples that survived are mere shadows of what they were in the original manuscript. We inform you of this in the hope of explaining why only some examples are given and why the discussion of them tends to be skeletal.

It should be noted that our aim is *not* to summarize or review studies on which we comment. Instead, we comment on specific aspects of a study or a measure for the purpose of illuminating points made with respect to a topic under consideration or as examples of mistakes that we hope you will learn from. As we keep reminding you in various places (e.g., Chapter 11), there is no substitute for reading the original report of an investigation.

We believe there is a powerful norm against criticizing fellow researchers. Without going far afield, we would like to sketch what are, in our opinion, some of its origins.

To begin with, criticism of fellow researchers is viewed as undermining the credibility of the discipline in the eyes of the public, not to mention granting agencies. In our opinion, it is the general reluctance on the part of sociobehavioral scientists to take a more critical posture concerning published research, especially wild claims based on highly questionable "findings," that has contributed to the erosion of the credibility of the sociobehavioral sciences.

Then there is the notion that to be constructive, criticism must be accompanied by proposed alternatives ("better" ones, of course). The roots of this can, in our opinion, be traced to, among other things, the reluctance to concede that, given the current state of knowledge and methodology, certain things may be undoable. Indeed, "there is no notion of the *undoable* if observation and measurement are possible" (Lieberson, 1985, p. 7).

Echoing Freedman's (1987b) exhortation "to start a new trend" (p. 213) of admitting to not knowing how to do something, we believe it is also necessary to acknowledge: (a) that certain questions are unanswerable, (b) that in the absence of appropriate conditions and means (e.g., settings, measures, analytic approaches) certain things are undoable, and (c) that cultural myths notwithstanding, mere effort does not necessarily pay off. Above all, it is important to recognize that something is *not* always better than nothing!

We would hasten to add that we do not claim to preach perfection. The adage that the perfect is the enemy of the good holds true also for the case of scientific research. There is no denying that preoccupation with perfection, that apprehension about not committing any errors, may lead to research paralysis. However, the recognition that perfection is unattainable does not constitute license that anything goes. Making a similar point in connection with controversies surrounding objectivity, Geertz (1973) remarked:

I have never been impressed by the argument that, as complete objectivity is impossible in these matters (as, of course, it is), one might as well let one's sentiments run loose. As Robert Solow has remarked, that is like saying that as a perfectly aseptic environment is impossible, one might as well conduct surgery in a sewer. (p. 30)

Had the kind of misconceptions and misapplications to which we allude been relatively rare, there would have been little reason for doing this in a book such as ours. It is because of their prevalence and their adverse effects that it is essential to confront them. Duncan (1984) expressed similar concerns most forcefully and graphically:

There would be no point in deploring such caricatures of the research enterprise if there were a clearly identifiable sector of social science research wherein such fallacies were clearly recognized and emphatically out of bounds. But in my discipline it just is not so. Individual articles of exemplary quality are published cheek-by-jowl with transparent exercises in statistical numerology. If the muck were ankle deep, we could wade through it. When it is at hip level, our most adroit and most fastidious workers can hardly avoid getting some of it on their product. It would be invidious as well as tedious to cite examples documenting this assessment. (pp. 226–227)

When even "most adroit and most fastidious" researchers are adversely affected by poor research practices, one can well envision the debilitating effects they are likely to have on novices and students.

THE REVIEW PROCESS

As we have already done earlier in this chapter, from time to time we allude to the review process leading to acceptance or rejection of papers by professional journals. Our remarks should not be construed as an attempt to join the controversy surrounding the review process (see Altman, 1989, for a news report of "the first-ever conference to review the review process"). Nor do we intend to offer alternative strategies and policies. Our aim is a much more modest one, that of alerting you that all is *not* well in the kingdom of peer review, thereby fostering in you a healthy skepticism toward what you are reading. Needless to say, such an orientation is inane, even harmful, if it is not grounded in knowledge and buttressed by clear thinking while reading.

We would like to stress that what is troubling us about the existing system is that gross errors and serious misconceptions that should have been detected even as a result of a cursory reading by a person with rudimentary knowledge appear to elude "expert" referees and editors. Regrettably, this happens with what is, in our opinion, an alarming frequency.

In sum, we are convinced that we would have done you a disservice had we presented a Panglossian view of the world of sociobehavioral sciences. More important, it is our sincere hope that our orientation will contribute toward your becoming a perceptive consumer of research as well as a proficient researcher.

PART 1
MEASUREMENT

Chapter 2
Measurement and Scientific Inquiry

Measurement pervades almost every facet of our lives and daily activities. We measure a great variety of things (e.g., weight, temperature, ingredients to be used in cooking, time, distance). At one time or another, we are measured by various people (e.g., physicians, teachers, supervisors, college admission officers, psychologists) on a wide range of things (e.g., blood pressure, achievement, productivity, aptitudes, attitudes, anxiety). In short, much of what we do, decisions we make, and decisions made about us involve measurement of one kind or another.

The orderliness and predictability of numerous activities and decisions in which we engage almost routinely—the very orderliness and functioning of society—are predicated, in large part, on the role measurement plays in our lives and in the society in which we live (for historical reviews of measurement, see DuBois, 1970; Wainer, 1987).

The considerable role measurement plays in modern times is attested to by, among other things, the existence of regulatory agencies and bureaus (e.g., the Bureau of Standards in the U.S.) that set standards for and monitor a vast assortment of measures. Indeed, "there is a federally mandated method for measuring almost every physical, chemical, or biological phenomenon" (Hunter, 1980, p. 869).

Despite its prevalence, or perhaps because of it, measurement means different things to different people in different contexts. The diversity of its meanings aside, measurement is not an end but a means in the process of description, differentiation, explanation, prediction, diagnosis, decision making, and the like. Scientists and laypersons alike seem agreed that science, however defined (see Chapter 7), is unthinkable in the absence of some sort of measurement (see, for example, Brodbeck, 1968, Part Seven; Campbell, 1952, Chapter VI; Churchman & Ratoosh, 1959; Feigl & Brodbeck, 1953; Kaplan, 1964, Part V; Nagel, 1931). Further, scientific advances are largely predicated on the measurement procedures used. Margenau, who offered an incisive elaboration of this view, asserted that measurement is "the scientist's ultimate appeal to Nature" (1950, p. 369). It stands "at the critical junction between theory and . . . experience . . . the contact of reason with Nature" (1959, pp. 163–164).

We turn first to a consideration of definition and benefits of measurement. This is followed by a presentation of two major topics: scales of measurement and the relation between measurement and statistics.

DEFINITION AND BENEFITS OF MEASUREMENT

As is the case with any concept, ambiguity, confusion, and disagreement are bound to surround the meaning of measurement when it is left undefined or when it is referred to without regard to a specific definition. Of various definitions of measurement in sociobehavioral sciences, the preeminent, although by no means universally accepted, is one offered and elaborated upon by Stevens (1951, 1959, 1968). Adapting and extending Campbell's (1928) formulations, Stevens (1968) defined measurement as "the assignment of numbers to aspects of objects or events according to one or another rule or convention" (p. 850).

Note that the numbers[1] are assigned to *aspects* of objects, not to the objects themselves. Thus, for example, one can measure the length, width, weight, volume, color, and so on of a box, but not the box *itself*. Similarly, one can measure a child's height, weight, mental ability, anxiety, motivation, and so on, but not the child *himself* or *herself*.

The realization that measurement is addressed to aspects of objects or people renders irrelevant persistent arguments that measurement in the sociobehavioral sciences is impossible or meaningless, at best, because of the uniqueness and great complexity of human beings. When a given aspect of objects is measured, all other aspects on which they may differ are ignored. Thus, when the weight of objects is measured, their differences in all other aspects (e.g., size, color, shape) are ignored because they are presumably irrelevant to the task at hand. For certain purposes, only the weight of objects may be relevant, whereas for others additional aspects may have to be attended to and measured. The complexity characteristic of attempts to explain human behavior inheres, in part, in the potentially large number of attributes one may have to attend to and measure.

What is relevant to measure can be determined only within an implicit or explicit theory about the phenomenon one wishes to study. Measurement, then, implies a theory about the operations of or the relations among a set of variables relevant to the phenomenon being investigated. It is meaningless to attempt to measure intelligence, say, in the absence of a theory of intelligence that, among other things, delineates its relations with other constructs and variables. When Guilford (1967), for example, rejected the "doctrine of one monolithic *intelligence*" (p. 27), he did so within the context of a theory of a multidimensional structure of intellect. Furthermore, it is within the context of his theory that he developed various measures of intellectual functioning. Theory not only determines what attributes or aspects are to be measured but also how they are to be measured. In other words, theory conceptualizes the aspects from which measurement operations follow (see Chapters 8 and 9).

ISOMORPHISM

The sine qua non of measurement is that the numbers assigned to objects reflect the relations among the objects with respect to the aspect being measured. This idea—referred to as isomorphism—means a one-to-one correspondence between elements of two classes.[2]

A prime example of isomorphism is that between a map and the geographic region it

---

[1]Stevens (1959, p. 19) pointed out that some authors distinguish between the assignment of "numerals" and "numbers" to aspects of objects, and discussed some of the ambiguities related to this distinction. Nevertheless, he admits to being himself inconsistent in this matter. See also, Stevens (1951, p. 22).

[2]For a more precise definition and discussions of isomorphism, see Brodbeck (1959), Cohen and Nagel (1934, pp. 137–141), and Stevens (1951, p. 23).

depicts. There is a one-to-one correspondence between, say, towns and the points used to represent them on the map, such that relations among the points on the map (e.g., distances) reflect relations among the geographic locations they represent. Hence, the great usefulness and convenience of maps. Measurement consists of mapping a set of objects onto a set of numbers, such that there is isomorphism between the objects measured and the numbers assigned to them. An obvious example is measurement of weight, where each of a set of objects is assigned a number such that the relations among the numbers reflect the relations among the objects with respect to weight (e.g., one object being twice as heavy as another).

BENEFITS OF MEASUREMENT

An appreciation of the benefits of measurement may be attained when it is contrasted with alternative approaches to the description of or the differentiation among a set of objects with respect to a given aspect. Contrast the limitations, ambiguities, and potential inconsistencies when attempting to describe verbally the weight of a set of objects (e.g., heavy, very heavy, very very heavy, not so heavy, light, lighter, much lighter) with statements about the numerical weights of the same objects.

A great advantage in using measurement is that one may apply the powerful tools of mathematics to the study of phenomena. Operating on sets of numbers that are isomorphic with aspects of sets of objects enables one to arrive at concise and precise statements of regularities, or laws, regarding phenomena to a degree unattainable without the benefits of measurement. Suppose, for example, that one wants to study and describe the relation between mental ability and achievement. Relying on observations and verbal descriptions, one is limited to unwieldy and potentially ambiguous statements (e.g., people high on mental ability generally manifest greater achievement than those low on mental ability). In contrast, measuring mental ability and achievement of a sample of people, one can calculate an index of the relation between the two variables (e.g., the correlation coefficient), and state the direction and strength of the relation with clarity and conciseness unattainable through verbal descriptions. Moreover, the index of the relation can in turn be used for various purposes (e.g., to determine whether and by how much the relation between mental ability and achievement differs across various racial groups), or, along with other statistics, it may be used to develop an equation to predict achievement from mental ability.

Because measurement constitutes a matching of numbers to aspects of objects, it is imperative to know "what was matched to what" (Stevens, 1968, p. 854) so as to be in a position to meaningfully interpret the numbers and to determine what mathematical manipulations may be meaningfully applied to them. What this boils down to is the scale type being used—a topic to which we now turn.

SCALES OF MEASUREMENT

Stevens (1951) proposed the following four types of measurement (also referred to as levels of measurement) in ascending order, from the crudest to the most elaborate: *nominal, ordinal, interval,* and *ratio*. Although this classification was extended and refined (e.g., Coombs, 1953; Stevens, 1959), it will suffice for present purposes. Stevens defined the scale types with reference to the kind of transformations under which they remain invariant. Invariance means no variance, no change. Bell (1945) adapted a statement by Keyser that conveys the idea of invariance forcefully and eloquently:

Invariance is changelessness in the midst of change, permanence in a world of flux, the persistence of configurations that remain the same despite the swirl and stress of countless hosts of curious transformations. (p. 420)

In the context of scale types, invariance refers to the kind of transformations that can be applied to the numbers without changing the meaning or the interpretation of the empirical relations to which the numbers refer. These are discussed and illustrated below under each of the four scale types.

NOMINAL SCALE

A nominal scale entails the assignment of numbers as labels to objects or classes of objects. In other words, numbers are used to substitute for names or any other symbols that identify objects or classes of objects.[3] The most basic example of a nominal scale is the assignment of identification numbers to a set of objects. The great convenience of identification numbers in many varied circumstances and settings is so obvious that it requires no elaboration or justification. Yet the importance of nominal scaling, from a measurement frame of reference, is not in the assignment of numbers to individual objects but rather to classes of objects.[4]

Classification and classification schemes play a central role in our daily lives and activities. Our ability to confront and deal with myriad stimuli impinging on us, to make sense of what would otherwise be a chaotic swirl of objects and events, is unimaginable without our resorting constantly, almost automatically, to classification. We classify people, objects, jobs, scientific disciplines, plants, events, or what have you, using a great variety of rules and criteria. Some appear simple, "obvious," even "natural." Others are highly sophisticated, extremely complex, not at all obvious, and are therefore frequently subject to disagreements, even great controversies.

When we classify people according to sex, for example, the rule is simple, natural, obvious. Contrast this with the rule the Lord gave Gideon for classifying his men into two camps: those he was to send home and those he was to lead in the attack on the Midianites. The Lord instructed Gideon to bring his men down to the water and classify them according to the way they were drinking:

"Make every man who laps the water with his tongue like a dog stand on one side, and on the other every man who goes down on his knees and drinks." . . . The Lord said to Gideon, "With the three hundred men who lapped I will save you and deliver Midian into your hands, and all the rest may go home." (*Judges*, 7:5–8)

A simple enough rule, but not at all obvious. The act of kneeling spontaneously was presumably meant to serve as an indicator of idol worshipping. Other interpretations are, of course, possible. In fact, it is the nature of indicators that they may be subject to different interpretations. Notions concerning relations of indicators and latent variables are introduced below.

Simple or complex, universally accepted or highly controversial, classifications reflect concepts, variables (e.g., socioeconomic class, race, political party affiliation, religious orientation), and are thus an integral part of an implicit or explicit frame of reference. When used in scientific research, classifications are integral parts of theoretical formulations.

Some authors deny classification the status of measurement. Referring to the nominal

---

[3]Stevens preferred to refer to them as numerals, because the numbers are used as labels. But see footnote 1, this chapter.

[4]Some authors distinguish between the two. Stevens (1951, p. 25) referred to the first as type *A* and to the second as type *B*. Nunnally (1978, pp. 13–14) referred to the first as labels and to the second as categories.

level of measurement, Coombs (1953) stated: "This level of measurement is so primitive that it is not always recognized as measurement, *but it is a necessary condition for all higher levels of measurement*" (p. 473).

To satisfy the requirements of nominal scaling, subjects have to be classified into a set of mutually exclusive and exhaustive categories. What this means is that each subject is assigned to one category only and that all subjects are classifiable into the categories used. For example, classifying people according to their political party affiliation, each person is classified as a member of one party only, and each person must fit into one of the categories used. In the event that certain people do not fit into any of the existing categories, new ones have to be added so that the requirement of exhaustiveness be met. Sometimes it is convenient to use a category such as "others," to which people who do not fit the categories of interest are assigned.

Whatever the classification rules, objects classified in different categories are treated as different in kind, not in degree. That is, classes of a nominal scale are not ordered. Democrats, for example, are not more than Republicans, or vice versa, on political party affiliation. They are *different* from each other. Another property of classification is that the objects classified in the same class are treated as being equal to each other regardless of how they may differ on aspects other than those used for the definition of the class. For example, if the definition of political party affiliation is that of being a registered member of a given party, then all registered Democrats are treated alike, although they may differ in commitment to the goals of the party, their voting record, contributions in money and services to the party, sex, race, occupation, and any other variable imaginable.

The question whether or not a given classification is meaningful or useful cannot be answered without considering why it is used in the first place and what has led to the specific definition of the variable. Classification is a form of measurement, and, as we said earlier, measurement is a means, not an end. The meaningfulness or usefulness of a given measure can be assessed only within a given theoretical or practical context.

It goes without saying that different definitions, resulting in different classification rules, may lead to different classifications of the same objects, people, and the like. For example, classification of people according to race depends on the definition of race in general and the categories used in particular. Issues regarding the definition of variables are discussed in Chapter 8 and will, therefore, not be pursued further here.

Whatever the definition of a nominal or categorical variable, the classes or categories used comprise a nominal scale. Each category may be assigned any number, as long as different numbers are assigned to different categories. The numbers assigned to the categories are but identification symbols; thus, scale invariance will be maintained under any one-to-one substitution. That is, any number can be substituted for any other number so long as distinct numbers are used to identify distinct categories. Despite the freedom to choose any set of numbers for the identification of distinct categories of a nominal scale, certain choices prove more convenient than others for specific purposes. For example, it is more convenient to use 1's and 0's to identify two categories of a nominal variable (e.g., male, female; black, white), although any two numbers (e.g., 1 and −22; .06 and 23.73) will do. In later chapters (see especially Chapter 19), we show that certain numbers are more useful for the coding of a nominal or categorical variable, because they facilitate analyses in which the variables are used, and because they lead to more direct interpretations of the results.

ORDINAL SCALE

An ordinal scale entails the assignment of numbers to persons or objects so that they reflect their rank ordering on an attribute in question. If person *A*, say, is viewed as kinder (or smarter, better looking) than person B, then he or she may be assigned a "2," whereas B may be assigned a "1." The numbers thus assigned do not reflect by how much A exceeds B on the attribute in question but rather the relation "greater than," or "more than," symbolized by $>$.

On an ordinal scale, it must be true that for any pair of objects, A and B, if A is greater than B, then B is not greater than A. This is referred to as an asymmetric, or nonsymmetric, relation. It is, of course, possible for A to be equal to B, reflecting a symmetric relation. Under such circumstances, A and B would be assigned the same number, referred to as a tied rank.

For any three objects, A, B, and C on an ordinal scale, it must be true that if $A > B$, and $B > C$, then $A > C$. This is referred to as transitivity. An asymmetric relation is not necessarily transitive. For example, person A may beat person B in a game of chess, and B may beat C. From this, it does *not* follow that A will beat C.

Because the numbers assigned to objects on an ordinal scale reflect only the relation "greater than," invariance will be maintained under any monotonic transformation of the scale values. A monotonic transformation is one in which the rank ordering of the numbers does not change. Following are examples of monotonic transformations: adding a constant to all the numbers, raising the numbers to any power, taking the square root of the numbers, and multiplying the numbers by a constant.

An ordinal scale can withstand the vagaries of a host of diverse transformations, because the information it conveys is rather crude and limited. Limitations of an ordinal scale as well as the potential for misinterpretation of the scale values will be illustrated through two examples.

Assume that two groups, each consisting of eight people, were rank ordered with respect to height. The results are depicted in Figure 2.1, where the letters above the line refer to the people, and the numbers below the line refer to their rank ordering on height; (a) and (b) refer to the two groups. Notice that the people are not evenly distributed on the height continuum. For example, A and C in (a) are relatively close on height, whereas C and D are relatively far apart, or D and B are closer on height than any other pair of people in (a). *Of course, this type*

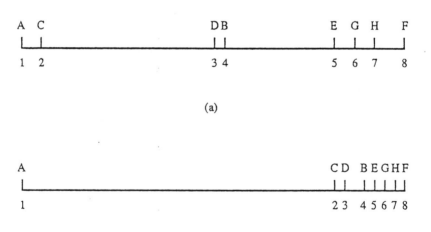

(a)

(b)

Figure 2.1

of information is lost when measures of height, which are on a ratio scale (see below), are converted into an ordinal scale. Given rank orders, it is not possible to tell, for example, whether person *A*, who is assigned a rank of 1, is relatively close in height to the person ranked 2 (*C* in our example) as in (*a*) or relatively far apart from him or her as in (*b*).

Turning now to the rank orders in the two groups, it is obvious that no meaningful comparisons can be made between ranks assigned in separate groups. The fact that two people have the same rank in distinct groups obviously does not mean that they are of the same height. It is possible, for example, for the person ranked as the shortest in group (*a*) to be taller than the person ranked as the tallest in group (*b*).

We now use Figure 2.1 to depict a different kind of situation in which ordinal scales are used. This time, *A* through *H* are eight objects (events, people, and the like). The two rank orders, (*a*) and (*b*), are those assigned to the *same* objects by two respondents. For example, *A* through *H* could be different kinds of foods, ranked by two individuals to indicate their preferences, or *A* through *H* could be TV advertisements ranked by two individuals with respect to their effectiveness. For the purpose of the present discussion, assume that the letters *A* through *H* stand for politicians running for office, who were rank ordered by two individuals with respect to sincerity. The letters are not evenly distributed so as to indicate scores the two individuals might have assigned the politicians had they been asked to rate each of them on a "scale of sincerity" instead of rank ordering them. *Obviously, this kind of information is not conveyed by the numbers one obtains when respondents rank order the politicians.*

Consider, first, the rankings under (*a*). Assume that the person who has assigned them feels that politician *A* is ever so slightly more sincere than *C* but that the two of them are much more sincere than the remaining ones. Also, *D* is slightly more sincere than *B*, and they in turn are more sincere than the remaining politicians, whose rank ordering is indicated in Figure 2.1 (*a*). Being limited to ranking, the respondent cannot convey this information. By their very nature, rankings convey intensity in a relative sense only. That is, *A* is perceived as more sincere than *C*, *C* more than *D*, and so on. What the rankings do *not* tell us is how sincere each politician is in the eyes of the person assigning the ranks. Thus, as another example, the person whose rankings are depicted under (*b*) may feel that politician *A* is relatively sincere, whereas the remaining ones are on the whole an insincere lot. Again the rankings do not provide this information.

Notice that the rank ordering of the politicians under (*a*) and (*b*) is the same. However, as should be clear on the basis of the foregoing assumptions, it would be a mistake to conclude that the two rank orders reflect equal degrees of perceived sincerity. It is even possible that in some "absolute," although unknown sense, the person whose rankings are depicted in (*b*) perceived politician *A* as less sincere than the lowest ranked politician by the person whose rankings are depicted in (*a*), i.e., politician *F*.

The gist of the preceding discussion is that measures that call for rank orderings by respondents may be useful for studying *intraindividual* hierarchies, preferences, and the like. Such measures should *not*, however, be used for the purpose of *interindividual* comparisons. Cattell (1944) coined the term "ipsative" to refer to measures that can be meaningfully interpreted *intra*individually, as contrasted with "normative" measures that can be interpreted *inter*individually.

INTERVAL SCALE

An interval level of measurement is achieved when numbers are assigned to objects so that, in addition to satisfying the requirements of the ordinal level, differences between the numbers may be meaningfully interpreted with respect to the attribute being measured. In other words, on an interval scale, constant units of measurement are used, affording meaningful expressions of differences between objects, comparisons of such differences, as well as the conversion of differences into ratios.

The example of an interval scale most often given is that of a measure of temperature. On a Celsius scale, for example, 60° centigrade is not merely more than 50°, but it is 10° more. Because the units on the scale are constant, it is also true that the difference between 60° and 50° is equal to the difference between, say, 90° and 80°, or the difference between 60° and 50° is twice that between 37° and 32°.

An interval scale is invariant under linear transformations:

$$X' = a + b\,X$$

where X' is the transformed score, a and b are constants, and X is the score to be transformed. In words: Multiplying scores on an interval scale by a constant (b) and/or adding a constant (a) to them does not alter the nature of the interpretation of differences or ratios of differences on the scale. As is well known, temperatures measured on a Celsius scale may be transformed into a Fahrenheit scale using the following:

$$F = 32 + 1.8C$$

where F and C are degrees Fahrenheit and Centigrade, respectively.

Note carefully that although it is meaningful to express *differences* in scores on an interval scale as ratios, it is *not* meaningful to do so for the scores themselves. The reason is that the zero point on an interval scale is arbitrary, hence the admissibility of adding a constant to scores on such a scale. To illustrate the fallacy of expressing scores on an interval scale as a ratio, consider the following: 80°C is twice as hot as 40°C. The statement is fallacious, because the zero point on the Celsius scale has been arbitrarily set at the freezing of water. A change in the definition of the zero point will result in a change of this ratio. This is also evident when the previously mentioned temperatures are transformed into a Fahrenheit scale and expressed as a ratio, as can be seen here:

$$\frac{80°C}{40°C} \neq \frac{176°F}{104°F}$$

Bearing in mind this characteristic of the interval scale should serve as a safeguard against committing fallacies exemplified by the following exchange between Alice and the Red Queen (from Carroll, 1960):

"Are five nights warmer than one night, then?" Alice ventured to ask.
  "Five times as warm, of course."
  "But they should be five times as *cold*, by the same rule—"
  "Just so!" cried the Red Queen. "Five times as warm, *and* five times as cold—just as I'm five times as rich as you are, *and* five times as clever!" (pp. 222–223)

Turning to examples of sociobehavioral measures, consider the following: (a) On an interval scale of intelligence, individual A has a score of 120 and individual B has a score of 60. The zero point on the intelligence scale is necessarily arbitrary (how would one define zero intelligence, in an absolute sense? As being dead?); thus, it is erroneous to conclude that person A is twice as intelligent as B. (b) On an interval scale of achievement in social studies, person A answered correctly 60 multiple-choice items and person B answered correctly 15 such items. Although it is true that person A answered correctly four times as many items as B, this *does not* mean that A knows four times as much in social studies as does B. For the latter conclusion to be valid, it would be necessary to demonstrate that a zero score on the measure (i.e., answering none of the items correctly) signifies zero knowledge in social studies. Needless to say, such a demonstration is impossible when items on a measure are meant to represent a domain, an almost infinite one, as is the case with most measures in the sociobehavioral sciences.

RATIO SCALE

A ratio level of measurement is achieved when, in addition to the requirements of the interval level, a true, or absolute, zero point can be determined. That is, zero means no amount of the attribute measured. The term ratio refers to the fact that, on such a scale, the ratio of any two scores is independent of the units of the scale. Stated differently, the ratio of any two scores is invariant when the scores are multiplied by a constant, thereby changing the units of the scale. Prime examples of ratio scales are measures of weight and height. On a measure of weight it is meaningful, for example, to say that an object weighing 30 pounds is three times as heavy as one weighing 10 pounds, and this ratio will not change when weight is expressed in other units (e.g., ounces, kilograms). Or, a person who is 6 feet tall is 1.2 times taller than one who is 5 feet tall, and this ratio is invariant under changes in the unit of length (e.g., inches, yards, meters). From the preceding, it follows that a ratio scale is invariant under the following transformation:

$$X' = a X$$

where X' is the transformed score, a is a positive constant, and X is the score to be transformed. Note that only such a transformation will not change the zero point and will preclude negative values. Addition of a constant, for example, will shift the zero point, thereby changing the ratio of transformed scores. Thus, a person weighing 180 pounds is twice as heavy as one weighing 90 pounds, and this ratio will not change when these weights are transformed as a result of multiplication by a constant. However, add a constant, say, 40 to the two weights, and their ratio will change. That is,

$$\frac{180}{90} \neq \frac{180 + 40}{90 + 40}$$

Ratio scales are not often encountered in sociobehavioral sciences, although they are not unheard of. The measurement of reaction time (e.g., on perceptual–motor tasks) is an example of a ratio scale used in psychological research.

INDICATORS AND LEVELS OF MEASUREMENT

Most measurement is indirect. That is, the phenomenon of interest is not measured directly but is instead inferred from an indicator it presumably affects or from one with which it is correlated. The use of the expansion of a column of mercury as an indicator of temperature is an example of the former. In sociobehavioral research, indicators are used extensively as measures of constructs (e.g., motivation, aggression, job satisfaction). It is because of such usage that a detailed discussion of indicators will have to await the presentation of construct validation (Chapter 4).

In the present context, we would like only to demonstrate that the determination of the measurement level of a construct is predicated *not* on the units of what is taken as its indicator but on the nature of the relation between the indicator and the construct. Thus, the units of an indicator may, for example, comprise an interval, or even a ratio, scale. However, when used as a measure of a given construct, the units of the indicator may constitute an ordinal scale only. Carter (1971), who provided an insightful discussion of this issue, used as an example income and education as measures of social status:

Certainly each, income and education, is a defensible measure (indeed a ratio one) of *something*. Income, as reported, is a measure of income; and education, as reported, is a measure of the number of years spent in approved classrooms. But how are these related to status? (p. 14)

Carter discussed in detail the untenable assumption underlying most uses of income and education as indicators of social status, namely that the relation between the latter and each of the former is linear. What this assumption amounts to is that equal differences in income, say, reflect equal differences in social status. However, to use Carter's example, the difference in social status between people whose income is $10,000 and $1,000 is not at all comparable to the difference between people whose income is $210,000 and $201,000. That the same holds true with respect to years of education is evident when one considers the potentially considerable differences in consequences (e.g., probability of employment, type of job, level of income) of, say, a one year difference in education at the following points: (a) between 10 and 11, (b) between 11 and 12 (the latter taken to mean graduation from high school), (c) between 15 and 16 (the latter taken to mean graduation from college).

In conclusion, our discussion of levels of measurement was limited to their relevance for the interpretation of scores. We cannot deal here with the very important issues and procedures regarding the determination of the level of measurement of a given approach, as this would require detailed discussions of measurement theories and scaling models. The literature in this area is extensive and mathematically sophisticated. Among other things, models and procedures have been developed in attempts to convert rank-order responses to an interval scale, or an interval scale to a ratio scale. For introductory presentations, see Allen and Yen (1979, Chapter 8); Anderson, Basilevsky, and Hum (1983); Nunnally (1978, Chapter 2). Following are some books devoted to scaling models and techniques in general or to their use in a specific area (e.g., attitude measurement): Andrich (1988), Bock and Jones (1968), Coombs (1964), Dunn-Rankin (1983), Dawes (1972), Edwards (1957b), Kruskal and Wish (1978), Maranell (1974b), Torgerson (1958), and van der Ven (1980). (See also Chapter 6 of this book and the references given therein.)

MEASUREMENT AND STATISTICS

People who have little knowledge of measurement and statistics tend to confuse or equate the two. This is particularly true of those who are uncomfortable with formulas, equations, numbers, and the like. Having endured a course in statistics, they not only do not see the need but also resist taking a course in measurement, which they perceive as a different name for the same drudgery. This attitude may explain, in part, the lack of understanding and almost utter disregard of the role of measurement in scientific inquiry manifested by many students and professionals in sociobehavioral sciences.

Two aspects of the relation between measurement and statistics will be considered: (a) measurement as a source of the numbers used in statistical analysis, and (b) levels of measurement and the method of statistical analysis.

MEASUREMENT AS SOURCE OF NUMBERS

Stated succinctly, measurement supplies the numbers used in statistical analyses. A researcher measures one or more variables (e.g., intelligence, socioeconomic status, race, sex) and uses the numbers thus obtained in simple or complex statistical analyses to describe or summarize phenomena, to estimate parameters, and test hypotheses regarding the phenomena under investigation. It should, therefore, come as no surprise that the nature and quality of measures affect various aspects of the statistical analysis (e.g., whether and to what extent estimates of parameters are biased). Above all, the interpretation and meaningfulness of results obtained in a statistical analysis cannot be divorced from the properties of the measures used to generate the numbers in the first place.

Although a truism, it appears necessary to remind researchers and consumers of research that when a set of meaningless numbers is subjected to a statistical analysis, the results are still meaningless. The danger of overlooking this truism is becoming increasingly greater as a result of the growing use of complex analytic techniques (e.g., factor analysis, discriminant analysis, multivariate analysis of variance) because of their ready availability to anyone possessing the rudimentary skills necessary to use various computer programs for data analysis. Faced with reams of output bristling with all sorts of indices and tests of statistical significance, it is very easy to become oblivious to the meaning of the numbers that were fed into the computer.[5]

Regrettably, the impression one might form on the basis of much of sociobehavioral research is that, regardless of how they were obtained and what they mean, the numbers are grist to a statistical mill. Moreover, one might even be led to believe that by the use of statistics one can somehow transform meaningless numbers into something meaningful and that the more complex and sophisticated the analysis, the more meaningful that something is bound to be. The deleterious consequences of such an orientation are incalculable. A researcher can mask, even bury beyond a trace, any and all deficiencies in data by subjecting them to a variety of sophisticated statistical analyses. The "results" thus obtained may have little or nothing to do with what it is the researcher claims to be studying, although this may not be apparent to him or her, nor to readers of the research report.

We believe that most researchers are not intent upon deceiving their readers; when they engage in statistical acrobatics to the point of self-delusion, they do so because of a lack of understanding of the role of measurement in research and/or because of mistaken beliefs in almost "magical" powers of statistical analysis. Be that as it may, the ready availability of computer programs for the performance of most complex statistical analyses has led to a sharp increase in their misapplication, often resulting in multilayers under which data of questionable quality, even meaningless data, are submerged. The impression that researchers and their readers roam in a fantasy world populated by factors, components, loadings, patterns, equations, functions, and so on is often inescapable.

Particularly troublesome are research reports in which data analysis is based on summary indices whose quality cannot be assessed, because little or no information is provided about the elements that went into each of the indices. A common occurrence is the use of total scores on multi-item measures in complex analyses (e.g., factor analysis, structural equation models—see Chapters 22 through 24) without providing information necessary to assess the value or meaningfulness of the total scores in the first place. The tendency to sum scores across items without checking whether or not one may be adding apples and oranges is

---

[5]This and related issues are discussed in Chapter 16.

unfortunately prevalent and is a consequence of the lack of attention to and concern with measurement issues of which we spoke previously.

Our purpose in the preceding was to draw your attention to the importance of carefully scrutinizing measures used in a research study. Effects of specific aspects of measures (e.g., validity, reliability) on statistical analyses are taken up, as necessary, in various parts of the book.

LEVELS OF MEASUREMENT AND METHOD OF ANALYSIS

We turn now to a consideration of measurement and statistics from another perspective—one that has generated a great deal of controversy, often emotionally charged, among psychometricians, statisticians, and authors concerned with design and analysis of research in sociobehavioral sciences. The controversy may be traced to the work of Stevens (e.g., 1951) in which he proposed a classification of "permissible statistics" (p. 25), depending on the level of measurement (see above) of the measures used. Thus, for example, he argued that means and standard deviations should not be calculated for measures that are on an ordinal level.

The literature on the relation between levels of measurement and statistics is extensive, with some authors strongly defending and expounding Stevens's position, and others rejecting it with varying degrees of acrimony or ridicule. Burke (1963) provided a good overview and discussion of the positions of the two camps—the "measurement directed," and the "measurement independent." Following are but a few examples from exchanges on this issue, aimed at conveying the emotional reactions it evokes among some of the disputants (see Stine, 1989, for a recent attempt to rebut Stevens's critics).

Introducing his discussion of "Scale dependent mistakes," Wolins (1982) wrote: "S.S. Stevens (1951), a famous psychologist, tore loose a concept from its roots in physics and laid it on to psychology. Without roots it rotted and made a big stink. We are still trying to clean up the mess" (p. 29). Reviewing a book on measurement and statistics structured along the lines of Stevens's classification of scales and statistics, Kaiser (1960b) concluded: "We have a carelessly written book with a density of errors . . . , confounded by a naive devotion to Stevens' scales of measurement, and apparently written in relatively thoroughgoing ignorance of modern statistical theory" (p. 413).

Lord (1953) used the form of a satirical tale to ridicule the "measurement-directed" position. Briefly, he told of a professor whose guilt feelings about his practice of calculating means and standard deviations on scores that were on an ordinal level led to a nervous breakdown and forced retirement. In appreciation for past services, the university gave the professor the concession for selling the "football numbers," along with a large supply of cloth numbers and a vending machine. All went well, until the machine was apparently tampered with, resulting in the freshman team being sold numbers that, they protested, were too low. In his efforts to determine what happened, the professor sought the help of a statistician, who without much ado proceeded to perform all sorts of calculations including the mean and standard deviations of the numbers. Horrified, the professor protested that, being football numbers, they did not even constitute an ordinal scale, to which the statistician responded: "The numbers don't know that" (p. 751). He went on, explaining: "Since the numbers don't remember where they came from, they always behave just the same way, regardless" (p. 751). As you have probably guessed, the encounter with the statistician led to a complete cure. The professor resumed his teaching, and calculated means and standard deviations of students' scores without the slightest reservation, not to mention guilt feelings.

The reason we repeated the story is that the statistician's line, quoted above, has become almost a battle cry for the "measurement-independent" position, usually taking the form: "the numbers do not know where they came from" (e.g., Gaito, 1980, p. 564). The truth of this statement is, of course, undeniable. This, however, does not mean that the person interpreting the numbers is absolved of the responsibility of knowing where the numbers came from. This is illustrated by the following anecdote related by Stamp (1929):

Harold Cox tells a story of his life as a young man in India. He quoted some statistics to a Judge, an Englishman, and a very good fellow. His friend said, "Cox, when you are a bit older, you will not quote Indian statistics with that assurance. The Government are very keen on amassing statistics—they collect them, add them, raise them to the *n*th power, take the cube root and prepare wonderful diagrams. But what you must never forget is that every one of those figures comes in the first instance from the *chowty dar* (village watchman), who just puts down what he damn pleases." (pp. 258–259)

Interestingly, "measurement-independent" authors, who almost invariably quote Lord to buttress their position, generally fail to mention his response to critics of his original statement. Referring to his original statement, Lord (1954) said: "It would be unfortunate if what has been written here were to lead anyone to ignore the very serious pitfalls actually present" (p. 265). After offering illustrations of statements that *do* and *do not* require assumptions about equal intervals, Lord wrote:

The conclusion to be drawn is that the utmost care must be exercised in interpreting the results of arithmetic operations upon nominal and ordinal numbers; nevertheless, in certain cases such results are capable of being rigorously and usefully interpreted, at least for the purpose of testing a null hypothesis. (p. 265)

One may manipulate numbers to one's heart's content, but substantive interpretation of results obtained by the manipulation of numbers is predicated on the meaning attached to the assignment of the numbers to the objects, that is, the measurement model. We strongly concur with Hays (1988), who said: "Only the users of the statistical result, the investigators and their readers, can judge the reinterpretability of the numerical result into a valid statement about the properties of things. . . . [S]tatistics as a discipline is quite neutral on this issue" (pp. 71–72).

As was pointed out earlier, the level of a scale is to be determined within a given substantive context. It is "not something that is decided by a commissar of scales on the basis of whether it feels right to him to call it one thing rather than another" (Cliff, 1982, p. 12). Nor, for that matter, is the appropriateness of a statistical analysis to be determined by a commissar of statistics.

The vast majority of researchers and their readers are probably not concerned at all with the issues we have been discussing. We believe this to be a consequence of the deplorable lack of attention to measurement issues that we discussed earlier. There is, however, a relatively large group of authors who, after careful and thoughtful consideration of the two positions discussed previously, conclude that strict adherence to either is neither warranted by the state of measurement in sociobehavioral sciences nor useful when considering consequences of violations of assumptions underlying specific statistical methods. We believe this pragmatic orientation is most reasonable and conclude this section with some comments about it.

We note, first, that in his later writings, even Stevens (1968) endorsed, to some extent, a pragmatic orientation. Dealing with the two positions under the heading: "Reconciliation and New Problems," Stevens spoke of "the pragmatic problem of appraising the wages of transgression" (p. 851) and concluded:

The question is thereby made to turn, not on whether the measurement scale determines the choice of a statistical procedure, but on how and to what degree an inappropriate statistic may lead to a deviant conclusion. . . . By spelling out the costs, we may convert the issue from a seeming proscription to a calculated risk. (p. 852)

The major source of the controversy regarding measurement and statistics in sociobehavioral research is whether most of the measures used are on an ordinal or an interval level. The pragmatists (e.g., Borgatta, 1968; Borgatta & Bohrnstedt, 1981; Gardner, 1975; Labovitz, 1967, 1972; Nunnally, 1978) argued cogently that, although most measures used in sociobehavioral research are not clearly on an interval level, they are not strictly on an ordinal level either. In other words, most of the measures used are not limited to signifying "more than," or "less than," as an ordinal scale is, but also signify degrees of differences, although these may not be expressible in equal interval units. Prime examples are summated measures of achievement, mental ability, attitudes, and the like. Such measures occupy an intermediate, "grey" (Gardner, 1975, p. 53) region between an interval and an ordinal level, and to treat them as if they were on an ordinal level may lead to a serious loss of information.

Some authors have addressed the issue of the relation between measurement and statistics from the perspective of the consequences of violating assumptions underlying the latter. For example, Nunnally (1978) argued and attempted to demonstrate that "usually no harm is done in most studies in the behavioral sciences by employing methods of mathematical and statistical analysis which take intervals seriously" (p. 17). Labovitz (1967, 1970, 1972), who is one of the most outspoken advocates of this orientation, stated:

Empirical evidence support the treatment of ordinal variables *as if* they conform to interval scales . . . . Although some small error may accompany the treatment of ordinal variables as interval, this is offset by the use of more powerful, more sensitive, better developed, and more clearly interpretable statistics with known sampling error. (1970, p. 515)

It is important to note that the orientation exemplified by Labovitz and Nunnally does not mean that "anything goes, regardless of the quality of the measures." Nevertheless, it is not without its critics (see, for example, Wilson, 1971). Regardless of one's position on this matter, it remains true that there is no substitute for high quality measures. The improvement of the quality of measures should be one of the top priorities in sociobehavioral sciences.

CONCLUDING REMARKS

We hope that this chapter has served to alert you to the crucial role of measurement in the scientific endeavor. This is particularly important, because the impression you might have gotten from reading research reports in sociobehavioral sciences is probably in sharp contrast to the one we have attempted to create. As indicated in Chapter 1, measurement issues are very frequently ignored, or treated cavalierly, almost mindlessly, in research reports. Measures seem to be used because they are "there," because someone else has used them, because nothing "better" is available. One cannot help but be amazed at the naive faith invested in what are at best crude measures by researchers who exhibit healthy skepticism, care, and sophistication with respect to other aspects of their studies (e.g., theoretical formulation, design, analysis).

Various authors have drawn attention to the lamentable state of measurement in research in diverse substantive areas. Referring to the indifference of many sociobehavioral scientists to measurement issues in the broad area of attitude research, Maranell (1974a) stated:

When measurement problems are ignored, the effects and the results are not unlike those that would be encountered by astronomers who are forced to use cracked lens and no calibration or surveyors who are forced to use rubber yardsticks or no yardsticks at all, or physicists with watches which run randomly fast and slow. (p. xii)

Reviewing the "state of the art" in consumer research, Jacoby (1978) declared:

Virtually no attempt has been made to identify the good measures and weed out the poor ones. . . . [M]ost of our measures are only measures because someone *says* that they are, not because they have been shown to satisfy standard measurement criteria (validity, reliability, and sensitivity). (p. 91)

Although research areas vary with respect to the quality of measures used in them, the foregoing observations are generally applicable to many, if not most, research areas in sociobehavioral sciences.

Chapter 3
Criterion-Related Validation

The present chapter and the next one are devoted to issues of validity in the broad context of measurement theory and practice. Following a brief overview of the meaning and definition of validity, the remainder of the chapter is addressed to criterion-related validation. The meaning of criterion and different types of criteria are discussed first. This is followed by a presentation of prediction, with special emphasis on predictive efficiency, differential prediction, and selection bias.

Validity: Meanings and Definitions

Even a cursory reading of books on measurement, research design, or reports of research studies in professional journals would suffice to see that the term validity is used differently by different authors and in different contexts. For example, the meaning of validity in a measurement context differs from that in a research design context (see Chapter 10). Moreover, within each of these contexts, one encounters different definitions of validity and distinctions among different types or kinds of validity.

It is interesting to note that a joint committee of several professional associations charged with the task of developing standards for educational and psychological measurement did not come up with a definition of validity. Instead, it offered what might be considered a characterization of validity, namely that it "refers to the appropriateness, meaningfulness, and usefulness of the specific inferences made from test scores. Test validation is the process of accumulating evidence to support such inferences" (American Psychological Association, 1985, p. 9).

A major difficulty with the preceding is in ascertaining what constitute "appropriate," "meaningful," and "useful" inferences—an almost impossible undertaking, requiring, among other things, definitions of these loaded terms and a delineation of conditions and means for their realization. Perhaps the best way to convey the complexity of such an endeavor is to point out that, notwithstanding the narrower terms "test scores" and "test validation," the committee's statement could be applied to the broad spectrum of scientific inquiry. In fact, as elaborated in this and the subsequent chapter, validation of measures is an instance of scientific inquiry, with all that it entails. Consequently much of what we say in Part 2 about science and scientific inquiry has direct bearing on what is entailed in the process of the validation of measures.

What does come through clearly from the committee's statement is that validity, or rather validation, refers *not* to a measure in question but to inferences made on the basis of scores obtained on it. In short, "One validates, not a test, but an *interpretation of data arising from a specified procedure*" (Cronbach, 1971, p. 447). (For a symposium on various aspects of the validation process, see Wainer & Braun, 1988.)

Accordingly, inferences may be more or less valid (appropriate, meaningful, useful), depending on the purpose, the respondents, and the circumstances for which they are made. For example, using scores on a given vocabulary test may afford more valid inferences about individuals' academic achievement than, say, predictions as to how well they will do in college or on a job. The validity of predictions will itself vary, depending on the type of college program or the type of job being considered. It is also clear that the same vocabulary test may be more or less valid, depending on respondents' age, ethnicity, race, educational background, to name but some factors. To minimize ambiguity, it is essential to specify, at the very least, for what, for whom, and under what circumstances are inferences from a set of scores being made.

Although the purposes for which a measure may be used may vary greatly, it is useful and possible to classify purposes into broad categories. A widely used tripartite classification related to validation of measures is: (a) content, (b) criterion, and (c) construct. Much of what follows in this and the subsequent chapter has to do with the meaning of these terms in the context of the validation process. Therefore, all we will do here is indicate what they refer to. Content refers to some domain of content (e.g., social studies, vocabulary, job performance). Criterion refers to some outcome (e.g., graduation from high school, absenteeism, delinquency). Construct refers to some trait or attribute (e.g., mental ability, attitude, motivation).

Whatever classification one chooses to adopt, it is important to bear in mind that validity is a "*unitary concept*" [italics added] (American Psychological Association, 1985, p. 9). Thus, although a classification according to types of inferences is convenient for organization and discussion purposes, it does not imply a set of mutually exclusive and exhaustive categories, *much less different types of validity.*

The last point bears emphasis in view of the fact that, until recently, discussions and reports of validity were couched in terms of *types*, with the above noted tripartite classification (content, criterion, and construct) being the dominant one for some time (see American Psychological Association, 1966, 1974). Even authors who disagreed with the conception of different types of validity reluctantly used them, because this is "what people in the field have traditionally done" (Ghiselli, Campbell, & Zedeck, 1981, p. 267).

Taking a strong stand against the notion of validity types, Dunnette and Borman (1979) warned that "the implication that validities come in different types leads to confusion and, in the face of confusion, oversimplification" (p. 483). In a perceptive discussion of validity, Guion (1980) asserted that the three "types" of validity are treated as "something of a holy trinity representing three different roads to psychometric salvation. If you cannot demonstrate one kind of validity, you have two more chances!" (p. 386).

Because the terms criterion and construct are currently used in connection with inferential and evidential validation processes, rather than for designation of types of validity, one runs the risk of slipping into the latter terminology.[1] Although we will try to guard against this, we

[1]For a comment on content and "content validity," see Chapter 4.

recognize that we may fail. In cases where our statements imply types of validity, we would like it understood that this was not our intention. *In sum, we believe that a classification of the validation process according to major purposes is convenient, provided the classification is not reified and provided one does not lose sight of the fact that the different purposes are interrelated facets of the same process.*

In view of the foregoing, you will probably not be surprised to learn that we were reluctant to present validity in two chapters. In the end, considerations of convenience have won out. We urge you to view this and the subsequent chapter as two aspects of the same unit.

CRITERION

Broadly speaking, a criterion is any variable (e.g., academic achievement, voting, aggression, productivity, drug use, absenteeism, delinquency) one wishes to explain and/or predict by resorting to information from another variable(s). Philosophers of science have been engaged in the study of explanation and prediction, with some (e.g., Hempel, 1965) maintaining that they are structurally and logically identical, and others (e.g., Scriven, 1959) contending that the two are distinct operations. Whatever one's stance on this issue, it remains true that there are circumstances in which one is able to predict a given phenomenon without being able to explain it and vice versa (for good discussions, see Doby, 1967, Chapter 4; Kaplan, 1964, Chapter IX).

Criterion-related validation focuses on prediction, the overriding concern being the degree of successful prediction of a criterion, regardless of whether or not it is possible to explain the process or processes leading to the phenomenon that is being predicted. Underscoring this point, Nunnally (1978) stated: "Thus if it were found that accuracy in horseshoe pitching correlated highly with success in college, horseshoe pitching would be a valid measure for predicting success in college" (p. 88; see also Cook & Campbell, 1979, p. 296).

The foregoing should not be construed as implying that a researcher or a practitioner interested in prediction is necessarily not interested in explanation. As Kaplan (1964) pointed out: "If we can predict successfully on the basis of a certain explanation we have good reason, and perhaps the best sort of reason, for accepting the explanation" (p. 350). Yet, as often happens in less developed sciences or in applied settings, it is possible and useful to predict phenomena, although explanations are either unattainable or are vague.

Applications of psychological measures for the purpose of prediction may be characterized as "psychotechnology" (Loevinger, 1957, p. 636) as contrasted with psychological theory. Examples of such applications abound. In work settings, for example, it is beneficial and useful for both employees and employers, although often in different degrees and for different reasons, to be able to predict who among applicants for a job are apt to succeed, accident prone, likely to be satisfied with the job, and the like. Such predictions are useful even when explanations of the phenomena are absent or elusive. In academic settings, it is useful and beneficial to predict for whom among applicants is there a higher probability of doing well in college, although the reasons for this may not be well understood, or even may be controversial. It may be worthwhile to use ear-canal hair and ear-lobe crease to predict coronary-artery disease (e.g., Elliott, 1983; Wagner et al., 1984), despite the diverse and contradictory explanations for the relations between the former and the latter.

The distinction between explanation and prediction should be borne in mind so as to avoid misinterpretations of research findings. This is especially true when results of a study designed for predictive purposes are interpreted as explanations of the phenomenon that is being predicted. This topic is discussed and illustrated in various chapters (e.g., Chapters 14 and 18). (See also, Pedhazur, 1982, Chapters 6–8.)

In sum, when the concern is with the use of predictors for the purpose of predicting criteria, issues of and approaches to criterion-related validation are preeminent. Before turning to these, it is necessary to discuss some aspects of the criterion.

NATURE AND TYPE OF CRITERIA

The selection of a specific criterion is determined largely by the values and goals of the person(s) making the selection. Whether it be productivity at a manufacturing plant, academic achievement, marital contentment, health, attitudes toward minorities, what counts is what is deemed important by the people who decide what the criterion is going to be in a given setting for given individuals.

Criteria permeate our lives. When we think about accomplishments or failures by ourselves or others, we are using, explicitly or implicitly, a criterion or criteria. This is most evident when we think about being successful at performing a given task or being good at a given job. Even when people appear to share a criterion, they often disagree about its definition. Thus, most people would probably agree that teachers, lawyers, doctors, judges, nurses, salespersons, truck drivers, and so on should be good, successful, effective at what they do. But there would probably be wide disagreement about the definitions of such adjectives.

It is probably because of the appearance of agreement about criteria, on the one hand, and the difficulty in defining them, on the other hand, that little attention is accorded them by individuals or institutions attempting to predict them. Fincher (1975) aptly labeled uncritical assumptions regarding the suitability of criteria as "audacious" (p. 495). And Jenkins (1946) noted that "psychologists in general tended to accept the tacit assumption that criteria were either given of God or just to be found lying about" (p. 93).

Regrettably, things have not changed much since Jenkins raised the question: "Validity for what?" Researchers still tend to specify a criterion in vague and global terms, and then search for predictors that will optimally predict it. When research thus conceived fails to live up to expectations, as it often does, it is usually the predictors that are faulted. It is, however, true that a program of prediction "can only be as good as [the] criterion" (Thorndike, 1949, p. 119). Moreover, "the Achilles' heel of criterion-related validity is, of course, the criterion" (Linn, 1984, p. 38).

The difficulties involved in attempts to arrive at an agreed upon definition of a criterion are well illustrated by the following incident. Some time ago, then Chief Justice Burger created a furor among lawyers when he stated that about half of the trial lawyers in the U.S. are inept and not qualified to represent their clients (see, for example, *The New York Times*, December 4, 1977). In an article entitled "Measuring competence: Debating an indefinable," Goldstein (1978) described the debates that took place at a convention of the American Bar Association in response to Burger's allegation. A motion calling upon the Chief Justice to either provide data in support of his allegation or to retract it was defeated at the convention. This was probably due to the realization by the majority of the delegates that no such data could be collected in the absence of an agreed upon quantifiable definition of competence.

It is not surprising that lawyers (or members of any profession that requires the performance of varied and complex tasks) cannot reach consensus about a definition of competence. Consider the following attempt by Simon H. Rifkind, a lawyer, to characterize a great trial lawyer. According to Rifkind, a great trial lawyer must have "an appetite for work, endurance, an elephantine memory, instant recall, uncanny perception of behavior, the gift of tongue, commanding presence and good voice" (quoted by Goldstein, 1978, p. E7).

Even if there were unanimity that Rifkind's characterization captures the essence of being a great trial lawyer, there would undoubtedly be considerable disagreement about the relative importance of its elements and even greater disagreement about the definition of each. Are, for example, "endurance," "uncanny perception of behavior," and "gift of tongue" equally important? Further, what is the definition of each? Although Rifkind's statement has a nice ring to it, its vagueness eludes a quantifiable definition.

The foregoing example can be multiplied with illustrations of attempts to define competence, success, effectiveness in other professions. It suffices, however, to explain why Rozeboom (1966) referred to the definition of the criterion as "a darkening mystery" (p. 194).

Because of difficulties in defining and quantifying criteria, individual researchers and institutions often resort to "criteria that are predictable rather than appropriate" (Wallace, 1965, p. 411). For example, there is a great deal of interest among educators, policy makers, and the public at large in what makes a "good" school. The same question is sometimes raised under the rubric of school effectiveness. Whatever the nomenclature, although all seem agreed that schools should be good or effective, there is little agreement about the definition of these terms, not to mention the efforts to measure good or effective schooling.

Many things about schools are relatively easy to observe and quantify; thus, they become, often by default, the criterion or criteria of good schooling. For example, it is more or less easy to observe the following: number of science laboratories in a school, number of books in the school library, class size, per pupil expenditure, teachers' salaries, number of administrators in the school, and mean scores on standardized achievement tests.

Note carefully that, in the preceding, reference was made only to some form of counting or quantification of the variables. Yet some of them are more accessible to quantification than others because of the potentially narrower range of definitions to which they are susceptible. Contrast, for example, number of books in the library and teachers' salaries. Clearly, the latter is open to a greater variety of definitions than the former.

Suppose now that one were not content with merely counting but were also to raise questions about, say, quality or utilization in reference to some or all of the variables noted above. This would lead to considerable complications. What, for example, makes for a good science laboratory? What good is it, if the teacher assigned to it is not qualified to use it properly? What good is a science laboratory, if it is not utilized or is underutilized? Then again, what constitutes utilization?

In the perennial search for the identification of good or effective schools, criteria vary and undergo changes not unlike those in fashions and fads in other spheres of society. Thus, in some places or at some times, the criterion of good schooling is students' performance on some cognitive variables (e.g., academic achievement), whereas at others it may be some indices of affective variables (e.g., motivation, attitudes).

Another area in which agreement about criteria is hard to come by is the outcome of therapy. Thus, Masters and Johnson, for example, have been criticized for their failure to delineate criteria of success of sex therapy. In response to critics, Dr. Masters is reported to have said: "I had to write the book in seven weeks and forgot to put in the final criteria" (Wolinsky, 1983, p. 2). Furthermore, at a news conference, Masters is reported to have stated:

The criteria applied to the cases presented in "Human Sexual Inadequacy" were actually that a woman needed to be orgasmic in at least 50 percent of her sexual opportunities to be considered a success.

For the treatment of impotence, the ability to get and keep erections on "more than 75 percent of coital occasions" was defined as successful therapy. (Brody, 1983b, p. A13)

It is not difficult to envision professionals and laypersons questioning such criteria in general as well as their specific aspects (e.g., the definition and measurement of being orgasmic).

RATING SCALES AS CRITERIA

Because of the difficulties in defining and measuring criteria, employers and researchers often resort to the use of rating scales. After all, what could be simpler than making up a few rating scales and asking supervisors to rate workers, students to rate professors, therapists to rate patients, patients to rate therapists, and so on? Among very serious problems frequently encountered in the use of rating scales as criteria are the following: (a) absence of definitions, or the presence of vague ones; (b) insufficient attention to, or utter disregard of, the perceptual processes underlying ratings; and (c) the manner in which ratings are combined to yield an overall index or several subindices. These and related issues are dealt with in Chapter 6 (see section on Rating Scales).

ULTIMATE AND INTERMEDIATE CRITERIA

From what was said thus far, it should be clear that the definition and measurement of criteria may be very difficult and are often elusive. This is particularly true of what may be termed ultimate criteria.

Ultimate Criteria.   Thorndike (1949, Chapter 5), who provided an excellent discussion of the criterion problem, had this to say about the ultimate criterion: "Such a criterion is ultimate in the sense that we cannot look beyond it for any higher or further standard in terms of which to judge the outcomes" (p. 121). An ultimate criterion is a final goal; it is what is deemed important in itself, hence warranting the efforts necessary to predict it. Thus, society considers it important to predict who, for example, will become a good (effective, sensitive) doctor (lawyer, pilot, teacher, secretary, administrator).

Even when a modicum of agreement about an ultimate criterion is reached, it should be recognized that criteria are multifaceted and dynamic. Hence, what might be considered good, or satisfactory, performance in reference to a given facet, in a given setting, at a given time, may be viewed as unsatisfactory in reference to another facet, in another setting, at another time.[2] For example, it is conceivable for the criterion of being a good physician to differ depending, among other things, on the time elapsed since graduation from medical school, type of specialty, and setting. In most instances, an ultimate criterion is a construct, an abstraction. Hence, what we say in the next chapter about constructs and construct validation applies equally to criteria that are constructs.

Because criteria are generally dynamic constructs, it is not surprising that a person judged high, successful, and the like at a given time and in a given setting may be judged as low, less successful, or failing at another time or in another setting. Indeed, conclusive judgment, if at all possible, of a person's status on an ultimate criterion may entail an assessment of the sum total of a lifetime's performance. As the poet Ovid put it:

No man should be called happy till his death;
Always we must await his final day,

---

[2]For discussions of the dynamic nature of job performance criteria, see Ghiselli and Haire (1960).

Reserving judgment till he's laid away.
(quoted by Montaigne, 1965, p. 54)

Intermediate Criteria. Because of the difficulties entailed in the definition and measurement of ultimate criteria, people frequently resort to what have been termed intermediate criteria (Cureton, 1951, pp. 634–635; Thorndike, 1949, Chapter 5). Notable examples of intermediate criteria are (a) grade-point average (GPA) in college; (b) graduation versus no graduation from college, a training program, and the like; and (c) performance on a certification examination.

As compared to ultimate criteria, intermediate criteria are (a) easier to define, (b) easier to measure, (c) more economical to obtain, and (d) require less time to wait for their assessment. Although these characteristics make intermediate criteria attractive, they should not be used without forethought and caution. The most important consideration in the choice of intermediate criteria is their relevance to the ultimate criteria of interest. Nevertheless, the use of intermediate criteria is frequently justified on the grounds that performance on them appears to be, or should be, related to performance on the ultimate criteria. Usually, such claims are based on logical analysis, or mere expectations, rather than on empirical evidence. It is important to bear in mind that a given intermediate criterion may have little or no relation with an ultimate criterion of interest. For example, it is possible that there is no relation between GPA in a professional school (e.g., law, medicine) and ultimate performance as a professional (whatever the specific definition). Whenever possible and feasible, data should be gathered in order to shed light on the relations between specific intermediate and ultimate criteria.

There are, however, situations in which intermediate criteria serve a useful purpose even when little is known about their relations with the ultimate criteria. This is the case when an intermediate criterion serves as a prerequisite for being qualified or permitted to practice in areas that constitute aspects of the ultimate criterion. Thus, because of the structure of accreditation and certification a person who fails to graduate from a medical school is prohibited from practicing medicine, regardless of his or her potential for becoming a "great" doctor. Similar examples come readily to mind. In the context of the present discussion, graduation versus no graduation from a professional school is the intermediate criterion one wishes to predict. This becomes particularly useful, even essential, when applicants compete for a limited number of openings or when training is costly in equipment, personnel, and time, to name but several factors.

Obviously, intermediate criteria may vary in importance, depending, among other things, on their costs, their relations to ultimate criteria, and whether they are prerequisites for practicing in a given profession or field. It is, therefore, important to always be mindful of the specific role an intermediate criterion is meant to play in a specific setting, thereby guarding against what might be an intermediate "tail" wagging an ultimate "dog."

We have concentrated on difficulties inherent in attempts to define and measure criteria in the hope of thereby underscoring that criterion-related validation depends, first and foremost, on a judicious selection of a criterion, as well as on a meaningful definition and measurement of it. Unfortunately, "it is very rare that the report of a criterion-related validity study says anything at all about the evaluation of the criterion measures themselves" (Guion, 1980, p. 395). As long as this state of affairs prevails, there is not much hope for criterion-related validation studies to make meaningful contributions in applied settings, much less to the development of theory in sociobehavioral sciences.

Earlier, it was pointed out that the criterion may be a construct. The same is true of the predictor. When either the predictor or the criterion or both are constructs, issues and procedures concerning constructs and construct validation (Chapter 4) become crucial in the process of criterion-related validation. This should serve as a reminder of what we said in the beginning of the chapter, namely that, although it is convenient to discuss aspects of the validation process separately, their interrelatedness should not be overlooked.

PREDICTION

Important and difficult problems concerning the definition and measurement of the criterion were discussed in preceding sections and will, therefore, not be repeated here. Instead, it will be *assumed* that a reasonable resolution of the criterion problem has been achieved and that it is desired to use one or more predictors to predict the criterion.

The basic approach in such situations is to study the relation between the predictor(s) and the criterion. For the case of a single predictor, the most frequently used index of the relation between it and a criterion is the Pearson product moment coefficient of correlation. Because our presentation is limited to the use of the Pearsonian correlation coefficient, it will be convenient to refer to it as the correlation coefficient or simply the correlation. In what follows, we assume that you have some familiarity with basic elements of correlation and simple regression analysis. These topics are presented in Chapter 17 to which you should refer whenever you are baffled by the presentation that follows or when you want an elaboration of it.

A correlation coefficient between a predictor and a criterion is referred to as a validity coefficient. Thus, having scores on a predictor X (e.g., mental ability, anxiety) and on a criterion Y (e.g., academic achievement, problem solving), r_{xy} is the validity coefficient. Although it is true that the higher the validity coefficient the "better," several points about the correlation coefficient that need to be borne in mind will be sketched.

As is discussed in Chapter 17, a major assumption underlying the correlation coefficient is that the relation between the variables under consideration is linear. What this means is that the points depicting scores of individuals on both variables follow a trend that can be characterized by a straight line. An example of a linear trend is given in (a) of Figure 3.1. In contrast, the trend in (b) is curvilinear. For illustrative purposes, assume that X = Anxiety, and Y = Problem Solving. Examine the two scattergrams of Figure 3.1 and notice that, if (a) were to reflect the situation, it would be concluded that increments in anxiety are associated with increments in problem solving. If, on the other hand, (b) were to reflect the situation, then it would be concluded that increments in anxiety are associated with increments in problem solving up to an optimal point (about a medium level of anxiety), beyond which increments in anxiety are associated with decrements in problem solving. Thus, moderate levels of anxiety appear to be beneficial for problem solving, whereas relatively high levels appear to be debilitating.

Using a Pearson correlation when data look like those in (b) of Figure 3.1 would result in a very low correlation, hence in an erroneous conclusion that anxiety and problem solving are not related. Clearly, the two variables are related, but the relation is not linear. The moral should be clear: At the very least, data should be plotted to note whether there is a serious departure from linearity (see Chapter 17). Methods of analysis of nonlinear relations are presented in Chapter 18, under the heading Curvilinear Regression Analysis.

A second point about the correlation coefficient to be borne in mind is that it is population specific. Other things being equal, the more homogeneous the population from which the sample under study was drawn, the lower the correlation. Conversely, the more hetero-

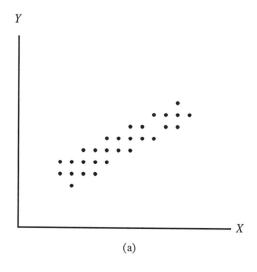

(a)

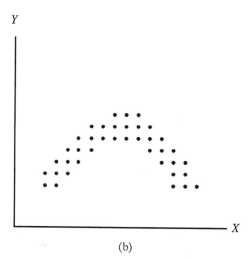

(b)

Figure 3.1

geneous the population from which the sample was drawn, the higher the correlation.[3] We return to this point below.

Finally, a correlation coefficient can be interpreted in a very general sense only. For example, assuming a positive correlation between two variables, it is possible to make general statements to the effect that those who are relatively high on one variable would probably be also relatively high on the other; those who are relatively low on one would probably be also relatively low on the other, and so forth. However, to be useful (e.g., for selection), a predictive system should enable one to make more specific predictions about expected status on the criterion, given status on the predictor. One of the most useful means

_____

[3]The validity of these statements is predicated on the use of probability sampling (see Chapter 15).

of accomplishing this is through the use of a prediction equation obtained in a regression analysis.

THE PREDICTION EQUATION

The distinction between regression and correlation models is discussed in Chapter 17. For present purposes, it will suffice to point out that it is only in the regression model that a distinction is made between a criterion and a predictor (or between a dependent and an independent variable),[4] leading, among other things, to a regression equation whereby a person's score on the criterion may be predicted on the basis of his or her score on the predictor. In the simplest case (i.e., linear regression with one predictor), the equation takes the following form:

$$Y' = a + bX \qquad (3.1)$$

where Y' is the predicted score; a is the intercept, that is, the point at which the regression line intercepts the Y ordinate; b is the regression coefficient or the slope of the regression line.

Following procedures we present in Chapter 17, the constants of the prediction equation (i.e., a and b) can be calculated and used to predict individuals' scores on the criterion on the basis of their scores on the predictor. In addition, it is possible to set confidence intervals around such predicted scores.

Our main concern here is with the use of the regression equation for the purpose of prediction. Assuming that Y is, for example, some index of productivity and that X is a score on an aptitude test, a selection officer may use the regression equation to predict applicants' Y scores on the basis of their X scores. Moreover, upon deciding on a minimum satisfactory performance on the criterion (Y), a cutting score on the predictor (X) can be determined, such that the probability of satisfactory performance for those selected (i.e., those scoring above the predictor cutting score) is maximized.

The preceding is not meant to imply that the determination of cutting scores on the predictor and the criterion is simple and straightforward. Various considerations, some of which are discussed in the next section, enter into such decisions. All we want to indicate here is that, given certain decisions, the regression equation may be used for the purpose of selection.

Before discussing some of the advantages of using regression equations instead of correlations in criterion validation studies, we comment on the concept of predictive efficiency, in the context of which we show how the choice of cutting scores affects the usefulness of the validity coefficient.

PREDICTIVE EFFICIENCY

Assume that Y is some criterion of interest (e.g., achievement, productivity, recovery) and that X is some relevant predictor (e.g., aptitude, personality trait, medical history). Assume also that all applicants, regardless of their status on X, were admitted (e.g., to college, a clinic) or hired. After the passage of some time (e.g., a year), scores on Y are also available. Accordingly, correlation and regression statistics can be calculated. In addition, applying the regression equation to X scores, predicted Y scores can be obtained.

---

[4]See Chapter 8 for definitions and classifications of variables.

You are probably wondering why one would bother to use a regression equation to predict Y scores when actual ones are available. This is done so that comparisons of actual and predicted performance may be made and predictive efficiency thereby ascertained. As is shown in Chapters 17 and 18, various results of regression analysis have bearing on this goal. The presentation here is limited to an introduction of basic concepts relevant to predictive efficiency. This will be done with the aid of Figure 3.2, where instead of plotting points depicting X and Y score combinations (i.e., scatterplot; see Chapter 17), ellipses are used. In other words, all the points are assumed to be enclosed in the ellipses.

Examine (a) of Figure 3.2 and notice the Y_c point on the ordinate. This is meant to represent the point above which performance on the criterion is deemed "satisfactory" (e.g., success, recovery, graduation). Look now at the abscissa and notice X_c, which is meant to represent a cutting score on the predictor. That is, if instead of admitting (hiring) all applicants a regression equation were to be used, then only those scoring above X_c would have been admitted (hired). Notice that by drawing lines emanating from the two cutting scores, the ellipse is divided into four areas, representing four possible combinations of predictor and criterion status.

In area A are people who on the basis of their scores on X would be predicted to be successful (i.e., above Y_c) and who are in fact successful. The term *valid positives* (VP) is used to refer to people in A. In area C are people who would be predicted to be not successful and who are in fact not successful. The term *valid negatives* (VN) is used to refer to people in C. Notice that both instances constitute what might be labeled "hits" when selection is based on the use of a regression equation.

The remaining two areas constitute "misses" when selection is based on the use of a regression equation. Specifically, people in B would be predicted to be successful but in fact are not successful. They are referred to as *false positives* (FP). People in D would be predicted to be not successful but in fact are successful. They are referred to as *false negatives* (FN).

In the following presentation, it will be convenient to work with proportions of people in a given area or combinations of areas. Thus, for example, when referring to people in $D + A$, we will speak of the proportion of people in these two areas, that is, $(D + A)/N$, where N is the total number of people (similarly for other areas or combinations of areas).

Now, $D + A$ indicates the proportion of people whose performance is "satisfactory" (i.e., above Y_c) when all applicants are admitted. This proportion is referred to as the *base rate* (BR), meaning the proportion of people who are "successful," regardless of their status on the predictor. Stated another way, BR is the proportion of people, from a given pool of applicants, expected to succeed when no selection, or random selection, is used. Because we are using proportions, $C + B$—the proportion of people expected not to succeed—is equal to $1 - BR$.

Assuming now that only applicants who score above X_c were selected, then $A + B$ would constitute the proportion selected and is referred to as the *selection ratio* (SR). The proportion of people not selected would, of course, be equal to $1 - SR$.

Taylor and Russell (1939), who were first to discuss predictive efficiency with reference to BR and SR, defined a success ratio as the ratio of A to $A + B$ [i.e., $A/(A + B)$], that is, the ratio of VP to applicants selected (i.e., $VP + FP$). Using the foregoing concepts, Taylor and Russell demonstrated that the same correlation coefficient may lead to greater or lesser predictive efficiency, depending on the BR, SR, or both. Also, that "very considerable improvement in selection efficiency . . . may be obtained with small correlation coefficients" (1939, p. 571).

The basic ideas advanced by Taylor and Russell are illustrated in Figure 3.2, where the

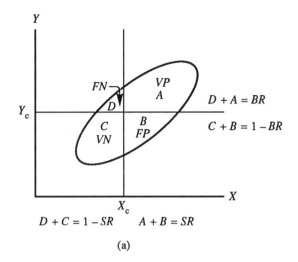

(a)

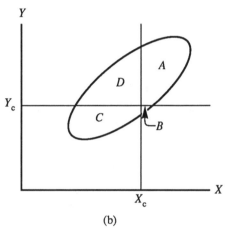

(b)

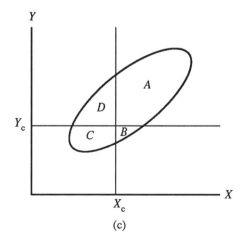

(c)

Figure 3.2

three ellipses are meant to depict the same scatterplot. The width of the ellipse signifies that the correlation between the predictor and the criterion (i.e., the validity coefficient) is relatively low. (Loosely speaking, the narrower the ellipse, the higher the correlation. When all the points fall on a straight line, the correlation is, of course, perfect. See Chapter 17.)

Consider, first, the effect of reducing the selection ratio (SR) while other things remain unchanged. An example of this can be seen by contrasting (a) and (b) of Figure 3.2, where A + B in the latter is smaller than in the former. Notice that this is accomplished by using a higher predictor cutting score in (b). As a result, the proportion of false positives (FP; area B) is smaller in (b) than in (a). Using Taylor and Russell's definition of the success ratio (see above), it is evident that the success ratio in (b) is larger than in (a).

By moving the cutting score on X farther to the right, that is by using an increasingly smaller SR, it is possible to eliminate false positives altogether, thereby achieving a 100% rate of success (i.e., a success ratio of 1.00). Of course, this may yield a considerably smaller number of applicants admitted, relative to the number sought in a given situation. Moreover, a reduction in the SR affects also the proportion of FN and VN. Note, in particular, that a reduction in SR leads to an increase in the proportion of FN—an issue discussed below.

Contrast now (a) with (c) of Figure 3.2 and notice that the SR is the same in both, but the BR is larger in the latter. This was accomplished by lowering the cutting score on Y (Y_c), which constitutes a less stringent definition of success. Recall that BR is the proportion of people who are successful when their status on the predictor is *not* used for the purpose of selection. Notice that the larger the BR (i.e., the larger the proportion of qualified applicants, or the lower the cutting score on Y), the smaller the proportion of FP (area B). However, there is an increase in the proportion of FN.

Notice also that the larger the BR, the less useful the predictor becomes. In the extreme case, when BR = 1.00 (i.e., all applicants are qualified, or when any performance, no matter how low, is deemed satisfactory), the predictor is not useful at all. If, under such circumstances, selection is necessary (e.g., when the number of openings is smaller than the number of applicants), then random selection would probably be fairest.

Assuming a bivariate normal distribution of X and Y scores, Taylor and Russell (1939) developed tables in which the success ratio (see above) is tabulated as a function of varying validity coefficients (r_{xy}), BR, and SR. Some examples excerpted from the Taylor and Russell tables are given in Table 3.1, where, under (a), SR and BR are constant whereas r_{xy} varies; under (b), SR and r_{xy} are constant whereas BR varies; under (c), BR and r_{xy} are constant whereas SR varies.

The figures in the body of the subtables are success ratios. For example, when SR = BR = .50, and r_{xy} = .20—see first row of subtable (a)—the success ratio is .56. This means an expected gain of .06, or 6%, in the success ratio as a result of using the predictor. (Without

Table 3.1

Excerpts from the Taylor and Russell Tables

	(a)		(b)		(c)
	SR = .50 BR = .50		SR = .50 r_{xy} = .40		BR = .50 r_{xy} = .40
r_{xy}		BR		SR	
0.20	0.56	0.10	0.16	0.10	0.78
0.30	0.60	0.30	0.41	0.30	0.69
0.60	0.70	0.70	0.81	0.70	0.58

Note: SR = Selection Ratio; BR = Base Rate; r_{xy} = validity coefficient. Figures in body of the subtables are success ratios. For explanations, see text.

the use of the predictor, the expected success ratio is equal to the *BR*—.50 in the present example.) Thus, even a relatively low validity coefficient yields an increase in the success ratio that would be deemed meaningful in various situations.

Compare now the first rows of (*a*) and (*b*). In both, the gain in the success ratio is .06. (Without the use of a predictor, the expected success ratio for a *BR* = .10 is .10.) But, whereas the validity coefficient in (*a*) is .2, that in (*b*) is .4. This, then, demonstrates what was said previously, namely that the predictive efficiency of a given validity coefficient depends on other factors (i.e., *BR* and *SR*). Other things being equal, the greatest gains in the success ratio will be obtained when *BR* = *SR* = .50.

When *SR* = .50, r_{xy} = .40, and *BR* = .30 (see *b*), the success ratio is .41—a gain of .11, or 11%, as compared with a selection process that is not based on the predictor. Notice that when *BR* and r_{xy} are constant (see *c*), a decrease in *SR* results in an increase in the success ratio. For example, the estimated success ratio is .58 when *SR* = .70, and .78 when *SR* = .10.[5]

Success, with respect to predictive efficiency, as defined by Taylor and Russell and as used in the preceding examples, refers to the gain in the proportion of *VP* that results from using a predictor in the selection process. This type of definition is probably most useful from the perspective of an employer or an institution interested in maximizing *VP*'s, but its use is not without costs.

Berkson (1947), for example, defined cost as the proportion of applicants who would be successful, although they score below the cutting score on the predictor and are, therefore, predicted to be not successful (i.e., False Negatives; see area *D* of Figure 3.2). It was pointed out earlier that when the success ratio is increased as a result of decreasing the *SR* (selection ratio), there is a concomitant increase in the proportion of *FN* (false negatives). Needless to say, *FN* are of particular concern for applicants who are rejected on the basis of their score on the predictor but who would have been successful had they been hired or admitted. Such individuals would certainly challenge Taylor and Russell's definition of success, as would people who are concerned with the cost to society as a consequence of underutilization of talent. It was also noted earlier that a reduction in *SR*, while holding other factors constant, results in an increase in *VN* (valid negatives), which Berkson (1947) labeled utility.

Depending on the specific purposes of a given study, it may be desired to direct efforts toward minimizing certain types of errors. For example, Loeber and Dishion (1983), who use the approach presented above in their review of studies dealing with the prediction of delinquency, point out that for judicial decisions about guilt, one would want to minimize false negatives, "that is, the predictors should not miss youths who are actual delinquents" (p. 70). If on the other hand, the concern is with treatment or prevention, one would want to minimize false positives, that is, those "seemingly at risk but who do not become delinquent" (p. 70).

The foregoing presentation was meant to serve as an introduction to the complex issues of prediction and definitions of outcomes of prediction. Our main aim was to demonstrate that it is unwise to rely solely on validity coefficients and that judgments about predictive efficiency and success depend on the specific definitions of these concepts. For additional discussions and extensions, see Cronbach (1971), Meehl and Rosen (1955), and Sechrest (1963). An extensive and sophisticated treatment of the role of tests in selection is given by Cronbach and Gleser (1965).

---

[5]The Taylor and Russell tables are reproduced in Ghiselli et al. (1981), who provide a good discussion of the concepts presented here. For additional discussions of these concepts, see Allen and Yen (1979, pp. 101–107), Wiggins (1973, pp. 240–250). In an extension of the concepts discussed here, Naylor and Shine (1965) provide tables for determining the increase in the mean on the criterion (instead of the proportion successful as given in the Taylor and Russell tables) as a result of using a predictor.

RANGE RESTRICTION

In order to elaborate on various possible outcomes of a selection process, it was assumed in the preceding sections that all applicants were admitted or hired. For obvious reasons, such studies are rarely carried out. In most instances, some selection takes place, and validity coefficients are calculated using scores for the select group. Because a select group is generally more homogeneous than the entire pool of applicants, validity coefficients calcu-lated using data obtained from the former are smaller (often considerably) than what they would be had data from the latter been used (for some examples, see Linn & Dunbar, 1982). This is illustrated in Figure 3.3, where X is the predictor, and Y is the criterion. The entire scatterplot is meant to depict the relation between the predictor and the criterion when data are available for all applicants. When, however, data are available only for applicants above a cutting score on the predictor, X_c, the scatterplot would look like the area to the right of the vertical line in Figure 3.3. The correlation based on the data in this area would be smaller than one based on the data in the entire scatterplot. Reduction in the magnitude of a correlation due to selection is generally referred to as the effect of range restriction on the correlation coefficient.

Broadly speaking, there are three kinds of range restriction: (a) direct, (b) indirect, and (c) ambiguous. Direct restriction occurs when selection is done on the basis of a cutting score on

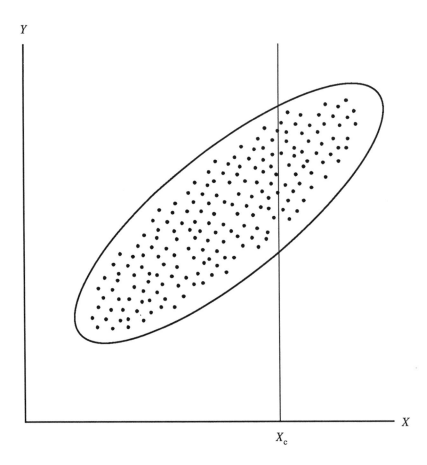

Figure 3.3

the predictor. For example, a college may admit only those students whose scores on the verbal part of the Scholastic Aptitude Test (SAT–V) are above a cutting score. This is the simplest form of range restriction (it is depicted in Figure 3.3). Consider now a situation in which a college admits students whose grade-point average (GPA) in high school is above a cutting score and that at a later date it is desired to study the validity of the SAT–V to predict GPA in college for those students who have been admitted. Because high school GPA and SAT–V tend to be positively correlated, a range restriction of the former tends to restrict the range of the latter, hence the term indirect restriction to refer to this process.

The most prevalent situation of range restriction, however, is one which was labeled above as ambiguous. This is meant to imply that, although one may have hunches or some knowledge about variables that are operating in a selection process, there is not sufficient valid information about the variables and about how they combine to produce the select group. A college may, for example, use a cutting score on SAT–V for admission but not adhere to it strictly. Exceptions may be made because of, say, minority status, extracurricular activities, relations to alumni of the college, and the like.

An even more intractable and frequently occurring situation is when a process of self-selection takes place. For example, a given college may adhere strictly to a cutting score on SAT–V but only some of the applicants who are notified that their applications have been approved choose to attend.

Although there are formulas available for correction for range restriction (see, for example, Ghiselli et al., 1981, pp. 296–306; Lord & Novick, 1968, pp. 140–148; Thorndike, 1982, pp. 208–215), they are applicable in very limited and simple situations. For example, Linn, who has written extensively on the topic of range restriction (e.g., 1968, 1983a, 1983b), has shown that attempts to correct the correlation coefficient under conditions labeled ambiguous above, may result in serious bias.

Finally, it is more meaningful to concentrate on the regression equation than on the validity coefficient. This issue is discussed in detail in the next section. For now, it will only be pointed out that under certain conditions (e.g., direct restriction) the validity coefficient will vary as a result of range restriction, whereas the regression equation will remain relatively stable. Look back at Figure 3.3 and try to visualize, or actually draw, the line for the regression of Y on X, and note that it will be about the same whether you do so for the entire scatterplot or only for the area above the cutting score. Actually, the formula for correcting the correlation coefficient for direct restriction of range is based on the assumption that the regression coefficient (b_{yx}) is unchanged when the range of the predictor is restricted (see, for example, Ghiselli et al., 1981, p. 296).

DIFFERENTIAL PREDICTION

The discussion of predictive efficiency in the preceding section was limited to situations in which all applicants are treated as if they belonged to the same group. Often, however, it is necessary or of interest to distinguish among applicants on the basis of their membership in some defined groups. For criterion-related validation, it may be desired to determine whether a predictor is equally predictive, for example, for males and females, or for whites, blacks, and Hispanics. This becomes particularly crucial when the purpose is to determine whether there is bias towards members of a given group in the selection process (see below). Thus, when applicants are viewed as belonging to more than one group, the concern becomes that of differential prediction.

There is an extensive literature dealing with what has been termed "single group validity" and "differential validity." Because the former concept was ill conceived (Cronbach, 1980), it will not be discussed. Differential validity refers to differences in validity coefficients obtained in different groups. The literature on differential validity will not be cited, because the validity coefficient is only one aspect of possible differences among groups that might lead to differential prediction. That this is so can be seen from the following expression of the regression equation to predict Y from X:

$$Y' = [\bar{Y} - r_{xy}\frac{s_y}{s_x}\bar{X}] + [r_{xy}\frac{s_y}{s_x}]X \qquad (3.2)$$

$$= \qquad a \qquad + \quad bX$$

where Y' = predicted Y score; $\bar{Y}$ and $\bar{X}$ = mean of Y and X respectively; r_{xy} = validity coefficient; s_y and s_x = standard deviation of Y and X respectively. As is indicated under (3.2), the first term (enclosed in the brackets) is the intercept (a), and the second term is the regression coefficient (b).[6] From (3.2), it is evident that the validity coefficient (r_{xy}) is only one of the elements of the regression equation for the prediction of scores on the criterion (Y) on the basis of scores on the predictor (X). Consequently, exclusive reliance on r_{xy}, as is done in studies of differential validity, is imprudent.

Differential prediction refers to differences in regression equations for different groups. Groups may differ in regression coefficients (b's) and/or intercepts (a's). From (3.2), it can be seen that, for two or more groups, the validity coefficients may, for example, be identical, and yet their regression coefficients may be more or less different, depending on the standard deviations. Conversely, the b's for different groups may be identical, but the validity coefficients may differ from one another. Since the intercepts (a's) are a function of the b's and the means, it follows that groups whose regression equations have identical intercepts may have different regression coefficients and/or validity coefficients.

In the hope of clarifying these ideas, we present a relatively simple example in Figure 3.4. Assume that the plots represent scores for females and males on a predictor (X) and a criterion (Y). Examine the two swarms of points and visualize two regression lines that fit

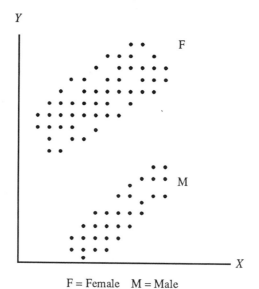

F = Female   M = Male

Figure 3.4

them (you may find it useful to actually insert such lines). Clearly, the regression coefficients (b's) are very similar in the two groups, whereas the intercepts (a's) are quite different. Further, the validity coefficient for females is smaller than that for males (the swarm of points for females is wider than that for males).

Now, relying exclusively on the validity coefficient, it would be concluded that X is a more valid predictor for males than for females, but using separate regression equations, females would be predicted to perform higher than their male counterparts. Assuming it is concluded that the b's are the same, then for any given X, the predicted Y for females will exceed that for males by an amount equal to the difference between the two intercepts (see next section, Comparing Regression Equations).

The example of Figure 3.4 also illustrates potential hazards of using a single correlation or a single regression equation when the subjects under study belong to groups that differ in some relevant ways on the variables under consideration (see The Nature of Groups Studied, and Selection Bias, below).

COMPARING REGRESSION EQUATIONS

In the preceding section, data for two groups were compared by inspection. Methods for testing differences among regression equations are presented in Chapter 21. For present purposes, a brief delineation of how this is done is given.[7] One begins by testing whether differences among the b's are statistically significant. Recalling that the b's indicate the slopes of the regression lines, it follows that a conclusion that differences among the b's are statistically not significant is tantamount to a conclusion that the regression lines are parallel. Under such circumstances, it makes sense to proceed to the second stage of the analysis, namely test differences among intercepts. If it is found that differences among intercepts are statistically significant, separate regression equations are developed, such that the b's are the same (i.e., a common, or pooled-within groups, b; see Chapter 21) for all groups whereas the a's differ for the different groups. If, on the other hand, it is concluded at the second stage of the analysis that differences among the a's are statistically not significant, a single regression equation is developed and used for members of all groups under consideration.

As discussed in Chapter 21, when it is concluded that differences among b's are statistically significant, it is not meaningful to test differences among intercepts. Instead, separate regression equations are developed for the groups involved. When it is desired to predict the criterion score for a given individual, the regression equation for the group to which he or she belongs is used.

To further explicate these ideas, we use Figure 3.5, where the points representing individual scores are not displayed so as not to clutter up the diagrams. Instead, regression lines are depicted. For ease of presentation, two groups and one predictor are used. As is discussed in Chapter 21, the approach described here applies to any number of groups and/or any number of predictors.

Some possible differences between regression equations are depicted in Figure 3.5. The labels A and B may refer to any two groups (e.g., males and females, blacks and whites, lawyers and police officers). In each case, the regression lines reflect the separate regression equations for the two groups. For the purpose of the discussion, predicted scores (Y'_A and Y'_B) for individuals who have identical scores on the predictor (X) are indicated. Using the separate regression lines to show the predicted scores for a given value of X is equivalent to

---

[7]Depending on your background, you may find the reading of relevant sections of Chapter 21 helpful for a better understanding of this section.

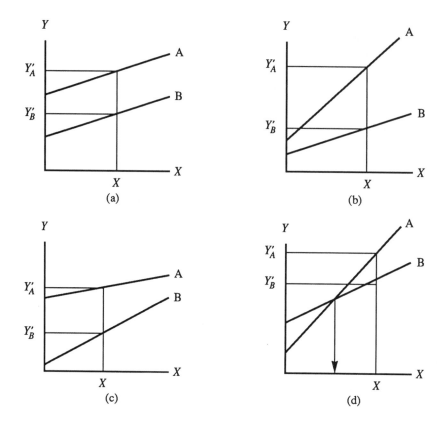

Figure 3.5

plugging X into the two separate regression equations for A and B in order to obtain Y'_A and Y'_B.

Look first at (a) of Figure 3.5 and notice that the regression lines are parallel, indicating that the two regression equations have identical regression coefficients (b's). The difference between the intercepts (a's), however, is relatively large. Under such circumstances, predicted scores for members of A will always be larger than those for members of B. The difference between the predicted scores for any given X will equal the difference between the two intercepts. This type of example was depicted in Figure 3.4 where it was also shown that the validity coefficients for two groups may differ.

Turn now to (b) and (c) of Figure 3.5 and notice that in both cases the regression line for A is above that for B. This, of course, means that predicted scores for any given X will be larger for members of A than for members of B. The magnitude of the difference between predicted scores will, however, depend on the specific X used. In (b), the difference between predicted scores will become increasingly larger with increasing values of X. The converse is true for the situation depicted in (c). Again, r_{xy} for A may or may not be different from r_{xy} for B.

Using terminology of Attribute–Treatment–Interaction (ATI) designs (see Chapters 12 and 21), the situations depicted in (b) and (c) would be referred to as ordinal interactions between the predictor and group membership. Briefly, this means that whereas predicted scores for members of one group are consistently larger than those for the other group, the magnitude of the difference depends on the specific values of the predictor (X). Contrast (b) and (c) with (a), where there is no interaction between the predictor and group membership.

This is why the difference between predicted scores in (a) is constant, whereas in (b) and (c) it varies, depending on the specific value of X.

Finally, turn to (d) of Figure 3.5 and notice that the regression lines intersect—a condition referred to as a disordinal interaction between the predictor and group membership (see Chapter 21). What this means is that, unlike the situations described thus far, predicted scores for one group will *not* be consistently larger than those for the other group. In (d), for example, predicted scores for people whose scores on the predictor are below the point corresponding to the intersection of the regression lines (indicated by the arrow) will be higher for members of B than for A. The converse is true of predicted scores for people whose scores on the predictor are above the point of intersection.

In discussing the situations depicted in Figure 3.5, attention was focused on the regression equation. It was pointed out that for specific comparisons between regression equations, the validity coefficient (r_{xy}) may or may not be equal. This should not be construed to mean that the magnitude of the correlation coefficient does not matter at all. First, it was shown above that r_{xy} is one of the elements that determines the magnitude of b. Second, the correlation coefficient plays a role in the determination of the standard error of estimate ($s_{y.x}$; see Chapter 17) and, consequently, in determining confidence intervals around predicted scores (for a discussion, illustrations, and references, see Pedhazur, 1982, pp. 143–147).

For present purposes, it will suffice to point out that, other things being equal, the smaller the correlation coefficient, the larger $s_{y.x}$ and, therefore, the wider the confidence interval around a predicted score. Roughly speaking, the wider the confidence interval around a predicted score, the less confidence one would have in decisions made on the basis of the predicted score (for a good discussion of this point, see Einhorn & Bass, 1971; see also, Barrett, 1974).

THE NATURE OF GROUPS STUDIED

People may be classified into a wide variety of groups; thus, the question arises: How does one decide what grouping, or classificatory, variables to use for the purpose of comparisons among regression equations? There is no simple answer to this question except to say that it depends on one's theoretical formulations and/or specific interests. For example, if one suspects that a selection procedure on the basis of a predictor is biased toward females, then a comparison of regression equations for males and females is called for.

SELECTION BIAS

When selection based on applicants' scores on the predictor(s) is challenged as favoring or discriminating against members of a given group (e.g., females, blacks), it is contended that the selection is biased. As a result of legislation, litigation, and general public concern (for a review, see Bersoff, 1981), issues of selection bias have been receiving increasing attention from sociobehavioral scientists in general and from measurement specialists in particular. As is true of other areas, there is no common, agreed-upon terminology (not to mention defini-tions of terms) regarding selection bias. For example, some authors use terms such as "selection bias," "test bias," "test fairness" interchangeably, whereas others make clear distinctions among them (see Petersen, 1980).

It is not our aim to review the extensive literature dealing with selection bias and related issues, nor is it our intention to discuss the various definitional, measurement, and statistical issues relevant to this topic (see, for example, Arvey & Faley, 1988; Berk, 1982; Cole, 1981; Cole & Moss, 1989; Equal Employment Opportunity Commission, Civil Service Commission, Department of Labor, and Department of Justice, 1978; Green, 1981a, 1981b; *Journal of Educational Measurement*, 1976, *13*, Spring issue; Pezzullo & Brittingham, 1979; Reynolds, 1982; Reynolds & Brown, 1984). Suffice it to point out that not only are some treatments of selection bias technically complex but also that they are all based on explicit or implicit value judgments (e.g., the meaning of "discrimination," "fairness"). (See, for example, Flaugher, 1978; Hunter & Schmidt, 1976; Petersen & Novick, 1976.) Our purpose, in addition to alerting you that selection bias is a complex topic, is limited to showing that one of the most popular approaches to the study of selection bias is based on the ideas presented above under the heading Differential Prediction.

Cleary (1968) offered the following definition:

A test is biased for members of a subgroup of the population if, in the prediction of a criterion for which the test was designed, consistent nonzero errors of prediction are made for members of the subgroup. In other words, the test is biased if the criterion score predicted from the common regression line is consistently too high or too low for members of the subgroup. (p. 115)

It should come as no surprise that Cleary's definition is referred to as the "regression model,"[8] as it is based on the comparison of regression equations as presented above. To clarify this, we refer you to Figure 3.5. Look first at (*a*) and notice that a common regression line would be one that is equidistant from lines *A* and *B* and parallel to them (you may find it helpful to insert such a line). Using a common regression line, instead of the separate ones, for selection would lead to consistent underpredictions for members of *A* and consistent overpredictions for members of group *B*, hence bias according to Cleary's definition.

Although somewhat more complicated, the use of a common regression line would also result in selection bias for the remaining cases depicted in Figure 3.5. In (*b*) and (*c*) too, a common regression line would lead to underprediction for members of *A* and to overpredictions for members of *B*. The degree of bias will, however, depend on the specific *X* score. In (*b*), the higher the *X*, the greater the bias. The converse is true for the situation depicted in (*c*). Finally, the use of a common regression equation for a situation like the one depicted in (*d*) will result in bias in favor of members of *B* and against members of *A* when their scores on *X* are below the point of intersection of the regression lines. The reverse will be true for people whose scores on *X* are above the point of intersection.

MULTIPLE PREDICTORS

The presentation in this chapter was limited to the case of a single predictor. In many instances, more than one predictor is used. Under such circumstances, multiple regression analysis (Chapter 18) is the analytic method most often resorted to. Among other things, various approaches to the selection of predictors have been developed (e.g., stepwise regression analysis). (For a review and relevant references, see Pedhazur, 1982, Chapter 6.)

CONCLUDING REMARKS

We believe it important to reiterate what we said in the beginning of this chapter, namely that, for convenience, criterion-related validation and construct validation are presented in separate chapters but that they constitute facets of the validation process. In addition, we

---

[8]What Cleary labeled test bias is referred to by some authors as selection bias. The absence of a common terminology was noted earlier.

would like to assure you again that various issues alluded to briefly in the present chapter, especially those concerning analytic approaches, are discussed in detail in subsequent chapters. Therefore, do not be concerned if some of the topics we have commented upon briefly are hazy. If at this time you would like clarification of a specific topic alluded to, we suggest that you read relevant explications in Part 3, especially in Chapters 17, 18, and 21.

Chapter 4
Construct Validation

The preceding chapter focused on issues concerning prediction of a criterion by resorting to information from one or more predictors. It was pointed out that whereas theoretical considerations are by no means irrelevant to such investigations, they do not play a central role in them. The perspective changes drastically when we turn to construct validation, as the definition and meaning of a construct emanate from the theoretical network in which it is embedded.

We begin with a consideration of the use of indicators for the purpose of making inferences about constructs. This is followed by a presentation of construct-validation approaches, under the headings of logical analysis, internal- and cross-structure analysis, and convergent and discriminant validation. The chapter concludes with a comment on content validity.

CONSTRUCTS AND INDICATORS

Constructs, which are synonymous with concepts, are theoretical constructions, abstractions, aimed at organizing and making sense of our environment. In other words, construct "is not a visual image, nor is it external to the mind; it is analogous to a piece in a game which thought plays" (Caws, 1959, p. 16). Examples of constructs are anxiety, motivation, mental ability, attitude, self-esteem, interest, frustration, and altruism.

Construct validation is concerned with validity of inferences about unobserved variables (the constructs) on the basis of observed variables (their presumed indicators). The reciprocity between constructs and indicators was enunciated by Immanuel Kant: "Concepts without factual content are empty; sense data without concepts are blind" (quoted by Mackay, 1977, p. 84). Construct validation is fraught with difficulties, ambiguities, even circularities. How, one might well wonder, is it possible to ascertain whether a given observed variable is an indicator of a variable that is unobservable in the first place? Further, in view of the fact that a given observed variable may reflect different constructs (e.g., the same behavior may reflect different motives), and the same construct may be manifested by different observed variables (e.g., the same motive may be reflected by different behaviors), how does one tell which is which?

Illustrating the inherent ambiguity in making inferences from an indicator to a construct is the following news item:

We hear of a museum in a certain Eastern city that was proud of its amazing attendance record. Recently a little stone building was erected nearby. Next year attendance at the museum mysteriously fell off by 100,000. What was the little stone building? A comfort station. (*This week*, April 17, 1948. Quoted by Wallis & Roberts, 1956, p. 133)

Complicating matters further is the fact that, in given situations, the interest is in studying an observed variable in its own right, whereas in others it is treated as an indicator of some construct. Thus, voting behavior, say, may be studied in its own right, or it may be used as an indicator of some construct, say, political involvement. Or, in a given study, the interest may be in the effect of education on income, whereas in another study both these variables may be taken as indicators of, say, socioeconomic status.

When observed variables are used as indicators of a construct, care should be exercised not to invest them with the meaning attributed to the construct, as this might lead to erroneous, even ludicrous conclusions. For example, in a reanalysis of data from the influential study of *Equality of educational opportunity* (Coleman et al., 1966, commonly referred to as the Coleman Report), Armor (1972) found correlations of about .7 between an index of ownership of nine household items (e.g., television set, vacuum cleaner, telephone, dictionary, refrigerator) and students' verbal achievement. Now, it may be meaningful to regard ownership of the aforementioned items as indicators of a construct (e.g., "family life style," "economic well-being of a family," Armor, p. 206) and to interpret the correlations accordingly. It is obviously quite a different matter to invest such indicators with the meaning of the construct they presumably represent, as this would lead to the conclusion that it is the owning of a telephone, a refrigerator, a vacuum cleaner, and the like that affects students' verbal achievement.

This example may appear so obvious as to not warrant mentioning. Yet misconceptions of this kind are all too common. For example, reporting on findings of a set of international studies of educational achievement (the IEA studies; see, for example, Peaker, 1975), Hechinger (1973) stated: "The number of books and magazines in a student's home had a greater effect on achievement in literature than income and education of the student's family." Without going far afield, it will be noted that it is conceivable for number of books and magazines in the home to be deemed indicators of parents' education or income, not to mention the possibility of all of the preceding being indicators of, say, socioeconomic status.

CONSIDERATIONS OF TIME, PLACE, AND CONTEXT

By their very nature, indicators may have different meanings in different places, cultures, subcultures, and the like. Moreover, within a given place, the meanings of indicators may change in the course of time because of historical events, changes in norms, economic conditions, to name but a few. This is particularly true when the indicators are responses to items, as in attitude or personality questionnaires. As an illustration, we turn to one of the most influential studies in social psychology—*The authoritarian personality* (Adorno, Frenkel-Brunswik, Levinson, & Sanford, 1950)—a major aspect of which was the development of the *F* (Fascism) Scale, which later came to be known as the Authoritarianism Scale. It is not possible, nor is it necessary, to deal here with the definition and the study of the construct of authoritarianism as used by the authors of *The authoritarian personality* (for some reviews and critiques, see Christie & Jahoda, 1954; Kirscht & Dillehay, 1967; Sanford, 1973).

For present purposes, it will suffice to draw attention to some sources of differences in meanings of the items of the *F* Scale. In one of the early studies of the *F* Scale, Christie and Garcia (1951) demonstrated that its items have different meanings for college students in different regions of the U.S. and attributed some of the differences to subcultural differences. More recently, Miller, Slomczynski, and Schoenberg (1981) showed that some items of the *F* Scale appear to tap the same dimension in the U.S. and in Poland, whereas others are more culture-specific.

The most obvious changes in meaning of *F* Scale items have come about as a result of major events in our society (e.g., Watergate, Iran-Contra affair, women's liberation, gay liberation). Following are some *F* Scale items whose meaning has undoubtedly changed because of such events:

Homosexuals are hardly better than criminals and ought to be severely punished.
Most people don't realize how much our lives are controlled by plots hatched in secret places.
The wild sex life of the old Greeks and Romans was tame compared to some of the goings-on in this country, even in places where people might least expect it. (Adorno et al., 1950, pp. 255–257)

Needless to say, interpretation of such items may vary in different parts of the country and in different segments of society. The main point, however, is that, even if one were to assume that inferences regarding authoritarianism on the basis of responses to the *F* Scale were valid at the time of its construction (an issue we are not addressing), it is safe to say that using it in its original form at the present time would result in the measurement of things, the nature of which may have little to do with the original conception of authoritarianism. Thus, even if a present-day researcher were to accept Adorno et al.'s formulation and definition of authoritarianism, he or she would be well advised to use a revision of the *F* Scale or devise a new scale.

REFLECTIVE AND FORMATIVE INDICATORS

A distinction is made between reflective and formative indicators (e.g., Bagozzi & Fornell, 1982). The former—also labeled "reflectors," (e.g., Costner, 1969) or "effect indicators" (e.g., Blalock, 1971)—refer to indicators taken as the effects of the construct in question. Formative indicators—also labeled "producers" (Costner, 1969), or "cause indicators" (Blalock, 1971)—are taken as causes of the construct in question.[1]

In most of the research concerning construct validation, indicators are treated as reflective. Some authors, notably Blalock (e.g., 1971), Costner (1969, 1971), Hauser (1972), Hauser and Goldberger (1971), Heise (1974), Jacobson (1973), and Jöreskog and Goldberger (1975), drew attention to situations in which indicators treated as reflective would more meaningfully be treated as formative. The choice is, of course, not arbitrary; rather it depends on the theoretical formulations about the construct. Using socioeconomic status (SES) as an example, Hauser (1972) pointed out that whereas education, income, and the like are most often treated as reflective indicators of SES, it would be more meaningful to treat them as formative indicators of SES. Indicators are clearly formative when they constitute manipulated variables hypothesized to affect unobserved variables (e.g., manipulation is said to affect anxiety, motivation, frustration; see below).

---

[1]Controversies regarding causation will not be addressed at this early stage. We examine them in the context of testing causal models (Chapter 24).

MODEL DIAGRAMS

Diagrams depicting relations between constructs and their indicators, as well as relations among the constructs, are very useful in showing, at a glance, theoretical formulations advanced with respect to them. Stripped of verbal baggage, a diagram will often reveal deficiencies, ambiguities, and inconsistencies in theoretical formulations that might otherwise go undetected or be not as apparent. Accordingly, we recommend that you get in the habit of using such diagrams whenever you are dealing with a theoretical formulation, be it your own or one advanced by others. Here we introduce only some of the conventions followed by most authors in drawing such diagrams. Other aspects are introduced and discussed in subsequent chapters.

Unobserved (latent) variables are depicted by circles, whereas observed (manifest) variables are depicted by squares. Unidirectional arrows are used to depict the direction of causation from variables conceived of as causes (or independent variables) to variables conceived of as effects (or dependent variables). Correlations among variables are depicted by curved bidirectional arrows.

The foregoing ideas as well as those concerning the two types of indicators are illustrated in Figure 4.1. Turning first to (*a*), it will be noted that X and Y are latent variables, whereas Z and W are manifest variables. Also, X is envisioned as a cause of Z, and Y as a cause of W. In the context of construct validation, X and Y may be two constructs (e.g., mental ability and motivation, anxiety and aggression), the former being reflected by Z and the latter being reflected by W. Finally, X and Y are said to be correlated.

Turning to (*b*) of Figure 4.1, it will be noted that, as in (*a*), X and Y are unobserved

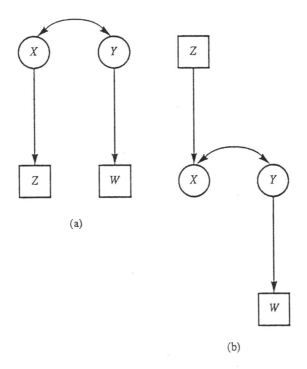

(a)

(b)

Figure 4.1

correlated variables, and W is a reflective indicator of Y. However, unlike in (a), Z in (b) is treated as a formative indicator of X.

SINGLE VERSUS MULTIPLE INDICATORS

The use of a single indicator for the measurement of a construct, as in Figure 4.1, almost always poses insurmountable problems, because it is not possible to identify and separate the different sources of variability of the indicator in question. Broadly speaking, variability of an indicator is composed of two major components: systematic and nonsystematic variance. Issues regarding the estimation of nonsystematic variance, also referred to as random error variance, are dealt with under the heading of reliability (see Chapter 5). Systematic variance may be due to various sources, among which are the latent variable that the indicator is presumed to reflect, other latent variables, the measurement method used (e.g., interview, multiple-choice items), and systematic errors (e.g., response set, social desirability).

A simple example will be used to illustrate the almost hopeless situation when single indicators are employed and also to bring to light the unrealistic assumptions, implicit or explicit, that are made when a solution to the problem is sought. Assume that one wishes to study the relation between two constructs, X and Y (e.g., anxiety and achievement, self-esteem and job satisfaction, frustration and aggression). Depending on what X and Y are, and on one's theoretical formulations, one may hypothesize that they are positively or negatively correlated. Alternatively, one may hypothesize that X affects Y, or that Y affects X, or that there are reciprocal effects between them. For present purposes, it will suffice to focus on the hypothesis that X and Y are correlated. The almost universal practice in sociobehavioral research is to use a single indicator, or measure, for each of the constructs and calculate the correlation (Chapter 17) between them. Referring to constructs mentioned above, one would, for example, calculate the correlation between self-ratings on self-esteem and on job satisfaction. This type of design is depicted in (a) of Figure 4.2, where X' and Y' are reflective indicators of X and Y respectively; $e_{X'}$ and $e_{Y'}$ refer to errors of measurement in X' and Y' respectively.

Because X and Y are unobservable, an inference about the relation between them is made on the basis of the relation between their presumed indicators. In other words, the correlation between X' and Y' is taken as representing that between X and Y. Note that such an inference is based on the implicit or explicit assumption of an identity between each indicator and the construct it presumably reflects. This assumption is shown in (a) of Figure 4.2 by the coefficients of 1.00 on the arrows leading from the constructs to their respective indicators and by coefficients of .00 on the arrows leading from the e's, the latter signifying that the measures are error-free.

When this assumption (or others regarding the relations between constructs and their indicators) is not made, one is faced with what is referred to as an underidentified model. What this essentially means is that one does not have sufficient information to solve for the unknown coefficients of the model (see Chapter 24). For present purposes, it will suffice to note that, if the coefficients on the arrows in (a) of Figure 4.2 were deleted, one would face the impossible task of using a single piece of information (the correlation between X' and Y') to solve for three unknown coefficients (the correlation between X and Y, and the coefficients connecting X with X', and Y with Y').

As is shown in Chapter 5, various approaches are available for the estimation of measurement errors. Using such estimates, one may then solve for the correlation between X and Y after correcting for measurement errors (this too is discussed in Chapter 5, under Correction for Attenuation). But note that when such an approach is taken with reference to a design

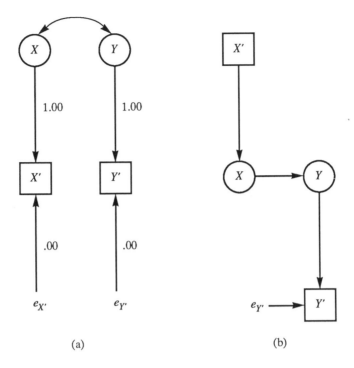

Figure 4.2

such as that depicted in (a) of Figure 4.2, it is necessarily assumed that, except for the variability accounted for by the construct, the remainder is due solely to random measurement errors. In many instances, this assumption is highly questionable.

In the preceding example, reflective indicators were used. It will be instructive now to present an example of a design in which a formative indicator is also used. This is done in (b) of Figure 4.2, where X' is taken as a formative indicator of X, whereas Y' is a reflective indicator of Y. Also, for the sake of illustration, the unobserved variable X is hypothesized to be a cause of the unobserved variable Y.

An example of such a research design would be one where X' is a manipulated variable assumed to affect some psychological construct (X),[2] which is hypothesized to affect the unobserved variable Y. Thus, X may be anxiety, and Y may be learning. X' represents some manipulation to induce anxiety, or different levels of anxiety. Or, X may be frustration, and Y may be aggression. X' would then be some manipulation aimed at inducing frustration. The main point is that the interest is not in the effect of the manipulation, X', on Y (the latter being measured by Y') but in the effect of the construct X on Y.[3]

As in (a) of Figure 4.2, model (b) is underidentified. Here too there is only a single piece of information, namely the relation between X' and Y', on the basis of which it is not possible to estimate the unknown coefficients.

---

[2]X' does not necessarily have to be a manipulation. Referring to an example given earlier, X' could be education and X SES.

[3]Issues concerning the relation between manipulation or measurement and constructs are addressed in Chapter 8 under the heading of Operational Definitions. Problems with designs exemplified by (b) of Figure 4.2 are discussed in Chapter 12 under the heading of Unintended Effects.

We hope that the preceding discussion has served to convince you of the untenable position and the consequent unrealistic assumptions one is forced into when resorting to single indicators in most areas of sociobehavioral research. The use of multiple indicators, to which we now turn, is one course of action aimed at coming to grips with some of the difficulties attendant with the use of single indicators.

Important advances in conceptualization and analyses of designs with multiple indicators have been made in recent years. Our purpose at this early stage is not to discuss these developments but merely to introduce on an intuitive level some basic ideas concerning their use. Ideas introduced here are explicated in several contexts in subsequent chapters (e.g., Chapters 5, 13, 23, and 24), where references are also given to relevant methodological and substantive studies dealing with multiple-indicator designs.

The term multiple indicators is used here to refer to different observed variables, or measures, believed to be either formative or reflective indicators of the same unobserved variable or construct. In the present context, a composite score based on responses to multiple items is treated as a single indicator. An example will be used to clarify our meaning. Father's education, mother's education, family income, father's occupation, and the like may be used as multiple indicators of socioeconomic status (SES). If, instead, such indicators were combined to form a single index of SES, it would, in the present context, be deemed a single indicator.

With the foregoing comments in mind, we turn to a very simple example of a design with multiple indicators, as depicted in Figure 4.3. Notice that the model consists of two con-structs, X and Y, each measured by two reflective indicators. Thus, X may be creativity (X_1 and X_2 are two measures of creativity), and Y may be intelligence (Y_1 and Y_2 are two measures of intelligence).

Figure 4.3 is similar to (a) of Figure 4.2 in that in both of them the interest is in the relation between the two constructs X and Y. However, whereas in (a) of Figure 4.2 single indicators of each construct were used, in Figure 4.3 two indicators of each construct are used. We showed earlier that the estimation of the relation between X and Y when single indicators are used is fraught with very serious problems, because in most instances it is based on untenable assumptions. The estimation of the relation between X and Y in Figure 4.3 is also based on a set of assumptions, which will not be gone into here except to note, by

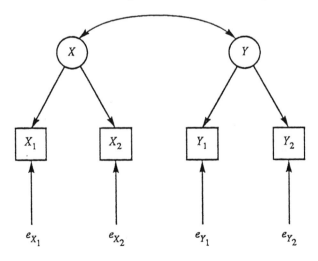

Figure 4.3

way of illustration, that the errors in the observed variables (i.e., the e's of Figure 4.3) are assumed to be not correlated among themselves (there are no lines connecting them).

All we will do for now is contrast Figures 4.2 (a) and 4.3 with respect to the number of pieces of information available for the estimation of unknown coefficients. For the design depicted in (a) of Figure 4.2, it was shown that one piece of information (i.e., the correlation between the two indicators X' and Y') was available for the estimation of three unknown coefficients. For the design in Figure 4.3, six pieces of information (there are six correlations when four indicators are correlated, two at a time) are available for the estimation of five unknown coefficients. Consequently, the model depicted in Figure 4.3 is said to be overidentified (see Chapter 24). Had three indicators been used for each of the latent variables of Figure 4.3, the assumptions for the estimation of unknown coefficients would have been less restrictive than those required for the case of two indicators for each latent variable.

CONSTRUCT VALIDATION APPROACHES

Construct validation is a never-ending enterprise. Gains, or losses, in credibility of inferences made on the basis of responses to (or status on) indicators of a construct depend on the nature and quality of the accumulated evidence involving the construct under consideration. Because tests of hypotheses involving the construct have bearing on its validation, it is clear that approaches to validation are limited only by the researcher's imagination and acumen, and the theoretical formulation and expectations regarding the construct under consideration.

For convenience, we discuss construct validation under three headings: (a) logical analysis, (b) internal-structure analysis, and (c) cross-structure analysis.

Logical Analysis

Clearly, logical analysis should be part of any aspect of the research activity. In the context of construct validation, a major aim of logical analysis is to generate counterhypotheses as alternative explanations regarding the construct presumably being measured, relations among constructs, and the like. Among sources of counterhypotheses are the definition of the construct, item content, method of measurement and the specific conditions under which it is used, directions to respondents, and scoring procedures. The preceding, and other facets not mentioned, are interrelated. Moreover, a given facet may be more or less relevant, depending on the specific conditions of a given study in which the measure is used.

Although it is true that "logical analysis of content cannot disprove a validity claim" (Cronbach, 1971, p. 475), there are instances when critical thinking would suffice to cast doubt about the validity of a measure or even lead to its rejection. As Cronbach (1971) stated: "When it is pointed out that hearing acuity makes the usual interpretation of the spelling test inappropriate for the hard-of-hearing child, no one is so pedantic as to insist on 'proof'" (p. 475).

Cronbach's example is so obvious as to elicit universal agreement. We would, therefore, like to present a research example, which, we believe, is obvious in that it does not require empirical "proof," yet many researchers seem to have thought otherwise. The Bem Sex-Role

Inventory (BSRI; Bem, 1974) is probably the most popular instrument used currently to measure masculinity and femininity. For present purposes, it will suffice to note that the BSRI consists of a set of adjectives (e.g., assertive, ambitious, warm) on which respondents are asked to rate themselves. Masculinity and femininity scores are obtained by summing the ratings on the "masculine" and the "feminine" traits respectively. Bem maintained that the masculine and feminine traits of the BSRI are positive, or desirable. Therefore, in order to check for the possibility of respondents giving socially desirable responses, Bem (1974) included what she considered a "completely neutral [scale] with respect to sex," half of whose items "were positive in value and half were negative" (p. 156).

Now, although the traits designated by Bem as masculine appear positive, some of the feminine traits cannot, by any stretch of the imagination, be construed as positive. Notable examples of such traits are Gullible and Flatterable. We believe that it would have been pedantic (in the sense used by Cronbach above) to require proof before being willing to concede that such traits are not positive. Yet it appears that only after it was shown (e.g., Pedhazur & Tetenbaum, 1979) that such traits were negative, some even more so than Bem's "neutral" negative traits, did some authors question their use, and did Bem omit them from the short form of the BSRI (see Beere, 1983, pp. 122–123, on this point).

Incidentally, a logical analysis of Bem's method of trait selection (see Pedhazur & Tetenbaum, 1979) would suffice to reveal how it could lead to the selection of negative traits. What we would like to stress here, in connection with logical analysis of construct validation, is that the relatively large number of authors whose work with the BSRI we have reviewed appear to have accepted Bem's assertion that the masculinity and femininity traits of the BSRI are all positive, socially desirable. We have not encountered even an allusion to the possibility that some of the feminine traits may be negative, socially undesirable. If anything, we came across authors who have unequivocally stated that the BSRI consists of desirable traits only. For example, Kelly, Caudill, Hathorn, and O'Brien (1977) stated: "Bem . . . has assessed only positive, socially desirable components of masculinity and femininity in her formulations" (p. 1185). *Because* of this, these authors conducted research whose sole purpose was to determine the effects of using, in addition to the BSRI, socially undesirable traits! Particularly disturbing is the fact that papers advancing the notion that the BSRI is comprised of positive traits only are still being published, even in the *same* journal in which much of the research and the controversy surrounding the BSRI appeared (for a couple of recent examples, see Larsen & Seidman, 1986; Paulhus & Martin, 1988).

We turn now to brief discussions and illustrations of some facets of logical analysis of construct validation listed above.

DEFINITION OF CONSTRUCT

Probably the most important, certainly the first, aspect of logical analysis is to scrutinize the definition of the construct. Philosophers of science have devoted a great deal of attention to the nature and role of definitions in scientific inquiry (see Chapter 8 and references given therein). For present purposes, we would like to stress the importance of examining the definition of the construct to determine whether it is vague, a tautology, logically consistent, consistent with the theoretical structure within which the construct is embedded, to name but some aspects.

It is a truism that sociobehavioral scientists use the same construct to mean different things to a greater or lesser degree. A prime example is the use of the construct "attitude." There are literally scores of definitions of attitude emanating explicitly or implicitly from a variety of theoretical orientations. For example, some general definitions of attitudes refer only to an evaluative component, whereas others refer also to cognitive and conative components. Some authors distinguish among constructs such as attitudes, beliefs, opinions, values, whereas others use them interchangeably (for some readings, see Fishbein, 1967; Greenwald, Brock, & Ostrom, 1968; Page, 1980).

Following is an example aimed at illustrating the importance of examining the definition of attitude in general as well as that of a specific attitude under consideration. Suppose one is describing the construction of a measure of Liberalism–Conservatism. It goes without saying that these constructs have to be defined. Is one concerned, for example, with political liberalism, economic liberalism, or both? Another issue might be whether Liberalism-Conservatism are to be assessed on an ideological or pragmatic level. For example, dealing with political beliefs, Free and Cantril (1967) found that the majority of Americans are conservative on an ideological level but liberal on a pragmatic level.

Yet another aspect of the definition might have to do with the relation between Liberalism and Conservatism. Some authors conceive of Liberalism–Conservatism as being on a bipolar continuum. What this essentially means is that being high on Liberalism implies being low on Conservatism and vice versa. Other authors conceive of Liberalism and Conservatism as independent of each other. Thus conceived, a person may, for example, be high on both Liberalism and Conservatism, or low on both (for a thorough discussion of these issues, see Kerlinger, 1984).

It goes without saying that a prerequisite for a critical evaluation of the definition of a construct is knowledge of theories and research findings relevant to the construct under consideration. A good means of developing a critical approach to construct definition, as well as other aspects of construct validation, is to study reviews of measures of constructs in specific areas. Notable among publications devoted to reviews of measures is the *Mental measurements yearbook*, currently published by the University of Nebraska Press. Some journals (e.g., *Educational and Psychological Measurement*, *Journal of Consulting and Clinical Psychology*) publish reviews on a regular basis.

ITEM CONTENT

Researchers and test constructors find it convenient to refer to a set of items as a sample from the domain of items that may serve as indicators of a given construct. In most instances, the domain does not exist in the sense of a population whose elements can be enumerated and sampled from. How, then, does one go about writing items designed to serve as indicators of a construct? At the stage of item writing, or selection from available items or other indicators, the most important guide is the definition of the construct. Similarly, to assess the appropriateness of items of an existing scale, one would first of all check whether they are consistent with the definition of the construct.[4]

MEASUREMENT PROCEDURES

By measurement procedures, we mean general methods of measurement (e.g., interview, summated rating scales, semantic differential, projective techniques); specific features of such methods (e.g., directions to respondents, item order, item wording); and conditions of

---

[4]We remind you that the presentation here is limited to the logical-analysis aspect of construct validation. Other approaches to the assessment of appropriateness of items are presented in subsequent sections (see especially internal-structure analysis).

administration (e.g., respondents are assured anonymity, the measure is administered together with what are presumably measures of other constructs).

The validity of a measure is adversely affected to the extent to which the obtained scores are due to the specific measurement procedure used. Certain aspects of the measurement procedure may play a greater or lesser role in subjects' responses, depending on the specific characteristic of the study in which the measure is used. Thus, for example, whether or not subjects are assured anonymity may become crucial in a study of attitudes toward "delicate" issues. Similarly, race of the interviewer may become crucial when the study is concerned with, say, desegregation policies.

The point we wish to emphasize here is that measurement procedures should be scrutinized in the context of the overall aim and setting of the study and in light of specific properties of the measures in question. In Chapter 6, we present some major measurement methods used in sociobehavioral research. Later in this chapter, we describe how the use of multiple methods to measure the same construct enables one to isolate variance due to a specific method from that due to a construct being measured. For now, we give only a couple of examples of examination of measurement procedures and counterhypotheses that may ensue.

Earlier in this chapter, the F Scale, or what has come to be known as the Authoritarianism Scale, was briefly described and discussed. The F Scale is an example of a summated-rating scale, often referred to as a Likert-type scale (see Chapter 6). For present purposes, it will be pointed out that, on a summated-rating scale, respondents are asked to indicate degrees of agreement or disagreement with a set of statements. Responses are then summed to yield an overall score. To obviate or lessen the effect of response sets, it is recommended that the scale be composed of both positively and negatively worded statements.

Soon after the publication of the F Scale, researchers pointed out that all of its statements were worded in the same direction and argued that higher scores do not reflect higher authoritarianism but rather an acquiescence or yeasaying tendency on the part of respondents (for a discussion of yeasaying and naysaying as a personality variable, see Couch & Keniston, 1960). Thus, logical analysis of a feature of the measurement method led to the questioning of the construct validity of the F Scale (e.g., Bass, 1955; Christie, Havel, & Seidenberg, 1958; Gage, Leavitt, & Stone, 1957).

For another example of logical analysis of measurement procedures, we turn to the Wilson-Patterson Attitude Inventory (WPAI; Wilson, 1975), which is presumably a measure of Conservatism, although it allegedly also yields a score on Liberalism and some other constructs (see section on Scoring, below). Here are the directions to respondents:

WHICH OF THE FOLLOWING DO YOU FAVOUR OR BELIEVE IN?
Circle 'Yes' or 'No'. If absolutely uncertain, circle '?'. There are no right or wrong answers; do not discuss; just give your first reaction. Please answer every item.

These directions are followed by 50 referents (e.g., Hanging thieves, Space travel, Bikinis).

Notice that a 'Yes' response is called for when a respondent is either in *favor* of or *believes* in a given referent; conversely, for a 'No' response. Although it is possible that, for certain referents, beliefs and evaluations go together, equating the two can be a source of ambiguity. Sources of even greater ambiguity are the item format and the response mode. Commenting on these issues in his review of the WPAI, Pedhazur (1978) stated:

Consider, for example, the item "smoking pot." A "yes" response may mean being in favor of decriminalization of the smoking of pot, but not being in favor of smoking it; being in favor of both decriminalization and smoking; being in favor of smoking despite, or because of, the laws that prohibit it. Still other meanings are conceivable. A "no" response to the same item may, similarly, have multiple meanings. (p. 1151)

SCORING PROCEDURES

Procedures used in scoring responses to a measure can also affect the validity of inferences made on the basis of them.[5] Critical evaluation of scoring procedures is, therefore, an important aspect of logical analysis. Issues concerning scoring may become complex, especially when the measure is designed to tap a multidimensional construct or when the responses elicited require classification and coding (e.g., projective techniques).

Complications may arise even when scoring appears straightforward. For example, it would appear that multiple-choice tests of achievement should pose no problems so far as scoring is concerned. Most users assign a 1 to each correct response, a 0 to each incorrect response, and sum the number of correct responses to arrive at a total score. Nevertheless, various decisions may be called for. For example, it may be necessary to decide whether or not, and in what manner, to correct for guessing (see Nunnally, 1978, pp. 642–655), or whether or not to assign differential weights to different items (e.g., Nunnally, 1978, pp. 296–297; Stanley & Wang, 1970; Wang & Stanley, 1970).

Our purpose is not to deal with scoring procedures on a technical level but rather to demonstrate that in this matter too, common sense can go a long way. We begin with the scoring of responses to a single item and then address issues of forming a composite score on the basis of two or more items.

Decisions regarding the scoring of an item cannot be made without a consideration of the construct of which the item is considered to be an indicator. For an example, we return to the WPAI (see above), this time to consider some issues of item scoring. It will be recalled that the WPAI is presumably a measure of Conservatism composed of 50 referents (e.g., School uniforms, Sunday school, Saluting the flag, Bikinis, Bearded men, Comics) to which respondents are asked to respond by circling 'Yes' or 'No' or '?'. A 'Yes' response to a "conservatism" referent is assigned a score of 2, whereas a 'No' response to such a referent is assigned a score of 0. Conversely, a 'Yes' response to a "liberalism" referent is scored 0, whereas a 'No' response is scored 2. A '?' response to any of the referents is scored 1.[6] The scores on the 50 items are added to yield a score on a Conservatism–Liberalism continuum, with higher scores indicating Conservatism and lower scores indicating Liberalism.

Notice that Wilson's scoring procedure is based on a conception of Conservatism–Liberalism comprising a bipolar continuum.[7] We are not concerned here with the merits or demerits of such a conception but with questionable, even strange, scoring procedures it has led to, in the light of the referents and response mode used. Consider, for example, the following referents: Pornography, Smoking pot, Hippies, Striptease shows, and Nude swimming. A 'No' response to each of these is scored 2, whereas a 'Yes' response is scored 0. Let us assume, for the sake of discussion, that a 'No' response to such referents reflects a Conservatism attitude. But why is it necessary to say 'Yes' to each of these referents in order for the responses to be scored in the direction of the Liberalism pole? As Pedhazur (1978) pointed out: "It is one thing to expect liberals to show tolerance toward such referents; it is quite another matter to expect them to say that they are in favor of or believe in them" (p. 1151).

Turning now to issues regarding composite scores, it will be noted that most measures of

---

[5]Scoring procedures can also affect the reliability of a measure. Reliability and its relation to validity is discussed in Chapter 5.

[6]Here is what Wilson (1975) said about the meaning and the scoring of this category: "The '?' category can be used to mean 'not understood', 'neutral', or 'indifferent', and it seems reasonable to give any of these responses an intermediate score" (p. 18). We will let you judge the "reasonableness" of Wilson's assumptions. Also, think about his use of "absolute uncertainty" (see instructions above) in connection with the kind of referents and the response mode he is calling for.

[7]See Definition of Construct, for a discussion and references on this point.

constructs are composed of multiple items, as the domain of a construct can rarely, if ever, be represented by a single item. In the next section (Internal-Structure Analysis), we discuss methods designed to determine whether or not it is meaningful to combine responses to a given set of items into a composite score. For now, however, we would like to stress that often it is not necessary to resort to complex analyses in order to pass judgment about the meaningfulness of combining scores on a set of items. All too frequently, the process of obtaining composite scores is done with utter disregard of elementary measurement principles and even common sense. As Duncan (1984) pointed out:

In a chemistry laboratory one learns to be a little cautious about "combining" substances. But, so far as I know, the somewhat analogous "combining" of information has not been widely recognized to have a property analogous to blowing up in the experimenter's face. (p. 227)

Following is an example illustrating such an occurrence. Earlier, we mentioned Armor's (1972) reanalysis of data from the Coleman Report. As one aspect of the reanalysis, Armor was interested in studying relations between teachers' responses to selected questions and students' achievement. For the former, Armor selected six questions asked of teachers and used the answers to obtain a composite index. Here is Armor's (1972) description:

The index was derived by scoring one point each for a teacher who would (1) definitely reenter teaching if they were deciding again; (2) not prefer to change schools; (3) express no preference for a particular ethnic composition [of the school]; (4) express no preference for a particular racial composition [of the school]; (5) expect to remain in teaching until retirement; and (6) prefer to see a black student go to a predominantly white college. (p. 228)

The preceding statements are paraphrases of the questions and response options. For example, the first question used by Armor read as follows:

Suppose you could go back in time and start college again; in view of your present knowledge, would you enter the teaching profession?
  (A) Definitely yes
  (B) Probably yes
  (C) Undecided
  (D) Probably no
  (E) Definitely no
(Coleman et al., 1966, p. 679; the entire Teacher Questionnaire, as well as other measures used in the study, are reproduced in the Report.)

Because our concern here is with the composite score, we will not dwell on Armor's item scoring strategy, although we have reservations about it. For example, in connection with the scoring of the above item, we wonder about the justification of treating "Definitely yes" as one category and lumping the remaining optional answers in another category. We invite you think about this and other matters concerning Armor's (1972) item scoring.

Here now is all that Armor (1972) said about his conception of the index: "Our a priori notion was that a good teacher attitude would be composed of strong commitment to teaching and to the school, and a tolerant attitude toward ethnic composition (with no objection to any racial or ethnic mixture)" (pp. 179–180). Overlooking the vagueness of the preceding statement and not addressing the issue of major aspects of teaching attitude not even alluded to, one has to question whether it is reasonable and meaningful to consider the three aspects mentioned earlier as parts of a single construct. It is possible, for example, that tolerance toward minority groups is related to teaching attitude. This, of course, is not the same as saying that tolerance toward minority groups is part of the construct teaching attitude.

Even if one were not to question Armor's claim of measuring commitment to teaching and to school (this is questioned below), one would have to question why these are necessarily related, not to mention being part of the same construct. Is it not possible for a teacher to be highly committed to teaching and yet for various reasons (e.g., convenience of transportation, prestige) wish to be transferred to another school? Actually, it is relatively easy to come up with examples of situations in which a teacher would seek a transfer *because* of his or her commitment to teaching.

Without going into the questionable practice of using one or two indicators to tap a complex construct, let us examine briefly a couple of them. Consider indicators that presumably reflect commitment to teaching (i.e., choosing teaching if given an opportunity to start again, and expecting to teach until retirement). It is rather easy to advance arguments in support of the notion that affirmative responses to these questions may reflect *lack* of commitment to teaching. At the very least, it is necessary to entertain the idea that they may reflect various other things (e.g., an assessment of one's chances to be admitted to, and to successfully complete, training in other, more preferred professions; the attractiveness of long vacations that coincide with those of one's children; job security; resignation to being in a rut). One could raise similar questions about Armor's interpretation of the responses to the other questions.

In view of the foregoing discussion, it is interesting to see what happened when Armor used the index to pursue the relation in which he was interested. Armor reported:

We found . . . that our index of good teaching attitudes was *inversely* related to average student achievement. In fact, the product-moment correlation between teacher attitude and student achievement for the nation as a whole was $-.42$. The higher the student achievement, the less tolerant and less committed the teachers (as measured by our index). It may be that our notion of good teaching attitude is wrong, but we prefer to believe that for some reason [!] the index is not adequate for assessing these attitudes. (1972, p. 180)

Armor decided, appropriately, not to use the index in his subsequent analyses of the Coleman Report data. Our presentation was designed to show why he should not have arrived at such an index in the first place.

We hope that the discussion of logical analysis served to illustrate the importance of the interplay among critical thinking, theory, knowledge of measurement, design, and analysis in the process of validation of a construct. We turn now to another aspect of the process of construct validation, namely internal-structure analysis.

Internal-Structure Analysis

Issues concerning the selection of indicators and the manner in which they are scored and combined were dealt with in the preceding section on a level of logical analysis. The present section is devoted to a description of analytic approaches aimed at assessing the validity of treating a set of indicators as reflecting the same construct. Much of the presentation constitutes an intuitive description of factor analytic approaches from the perspective of construct validation. Chapters 22 and 23 are devoted to factor analysis. Depending on your background and specific aims and needs, you may find it useful or even essential to study these chapters in conjunction with the presentation that follows.

Consider Figure 4.4, where C stands for a construct (e.g., intelligence, aggression, attitude); the X's stand for indicators (e.g., measures of intelligence, striking a person or an object, using abusive language, items on a measure of attitudes); the e's stand for errors, or

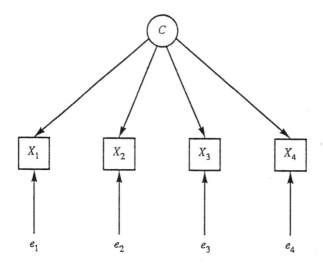

Figure 4.4

aspects unique to a given indicator. As depicted in the figure, each indicator is composed of two components: (a) due to the construct, and (b) due to errors or other factors unique to the indicator, as is evidenced by the absence of lines connecting e's.[8]

From the preceding, it follows that the correlations among the indicators in Figure 4.4 are attributed to the construct they are said to reflect. Therefore, to accept the validity of the model, hence the validity of the indicators of the construct, it is necessary, although not sufficient, to demonstrate that it is consistent with the data. Essentially, this means that the relations among the indicators are reasonably accounted for by the model.[9]

At a minimum, it is necessary to demonstrate that reflective indicators of a construct (e.g., items, subtests) "hang together;" that they are homogeneous. Needless to say, a set of heterogeneous indicators cannot be measuring the same thing, and it, therefore, makes no sense to combine them into a composite index.

FACTOR ANALYSIS AND INTERNAL STRUCTURE

Of various approaches for studying the internal structure of a set of indicators, probably the most useful is some variant of factor analysis—a topic to which Chapters 22 and 23 are devoted. For present purposes, only a general delineation of this approach and its potential uses in the process of construct validation will be given.

Factor analysis refers to a family of analytic techniques designed to identify factors, or dimensions, that underlie the relations among a set of observed variables. In the present context, the observed variables are the indicators (measures, items) presumed to reflect the construct (i.e., the factor).

In most instances, factor analysis is applied to the correlations among indicators. An estimate of the relation between each indicator and a factor—referred to as a factor

---

[8]It is possible to formulate models in which errors are correlated (see Chapter 23).

[9]The fact that alternative models may also be consistent with the data is discussed in other chapters, especially Chapters 22, 23, and 24.

loading—is obtained. Loosely speaking, a factor loading is the weight of an indicator on the factor, much like a standardized regression coefficient (β) in a regression analysis (see Chapters 17 and 18). For certain kinds of factor-analytic solutions, the factor loading is the correlation between the indicator and the factor. Under such circumstances, a factor loading may vary from zero (no relation between the indicator and the factor) to plus or minus one (perfect relation between the indicator and the factor).

Generally speaking, the higher the factor loading, the more meaningful it is, or the greater is the impact of the factor on the indicator. Consistent with the interpretation of a correlation coefficient (see Chapter 17), the square of such factor loadings indicates the proportion of variance of a given indicator accounted for by the factor. For example, a loading of .4 means that .16 ($.4^2$), or 16% ($.16 \times 100$), of the variance of the indicator is accounted for by the factor.

A distinction is made between *exploratory* and *confirmatory* factor analysis. Loosely speaking, exploratory factor analysis is concerned with the question of how many factors are necessary to explain the relations among a set of indicators and with the estimation of the factor loadings. Confirmatory factor analysis, as the name implies, is concerned with parameter estimation and tests of hypotheses regarding, for example, the number of factors underlying the relations among a set of indicators.

In what follows, we will attempt to clarify the meaning of the two approaches by way of general descriptions and illustrations of their use for the purpose of construct validation. Before doing this, two comments will be made. One, as we discuss and illustrate in Chapters 22 and 23, there is much more to the two broad approaches than we can even begin to hint at here. Two, we are acutely aware of the likelihood that you may find our sketchy descriptions confusing, even frustrating. Worse yet, we know that, in offering loose descriptions of extremely complex analytic approaches, we run a high risk of misinforming and of leading to misconceptions. Therefore, *before you form an opinion about factor analysis, not to mention before you attempt to interpret factor-analytic results, you should, at the very least, study Chapters 22 and 23.*

EXPLORATORY FACTOR ANALYSIS

Suppose, for the sake of illustration, that a researcher is interested in constructing a measure of self-concept and that he or she writes (or selects from the literature) 20 items on which respondents are to be asked to rate themselves. Assume further that the researcher wishes to add the ratings on the 20 items in order to arrive at a total self-concept score. It stands to reason that, for a total score to be meaningful, it is essential for the items to "hang together;" to tap the same dimension.

One can, of course, study the correlation of each item with every other item. However, it is generally difficult to arrive at an overall picture, even with a relatively small number of items. The number of correlations one would have to examine and summarize is equal to

$$\frac{k\,(k-1)}{2}$$

where k is the number of items. Thus, for the 20 items being considered here, one would have to examine: $[(20)(19)]/2 = 190$ correlations. If, instead, the correlation matrix is factor analyzed, and only the first factor is retained (see discussion of this point below), then only 20 factor loadings would have to be examined.

The factor loadings are examined in order to determine which of them are meaningfully correlated with the factor. As is discussed in various subsequent chapters (e.g., Chapters 9 and 15), a decision regarding the meaningfulness of statistics (correlations, in the present case) depends on various considerations, primary among them being substantive aspects of the research. In applications of factor analysis, researchers often treat loadings exceeding .4 or .5 as meaningful. Using criteria such as these, the researcher may decide to include in the scale only the items with meaningful loadings.

When the number of items whose loadings meet the criterion of meaningfulness is deemed insufficient, new items are added, or items whose loadings did not meet the criterion are revised. The new set of items, those whose loadings met the criterion and those that were added or revised, are subjected to factor analysis. The process may be repeated until the researcher is satisfied with the set of items that is to comprise the measure of self-concept.

To obviate the need for repetitious attempts, the practice most often followed is to begin with a larger pool of items from which those to be used in the scale are to be selected. A factor analysis of the larger pool of items helps one decide which of them are to be retained, discarded, revised, or what have you. You will find useful discussions of applications of factor analysis in the process of scale construction in Gorsuch (1983, Chapter 17), Marradi (1981), and Zeller and Carmines (1980, Chapter 4).

The preceding discussion was necessarily predicated on several implicit assumptions, the most important of which will now be stated and briefly discussed. As was stated several times earlier, it is necessary to define the construct in order to be in a position to search for relevant indicators, to write or select items, and the like. In the previous discussion, it was assumed that self-concept is conceived as a unidimensional construct. Suppose, instead, that it is conceived as a multidimensional, multifaceted construct (Shavelson & Bolus, 1982, for example, speak of Academic Self-Concept, Social Self-Concept, and the like). Under such circumstances, one would write or select items presumed to be tapping each of the facets. When subjecting the correlation matrix of all the items to a factor analysis, one would expect items meant to tap different facets of self-concept to have meaningful loadings on different factors. However, if the different facets are conceived of as dimensions of a general self-concept, the factors reflecting these dimensions would be expected to be intercorrelated.

Another assumption implicitly made in the previous discussion is that only one meaningful factor has "emerged" from the analysis.[10] Suppose now that a researcher defined self-concept as a unidimensional construct, but when the correlation matrix of the items meant to measure this construct is factor analyzed, there is a strong indication that two relatively independent factors underlie the relations among the items. Faced with such results, the researcher may stick to the original conception of unidimensionality of self-concept and conclude that the attempted scale development failed or was only partially successful. In light of such a conclusion, the researcher may decide to retain items that have meaningful loadings on only one of the factors that he or she deems to be consistent with the definition of self-concept.

When necessary, items are revised, new items written or selected, and the process outlined above is repeated. Suppose that this is done, and again more than one meaningful factor "emerges." In principle, there is nothing to stop a researcher from persisting in efforts to create a measure of what he or she conceives as a unidimensional construct. It stands to reason, however, that when faced with repeated failures to develop a measure that is consistent with the definition of the construct, a researcher would have to resort to other courses of action. Depending, among many other things, on the researcher's convictions, theoretical formulations, and tenacity, he or she may abandon efforts to develop the measure, resort to

---

[10]The issue of criteria for the number of factors to be retained is complex and controversial. For a discussion, see Chapter 22.

different methods of measurement, search for contaminating variables, revise the definition of the construct, to name but some alternatives.

Whatever the course of action, researchers and consumers of research should beware of the reification trap, which is exemplified by queries as to whether a specific scale *really* measures the construct under consideration (e.g., Does the Wechsler Intelligence Scale *really* measure intelligence?). This is a wrong question to ask, as it overlooks the fact that one is dealing with an abstraction, not with some object against which the measure can be applied in order to ascertain whether it "fits."

A meaningful and essential question to raise about a measure is whether it is consistent with the definition of the construct it is meant to be tapping. When considering, for example, a measure of intelligence, it is necessary to examine whether it is consistent with the definition of intelligence that the measure is said to be tapping or reflecting. Factor analysis is one of the most powerful analytic approaches that may be used for this purpose. In fact, the history of measurement of mental abilities and the controversies surrounding such attempts is part and parcel of the history of developments in factor analysis, of its extensive applications, and of controversies surrounding it.

Spearman (1904), who laid the foundations of factor analysis, used it in his persistent efforts to lend support to his two-factor theory of intelligence, according to which a common (or general) factor, *g*, underlies measures of mental ability, and a unique (or specific) factor, *s*, underlies each of the measures. Similarly, Thurstone (1947), who conceived of intelligence as comprised of relatively differentiated mental abilities, resorted to factor analysis in the development of a measure of primary mental abilities. The role of factor analysis in theoretical development and construct validation of measures of mental abilities is epitomized in Guilford's extensive work on the "structure of intellect" (for a summary, as well as an historical background of the development of mental testing, see Guilford, 1967).

In the course of reading the preceding discussion, you have probably wondered how, in view of differences in construct definitions and measurement approaches, one goes about determining who is "correct." We would, therefore, like to remind you of what we said earlier, namely that a construct by itself is not meaningful. A construct derives its meaning and relevance from the theoretical context, the nomological network, within which it is embedded—a topic to which we return in the section entitled Cross-Structure Analysis.

In sum, exploratory factor analysis can be invaluable at the stage of the construction of a measure. A researcher who, for example, believes that he or she has constructed a unidimensional measure, may find, upon factor analyzing it, that it is multidimensional and that a single total score on the scale is not tenable. Conversely, presuming to have constructed a multidimensional measure, a researcher may discover that it is unidimensional.

Factor analysis may also be invaluable to a person contemplating the use of an existing measure. Following are but some examples when factor analysis of an existing scale may prove essential or extremely useful:

1. When no information regarding the internal structure of the measure is available—an all too common occurrence in sociobehavioral research. On the basis of the factor loadings, it may, for example, be concluded that certain items are irrelevant (e.g., they have very low loadings) or that they even go counter to the definition of the construct the scale is presumably measuring (e.g., their loadings have the "wrong" sign; they have meaningful loadings on the "wrong" factor, or on more than one factor.)

2. When it appears or is even expected that the factor structure may be different from the one reported by the author of the measure. This may happen, among other things, because a different type of respondent is being used (e.g., males versus females, young versus old), changes due to history (e.g., prewar versus postwar conditions).

3. When the prospective user has reservations about the adequacy of factor analyses of the scale (e.g., the sampling and/or the size of the sample, the number of factors retained, the method of extraction or rotation of factors). We discuss and illustrate some such issues in Chapter 22.

CONFIRMATORY FACTOR ANALYSIS

Earlier, we said that confirmatory factor analysis is addressed to parameter estimation and to the testing of hypotheses. Our aim in the present section is very modest. All we will do is describe, in very general terms, what the application of confirmatory factor analysis means and what it entails. To this end, we will use the same substantive example we have used when we introduced exploratory factor analysis, namely the measurement of Self-Concept. We leave an elaboration of contrasts between exploratory and confirmatory factor analysis to Chapters 22 and 23, where we apply both to the same sets of illustrative data, using the substantive example described here.

Suppose, then, that it is desired to carry out a confirmatory factor analysis of indicators (e.g., items) of Self-Concept. Unlike exploratory factor analysis, in confirmatory factor analysis it is, obviously, necessary to advance hypotheses to be tested. For illustrative purposes, it will be assumed that Self-Concept is hypothesized to be comprised of two correlated dimensions—Academic and Social—each being tapped by three indicators, as depicted in Figure 4.5.

Following the conventions described earlier in this chapter, the constructs (factors, latent variables) are depicted by circles, whereas the indicators (manifest variables) are depicted by squares. In Figure 4.5, A = Academic Self-Concept, S = Social Self-Concept, and the X's are their indicators. The curved bidirectional arrow indicates that the two dimensions of Self-Concept are said to be correlated. Notice that, according to this model, each indicator reflects (has a loading on) one factor only. Also, the errors (i.e., the e's) are said to be not correlated. Using correlations, or covariances, among the indicators, confirmatory factor analysis is

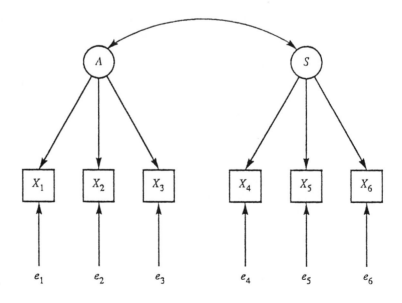

Figure 4.5

applied to estimate the weights of the indicators on the factors, the correlation, or covariance, between the factors, and the errors.[11]

Broadly speaking, the test of the model consists of determining whether the observed relations (correlations or covariances) among the indicators can be reproduced or closely approximated by using the parameter estimates. Referring to Figure 4.5, if the model fits the data, it should be possible to reproduce or closely approximate the correlation between X_1 and X_2, for example, by using (multiplying) their weights on A, as this is the only thing they are said, according to the model, to have in common. In contrast, the only thing X_1 and X_4, say, share, is that the respective factors that they reflect (A and S) are correlated. Accordingly, the correlation between the factors and the weights of the indicators on the factors would have to be used (multiplied) when attempting to reproduce the correlation between these indicators.

We are very anxious not to create the false impression that the process of confirmatory factor analysis is straightforward and incontestable. We believe, however, that it would be ill advised to attempt to discuss here various issues that make for the complexity and ambiguity of the process, as the issues themselves are complex and are, therefore, given detailed treatments in subsequent chapters.

Among issues that play a major role in the process of confirmatory factor analysis and that are discussed in detail in subsequent chapters are:

1. Model specification. Thus, when a model such as the one under consideration is tested, it is assumed that it is correctly specified.

2. The logic of hypothesis testing. Strictly speaking, an hypothesis cannot be confirmed. All one can do is reject or fail to reject it. Failure to reject a model leads to the conclusion that it has been confirmed. That this is a misnomer becomes clear when it is recognized that various other models may be shown to fit the data.

3. The difference between statistical significance and substantive importance, and related issues of sample size, effect size, power of statistical tests of significance.

Rest assured that the preceding was *not* intended to confuse or intimidate you, although it may have had such an effect. We were faced with the dilemma of either glossing over the complexities and running the risk of launching you on the road of misapplications and misinterpretations, or of hinting at the complexities and running the risk of confusing and intimidating you. We feel strongly that it is far better to run the latter risk.

Whatever your reaction to the issues listed above, we urge you not to worry about them at this stage. As we said, they are dealt with in detail in subsequent chapters. All we wanted to do is put you on notice that you will have to become familiar with them in order to be an intelligent consumer or user of confirmatory factor analysis.

Cross-Structure Analysis

Internal-structure analysis, discussed and illustrated in the preceding section, is necessary in order to determine whether there is correspondence between the structure of a set of indicators and the construct they are said to reflect. It is important, however, to recognize that evidence from internal-structure analysis is necessary but not sufficient to lend support to the construct validity of a measure or a set of indicators. The reason is that a given internal structure may be consistent with definitions of different constructs. Thus, for example, when

---

[11]How this is accomplished, is explained and illustrated in Chapter 23.

a construct is defined as unidimensional, it is necessary to demonstrate that the structure of the measure, or the indicators, designed to tap the construct is unidimensional. However, such evidence does not preclude the possibility that a unidimensional construct different from the one the researcher has in mind is being tapped. Moreover, the structure may be a consequence of aspects specific to the method of measurement being used (see discussion of method factors under Convergent and Discriminant Validity, below).

Earlier in this chapter, it was said that the meaning of a construct inheres in its relations with other constructs in a nomological network. Consequently, construct validation ultimately rests on studying relations between the construct in question and other constructs or variables in a theoretical context. Hence, the label nomological validity (Campbell, 1960; Cronbach & Meehl, 1955) used to refer to this approach.

Cross-structure analysis amounts to tests of hypotheses in which the construct in question is one of the variables. For example, assume that one is concerned with two constructs, X and Y, and that multiple indicators are used to measure each of them. Following procedures discussed in the preceding section, one would study the internal structure of the indicators of each of the constructs. But, in addition, it would be necessary to do a cross-structure analysis. Note that we are using the term cross-structure analysis in the broad sense of studying relations among indicators of two or more constructs. Using a theoretical framework, one may, for example, hypothesize that X and Y are positively correlated, or that X affects Y, or that Y affects X. Whatever the hypothesis, X and Y are unobservable (latent) variables. The hypothesis is, therefore, tested by studying the relations among the indicators that presumably manifest the constructs in question.

Support of the hypothesis lends support to the validity of the indicators (measures) of X, Y, or both. Failure to support the hypothesis (see discussion of hypothesis testing in Chapter 9) does not necessarily mean that the indicators of X, say, are not valid. Alternative explanations for the failure to support the hypothesis include (a) questionable theoretical framework, (b) dubious validity of the indicators of Y, and (c) deficiencies in the research design or the analysis. (For implications of negative evidence, see Cronbach & Meehl, 1955, pp. 295–296.)

Important as cross-structure analysis is for construct validation, it is necessary to always bear in mind that alternative explanations and models are possible even when the model tested fits the data well. Assume, for example, that a model consisting of multiple indicators of two constructs has been found to fit the data. It is possible that what are conceived of as two constructs are two aspects of the same construct (as in the example given in connection with Figure 4.5).

There is no simple answer to the question of how one selects from among alternative models that fit the data equally well (see Tesser & Krauss, 1976, for a discussion of such issues and suggested solutions). Testing the fit of a model is but one aspect of the interplay between theory and observed phenomena. In general, the more articulated the theory and the model derived from it, the more confidence one would have in one's conclusions when the model is found to fit the data. Yet finding that a given model fits a given set of data does not constitute unequivocal evidence that it is the "true" model. It is always possible for another model, derived from a different theoretical framework, to also fit the data. Considerations of the logic and meaning of hypothesis testing (Chapter 9) are directly relevant to the issues raised here.

The discussion thus far has dealt with relations among constructs. In certain situations, a study may be concerned with the relation between a construct and an observed variable. For example, one may wish to study the relation between conservatism and age, or between self-esteem and sex. A special case of the situation in which the relation between a construct and an observed variable is studied within the context of construct validation is what has been referred to as the "known groups" approach. Cronbach and Meehl (1955), who referred to this approach as "group differences," described it as follows: "If our understanding of a construct leads us to expect two groups to differ on the test, this expectation may be tested directly" (p. 287). Support of the hypothesis (i.e., the expectation) would lend support to the validity of inferences made on the basis of responses to the measurement of the construct.

Using the known groups approach in the process of construct validation is particularly prone to an error referred to by logicians as the fallacy of affirming the consequent (see Chapter 9). In the context of construct validation, the fallacy of affirming the consequent is committed when differences of known groups on a given measure are construed as evidence of the validity of the measure to tap a construct in question. Probably the most flagrant example of the fallacy is selecting items for a scale, because they discriminate among known groups, and then using differences among the groups on the scale as evidence of construct validity. Unfortunately, one often encounters such practices in sociobehavioral research. For example, item selection for many sex-role instruments was based on their ability to discriminate between males and females (see Constantinople, 1973, for a review). Now, it is one thing to maintain that a given scale measures masculinity, say, and hypothesize that males will score higher than females on this scale. It is quite another thing and a fallacy to maintain that a scale measures masculinity, *because* males score higher on it than do females. As Constantinople (1973) pointed out:

In all probability, the length of the big toe would discriminate men and women, but does having a longer toe than most women make a woman less "feminine," and can one have more confidence that she is less "feminine" because she scores deviantly on a number of items with similarly critical content? (p. 405)

CONVERGENT AND DISCRIMINANT VALIDATION

A researcher who is planning to measure a construct is faced with a choice from a wide array of different, often bewildering methods and approaches to measurement. For example, when attempting to measure attitudes, one may choose to do this by resorting to self-reports, projective techniques, inferences on the basis of observed behavior, physiological reactions, sociometry, to name but a few broad approaches.[12]

Even after an approach has been decided upon, one is still faced with a variety of methods to choose from. Suppose one decides to use self-reports to measure attitudes; should one use a summated-rating scale, an equal-appearing interval scale, a Guttman scale, a Q–sort, a check list, or an open-ended questionnaire? (See Chapter 6, for a description of some major approaches to measurement.)

The validity of any method of measurement, or technique of data collection, is potentially threatened by a host of factors related to the subjects, the researcher, and the research settings. When a single method is used to measure a construct, it is not possible to determine whether and to what extent subjects' responses are a result of, say, response set, reactivity to researcher's expectations, the specific research settings, to name but a few.[13]

Researchers often use a single method (e.g., summated-rating scale; see Chapter 6) to measure several constructs (e.g., attitudes toward blacks, self-concept, conservatism) and then intercorrelate the scores in order to study the relations among the constructs. Under such

---

[12]For a very good discussion of different approaches to the measurement of attitudes and the importance of using more than one approach, see Cook and Selltiz (1964).

[13]These and related issues are discussed in Chapters 10 and 11.

circumstances, the observed correlations may be largely, even solely, due to the specific method used to measure the constructs.

An example of the hazard of relying on a single method of measurement will be given from the area of intergroup stereotypes. There is a relatively large research literature in which different researchers claim to have found high agreement and stability among different respondents, at different times, regarding stereotypes of various groups (e.g., Turks, Jews, blacks). In a critique of this research area, Ehrlich and Rinehart (1965) maintained that the consistency of the findings in the various studies was due largely to their reliance on the "stereotype check list." In support of their claim, Ehrlich and Rinehart (1965) demonstrated important differences in responses, depending on whether subjects were given a stereotype check list or an open-ended questionnaire. For example, respondents using the check list attributed larger numbers of traits to the target groups and exhibited greater consensus than did respondents using the open-ended questionnaire. Moreover, the trait list generated by respondents using the open-ended format was markedly different from the one used in the check-list format.

In order to overcome problems and biases inherent in the use of a single method, various authors have advocated the use of multiple methods for the measurement of a construct. Some authors (e.g., Garner, Hake, & Erikson, 1956) referred to such an approach as multiple operationalism. Others (e.g., Denzin, 1978, Chapter 10) referred to it as triangulation. Still others (Campbell & Fiske, 1959) referred to it as a multimethod approach. Whatever the specific term, it is such an approach that holds promise of detecting biases due to a specific method or to an interaction between a method and other factors.

In a seminal paper, Campbell and Fiske (1959) proposed the concepts convergent and discriminant validity. *Convergent validity* refers to a convergence among different methods (preferably maximally different ones) designed to measure the same construct. For example, a high correlation between a paper-and-pencil measure and a projective technique, both designed to measure anxiety, say, constitutes evidence of convergent validity. In other words, convergent validity refers to the confirmation of the measurement of a construct by the use of multiple methods.

Discriminant validity refers to the distinctiveness of constructs, demonstrated by the divergence of methods designed to measure different constructs. Thus, for example, the correlation between two scales said to measure two distinct constructs (e.g., anxiety and introversion) should be not so high as to raise doubt whether distinct constructs are being measured.

Fallacies concerning distinctiveness or the lack thereof of constructs have been discussed under such labels as jingle and jangle fallacies. The jingle fallacy refers to the belief that, *because* different things are called by the same name, they are the same thing. Conversely, the jangle fallacy refers to the belief that things are different from each other, *because* they are called by different names. Examples of jingle and/or jangle fallacies abound in sociobehavioral research literature. For interesting discussions and examples, see Kelley (1927, pp. 62–64) and Hartley (1967).

In the context of measurement of constructs, jingle fallacies are often encountered in the form of low correlations among instruments said to be measuring the same construct. Conversely, jangle fallacies are encountered in the form of correlations too high for comfort among measures said to be measuring distinct constructs. A case in point are the various measures used to measure a "perceptual style" referred to as field dependence–independence (FDI). Correlations among various measures presumably measuring FDI range from moderately negative to moderately positive, with a median of about .4 (see, for example, Arbuthnot, 1972; Witkin, Dyk, Faterson, Goodenough, & Karp, 1962, pp. 44–45), leading Cronbach (1970) to comment: "When tests supposed to measure the same thing correlate zero or even negatively in some groups, it is clear that no one task can be relied on" (p. 628; see also, Arbuthnot, 1972).

Without going into details, we note that FDI was conceived as a personality construct distinct from ability constructs. Consequently, correlations between FDI measures and ability measures should not be too high, thereby providing evidence of discriminant validity. Because of the lack of convergent validity, noted above, it is not possible to make a blanket statement about the correlations between FDI measures and measures of ability. It has, however, been demonstrated that some FDI measures correlate highly with ability measures, leading Vernon (1972) to comment: "The strong positive correlation with such a wide range of spatial tests is almost embarrassing" (p. 368).

Turning to another example: citing Wylie's (1974) review of 93 attempts to study convergent validity of various measures of Self-Esteem, Briggs and Cheek (1986) stated: "Correlations between various scales constructed to assess global self-esteem have ranged from zero to .8, with an average correlation of only .4" (p. 131). Not surprisingly, they concluded: "The status of self-esteem measurement research had become something of an embarrassment to the field of personality psychology" (p. 131).

In discussions of convergent and discriminant validity, reference is frequently made to "high" and "low" correlations without specifying what these terms mean (we have done this earlier). Needless to say, absence of criteria for what are to be deemed high and low correlations opens the door to ambiguities, disagreements among researchers, and even inconsistencies in the work of single researchers. An example of the latter comes from a study of superior, peer, and self-ratings of job performance. Reporting correlations of .52, .53, and .65 between superior and peer ratings of three aspects of job performance, Lawler (1967) concluded that these indicate "good convergent validity" (p. 374). However, reporting on what appears to be another aspect of the same study, Lawler (1966) stated that the correlation between superiors' rankings of two aspects of job performance is .56. This time, the following interpretation was offered: "The correlation coefficient was not so large as to indicate that managers were unable to discriminate between performance and ability factors" (p. 158).

MULTITRAIT-MULTIMETHOD MATRIX

Campbell and Fiske (1959) proposed the analysis of a multitrait-multimethod (MTMM) matrix for the purpose of studying convergent and discriminant validity of measures. A MTMM matrix is a matrix of correlations among two or more traits measured by two or more distinct methods. Such a matrix for three traits and three methods is depicted in Figure 4.6.

We indicate correlations only in certain parts of the figure so that we may use other parts to label different segments of the MTMM matrix. For illustrative purposes, think of A as standing for Anxiety, B for Bashfulness, and C for Cheerfulness. Think of Method 1 as a paper-and-pencil questionnaire, of Method 2 as some kind of projective technique, and of Method 3 as ratings by a clinical psychologist. Thus A_1 indicates anxiety as measured by a paper-and-pencil questionnaire; B_1 is bashfulness as measured by a paper-and-pencil questionnaire; and so forth up to C_3, which stands for cheerfulness as measured by ratings of a clinical psychologist.[14]

The correlations along the principal diagonal (from upper left to lower right) are the reliabilities of each of the measures (e.g., $r_{A_1 A_1}$ is the reliability of anxiety as measured by a paper-and-pencil questionnaire; see Chapter 5 for a discussion of reliability).

Correlations enclosed in solid triangles are between different traits measured by the same

---

[14]The issue of what constitute different methods is discussed below.

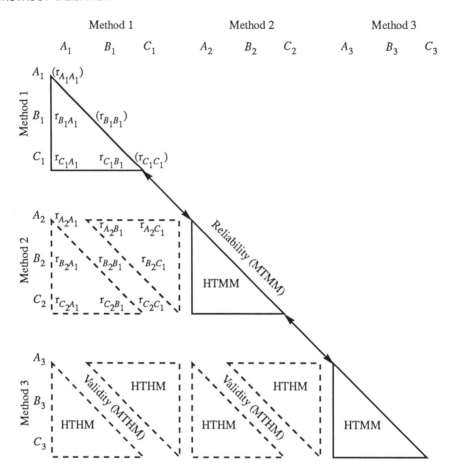

Figure 4.6

method, hence *heterotrait-monomethod* (HTMM) triangles. For example, $r_{B_1A_1}$ is the correlation between bashfulness and anxiety as measured by a paper-and-pencil questionnaire.

Correlations enclosed in dashed triangles are between different traits measured by different methods, hence *heterotrait-heteromethod* (HTHM) triangles. For example, $r_{C_2A_1}$ is the correlation between cheerfulness as measured by a projective technique and anxiety as measured by a paper-and-pencil questionnaire.

Correlations on the diagonal between two HTHM triangles are between the same trait measured by different methods, hence *monotrait-heteromethod* (MTHM) diagonal. For example, $r_{C_2C_1}$ is the correlation between cheerfulness as measured by a projective technique and cheerfulness as measured by a paper-and-pencil questionnaire. The MTHM diagonal is referred to as the validity diagonal.

Some aspects of the information that may be gleaned from the MTMM matrix will now be indicated. Contrast, for example, $r_{B_1A_1}$ with $r_{B_2A_1}$. In both cases, we are dealing with a correlation between bashfulness and anxiety. But $r_{B_1A_1}$ indicates the correlation between these traits when both are measured by the *same* method (i.e., Method 1), whereas $r_{B_2A_1}$ indicates the correlation between bashfulness and anxiety as measured by two *different* methods (i.e., B is measured by Method 2, and A is measured by Method 1). If $r_{B_1A_1}$ is larger than $r_{B_2A_1}$, it may be concluded that this is due to the effect of a common method (Method 1) used for the measurement of B and A when the former is calculated.

Look now at the MTHM diagonals (i.e., validity diagonals). Because these represent correlations between the *same* traits when measured by *different* methods (e.g., $r_{A_2A_1}$), one would require that they be high, thereby indicating convergent validity. Contrast now a given correlation in a MTHM diagonal with correlations in either the row or the column of the HTHM triangles corresponding to it. For example, contrast $r_{A_2A_1}$ with $r_{A_2B_2}$ or with $r_{B_2A_1}$ and notice that, in all instances, the *same* two methods are used (i.e., Methods 1 and 2). But $r_{A_2A_1}$ indicates the correlation between two methods used to measure the *same* trait, whereas the other correlations are between the same two methods when used to measure *different* traits. Consequently, one would expect $r_{A_2A_1}$ to be higher than correlations in its row or column (e.g., $r_{A_2B_1}$), otherwise the validity of the measures involved would have to be questioned.

Reasoning along lines indicated in the preceding paragraphs, Campbell and Fiske (1959) arrived at a set of guidelines and criteria for studying convergent and discriminant validity in the MTMM matrix. Their guidelines and criteria were, however, criticized as being limited, ambiguous, and based on questionable assumptions (see, for example, Althauser & Heberlein, 1970; Jackson, 1969; see also Alwin's, 1974, comments on Althauser & Heberlein, and Althauser's, 1974, reply). Various other approaches to the analysis of the MTMM matrix have been proposed (for reviews, see Alwin, 1974; Schmitt, Coyle, & Saari, 1977; Schmitt & Stults, 1986). There appears to be agreement that the most informative approach is confirmatory factor analysis (*CFA*). Applying *CFA* to a MTMM matrix one can study, among other things, the effects of traits, methods, and correlations among them. In Chapter 23, we illustrate the application of *CFA* to the MTMM matrix and offer references to studies in which this approach has been used.

WHAT ARE DIFFERENT METHODS?

Recall that Campbell and Fiske (1959) referred to convergent validity as a high correlation between maximally different methods used to measure the same trait. There are, however, no clear criteria for what constitute different methods, not to mention *maximally* different ones. Part of the problem is that methods that appear to be different may be intercorrelated because of specific traits, settings, subjects, and the like used in a given study. For example, different methods of measurement of specific traits in a specific setting may be affected by halo, social desirability, and the like, thereby making the methods less different from each other than they appear to be (see Jackson, 1969, for a discussion of this point).

Various authors appear to be using different criteria for what they consider different methods in a MTMM matrix. Because of the implications this has for the analysis and interpretation of MTMM matrices, several examples of the substantial variability in what are considered different methods will be given. Following is a description of a MTMM matrix that Avison (1978) analyzed:

The three traits were the subjects' sense of participation in decision-making in the home (as a child), in the school (as a student), and on the job (as an employee). Each trait was measured by three methods: perceived freedom to participate, perceived impact of participation, and actual frequency of participation. (p. 441)

It will be noted that Avison (1978) himself conceded that "the data differed somewhat from more standard examples of MTMM situations" (p. 441). Yet treating questions about one's *perceptions* of participation in decision-making and the *perceived* impact of the *perceived* participation as distinct methods of measurement is, to say the least, questionable.

Another example of a questionable conception of what are different methods comes from a study by Wanous and Lawler (1972), who used a MTMM matrix to study the measurement and meaning of job satisfaction. Essentially, employees were asked to rate their job on 23 items five times, each time using a different frame of reference (e.g., "How much each quality or characteristic is present on your job?" "How much each quality or characteristic do you think should be associated with your job?" p. 98). Using these ratings, the authors derived several indices (e.g., the difference between rating of the job as it is now and as it should be) and used the following four "methods" in a MTMM matrix: (a) Satisfaction, (b) Is Now, (c) Would Like minus Is Now, and (d) Should Be minus Is Now.[15]

It should be noted that Wanous and Lawler equated operational definitions with methods (see, for example, pp. 98 and 102).[16] In a reanalysis of Wanous and Lawler's data, Kalleberg and Kluegel (1975) repeated this, as is evidenced by the following statement: "Four traits or facets of job satisfaction were measured by each of *four methods or operational definitions* [italics added]" (p. 6). Be that as it may, Kalleberg and Kluegel (1975) maintained that Wanous and Lawler drew "faulty inferences" (p. 1) from their data.

Using *CFA*, Kalleberg and Kluegel (1975) found, among other things, that the four "methods" used by Wanous and Lawler are "highly intercorrelated; in fact, the third and fourth methods of measurement are so highly intercorrelated (.96) that they are best considered as one method of measurement" (p. 7). The high correlations are not surprising when one bears in mind what Wanous and Lawler viewed as different methods of measurement. For example, the aforementioned .96 correlation is between an index based on the difference in rating the job as one "Would Like" it to be and as it "Is Now," and an index based on the difference of "Should Be" and "Is Now."

The MTMM matrix has frequently been used in attitude research. For example, Ostrom (1969) used four methods (e.g., summated-rating scales, equal-appearing interval scales) to measure affective, behavioral, and cognitive components of attitudes toward the church. Bagozzi (1980a, pp. 136–146), who reanalyzed Ostrom's data using *CFA*, found, among other things, that the correlation between two of the measures was "nearly unity" (p. 142) and that "one may not reject the hypothesis that the two methods are equivalent" (p. 144).

It is not possible to attempt to explain such findings without going into substantive and measurement issues. Recall, however, that our purpose here is limited to the issue of what are considered different methods by various researchers. Suffice it to point out that, whereas Ostrom (1969) used different methods to measure attitudes toward the church, they share common elements (e.g., self-report, paper-and-pencil measures, some form of indication of agreement-disagreement with attitude statements).

Ratings from different sources (e.g., self-ratings, ratings by peers, ratings by superiors) are very often treated as different methods in MTMM matrices (e.g., Fiske, 1949; Schneider, 1970). Kavanagh, MacKinney, and Wolins (1971) "question the value of including self-ratings in a multitrait-multimethod analysis" on the grounds that "a particular bit of behavior may have a different meaning for the actor (act meaning) than for the observer (action meaning)" (p. 36). What is one to conclude from the preceding? Are self-ratings addressed to different aspects of what is being rated than are ratings by superiors, say, and should they, therefore, not be treated as different methods? On the other hand, do self-ratings and ratings by staff, for example, constitute the same method of measurement? There are no simple answers to these questions. In effect, we have come full circle in our quest for criteria for the determination of what are to be considered different methods of measurement. Wolins (1982), who grappled with the issue of what constitute different methods, commented: "Although it makes sense to think of traits being correlated, I cannot get a cognitive grip on the idea of methods being correlated" (p. 63).

---

[15]Problems concerning the use of difference scores are discussed in Chapters 13 and 21.

[16]Operational definitions are discussed in Chapter 8.

In sum, we hope that the preceding discussion served to underscore the complexities inherent in the use, analysis, and interpretation of the MTMM matrix. Commenting on the use of the MTMM matrix to evaluate measures, Campbell (1960) observed that it is "a humbling experience, generating modesty and caution" (p. 552). As was stated earlier, analysis of the MTMM matrix is illustrated in Chapter 23.

A NOTE ON CONTENT VALIDITY

When the concept of validity was introduced in Chapter 3, it was pointed out that, whereas it is convenient to discuss different aspects of the validation process separately, there is a danger that this may lead to oversimplification and confusion. In particular, this may contribute to the perpetuation of the mistaken notion of different "types" of validity. Nowhere is the confusion more evident than in discussions of content validity, and in attempts to distinguish between it and construct validity. The reason for the confusion is that content validity is not a type of validity at all.

In order to clarify its current status, it is worthwhile to note that, until recently, content validity has been almost the sole province of educational psychologists and educators concerned with measurement of achievement. Demonstration of content validity was, ipso facto, expected when a measure of achievement was concerned, whereas demonstration of construct validity was expected when a measure of traits, attributes, and the like was concerned. Textbooks in measurement have, by and large, reinforced this conception. Thorndike and Hagen (1977), for example, stated: "It should be clear that rational or content validity, is important primarily for measures of achievement" (p. 58).

In recent years, notions about content validity have come to play a prominent role in the work of agencies and professionals concerned with employee selection and equal employment opportunity. This interest in content validity was largely stimulated by judicial decrees regarding the use of tests in selection, certification, and the like, and by guidelines on employee selection issued by federal agencies. For example, in "uniform guidelines on employee selection" adopted by the Equal Employment Opportunity Commission, Civil Service Commission, Department of Labor, and Department of Justice (1978), standards for demonstrating content validity are delineated. Among other things, it is pointed out that:

To demonstrate the content validity of a selection procedure, a user should show that the behavior(s) demonstrated in the selection procedure are a representative sample of the behavior(s) of the job in question or that the selection procedure provides a representative sample of the work product of the job. (p. 38302)

The most important thing to note about statements such as the preceding, be they made in the context of achievement testing or selection procedures, is that they are inconsistent with the definition of validity. As discussed in the beginning of Chapter 3, validity refers to inferences made about scores, not to an assessment of the content of an instrument. This is not to say that the content of an instrument is irrelevant. Clearly, it is paramount, but it does not constitute evidence of the validity of the instrument.

It remains true that, except for people expressly concerned with what has been labeled content validity, most sociobehavioral scientists have manifested a cavalier attitude concerning the domain of content they were presumably measuring (see Bohrnstedt, 1983, p. 98).

Contrary to the impression one may form on the basis of what has been written about content validity, content relevance is not confined to measures of achievement. How can one conceive of a construct and proceed to develop a measure of it in the absence of a domain of content? The very definition of a construct implies a domain of content. Consider, for example, the construct of conservatism. Is one concerned with "temperamental conservatism," "situational conservatism," "political conservatism," "conservatism as a philosophy?" (see Rossiter, 1968). Needless to say, the content of a specific measure of conservatism will depend on which of the preceding or other conceptions of conservatism one wishes to measure. Earlier in this chapter (see, in particular, the section entitled Logical Analysis), the requirement that the content of a measure be consistent with the definition of the construct was discussed in detail and will, therefore, not be repeated here.

It is considerations such as the preceding that have prompted various authors to argue against the notion of content validity (see, for example, Fitzpatrick, 1983; Guion, 1977, 1978; Messick, 1975, 1980, 1981; Tenopyr, 1977). Moreover, these authors and others have stressed the idea that all measures have to be assessed from the perspective of the construct they are said to be tapping. Thus, Messick (1975) maintained that "*all measurement should be construct-referenced*" (p. 957). Tenopyr (1977) contended that "any inference relative to prediction and, furthermore, all inferences relative to test scores, are based upon underlying constructs" (p. 48). And Guion (1978) declared that "*the evaluation of the score assigned to performance . . . must be evaluated according to that principle of construct validity concerning alternative interpretations of scores*" (p. 209).

Responding to arguments such as those quoted in the preceding paragraph, the most recent revision of the *Standards for educational and psychological testing* (American Psychological Association, 1985) stated:

Methods classed in the content-related category thus should often be concerned with the psychological construct underlying the test as well as with the character of test content. *There is often no sharp distinction between test content and test construct* [italics added]. (pp. 11)

CONCLUDING REMARKS

Much has been said in this and the preceding chapter about the validation process—that there is a clear danger of losing the forest for the trees. Therefore, we feel it important to stress that the gist of the message we tried to convey is that the validation process is part and parcel of scientific inquiry. From this several things ensue.

Theory, research design, and analysis have direct bearing on the validation process, just as the validation process has direct bearing on them. Consequently, construction of measures without regard to or knowledge of other aspects of the research endeavor is bound to be abortive. It is for this reason that we kept referring you to other chapters in the book, all the while being acutely aware of the frustration such monotonous suggestions may engender.

Being a complex and ongoing endeavor, validation requires serious and sustained efforts. In the foreword to a book devoted to current issues in social measurement, the editors (Bohrnstedt & Borgatta, 1981) pointed out that "the quality of the models available to evaluate measures far outstrip the quality of the measures themselves" (p. 14). Bohrnstedt and Borgatta did not mean that measurement models are not important but that, in view of the state of measurement in the sociobehavioral sciences, what is probably more important is for researchers "to approach development of measures with more care and forethought. *Good measures may take years to develop, not days or weeks* [italics added]" (p. 14).

In view of the cavalier manner in which measures are constructed and used in sociobehavioral research, we believe it fitting to conclude with Crandall's (1973) indictment that "the casual generation of new scales is professionally irresponsible" (p. 52).

In the present chapter, we address the broad topic of measurement precision. After some general observations about the status of reliability in measurement and research, we turn to a consideration of different types and sources of measurement errors, and how they relate to conceptions and definitions of reliability. Classical test theory is then presented as an example of reliability theories that have been advanced and as a means of introducing fundamental concepts of reliability. This is followed by a review of some of the most common approaches to the estimation of reliability, with an emphasis on internal-consistency estimates, in the context of which numerical examples are analyzed by hand and/or through the use of a computer program. Considerations in the selection of a reliability estimate are then reviewed. The chapter concludes with some selected topics, among which are standards for reliability, relation between reliability and validity, effects of unreliability on statistical estimation.

STATUS OF RELIABILITY IN MEASUREMENT AND RESEARCH

Judging by the comparatively greater amount of attention devoted to reliability (as opposed to validity) in measurement and research in sociobehavioral sciences, it would appear that many consider it to be *the* paramount measurement problem. This is a misconception whose deleterious consequences may be far reaching.

Because reliability lends itself more easily to mathematical formulations than does validity, and because high reliability coefficients are attainable with relative ease, many researchers and consumers of research appear to overlook the fact that *reliability is a necessary but not a sufficient condition for validity*. That is, a measure cannot be valid, if it is not reliable, but being reliable it is not necessarily valid for the purpose its author or a user has in mind. High reliability coefficients can be so alluring that the danger of erroneously treating them as evidence of validity is ever present. This is probably why Rozeboom (1966) labeled reliability as "the poor man's validity coefficient" or "instant validity" (p. 375).

The foregoing should not be construed as implying that reliability is not that important, that one need not be concerned about the reliability of measures one is using or of those used by others. On the contrary, as will be amply shown in this chapter, reliability of measures is of utmost importance and has to be an integral part of any research undertaking. Our aim in making the above remarks was to place reliability in a proper perspective.

SYSTEMATIC AND UNSYSTEMATIC ERRORS

In a most general sense, "*Reliability* refers to the degree to which test scores are free from errors of measurement" (American Psychological Association, 1985, p. 19). Broadly, two kinds of errors may occur in the process of measurement: systematic and unsystematic. As these labels imply, systematic errors are ones that recur upon repeated measurements, whereas unsystematic or random errors are ones that vary in unpredictable ways upon repeated measurements.

As an example, assume one is measuring the length of a table with a ruler. To assess precision, repeated measurements may be taken so as to note how consistent they are. Although a considerable degree of consistency in such repeated measurements would be expected, some variability would be inevitable. It could be that the ruler was not placed in the same exact location each time or that readings varied from one measurement to another. To the extent that such errors are random, they would vary inconsistently and unpredictably upon repeated measurements, thus, adversely affecting reliability.

Constant or systematic errors may also occur in the course of measuring the length of the table. For example, unknowingly one may be using a ruler that begins not at 0 but rather at 1 inch. Clearly, this type of error will not vary, no matter how many times the measurement is repeated. Thus, so far as systematic errors are concerned, results of repeated measurements will be consistent, hence contributing to reliability of measurement. It is, however, very important to recognize that systematic errors have negative effects on validity. Detailed presentations of sources of unsystematic and systematic errors in sociobehavioral measurements will be found in Ghiselli et al. (1981, pp. 242–247), Nunnally (1978, pp. 225–229), Stanley (1971), and Thorndike (1951).

ON CONCEPTIONS OF RELIABILITY

Writing over three decades ago, Tryon (1957) stated that an investigator turning to any scholarly work for guidance on how to estimate the reliability of a measure

would confront such an array of different formulations that he would be unsure about how to proceed. After fifty years of psychological testing, the problem of discovering the degree to which an objective measure of behavior reliably differentiates individuals is still confused. (p. 229)

In view of many new formulations (including Tryon's), the current status of reliability estimation is considerably more confused or rather more complex. The complexity stems from different theoretical formulations of reliability, based on different assumptions regarding such issues as true scores and errors. As is shown below, different approaches to reliability estimation attend to different sources of errors. Thus, what is viewed as random error from the perspective of one approach may be viewed as systematic error or ignored altogether from another perspective. Statements about *the* reliability of a measure are, therefore, inappropriate and potentially misleading. Instead, "reliability" and "reliability coefficient" need to be regarded as generic terms (American Psychological Association, 1985, p. 19).

PROBLEMS WITH THE NOTION OF REPEATED MEASUREMENTS

Taking repeated measurements of an object enables the physical scientist to assess the precision with which it is measured. The situation is not as simple in sociobehavioral sciences, where most of the variables of interest are not meaningfully susceptible to repeated measurements, not to mention the practical problems inherent in attempts to do this.

The very act of measurement changes the people being measured, to a greater or lesser extent. Thus, answering questions on, say, an achievement test, constitutes learning and practice, and may lead to other changes that would then affect responses on what is believed to be a remeasurement. Or, an individual's consistent responses to an attitude survey administered at two points in time may be due, at least in part, *not* to consistency of attitudes but to the recall of specific responses given at time 1. In short, it is almost always a misnomer to speak of remeasurement, not to mention repeated measurements.

Because of these and other problems, reliability of measures in sociobehavioral sciences is usually estimated by studying the extent to which individuals retain their relative positions in a group. This is generally a reasonable approach, as the interest is most often in interindividual differences (e.g., differences among individuals on particular traits or characteristics), as contrasted with intraindividual differences (e.g., differences within individuals on a particular trait at several points in time or under different circumstances).

When it is desired to make comparative statements about individuals or to make decisions about them on the basis of their scores on some measure, it is essential to know how much confidence may be placed in the scores. Generally speaking, the more reliable a measure is, the greater the confidence one would have in the scores obtained on it (see Standard Error of Measurement, later in this chapter).

CLASSICAL TEST THEORY

Various theories of reliability have been formulated. Because our focus is on the role of reliability in the research context, we do not review these theories but concentrate instead on procedures for the estimation of reliability and implications of reliability for, among other things, validity and statistical analysis. We believe, however, that an illustration of how theories of reliability are formulated will enhance your understanding of theoretical conceptions of reliability as well as estimation procedures derived from them. For historical reasons, and because it served as a point of departure for most of the other theories, we use classical test theory as our illustration.

Since it was proposed by Spearman (1904), the true-score model, or what has come to be known as classical test theory, has been the dominant theory guiding estimation of reliability. The model has undergone both change and expansion, with few people today accepting it in its original form. We present the basic elements and assumptions of the theory (for a detailed presentation of classical test theory, see, Gulliksen, 1950; Lord & Novick, 1968) in order to introduce some fundamental concepts and show how they lead to a definition of reliability. Generalizations and alternative conceptions that have been proposed in order to deal with some of the difficulties or problems inherent in the model will be referred to as needed.

According to the true-score model, an observed score is conceived of as consisting of two components—a true component and an error component. In symbols:

$$X = T + E \qquad (5.1)$$

where X is the fallible, observed score; T is the true score; and E is random error.

Conceptually, the true score can be thought of as the score that would be obtained under ideal or perfect conditions of measurement. Because such conditions never exist, the observed score always contains a certain amount of error.

Although (5.1) is theoretically meaningful, it cannot be used for the purpose of estimating the amount of error contained in an observed score or conversely the precision of such a score. The reason is that (5.1) contains two unknowns (i.e., T and E), and, thus, no solution is possible without further assumptions. In classical test theory, it is assumed that the traits measured are constant and that measurement errors are random. Accordingly, if any individual were to be measured many times, assuming for the moment that he or she remains unchanged, a series of equations such as (5.1) would be obtained, each consisting of the same true score (because it is assumed to be constant) but differing observed scores because of variations in errors. Being random, the mean of measurement errors over many repeated measurements is expected to be zero, that is,

$$E(E) = 0 \tag{5.2}$$

where $E(\ )$ refers to the expectation operator, indicating the expected value, of the random variable E. The expected value of a random variable is its long-run average over an indefinite number of repeated random samples (for a discussion of expectations and their place in statistical and probability theory, see, for example, Edwards, 1964; Hays, 1988, pp. 164–166, 866–872). The true score is, therefore, equal to the expectation of the observed scores, that is, the mean of the observed scores over an indefinite number of repeated measurements:

$$T = E(X) \tag{5.3}$$

This conception is based on the untenable assumption that, when individuals are measured repeatedly, their true scores remain unchanged. Therefore, as was pointed out earlier, a different approach to the estimation of reliability is taken. Instead of measuring one individual repeatedly, many individuals are measured once or twice on the same scale, or on parallel forms (see below), and the information thus obtained is used in the estimation of the reliability of the scale.

With no loss of generality, in the ensuing presentation we will use deviation scores rather than raw scores. Thus (5.1) is restated as:

$$x = t + e \tag{5.1'}$$

where $x = X - \bar{X}$; $t = T - \bar{T}$; $e = E - \bar{E}$; that is, raw scores minus their respective means.

Broadly speaking, differences among individuals in observed scores may be due to true differences among them on the attribute being measured or due to errors (e.g., guessing, inattentiveness, carelessness). Thus conceived, the aim becomes one of partitioning the observed-score variance into true and error components. Before seeing how this may be done, it is necessary to examine the relation between true and error scores. Recalling that errors are conceived to be random, it follows that the expected correlation between true and error scores is zero. It also follows that, when scores across many individuals are averaged, the errors would cancel out (the average of the errors being zero), and, therefore, the average of the observed scores would be expected to equal the average of the true scores. That is,

$$E(X) = E(T) \tag{5.4}$$

Recalling that an observed score is a composite of true and error scores, the observed-score variance can be expressed as the variance of the sum of true and error scores[1]

---

[1]Variance of a composite score is discussed later in this chapter, under Coefficient α.

$$\sigma_x^2 = \sigma_{(t + e)}^2$$
$$= \sigma_t^2 + 2\sigma_{te} + \sigma_e^2 \qquad (5.5)$$

where σ_t^2 = variance of true scores; σ_e^2 = variance of errors; σ_{te} = covariance of true and error scores. However, because the correlation (therefore, the covariance)[2] between true and error scores is zero (see above), the observed-score variance is equal to the sum of true-score and error-score variances

$$\sigma_x^2 = \sigma_t^2 + \sigma_e^2 \qquad (5.6)$$

We examine now the properties of the correlation between observed scores (i.e., $t + e$) and true scores (t):[3]

$$r_{xt} = \frac{\Sigma(t + e)t}{N \, \sigma_x \, \sigma_t}$$

$$= \frac{\Sigma t^2 + \Sigma te}{N \, \sigma_x \, \sigma_t}$$

$$= \frac{\sigma_t^2 + \sigma_{te}}{\sigma_t \, \sigma_x}$$

[because $\sigma_{te} = 0$]

$$= \frac{\sigma_t^2}{\sigma_t \, \sigma_x} = \frac{\sigma_t}{\sigma_x} \qquad (5.7)$$

In words: the correlation between observed scores and true scores is equal to the ratio of the standard deviation of true scores to the standard deviation of observed scores.

Now, the square of the correlation coefficient (r) indicates the proportion of variance shared by the variables being correlated, or the proportion of variance in one variable accounted for by another variable (see Chapter 17). In the present context, the squared correlation indicates the proportion of variance in the observed scores that is due to true differences among the people being measured. That is,

$$r_{xt}^2 = r_{xx} = \frac{\sigma_t^2}{\sigma_x^2} \qquad (5.8)$$

where r_{xx} = reliability of measure X. *This, then, is the definition of reliability of a measure: It is the ratio of true-score variance to observed-score variance.*

From the definition of the *reliability coefficient* (5.8), it follows that its square root is equal to the correlation between observed and true scores (5.7)—referred to as the *reliability index*. Because it refers to a relation between observed scores and scores on a latent variable, or a construct, the reliability index has also been labeled the theoretical validity of a measure (Lord & Novick, 1968, p. 261), or an epistemic correlation (Northrop, 1947, Chapter VII).

Using (5.6), the variance of true scores may be expressed as: $\sigma_t^2 = \sigma_x^2 - \sigma_e^2$. Substituting the preceding for the numerator of (5.8), an alternative expression of reliability is:

---

[2]Variance, covariance, and correlation are discussed in Chapter 17.

[3]In presenting and deriving various correlation equations within the framework of reliability theory, some authors (e.g., Ghiselli et al., 1981; Gulliksen, 1950; Nunnally, 1978; Thorndike, 1982) use r (the sample statistic), whereas others (e.g., Allen & Yen, 1979; Lord & Novick, 1968; Zeller & Carmines, 1980) use ρ (the parameter). We use r in order to be consistent with our usage in subsequent chapters.

$$r_{xt}^2 = r_{xx} = \frac{\sigma_x^2 - \sigma_e^2}{\sigma_x^2}$$

$$= 1 - \frac{\sigma_e^2}{\sigma_x^2} \tag{5.9}$$

From this it can be seen that the reliability can range from 0 to 1. It is 1, when all the observed variance is due to true-score variance; that is, when there are no random errors of measurement. At the other extreme, when all the observed variance is due to random errors of measurement, the reliability is 0.

Note that the model does not distinguish between true variance and systematic error variance (e.g., response style, variance due to the specific method of measurement used). (For the latter, see Chapter 4, Convergent and Discriminant Validation.) In other words, reliability, as defined above, is actually the proportion of observed variance that is systematic. Note also that the definition of reliability, r_{xx}, refers to a squared correlation (i.e., the squared correlation between observed and true scores). Therefore, the reliability coefficient, *not* its square, is interpreted as the proportion of systematic variance in the observed scores. For example, $r_{xx} = .8$ means that .8, or 80%, of the variance of the observed scores is systematic; $1 - .8 = .2$ is the proportion of variance due to random errors.

Earlier, it was pointed out that, because one may attend to different sources of error when estimating reliability, it is more appropriate to use the term reliability generically. Now that it was shown that reliability estimates are essentially squared correlation coefficients, there is another sense in which one should avoid speaking of *the* reliability of a given instrument, without specifying the population from which the sample used for its estimation was drawn.

As was pointed out in Chapter 3, the correlation coefficient is population specific. It follows that, the same instrument may be more or less reliable, depending on the variability of the population of interest. Researchers who bother at all to report reliability estimates for the instruments they use (many do not) frequently report only reliability estimates contained in the manuals of the instruments or estimates reported by other researchers. Such information may be useful for comparative purposes, but it is imperative to recognize that the *relevant reliability estimate is the one obtained for the sample used in the study under consideration*. It is this reliability coefficient that has to be used when calculating other statistics (e.g., standard errors of measurement; see below), and it is this estimate that may help explain certain findings (e.g., lower than expected correlation between variables under study; see "correction" for attenuation, below).

THE NOTION OF PARALLEL MEASURES

Despite their interesting properties, the equations developed above cannot be used for the estimation of reliability, because they include an element that refers to an unobservable—true-score variance. One suggested solution is to use the correlation between two measures of the attribute under study as an estimate of the reliability of either one of them. Clearly, the two measures should be alike, which in the context of classical test theory means that they should be parallel.

Parallel Measures.   Two measures, X_1 and X_2, are said to be parallel if

$$X_1 = T + E_1$$
$$X_2 = T + E_2$$
$$\sigma_{e_1}^2 = \sigma_{e_2}^2 \tag{5.10}$$

That is, two measures are parallel, if they have identical true scores and equal error variances (Novick, 1966). As a consequence, the means and variances of both measures are also equal. Recalling the assumption that errors are random, it follows that errors associated with parallel measures are not correlated among themselves, nor are they correlated with true scores, be they on the same measure or on a parallel one. That is,

$$r_{e_1 e_2} = 0 \tag{5.11}$$

$$r_{e_1 t_1} = r_{e_1 t_2} = r_{e_2 t_2} = r_{e_2 t_1} = 0 \tag{5.12}$$

Using the preceding, it can be shown that the correlation between two parallel measures is an estimate of the reliability of either one of them. Expressing observed scores on each form as composites of true and error scores, the correlation between two parallel forms is:

$$
\begin{aligned}
r_{x_1 x_2} &= \frac{\Sigma(t + e_1)(t + e_2)}{N \, \sigma_{x_1} \sigma_{x_2}} \\
&= \frac{\Sigma t^2 + \Sigma t e_1 + \Sigma t e_2 + \Sigma e_1 e_2}{N \, \sigma_{x_1} \sigma_{x_2}} \\
&= \frac{\sigma_t^2 + \sigma_{te_1} + \sigma_{te_2} + + \sigma_{e_1 e_2}}{\sigma_{x_1} \, \sigma_{x_2}}
\end{aligned} \tag{5.13}
$$

[because the last three terms of the numerator equal zero, and because $\sigma_{x_1} = \sigma_{x_2}$]

$$r_{x_1 x_2} = \frac{\sigma_t^2}{\sigma_x^2}$$

which is consistent with the definition of reliability given earlier.

Adopting the parallel-measures model, one would administer two parallel measures of the attribute in question and use the correlation between them as the estimate of the reliability of either. This, however, implies that the very restrictive assumptions regarding parallel forms are met, which is rarely the case. Because of this and other considerations, the true-score model as originally formulated was found lacking and severely limited.

VARIATIONS ON THE TRUE-SCORE MODEL

Different formulations that may be viewed as variations on the true-score model have been proposed. They all share a basic aim, namely the construction of measures designed to "measure the same phenomenon." The models differ with respect to specific assumptions of the parallel-measures model that are relaxed. At this stage, we offer a brief characterization of some such models. In Chapter 23 (Measurement Models), we show how, through the application of confirmatory factor analysis, it is possible to ascertain the fit of each of these models to data.

Tau-Equivalent Measures.   Two measures are said to be tau-equivalent, if they have identical true scores. Although this is an assumption shared with the parallel-measures model, tau-equivalent measures need not have equal error variances (Novick & Lewis, 1967).

Essentially Tau-Equivalent Measures.   Relaxing the assumptions further, in addition to unequal error variances, true scores on essentially tau-equivalent measures may differ by an additive constant (Novick & Lewis, 1967)—yielding unequal true-score means.

Congeneric Measures.   This least restrictive model within the framework of classical test theory requires only that true scores on measures said to be measuring the same phenomenon be perfectly correlated (Jöreskog, 1971b). Consequently, on congeneric measures, error variances, true-score means, and true-score variances may be unequal.

APPROACHES TO THE ESTIMATION OF RELIABILITY

Reliability may be characterized as a theory of error or, more appropriately, theories of errors. It was noted earlier that measurement errors may emanate from various sources and that what is considered error from one frame of reference may not be considered thus from another frame of reference. Not surprisingly, different definitions and conceptions of error have led to different approaches to the estimation of reliability. This is why it was said earlier that it is misleading to speak of *the* reliability of a measure. Estimates of reliability will differ, to a greater or lesser extent, depending on the specific sources of error being addressed. *It is, therefore, imperative that reports of reliability include sufficient information about the procedure used in its estimation so that readers can ascertain the sources of error that have been addressed.* The most commonly used approaches to the estimation of reliability are presented below in three broad categories.

Test Retest

Conceptually and intuitively, the simplest approach—one corresponding most closely to a view of reliability as consistency or repeatability of measurement—is the test–retest method. According to this approach, a group of people is measured twice, using the same measure, and the two sets of scores thus obtained are correlated. The correlation coefficient is taken as an estimate of the reliability of the measure. Some authors refer to the correlation thus obtained as a coefficient of stability.

The assumption underlying this approach is that the correlation between the two sets of observed scores is due to underlying unobservable true scores that are constant and that the correlation will be less than perfect to the extent that random errors of measurement have occurred. Clearly, this is an unrealistic assumption with respect to most variables of interest in sociobehavioral research (e.g., attitudes, motivation, interests, achievement). It has already been argued that it is a misnomer to speak of remeasurement with respect to most, if not all, such attributes. Suffice it, therefore, to point out here that measuring people twice in a row with the same measure is particularly prone to biases due to carry-over effects, where the mere act of responding to a set of items the first time influences the responses given the second time around. Generally speaking, carry-over effects tend to lead to overestimates of stability from one period to another, hence to inflated estimates of reliability.

One way to minimize carry-over effects is to increase the time interval between two administrations of the same measure. Although this solves some of the problems, it creates others. It is true that the longer the time interval between two administrations of a measure, the lower the probability of carry-over effects. However, it is also true that the longer the time interval, the higher the probability for individuals to undergo real changes in the trait or characteristic under study. Therefore, a low test–retest correlation, for example, may be indicative of a measure with low reliability, of true changes in the individuals measured, or a combination of both. The point is that, in the test–retest model, it is not possible to separate the reliability of a measure from its stability.[4] This is why it is generally suggested that the interval between the two administrations be relatively short, say, a week to two weeks, thereby hoping to tap only random measurement error and not true changes. Because of the serious deficiencies of the test–retest approach, it is recommended that it not be used or that it be used with caution.

Equivalent Forms

In an attempt to avoid some of the problems inherent in the test–retest approach, it has been suggested that reliability be estimated by correlating scores on two different forms of a measure designed to "measure the same phenomenon." Ideally, the two forms should be parallel. But because the very restrictive assumptions underlying parallel measures are rarely met (see above), equivalent, or alternate, forms that depart more or less from parallelism are often used. The correlation between the two forms is taken as an estimate of the reliability of either of them and is also referred to as a coefficient of equivalence, or as alternate-forms reliability.

Coefficients of equivalence reflect not only reliability but also the extent to which the two forms measure the same attribute. Moreover, depending on the time interval between the administration of the two forms, coefficients of equivalence may also reflect temporary as well as lasting changes individuals have undergone. An example of the former may be changes in individuals' mood from one administration to another. An example of the latter may be individuals acquiring, in the interim, information relevant to the phenomenon being measured. It is generally recommended that equivalent forms be administered several days apart, thereby affording an opportunity of tapping errors that emanate from the specific forms used as well as from temporary changes respondents may undergo. For obvious reasons, the coefficient thus obtained is referred to as a coefficient of equivalence and stability.

Although the rationale underlying the use of equivalent forms for the estimation of reliability is intuitively appealing, the usefulness of this approach is limited primarily by difficulties in constructing equivalent forms and in determining whether they are in fact equivalent.

Internal Consistency

It seems unnecessary to elaborate on the practical problems attendant with attempts to contact the same individuals twice, not to mention securing their cooperation in responding to the same measure again (in the case of test retest) or to a measure similar to the one they have responded to earlier (when alternate forms are used). It is, however, necessary to recognize that subject attrition and self-selection are almost unavoidable under such circumstances,

---

[4]Procedures have been developed to separate estimates of reliability from those of stability of measures (e.g., Heise, 1969a; Werts, Breland, Grandy, & Rock, 1980; Werts, Jöreskog, & Linn, 1971; Wheaton, Muthen, Alwin, & Summers, 1977; Wiley & Wiley, 1970). These require a minimum of three administrations of the same measure.

particularly when the interval between two administrations is relatively long. Threats to the validity of a study as a result of subject attrition or self-selection are dealt with in several places in Part 2 of this book.

Partly because of the previously noted problems and partly in response to some of the concerns raised in the preceding sections in connection with the test–retest and alternate-forms approaches, a conception of reliability that is based on a single administration of a measure—referred to as internal consistency reliability—has been proposed.

Before presenting this approach, it is necessary to comment briefly on the distinction between measures consisting of single items and ones composed of multiple items. This distinction was not mentioned earlier in this chapter, because, issues of validity aside, test–retest or alternate-forms reliability are equally applicable to either type of measure. Thus, for example, one may use a single indicator of socioeconomic status (SES), say, income or one may arrive at a composite SES index on the basis of multiple indicators (e.g., income, education, occupation). In either case, test–retest reliability may be estimated by obtaining responses at two points in time; likewise for alternate-forms reliability estimates, be they based on single items or on, what is generally the case, forms composed of multiple items.

To be substantively meaningful, a composite score has to be based on items "measuring the same phenomenon." In other words, responses to items comprising a measure of an attribute, a construct, are expected to be internally consistent. It is on this notion that internal-consistency reliability estimates are based.

SPLIT-HALF RELIABILITY ESTIMATES

The earliest example of the internal-consistency approach to the estimation of reliability is what has come to be known as split-half reliability estimates. Although, as is discussed below, this approach is severely limited and should, therefore, be avoided, we present it for historical reasons and because it is easy to grasp and can, thus, serve as a useful introduction to other internal-consistency approaches. Most important, however, because it is widely used, we believe attention has to be drawn to its limitations.

The split-half approach can be viewed as a variation on the alternate-forms estimate of reliability. The items that comprise a given measure are split in half, and each half is treated as if it were an alternate form for the other, thereby obviating the need to construct two forms of the same measure. As with alternate-forms reliability estimates, scores on the two halves of the measure are correlated. This correlation, however, is based on measures that are half as long as the original one. Thus, for example, if the original measure consisted of 10 items, the correlation between the two halves, each consisting of 5 items, would be an estimate of the reliability of a measure 5 items in length. In order to estimate the reliability of a measure twice as long as each half (i.e., the length of the original measure), split-half correlations are traditionally stepped up by the Spearman-Brown formula (so named for the two men who independently derived it in 1910):

$$r_{xx} = \frac{2r_{1/2\ 1/2}}{1 + r_{1/2\ 1/2}} \tag{5.14}$$

where r_{xx} = the reliability of a measure, and $r_{1/2\ 1/2}$ = the correlation between its two halves. Thus, if, for the example given above, the correlation between the two halves of an instrument (each consisting of 5 items) was .62, the estimate of the reliability of the instrument would be

$$\frac{2(.62)}{1 + .62} = .765$$

Formula (5.14) is a special case of the general Spearman–Brown formula:

$$r_{kk} = \frac{kr_{xx}}{1 + (k - 1)r_{xx}} \qquad (5.15)$$

where k is the factor by which the instrument is increased or decreased; r_{kk} is the estimated reliability of an instrument k times longer (or shorter) than the existing one; r_{xx} is the reliability of the existing instrument, that is, prior to the change in its size. Note that the Spearman–Brown formulation is based on the intuitively reasonable expectation that increases in the size of an instrument would lead to increases in its reliability and that decreases in its size would lead to decreases in its reliability.

The validity of the Spearman–Brown formula is, however, predicated on the assumption that the parts added to an instrument or the parts subtracted from it are strictly parallel; that is, they are assumed to have identical true scores and equal error variances (see earlier discussion of parallel measures). When, for example, a test is doubled in length, it is assumed that the part added is parallel to the original instrument. To the extent to which this assumption is not met, the Spearman–Brown formula will lead to biased estimates. As is shown later in this chapter, other approaches are based on less restrictive assumptions and are, therefore, more realistic for estimating the reliability of many, if not most, sociobehavioral measures.

Before returning to the split-half approach, we illustrate the application of the Spearman–Brown formula. Assume that one has constructed a measure consisting of 5 items and has estimated its reliability to be .40. What would be the estimated reliability of a measure twice as long? That is, a measure consisting of 10 items. In the present case, k is 2, and r_{xx} is .40. Applying (5.15):

$$r_{kk} = \frac{2(.40)}{1 + (2 - 1)(.40)} = .57$$

As another example, assume now that having an instrument consisting of 5 items with a reliability of .40, the researcher wishes to estimate the reliability of an instrument three times as long (i.e., 15 items). In this case, k is 3, and r_{xx} is .40. Applying (5.15) yields an estimated reliability of *.67*.

A couple of things will be noted: (a) Doubling the size of an instrument will not double its reliability, and (b) increases in the size of the instrument lead to diminishing returns. That is, as one continues to increase the size of the instrument, the estimated gains become increasingly smaller. The specific magnitudes of the gains will depend, among other things, on the reliability of the original instrument. Although the topic of desired levels of reliability is discussed later in this chapter, it will be noted here that (5.15) can be used to solve for k, thereby estimating by how much an instrument should be increased or decreased in order to obtain a desired level of reliability. Specifically,

$$k = \frac{r_{kk}(1 - r_{xx})}{r_{xx}(1 - r_{kk})} \qquad (5.16)$$

where k is the factor by which the instrument should be increased or decreased in size; r_{kk} is the desired reliability; r_{xx} is the reliability of the existing instrument.

Returning now to the split-half approach for the estimation of reliability, it will be noted that probably its sole advantage is convenience. Instead of constructing alternate forms, one pretends to have them by splitting an existing instrument. Scores on the two halves are correlated, and then the Spearman–Brown formula is used to estimate the reliability of an instrument twice the size of the halves.

Needless to say, there are many ways in which an instrument may be split in half. For example, there are 126 different ways to split a measure consisting of 10 items.[5] It is clear that the probability of various split-halves yielding equal correlations between the halves is very low (later in this chapter, we illustrate how diverse correlations are obtained from different splits of an instrument). How, then, does one decide which is the "correct" split? The answer is that, consistent with the assumptions underlying the Spearman–Brown formula (see above), the two halves should be parallel. Because this is easier said than done, researchers generally follow ad hoc approaches in splitting a measure, the two most popular ones being (a) forming two halves by placing all odd-numbered items in one half and all even-numbered items in the other half (i.e., odd-even), and (b) placing the first half of the items in one part and the remaining items in the other part (i.e., first-second). Potential problems with such approaches are obvious. As one example, suppose that a measure of achievement is used in which the items are ordered in ascending difficulties. Following the first-second approach, under such circumstances, will obviously yield two halves that are *not* parallel.

COEFFICIENT α (ALPHA)

Earlier, we stated that the internal-consistency approach to the estimation of reliability is based on the notion that the items, or subparts, of the instrument measure the same phenomenon. Broadly speaking, this means that the items are homogeneous. We said "broadly," because there is no "general agreement as to just what this term should mean and how homogeneity should be measured" (Lord & Novick, 1968, p. 95). (See also, Coombs, 1950; Green, Lissitz, & Mulaik, 1977; Loevinger, 1948; Scott, 1960; Terwilliger & Lele, 1979; Weiss & Davison, 1981.) We return to this issue later in this chapter. Suffice it to note for now that, despite the lack of agreement about its meaning, homogeneity of items is an intuitively meaningful and appealing term when dealing with measures of phenomena that are derived from a theoretical frame of reference and are of interest on substantive grounds (e.g., traits, characteristics, attributes).

Various theoretical formulations regarding approaches to internal-consistency estimation of reliability have been advanced. To some extent, all are concerned with homogeneity in the broad sense referred to above. That is, they focus on what the items, or components, that comprise a scale share. This is generally accomplished by essentially splitting the scale into as many parts as it has items and studying the relations among them. Note that this may be viewed as a logical extension of the split-half approach in which the arbitrariness of splitting a measure in halves is obviated (see discussion of split-half, above).

Although they begin with different assumptions and use different analytic approaches in studying the relations among the items, the different theoretical orientations arrive at essentially the same estimates of reliability. In fact, although some of the analytic approaches appear to differ greatly from each other, it may be shown that they use formulas that are algebraically identical. In view of the foregoing, we concentrate on a formula that is probably used most often in the estimation of internal-consistency reliability, namely alpha coefficient, α, often referred to as Cronbach's alpha because of the classic presentation and

---

[5]Number of possible split halves = $(2n!)/2(n!)^2$, where $2n$ = the number of items, and ! denotes the factorial.

elaboration of this approach by Cronbach (1951). In a later section, we comment on other approaches that are shown to be either subsumed under alpha or similar to it.

Various algebraically identical expressions of alpha exist; the one most often used being

$$\alpha = \frac{k}{k-1}\left[1 - \frac{\Sigma\sigma_i^2}{\sigma_x^2}\right] \qquad (5.17)$$

where k = the number of items; $\Sigma\sigma_i^2$ = the sum of the variances of the items; and σ_x^2 = the variance of the total score, that is, the composite score.

Variance of a Composite Score.   Earlier in this chapter, an observed score was conceived as composed of a true and an error component. It was shown—see (5.5) and the discussion related to it—that the variance of the composite is equal to the sum of the variances of its components plus twice the covariance of its components. Although in the case of (5.5) there were only two components, the same holds true for any composite score regardless of the number of components. That is, *the variance of a composite score is equal to the sum of the variances of its components plus twice the sum of the covariances of all possible pairs of its components*:

$$\sigma_x^2 = \Sigma\sigma_i^2 + 2\Sigma\sigma_{ij} \qquad (5.18)$$

where σ_{ij} = the covariance of items i and j $(i \neq j)$.

Covariance and correlation are discussed in Chapter 17. For present purposes, we wish only to show how the covariance between two variables, X and Y, can be expressed as a product of their standard deviations and the correlation between them. The correlation between X and Y can be expressed as

$$r_{xy} = \frac{\Sigma xy}{N\sigma_x\sigma_y} \qquad (5.19)$$

where Σxy is the sum of the products of the deviations of X from the mean of X, and Y from the mean of Y; N is the number of people; σ_x and σ_y are the standard deviations of X and Y respectively. Now, the covariance between two variables, X and Y, may be expressed as

$$\sigma_{xy} = \frac{\Sigma xy}{N} \qquad (5.20)$$

where σ_{xy} is the covariance between X and Y, and the other terms are as defined under (5.19). Using (5.19), the covariance can, therefore, be expressed thus:

$$\sigma_{xy} = r_{xy}\,\sigma_x\sigma_y \qquad (5.21)$$

A couple of points will be made about (5.21). When the scores on X and Y are standardized (i.e., z scores; see Chapter 17), their standard deviations equal 1.00, and (5.21) reduces to r_{xy}. That is, the correlation coefficient is a covariance between standard scores. From the preceding and from (5.21), it is obvious that, when the correlation between two variables is zero, so is the covariance between them. Also, other things being equal, the larger the correlation between two variables, the larger their covariance.

With the preceding observations in mind, we return to a discussion of the formula for the calculation of alpha (5.17). Recall that k is the number of items. The first term in (5.17) [i.e., $k/(k-1)$] is close to one, particularly when the number of items is relatively large, and we will, therefore, not be concerned with it. Instead we concentrate on the key term of (5.17), that is, on the ratio of the sum of the variances of the items to the total variance. Note that this ratio is subtracted from one, and, therefore, the smaller it is, the higher the resulting reliability estimate. Conversely, the larger this ratio, the smaller the reliability. Now, it was noted previously that the total variance is equal to the sum of the variances of the items plus twice the covariances of all possible paired items. Using this conception, it will be instructive to provide an alternative expression of (5.17)

$$\alpha = \frac{k}{k-1} \left[1 - \frac{\Sigma\sigma_i^2}{\Sigma\sigma_i^2 + 2(\Sigma\sigma_{ij})} \right] \qquad (5.17')$$

where σ_i^2 is the variance of item i, and σ_{ij} is the covariance between item i and j.

From (5.17'), it is clear that the two terms of the ratio under consideration will differ only when items comprising the total score are correlated. In the extreme case, when the correlation between all possible pairs of items is zero, the total variance will equal the sum of the variances of the items. Under such circumstances, the ratio of the sum of the variances of the items to the total variance will equal 1.00, and the reliability coefficient will equal 0. This makes sense, because the absence of correlations among the items means that they share nothing in common, which goes counter to the conception of internal-consistency reliability, namely that the items measure the same thing.

Having shown the role played by correlations among items in the estimation of alpha, it will be instructive to contrast the role of the covariances with that of the variances in the variance of the composite, that is, the total score. Recall that the number of possible pairings of a set of k items is equal to $[k(k-1)]/2$. Thus, for example, when k is 10, there are 45 pairings of items. Therefore, the variance of total scores using 10 items is based on 10 variances (i.e., the sum of the variances of the items) and 90 elements due to the covariances between items (i.e., twice the sum of the covariances between all pairs of items). Although the specific magnitudes of the covariances depend on the specific standard deviations and correlations between the items, it is evident that as the number of items is increased, the covariances among them play an increasingly larger role, as contrasted with the variances, in the determination of the variance of the total.

Contrast the example used above, where the total score was based on 10 items, with a measure whose total score is based on 40 items. In the latter case, the total variance will be equal to the sum of 40 variances of the items plus twice 780 covariances between pairs of items (i.e., 1560 elements). For 10 items, we have a ratio of 10 to 90 variances to covariances, whereas for 40 items, this ratio is 40 to 1560. What all this boils down to is that, even when the correlations among pairs of items are relatively small, the total variance will become increasingly larger, as compared to the sum of the variances of the items, as the number of items becomes larger. Hence, alpha will become increasingly larger. Finally, other things being equal, the larger the correlations among items, the larger the covariances among them and, hence, the reliability of the measure of the composite score. We return to some of these issues later.

A NUMERICAL EXAMPLE

We illustrate the calculation of alpha using the illustrative data reported in Table 5.1. As is our practice with other numerical examples, we are using a small data set, so that all the calculations may be done with relative ease by hand or with a calculator. We feel it important for you to do the calculations, particularly because we use summary results in some parts of the illustration. For example, we report the variances of the items, or the correlations among them, without going through the calculations. We suggest that you do them all. If you are encountering any difficulties, refer to Chapter 17, where calculations of the various statistics presented here are discussed. After you master the basic approach, you can leave the calculations to the computer. Later in this chapter, we discuss and illustrate the use of a computer program for the estimation of reliability.

The illustrative data reported in Table 5.1 are responses of 20 individuals to a measure composed of 4 items. Also included in the table are total scores, which are the sums of the scores on the 4 items for each respondent. The measure may be thought of, for example, as one of attitudes toward abortion or toward nuclear disarmament. Respondents are asked to indicate the extent to which they agree or disagree with each of the 4 statements, using a scale ranging from 1 to 7, where 1 = disagree very strongly, and 7 = agree very strongly. Alternatively, the items of Table 5.1 may be thought of as coming from a self-report inventory, where subjects are asked to indicate, on a 7-point scale, how frequently they exhibit a particular behavior (with 1 = not at all, and 7 = very frequently). (See Chapter 6, for a presentation of selected approaches to measurement in sociobehavioral sciences, including a discussion of summated-rating scales and self-report inventories.) You may find it helpful to think of examples from your field of interest.

In the row before last of Table 5.1 are reported the item means as well as the mean of the total scores. It will be noted in passing that the mean of a composite score is equal to the sum of the means of its components. In the present example, the mean of the total score is equal to the sum of the means of the four items ($11.10 = 2.35 + 2.65 + 3.45 + 2.65$).

Our concern here is with the last row of Table 5.1, where the item variances and the variance of the total scores are reported. As was discussed earlier, only when all the covariances among

Table 5.1
Scores on Four Items and the Total (N = 20)

X1	X2	X3	X4	Total
3	2	6	3	14
3	5	6	2	16
1	2	1	3	7
5	2	3	2	12
1	2	2	5	10
6	5	7	5	23
5	3	5	6	19
1	1	3	1	6
1	1	3	1	6
5	6	6	3	20
2	1	3	2	8
3	2	5	1	11
2	5	5	5	17
1	1	1	1	4
2	2	1	2	7
2	5	3	3	13
1	2	5	2	10
1	2	1	1	5
1	1	1	4	7
1	3	2	1	7
Σ: 47	53	69	53	222
$\bar{X}$: 2.35	2.65	3.45	2.65	11.10
σ^2: 2.628	2.527	3.847	2.428	28.690

Table 5.2

Covariances (above diagonal), Variances (diagonal), Correlations (below diagonal). Four Items. Data from Table 5.1.

	X1	X2	X3	X4
X1	2.628	1.423	2.194	1.074
X2	0.552	2.527	1.908	1.028
X3	0.690	0.612	3.847	1.009
X4	0.425	0.415	0.330	2.428

Note: Sum of diagonal elements is 11.43. Sum of elements above diagonal is 8.636.

the items equal zero (i.e., when there are no correlations among the items) will the total variance equal the sum of the variances of the items. In the present example, the sum of the item variances is 11.43, and the total variance is 28.69. From (5.18), it follows that 17.26 (28.69 − 11.43) is equal to twice the sum of the covariances among the items. We will now calculate the total variance using (5.18). As will become evident, this involves a relatively large number of calculations even when the number of items is small. Needless to say, one would generally *not* use (5.18) to calculate the variance of composite scores. We do this here to show clearly the components that make up the variance of the composite.

To apply (5.18), it is necessary first to calculate the variances of the items as well as the covariances between all pairings of the items. In the present case, four variances and six covariances have to be calculated. These are reported in Table 5.2. (We remind you of our suggestion that you do the calculations.)[6]

On the diagonal of Table 5.2 are reported the variances of the items (compare with the last row of Table 5.1). Above the diagonal are reported the covariances among the items. Thus, for example, 1.423 is the covariance between items 1 and 2. A covariance is a symmetric index. That is, the covariance between items 1 and 2, say, is the same as the covariance between 2 and 1. Therefore, normally, covariances would also be reported below the diagonal. We do not do this in Table 5.2, because we want to report the correlations among the items, which is what the elements below the diagonal are. Below, we use the correlations to illustrate some points discussed earlier.

When, *unlike* Table 5.2, the covariances are reported above and below the diagonal, the table is referred to as a covariance matrix (or a variance-covariance matrix. Notice that the variance of an item can be conceived of as its covariance with itself). Using a covariance matrix, one would add all of its elements to obtain the variance of a composite based on the items, or components, that comprise the matrix. Adding all the elements is tantamount to adding the variances (i.e., the diagonal elements) plus twice the sum of the covariances (because in a covariance matrix, the triangle below the diagonal is a mirror image of the one above the diagonal). In the case of Table 5.2, however, the total variance (i.e., 28.70) is equal the sum of the diagonal elements (2.628 + 2.527 + 3.847 + 2.428 = 11.43) plus *twice* the sum of the elements *above* the diagonal [2 (1.423 + 2.194 + 1.074 + 1.908 + 1.028 + 1.009) = 17.272]. This is, within errors of rounding, the same as the value reported in Table 5.1.

Before using the results reported in Table 5.2 for the calculation of alpha, we comment briefly on the correlations among the four items, reported below the diagonal. Note that the correlations are all positive and of moderate magnitudes, indicating that the items share some common elements. Specifically, items 3 and 4, for example, share about .11 of the variance

---

[6]Use *N*, not *N* − 1, when calculating variances and covariances in this chapter.

(i.e., .33^2), whereas items 1 and 3 share about .48 of the variance (i.e., .69^2). Because covariances are affected by the units of the scales of the measures used, they are generally not as easily interpretable. Using the standard deviations of any two items and the correlation between them, the covariance between the items may be calculated (see 5.21). For example, the covariance between items 2 and 3 is

$$(.612) \sqrt{2.527} \sqrt{3.847} = 1.908$$

Try calculating the other covariances in the same manner. The preceding demonstrates what we have said earlier: Other things being equal, the higher the correlations among the items, the larger their covariances, hence, the larger the variance of the composite based on the items.

We return now to the main purpose of this section—the calculation of coefficient alpha for the four items reported in Table 5.1. To this end, we can use either (5.17) or (5.17'). We use the latter, because it shows clearly the role played by the correlations, hence the covariances, among the items comprising the scale. Using results reported in Table 5.2, alpha for the data of Table 5.1 is

$$\alpha = \frac{4}{4-1} \left[1 - \frac{11.43}{11.43 + 17.27} \right] = .80$$

Thus, using α, the estimated reliability of the measure based on the four items under consideration is .80. It could, therefore, be stated that .8, or 80%, of the variance of the total scores is reliable, or systematic, variance. Note again that, had all the correlations among the items been zero, the ratio of the sum of the variances of the items to the total variance would have been 1.00 (both the numerator and the denominator in the bracket would have been 11.43), and the reliability would have, therefore, been .00. Before discussing properties of and assumptions underlying α, its application to measures in which the items are scored dichotomously will be illustrated.

ALPHA FOR DICHOTOMOUSLY SCORED ITEMS

For the illustrative data given in Table 5.1, we used items whose scores could range from 1 to 7. This type of scoring is most often used for measures of attitudes, interests, and the like. Some types of measures consist of items that are scored dichotomously (also referred to as binary scored items, or binary items). That is, the score on an item can take only one of two values. Multiple-choice items on measures of achievement are prime examples of dichotomously scored items. Regardless of the number of choices, responses to such items are generally scored as either correct (usually assigned a score of 1) or incorrect (usually assigned a score of 0). Other examples of dichotomously scored items are ones to which only one of two responses are elicited (e.g., agree/disagree, true/false). Issues concerning advantages or disadvantages of the two types of scoring are discussed in Chapter 6.

It will be noted first that (5.17) is a general formula for the calculation of alpha, and it is, therefore, also applicable to measures whose items are scored dichotomously. We introduce a special case of (5.17), because this affords an opportunity to (a) comment on some properties of binary items; (b) show that calculations are considerably simplified, which is particularly useful when they are done by hand; and most important (c) show its identity with a very popular formula, namely Kuder–Richardson 20 (see below).

Although any two scores may be used to score responses to a binary item, or variable, it is very often useful to use 1's and 0's for this purpose. It is particularly natural to assign a 1 to a correct response to an item on an achievement or ability measure and a 0 to an incorrect response. This is what one does when one counts the number of correct responses on a multiple-choice test in order to arrive at a total score.

Mean of a Binary Item.   When 1's and 0's are used as scores for a binary item, the mean of the item is equal to the proportion of people who received a score of 1 on the item. This is because, in the calculation of the mean, we sum the scores, which, in the present case, are all 1's, and divide by the number of people, thereby obtaining the proportion of 1's. Because of this, p is often used to represent the mean of a binary item. It is noted in passing that, when dealing with measures of achievement or ability, p is also referred to as the item difficulty index, because it indicates the proportion of people who passed a given item. Note that the larger the p, the easier the item for the specific group of examinees.

Variance of a Binary Item.   The general formula for the calculation of variance (see Chapter 17) can be used for the calculation of the variance of a binary item. However, it can be shown that, for a binary item, the variance is equal to pq, where p is the proportion of people who have a score of 1 on the item (i.e., the mean of the item; see above), and $q = 1 - p$, that is, the proportion of people who have a score of 0 on the item. The standard deviation of a binary item is equal to the square root of its variance, that is, $\sqrt{pq}$. Note that the variance of a binary item, and its standard deviation, are at a maximum (.25 and .5 respectively) when $p = .5$.

With the foregoing in mind, alpha, for a measure whose items are dichotomously scored, is

$$\alpha = \frac{k}{k-1}\left[1 - \frac{\Sigma p_i q_i}{\sigma_x^2}\right] \tag{5.22}$$

where p and q are as defined above, and i refers to item i. Compare (5.22) with (5.17) and notice that they are identical, except that, in the former, the sum of the variances of the items (the numerator inside the brackets) is expressed as the sum of the pq's for the items, because it refers to measures whose items are dichotomously scored. In short, (5.22) is a special case of (5.17).

For illustrative purposes, we dichotomized the scores on the four items reported in Table 5.1 and used earlier for the calculation of alpha. Specifically, scores equal to 1, 2, or 3 were recoded as 0, whereas scores of 4 through 7 were recoded as 1. *It is very important to recognize that we do not recommend such practices.* On the contrary, we argue against them in various parts of the book, because, among other things, they lead to loss of information. For the sake of illustration, suppose that the scores in Table 5.1 refer to degrees of agreement with attitude statements. By recoding the scores, as indicated above, distinctions among people whose scores were 1 through 3 are lost, as are those among people whose scores were 4 through 7. Actually, we decided to use this example to demonstrate that the loss of information leads to a lower reliability estimate for the four items, as compared with the one obtained earlier. This should not come as a surprise, as reliability reflects systematic distinctions among people, and the recoding eliminated some of the distinctions. *In sum, do not dichotomize items or variables that are scored on a continuum. Use (5.22) only when the items are indeed binary.*

The recoded scores of Table 5.1 are reported in Table 5.3. Note that (a) the sum of scores for each item is the number of 1's, (b) the mean of each item is equal to the proportion of people who have a score of 1 on the item (i.e., p), (c) the variance of each item is equal to pq,

Table 5.3
Scores on Four Dichotomously Scored Items and the
Total (N = 20)

X1	X2	X3	X4	Total
0	0	1	0	1
0	1	1	0	2
0	0	0	0	0
1	0	0	0	1
0	0	0	1	1
1	1	1	1	4
1	0	1	1	3
0	0	0	0	0
0	0	0	0	0
1	1	1	0	3
0	0	0	0	0
0	0	1	0	1
0	1	1	1	3
0	0	0	0	0
0	0	0	0	0
0	1	0	0	1
0	0	1	0	1
0	0	0	0	0
0	0	0	1	1
0	0	0	0	0
Σ: 4	5	8	5	22
$\bar{X}$: 0.20	0.25	0.40	0.25	1.10
σ^2: 0.160	0.188	0.240	0.188	1.490

Note: For each item $\bar{X} = p$; $\sigma^2 = pq$. For an explanation, see text.

and (d) the mean of the total scores is equal to the sum of the means of the items (i.e., Σp_i; see discussion of these points earlier in this chapter).

Analogous to Table 5.2, we report item variances, and item intercorrelations and covariances in Table 5.4, where the sum of the item variances (i.e., the diagonal elements) is .776, and twice the sum of the elements above the diagonal is .716. The variance of the total scores, therefore, is 1.492.

Contrast Table 5.2 with Table 5.4. Notice that the values reported in the latter table are considerably smaller than those reported in the former. This is a direct result of the dichotomization of the scores and serves to underscore our admonition against engaging in such practices.

Table 5.4
Covariances (above diagonal), Variances
(diagonal), Correlations (below diagonal).
Four Items. Data from Table 5.3.

	X1	X2	X3	X4
X1	0.160	0.050	0.070	0.050
X2	0.289	0.188	0.100	0.038
X3	0.357	0.471	0.240	0.050
X4	0.289	0.200	0.236	0.188

Note: Sum of diagonal elements is .776. Sum of elements above diagonal is .358.

Using the values obtained above, the estimated reliability of a measure composed of the four items reported in Table 5.3 is

$$\alpha = \frac{4}{4 - 1} \left[1 - \frac{.776}{1.492} \right] = .64$$

As anticipated, the reliability of a measure whose item scores were dichotomized is lower than the one estimated for the same measure prior to the dichotomization: .64 as compared with .80.

INTERNAL CONSISTENCY: THEORETICAL ORIENTATIONS AND ASSUMPTIONS

Novick and Lewis (1967) showed that, for alpha to equal the reliability of a measure, the items comprising it have to be at least essentially tau-equivalent. This means that true scores on the items are assumed to differ from each other by no more than a constant. When this assumption is not met, alpha is a lower bound estimate of reliability. Stated differently, coefficient alpha will underestimate the reliability of a measure when its items are not at least essentially tau-equivalent.

In the previous section, a form of alpha particularly useful for calculations with dichotomous items was introduced—see (5.22). The identical formula also goes under the name of Kuder-Richardson 20, or KR–20, thus named after the two authors who developed it (20 is simply the number attached to the formula in a paper by Kuder & Richardson, 1937). It will be noted that, although alpha and KR–20 are identical, the latter is based on stricter assumptions than the former. Specifically, KR–20 is based on the assumption that the items comprising a measure are parallel. This, it will be recalled, means that true scores on all the items are identical, as are all errors. Needless to say, these are much more unrealistic assumptions than those indicated above regarding alpha. Yet, to repeat, the estimation of the reliability using alpha or KR–20 is the same, as the two formulas are identical.

When item variances are all equal, alpha can be expressed as follows:

$$\alpha = \frac{k\bar{r}_{ij}}{1 + (k - 1)\bar{r}_{ij}} \tag{5.23}$$

where $\bar{r}_{ij}$ = the average correlation among the k items.

For obvious reasons, (5.23) is referred to as average r estimate of reliability. Now, recall that standard scores (z scores) have a mean of zero and a standard deviation of one, from which it follows that, when item scores are standardized, (5.23) will yield alpha, sometimes referred to as standardized item alpha (see estimation of reliability by computer, below).

We introduced (5.23) neither because we believe that the assumption of equal item variances is a realistic one, nor because we recommend that item scores be standardized, but in order to relate alpha to the Spearman–Brown approach to the estimation of reliability. Earlier in this chapter, it was pointed out that the Spearman–Brown approach to the estimation of reliability—see (5.15)—is based on the very restrictive assumption that the items, or components, that make up a measure are parallel. It can be shown that (5.23) is an expression of the general Spearman–Brown formula (5.15). However, because (5.23) was shown to be a special case of alpha, it follows that it is based on less restrictive assumptions than (5.15). Once again, we encounter two identical formulas based on different assumptions.

Recall that the split-half approach to the estimation of reliability was shown to be a special case of the Spearman–Brown approach. It was, however, noted that split-half methods are seriously flawed, because a measure may be split in many different ways, thereby potentially leading to many different estimates of its reliability. Because alpha is based on the notion of splitting a measure into as many parts as its number of items, this problem is avoided. Moreover, Cronbach (1951) demonstrated that alpha is the average of all possible split-half reliability coefficients of a given measure.

Tryon (1957) criticized classical test theory and its variants as being based on highly restrictive and unrealistic assumptions, and offered an alternative theoretical orientation— that of domain sampling. (In addition to Tryon's paper, you will find very good discussions of domain sampling in Ghiselli et al., 1981, Chapter 8; Nunnally, 1978, Chapter 6.) It also leads to the same formula as alpha (5.17) for the estimation of reliability, but it does so within the context of a more realistic conception and, hence, less restrictive assumptions regarding the type of measures used in sociobehavioral sciences than that advanced by classical test theory and its variants.

We are certain that you are wondering what, if any, are the practical implications for the estimation of reliability when different theoretical orientations lead to the same formula. The answer to this question will be more meaningful after we consider, in turn, relations of length and homogeneity of measures to internal-consistency reliability.

TEST LENGTH AND INTERNAL-CONSISTENCY RELIABILITY

It stands to reason that, when scores on items of a given instrument are conceived as being composed of true and random error components, the reliability of the instrument will increase as a result of adding items that measure the same phenomenon. This, for example, is what is behind the rationale of the Spearman–Brown approach.

It should, however, be recognized that internal-consistency reliability estimates are a result of an interplay between the number of items comprising the instrument and the interrelations among the items—see (5.17), (5.17′), and (5.18), and the detailed discussion related to these formulas. Even when relations among items of a measure tend to be low, indicating that, by and large, they appear to be measuring different things, the total variance will become increasingly larger, relative to the sum of the variances of the items, as the number of such items is increased. Stated differently, given a sufficiently large number of items, a measure may be shown to have high internal-consistency reliability, even when it is composed of items that share little among themselves. It can be shown that, when the interitem correlations are about the same, alpha approaches 1 as the number of items approaches infinity.

However, it is also the case that the reliability is expected to be high even when the number of items is relatively small, provided the correlations among them are high. For example, a measure composed of 3 items whose average intercorrelation is .50 is expected to have an alpha of .75. The same alpha is expected for a measure composed of 9 items when the average intercorrelation among them is .25, and of 27 items when the average intercorrelation among them is .10.

HOMOGENEITY AND INTERNAL-CONSISTENCY RELIABILITY

Earlier, we pointed out that there is no agreement about the meaning of homogeneity. Rozeboom (1966), who offered a perceptive discussion and formulas for the estimation of homogeneity, maintained that homogeneity is "basically an average correlation" (p. 321). Lord and Novick (1968), on the other hand, stated: "Thus a homogeneous test is one whose components all *'measure the same thing'* [italics added] in their true-score components" (p. 95). Although Lord and Novick did not offer a criterion for what constitutes "measuring the same thing," various authors (see, in particular, Green et al., 1977) understand it to mean unidimensionality, or single-factoredness. These terms come from the area of factor analysis—a topic to which Chapters 22 and 23 are devoted (for an intuitive introduction to factor analysis, see Chapter 4).

When homogeneity is understood to mean unidimensionality, it means that, for an instrument to be viewed of as consisting of homogeneous items, it has to be demonstrated that a general factor is sufficient to account for the relations among them. It follows that a homogeneous instrument is also internally consistent. The converse does not, however, follow. *An instrument that is internally consistent is not necessarily homogeneous.*

Cronbach (1951) did not limit alpha to an instrument that is unidimensional: "α estimates the proportion of the test variance due to *all common factors among the items* [italics added]. That is, it reports how much the test score depends upon *general and group* [italics added], rather than item specific factors" (p. 320).

Two things will be noted: (a) Cronbach used the term "general" factor to refer also to the first factor, and, most important for present concerns, (b) alpha can be high even when no general factor underlies the relations among the items. This will happen when two or more common, or group, factors underlie the relations among the items. This should be, at least to some extent, evident from the previous discussion regarding the interplay between the average intercorrelation among the items and the number of items in determining alpha. It can, perhaps, be most clearly seen by studying (5.23), in which alpha is based on the average intercorrelation among the items. When an instrument is composed of distinct sets of items, the average intercorrelation among the items may still be relatively large (depending on the magnitude of the relations among the items within a given set and on the number of sets) for a given number of items to yield a high alpha. Moreover, even when the average interitem correlation is small, alpha will be high, given a sufficiently large number of items (see earlier discussion and illustrations of this point).

The most important lesson to be learned from the preceding discussion is that alpha *should not* be taken as an index of the homogeneity of an instrument. Even from a cursory reading of the literature on measurement and substantive research reports, it will be evident that many people use internal-consistency reliability estimates as indices of homogeneity or unidimensionality of an instrument (for some examples and a very good discussion, see Green et al., 1977).

HOMOGENEITY, INTERNAL-CONSISTENCY, AND VALIDITY

The validity of a total score is predicated on the extent to which the items of which it is comprised measure the same thing. However, as was demonstrated above, alpha may be high even in the absence of a general factor or when such a factor does not account for much of the test variance. Consequently, total scores that are high on reliability may be of dubious validity.

Interestingly, one encounters instances in which researchers set out to devise measures composed of heterogeneous items. Moreover, such researchers not only indicate that they expect low internal-consistency reliability estimates for their measures but also use low reliability estimates (e.g., low alphas) as evidence of their success in the construction of the measures. Because this issue is of utmost importance for validity and its relation to reliability we consider an example of it.

In selecting items for their measure of internal-external control, Mischel, Zeiss, and Zeiss (1974) stated that, because they deliberately "attempted to sample as diverse a range of situations and outcomes as possible. . . . *inevitably, low internal consistency was expected*" [italics added] (p. 267). Briefly, Mischel et al. constructed a 14-item scale that yields 3 scores—a total score, a positive outcomes subscale score, and a negative outcomes subscale score. Split-half correlations, followed by the application of the Spearman–Brown formula, produced the following estimates of reliability: .14 for the positive subscale, .20 for the negative subscale, and .04 for the total scale.[7]

The use of items for purely predictive purposes should be distinguished from their use for the measurement of a construct. Summing scores on heterogeneous items may be useful for predictive purposes in an atheoretical context, although chances are that employing such items separately in, say, a regression analysis would enhance prediction. Be that as it may, summing scores on heterogeneous items and claiming, as Mischel et al. did, that the summed score reflects a construct is a contradiction in terms.[8]

It is, of course, possible to conceive of locus of control (the construct Mischel et al. claimed to have been measuring) as being multidimensional. Accordingly, it may be necessary to construct several subscales to measure this construct. However, for scores on the subscales to be meaningful, the items of which each would be comprised would have to be homogeneous. (These issues were discussed in Chapter 4.)

Finally, when the focus is on the measurement of a construct, a relatively low internal-consistency reliability serves as negative evidence. That is, although, as we have said repeatedly, a high internal-consistency reliability does not constitute evidence of homogeneity of a measure, a low internal-consistency reliability constitutes evidence that the measure is not homogeneous.

CONSIDERATIONS IN SELECTING A RELIABILITY ESTIMATE

In view of the different approaches to the estimation of reliability and in view of the fact that different conceptions of reliability lead to the same formula (see discussion of alpha and its variants, above), it is necessary to consider criteria for the selection of a specific approach. These have to do with two related issues: (a) the nature of the attribute being measured, and (b) sources of error deemed important to address with respect to the attribute being measured.

Recall that different approaches to the estimation of reliability differ primarily with respect to the sources of error being addressed or the components of variability that are treated as random error. For example, in the test–retest approach, all changes from one testing period

---

[7]Note that neither split-half nor other internal-consistency reliability estimates are valid for present purposes.
[8]See adverse effects of unreliability on the correlation coefficient later in this chapter, where we comment further on this study.

to another are treated as random errors. This may be tenable for relatively stable attributes (e.g., mental ability) but untenable for relatively unstable ones (e.g., mood).

Internal-consistency estimates of reliability, on the other hand, primarily address errors due to sampling of content. That is, the degree to which the items on a measure are representative of the domain of the construct being measured. It is, therefore, not surprising that this approach is most meaningfully derived from the domain-sampling conception of measurement. In addition to errors due to sampling of content, internal-consistency reliability addresses errors due to temporary fluctuations within a single occasion (e.g., fatigue, mood, attentiveness, guessing).

Needless to say, the foregoing remarks were not meant to be exhaustive but rather indicative of some of the elements that need to be taken into account when choosing from among different approaches to reliability estimation (for a more detailed discussion, see Nunnally, 1978, Chapter 7). Although alpha is generally the estimate of choice when measuring constructs, other estimates may be deemed more relevant for a given construct in given circumstances. As in most other matters, theoretical and practical considerations concerning a specific research study are essential for a decision regarding the choice of reliability estimates.

COMPUTER PROGRAMS FOR RELIABILITY

A general orientation to computer packages for statistical analysis and our criteria for the selection of specific programs for illustrative applications are given in Chapter 16. Interestingly, although very comprehensive computer packages for almost any statistical analysis imaginable are available, some of them (e.g., BMDP, MINITAB) do not include a procedure for the estimation of reliability. Only very recently has SAS included in its PC version an option for the calculation of alpha as part of PROC CORR. The mainframe version does not yet include such an option. Such an omission may seem puzzling, especially when it is recognized that, compared with extremely complex procedures included in the aforementioned packages, the reliability procedure is relatively simple to program. Might this omission be rooted in perceived and/or expressed lack of interest in reliability estimates on the part of customers of a given package?

For the following demonstration, we will use the RELIABILITY procedure of SPSS.

SPSS

We assume that you have some familiarity with the control language of SPSS, and, therefore, we comment only briefly on some of the input statements. If you are not familiar with this package or with packaged computer programs in general, you may want to read relevant sections of Chapter 16.

THE DATA

The illustrative data to be used in this analysis are reported in Table 5.5, whose layout is identical to that of Table 5.1, except that here we present responses of 20 individuals to 10

Table 5.5
Scores on Ten Items and the Total (N = 20)

X1	X2	X3	X4	X5	X6	X7	X8	X9	X10	Total
3	2	6	3	3	3	3	5	2	5	35
3	5	6	2	1	2	5	6	2	3	35
1	2	1	3	2	3	1	2	2	1	18
5	2	3	2	1	5	1	2	2	2	25
1	2	2	5	1	1	1	3	3	1	20
6	5	7	5	3	3	2	2	1	5	39
5	3	5	6	5	5	7	5	6	6	53
1	1	3	1	4	5	7	2	2	2	28
1	1	3	1	2	1	2	1	3	5	20
5	6	6	3	5	5	3	5	3	1	42
2	1	3	2	1	2	1	1	2	3	18
3	2	5	1	1	3	3	1	3	3	25
2	5	5	5	3	1	3	1	5	1	31
1	1	1	1	1	2	1	3	2	1	14
2	2	1	2	2	3	2	2	1	3	20
2	5	3	3	2	3	3	5	3	7	36
1	2	5	2	3	1	2	3	2	3	24
1	2	1	1	1	1	2	5	1	2	17
1	1	1	4	1	5	1	3	5	2	24
1	3	2	1	7	5	3	1	2	5	30
Σ: 47	53	69	53	49	59	53	58	52	61	554
$\bar{X}$: 2.35	2.65	3.45	2.65	2.45	2.95	2.65	2.90	2.60	3.05	27.70
σ^2: 2.628	2.527	3.847	2.428	2.747	2.348	3.127	2.690	1.740	3.247	93.710

Note: The first four items are the same as those given in Table 5.1.

items, whereas Table 5.1 consisted of responses of 20 individuals to 4 items. Moreover, as indicated in the note to Table 5.5, the first 4 items are the same as those given in Table 5.1. In the course of the analysis, it will become clear why we chose to do this. For comparisons with the computer output, means and variances are also reported in Table 5.5.

Input

```
SET LISTING='T55SPS.LIS'.
TITLE RELIABILITY ESTIMATES. DATA OF TABLE 5.5.
DATA LIST FREE/X1 TO X10.
BEGIN DATA.
3 2 6 3 3 3 3 5 2 5   [data for the first subject]
. . . . . . . . . .
1 3 2 1 7 5 3 1 2 5   [data for the last subject]
END DATA.
LIST.
RELIABILITY VARIABLES=ALL/
   SCALE(ATTIT)=ALL/
   SCALE(ATTIT)=ALL/MODEL=SPLIT/
   STATISTICS ALL/SUMMARY ALL.
```

Commentary

This job was run on the PC version of SPSS. See Chapter 16, for an explanation of similarities and differences between the mainframe and the PC versions of SPSS.

We are using small data sets; therefore, we follow the practice of including them as part of the command file. As you can see, we are using a free format input, requiring only that data values be separated by at least one blank or by a comma. The specification X1 TO X10 provides names for the 10 variables (10 items in this case). As explained in Chapter 16, we include the LIST procedure in our sample runs so that a record of the raw data be part of the output.

The RELIABILITY procedure requires that variables one contemplates using in the analysis be specified on a VARIABLES subcommand; ALL is acceptable. Having done this, it is possible to do analyses using all the items or any combinations of interest. Each set of items comprising a scale or a subscale is indicated on the SCALE subcommand. In the present case, all items are used in one scale named, in parentheses, ATTIT for attitudes.

RELIABILITY affords the use of several models for the estimation of reliability. When none is specified on the MODEL subcommand, as is the case in the first SCALE subcommand, ALPHA is used by default. For comparative and illustrative purposes, we also analyze the data using MODEL=SPLIT, that is, split-half reliability estimate. Note that SPSS performs a first–second split by placing the first $k/2$ items in the first half and the remaining items in the second half.

A variety of item and scale statistics (e.g., means, standard deviations, inter-item variance-covariance matrix, inter-item correlation matrix, item-total correlations) may be specified on the STATISTICS and SUMMARY subcommands. The specification ALL is also accepted.

Output

```
RELIABILITY COEFFICIENTS        10 ITEMS
ALPHA = .7871   STANDARDIZED ITEM ALPHA = .7846
```

Commentary

Alpha of .79 indicates that about 79% of the variance of the scale is systematic. This value is obtained by applying (5.17). The standardized item alpha is estimated using standard scores on the items or equivalently by applying (5.23) in which the average correlation among the items is used. As an exercise, we recommend that you calculate the standardized item alpha using the values reported in Table 5.6, below the diagonal. Because the item variances in the present example are similar to each other, the two estimates of alpha are almost identical— see discussion associated with (5.23).

Output

CORRELATION BETWEEN FORMS = .5437
EQUAL LENGTH SPEARMAN–BROWN = .7044

Commentary

These are excerpts of the results obtained from the analysis in which MODEL=SPLIT was specified (see input statements). The correlation between the two halves is .5437. Applying the Spearman–Brown formula for the case of split-half—see (5.14) and discussion related to it—the estimated reliability for the present scale is .7044. As was pointed out earlier, when MODEL=SPLIT is specified, SPSS splits the test into first and second halves. As an exercise, we suggest that you calculate the split-half correlation based on odd-even halves, which you will find to be .723. When stepped up by the Spearman-Brown formula (5.14) the estimate is .839. Note the considerable difference between the two split-half estimates, reinforcing our recommendation that this approach not be used for the estimation of reliability.

ALPHA FOR DICHOTOMOUSLY SCORED ITEMS

Earlier, it was stated that alpha is also applicable when items are dichotomously scored—see (5.22) and discussion related to it—and that, under such circumstances, the formula for alpha and KR–20 yield identical results. As an exercise, you may wish to dichotomize the data of Table 5.5. It is not necessary to go through the mechanics of the conversion, as this can be accomplished by using the following RECODE command, to be placed after the DATA LIST command.

RECODE X1 TO X10 (1 THRU 3=0) (4 THRU 7=1).

All other input statements given previously are not affected. If you ran the data of Table 5.5 in this recoded form, you would find that alpha is .718. We remind you of our exhortation *not* to dichotomize items scored on a continuum. The preceding was only meant to demonstrate that RELIABILITY of SPSS will yield the same results as KR–20 when the items are scored dichotomously, as is most often done on measures of achievement or ability.

A CLOSER LOOK AT THE DATA OF TABLE 5.5

Recall that the first 4 items in Table 5.5 are the same as those used in Table 5.1. Earlier, alpha for these first 4 items was estimated to be .80. Thus, after adding 6 items the reliability of the longer scale is slightly lower (.79; see above). It would appear, therefore, that the items that were added are not essentially tau-equivalent with the first 4; they are not measuring the same thing (see detailed discussion earlier in the chapter).

Had the number of subjects been sufficient, it would have been useful to do a factor analysis in order to note the structure that underlies the responses to the items. For present purposes, however, a less rigorous approach will suffice. What we are in effect going to do is an "eyeball" factor analysis of the correlation matrix of the 10 items.

The matrix of the correlations among the 10 items, as obtained from the SPSS output, is reproduced below the diagonal in Table 5.6. To facilitate inspection, we enclose two clusters of variables in the table. The first cluster consists of items $X1$ through $X4$, and the second cluster consists of items $X5$ through $X7$. Note that the correlations among the items in the first cluster range from .33 to .69, and those among the items in the second cluster range from .36 to .51. With some exceptions (e.g., the correlation between $X1$ and $X6$), the correlations between items across the clusters are generally lower than those between items within a given cluster. Also, with a few exceptions (e.g., the correlation between $X4$ and $X9$), the correlations between items $X8$ through $X10$ and the items in the previously noted clusters are generally low. In short, the two clusters of items appear to be measuring somewhat different things.

We remind you that our purpose was to do a very rough approximation to a factor analysis. What we have done should also serve to illustrate that attempts to discern a pattern of relations among items or variables, even for a relatively small correlation matrix, can become quite unwieldy. Hence, the virtue of methods such as factor analysis, presented in Chapters 22 and 23.

From an earlier analysis, we know that alpha for items $X1$ through $X4$ is .80. The alpha for items $X5$ through $X7$ is .72. It is relatively easy to calculate these alphas, using relevant elements from the diagonal and above the diagonal of Table 5.6 and applying Formula (5.17). If you wish to obtain these alphas through RELIABILITY of SPSS, all you have to do is add the following two subcommands to the input statements given earlier.

```
SCALE(ATTIT1)=X1 TO X4/
SCALE(ATTIT2)=X5 TO X7/
```

For purposes of identification, we label the first cluster ATTIT1 and the second ATTIT2. In a real study, one would use labels that reflect what it is one believes each cluster of items is measuring. Various other decisions would be called for in a real study. For example, one would have to decide whether to discard items $X8$ through $X10$, whether to add items to the second cluster, and so on. Our aim here was limited to illustrating that sole reliance on alpha is not sufficiently informative and may be misleading. Many researchers would view an alpha of .79 for 10 items as indicating homogeneity or unidimensionality. Yet, as our very rough inspection has shown, this would be a mistaken conclusion.

Table 5.6

Covariances (above diagonal), Variances (diagonal), Correlations (below diagonal). Ten Items. Data from Table 5.5

	X1	X2	X3	X4	X5	X6	X7	X8	X9	X10
X1	2.628	1.423	2.194	1.074	0.543	1.018	0.673	0.635	0.190	0.733
X2	0.552	2.527	1.908	1.028	0.908	0.182	0.728	1.015	0.260	0.517
X3	0.690	0.612	3.847	1.009	0.948	0.072	1.457	0.795	0.330	1.077
X4	0.425	0.415	0.330	2.428	0.357	0.182	0.277	0.515	1.210	0.268
X5	0.202	0.344	0.291	0.138	2.747	1.273	1.507	−0.005	0.380	0.977
X6	0.410	0.075	0.024	0.076	0.501	2.348	0.982	0.145	0.430	0.403
X7	0.235	0.259	0.420	0.101	0.514	0.363	3.127	0.965	0.710	1.068
X8	0.239	0.389	0.247	0.202	−0.002	0.058	0.333	2.690	0.160	0.505
X9	0.089	0.124	0.128	0.589	0.174	0.213	0.304	0.074	1.740	0.170
X10	0.251	0.181	0.305	0.095	0.327	0.146	0.335	0.171	0.072	3.247

Note: This table is a composite of two pieces of SPSS RELIABILITY output: COVARIANCE MATRIX and CORRELATION MATRIX. Sum of diagonal elements is 27.329. Sum of elements above diagonal is 93.710. See text for a discussion of the two enclosed clusters of items.

SELECTED TOPICS

We conclude this chapter with a presentation of selected topics related to reliability. Coverage of these topics varies: Some are presented with a fair degree of detail, whereas others are only commented upon briefly for the purpose of acquainting you with them and providing you with references where detailed presentations of them are given. Keep in mind that the term reliability (e.g., in the various formulas) is used generically and that the answer to the question "Which estimate of reliability?" depends on the specifics of the situation.

"STANDARDS" OF RELIABILITY

How high should the reliability of a measure be? Obviously, other things being equal, the higher the reliability, the better. It stands to reason, however, for a given magnitude of a reliability coefficient to be deemed acceptable in one set of circumstances and unacceptable in another set of circumstances. Of various considerations in the determination of acceptability of a given reliability coefficient, the most important one has to do with the type of decisions made on the basis of the scores and the possible consequences of the decisions. With this in mind, various authors have offered guidelines or rules of thumb regarding standards or minimum levels of acceptable reliability coefficients (e.g., Nunnally, 1967, pp. 226, 1978, pp. 245–246; Thorndike & Hagen, 1977, pp. 92–94). For example, it has been argued (e.g., Nunnally, 1967, 1978) that relatively low reliability coefficients are tolerable in early stages of research, that higher reliabilities are required when the measure is used to determine differences among groups, and that very high reliabilities are essential when the scores are used for making important decisions about individuals (e.g., selection and placement decisions).

Although such recommendations are based on sound reasoning, we question the wisdom of proposing specific values as standards of reliability, because they tend to develop a life of their own and are frequently applied without concern to the ideas that led to them. This is exemplified by their continued use even when the author who proposed them has apparently changed his or her mind. A case in point is the following rule of thumb proposed by Nunnally (1967): "In the early stages of research on predictor tests or hypothesized measures of a construct, one saves time and energy by working with instruments that have only modest reliability, for which purpose reliabilities of .60 or .50 will suffice" (p. 226). Nunnally (1978) repeated the preceding statement with one modification, namely that "reliabilities of .7 or higher will suffice" (p. 245). Because researchers seem to have the need to refer to an authoritative source as "justification" for their use of measures with relatively low reliability coefficients, they may be inclined to refer to the "standard" that best suits their purposes. For example, *referring to Nunnally (1967)*, Caplan, Naidu, and Tripathi (1984) said: "Alphas of .50 or higher are judged *adequate* [italics added] for research purposes" (p. 306). Interestingly, Ellis (1988) *referred to Nunnally (1978)* and concluded that all his measures reached "*acceptable* [italics added] levels of reliability" (p. 685), despite the fact that several of them were lower than the .7 standard set by Nunnally in the reference cited.

When approached by colleagues or students with a request for a reference in which they might find justification for the use of their reliability estimates, we suggest facetiously that, if their estimates are about .7, they use Nunnally (1978) but that, if they are about .5, they use Nunnally (1967). In a more serious vein, we point out to the inquirer that the matter is not one to be resolved by an authority decreeing that a given reliability coefficient is Kosher or not Kosher. For added effect, we relate the story of the woman who sought a Rabbi's determination as to whether her chicken was Kosher. When, after inspecting the chicken, the Rabbi proceeded to smell it—an act that struck the woman as rather peculiar under the circumstances—she could not contain herself and implored: "Rabbi, is it Kosher?" "Yes," he replied, "but it stinks!" Is it Kosher to use a measure whose reliability coefficient is .5 or whatever? Of course it is! Does a .5 reliability coefficient stink? To answer this question, no authoritative source will do. Rather, *it is for the user to determine what amount of error he or she is willing to tolerate, given the specific circumstances of the study* (e.g., what the scores are to be used for, cost of the study).

PREDICTED TRUE SCORES

Earlier in this chapter, it was pointed out that the observed score is conceived as composed of true and error components—see (5.1) and the discussion related to it. Using conceptions and assumptions of linear regression analysis (see Chapter 17), the equation for predicting true scores from observed scores is:

$$
\begin{aligned}
T' &= \quad a \quad + \quad bX \\
&= (1 - r_{xx})\bar{X} + r_{xx}X
\end{aligned}
\tag{5.24}
$$

where T' = predicted true score; a = intercept; b = regression coefficient; X = observed score; r_{xx} = reliability coefficient; $\bar{X}$ = mean of observed scores for the group.

Depending on your background, you may wish to study relevant sections of Chapter 17 in conjunction with the present section. For present purposes, we would like to draw your attention to the special expression of the regression equation for the regression of true scores on observed scores—i.e., the second expression of (5.24). As you can see, the first term is the intercept (a), and the reliability coefficient is the regression coefficient (b).

The interplay between the two terms in yielding predicted true scores warrants careful examination. Note, for example, that, when the reliability is perfect (i.e., 1.00), predicted true scores are equal to the observed scores. This makes sense, as perfect reliability means no errors of measurement. Conversely, when the reliability is .00 (i.e., all the variance is due to errors of measurement), predicted true scores equal the mean of the group, regardless of the value of the observed score. This too makes sense, as under such circumstances the best prediction, from a least-squares perspective, is the mean of the group. Finally, when the reliability is not perfect (which is almost always the case), the predicted true score is closer to the mean of the group than is the observed score. This is the phenomenon of regression toward the mean due to measurement errors—a topic discussed in Chapter 10.

Following are some of the circumstances under which true scores are of special interest.

1. When it is desired to match subjects who belong to different groups that differ in their means and/or the reliability of the measure used (see Stanley, 1971, p. 376).

2. When subjects are to be classified in different categories on the basis of different cutoff scores (see Crocker & Algina, 1986, pp. 147–148).

3. When it is desired to correct for measurement errors prior to the application of a statistical analysis. For example, as is discussed in Chapter 21, when analysis of covariance is applied to nonequivalent groups, measurement errors may lead to serious bias and, hence, to erroneous conclusions. Among suggested solutions is that the analysis be applied to predicted true scores rather than the observed scores (for a discussion and a numerical example, see Huitema, 1980, pp. 311–321).

4. For use with a standard error to set confidence intervals around the predicted true score. This point is discussed in the section on standard errors to which we now turn.

STANDARD ERRORS AND CONFIDENCE INTERVALS

Broadly speaking, a standard error is a standard deviation of a sampling distribution of a statistic. For example, the standard error of the mean is the standard deviation of the distribution of many means obtained through random sampling from a given population (see Chapter 15 for a discussion of sampling distributions). Using the standard error, one may set a confidence interval, with a given probability, around the mean (see Hays, 1988, Chapter 6, for a discussion of confidence intervals).

In the context of reliability, three different standard errors have been defined. As Stanley (1971, p. 381) pointed out: "There is some confusion in the literature" regarding their use (see also, Dudek, 1979; Lord & Novick, 1968, pp. 66–69; McHugh, 1957). Two of the three standard errors will be presented here.

In the present context, the *standard error of estimate*, s_e, is the standard deviation of predicted true scores for a given observed score:

$$s_e = s_x \sqrt{r_{xx} (1 - r_{xx})} \tag{5.25}$$

where s_x = standard deviation of the measure for a given group; r_{xx} = reliability coefficient for the group in question.

Assume that for a given group of subjects, the relevant data are

$$\bar{X} = 80 \qquad s_x = 10 \qquad r_{xx} = .84$$

Applying (5.25)

$$s_e = 10\sqrt{(.84)(1 - .84)} = 3.67$$

For illustrative purposes, two observed scores will be used: 75 and 85. Applying (5.24), the predicted true scores for these observed scores are

$$(1 - .84) (80) + (.84) (75) = 75.80$$

and,

$$(1 - .84) (80) + (.84) (85) = 84.20$$

As was pointed out above, the predicted true scores are closer to the mean than their respective observed scores.

Assume that one wants to construct the 90% confidence interval for the two predicted true scores. From the areas under the normal curve, the z corresponding to the area encompassing the middle 90% (i.e., leaving 5% in each tail) is 1.65. Accordingly, the confidence intervals for the scores under consideration are:

$$75.80 \pm (1.65) (3.67)$$

$$84.20 \pm (1.65) (3.67)$$

Thus, for people whose observed score is 75, the best prediction is a true score of 75.80. About 90% of their true scores are in the interval ranging from 69.74 (75.80 − 6.06) to 81.86 (75.80 + 6.06). For people scoring 85, the best prediction is a true score of 84.20. About 90% of their true scores are in the interval ranging from 78.14 to 90.26. Several points will be made.

1. The true score for any given individual is unknown, hence, it is not possible to tell whether or not it is included in the confidence interval.

2. The confidence interval is symmetric around the predicted true score, *not* around the observed score.

3. Instead of z values, some authors use t values for the purpose of setting confidence intervals. When the number of people in the group is, say, 30 or greater, it makes practically no difference whether z or t values are used.

4. It is assumed that errors are normally distributed and that their variability is constant for all observed scores. The latter assumption, referred to as *homoscedasticity*, is discussed in Chapter 17.

The more common practice when setting confidence intervals around predicted true scores is to use the *standard error of measurement*, s_m (e.g., Nunnally, 1978, pp., 239–241):

$$s_m = s_x \sqrt{(1 - r_{xx})} \qquad (5.26)$$

The s_m is an estimate of the standard deviation "expected for observed scores when the true score is held constant" (Dudek, 1979, p. 335). Compare (5.25) with (5.26) and notice that the difference between the two is that the former includes one additional term under the radical (i.e., r_{xx}). Two things will be noted: (a) Because r_{xx} is almost always a fraction, the standard error of estimate is smaller than the standard error of measurement; and (b) when the reliability is high, the two standard errors are fairly similar to each other. In any case, using the standard error of measurement instead of the standard error of estimate will result in a wider confidence interval. What is important to bear in mind, however, is that, whichever standard error is used, the confidence interval should be set around the predicted true scores, *not* around observed scores.

For comparative purposes with the calculations done above, we use the same data to calculate the standard error of measurement and then use it to set confidence intervals for the same observed scores as those used previously.

$$s_m = 10\sqrt{(1 - .84)} = 4.00$$

As indicated above, the standard error of measurement is larger than the standard error of estimate (3.67).

The predicted true scores for the observed scores used above (75 and 85) are, of course, the same as obtained earlier: 75.80 and 84.20 respectively. Using the s_m, the 90% confidence intervals for these scores are:

$$75.80 \pm (1.65)\ (4.00)$$

$$84.20 \pm (1.65)\ (4.00)$$

For the data under consideration, the size of the confidence interval when using s_m is 13.20—(2)(1.65)(4.00)—as compared with 12.11—(2)(1.65)(3.67)—which is the size of the interval when s_e was used (see above).

Although the reliability coefficient is useful as an overall index of precision of a measure, it is the standard error of estimate (or measurement) and confidence intervals that are of interest when one's aim is to assess the precision of given scores. Confidence intervals serve as reminders that the observed scores are not error free and that differences between observed scores should be treated with due circumspection.

Finally, it will be recalled that, other things being equal, the greater the variability of the group, the higher the reliability coefficient. However, as an examination of the formulas for the standard errors will show, an increase in reliability as a result of greater variability is offset, so to speak, by a corresponding increase in the standard errors. What this amounts to is that, whereas reliability coefficients may vary greatly across groups, the standard errors are, generally speaking, similar across groups, thus, serving as a more realistic means for comparisons across groups differing in variability.

ADVERSE EFFECTS OF UNRELIABILITY

A good deal of effort has been devoted to ascertain the manner and extent of effects of random measurement errors on specific aspects (e.g., parameter estimation, tests of significance), designs (e.g., experimental, quasi-experimental), and analytic approaches (e.g., regression analysis, analysis of covariance). For a very good review of the effects of measurement errors on statistical analysis, see Cochran (1968).

Knowledge of the effects of unreliability is important so that corrective action be taken, when possible, or the effects be considered when drawing conclusions and interpreting results of analyses. Here, we discuss only the effects of unreliability on the correlation coefficient. Adverse effects of unreliability in more complex situations are not only more complex but may even "become devastating" (Fleiss & Shrout, 1977, p. 1190). Some of the complications are discussed in later chapters (e.g., Chapters 15, 17, and 21), where relevant references are also provided.

CORRELATION COEFFICIENT

As you are surely aware, the Pearson correlation coefficient is one of the most frequently used measures of association between two variables. In preceding chapters, its use was discussed in the context of validity. In the present chapter, it has been used in the context of reliability.

Assume that we are interested in the correlation between two variables, X and Y, and that we have reliability estimates of the measures of these variables, designated as r_{xx} and r_{yy}. It can be shown that

$$r_{xy} = r^*_{xy} \sqrt{r_{xx}r_{yy}} \qquad (5.27)$$

where r_{xy} = observed correlation between X and Y; r^*_{xy} = correlation between the true scores of X and Y.

Examine (5.27) and notice that r_{xy} will equal r^*_{xy} only when the reliabilities of the two measures are perfect (i.e., 1.00). As you can see, unreliability of the measure of one or both variables leads to a downward bias, or an attenuation, of the correlation coefficient. Clearly, the lower the reliabilities, the lower the estimate of the true correlation between the variables will be.

In Chapter 4, attention was drawn to the predicament, even embarrassment, posed by low correlations between instruments presumably measuring the same construct. Validity issues aside, from (5.27) it can be seen that low correlations between instruments meant to measure the same construct may be due, at least in part, to low reliabilities. The same holds true when the correlation between two constructs is considerably lower than expected on the basis of theoretical considerations (see Cross-Structure Analysis in Chapter 4).

As an example, we return to a study by Mischel et al. (1974), upon which we commented earlier in this chapter. Recall that the authors constructed a measure of locus of control consisting of two subscales for which they obtained extremely low reliability estimates (.14 and .20). It, therefore, comes as no surprise when reported correlations between the subscales are close to zero (".03, −.06, and −.02 for males, females, and the total sample, respectively" p. 270). Also not surprising are the findings that the correlations between the subscales and other variables are, by and large, extremely low.

"CORRECTION" FOR ATTENUATION

Using (5.27), a "correction" for attenuation has been suggested:

$$r_{xy}^* = \frac{r_{xy}}{\sqrt{r_{xx}r_{yy}}} \tag{5.28}$$

where the terms are as defined under (5.27). Rather than a correction for attenuation formula, (5.28) is more appropriately characterized as an estimate of the correlation coefficient when the measures of both variables are perfectly reliable.

For the sake of illustration, assume that $r_{xy} = .6$, and $r_{xx} = r_{yy} = .75$. Applying (5.28)

$$r_{xy}^* = \frac{r_{xy}}{\sqrt{r_{xx}r_{yy}}} = \frac{.6}{\sqrt{(.75)(.75)}} = .8$$

Thus, given that the correlation between X and Y is .6, it is estimated that, with perfectly reliable measures, the correlation between these variables would be .8.

Equation (5.28) may be adapted to correct for the unreliability of the measure of only one of the variables, say Y, by using only an estimate of its reliability in the denominator. Such a correction may be applied in, for example, criterion-related validation studies, as it would be inappropriate to correct for the unreliability of the predictor (see Ghiselli et al., 1981, pp. 290–291; Nunnally, 1978, p. 238), because decisions (e.g., selection) have to be made on the basis of the available, fallible predictor scores.

As Nunnally (1978) pointed out, rather than resorting to the fiction of perfect reliabilities, it is frequently more meaningful to estimate what the correlation between two variables would be, if the reliability of one or both of their measures were increased by a specified amount. Equation (5.28) is adaptable for such situations as well (see Nunnally, 1978, pp. 238–239).

Although (5.28) is quite versatile, and its application straightforward, its validity has been questioned (e.g., Johnson, 1950; Winne & Belfry, 1982). When underestimates of reliability are used, the disattenuated correlation is overestimated and may even exceed 1.00! Undue reliance on disattenuated correlations may not only lead one into a fantasy world but may also deflect one's attention from the pressing need of improving the reliability of the measures used.

INTEROBSERVER AGREEMENT AND RELIABILITY

The use of observers as a method of measurement is prevalent in various disciplines and professions (e.g., psychology, anthropology, education, marketing). Observation is dealt with in Chapter 6, where we also comment on reliability and provide relevant references. Accordingly, it will only be pointed out here that an important distinction is made between interobserver agreement and interobserver reliability (referred to by some as interrater agreement and interrater reliability) and that various methods have been proposed to assess each of them.

GENERALIZABILITY THEORY

One of the difficulties with traditional approaches to the estimation of reliability is that, although it is recognized that measurement errors may emanate from different sources, they are lumped together in the estimation process. In a sweeping reformulation, Cronbach and associates (e.g., Cronbach, Gleser, Nanda, & Rajaratnam, 1972) advanced generalizability theory. Instead of the true score of classical test theory, in generalizability theory "the investigator uses the observed score or some function of it as if it were the universe score. That is, he generalizes from sample to universe. *The question of 'reliability' thus resolves into a question of accuracy of generalization, or generalizability*" (Cronbach et al., 1972, p. 15).

Utilizing complex analysis-of-variance designs, generalizability theory enables one to simultaneously identify and distinguish among different sources of error (e.g., subjects, occasions, raters, items, time). A thorough familiarity with the analysis of variance is necessary for the application of generalizability theory. In addition, it should be clear that the greater the number of sources of error one wishes to address, the more complex the design and the more demanding is its execution. This is probably why generalizability theory has been applied infrequently.

If you are interested in learning about generalizability theory, we suggest that you begin *not* with Cronbach et al.'s work, which is very complex, but rather with some introduction. Probably the best introduction, which is also tied in with a computer program for the analysis of designs according to generalizability theory, is that of Brennan (1983; see also Crocker & Algina, 1986, Chapter 8; Feldt & Brennan, 1989; Shavelson, Webb, & Burstein, 1986; Webb, Rowley, & Shavelson, 1988).

STUDY SUGGESTIONS

1. The error and total variance of a measure are respectively 11.58 and 73.62. What is its estimated reliability?
2. The reliability of a measure consisting of 10 items was estimated to be .50. What is the expected reliability, if the measure is increased in length to:
   (a) 20 items.
   (b) 30 items.
3. A test consisting of 100 items has an estimated reliability of .92. Assume that it is desired to shorten the test so that the estimated reliability of the shorter version be .82. How many items should the shorter version of the test include?
4. For a test consisting of 15 items, the sum of the variances of the items is 8.36, and the total variance is 23.61.
   (a) What is its estimated α reliability?
   (b) What proportion of variance of the test is due to error?

5. The following are responses of 10 subjects to 8 dichotomously scored items (i.e., 1 = correct response; 0 = incorrect response).

```
1 1 1 1 1 1 1 0
1 1 1 1 1 0 1 1
1 0 1 0 0 0 0 0
1 0 1 0 0 0 1 1
0 0 1 0 0 0 0 0
1 0 1 1 1 1 0 1
1 0 0 0 1 0 0 0
1 0 0 1 0 0 1 0
0 1 0 1 0 1 0 0
0 0 1 1 1 0 1 0
```

What is (are) the:

(a) item means?

(b) item variances?

(c) mean of the total scores? Verify that it is equal to the sum of the item means.

(d) variance of the total scores?

(e) reliability of the test using coefficient α?

If you have access to a computer program for reliability (e.g., SPSS), we suggest you run the example and compare the results with your hand calculations (examples of SPSS control statements were given in the chapter).

6. Assume the following were estimated for a relatively large sample:

$$\bar{X} = 62 \qquad s_x = 7.63 \qquad r_{xx} = .75$$

(a) Estimate the predicted true score for a person whose observed score is 65.

(b) What is the standard error of estimate?

(c) What is the standard error of measurement?

(d) Using the standard error of estimate, calculate the 68% confidence interval for the predicted true score.

(e) Using the standard error of measurement, calculate the 68% confidence interval for the predicted true score.

7. The correlation between X and Y is .62. Estimated reliabilities of X and Y respectively are .82 and .73. Estimate the correlation between X and Y, assuming the measures of both variables are perfectly reliable.

Answers

1. .84
2. (a) .67—see (5.15)
   (b) .75
3. 40 items—see (5.16)
4. (a) .69
   (b) .31
5. (a) .7 .3 .7 .6 .5 .3 .5 .3
   (b) .21 .21 .21 .24 .25 .21 .25 .21
   (c) 3.9 = .7 + .3 + .7 + .6 + .5 + .3 + .5 + .3

    (d) 4.09

    (e) .64

6. (a) 64.25

    (b) 3.30

    (c) 3.82

    (d) $60.95 - 67.55$

    (e) $60.43 - 68.07$

7. $r_{xy}^{*} = .80$—see (5.28)

Chapter 6
Selected Approaches to Measurement in Sociobehavioral Research

Many books and numerous articles have been devoted to measurement approaches in sociobehavioral research (e.g., multiple-choice tests, rating scales, projective techniques, interviewing, observational methods) or even to specific aspects of a given approach (e.g., item characteristics, test equating, norms, response styles). Certain approaches have been developed and used primarily in the context of specific substantive areas (e.g., attitudes, achievement, mental abilities, personality, interests). Some approaches—generally referred to as measurement models—focus on differentiations among people, whereas others—generally referred to as scaling models—focus on differentiations among stimuli. Following is a small selection of books that address issues of measurement, scaling, or both: Coombs (1964), Coxon (1982), Edwards (1957b), Guilford (1954), Kruskal and Wish (1978), Maranell (1974b), McIver and Carmines (1981), Nunnally (1978), Torgerson (1958), and van der Ven (1980).

In the confines of a chapter, it is obviously impossible to give even a rough overview of this vast area. Our very limited aim is to introduce *some* approaches and discuss *some* issues related to them. Our sole justification for the choice of approaches to be presented is that they are among the more popular ones, in part because of their applicability for diverse purposes.

We begin with a presentation of rating scales in general, followed by summated rating scales and semantic differential scales. Next, we turn to a presentation of interviews stressing their structure and interviewer effects. Selected issues of task and respondent effects are also commented upon in separate sections, as their effects are not confined to interviews. A section on observations concludes the chapter.[1]

---

[1]As you read the current chapter, in particular the sections addressed to interviewer, task, and respondent effects, you may find it helpful to review relevant sections in Chapter 11, which in many ways complements the present chapter.

RATING SCALES

The "ubiquitous" (Dawes, 1972, p. 93) and beguiling rating scales have been around for a long time. References to their use have been traced "back to at least 150 B.C. when Hipparchus used a six-point scale to judge the brightness of stars" (Lodge, 1981, p. 5).

We believe it safe to assume that not only have you encountered various forms of rating scales but that you have also at one time or another responded to rating scales. Perhaps you have even used rating scales to elicit responses from other people. Be that as it may, you surely know that rating scales are used to quantify evaluations, impressions, judgments, perceptions, and the like, of self, others, objects, settings, to name but some general areas.

The great popularity of rating scales is probably due to the relative ease with which they can be constructed and administered, and to their seeming applicability for the measurement of almost anything imaginable. Although rating scales may take different formats, they share a common approach in that respondents are instructed to indicate their position, in the broadest sense of this term, with respect to the referent of the rating (e.g., degree of agreement with an attitude statement, frequency with which a given behavior has been manifested, quality of a product).

SCALE FORMAT

Different formats of rating scales are in use. Following are examples of and brief comments on some popular formats (for more detailed treatments, see Aaker & Day, 1983; Dawes, 1972; Dawes & Smith, 1985; Gable, 1986; Guilford, 1954; Lemon, 1973; Lin, 1976; Nunnally, 1978; Saal, Downey, & Lahey, 1980).

Probably the most popular is the graphic rating scale, as it resembles measurement strategies with which respondents are typically familiar (e.g., length with a yardstick, temperature with a thermometer). A graphic scale consists of a straight line with its end points labeled to serve as anchors (e.g., lazy—industrious; warm—cold; agree strongly—disagree strongly; never—always). Respondents are instructed to mark the point on the line corresponding to or reflecting their position. Most often, the line is broken or divided into segments, as illustrated by the following.

Warm __ __ __ __ __ __ __ Cold

Never ___|___|___|___|___|___ Always

Although a mark may be placed at any point within a segment, typically marks within a given segment are treated alike. Thus, the previous scales are generally treated as consisting of seven points or steps (the question of the optimal number of points is addressed in a later section). Accordingly, responses would be scored on a scale ranging from 1 to 7, with 1 representing one end point (e.g., Never) and 7 representing the other (e.g., Always).

In the preceding examples the numbers were implied. Instead, they may be included in the scale, as in the following example:

Agree Very Strongly ___|___|___|___|___|___| Disagree Very Strongly

          1   2   3   4   5   6

Descriptors or definitions may be provided not only for the end points of the scale but also for some or all the intermediate ones, with or without numbers. For example:

1	2	3	4

Never   Rarely   Frequently   Always

In many instances, it is more convenient to provide respondents with a set of defined response categories that they are to use to indicate their position with respect to a set of statements, behaviors, traits, and the like. For example, each of a set of attitude items may be preceded with a short line on which respondents are instructed to record the response reflecting their degree of agreement or disagreement. Following are examples of three alternative formats of such response categories, along with their definitions:

(a)	(b)	(c)
+3: Agree Very Strongly	6: Agree Very Strongly	AVS: Agree Very Strongly
+2: Agree Strongly	5: Agree Strongly	AS: Agree Strongly
+1: Agree	4: Agree	A: Agree
−1: Disagree	3: Disagree	D: Disagree
−2: Disagree Strongly	2: Disagree Strongly	DS: Disagree Strongly
−3: Disagree Very Strongly	1: Disagree Very Strongly	DVS: Disagree Very Strongly

A choice from among these or other possible formats depends on various factors. For example, format (a) is generally preferable when respondents are relatively sophisticated. The tendency to associate agreement with positive signs and disagreement with negative signs helps maintain consistency in the use of categories as defined. Format (a) may, however, be deemed inappropriate for certain kinds of subjects (e.g., persons with little education, young children).

Some Common Characteristics of Rating Scales

Unique features and formats of rating scales aside, they share a major characteristic, namely the person doing the rating serves as the measuring instrument. It follows that validity and reliability of ratings are predicated on the "assumption that the human observer is a good instrument of quantitative observation . . . capable of some degree of precision and some degree of objectivity" (Guilford, 1954, p. 278). Not unexpectedly, then, validity and reliability of ratings may vary greatly, depending on who does the ratings, with what frame of reference, for what purposes, in what settings, and the like. This has led to concerns, even strong skepticism, among some authors (e.g., Oppenheim, 1966) about the usefulness of rating scales.

In what follows, we comment briefly on some major issues in the use of rating scales.

RATINGS AND PERCEPTION

Probably the major reason why rating scales are vulnerable to misuse and misinterpretation stems from the fact that they reflect a perceptual process. The literature on perception in general and person perception in particular (e.g., Markus & Zajonc, 1985; Schneider, Hastorf, & Ellsworth, 1979; Warr & Knapper, 1968) is replete with examples of effects of perceivers' attitudes, values, motives, and the like, on their perceptions. It is, therefore, not surprising that ratings often tell more about the raters than about the objects they rate.

The vulnerability of ratings to various sources of rater biases and response sets is well documented (e.g., Guilford, 1954; Landy & Farr, 1980; Saal et al., 1980). One of the most common sources of bias is the halo effect, a constant error that occurs when raters' general impressions bias their ratings of distinct aspects of the ratees. Another is the tendency on the part of some raters to give ratings that are consistently too high or too low (leniency/severity errors). Some raters tend to avoid extreme categories, concentrating instead on categories around the midpoint of the scales (error of central tendency). Among strategies aimed at minimizing raters' biases are training in the application of the specific scales, clear definitions of referents and the scales used. We comment only on the latter.

DEFINITIONS

General issues concerning definitions are discussed in other chapters (e.g., Chapters 3, 4, and 8). In the present context, we would like to stress that clear definitions of the referents to be rated as well as categories of the rating scale used are imperative. The degree of elaboration necessary will vary with the specific referents, type of scale, respondents, circumstances, and the like.

Unfortunately, rating scales are frequently employed without providing raters with any definitions. In the extreme case, global ratings on broad aspects (such as how "good" a worker is, how "effective" a professor is, how "democratic" a leader is) are elicited without any attempt at definitions of the relevant terms. It is clear that, in the absence of definitions, raters necessarily resort to their own definitions or conceptions. Not surprisingly, validity and reliability of ratings tend to be very low under such circumstances.

Even when ratings are elicited for more specific attributes or aspects, definitions are often absent or vague, as is exemplified by the 30 item "staff evaluation form" President Carter's chief of staff, Hamilton Jordan, expected Cabinet officers and White House staff members to use in rating their subordinates. Here are several examples: (a) How confident is the ratee (on a scale ranging from "self-doubting" to "cocky," with "confident" occupying the middle range)? (b) How stable is he or she (ranging from "erratic" to "steady")? (c) What is the range of his or her information (ranging from "narrow" to "broad")? For a copy of the form, see *The New York Times*, July 19, 1979, p. A16.

Jordan's approach is not unlike the one used widely in private industry and in academia. Following is an almost random selection of items from various scales used by students to rate their professors: (a) original–conventional, (b) creative–routinized, (c) receptive to new ideas, (d) interested in teaching, (e) concerned about student, (f) ability to explain, and (g) fair in evaluation of students (see examples of scales from which the preceding have been excerpted, and other scales, in Elmore & LaPointe, 1975; Marsh, 1982; Sockloff, n.d.).

Definitions of Categories.   It has been shown (e.g., Goocher, 1965, 1969; Hakel, 1968; Simpson, 1944) that apparently unambiguous terms used as categories of rating scales (e.g., frequently, often, occasionally, sometimes) are interpreted differently by different raters and also have different meanings for the same rater in different contexts.

A more specific definitional concern, often referred to as anchoring, relates to whether all or some of the categories should be defined and which is the best pattern of definition (e.g., end, middle). Results of studies addressing such questions have been inconsistent. At the present time, it is not clear what degree of category definition (e.g., all-category-defined, some-category-defined, end-category-defined) is optimal (see Dixon, Bobo, & Stevick, 1984, for a review). As Landy and Farr (1980) pointed out:

The importance of the type and number of anchors probably covaries with the adequacy of the dimension definition. In the absence of adequate definitions of the dimensions to be rated, the rater must depend on the anchors to supply the meaning of the scale. (p. 88)

COMPOSITES OF RATINGS

In an attempt to facilitate decisions about individuals being rated (e.g., who should be promoted, fired, awarded tenure), scores on several rating scales are often combined into a composite score. It goes without saying that the separate ratings should be addressed to the same criterion or aspects of the same criterion; otherwise the composite score is bound to be meaningless or misleading. But even when the separate ratings appear to be addressing the same overall criterion, there remains the very difficult question of how to weight each of them in the process of arriving at the overall score.

Adding, or averaging, the ratings, thereby giving each an equal weight, is probably the most frequent, although very often inappropriate, approach taken. It is safe to say that on very rare occasions will an employer consider being on time, following instructions, keeping work area clean, being accurate, productive, and so on, equally important in assessing employees. The relative importance of each aspect will depend on the specific definition of the criterion (assuming one has been attempted) which, in turn, will depend on the specific job and the specific setting.

Examples of combinations of ratings for which little or no justification is given and that appear inappropriate even by inspection only unfortunately abound. Table 6.1 is a caricature of rating systems that was probably designed to serve as an antidote against the very frequent abuses of ratings. We regret that we do not know the identity of the author(s).

Summated Rating Scales

As has already been pointed out in earlier chapters, single-item measures are generally deficient both with respect to validity and reliability. Because of this, multi-item scales are often resorted to, as is exemplified by measures of achievement, aptitudes, personality, and attitudes.

Broadly speaking, a summated rating scale is one that consists of several items, responses to which are summed to yield a single score. Perhaps one of the most popular forms of such scaling currently in use is that referred to as a Likert-type scale, so named after Likert (1932) who first proposed this method of scale construction.

The first phase in Likert scaling is the generation of an item pool. This is done by writing items and/or culling statements from various sources (e.g., literature, mass media, people's utterances) concerning the referent in question. In order to minimize response sets, such as agreement with items regardless of their content,[2] both favorable and unfavorable statements (approximately in equal numbers) regarding the referent in question are assembled.

Prior to summing responses to items in order to arrive at total scores, scoring of either

_____

[2]See Response Styles, later in this chapter.

Table 6.1
Employee Performance Appraisal

Area of Performance	Degree of Performance				
	Far exceeds job requirements	Exceeds job requirements	Meets job requirements	Needs Improvement	Does not meet minimum requirements
Quality of work	Leaps tall buildings in a single bound	Leaps tall buildings with a running start	Can leap short buildings with prodding	Bumps into buildings	Cannot recognize buildings
Promptness	Is faster than a speeding bullet	Is as fast as a speeding bullet	Would you believe a slow bullet?	Misfires frequently	Wounds self when handling guns
Adaptability	Walks on water	Keeps head above water under stress	Washes with water	Drinks water	Passes water in emergencies
Communication	Talks with God	Talks with the angels	Talks to himself	Argues with himself	Loses arguments with himself

positively worded (favorable) or negatively worded (unfavorable) items has to be reversed or reflected so that *agreement* with a positively worded item will be assigned the same score as *disagreement* with a negatively worded item. For example, if Agree Very Strongly with a positively worded item is scored as 6, then Disagree Very Strongly with a negatively worded item is also scored as 6.

ITEM ANALYSIS

The pool of items is administered to a screening sample comprised of subjects similar to those for whom the scale is intended, who respond to each item on a scale indicating varying intensities of approval/disapproval, agreement/disagreement, and the like. Although originally Likert used a 5-point scale (i.e., strongly approve, approve, undecided, disapprove, strongly disapprove), various numbers of response alternatives (including or excluding an "undecided" category) are used in such scales (see Task Effects, later in this chapter).

The responses of the screening sample are subjected to an item analysis in order to determine the adequacy of the individual items so that the "best" ones may be selected for inclusion in the scale. Two approaches to item selection were proposed by Likert: (a) Items that discriminate between groups identified as scoring "high" or "low"[3] are selected (see Edwards, 1957b, Chapter 6, for details of tests of item discrimination); or (b) items whose correlations with total scores are relatively high are selected. Because the item is part of the total score, item-total correlations are inflated to a certain extent. It has, therefore, been suggested that such correlations be corrected. In the past, this was done by applying an estimation formula (see Nunnally, 1978, p. 281). Nowadays, computer program procedures are available (e.g., RELIABILITY of SPSS) to exclude from the total score a given item when its correlation with the total is calculated. Such corrections are especially important when the number of items is relatively small.

DIMENSIONALITY

When a total score is meant to reflect a construct, all issues concerning construct validation (see Chapter 4) are directly relevant. A notable case in point is the issue of dimensionality. As was pointed out in Chapter 4, the validity of summing scores on items is predicated on them tapping the same dimension. Further, item analysis of the kind described in the preceding section is of limited usefulness so far as determination of dimensionality of a scale is concerned.

One of the means of studying dimensions underlying relations among a set of items is factor analysis (see Chapter 4 for an intuitive introduction, and Chapters 22 and 23 for detailed discussions along with illustrative analyses). In the present context, therefore, probably the best approach to the selection of items from the pool administered to the screening sample (see above) is to factor analyze the correlation matrix among all the items. Items having "high" loadings on the same factor and "low" loadings on all other factors would be considered good candidates for inclusion in a scale for the measurement of the dimension in question. Using this approach, one may produce and validate a scale aimed at measuring a unidimensional or a multidimensional construct. In the former case, items loading on a single factor would be selected for inclusion in the scale. In the latter case, items loading on

---

[3]Based on their total scores, approximately 25% are selected for each group.

different factors would be selected to comprise subscales that would yield summated scores for each dimension of interest.

SCORING OF ITEMS

Originally, Likert proposed a somewhat complex way of scoring each item based on normal deviates. However, it has been shown that the much simpler method of assigning integers to each category (e.g., 1 to disagree strongly, 2 to disagree, and so on) produces results very similar to those obtained by the more laborious procedure.

TOTAL SCORE AND ITS INTERPRETATION

Although differential weights may be applied to the separate items (as in assigning weights from a factor analysis in producing factor scores), for most purposes, unit weighting (i.e., merely summing the separate responses, thus, weighting each of the items equally) has been shown to produce satisfactory results.

Instead of expressing the total score as a sum of the individual items, it is more useful to express it as an average, that is, dividing the total score by the number of items. Assume, for example, that a measure consists of 20 items and that the response categories range from 1 = disagree very strongly to 6 = agree very strongly. Assume further that a given individual has a total score of 96. It is rather difficult to develop a feel for the meaning of such a total score. Dividing it by 20 (number of items) yields a score of 4.8 on the continuum indicated above, rendering it somewhat easier to interpret.

It should, however, be noted that, whether expressed as a total or an average, comparisons of scores on summated scales are relative in nature. Thus, an individual's standing may be compared to his or her group or to some other norm; groups may be compared to each other.

SEMANTIC DIFFERENTIAL

Stimuli, be they concepts, objects, or people, evoke a variety of responses. The Semantic Differential (SD) technique was developed to assess some such responses. As originally conceived by Osgood (1952) and later expanded upon by Osgood, Suci, and Tannenbaum (1957), the SD[4] was meant to assess connotative or metaphorical meaning of a wide range of concepts. Its use is based on two basic notions: (a) that concepts differ (hence can be "differentiated") with respect to the meaning(s) they convey or evoke, and (b) that the meaning of most concepts can be captured by a relatively small number of dimensions (these are discussed below).

Concepts are rated on a set of bipolar adjective scales. Except for cases where the scale structure is decided upon a priori (see below), typically the goals of using the SD are two-fold: (a) to investigate the meaning of the scales by examining relations among them, and (b) to assess the meaning of the concepts or differences among concepts.

The format most often used in the SD is illustrated in Table 6.2, where the concept

---

[4]For convenience, we speak of the SD, but we do not mean to imply that it is a measure. Rather it is a technique of wide applicability.

Table 6.2

Sample Semantic Differential Concept and Scales

				COMPUTER				
good	——	——	——	——	——	——	——	bad
slow	——	——	——	——	——	——	——	fast
ugly	——	——	——	——	——	——	——	beautiful
active	——	——	——	——	——	——	——	passive
large	——	——	——	——	——	——	——	small
weak	——	——	——	——	——	——	——	strong
valuable	——	——	——	——	——	——	——	worthless
powerless	——	——	——	——	——	——	——	powerful
sharp	——	——	——	——	——	——	——	dull

COMPUTER[5] is to be rated on nine bipolar scales. These 7-point scales are designed to assess both directionality (e.g., is it good or bad?) and intensity (e.g., how good or how bad?). Clearly, SD is a special kind of a rating scale. Hence, problems and concerns discussed earlier in connection with rating scales in general (e.g., definitions, composite scores) apply to it as well.

Examine the scales in Table 6.2 and notice that, although each has its own nuances, they do not convey nine distinct dimensions of meaning. Little effort is required to group the scales into subsets, each reflecting some common dimension of meaning. For example, good–bad and beautiful–ugly seem to share some common meaning, as do slow–fast and active–passive.

In fact, factor analyses of relations among scales such as those under consideration (Osgood et al., 1957) have repeatedly yielded the following three primary dimensions: (a) Evaluative (E), generally the most dominant one, is concerned with the favorableness of the reaction, that is, "the *attitudinal* variable in human thinking;" (b) Potency (P) is "concerned with power and the things associated with it, size, weight, toughness, and the like;" and (c) Activity (A) involves "quickness, excitement, warmth, agitation and the like" (pp. 72–73).

Referring to the scales given in Table 6.2: the E(valuative) dimension is reflected by good–bad, beautiful–ugly, valuable–worthless; the P(otency) dimension by large–small, weak–strong, and powerless–powerful; the A(ctivity) dimension by slow–fast, active–passive, and sharp–dull. Assuming for the moment the validity of these three dimensions, scores on each would be arrived at by summing the responses for each of the scales comprising a particular dimension.

To minimize response set, scales are typically presented so that adjectives of a given pole (e.g., positive) are counterbalanced (see Table 6.2 where, for example, "good" and "ugly" are on the left). Accordingly, as explained earlier in connection with summated rating scales, scoring of relevant scales has to be reflected or reversed prior to the summation. Differences between two or more concepts (as well as between two or more groups) can then be assessed through the use of a variety of univariate and multivariate analyses.

Despite problems and concerns raised in connection with the use of the SD (see below), it has endured partly because of the relative consistency with which the EPA dimensions, which appear to account for much of the covariation in ratings, have been obtained in diverse studies with disparate populations.[6]

---

[5]For illustrative purposes, only one concept is given. Issues concerning choice of concepts and scales are discussed below.

[6]The three dimensions have been replicated in cross-cultural research as well (e.g., Osgood, May, & Miron, 1975; Snider & Osgood, 1969, Part V). The edited compilation of Snider and Osgood (1969) constitutes a good

The SD enjoys a great deal of popularity, because it is easy to administer, the responses required of subjects are fairly simple, and it is adaptable to a wide range of topics. It is, however, these very aspects that have also contributed to much of the confusion and misunderstanding surrounding applications of SD, analyses of data it yields, and interpretations of results.

As in the case of summated rating scales, many researchers seem to think that, by attaching an assortment of bipolar rating scales to a set of concepts, they are ipso facto applying the SD approach. It should also be noted that different types of scales, some of which are not truly bipolar in nature, have been used in alleged applications of the SD.

Originally, the SD was designed to ascertain meaning across a wide array of concepts. Accordingly, diverse concepts were intentionally used. Subsequently, many, if not most, applications have focused on the meaning of and/or attitudes toward some specific concept domain (e.g., ethnic groups, aspects of the self).

An exhaustive treatment of the SD is beyond the scope of this presentation. General expositions of the SD, discussions of its assumptions, and of problems that often arise in its use can be found, for example, in Bynner and Coxhead (1979), Heise (1969b, 1970), Maguire (1973), Mann, Phillips, and Thompson (1979), Mayerberg and Bean (1978), Miron (1972), Miron and Osgood (1966), Osgood et al. (1957), and Snider and Osgood (1969).

In the remainder of this section, we address some issues related to the selection of scales and concepts, concept-scale interaction, and analytic approaches.

SELECTION OF SCALES

Initially, Osgood and his associates constructed 50 7-point rating scales whose end points were anchored by frequently used bipolar adjective pairs (e.g., good–bad, large–small, beautiful–ugly, hard–soft, sweet–sour, strong–weak, clean–dirty, high–low, calm–agitated). Subjects used these 50 scales to rate 20 diverse concepts (see below). The focus was on the dimensions underlying the scales; thus, a 50×50 correlation matrix among all scales was constructed by summing over all subjects and concepts (this and alternative ways of constructing correlation matrices as well as methods of analysis are discussed below).

A factor analysis of the 50×50 correlation matrix yielded the three major factors referred to earlier (i.e., EPA), with some scales being more or less pure measures of a given dimension (e.g., good–bad for E, powerful–powerless for P, fast–slow for A). Factor loadings for each of the 50 scales are presented in Osgood et al. (1957), where summaries of other studies, differing to a greater or lesser extent in the scales, concepts, and subjects used, are also given.

In subsequent research, three or four representative scales per dimension have often been used, generally yielding adequate reliability of the factor scores. Because Osgood et al.'s primary purpose was to investigate the dimensionality of the scales, the selection of scales was of necessity more structured and rigorous than the selection of concepts.

Criteria for scale selection include factorial composition, relevance to the concepts, and semantic stability. The use of a subset of scales from Osgood et al.'s original list of 50 (or, for that matter, from any other list) for the purpose of obtaining subscale scores on EPA is predicated on the assumption that the scales indeed reflect these three dimensions. The relative durability and stability of the three dimensions notwithstanding, it is necessary to

---

sampling of SD applications in diverse settings and in various substantive areas (e.g., social psychology, personality, esthetics, advertising).

investigate the factorial structure of the scale and concept combinations used in a given study. Failure to ascertain that the EPA structure is applicable and that scales assumed to tap a given dimension indeed do so has led to many difficulties (some are discussed below). This is particularly true of research conducted in narrowly defined concept domains "for which the usual correlational structure breaks down" (Kahneman, 1963, p. 554).

We do not mean to imply that the selection of scales should not be guided by previous research with the SD. What we would like to stress, however, is that you would do well to adhere to Mayerberg and Bean's (1978) following "don'ts":

(1) Don't *presume* [italics added] the meaning of scales on the basis of previous research; (2) don't sum across scales presumably reflecting the same meaning dimension without evidence that the scales do, in fact, represent a unidimensional factor. (p. 479)

SELECTION OF CONCEPTS

Recall that in the original conceptualization of the SD, primary emphasis was placed on the meaning of the scales. As a result, selection of concepts was not as structured as that of scales. Maximum diversity of concepts and respondents' familiarity with them were the criteria for concept selection. According to Osgood et al. (1957): "On these bases the experimenters simply selected the following 20 concepts: LADY, BOULDER, SIN, FATHER, LAKE, SYMPHONY, RUSSIAN, FEATHER, ME, FIRE, BABY, FRAUD, GOD, PATRIOT, TORNADO, SWORD, MOTHER, STATUE, COP, AMERICA" (p. 34).

It has already been pointed out that, in most applications of the SD, the interest is in particular substantive areas. Obviously, in such applications, concepts should be "representative" of the domain of interest as well as ones with which respondents are familiar. The concepts should, however, not be too circumscribed as to evoke the same, or nearly the same, reaction from all subjects on all scales.[7] The reason is that limited variability severely restricts the correlation coefficient (see Chapter 3, Range Restriction). Because the correlations are subjected to factor analysis, it follows that, under such circumstances, it is highly unlikely for any structure to emerge.

Other issues relevant to concept (and scale) selection are presented below (e.g., under concept-scale interaction). For now, we quote Mayerberg and Bean's (1978) remaining "don'ts":

(3) Don't sum across concepts within a concept domain unless there is evidence that the responses to the various concepts are highly similar; and (4) don't sum across concepts reflecting different concept domains. (p. 479)

CONCEPT-SCALE INTERACTION

Two scales may be related, because they share a common component of meaning, independent of the concepts being rated. Alternatively, the concepts (the stimuli themselves) may, in part, determine the relationship between the scales (Bynner & Coxhead, 1979). In other words, scales may be differentially relevant to the concepts and/or the concepts may "instigate semantic shifts in adjectives" (Heise, 1969b, p. 416), leading to differences in the

---

[7]See Heise (1970), for examples of concepts that are generally rated near the extremes of the EPA dimensions (e.g., positive evaluation: family, church, truth; negative activity: snail, stone, sleep).

relations among the same scales, depending on the concepts to which they are applied. As a consequence of this phenomenon, called concept-scale interaction, a different set of factors (differing in number and/or nature) may result depending on the concept(s) in question. This is particularly prone to occur when only one or a few concepts are used, as factor analyses under these conditions "are highly wrought with hazards" (Heise, 1969b, p. 421).

The notion of concept-scale interactions is by no means new. In fact, on the basis of studies conducted at the early stages of the development of the SD, Osgood et al. (1957) concluded: "It is clear that there is a high degree of concept-scale interaction; the meanings of scales and their relations to other scales vary considerably with the concept being judged" (p. 187). They continued: "Obviously these results raise serious practical problems in connection with the construction of generalized semantic measuring instruments. . . . In the last analysis it may prove necessary to construct separate measuring instruments for each class of concepts being judged" (p. 188).

Osgood et al.'s exhortations have unfortunately been generally unheeded. Subsequent ample evidence of concept-scale interactions and elaborations of problems to which they lead (e.g., Bynner & Coxhead, 1979; Heise, 1969b, 1970; Kubiniec & Farr, 1971; Maguire, 1973; Mann et al., 1979; Mayerberg & Bean, 1978; Miron, 1972) have not fared any better.

Although some concept-scale interactions may be methodological artifacts that could conceivably be reduced or eliminated altogether (e.g., by appropriate selection of scales, the use of the appropriate unit of analysis; see Heise, 1969b), many genuine instances abound. In view of the fact that correlations among scales may differ, depending on the concepts being rated, it follows that factor structures may differ to a greater or lesser extent. Therefore, reliance on a commonly accepted factor structure when deriving scores on dimensions of the SD may lead to irrelevant comparisons (e.g., among concepts), at best, and to erroneous ones, at worst.

In most applications of the SD, the possibility of assessing a potential concept-scale interaction is not even entertained. The EPA structure is accepted a priori and all concepts are scored accordingly. Even when factor analysis is applied, the possibility of detecting concept-scale interactions is often precluded, because of the manner in which the correlation matrix among the scales is generated (see explanation, below).

In sum, it is essential that the structure of every new concept domain be investigated, utilizing a methodology suitable for detecting the occurrence of concept-scale interactions.

ANALYSIS OF SD DATA

Analysis of SD data is a rather complex undertaking. We comment first on major factors that contribute to the complexity. Some analytic approaches are then outlined and commented upon.

Recall that the SD was designed to serve two basic purposes: (a) to investigate the structure of the meaning of the scales, and (b) to use this structure to assess the differential meaning of concepts.[8] Unlike more conventional types of data, SD data contain three dimensions or modes: concepts, scales, and persons.[9] The structure of the scales is typically

---

[8]The investigation of concept differences is necessarily dependent on the scale structure; thus, we limit our presentation to analytic approaches used to investigate the latter.

[9]Variation in SD data can be attributed to the three modes and to the interactions among them. See Maguire (1973) and Bynner and Coxhead (1979) for comprehensive presentations of the linear model underlying SD data. A more restricted model was given by Kahnemann (1963).

explored through factor analysis. Now, most factor analytic approaches are applicable to data arranged in two modes (e.g., subjects by variables; see Chapters 22 and 23). Therefore, application of traditional factor analysis to SD data requires that the three-mode structure be collapsed, in some sense, into a two-mode structure.[10] Following Bynner and Coxhead (1979), we present five basic approaches for accomplishing this.[11] As will be shown, they differ in the sources of variations on which they focus. Consequently, factor-analytic results applied to data collapsed according to different strategies may differ dramatically from each other.

1. Persons by Scales. In this approach, referred to as the summation method by Maguire (1973) and Miron and Osgood (1966), the two modes are derived by generating an average score over all concepts for each person on each scale. Correlations among the scales are then calculated from the persons by scales matrix. Essentially, the concept mode is treated as the least important one with differences between concepts being ignored. "This method appears appropriate in the original Osgoodian context, where genuinely concept-independent components of meaning are sought using a very wide range of concepts" (Bynner & Coxhead, 1979, p. 376). Because the data are collapsed across concepts, attempts to study concept-scale interaction are precluded.

2. Concepts by Scales. Like the preceding, this is a summation method, except that the averaging is done over all individuals for each concept-scale combination. Correlations among scales, calculated from the matrix of concepts by scales, are then factor analyzed. Clearly, individuals are viewed as the least important mode, as differences among them are ignored. This approach may be appropriate when group perceptions are of primary interest.

Notice that, analogous to subjects in most applications of factor analysis, concepts constitute the rows in the reduced data matrix. Therefore, a relatively large number of concepts is required for a stable solution. Bynner and Coxhead (1979) recommended that a minimum of 30 concepts be used, whereas Heise (1969b) maintained that "40 appears to be a reasonable lower bound" (p. 419).

3. Persons by Scales—Separate Concepts. Dealing with each concept separately, interscale correlations are calculated for each of the persons by scales matrices. That is, as many such matrices are formed as there are concepts. Maguire (1973) and Miron and Osgood (1966) recommended that the correlations from the separate matrices be averaged and the resulting matrix of persons by scales be factor analyzed. But doing this is tantamount to ignoring the question of concept-scale interaction. Therefore, it is recommended that the separate correlation matrices be examined first for concept-scale interaction, which would be indicated when correlations among scales differ from concept to concept. In the absence of concept-scale interaction, correlations would be averaged and the resulting matrix factor analyzed. In the event that concept-scale interaction is detected, other analytic approaches would be more appropriate (e.g., factor analyzing each concept separately).

4. Concepts by Scales—Separate Individuals. Whereas in the preceding approach each concept was dealt with separately, in the present approach each person is dealt with separately. That is, interscale correlations are calculated for each individual's concepts by scales data matrix. This enables detection of person–scale interaction, which would be indicated, if the correlations among the scales differed from person to person. Although the matrices can subsequently be averaged over people (if no person–scale interaction exists), this approach suffers from the same limitation as the second one, namely that a relatively large number of concepts is required for a stable solution.

5. "String Out." In this approach, any combination of two of the three modes is treated as a separate observation. These are then "strung out" to form a single data matrix. The most common method of "stringing out" is one in which each person–concept response is treated as a separate observation. Interscale correlations are then calculated for the person–concept (the strung out mode) by scales data matrix. Maguire concluded that this was the best and most convenient method for calculat-

---

[10]Although a three-mode factor analysis, developed by Tucker (1966), can deal directly with SD data, this type of analysis has generally been applied very infrequently.

[11]You may find the schematic display, presented by Bynner and Coxhead on p. 375, of help in clarifying the five methods.

ing interscale correlations. However, as was pointed out by Kubiniec and Farr (1971), because "covariation over subject–concept observations is studied, preventing consideration of structure differences among concepts" (p. 533), concept–scale interaction is ignored. Moreover, using two different approaches of stringing out (the one described above, and one in which each concept–scale combination is treated as a separate observation), Mayerberg and Bean (1978) have showed that different types of factors were obtained for the same data.

From the review of approaches to the reduction of SD data, it should be clear that, depending on the approach used, certain sources of variations are excluded from consideration. In addition, the units of analysis (e.g., subjects, concepts) may differ from one approach to another. Not surprisingly, the different approaches can and do produce correlations that differ dramatically from one another, even to the extent of a change in sign (Bynner & Coxhead, 1979). Consequently, conclusions regarding the structure of meaning of scales used in the SD are dependent, in large part, on the specific approach used. The illustrative examples of Maguire (1973), Bynner and Coxhead (1979), Coxhead and Bynner (1981), and Mayerberg and Bean (1978) provide striking evidence of this state of affairs.

CONCLUDING COMMENT

We hope that, if nothing else, our rather limited overview has served to alert you to the complexities attendant with a valid and meaningful application of the SD. The case under consideration illustrates forcefully that a meaningful application of any technique requires much more than knowledge of the mechanics of its construction and administration. On the level of mechanics, there are few techniques that are simpler than the SD. This is probably why it is so frequently misapplied.

Complexities arise, because it is essential to determine, among other things, the dimensions underlying the scales used and the type of analysis most appropriate to answer the specific questions addressed. From our overview, it should be clear that a basic understanding of factor analysis is essential for the assessment of reports on applications of SD and that a more thorough knowledge is required when one wishes to apply the SD. Further, although our comments on analytic approaches were brief, we hope that they have conveyed the message that an intelligent choice from among an array of data reduction procedures cannot be made without a thorough understanding of the substantive questions the SD is meant to shed light upon, knowledge of relevant measurement principles, and familiarity with the relevant analytic techniques.

INTERVIEWS

In light of their pervasive role in our daily lives, it is only natural that questions and answers be resorted to in the course of gathering information in the research context. Interviews are commonly used for the gathering of information about "facts," opinions, attitudes, behaviors, and the like. Although the question–answer sequence in the course of interviewing is subject to a host of special rules whose structure and possible effects are not readily obvious to the untrained, the great popularity of interviewing rests, in part, on the perceived similarity between it and the everyday activity of asking questions and/or providing answers. Bingham and Moore (1941) characterized the interview as a "conversation with a purpose" (p. 1).

Exemplifying the essence of most current definitions of an interview is one proposed by Kahn and Cannell (1957), namely it is:

a specialized pattern of verbal interaction—initiated for a specific purpose, and focused on some specific content area, with consequent elimination of extraneous material. Moreover, the interview is a pattern of interaction in which the role relationship of interviewer and respondent is highly specialized, its specific characteristics depending somewhat on the purpose and character of the interview. (p. 16)

The interview may serve diverse purposes, hence, its schedule or format vary accordingly. Following are but some major areas along with some illustrative purposes suggesting different formats an interview may take: personnel (e.g., selection, appraisal); health (e.g., medical history, diagnosis); journalism (e.g., news gathering, opinion polls); law (e.g., depositions); marketing (e.g., shopping habits, product preferences); sociobehavioral research (e.g., surveys of attitudes, aspirations, sexual practices).

Our discussion of interviews and interviewing will focus on its use in research in the broadest sense of the term (e.g., theory testing, opinion polls, program evaluation, marketing). As with other methods addressed in this chapter, the presentation is introductory and by no means exhaustive. You will find useful discussions of interviews in general as well as of specialized approaches, in the following: Bradburn et al. (1979); Brenner (1978, 1981b); Cannell and Kahn (1968); Cannell, Miller, and Oksenberg (1981); Gorden (1975); Kahn and Cannell (1957); and Miller and Cannell (1988).

Interviewing can be carried out face to face or through the telephone. The use of the latter has increased dramatically in recent years and will no doubt continue to do so. This is due, in part, to technological advances; to the fact that telephone interviewing is more economical; and that it can be accomplished more quickly, thus enabling one to address "hot" issues (e.g., polls on expected voting behavior) in a more timely fashion.

As telephone communication is generally more constrained, devoid of the nuances, notably nonverbal cues, face-to-face interviewing is generally preferable when addressing complex or intimate issues requiring in depth probing. Moreover, response rates for face-to-face interviews are usually several percentage points higher than for telephone interviews. We focus on face-to-face interviewing. For information about specifics of telephone interviewing as well as comparisons with face-to-face interviewing, see, for example, Cannell (1985b), Frey (1989), Groves and Kahn (1979), Lavrakas (1987), Schuman and Kalton (1985), and Weinberg (1983).

INTERVIEWS VERSUS QUESTIONNAIRES

It is worthwhile to contrast interviews with their most common alternative, namely questionnaires. We use the term questionnaire to refer to any paper-and-pencil, information-gathering instrument that is largely self-administered.

Beginning with some advantages of questionnaires over interviews, it will be noted that they are generally less costly, less time consuming, and considerably less demanding with respect to such matters as selection, training, and supervision of personnel. Also, mail questionnaires can generally provide for wider coverage of the population of interest than do interviews. Sometimes, mail questionnaires are the only means of reaching respondents in remote locations or of special populations.

Being generally more uniform and standardized than interviews, questionnaires are less susceptible to biases due to deviations from instructions and method of administration (a rather common occurrence in some types of interviews), not to mention potential bias associated with interviewer effects (see below). Finally, confidentiality and anonymity can be more effectively insured through the use of questionnaires.

Turning to some advantages of interviews over questionnaires, it will be noted that certain areas of study and certain types of information may lend themselves more naturally to the use of interviews. Whereas written questions, statements, and responses may be limited and limiting, an interview can potentially address more complex issues, be of greater length, provide opportunity for probing deeper into participants' responses, and be more flexible and spontaneous in exploring new lines of inquiry. In some circumstances, interviews are the only viable mode of obtaining the information sought (e.g., from children or from people with little education).

The interaction that takes place between interviewer and interviewee affords greater opportunities for motivating the latter to provide more accurate responses, and for coping with sources of errors that generally go undetected when using questionnaires (e.g., misunderstanding instructions, question wording, definitions of terms). Also, the interview setting makes it more difficult for respondents to avoid answering certain questions or to terminate their participation altogether.

Further, the interviewer can exert more control in the presentation of the questions, their order, the elimination of irrelevant questions, and the like. Finally, observation of respondents in an interview setting may provide valuable information and insights generally not available when questionnaires are used.

In sum, each approach has unique strengths and weaknesses, making it more or less suitable for studying certain phenomena, for specific purposes, in given settings, with specific resources, respondents, and the like.

INTERVIEW STRUCTURE

Unlike other types of face-to-face communications, the interview is governed by certain rules of initiation, conduct, and termination that, in most instances, are set explicitly or implicitly by the interviewer. This is especially true of the research interview, which is, in the main, an encounter between strangers for a specific purpose set by the interviewer. The interviewer has not only to secure the cooperation of the interviewees but also to motivate them to respond honestly and to the best of their abilities to the questions posed to them. Moreover, it is the interviewer who is expected to control the encounter, probing, directing and redirecting, rewarding "appropriate" responses, discouraging "irrelevant" ones as the situation may require.

Yet interviews can vary greatly in structure. Thus, questions can range from very unstructured, loose, and nondirective to very directive and closed. Likewise, responses can vary from open-ended and free-form to highly structured, forced-choice. The more structured the interview, the greater the likelihood of unambiguous and focused communication. Our presentation is concerned primarily with fairly structured interviews, referred to also as standardized or directed interviews.[12]

MEASUREMENT ERRORS AND RESPONSE EFFECTS

As with any measurement instrument, assessment of validity and reliability of interviews is based on attempts to identify various sources of systematic and nonsystematic errors (see Chapter 5, for detailed discussions). Nonsystematic errors aside, potential sources of systematic errors in interviews may be grouped under three main headings: interviewer (e.g.,

---

[12]For some examples of unstructured interviews, see Lofland (1971) and Mishler (1986).

background variables, expectations, errors in probing); task (e.g., question wording, format); and respondent (e.g., background, attitudes, response styles). It is, of course, possible for these factors to interact in their effects on responses.

Interviewer effects are addressed in the next section. Because much about respondent and task effects is also relevant, to a greater or lesser degree, to other modes of data gathering (e.g., questionnaires), their potential effects are discussed more generally in sections that follow.

Interviewer Effects

Interviewer effects are inevitable, for as Kahn and Cannell (1957) stated:

> It is impossible to conceive of an interview as anything else but a process of interaction, and interaction means by definition that each individual is influencing the other and reacting to the other in a variety of ways. To say, therefore, that we want an interview without interviewer influence is a contradiction in terms. (p. 195)

The question, thus, is not whether interviewer effects exist but rather what they are. Further, can different types of interviewer effects be identified? Are there ways of minimizing some or all of them?[13]

Broadly speaking, a distinction can be made between role-dependent and role-independent effects. As these names imply, the former refer to effects of particular aspects of the interviewer's role as well as the manner in which the role is executed. Role-independent effects, on the other hand, stem primarily from interviewer attributes in the broadest sense of this term. We address each of these separately.

ROLE-DEPENDENT EFFECTS

Appearances to the contrary, the interviewer's role is generally fairly prescribed and delineated (see Brenner 1978, 1981a, 1982, for detailed discussions of interviewers' and respondents' roles). For the most part, the interviewer is expected to adhere to the standardized structure of the interview;[14] his or her primary role being that of creating optimal conditions that would stimulate and motivate the respondent to provide relevant and accurate responses.

Nevertheless, as Cannell et al. (1981) wrote, the "interviewer's potential for manipulating or distorting responses has generated numerous approaches aimed at controlling the interviewer's influence on responses" (p. 389). Among these are rules of behavior, types of feedback and the conditions under which they are applicable, probing strategies, appropriate use of instructions (see, for example, Brenner, 1982; Cannell, 1985a; Cannell et al., 1981; Fowler & Mangione, 1990; O'Muircheartaigh, 1977; Sudman & Bradburn, 1974).

Response effects due to interviewer role behavior concern divergence between the interviewer's role demands and the actual behavior engaged in. To some extent, this has to do with interviewer competency and/or propensity to carry out the prescribed role (Brenner,

---

[13]We remind you of our suggestion (footnote 1) that you read relevant sections of Chapter 11 in conjunction with the present chapter. For a particularly relevant section in connection with interviewer effects, we suggest that you read the one entitled Researcher in Chapter 11.

[14]This, of course, is not an all or none situation but varies depending on how structured the interview is. In the extreme case, a highly structured interview may resemble a stimulus-response situation (Brenner, 1982).

1981a; Sudman & Bradburn, 1974). Among other things, the following have been found: (a) Questions are often altered and not posed as written (e.g., Bradburn et al., 1979; Brenner, 1982; Martin, 1983; Schuman & Kalton, 1985); (b) interviewers may probe and react to answers differently (Cannell & Kahn, 1968; Martin, 1983); and (c) feedback is often used ineffectively, in that positive feedback is given indiscriminately (Martin, 1983). Other illustrations of biasing effects may be found in Kahn and Cannell (1957) and in Hyman, Cobb, Feldman, Hart, and Stember (1954).

On balance, Sudman and Bradburn (1974) maintained that interviewer and respondent effects are less important than task effects. However, Brenner (1982), who reviewed the evidence with respect to role-restricted interviewer characteristics, concluded that the potential for bias is such that "it is necessary, in any particular survey, to assess the degree to which interviewers are likely to have biased the response process" (p. 135).

ROLE-INDEPENDENT EFFECTS

Role-independent effects are those stemming from interviewer background and psychological attributes.

BACKGROUND ATTRIBUTES

Effects of interviewers' background attributes that have been studied most frequently include race, sex, age, and socioeconomic status (SES). In the main, age and SES seem not to affect the responses, although the effects of the latter are sometimes ambiguous, especially because they tend to be confounded with race (Hagenaars & Heinen, 1982).

Race and sex, on the other hand, have been found to affect responses when the questions are germane to these characteristics (e.g., racial attitudes, sexual stereotypes). (For reviews, see Cannell & Kahn, 1968; Hagenaars & Heinen, 1982; Schuman & Kalton, 1985; Sudman & Bradburn, 1974.)

PSYCHOLOGICAL ATTRIBUTES

Grouped under psychological attributes are effects of interviewers' personality traits, attitudes, values, opinions, expectations, and the like. It is often claimed that interviewers' attitudes, values, and opinions affect responses either directly or have indirect effects manifested through recording and transcribing errors. At the very least, there is some evidence that, for certain questions, a relation exists between interviewers' opinions and interviewees' responses (e.g., Bingham & Moore, 1941; Cannell & Kahn, 1968; Cantril, 1944; Erdos, 1970). However, Schuman and Kalton (1985) maintained that there is little direct evidence of bias due to interviewer ideology.

The literature dealing with interviewer selection contains many suggestions regarding desirable personality traits, such as honesty, adaptability, and appropriate temperament (e.g., Gorden, 1975; Lin, 1976; Sheatsley, 1951; Weinberg, 1983). For the most part, however, these common-sense based recommendations appear to be anecdotal with little systematic research to back them up.

In an extensive review, Hagenaars and Heinen (1982) concluded that "in general, there are no response effects of the interviewers' role-independent characteristics; only under rather specific circumstances are they to be expected" (p. 126).

TASK EFFECTS

Subsumed under task are aspects of the following: questions or stimuli (e.g., how they are presented, phrased); responses (e.g., open–closed, number of response alternatives); administration procedures (e.g., feedback, how to deal with reluctant participants).

Much has been written about these and related topics (see Chapter 11). In the hope of avoiding an extremely disjointed presentation, we decided to concentrate on some issues concerning question and response modes. Underscoring the magnitude of the subject under consideration is the fact that, even after this strict limitation, we could barely scratch the surface. For more detailed discussions of issues covered here and others, see Cannell and Kahn (1968), Cantril (1944), Converse and Presser (1986), Gable (1986), Kahn and Cannell (1957), Molenaar (1982), Nunnally (1978), Schuman and Kalton (1985), Schuman and Presser (1981), and Sudman and Bradburn (1974).

Question and Response Modes

Because of the crucial role of question wording, we begin with general observations on this topic. This is followed by a presentation of some specific aspects of question and/or response modes.

QUESTION WORDING

It is a truism that the wording of a question largely determines the kind of answer that will be given. This is illustrated in the following well-known anecdote recounted by Sudman and Bradburn (1982):

Two priests, a Dominican and a Jesuit, are discussing whether it is a sin to smoke and pray at the same time. After failing to reach a conclusion, each goes off to consult his respective superior. The next week they meet again. The Dominican says "Well, what did your superior say?" The Jesuit responds "He said it was all right." "That's funny," the Dominican replies, "my superior said it was a sin." Jesuit: "What did you ask him?" Reply: "I asked him if it was all right to smoke while praying." "Oh," says the Jesuit, "I asked my superior if it was all right to pray while smoking." (p. 1)

There is an extensive literature dealing with item writing and elements of good question wording (e.g., Cantril, 1944; Converse & Presser, 1986; Converse & Schuman, 1984; Hogarth, 1982; Miller, 1983; Oppenheim, 1966; Payne, 1951; Sheatsley, 1983; Sudman & Bradburn, 1982; Turner & Martin, 1984, Vol. 1, Chapter 9). Nevertheless, as conveyed by the title of Payne's (1951) classic *The art of asking questions*, a fair amount of art goes into item writing or question wording. The well-written item or the well-worded question is unimaginable without an element of creativity, an ability to make inferential leaps, and to communicate clearly and succinctly.

The overriding factor affecting responses is the meaning specific words, phrases, or their juxtaposition have for the respondents. Words or questions whose meanings are "perfectly clear" to the researcher may be unintelligible to respondents or have different meanings for them.

An interesting example of this is related by Schuman and Kalton (1985; taken from a study by the first author). Among items presented in the course of an interview, subjects were asked to indicate agreement or disagreement with the following item: "In spite of what people say, the lot of the average man is getting worse, not better" (p. 642). "Because the item had been used many times before by others,[15] it was assumed to be unproblematic and placed in the final interview schedule without pretesting" (p. 642). As it turned out, interviewers pointed to

the "lot of the average man" question as far and away the most problematic in the entire hour-long interview, mainly because this usage of *lot* is not familiar to many Americans. The question was variously interpreted to refer to a lot of average men, to the size of housing lots, and even in one case to cemetery lots! (pp. 642–643)

The preceding example concerned meaning or interpretation of the same question. Needless to say, the situation is generally much more complex when question wording is varied. Because wording effects can work in subtle and unpredictable ways "it may be incorrect to think that it is possible to have alternative wordings of the 'same' item. Any change in wording can change the meaning of the questions" (DeLamater, 1982, p. 23). Meaning may even be affected when the same response categories are used, but their order is varied. Examples of each—taken from Schuman and Presser's (1981) excellent book, where you will find a wealth of information on experiments on format, wording, and context of questions—follow.

Two forms of the "same" question (p. 281):

"Forbid" form	"Allow" form
Do you think the United States should forbid public speeches in favor of communism?	*Do you think the United States should allow public speeches in favor of communism?*

Different ordering of response categories (p. 60):

"Plenty" first	"Plenty" last
Some people say that we will still have plenty of oil 25 years from now. Others say that at the rate we are using our oil, it will be used up in about 15 years. Which of these ideas would you guess is most right?	*Some people say that at the rate we are using our oil, it will be used up in about 15 years. Others say that we will still have plenty of oil 25 years from now. Which of these ideas would you guess is most right?*

Without going into the details, it will be pointed out that response patterns (e.g., percent agree/disagree) differed for each of the preceding.

Focusing on the direction of item wording, Reiser, Wallace, and Schuessler (1986) showed that people are more prone to *agree* with negatively worded statements than to *disagree* with positively worded statements that express the same idea (e.g., agreeing with "Most people cannot be trusted" than disagreeing with "Most people can be trusted").

That preferences and decisions are affected by the format in which information is presented is illustrated in a study by McNeil, Pauker, Sox, and Tversky (1982). Patients, physicians, and graduate students in business with a sound background in statistics and decision theory were asked to imagine that they had lung cancer and to choose between two therapies on the basis of information provided about them. One aspect of the information was provided in terms of either mortality or survival rates (e.g., 10% mortality rate or 90% survival rate). Regardless of background, more subjects preferred the treatment whose effectiveness was couched "in terms of the probability of living rather than in terms of the probability of dying" (p. 1259).

---

[15]Incidentally, this item is from Srole's (1956) popular Anomia Scale.

OPEN–CLOSED DIVIDE

A primary aspect of question structure concerns the response mode called for. At one extreme is the open question (also named free-form or unstructured) calling for open-ended responses. At the other extreme is the closed question (also named forced-choice) requiring respondents to select from a set of responses provided. Forced-choice responses can be elicited by various formats, including yes/no, multiple choice, checklist, rating scale, variants of agreement–disagreement forms. Structure may, of course, vary between the two extremes indicated.

Whether to use open or closed questions is a subject of much debate and controversy. Partly this is because some authors and researchers tend to associate these two types of questions with different research orientations. Open questions are claimed to be appropriate for qualitative research, whereas closed questions are deemed more suitable for quantitative research. For some attempts to determine whether and under what circumstances is one format preferable to the other, see Schuman and Presser (1981), and Converse and Presser (1986).

NUMBER OF RESPONSE CATEGORIES

The bulk of the research on this issue focused on rating scales, although some of the conclusions may apply also to other types of questions as well. The number of response alternatives used in rating scales has varied considerably, with suggested numbers ranging from two or three (e.g., Jacoby & Matell, 1971) to 25 under certain conditions (e.g., Guilford, 1954). It is even not uncommon to encounter scales with 100 potential response alternatives (e.g., scales based on percentages) or ones that place no limit on the number of alternatives.

The effect of the number of scale points on, among other things, reliability, validity, recoverability, and respondent preference was examined by many researchers (e.g., Comrey & Montag, 1982; Garner, 1960; Green & Rao, 1970; Komorita & Graham, 1965; Lissitz & Green, 1975; Matell & Jacoby, 1971, 1972; McKelvie, 1978; Ramsay, 1973). Although results have been inconsistent and somewhat controversial, it appears that most general recommendations are for scales consisting of five to nine points (e.g., Cox, 1980; Gable, 1986; Molenaar, 1982; Nunnally, 1978).

AN INTERMEDIATE CATEGORY

Whether or not to include an intermediate category as one of the response alternatives is a question to which no clear answer can be given. To begin with, the meaning of an intermediate category differs for different people, for different types of items, and in different substantive contexts. Following are some ways in which this term or terms like it (e.g., middle alternative) have been used: Don't Know, Neutral, Undecided, No Opinion, Indifference, No Comment, No Commitment, Middle Position. Clearly, the preceding are not synonymous. In what follows, we briefly summarize findings regarding the use of some of the preceding terms.

A LOGICAL MIDDLE POSITION

For certain kinds of questions, a middle position seems logical. Questions to which responses such as "right amount," "about the same as now," "middle of the road," "neither too heavy nor too light," are logical come readily to mind. It was found (e.g., Gable, 1986; Molenaar, 1982; Schuman & Presser, 1981) that the percent of respondents using a middle position, when it is offered as one of the response alternatives, is larger (frequently considerably so) than the percent of respondents volunteering such a response when it is not offered.

It should be recognized that, when offered, the middle position may be chosen for a variety of reasons. Some may choose it as an easy or fast way out. For others, this choice may serve as a means of coping with anxiety engendered by being expected to respond to a question about which they happen to have little or no knowledge, or one to which they have devoted little thought. Still others may choose the middle position, because they do not understand the question. This state of affairs poses difficulties for the analysis and interpretation of results (see Schuman & Presser, 1981, Chapter 6, for a thorough discussion of the middle position).

DON'T KNOW OR NO OPINION

The inclusion of an option "Don't Know" (DK) or "No Opinion" (NO) is motivated largely by an attempt to deal with what have been labeled "nonattitudes" (Converse, 1970) or "pseudo opinions" (e.g., Bishop, Oldendick, Tuchfarber, & Bennett, 1980). These refer to people's willingness to voice opinions and express attitudes about referents and issues with which they are not familiar at all. A dramatic manifestation of this is the tendency of people to offer an opinion about or express an attitude toward nonexisting referents and issues. It has been shown, for example, that relatively large proportions of people surveyed expressed attitudes towards fictitious: (a) ethnic groups, (b) congressional acts, and (c) constitutional amendments. (For a recent study, see Bishop, Tuchfarber, & Oldendick, 1986. For a review and evaluation of the debate and research on nonattitudes, see Smith, 1984.)

It has been shown that when DK is *not* included as a possible response, about 10% of respondents choose to say that they do not know. When, however, DK is offered as a possible response to the *same* items or questions, about 30% tend to choose it. Similarly, a middle category on a rating scale (e.g., 4 on a 7-point scale) tends to attract a relatively large number of respondents (Aldrich, Niemi, Rabinowitz, & Rohde, 1982).

The choice of DK has been shown to be related to a variety of subject variables (e.g., level of education; see, for example, Converse, 1976), item ambiguity (e.g., Coombs & Coombs, 1976) as well as the specific topic. (For a thorough treatment of these issues as well as the broader issue of question wording, see Schuman & Presser, 1981.)

It is important to bear in mind that DK may mean different things to different respondents as well as to different researchers. Among meanings attached to it are: no knowledge, ignorance, indifference, ambivalence. Matters are even more complicated in view of the fact that although most authors use DK and "No Opinion" (NO) interchangeably, others distinguish between them.

No wonder various authors (e.g., Andrich, 1978; Bock & Jones, 1968; Converse & Presser, 1986) suggested that, in general, an intermediate category not be used or be used with caution.

QUESTION ORDER

Another controversial issue pertains to potential effects of the order of questions, also referred to as sequencing effects. On the one hand, simply varying the overall position of a question in a questionnaire or interview schedule does not appear to produce any major effects (Molenaar, 1982). On the other hand, when the context within which questions are placed is considered, order effects, such as saliency, consistency, and contrast, become more evident (Cantril, 1944; Kahn & Cannell, 1957; Molenaar, 1982; Schuman & Presser, 1981).

As Schuman and Presser (1981) pointed out, order effects, or more specifically context order effects, are likely to occur when the questions involved deal with closely related issues. This is compounded by the fact that questions on a questionnaire are typically arranged by topic. In addition, general questions appear to be more sensitive to order effects than are specific questions. Drawing attention to the fact that survey researchers act as if question ordering has little or no effect, Schuman and Presser (1981) cautioned: "These convenient assumptions must be challenged in the light of both past research and our own experiments" (p. 74).

RESPONDENT EFFECTS

As was pointed out earlier, respondent effects can be discussed in the more general context of subject effects. The latter are dealt with in detail in Chapter 11; therefore, only some general observations about respondent effects, with special reference to responding to questions (be they in interviews or on questionnaires), will be made here.

To begin with, we would like to remind you of our remarks to the effect that certain aspects of the interview process are not clearly classifiable into one of the three major categories (i.e., interviewer, task, and respondent) with which we are concerned. Further, there may be an interaction among the different categories in their effect on the response. Without going into the details of the meaning of interaction,[16] it will suffice for present purposes to point out that it refers to joint effects of two or more variables. An example of this would be that, when faced with a complex question, an inordinate proportion of respondents with a grade school education but not those with a college education would select a "Don't Know" response.

Of various aspects of respondent role-enactment, probably the most important and pervasive is that of *self-presentation*, which refers to the desire on the part of the respondent to present him or herself to the researcher in a particular light, to make a particular impression. Although "it is generally assumed that, other things being equal, people will act in such a way as to reduce personal or social discomfort or to make as good an impression on other people as possible" (Sudman & Bradburn, 1974, p. 9), self-presentation need not always be positive (for an example, see discussion of the negativistic subject in Chapter 11).

It stands to reason for the concern with self-presentation to be affected by the specifics of the context. Thus, respondents might be concerned with the image they are projecting when responding in a face-to-face situation but not when responding anonymously to a mail questionnaire. However, this in turn would depend on task factors. For example, differences between responses to face-to-face interviews and to questionnaires administered anony-

---

[16]See Chapter 10, for an intuitive introduction, and Chapters 20 and 21, for detailed discussions.

mously would depend on the nature of the questions. Fairly innocuous questions would probably elicit similar responses in both contexts, whereas "embarrassing" questions would probably elicit radically different responses in the two settings. But, although embarrassing questions are more likely to elicit socially desirable answers in a face-to-face interview, the specific effect may depend on the status of the interviewer (e.g., one's teacher, one's psychiatrist, a graduate assistant).

As if the preceding were not complex enough, the fact that respondents may assume multiple roles and that these may even be in conflict leads to further complications. For a discussion of how this may occur and what the consequences may be, see Chapter 11.

That the nature of the response may be affected by the respondent's comprehension of the question has already been discussed in an earlier section (see also Chapter 11 on Comprehension Artifact). Responses may also be affected by how accessible to the respondent is the information being sought (Cannell et al., 1981; Cannell & Kahn 1968; Converse & Presser, 1986; DeLamater, 1982; Kahn & Cannell 1957; Sudman & Bradburn, 1974). Of course, information may be more or less accessible, even totally inaccessible, for a variety of reasons, among which are "forgetfulness," repression, inability or reluctance to verbalize. Among potential consequences of this are underreporting (false negatives), overreporting (false positives), and distortion of responses.

RESPONSE STYLES

A response style, also referred to as response set, is the tendency to provide responses independent of item content. The two response styles that have been the subject of the greatest amount of research activity are acquiescence and social desirability.

Acquiescence. Originally introduced by Cronbach (1946), acquiescence, or yeasaying (Couch & Keniston, 1960), refers to the tendency of respondents to agree more than to disagree. Couch and Keniston (1960) wrote: "As a consequence questionnaire items seem almost 'possessed' by a tendency to correlate positively with one another regardless of content" (p. 169). Reference to studies concerned with this type of response style have been given in Chapter 4 in connection with a discussion of a measure of authoritarianism (*F* Scale).

Generally speaking, acquiescence can act as a source of confounding error, especially if the question or stimulus is ambiguous (e.g., Brenner, 1981a; Cannell et al., 1981; Converse & Presser, 1986; DeLamater, 1982; Jackson, 1967; Messick, 1967; Schuman & Presser, 1981; Wiggins, 1973).[17] In addition, there is some tentative evidence that it occurs somewhat more frequently among the less educated and among those less intensely involved in the task (Schuman & Presser, 1981).

Social Desirability. The social desirability response style was originally proposed by Edwards (1957a). It refers to the tendency to present oneself in a good light to the researcher or interviewer; therefore, it has also been called self-desirability (Nunnally, 1978). Social desirability has been found to affect responses on questionnaires and interviews, although the size of the effect and its consistency is a subject of debate (e.g., Brenner, 1981a; Cannell & Kahn, 1968; Cannell et al., 1981; DeLamater, 1982; Edwards, 1967a, 1967b; Sudman & Bradburn, 1974; Wiggins, 1973).

[17]But see Nunnally (1978), who maintained that "the agreement tendency is of very little importance either as a measure of personality or as a source of systematic invalidity in measures of personality and sentiments" (p. 669).

OBSERVATION

It is a truism that we learn about our physical and social environment through observation. However, whether they be everyday tacit and seemingly haphazard observations or deliberate and systematic ones of scientific inquiry, it is important to recognize that observation is an active process. This implies a specific frame of reference, which entails selectivity in the "what" as well as the "how" of observation. In order to demonstrate this, Popper (1972) asked his readers to participate in an experiment that consisted in his telling them to "*observe*, here and now" (p. 259). He then said:

I hope you are all co-operating, and observing! However, I fear that at least some of you, instead of observing, will feel a strong urge to ask: "WHAT do you want me to observe?" If this is your response, then my experiment was successful. For what I am trying to illustrate is that, in order to observe, we must have in mind a definite question which we might be able to decide by observation. Darwin knew this when he wrote: "How odd it is that anyone should not see that all observation must be for or against some point of view." (p. 259)

It was all summed up by Confucius: "For one who has no objective, nothing is relevant" (quoted by Armstrong, 1985, p. xi).

Although some consider observation "the fundamental basis of any science" (Brandt, 1972, p. 22), others see it more as the cornerstone of certain research strategies (e.g., Bogdan & Taylor, 1975; Erickson, 1986). Indeed, the term observational research is often used interchangeably with such terms as naturalistic inquiry, field-based research, ethnography, anthropological research, nonexperimental research, quasi-experimental research, to name but a few.[18] This has led to mistaken notions, the primary one being a division between observational and experimental research (e.g., Weick, 1968).

We believe the term "observational research" is a misnomer, as it erroneously places a method of data collection (i.e., observation) on par with such research approaches or research designs as experimental (see Chapter 12), quasi-experimental (see Chapter 13), and nonexperimental (see Chapter 14). In sum, observation is but one of many data collection and measurement procedures, and as such it "belongs to the same class of scientific activities as using a ruler, measuring electrical current or weighing chemicals" (Fassnacht, 1982, p. 39).

As typically utilized in sociobehavioral research, observations focus on verbal or linguistic behavior, probably because it is easier to codify than other behaviors, such as extralinguistic elements (e.g., vocal pitch, duration), facial expressions, body movements, and personal space. Although most often applied in "natural habitats,"[19] there is nothing inherent in observation that limits it to such settings. It may seem superfluous to state that behavior can also be observed in the laboratory, under experimental conditions, in simulated settings, and the like. Yet such statements are necessary in view of misconceived notions regarding observational research alluded to above.

As might be expected, observational procedures are not without problems. To begin with, they are generally expensive. In addition, they are vulnerable to observer effects (e.g., expectancies, halo, recording errors) and to reactivity on the part of people being observed. Frequently, the privacy of those being observed is compromised (see Fassnacht, 1982, for a summary of both the pro and con arguments).

To bring order into the diversity of aims, settings, and objects of observations, assorted taxonomies have been proposed (for some examples, see Brandt, 1972; Evertson & Green,

---

[18]See also Chapters 13 and 14.

[19]In fact "in situ" is a part of some definitions of observation (e.g., Weick, 1968).

1986; Medley, 1982; Weick, 1985; Wiggins, 1973). Perhaps the most differentiated taxonomy was proposed by Fassnacht (1982). You may find it helpful to consult criteria (e.g., purpose, content, definition, reliability, validity, practicality) developed by Herbert and Attridge (1975) to guide users and developers of observational systems.

As with other approaches presented in earlier sections, our treatment of observation is necessarily limited. In fact, we address only some issues concerning systematic observation.[20] To indicate what this means and how it is distinguished from other forms of observation, it will be helpful to use Weick's (1985) following definition:

Systematic observation is defined as *sustained, explicit, methodical observing and paraphrasing of social situations in relation to their naturally occurring contexts.* (p. 568)

Several points will be made about this definition. Clearly excluded from consideration are fleeting, unconscious, unplanned, unorganized observations. By paraphrasing, it is meant that the observer is selective and actively interprets what is observed. Social situations imply that the object of observation consists of three elements—actors, settings, and the activities engaged in. You would do well to read Weick's detailed presentation of each of the seven elements embedded in his definition (see also Weick, 1968). With the foregoing in mind, we turn to a discussion of the data.

OBSERVATIONAL DATA[21]

The types of data that can be collected and the instruments used to record them are almost as diverse as the actors, settings, objects, contents, and substance involved in observation. Brandt (1972), who provided one of the most comprehensive presentations of this topic, proposed a classification that includes the following categories.

1. Narratives: comprise data "that merely reproduce behavioral events in much the same fashion and sequence as in their original occurrence" (p. 80), exemplified by such things as anecdotes, specimen records, field notes, ecological descriptions, letters, diaries.

2. Ratings (e.g., numerical, graphic).

3. Checklists: "limited in scope to those specific aspects of behaviors and situations on which observers can readily agree" (p. 81), consisting of such things as static descriptors (e.g., age, sex), action checklists (e.g., interaction analysis, category systems, sign systems), activity logs, discrete event records, trait indicator checklists.

As our presentation is limited to some aspects of systematic observation, we address only ratings and checklists.

RATINGS

In view of the great popularity of rating scales in sociobehavioral research (see beginning of this chapter), their pervasive use in observational schedules is not surprising (Brandt, 1972; Fassnacht, 1982). Among typical utilizations of rating scales in observational schedules are ratings of behaviors (e.g., their intensity, frequency); assessments of interactions in terms of

---

[20]For presentations that specifically contrast systematic observation with other forms of observation (e.g., ecological, ethnographic) see, for example, Evertson and Green (1986), and Medley (1982).

[21]Leamer (1988) remarked: "I really dislike the word pair *observational data*. Isn't it equivalent to *observational observations*?" (p. 493). Although we agree, we use this nomenclature because of its wide currency.

various criteria; and evaluations of environments or settings (e.g., work setting, playground, classroom).

Issues concerning the use of rating scales were discussed earlier in this chapter. Instead of repeating the discussion, we would only like to remind you of the pivotal role played by the rater (e.g., background characteristics, frame of reference, bias, halo effect). General difficulties attendant with the use of rating scales are exacerbated when, as commonly applied, ratings are made at the end of the observation period rather than throughout. Further, the frequent use of overall ratings based on brief samplings of behavior is also problematic (Foster & Cone, 1986).

CHECKLISTS

Checklists have "been used for centuries as a means to ensure noticing and recording of specific items in particular situations" (Brandt, 1972, p. 94). As an observational procedure, they are used to record the occurrence and at times the frequency of prespecified behaviors and interactions. Although there is considerable diversity in the kind and format of checklists, the most commonly used ones consist of either sign systems or category systems (Medley & Mitzel, 1963).

SIGN SYSTEMS

A sign system, also called a distinctive features system (e.g., Fassnacht, 1982), contains a list of behaviors, incidents, or events of interest. During a given period of observation, observers are asked to record the occurrence and sometimes the frequency of behaviors, if they correspond to an item on the list. The underlying assumption is that the observed behavior or "event is regarded as indicative of the presence or absence of some characteristic of interest to the user of the system" (Medley, 1982, p. 1842). As such, "signs function much as do pass-fail items on objective tests" (Medley, 1982, p. 1842).

The observer's task is to record behaviors corresponding to those on the checklist. Behaviors not on the list are not tallied. Sign systems can consist of a fairly extensive list of behaviors; indeed, several behavioral domains can be accommodated at one time. Consequently, observers need to be cognizant of and attend to the entire range of behaviors at all times. Nevertheless, a list that spans a wide array of behaviors does not necessarily impose an undue burden on the observer, as signs are generally narrowly defined and explicit enough so that they are quickly and easily identifiable. Further, behaviors that are relatively infrequent are often chosen for inclusion in the checklist. As a result, there may be intervals of time where none of the observed behaviors is relevant. This situation can be disconcerting to some observers, making them more susceptible to distractions and observer drift (Foster & Cone, 1986; Medley & Mitzel, 1963).[22]

CATEGORY SYSTEMS

A category system consists of a set of mutually exclusive and exhaustive categories that are to be used to classify *each* and *every* observed behavior from *a single domain*. Essentially,

---

[22]Observer drift "refers to the tendency of observers to change the manner in which they apply the definitions of behavior over time" (Kazdin, 1977, p. 143).

the task of the observer is to assign relevant behaviors to the categories provided in the schedule. It is assumed that, during the period of observation, every occurrence of such behaviors is observed and classified into one and only one category.

The categories are necessarily few in number (e.g., less than 10; Medley & Mitzel, 1963); they are limited in scope and explicit enough so that observers can readily identify relevant behaviors and classify them promptly and with relative ease. Needless to say, selection must take place, but keep in mind that the categories are provided to the observers, thereby limiting the recording only to behaviors that are classifiable into one of them.

Category systems are typically more developed and theory-based than are sign systems, and they are generally more difficult to construct. The assumption of exhaustiveness of the categories and the requirement that they be explicit necessitates a very clear understanding of the domain of interest on the part of the constructor of such systems.

RELIABILITY

As is the case with any measure, the reliability of observational measures needs to be assessed. A general overview of reliability was presented in Chapter 5 with special emphasis on classical test theory. Reliability of observational data has been the subject of much discussion and debate (e.g., Berk, 1979; Fleiss, 1986, Chapter 1; Frick & Semmel, 1978; McGaw, Wardrop, & Bunda, 1972; Medley & Mitzel, 1963; Mitchell, 1979; Robinson, 1957; Rowley, 1976; Sackett, 1978; Tinsley & Weiss, 1975; Towstopiat, 1984; Weick, 1968). It is not our intention to review the specifics of the debate. Rather, our aim is to provide you with an introduction to some of the problems and issues involved. For more information, see the references cited above.

The most prevalent approach to assessing the reliability of observational measures is to calculate interobserver agreement (also called interrater agreement).[23] The problem, as we shall see, is that, although interobserver agreement addresses a particular source of error and may be important in its own right, it is not an index of reliability at all. Yet despite repeated attempts to alert researchers to this problem (see references cited above),[24] interobserver agreement continues to be the most frequently estimated index. In many instances, it is the only index reported.

Generally speaking, interobserver agreement consists of assessing the extent to which two (or more) observers agree in their codings, ratings, categorizations, and the like. Although many interobserver agreement indices have been proposed, they are basically aimed at estimating percentage of agreement among observers. Specific indices do differ, among other things, in whether or not they: (a) are sensitive to degrees of agreement, and (b) correct for chance agreement.

Recall that, in classical test theory, reliability is defined as the ratio of true score variance to observed score variance (see Chapter 5). Because of the amount and type of data collected through observations, reliability estimates are complicated. Complexity arises, in part, because behavior is frequently sampled more than once during any particular period of observation; more than one observer may be used at any one time; and several observational periods may be scheduled. As a result, measurement errors in the observations may emanate from many sources. For example, the observers may disagree as to the behavior of interest; the

---

[23]See Frick and Semmel (1978), for distinctions among criterion related agreement, intraobserver agreement, and interobserver agreement.

[24]But see Fassnacht (1982), who maintained that classical test theory reliability is of questionable value for observational data and that interobserver agreement is sufficient.

sample of behaviors may be inappropriate; the behaviors themselves may vary randomly; the person(s) being observed may have changed from one occasion to the next; and there may be changes in the circumstances of observation, and so forth.

Interobserver agreement indices only address potential errors among the observers. Moreover, these errors reflect observer differences in the *use* of the observation instrument, in its scoring perhaps, rather than in the behaviors themselves. Although agreement among observers is certainly important and should be assessed, it does not address broader concerns. As it turns out, interobserver agreement may be quite high, and yet reliability may be low. Potential contributors to low reliability under these conditions include the following: disagreement on individual items, although the total scores are equal to each other; variations in behaviors from one occasion to another; the group being observed is relatively homogeneous with respect to the phenomena of interest; and observer drift.

Several approaches (both correlational as well as those relying on analysis of variances procedures) have been proposed for the assessment of interobserver reliability (see, for example, Berk, 1979; Tinsley & Weiss, 1975). They share a common deficiency in that they yield a single index, thereby ignoring the multiplicity of potential sources of errors in observational data (see above). It has, therefore, been argued (e.g., Berk, 1979; McGaw et al., 1972; Mitchell, 1979) that generalizability theory (see Chapter 5, for a very brief introduction and references) with its capacity to distinguish among different sources of variability (e.g., occasions, observers, subjects, behaviors) is eminently suited for assessment of interobserver reliability.

CONCLUDING REMARKS

In this chapter, we have reviewed various approaches to measurement in sociobehavioral research. The approaches presented were chosen because of the prevalence of their use as well as to provide you with an inkling of the diversity that exists. We remind you that our presentation was necessarily limited, being neither exhaustive in the approaches reviewed nor in the issues raised.

This chapter concludes Part 1. Although we have repeatedly referred you to related design and analysis considerations that appear in other parts, our focus in this part has been primarily on measurement concerns. Beginning with the next chapter, we turn our attention to design issues. But because of the inherent interrelations among the various aspects of research, we will return to some of the issues raised in Part 1, as we will also continue to make reference to Part 3 for presentations of relevant analytic techniques.

PART 2
DESIGN

Chapter 7
Science and Scientific Inquiry

Derived from the Latin scientia, meaning knowledge, science has come to mean different things to different people at different times and in different contexts. Among other things, it is used to refer to knowledge as contrasted with intuition or belief; facts as contrasted with fiction; truth as contrasted with falsehood; accumulated knowledge about nature and the physical world as contrasted with myths and legends; different branches of knowledge, particularly those based on laboratory work and experimentation; and the method by which knowledge is arrived at.

Not surprisingly, Peirce (1958) asserted that science cannot be defined "with . . . precision . . . any more than we can so define *Money, Government, Stone, Life*. The idea, like these, and more than some of them, is too vastly diversified. It embodies the epitome of man's intellectual development" (p. 37). Ziman (1968) similarly maintained that to attempt "to answer the question 'What is Science?' is almost as presumptuous as to try to state the meaning of Life itself" (p. 1).

Following are but a few, almost randomly selected, statements illustrating the diversity of conceptions of science. Science is (a) "the criticism of Myths" (Yeats; quoted by Ellmann, 1964, p. 234); (b) *The art of the soluble* (Medawar, 1967); (c) "a system of beliefs to which we are committed" (Polanyi, 1964, p. 171); (d) "nothing else than the search to discover unity in the wild variety of nature—or more exactly, in the variety of our experience" (Bronowski, 1965, p. 16); (e) "nothing but *trained and organized common sense*" (Huxley, 1895, p. 45); and (f) "what scientists do" (Bridgman, 1959, p. 128).[1]

Attempts to articulate the aim of science cannot fare better, because (paraphrasing Dewey's, 1916, p. 125, statement about aims of education) science as such has no aims. Scientists, philosophers, policy makers, and so forth, have aims, not an abstract idea like science. Although admitting that to speak of the aim of science "may perhaps sound a little naive," Popper (1972, p. 191) said: "I suggest that it is the aim of science to find *satisfactory explanations*, of whatever strikes us as being in need of explanation."

---

[1]If the last statement strikes you as an operational definition, you may be interested to know that it was Bridgman (1927) who formulated the notion of operational definition (see Chapter 8).

It is important to bear in mind that science is but one of various perspectives in the attempts to explain nature and the place of humankind in it. Religion, mythology, philosophy, art, literature, have each in its own way been offering answers to questions that have been puzzling humankind from time immemorial. What is it, therefore, that distinguishes science from other perspectives? It is safe to say that most people would agree that science is distinguished by the method scientists use in arriving at answers.

Obviously, it is not possible to do justice to this complex topic in the brief space of a chapter. All we will attempt is a sketch, in broad strokes, of some major issues. What follows is, needless to say, *our* conception of scientific inquiry, based on *our* understanding of what it is scientists and philosophers say about this topic. Although we will not keep reminding you of this, we hope you will bear it in mind when reading our comments and interpretations, especially when you disagree with them. Our aim is not to proselytize but rather to present an orientation whose very essence is based on the notion of diversity of interpretations and potential disagreement.

We begin with a discussion of some misconceptions about scientific method and the role of facts in scientific inquiry. This is followed by a characterization of what we refer to as a scientific orientation. The chapter concludes with a discussion of two controversial topics: Basic and Applied Research; Natural and Sociobehavioral Sciences.

SCIENTIFIC INQUIRY

The notion that the royal road to *Truth*, to discovery of the Laws of Nature, is through *The Scientific Method* has until recently been part of the vision of scientific inquiry, as is exemplified by Pearson's (1911) assertion: "There is no short cut to truth, no way to gain a knowledge of the universe except through the gateway of scientific method" (p. 17). The picture of the scientist that emerges from such pronouncements is one of an objective observer who approaches phenomena without preconceptions, examines the facts, accumulates evidence in a detached, dispassionate and methodical manner, and arrives at conclusions (truth?) by resorting to reason and logic, letting the chips fall where they may. Nothing is, of course, farther from the truth.

Scientific inquiry is not a search after truth, eternal and absolute. Nor is it a search after laws of nature, waiting to be discovered. "A scientific law is not part of nature. It is only a way of comprehending nature" (Thurstone, 1947, p. 51). Truth is a working hypothesis held until further notice, until it is replaced by another hypothesis. What is considered true from one conceptual framework, for a given purpose, and under given conditions, may be deemed not true from another conceptual framework, for a different purpose, and under different circumstances. Thus, Niels Bohr spoke of "two sort of truths, profound truths recognized by the fact that the opposite is also a profound truth, in contrast to trivialities where opposites are obviously absurd" (quoted by Bohr, H., 1967, p. 328).

Formulations regarding the scientific method were advanced primarily by philosophers, not by scientists. Many, if not all, practicing physical scientists would probably agree with Beveridge's (1980) characterization of the scientific method as "the philosophers' myth" (p. 54). At best, physical scientists seem to view assertions by philosophers of science as "irrelevant" to their scientific activities. At worst, they manifest a "disdainful attitude toward the activities of the philosopher" (Gale, 1984, p. 491). Following is Medawar's (1982) depiction of natural scientists' posture concerning the scientific method:

Ask a scientist what he conceives the scientific method to be, and he will adopt an expression that is at once solemn and shifty-eyed; solemn, because he feels he ought to declare an opinion; shifty-eyed, because he is wondering how to conceal the fact that he has no opinion to declare. (p. 80)

The situation is radically different when one considers what appears to be sociobehavioral scientists' obsession with dicta of philosophers of science regarding the "correct" way of doing science. Failure of sociobehavioral scientists to match the achievement of physical scientists is attributed, largely, to their lack of adherence to the precepts set forth by philosophers of science. This orientation has had "destructive" (Polanyi, 1964, p. xiii), "disastrous" (Cook & Campbell, 1979, p. 92) effects on the sociobehavioral sciences.

THE ROLE OF FACTS

Misconceptions about science, or what may be characterized as naive scientism, are nowhere more evident than in the role assigned to facts. In what follows, we make some general observations about the role of facts. We return to this topic in Chapter 9, where we consider it in relation to theory.

In his account of *The grammar of science*, Pearson (1911) maintained that judgment based on facts "ought to be independent of the individual mind which examines them" (p. 6). Furthermore, *"The classification of facts, the recognition of their sequence and relative significance, is the function of science"* (p. 6). Similarly, in an explication of *The rules of sociological method*, Durkheim (1938) insisted: *"All preconceptions must be eradicated"* (p. 31) when observing "social facts." Durkheim even maintained that "a special demonstration of this rule is unnecessary," as it is "the basis of all scientific method" (p. 31).

The preceding will probably strike some as "quaint," "naive," conceptions characteristic of a bygone era. Yet the same orientation is, we believe, embodied in the oft repeated dictum by current researchers: "Let the facts speak for themselves!" This is an empty phrase. "Facts are ventriloquist's dummies. Sitting on a wise man's knee they may be made to utter words of wisdom; elsewhere, they say nothing, or talk nonsense, or indulge in sheer diabolism" (Huxley, 1944, p. 301).

Its Latin origin meaning "given" notwithstanding, data are not *given*; they are "constructed" (Bateson, 1984). The notion that facts are "out there" to be inspected, studied, accumulated, and used in the formulation of theory has its roots in the conception of "pure," unmediated, perception—a conception branded by Nietzsche as "the dogma of immaculate perception." "Everything of which we become conscious is arranged, simplified, schematized, interpreted through and through. . . . We never encounter 'facts'" (1968, pp. 263–264).

Carr (1967), who presented a penetrating discussion of facts in history, wrote:

The facts are really not at all like fish on the fishmonger's slab. They are like fish swimming about in a vast and sometimes inaccessible ocean; and what the historian catches will depend partly on chance, but mainly on what part of the ocean he chooses to fish in and what tackle he chooses to use—these two factors being, of course, determined by the kind of fish he wants to catch. By and large, the historian will get the kind of facts he wants. (p. 26)

What we see—the facts—is largely determined by what we are looking for, by our beliefs, expectations, orientations, by our theories. Bronowski (1965), who ridiculed the "foolish picture of the scientist fixing by some mechanical process the facts of nature" (p. 11), pointed out that one of the aims of the physical sciences "has been to give an exact picture of the material world. One achievement of physics in the twentieth century has been to prove that that aim is unattainable" (1973, p. 353).

SCIENTIFIC ORIENTATION

If, as was contended in the preceding section, there is no such thing as the scientific method, then what is it that distinguishes science from other modes of explanation? An answer may be gleaned when it is recognized that

the scientific enterprise is corporate. . . . Every scientist sees through his own eyes—and also through the eyes of his predecessors and colleagues. It is never one individual that goes through all the steps . . . ; it is a group of individuals, dividing their labour but continuously and jealously checking each other's contributions. (Ziman, 1968, p. 9)

The essence of such an orientation is a critical attitude towards findings and assertions based on them; an active search for flaws in one's work, for weaknesses and inconsistencies in one's reasoning; and the viewing of explanations as tentative stages in a never-ending process of successive approximations.

We are well aware that the preceding may strike you as a portrayal of a world of fantasy populated by imaginary beings. After all, scientists are human. They strive for status, compete for grant money, guard zealously their turf, and forge friendships or sever them, depending on whether fellow scientists agree or disagree with their viewpoint. Who among us cannot come up with examples of scientists' petty rivalries, acrimonious and illogical debates, hostility, closed-mindedness, intellectual dishonesty, even outright fraud in the service of personal advancement or that of pet ideas or beliefs? Indeed, one is not surprised at Gouldner's (1970) urging sociologists to "surrender the human but elitist assumption that *others* believe out of need whereas *they* believe because of the dictates of logic and reason" (p. 26).

As is true of any community, the scientific community is not monolithic. The vast majority of scientists are honest, intellectually curious, and aware that their work is part of an ever-changing scientific scene. This is not to say that they find it easy to revise their formulations, especially when this requires a major shift in thought patterns or in conceptions that play a central role in their view of the phenomenon under study. In the light of this, it is remarkable that some scientists, admittedly a small minority, expect, even hope, that their work would become obsolete as a result of further research and developments of new theories. As Franks (1981) pointed out: "Michael Faraday once expressed the hope that 50 years after his death nothing he had ever written would still be considered true" (p. 190).

The public nature of the scientific enterprise makes it susceptible to the scrutiny of anyone who cares to do so, thereby making it more probable for inappropriate practices to be detected and exposed. This is not to say that the process is a simple one or that inappropriate practices may not go undetected for a long time.[2] There is a Hebrew saying that The Lie has no legs to stand on, to which someone has added that it, however, can crawl for long distances.

Detection of outright fraud in science depends largely on the stage of development of a

---

[2]For a very interesting study of fraud, misrepresentation, and flaws in medical research, see Stewart and Feder (1987). See also, an editorial in the same issue (pp. 181–182) describing the many obstacles to the publication of the paper, including threats of suits for libel, acrimonious accusations and counter accusations, controversy among reviewers, disagreements between the authors and the editors, all of which led not only to considerable delays in the publication of the paper but also to drastic revisions of it. See also, Braunwald (1987) for a rebuttal.

given discipline. Generally speaking, the less developed a discipline, the lower the probability of detection. The same holds true when some artifactual process, of which the researcher himself or herself is not aware, is responsible for the results. In more advanced sciences, the failure to replicate findings would constitute a serious, in many instances the ultimate, challenge to the validity of a study.[3] Not so in most research areas in sociobehavioral sciences, where it is relatively easy for a researcher to dismiss failure by others to replicate his or her findings by attributing it to the use of different measures, settings, samples, experimenters, procedures, to name but some.[4]

Lest we create the wrong impression that more advanced sciences are immune to artifactual findings, we will draw attention to a fascinating example. In 1962, a Russian scientist claimed that, using ordinary water, he produced a new form of water, one that does not behave like ordinary water. The new fluid was first named anomalous water and subsequently polywater. As related by Franks (1981), in the 11 years that followed, about 400 scientists conducted research in polywater, and 500 publications related to this research appeared, many of them in influential scientific journals. "Eventually polywater was recognized for what it was: a nondiscovery, an artifact" (Franks, 1981, p. 3), having to do with impurities that were overlooked.

A scientific orientation is, further, characterized by a fair degree of tolerance for ambiguity that is manifested, among other things, by a recognition that there are no "rules" and "prescriptions" leading to discovery; a willingness to do without answers when satisfactory ones are not available; and an appreciation that "doubt is not a pleasant condition, but certainty is an absurd one" (Voltaire; quoted by Mahoney, 1976, p. 168).

A scientific orientation also implies willingness and ability to question "obvious" answers. One of the major obstacles to scientific progress is the acceptance of obvious answers without questioning—the preservation of the status quo in the name of "conventional wisdom," not to mention active resistance to attempts to make it the subject of scientific study.

The history of science is replete with examples of attempts to curb efforts to question obvious answers. One of the most celebrated cases is, of course, that of Galileo's. As is discussed below, the very viability or need for sociobehavioral sciences is questioned by many. This is due, in part, to the conviction that we do not need sociobehavioral scientists to tell us what we know from our own experience and observations. Responding to reporters' criticisms about expenditures on studies that "confirmed what most laymen already knew," Thorndike is reported to have said: "That is the fate of educational research. I[f] it comes out the way people thought it should, they ask, 'What is the point'. If start[l]ing conclusions emerge, people say, 'I do not believe it.'" (*The New York Times*, May 25, 1973, p. 11).

Another important aspect of a scientific orientation is the ability to entertain competing answers to a question and to test among them. Obviously, this is inconceivable in the absence of a degree of tolerance for ambiguity. People who are intolerant of ambiguity are not merely unwilling but are actually unable to entertain competing answers.

In sum, we believe that whereas advancing the notion of the scientific method is bound to lead to confusion and misunderstanding, it is meaningful to speak of a scientific orientation, some of whose characteristics we have sketched above (for similar views, see Kaplan's, 1964, discussion of "the scientific habit of mind," p. 380). As Bridgman (1980) observed: "The scientific method, as far as it is a method, is nothing more than doing one's damnedest with one's mind, no holds barred" (p. 535).

---

[3]But see discussion of falsification and the status of theory in Chapter 9.

[4]For a discussion of replications and difficulties in interpreting unsuccessful ones, see Aronson, Brewer, and Carlsmith (1985, pp. 480–481).

BASIC AND APPLIED RESEARCH

Attempts to distinguish between basic and applied research have been and continue to be a source of controversy among scientists, policy makers, and the public at large. This is because there is a lot at stake, not the least being the prestige and status of scientists and their claim for public support, particularly financial support. The value-laden nature of the controversy is graphically manifested in the use of "pure" as a synonym for basic.

Definitions of basic and applied research vary and could fill many pages (Klopsteg, 1959). In a summary of a symposium on basic research, Wolfle (1959) reported that there were two opposing views among the participants regarding attempts to define basic and applied research. "One group thought the effort to agree upon a precise definition would be very difficult but thoroughly worth while. The other group thought the effort not worth while. The latter point of view prevailed" (p. 257).

In its attempts to identify projects dealing with basic research, the National Science Foundation (in Klopsteg, 1959) adopted the following "working" definition:

Basic research is that type of research which is directed towards increase of knowledge in science. It is research where the primary aim of the investigator is a fuller knowledge or understanding of the subject under study, rather than a practical application thereof. (p. 186)

Questioning the meaningfulness of the distinction between basic and applied research, Reagan (1967) cited the following definitions or characterizations of basic research offered by leading scientists in hearings before Congressional Subcommittees. According to Edward Teller, pure research "is a game, is play, led by curiosity, by taste, style, judgment, intangibles" (p. 1383). For Leland J. Haworth, basic research "seeks an understanding of the laws of nature without regard to the ultimate applicability of the results" (p. 1383). And according to Glenn T. Seaborg, the foundation of basic research is "intellectual curiosity. [T]he motivating force is not utilitarian goals, but a search for a deeper understanding of the universe and the phenomena within it" (p. 1383).

Shades of differences in distinctions between basic and applied research aside, most of them revolve around the motivation of the scientist.[5] Stated bluntly: Research in the pursuit of knowledge and understanding is viewed as basic, whereas research carried out for the purpose of solving practical problems is considered applied.

How and by whom are the motives of the scientist to be determined? Various people have attempted to answer this question. By and large, the answers are, in our opinion, too pat, simplistic; some are even flippant. Here are a couple of examples of the latter. Waterman (1959) wrote: "The simplest answer is that if one feels he must make a psychiatric test of an individual to determine why he wants to do a piece of research, then it is undoubtedly basic" (p. 20). Bridgman (1980) likened the scientist's motive to do basic research to that of the mountain climber's: "Because it is there." As an antidote to such a conception, one would do well to remember that, when the notorious bank robber Willie Sutton was asked why he robbed banks, he responded quite naturally: "Because that's where the money is." Persistence in search of motives, and where this might lead is illustrated by the following anecdote. Upon being informed of the death of the Czar of Russia, Metternich is reported to have stated: "I wonder what his motive could have been."

---

[5]Other criteria for the distinction between basic and applied research have been proposed. For example, Storer (1966) maintained that "at the heart of the distinction is the question: Which audience is more important to the researcher?" (p. 110). For a scientist doing basic research, the more important audience is composed of scientists or colleagues, whereas for a scientist doing applied research, it is employers or the lay public.

It is interesting to note that, in a report sponsored by several organizations and commissions under the auspices of the National Academy of Sciences, it was asserted that "basic research can be most simply defined as the discovery of new knowledge" (Adams, Smelser, & Treiman, 1982a, p. 2). Yet it is the potential for applications of basic research that is repeatedly given for its justification, as is illustrated by the following:

In short, the justification for basic research in all fields lies in the knowledge-generating utility of scientific discoveries and in the well-founded anticipation—but not guarantee—that some of those discoveries will in the long run prove to be of great practical benefit. (p. 3)

Debates regarding basic research are reminiscent of more general ones about knowledge for the sake of knowledge, art for the sake of art, truth for the sake of truth. We agree with de Unamuno's (1954) assertion: "All knowledge has an ultimate object. Knowledge for the sake of knowledge is, say what you will, nothing but a dismal begging of the question" (p. 15). Further, "This is inhuman" (p. 29). As Bronowski (1965) pointed out: "What a scientist does is compounded of two interests: the interest of his time and his own interest. In this his behavior is no different from any other man's. The need of the age gives its shape to scientific progress as a whole" (p. 8).

Some authors (e.g., Bridgman, 1980, pp. 441–451) attributed the lack of progress in sociobehavioral sciences largely to their exclusive concern with practical problems. Others (e.g., Proshansky, 1981; Reagan, 1967) contended that sociobehavioral sciences are inherently applied. The preceding implies, erroneously we believe, that, in the natural sciences, it is possible to foretell which kind of research will lead to practical applications and which will not. The history of science abounds with examples of research of the most basic kind transforming the world of applications and practicalities. Suffice it to mention what basic research in nuclear physics or on the transistor has engendered. As with motives, the scientist is not necessarily in a better position to predict the practical outcomes of basic research. This is well exemplified by what Rutherford is reported to have said in 1933: "Anyone who expects a source of power from the transformation of these atoms is talking moonshine" (quoted in Weisskopf, 1972, p. 139).

In the course of reporting on their finding that the notion that "tongues of frogs work like a crossbow when they feed on insects" (*The New York Times*, September 18, 1983, p. 49) was erroneous, the researchers were asked what were the practical implications of their research. "One of the researchers, Dr. Carl Gans, responds that 'first of all, my mother, who is 83 years old, was very pleased' when she read about it" (p. 49). Although Dr. Gans then proceeded "in a more serious vein" to discuss some practical applications, we rather like his initial reaction, because it exhibits an awareness of the tenuous nature, even pomposity, of prognostications about the practical effects of basic research.

In what, we believe, are some of the most perceptive statements about the presumed distinction between basic and applied research, Medawar (1982, pp. 29–41) pointed out that neither purity nor usefulness are alluded to when scientists evaluate research. "'How neat!' one scientist might say of another's work—or 'How ingenious!'—or 'How very illuminating!'—but never, in my hearing anyway, 'How pure!'" (p. 38).

Believing, as we do, that the distinction between basic and applied research is not meaningful and that it may even have adverse effects (see below), should not be construed to imply that research studies do not differ in quality and potential impact or benefits, or that it is not possible to identify studies designed to solve specific practical problems and others that appear to be not concerned with practical problems. What we object to is the dichotomy of basic versus applied and, more importantly, to its use for the assessment of the worth of a study or of its potential practical implications, not to mention the worth of the scientist carrying out the study.

Anyone familiar with academia could not but have encountered the class distinction between the "elite pure researchers," and the "downtrodden applied researchers." Storer (1966), who referred to the distinction between basic and applied research as being "invidious" (p. 106), tried to convey the flavor of the arguments one might hear from members of the two camps:

> The basic scientist feels that applied scientists are not creative, that applied work attracts only mediocre men, and that applied research is like working from a cookbook. For his part, the applied scientist might well counter with the imprecation: The basic scientist is a snob, working in his ivory tower and afraid to put his findings to a real test; he is like Bacon's spider, spinning webs out of his own substance while we in applied research are making real progress. (p. 108)

Although admittedly expressed "in exaggerated form" (Storer, 1966, p. 108), such attitudes inevitably have deleterious effects on the people directly involved as well as on society at large and, therefore, deserve careful attention by academic institutions as well as by government agencies and private foundations.

We would like to conclude our discussion by noting that the distinction between basic and applied research has important implications for the question of the scientist's responsibility for the consequences of his or her research. Without going into the details of the very complex debate about science and values, or the ethical responsibilities of the scientist (see, for example, Glass, 1965), it will be pointed out that, generally speaking, those who insist on the distinction between basic and applied research tend to advance the view that the scientist should not be held accountable for the consequences of his or her work. (For discussions in the context of sociobehavioral research, see Beauchamp, Faden, Wallace, & Walters, 1982; Brodbeck, 1968, Part Two; Frankel, 1976; Kaplan, 1964, Chapter X; Lindblom & Cohen, 1979; Reynolds, 1979.)

Needless to say, such an orientation may have far-reaching consequences, particularly in view of the increasing dependency of the public and decision makers on the new priesthood of scientists for explanations, analyses, and recommendations. In an era of "Star Wars," at a time when humankind has the means to destroy the planet, this state of affairs should be of grave concern to us all. Fortunately, attitudes have been changing, as is attested to by, among other things, citizens' vociferous concerns and governmental partial responsiveness regarding the arms race, construction and control of nuclear power plants, disposal of nuclear waste, pollution, population explosion, acid rain, toxic wastes, to name but some of the most important ones.

NATURAL AND SOCIOBEHAVIORAL SCIENCES

Distinctions between natural and sociobehavioral sciences are another source of controversy among scientists, philosophers, artists, and the public at large. Conceptions of and attitudes towards what are referred to as social or behavioral sciences run the gamut, from denying them the status of science, through suspicion, fear, mistrust, indifference, to full acceptance. The controversy revolves around two major issues: (a) the "findings" of sociobehavioral research and the role of sociobehavioral scientists in promoting them as policy guides, and (b) the substance and methods of sociobehavioral research. We treat each in turn.

Sociobehavioral Research Findings and Policy Advocacy

Opposition to, even outright rejection of, sociobehavioral sciences is in no small measure due to sociobehavioral scientists' pronouncements regarding their findings and their strong advocacy that they be used as guides for policy decisions. Stouffer (1950) attributed the troubles of sociobehavioral sciences to "our own bad work habits" and to the "implicit assumption that anybody with a little common sense and a few facts can come up at once with the correct answer on any subject" (p. 355). Stouffer maintained that sociobehavioral scientists respond to societal rewards for quick and confident answers, without regard to how these were arrived at. As a result, "much social science is merely rather dull and obscure journalism" (p. 355), where the absence of evidence for its "interpretations" and recommendations is masked by "academic jargon. If the stuff is hard to read, it has a chance of being acclaimed as profound" (p. 356).

Some twenty years later, Frankel (1973) wrote that sociobehavioral scientists "exaggerate the amount of sound and applicable knowledge they have and . . . offer confident solutions to social problems—solutions that, when tried, turn out to be only a mixture of pious hope and insular moral judgments" (p. 931). Repeated failures of quick fixes offered rashly, even recklessly, by sociobehavioral scientists have, unavoidably, led to negative attitudes towards sociobehavioral sciences by large segments of society.

The question whether scientists should limit themselves to the presentation of their findings or also act as advocates for policies they presumably support is a source of "endless debate" (Hammond & Adelman, 1976, p. 389). We will not review here the various arguments and proposals aimed at coming to grips with this complex issue. (For some notable examples, see the symposium edited by Frankel, 1976. See also, Hammond & Adelman, 1976, and references given in the preceding section in connection with remarks about the responsibility and accountability of scientists for their research results.) Instead, we would like to draw attention to the serious damage done by what we believe is a cavalier, at times outright irresponsible, attitude on the part of sociobehavioral scientists who, despite their awareness of the shortcomings of their research, rush to disseminate their findings with an air of certainty, claiming that they provide evidence in support of the implementation of policies they favor. In view of this, it is not surprising that some deem sociobehavioral sciences as nothing short of sin. Auden (1950) gave a witty expression to this very serious attitude towards sociobehavioral sciences:

> Thou shalt not answer questionnaires
> Or quizzes upon World-Affairs,
> Nor with compliance
> Take any test. Thou shalt not sit
> With statisticians nor commit
> A social science (pp. 69–70)

We are very anxious not to create the false impression that other scientists do not engage in questionable, even reprehensible, practices. We focus on sociobehavioral scientists, because our book is about sociobehavioral science. Some of the most visible and outspoken sociobehavioral scientists have been making grandiose claims for their research—this despite their awareness that their tenuous findings will be used for partisan purposes. A notable example is James Coleman (quoted by Fiske, 1980), who is reported to have said: "You have to look at social science results not so much as something that will inform a decision but *as weapons in a political debate. They are weapons that will be used by whichever side they will favor* [italics added]" (p. C1). This is the same Coleman who led the research on *Equality of educational opportunity* (Coleman et al., 1966). It is not necessary in the present context to review the study and its impact on the courts and the legislature, particularly with respect to school desegregation policies and programs (for a critique of the study and references to the debates that it engendered, see Pedhazur, 1982, pp. 189–193, 263–267). It will be noted, however, that Coleman himself was actively involved in promoting policies based on findings that he later disavowed or viewed with considerable reservations. Retracting some of its major conclusions, Coleman (in Fiske, 1980) acknowledged, among other things, that "some of the methods used in preparing the 1966 report can now be viewed as inadequate." He is then reported to have said: "We didn't know enough at the time" (p. C4).

Although it is not clear whether the "we" in the preceding sentence refers to Coleman and his associates or to sociobehavioral scientists in general, it will be pointed out that the methods Coleman and his associates used were not novel ones. Quite a bit was known about their properties at the time Coleman and his associates applied them. Instead of providing documentation in support of this assertion, it will suffice to point out that soon after the report was published, various authors were in a position to critically evaluate the applications, or misapplications, of the methods used in it.

Remarkably, experience appears to have had no impact on Coleman's subsequent behavior. No sooner did he and his associates (Coleman, Hoffer, & Kilgore, 1982) publish another controversial report—this time claiming that private schools are more effective than public schools—than the retractions followed. Following are some illustrations of what the popular media had to say about Coleman's retractions (for references to professional literature in which various aspects of the report were debated, see Chapter 13). Under the banner: "School Study Said to Fail To Emphasize Main Point," we are told that Coleman "now says that the document published two weeks ago did not emphasize the most significant conclusions of his study and that the data on which it was based were flawed" (Fiske, 1981). Commenting on "Professor Coleman's troubles," Hechinger (1981) noted:

Responding more quickly this time than before to his critics who questioned his methods and findings, Mr. Coleman has already rephrased some of his conclusions. . . . But in reconsidering his report, Mr. Coleman also conceded that he "wanted to address the policy issue whether public funds should be used to encourage private education." (p. A18)

Another example of the wide dissemination of a policy recommendation based on research findings that have been questioned has to do with what has come to be known as the "bonding" theory, according to which there is a special, relatively short, period right after birth when contact between parents and their baby is essential for the establishment of an emotional attachment, a bond, between parents and child that has lasting effects on their relationships and on the development of the child. In the context of the present discussion, we are not concerned with the merits or demerits of the research that has led to these conclusions.[6] Instead, we would like to indicate how it was mirrored in the news media, particularly the changes in the authors' pronouncements about their "theory."

Reviewing the controversy in *The New York Times* under the banner: "Influential Theory On 'Bonding' at Birth Is Now Questioned," Brody (1983a) wrote that the theory "has prompted many hospitals to allow, even encourage, mothers and fathers to have immediate

---

[6]For critical reviews of the research literature on mother–infant and father–infant bonding respectively, see Goldberg (1983), and Palkovitz (1985). Both authors concluded that the concept of bonding has not been adequately tested.

and prolonged contact with their newborn babies" (p. C1). Brody quoted from a book entitled *Parent–infant bonding*, in which the authors wrote: "Sadly, some parents who missed the bonding experience have felt that all was lost for their future relationships. *This was (and is) completely incorrect* [italics added]" (p. C8). However, this was stated by the *very same* authors of the bonding theory who in the earlier edition of the book said: "There is a sensitive period in the first minutes and hours of life during which it is necessary that the mother and father have close contact with their neonate for later development to be optimal" (p. C8). Regarding the latter statement, one of the authors is reported to have said in an interview: "*I wish we'd never written the statement* [italics added]" (p. C8).

We are very eager to avoid misunderstanding our reasons for citing this study. We *do not* wish to create the impression that authors of a theory must be wedded to it for life, and that we are criticizing the authors of the bonding theory for changing their minds. Quite the contrary, on the basis of what we have said thus far, it should be clear that any scientific theory, and implications from it, is accepted provisionally, subject to modification, even rejection, as a result of subsequent formulations and research. But we suspect this was not the case for the theory under consideration. It does not appear that the authors have come by new evidence, or interpretation of "old" evidence that was not available when the initial statements were made. At the very least, we believe that greater care is called for in disseminating findings that may lead to policies that, as in the case under consideration, have potential adverse effects. As Brody (1983a, p. C1) noted: "Critics say that premature enthusiasm and publicity . . . has prompted feelings of guilt and fear of failure in parents who did not share the first minutes and hours of life with their infants."

It is the wide dissemination of questionable findings, of which the above are but some examples, that prompts the popular media to question the wisdom of relying on sociobehavioral research when it comes to policy decisions, not to mention providing financial support for such research efforts (see, for example, Britell, 1980).

Our aim in the preceding discussion was not to assess the accomplishments or the promise of sociobehavioral sciences,[7] but rather to alert you to the incalculable costs to society and to the profession of lax practices in the dissemination of and claims made for sociobehavioral research findings. We cannot agree more with Kitcher's (1985) statement: "When scientific claims bear on matters of social policy, the standards of evidence and of self-criticism must be extremely high" (p. 3).

Our discussion thus far dealt with adverse effects of exaggerated or unfounded claims by sociobehavioral scientists on the credibility and status of sociobehavioral sciences in society. We turn now to the other aspect of the debate regarding distinctions between natural and sociobehavioral sciences—that concerning substance and methods.

Substance and Methods in Sociobehavioral Sciences

Are the approach and methods used in the study of inanimate objects applicable to the study of living organisms, especially humans? This, in a nutshell, is the essence of the perennial debates as to whether it is necessary to distinguish between natural and sociobehavioral sciences and, furthermore, whether the latter deserve to be accorded the status of science

---

[7]For an extensive report of a committee of the National Academy of Sciences on the role and accomplishments of sociobehavioral research in various areas (e.g., racial attitudes, survey research, voting, behavior and health) see Adams, Smelser, and Treiman (1982a, 1982b).

altogether. That there cannot be consensus about these issues should be evident from the great diversity of philosophical orientations leading, among other things, to diverse conceptions of science, scientific methods, and scientific inquiry. It can even be asserted that disputants promulgating opposing views are not using the same language, in the sense that they invest the same terms with different meanings.

At one end of the continuum are those who see no difference *in principle* between natural and sociobehavioral sciences, although they do see differences *in practice* between the two domains because of the differences in their subject matter (e.g., Bhaskar, 1978; Cohen, 1953, Book III; Kaplan, 1964, pp. 27–33; Kemeny, 1959, Chapter 15; Knorr, 1981; Nagel, 1961, Chapter 13). At the other end of the continuum are those who deny the possibility of sociobehavioral science altogether or at least when addressing specific phenomena (e.g., Almond & Genco, 1977; Gergen, 1973, 1982; Winch, 1958). For readings and exchanges expressing different points of view on this issue, see Krimerman (1969, Parts III and IV). For an important set of papers in which authors from various disciplines (psychology, sociology, psychiatry, anthropology, philosophy, and geophysics) reflect on the current status of sociobehavioral sciences, see Fiske and Shweder (1986b).

Our aim here is not to review this controversy but rather to provide an overview of some aspects of sociobehavioral research that play a central role in it. Many of the topics commented upon briefly here are dealt with in various places in this book.

Although debates regarding the status of sociobehavioral sciences differ in emphases, depending on the specific context,[8] they revolve around conceptions of the human condition that include: (a) free will and how it relates to the formulation of laws governing human behavior, (b) cultural and temporal relativity of laws of human behavior, (c) uniqueness of the individual and nonrepeatability of experience, (d) complexity of phenomena and the attendant difficulties in controlling the myriad variables involved, (e) distortion of phenomena studied as a consequence of controls instituted by the researcher, (f) ethical issues of experimenting with humans, and (g) reactivity and reflexivity of humans, which may lead, among other things, to the validation or invalidation of an hypothesis, because the subjects were informed of it (i.e., the self-fulfilling prophecy; Merton, 1948) or because of what they surmise the hypothesis to be (e.g., demand characteristics; see Chapter 11).

Those who deny the possibility of sociobehavioral science attribute this to the difficulty (some say impossibility) of separating what "is" from what "ought" to be, the "descriptive" from the "prescriptive," when studying humans. Northrop (1947) highlighted these issues, saying:

> In natural science there are only problems of fact. Having found, upon the verification of Kepler's three laws of planetary motion, that planets move in an orbit which is an ellipse, astronomers do not face the normative problem concerning whether the planets should not do squads right in an orbit which is rectangle.
>
> But social institutions, being in part at least man-made, confront the scientist with two quite different questions: (1) What is the character of social institutions in fact? This is a question comparable to the astronomer's question with respect to the solar system; and (2) How ought social institutions to be? (p. 255)

We comment on Northrop's statement as it affords an opportunity to underscore some points discussed earlier in this chapter as well as to mention some issues discussed below.

---

[8]For examples of exchanges in the context of social psychology, instigated by Gergen's (1973) view of social psychology as history, see Gergen (1982), Manis (1975), Schlenker (1974), Thorngate (1975). See also, *Personality and Social Psychology Bulletin*, 1976, *2*, 371–465, for a symposium on social psychology and history.

What we say about Northrop's position applies, we believe, generally to positions that question the viability of sociobehavioral science.

First, Northrop depicted a world of extremes: on the one hand the closed system of astronomy and on the other hand the open system of social institutions. Comparisons of this kind are "invidious" (Secord, 1986, p. 199), as they even overlook the great diversity in the natural sciences. Moreover, as Secord pointed out, even physics, to which sociobehavioral sciences are most often compared, is not "fairly represented" (p. 199) in such comparisons.

Second, Northrop's conception of facts and their role in invalidating theory has been found wanting not only in the sociobehavioral sciences but also in the natural sciences (see The Role of Facts earlier in this chapter, and Theory and Facts in Chapter 9).

Third, Northrop's picture of value-free natural science and "factual social theory" is a relic of positivist thinking characteristic of a bygone era. Scriven (1983), who argued cogently against the notion of value-free science, regarded it as the "most significant of all the bad debts inherited" (p. 76) from positivism. He pointed out that: "The scientist's task is not to find just any explanation but the best explanation; not to use some experimental design but the best one that is feasible—and that one only if it is good enough to establish a worthwhile conclusion" (p.76). Indeed, "Science is about as value-free as buying hogs or playing chess" (p. 79).

The choice of problems to be studied, the formulation of hypotheses, the type of evidence sought, the method of obtaining it, the manner in which hypotheses are tested, and decisions regarding their rejection or acceptance are not value-free (see Chapter 9, for a discussion of decisions regarding effect size, and Type I and Type II errors in the context of hypothesis testing).

To deny that values play a role in scientific inquiry is to deny our very humanness (for some discussions, see Gouldner, 1962; Hesse, 1978; Homans, 1978; Howard, 1985; Nagel, 1961, Chapter 13; Rudner, 1953). There is also no denying that values play a more pronounced role in sociobehavioral research. To appreciate that this is so, it would suffice to mention, almost at random, some research areas: leadership, conformity, social status, authoritarianism, risk taking, locus of control, attraction, attribution, achievement motivation, liberalism, conservatism, intelligence, aggression, persuasibility. Not only are definitions and meanings of the preceding affected by the researcher's values but so is the *value* of studying them in the first place.

Cogent arguments have also been advanced concerning the effects of researchers' values and ideologies, their views of nature, society and humankind, on their choice of a discipline (e.g., sociology, political science, psychology) and of a specific orientation within it (see, for example, Gouldner, 1970; Lipset, 1983). Thus, writing about personality theories, Allport (1961) asserted:

All books on the psychology of personality are at the same time books on the philosophy of the person. It could not be otherwise. A writer who decides that one theory of learning, or of motivation, is better than another is thereby endorsing one view of the nature of man at the expense of other views. (p. xi)

Theories of learning (like much else in psychology) rest on the investigator's conception of the *nature of man*. In other words, every learning theorist is a philosopher, though he may not know it. (p. 84)

The realization that values play a role in scientific inquiry is an important first step toward taking them into account when examining the results, when entertaining alternative explanations and hypotheses, and when considering implications and advancing recommendations. "Freedom from bias means having an open mind, not an empty one" (Kaplan, 1964, p. 375).

Needless to say, there is a great deal of variability in sociobehavioral researchers' awareness, not to mention acknowledgment, of the role values play in their own theoretical formulations and research. Following are some examples.

In an autobiographical note about becoming a sociologist, Homans (1962) explained his acceptance of Pareto's views: "As a Republican Bostonian who had not rejected his comparatively wealthy family, I felt during the thirties that I was under personal attack, above all from the Marxists. I was ready to believe Pareto because he provided me with a defense" (p. 4).

Contrast the preceding with a statement by Lewontin, Rose, and Kamin (1984)—an evolutionary geneticist, a neurobiologist, and a psychologist respectively—in introducing their treatise against genetic determinism.

We share a commitment to the prospect of the creation of a more socially just—a socialist—society. And we recognize that a critical science is an integral part of the struggle to create that society, just as we also believe that the social function of much of today's science is to hinder the creation of that society by acting to preserve the interests of the dominant class, gender, and race. (pp. ix–x)

Lewontin et al.'s orientation should be viewed in the context of the controversies surrounding mental testing and contrasting conceptions regarding causes of racial differences in intelligence. You are probably familiar with what has come to be known as the "Jensen controversy" in connection with the latter. For penetrating discussions and illustrations see Cronbach (1976a) and Ezrahi (1976).[9]

In a review of research on school vandalism, Zwier and Vaughan (1984) illustrated how different ideologies—conservative, liberal, and radical—affect the overall approach as well as specific aspects of studies. Regarding the former, they said: "The conservatives will show that school vandalism is due to deviant individuals, who must be deterred; the liberals will produce evidence blaming the school; the radicals will contend that the disinterest of the whole community is at fault" (p. 270). Many other examples of the role of ideologies in the identification of social problems, planning and execution of research to study them, and policy recommendations derived from them (e.g., affirmative action, unemployment, rape, compensatory education) will be found in a book devoted in its entirety to such issues (Shotland & Mark, 1985).

It is fair to say that the very stand regarding the possibility of sociobehavioral science is largely determined by one's conception of the role values play in it and the implications this has for generalizations and policy recommendations. Generally speaking, those who accept the notion of sociobehavioral science acknowledge the role played by such factors as values, ideologies, and philosophies but maintain that, by being cognizant of them and by using appropriate controls, it is still possible to arrive at relatively valid conclusions. Moreover, they point to the public aspect of scientific research, and to the "organized skepticism" (Merton, 1982, pp. 12–13) that characterizes it, as safeguards against its total subordination to values and ideologies. Those who reject the notion of sociobehavioral science do so, in part, because of what they believe is the overwhelming role of values, ideologies, and the like in the work of sociobehavioral scientists.

We turn now to a consideration of some aspects of sociobehavioral research that are unique to it and the implications that follow therefrom. A note of caution is appropriate: We are addressing the issues broadly, as if the sociobehavioral sciences are "of one piece." Obviously, they are not, and you are urged to bear this in mind when considering what follows.

The overriding aspect unique to sociobehavioral sciences, from which ensue implications and complications discussed below, is that researchers study beings like themselves. One of

---

[9]For accusations of fraud committed by Burt, on whose data Jensen and others have relied, see Chapter 11.

the most important characteristics of this condition is the communication by means of language between the scientist and the subjects he or she studies. Here is how Kaplan (1964) introduced this topic:

Kenneth Colby tells the fable of an object that arrives from outer space and that resists all efforts by the physicists and astronomers to determine its composition, structure, or function, till at last a psychologist has the happy thought of asking, "What is your name?" and the object replies, "Ralph"! The circumstance that behavior includes speech allows to the behavioral scientist precious techniques denied to other scientists. But for that matter, each science—and indeed, each inquiry—finds some techniques appropriate and others inappropriate and even impossible. (p. 31)

THE ROLE OF LANGUAGE

Needless to say, most techniques used in sociobehavioral research would be unimaginable without the use of language. However, the role of language in each technique varies, having unique strengths and weaknesses. Problems of meaning, of interpretation, generally difficult, become particularly acute when attempting to elicit and interpret responses regarding, say, people's thoughts, feelings, experiences, perceptions, attitudes, and intentions. Not only is the researcher faced with the task of interpreting responses, but the respondent too is engaged in interpreting what the researcher says as well as his or her own states.

Whether or not one accepts what has come to be known as the Whorfian hypothesis, namely that language molds the way we perceive, think, and remember (see, Whorf, 1956), the pervasive role of language in every facet of our lives requires no comment. Examples of the effects of language on the conduct of and conclusions drawn from sociobehavioral research abound. In various places, we address effects of language in some specific research areas (e.g., in Chapter 6, we discuss effects of question-wording in questionnaires and interviews; Chapter 11, we discuss Comprehension Artifacts in research). For now, we will only note that some of the most controversial issues in sociobehavioral research (e.g., test bias, attitudes and behavior, verbal reinforcement, the validity of cross-cultural comparisons) are largely predicated on issues of language usage and interpretation.

OBSERVER AND ACTOR

As discussed in detail by Kaplan (1964), "behavioral science is involved in a double process of interpretation, and it is this which is responsible for such of its techniques as are distinctive" (p. 32). The double process has to do with the distinction between "*act meaning* and *action meaning*" (p. 32), the former referring to the meaning an act has for the actor, and the latter to the meaning it has as subject matter the scientist attempts to explain. But the scientist engaged in a search for action meaning is also an actor. In the broadest sense, we are confronting here in full force the perceptual process we have discussed earlier in connection with the meaning of facts. We are faced with an observer using a specific frame of reference in the process of observing an observer. The difficulties inherent in the scientist-observer's attempts to observe him or herself cannot be overestimated. They are, borrowing a phrase from Berger and Luckmann (1967, p. 13), akin to "trying to push a bus in which one is riding." In short, we are dealing with processes that are not only extremely complex but also bear the seeds of infinite regress. Interestingly, sociobehavioral scientists generally operate as if they are not subject to the same forces and constraints they claim affect the people they study.

As if the preceding were not problems enough, it is necessary to recognize that, in sociobehavioral research, subjects are engaged, to a greater or lesser extent, in defining the situation in which the research takes place. From this ensue a host of problems and issues that will occupy us in various chapters. For now, it will suffice to point out that such issues as the relative advantages and disadvantages of different research designs (e.g., laboratory experiments, field experiments, quasi-experiments) and problems attendant with them (e.g., reflexivity and reactivity of the subject, demand characteristics, effects of experimenter's expectations, sensitization) are aspects of this process.

THE ROLE OF MEASUREMENT

The role and status of measurement in scientific inquiry was discussed in Chapter 2, where it was argued that progress in science is largely dependent on the measurement procedures used. In the present context, it will be pointed out that, in the natural sciences, there is, generally speaking, agreement not only about the importance of measurement but also about the specifics of measurement procedures. We cannot resist the temptation to say: Measurement comes naturally to natural scientists. That this is far from being the case in sociobehavioral sciences should be evident from Part 1 of this book.

SAMPLES, SETTINGS, AND THE INDIVIDUAL

Other areas about which there is little agreement among sociobehavioral scientists concern what, if anything, has been accomplished in the sociobehavioral sciences; what areas hold greatest promise and should, therefore, be pursued. These issues are discussed in Chapter 9. We conclude with some remarks about the conduct of sociobehavioral research that, we believe, has contributed to skepticism about its usefulness and status. Again, some of these issues are discussed in detail in other chapters.

Earlier, we noted that one of the issues in the debate about the status of sociobehavioral science concerns the temporal and cultural relativity of its laws. It is, therefore, not surprising that generalizations of sociobehavioral research findings are, to a large extent, culture- and time-bound. Only absolutists seeking eternal truths are surprised or unsettled by this. What should be truly unsettling to us all are the routine generalizations to all humankind, past, present, and future, on the basis of what are euphemistically referred to as samples of convenience.

Issues of sampling and generalization from specific research settings are dealt with in subsequent chapters (e.g., Chapter 15). What concerns us here is that, although practice varies with specific disciplines, many, if not most, sociobehavioral researchers are oblivious to the role of sampling and specific settings in their research, or flagrantly ignore them, all the while making the broadest generalizations imaginable. Why should one expect to generalize to all American college students, not to mention all Americans and all humankind, on the basis of one's proverbial sophomores who were invited, persuaded, or coerced to take part in a study? Why should one expect to make generalizations about group processes on the basis of a short-term study for which the aggregate of individuals assembled do not meet minimal criteria of what generally is taken to constitute a group? What is the validity of publishing average responses of some classes in a given college as "norms," and why do researchers then use such norms in the interpretation of results of their own classes? Such questions could be multiplied almost indefinitely. However, these should suffice to indicate why it is that results from what are presumably the same studies differ greatly, leading critics to question the validity of sociobehavioral research. We invite you to examine the professional literature in your field of interest and note how often are samples and settings taken seriously into account when generalizations are made.

CONCLUDING REMARKS

We are aware that much of our discussion in this chapter will probably leave you uncomfortable, perhaps baffled, even annoyed. This would be particularly true, if you approached this chapter with the expectation of learning the "rules" of the "correct" method for doing scientific research. Our aim was to raise questions, to provoke thought, to raise doubts in your mind. With de Unamuno (1954), we believe that: "True science teaches, above all, to doubt and to be ignorant; advocacy neither doubts nor believes that it does not know" (p. 93). But the ignorance referred to here emanates from knowledge. As Montaigne (1965) pointed out: "There is an abecedarian ignorance that comes before knowledge, and another, doctoral ignorance that comes after knowledge: an ignorance that knowledge creates and engenders, just as it undoes and destroys the first" (p. 227). It is all encapsulated in Socrates' incomparable phrase: "I know that I don't know."

Chapter 8
Definitions and Variables

It is a truism that meaningful communication is unthinkable in the absence of agreement regarding the meaning of the words used by the communicators. The potency of communicators understanding one another's language and the deleterious consequences of the absence of such understanding are well illustrated in the biblical story of the Tower of Babel. As related in *Genesis*, Chapter 11, the people of the earth had one language, and they said: "Come, let us build ourselves a city, and a tower with its top in the heavens, and let us make a name for ourselves, lest we be scattered abroad upon the face of the whole earth." When the Lord saw what they were up to, he said: "Behold, they are one people, and they have all one language; . . . and nothing that they propose to do will now be impossible for them. Come, let us . . . confuse their language, that they may not understand one another's speech." As a result, the building of the city was abandoned, and the people were scattered over all the earth.

Even for people who speak the same language, words have different meanings, depending on, among other things, who speaks, to whom, in what context, at what time, and with what purpose. Words, particularly those referring to important aspects of our lives and environment, are loaded with connotations, nuances, "emotive meaning" (Kahane, 1973, p. 187). Are, for example, people of a given age "elderly," "old," "senior citizens," "gray panthers?" Are certain countries "poor," "underdeveloped," "developing," "backward?" Is one "pro life" or against "abortion?"; for "abortion" or for "freedom of choice?" The list could be extended almost indefinitely. The point is that the different terms reflect different outlooks, values, attitudes, and the like. Indeed, there is a sense in which "A rose by any other name would *not* smell just as sweet" (Kahane, 1973, p. 187).

When sociobehavioral scientists use terms that have been part of the language for a long time and have gathered multiple meaning (e.g., alienation, anxiety, motive, attitude, power, leadership), they run the risk of being misunderstood. When they choose instead to invent their own terminology, they are often accused of resorting to jargon that is variously perceived as an attempt to achieve scientific respectability, to mislead, or even to deceive.

Nevertheless, most people tend to fault themselves when they are unable to make sense of what are essentially meaningless statements, particularly when the statements are made by recognized authorities or published under prestigious auspices. Because of frequent exposure to technical language, some of it essential for precise communication, professionals too run the risk of being lulled into accepting gibberish as profound statements. Andreski (1972) offered perceptive discussions and illustrations of "The Smoke Screen of Jargon" (p. 59). Being critical of such concepts as '*n* Ach' (need Achievement) and '*n* Aff' (need Affiliation), Andreski stated that in order to prove to himself that he "too can make such discoveries" (p. 67), he invented the concept 'N. Bam,' which he used in the following statement:

In connection with David McClelland's article it might be relevant to report that the preliminary results of our research project into the encoding processes in communication flow indicate that (owing to their multiplex permutations) it is difficult to ascertain direct correlates of '*n* Aff'. On the other hand, when on the encephalogram 'dy' divided by 'dx' is less than '0', '*n* Ach' attains a significantly high positive correlation with '*n* Bam', notwithstanding the partially stochastic nature of the connection between these two variables. (p. 68)

Following is Andreski's translation of his passage in plain English, which he suggests be read after the reader's own attempts to decipher the original statement:

Owing to the waywardness of human nature, it is difficult to find out why people join a given group, but observation of how people speak and write clearly suggests that, when the brain is slowing down, a desire to achieve often gives rise to a need to bamboozle. (p. 68)

We are not concerned here with the validity of Andreski's critique of the concept of '*n* Ach' and '*n* Aff' but rather with the fact that not only was his statement published in a sociological journal but that, after its publication, he was "approached by some industrial research organisations who offered co-operation" (p. 68).

Often, it takes an "outsider" to recognize the Emperor's new clothes for what they are. Witness the following statements taken from a review of a remedial reading program carried out by the Department of Health, Education, and Welfare:

The objectivities did not specify to the quantifiable of the success of the proposed program. . . . There is no realistically promises that addresses the needs identified in the proposed program. (*The New York Times*, May 26, 1978)

Statements such as the preceding ones prompted Representative Robert Daniel of Virginia to suggest that the author of the report himself be enrolled in a remedial reading program, and *The New York Times'* commentator wondered whether the officials who reviewed the report prior to its circulation "need remedial training too, or just something to keep them awake on the job?"

The use of gobbledegook is by no means limited to the sociobehavioral sciences. A case in point is the concern expressed in the *Oil and Gas Journal* (Ralph, 1967, p. 61) about "computermen" and top management not speaking the same language. "To bridge the language barrier" the journal reprinted "The Buzzphrase Generator," which was said to have appeared originally in "Scientific Sales Co." Here is a reproduction of The Buzzphrase Generator, followed by directions for use:

Column 1	Column 2	Column 3
0. integrated	0. management	0. options
1. total	1. organizational	1. flexibility
2. systematized	2. monitored	2. capability
3. parallel	3. reciprocal	3. mobility
4. functional	4. digital	4. programming
5. responsive	5. logistical	5. concept

6. optimal	6. transitional	6. time-phase
7. synchronized	7. incremental	7. projection
8. compatible	8. third-generation	8. hardware
9. balanced	9. policy	9. contingency

To use the Generator, randomly select a three-digit number to arrive at a three-word combination by using the numbered words from the corresponding columns. Thus, for example, if you randomly selected the number 763, you would arrive at the phrase "synchronized transitional mobility." The number 320 would yield "parallel monitored options." As you can easily prove to yourself, use of the Generator will yield phrases that are bound to impress even experts in various fields.

An important safeguard, although by no means a guarantee, against ambiguity and vagueness is the definition of the major terms being used. In the next section, we sketch some characteristics and types of definitions and then address two types—theoretical and empirical—that are particularly important in the context of scientific inquiry and in the communication of scientific findings. Following this, we turn to an explication of the term "variable" and to some classifications of variables.

DEFINITIONS

Broadly speaking, a definition is a statement about the meaning of a word, a term, or a phrase. Stated differently, a definition is a statement about the use of words. Acceptance of a definition of a given word is an agreement to use it according to the definition. Consequently, it is not meaningful to question the truth or falsity of a definition, but rather its clarity, meaningfulness, acceptability, usefulness, and the like. Philosophers, logicians, and linguists, who are among those most notably concerned with explicating the meaning of definition, have advanced classifications of definitions according to their nature and function, and have formulated criteria for good definitions (see, for example, Cohen & Nagel, 1934, Chapter XII; Copi, 1972, Chapter 4; Kahane, 1973, Chapter 10; Kaplan, 1946, 1964, Chapter II).

The most prevalent type of definition is the *lexical*, namely a definition of the linguistic usage of words, prime examples of which are dictionary definitions. In contradistinction to a lexical definition is a *stipulative* definition, that is, a definition that specifies the meaning assigned to a word by the person or persons using it. In essence, a stipulative definition is a statement having the following structure: "By (such and such a word) I mean (such and such)." Humpty Dumpty claimed to have used words in this sense only:

"When *I* use a word," Humpty Dumpty said, in a rather scornful tone, "it means just what I choose it to mean—neither more nor less."
"The question is," said Alice, "whether you *can* make words mean so many different things."
"The question is," said Humpty Dumpty, "which is to be master—that's all." (Carroll, 1960, p. 186)

Humpty Dumpty's capriciousness notwithstanding, stipulative definitions are essential for the smooth functioning of society. Larceny, minor, poverty, urban, unemployment, household, family, and skyscraper are but some of the myriad terms that require stipulative definitions in the course of legislation, implementation, and administration of government policies and programs. Such definitions are generally arrived at as a result of a confluence of political, legal, social, economic, and ethical considerations at a given point in time and place.

We are often jolted when we become aware of "outdated" stipulative definitions. For example, discussing the urban–rural concepts, Bradburn (1982) made the interesting point that, although it was "obvious" that our society was becoming increasingly urbanized, it came as a surprise to him, as he believed it would to his readers, to discover that the definition of "urban" used by the Census Bureau, namely "the proportion living in places of 2,500 inhabitants or more" dates back to 1900. Bradburn noted that, for him, "the concept conjures up a different image than that conveyed by a place having 2,500 inhabitants" (p. 138), as it surely does for most of us.

Obviously, stipulative definitions, be they for new terms or for ones borrowed from everyday language, are also an integral part of science.

Theoretical Definitions

To be scientifically meaningful, a concept, or a construct, has to be part of an implicit or explicit theoretical framework that explicates its relations with other concepts, be they antecedents, consequents, or concomitant ones. Generally, a theoretical definition of a construct entails the use of terms that may also require definition, thus, carrying the seeds of infinite regress. Not surprisingly, J. Rousseau (quoted by Thomas, 1976) remarked: "Definitions would be good things if we did not use words to make them" (p. 209). As Bertrand Russell pointed out:

Since all terms that are defined are defined by means of other terms, it is clear that human knowledge must always be content to accept some terms as intelligible without definition, in order to have a starting-point for its definitions. (quoted by Copi, 1972, p. 108)

But the question still remains: "Which terms may be left undefined?" Brodbeck (1963), who offered a very good discussion of definitions and theoretical meanings of concepts, suggested that one stops defining terms used in a definition "when there is no longer ambiguity or disagreement about the referent of the term" (p. 48) being defined. Stated differently, a term is adequately defined when people using the definition know and are in agreement about what to look for.

The preceding statements address the question of what is an adequate definition, but they are not of much help to the person seeking guidance as to how to arrive at such definitions. Various criteria for good definitions have been advanced by philosophers and logicians. Although there is a good deal of agreement about criteria for certain types of definitions (e.g., lexical), there is considerable disagreement regarding other types (e.g., theoretical definitions). In what follows, we introduce some criteria about which various authors seem agreed. (For detailed presentations, see references cited below as well as ones cited earlier in this chapter.)

CRITERIA FOR GOOD DEFINITIONS

1. A definition must not be too broad or too narrow. This is, admittedly, a vague criterion. Generally speaking, however, a definition is too broad when it leads to the inclusion of things that one does not wish the definition to refer to, and it is too narrow when it leads to the exclusion of things one wishes the definition to refer to. Most authors attempt to clarify the meaning of this criterion by way of examples. As an illustration of a definition that is too broad, Copi (1972) related the following anecdote:

Plato's successors in the Academy at Athens spent much time and thought on the problem of defining the word "man." Finally they decided that it meant *featherless biped*. They were much pleased with the definition, until Diogenes plucked a chicken and threw it over the wall into the Academy. Here was a featherless biped, surely, but just as surely it was not a man. (p. 138)

2. *A definition should not contain vague, ambiguous, obscure, or figurative language.* As an example, Kahane (1973) noted that, although the expression "ship of the desert" indicates the "main use to which camels are put in dry areas, it hardly is an adequate definition of the term 'camel'" (p. 182).

3. *A definition should not be circular*; that is, the term to be defined, or a grammatical variant of it, should not be part of the definition.

4. *A definition should "state the essential properties of the things named"* (Kahane, 1973, p. 182) by the term being defined. As Kahane pointed out, this criterion is controversial, especially because it calls for a distinction between essential and accidental properties—a notion rejected by many philosophers.

THEORETICAL DEFINITIONS IN SOCIOBEHAVIORAL RESEARCH

With the previous considerations in mind, we comment briefly on the state and some aspects of theoretical definitions in sociobehavioral research. Bear in mind that, as with other issues we have been discussing, sociobehavioral science disciplines vary considerably with respect to attention being paid to theoretical definitions.

In Chapter 4, reference was made to jingle and jangle fallacies, the former referring to situations where things that are different from each other are treated as being alike, *because* they are called by the same name; the latter referring to the converse situation where things are believed to be different from each other, *because* they are called by different names. A serious problem attendant with the jangle fallacy is that it creates the mistaken impression that a new field of study is being inaugurated or that a novel theoretical formulation is being advanced, thereby seeming to absolve its advocates from paying attention to literature about the phenomenon in question on the grounds of it being irrelevant. Following is an example:

WHAT'S IN A NAME?
Cardiologists Meyer Friedman and Ray Rosenman applied twice to the National Institutes of Health (NIH) for a research grant to study the relationship between coronary heart disease and "emotional stress," and were turned down both times. Because they used the term "emotional stress," an NIH official told them, their applications were sent for review to psychiatrists, who were skeptical that cardiologists were competent to investigate emotions. The official suggested that the team might get a more favorable hearing if they referred to the "Type A behavior pattern," a new research area in which no one could claim expertise. Friedman and Rosenman made the change, their next proposal was accepted and a new term entered the medical and popular vocabulary. (*Psychology Today*, 1987, *21*(2), 50)

DISPOSITIONAL CONCEPTS

Most concepts used in science are dispositional; that is, they do not refer to states or conditions of objects, people, or what have you but rather to their dispositions, or tendencies, to behave or react in a certain way given certain conditions. Examples of dispositional concepts are magnetism, brittleness, aggression, intelligence, conservatism, and flexibility. What they have in common is that they are not observable but are rather constructs inferred from observations.

Problems attendant with definitions of dispositional concepts are complex and controversial (for a good discussion, see Rosenberg, 1979). In part, the state of theory in a given field or discipline determines the scope of problems and difficulties in defining dispositional concepts, and the degree of agreement among scientists with respect to such definitions. In addition, as is discussed in the next section (Empirical Definitions), the state of measurement in a given discipline affects the degree of agreement attainable among researchers. On both counts, it stands to reason for controversies and disagreements about the meaning of dispositional concepts to be much greater in sociobehavioral than in natural sciences. Following are a couple of examples of concepts about which definitions abound and agreement is nowhere in sight.

A notable example of a dispositional concept is attitude (see Fleming, 1967, for a fascinating historical review of the concept attitude). Although there are literally scores of definitions of attitude, they share the conception that it is a predisposition. The definitions do, however, differ in, among other things, the nature of the dispositions (e.g., evaluating the object of the attitude, having behavior tendencies toward it). (For some reviews and examples, see Allport, 1985; Fishbein & Ajzen, 1975; Greenwald, 1968.) Also, as was noted in Chapter 4, some use terms such as attitude, belief, value, interest, sentiment, and opinion interchangeably whereas others distinguish among them. And then there are those who claim to be doing research on attitude but do not bother to even comment about what they mean by the term. As Dawes and Smith (1985) observed:

It is not uncommon for psychologists and other social scientists to investigate a phenomenon at great length without knowing what they're talking about. So it is with *attitude*. While 20,209 articles and books are listed under the rubric "attitude" in the *Psychological Abstracts* from 1970 through 1979, there is little agreement about the definition of *attitude*. (p. 509)

Aggression is another example of a dispositional concept that has been defined variously by different researchers in different research settings (e.g., in laboratory experiments, field studies). In a recent review of altruism and aggression, Krebs and Miller (1985) commented on the "considerable diversity in the definitions" (p. 1) of these terms and traced the sources of the diversity to, among other things, conceptions regarding human nature and morality. Reporting on their study of television and aggression, Milavsky et al. (1982) said:

We decided that the most appropriate definition of aggression for studying the effects of televised violence was: physical or verbal acts intended or known in advance to cause injury to others. Intentional harm to others was the essential consideration, because this was and remains the key element in the social concern about violence. (p. 47)

But according to Tedeschi (1983): "It is not the action or the intent . . . that identifies the action as aggression, but rather the lack of justification that does so" (p. 138). Tedeschi pointed out that, after commenting on problems with the various definitions of aggression, many writers

tend to shrug their shoulders and comment that we all know what we want to study . . . and then settle for one or the other inadequate concept. *The present approach is to reject every definition of aggression as inadequate* [italics added] and to provide an alternative way of conceptualizing the relevant behaviors. (p. 138)

We could go on almost indefinitely with examples of other concepts whose definitions vary so greatly as to not even qualify them as referring to the same phenomenon. We believe, however, that our illustrations will suffice to point out that one of the major impediments to cumulative knowledge in sociobehavioral sciences is the "loose" state of theoretical definitions. In many instances, researchers *do* speak of *different* things, although they call them by the same name. And in equally many other instances, researchers *do* speak of the *same* thing, although they call it by different names.

We turn now to a consideration of empirical definitions and their relations to theoretical ones.

Empirical Definitions

In our discussion of theoretical definitions (preceding section), we stated that a construct derives its meaning from its relations with other constructs in a theoretical context. In order to test hypotheses derived from theory, however, it is necessary to relate constructs to observed phenomena.[1] This is accomplished by means of empirical definitions of constructs. Note that, although all constructs have to be theoretically defined, not all of them have to be empirically defined. Constructs not empirically defined are related to observed phenomena through their relations with other constructs that have been empirically defined.[2]

Empirical definitions have been variously labeled epistemic definitions, rules of correspondence, and operational definitions (e.g., Margenau, 1950, Chapter 12). This is not to say that all writers use the terms synonymously. Nor does it mean that there is universal agreement about the meaning of any of these terms. A notable case in point is the controversy surrounding the meaning of operational definition (see below).

Broadly speaking, an empirical definition relates a construct to reflective or formative indicators. From the presentation in Chapter 4, it will be recalled that reflective indicators are conceived of as being caused by the construct under consideration, whereas formative indicators are conceived of as causing or affecting the construct. Notable examples of reflective indicators are measures (e.g., of liberalism, intelligence), whereas notable examples of formative indicators are manipulations designed to induce some state (e.g., anxiety, fear, motivation).

Attempts to arrive at empirical definitions in sociobehavioral sciences very often lead to a rude awakening that one really does not know what one is talking about, at least that one's conceptions are hazy. Underscoring the role of measurement in the clarification of constructs, Thomson (Lord Kelvin, 1891) stated:

> I often say that when you can measure what you are speaking about and express it in numbers you know something about it; but when you cannot measure it, when you cannot express it in numbers, your knowledge is of a meagre and unsatisfactory kind: it may be the beginning of knowledge, but you have scarcely, in your thoughts, advanced to the stage of *science*, whatever the matter may be. (pp. 80–81)

Stressing the role of theory in measurement, Pawson (1989) proposed "an amended version of Kelvin's dictum: 'If you cannot theorize, your measurement is meagre and unsatisfactory'" (p. 73). The paramount role of the theoretical conception of a construct as a

---

[1]Hypothesis testing and its relation to theory is discussed in Chapter 9.

[2]For good discussions of this and related issues, see Margenau (1950, Chapter 12), Northrop (1947, Chapter 7), and also see Torgerson (1958, Chapter 1), who elaborated on Margenau's ideas in the context of sociobehavioral sciences.

guide to the type of indicators that may be reflecting it was discussed in detail in Chapter 4. In the present context, therefore, we only use a research example illustrating this. Galle, Gove, and McPherson (1972) were interested in studying whether the relation between population density and pathology that has been demonstrated among various species of animals holds also for humans. Following animal ecologists, they defined density as persons per acre.

Having found density, thus defined, and pathology (e.g., mortality rate, fertility rate, juvenile delinquency) not related, Galle et al. (1972) reasoned that "in the case of human populations, the situation is substantially more complex, especially in an urban setting" (p. 26). Among other things, they spoke of "interpersonal press" (comprised of number of persons per room and number of rooms per housing unit), and of "structural" factors, namely the type of structures in which people live and the spacing among them (e.g., high-rise luxury apartments versus public housing). Taking aspects such as these into consideration, they arrived at a different empirical definition of density and showed the index based on it to be related to social pathologies.

We are not concerned here with the validity of Galle et al.'s index of density nor, for that matter, with the validity of their measures of pathology. Our sole purpose in using this example is to illustrate that the empirical definition of density was revised on the basis of theoretical considerations. It is, however, important to bear in mind that this appears to have been done *after the fact*—after the results obtained on the basis of the first empirical definition did not "pan" out or were, perhaps, disappointing to the researchers. One cannot but wonder what direction their research, theoretical formulations, and conclusions would have taken had Galle et al. found that people per acre and pathology *were* related.[3]

In the preceding section, we commented on the great diversity of theoretical definitions of constructs in sociobehavioral sciences (e.g., attitude, aggression). The problem is probably even more serious with respect to empirical definitions. For example, reviewing the literature on attitudes and opinions, Fishbein and Ajzen (1972) found "almost 500 different operations designed to measure 'attitude'" (p. 492). They then pointed out that over 200 studies that they reviewed used "more than one measure of an 'attitudinal' variable, and about 70 percent obtained different results when different measures of 'attitude' were used" (p. 493).

Contributing further to the confusion is the fact that, in many instances, empirical definitions are not related to theoretical definitions of their respective constructs, or even go counter to them. Thus, for example, although an author may define attitude as being composed of affective, cognitive, and conative components, the empirical definition the author is using may address affect only (i.e., being in favor or against the object of the attitude). Similarly, an author may go to great lengths in defining a given attitude as being multidimensional, or multifaceted, and yet use a measure that is unidimensional.

Earlier, when we commented on theoretical definitions of aggression, we made reference to Milavsky et al.'s (1982) study of television and aggression. Moving from their theoretical considerations of aggression to its empirical definition, Milavsky et al. stated that they decided to study aggressive behavior in the context of daily life. Explaining their decision, they said:

Surrogate measures of aggression—such as hitting dolls, punching padded boards, or pressing buttons and turning dials that supposedly inflict noxious stimuli—were rejected as inadequate, primarily because the degree to which they accurately measure real antisocial aggression is open to question. (pp. 47–48)

---

[3]For a discussion of the perils of post factum theorizing, see Chapter 9.

Note, however, that Milavsky et al. used a measure of aggression based on peer nomina-tions obtained in classroom settings. Essentially, children answered such questions as "Who does not obey the teacher?"; "Who does things that bother others?"; "Who starts a fight over nothing?"; "Who pushes and shoves children?"; "Who says mean things?" (p. 52). The authors themselves acknowledged that, without further research, it is not possible to tell whether these are valid indicators of antisocial behavior in other settings. Further, they drew attention to questions raised regarding "long-term social consequences of this sort of antiso-cial behavior" (p. 48).

If we were to point to a single notion that has been most responsible for the proliferation of empirical definitions and for their divorcement from theoretical ones in sociobehavioral research, we believe it would be that of operational definition. We briefly review this issue because of the adverse effects it had on sociobehavioral sciences, lulling some researchers into an "uncritical complacency and reification of test scores" (Campbell, 1969a, p. 351).

OPERATIONAL DEFINITION

The idea of operational definition is most closely associated with the name of the physicist Bridgman (1927), according to whom a *"concept is synonymous with the corresponding set of operations"* (p. 5).

Under the impact of Bridgman's ideas "the cry for 'operational definitions', especially in psychology, rose almost to a clamor" (Kaplan, 1964, p. 39). Many viewed it as a panacea for the ills that plagued the sociobehavioral sciences. "Some psychologists in their enthusiasm mistook the operationist footnote for the whole philosophy of science, if not for the whole of philosophy" (Bergmann, 1954, p. 48). Although Bridgman revised his original position—some (e.g., Margenau, 1950, p. 232) viewed it as a retreat—he maintained that he never meant it to be a philosophical orientation. In a symposium on "The present state of opera-tionalism," Bridgman (1954) stated:

I feel that I have created a Frankenstein, which has certainly got away from me. I abhor the word *operationalism* or *operationism*, which seems to imply a dogma, or at least a thesis of some kind. The thing I have envisaged is too simple to be dignified by so pretentious a name. (pp. 74–75)

The degeneration of the idea that a concept is synonymous with a specific set of operations is probably best exemplified by the oft repeated statement "intelligence is what intelligence tests test." As various authors have pointed out (e.g., Adler, 1947; Allport, 1940, pp. 20–21; MacIver, 1942, pp. 157–158), in order to develop a measure of intelligence or, for that matter, of any construct, it is necessary to know what is that "what" one wishes to measure. Or, in Bridgman's (1945) words: "With regard to the intelligence test, the assertion as it stands begs the question. The question-begging word is the humble 'what.'" (p. 249). It is one's theory that serves as a guide to operations; not the other way around.

The perversion of the notion of operational definition and the mindlessness with which it is often applied is exemplified by researchers' response to criticism of their work with the retort: "But this is my operational definition of . . . " (anxiety, intelligence, or what have you), as if all that is required is their say so. Adler (1947), who satirized this state of affairs, offered the following test (p. 439):

THE C_N TEST

1. How many hours did you sleep last night?   —
2. Estimate the length of your nose in inches and multiply by 2.   —
3. Do you like fried liver? (Mark 1 for Yes, −1 for No.)   —

4. How many feet are there in a yard?   —
5. Estimate the number of glasses of ginger ale the inventor of this test drank while
    inventing it.   —
Add the above items. The sum is your crude C_N score.   —

Adler then presented a formula to be used in calculating a "refined C_N rate" on the basis of taking the test daily at the same hour of the day for as long as one can take it. In a more serious vein, Adler asked the reader to imagine that he or she was sent to bring home some C_N. Using the previous definition, what would he or she look for?

The strict operationists equated the operational definition with the concept that it was said to define. Accordingly, it was argued, different definitions (e.g., of length) refer to different concepts. Moreover, as Bergmann (1954) noted, some operationists even "refused, presumably on operationist principles, to 'generalize' from one instance of an experiment to the next if the apparatus had in the meantime been moved to another corner of the room" (p. 49).

In earlier chapters (especially Chapter 4), we discussed and illustrated the use of multiple indicators of a construct. The very idea of multiple indicators is an assertion that the construct and its empirical definition (e.g., measure) are *not* synonymous. It is an assertion that measures, especially in the sociobehavioral sciences, contain all sorts of irrelevancies (e.g., random errors, response sets), and that only by resorting to "heterogeneity of irrelevancies" (Kiesler, Collins, & Miller, 1969, p. 71) or "multiplism" (Cook, 1985) can we hope to distinguish between what is relevant and what is irrelevant, or biasing, in the measures of given traits. It should be clear that this approach is antithetical to the one taken by the strict operationist. Bergmann (1954), who noted that, in the context of operationism, there was no *a priori* rule that would enable one to distinguish between relevant and irrelevant variables, concluded: "Generally, the operationist fashion provided some specious arguments to those who disliked all sorts of theorizing or, even, conceptualizing" (p. 49).

In conclusion, it will be pointed out that the emphasis on "operations has tended to solve very few problems and to introduce more and more rhetoric and less and less science into the subject matter" (Northrop, 1947, p. 125). Although the heyday of operationalism is long over, simplistic notions about empirical definitions linger is some quarters.

VARIABLES

Broadly conceived, scientific inquiry is the pursuit of relations among variables. It is variability of phenomena that attracts our attention, arouses our curiosity, and often impels us to seek explanations for it. Essentially, scientists attempt to explain or predict variability of a given variable by studying its relations with other variables. We are using the term "relation" to refer not only to research in which no distinction is made between types of variables studied (e.g., independent, dependent; see below) but also to research in which such distinctions are made.[4]

The term variable is "highly ambiguous" (Rozeboom, 1966, p. 8) and is used variously in different contexts (e.g., logic, mathematics). Even in science, where variable is "probably the basic methodological concept" (Rozeboom, 1961, p. 340), its meaning is neither unambiguous, nor is its use consistent. This is due, in part, to the different types of variables and the different functions they may serve in a given study. In what follows, we first address the

---

[4]This point is discussed, along with illustrations, in Chapter 9 under Problem Characterization and Format.

definition of variable. This is followed by a discussion of some basic classifications of variables from different perspectives.

DEFINITION OF VARIABLE

A variable is any attribute or property in which organisms (objects, events, people) vary. More formally, "a 'variable' (in the scientific sense) over a population *P* is *a set of properties or attributes which are mutually exclusive and exhaustive within P*" (Rozeboom, 1966, p. 9). Examples of variables are height, weight, sex, mental ability, temperature, race, religious affiliation, and aggression.

Note that, to qualify as a variable, the attribute or property under consideration must consist of at least two values, for example, male and female. Studying males or females only converts the variable sex into a constant. Further, *at any given time*, it must be possible to assign to each element in the population *one and only one* value on the variable under consideration. This notion was discussed in Chapter 2 (Nominal Scale), where issues of classification were also commented upon. It was pointed out, among other things, that no object under consideration can be classified into more than one category of the variable (mutual exclusiveness) and that all objects under consideration must be classifiable into one of the categories (exhaustiveness). Although, in the preceding, reference was made to categorical, or classification, variables, the same hold true for continuous variables (see below). For example, *at any given time*, a person can be assigned *one and only one* value on height, weight, age, intelligence, anxiety, motivation, and the like.

The foregoing examples warrant some comments. First, they illustrate what we said earlier about empirical definitions, namely that they are very often measures of the variable being defined. Second, specific values assigned to objects or people are predicated on the method of measurement. Third, and most important, the variables used as examples bring out in strong relief the predicament of sociobehavioral sciences, as contrasted with natural sciences, notably the more advanced among them. Generally speaking, when in the natural sciences an object or an individual can be assigned more than one value or score at the same time, it is a sure sign that he or she is being measured on more than one variable. A person cannot be six and five feet tall, say, at the same time, but he or she can be six feet tall and weigh 180 pounds at a given time.

Does the same hold true with respect to such variables as intelligence, anxiety, and motivation? The answer is, of course, a resounding no, at least as long as there is no agreement about theoretical and empirical definitions of these constructs. At the current state of formulations and definitions of intelligence, say, an individual may, at any given time, not only have many scores on intelligence, depending on the number of scales used and their specific properties, but he or she may even be viewed as more intelligent on the basis of some of the scales and less intelligent on the basis of others.

Classification of Variables

Classifications of variables can serve useful purposes, provided it is recognized that, as in other instances, various classification systems may be arrived at and that some may be more meaningful or useful than others in given contexts and for given purposes. In what follows, we discuss some broad classifications of variables that are helpful when designing or evaluating research studies. We would like to stress that the classifications we present are neither exhaustive nor mutually exclusive. Also, at this stage, we refrain from addressing subtleties lest this may confuse rather than enlighten. Various aspects and types of variables introduced here are discussed and elaborated upon in subsequent chapters, in the context of specific designs and analyses.

MEASUREMENT PERSPECTIVE

Of various classification schemes that may be used from a measurement perspective, we present one consisting of two classes, namely categorical and continuous variables.

A *categorical variable*, also referred to as a qualitative or grouping variable, is one in which objects (people, events) are assigned to a set of mutually exclusive and exhaustive categories. Stated differently, a categorical variable is a classificatory variable on which objects (people, events) classified differ in kind, not in degree. A categorical variable, then, reflects the condition of "either/or." A person (object, event) either belongs to a given category or does not belong to it.

Examples of categorical variables are sex, race, different methods of teaching, and different drugs. We will use these variables to illustrate what was said above, namely that different schemes for the classification of variables are possible. For example, from a research design perspective (see below) one may classify sex and race as attribute variables; that is, they refer to attributes of the subjects being studied. Different methods of teaching and different drugs, on the other hand, are manipulated variables or susceptible of being manipulated by a researcher for the purpose of a given study.

Although subjects taught by a given method or administered a specific drug are equal with respect to the treatment to which they are exposed, they may differ widely on a host of attribute variables (e.g., sex, race, age, motivation). As we will see in later chapters, one of the concerns of research design is how to control for such individual differences in order to arrive at valid conclusions about the effects of the manipulated variables. The point we wish to make here, however, is that, whereas from a research design perspective the four variables under consideration may be classified into different categories, from a measurement perspective they are alike; that is, they are categorical variables.

Many of the variables used in research are categorical. For example, whenever a researcher studies the effects of different methods (e.g., of production, communication, counseling) on one or more variables (e.g., output, attitude change, adjustment), the different methods comprise a categorical variable—similarly, when the interest is in studying differences among preexisting groups (e.g., males, females; married, divorced, single) on one or more variables (e.g., attitudes toward arms control, verbal fluency). In later chapters, we treat such variables in great detail. Chapters 19 and 20, for example, are devoted in their entirety to designs consisting of categorical independent variables.

The decision whether to include attribute categorical variables in a study should not be made lightly. In particular, one should resist the temptation to include broad categorical variables, just because they are readily available, or because other researchers have included them in their studies. What we have in mind are such variables as sex, race, country of origin, place of residence, political party affiliation, and religious affiliation.

Being broad, such variables are bound to be comprised of widely heterogeneous groups with respect to myriad variables. In the absence of a clear reason for doing so, inclusion of broad categorical variables in a study is likely to deflect attention from the variable(s) that should be the focus of study. Thus, it is easy to fall into the trap of "explaining" differences among people on some phenomenon of interest on the basis of sex, say, when what is called for is to determine what specific variable(s) on which males and females differ affect the phenomenon under study.

A *continuous variable* is one on which objects (people, events) differ in degree, not in kind. On continuous variables, then, distinctions among objects, people, and the like are made on the basis of being "more" or "less" on whatever the variable refers to (e.g., more or less liberal, masculine, aggressive). Some authors refer to such variables as *quantitative* variables; others refer to them as *numerical* variables.

The degree of refinement of distinctions among objects being measured on a continuous variable is, admittedly, predicated on the level of measurement.[5] Moreover, strictly speaking, a continuous variable is one that is susceptible to infinite gradations. That is, the choice of gradations is arbitrary and can be made ever finer if deemed necessary or useful. For example, weight can be measured to the nearest ton, pound, ounce, and so on, depending on what is being weighed and for what purpose. Certain variables can take discrete values only (e.g., number of children in a family, number of rooms in a housing unit). For present purposes, therefore, whether a variable is susceptible of ever finer gradations of its units or whether it is one whose units are discrete, it will be referred to as a continuous variable.

Examples of continuous variables are practice time, reaction time, mental ability, and locus of control. As with categorical variables, continuous variables may be classified differently from different perspectives. From a research design perspective (see below), for example, practice time, mental ability, and locus of control may be the independent variables, whereas reaction time may be the dependent variable. Different designations are, of course, possible and will be determined by the specific research design. For example, mental ability may be treated as a control variable. Be that as it may, from a measurement perspective, the four variables under consideration are alike in that they are continuous.

To illustrate once more that variables may be classified differently from different perspectives, we will consider the variable drug as employed in two studies. In one, effects of *different* drugs on, say, blood pressure are studied; in the other, effects of different dosages of the *same* drug on blood pressure are studied. Although in both studies drug is a manipulated independent variable (see below), it is a categorical variable in one of them and a continuous variable in the other.

Before turning to considerations of classification of variables from a research design perspective, it should be noted that classification schemes other than the one we have discussed are possible from a measurement perspective (e.g., latent and manifest variables; see Chapter 4).

RESEARCH DESIGN PERSPECTIVE

As with the measurement perspective, our presentation of classification of variables from a research design perspective is neither exhaustive nor detailed.

In Chapter 3, a distinction was made between predictive and explanatory studies. Because the focus of these types of studies is quite different, it is advisable to use different labels for the variables employed in them. Specifically, we propose that, in predictive studies, variables be designated as predictors and criteria, whereas in explanatory studies they be designated as independent and dependent. We believe that doing this will help avoid confusion,

---

[5]For example, on an ordinal scale, we can only state that one person is more than another but not by how much more. See Chapter 2, for detailed discussions of this and related points.

misapplication of analytic methods, and misinterpretation of findings. Following is an example of what we have in mind.

Assume that a researcher uses mental ability, years of education, motivation, socioeconomic status, age, and sex, to name but a few variables, to predict income. Under such circumstances, the researcher is at liberty to try out different analytic approaches for the selection of a smaller set of variables and then decide to use the one set he or she deems optimal in light of various considerations (e.g., efficiency of prediction, cost, availability). It is very important that results of such a study *not* be used for explanatory purposes (e.g., attempts to determine relative importance of the variables under consideration in their effects on income).

The situation is radically different when the researcher uses the aforementioned variables to explain variability in income. That is, the researcher wishes to study the effects of these variables on income. Without going into the details here, it will be pointed out that variable selection procedures, appropriate and potentially useful in predictive research, are inappropriate in explanatory research. Moreover, in an explanatory study, the choice of the variables and the analytic approach are predicated on the theoretical formulations advanced by the researcher. For example, the researcher may hypothesize that socioeconomic status affects education and motivation, which in turn affect income. This would require a different analytic approach and lead to different interpretations than a formulation in which the three aforementioned variables are treated as being on the same level.

The remainder of this section is devoted to broad classifications of variables in explanatory studies. Probably the most common classification of variables in such studies is that of independent and dependent variables. An *independent* variable is the presumed cause, whereas a *dependent* variable is the presumed effect. Stated differently, the independent variable is free to vary independently of the dependent variable, or its variability may be determined by the researcher, whereas the variability of the dependent variable *depends*, in part at least, on the effect of the independent variable.

It is useful to further classify independent variables into manipulated and nonmanipulated ones. This classification stems from the important distinction between experimental and nonexperimental research to which we devote several chapters (see Chapters 12–14). For now, it will only be noted that, in experimental research, the researcher manipulates one or more variables (independent) believed to be affecting the phenomenon to be explained (the dependent variable) and observes whether the former led to variability of the latter. In contrast, in nonexperimental research, the researcher observes variability in the phenomenon to be explained (the dependent variable) and collects information about variables (independent) presumed to have led to it.

Depending on the specific research design, the "same" independent variable may be manipulated or not. For example, assume that a medical researcher hypothesized that diet is a major cause of variability in blood pressure. Broadly speaking, two alternative approaches may be taken to test this hypothesis. An experiment may be conducted in which subjects are randomly assigned (see Chapter 10) to different diets. After a given period of time, differences in blood pressure among the groups are studied. Alternatively, in a nonexperimental study, measures of blood pressure and information about dietary habits of patients are collected and the relation between the two studied in an attempt to infer whether the latter affected the former.

In line with our discussion of different types of classifications, it will be noted that independent variables (manipulated or nonmanipulated) may be continuous or categorical. Returning to an earlier example, a researcher may administer *different* drugs (independent categorical variable) or different dosages of the *same* drug (independent continuous variable) in an attempt to study effects on blood pressure (the dependent variable). Examples of nonmanipulated categorical and continuous independent variables that might be used in the study of blood pressure are sex and age.

Variables are not inherently independent or dependent, manipulable or nonmanipulable. The same variable may be conceived of as independent in one study, or even in one phase of the same study, and as dependent in another study, or in another phase of the same study. The same applies to manipulation versus nonmanipulation of variables. We purposely choose the variable sex, which most people are prone to think of as a nonmanipulated independent variable, to illustrate first how it may be used as a dependent variable and then how it may be manipulated.

Assume that a researcher claims to have developed a drug that, if taken by a woman before sexual intercourse, would increase the probability of her giving birth to one sex or the other. If one were to design a study to test the effectiveness of the drug, sex of the newborn would be the dependent variable.

For an example of a design in which sex may be a manipulated variable, we will assume that it is of interest to study whether colleges engage in admission policies that are discriminatory against women. For such a problem, a nonexperimental design comes readily to mind: determine whether college admission rates differ for males and females. Without going into the validity problems that may arise in such a design (see Chapter 14), it will be pointed out that the researcher may choose to manipulate the sex of the applicants by, for example, submitting identical applications in all respects, except for the sex of the applicant, to different colleges and then studying the admission rates for males and females. An example of a study in which race, sex, and ability of applicants were thus manipulated will be found in Walster, Cleary, and Clifford (1970).

The various examples given above were purposely simple, because our sole objective was to acquaint you with the basic ideas concerning variables and how they relate to the research design. As will become evident in subsequent chapters, research designs most often consist of more than one independent variable and may also have more than one dependent variable. In some designs, all the independent variables are manipulated; in others, some are manipulated and some are not, and in still others, all the variables are nonmanipulated.

Sometimes, it is convenient to use special labels for variables that play a special role in the research design. For example, a variable used for purposes of control is sometimes referred to as a control variable to distinguish it from the independent variables whose effects on the dependent variable are the focus of study. Similarly, in later chapters, we may find it convenient to refer to certain variables as moderators, suppressors, covariates, proxies, depending on their function in the design.

Clear designations of the roles of the variables when designing a study or when evaluating a report of a study is an important safeguard against the application of inappropriate analyses and the drawing of erroneous conclusions and implications. We, therefore, suggest that you get in the habit of being clear about the status of each variable in your own research or in that reported by others. Frequently, this would suffice to alert you to ambiguities in your thinking or in that of others, not to mention more serious problems that may cast doubt on the validity of the study under consideration.

As a simple example of what we mean by clear designation of variables, we will describe an aspect of a study by McGee and Snyder (1975) designed to study the "relationship between self-perceptions of situational versus dispositional causation of behavior and situational versus dispositional control of actual observed behavior" (p. 185). For present purposes, it is not necessary to go into the theoretical formulations advanced by the authors. Instead, we will note that people were observed in restaurants to identify those who salted their food before tasting it and those who salted it after tasting it. They were then approached by the researchers who requested their participation in a study by responding to a questionnaire on which they were to indicate which of a set of traits described them. McGee and Snyder (1975) hypothesized that

individuals who ascribed relatively few traits to themselves on the perceptual measure would be particularly likely to salt their food after tasting it. In contrast, those who ascribed relatively many traits to themselves would be particularly likely to salt their food before tasting it. (pp. 186–187)

We comment briefly on the variable names used in the hypothesis and on the analytic approach taken. Beginning with the variable names, it will be noted that food salting and trait ascriptions are probably indicators of variables in which the authors are interested; not the variables themselves. It is safe to say, for example, that the authors are not interested in people's proclivities to salt their food before or after tasting it but rather in what they believe such behavior represents, reflects, indicates. Consequently, it is conceivable that, in another study, the same authors would find it more meaningful to use another indicator(s) of the same variable. The hypothesis should refer to the variables of interest, *not* to the specific indicators, or the specific empirical definition, used. Because issues of hypothesis formulation are discussed in Chapter 9, we will not pursue them further here. Moreover, despite the reservations just expressed, we will refer to the variable names used by McGee and Snyder when we comment on their analytic approach.

From the hypothesis stated above it seems clear that the independent variable is conceived to be trait ascription and the dependent variable is conceived to be food-salting behavior. This becomes particularly evident when, in introducing their results section, McGee and Snyder (1975) stated: "It was predicted that the more likely an individual was to ascribe personality traits to himself, the more likely he was to salt his food before tasting it" (p. 187). Yet the roles of the variables are reversed in the analysis. Specifically, the authors claim to have supported their hypothesis by demonstrating a statistically significant difference between the means of trait ascriptions of those who salted their food before tasting it and those who salted it after tasting it. This goes counter to the logic of hypothesis testing (see Chapter 9). Without going into the details, it will suffice to point out that the authors themselves appear to sense that their analytic approach is questionable, as is evidenced by their reporting that they found no significant differences between those who salted before tasting the food and those who salted after tasting it on such variables as sex, smoker versus nonsmoker, eating alone versus not eating alone, age, and weight.

CONCLUDING REMARKS

We hope that our discussion of definitions and variables has clarified the relations between them and has shown how intimately they are tied to measurement approaches. When reading the next chapter—devoted to theory, problems, and hypotheses—you are urged to bear in mind that, no matter how sophisticated the theory, how elaborate the hypotheses derived from it, how intricate the research design, and how fancy the analysis, little that is meaningful can be accomplished when the variables are poorly defined theoretically and/or empirically.

Chapter 9
Theories, Problems, and Hypotheses

Originally used to refer to a mental viewing, a vision, the word theory has come to have diverse meanings, leading Merton (1968) to assert that the "use of the word often obscures rather than creates understanding" (p. 39). Introducing a symposium devoted to the explication of the structure of scientific theories, Suppe (1977b) observed that "philosophers of science still are searching for an analysis of theories which will provide an adequate philosophical understanding of theories" (p. 233).

We begin with some observations about definitions of theory and the relation between theory and facts. This is followed by some considerations of the role of theory in scientific research. After some comments about theory testing, the balance of the chapter is devoted to issues concerning formulation of problems and hypotheses, and the logic of hypothesis testing.

DEFINITIONS AND ROLE OF THEORY

Despite a plethora of definitions of theory, most share a common core: Theory is an invention aimed at organizing and explaining specific aspects of the environment. A major characteristic of a scientific theory—one that distinguishes it from other forms of explanations—is that testable hypotheses may be derived from it. More formally:

Theory means . . . *a system of logically interrelated, specifically non-contradictory, statements, ideas, and concepts relating to an area of reality, formulated in such a way that testable hypotheses can be derived from them.* (de Groot, 1969, p. 40)

de Groot pointed out that he opted for a definition that is not as rigorous and as rigid as ones advanced in the context of the physical sciences, because adopting the latter orientation for sociobehavioral sciences would "introduce an 'ideal' which, in most cases, is unattainable either for the time being or on principle" (p. 40).

THEORY AND FACTS

Issues concerning the meaning of facts were commented upon in Chapter 7. Until recently, a predominant theme in scientific inquiry and in philosophies of science has been that of the use of independently existing facts to test the truth or falsity of hypotheses derived from theory. The essence of this orientation was expressed by Huxley (n.d.): "The great tragedy of Science—the slaying of a beautiful hypothesis by an ugly fact" (p. 247).

Current conceptions more realistically view facts as deriving specific meanings and relevance from a given theoretical orientation. Here is how Weimer (1977) put it: "To state a fact is to argue for the warrant of the theory which necessitates it, and to teach others that it is a fact is to enjoin them to see reality as that theory commands one to see it" (p. 14). In short, a theory "makes it possible to observe phenomena as being of a certain sort, and as related to other phenomena" (Hanson, 1958, p. 90).

To better understand the status of facts and the role they play in scientific inquiry, it is useful to distinguish between facts as sense perceptions and observations. Consider Popper's (1972) analysis:

In science it is *observation* rather than perception which plays the decisive part. But observation is a process in which we play an intensely *active* part. An observation is a perception, but one which is planned and prepared: We do not 'have' an observation [as we may 'have' a sense experience] but we 'make' an observation. . . . An observation is always preceded by a particular interest, a question, a problem—in short, by something theoretical. (Popper, 1972, p. 342)

In what are probably the most perceptive discussions of theory and facts from a scientific perspective, Whewell (1847) argued that the distinction between the two is "untenable" and leads to "endless perplexity and debate. . . . There are . . . no special attributes of Theory and Fact which distinguish them from one another. Facts are phenomena apprehended by the aid of conceptions and mental acts, as Theories also are" (Vol. 2, p. 94). Further, Whewell (1847) wrote: "There is a mask of theory over the whole face of nature" (Vol. 1, p. 42). In sum, then, observations are "theory-laden" (Hanson, 1958, p. 19), or, as Johnson (1953) put it: "Believing is seeing" (p. 79).

THEORY AS FRAME OF REFERENCE

Theory provides the researcher with a "selective point of view" without which research would be "the ditty bag of an idiot, filled with bits of pebbles, straws, feathers, and other random hoardings" (Lynd, 1939, p. 183). By providing an orientation for what to look for, theory also helps determine which variables are relevant and which are not relevant. Moreover, as is discussed below and in subsequent chapters, through problems and hypotheses derived from it, theory determines largely the type of research design, the analytic approach, and the interpretation of the results.

Not surprisingly, attempts to explain the "same" phenomenon from different theoretical orientations may lead to the selection of different variables, to differences in conceptualizations, definitions, and measurement of the same variables (see Chapters 4 and 8), and to differences in the interpretation of the same results. This is particularly evident when the same phenomenon is studied from theoretical perspectives of different disciplines. As an example of this, Adams et al. (1982a) used attempts of sociobehavioral scientists from different disciplines to explain why some women choose to work outside the home, and why the number of such women has been on the increase. Economists might look for such things as demand for labor, increase in pay rates. Sociologists might search for the answer in changes in the types of jobs available to women and in the patterns of family living. Psychologists might be concerned with roles, with self-image. Demographers might focus on birth rates and their effects on demands for certain goods and services, and on the supply of labor. Adams et al. (1982a) concluded: "In short, what mainly distinguishes academic disciplines from one another is not that they focus on different kinds of facts but rather that they interpret the same facts within distinctive conceptual frameworks" (p. 9).

THEORY AS BIAS

Being a way of seeing, a theory is also a way of not seeing. Implications this has for theory and hypothesis testing are taken up later on. For now, we would like to stress the importance of being alert to potential biasing, even "blinding," effects of theory.

A researcher may, for example, not "see" evidence that is contrary to his or her theory, or "seeing" it, he or she may come up with all sorts of explanations (rationalizations?) why the evidence should not be viewed as challenging the theory. Often such explanations consist of attributing deviant results to various possible deficiencies in the design and execution of the study (e.g., sampling errors, measurement errors, weak manipulations). Following are some examples of biasing effects of theory.

Barber and Fox (1958) reported on interviews with two "distinguished" medical scientists who "independently observed the same phenomenon in the course of their research: reversible collapse of rabbits' ears after injection of the enzyme papain. One went on to make a discovery based on this serendipitous or chance occurrence; the other did not" (p. 128). What emerges from the interviews is that the researchers' preconceptions, their theoretical orientations and interests, determined how they perceived the phenomenon. Witness a statement by the researcher for whom this was a "serendipity-lost experience":

Since I was primarily interested in research questions having to do with the muscles of the heart, I was thinking in terms of muscle. That blinded me, so that changes in the cartilage didn't occur to me as a possibility. I was looking for muscles in the sections, and I never dreamed it was cartilage. (p. 135)

You are probably familiar with controversies surrounding reliance of editors of professional journals on referees' recommendations regarding acceptance, revision, or rejection of manuscripts submitted for publication. Accusations of all sorts of biases have been made (e.g., that those involved are: against women authors, in favor of prestigious authors or pet theories). Following are a couple of examples of research in this broad area.

Peters and Ceci (1982) altered the institutional affiliations and the names of the authors of 12 published research articles and resubmitted them to the 12 journals in which they had originally appeared. Three of the 12 articles were detected as having been published. Eight of the remaining nine were rejected, frequently because of what the referees deemed "serious methodological flaws" (p. 190). For extensive and diverse commentaries by, among others, current and former journal editors, and Peters and Ceci's response, see *The Behavioral and Brain Science*, 1982, *5*, 196–255. This issue was subsequently published in book form (Harnad, 1983).[1]

---

[1]*The Behavioral and Brain Sciences* is one of a small number of journals that follow a policy of inviting authorities in the given field to comment on articles accepted for publication. We believe you will benefit from studying different, often contradictory, views of the same(?) paper published in this journal.

Mahoney (1977c) conducted a study aimed at investigating referees' *"confirmatory bias"*—*"the tendency to emphasize and believe experiences which support one's views and to ignore or discredit those which do not"* (p. 161). Seventy-five referees were invited to review an article, purportedly submitted for publication, that addressed current issues in behavior modification.

Of five groups of referees, we are concerned here with two who saw identical manuscripts, except for the results section. Referees in one of the groups saw positive results consistent with their presumed theoretical orientation, whereas referees in the other group saw negative results inconsistent with their presumed theoretical orientation. Among the findings were the following:

1. By and large, referees who received the manuscript with the positive results recommended that it be published, whereas those who received the manuscript with the negative results recommended that it be rejected.

2. Despite the fact that the papers were identical in all other respects, referees who received the one with the positive results tended to give it high ratings on writing, relevance, scientific contribution, methodology, and the like, whereas the converse was true for referees who received the paper with the negative results.

What the preceding examples amount to is that "it is not simply that scientific theories are tested by observations—the observations are also tested" (Singh, 1985, p. 157). Not as "flippantly" as some view it, Sir Arthur Eddington is reported to have remarked: "Never trust an experimental result until it has been confirmed by theory" (Chernoff, 1978, p. A23). This attitude is well illustrated in the following story related by Einstein's student Ilse Rosenthal-Schneider in a manuscript entitled "Reminiscences of conversation with Einstein," dated 23 July 1957 and quoted by Holton (1972):

Once when I was with Einstein in order to read with him a work that contained many objections against his theory . . . he suddenly interrupted the discussion of the book, reached for a telegram that was lying on the windowsill, and handed it to me with the words, "Here, this will perhaps interest you." It was Eddington's cable with the results of measurement of the eclipse expedition [1919]. When I was giving expression to my joy that the results coincided with his calculations, he said quite unmoved, "But I knew that the theory is correct"; and when I asked, what if there had been no confirmation of his prediction, he countered: "Then I would have been sorry for the dear Lord—the theory *is* correct." (p. 361)

THEORY TESTING

Positivism in its various manifestations has, until recently, been the predominant orientation concerning theory testing. Few have questioned its basic tenets about the use of "objective" evidence for the purpose of theory confirmation. In recent years, however, the demise of positivism and the heralding of the present post-positivist era have become major themes in the writings of philosophers of science and sociobehavioral scientists alike (e.g., Fiske & Shweder, 1986b; Suppe, 1977a).

Renunciation of positivism has become so widespread that Marsh (1982) was moved to observe: "Positivism is, in fact, like sin: everyone is against it" (p. 51). Furthermore, so strong was the reaction to positivism that Stent (1975) puzzled, in retrospect, how it managed to "gain such a hold over the human sciences" (p. 1054).

It is not our aim to review the vast literature that has led to the dethronement of positivism. Nor can we deal here adequately with the complex formulations regarding theory testing and the choice from among rival theories of the "same" phenomenon. All we will attempt is a very modest sketch of this topic and provide some references.

Among notable contributors to current conceptions about theory and theory testing are Feyerabend (1978), Kuhn (1970), Lakatos (1978), and Popper (1959, 1968, 1972). Popper argued persuasively that hypotheses and theories cannot be confirmed or proven, no matter how much evidence is marshaled in support of their assertions. Instead, they may be falsified. Contrary to some misconceptions and misinterpretations, Popper (1959) did not accord the status of certainty to the disproof of scientific theories, as is illustrated by the following:

In point of fact, no conclusive disproof of a theory can ever be produced; for it is always possible to say that the experimental results are not reliable, or that the discrepancies which are asserted to exist between the experimental results and the theory are only apparent and that they will disappear with the advance of our understanding. . . . If you insist on strict proof (or strict disproof) in empirical sciences, you will never benefit from experience, and never learn from it how wrong you are. (p. 50)

Lakatos (1978), who distinguished among three modes of falsification (dogmatic, methodological, and sophisticated), argued cogently that "no experimental result can ever kill a theory: any theory can be saved from counterinstances either by some auxiliary hypothesis or by a suitable reinterpretation of its terms" (p. 32). Lakatos distinguished between the "hard core" of a theory, consisting of a set of central principles impervious to challenge, and the "protective belt" surrounding it. Progressive adjustments are made in the theory's protective belt in attempts to withstand the onslaught of anomalies and counterinstances.

New theories do not replace old ones, because the latter have been shown to be false, but rather because the former have proven to be more adequate, offering a more comprehensive, more parsimonious, and a more integrative explanation of phenomena. Or could the process be more in line with Max Planck's (1968)[2] observation that "a new scientific truth does not triumph by convincing its opponents and making them see the light, but rather because its opponents eventually die" (pp. 33–34)?

Be that as it may, the relation between old and new theories was aptly characterized by Einstein and Infeld (1961):

Creating a new theory is not like destroying an old barn and erecting a skyscraper in its place. It is rather like climbing a mountain, gaining new and wider views, discovering unexpected connections between our starting point and its rich environment. But the point from which we started out still exists and can be seen, although it appears smaller and forms a tiny part of our broad view gained by the mastery of the obstacles on our adventurous way up. (p. 152)

POST HOC THEORIZING

Instead of being guided by theory, researchers frequently gather data or use available data and attempt to come up with a theory to explain them—a practice referred to as post hoc theorizing. It is important to recognize that finding agreement between the data and a theory thus devised does not constitute a test of it. As Peirce (1932) pointed out, "if we look over the phenomena to find agreement with theory, it is a mere question of ingenuity and industry how many we shall find" (p. 496).

Here is an amusing example of post hoc explanation. Commenting on an article in *Science* about differential effects of strategies for the control of gonorrhea in Sweden and in

---

[2]Eminent physicist, originator of quantum theory, and Nobel laureate.

Denmark—according to which a sharp decline in the incidence of gonorrhea was observed in the former but not in the latter—Healey (1976) offered a "linguistic deterrent" explanation for the results. Healey pointed out that protective devices are referred to as *kondoms* in Sweden, whereas in Denmark they are referred to as *svangerskabsforebyggende middel.* "The sheer effort of uttering all ten syllables must surely be a deterrent to their purchase and use" (p. 98). Indeed, given sufficient ingenuity, one can come up with explanations that fit any result (for a good discussion and examples of post hoc theorizing in a more serious vein, see Merton, 1968, pp. 147–149).

Post hoc theorizing should not be confused with the meaningful and necessary process of theory refinement, revision, reformulation, or whatever the case may be, in light of research findings. The key difference between the two approaches is that, unlike post hoc theorizing, existing data are *not* used to test hypotheses that were formulated to fit the data to begin with but rather that *newly designed studies* are used to test hypotheses derived from the reformulated theory.

STATE OF THEORY IN SOCIOBEHAVIORAL SCIENCES

Most conceptions regarding theory testing and choice from among rival theories were advanced in the context of the physical sciences. It should come as no surprise that the state of theory is in much greater flux and is considerably more controversial in sociobehavioral sciences. Suffice it to recall that there are those who deny the very viability of sociobehavioral science (see Chapter 7). In addition, as discussed in detail in Part 1, the generally primitive nature of measurement in sociobehavioral sciences is an impediment to the development of elaborate theories.

Conceptions of theory in sociobehavioral sciences run the gamut from those circumscribing it, for the time being, to tests of single hypotheses, through those calling for the construction of "mini" theories, theories of middle-range (Merton, 1968), to those maintaining that attempts should be directed towards the construction of grand theories. The differences are primarily due to differences in the perceived state of the sociobehavioral sciences and the consequent expectations regarding the most promising route toward maturity on par with the natural sciences.

Those who maintain that efforts should be directed towards the testing of single hypotheses believe that, because of the primitive state of the sociobehavioral sciences, it is premature and unproductive to engage in theory construction. This view of tests of single hypotheses serving as building blocks for the accumulation of knowledge that will ultimately lead to the construction of theories is, we believe, as sterile as the hope that an accumulation of facts will lead to a meaningful theory. Meaningful hypotheses cannot emerge in a theoretical vacuum. Admittedly, the theory from which a given hypothesis was derived is frequently implicit. The researcher may not even be aware of the theoretical orientation that has led him or her to advance and test a given hypothesis. Yet it is theory that renders the hypothesis and the variables that it refers to, relevant to attempts to explain a given phenomenon. Moreover, it is theory that gives coherence and integration to a set of hypotheses designed to explain given phenomena.

We do not think it necessary to document in detail the volatile and ephemeral nature of research in sociobehavioral sciences but feel that some general comments and examples are called for. Turn, almost at random, to a report on some research area, particularly to a review article, and you are bound to find the obligatory opening remarks to the effect that what was done thus far in the area under consideration is deficient and questionable, and that inconsistency of findings from different studies is probably the only consistent result.

Even a cursory inspection of tables of contents of journals, or of books that have appeared in two or more editions (e.g., textbooks, handbooks), or of annual reviews will suffice to convince one of the ever-changing scene of topics, of the ebb and flow of research areas. In social psychology, for example, one encounters a tide of papers on authoritarianism, which is replaced by one on cognitive dissonance, which in turn is replaced by one on risky-shift (or locus of control, sex roles, learned helplessness, attribution). Is there any wonder that Meehl (1978) declared that like old generals, theories in "soft" areas of psychology "never die, they just slowly fade away" (p. 807; see also, Berkowitz, 1983; Travers, 1973)?

There are, of course, many reasons for this state of affairs. That many of the difficulties stem from deficiencies in measurement, design, and analysis is, we trust, amply demonstrated throughout this book. In the present context, however, we would like to point out that one of the major sources of the difficulties has to do with unrealistic expectations and aspirations regarding the capacity of sociobehavioral research to arrive at explanations of social phenomena and at solutions to social problems.

For a long time, sociobehavioral researchers exuded naive confidence in their ability to arrive at facile solutions to social problems regardless of their complexity. It is only in recent years that some have come to recognize the wisdom of Mencken's observation that "there is always an easy solution to every human problem—neat, plausible and wrong" (quoted by Thomas, 1976, p. 181). In addition, it is only in recent years that some leading authors and researchers have been advocating a more realistic appraisal of the potential and promise of sociobehavioral research. (Ironically, it is earlier writings of some of the same authors that have contributed unwittingly to unrealistic aspirations and expectations among sociobehavioral researchers.)

In a paper entitled "Prudent aspirations for social inquiry," presented at a symposium on the occasion of celebrating the fiftieth anniversary of the Social Science Research building at the University of Chicago, Cronbach (1982) declared:

> Fortunately, today's profession is coming to see the rationalist, scientistic ideal as no more than an infantile dream of omnipotence. The present mood, one hopes, bespeaks an institution on the brink of adulthood, ready to claim a role within its capabilities and aware that waiting for its Newton is as pointless as waiting for Godot. (p. 61)

The editors of a more recent symposium on the state of sociobehavioral research, Fiske and Shweder (1986a), used the subtitle "uneasy social science" for their introduction. We believe that Cronbach (1986), who was a participant in this symposium too, captured its theme and mood in the title of his paper: "Social inquiry by and for earthlings."

Similar themes were sounded in a symposium on the state of sociobehavioral sciences (Smelser & Gerstein, 1986) on the occasion of the fiftieth anniversary of the publication of a report on social trends in the United States by a committee commissioned by President Hoover. Concluding his examination of major themes in the earlier report (e.g., science and its role in social change, theory and facts), Smelser (1986) stated: "As a result of change in our thinking about the relations between science and society, I believe we have become, paradoxically, both more sophisticated in our research design and measures and less pretentious in our aspirations than we were 50 years ago" (p. 34).

That the more judicious and realistic conception of sociobehavioral research reflected in the foregoing statements is not yet shared by the vast majority of sociobehavioral researchers is evident from the almost continuous stream of solutions to the most complex of social problems presented with a degree of certitude that frequently borders on irresponsibility.

PROBLEMS

"In the beginning was not the 'word' but a problem" (Kempthorne, 1980, p. 17). Although this may not hold true for The Creation, it aptly portrays how a scientific inquiry is initiated. You are probably familiar with the saying: "A problem well put is half solved." Here is how Einstein and Infeld (1961) viewed the role of problem formulation in scientific inquiry:

The formulation of a problem is often more essential than its solution, which may be merely a matter of mathematical or experimental skill. To raise new questions, new possibilities, to regard old problems from a new angle, requires creative imagination and marks real advance in science. (p. 92)

It takes an imaginative mind to structure a new reality from phenomena that appear hackneyed to most people; to see order in what appears to be chaotic and disjointed. This is exemplified by the use of novel concepts in familiar settings, by asking novel questions that place old phenomena in a new light, creating a new context. As Heisenberg (1962) reminded us: "What we observe is not nature in itself but nature exposed to our method of questioning" (p. 58).

PROBLEM CHARACTERIZATION AND FORMAT

In a most general sense, a problem is a statement, usually interrogative, about a relation between two or more variables. Two things will be noted:

1. To qualify as a problem, as used in this book, the statement must make reference to some kind of relation (see below) between at least two variables. Excluded from consideration are what are viewed by some as "problems," perhaps because of difficulties entailed (e.g., constructing a measure, obtaining a probability sample).

2. As in Chapter 8, our use of the term "relation" is not limited to situations in which no distinction is made between independent and dependent variables (e.g., when the correlation between two variables is calculated) but includes also statements that refer to or imply effects of independent variables on dependent variables.[3]

To clarify our meaning, the same variables will be used in three possible formats of problem statement. The formats are numbered for convenience of reference in the discussion that follows.

Format 1: What is the relation between mental ability and academic achievement?
What is the relation between sex and aggression?
What is the relation between teaching style and student academic achievement?

Format 2: How do students of differing levels of mental ability differ in academic achievement?
How do males and females differ in aggression?
How do students exposed to different teaching styles differ in academic achievement?

Format 3: What is the effect of mental ability on academic achievement?
What is the effect of sex on aggression?
What is the effect of teaching style on students' academic achievement?

Note that in Format 1, the statements are "noncommittal" in the sense that there is no explicit or implicit indication of a distinction between an independent and a dependent variable. This is not to say that the person who formulates such problems may not have such a distinction in mind, or that a reader may not make an inference whether a distinction is

---

[3]For definitions and classifications of variables, see Chapter 8.

intended and, if so, which of the variables is meant to be the independent and which the dependent.

In Format 2, distinctions between independent and dependent variables are implied. Ignoring for now the awkward wording concerning mental ability (i.e., "students of differing levels of mental ability"), it appears that mental ability, sex, and teaching style, are meant to be the independent variables in the three problem statements. Note, however, that, of the three, only teaching style is *perhaps* a manipulated variable (see below). In other words, the first two problem statements probably refer to nonexperimental designs (see Chapter 14), whereas the third *may* be referring to an experimental or a quasi-experimental design (see Chapters 12 and 13). Be that as it may, the statements of the problems are ambiguous in the sense of not explicitly stating that differences in performance on the dependent variables are due, albeit in part, to the effects of the implied independent variables. Thus, for example, although males and females may differ in aggression, the difference may be due *not* to sex but to another variable or variables correlated with sex.

To show more clearly the ambiguity of Format 2, we examine the third statement, namely the one dealing with teaching style and student academic achievement. We said above that teaching style is probably a manipulated variable. That is, one may design an experiment in which students are randomly assigned to different teaching styles and note their effects on academic achievement.

It is, however, possible for the problem to be formulated in a nonexperimental design setting. That is, assume that the researcher attempts to explain why certain groups of students differ in academic achievement. Assume further that the researcher has observed that teachers use different styles in their teaching and that he or she wishes to determine whether classes taught by different styles manifest different levels of academic achievement. It is clear that, even if this is found to be the case, the differences in academic achievement may be due *not* to teaching styles but to a host of other variables.

To underscore the ambiguity, it will be pointed out that, assuming a nonexperimental design, it is even conceivable for teaching style to be the *dependent* variable. For example, students of certain levels of ability, motivation, or what have you, *who as a result achieve differently*, may elicit different teaching styles, presumably to best fit their needs and achievement levels.

Our sole purpose here was to illustrate potential ambiguities emanating from the problem statement. Distinctions among different kinds of designs, and controls a researcher may exercise in each in an attempt to arrive at reasonably valid conclusions, are discussed in detail in subsequent chapters (see, in particular, Chapters 12–14).

In contrast to Formats 1 and 2, in Format 3, it is clear which is the independent and which is the dependent variable in each of the problems. Again, we are not concerned here with the validity of the design, the measures used, and the theoretical orientation of the researcher. It is quite possible that, on these grounds, one would dismiss or seriously question the findings. What we do wish to stress is that the problem statement largely determines the analytic approach. This will be illustrated by using the first problem in each of the three sets.

In Format 1, the question raised is about the relation between mental ability and academic achievement. Therefore, a correlation coefficient appears to be called for. Note that, in the absence of a statement of hypothesis (see below), it is not possible to be more specific about the appropriate analytic method. Thus, for example, if it were hypothesized that the relation between mental ability and achievement is curvilinear (see Chapter 18), then it would be inappropriate to calculate, say, the Pearson correlation coefficient, as it is based on the assumption that the relation between the variables being correlated is linear (see Chapter 17).

Above, we alluded to awkward wording in Format 2. This is because mental ability is a continuous variable (see Chapter 8). Not only is the statement awkward, but it also is prone to lead to a choice of an inappropriate analytic approach. Assume, for the sake of illustration, that the researcher intends to hypothesize that students of high mental ability tend to be high in academic achievement, those of low mental ability tend to be low in academic achievement, those of average mental ability tend to be average in academic achievement, and so forth. Using Format 2, the researcher may even be inclined to form distinct groups on the basis of mental ability (e.g., high, average, low) and to treat mental ability as if it were a categorical variable (see Chapter 8). As is discussed in later chapters (especially Chapter 20) such an approach would, at best, lead to loss of information, but it could also lead to erroneous conclusions.

Turning to Format 3, a simple regression analysis appears to be the appropriate analytic approach, assuming the relation is linear (see Chapter 17). Note that, although Format 1 calls for the calculation and interpretation of a correlation coefficient, Format 3 calls for the calculation and interpretation of a regression coefficient. Also, a finding that the regression coefficient is positive will indicate that increments in mental ability are expected to be associated with increments of a given magnitude in academic achievement—a statement that would be made much more awkwardly and not as clearly, if one were to use Format 2 as a basis for the hypothesis statement.

We hope the foregoing discussion would suffice to serve as an introduction, a first approximation, to the crucial role of problem statement. We say more about this topic below, in our discussion of relations between problems and analytic methods. In addition, we illustrate and comment upon problem statements when we discuss hypothesis statements (later in this chapter) and different analytic approaches (in various other chapters). Clearly, format is but an aspect of problem statement. The primary concern should, of course, be with the substantive issues the problem addresses—a topic to which we now turn.

PROBLEMS AND SUBSTANCE

Various authors urge researchers to avoid "trivial" problems. Thus, Box (1976) declared: "It is inappropriate to be concerned about mice when there are tigers abroad" (p. 792). Speaking of amassing data and of using fancy methodology in support of trivial hypotheses, McGuire (1973) paraphrased Maslow, saying: "What is not worth doing, is not worth doing well" (p.450). Some authors resort to humor and satire to ridicule research directed toward the "obvious" or the inane (e.g., why the utterance, "Please pass the salt," should be associated with salt passage, Pencil, 1976; Do Chicken Have Lips? Zaltman, Lemasters, & Heffring, 1982, pp. 157–159).

However, what makes a problem important and worth pursuing? This question baffles professionals and is a source of confusion, even despair, to students. It is not uncommon for students, when peddling their dissertation problem to different faculty members in search of a sponsoring committee, to encounter those who view their problem as important, meaningful, "doable," and those who brand it as trite, meaningless, not "doable." This should not come as a surprise, considering that the problem encapsulates the puzzle one feels impelled to solve. What is puzzling for one person may go unnoticed by another person or leave him or her unperturbed. Einstein and Infeld (1961) pointed out that, although there are some similarities between the detective and the scientist, they differ in a fundamental way. "For the detective the crime is given, the problem formulated . . . The scientist must, at least in part, commit his own crime, as well as carry out the investigation" (p. 76).

The formulation of a scientific problem constitutes a creative act. What is viewed as creative, important, meaningful, depends on the values of a specific culture or subculture, at a given time, in a given context. This, of course, applies also to the subculture(s) of science. Indeed, the annals of science are replete with examples of initial dismissal of some of the greatest discoveries and contributions as being trivial, irrelevant, downright wrong, even fraudulent. (For a very interesting review and analysis of sources of resistance by scientists to scientific discovery, see Barber, 1961.)

Planck (1968) provided the following account of his experience when working on his doctoral dissertation, in which he reformulated the second law of thermodynamics.

The effect of my dissertation on the physicists of those days was nil. None of my professors at the University had any understanding for its contents, as I learned for a fact in my conversations with them. They doubtless permitted it to pass as a doctoral dissertation only because they knew me by my other activities in the physical laboratory and in the mathematical seminar. But I found no interest, let alone approval, even among the very physicists who were closely concerned with the topic. Helmholtz probably did not even read my paper at all. Kirchhoff expressly disapproved of its contents. (pp. 18–19)

In view of the relatively loose and primitive state of theory, measurement, design, and analysis in sociobehavioral sciences, there is considerably more room for questioning and disagreement regarding the validity and worth of a study than in the natural sciences. Accordingly, one is not surprised when Lindsey (1977) asked: "How is it that so much triviality, illiteracy, and dullness is yearly entered into the scientific publication stream?" (p. 579), or when Kupfersmid (1988) asserted *"Many articles focus on irrelevant topics"* (p. 635).

Public opposition to sociobehavioral sciences (see Chapter 7) is largely determined by what is viewed as being in the purview of science. Thus, attempts to study, say, romantic love, sexual attraction, have, until recently, been viewed with suspicion, disdain, ridicule, depending on the viewer's values and attitudes. Senator Proxmire has often awarded his well-known Golden Fleece award to sociobehavioral scientists whom he considered wasting taxpayers' money in their attempts to study what he deemed trivial problems or ones not susceptible to scientific study, as the case may be.

In view of the foregoing, what is the researcher to do? To begin with, he or she would do well to heed Lynd's (1939) advice to the scientist to "continually ask himself . . . 'Why do I pose a given problem and ask the questions I do regarding it?'" (p. 203), or, following Stouffer's (1950) advice, the researcher contemplating a research question should ask: "What of it?" (p. 359). Such self-questioning may serve as an antidote to becoming so involved with the research, the data, the fancy analyses carried out by powerful computers, so as to be blind to the triviality or vacuousness of the problem. Worse yet, the risk of not thinking at all about what one is doing is ever present in such situations. In connection with his discussion of the scientific specialist's process of thinking, Stamp (1937, p. 17) quoted Anatole France's aphorism: "The worst of science is, it stops you thinking."

However, you are undoubtedly wondering, how does one find a problem in the first place? Some authors (e.g., Popper, 1959; Reichenbach, 1938) argued that this question belongs to the context of discovery, as distinct from the context of justification and that it, therefore, is not susceptible to a statement of rules and principles to be followed. Others maintain, explicitly or implicitly, that a systematic approach to problem formulation is possible or that general principles can be delineated. There is a germ of truth in both positions. Although it is true that problem formulation entails a creative process the nature of which is, to say the least, not well understood, it is also true that certain principles may be formulated as aids in the search for and formulation of problems that are more amenable to solutions (for a good discussion of this topic, see McGuire, 1983).

In the following sections, we *sketch* some of the issues relevant to problem formulation and some of the suggested approaches aimed at promoting formulation of what are considered meaningful and soluble problems. It is important to recognize that the issues we discuss are neither mutually exclusive nor exhaustive. Also, we cannot emphasize too strongly that our presentation is *not* meant to serve as a set of recipes that when followed will ensure success. As best, we hope that it will provide a frame of reference for thinking about the process of problem formulation.

SCOPE OF PROBLEM

Probably the most obvious aspect of problem formulation is its scope. Problems that are all encompassing, or too broad, elude meaningful solutions. Broad questions (e.g., "What are the causes of crime, delinquency, happiness, poverty, aggression?") are bound to lead to vague answers. Moreover, attempts to design research to investigate such questions may engender a sense of frustration, even a feeling of helplessness, that may lead to immobilization. We believe this to be a major cause of a permanent state of a large segment of doctoral students, namely the ABD (All But Dissertation).

We said earlier that a problem refers to relations among variables. Thus, although one's initial interest in a given phenomenon and the motivation to study it are probably on the level of the preceding global questions, it is necessary to reduce such questions to workable and soluble problems by focusing on relations among specific variables deemed to be operating.

Commenting on issues regarding problem formulation, a departing editor (Campbell, 1982) of the *Journal of Applied Psychology* said, among other things:

Another strong impression I have is that there are certain forms of research questions that are best to avoid. They tend to lead to studies that are not very useful or that at least yield a very small return of information. One such question is the tendency to pose a general question with the expectation that a general answer is possible. Examples would be: Is a training program effective? How should performance be measured? What makes organizations effective? Are the people in the organization motivated? If the investigator stays at this level too long, what tends to come out is a rather bland set of mixed results that at best suggest the need for further research. (p. 697)

Not only are Campbell's examples of questions too broad, but some also do not qualify as problems in the sense defined earlier. For example, whereas the question regarding the effectiveness of a training program has to be restated and focused on specific variables, it does imply an interest in studying the effect of some independent variable(s) on some dependent variable(s). Contrast this with the questions concerning how performance should be measured or whether the people in the organization are motivated. These questions refer to measurement of specific variables, not to relations between variables.

PAST RESEARCH AND LITERATURE REVIEW

It is a truism that past research on the phenomenon under investigation should play a key role in the process of problem formulation and the design of a study—hence, the importance of a thorough review of the relevant literature. Unfortunately, what is served in the guise of a literature review is, in many instances, little more than a tiresome listing of studies and findings without even a hint that the author has been thinking when reading the literature, not to mention critically evaluating what he or she has been reading. One frequently gets the strong impression that the "review" was done *after* the study was completed. In fact, we have encountered students who, while collecting data or analyzing data for their dissertation, told us that they have not yet reviewed the literature but assured us, with an air of checking off things to do, that they were going to do this in the near future.

The inaneness characteristic of many literature reviews is exemplified by Phillips's (1978) account about references to his work. Phillips reported that he published several papers in which he used a given instrument *"without any real questions about its validity"* [italics added] (p. 229). Subsequently, however, he published several additional papers in which he questioned the adequacy and validity of the instrument. Phillips pointed out that the latter papers were not ignored by sociologists who used the same instrument but that they were cited uncritically along with the earlier papers. Referring to authors who have cited his work, Phillips said:

> They fail to acknowledge that some of these articles of mine call into question the inventory's adequacy and, *if taken seriously*, the very utilization of such a measuring device. It is not that they attend to, and rebut, my criticisms, but they ignore them altogether. In other words, they pay lip-service to the scientific norm of covering the relevant literature without acknowledging that part of that very literature has the consequence of undermining their own research aims and assumptions. (p. 229)[4]

At the very least, a review of the literature should serve as a safeguard against attempts to reinvent the wheel. To this end, it is crucial to break out of the almost inevitable parochialism that training and specialization engender. Not only do psychologists, sociologists, political scientists, and the like tend to read literature only in their own discipline, but they further limit such reading to some subdiscipline. Needless to say, this fosters tunnel vision.

In an address to the Society for the Psychological Study of Social Issues, Murphy (1939) related with remarkable candor his feelings when he stumbled upon a book by medical researchers who dealt with topics he had been actively pursuing for some time.

> I had indeed to blush when I thought of the emptiness and ineptitude of many of my own discussions of motives, the learning process, and the integration of attitudes, when I discovered that problems which I had only vaguely sensed had long been the subject of exact research by medical men, but not by us social psychologists. (p. 112)

Discussing "The dilemma of specialization," Hayek (1956) maintained that although specialization may be useful in certain fields (e.g., chemistry, physiology, physics), it has a pernicious effect in sociobehavioral sciences. Using economics as a frame of reference, he said: "Nobody can be a great economist who is only an economist—and I am even tempted to add that the economist who is only an economist is likely to become a nuisance if not a positive danger" (p. 463). Similarly, Ortega y Gasset (1932, Chapter 12) lamented the "barbarism" of specialization.

It goes without saying that rampant parochialism and specialization in sociobehavioral sciences are inimical to cumulative knowledge. As Kaplan (1964) observed: "Much of the theorizing in behavioral science is not building on what has already been established so much as laying out new foundations, or even worse, producing only another set of blueprints" (p. 304). Zeaman (1959) expressed the same thought more bluntly:

> One of the differences between the natural and the social sciences is that in the natural sciences, each succeeding generation stands on the shoulders of those that have gone before, while in the social sciences, each generation steps in the faces of its predecessors. (p. 167)

---

[4]In Chapter 4, we discussed deleterious consequences of utilizing instruments without any attention to their validity and offered examples not unlike the one related by Phillips.

In a book devoted to the presentation of a systematic approach to the reviewing of past research, Cooper (1984) stated: "Research methods textbooks in the social sciences show a remarkable lack of attention to how an inquirer finds, evaluates, and integrates past research" (p. 9). Perhaps this is due to the fact that a meaningful treatment of this broad topic would require more space than can be accorded to it in such textbooks.

Be that as it may, a brief discussion of this topic has become even more onerous in view of recent developments in and increasing reliance on meta-analytic techniques that employ quantitative methods of varying degrees of sophistication and complexity in summaries of research literature. For present purposes, it would suffice to point out that, loosely speaking, meta-analysis refers "to the analysis of analyses," or "to the statistical analysis of a large collection of analysis results from individual studies for the purpose of integrating the findings" (Glass, 1976, p. 3). Introductions to meta-analysis will be found in Glass, McGaw, and Smith (1981); Hedges and Olkin (1985); Hunter, Schmidt, and Jackson (1982); Light and Pillemer (1984); Rosenthal (1984); Wolf (1986); Yeaton and Wortman (1984). For a review of several books on meta-analysis, see Hedges and Olkin (1986). Various computer programs for meta-analysis have also been developed (e.g., Mullen & Rosenthal, 1985). This approach has by no means escaped controversy. For an example of an exchange of views on the use of meta-analysis in education, see *Educational Researcher*, 1984, *13*(8), 6–27. See also, *Journal of Consulting and Clinical Psychology*, 1983, *51*, 3–75, for a special section on meta-analysis. For a general review of meta-analysis, see Green and Hall (1984).

From the foregoing, it should be clear that we cannot present here a detailed treatment of how to go about reviewing the literature. Instead, we limit ourselves to some general observations about the process.

There is no denying that, because of the publication explosion, one can hardly keep apace with what is being published in one's own area of specialization, let alone the broader spectrum of sociobehavioral research. Yet, as we asserted earlier, it is of utmost importance to be familiar, albeit superficially, with what is going on in areas other than one's own. We recommend that you begin by systematically following annual reviews and handbooks in the various disciplines. There are, for example, annual reviews of psychology, sociology, and anthropology. There are handbooks of social psychology, sociology, communication, personality, child development, school psychology, marketing, consumer behavior, to name but a few. In addition, encyclopedias (e.g., of the social sciences, of educational research) can serve as an introduction to a specific area and provide you with some of the major references. Limiting yourself to reading such sources in disciplines other than your own is admittedly not without risks. Simplification, perhaps even oversimplification and distortion, are almost inevitable when one attempts to provide an overview of research in, say, an annual review. It is, therefore, important that you read at least some of the original sources to which a review makes reference. Finally, we believe you will benefit from perusing some major journals in areas other than your own to keep abreast of what people in related disciplines may be thinking and doing about the very same issues in which you are interested.

When reading a report of a study, it is important that you critically evaluate all of its aspects (e.g., the theoretical rationale, the design, the measures used, the analysis, the inferences and implications made by the author). This may lead to "surprising" revelations that authors, even eminent ones, wittingly or unwittingly misinterpret their "findings," utilize scales of questionable validity and reliability, engage in linguistic acrobatics, and the like.

Deficiencies in reviews of past research are due, among other things, to lack of training in this area as well as to lack of knowledge in matters of design, measurement, and analysis. The reluctance to evaluate critically published research tends to increase as a function of the complexity of the design, measures, and analysis being used. Many readers who lack the necessary training read *around* the tables, formulas, figures, and the like. Consequently, they are forced to either accept without questioning the author's summary and conclusions or to reject them. In either case, this is done largely on the basis of irrelevant factors (e.g., the author's and/or the journal's reputation, the consistency of the "findings" with one's expectations or intuition).

PROBLEMS AND METHODS

Many critics maintain that a major cause of the poor state and meager accomplishments of research in the sociobehavioral sciences is the emphasis on and preoccupation with methods at the expense of substance. In an address to the Society for the Psychological Study of Social Issues, Murphy attributed "a large part of our trouble" to the "over-rapid development of research techniques which can be applied to the surface aspects of almost any social response, and are reasonably sure to give a publishable numerical answer to almost any casual question" (1939, p. 114). Murphy went on to say: "Woe to that science whose methods are developed in advance of its problems, so that the experimenter can see only those phases of a problem for which a method is already at hand" (p. 114).

About thirty years later, McGuire (1973), in a wide-ranging critique of the progress of social psychology, depicted much of the research in the area as stage management designed to demonstrate the obvious or the trivial. Among other things, he faulted the training of sociobehavioral scientists, venturing a guess that "at least 90% of the time in our current courses on methodology is devoted to presenting ways of testing hypotheses and that little time is spent on the prior and more important process of how one creates these hypotheses in the first place" (p. 450; for similar views, see Travers, 1973).

In an insightful discussion of the role of methodology in sociobehavioral sciences, Kaplan (1964) drew attention to the danger of techniques determining the choice of the research problem to be investigated. Speaking of what he called *"the law of the instrument,"* he said:

Give a small boy a hammer, and he will find that everything he encounters needs pounding. It comes as no surprise to discover that a scientist formulates problems in a way which requires for their solution just those techniques in which he himself is especially skilled. (p. 28)

Although we have no quarrel with the preceding statements, and although we wholeheartedly endorse Tukey's (1954) dictum that "the important question about methods is not 'How' but 'Why'" (p. 36), we would like to caution against a conclusion that methods are of no use at the problem-formulation stage. The choice of a method (e.g., analysis, measurement) is obviously determined largely by one's familiarity with it. It, therefore, stands to reason that the more limited the researcher's exposure to methods, the greater the likelihood of his or her research being method-driven. Indeed, "the man of one method or one instrument . . . tends to become method-oriented rather than problem-oriented" (Platt, 1964, p. 351). The benefits of exposure to a wide range of methods can, therefore, not be overestimated.

HYPOTHESES

An hypothesis is a conjectural statement about a relation between two or more variables. As in the case of problem definition, given earlier in this chapter, we use the term "relation" broadly to refer to designs in which no distinction is made between independent and dependent variables as well as in ones where such distinctions are made. To clarify our meaning and to demonstrate the correspondence between problem and hypothesis statements, we will give alternative versions of hypotheses corresponding to some of the problem statements presented earlier in this chapter (see Problem Characterization and Format).

We repeat two versions of one of the problems given earlier:

Format 1. What is the relation between mental ability and academic achievement?
Format 3. What is the effect of mental ability on academic achievement?

Consistent with Format 1 and assuming that the hypothesized relation is positive, the hypothesis statement might be: "There is a positive relation (or correlation) between mental ability and academic achievement." An alternative statement might be: "Mental ability and academic achievement are positively correlated." Several points will be made about these statements.

1. There is no explicit distinction between an independent variable and a dependent variable.

2. It is assumed that the relation between the two variables is linear.

3. No mention is made of the measures of the variables. That is, it is *not* stated that there is a positive correlation between performance on, say, the Wechsler Intelligence Scale and on the Metropolitan Achievement Test. Hypotheses should refer to relations among variables, *not* among measures, indicators, or definitions of variables. This point relates to our earlier discussions regarding definitions and measures of constructs, and deleterious consequences of treating measures, indicators, or definitions as if they were the constructs (see, in particular, Chapters 4 and 8).

To further clarify this point, another example will be offered. Suppose that a researcher wished to study the effect of anxiety on fear of failure. Assume that he or she manipulates anxiety by giving different instructions to different groups. Also, fear of failure is measured on some scale the researcher has constructed. Clearly, the researcher is interested in the effect of anxiety, *not instructions*, on fear of failure, *not on a scale of fear of failure*.

4. The hypothesis statement *does not* include any reference to statistical significance. It is *not* stated, for example, that there is a statistically significant correlation between the two variables. The logic of hypothesis testing is discussed later in this chapter. In the present context, therefore, it will only be noted that, because a statistical test of significance is used for the purpose of determining whether or not to reject a null hypothesis (e.g., that the variables are not correlated) at a given probability level, reference to the test does not belong in the hypothesis.

5. The hypothesis stated above is very crude in that the conjecture is only with respect to the direction of the relation between the variables (i.e., positive), without any regard to its magnitude. (An even cruder hypothesis would be one in which the direction of the correlation is not hypothesized. That is, all that would be hypothesized is that the variables under consideration are correlated.) Issues of statistical significance versus substantive meaningfulness are taken up later in this chapter and in various other chapters (especially Chapter 15). For now, it will be pointed out that no matter how minuscule and meaningless, from a substantive view, the relation between the variables may be, the hypothesis may be said to have been supported when the null hypothesis is rejected.

Turning now to Format 3 of the problem statement, the corresponding hypothesis statement might be: "Mental ability has a positive effect on academic achievement." Variations on the wording of this statement are, of course, possible.

Several points will be made with respect to this hypothesis statement and in contrast with the one stated above.

1. Consistent with the problem statement, mental ability is treated as the independent variable and academic achievement as the dependent variable. Needless to say, this is not an arbitrary decision but rather one derived from some theoretical formulation about the process of academic achievement.

2. As with the hypothesis about the correlation between these variables (see above), the present hypothesis is based on the assumption that the regression of academic achievement on mental ability is linear.[5] A major consequence of the difference between the two hypotheses, however, is that, although for the preceding one, a correlation coefficient would be used as an index of the relation between mental ability and academic achievement, for the present hypothesis, the regression coefficient associated with mental ability would be taken as indicating the effect of this variable on academic achievement.

3. The hypothesis is stated with respect to variables, *not* measures, indicators, or definitions of variables (see discussion above).

4. As with the earlier hypothesis, the present one is crude. Notwithstanding the magnitude of the regression coefficient, the hypothesis would be deemed supported, if the null hypothesis that the regression coefficient is zero is rejected. A more meaningful statement of the hypothesis would, of course, be one that specifies the magnitude of the effect of mental ability on academic achievement (i.e., the magnitude of the regression coefficient). However, this is predicated, among other things, on a thorough understanding of the properties of the measures used.

We hope that even the very simple examples of hypothesis statements we have given served to illustrate the role of theory in their formulation and in turn their effects on the design of the research, measurement, data analysis, interpretation of results, and implications thereof.

Finally, some researchers mistakenly think that there must be an exact correspondence between the number of problems and the number of hypotheses. That this is not so will be shown by way of an example. Assume that the independent variable is political party affiliation and the dependent variable is attitudes toward the Equal Rights Amendment (ERA). The problem statement might be: "What is the effect of political party affiliation on attitudes toward the ERA?"[6] If the independent variable consists of only two categories (e.g., Democrat and Republican), then a single hypothesis would suffice. For example: "Democrats are more favorable toward ERA than are Republicans."

Suppose, however, that the independent variable consisted of four categories (e.g., Conservative, Democrat, Republican, and Liberal). Under such circumstances, the problem statement will still be as above. However, the researcher may have several hypotheses regarding differences among the political parties. For example between: (a) Democrats and Liberals, (b) Conservatives and Republicans, and (c) Democrats and Liberals versus Conservatives and Republicans. Such comparisons—referred to as multiple comparisons among means—are discussed in Chapter 19.

The preceding also illustrates a point discussed several times earlier, namely that lack of knowledge of a specific method (multiple comparisons among means in the present case) may preclude the possibility of testing multiple hypotheses or even entertaining them. The same applies, with even greater force, to multiple hypotheses in more complex designs.

HYPOTHESES AS GUIDES AND MISGUIDES

The guiding force of hypotheses in determining what to observe, what variables to relate, how to relate them, is undeniable. Indeed, as Hutten (1962) wrote: "We make hypotheses about what we are going to search for, otherwise we would not find anything" (p. 215). Equally undeniable is the force of hypotheses to misguide by serving as blinders, so to speak, on one's eyes and mind.[7]

---

[5]Of course, linearity should not be assumed. Methods are available for determining not only whether the regression departs from linearity but also the form of a curvilinear regression (see Chapter 18).

[6]Although we are using an example of a nonexperimental design (see Chapter 14), our comments apply equally to other types of designs (see Chapters 12 and 13).

[7]See earlier discussions and illustrations in this chapter, especially Biasing Effects of Theory.

Francis Bacon (1870), whose writings on the philosophy of science in the seventeenth century have had a strong impact on scientists and philosophers of science alike, stated it thus:

The human understanding when it has once adopted an opinion (either as being the received opinion or as being agreeable to itself) draws all things else to support and agree with it. And though there be a greater number and weight of instances to be found on the other side, yet these it either neglects and despises, or else by some distinction sets aside and rejects; in order that by this great and pernicious predetermination the authority of its former conclusion may remain inviolate. (p. 56)

Various scientists have recognized the importance of entertaining multiple alternative hypotheses about a phenomenon of interest. Thus, Darwin kept copious notes of hypotheses and findings that were contrary to his own. Kepler "made nineteen hypotheses with regard to the motion of Mars, and calculated the results of each, before he established the true doctrine, that the planet's path is an ellipse" (Whewell, 1847, Vol. 2, p. 42). Webb and Webb (1968) reported that they "have found it useful, in the early stages of an investigation, deliberately to 'make a collection' of all the hypotheses we could at that stage imagine which seemed to have relevance whatever to the special kind of social institution that we were dealing with" (p. 61).

Chamberlin (1890/1965) proposed the method of multiple working hypotheses as an antidote against biasing effects of entertaining a single hypothesis. In a thought provoking paper, Platt (1964) asserted that a major factor in scientific progress is the resorting to "strong inference," which he characterized as follows:

1) Devising alternative hypotheses;
2) Devising a crucial experiment (or several of them), with alternative possible outcomes, each of which will, as nearly as possible, exclude one or more of the hypotheses;
3) Carrying out the experiment so as to get a clean result;
1') Recycling the procedure, making subhypotheses or sequential hypotheses to refine the possibilities that remain; and so on. (p. 347)

Platt's proposals were made in the context of advanced sciences where strong inference is viable in principle. The situation in sociobehavioral sciences is much more nebulous, partly because of the lack of systematization and standardization of measurement, sampling, and methods of investigation. Nevertheless, sociobehavioral researchers should at least adopt the frame of mind of strong inference by actively searching for alternative explanations of the phenomenon they study. Discussing the construction of social theories and the training of sociobehavioral scientists, Stinchcombe (1968) asserted: "A student who has difficulty thinking of at least three sensible explanations for any correlation that he is really interested in should probably choose another profession" (p. 13).

HYPOTHESIS TESTING

Before discussing matters pertaining to hypothesis testing, a comment about terminology is in order. Some authors use the terms hypothesis testing and significance testing interchangeably, whereas others distinguish between them (see Huberty, 1987, for a discussion and references). We use the term hypothesis testing to refer to the logic involved in the process as well as to statistical testing (see below).

Hypotheses are tested by examining evidence implied by them. Broadly speaking, an hypothesis is rejected when the evidence is inconsistent with it. In line with the earlier discussion regarding falsification and confirmation of theory, it should be clear that an hypothesis cannot be confirmed. Accordingly, *a statement about confirmation of an hypothesis is to be understood as shorthand for a statement to the effect that the evidence did not lead to its rejection.* An hypothesis gains credibility largely when rival hypotheses that would otherwise serve as plausible explanations of the phenomenon under study are rejected.

FALLACY OF AFFIRMING THE CONSEQUENT

Hypothesis confirmation involves what logicians have labeled the fallacy of affirming the consequent. Hamblin (1970) explained the fallacy thus:

The ordinary form of reasoning from *S implies T and S is true* to *T is true* is commonly called *modus ponens*; and the Fallacy of the Consequent is generally regarded as a backwards version of this, from *S implies T and T is true* to *S is true*. (p. 35)

Following (from Cohen & Nagel, 1934) is an example of this type of fallacy:

Suppose we know that *If there is a total eclipse of the sun, the streets are dark* is true. May we then offer as conclusive evidence for *There is total eclipse of the sun* the proposition *The streets are dark*? If we did, the inference would be fallacious. For the hypothetical simply asserts that if the antecedent is true, the consequent must also be true; it does not assert that the consequent is true *only on the condition* that the antecedent is true. Thus the streets may be dark at night or on cloudy days, as well as during a total eclipse. It is therefore a fallacy to affirm the consequent and infer the truth of the antecedent. (p. 98)

Although the fallacy is fairly evident when stated in a format such as the preceding, it is much less so when committed in the process of hypothesis confirmation. Consider the typical strategy: (a) An hypothesis is formulated from which certain consequences ensue; (b) observations are made (data are collected) to ascertain the outcomes; and (c) the hypothesis is deemed confirmed when the data are consistent with it. This inductive reasoning employed in the process of hypothesis confirmation was cogently criticized by Johnson (1954), who also offered some amusing examples of it, among which is the following:

Uncle Heeb became bored with reading about the preparations for the Byrd expedition to the South Pole, especially by the precautions taken against the cold. They were, in his opinion, the silliest lot of men he had ever heard of. He himself had received little formal schooling because he was orphaned during the siege of Vicksburg; but he had tried to make good use of what he had by noticing what went on about him. As a buyer of cattle, he had traveled as far north as central Saskatchewan Province, Canada, and as far south as Old Mexico. The farther north he went, the colder it got; the farther south he went, the hotter it got. Everybody knows that the North pole is the coldest spot on earth; the South Pole must, therefore, be the hottest. (p. 726)

Statistical Tests

Broadly conceived, statistical tests are tools used in the assessment of evidence contained in data with respect to the tenability of an hypothesis under consideration. Probably very few methodological issues have generated as much controversy among sociobehavioral scientists as did the use of such tests (see Morrison & Henkel, 1970, for a compilation of papers on this topic). This is largely due to widespread misapplications and misinterpretations of statistical tests, even to the extent of investing them with what appear to be magical powers. One is, therefore, not surprised when reading Bakan's (1966) assertion that the prevalent abuse of tests of significance "may be taken as an instance of a kind of essential mindlessness in the conduct of research" (p. 436), or Carver's (1978) claim that the use of such tests constitutes a "corrupt form of the scientific method" (p. 378). Depicting misuses of statistics, Andrew Lang is reported to have said: "He uses statistics as a drunken man uses lamp-posts—for support rather than illumination" (quoted by Mackay, 1977, p. 91).[8]

It is not our intention to give a detailed formal discussion of statistical tests. Such presentations will be found in statistics textbooks (e.g., Hays, 1988, Chapter 7; Moore, 1979, Chapter 8). (For an extensive review of issues concerning statistical tests, as well as controversies surrounding them, see Oaks, 1986. For good readable overviews, see Henkel, 1976; Huberty, 1987.) All we will attempt is an overview of reasoning behind such tests, misconceptions about them, and controversies surrounding their use, in the hope of thereby providing a realistic characterization of their role in the context of hypothesis testing.

To begin with, it should be noted that, when people speak of statistical tests they may have different approaches in mind. The two most popular ones are discussed below under: (a) significance testing; and (b) a decision-based strategy. A different approach, referred to as Bayesian statistical inference (Edwards, Lindman, & Savage, 1963; see also, Iverson, 1970; Morgan, 1968; Novick & Jackson, 1974; Phillips, 1974; Winkler, 1972) has been advocated but, for reasons that will not be gone into here, was virtually ignored by sociobehavioral researchers.

Although statistics can be used for descriptive purposes, they are particularly useful for making inferences, generalizations, about a population on the basis of a sample drawn from it. The usefulness of such generalizations has become a truism, and reliance upon them touches directly or indirectly on many facets of our lives. Stripped of surplus meaning and myths surrounding them, statistical tests use sample statistics (e.g., mean, correlation) for the purpose of making probabilistic inferences about parameters (corresponding indices for the population). To be validly applied, therefore, such tests have to be based on statistics obtained from "representative" samples (see Chapter 15). This seems so obvious as to not warrant mentioning (but see comment below).

Assume it is of interest to determine whether two groups (e.g., males and females, blacks and whites) differ (e.g., in mental ability, income, height, attitudes, aggression). If all the people in the populations of interest[9] were measured, it would be a matter of observation whether they differ on the parameters of interest (e.g., mean income). Assuming the populations do differ, it would still be necessary to entertain the possibility that the observed differences are due, solely or in part, to all sorts of errors (e.g., measurement, recording, calculation). A source of error that could, however, be ruled out is that of sampling, because none took place. For a variety of reasons (e.g., feasibility, economy; see Chapter 15), samples are studied, and on the basis of their statistics, generalizations are made to the populations from which they were drawn. It is in such generalizations that statistical tests play a role.

As with most aspects of the application and interpretation of statistical tests, there is by no means agreement regarding the requirement for representative samples. In addition, some authors who argue for the requirement of representative samples maintain, correctly we believe, that statistical tests can be validly applied in situations when no sampling has taken

---

[8]Although Mackay gave references to most of the quotations, he did not give one to Lang's quotation. As frequently happens, it is difficult to establish authorship. A case in point is the following statement in a recent *New York Times* editorial, entitled The Bricks of Scholarship (1988, January 21): "A. E. Housman, the poet and classical scholar, once assailed a German rival for relying on manuscripts 'as a drunkard relies on lampposts, for support rather than illumination'" (p. A20).

[9]Note that it is necessary to define the populations of interest. Is one interested in studying, for example, all males and females in a given city, state, country, continent, the world?

place but when subjects have been randomly assigned to different treatments. (The controversy surrounding the requirement of representative samples is reviewed by Oaks, 1986. See also, Morrison & Henkel, 1970. Randomization and its role in research design are discussed in the next chapter.)

Significance Testing: *P* Values

Tests of statistical significance were designed to serve as an aid in assessing evidence with respect to the probability of it having arisen because of sampling errors, *assuming that the hypothesis being tested is true*. The hypothesis being tested is referred to as the null hypothesis. Although researchers most often interpret "null" to mean "zero" (e.g., no difference between two means, zero correlation between two variables), it actually means the hypothesis to be nullified, rejected, challenged. As is pointed out by many writers, null hypotheses of zero differences or zero relations—"the nullest of null hypotheses," Kish (1959, p. 337)— are in many instances not meaningful, even "preposterous" (Edwards, 1965, p. 402).

THE INTERPRETATION OF *P* VALUES

A *P* value refers to the probability of the evidence having arisen as a result of sampling errors, *given that the null hypothesis is true*. A *P* value that is deemed "small" would lead to the rejection of the null hypothesis. Thus, significance testing is used to assess the evidence against the null hypothesis. This was stated forcefully by Fisher (1966), whose name is most closely associated with this approach: "Every experiment may be said to exist only in order to give the facts a chance of disproving the null hypothesis" (p. 16). Further, Fisher (1966) said: "In relation to the test of significance, we may say that a phenomenon is experimentally demonstrable when we know how to conduct an experiment which will rarely fail to give us a statistically significant result" (p. 14).

From the preceding, it follows that someone (the researcher, the consumer) must decide when a given *P* value is sufficiently small so that an observed event may be treated "not to be reasonably believable. No rule can decide this. The decision must be arrived at under the discipline of a grim personal responsibility. It must rely on an ultimate power of the mind" (Polanyi, 1968, p. 29). Lehmann (1968) suggested that the *P* value be interpreted as an index of surprise. The smaller the *P* value, "the more surprising it is to get this extreme" (p. 43) a result under the null hypothesis, hence the stronger the evidence against it (for discussions of *P* values and suggestions for their use, see Gibbons & Pratt, 1975; Stallings, 1985).

It is considerations such as the foregoing that have led to the recommendation that *P* values be included in research reports. As proponents of this practice point out, it can be easily adhered to as output of computer programs include probability levels for the statistical tests used. Essentially, this approach is followed in most of the sociobehavioral research literature. Most often it takes the form of using different numbers of stars or asterisks to indicate different levels of significance (e.g., one star for the .05 level, two stars for .01), which prompted McDonald (1985) to compare this practice to that of "grading of hotels in guidebooks" (p. 20).

In his most insightful discussion of "What is not what in statistics," Guttman (1981) asked:

How can authors and editors of scientific journals be made to realize that when they fill their data tables with a galaxy of stars, double stars, and even triple stars, they are not testing hypotheses but are merely rejecting statistical inference itself? (p. 26)

Significance testing is apparently so entrenched that even authors who reject it or question the exclusive reliance on it use it themselves. Thus, Mahoney (1976) pointed out:

Even though I am very critical of statistical inference . . . I shall probably continue to pay homage to "tests of significance" in the papers I submit to psychological journals. My rationale for this admitted hypocrisy is straightforward: until the rules of the science game are changed, one must abide by at least some of the old rules or drop out of the game. (p. xiii)

What we find especially interesting is that Mahoney was editor of *Cognitive Therapy and Research* for five years, from its inception in 1977. On the basis of an admittedly cursory examination of the five volumes under his editorship, we could not discern a noticeable departure from the prevailing practices of relying on significance testing.

Indeed, even almighty journal editors seem unable to change the rules of the game, at least so far as significance testing is concerned. Here is what Campbell (1982) had to say on the occasion of his departure as editor of the *Journal of Applied Psychology*:

It is almost impossible to drag authors away from their *p* values, and the more zeros after the decimal point the harder they cling to them. . . . Perhaps *p* values are like mosquitos. They have an evolutionary niche somewhere and no amount of scratching, swatting, or spraying will dislodge them. (p. 698)

Two issues deserve special attention: One has to do with widespread misinterpretation of *P* values; the other concerns the distinction between statistical significance and substantive importance. These issues will be considered in turn, beginning with the former.

MISINTERPRETATIONS OF *P* VALUES

Various writers have drawn attention to what is "perhaps the most important and least understood principle of statistical significance testing" (Carver, 1978, p. 384), namely the meaning of the *p* value with respect to the rejection of the null hypothesis. Cronbach and Snow (1977) stated this succinctly:

A *p* value reached by classical methods is not a summary of the data. Nor does the *p* attached to a result tell how strong or dependable the particular result is. . . . Writers and readers are all too likely to read .05 as *p* (*H:E*), "the probability that the *H*ypothesis is true given the *E*vidence." As textbooks on statistics reiterate almost in vain, *p* is *p* (*E:H*), the probability that this *E*vidence would arise if the [null] *H*ypothesis is true. (p. 52)

Carver (1978) offered the following as an illustration of erroneous interpretation of *p*:

What is the probability of obtaining a dead person (label this part *D*) given that the person was hanged (label this part *H*); that is, in symbol form, what is *p* (*D:H*)? Obviously, it is very high, perhaps .97 or higher. Now, let us reverse the question. What is the probability that a person has been hanged (*H*) given that the person is dead (*D*); that is, what is *p* (*H:D*)? This time the probability will undoubtedly be very low, perhaps .01 or lower. No one would be likely to make the mistake of substituting the first estimate (.97) for the second (.01); that is, to accept .97 as the probability that a person has been hanged given that the person is dead. Even though this seems to be an unlikely mistake, it is exactly the kind of mistake that is made with interpretations of statistical significance testing. (pp. 384–385)

A related misconception is that $1 - p$ indicates the probability of successful replication of the findings in future studies. In other words, the *p* value is erroneously interpreted as the probability of the results having arisen by chance. As Carver (1978), who labeled this the "Odds-Against-Chance Fantasy" (p. 383), points out: "(a) The p value was calculated by assuming that the probability was 1.00 that chance did cause the . . . difference, and (b) the p value is used to decide whether to accept or reject the idea that the probability is 1.00 that chance caused the . . . difference" (p. 383).

One of the consequences of this type of misinterpretation is the treatment of smaller probability levels as indicating greater significance, hence greater confidence, in the alternative hypothesis when the null hypothesis is rejected (e.g., that $p < .01$ is more significant than $p < .05$). When a researcher labels test results as "significant," "very significant," or "highly significant," depending on the level of p at which the null hypothesis was rejected, it is as if he or she assumes that the probability of supporting the alternative hypothesis is equal to $1 - p$.[10]

STATISTICAL SIGNIFICANCE AND SUBSTANTIVE IMPORTANCE

A very common error, committed despite numerous warnings in the literature, is the confounding of statistical significance with substantive meaningfulness. This is probably due to the positive connotations of the word significance. Not only were attempts by various authors to offer a more neutral terminology to no avail,[11] but the situation has worsened considerably as it has become common practice to drop the word "statistical," and speak instead of "significant differences," "significant correlations," and the like. This practice appears to be condoned by various professional organizations as attested to by the format used in their journals. In some instances, authors may even be misled into believing this to be the preferred format for reporting results. Cases in point are examples given in the *Publication manual* of the American Psychological Association (1983), including the sample paper, where the word "statistical" is not used when results of statistical tests of significance are referred to. For example: "The analysis of variance indicated a significant retention . . . " (p. 81). "Type of processor was again found to be significant . . . " (p. 151).

As was indicated earlier, all that statistical significance means is rareness. Thus, for example, to state that a correlation of .02 is statistically significant beyond the .01 level of significance (i.e., $p < .01$) means that, *assuming that the correlation between the variables under consideration is zero in the population* (i.e., the null hypothesis), the probability of obtaining a correlation of .02 or larger in the sample is less than one in a hundred. What is very important to note about the preceding is that it implies nothing regarding the substantive meaning of the correlation. We purposely chose to present a correlation that is close to zero so as to not get sidetracked here by issues concerning the interpretation of the correlation coefficient within a given substantive area (see Chapter 17).

The point we wish to stress is that tests of statistical significance have become a blind ritual, which led Tukey (1969) to urge researchers to refrain from statistical "sanctification" of data. What is essential is to distinguish between statistical significance and substantive importance or meaningfulness of results. Concern with the latter has been discussed variously under the headings of the magnitude of the relation, effect size, magnitude of the effect. These are discussed below and in Chapter 15, where relevant references are also

---

[10]Issues concerning alternative hypotheses are discussed in the next section.

[11]Kish (1959, p. 337), for example, proposed the phrase "test against the null hypothesis or the abbreviation TANH."

given. For present purposes, a statement attributed to Gertrude Stein (quoted by Shindell, 1964) will serve admirably: "A difference to be a difference must make a difference" (p. 30). Interestingly, Huff (1954) spoke of "the fine old saying that a difference is a difference only if it makes a difference" (p. 58).

The idea that findings be examined in light of their substantive importance and meaningfulness is so self-evident that one cannot help but wonder why various authors find it necessary to remind researchers of it. What may be even more puzzling is that most researchers do not heed exhortations to be concerned primarily with magnitudes of effects or relations, and they instead persist in relying almost exclusively on significance testing. This is manifested, among other things, in research reports replete with t ratios, F ratios, probability levels, and the like, often to the exclusion of any descriptive statistics. Even when descriptive statistics are reported, they are most often not interpreted, despite the fact that it is *they* that constitute the results about which the researcher speaks with unwarranted finality of tests of significance.

We believe that there is a simple explanation for this state of affairs. Although the choice and application of tests of significance are relatively simple, a decision regarding the substantive meaningfulness of findings is complex. It requires little training and, in view of the widespread availability of computing facilities, even less effort to obtain a t ratio, say, and declare that the difference between two means is, or is not, statistically significant. However, it requires a good deal of knowledge and hard thinking to decide whether a given finding is substantively meaningful. As this topic is discussed below under effect size, we will not comment further on it here.

A Decision-Based Strategy

In significance testing (see preceding section), an exact null hypothesis (e.g., that the means of two groups are not different from each other) is pitted against an inexact alternative hypothesis. That is, any departure from the null hypothesis is subsumed under the alternative hypothesis that is accepted in the event the former is rejected. Following this approach, researchers run the risk of failing to bear in mind the very important distinction between statistically significant and substantively meaningful results discussed in the preceding section. However, it is probably a failure to bear this distinction in mind that leads researchers to apply this model in the first place.

In the present section, we describe a decision-based strategy for hypothesis testing that stems from the work of Neyman and Pearson. According to this approach, the alternative hypothesis is some exact value specified by the researcher. For example, if, according to the null hypothesis, the correlation between two variables is zero, the alternative hypothesis might be that the correlation is .40. Similarly, when testing the difference between two means, the alternative hypothesis would refer to a specific magnitude by which one of the means exceeds the other.

ELEMENTS OF THE DECISION-BASED STRATEGY

Four elements are involved in this strategy: (a) Effect size, (b) Type I error, (c) Type II error, and (d) sample size. The first three elements will be described and interrelations among the four elements then be sketched to a degree necessary to understand the reasoning behind the present strategy (these topics are also discussed in Chapter 15).

Effect Size.   The notion of effect size was alluded to earlier in connection with the distinction between statistical significance and substantive importance of results. Ideas concerning effect size will be presented here on an intuitive level. This topic is dealt with more formally in Chapter 15 in connection with the determination of sample size. Loosely speaking, effect size refers to magnitude of findings (e.g., a correlation between two variables, the difference between two means).

Interest in effect size implies an interest in strength, importance, meaningfulness of findings. Needless to say, the preceding terms are not synonymous, not to mention the connotations of each of them. However, because they are used almost interchangeably in connection with attempts to define effect size, ambiguities abound. Consider strength and importance. It is possible, for example, for a relation between two variables to be deemed strong and yet not substantively important. The converse is, of course, also true. Moreover, the meaning of the aforementioned terms is predicated, among other things, on one's values, the research context, and costs in the broadest sense of these terms.

It seems trite to state that what is deemed strong, important, and meaningful by one person may be deemed weak, unimportant, and meaningless by another person or by the same person at another time or in another context. Yet it needs to be stated, especially because of various prevalent conventions regarding effect size. These are commented upon below and discussed in greater detail in Chapter 15. For now, the following statement by Bickman (1988), *which was made without elaboration*, will suffice to make the point: "A statistically significant effect is sufficient for theoretical work, but a strong effect in needed for applied work" (p. 68). Although we question the wisdom of this statement and believe that many would, we can well envision researchers using Bickman's statement as justification for their lack of concern with effect size in their "theoretical work."

Probably the most frequent criticism of emphasis or exclusive reliance on significance testing is that little or no attention is paid to effect size (for a critique of medical research on these grounds, see Pocock, Hughes, & Lee, 1987). The importance of distinguishing between statistical significance and effect size will be illustrated by means of a research example as reported on in the popular media.

Under the heading "It Couldn't Hurt," Haberman and Krebs (*The New York Times*, May 19, 1979, p. 12) reported on research supporting the claim of millions of mothers about the medicinal powers of chicken soup, particularly for the treatment of colds. They cited a paper published in *Chest*, a journal specializing in pulmonary diseases, in which Dr. Marvin A. Sackner reported that "fresh chicken soup clears mucus from the nasal passages at the rate of 9.2 millimeters per minute, compared with 8.4 for hot water and 4.5 for cold water." Haberman and Krebs further reported that "a peer review of Dr. Sackner's findings pronounced them 'statistically significant.'"

We do not have the foggiest idea whether the differences are meaningful, especially whether the eating of chicken soup would lead to a greater sense of relief from a cold than would the drinking of hot water. We assume, at least we hope, that researchers in this field can and do assess the meaningfulness of the differences. We would, however, like to point out that the report also states that "It seems that for the chicken soup to work, the patient *must ingest some every half hour* [italics added], since its curative powers wear off quickly." We invite you to ponder whether, in view of the preceding, you would avail yourself of this medicine when you suffer from a cold. Your decision for or against using it would, wittingly or unwittingly, be based on your impression (assessment) of the effect size, of the importance or meaningfulness of the results.

The decision regarding effect size is especially onerous in sociobehavioral research, as the generally crude state of measurement in many research areas renders interpretation of effects (relations) from a substantive frame of reference very difficult. What, for example, is the meaning of a two-point difference on a scale of altruism (or warmth, aggression, locus of control) developed for the purpose of a given study in a given setting?

Even when measures developed by professional organizations (e.g., standardized achievement tests) are used, a decision regarding effect size is by no means simple. Suppose, for example, that one wishes to assess the difference between two teaching methods and that a standardized achievement test is used as a measure of the dependent variable. To be meaningful, the interpretation of the difference between means, say, of groups taught by the different methods, must be made within the context of a host of factors (e.g., costs; demands on students, teachers, school administration, and parents; duration of the effects; effects of the program on variables other than the dependent variable under study).

The fact that an informed decision about effect size in sociobehavioral research is frequently a very difficult, even unattainable, goal has prompted various authors to propose conventional effect sizes. Notable among such authors is Cohen (1988) who proposed conventions for small, average, and large effect sizes for correlations, differences between means, and so forth (see Chapter 15). We would like to stress that we do not fault Cohen—who has made very important contributions in alerting sociobehavioral researchers to issues concerning effect size and statistical power analysis—for offering his guidelines. Commendably, Cohen (1988) acknowledges that "this is an operation fraught with many dangers: The definitions are arbitrary, such qualitative concepts as 'large' are sometimes understood as absolute, sometimes as relative; and thus they run a risk of being misunderstood" (p. 12).

However, it is important to stress that, although *unintended*, proposals of conventional effect sizes tend to blur the distinction between magnitude of effect and its substantive importance. What is deemed "strong" or "large," say, tends also to be interpreted as "important," "meaningful." In addition, as is true of any rule of thumb, conventions for effect sizes have the *unintended* effect of deflecting researchers' attention from the need to come to grips with the problem of what is a meaningful effect size in a given context, for a given study.[12] This at least is the impression we get from reading literature in various areas. Many of the researchers who make reference to effect size (most do not bother at all) appear to believe that, by making some remark about the effect size being "average," "large," or whatever, according to some convention, they have discharged their "duty" in this regard.

As was pointed out above, effect size is discussed further in Chapter 15, where some of the proposed indices of effect size are also presented. In concluding the present discussion of this topic, we would like to stress that knowledge of the subject matter under study, the properties of the measures used, and hard thinking are the most important ingredients for making informed decisions regarding effect size.

Type I error refers to the error of rejecting the null hypothesis when it should not have been rejected. That is, rejecting the null hypothesis when it is true for the population from which the sample was drawn. The magnitude of Type I error is determined by the rejection region, which is a function of the level of α (alpha) the researcher decides upon. In an attempt to clarify this point, various authors (e.g., Schroeder, Sjoquist, & Stephan, 1986) used the analogy of a jury's decision regarding the guilt of a defendant. The assumption that the defendant is innocent is analogous to the null hypothesis. In order to declare the defendant guilty, it is necessary that the assumption of innocence be rejected "beyond a shadow of doubt." In the context of hypothesis testing, the specification of α is tantamount to a

---

[12]In Chapter 5, we discuss similar difficulties in connection with standards of reliability.

specification of "the exact probability of making an inferential error—that is [defining] how big the 'shadow of doubt is'" (Schroeder et al., 1986, p. 39).[13]

Rejection of the null hypothesis leads to the conclusion that the alternative hypothesis is tenable; therefore, it follows that Type I error leads to a false positive decision.

Type II error, symbolized by β (beta), refers to failure to reject the null hypothesis when it should have been rejected, because it is not true in the population from which the sample was drawn. $1 - \beta$ has been labeled the *power* of the statistical test, that is, the power of the test to reject the null hypothesis when it should be rejected. Type II error leads to the conclusion that the alternative hypothesis is not tenable; thus, it follows that it leads to a false negative decision.

RELATIONS AMONG THE FOUR ELEMENTS

The four elements under consideration are interrelated. A selection of any three of them determines the fourth. Thus, for example, selecting α, effect size, and N, determines β and, hence the power of the test (i.e., $1 - \beta$). From the preceding it also follows that holding two elements constant and varying a third will determine the fourth. This is particularly interesting with respect to the relation between α and β. Holding effect size and N constant, an inverse relation between α and β ensues. That is, decreases in α lead to increases in β and consequently to decreases in the power of the test. Conversely, increases in α lead to decreases in β and consequently to increases in the power of the test. Analogous statements can, of course, be made with respect to the effect of varying β on the level of α. What this boils down to is that decreasing the probability of false positive decisions increases the probability of false negative ones and vice versa.

Varying effect size, while holding α and sample size constant, affects β, hence, the power of the test. Specifically, the larger the effect size considered meaningful within a given study, the greater the power of the test and vice versa. This makes sense intuitively, as large effects should be easier to detect, to notice with the naked eye, so to speak.

Varying sample size, while holding α and effect size constant, affects β, hence, the power of the test. Specifically, the larger the sample size the greater the power of the test.[14]

THE DECISION PROCESS

If, in view of the preceding presentation, you are wondering as to how one decides about magnitudes of the elements involved in the approach under consideration, then our major aim of alerting you that decisions are called for has been achieved. Before turning to a consideration of such decisions, several things will be pointed out: (a) Regrettably, the majority of researchers make no decision regarding any of the four elements; (b) some researchers make a decision regarding the magnitude of α, although many of them end up not adhering to it;

---

[13]As an aside, it is interesting to note that the New Jersey Supreme Court ruled 7-to-0 that "Juries deciding whether a convicted murderer should receive the death penalty or life in prison can consider statistics that show whether defendants of similar backgrounds are likely to kill again after long prison terms" (*The New York Times*, June 27, 1984, p. A24).

[14]β can be decreased, hence power increased, by means other than varying one or more of the elements under discussion (e.g., by increasing the reliability of the measures used, improving control over the variables involved). These issues are discussed in Chapter 15.

and (c) whatever the decisions, they are arrived at subjectively (see, e.g., Neyman, 1950, p. 262). This underscores what we said in Chapter 7 and in this chapter regarding the role of the researcher's theoretical frame of reference and values in the research endeavor.

Needless to say, the decision process is by no means simple and straightforward. Consequently, it would be foolhardy to attempt to offer a set of prescriptions. What follows should be viewed as general comments and recommendations the researcher would be advised to consider in the decision process.

We believe the most logical place to begin is to decide on the effect size. In view of what was said earlier, it should be clear that this is also the most difficult decision. Yet it has to be made, even if this entails employing conventional effect sizes despite their serious shortcomings (see above). It is, however, hoped that the researcher who finds it necessary to resort to conventional effect sizes will be cognizant of the need for tempering conclusions and implications reached on the basis of statistical testing.

Having decided on effect size, α and β (hence, the power of the test) should be decided upon. As a result, the necessary sample size is determined (see Chapter 15). Assuming one proceeds in the manner recommended here, are there criteria for choices of α and β? What follows constitutes an answer, in general terms, to this question.

As you undoubtedly know, most sociobehavioral researchers choose α by convention, usually .05 or .01 (see Cowles & Davis, 1982, for a review of the origins of .05 level as a criterion). Although, generally speaking, there is good reason for the selection of a relatively small α so as to guard against false positive findings, blind adherence to convention is clearly unwise. Suffice it to point out that the consequences of false positive findings may vary greatly depending, among other things, on the area of study and the costs (in the broadest sense) involved.

Many authors (e.g., Labovitz, 1968, 1972; Rozeboom, 1960) have spoken against the "sacredness" or "dogma" surrounding the choice of conventional α's and have drawn attention to prevalent abuses and misinterpretations that ensued. Some of these will be sketched now.

The most serious abuse has to do with the rather common practice of not publishing studies in which the results were found to be *not* statistically significant at a conventional α level, which prompted Gurel (1968) to complain "of the fallacy of the .05 as the pearly gates through which we pass from despondency to exultation" (p. 129).

The research literature is replete with charges of prejudice against the null hypothesis (for a thorough treatment, see Greenwald, 1975) or against negative results. Furedy (1978) even asserted that the effects of this prejudice are "every bit as devastating as the effects of racial prejudice on the life of a political community" (p. 169). Without going into the details of the controversy, some of its aspects will be noted.

As has been argued by many authors (see, for example, Meehl, 1967), the point null hypothesis is almost always false. This is why many maintain that failure to reject such an hypothesis is a reflection of weaknesses in the design and/or in the execution of the study (e.g., large Type II errors, errors of measurement, poor controls). It has, therefore, been contended that all one has to do in order to "support" the null hypothesis is to do sloppy research. Do you wish, for example, to demonstrate that boys do *not* differ "significantly" in height from girls? Easy! Take very small samples of boys and girls (e.g., four boys and four girls) and apply a *t* test to the difference between their means on height. The probability is very high that you will have to declare even a large difference as being statistically *not* significant at conventional α levels.

Understandably, it has, therefore, become customary to expect authors who wish to support the null hypothesis[15] to demonstrate that their design and measures are sensitive enough to detect an effect size they consider meaningful. Note carefully the implications of the preceding statement. First, it implies that one is *not* seeking to test the degenerate null hypothesis of a zero difference, a zero correlation, and the like. Second, a meaningful effect size has been specified. Third, α and β have been selected. Fourth, sample size was determined on the basis of the aforementioned decisions.

Rarely are decisions outlined in the preceding paragraphs made by researchers, in private or in public, whether or not their aim is to reject or support the null hypothesis. In the vast majority of cases, the concern is only with the rejection of the null hypothesis. It has been asserted that not only are journal editors reluctant to publish results that are not statistically significant but that, probably because of this, many authors do not even bother to write up such results. This state of affairs is illustrated by the following parable related in a novel by Hudson (1968):

> There's this desert prison, see, with an old prisoner, resigned to his life, and a young one just arrived. The young one talks constantly of escape, and, after a few months, he makes a break. He's gone a week, and then he's brought back by the guards. He's half dead, crazy with hunger and thirst. He describes how awful it was to the old prisoner. The endless stretches of sand, no oasis, no signs of life anywhere. The old prisoner listens for a while, then says, 'Yep. I know. I tried to escape myself, twenty years ago.' The young prisoner says, 'You did? Why didn't you tell me, all these months I was planning my escape? Why didn't you let me know it was impossible?' And the old prisoner shrugs, and says, 'So who publishes negative results?' (p. 121)

That this attitude is probably held strongly by many researchers may be gleaned from the following. In an editorial to the first issue of *Cognitive Therapy and Research*, Mahoney (1977a) stated: "The journal will welcome the submission of negative results from methodologically adequate experiments" (p. 3). Nevertheless, Mahoney (1977b) reported that "negative results manuscripts were sparse" (p. 365).

From the discussion of the strategy under consideration, it should be clear that α has to be decided upon a priori. It is a violation of the inferential model under consideration to first do the analysis and then, on the basis of tabled probabilities associated with a given test (e.g., F ratio), or associated P values reported in computer outputs, to determine the level of significance. Shine (1980), who discussed the fallacy of replacing an a priori significance level with an a posteriori one, goes so far as to state that when a researcher "selects a final value for α . . . he enters into a covenant with the scientific community by which he agrees to reject H_o [the null hypothesis] if, and only if, $p < \alpha$" (p. 332). Replacing an a priori α level by another one is, according to Shine, an "unethical procedure" (p. 334).

It was noted earlier that the concern about the commission of Type I errors is motivated by a concern about possible adverse effects of false positive claims. Of course, the potential for deleterious consequences of such claims depends on their costs in the most general sense of this term (e.g., is the false claim being made with respect to a relatively benign treatment or one that may have harmful side effects?) and should be weighed accordingly in the decision about α.

The costs of making false negative claims (i.e., committing Type II errors) should be similarly weighed (e.g., might the failure to reject the null hypothesis lead to the abandonment of research with a method that appears to hold great promise?). Thus, in certain fields of study, false negatives may be deemed as damaging as false positives (Type I errors) or even more so. Consider medical research: Would it be more harmful to erroneously conclude

---

[15]For discussions of problems in attempts to support the null hypothesis, see Cook and Campbell (1979, pp. 44–50); Cook, Gruder, Hennigan, and Flay (1979); Julnes and Mohr (1989).

that a particular treatment did or that it did not produce serious side effects? Or, to use the criminal justice analogy, is it more serious to jail an innocent person or to free a guilty one? Obviously, no simple answer can be given to these questions. That, however, does not obviate the need to address the issues.

As in the case of α, conventions have been proposed regarding the selection of β. Most authors recommend that a β of .2 be used, leading to power of .8 to reject the null hypothesis at a given α for a given effect size. Discussing decisions regarding magnitudes of α and β, Tatsuoka (1982) advised flexibility "within reasonable limits." To the question "What *are* reasonable limits?" he responded: "Unfortunately there is no answer to this other than 'Let common sense and your set of values be the judge!'" (p. 1782). In the final analysis, then, it is the researcher, guided by his or her values, who must decide what effect size, α, and β are most meaningful within the context of his or her specific study.

You will surely not be surprised to learn that, like significance testing, the decision-based strategy outlined in this section has come under varying degrees of criticisms. Rozeboom (1960), for example, maintained that, whereas this approach suffers from various serious shortcomings, "its most basic error lies in mistaking the aim of a scientific investigation to be a *decision*, rather than a *cognitive* evaluation of propositions" (p. 428). Guttman (1985), who was even more critical, declared: "The idea of accepting or rejecting a null hypothesis on the basis of a single experiment—which is the crux of Neyman–Pearson theory—is antithetical to science" (pp. 4–5).

Incidentally, Guttman rejected the usefulness of statistical tests in scientific inquiry and stressed instead the importance of replication, which is "a major concern of empirical science" (p. 5). The importance of replication is, of course, incontestable. Yet, as is well known, replications are extremely rare in sociobehavioral sciences. Among explanations that have been advanced for this state of affairs is the very low probability that reports of replications would be accepted for publication.

In light of the preceding, it is interesting to point out that, in his editorial at the inception of *Cognitive Therapy and Research* (referred to above in connection with the discussion of "negative results"), Mahoney (1977a) also invited submission of replications, but few were submitted (see Mahoney, 1977b). We believe this can be traced to the education of professionals, especially to the expectation that their doctoral dissertation be an "original" contribution. Although we will not elaborate, we believe this expectation to be ill-advised. In any event, that doctoral dissertations often are not only far from being original contributions but hardly even meet standards of a worthwhile exercise can be verified by anyone who cares to look into this matter.

We believe that we will not be much off the mark, if we said that by now you are probably totally confused by the dizzying array of arguments regarding the use of statistical tests and that you are probably wondering whether they are of any use. As was pointed out, some authors (e.g., Carver, 1978; Guttman, 1985) indeed argued that they should be abandoned altogether. Many other authors believe that, appropriately used and interpreted, statistical tests may serve a useful, although limited, purpose. Thus, Cronbach and Snow (1977, p. 53) maintained that such tests can serve to "discipline" the researcher "and to help readers focus their attention." Edwards et al. (1963) correctly extolled the virtue of the "interocular traumatic test"—attributed to Berkson—according to which "you know what the data mean when the conclusion hits you between the eyes" (p. 217). They added, however, that "the enthusiast's interocular trauma may be the skeptic's random error. A little arithmetic to verify the extent of the trauma can yield great peace of mind for little cost" (p. 217).

We, too, are of the opinion that statistical tests may be of limited use. To appreciate that this is the case, it is necessary to recognize that statistical tests have bearing on only one alternative hypothesis, namely that the results may be due to sampling fluctuations. It goes without saying that many other, more serious alternative hypotheses to the rejected null hypothesis are frequently tenable and need to be addressed, if one is to have a reasonable degree of confidence in one's conclusions. Threats to internal and external validity of studies are introduced in Chapter 10 and further elaborated upon in subsequent chapters. For now, it will only be pointed out that statistical tests address only one of the many threats to the validity of a study (Winch & Campbell, 1969).

Discussing the role of statistics in psychology, Nunnally (1960) offered advice to psychologists that, we believe, bears repeating, because it should be taken to heart by all researchers and consumers of research:

We should not feel proud when we see the psychologist smile and say "the correlation is significant beyond the .01 level." Perhaps this is the most that he can say, but he has no reason to smile. (p. 649)

CONCLUDING REMARKS

We would like to conclude this chapter with a comment on the "obvious" interdependence of issues raised and discussed in it and those dealt with in Chapters 7 and 8. Indeed, we recognize that a sense of circularity is unavoidable when reading these chapters. Suffice it to mention such issues as the relation between theory and facts, concepts and theory, to realize that one cannot avoid being nagged by the proverbial chicken and egg question. Thus, for example, theory determines what the "facts" are, but these in turn are used to test hypotheses derived from theory (see Hesse, 1974, pp. 33–37, for a perceptive discussion of this issue, which has been referred to as the circularity objection). As Harré (1972) maintained: "What we cannot do is describe the world in the absence of any prior understanding of it, and in the absence of any theory" (p. 163). How, one cannot but wonder, does one arrive at the *prior* understanding of the world? Is it conceivable that it is accomplished in the absence of encounters with the world one wishes to describe—encounters that shape one's understanding of what one is attempting to describe?

Addressing the issue regarding the relation between concepts and theory, Kaplan (1964) drew attention to what he labeled "*the paradox of conceptualization*. The proper concepts are needed to formulate a good theory, but we need a good theory to arrive at proper concepts" (p. 53). Is there any wonder that Jones (1974) found that we are caught in "Catch–23"?

In Plato's Meno, Socrates argued that, in order to know something one has to know everything. Barring this, we go on living in a "world of speculation," engaged in what we believe is a "spiraling approximation" (Bridgman, 1959, p. 40) toward the "truth." Could we be all wrong in our views of the universe, in our scientific theories? Of course! However, this is the essence of our all too human condition, and with the poet and mathematician Clarence R. Wylie (quoted by Weaver, 1961), we may declare:

Not truth, nor certainty. These I foreswore
In my novitiate, as young men called
To holy orders must abjure the world.
"If . . . , then . . . ," this only I assert;
And my successes are but pretty chains
Linking twin doubts, for it is vain to ask
If what I postulate be justified,
Or what I prove possess the stamp of fact.

Yet bridges stand, and men no longer crawl
In two dimensions. And such triumphs stem
In no small measure from the power this game,
Played with the thrice-attenuated shades
Of things, has over their originals.
How frail the wand, but how profound the spell!
(p. 113)

Chapter 10
Research Design:
Basic Principles and Concepts

As is true of many of the concepts and terms we introduced in preceding chapters, terms such as "design," "research design," "experimental design," and "survey design" are used differently by different authors and researchers. Some use them "narrowly," almost synonymously with the term "analysis," whereas others use them "broadly" to refer to all aspects of the research, including measurement, sampling, setting, data collection, analysis, and theoretical formulations. Understandably, therefore, books devoted to research design vary widely in topics covered as well as in specific emphases.

As was stated repeatedly in preceding chapters, all aspects of research are interrelated and bear on one another. It is to underscore the role of philosophical underpinnings and theoretical perspectives in the design or evaluation of research that we opened this part of the book with discussions of science and scientific inquiry. Beginning with this chapter, we turn to topics considered fundamental to the domain of research design by many authors and researchers. Specifically, in this chapter we address two broad issues central to any type of research design: (a) Control and (b) Validity. The next chapter is devoted to artifacts and pitfalls in research. Subsequent chapters deal with different types of designs (e.g., experimental, nonexperimental). As will become evident from these chapters, strengths and weaknesses of different types of designs, even the very distinctions among them, revolve largely around issues of control and validity. Consequently, topics introduced in this chapter are referred to and, when needed, elaborated upon in connection with discussions of specific designs in this part of the book as well as in connection with specific analytic approaches presented in Part 3.

CONTROL

A major portion of Chapter 8 was devoted to definitions of variables and to their classifications from different perspectives (e.g., measurement, research). In the context of that presentation, a distinction was made between predictive and explanatory research. Issues pertaining to predictive research were discussed in Chapter 3. In the present and the following four chapters, we focus on designs for explanatory research.

In the broadest sense, explanatory research can be conceived of as an attempt to explain variability of the phenomena of interest (the dependent variables) by attributing it to its presumed causes (the independent variables).[1] It is, however, necessary to recognize that countless variables, in addition to the ones the researcher is studying, may be affecting, to a greater or lesser extent, the phenomenon under investigation, thereby posing potential threats to the validity of findings and to inferences made from them. Anticipating such threats is, therefore, a major aspect of the design and execution of research. In other words, scientists attempt to design and carry out research with the view of ruling out alternative plausible explanations for the findings. It is in attempts towards achieving this goal that the concept of control plays a central role.

Probably the most important sense in which the term control is used in scientific research relates to its original meaning (see Boring, 1954): a check or a comparison. The reason is that at least one comparison is necessary in order to assess the validity of a finding or an inference made from it. This is also why control connotes in the minds of many modern-day researchers and readers the use of a "control group," one that did not receive the treatment being credited with affecting the dependent variable.

The present section is limited to an overview of major types of controls and their roles in the research design. To this end, it is convenient to resort to yet another broad classification of variables, one suggested by Kish (1959, 1975): (a) *Explanatory*, (b) *Controlled*, (c) *Confounded*, and (d) *Randomized*. Explanatory variables are the independent and the dependent variables, that is, the variables that are the focus of the study. The remaining three types of variables, subsumed under the heading "extraneous" (Kish, 1959, p. 329) or nuisance variables, differ from each other with respect to whether and how they are controlled. Various kinds of controls are the subject of the remainder of this section; thus, we will only note here that "confounded" refers to extraneous variables that remain uncontrolled and are confounded with the explanatory variables, thereby casting doubt about the validity of inferences made with respect to the latter. Obviously, one would want to eliminate such variables from the design. How this may be accomplished is discussed below.

When studying a given phenomenon, the same variable may be viewed as explanatory from one theoretical perspective and extraneous from another. This is part of the essence of differences among theoretical orientations that occupied us in preceding chapters (particularly Chapters 7–9). In sum, then, the decision what and how to control is "not automatic" (Kish, 1959, p. 333). Rather, it depends on logical considerations, the theoretical frame of reference, and technical issues relevant to a specific design and to specific types of controls.

Forms of Control

Of various forms of control, we review here: (a) manipulation, (b) elimination or inclusion, (c) statistical, and (d) randomization.

---

[1]As a safeguard against ambiguity, it was proposed in Chapter 8 that the terms independent and dependent variables be reserved for explanatory research whereas the terms predictors and criteria be used to refer to corresponding variables in predictive research.

MANIPULATION

Control through *manipulation* refers to control the researcher exercises in manipulating the independent variables. Examples are choices of types of drugs to be used, or dosages of the same drug; different types of reinforcers, or different degrees of the same reinforcer; different sources of communication; different teaching methods; different leadership styles. From the preceding, several things follow.

First, this type of control can be exercised only in experimental or quasi-experimental research. In fact, as discussed in subsequent chapters, this is one of the characteristics that distinguishes these types of designs from nonexperimental ones.

Second, decisions regarding, say, choice of specific treatments, their intensity and duration, depend on a variety of factors, among which are theoretical formulations regarding the phenomenon being studied, the factors that may be affecting it, expectations regarding the potency of such factors, and costs and consequences in the broadest sense of these terms. We comment on some of these issues in subsequent chapters.

Third, recalling our discussions of constructs, latent and observed variables (Chapter 4), and definitions (Chapter 8), it should come as no surprise that different researchers may resort to different definitions of the "same" variable, or that they may use different manipulations of a variable on whose definition they agree, or that they may claim to be affecting different latent variables while using the same manipulations.

Fourth, an integral part of control through manipulation is uniformity or constancy in its implementation. Examples are calibration and standardization of instruments, equipment, instructions, procedures of administration, and the like used in the process of variable manipulation. Hazards of lack of uniformity in implementation of a manipulation lurk at almost every step of the research. This is particularly true when more than one person administer the treatments or even when the same person does so but over relatively long periods of time. The subtleties of things that may go wrong are so varied as to elude even vigilant researchers with keen minds.

There is, however, another side to this coin, particularly when the manipulation involves relatively complex instructions to the subjects. Under such circumstances, subjects may vary greatly in their comprehension of the instructions. Some may not comprehend them at all. Consequently, whereas the researcher may be satisfied that the treatment was uniformly administered, he or she may be unaware that it was not uniformly received. This issue is discussed in Chapter 11 under Comprehension Artifact.

ELIMINATION OR INCLUSION

Scientists are constantly trying to identify and isolate extraneous variables that may confound the effects of the independent variables. Such variables are then controlled either by eliminating them from the design or by including them in it so that their effects on the dependent variable may be estimated and separated from the effects of the independent variables under study.[2]

By *elimination*, we mean that variables are converted to constants. For example, variables such as noise, lighting, sex, race, socioeconomic status, and the settings in which the study is conducted may be eliminated by holding them "constant." Studying, say, black males, at the

---

[2]Another form of control of extraneous variables, through randomization, is presented in the next section, where we also offer a contrast between it and the forms of control considered here.

same time of day, under the same conditions of temperature and lighting, will convert race, sex, time, temperature, and lighting to "constants." We put the term constant in quotation marks as shorthand for "constant for all intents and purposes with respect to a given variable in a given study." To clarify, let us consider the meaning of holding noise constant. In some studies, this may mean a "quiet" environment in which the people being studied are not distracted by "all sorts of loud noises." In other studies, on the other hand, holding noise constant may require a soundproof room. In short, what is regarded "constant" depends on the specifics of the study. For convenience, we will not continue to use quotation marks around the term constant.

By control through *inclusion*, we mean that an extraneous variable is included in the design so that its potential effects on the dependent variable may be studied. The preceding statement and its implications cannot be well understood without knowledge and understanding of different designs and the analytic approaches associated with them. Some of these are dealt with in subsequent chapters. For now, we will attempt to offer an intuitive explanation through an example. Assume that a researcher wishes to study the effects of different sources of communication on attitude change. Assume also that, within the context of his or her theoretical formulation, the researcher views sex as an extraneous variable that he or she wishes to control. Now, to control sex through elimination would mean that males only or females only would be studied. To control sex through inclusion, on the other hand, would mean to study both males and females in a factorial design.

Factorial designs—how they are analyzed and interpreted—are discussed in various chapters (see, in particular, Chapters 12 and 19). For now, all we will note is that, in such a design, one studies the effects of each of the variables (referred to as the main effects) and the interactions between them, that is, their joint effects on the dependent variable. Referring to the example about attitude change, the researcher will study how it is affected by different sources of communication, by sex, and by the interaction between sources of communication and sex. The absence of an interaction means that the differences among sources of communication are the same regardless of the sex of the people studied. The presence of an interaction means that the effectiveness of a given communication source in changing attitudes depends on the sex of the people being addressed.

The decision whether to control an extraneous variable through elimination or by inclusion has implications for generalizations that may be validly made from the findings.[3] When an extraneous variable is eliminated, valid generalizations may be made only to the level, or category, of the extraneous variable used in the study (e.g., males). When, on the other hand, an extraneous variable is included in the design, generalizations may be made to the various categories it consists of (e.g., males and females). As was alluded to above, the nature of the generalizations depends on whether or not there is an interaction between the extraneous variable and the treatments.

Clearly, controlling extraneous variables through inclusion affords wider generalizability of findings. Inevitably, issues such as availability, feasibility, and costs play a part in the choice between the two types of controls. In addition, the choice depends also on one's theoretical expectations regarding the operation of the extraneous variable under consideration. Thus, for example, when a researcher has a hunch that a variable he or she views as extraneous may interact with the explanatory variable(s), it would be preferable to control for it through inclusion.

Generally speaking, when an interaction is detected, it is more meaningful to conceive of

---

[3]The type of generalizations we have in mind are subsumed under external validity discussed later in this chapter.

the variable in question as explanatory rather than extraneous. Doing this may lead to a reformulation of one's theory regarding the phenomenon being studied as well as to the designing of a new study in which the role of the variable is altered accordingly.

STATISTICAL CONTROLS

For convenience, categorical variables were used to explain and illustrate the meaning of control of extraneous variables. The logic applies equally to control of continuous extraneous variables. A couple of examples will be used in the hope of clarifying the meaning of statistical control. Bear in mind that the purpose here is illustrative, *not* to explain the analytic approaches referred to in the examples.

A prime example of statistical control of extraneous continuous variables is their use as covariates in the Analysis of Covariance (ANCOVA)—an analytic approach presented in Chapter 21 (see also, Chapter 13). For present purposes, it will only be pointed out that, if, for example, it is desired to assess differences among treatments (e.g., teaching methods, therapies) while controlling for extraneous continuous variables (e.g., mental ability, motivation), then these variables would be treated as covariates in the analysis. The purpose of doing this is to decrease the error term, thereby increasing the sensitivity of the analysis.

Another analytic approach designed to exercise statistical control is partial correlation. We describe it briefly in order to illustrate that controls cannot be applied automatically, not to mention mindlessly (see Pedhazur, 1982, Chapter 5, for a more formal presentation of partial correlation).

Essentially, a partial correlation is the correlation between two variables after one or more variables have been controlled or their effects partialed out. This is why a partial correlation is often described as the correlation between two primary variables while partialing out control variables. An example will be used to clarify this.

Assume that one's aim is to determine whether height and academic achievement are correlated. Also, the sample used varies in age from 7 to 15. Because the older the children, the taller they tend to be, and the higher they tend to be on academic achievement, the correlation between these two variables is bound to be positive and relatively high. For that matter, any two variables that are affected by maturation will be highly correlated when the sample of children is heterogeneous in age.

Correlations between two variables that are largely or entirely due to some common cause, or an extraneous variable, are referred to as spurious correlations. In (a) of Figure 10.1, we depict the general case of a spurious correlation between X_1 and X_3, which is due to the fact that both variables are affected by X_2. Referring to our example, X_2 may be age and X_1 and X_3 may be height and academic achievement respectively. To study the relation between height and academic achievement while controlling for age, one can either calculate the correlation between the primary variables within narrow ranges of age or calculate the correlation while partialing out age. Assuming the latter is done, if the model depicted in (a) is "correct," then the partial correlation should be zero or, because of sampling fluctuations, close to zero.

Contrast the model depicted in (a) with the one depicted in (b) and note that the same variables are used in both, except that in the latter, X_1 is said to affect X_2, which in turn is said to affect X_3. For example, X_1 may be socioeconomic status (SES), X_2 motivation, and X_3 academic achievement. According to (b), then, none of the variables is extraneous. We discuss analyses of such models in Chapter 24. For present purposes, however, we would only like to point out that, if the model depicted in (b) were correct, then, in this case too, the

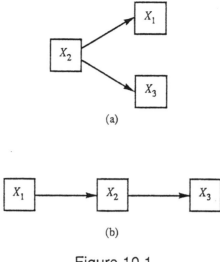

(a)

(b)

Figure 10.1

partial correlation between X_1 and X_3, partialing out X_2, would be expected to be zero. Clearly, however, the two models differ drastically.

RANDOMIZATION

Obviously, the number of extraneous variables that can be controlled directly (e.g., through inclusion; see preceding section) is relatively small. What, then, about the countless other extraneous variables, many of which the researcher is not even aware of, that may cause the things being compared to be unequal or to confound the effects of the independent variables? It is the ingenious idea of randomization that comes to the rescue, so to speak.

While conducting agricultural experiments, Fisher faced the difficult task of "equating" plots of land that may have differed in many ways, some unknown to him. Being concerned about the potential for conscious or unconscious bias if the decision which plots are to be treated with which fertilizers, say, were left to the researcher, Fisher struck upon the idea of leaving the choice to chance. This, in essence, is the idea of *randomization*, which although it may appear simple and obvious, "is one of the few characteristics of modern experimental design that appears to be really modern" (Cochran & Cox, 1950, p. 7). Being constantly amazed by what randomization accomplishes, Zeisel (1985) referred to it as "miraculous" (p. 133).

The reliance on the drawing of lots as a means of avoiding bias, of achieving fairness in the allocation of resources or rewards, in the assignment of duties, and the like goes back to ancient times (for a review and some examples, see Fienberg, 1971). For lack of better alternatives, people appear inclined to let "chance" determine not only who will win the lottery but also who will be drafted, who of a pool of "equally" qualified applicants will be hired, admitted to a selective program of studies, to name but some examples.

Although the concept of randomness appears intuitively clear, it is not easy to define, because it implies a definition of chance. As popularly conceived, random refers to occurrences taking place "without definite aim, direction, rule, or method" (Webster, 1981). In contrast, in the context of statistics, randomness is "attained" by following a careful plan, by resorting to random methods or procedures.

To understand the preceding, it is necessary to distinguish between randomness as a process and as a product. The process refers to the method used to attain randomness (e.g., tossing a coin, rolling a die). The product is, of course, the result. Now, in the context of statistics, it is *not* possible to determine whether a product is random. It *is* possible, however, to estimate the probability of obtaining the product, given the process used to generate it. For example, it is not possible to determine whether an observed result of 60 heads and 40 tails in 100 tosses of a coin constitutes randomness. It is possible, however, to calculate the probability of obtaining such a result, assuming that a fair coin has been tossed in a fair manner.[4]

The concept of randomness plays a central role in research design and statistical analysis. It is the resorting to a random process that justifies the application of the mathematics of probability when making generalizations from sample statistics to parameters, when performing statistical tests of significance.

The use of a random process for the purpose of obtaining "representative" samples from defined populations is well known, as is attested to by references to the use of random samples when survey results are reported in the mass media. It has even become customary for TV stations, newspapers, and magazines to offer a disclaimer to the effect that a nonscientific sample was used when results obtained from a nonprobability sample are reported.

Less well known is the use of random processes for the purpose of controlling extraneous variables, be they viewed as "chance" factors or as the multitude of factors one cannot even enumerate, let alone control for by other means (e.g., elimination, inclusion; see preceding section). It is useful to distinguish between the two uses of randomness by referring to its use in sampling as random selection and to its use for control purposes as random assignment. Random selection is discussed in Chapter 15. Here we focus on random assignment or randomization.

Essentially, randomization is designed to "equate" on all extraneous variables things that are being compared (e.g., groups exposed to different treatments). This is accomplished by using a random process in assigning units being studied to different treatments or conditions. Stated differently, randomization is designed to give each unit an equal probability of being assigned to one of the treatments under consideration. We used the general term "units," rather than persons, because, depending on the design, the units that are randomly assigned may be aggregates of people, organisms, objects (e.g., organizations, classrooms, factories).

The use of mechanical devices (e.g., tossing coins, rolling dice, pulling names out of a hat) for the purpose of randomization comes readily to mind. Yet such devices are not only cumbersome when the number of units is relatively large, they also tend to fail, because of difficulties in mixing well many slips of papers, capsules, numbered ping-pong balls, or what have you and because of potential biases due to the manner in which these are then pulled out from a hat, a drum, a fishbowl.

A dramatic example of this is the 1970 draft lottery, the results of which were challenged by statisticians and others on the ground that the mechanical devices used in the selection of dates of birth for the purpose of determining the order of who would be drafted into the service resulted in a nonrandom selection. Under the banner "Statisticians Charge Draft Lottery Was Not Random," Rosenbaum (1970) described the selection process as well as challenges to it. As to the selection process, it was done by using 366 capsules that contained the dates of the year. First, the 31 January dates were placed in a wooden box. The 29 February dates were then added and mixed with the January dates. The March dates were then added and mixed with those of the preceding months, and so forth. Consequently, capsules for different months were mixed a different number of times. For example, the

---

[4]For illustrative purposes, we assume the use of a fair coin (i.e., a coin for which the probability of coming up head is .5). It is, of course, possible to estimate the probability of the results, given other assumptions (e.g., that the coin is biased; for example, that the probability of it coming up head is .6).

January capsules were mixed 11 times whereas those of December were mixed only once. As to the drawing itself, Rosenbaum reported that the "persons who drew the capsules . . . generally picked ones from the top, although once in a while they would reach their hand to the middle or the bottom of the bowl" (p. 66). Not surprisingly, a systematic pattern emerged, with the likelihood of being drafted being greater for those who were born in the later months of the year.

It is important to address the question of whether a random process could have led to the kind of results obtained in the 1970 draft lottery. The answer is unequivocally yes. Recall the distinction made above between a random process and a random product. It is in the utilization of a random process that we resort to the concept of probability, which refers to the occurrence of events *on the average*, "in the long run"—*not* to a specific event. We are reminded of the anxious patient who sought reassurances regarding the risk of an operation he was to undergo. When, in an attempt to allay his anxiety, the surgeon informed him that the rate of mortality is 2%, the patient asked for an explanation. Whereupon the surgeon said: "Out of every 100 operations, about two patients die." To which the patient responded: "And did the two die already?"

It is the essence of probability for improbable events to occur. As Aristotle (1962), quoting Agathon, said: "We must expect the unexpected often to happen" (p. 43). As any result is probable, the virtue of using a random process is that it justifies the calculation of the probability of obtaining a given result. At the risk of being repetitive, it will be noted that events whose probability of occurrence is very low could have been generated by a random process. However, when one suspects that a given process may not have been random, as appears to be the case in the 1970 draft lottery, one can then calculate the probability of obtaining the specific results, assuming a random process was used. A very low probability associated with the observed results casts doubts about the randomness of the process that generated them. This is what Fienberg (1971) attempted to demonstrate in connection with the 1970 draft lottery.

RANDOM NUMBERS TABLE

Because of the potential problems in using mechanical devices for randomization, it is recommended that they be avoided and that a table of random numbers be used instead. Briefly, such a table consists of integers, ranging from 0 to 9, each occurring with approximately the same frequency but in no systematic pattern.[5] Many statistics books contain excerpts from larger tables of random numbers. Also, many computer packages and even some calculators have routines for generating random numbers. For illustrative purposes, MINITAB will be used to generate 1000 random integers ranging from 0 to 9.

MINITAB

Input

```
OH=0
OUTFILE 'RANDOM';   [Output file name. Manual, p. 273]
RANDOM 1000 C1;     [Generate 1000 random numbers, place in C1]
   INTEGER 0 9.     [Subcommand. Manual, p. 249]
PRINT C1            [Manual, p. 40]
HISTOGRAM C1        [Manual, p. 69]
```

[5]For an extensive discussion of the process of creating a table of a million random digits and the tests used in the process, see Rand Corporation (1955). For a recent description of the use of computers to generate random numbers, see Gleick (1988). In Chapter 15, we illustrate how such tables are used in sampling.

Commentary

See Chapter 16, for a general introduction to computers, a description of the programs we use, and our practice in reporting and commenting on input and output. As explained in Chapter 16, the italicized comments in the brackets are *not* part of the program input.

Output

	1–5	6–10	11–15	16–20	21–25	26–30
1	27454	50023	00605	58575	92104	99587
2	47602	83534	93371	06447	79289	33827
3	04084	18953	40323	47811	57679	43601
4	39953	80203	08453	15107	70244	09696
5	67348	94196	19842	39642	50094	47214
6	74524	49759	12658	22959	26791	83938
7	45683	39192	96268	98312	44852	30895
8	85500	64696	64441	56684	75640	68509
9	14136	63511	03683	35847	69161	89825
10	45814	26417	98936	30387	64399	74921

Histogram of C1   N = 1000
Each * represents 5 obs.

Midpoint	Count	
0	92	******************
1	100	********************
2	97	********************
3	101	*********************
4	104	*********************
5	95	******************
6	101	*********************
7	98	********************
8	103	*********************
9	109	**********************

Commentary

To demonstrate the use of a table of random numbers in random assignment, we report above the first 300 integers generated by MINITAB. Three things will be noted about the output.

1. The numbers are reported in single columns. For convenience, *we grouped them in blocks of five columns and added row and column numbers*. This is how such tables are generally presented in the back of statistics books, but any arrangement will do, so long as one does not introduce a systematic pattern in arriving at it.

2. As explained below, we have underlined certain numbers. In other words, the underlines are *not* part of the output.

3. A table of random numbers consists, *in the long run*, of equal frequencies of the numbers 0 to 9. If we were to report the 1000 integers generated by MINITAB, we would expect each integer to appear, in no systematic order, *about* 100 times in the table. We used MINITAB to plot a histogram of the *1000* integers from which the first 300 were taken and reported above. As you can see, the frequency of each integer hovers around 100.

Assume now that 40 people are to be randomly assigned to two groups (e.g., two treatments, a treatment and a control). First, they are given identification numbers (ID's) ranging from 1 to 40. Second, entering the table of random numbers (see below), the first 20 people whose ID's come up are assigned to one of the groups and the remaining 20 to the other group. To insure that each person has an equal probability of being selected to one group or the other, two digit numbers have to be selected from the random numbers table. Had the number of people to be assigned been greater than 99, it would have been necessary to select three digit numbers. In such a case, a 002, for example, would mean the person whose ID is 2.

Depending on the size of the table, random numbers tables may consist of several, even many, pages and may be variously arranged in blocks. It is necessary, therefore, to decide where in the table to begin, and how to proceed from the point of entry. That is, on what page, row, and column to begin and in which direction to move from the point of entry (e.g., upwards, downwards, sideways). Although there are various ways of doing this, one of which is to select a number(s) randomly to indicate page, row, column, we will not be concerned with this issue here. For present purposes, it will suffice to shut one's eyes and stick a pencil, say, anywhere in the table. We did this and came up with the 0 digit in row 3 and column 12. One can now begin reading two-digit numbers, moving in any direction (up, down, left, right, diagonally) in the table. For the present illustration, we decided to take the digit to the right of the 0 as the second digit, to move downwards in the columns, and to move to the top of the next two columns to the right when the bottom of any two columns was reached.

Our first two-digit number, then, is 03. Thus, the person whose ID is 3 is selected. For convenience, we underlined all the numbers that were selected (the number adjacent to 03, 23, is also underlined, because it is one of the 20 that qualified for the present purposes). Thus, the 20 two-digit numbers underlined were selected to comprise one of the groups, with the remaining 20 people comprising the other. The numbers, in the order in which they were selected, are: 03, 26, 36, 05, 23, 06, 15, 39, 22, 35, 30, 10, 31, 38, 25, 24, 21, 02, 04, 40. Note the following: (a) Numbers larger than 40 were ignored; (b) when a number came up again, it was ignored (for example, 36 came up again when the bottom of columns 14–15 was reached); and (c) when the bottom of columns 18–19 was reached, we moved to the top of columns 20–21. The fact that these columns are in two separate blocks is, as noted earlier, immaterial.

Because of the random assignment, the two groups are expected to be equally distributed with respect to all variables (e.g., sex, race, mental ability, motivation). As discussed above, however (see also discussion of replications below), *this expectation refers to the long run, not to a specific event.* Nevertheless, for illustrative purposes only, it would be useful to demonstrate what is meant by equating the groups on extraneous variables. Assume that, of the 40 people we have used above, 20 were males and 20 females. Also, males have odd ID's, whereas females have even ID's. Note that, of the 20 numbers randomly selected, 9 are odd, and 11 are even. That is, the first group would consist of 9 males and 11 females; the second group would be comprised of 11 males and 9 females. In the present case, the random assignment resulted in *about* an equal number of males and females in each of the groups. An assignment of *equal* numbers of males and females to the two groups will, of course, not always take place.

Although randomization to two groups was illustrated, the same approach is applicable for randomization to more than two groups. For example, to randomly assign the 40 people in question to four groups, the 10 people whose ID's came up first would be assigned to the first group, the second 10 to the second, and so on. The groups thus composed can further be randomly assigned to various treatments.

RANDOM PERMUTATIONS

As was demonstrated above, the use of a table of random numbers for random assignment is straightforward, except that certain numbers selected have to be discarded, either because they are too high for the purposes at hand, or because they have already come up earlier. An alternative approach in which this is avoided is to use random permutations. Permutations are all possible, ordered arrangements of a set of objects. For example, the numbers 1, 2, and 3 can be arranged in 6 different orders, that is, 6 permutations, as follows:

(1 2 3) (1 3 2) (2 1 3) (2 3 1) (3 1 2) (3 2 1)

In general, the number of permutations is equal to $N!$, referred to as "N factorial." For the three numbers considered here, this means $3! = 3 \times 2 \times 1 = 6$. For 4 numbers, the permutations are $4! = 4 \times 3 \times 2 \times 1 = 24$. An unbiased selection is one in which each permutation has an equal and independent probability of being selected. For the three numbers under consideration, this means that each permutation has a $1/6$ probability of being selected and that the selection of each permutation is independent of the selection of any other permutation.

Tables of random permutations are available (e.g., Fisher & Yates, 1963; Moses & Oakford, 1963). Also available are computer programs for generating random permutations of any size needed. For illustrative purposes, we will use MINITAB.[6]

MINITAB

Input

```
OH=0
OUTFILE 'PERMUTE'
SET C1          [See Manual, p. 33]
1:40
END
SAMPLE 40 C1 C2
PRINT C2
```

Commentary

As you can see, the SET command is used to place integers from 1 to 40 in C(olumn) 1. SAMPLE is then used to sample without replacement 40 numbers from column 1 and place them in C(olumn) 2, which is then printed.[7]

Output

```
34 38  4 11 33  1 32 19  5 37 20  7 12  3 17 14 40 39 21 35
27  6 16  8 26 28 29 30 36  9 23 13 15 10 24 22 31 25 18  2
```

Commentary

People whose ID's correspond to the first 20 numbers (the first row) would be assigned to one group and the remainder to the other group.

---

[6]Also applicable is PROC PLAN of SAS (see Chapter 16, for a description of SAS).

[7]The use of MINITAB in this format was described in Minitab Users' Group (MUG) *Newsletter* (July 1988, p. 7). If you are using MINITAB, you will find the MUG *Newsletter* a valuable source of information.

GIVE RANDOMIZATION A CHANCE

By "giving randomization a chance," we mean that a "sufficient" number of replications has to be used for there to be a high probability that randomization has accomplished its task of equating the groups on all variables. Perhaps the best way to explain what we mean is to consider a couple of extreme examples. Suppose that it is desired to study the reaction of two people to different stimuli, and suppose that one of them is male and the other female. Obviously, randomly assigning the two people to the two stimuli *will not* equate them with respect to sex or anything else. Similarly, randomly assigning two teachers who differ in, say, ability, motivation, sensitivity, to use two different teaching methods will in no way enable one to determine whether observed differences among students are due to differences between the teachers, the methods, or both. We repeat: "sufficient" replications are necessary for randomization to take effect. We have placed the term sufficient in quotation marks, because the specific number will depend on a variety of factors (e.g., variability of the people on what are perceived to be important factors relevant to what is being studied, substantive considerations, measurement, tests of significance. Some of these were discussed in Chapter 9. See also, Chapter 15).

However, even when "sufficient" replications are used, the groups may still differ after randomization because of the "luck of the draw," although the probability of this happening is increasingly smaller with increasing numbers of replications. What, then, is one to do when randomization fails? In an attempt to answer this question, it is necessary to consider, first, how one goes about determining whether randomization has failed. It goes without saying that one cannot and need not attempt to determine whether the groups differ on the infinite number of variables on which randomization was expected to equate them. Instead, one would focus on *relevant* extraneous variables. What is relevant depends, of course, on the specifics of the study. Thus, for example, if, for whatever reason, a researcher has decided not to directly control a major extraneous variable, then checking whether the groups differ on it after randomization would make sense.[8] In general, concern about whether randomization has failed is greater when the number of units being randomly assigned is relatively small.

What one does when one suspects that randomization has failed depends on the specifics of the study and on the gravity of one's suspicions. In certain instances, it may be possible to rectify the problem by resorting to "post stratification with respect to known variables and statistical analysis" (Cornfield, 1971, p. 1676). In others, it may be best, when feasible, to go through another process of randomization. Temptations to equate the groups on variables of interest by, for example, shifting people from one group to another should, however, be resisted, as it is never possible to tell what biases, conscious or unconscious, may be introduced in such equating processes. It is because of such potential problems that we resort to randomization in the first place.

Finally, it should be clear that randomization does not eliminate or help identify variability due to extraneous variables. Instead, it is designed to eliminate bias by spreading variability due to extraneous variables equally across groups being studied. Recall the distinction between systematic and nonsystematic variance (see Chapters 2, 4, and particularly 5). Systematic variance in the dependent variable is attributed to the independent variables and to extraneous variables that are controlled directly. Nonsystematic variance is variance at-

---

[8]It is almost certain that groups will differ on any variable. The question, therefore, becomes whether the difference is meaningful, which brings up such issues as effect size, tests of statistical significance, power of the statistical test of significance. These and related topics were discussed in Chapter 9. See also Chapter 15.

tributed to random errors. Variance due to extraneous variables that are controlled through randomization is, in effect, treated as random error. The larger this type of variability, the less sensitive the statistical analysis. In sum, although both direct control of extraneous variables and randomization are designed to reduce bias, the former has the additional benefit of leading to a more precise analysis.

Recommendations

It is recommended that extraneous variables viewed as playing a major role in one's study be controlled directly, as this would lead to the identification and separation of systematic variance in the dependent variable due to them, thereby reducing the error term and increasing the sensitivity of the analysis. Also, depending on the type of control used, one may discover whether the treatments under consideration interact with the variable being directly controlled.

When extraneous variables are controlled by inclusion, as in factorial designs, one resorts to stratified randomization. That is, one introduces random assignment within the strata of the extraneous variable(s). For example, if, in a study of the effects of different treatments, one includes sex as an extraneous variable to be controlled directly, males and females (the strata) are randomly assigned separately to the different treatments.

Whatever the direct controls used, the myriad variables not controlled directly are controlled by randomization, relegating the variance due to such variables to the status of nonsystematic variability, that is, random errors, thereby eliminating confounded variables (see above).

We turn now to a discussion of validity, which, as will become evident, is intimately related to control.

VALIDITY

Volatility of validity classifications, even within the research design context,[9] is best exemplified by the work of the leading and most influential exponents of this subject. Through a series of publications that had a profound effect on sociobehavioral researchers, Campbell and his associates (e.g., Campbell, 1957, 1969a; Campbell & Stanley, 1963; Cook & Campbell, 1976, 1979) expounded on validity and threats posed to it in different research designs. Authors who discuss the topic of validity within the context of research design typically either adopt the formulations of Campbell and his associates or use them as the point of departure. *This is certainly the case with our presentation*, and we would, therefore, like to acknowledge our indebtedness to Campbell and his associates.

In earlier treatments of the topic (Campbell, 1957; Campbell & Stanley, 1963), two types of validity were distinguished and discussed: *internal and external validity*. In subsequent formulations (Cook & Campbell, 1976, 1979), the classification was expanded to four types: (a) *statistical conclusion validity*, (b) *construct validity*, (c) *internal validity*, and (d) *external validity*.

---

[9]See Chapter 3 for a discussion of validity classifications in the context of measurement.

By *statistical conclusion validity*, Campbell and his associates meant the validity of conclusions, or inferences, based on statistical tests of significance. Consequently, their discussion of this type of validity (e.g., Cook & Campbell, 1979, pp. 39–50) included such issues as effect size, Type I and Type II errors, power of the statistical test, "acceptance" of the Null hypothesis. It will be recalled that we discussed these topics in the context of hypothesis testing (See Chapter 9; they are also discussed in Chapter 15, in the context of sampling).

Construct validity was used by Campbell and his associates to refer to the correspondence between a measure or a manipulation and the construct that is presumably being measured or manipulated. Therefore, in their discussion of this type of validity they included *convergent* and *discriminant* validity, and *multitrait-multimethod* approaches (e.g., Cook & Campbell, 1979, pp. 59–70)—topics discussed in Chapter 4. Cook and Campbell included in their discussion of construct validity other topics as well (e.g., experimenter expectancies, demand characteristics). We discuss such topics in subsequent chapters (particularly Chapter 11).

Our own orientation with respect to validity typologies may be easily discerned from the manner in which we have organized our presentation. We felt that a discussion of construct validity is best placed within the context of measurement, especially when, as in our case, an attempt is made to cover this topic in greater detail than is usually accorded it within the research-design context. Similarly, we felt that presentations of statistical conclusion validity belong more naturally in the context of hypothesis testing and sampling.

Accordingly, the presentation that follows is limited to internal and external validity, where we adopt the format used by Campbell and his associates. Specifically, pursuant to a description of the type of validity being considered, some threats to it are briefly discussed. The specifics of what can be done in order to avoid or cope with a given threat to internal or external validity depend on the kind of design used. Therefore, they are discussed in appropriate places in subsequent chapters.

Keep in mind that the list of threats to validity is not exhaustive. In fact, it *cannot* be exhaustive, as it depends on what a researcher suspects are factors that may have invalidated whatever he or she claims has taken place in the specific study involved. The list most authors, ourselves included, present or select from is one comprised of major threats identified by Campbell and his associates. That this is not meant to be a sacred check list, it would suffice to point out that whereas in earlier publications (e.g., Campbell & Stanley, 1963, p. 175) the list of threats to internal validity consisted of eight headings, in later publications (e.g., Cook & Campbell, 1979, pp. 51–55) it was extended to 13. The added threats (e.g., Diffusion or Imitation of Treatments, see below) came to the fore as a result of growth in large-scale research studies (e.g., Head Start) and concerns attendant with them. Other threats to validity may become of major concern, and, therefore, be included in someone's list as a result of specific developments or emphases in some research programs, measurement, analysis, and the like.

Internal Validity

Internal validity refers to the validity of assertions regarding the effects of the independent variable(s) on the dependent variable(s). In the broadest sense, this can be stated in the form of the question: Is what has taken place (i.e., the phenomenon observed) due to the variables the researcher claims to be operating (e.g., manipulated variables), or can it be attributed to other variables? In essence, the validity of the answer to this question depends on the plausibility of alternative answers, that is, alternative explanations. It follows that internal validity is the *sine qua non* of meaningful research.

In view of our discussion of control earlier in this chapter, its central role in attempts to maximize internal validity should be evident. Other things equal, the more powerful the controls one exercises, the more internally valid the study. As we discuss in Chapter 12, the two major reasons why experimental research is generally more internally valid than nonexperimental research is that, in the former, independent variables are manipulated and units are randomly assigned to the levels of the independent variables.

Attempts to assess internal validity involve "a deductive process in which the investigator has to be his own most trenchant critic" (Cook & Campbell, 1976, p. 229). Needless to say, this is easier said than done. As discussed in Chapter 9, the tendency to overlook evidence that goes counter to one's expectations and hypotheses, or to misinterpret, even rationalize, such evidence, is quite common.

We turn now to a description of some of the major threats to internal validity.

History. Subsumed under this heading are events that took place in the course of a study and that might have affected its outcome. For example, suppose that, in the course of a study of determinants of attitudes toward the Equal Rights Amendment (ERA), the legislature passes or defeats the ERA. The internal validity of the study would be jeopardized to the extent that the people in the study are aware of the debate and actions of the legislature and to the extent that these have affected their attitudes. Whether a given event poses a threat to the internal validity of a study depends on the specifics of the study.

Maturation refers to changes that people being studied undergo with the passage of time, including growing older, gaining experience, becoming tired, hungry, and the like. The concern is that responses (e.g., learning, motivation, aggression, concentration) attributed to treatments may be, in part or wholly, due to such maturational processes. It is also possible for maturation to interact with treatments.

Testing. When people are measured several times on the same variable, their performance may be affected by, among other things, practice, memory of earlier responses, sensitization and/or conjectures regarding the purpose of the research and the expectations of the researcher. For example, given a pretest, followed by some treatments, and then a posttest, observed changes in, say, learning, attitudes, empathy, and altruism, may be a consequence of the pretest and/or the interaction between the pretest and the treatments.

Instrumentation. Internal validity is compromised when differences in outcomes of different treatments may be attributed, to a greater or lesser extent, to aspects of the instruments used. This may occur when, for example, measures believed to be equivalent are not equivalent (e.g., they tap somewhat different competencies, orientations, or they differ in difficulty, in appeal). Another example would be cosmetic changes in instruments, which in actuality constitute changes in what they are measuring. A related example is one in which no changes are made in the instruments, but the researchers become more proficient in using them in the course of the study.

Regression Toward the Mean (RTM). Unlike the preceding threats to internal validity, this one is much more complex. In her discussion of RTM within the context of developmental research, Furby (1973) demonstrated that it is not only "often neglected, but it is also seriously misinterpreted" (p. 179), despite detailed discussions available in the literature. Focusing on research mistakes in the sociobehavioral sciences, Wolins (1982) contended that "Regression Toward the Mean Mistake . . . is the most persistent, complex, and insidious of all mistakes" (p. 13; see also Campbell, 1969b; Campbell & Erlebacher, 1970; Wallis & Roberts, 1956, pp. 258–263). In view of the preceding, one is not surprised at Roberts' (1980) assertion: "Perhaps every applied statistician worth his salt has said to himself at some time, 'I understand regression-towards-the-mean; others only think they do'" (p. 59).

A good grasp of regression, measurement, and the relation between them is necessary, although not sufficient, for an understanding of RTM. Consequently, we cannot even begin to do justice to RTM in the present discussion. Our aim is limited to providing an intuitive flavor of the topic within the context of internal validity. Study of regression analysis (particularly Chapters 17 and 18) in conjunction with the references cited in the preceding paragraph is strongly recommended.

In his extensive studies of heredity, Sir Francis Galton drew attention to RTM, or what he referred to as "reversion" or "regression towards mediocrity."[10] As one example, Galton noted that children of very tall parents were, on the average, shorter than their parents. Conversely, children of very short parents were, on the average, taller than their parents. The same phenomenon occurs with other variables. For example, students who do very well on a midterm examination do, on the average, less well on the final. Conversely, those who do very poorly on the midterm do, on the average, not as poorly on the final.

In general, RTM occurs whenever two variables are not perfectly correlated. Assuming, for the sake of illustration, that two variables are positively but not perfectly correlated, then people who are high on one of the variables will also tend to be high on the other variable, but relatively less so. Similarly, people who are low on one of the variables will also tend to be low on the other variable, but relatively less so.

As was noted above, mistaken notions and confusion about RTM are prevalent. Galton's studies, for example, have created the wrong impression that variability of height, say, decreases with time. This has led some people, notably advocates of eugenics, to use RTM to buttress their calls for action to stem the tide of "regression towards mediocrity." The fallacy in this kind of interpretation of RTM is easily exposed when it is recognized that using a regression equation in which the direction of the prediction is reversed (i.e., using the criterion to predict the predictor), it may be erroneously claimed that the converse of regression towards mediocrity is taking place.

To clarify this point, we return to the example of performance on midterm and final examinations used above. It can be shown that students who performed exceptionally well on the final did, on the average, not do as well on the midterm; students who performed exceptionally poorly did, on the average, not as poorly on the midterm. Thus, using performance on the midterm to predict performance on the final would seem to support the notion of regression towards mediocrity—the best students get worse, and the worst students get better. However, using the final to predict the midterm would seem to lend support to the opposite view, namely better students get even better, and the poorer ones get even poorer. The point, however, is that both trends are regression tautologies.

As to the why of RTM, it is convenient to begin by considering the effects of measurement errors (see Chapter 5). For present purposes, it will suffice to note that we are concerned with random measurement errors. Random errors attenuate (i.e., lower; see Chapter 5) the correlation between two variables or between scores on the same variable measured at two points in time. It follows, then, that the greater the random errors, the greater the RTM. This becomes particularly clear when one thinks of people who have extreme scores—very low or very high. For example, on measures of achievement that are not perfectly reliable (none are), very high and very low scores are, in part, due to having an exceptionally "good" or "poor" day, making "lucky" or "unlucky" guesses, and the like. Consequently, one would expect people who did extremely well or extremely poorly to be, on the average, closer to the mean when they are measured a second time. The same reasoning applies when measures on

---

[10]The symbol r for the correlation coefficient has its origin in the term "reversion." For some historical notes regarding regression theory, see Roberts (1980).

two different variables are given at the same time. People whose extreme scores on one of the variables is due, in part, to large random errors would not be expected to have the same magnitude of random errors in the same direction on the other variable, assuming one is dealing with positively correlated variables.

Most discussions of RTM explain it solely with reference to errors of measurement. However, to repeat, RTM occurs whenever two variables are not perfectly correlated. When two errorless variables are not perfectly correlated, it follows that scores on each are, loosely speaking, comprised in part of elements or factors common to the two variables, and in part of elements or factors unique to each variable. Now, people who score at the extremes of one variable do so, in part, because of a rare combination of factors that is not expected to be repeated when the other variable is being measured.

In the context of RTM, measurement errors "can be considered as just a specific case of the more general 'factors determining a score'" (Furby, 1973, p. 175) explanation. In sum, RTM occurs when the correlation between two variables is not perfect, which may be due to measurement errors and/or factors or elements unique to each of the variables.

From the preceding discussion, it follows that threats to internal validity from RTM are particularly critical when people are chosen for study because of their extreme standing on some variable (reading, aggression), as in the case of compensatory programs (e.g., for educationally disadvantaged, chronic juvenile offenders, recidivists). Under such circumstance, observed improvements on a posttest (e.g., in reading) may be in part, or even all, due to RTM. Not surprisingly, controversies regarding biasing effects of RTM have been particularly intense in connection with compensatory programs.

Tversky and Kahneman (1974; see also, Kahneman & Tversky, 1973) drew attention to "pernicious consequences" of "failure to recognize the import of regression" (p. 1127) that is "all about us" (Kahneman & Tversky, 1973, p. 249). As one of their illustrations, they related how flight instructors concluded that "verbal rewards are detrimental to learning, while verbal punishments are beneficial" (p. 1127). As evidence, the instructors pointed out that praise for an exceptionally good landing was generally followed by a poorer landing, whereas harsh criticism of an extremely poor landing was generally followed by a smoother landing. Kahneman and Tversky (1973) observed:

This true story illustrates a saddening aspect of the human condition. We normally reinforce others when their behavior is good and punish them when their behavior is bad. By regression alone, therefore, they are most likely to improve after being punished and most likely to deteriorate after being rewarded. (p. 251)

Selection refers to the process used in assigning individuals (or other units) to different treatments or control groups. The crucial role of randomization in equating groups probabilistically was discussed earlier in this chapter. For a variety of reasons (see Chapter 13), experiments are often conducted with preexisting groups or when the assignment of units to treatments is nonrandom. In such designs, referred to as quasi-experiments, threats to internal validity loom large. Because it is impossible to determine and take into account all the relevant variables on which the groups differ *prior* to the administration of the treatments, it is extremely difficult, some say impossible, to tell whether observed differences among groups on the dependent variable are due to the treatments, to prior differences among the groups, a combination of the two, or interactions between treatments and variables on which the groups differed prior to the administration of the treatments. We return to these issues in Chapter 13, where we comment on designs with nonequivalent groups as well as on selectivity bias.

Mortality refers to attrition of people or other units in the course of the study. This is particularly prone to happen when the study is of relatively long duration. People may drop out, rats may die, and organizations may withdraw or even cease to exist. Unless it is assumed that mortality is due to a random process—a highly untenable assumption in most instances—it is clear that it vitiates the effects of randomization. Mortality may be characterized as a self-selection process, the reasons for which are generally very difficult, if not impossible, to discern. The people who drop out are often of no help in this matter, not only because they may refuse to respond to the researcher's queries about their motives for dropping out, but also because they may conceal their motives, or they may be unsure about them, not to mention being unconscious of them.

Diffusion or Imitation of Treatments.   When people who are exposed to a given treatment or who serve as controls can learn about another treatment *not* meant for them (e.g., through communication with those exposed to such a treatment or from reports in the media), they may, if they deem it desirable, and when feasible, avail themselves of the treatment (e.g., adopt an experimental teaching method, use medication and/or a diet whose effects are being studied). At the very least, knowledge about other treatments may affect people's responses to a treatment meant for them or alter their behavior when they are meant to serve as controls (see below). Diffusion of information may invalidate, generally to an unknown extent, comparisons among groups for the purpose of assessing treatment effects.

Compensatory Rivalry or Resentful Demoralization.   These are two kinds of effects that diffusion of information about the different treatments in a study may have. When people are exposed to a treatment that is, or that they perceive as, less desirable than other treatments, they may engage in compensatory rivalry. They may, for example, work harder, be more punctual, be more sensitive to needs of subordinates, cut down on absenteeism, study harder, or do whatever it is they feel it takes to counteract the expected superiority of the more desirable treatments. The same may hold true for people in a control group, particularly when they believe that demonstrated success of a treatment will adversely affect their working conditions, careers, or whatever may be at stake. Cook and Campbell (1979) cited Saretsky (1972) as offering several examples of controls exerting special efforts and as labeling this phenomenon a "'John Henry effect' in honor of the steel driver who, when he knew his output was to be compared to that of a steam drill, worked so hard that he outperformed the drill and died of overexertion" (p. 55).

Instead of engaging in compensatory rivalry, groups receiving less desirable treatments or no treatment may, as a result of becoming resentful and demoralized, perform more poorly than they normally do. Clearly, internal validity may be seriously compromised when this occurs.

INTERNAL VALIDITY: CONCLUDING REMARKS

In conclusion, we would like to reiterate that the list of threats given above is not exhaustive. Also, internal validity may be threatened from more than one source. Depending on the specifics of a study, several threats may operate simultaneously. Threats may also interact with one another and/or with treatments, rendering interpretations of results almost impossible.

Finally, we would like to repeat that *the distinction among different types of validity should not be overstated.* Many of the threats discussed below under external validity could also have been discussed under internal validity. For example, Multiple-Treatments Interference (see below) may also pose potential threats to internal validity. To underscore the hazards of overstating distinctions among the different types of validity, it will be pointed out that some of the threats that we and other authors (e.g., Bracht & Glass, 1968) discussed under the heading of external validity, Cook and Campbell (1979) and others discussed under the heading of construct validity. We return to issues concerning relations among different types of validity in the concluding section of this chapter.

External Validity

External validity refers to generalizability of findings *to* or *across* target populations, settings, times, and the like. Before turning to these two types of generalizations, it will be noted that internal validity is a necessary, although not sufficient, condition for external validity. Clearly, when internal validity of a study is in doubt, it makes little sense to inquire *to* what, or *across* what, are its findings generalizable. Also, because external validation entails inductive inference, it "is inherently more problematic than even internal validity whose bases are more obviously deductive" (Cook & Campbell, 1979, p. 86).

The term *generalizing to* concerns validity of generalizations from samples to populations of which the samples are presumably "representative." Consequently, whatever the target population (e.g., people, times, settings), the validity of this type of generalization is predicated on the sample-selection procedures. In Chapter 15, we discuss the distinction between probability and nonprobability, or judgment, sampling and present selected probability sampling approaches. For now, therefore, we will only note that because sampling errors cannot be estimated for judgment sampling, inferences based on it are speculations, no matter how sophisticated, and hence constitute the converse of sampling, that is, "populationing" (Ackoff, 1953, pp. 121–123).

Generalizing across concerns the validity of generalizations *across* populations. For example, results obtained with a sample from a given population (e.g., males, blacks, blue-collar workers) are generalized to other populations (e.g., females, whites, white-collar workers), or results obtained in one setting (e.g., classroom, laboratory) are generalized to another setting (e.g., playground).

As Cook and Campbell (1979, p. 72) pointed out, although the distinction between the two types of generalizations is "useful," it should not be "overstressed," as generalizing *across* "logically presupposes" (p. 72) validity of generalizing *to*. Yet Cook and Campbell not only noted that some researchers and authors have been concerned primarily with one type of generalization or the other, but they themselves have chosen to concentrate on threats to the validity of generalizations *across*. Essentially, they reasoned that probability sampling is uncommon in field research and that, therefore, "strict generalizing to targets of external validity is rare" (Cook & Campbell, 1979, p. 73). Contending, further, that, even when one begins with a probability sample, "attrition is almost inevitable" (p. 73) and may render initial sampling useless, they concluded: "A case can be made, therefore, that external validity is enhanced more by a number of smaller studies with haphazard samples than by a single study with initially representative samples if the latter could be implemented" (p. 73). However, they reminded the reader that people or settings in haphazard samples being studied should belong to the classes of people or settings to which one wishes to generalize.

If the preceding left you uncomfortable, even confused, then we have accomplished our aim of alerting you to the fact that generalizations across populations cannot be codified. Although we discuss below some major threats to external validity, these are *not* meant to serve as a check list but as general ideas that will, we hope, stimulate your thinking when you are concerned with generalizations, be they from your own research findings or from those of others.

Earlier treatments of external validity (e.g., Campbell & Stanley, 1963) were far less detailed than those of internal validity. Perhaps this was, in part, due to (a) the greater difficulty of delineating the various things that can go wrong with the former as compared to the latter, and (b) internal validity being a necessary condition for external validity. Be that as it may, other authors have extended the treatment of external validity. Notable among these are Bracht and Glass (1968), who offered a detailed discussion of external validity under two broad headings: *population validity* and *ecological validity*.[11] In what follows, we borrow primarily from Bracht and Glass (1968) and from Cook and Campbell (1979).

THE MEANING OF INTERACTION: A REMINDER

Many of the threats to external validity can be best understood when cast in the form of an interaction—an intuitive explanation of which was given earlier in this chapter (for detailed discussions of interaction, see Chapters 20 and 21). Thus, when it is concluded that treatments, or independent variables, interact with attributes of the people being studied or the settings, to name but two factors, generalizations are limited accordingly. For example, when modes of communication interact with race of the receiver of the communication, a blanket statement about the effects of the modes of communications is inappropriate. Instead, it is necessary to specify the effects of each mode of communication for a given racial group.

Treatments-Attributes Interaction.   We use the term attribute in a general sense to refer to variables on which the people studied may differ (e.g., sex, education, personality characteristics). When the goal is to generalize *across* levels of attribute variables, it is necessary that they be included in the design. Generalizations across levels of an attribute may be made when it does not interact with the treatments. When, on the other hand, an interaction is detected, generalizations have to be qualified accordingly (see Chapters 12, 20, and 21 for interpretations of interactions).

Treatments-Settings Interaction.   Settings refer to the environments in which a study is conducted. Distinctions among settings may vary from "narrow" (e.g., a laboratory experiment conducted in a school or a factory) to "broad" (e.g., an experiment conducted in a laboratory as contrasted with one conducted in the field). We inserted narrow and broad in quotation marks to indicate that distinctions among the same settings may be viewed as narrow or broad, depending on the specific phenomenon being studied, the theoretical expectations, the kind of treatments, to name but some of the major factors.

Setting is discussed in Chapter 12 in connection with attempts to distinguish between laboratory and field experiments. For now, therefore, we will only note that a treatment–setting interaction places limits on the generalizability of findings.

Multiple-Treatment Interference refers broadly to research in which subjects are administered more than one treatment or when the same people participate in more than one experiment. Referring to the first situation, treatments administered simultaneously may interact with each other. Alternatively, when treatments are administered sequentially, they

---

[11]For a five-category classification of threats to external validity within the context of evaluation research, see Bernstein, Bohrnstedt, and Borgatta (1975).

may have what are referred to as crossover effects. That is, treatments administered at earlier stages of the study may affect the performance of those administered at later stages (see, for example, Cox, 1958, Chapter 13; Fleiss, 1986, Chapter 10). In either case, generalizations to field settings, in which single treatments are generally used, are questionable.

The second situation refers to the broad distinction between naive and experienced subjects—the former having little or no experience as subjects in scientific research; the latter having been subjects in multiple studies. Experienced subjects tend to be "research wise" not only because of having taken part in multiple studies but also because of the likelihood of having been debriefed at the conclusion of studies in which they participated. Although the nature of debriefings necessarily vary, chances are that, in the course of several debriefings, subjects would be informed of, perhaps even be invited to discuss, research aspects such as deception, concealment, the use of stooges. Clearly, such experiences are bound to affect their behavior and responses when they serve as subjects in some subsequent study.

Pretest Sensitization.   In various situations, particularly when the researcher wishes to measure the effects of treatments in changing some dependent variable (e.g., attitudes, achievement, motivation, anxiety), subjects are measured prior to the administration of the treatments. Our concern here is not with the very complex problems attendant with measurement of change (see Chapters 13 and 21) but with the effects a pretest may have on the behavior and responses of the subjects. Exposure to a pretest may interact with the treatments or may even be the sole cause of observed changes on some measure of interest. For example, measuring subjects' attitudes toward China prior to subjecting them to a treatment designed to change their attitude toward China (e.g., showing them a film about China) may not only sensitize them to respond differently to the treatment but also affect their responses to the measure of attitudes toward China administered subsequently.

It is clear that, depending on its nature and magnitude, pretest sensitization may render invalid generalization about the effect of a treatment in situations in which a pretest is not used. In most instances, it is the application of a treatment without a pretest that is of interest, because this is what takes place in field applications. For a detailed discussion and a review of studies dealing with pretest sensitization, see Lana (1969). We return to pretest sensitization in Chapter 12, where we discuss examples of designs in which its effects may be assessed.

Posttest Sensitization.   When an experiment is conducted for the purpose of assessing the effect(s) of a treatment(s), it is necessary to obtain some index of the phenomenon that is presumably affected in order to determine magnitudes of differences among treatments (or a treatment and a control) and also whether the differences are statistically significant. Most often this is accomplished by administering some post-treatment measure(s).

When, on the basis of the analyses performed on the posttest measure(s), a treatment is chosen to be implemented, it is generally used without resorting to postmeasures. For example, an experiment may have been conducted to study the effects of different formats for the advertisement of a product and posttests used to determine which of them is most effective. However, when, on the basis of the results of the experiment a given format is chosen, it is generally used (e.g., on TV, in newspapers) without any posttest measures. As Bracht and Glass (1968) pointed out, when a treatment effect is latent or incomplete, the administration of a posttest to measure its effect may sensitize subjects, thereby leading to responses that the treatment by itself would not have elicited. When this happens, external validity of the findings is jeopardized.

EXTERNAL VALIDITY: CONCLUDING REMARKS

When we began the discussion of external validity, we said that our purpose was not to provide an exhaustive list of threats to it. It should be clear by now that such a list cannot be compiled. Questions regarding specific threats to external validity depend on the specifics of a study and the kind of generalizations the researcher wishes to make. Moreover, although it was convenient to discuss different kinds of threats to external validity separately, it should be borne in mind that various threats may interact.

Further, threats listed under external validity may also pose threats to other types of validity. For example, although samples of convenience jeopardize external validity, they may also jeopardize the internal validity of studies. The foregoing concerns serve as a prelude to our concluding discussion in which we address issues of relations among different types of validity as well as the debate surrounding hierarchies and priorities among them.

Relations and Priorities Among Validity Types

It will be recalled that our treatment of validity in this chapter was limited to two of the four types—internal and external. The other two—statistical conclusion and construct—were dealt with in other chapters. Various authors (e.g., Cook & Campbell, 1979, pp. 80–82; Judd & Kenny, 1981, pp. 42–44) drew attention to relations and conflicts among different validity types. For example, in the interest of maximizing statistical conclusion and internal validity, the researcher would be well advised to maximize homogeneity of participants, settings, times, and the like. However, increases in statistical conclusion and internal validity that may, thus, ensue would be at the expense of external validity, that is, in limiting generalizability.

This raises the issue of priorities among different validity types. Decisions regarding such priorities can be viewed as instances of the countless decisions a researcher has to make when designing a study—balancing, in the process, such factors as aims, costs, and consequences of the research. Some authors have, however, elevated priorities among validity types to a philosophical plane.

Broadly speaking, two schools of thought may be identified. According to one school of thought, priorities among validity types are predicated on the kind of research being contemplated. The other school of thought rejects the notion of priorities among validity types. Some authors (e.g., Olson & Peter, 1984) even questioned the merit of validity types classifications altogether.

Authors who proposed priorities among validity types did so explicitly or implicitly with the distinction between basic and applied research in mind (see Chapter 7). Thus, when they discussed issues of priorities among validity types, Cook and Campbell (1979) stated: "For investigators with theoretical interests our estimate is that the types of validity, in order of importance, are probably internal, construct, statistical conclusion, and external validity" (p. 83). In contrast, "the priority ordering for many applied researchers is something like internal validity, external validity, construct validity of the effect, statistical conclusion validity, and construct validity of the cause" (p. 83).

Judd and Kenny (1981), on the other hand, maintained that, although priorities among validity types for laboratory experiments "have been established by a research tradition" (p. 44), this is not the case for applied research. They further contended that the applied researcher faces greater conflicts than does the laboratory researcher, because all the validity types are likely to claim the former's attention. Judd and Kenny "[took] no final position concerning which of these claims should be heeded most closely" (p. 44).

CONCLUDING REMARKS

Two major constituents of research design—control and validity—were introduced in this chapter. As was stated several times in the course of the presentation, various issues alluded to in the present chapter we elaborate upon in subsequent chapters in the context of specific research designs and/or specific analytic techniques. Before turning to specific research designs, however, we address in the next chapter some major potential sources of invalidity not dealt with in the present one.

Chapter 11
Artifacts and Pitfalls in Research

A major portion of the preceding chapter was devoted to potential threats to internal and external validity of research. The present chapter also deals with this broad topic, except that the focus is on artifacts and pitfalls emanating from the participants (i.e., researcher and subject). We realize that you may think that we dwell too much on things that may go wrong in sociobehavioral research. Yet becoming aware of what may go wrong is essential for planning and execution of research as well as for interpretation of results, be they one's own or those of others.

The issues dealt with in this chapter were, until recently, ignored or glossed over by sociobehavioral scientists, largely because of naive notions about objectivity of researchers and passivity of subjects. Attesting to the growing concern about artifacts and pitfalls emanating from research participants is an extensive literature addressed to such broad aspects as the social nature of research (e.g., Brenner, 1981b; Brenner, Marsh, & Brenner, 1978; Friedman, 1967; Wuebben, Straits, & Schulman, 1974a); research with human subjects (e.g., Adair, 1973; Barber, 1976; Silverman, 1977); experimenter effects (e.g., Rosenthal, 1966); and general treatises on artifacts and pitfalls (e.g., Barber, 1976; Rosenthal & Rosnow, 1969a).

Adair (1973) raised the question: "For scientific purposes, which view of the experiment is more valid, the subject's or the experimenter's?" (p. 21). We believe the issue is not which view is more valid but rather that there *are two views*: the researcher's and the subject's. *Both* are engaged in an ongoing perceptual process that is shaped by their differing perspectives, roles, backgrounds, expectations, and events occurring in the course of the conduct of the study, to name but some of the factors.

The two perceptual processes are not independent. For example, a subject may perceive the experimenter as being deceitful. This may affect the subject's behavior, attitude, responses to the experimenter, including deception. These in turn would affect the experimenter's perception of the subject, probably leading to some conscious or unconscious changes in the experimenter's behavior. These would then affect the subject's perception, which would . . . .

The preceding is admittedly a rather lame attempt to convey some of the complexity of perceptual processes that may take place in the course of a study. Obviously, we cannot address here the extremely complex phenomena of perception, its antecedents and its effects. Philosophers as well as sociobehavioral scientists have been grappling with these issues from a wide array of theoretical frameworks (see, for example, Allport, 1955; Ross & Fletcher, 1985).

It should be clear that the perceptual processes with which we are concerned are *not* limited to experiments. They occur to a greater or lesser degree in all research with humans. For example, when, in a nonexperimental study, data are collected through interviews, both interviewer and interviewee are engaged in perceptual processes, which include perceptions of each other as well as the setting, what is being said and how, and the like (see Chapter 6). Accordingly, when we use examples within a given context (e.g., an experiment), it should be understood that the points made apply in a general sense to other contexts as well.

What follows is but an outline of some major artifacts and pitfalls, organized under two main headings: (a) Subject, and (b) Researcher. A third, equally important source of potential artifacts and pitfalls, namely setting (e.g., laboratory, factory, classroom) is not dealt with here, because we felt it more meaningful to address it in connection with the different types of designs (see especially Chapter 12).

SUBJECT

Presaging current concerns about artifacts and pitfalls emanating from subjects, Rosenzweig (1933) stated:

But when one works with human materials one must reckon with the fact that everyone is a psychologist. How many subjects in a psychological experiment are purely receptive? How many are willing fully to adopt the humble role of subject in an investigation of their motives, aims and thoughts? Most, as a matter of fact, are carrying on a train of psychological activity that is rather about the experiment than a part of it by intention of the Er [Experimenter]. "Where did I see that man before?—What is he getting at anyhow?—I wonder if he will ask me about this?—I won't tell him about that.—Could H. have been here for the same test?—How stupid that experimenter looks!—What a loud necktie!—How stupid he must think I am!—When will this be over?" (p. 342)

Suffice it to note that not only does the subject's background, in the broadest sense of this term (e.g., sex, race, education, experience, personality, attitudes toward scientific inquiry, motivation, anxiety), affect his or her perception of the study and his or her role in it, but so do also myriad factors associated with the setting and the researcher (e.g., whether a treatment is administered individually or in a group; the status, personality, and behavior of the researcher; the instructions; the nature of the task). In short, the subject is engaged in an ongoing process of defining the situation that, among other things, determines the role(s) he or she assumes.

ROLES

An extensive literature exists about subject roles in scientific research. Different terms have sometimes been used by different authors to refer to the same or very similar roles. Following Weber and Cook (1972), who offered a thorough review of this literature (for other reviews, see Adair, 1973; Silverman, 1977), we discuss "the good subject, the faithful subject, the negativistic subject, and the apprehensive subject" (p. 274).

The "Good" Subject.   Orne (1962, 1969) offered insightful portrayals of the good subject who holds science and experimentation in high regard, and attempts to act in a manner that will confirm what he or she perceives the experimenter's hypothesis to be. The good subject is willing to comply with almost any request by the experimenter, regardless of how bizarre or dangerous it may appear, because he or she believes that, being part of an experiment, not only is there a good reason for the request but also that the experimenter will not ask him or her to do anything that is harmful to oneself or to others.

The good subject takes great pains not to spoil the experiment. In order to be in a position to help *"validate the experimental hypothesis"* (Orne, 1962, p. 778), it is necessary that he or she know the hypothesis. The fact that researchers frequently attempt to conceal their hypotheses does not prevent subjects from attempting to guess what they might be. Among other things, they do this by (a) interpreting explicit and implicit instructions, (b) attending to verbal and nonverbal cues emitted by the experimenter and/or by fellow participants, and (c) taking notice of specific aspects and characteristics of the settings. Orne (1962, 1969) coined the term *"demand characteristics of the experimental situation"* (1962, p. 779)—"demand characteristics" in short—to refer to "the totality of cues which convey an experimental hypothesis to the subject" (p. 779) and function as "significant determinants" (p. 779) of his or her behavior.

An early example of the good—nay, *benevolent*—subject who is not only willing to perform under what will surely strike many a reader as bizarre circumstances but is also probably making every effort to support what appeared to be the researcher's hypothesis comes from a study of the effects of distraction on higher thought processes (Hovey, 1928). As part of the directions for a measure of mental ability, subjects "were told that there would be distractions and that they were to do their best regardless" (p. 586). Here is how the author described the distractions.

One professor and 8 advanced students in psychology assisted. The first took charge of the testing. Four of the students assisted in the operation of the mechanical distractors. The other 4 students served as distractors themselves by performing specified stunts. The distractors used were: 7 bells and 5 buzzers; 5500-watt spotlight; 90,000-volt rotary spark gap; phonograph; two adjustable organ pipes and three metal whistles, 14, 24, and 26 in. long; 55-pound circular saw (36 in. in diam.) mounted on a wooden frame; mounted camera operated by a well known photographer; and the four students performing stunts. (pp. 586–587)

Hovey (1928), who pointed out that "several distractors were often used simultaneously" (p. 587), concluded, among other things, that subjects do not differ in their susceptibility to distraction and that performance on a mental test is not affected adversely by distraction. Moreover, Hovey stated: "True mental ability is more nearly approximated under distraction than under standard conditions" [!] (p. 591).

Lest you be inclined to think that Hovey's research belongs to a bygone era characterized by naive conceptions of what takes place during an experiment, we would like to point out that current research literature is littered with instances in which researchers appear to be unaware of or oblivious to conscious and/or unconscious cues they give the subjects. A case in point is Bem's (1975) research on "sex-role adaptability." Briefly, Bem was interested to see whether "androgynous" subjects are more adaptable than "masculine" and "feminine" ones to the specific requirements of a situation, displaying masculine or feminine behaviors depending on what is called for.[1]

---

[1]We remind you that, in Chapter 4, we have expressed serious reservations about the inventory (BSRI) Bem used to measure sex roles. Nevertheless, we chose to use an example from sex-role research, because it is currently very popular.

Stanford University students were told that they were taking part in an experiment on mood. Each student was asked to engage in four different activities (e.g., building something with plastic disks, "interacting with a tiny kitten," p. 634) and to respond to a mood questionnaire after each activity. In one segment of the experiment, a kitten was placed in a completely enclosed playpen. The student was shown how to open the playpen and was instructed to interact with the kitten (this was viewed as a period of "forced play," p. 640). After engaging in another activity, during which time the kitten was removed from the room, the kitten was again placed in the playpen, but this time the student was free to choose whatever he or she wished to do (e.g., play games available in the room, play with the kitten). Bem was, of course, interested to see who would choose to play with the kitten (this period was viewed as "spontaneous play," p. 640).

As if the preceding were not enough to provide all sorts of cues, the students were

told that they would be left alone in the room . . . so that they could "really get involved with each activity," and that the experimenter would "*keep an eye on things from behind the one-way mirror, just to make sure that nothing was going wrong*" [italics added]. (p. 639)

We will let you ponder about the effect, not to mention the sense, of informing the subject that he or she would be observed through a one-way mirror, about what might "go wrong" when an adult is left in a room to build something from plastic disks or to play with a "tiny kitten." Finally, we believe it will not be farfetched to venture a guess that most, if not all, of the subjects were Bem's students and that they were, therefore, familiar with her work in the area of sex roles. Some may have even taken part in her other studies in this area. It would be the height of naivete to assume that subjects' behaviors and responses were not affected by these and other similar factors.

The "Faithful" Subject.   The "faithful" subject (Fillenbaum, 1966; Fillenbaum & Frey, 1970) leans over backwards not to let knowledge or suspicion about the researcher's hypothesis affect his or her behavior. In essence, the subject attempts to act as if he or she had no inkling what the researcher was after. Rosenzweig (1933), who anticipated this role too, quoted one of his subjects as telling him the following after an experiment: "At first I tried to figure out what you were getting at but then I realized this would be unfair. I tried to act from then on as a subject ought to act" (p. 347). Needless to say, conceptions of how "a subject ought to act" may vary, depending on various characteristics of the subject, the researcher, and the setting.

The "Negativistic" Subject.   In contrast to the cooperative orientation of the good or faithful subject, the "negativistic" ("perverse," Silverman, 1977) subject may be not only uncooperative and indifferent but also downright hostile and actively engaged in undermining the research. The mood, attitude, and behavior of this type of subject are well captured in a fictitious letter from subject to experimenter, composed by Jourard (1968) on the basis of his conversations with people who served as subjects in psychological experiments. Following are some excerpts.

I lie to you a lot of the time, even on anonymous questionnaires. When I don't lie, I will sometimes just answer at random, anything to get through with the hour, and back to my own affairs.

I feel used, and I don't like it. But I protect myself by not showing you my whole self, or by lying. Did you ever stop to think that your articles, and the textbooks you write, the theories you spin—all based on your data (my disclosures to you)—may actually be a tissue of lies and half-truths (my lies and half-truths) or a joke I've played on you because I don't like you or trust you?

Another thing. Those tests of yours that have built-in gimmicks to see if I'm being consistent, or deliberately lying, or just answering at random—they don't fool me. (pp. 9–12)

Masling (1966) referred to consequences of the negativistic subject's behavior as the "The Screw You Effect" (p. 96), an example of which may be found in Goldberg (1965). In a post-experiment interview, a female sophomore art major

told the experimenter that she did not like psychology or psychologists. She resented, she said, brainwashing and attempts by psychologists to control the minds of other people. Consequently, "I chose the tastes, because I knew you wanted me to pick the weights." (p. 897)

The "Apprehensive" Subject.   The "apprehensive" subject (Rosenberg, 1965, 1969) is concerned about the experimenter's impression of him or her as a person (Silverman, 1977, spoke of the "prideful" subject).[2] The likelihood that subjects will assume the apprehensive role and act accordingly is particularly high when they perceive the researcher as having high status (e.g., professional), having special training in evaluating people (e.g., psychologist), and/or when performance on the task appears to reflect on one's ability or personality (e.g, being told or discerning that the research is about one's reasoning ability or one's altruism).

As with the other roles, the apprehensive role is not limited to experiments. Thus, for example, in surveys or opinion polls, subjects may be apprehensive about being perceived as ignorant, uninvolved in civic affairs, uncooperative, or what have you, and respond accordingly. A case in point is the extensive literature dealing with what Converse (1970) labeled "non-attitudes."[3]

ROLE MULTIPLICITY AND CONFLICT

As in other settings, subjects in scientific research may assume multiple roles. Moreover, depending on the specifics of the research, certain roles may be in conflict. There may, for example, be a conflict between the good and apprehensive roles, such that a subject may become apprehensive about the image he or she will be projecting, if he or she were to assume the role of the good subject (see Weber & Cook, 1972). Fillenbaum and Frey (1970), who advanced the notion of the faithful subject, pointed out that subjects may be inclined to assume such a role when mild deception is used but that "severe deception (e.g., one hurtful to self or one that forces the subject to harm others) or an illegitimate one may elicit quite different roles" (p. 48).

The issue of role assumption is very complex, because it is affected by a multitude of situational variables, subject attributes, and interactions among them. When Orne (1962) wrote about the good subject, there prevailed a generally favorable climate about science and optimism about the promise of scientific inquiry to help solve the great problems facing humankind. In such a climate, it is not surprising that people, particularly college students, are willing to assume the role of the good subject. However, by the same token, it is not surprising when a change in attitudes towards science and scientific inquiry, such as had taken place in the late 1960's, leads many people to assume the role of the negativistic subject.

Contrary to what some researchers may wish or think, subjects are not perfect servants (see Lyons, 1964), nor are they passive. They define the situation, they speak to themselves, and this affects what roles they assume, how they react to researcher's instructions. It is a truism that people will define the situation differently, depending on myriad variables. Farber (1963) offered admirable examples of different subjects reporting about their perceptions and reactions to a verbal conditioning experiment. Following are but a couple of excerpts.

---

[2]Rosenberg's formulations of evaluation apprehension are discussed in Chapter 12, under Manipulation Strength, in connection with the use of monetary rewards in experiments.

[3]See Chapter 6, where this and issues concerning "Don't Know" responses are discussed.

The first subject answered the question "How did you react?" as follows: "Every time I said 'you' he [the experimenter] said 'good' so naturally I said 'you' most of the time, but now and then I said something else just to break the monotony." (p. 191)

"At first I purposely avoided using 'you' any more than any other pronoun because I felt like I was being conditioned into saying it. Finally on the last five cards I purposely used 'you' because I felt that possibly by not using it they would feel I had missed the whole point of the experiment." (p. 192)

Is there any wonder that some authors have been questioning who is conditioning whom? Some years ago, a cartoon appeared in one of the professional journals depicting one rat telling another that he has conditioned the researcher so well that whenever he presses the bar the researcher gives him food.

Similar concerns have been raised with respect to deception. Brown (1965), for example, noted the following: "The trouble with deception, morality aside, which it usually is, is that one cannot be sure who is being deceived" (p. 580). And discussing the human subject, Schultz (1969) concluded: "We cannot continue to design elaborate studies based on deception when we may be the only ones being deceived" (p. 224). Indeed, there is research evidence of subjects deceiving the researcher. Newberry (1973), for example, used a confederate to inform prospective subjects of solutions to some of the problems they will be asked to solve in an experiment. Not only did many of the subjects utilize the information, but also in post-experimental queries a large proportion of them denied having had any prior knowledge about the experiment, this even when the demand characteristics were designed to encourage the subject to admit that he or she heard about it through the rumor mill on campus. Not surprisingly, deception rates varied, depending on conditions under which subjects were questioned (e.g., a questionnaire administered under anonymous conditions, an interview conducted by the experimenter).

The phenomenon of subjects defining the situation was superbly summarized by Farber (1963):

Subjects may not know exactly what is going on in an experiment or, for that matter, in a therapeutic session, but very few have no ideas at all. They may be mistaken, or they may be concerned with irrelevant matters, such as whether participation in the experiment is worth the time and trouble, or whether the counselor is as blase as he seems, or what's for lunch. The one thing psychologists can count on is that their subjects or clients will talk, if only to themselves. And, not infrequently, whether relevant or irrelevant, the things people say to themselves determine the rest of the things they do. (p. 196)

ATTRIBUTES

Issues of sampling and representativeness aside,[4] it is obvious that subjects' attributes (e.g., sex, mental ability, motivation, experience) are bound to affect, to a greater or lesser extent, their definitions of the situation, their reactions to the experimenter, instructions, tasks, to name but a few. It goes without saying that it is neither possible nor necessary for a researcher to offer exhaustive information about subjects' attributes. It is *relevant* information about subjects' attributes that matters. Relevance is, of course, dependent on the context of the study—in the broadest sense of this term (e.g., theoretical framework, topic being studied, setting, experimenter attributes).

We recognize that we are running the risk of appearing to belabor the obvious. Yet, in

---

[4]That such issues should never be set aside should be clear, we hope, from our discussions of the crucial role they play in the validity of analyses and generalizations (e.g., Chapters 10 and 15). In the context of the present discussion we are concerned with the need for information about subjects' attributes even when probability sampling was not carried out.

view of current practices in research reports, we believe it important to make these points. Suffice it to note that many researchers provide no information about their subjects' attributes. But even when some such information is provided, it tends, in the majority of cases, to be perfunctory. The unavoidable impression is that subjects' attributes reported are the ones that are readily available, regardless of their relevance. Notable among attributes most frequently reported are sex, age, and race. However, is, for example, the sex of the subjects relevant? Although it may sound trite, we cannot refrain from stating: It depends!

And what does one learn when informed that the proverbial sophomores served as subjects? It does not require much insight to recognize that sophomores from, say, an Ivy League institution, differ in many ways from sophomores in, say, a state institution in which an open-enrollment policy is practiced and that given differences between sophomores from the two institutions may be relevant in certain studies. Similar statements could be made with respect to sophomores from different geographic regions, from institutions varying in size, and so forth.

Furthermore, it does not require great wisdom or effort to come up with numerous questions about specific attributes of sophomores that may be paramount in given contexts. Following are but some illustrative questions, along with illustrative references in which they were addressed. Are they naive or experienced subjects? If the latter, what sort of experiences (e.g., positive, negative) did they have in other studies in which they served as subjects? (See Christensen, 1977; Holmes & Appelbaum, 1970.) What are their attitudes toward, say, psychology and psychological research? (See Adair & Fenton, 1971.) Are they volunteers, or is their participation part of a course requirement? (See Rosenthal & Rosnow, 1969b; Rosnow & Rosenthal, 1976.) Tolman (quoted by Hovland, 1959) captured the essence of the problem, saying, "college sophomores may not be people" (p. 10).

Problems concerning the nature of subjects are by no means limited to research with humans. An intriguing illustration that *Rat is not* a rat is *not* a rat is *not* a rat comes from work by Jones and Fennell (1965). Addressing the dispute between followers of Hull and followers of Tolman "over the nature of learning" (p. 289), in particular Tolman's concept of "latent learning," Jones and Fennell pointed out that the two camps were "strikingly distinct in many ways" (p. 289; e.g., their approach to theory, methodology, the kind of experiments they performed). However, what was apparently overlooked is that they also "*used two different strains of rats* [italics added]" (p. 289)—one bred in Iowa and one in California. As you may have guessed, Jones and Fennell used what were essentially rats from the two strains and demonstrated that the runway performance of each strain was consistent with the respective theory championed by the camp that studied it.

Another example comes from the work of biologists at the University of Wisconsin, who discovered that many of the mice they obtained from a breeding laboratory were incorrectly identified and had nonstandard genes. The researchers concluded that the seriousness of this matter "cannot be overemphasized" (Kahan, Auerbach, Alter, & Bach, 1982, p. 381). Among other things, they raised the possibility that failure of some of their experiments may have been due to the lack of genetic integrity of the mice they used.

Commenting on this report under the title "Blind Mice and Men," a *New York Times* (July 22, 1982) "Topics" author disclosed that the news "failed to amaze a biologist friend at one of the National Institutes of Health." It appeared that this friend had been wondering about the breeding practices of mice after having noticed that most of the mice in one colony "were as blind as bats." He even arrived at a "theory" of how this has occurred:

[A]t breeding time the caretaker would pull up a handful of mice to serve as the parents for the next generation. Cycle after cycle, they passed an ever worse blindness forward because they tended to be the mice least able to see the caretaker's descending hand.

The seriousness with which this theory was advanced notwithstanding, the anecdote does illustrate the consequences of overlooking the possibility that one's subjects do not possess the attributes they are believed to possess.

COMPREHENSION ARTIFACT

Several times earlier, we alluded to the problem of subjects not comprehending the experimenter's instructions. In their discussion of comprehension artifacts, Crano and Messé (1985) gave examples of differential effects of treatments among those who have and those who have not comprehended the instructions (for another example, see Nicholson & Wright, 1977).

Needless to say, comprehension artifacts are not limited to the treatment. They may, for example, occur with respect to the measurement of the dependent variable (see, for example, Chapter 6, Task Effects). Moreover, such problems may occur in any kind of research (e.g., nonexperimental).

Comprehension artifacts raise questions about the norm of strict adherence to standardization of treatment administration, especially when it involves complex instructions. In their eagerness to standardize treatment administration, some authors and researchers even resort to mechanical devices (e.g., tape recorders for the administration of instructions).

When instructions are relatively complex, the researcher who is uncompromising about uniformity of treatment administration runs the risk of lack of uniformity in its reception by the subjects. The preceding is not meant to make light of the aim of standardization but rather to remind you that here, as in any aspect of the research, the researcher should not take leave of his or her senses. If subjects seem not to comprehend the instructions, would it not be preferable to do something about it (e.g., to rephrase) than to pretend that one has not noticed it and devoutly follow the standardization commandment?

As is true for scale development, the best safeguard against comprehension artifacts is to develop and test instructions and procedures for treatment administration in pilot studies. Using subjects similar to those who will be used in the study proper would enable the researcher to make the necessary revisions so as to minimize comprehension artifacts even when standardization is strictly adhered to. Following such a procedure, a researcher could be fairly confident that the study proper is relatively free of comprehension artifacts.

We hope that our brief overview of the subject will suffice to remind you that, when people become subjects—be it in a laboratory experiment, a survey, or what have you—they do not leave behind their personalities, experiences, and the like. What they are, especially with respect to attributes relevant to the study, has bearing on how they respond to treatments, instructions, and the like. In sum, being oblivious to the possibility of interactions between subjects' attributes and treatments, settings, researchers is tantamount to viewing people as being interchangeable.

RESEARCHER

We use the term researcher to refer also to such roles as theorist, experimenter, test administrator, data analyst. The importance of recognizing that artifacts and pitfalls may emanate from different roles a researcher may assume was stressed by Barber (1976), who drew attention to the imbalance in most treatments of this topic in that they address almost exclusively the role of the experimenter. One of Barber's "major contentions" was that "the bias that has often been attributed to the lowly experimenter who runs the study is at times actually due to the high status investigator who has major responsibility for the study" (p. 45).

As in the case of the subject, we do not strive to be exhaustive in our discussion of artifacts and pitfalls emanating from the researcher. All we will do is make some broad comments, accompanied by some illustrative research and selected references to the literature. Although some of the artifacts and pitfalls may be more relevant, even unique, to a given role, most of them are not limited to the specific role in connection with which we may be mentioning them (e.g., effects of expectancies are not limited to experimenter role, even though we may mention them primarily in connection with it).

We know of no better statement that conveys the idea of artifacts and pitfalls emanating from the researcher than Mark Twain's (1935) delightful description of an experiment he had conducted, which "proved that the ant is peculiarly intelligent in the higher concerns of life" (p. 284).[5]

I constructed four miniature houses of worship—a Mohammedan mosque, a Hindu temple, a Jewish synagogue, a Christian cathedral, and placed them in a row. I then marked 15 ants with red paint and turned them loose. They made several trips to and fro, glancing in at the several places of worship, but not entering. I turned loose 15 more, painted blue. They acted just as the red ones had done. I now gilded 15 and turned them loose. No change in the result: the 45 traveled back and forth in an eager hurry, persistently and continuously, visiting each fane, but never entering. This satisfied me that these ants were without religious prejudices—just what I wished; for under no other condition would my next and greater experiment be valuable. I now placed a small square of white paper within the door of each fane; and upon the mosque paper I put a pinch of putty, upon the temple paper a dab of tar, upon the synagogue paper a trifle of turpentine, and upon the cathedral paper a small cube of sugar. First I liberated the red ants. They examined and rejected the putty, the tar, and the turpentine, and then took to the sugar with zeal and apparently sincere conviction. I next liberated the blue ants, they did exactly as the red ones had done. The gilded ants followed. The preceding results were precisely repeated. This seemed to prove beyond question that ants destitute of religious prejudices will always prefer Christianity to any of the other great creeds. However, to make sure I removed the ants and put the putty in the cathedral and sugar in the mosque. I now liberated the ants in a body and they rushed tumultuously to the cathedral. I was very much touched and gratified, and went in the back room to write down the event; but when I came back the ants had all apostatized and had gone over to the Mohammedan communion. I said that I had been too hasty in my conclusions, and naturally felt rebuked and humbled. With diminished confidence I went on with the test to the finish. I placed the sugar first in one house of worship, then another, till I had tried them all. With the result: that whatever church I put the sugar in, that was the one the ants straightway joined. This was true, beyond shadow of a doubt, that in religious matters the ant is the opposite of man: for man cares for but one thing, to find the Only True Church; whereas the ant hunts for the one with the sugar in it. (pp. 284–285)

Although researchers have by and large come to recognize the requirement to describe their subjects, albeit frequently inadequately (see discussion of subject attributes, above), information about researchers is conspicuously absent in most research reports. It is as if researchers deem such information irrelevant, perhaps even intrusive and presumptuous. Clearly, acknowledging the need to describe the researcher is tantamount to an admission that certain things about the researcher, or about what he or she does, may affect the findings. This, of course, goes counter to the conception of the impartial, objective researcher. Friedman (1967) captured this orientation among psychologists, saying that they

---

[5]We are grateful to Ms. Sunny Gottberg of the Mark Twain Project at the University of California, Berkeley, for her help in locating this reference.

subscribed to the democratic notion that all *experimenters* are created equal; that they have been endowed by their graduate training with certain interchangeable properties; that among these properties are the anonymity and impersonality which allow them to elicit from the same subject identical data which they then identically observe and record. (pp. 3–4)

And Gouldner (1970) characterized sociologists' conceptions of themselves, as contrasted with those of the people they were studying, thus:

The *operating* premise of the sociologist claiming autonomy for his discipline is that he is free from the very social pressures whose importance he affirms when thinking about other men. In effect, the sociologist conjugates his basic domain assumptions by saying: *they* are bound by society; *I* am free of it. (p. 54)

Focusing on psychologists, Mahoney (1976) pointed out the following:

Notwithstanding their seemingly voracious scrutiny of everything from planaria to the behavior of crowds, psychologists have granted a mysterious research exemption to *homo scientus* . . . . Does the psychologist assume that we already know how scientists think, feel, and behave? Or is he reluctant to expose some of the elements he suspects he would find? Is he protecting either the scientist or the public from the destruction of their palliative image of the truth seeker? (p. 28)

We strongly recommend that you read Mahoney's book, as it contains not only insightful and interesting discussions of psychologists as scientists but also absorbing descriptions and discussions of the rites of passage of graduate education, games scientists play, the quest for publication, to name but some of the topics.

Despite recent concerns and evidence about artifacts and pitfalls emanating from the researcher, virtually all research reports contain no information about the researcher. A small portion of reports contain some information about experimenters only. However, as in the case of subjects (see above), the information is generally perfunctory (e.g., experimenters were 10 male and 10 female graduate students).

Here is but one example of researchers *not* reporting about themselves information they apparently feel is relevant when it concerns others performing the same task in the study. Breast cancer patients were interviewed in an attempt to study their attributions, beliefs about control, and adjustment. Following is *all* the information given about the interviewers: "The interviewers were the three authors plus two other women in their 40s who had prior interviewing experience" (Taylor, Lichtman, & Wood, 1984, p. 491). Evidently, researchers' expertise is expected to be taken for granted.

ATTRIBUTES

In recent years, a wide range of researcher's attributes—we are tempted to say every conceivable attribute—have come under scrutiny with respect to their effects on the outcomes of research. Among these are sex, race, age, mental abilities, status, warmth, experience, education, attitudes toward research, religion, authoritarianism, hostility, anxiety, and dominance. The range of phenomena in which effects of researcher's attributes were investigated is equally wide (e.g., learning, attitude change, person and object perception, problem solving).

To reiterate: The attributes we have mentioned and others may be relevant to more than one of the researcher's roles. For example, there is a fair amount of evidence on the effects of examiner's (interviewer, test administrator) sex, race, warmth, on subjects' responses to measures of mental ability, attitudes, interests, to name but a few.

Reviews and summaries of the voluminous literature dealing with effects of researcher's attributes will be found in the following: Adair (1973); Barber (1976); Friedman (1967); Mahoney (1976); Rosenthal (1966); and Rosenthal and Rosnow (1969a). In view of what we have been saying all along about factors affecting findings in sociobehavioral research, we hope it will not come as a surprise to you when we note that there is a good deal of inconsistency and disagreement regarding the effects of various attributes of the researcher. Actually, high consistency among the various studies would be surprising, if not suspect, in view of their variability on such aspects as subjects (virtually all comprising samples of convenience), experimenters, testers, phenomena studied, measurement, and analytic approaches.

EXPECTANCIES

The fact that different experimenters obtain different results in what appear to be similar studies has led some authors to suspect that experimenters communicate unconsciously (e.g., by tone of voice, gestures, facial expressions) their expectations to their subjects. As with other artifacts, Rosenzweig (1933) anticipated this one also, stating: "It is not difficult to see how an unguarded word, nod or glance from the Er [Experimenter] may have a suggestive significance of marked consequence to certain experimental results" (p. 352). However, as was noted earlier, the prevailing climate was not favorable for the kind of concerns Rosenzweig was voicing. With the change in the climate came a heightened awareness of and research on the effects of experimenter expectancies—also referred to as experimenter bias, effects of experimenter's hypothesis—on results of research.

Recent concerns and research about experimenter expectancies are in no small measure due to Rosenthal's contributions (e.g., 1963, 1966, 1969b). Whereas he addressed himself to various experimenter effects (e.g., as observer, data analyst, interpreter), it is to experimenter expectancies that he devoted most of his energies and in which he has had the greatest impact, as attested, among other things, by the fact that some authors refer to experimenter expectancies as the "Rosenthal Effect."

Rosenthal and his associates, and many other researchers who were influenced by them, investigated effects of experimenter expectancies in research with animals and with humans, dealing with a wide array of phenomena (e.g., rats' maze learning, human perceptions and judgments, student achievement). Summarizing "the first 345 studies" on expectancy effects, Rosenthal and Rubin (1978) declared: "The reality of the phenomenon is beyond doubt and the mean size of the effect is clearly not trivial" (p. 385).

The work by Rosenthal and his associates did not escape criticisms, even rejection. A wide sampling of commentaries on the research summarized by Rosenthal and Rubin, and their response to the commentaries, will be found following their original statement in *The Behavioral and Brain Sciences*, 1978, *3*, 386–415.

As you probably have guessed, the commentaries on Rosenthal and Rubin's paper run the gamut from approval and acceptance to disapproval and rejection. Following are some of the major themes in the commentaries:

1. The reality of experimenter expectancy effects is irrefutable. Those who question it do so, because they feel threatened by it (e.g., Babad, pp. 387–388).[6]

2. What is needed is not another statistical summary of studies demonstrating experimenter expectancy effects but a theoretical formulation of the phenomenon that will, among other things, help

---

[6]Page numbers in this section refer to *The Behavioral and Brain Sciences*, 1978, *3*.

explain why it is observed in certain studies and not in others (e.g., Adair, pp. 386–387; Ellsworth, pp. 392–393).

3. Rosenthal and Rubin's statistical summaries are questionable and/or ignore the quality of studies being summarized (e.g., Fiske, pp. 393–394; Kruglanski, pp. 399–400; Mayo, pp. 400–401).

4. Researchers who expect to demonstrate effects of experimenter expectancies are bound to find them. Moreover: "The nice thing about being a proponent of the importance of interpersonal expectancy effects is that one's own articles, even when criticized for biases they reveal, provide further confirmation of the hypotheses on which one's research is based" (Gadlin, p. 394).

5. In their eagerness to demonstrate experimenter expectancy effects, Rosenthal and his associates introduced all sorts of biases (e.g., in data analysis, changing hypotheses after failing to confirm them). Notable among critics advancing such arguments is Barber (pp. 388–390), who is probably the most persistent and trenchant of Rosenthal's critics (for an exchange with Rosenthal, see Barber & Silver, 1968a, 1968b; Rosenthal, 1968. See also Barber, 1976, pp. 64–83).

As you must have gathered even from the brief overview given above, experimenter expectancy is a much more complex phenomenon than one may be led to believe it to be on the basis of presentations by some authors. Some of the most heated exchanges regarding expectancy effects were sparked by the publication of a book by Rosenthal and Jacobson (1968) entitled *Pygmalion in the classroom* in which they claimed to have demonstrated teacher expectancy effects, similar to those of experimenter expectancies. Briefly, teachers were led to believe that some of their students (randomly selected by the researchers) were late bloomers, who, in the course of the academic year, were expected to manifest a "spurt" (p. 66) in their intellectual development. According to Rosenthal and Jacobson, this sufficed for teachers to communicate indirectly (e.g., by tone of voice, types of questions, reinforcement) their expectations to the students, who, as a result, manifested marked increases in performance on a mental ability test. Note that the expectancy effect we are dealing with here is referred to in various areas as the self-fulfilling prophecy (Merton, 1948).

In a very strong critique of Rosenthal and Jacobson's book, Thorndike (1968) deplored its publication, because "it is so defective technically" (p. 708). Thorndike pointed out that "the general reasonableness of the 'self-fulfilling prophecy effect' is not at issue" (p. 708) but rather the data and the analyses purporting to have demonstrated the phenomenon.

Needless to say, Rosenthal (1969a) responded to Thorndike's critique, to which Thorndike (1969) then responded. Snow (1969), who also found *Pygmalion in the classroom* seriously flawed, stated that, in his "considered opinion . . . the research would have been judged unacceptable if submitted to an APA [American Psychological Association] journal in its present form" (p. 197). Because of the important implications of what has come to be known as the Pygmalion Effect, many other authors have joined the fray. (For a reanalysis of the Rosenthal-Jacobson data, reviews by several other authors, and an exchange with Rosenthal & Rubin, see Elashoff & Snow, 1971. For a recent exchange, see Rist, 1987; Rosenthal, 1987; Wineburg, 1987a, 1987b. For a book dealing with teacher expectancies, see Dusek, 1985.)

In various places (e.g., Chapter 9, Past Research and Literature Review), we cautioned against exclusive reliance on secondary sources. In the context of the present discussion, we would like to single out what we believe to be a remarkable example of questionable reporting by textbook authors that may in itself be taken as an instance of expectancy effects. Introducing their discussion of "The Pygmalion Effect" (pp. 127–129) in the context of their treatment of discrimination, Gergen and Gergen (1981) said the following: "Since demonstrating the negative effects of prejudicial expectancies would be unethical, researchers have furnished a *dramatic* [italics added] illustration of positive effects" (p. 128). They then described Rosenthal and Jacobson's (1968) study and reported their findings.

Before telling you what Gergen and Gergen said, it is necessary for you to know that Rosenthal and Jacobson's study involved students in grades one through six. Criticism of this study aside (see above), it will be pointed out that only for grades one and two were there meaningful and statistically significant "gains." For grades three through six, there were virtually no differences between the experimental and control groups.

Now, reporting on Rosenthal and Jacobson's results, *Gergen and Gergen limited themselves to grades one and two*. In fact, they even presented a figure (p. 129) that referred to these two classes only. This is particularly noteworthy in view of the fact that Rosenthal and Jacobson (1968, p. 75) presented a similar figure, but one that included the six grades and from which it is very clear that there were no differences to speak of for the grades omitted by Gergen and Gergen. Here now is some of what Gergen and Gergen (1981) said about the results: "The difference between the two groups continued to increase, and by the end of the year it *truly was impressive* [italics added] (see Figure 4-1)" (p. 128).

We believe it worthwhile to tell you something about the first author (K. J. Gergen). It will be recalled that, in Chapter 7, we discussed the controversy surrounding the viability of sociobehavioral sciences (see Substance and Methods in Sociobehavioral Sciences). In the context of that discussion, we pointed out that Gergen's work, in which he rejected the notion of sociobehavioral science, instigated heated exchanges. Viewing "Social psychology as history," Gergen (1973) said: "We are essentially engaged in a systematic account of contemporary affairs" (p. 316). Accordingly, he asserted:

Perhaps our best option is to maintain as much sensitivity as possible to our biases and to communicate them as openly as possible. Value commitments may be unavoidable, but we can avoid masquerading them as objective reflections of truth. (p. 312)

Juxtaposition of the statements by Gergen and Gergen and those by Gergen should give one pause about the vagaries of some of the reporting in sociobehavioral research literature. Indeed, it is for this very reason that we bothered to present this example.

Underscoring complexities attendant with disputes surrounding expectancy effects is a recent paper by Reichardt (1985) in which he argued that purported teacher expectancy effects in a "highly acclaimed study" by Seaver (1973) "probably are due in large part to a regression artifact" (p. 231). Furthermore, why was this alternative explanation for Seaver's findings overlooked "by his dissertation committee, by the reviewers of the journal in which the paper was published, or by the many authors who have prominently and favorably cited Seaver's study" (p. 233)? Reichardt's answer was that this was "probably due to the effects of researcher expectancies"[!] (p. 231).

DESIGNER, OBSERVER, AND INTERPRETER

Various pitfalls inhere in the researcher's roles as the designer of the study, as an observer, and interpreter. What is to be investigated, and how is it to be done? What are the "facts"? What hypotheses are to be tested? What design appears most appropriate for testing them? What are the findings, and what is their meaning? That answers to these and related questions depend, to a greater or lesser extent, on who is asking them, with what frame of reference, and towards what end should, we hope, be clear from our discussions in Chapters 7 and 9. Large segments of these chapters can be viewed as elaborations on themes raised by questions such as the preceding ones. Consequently, we will not elaborate on these topics here.

DATA ANALYST

Pitfalls and artifacts in the analysis and interpretation of results are so pervasive that we found it necessary to discuss them in various places in earlier chapters. An integral part of understanding a given research design and data analysis is knowledge and appreciation of the potential artifacts and pitfalls related to them. Accordingly, when we present different designs and analytic approaches in subsequent chapters, we comment on and illustrate pitfalls and artifacts related to them. The presentation here is, therefore, limited to some general comments about artifacts and pitfalls in statistical data analysis.

Misapplications, misinterpretations, and abuses of statistical analysis are so prevalent that not only do most books on research design and statistics address them, but there are also books devoted almost in their entirety to such topics (e.g., Hooke, 1983; Huff, 1954; Kimble, 1978).

Other indications of pervasive concerns about pitfalls and artifacts in data analysis are (a) the prominence of discussions of these issues in evaluations and critiques of research reports, and (b) the numerous reanalyses of data used in original reports, usually with the aim of demonstrating that different conclusions are reached when the "correct" or more "appropriate" analysis is applied. What is correct and appropriate is, in certain situations, determined by the researcher's frame of reference, in the broadest sense of the term. Hence, the quotation marks.

Numerous errors in analysis about which there can be no disagreement are also committed. The kind of errors we have in mind are the use of a wrong formula, the wrong number of degrees of freedom or error term for an F ratio, and the inappropriate application of an analytic technique. Such errors may not only lead to erroneous conclusions but also to ones diametrically opposed to those that would have been obtained had the correct analysis been applied. In subsequent chapters, we discuss and illustrate the latter.

Finally, there are computational errors. Although such errors are bound to occur in data analysis, it has been noted that they, as well as errors of observing and recording, are more often made in the direction of the researcher's expectations and hypotheses (see, for example, Rosenthal, 1966, pp. 12–14, 217–218).

In a very interesting paper, Gould (1978) reanalyzed data presented by Morton in support of his views regarding Caucasians' superiority in mental ability. Gould's exercise exemplifies the virtue of scrutinizing the original sources—a point stressed in earlier chapters. Several things will be pointed out:

1. Because Morton reported the original data, Gould was able to determine that, in the process of arriving at his results, Morton engaged in all sorts of machinations (e.g., excluding cases that did not fit his expectations) and also committed computational errors that were in the direction of his expectations.

2. Gould stated his belief that Morton did not commit deception consciously but rather that he was finagling unconsciously.

3. Further, "once he [Morton] finagled the 'right' result, he regarded his work as complete," (p. 200) and did not entertain alternative hypotheses.

It is important to recognize Gould's aims in writing the paper. To begin with, he pointed out the following:

No scientific falsehood is more difficult to expunge than textbook dogma endlessly repeated in tabular epitome without the original data. Morton's tables enjoyed this brand of immortality and remained in the literature without serious challenge. (p. 504)[7]

---

[7]As you may recall, we have cautioned repeatedly against undue, not to mention exclusive, reliance on secondary sources. Another example of hazards of relying on secondary sources is given below.

Second, Gould expressed his suspicion

that unconscious or dimly perceived finagling, doctoring, and massaging are rampant, endemic, and unavoidable in a profession that awards status and power for clean and unambiguous discovery. . . . The point is this: unconscious finagling is probably a norm. (p. 504)

Finally, Gould stated that he was not proposing a cure for the problem but rather that he wrote the "article to argue that it is not a disease. The only palliations I know are vigilance and scrutiny" (p. 509).

The "rewards" of "vigilance and scrutiny" are well illustrated by Friedlander (1964), who recounts how disappointment at obtaining low reliability coefficients for his measures led him to repeat the calculations. As a result, he detected computational errors and was "rewarded" with reliabilities that were higher than those he obtained earlier. The important thing to note is Friedlander's admission that had he "not been displeased and surprised with the low reliability coefficients, it is doubtful that he would have repeated his calculations" (p. 198).

Friedlander related his personal experience in order to draw attention to two kinds of biases: (a) Results *inconsistent* with one's theoretical expectation will probably be checked carefully (it is even likely for the researcher to conclude that another "more appropriate" analysis is called for), and (b) results *consistent* with one's theoretical expectations will probably be trusted, leading to a lower probability of detecting computational errors. Friedlander concluded:

Hope springs eternal—and is evidently expressed through "subjective arithmetic" and through the functional adage: "If you don't succeed at first, try and try again." And, let us add: "If you *do* succeed at first, do not try again." (p. 199)

The preceding examples dealt with errors committed unintentionally. Unfortunately, outright fraud in scientific reports is not unheard of. In many instances, it may be difficult, if not impossible, to detect it. Nevertheless, even in cases of fraud, careful scrutiny may pay off, as is illustrated by the following example.

You are probably familiar with the controversy surrounding the role of heredity and environment in mental abilities. Our aim here is not to review the debate but rather to point out that one of the leading exponents of the hereditary point of view was the prominent British psychologist Cyril Burt. Now, although various authors have taken issue or even totally rejected Burt's position, none seemed to question his data on which it was allegedly based. In fact, many researchers cited Burt's data as the most comprehensive and representative available (e.g., Jensen, 1972).

Scrutiny of Burt's reports, however, led some authors, notably Kamin (1974), to suspect the veracity of his data. Among other things, Kamin noticed that the results from what Burt claimed to be different studies were too good to be true (e.g., identical correlation coefficients to the third decimal place). For a statistical analysis that attempts to show that the results reported by Burt are highly improbable, see Dorfman (1978).

Although the evidence that Burt has indeed engaged in fraud is incontrovertible (see, for example, Evans, 1976; Wade, 1976), it is sad to report that textbooks continue to use his data as evidence in support of heritability of intelligence. In a revealing analysis of biology textbooks, Paul (1985, 1987) showed that authors of textbooks in genetics responded in a "curious way" to the revelations about Burt's fraud: "They stopped citing Burt as an authority, but many continued to cite his results" (1987, p. 26). Indeed, "some, because they are familiar with the Cyril Burt scandal, end up actually denouncing the same data they are reporting" (1987, p. 30).

Under tester, we subsume pitfalls and artifacts emanating from researchers' decisions and/or actions related to the measurement process (e.g., construction, selection, administration, evaluation, of measures). Because Part 1 is devoted to measurement, we limit ourselves here to some general comments.

Validity (Chapters 3 and 4) is, obviously, the single most important aspect requiring the closest attention in attempts to guard against pitfalls and artifacts that emanate from the measurement. When measures of questionable validity are used for the independent and/or the dependent variable, one's claims regarding, say, the effects of certain treatments may be entirely invalid. Particularly pertinent to present concerns are our discussions of definitions and measurement of criteria (Chapter 3) and of variance attributable to the method of measurement (Chapter 4).

Reliability is the second aspect of measurement requiring special attention in connection with pitfalls and artifacts. For example, in Chapter 21, under Regression Adjustment, we illustrate how errors of measurement in a pretest lead to biased estimates of the regression coefficient associated with it and thereby to an underadjustment for initial differences between nonequivalent groups on the pretest. As a result, it is concluded that there is a difference between the treatment group and the nonequivalent control group when in fact this is *not* the case (see discussion in connection with Figure 21.3).

Other kinds of examples of pitfalls and artifacts that are mainly due to inadequate or deficient measures, or measurement procedures, are given in various sections of the next chapter (see especially Treatment Effectiveness; also Manipulation Checks).

CONCLUDING REMARKS

In conclusion, we reiterate what was said in the beginning of this chapter: (a) Because many things may and do go wrong in research, we felt it important to alert you to major sources of potential artifacts and pitfalls, and (b) the presentation was of a general kind. Hence, certain issues may be more or less applicable, depending on the specifics of the design.

Beginning with the next chapter, we address specific research designs, their unique features, advantages and disadvantages, and outline analytic methods associated with them. In the context of these presentations, we return to some of the issues introduced in this and the preceding chapter.

The notion of experiment is so ingrained in thinking and writing about science that many view the two as synonymous. Even those who do not go so far consider the experimental method as "the cornerstone of scientific research" (Ingersoll, 1982, p. 625); "the scientific method par excellence" (Kish, 1975, p. 268). This is not to say that the value of experiment is acknowledged by all. In fact, experimental research in sociobehavioral sciences has come under severe attack in recent years. Foremost among diverse reasons for objections to, or rejection of, experimental research in sociobehavioral sciences are ethical concerns about manipulation, deception, concealment, and the like resorted to in the course of experimentation with humans. Another major reason, mentioned particularly in connection with laboratory experiments, is that, being conducted in artificial and exceedingly controlled settings, "findings" from such studies have no bearing on "real life" situations. This, it will be recalled, is the issue of external validity that occupied us in Chapter 10 and to some aspects of which we return below.

After a brief consideration of definition of experiment, we review some major elements of experimental design, with an emphasis on their relevance to internal and external validity. Next, some elementary experimental designs are presented, strengths and weaknesses of each are indicated, and analytic approaches that may be used with each are sketched.

Definition of Experiment

Experiment is popularly conceived as "a test or a trial" (Webster, 1981) of something in order to determine whether it "works." This is exemplified by governmental or organizational "experimental" programs (more appropriately referred to as "pilot" programs) designed to determine whether efforts and expenditures are warranted to implement them on a wider scale. Similar loose notions are revealed when a study is characterized as being "just an experiment."

As was discussed in Chapter 10, a major problem in sociobehavioral research is how to "equate" groups exposed to, say, different treatments. It is because of the impossibility of accomplishing this through direct control of all the relevant variables that randomization is resorted to. With this in mind, the following definition is offered:

An experiment is a study in which at least one variable is manipulated and units are randomly assigned to the different levels or categories of the manipulated variable(s).

To qualify as an experiment, therefore, a study must not only involve manipulation of a variable(s) but must also entail random assignment of units (e.g., people, households, groups, schools, factories) to the levels, or categories, of the manipulated variable(s). Some authors (e.g., Cook & Campbell, 1979, p. 224) referred to such designs as "*true*" experiments, as contrasted with "*quasi*" experiments (see Chapter 13). Other authors (Anderson et al., 1980, Chapter 4) distinguished between randomized and nonrandomized studies.

ELEMENTS OF EXPERIMENTAL RESEARCH

In this section, some major elements of experimental research are presented. We begin with a discussion of the setting in which the experiment is conducted, in the context of which we discuss such issues as comparability of settings, contrasts between laboratory and field experiments, and controversies surrounding them. We then turn to issues concerning manipulation of variables and manipulation checks.

Setting

Broadly, a distinction can be made between experiments conducted in settings expressly created for the purpose of the study (i.e., laboratory experiments) and ones conducted in existing settings (i.e., field experiments). Controversies concerning aims, advantages, and disadvantages of laboratory versus field experiments abound. Before addressing them, we comment on issues frequently overlooked when settings are being compared.

COMPARABILITY ACROSS SETTINGS

Advocates of a clear distinction between laboratory and field experiments, particularly those who question the value of the former, frequently point to inconsistent, even contradictory, findings yielded by the "same" studies conducted in the two settings. Generally, this is presented as evidence of the futility of laboratory experiments. But what is being overlooked is that, in many instances, studies considered to differ in setting only (i.e., laboratory versus field) actually differ in many subtle and not so subtle ways. Among these are differences in types of respondents, in the integrity of randomization of respondents, and duration of the study. In addition, the nature of the manipulation of the independent variables and the definitions and measures of the dependent variables frequently differ in the two settings.

LABORATORY VERSUS FIELD EXPERIMENTS

Most authors and researchers would probably agree that, because of the potential for utmost control, internal validity of laboratory experiments is potentially high. Many would, however, add that the high internal validity of the laboratory experiment is achieved at the expense of low external validity, that is, low generalizability.[1] Indeed, the common belief seems to be that, by its very nature, field research is more externally valid than laboratory research. In an attempt to determine whether this is supported by research in industrial and organizational psychology, Dipboye and Flanagan (1979) analyzed several journals in these areas (e.g., *Journal of Applied Psychology*) and concluded "that blanket statements concerning the inherent external validity of field research are not only inaccurate but serve to hinder the development of industrial and organizational psychology as a field of study" (p. 149). (For a comment and a reply respectively, see Willems & Howard, 1980; Dipboye & Flanagan, 1980.) Nevertheless, it is the issue of generalizability, or the lack of it, that is a focal point for the contradictory claims about the value of laboratory experiments.

ARTIFICIALITY VERSUS REALISM

A major issue in the debate regarding distinctions between laboratory and field experimentation in sociobehavioral sciences has to do with what is perceived to be the "artificiality" of laboratory settings versus the "naturalness" of field settings. Some have argued that nothing useful can be learned in the former and that only field studies, that is, studies in the "real world," can yield meaningful information about human behavior. Following are some statements exemplifying this view.

In a foreword to a book of readings on field research in social psychology entitled *Beyond the laboratory* (Bickman & Henchy, 1972), Secord (1972) asserted that in laboratory experiments:

fragments of behavior, torn from their larger context in everyday life, are often the focus of study. . . . It could thus be argued that contemporary social psychology pertains largely to esoteric behavior in a never-never land—artificial behavior in the culture of the laboratory—yielding knowledge that is difficult to generalize to the world outside the laboratory. (p. xi; see also Secord, 1986)

Arguing along similar lines, Argyle (1969) asserted that experiments in social psychology have sometimes "compelled people to behave not only like rats but like *solitary* rats" (p. 18). Further,

when a subject steps inside a psychological laboratory he steps out of culture, and all the normal rules and conventions are temporarily discarded and replaced by the single rule of the laboratory culture—'do what the experimenter says, no matter how absurd or unethical it may be'. (pp. 19–20)[2]

In a guest editorial on research in developmental psychology, Bronfenbrenner (1974) made the following statement, which has been frequently quoted by authors who question the value of laboratory experiments: "Indeed, it can be said that *much of American developmental psychology is the science of the behavior of children in strange situations with strange adults*" (p. 3). It should be noted, however, that the same author (Bronfenbrenner, 1979) warned against arbitrary claims of superiority of research on the basis of the setting in which it is conducted. He went on to point out that, depending on the problem being investigated, "the laboratory may be an altogether appropriate setting . . . and certain real-life environments may be highly inappropriate" (p. 34). As an example, Bronfenbrenner noted that, if one's aim is to study interactions between mother and child in strange and unfamiliar

---

[1]For detailed discussions of internal and external validity, see Chapter 10.
[2]See discussion of The "Good" Subject in Chapter 11.

situations, then a laboratory experiment "approximates this condition far better than the home" (p. 34).

Addressing the distinction between laboratory and field experiments, Aronson, Brewer, and Carlsmith (1985) contended that, whereas it is superficially reasonable, it is a "vast oversimplification" (p. 443); "it is almost certainly the case that we are not talking about a dichotomy at all" (p. 444). Further, "the value of field experimentation rests not on its being more 'real' than laboratory research but on its being 'more different'" (p. 481). In this connection, Aronson et al. (1985) distinguished between two kinds of realism: (a) "*experimental realism*," that is, an experimental setting in which respondents become involved, one that they take seriously, and which "has impact on them" (p. 482); and (b) "*mundane realism*"—research setting that is "likely to occur in the normal course of the subjects' lives, that is, the 'real world'" (p. 482). They then stated:

The fact that an event is similar to events that occur in the real world does not endow it with importance. Many events that occur in the real world are boring and unimportant in the lives of the actors or observers. Thus, it is possible to put subjects to sleep if an experimental event is high on mundane realism but remains low on experimental realism.

Mundane realism and experimental realism are not polar concepts; a particular technique may be high on both mundane realism and experimental realism, low on both, or high on one and low on the other. (p. 482)

To the preceding, we would add that what is viewed as real or artificial depends, among other things, on the specifics of the problem being studied, the culture or subculture in which it is studied, and the historical context. Suffice it to contrast an urban technological society with a rural one that has been little affected by modern technology to realize how radically different are some of the "natural" and "artificial" settings in the two. In sum, then, there is no clear dividing line between the "artificiality" of the laboratory and the "realism" of the field experiment.

DIVERGENT PURPOSES

Diverse views about the distinction between laboratory and field experiment, and advantages and disadvantages of each, also emanate from different conceptions regarding the purposes of research in the two settings. These in turn are related to broader issues discussed in preceding chapters, particularly: (a) basic versus applied research (Chapter 7), and (b) relations and priorities among validity types (Chapter 10). It will be recalled that those who advocate a distinction between basic and applied research also tend to advance views about priorities among validity types, depending on the type of research being conducted. Thus, for example, while deploring the undue reliance on laboratory experiments in social psychological research, McGuire (1969b) nevertheless asserted: "The manipulational laboratory experiment is and probably ought to be the most commonly used method in basic research" (p. 35).

Although some authors fault and even reject the laboratory experiment, because it does not reflect the "real world," others argue that it is not designed to reflect the real world. Thus, Festinger (1953) asserted: "A laboratory experiment need not, and should not, be an attempt to duplicate a real-life situation" (p. 139; see also, Berkowitz & Donnerstein, 1982). And Wuebben, Straits, and Schulman (1974b) declared that "from the scientist's point of view the experiment is particularly attractive *because* it is contrived, *because* it is artificial and *because* it is therefore devoid of all the confounding variables that exist in the real world" (p. 16).

Extolling the "virtues of deliberate artificiality" and of "unnatural experimentation," Henshel (1980a, 1980b) made a strong case for the laboratory experiment and deplored the fact that, in reaction to criticism, laboratory experiments in sociobehavioral sciences had become "less laboratory-like" (1980a, p. 476). Henshel advanced the concept of "inoperative ·law," which refers to "regularities that, although real, are never found outside especially created systems, because the requisite conditions are never met elsewhere" (1980b, p. 178). He then offered various examples of laws in the natural sciences that "appear to apply only under *artificial conditions*" (1980b, p. 179).

The position that it is not the purpose of the experiment to duplicate the external world, that it "*demands* artificiality" (Henshel, 1980b, p. 191), led Henshel to conclude: "Its purpose—presuming the experimenter finds something of value—is to *remake the outside world* so that it duplicates as closely as possible the experimental world" (1980b, p. 191; see also Mook, 1983). Advancing similar arguments against the abandonment of the laboratory in favor of naturalistic research, Bugelski (1981) said: "If we do that we will see cannon balls falling faster than feathers and will never find out about gravity, vacuums, outer space, and weightlessness" (p. 63). Hutten (1962) summarized this orientation well:

The scientist works in the laboratory or within a circumscribed situation. Experimentation allows him to push his hypothesis beyond the realm of everyday things and to advance. This means to employ instruments, to isolate phenomena, to create artificial conditions in which things happen which would not otherwise happen. The creative power of the scientist so becomes manifest. For the artifact of the laboratory of today becomes the reality of everybody tomorrow. (p. 216)

Variable Manipulation

In this section, we discuss some aspects of the manipulation of variables. First, we address issues concerning strength of manipulation of variables. We then comment on integrity and effectiveness of manipulation. Finally, we examine problems concerning manipulation checks.

MANIPULATION STRENGTH

Following Yeaton and Sechrest (1981), we use strength to mean "the a priori likelihood that the treatment could have its intended outcome" (p. 156). Note that the assessment of manipulation strength is made independently of the *actual* effect of the treatment on the dependent variable. Thus, a treatment judged as being weak may have a strong effect on the dependent variable and vice versa (e.g., what is deemed a strong dosage of a drug may have a weak or even no discernable effect). As is elaborated below, because of weaknesses in theoretical formulations, especially as they relate to definitions and measurement of variables, it is virtually impossible to specify manipulation strength with respect to many of the variables used in sociobehavioral sciences.

Depending on the specifics of the design, the manipulated variables may be categorical and/or continuous.[3] Assessment of manipulation strength is particularly troublesome for categorical variables, because the categories tend to be global, hence vaguely defined. As a

---

[3]For a discussion of types of variables, see Chapter 8. For convenience, we limit the discussion to designs consisting of a single variable, be it categorical or continuous.

result, it is frequently very difficult to tell what is being manipulated, not to mention the strength of the manipulation.

An example will illustrate what we have in mind. Consider the standard teacher-centered versus student-centered teaching styles. What do these actually mean? Even a cursory glance at the research literature will show that many different treatments go under these names. The converse is also true—treatments called by different names may refer to the same variable. For example, are student-centered and teacher-centered teaching styles the same as democratic and autocratic teaching styles respectively, or as Progressivism and Traditionalism (Conservatism?) respectively? It depends on whose research one is looking at.[4] Other examples of treatments of categorical variables that tend to be global are leadership styles (e.g., democratic, authoritarian, laissez-faire), psychotherapies (e.g., cognitive, behavior).

Assessment of manipulation strength may be complicated even when the manipulation is ostensibly "simple" and circumscribed. Consider the simple situation of varying the sum of money participants in an experiment are paid. What could be simpler than dealing in dollars and cents? Yet the determination of what constitute, say, "large" and "small" payments is far from simple. Clearly, it depends, among other things, on who is paying, to whom, under what circumstances, for what task, and at what point in the experiment. Lest you think this so obvious as to not warrant mentioning, following are some research examples.

We begin with an example from a classic study by Festinger and Carlsmith (1959) in which college students who performed very dull tasks for an hour (e.g., putting spools in a tray, emptying the tray and refilling it, repeatedly) were then paid either $1.00 or $20.00 to lie to a prospective participant in the study, telling him or her that the tasks are interesting, enjoyable, and intriguing. Actually, the prospective participants were accomplices of the researchers. The purpose of the study was to determine whether the different payments would have different effects on the liars' attitudes toward the tasks they had performed. Deriving the hypothesis from Festinger's (1957) theory of cognitive dissonance, it was predicted and demonstrated that those who were paid $1.00 rated the tasks (in a survey administered at a later stage and designed to appear unrelated to the experiment) as being more enjoyable than did those who were paid $20.00.

For present purposes, it is not necessary to go into the details of Festinger and Carlsmith's explanation for their findings, except to note that they maintained that participants who were paid a small sum (i.e., $1.00) experienced cognitive dissonance, which they resolved by changing their attitudes toward the tasks, perceiving them as not so boring, perhaps even enjoyable. In contrast, it was claimed that those who were paid a large sum (i.e., $20.00) did not experience cognitive dissonance, and, therefore, no change in their attitudes ensued.

This study launched what has come to be known as the forced compliance paradigm (for a review, see Kiesler et al., 1969). For present purposes, it will only be pointed out that, in the many studies of forced compliance, payment to what were presumably the same type of participants (i.e., college students) varied (e.g., $.50, $1.00, $5.00, $10.00), and a payment deemed large, say, by one researcher, may have been deemed small or average by another. Particularly pertinent to the present discussion is Rosenberg's (1965) argument that, in some of the studies, the "use of surprisingly large monetary rewards for eliciting counterattitudinal arguments may seem quite strange to the subject, may suggest that he is being treated disingenuously" (p. 29). Under such circumstances, Rosenberg argued, "the typical subject will be likely to experience *evaluation apprehension*" (p. 29), that is, "an anxiety-toned concern" (Duncan, Rosenberg, & Finkelstein, 1969, p. 212) to be evaluated positively by the experimenter (usually a psychologist). Rosenberg speculated that participants who were paid

---

[4]See Chapter 4, for a discussion of jingle and jangle fallacies.

large sums for lying reasoned about the aims of the researchers somewhat as follows: "They probably want to see whether getting paid so much will affect my attitude, whether it will influence me, whether I am the kind of person whose views can be changed by buying him off" (p. 29).

In a similar vein, Chapanis and Chapanis (1964) contended that Festinger and Carlsmith's experiment "could be more appropriately entitled 'The Effect of a Plausible and Implausible Reward in Task Evaluation'" (p. 6). They maintained that

$20.00 is a lot of money for an undergraduate even when it represents a whole day's work. When it is offered for something that must be less than 30 minutes work, it is difficult to imagine a student accepting the money without becoming wary and alert to possible tricks. (p. 6)

As a contrast to the preceding, we will describe a study in which minuscule payments were used. We will not speculate about the reactions such payments might have elicited among participants, as our sole aim in using this example is to illustrate what the researchers (presumably also the referees and the editor of the journal in which the article appeared) have deemed differential "monetary rewards." The study we have in mind is one conducted by Bem and Lenney (1976), who claimed to have demonstrated that "cross-sex behavior is motivationally problematic for sex-typed individuals" and that they, therefore, try to avoid it. Sex-typed subjects were said to "prefer sex-appropriate activity and resist sex-inappropriate activity, *even though such choices cost them money* [italics added]" (p. 48).[5]

The preceding, taken from the abstract, may lead readers who confine themselves to the reading of journal abstracts and perhaps summaries to form an impression that the sums of money involved mattered. Essentially, students in introductory psychology at Stanford University were asked to indicate which from among a set of activities (presumably masculine, feminine, and neutral) they would prefer to perform for the purpose of photographs the researchers needed. Activities were presented in pairs, "and the less sex-appropriate activities were always the *more highly rewarded* [italics added]" (p. 49). Now, what do you suppose was the researchers' conception of what constituted a higher reward for *Stanford University students*? We will let them tell you.

The specific payments for all of these activities varied from 2¢ to 6¢, and the payment difference between members of a pair varied from 1¢ to 3¢. Across all 30 pairs, then, a subject could earn *as much as $1.44 or as little as 90¢* [italics added]. (p. 51)

In sum, therefore, it cost a participant who chose *only* "sex-appropriate" activities *all of 54¢*! We believe it is not necessary to comment on this any further. We would, however, like to point out that although a reader of the study is at least in a position to see what the "differential rewards" were and make an informed judgment, this is not the case when one reads papers in which the results of this study are mentioned or when one reads reviews of the literature in the area of sex roles. All one is told is that sex-typed individuals preferred sex-appropriate activities even though it cost them money. Information essential for the evaluation of validity of findings and claims based on them unfortunately is generally missing in literature reviews. We will not venture a guess as to how many readers go back to the original papers. Instead, we hope that this example has helped convince you of the importance of doing just that.

Attempts to assess treatment strength are admittedly complex. Nevertheless, a researcher who is unable to make a reasonable statement about treatment strength probably has no idea

---

[5]For critical comments about the scale Bem and Lenney used to measure sex roles (i.e., the BSRI), see Chapter 4.

as to the expected effect of the treatment on the dependent variable. Regrettably, researchers in some areas appear to hold unrealistic, even foolhardy, expectations regarding effects of their treatments. The broad area of compensatory education programs is replete with examples in which researchers expected to achieve strong and lasting effects as a result of what may at best be viewed as a weak treatment. For example, some researchers appear to have expected brief periods of remedial reading for disadvantaged children (e.g., a couple of hours a day during a two-week summer camp) to lead to substantial gains in their mental abilities and, for good measure, also improve their study habits, enhance their self-image, or some such laudable goals. Similar unrealistic expectations can be found in other areas where, for example, by having participants read some brief vignette, the researcher believes to be manipulating and inducing changes in complex and strongly held beliefs, attitudes, values, to name but some. One cannot but be baffled when researchers express disappointment at having failed to achieve such lofty goals through such lowly means.

TREATMENT INTEGRITY

It goes without saying that the treatment should be delivered as intended. In many instances, however, this is easier said than done. This is especially true when the treatment is complex, vaguely defined, of relatively long duration, administered by multiple experimenters, to name but some factors. Difficulties in maintaining treatment integrity are particularly pronounced in studies in which the investigator (usually a professor) delegates the task of administering the treatments to assistants (usually students). Roth (1966) likened experimenters (more generally, people who are engaged by a senior investigator to collect data, conduct interviews, code, tabulate, analyze data, and carry out similar tasks) to "hired hands" in industry. "A hired hand is a person who feels that he has no stake in the research that he is working on, that he is simply expected to carry out assigned tasks and turn in results which will 'pass inspection'" (Roth, 1966, p. 195). Much like the hired hand in industry, the hired hand experimenter tends to "cut corners" and restrict productivity within the limits of formal or informal "quotas." In the process, he or she may deviate from instructions for the administration of treatments, completely ignore them, or even cheat.

Roth pointed out that, in factory production, there is at least some limitation on deviations from prescribed procedures, because it is expected that a high proportion of the products "'work' reasonably well" (p. 193). In contrast, in sociobehavioral research, "the product is usually so ambiguous and the field of study so lacking in standards of performance, that it is difficult for anyone to say whether it 'works' or not" (p. 193).

Attempts to catch cheaters in hired hand research will probably succeed only for "cruder, more obvious" (p. 194) forms of cheating. The more common subtle deviations and transgressions not only elude detection, but certain kinds of "gimmicks for catching cheaters may even put the finger on the wrong person" (p. 194). Roth offered anecdotal evidence of honest interviewers having been criticized for failing to come up with the same number or type of answers provided by the majority of interviewers who, unbeknownst to the investigator, made them up.

Attempts to maintain integrity of treatment include standardization of measures, instruments, instructions, settings, and training in the administration of treatments (but see Comprehension Artifact in Chapter 11). Very important also is monitoring to insure that treatments are administered as prescribed. Doing this is, however, neither easy nor free of problems. For example, Roth (1966) reported how attempts by an investigator to check on interrater reliability were foiled by the raters who "learned to loathe these checks" (p. 190).

Because many facets of treatment-integrity violations may be subsumed under various other aspects of the research endeavor (e.g., experimenter expectancies, see Chapter 11), we will not continue to elaborate on them here. We cannot, however, agree more with Yeaton and Sechrest's (1981) admonition that "no amount of care in research design and statistical analysis can compensate for carelessness in planning and implementing treatments" (p. 161).

TREATMENT EFFECTIVENESS

Treatment effectiveness refers to the effects treatments have on the dependent variable. Because this may be subsumed under the general heading of effect size—a complex topic discussed in various chapters (see, in particular, Chapters 9 and 15)—we do not comment on it here.

MANIPULATION CHECKS

It is very important to check whether the manipulation had its intended effect. This is especially true in sociobehavioral research where very frequently the manipulation is meant to affect some construct (e.g., anxiety, motivation, aspirations). An aspect of checking whether the manipulation had its intended effect is the determination of whether it did so with the intended strength.

Manipulation checks are also aimed at uncovering whether a manipulation had unintended effects, that is, whether it affected other variables in addition to, or in lieu of, the intended one. Further, it is also possible for the *manipulation check itself* to have unintended effects.

Before turning to a consideration of each of the preceding points, a comment about measurement is in order. As was noted above, in much of the research in sociobehavioral sciences, manipulations are aimed at producing variations in constructs. Consequently, measurement issues, particularly those concerning construct validation (see Chapter 4), are central to the process of manipulation checks. Using measures of dubious validity and/or of low reliability to check on the manipulations, researchers run the risk of arriving at erroneous conclusions regarding the effectiveness of their manipulations (e.g., concluding that the manipulations did not have the desired effects when more valid measures would have indicated the opposite).

INTENDED EFFECTS

To begin with, it is necessary to recognize that the same manipulation may have different effects on different kinds of people, in different settings, and the like. Thus, Aronson et al. (1985, p. 478) suggested that telling Princeton sophomores that they had failed on a test of creative problem-solving may have the intended effect of lowering their self-esteem. The same manipulation may, however, have little effect on working-class immigrants. As another example, assume that a researcher wishes to manipulate different levels of the *same* reinforcer or to use *different* reinforcers. It is well known that what serves as a reinforcer for certain people (e.g., executives) may not serve as a reinforcer for others (e.g., blue-collar workers). More generally, the role of culture in what constitute reinforcers is well known (e.g., Havighurst, 1970).

An example of the "same" manipulation having different effects comes from Schachter's work. In a set of studies on *The psychology of affiliation*, Schachter (1959) attempted to manipulate anxiety of participants by varying instructions given them. Checking on the effects of the manipulations, it was found that anxiety of participants in one of the studies was "noticeably lower" (p. 23) than that in another, despite the fact that "the anxiety-producing instructions were precisely the same" (p. 23) in both. Although Schachter attributed the difference to "differential rapport between the experimenter and the subject" (p. 23; in one of the studies, the manipulation was administered in a group setting, whereas in the other it was administered individually), other explanations are possible.[6]

Even when the manipulation is applied to relatively homogenous groups (e.g., coming from the same subculture), it may not have the desired effect on all participants. This may occur because of individual differences—a term often used as a "grab bag" for a host of variables that the researcher is unable to identify and pin down. This too is illustrated in Schachter's (1959) attempts to manipulate anxiety of participants. Upon checking on the effectiveness of the manipulation, Schachter found that some participants in the high anxiety condition had lower levels of anxiety than those in the low anxiety condition (e.g., pp. 34–35).

For the purpose of hypothesis testing, Schachter regrouped participants according to the level of their measured anxiety at the stage of the manipulation checks. Consequently, some of the participants who were exposed to high anxiety manipulation were placed in the low anxiety group and vice versa. Doing this voided the effects of randomization. That is, attempts to "equate" the groups on all variables, except for the manipulations, were thereby negated.[7] The newly constituted "high" and "low" anxiety groups were composed of different kinds of people, raising serious questions about the internal validity of the study.

The preceding is not meant as a criticism of Schachter's work. To begin with, in checking on the effectiveness of his manipulation, he did more than most researchers do, and having done this, he could not ignore what he found. Yet the problem of voiding the effects of randomization cannot be ignored either. We are not going to comment on alternative actions to the one taken by Schachter, because, as we discuss in the next section, there are good reasons for *not* checking on the effectiveness of the manipulations using the same people for whom the effects of the treatments on the dependent variable are also examined.

UNINTENDED EFFECTS

Manipulation checks are also aimed at determining whether the manipulation had unintended effects that may have jeopardized the validity of an experiment. Unintended manipulation effects can be conceived of as aspects of artifacts and pitfalls of the research process. Because these were broadly addressed in Chapter 11, the present discussion is limited to some unintended effects of manipulations requiring special attention in diverse research areas. What we have in mind is the likelihood of manipulations directly affecting the dependent variable and/or its indicator. In addition, possible unintended effects of the manipulation check itself will also be considered.

For simplicity of presentation and discussion, we use a design in which one unobserved independent variable, X, is hypothesized to affect one unobserved dependent variable, Y. Several models using these two variables are depicted in Figure 12.1. Note that, in all of them, X' is taken as a formative indicator of X, and Y' is taken as a reflective indicator of Y.

---

[6]See Treatment Integrity, above.

[7]For a related discussion, see Chapter 11, Comprehension Artifact.

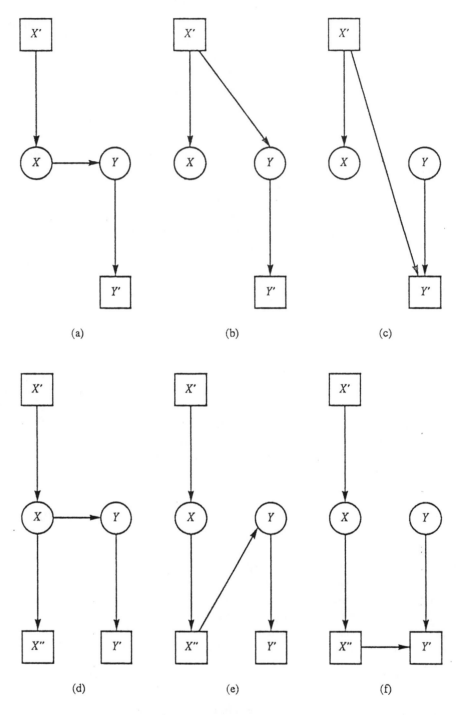

Figure 12.1

The meaning of X'' is discussed below. *To avoid clutter, no arrows are included to signify errors.*

Model (a), according to which construct X affects construct Y, is the one the researcher wishes to test. This model was used in Chapter 4—Figure 4.2, (b)—where, for illustrative purposes, X was designated as frustration and Y as aggression. In Chapter 4, it was pointed out that inferences about the effect of the former on the latter are made on the basis of the relation between their indicators (X' and Y'). Attention was also drawn to difficulties in doing this, because single indicators are used (if necessary, review the relevant section in Chapter 4).

Examine now (b) and (c) and notice that they may serve as two possible alternative explanations for the observed relation between X' and Y'. Thus, according to (b), X' and Y' are related, because the former (i.e., the manipulation) affects the dependent variable, Y, that is reflected by the latter. According to (c), the two indicators are correlated, because X' affects Y'. Various other models are possible. In any event, note that, because the three models are underidentified (see Chapter 4), it is not possible to tell whether any one of them constitutes a tenable explanation of the observed relation between X' and Y'.[8]

In the models discussed thus far, there has been no indication of a manipulation check. It is to such models, depicted in the bottom half of Figure 12.1, that we now turn. Note that, in the three illustrative models, (d), (e), and (f), X'' is a reflective indicator of X, which in the present context is a check on the effectiveness of the manipulation. Referring to the example given above, X'' may be a measure of frustration to determine whether X', the manipulation, had the intended effect on X, the construct frustration.

Note that three observed relations among the three indicators may be obtained for model (d). However, although (d) includes several simplifying assumptions (e.g., it is assumed that X does *not* affect Y'), it is underidentified as it contains four unknown coefficients.

From a variety of alternative models, we have chosen to depict two, (e) and (f), that are of special interest in the context of the present discussion. According to both these models, the construct X plays no role, so far as the dependent variable is concerned. Instead, it is the manipulation check, X'', that plays the determining role. In either (e) or (f), a relation between the manipulation, X', and the measure of the dependent variable, Y', would be observed because of the introduction of the manipulation check, X''. If (e) were tenable, the relation would be observed because X'' is said to affect Y, which is, in turn, said to be reflected by Y'. If, on the other hand, (f) were tenable, the relation would be observed, because the manipulation check, X'', is said to affect Y' directly. Under either (e) or (f), therefore, a researcher would be inclined to conclude *erroneously* that X *does* affect Y.

Because these models too are underidentified, there is no way of determining which of them, and various others not depicted here, is tenable. Nevertheless, models (e) and (f) serve to bring out the important point that the manipulation check itself may lead to results that would appear to confirm one's hypothesis. Had no manipulation check been included, no relation would have been observed between X', the manipulation, and Y', the measure of the dependent variable. Under such circumstances, the plausible conclusion would have been that X does *not* affect Y.[9] A brief explanation of how a manipulation check may lead to such results will be given, along with some illustrations.

---

[8]For an interesting discussion relevant to issues discussed here as well as in preceding sections, see Pastore's (1950) critique of studies of frustration and aggression in which he argued that not only was treatment integrity compromised but also that aggression may have been a reaction to "an unreasonable situation rather than to underlying frustration *per se*" (p. 273).

[9]We remind you, however, that the situation is more complex because of the use of single indicators (see above). Of course, it is desirable to use multiple indicators in manipulation checks. For some examples, see Bagozzi (1980a, Chapter 7) and Blalock (1985a).

In the relatively small number of studies in which manipulation checks are carried out, this is usually done using the same people for whom the effect of the independent variable on the dependent variable is also investigated. In some, the checks are made prior to the observation of behavior or measurement of the dependent variable, whereas in others they are done after having observed behavior or having measured the dependent variable. Depending primarily on whether reactive or nonreactive indicators or measures are used in the assessment of the effectiveness of the manipulation, either of these approaches to manipulation checks may seriously jeopardize the validity of the research.

REACTIVITY IN MANIPULATION CHECKS

The important distinction between *reactive* and *nonreactive* measures was introduced by Campbell (1957) in the context of his discussion of factors affecting the validity of experiments in social settings.

A reactive measure is one which modifies the phenomenon under study, which changes the very thing that one is trying to measure. In general, any measurement procedure which makes the subject self-conscious or aware of the fact of the experiment can be suspected of being a reactive measurement. Whenever the measurement process is *not* a part of the normal environment it is probably reactive. Whenever measurement exercises the process under study, it is almost certainly reactive. (pp. 298–299)

From the preceding, it follows that the same measure or indicator may be more or less reactive, depending on the circumstances in which it is obtained. (See Campbell, 1957, p. 299, for some interesting examples of the same measure or indicator being either reactive or nonreactive. For a detailed treatment of nonreactive measures, see Webb, Campbell, Schwartz, Sechrest, & Grove, 1981.)

In the preceding, we spoke of "indicators" or "measures" in order to signify that either (or both) may be used for manipulation checks. Thus, participants' behaviors (e.g., whether or not they appear nervous, offer assistance to someone, make a telephone call) or their responses to a measure (e.g., a questionnaire about how they feel) may be used for manipulation checks. Two points will be made: (a) Observations of behaviors or responses to some measure are not in and of themselves reactive or nonreactive, and (b) in a broader sense, behaviors as indicators of a construct *are* measures (see Chapter 2). In the discussion that follows, we use the term measures of the effectiveness of the manipulation in this broad sense. The same holds true for the dependent variable. Thus, when we speak of responses to measures of the dependent variable, we also mean behaviors that are used as indicators of the dependent variable (e.g., inviting a member of a minority group to participate in some activity, mailing in a donation to some organization, buying a product).

Now, using reactive measures in checking on the manipulation prior to measuring the dependent variable is bound to intensify participants' efforts to discern the aims of the manipulation, which in turn is likely to affect their responses to the measure of the dependent variable. We are not suggesting that, in the absence of a manipulation check, participants do not engage in guessing about the aim of the research and that their guesses do not affect their responses to the measure of the dependent variable.[10] Nor does it matter whether or not participants make "correct" guesses. In fact, it is possible that, because of "wrong" guesses, most participants would give responses opposite to the ones they would have given had a manipulation check not been obtained. All that matters is that the manipulation check may

---

[10]As was discussed in Chapter 11, participants almost always attempt to guess what the research is about.

trigger specific kinds of guesses on the part of the participants and that the guesses may affect their responses to the measure of the dependent variable.

Carrying out manipulation checks after the measurement of the dependent variable may create its own set of problems. Specifically, responses to manipulation checks may be colored by the manner in which participants responded to the measure of the dependent variable, thereby affecting the validity of the manipulation check. Participants may, for example, engage in rationalizations with respect to their perceptions of the manipulation so as to not appear inconsistent, irrational, selfish, foolish, or whatever the specific case may be. For example, having changed their attitudes, they may feel a need to say that the communicator was highly credible and vice versa. In short, depending on the specifics of the research, manipulation checks taken after measuring the dependent variable may lead a researcher to conclude *erroneously* that the manipulation did (did not) have its intended effect.

RESEARCH EXAMPLES

Before suggesting an approach to manipulation checks that is preferable to the two discussed above, a research area will be briefly reviewed to illustrate problems that may arise from manipulation checks taken prior to the measurement of the dependent variable. The same research area will also serve to illustrate some issues with which we were concerned in earlier sections of this chapter. We have in mind studies of effects of fear arousal, or fear appeals, on persuasion. Simply stated, it is research concerned with the effectiveness of fear arousal in changing attitudes, opinions, and behaviors.

Janis and Feshbach (1953) exposed high school students to a lecture regarding the importance of dental hygiene. One group was given a "strong" fear appeal, emphasizing and illustrating threats of pain, tooth decay, disease. A second group was given a "moderate" appeal, which "described the same dangers in a milder and more factual manner" (p. 91). A third group was given a "minimal" appeal that "rarely referred to the unpleasant consequences of improper dental hygiene" (p. 91). Although "the three forms of communication contained the same essential information and the same set of recommendations" (p. 91), it was found that the minimal appeal was the most effective and the strong appeal the least effective.

The implications of such findings for various aspects of our lives (e.g., health care, politics, education) are evident. Not surprisingly, the study stimulated a good deal of research on a variety of topics (e.g., anti-smoking, safe driving), which led McGuire (1969a) to comment: "One of the most interesting and provocative lines of research on message factors is that initiated by the work of Janis and Feshbach (1953) on fear appeals in persuasion" (p. 203).

It is not our aim to review the many studies that followed the one conducted by Janis and Feshbach. We will only note that they yielded conflicting results, some replicating Janis and Feshbach's findings, others failing to replicate them, and still others reporting results in the opposite direction, that is, the stronger the fear arousal, the more effective the message (see Higbee, 1969, for a review of much of the research, along with an attempt to account for the conflicting findings. The latter is discussed below).

Our primary concern is with manipulation checks and with strength of manipulation. Turning first to manipulation checks, it will be noted that researchers who did attempt to check on the effectiveness of the manipulation did so prior to or simultaneous with the measurement of the dependent variable. To the best of our knowledge, in all instances this was done by administering a short instrument designed to measure participants' fear or anxiety (e.g., Janis & Feshbach, 1953; Rogers & Mewborn, 1976). In some cases (e.g., Evans, Rozelle, Lasater, Dembroski, & Allen, 1970), the same instrument was administered several times in the course of several weeks.

The type of measures used for checks on the manipulation of fear have almost certainly led to reactivity on the part of the participants and have, therefore, affected, to an unknown degree, their responses to measures of the dependent variable. An indication of what the effect of reactivity might have been comes from a study by Wuebben (1968) on the effects of high versus low threat messages (regarding the probability of contracting a disease) on action taken by participants. The specific action was telephoning "for an appointment with a doctor who specialized in teaching people how to prevent the disease" (p. 91). For theoretical reasons that he did not detail, Wuebben hypothesized that participants in the high threat condition would be more likely to call for an appointment with the doctor than those in the low threat condition.

In an attempt to check on the effectiveness of the manipulation, Wuebben asked approximately one half of the participants to respond to "relevant attitude scales immediately after their exposure to the message" (p. 91). Interestingly, *Wuebben's hypothesis was supported only in the manipulation-check condition.* In this condition, 44% and 11% of those who received the high and low threat messages respectively called for an appointment. In contrast, in the *no*-manipulation-check condition, 21% and 36% of those who received the high and low threat messages respectively called for an appointment.

It will be noted that the results for the *no*-manipulation-check condition are statistically not significant. We remind you, however, of the distinction between meaningfulness and statistical significance (e.g., Chapters 9 and 15). Without going far afield it will only be pointed out that it is conceivable that researchers working in this area would consider the difference of 15% in response rate between the high and the low threat conditions, *which incidentally is in the direction opposite to the one predicted*, meaningful. Such researchers would probably attribute the failure to reject the null hypothesis to the relatively small number of participants (62 and 61, for the manipulation-check and *no*-manipulation-check conditions respectively).

Be that as it may, the main point is that the effects observed in Wuebben's study are probably due mainly, if not solely, to the manipulation check itself operating perhaps in a manner depicted in (*e*) or (*f*) of Figure 12.1. Had Wuebben checked on the effectiveness of the manipulation using *all* the participants, chances are that he would have arrived at the conclusion that the hypothesis was supported (i.e., a high threat message is more effective than a low one).

MANIPULATION CHECKS IN PILOT STUDY

We hope that the discussion and illustration in the preceding section would suffice to alert you to the potential problems of doing manipulation checks prior to, or after, the measurement of the dependent variable. This is particularly true when reactive measures are used for the manipulation checks. A preferable approach is to check on the effectiveness of the manipulation in a pilot study.[11] This has the added advantage of enabling the researcher to determine whether or not a desired level of strength has been achieved through the manipula-

---

[11]Wuebben suggested some alternative designs and discussed advantages of each. See also Kidd (1976, 1977) and Wetzel (1977).

tion. We comment briefly on this important, although frequently neglected, aspect of manipulation checks.

Earlier in this chapter, the importance of determining the strength of the manipulation was stressed. In the absence of manipulation checks, it is difficult to resist the temptation to attribute failure to support one's hypothesis to the fact that the manipulation did not have its intended effects (e.g., it was not strong enough or it was too strong).

To be meaningful, a check on the strength of a manipulation requires a clear definition of what is meant by terms such as "strong," "weak," "high," "low," as well as the availability of the means for assessing them. This brings us back to our earlier discussion of the role of measurement in the assessment of manipulation strength (see above). Problems of checking on the effectiveness of the manipulation in the study proper aside (see above), even in the minority of studies in which a manipulation check is done, strength is generally determined by demonstrating that the group given the "high" threat message has a higher mean on some measure (e.g., fear, anxiety) than the group given the "low" threat message. However, what is "high" and what is "low" is generally not clear, because measures whose psychometric properties are not known are commonly used in such assessments. Most often, such measures consist of some rating scales thrown together by a researcher for use in his or her study and used by no one else. Small wonder that, in his review of research on fear arousal, Higbee (1969) noted: "Unfortunately, there is no accurate way of determining comparability of fear levels from one study to another" (p. 439). Drawing attention to the variety of terms used in different research studies (e.g., high, strong, threatening, medium, mild, minimal, optimistic), Higbee raised the real question whether what was considered high fear in one study may have been viewed as low fear in another study, assuming the kinds of fear being measured in the different studies were even equivalent.[12]

SOME ELEMENTARY DESIGNS

In this section, we introduce some elementary designs, indicate some of their properties, and comment briefly on analytic approaches appropriate for each. First, however, some general observations will be made.

1. Notational System. By and large, we follow, as do most authors, terminology and notation introduced by Campbell and his associates (e.g., Campbell & Stanley, 1963; Cook & Campbell, 1979). Specifically, *O* stands for an observation, a measurement; *X* stands for a treatment, an intervention. A temporal sequence is indicated by the dimension going from left to right. Thus, for example, *O X O* means an observation, followed by a treatment, which is followed by another observation.

Symbols in a given row refer to the same group, whereas separate rows refer to different groups.[13] A vertical alignment of symbols signifies simultaneous events (i.e., observations, treatments) across groups. We use numbered subscripts where and when this facilitates the discussion. If you read work by Campbell and his associates (we strongly recommend that you do), you would notice that, in some designs, they use *R* to indicate that subjects were randomly assigned to groups, thereby differentiating such designs from quasi-experimental ones that they discuss in the same presentations. We do *not* use *R* because all the designs discussed in this chapter are experimental. Hence, it is assumed that subjects are randomly assigned to the different treatments.[14]

---

[12]See Higbee (1969, pp. 433–435) for a discussion of "Fear of What?"

[13]Our discussion focuses on comparisons among groups, because this is what most often takes place in experimental research. It should, however, be understood that units other than subjects (e.g., classrooms, factories, households, school districts) may be randomly assigned to different treatments.

[14]See definition of experiment in the beginning of the chapter.

2. Numbering and Naming. We number the designs *solely for convenience of reference*, not to imply any order of importance or preference. We also name the designs in order to convey some of their general characteristics. As will become clear, however, the names we use do not capture all the nuances and possible variations on given designs.

3. Application and Analysis. For each design, we make some observations regarding its application and suggested analytic approaches. These remarks are necessarily brief and general. When a specific analytic approach is mentioned, it is commented upon briefly and references are given to chapters in Part 3 in which it is presented and illustrated. Needless to say, if you have little or no familiarity with an analysis mentioned, our comments may be of no use to you. Worse, you may find them confusing. As a partial remedy for this unavoidable consequence of the organization of this book, all we can do is recommend that you turn to the relevant chapter(s), even if just for a skimming, whenever you are at a loss. In addition, we recommend that when you study Part 3, you reread relevant sections of chapters on research designs in Part 2.

4. Validity. Detailed discussions of threats to internal and external validity were given in Chapter 10. It will be recalled that two other types of validity (construct and statistical conclusion) were only mentioned in passing in Chapter 10, because the former was discussed in detail in Part 1, especially Chapter 4, whereas the latter is discussed under hypothesis testing (Chapter 9) and under sampling (Chapter 15). We mention this here to stress that meaningful statements about such complex and wide-ranging topics with respect to a given design cannot be made in the absence of a detailed description of the study.

In view of the foregoing, it is with great hesitation that we decided to make some very general comments about internal and external validity in connection with some of the designs we present. *We do this in the hope that the comments will serve as reminders of discussions of relevant topics, as hints of things to consider and think about when evaluating a specific design.* You are urged to bear this in mind when reading the comments about validity and to consult relevant chapters for discussions of specific issues with which you may be concerned when evaluating a specific study. Because we make no mention of measures and samples when we present the different designs, we cannot, needless to say, make any comments about construct and statistical conclusion validity.

5. Caveat. Schematic depictions of designs have a certain allure that may create the *wrong* impression that the choice of a design is a rather routine affair. In fact, as a result of the great impact of the work by Campbell and his associates, including the adoption of their notational system, it has been maintained that, for many researchers, the selection of a design has become something akin to a game of tick-tack-toe. We trust that we have made it clear that the choice of a design should be based on overall considerations of the study, that is, the theoretical framework, the problem, the hypotheses, the treatments, measures, settings, cost, feasibility, time, to name but some.

1. Treatment-Control.   Postmeasure Only

$$X \; O_1$$

$$O_2$$

In this design, one group receives a treatment, X, whereas another group that receives no treatment serves as a control. At the termination of the study, both groups are measured on the dependent variable, designated by O. O may stand for more than one measure of the dependent variable (i.e., multiple indicators; see Chapter 4) and/or for more than one dependent variable (e.g., interests, motives, attitudes). In order not to complicate matters, we will assume in this section that a single dependent variable, measured by a single indicator, is used. Also, whereas the dependent variable may be categorical or continuous, our presentation is limited to the latter. We do this because, in Part 3, we present only analytic approaches for the case of a continuous dependent variable. (For some introductions to analytic approaches when the dependent variable is categorical, see Aldrich & Nelson, 1984; Berry & Lewis-Beck, 1986, Part II; Fienberg, 1980; Forthofer & Lehnen, 1981; Reynolds, 1977; Swaford, 1980.)

Because subjects are randomly assigned to treatment and control, it may be assumed that the groups are equivalent, in the probabilistic sense, on all variables except for the treatment.[15] Consequently, a statistically significant difference between O_1 and O_2 is taken as indicating that the difference between the groups is due to the treatment. Before commenting on the analytic approach, several issues regarding the use of a control group will be addressed.

It will be noted that it is not always feasible, ethical, appropriate, or necessary to use a control group that has received no treatment. In experiments on the effectiveness of a new drug or a new surgical technique, for example, it may be unacceptable, even unethical, to withhold treatment from certain patients. In a study of nutrition, a control group on starvation is neither feasible nor appropriate (Riecken & Boruch, 1974, p. 46). When attempting to determine the effect of a teaching method, the interest is generally *not* in how effective it is as compared to no teaching at all. Other examples come readily to mind.

It may, however, be argued with equal force that it is inappropriate, even unethical, to institute a medical treatment, say, or approve a new drug without having compared its effectiveness to no treatment or no drug. In essence, the argument boils down to the need of a base line for comparison.

The dilemma of whether or not to use a control group that has received no treatment is graphically illustrated in the following episode related by Dr. E. E. Peacock:

One day when I was a junior medical student, a very important Boston surgeon visited the school and delivered a great treatise on a large number of patients who had undergone successful operations for vascular reconstruction. At the end of the lecture, a young student at the back of the room timidly asked, "Do you have any controls?" Well, the great surgeon drew himself up to his full height, hit the desk, and said, "Do you mean did I not operate on half the patients?" The hall grew very quiet then. The voice at the back of the room very hesitantly replied, "Yes, that's what I had in mind." Then the visitor's fist really came down as he thundered, "Of course not. That would have doomed half of them to their death." God, it was quiet then, and one could scarcely hear the small voice ask, "Which half?" (originally reported in *Medical World News*, September 1, 1972, p. 45; reprinted in Tufte, 1974, p. 4)

Focusing on medical research, Rutstein (1969) noted that, in very few instances, a base line for comparison is not necessary. For "a disease such as human rabies, which is practically 100 per cent fatal, controlled observations are not needed because any recovery of treated patients is an obvious benefit" (p. 530). However, as Rutstein also noted, "most diseases do not fall in such a clear-cut category" (p. 530).

Among control groups that may be used in lieu of, or in addition to, a no-treatment group are placebo control groups, and "current," "status quo," or "standard" treatment control groups.

We cannot address the complex issues concerning the definition and use of placebo. Following is but a small selection of references in which they are addressed: Grünbaum (1981), Prioleau, Murdock, and Brody (1983; a wide range of commentaries on Prioleau et al.'s work and a response to the commentaries will be found in *The Behavioral and Brain Sciences*, 1983, *6*, 285–310), Shapiro (1960, 1964), Shorter (1985), and White, Tursky, and Schwartz (1985).

In many instances, the primary interest is in comparing an innovative treatment with treatments currently used or what are viewed as standard treatments. The need and benefits of doing this are well illustrated by Gilbert, McPeek, and Mosteller (1977), who analyzed reports of research in surgery and anesthesia in which innovative approaches were compared

---

[15]See Chapter 10 for a detailed discussion of randomization.

to standard ones. They found that the innovations resulted in improvements in approximately half the studies and concluded, among other things, that "the experimental group is neither much better nor much worse off than the control in most trials, and *we have little basis for selecting between them prior to the trial* [italics added]" (p. 689). For similar conclusions, see Mosteller's (1981) evaluation of social, medical, and technological innovations. For recent critiques of medical research on the grounds of, among other things, absence of controls or the use of inadequate controls, see Lipton and Hershaft (1985) and references to other critiques given therein.[16]

When a current or standard treatment is used as a control, it is important that a clear description of its salient factors be given. Regrettably, in many research areas (e.g., education, psychotherapy), the description of the standard treatment is reminiscent of commercials in which the advertised product was compared to Brand X. In educational research, for example, one encounters references to control groups taught by the traditional or conventional method that, loosely translated, means anything done by others. Nothing much can be gained from comparisons with such "treatments."

In sum, the decision regarding the type of control group to be used is neither simple nor routine. It requires that all aspects of the study be taken into account.

Analysis.   One would analyze data from Design 1 by applying a simple regression analysis, where the independent categorical variable is represented by a coded vector. Measures of the dependent variable, O, for the two groups are contained in a single vector that is regressed on the coded vector (see Chapter 19). Equivalently, a t ratio may be calculated. When more than one treatment and/or control group are used, the analysis proceeds as in Design 2 (below).

Validity.   Generally speaking (see introductory comments about validity, above), major threats to internal validity (e.g., History, Maturation; see Chapter 10) are controlled by the inclusion of a control group. As to external validity, because no premeasure is used, it follows that threats due to sensitization of pretesting or interaction of pretesting with the treatments are eliminated (contrast with Design 3, below). Without additional information, little else can be said about external validity.

2. Categorical or Continuous Independent Variable.

Postmeasure Only

$$X_1 \ O$$

$$X_2 \ O$$

$$X_3 \ O$$

X, the independent variable, may be categorical or continuous. That is, it may consist of multiple categories (e.g., different drugs, different teaching methods) or multiple levels (e.g., different dosages of the *same* drug, different lengths of time of exposure to the *same* teaching method).[17] Although, for convenience, we use three categories or levels, it should be clear that this design is applicable when the independent variable is comprised of any number of categories or levels.

---

[16]Various examples and strong arguments against claimed benefits on behalf of the medical profession will be found in George Bernard Shaw (1930). Although neither a scientific researcher nor a statistician, Shaw manifested greater insights into the logic of research and the interpretation of statistics than many practicing researchers and statisticians.

[17]See Chapter 8 for a detailed discussion of variables.

This design is useful whenever the aim is to compare the effects of different categories of a categorical variable or the effects of a continuous variable. Note that control is exercised by randomly assigning subjects to the different categories or levels, thereby equating the groups on all variables, except for the independent variable. Consequently, differences among categories (i.e., treatments) or levels on the dependent variable may be attributed to whatever the categories or levels represent.

From the preceding, it follows that it is not necessary to include a no-treatment control or placebo group in Design 2. In fact, for many research problems, comparisons with such control groups is either of no interest or not feasible. (See discussion under Design 1. For a recent argument against the use of such control groups in research on the outcome of psychotherapy, see Basham, 1986.)

Design 2 does not, however, preclude the use of control groups. Actually, Design 1, and extensions of it, may be subsumed under Design 2. Thus, for example, X_1 may be a given treatment, X_2 a no-treatment control group, and X_3 a placebo control group. Another example would be a design consisting of several treatments as well as one or more control groups.

Analysis.   We comment separately on the suggested analysis when the independent variable is categorical and when it is continuous.

When the independent variable is categorical, one would do a multiple regression analysis in which the dependent variable, O, is regressed on a set of coded vectors representing the categories of the independent variable, X. Because multiple categories are used, it is of interest to focus on differences between effects of specific categories or combination of categories. This is accomplished by calculating what are referred to as a priori or post hoc multiple comparisons. For a presentation of this type of analysis, see Chapter 19, where it is also pointed out that the data could be equivalently analyzed through a one-way, or simple, analysis of variance.

When the independent variable is continuous, the interest is in determining the nature of the regression of the dependent variable on the independent variable. That is, the aim is to determine whether the regression is linear or curvilinear and, if the latter, what its specific shape is. This type of analysis is described in Chapter 18.

3. Treatment-Control.   Premeasures and Postmeasures

$$O_1 \ X \ O_2$$

$$O_3 \ \ \ O_4$$

This design differs from Design 1 in that a premeasure—O_1 and O_3 for the treatment and the control group respectively—is obtained. The treatment, X, is then administered to one of the groups, after which a postmeasure is obtained for both.

Although we could present this design as a special case of Design 4, below, we choose to present it in its present format for the following reasons: (a) We wish to contrast it with Design 1, (b) various authors offer detailed discussions of the design in its present format (see especially Campbell & Stanley, 1963, pp. 183–194; Namboodiri, 1970), and (c) an important extension of it is presented as Design 6, below.

Because the premeasure is the same as the measure of the dependent variable,[18] the design is frequently referred to as "Pretest–Posttest" or "Before–After" to distinguish it from Design 1, which is referred to as "Posttest-Only" or "After-Only." The reason researchers

---

[18]One can, of course, use an equivalent or parallel form of the same measure. For certain problems, this would be preferable.

give most frequently for using this design is that they are interested in assessing change (i.e., gains or losses from the pretest to the posttest) as a result of the treatment.

The common-sense appeal of a measure of change notwithstanding, its properties are very complex. It is neither possible nor necessary to discuss here complications arising when attempting to measure change. Some difficulties in the use and interpretation of change scores are discussed in Chapter 13, where references are also given. For present purposes, it will only be pointed out that very often researchers resort to change scores when these are not necessary. For example, when one is interested in the differential effects of several treatments or the effect of a treatment as compared with some controls, there is no need to resort to change scores.

Analysis.   The appropriate analysis for this design is the analysis of covariance (AN-COVA), where the pretest is treated as the covariate. ANCOVA is presented and illustrated in Chapter 21. It will be noted in passing that, under some restrictive assumptions,[19] difference scores (i.e., for each subject, the pretest is subtracted from the posttest) could be obtained instead and then analyzed in the manner indicated for Design 1 (i.e., regress the difference scores on a coded vector).

Validity.   The internal validity of this design is the same as Design 1. The two differ with respect to external validity. Because a premeasure is used in the present design, it is not possible to surmise how subjects might react in situations where premeasures are not taken. A researcher may, for example, wish to study the effect of a persuasive communication, X, on attitudes. Measuring subjects' attitudes prior to the administration of the treatment may sensitize them, thereby leading them to respond differently to the communication than they might have done in the absence of a premeasure. Under such circumstances, it would be highly questionable to generalize to real life situations in which premeasures are generally not used.

Premeasures can affect subjects' performance on the posttest in the following two ways: (a) directly, as a result of sensitizing them, serving as a warm up, and the like; and (b) by interacting with the treatment, thereby facilitating or inhibiting its effect, depending on the specifics of the problem being investigated (e.g., attitudes, learning, motivation). We return to these issues in Design 6, where it is shown how one may assess the pattern and magnitudes of premeasure effects.

4. Treatments And Concomitant Variables

$$C\ X_1\ O$$

$$C\ X_2\ O$$

$$C\ X_3\ O$$

Note that, except for the addition of C, this design is the same as Design 2. C stands for a concomitant variable(s), that is, a variable(s) that is related to the dependent variable. Generally speaking, concomitant variables are subjects' attributes relevant to phenomena being studied. For example, in a study of the effects of different methods of teaching on academic achievement, some concomitant variables that come immediately to mind are mental ability, motivation, and anxiety.

In many research areas, the bulk of the variance of the dependent variable is due to what are generally termed individual differences. When such differences are not taken into ac-

---

[19]See comment on difference scores in Chapter 21.

count, they are relegated to the error term, thereby leading to a relatively insensitive statistical analysis of the results. The design under consideration is meant to remedy this by controlling for relevant concomitant variable(s). Thus, for example, in an experiment on the effects of career counseling, it may be advisable to use interests and/or attitudes, to name but two potentially relevant variables, as concomitant variables.

By using a concomitant variable(s), variance due to it can be separated from the error term, thereby leading to a more sensitive statistical analysis. It stands to reason that an attribute has to be relevant to the phenomenon being studied, if it is to serve as a useful concomitant variable in the sense that its inclusion in the design will result in a meaningful reduction of the error term. Whether a given attribute is relevant or not depends, of course, on what is being studied.

As you might have discerned, the concomitant variable can be the same as the dependent variable. That is, when studying reading achievement, say, one may take into account prior achievement in reading. Note that what we are talking about is the use of a premeasure(s) as a concomitant variable(s). Accordingly, just as Design 1 was viewed as a special case of Design 2, so can Design 3 be viewed as a special case of Design 4. Because the comments we made about Design 2 in relation to Design 1 apply equally to the relation between Design 4 and 3, we will not repeat them here.

For Design 4 to be validly applied, it is required that the concomitant variable(s) *not* be affected by the independent variable, that is, by the treatments. The best way to insure this is to obtain measures of the concomitant variable(s) *prior* to the administration of the treatments. There are, however, variables and/or situations for which the requirement will be met, even if the measure of the concomitant variable is taken after the administration of the treatments. Age, for example, is obviously not affected by treatments and can, therefore, be obtained even after they have been administered. Similarly, when treatments designed to affect short-term memory, say, are viewed as not effecting subjects' mental ability, then the use of mental ability as a concomitant variable, even though it was measured after the treatments were administered, may pose no problems. Nevertheless, to repeat, it is best to measure the concomitant variable prior to the administration of the treatments.

The use of a concomitant variable is not limited to designs with a single categorical variable as Design 4 is. It can be equally useful in designs with multiple independent variables, as in factorial designs, discussed under Design 5.

Analysis. As in the case of Design 3, the analysis for the design under consideration is the ANCOVA, with the concomitant variable(s) used as a covariate(s). As was pointed out above, this type of analysis is presented in Chapter 21.

5. Factorial Designs

$$A_1 B_1 \ O_1$$

$$A_1 B_2 \ O_2$$

$$A_2 B_1 \ O_3$$

$$A_2 B_2 \ O_4$$

A factorial design is one in which more than one factor is used. We have commented on such designs several times earlier (e.g., Chapter 10, under Forms of Control; Elimination or Inclusion). For this design, we switch to a notation that facilitates depiction of designs of any size and complexity as well as references to specific segments of such designs. Letters refer to factors, and subscripts refer to categories within a factor. For example, $A_1 B_1$ refers to

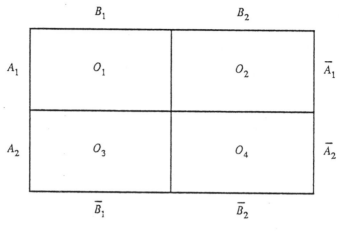

Figure 12.2

category 1 of factors A and B. It is this notation that we use also in subsequent chapters to depict factorial designs. As before, O's stand for measures of the dependent variable.

For ease of presentation here, we use the simplest factorial design possible, that is, one consisting of two factors, A and B, each with two categories. For example, A may be two methods of teaching, two types of communications; B may be two kinds of rewards, two channels of communication. Or, A may be two leadership styles, and B may be sex of the subjects. Note that, in the first two examples, both variables are manipulated, whereas in the last example, one variable is manipulated, and one is not.

It will be recalled that to qualify as an experiment (see definition in the beginning of this chapter), at least one variable must be manipulated and subjects have to be randomly assigned to treatments. When, in addition to the manipulated variable(s), attributes (e.g., sex, race, religious affiliation, political party affiliation) are used in the study, stratified randomization is generally resorted to so as to ensure that equal numbers of people within categories of the attributes are randomly assigned to the different treatments.[20] For the example given previously, therefore, males and females would be *separately* randomly assigned in equal numbers to the different categories of the manipulated variable. The same is true when more than one attribute is used. Thus, assuming that race (e.g., black and white) and sex are introduced in the design, then stratified randomization to treatments would be carried out *separately* for cross classifications of these variables. Thus, black males, black females, white males, and white females would be randomly assigned in equal numbers to the different treatments.

It is helpful to depict factorial designs as in Figure 12.2. The values that go in the cells are means on the dependent variable under different treatment combinations. For example, O_1 represents the mean for subjects who were given treatment combination A_1 and B_1—similarly for the other cells.

Analysis.   The analysis of factorial designs is presented and illustrated in Chapter 20. For now, therefore, we will only make some general comments along lines similar to those we have used earlier when we mentioned such designs. In a factorial design, one estimates what

---

[20]The desirability of having equal numbers of people in the different treatment categories and the difficulties that arise when there are unequal cell frequencies in factorial designs are commented upon in Chapter 20.

are referred to as main effects and interaction effects. Using Figure 12.2, for illustrative purposes, the main effect for A refers to the difference between A_1 and A_2, ignoring factor B. That is, one would look at the difference between the means of the rows, as if the columns did not exist. Similarly, the main effect for B refers to the difference between the column means, as if there were no rows. The interaction, on the other hand, refers to joint effects of categories of the two factors. In essence, it is the combined effects of factors, independent of their separate effects (i.e., their main effects). We realize that, depending on your background, you may find the preceding comments not meaningful, perhaps even confusing. All we can do is remind you of our introductory comments about analysis. You may either want to consult now Chapter 20, where we elaborate on the meaning of main effects and interactions and illustrate them. Alternatively, you may decide to live with the ambiguities, for the time being, and forge ahead.

Factors in factorial designs can consist of any number of categories. For example, a 4 by 5 factorial design means that one of the factors consists of 4 categories and the other of 5 categories. Further, factorial designs can be extended so that they consist of more than two factors, each with as many categories deemed necessary and feasible in a given study. Thus, a 3 by 4 by 2 means a factorial design consisting of 3 factors, the first comprised of 3 categories, the second of 4, and the third of 2.

6. Solomon Four-Group Design

$$O_1 \ X \ O_2$$

$$O_3 \quad O_4$$

$$X \ O_5$$

$$O_6$$

This design is named after Solomon (1949), who proposed it. Note that it is a composite of Design 3 (the first two rows) and Design 1 (the last two rows).

Analysis. This design yields quite a bit of information that cannot be extracted in a single analysis. One piece of important information yielded is whether the pretest acts as a sensitizer (see below). Another piece of important information is based on the fact that

the effect of X is replicated in four different fashions: $O_2 > O_1$, $O_2 > O_4$, $O_5 > O_6$, and $O_5 > O_3$. The actual instabilities of experimentation are such that if these comparisons are in agreement, the strength of the inference is greatly increased. (Campbell & Stanley, 1963, p. 195)

From the various possible analyses for this design, we will comment only on the one aimed at determining whether the pretest acts as a sensitizer. For this purpose, a portion of the data is used and cast in a factorial design, as indicated in Figure 12.3. Note that the design is composed of two factors, each consisting of two categories: (a) whether the treatment, X, was administered or not, (b) whether a pretest was administered or not. As discussed briefly under design 5, one obtains the main effects for the two factors and the effect of their interaction. If the pretest main effect is statistically significant, it means that the mere fact of pretesting affects subjects' responses to the dependent variable, regardless of whether or not they received the treatment. A statistically significant interaction means that the effect of the treatment depends on whether or not it was combined with a pretest.

As is discussed in Chapter 20, in the presence of an interaction, the interpretation of main effects is not meaningful. Instead, one performs tests of simple main effects, thereby pinpointing the nature of the interaction. Referring to Figure 12.3, examples of tests of simple main effects that can be performed pursuant to a significant interaction are: (a) between O_2

	Treatment X	No Treatment $\sim X$
Pretest	O_2	O_4
No Pretest	O_5	O_6

Figure 12.3

and O_5, thereby determining whether there is a difference between two groups both of whom received the treatment, but only one of them was pretested, and (b) between O_4 and O_6, thereby determining whether the pretest had an effect in the absence of a treatment.

7. Attribute–Treatment–Interactions (ATI)

$$A \; X_1 \; O$$

$$A \; X_2 \; O$$

$$A \; X_3 \; O$$

In this design, A stands for an attribute(s) or an aptitude(s). As before, X stands for treatment and O for a measure of the dependent variable.

A Comment on Terminology.   Cronbach and Snow (1977), who have been most influential in conceptualizing and promoting ATI research, used the term "aptitude." They stressed, however, that their use of this term was not confined to what is usually considered the domain of aptitude testing but referred to "any characteristic of a person that forecasts his probability of success under a given treatment" (p. 6; see also Corno & Snow, 1986, p. 605). Some authors (e.g., Berliner & Cahen, 1973; Hills, 1971) preferred to speak of Trait–Treatment–Interaction (TTI), because they believed the term "trait" to be less restrictive than aptitude. Because most people, we believe, tend to think of aptitudes in a narrow sense of specific abilities and of traits as personality characteristics, we prefer the term attribute, in the sense of "a quality, character, or characteristic ascribed" (Webster, 1981). We note, however, that some authors (e.g., Miller & Wilson, 1983; Theodorson & Theodorson, 1969) used the term attribute in a more restrictive sense to refer to categorical or qualitative variables. In the final analysis, we agree with Cronbach and Snow (1977) that "the world will be as well served by any label, so long as the research itself goes forward" (p. 6).

There are two reasons for taking individual differences into account when studying treatment effects:

1. To separate variance due to individual differences from the error term, thereby increasing the sensitivity of the analysis. Design 4 in which a concomitant variable(s) is used is meant to accomplish this goal.

2. To identify treatments optimal for given individuals. This, because not all individuals respond equally to the same treatment. Moreover, a given treatment, particularly beneficial to certain kinds of people, may be useless or even harmful to other kinds of people. When feasible, it is desirable to adapt treatments to individual differences among people. The ATI design is an important tool in attempts toward achieving this goal.

The attribute(s) used in an ATI design is one deemed relevant to the treatments and the phenomenon under study. Relevance depends on theoretical and practical considerations, and expectations that the attribute will interact with treatments; that is, subjects along the continuum of the attribute would respond differently to a given treatment.

Subjects are randomly assigned to the treatments or to treatments and controls. As in Design 4, where a concomitant variable is used, it is important that the treatments not affect the attribute. The best way to insure this is to measure the attribute prior to the administration of the treatments.

The similarity of Design 4 and the present one does not stop here. Generically, both designs are the same, in that they are aimed at taking individual differences into account. The distinction between them stems from the researcher's conception regarding the role of the individual differences in the design. In Design 4, individual differences, in the form of a concomitant variable(s), are used for control purposes. In the present design, individual differences, in the form of an attribute(s), are used to determine whether they interact with the treatments.

Clearly, depending on the researcher's frame of reference, the same attribute (e.g., mental ability, anxiety, attitude, locus of control) may in one context be conceived of as a concomitant variable to be controlled and in another context as one whose interaction with treatments is sought.

Analysis.   The analytic approach is the same as that taken in Design 4, except that, in Design 4, it is necessary to demonstrate that the treatments *do not* interact with the attribute (i.e., the covariate) in order to apply ANCOVA, whereas in the present design such an interaction is expected and is the focus of the study. When, in Design 4, it is found that the covariate *does* interact with the treatments, the design is in effect treated as an ATI.

In essence, the analysis is aimed at answering the question whether the regression of the dependent variable on an attribute(s) is the same for two or more groups that have been exposed to different treatments, or to treatments and controls. For a detailed discussion and numerical examples, see Chapter 21.

CONCLUDING REMARKS

In the beginning of this chapter, it was pointed out that the conduct of experiments in sociobehavioral sciences is controversial, with some authors rejecting experiments as totally inappropriate. It was further pointed out that, even among authors who endorse the use of experiment, some reject the laboratory experiment because of its artificiality and insist that only field experiment has the potential of providing knowledge that is generalizable to real life.

The controversy is rooted in philosophical and theoretical orientations as well as in misconceptions regarding the role of experiments in general and laboratory experiments in particular. Not unexpectedly, researchers who have different conceptions about the nature of reality and/or theories of human behavior tend to disagree with respect to the use of experiments. For example, focusing on the debate between situationists (those advancing the notion that much of behavior is situation specific) and traitists (those asserting that much of behavior is trait determined), Bowers (1973) pointed out that the former favor experimental research whereas the latter favor nonexperimental research.

Misconceptions about the role of experiment abound. Over 50 years ago, Thurstone (1937) found it necessary to remind psychologists "that an experiment is not good just because it involves ingenious apparatus" (p. 232). More recently, Bugelski (1981) reminded researchers that "the laboratory is not a building or a room with fixed walls and do-not-disturb signs" (p. 63). And Weick (1967) chose to begin his incisive discussion of the "promise and limitations of laboratory experiment" by stating his conclusion, namely "there are *NO* limitations to experiments. The limitations instead involve laboratory *experimenters*, their decisions and their concerns" (p. 52; see also, Boruch, 1975, for a very good discussion of mistaken notions about experiment and the consequent resistance to it).

Being a method, advantages and disadvantages of experiment, be it in the laboratory or in field setting, depend on the specific questions asked within a given set of circumstances and on the kind of answers sought. In short, experiment is neither good nor bad. Rather, it is the researcher who may put it to good or bad use. As with all decisions regarding research design, it is the researcher's obligation to decide which method is best suited under the given circumstances.

This is not to say that different methods may not lead to different findings. But, then, this is why we have been stressing the importance of using more than one method (see Chapter 4). It is only a multimethod approach that holds the promise of separating effects due to methods from those that appear to be due to the independent variables of interest.

Chapter 13
Quasi-Experimental Designs

This chapter is about designs that suffer, to a greater or lesser extent, from serious shortcomings and pitfalls. It is, therefore, recommended that they be used only *"where better designs are not feasible"* (Campbell & Stanley, 1963, p. 204), that utmost circumspection be exercised in the interpretation of the results, and in conclusions and recommendations based on them.

The reason we opened with this admonition is that quasi-experimental designs have acquired respectability far beyond what they deserve. This is largely due to the prestige and authority of Campbell and his associates, who have been most influential in elucidating them. However, elucidation does not constitute advocacy. Campbell and his associates consistently drew attention to sources of invalidity in such designs, and urged that "true" experiments be carried out whenever possible. Indeed, in a statement by Campbell and Boruch (1975), aimed at highlighting weaknesses of quasi-experimental designs, they asserted that Campbell and Stanley's "presentation of quasi-experimental designs could as well be read as laborious arguments in favor of doing randomized assignment to treatment whenever possible" (p. 202).

Evidently, many researchers and authors have ignored the detailed discussions and caveats concerning the use of quasi-experiments. Deploring the tendency of some researchers to proclaim proudly that theirs was a *quasi*-experimental design, Campbell and Boruch (1975) stated: "It may be that Campbell and Stanley . . . should feel guilty for having contributed to giving quasi-experimental designs a good name" (p. 202). It is perhaps continued and widespread misuse of quasi-experimental designs that prompted Campbell (1984a) to complain that "experiments move to quasi-experiments, and on into queasy experiments, all too easily" (p. 33). And Stanley (1966) found it necessary to warn against the drift from "quasi-experimental" to "pseudo-experimental" (p. 83) designs.

What is a quasi-experiment? It is an investigation that has all the elements of an experiment, *except that subjects are not randomly assigned to groups*. In the absence of randomization, the researcher is faced with the task of identifying and separating the effects of the treatments from the effects of all other factors affecting the dependent variable. "In a sense, quasi-experiments require making explicit the irrelevant causal forces hidden within the

277

ceteris paribus of random assignment" (Cook & Campbell, 1979, p. 6). But it is because of the impossibility of this task that randomization is resorted to in the first place (see Chapter 10).

Because of potential misinterpretations of the term quasi-experiment, various authors have refrained from using it, preferring instead less "loaded" terms. Thus, being reluctant "to borrow the prestige word 'experiment'" (p. 270) for designs of the kind to be presented in this chapter, Kish (1975) preferred the term "controlled investigations" (p. 270). Cochran (1983) used the term "observational studies" (p. 2).

We believe it worthwhile to use the designation quasi-experimental designs to refer to investigations in which treatments are administered but randomization is absent, and the designation nonexperimental designs to refer to investigations that do not include a discernable treatment (see Chapter 14). Thus, when, *in the absence of randomization*, it is desired to assess the effects of, say, teaching methods on academic achievement, drugs on blood pressure, diets on weight loss, and so forth, it is useful to refer to the design as quasi-experimental. When, on the other hand, the aim is to explain differences between groups (e.g., males and females, brain damaged and normals) in, say, mechanical aptitude or locus of control, then it is useful to refer to the design as nonexperimental—similarly, when it is desired to determine the effect of, say, parents' socioeconomic status on their children's motivation or the effect of education on income.

The distinguishing characteristic between the two types of designs, therefore, is whether or not a treatment(s) was administered. We must hasten and add that there is no consensus regarding the definition of quasi-experiment. This is due, in part, to diverse meanings of the term treatment (see below). Illustrating a looser use of the term quasi-experiment is the sole example given in connection with its definition in *A dictionary of social science methods* (Miller & Wilson, 1983). The authors noted that, if one wished to study whether broken homes lead to juvenile delinquency, it would of course be impossible to randomly assign couples to separate and others to stay married regardless of their wishes, and then study the rate of delinquency among the children of the two groups. Consequently, "the best that can be done is a quasi-experiment in which couples are selected who fit into the two groupings" (pp. 89–90). We believe many authors would not consider this an example of a quasi-experiment. In any case, we do not.

To clarify our objection, we note that, in line with what we said previously, a quasi-experiment may be characterized as an investigation that would become an experiment, if subjects or other relevant units *assigned to treatments in a nonrandom manner were to be assigned randomly*. The preceding example does not, in our opinion, qualify as a quasi-experiment on the grounds that the nature of the treatment is not at all clear, although superficially it is broken homes versus intact ones. Moreover, it is not as if people are assigned, *albeit not randomly*, to the different treatments.

THE MEANING OF TREATMENT

The term treatment is used variously by different authors, some restricting it to a deliberate intervention, a manipulation, preferably under the control of the researcher, others using it more broadly. Cook and Campbell (1979), for example, would regard naturally occurring events (e.g., natural disasters) as treatments, provided they are "abrupt and precisely dated" (p. 296). Further, they would "tolerate" considering "'treatments,' such as attending a particular training program, even where the program was a permanent institution and where the researcher did not manipulate anything" (p. 296). They did, however, note the importance of identifying what it is about the treatment that presumably caused group differences on the phenomenon of interest.

The potential for clarity about the treatment is generally greatest when the researcher is involved in its conception and administration.[1] Note carefully that we said clarity, *not* validity. A researcher may state clearly what the treatment is, and yet its validity may be dubious. The probability for this to occur is particularly high when it is claimed that the treatment affects a construct. Validity claims, it will be recalled, depend on theoretical and practical considerations relevant to the phenomenon being studied. These include issues concerning variables and their definitions (e.g., theoretical and empirical definitions; Chapter 8), artifacts and pitfalls (e.g., researcher expectancies; Chapter 11), various aspects of variable manipulation (e.g., strength, integrity, intended and unintended effects; Chapter 12).

In many instances, the researcher is not involved in the design and administration of the treatment. Often, the researcher appears on the scene after the treatment has already been administered. Thus, for example, in what is referred to as evaluation research, evaluators frequently attempt to assess the effect of some treatment or program in whose planning and administration they did not participate. Under such circumstances, the clarity with which the treatment may be ascertained depends on the specifics of the study. Examples where the nature of the treatment is relatively clear are attempts to study the effect of (a) fluoridation of water on tooth decay, (b) the 55 mile per hour speed limit on traffic accidents, (c) the ban on TV advertisement of cigarettes on consumption of cigarettes, and (d) a no-fault divorce law on divorce rates. *We are not concerned here with validity considerations of such studies (e.g., controls). All we are saying is that, although not involved in its conception and administration, the researcher may have a clear idea of the nature of the treatment whose effects he or she wishes to assess.*

Contrast the preceding examples with the common circumstance of considering some global settings as constituting treatments that have led to observed differences among groups "exposed" to them. Examples that come to mind are attempts to determine the effects of compensatory education programs (e.g., Head Start) or of institutions (e.g., private versus public schools). Considering such global settings as treatments is generally uninformative. What is necessary is to identify what it is about the settings that make for the differences in the phenomena being investigated. For example, are differences in achievement of students attending private or public schools due to differences in teaching methods, homework assignments, and/or discipline?

We turn now to a brief discussion aimed at highlighting the contrast between experiment and quasi-experiment. This is followed by a presentation of some major designs proposed for the latter.

Experiment Versus Quasi-Experiment

The contrast between experiments and quasi-experiments is depicted in Figure 13.1 for the simplest design possible—one comprised of a single independent variable and a single dependent variable.

Note that the model portrayed in (*a*) is an experiment in which treatment X is hypothesized to affect the dependent variable Y. For example, X may be communicator status (e.g., high,

---

[1]Note that, by involvement, we *do not* mean that the researcher necessarily administers the treatment. We remind you that we use the term researcher in a broad sense to subsume such roles as designer of the study, experimenter, test administrator, data analyst (see Chapter 11).

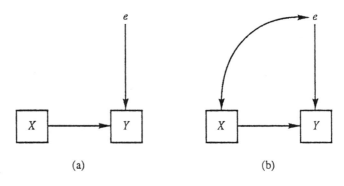

Figure 13.1

low), and Y may be attitude. Because subjects were randomly assigned to the different categories of X, the groups may be assumed equal, in a probabilistic sense, on all other variables affecting Y and that are subsumed under e. As a result, no correlation is expected between X and e.

In (b) of Figure 13.1, a quasi-experiment is depicted. Here too the interest is in the effect of X on Y. However, because randomization was *not* resorted to in the assignment of subjects to the different categories of X, the groups differ, in addition to being exposed to different treatments, in many unknown and unknowable ways. Omission of relevant variables correlated with the independent variable constitutes specification error, leading to biased estimates of the effects of the independent variable.

It should be noted that (b) of Figure 13.1 is a broad schematization of the problem of omitted variables. All that is indicated by the curved bidirectional arrow connecting e and X is that omitted variables are correlated with the independent variable. Such correlations may be due to different, even antithetical, processes. For example, the independent variable may be correlated with an omitted variable because (a) the former affects the latter, (b) the latter affects the former, or (c) both are affected by another variable. Clearly, when omitted variables are to be included in the design, in an attempt to avoid their biasing effects, it is imperative that the model of the pattern of relations among the variables be explicated. The absence of such a theoretical model precludes rational decisions regarding the analytic approach to be taken. This, as is discussed below, has important implications regarding attempts to adjust for initial differences among groups receiving different treatments.

Lack or insufficient researcher control in the assignment of subjects may occur for a variety of reasons (e.g., the researcher appears on the scene when the study is over or is already in progress, institutional constraints, political pressures, ethical considerations, economic factors). In many instances, participation in a quasi-experiment and exposure to specific treatments is determined by a process of self-selection, usually on the basis of status on the dependent variable. People who choose to go on a diet, say, may be the heavier ones; people who seek therapy may be the ones who are more disturbed; students selecting to attend private schools may be higher on the dependent variable (e.g., academic achievement) than those selecting to attend public schools. The same holds true about nonrandom assignment. Thus, for example, people may be assigned to treatments, because, on the basis of their status on the dependent variable (e.g., weight, alcoholism, psychological adjustment, academic achievement), they are deemed the most deserving (as having a better chance to benefit from the treatment or what have you).

Whatever the reasons for self-selection or nonrandom assignment, it is obvious that, unless it were possible to take all the relevant variables into account—a task that may be more or less approximated but never accomplished—conclusions may not only be erroneous but also counterintuitive. Thus, for example, Zeisel (1985, p. 143) pointed out that, according to an old Chinese statistical joke, the rate of mortality among people who are visited by a doctor is much higher than among those who are not visited by a doctor! In a more serious vein, Campbell and Boruch (1975) stated:

If a quasi-experimental study shows that people who have had psychotherapy have a higher suicide rate than matched cases who have not had psychotherapy, one is correctly reluctant to conclude that psychotherapy causes suicide. It is clear that no amount of matching can completely correct for the fact that those seeking psychotherapy are more suicide prone. (p. 203)

Similar examples abound. Thus, children who have been exposed to a compensatory program (e.g., Head Start) may still manifest lower achievement than a comparison group; alcoholics exposed to treatment may manifest poorer progress than a control group. Such results cannot, however, be construed as indicating that the program did not have a positive effect, not to mention the potential of erroneously concluding that it had a negative effect. The program may have been shown to have a positive effect, if it were possible to compare the group exposed to it with an equivalent group not exposed to it. This, as we said repeatedly, is best accomplished when subjects are randomly assigned to treatment and control groups. In the absence of randomization, one is faced with comparisons of nonequivalent groups, which no amount of adjustment may render "equal." As is discussed below in connection with different quasi-experimental designs, some efforts to accomplish a valid comparison may be more successful than others.

It should be noted that even when self-selection or nonrandom assignment to groups results in no differences on the dependent variable prior to exposure to treatments, the groups may differ on an assortment of variables that affect the dependent variable or that affect subjects' susceptibility to benefit, say, from a given treatment. The latter is another way of saying that there is a selection–treatment interaction.

THREE QUASI-EXPERIMENTAL DESIGNS

In what follows, we present three types of quasi-experimental designs. The notational system used is the same as that introduced in Chapter 12 (see Some Elementary Designs), except that a dashed line is added to indicate that the groups are nonequivalent.

The presentation follows a pattern similar to that of Chapter 12. For each design, some general comments about purpose, strengths, and weaknesses are made. Also some variations and extensions of the basic designs presented are noted. As in Chapter 12, analysis sections are limited to general remarks and references to chapters where the analytic approaches are presented and illustrated. However, because of complexities arising as a result of nonrandomization, observations about analysis are inevitably more complex than those made in Chapter 12. In fact, we feel it prudent to refrain from commenting here on some suggested analytic approaches (e.g., structural equation modeling) because of their much greater complexity. Accordingly, what we said in Chapter 12 about analysis applies with greater force to this chapter: The degree to which you may benefit from our comments depends on your familiarity with the methods in question. When reading about suggested analytic approaches, you may wish to consult, albeit superficially, relevant sections of chapters referred to.

1. Nonequivalent Control Group

O X O

O   O

In this design, a pretest is used in an attempt to take into account, adjust for, initial differences between the treatment and the control group. As Cook and Campbell (1979, p. 103; see also, Mohr, 1982) noted, this is the most popular design when randomization is not resorted to. They recommended it, however, for situations "where nothing better is available" (p. 104).

The present design is *superficially* similar to Design 3 of Chapter 12. The difference between them is, of course, that randomization was used in the latter. It is instructive to recall that, in our comments on Design 3 of Chapter 12, we pointed out that it is frequently used for the wrong reasons and that, in most situations, a design without a pretest (see Chapter 12, Design 1) is preferable. In contrast with experimental design, the pretest is an integral part of the quasi-experimental design under consideration.

In our discussion of experimental designs (Chapter 12), we also said that, in the absence of information about the specifics of a study, statements about internal validity are necessarily equivocal. This is even more so with respect to quasi-experimental designs, because of the "crippling threat" (Mohr, 1982, p. 55) of selection. For illustrative purposes, let us consider the threat of history. Although superficially it appears to be controlled in the present design, it is really not possible to even speculate about this in the absence of information about how the treatment and control groups were formed. Were they, for example, intact groups selected from the same setting (e.g., school, factory)? Were they intact groups selected from what the researcher believed to be similar settings (e.g., school districts, hospitals, factories, geographic regions)? Was the treatment group composed of volunteers and the control group of people deemed similar to them? Generally speaking, it is probably more plausible to assume that history was controlled when intact groups are selected from the same setting. Yet, to repeat, information about the specifics of the study is essential for making a judgment.

Other aspects of validity (e.g., maturation, instrumentation, regression) are equally vulnerable to threats of nonrandom selection. Because these problems are intertwined with those of analysis, they are discussed below. In general, however, the farther apart the treatment and the control group are on the pretest, the greater the probability for invalidating effects of selection or interaction of selection with other factors (for detailed discussions and illustrations of various outcomes due to the effects of different factors, see Cook & Campbell, 1979, pp. 104–112).

Analyses

The literature devoted to analysis of data from the nonequivalent-control-group design is extensive. This is not because authors who write on this topic prefer this design. On the contrary, most presentations stress the very serious sources of bias in this design and the difficulties in deciding what type of analysis is most appropriate for it. For example, Huitema (1980), who devoted several chapters to analytic approaches for this design, explained that he did this "because the analysis in this design is so messy" (p. 298). Reichardt (1979), who offered an excellent discussion of this topic, arrived at similar conclusions.

Probably the only point about which there is agreement is that there is no single, preferred approach to the analysis of data from the nonequivalent-control-group design. Some authors (e.g., Mark & Cook, 1984; Porter & Chibucos, 1975) recommended that multiple analyses be performed so as to take advantage of unique strengths of each and to control for unique weaknesses of each. Others (e.g., Anderson et al., 1980, Chapter 12; Judd & Kenny, 1981, Chapter 6; Reichardt, 1979; Weisberg, 1979) stressed the importance of correct model specification as a guide in the selection of the analytic approach. They did, however, acknowledge and discuss the difficulties in accomplishing this.

Introducing a recent compilation on quasi-experiments, Trochim (1986) gave what we believe is an apt characterization of current orientations to the analysis of such designs: "We have virtually abandoned the hope of a single correct analysis, and we have accordingly moved to multiple analyses that are based on systematically distinct assumptional frameworks and that rely in an increasingly direct way on the role of judgment" (p. 6).

In what follows, two broad analytic approaches are outlined: (a) regression adjustment, and (b) difference scores.[2] In addition, we comment briefly on selectivity bias.

Regression Adjustment

The use of regression analysis for comparisons of regression equations from different groups was described in Chapter 3 in connection with differential prediction and selection or test bias (see Comparing Regression Equations). Essentially, the same approach, usually referred to as the analysis of covariance (ANCOVA), is recommended by some authors for the purpose of adjusting for initial differences between nonequivalent groups on the pretest. It should be noted that ANCOVA was recommended for a radically different purpose (that of taking individual differences into account, thereby increasing the sensitivity of the analysis) in experimental designs (see Chapter 12, Design 4). Although the application of ANCOVA in experimental designs is, generally speaking, potentially useful, its application for the purpose of adjusting for initial group differences, as in the present design, is fraught with serious biases and threats to validity. We comment briefly on some major ones under separate headings. (For detailed discussions and illustrative analyses, see Chapter 21. See also, the references given previously.)

MEASUREMENT

To begin with, the validity of a regression adjustment is predicated on the assumption that the factor structures of the pretest and posttest within and across the two comparison groups are equal. Loosely speaking, what the preceding means is that (a) the pretest measures the same construct in both groups, (b) the posttest measures the same construct in both groups, and (c) the pretest and the posttest measure the same construct.[3] One or more of these assumptions is dubious, especially when the nonequivalent groups are far apart on the pretest. Moreover, the treatment itself may lead not only to a change in mean performance, which is presumably the

---

[2]For good discussions of analyses of quasi-experimental designs, including approaches not dealt with here, see Achen (1986).

[3]An introduction to factor analysis is given in Chapter 22.

researcher's aim, but also to a posttest structure that is different from that of the pretest and/or to different posttest structures for the treatment and the control group.

Finally, depending on what is being measured, even the mere taking of the pretest and/or passage of time between the pretest and the posttest may result in differences in their factor structures (e.g., Fleishman & Hempel, 1954). What the preceding boils down to is that, when the assumptions mentioned above are not met, the validity of the adjustment for initial differences becomes questionable.

Even if it were tenable to assume that the pretest and the posttest measure the same constructs in both groups, it is necessary to address the question of errors of measurement in the pretest. When random assignment is used, random measurement errors reduce the power of the statistical test,[4] but they do not lead to bias in the estimates of the treatment effects. The situation is radically different in the case of nonequivalent groups, where random measurement errors lead also to bias in the estimation of treatment effects. Biasing effects of measurement errors are discussed and illustrated in Chapter 21, where it is shown that they may even lead to the erroneous conclusion that a treatment has harmful effects.[5]

EXTRAPOLATION

In the context of regression analysis, extrapolation means extending the regression line, or applying the regression equation, beyond the range of the scores on the pretest (predictor, independent variable) used in the estimation of the regression equation. Extrapolation can best be illustrated graphically. In Figure 13.2 (a), a linear regression of Y on X is depicted for observed scores ranging between X_1 and X_2 (the solid line). The dashed lines beyond the range of the observed scores in both directions are but some examples of innumerable possible extrapolations. They suffice, however, to illustrate the hazards of extrapolation. For example, a researcher may act as if the regression continues to be linear, as is indicated by the middle dashed line, when in fact it is curvilinear, as is exemplified by the other dashed lines.

Now, when a regression adjustment is carried out in the present design, it is very often based on extrapolation of the regression lines for the treatment and the control groups. This becomes particularly risky when the groups are far apart on the pretest so that there is a range of scores where no observations are available at all. Such a case is depicted in (b) of Figure 13.2. The application of ANCOVA under such circumstances is based on extrapolating the two regression lines, as indicated by the dashed lines.

REGRESSION ARTIFACTS

In our discussion of threats to internal validity in Chapter 10, a relatively detailed description of regression toward the mean (RTM) was given. Consequently, in the present context it will only be pointed out that RTM poses a serious threat to validity when the pretest is measured with error (which is virtually always the case), and when the pretest and the posttest do not measure the same constructs (see Measurement, above). The latter becomes particularly problematic when proxy variables are used for the pretest (see below). Generally speaking, the farther apart the two groups are on the pretest, the greater the RTM threat.

---

[4]Power of the statistical test is discussed in Chapter 15.

[5]For a good introduction to the biasing effects of measurement errors, see Reichardt and Gollob (1986).

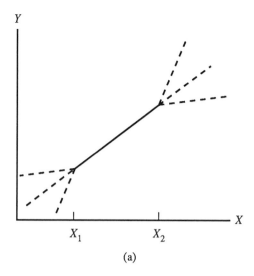

(a)

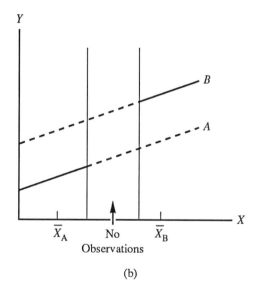

(b)

Figure 13.2

Figure 13.2 (*b*) can be used to illustrate the RTM threat. Assume, for illustrative purposes, that subjects in groups *A* and *B* come from different populations. Further, subjects in *A* are *above* the mean of their population, whereas subjects in *B* are *below* the mean of their population. Because of measurement errors and/or the possibility that the pretest and the posttest do not measure the same thing, the groups will regress toward their respective population means.

Consider first the situation where a treatment is *not* administered. Under such circumstances, a valid adjustment for initial differences on the pretest should result in equal posttest means for the two groups. However, because of RTM, this will not occur. Given the assumptions in the preceding paragraph, the adjusted mean for B will be higher than that for A.[6] Assume now that B was administered a treatment and that A served as a nonequivalent control group, and that the treatment had *no* effect at all. Because of RTM, it will be concluded *erroneously* that the treatment had a positive effect (assuming that higher scores indicate improved performance), after adjusting for initial differences on the pretest. If, on the other hand, A were administered the totally ineffective treatment, it would be concluded *erroneously* that the treatment had a negative effect.

Although extreme examples were used for illustrative purposes, it should be clear that RTM poses a threat even when treatments are effective. For example, the treatment and RTM may be operating in the same direction, leading to the conclusion that the effect is larger than it really is. The converse conclusion would be reached when the treatment and RTM operate in opposite directions. Other examples come readily to mind. The main point is that treatment and RTM effects are confounded.

EXTENSIONS AND VARIATIONS

As with Design 3 of Chapter 12, extensions of and variations on the present design are possible. For example, instead of using a treatment and a control group, two treatments or several treatments and several controls can be used. The difficulties outlined above apply equally to such extensions.

Cook and Campbell (1979, Chapter 3) discussed various other extensions, some of which constitute an improvement on the design we have been discussing. A case in point is the following design:

$$O_1\ O_2\ X\ O_3$$

$$\text{---------}$$

$$O_1\ O_2\quad O_3$$

The difference between this design and the one we have been discussing is that two pretests are taken at two points in time, prior to the administration of the treatment, X. "The advantages of pretests at two (or more) time points are considerable" (Cook & Campbell, p. 117). This is primarily because such a design affords an opportunity to study the growth rates for the two groups. However, as Cook and Campbell pointed out, caution has to be exercised because of, for example, fallibility of measures, lack of equal intervals in the measure used (see Difference Scores, below). In addition, because of the administration of the treatment, inferences about growth for the treated group are based on extrapolation. That is, assumptions are made about what the pattern of growth would have been had a treatment not been administered.

Before turning to the next topic, two points will be made. One, the two designs presented in this section can be viewed as special cases of interrupted time-series designs with a nonequivalent control group (see below). Two, our presentation was not meant to be exhaustive. We recommend that you read Cook and Campbell's (Chapter 3) presentation of other extensions and variations on the basic design with which we were concerned.

---

[6]For a discussion of adjusted means and illustrative calculations, see ANCOVA in Chapter 21.

PROXY VARIABLES

In econometrics, "the variable used as a substitute for the theoretically specified variable is called a *proxy variable*" (Rao & Miller, 1971, p. 82). In an effort to counteract bias that may ensue because of the omission of a relevant variable from a regression equation, say, researchers resort to a proxy variable "considered to be a 'close substitute'" (Rao & Miller, p. 82) for it. As an example, Rao and Miller said that an economist developing a production function may use "rainfall" as a proxy for "weather," because the latter "cannot be measured with any one quantity" (p. 82). A proxy, then, is a surrogate for an omitted variable.

From the preceding, it may appear that a proxy variable is synonymous with the term indicator used in various chapters (see especially Chapter 4). However, the proxy may represent, in addition to the omitted variable the researcher has in mind, other omitted variables (see Rao & Miller, 1971, pp. 82–88). Judd and Kenny (1981, p. 191) distinguished between an indicator and a proxy on the basis of the types of errors they may contain. An indicator "measures *only* the theoretical construct of interest but contains in addition random error" (p. 191). Errors in a proxy, on the other hand, are comprised of both random and systematic components. Consequently, "the proxy variable reflects not only the theoretical construct of interest, but also other constructs as well" (Judd & Kenny, p. 191).

The situation is not as simple and as clear-cut as may appear from the preceding. The problem stems from different conceptions regarding what the systematic errors reflect. For example, systematic errors may reflect *not* another construct but rather the method of measurement used (i.e., a method factor; see Chapter 4, Multitrait-Multimethod Matrix). Other sources of systematic error have been formulated in the context of different measurement models (see Alwin & Jackson, 1979).

We introduced the concept of proxy variable in the present discussion, because such variables are used frequently in lieu of, or in addition to, pretests in attempts to equate nonequivalent groups. But, as should be clear from our introductory remarks, the use of proxy variables is by no means limited to such situations. Because proxy variables are used very often in other contexts, and because they are open to very serious misinterpretations in the hands of an inexperienced or an imprudent researcher, we feel it important to comment, albeit briefly, on their general use before dealing with their specific role in the design under consideration.

USE AND INTERPRETATION OF PROXY VARIABLES

Although it may seem obvious, it will nevertheless be pointed out that it makes little sense to use a proxy when the variable it is supposed to represent is readily available. Consider the following example. Reporting on a sex-discrimination case brought against the City University of New York by female faculty members, Bodner (1983) pointed out, among other things, that

pre-hire years of teaching experience and pre-hire publications, both clearly relevant and important factors [in salary decisions], are left out [from the regression equation] because, as the statistician for the plaintiff suggests, with the court's acquiescence, they are "adequately accounted for by variables for age; degrees and years between degrees." (p. 56)

Frivolous decisions of this kind aside, it should be noted that the use of a proxy variable may sometimes exacerbate the problem it was meant to solve by leading to even greater bias in parameter estimation (see Rao & Miller, 1971, pp. 81–88). It is concern with such potential problems that prompted Levin (1970) to recommend: "In many cases it may be wise to acknowledge the omission and to speculate on the resulting bias rather than to use a questionable proxy" (p. 59).

An even more grievous problem is the potential for misinterpreting the results by attributing an observed effect to the proxy variable rather than to the variable for which it presumably acts as a substitute. To borrow an example from Robins and Greenland (1986, p. 398), using match carrying as a proxy for smoking is likely to lead to the conclusion that it has a strong effect on lung cancer. Misinterpretations of proxy variables may lead to erroneous, even ludicrous, expectations that manipulation of the proxy will have the same effect as the manipulation of the variable for which it serves as a substitute.

PROXY VARIABLES IN NONEQUIVALENT-CONTROL-GROUP DESIGN

A researcher may, for a variety of reasons, not be in a position to obtain a pretest. Obvious examples are situations in which the researcher becomes involved after the study has begun or when it is already over. Under such circumstances, the researcher may look for some proxy variables to use in an attempt to equate the treatment and the control groups.

In some instances, what are ostensibly pretest data may be available. For example, scores on the same measure of academic achievement used for the posttest may be available in student files. Complications and potential biases arise when such archival pretest data are used in lieu of ones obtained just prior to the administration of the treatment. These stem from changes that may have taken place from the time the "pretest" was administered to the time the study was initiated. Depending on the stability of the attribute measured, it is possible that equating the groups on pretests available in the records may *not* equate them with respect to their status just prior to the initiation of the study (for a discussion of this topic in the context of contrasting causal models, see Judd & Kenny, 1981, pp. 125–126). In essence, archival pretest data may be conceived of as proxy measures, posing problems similar to those attendant with the use of proxy variables.

For some research problems, a pretest may not make sense. Notable examples are situations in which the treatment is aimed at teaching new subject matter or training in the performance of tasks with which the subjects are not familiar. When, for example, a study is aimed at comparing two methods of teaching introductory calculus, it does not make sense to equate the students on a pretest in calculus.

For some of the reasons mentioned above, and others, researchers frequently use proxy variables in regression adjustment for the design under consideration. Generally, such studies are couched in the language of ANCOVA. Researchers tend to speak of effects of different treatments, institutions, programs, after adjusting for initial differences on a covariate(s). Although the analysis proceeds in the same way as indicated previously for the case of a pretest, it should be clear from our general remarks about proxy variables that the problems discussed in connection with the use of a pretest (e.g., errors of measurement, RTM) are potentially even more serious when a proxy variable(s) is used.[7]

---

[7]As is discussed below (see Selection Models), the most important threat to the validity of the present design, that of selection, applies to designs with pretests as well as with proxy variables.

THE LOGIC OF STATISTICAL CONTROLS

Difficulties with the use of proxy variables for the purpose of adjusting for initial differences between groups aside, it is required that they *not* be affected by the treatment. This is because only when the treatment and the control groups are deemed to have been equal *prior* to the administration of the treatment—in the present case, as a result of the adjustment on the proxy variable(s)—that a difference between them on the dependent variable may be validly attributed to the treatment.

More generally, the present requirement has to do with the logic and validity of statistical controls. As discussed in Chapter 10 (see Statistical Controls), meaningful decisions regarding the variable(s) to be controlled, and the interpretation of the results obtained once the controls have been executed, cannot be made in the absence of a theory about the relations among the variables under consideration (see, for example, the discussion in connection with Figure 10.1). Important discussions of the hazards of controlling variables in a theoretical vacuum will be found in Meehl (1970, 1971). Cohen and Cohen (1983) concluded their discussion of the role of theory in the determination of controls thus:

Consider the fact that the difference in the mean height between the mountains of the Himalayan and the Catskill ranges, adjusting for differences in atmospheric pressure, is zero! This is worth pondering. (p. 425)

We use now the very simple models depicted in Figure 13.3 to illustrate the role played by the theoretical model in the context of attempts to adjust for initial differences between nonequivalent groups. For generality, the variable for which the adjustment is made (the control variable) will be referred to as C (e.g., pretest, attribute, covariate, proxy); the treatment (e.g., treatment versus control, two or more treatments) as T; and the dependent variable as Y.

In (a), C is not correlated with T. Under such circumstances, the estimate of T is not affected by the inclusion or omission of C. This, it will be recalled, is the expectation in experimental design. As discussed in Chapter 12 (see Design 4), control for C (frequently some relevant aspect of individual differences) is aimed at increasing the precision or sensitivity of the analysis.

In quasi-experiments, C and T tend to be correlated, to a greater or lesser degree, as is indicated in (b). Note carefully that the correlation is taken as given; that is, there is no indication as to why the two variables are correlated. Two contrary conceptions of why C and T are correlated are depicted in (c) and (d).[8] Clearly, the nature and meaning of controlling for C depends on which of the models depicted in Figure 13.3 is being tested.

When C stands for a pretest or a proxy variable measured prior to the introduction of the treatment, (d) and (e) can be ruled out, as an effect of T on C is untenable. Although there is a crucial difference between (b) and (c), the estimate of the effect of T on Y, after controlling for C, will be the same in both models. Note very carefully that we are not saying that the estimate of the effect of T will be unbiased. It will, in all probability, be biased because of omitted variables affecting Y that are correlated with C and T. This, of course, is the almost intractable problem of selectivity in quasi-experiments (see Selectivity Bias, below).

In many research situations, the proxy variable is measured concurrently with the treatment administration or even after the treatment has been administered. Under such circums-

---

[8]Other conceptions are possible, but these two will suffice for present purposes.

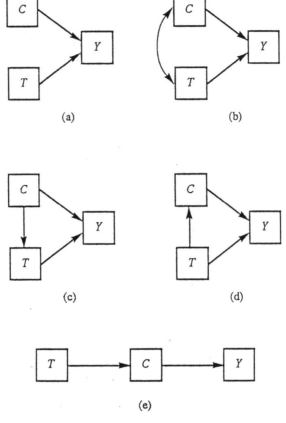

(a)   (b)

(c)   (d)

(e)

Figure 13.3

tances, models such as (d) and (e) become plausible. Controlling for C when it is affected by T, as in (d) and (e), one may answer questions as to whether T has a direct as well as an indirect effect (via C) on Y, as in (d), or only an indirect effect, as in (e). Clearly, these answers have no bearing on the question posed in the design under consideration. In sum, controlling for C when it is affected by T does not provide a valid estimate of the effect of T in the nonequivalent-control-group design.

Researchers frequently attempt to cope with the problem of lack of data on pretests or proxy variables prior to the administration of the treatment by collecting data on such variables retrospectively. Subjects are asked, for example, how they felt before the treatment was administered; what were their plans, aspirations, or what have you before they entered a course of study in college; what their income was before they began the program of training whose effect is being evaluated. We believe it not necessary to discuss here the additional diverse hazards (e.g., forgetting, distortion) in using such data for equating nonequivalent groups.[9]

In concluding this section, we would like to point out that studies in which one or more of

---

[9]Retrospective data are also used widely in nonexperimental designs. For a book devoted to this topic, see Moss and Goldstein (1979).

the problems and pitfalls discussed above have been overlooked are unfortunately abundant in sociobehavioral research. Therefore, vigilance is very important when reading reports of quasi-experimental studies.

Regardless of the areas of your substantive interest, we believe you will gain insight into the various issues we have raised by studying the controversy surrounding the study of the effects of private versus public schools (Coleman et al., 1982). For a review essay of the controversy surrounding Coleman et al.'s study, see Murnane (1984). *Sociology of Education* devoted several issues to this debate (e.g., 1982, *55*, April/July; 1983, *56*, October; 1985, *58*, April). You will find that practically every point we have mentioned in this section (e.g., use of proxy variables, treatment affecting the proxy variables, omitted variables, retrospective data, measurement) has been debated in connection with this study.

Difference Scores

In its most rudimentary form, the use of difference scores for comparing an experimental and a control group entails the following steps:

1. For each subject, the pretest score is subtracted from the posttest. This is referred to as a raw score (simple) difference (change, gain) to distinguish it from other forms (e.g., standardized difference; see below).

2. Means of difference scores thus obtained are calculated for the experimental and control groups.

3. The difference between the means of the difference scores is tested for significance (e.g., *t* ratio).

The use of raw difference scores is shown in Chapter 21 to be a special case of the regression adjustment (see ANCOVA section of Chapter 21). Therefore, the various issues and difficulties that were mentioned and discussed in connection with regression adjustment apply also to the use of difference scores. For example, it is required that the pretest and the posttest have the same factor structure. Clearly, it does not makes sense to subtract a score on a pretest from that on a posttest when the two tests measure different things. Instead of repeating what was said earlier in connection with regression adjustment, we discuss briefly some specific aspects of raw difference scores as they relate to the design under consideration. Subsequently, we comment on some suggested alternatives to raw difference scores.

INTERPRETIVE AND ANALYTIC DIFFICULTIES

Difficulties in comparing differences (gains, improvements) at different points on a continuum of a given measure are well illustrated in the following:

An instructor may grade physical education students on their improvement in running the mile. All of the students running an eight-minute mile at the beginning of the course may cut more than a minute out of their times; none of the four-minute milers are likely to improve by more than a few seconds. Clearly, the eight-minute milers "improved" their time by more seconds than did the four-minute milers. Yet no instructor would give A's to the slowest runners and F's to the fastest, regardless of his commitment to the concept of grading on improvement. Somehow these "improvements" are not comparable for the purpose of evaluation. This inability to directly compare changes at different points of the scale, *even with ratio scales*, is the fundamental problem of the measurement of change. (O'Connor, 1972a, p. 73)

In the context of the present design, such difficulties will arise when subjects in the experimental and the control groups grow at different rates. The farther apart the two groups are on the initial measure, the potentially more severe the interpretive difficulties. Note that difficulties in interpretations of differences arise even when the measure used is on a ratio or interval level.

Sensitivity and difficulty level of the pretest and/or the posttest also play a crucial role in the degree to which analysis of difference scores may be biased. Sensitivity and difficulty level of a measure (or items within a measure) are determined by the subjects' responses to it. Therefore, a given measure deemed relatively difficult for one group may be regarded as relatively easy for another group. Now, when a measure is difficult, a floor effect is observed. That is, many of the subjects have very low scores, close to or at the minimum score possible. If, on the other hand, the measure is easy, a ceiling effect is observed. That is, many of the subjects have high scores close to or at the maximum score possible. In either case, the measure is not sensitive to validly differentiate among the subjects on the construct of interest (e.g., achievement, aptitude). When there is a ceiling and/or a floor effect on the pretest and/or the posttest, difference scores are not meaningful.[10]

When nonequivalent groups are used, it may even happen that there is a ceiling effect for one of the groups and a floor effect for the other. In compensatory education programs, for example, it often happens that the pretest is relatively difficult for the subjects participating in the program and relatively easy for the comparison (control) group, indicating a probability of a floor effect for the former and a ceiling effect for the latter. Under such circumstances, the use of difference scores will lead to serious bias in estimating treatment effects (for a good discussion and illustrations of biases resulting from ceiling and floor effects, see Campbell & Boruch, 1975, pp. 268–272).

RELIABILITY AND CORRELATION
WITH INITIAL STATUS

There is an extensive literature addressed to substantive and analytic difficulties with the use of difference scores (see, for example, Bohrnstedt, 1969; Cronbach & Furby, 1970; Harris, 1963; Linn, 1981; Linn & Slinde, 1977; O'Connor, 1972a, 1972b; Plewis, 1985; Rogosa, Brandt, & Zimowski, 1982; Rogosa & Willett, 1983; Willett, 1988). Among issues that have received special attention in this literature are reliability of difference scores and the correlation between initial status (i.e., scores on the pretest) and gain (difference) scores (i.e., posttest minus pretest). Because difficulties with reliability of difference scores are of special concern when interpreting individual scores, we will not deal with them here. Instead, we will comment on the correlation between pretest (X) and gain scores ($Y - X$),[11] and on what implications this might have for the design under consideration. The correlation between pretest and gain scores is:

$$\rho_{X,Y-X} = \frac{\rho_{XY}\sigma_Y - \sigma_X}{\sqrt{\sigma_X^2 + \sigma_Y^2 - 2\rho_{XY}\sigma_X\,\sigma_Y}} \tag{13.1}$$

where X = pretest; Y = posttest; ρ = correlation coefficient; σ = standard deviation; σ^2 = variance.

---

[10]Ceiling and/or floor effects also distort results of analysis through regression adjustment, described in the preceding section.

[11]We use the term gains or gain scores for convenience. Our statements about gains apply also to other kinds of difference scores.

Table 13.1

Illustrative Data for Pretest (X) and Posttest(Y)

	X	Y	$Y - X$
	1	5	4
	2	2	0
	3	4	1
	4	6	2
	5	3	-2
M:	3.00	4.00	1.00
σ:	1.41	1.41	2.24

$$\rho_{XY} = .00 \qquad \rho_{X,Y-X} = -.707$$

In order to highlight salient properties of (13.1), we have devised the numerical example reported in Table 13.1. After applying (13.1) to the data in this table, we comment on the relevance of this formula to designs with nonequivalent groups.

The table consists of scores for five subjects on a pretest (X); a posttest (Y); and gains $(Y - X)$. In addition, we report means, standard deviations, and correlations. Note that the correlation between X and Y is zero and that the $\sigma_X = \sigma_Y$. Look now at (13.1) and note that, under such circumstances, it reduces to $-\sqrt{1/2} = -.707$, which is the value reported for the correlation between X and $Y - X$.[12]

This numerical example is, admittedly, extreme. In fact, obtaining gain scores when the correlation between the pretest and the posttest is zero makes as much sense as the proverbial addition or subtraction of apples and oranges. Yet the example serves to underscore the point that, even under such extreme circumstances, the correlation between initial status and gains is *not* zero.

Let us now consider some more realistic situations in designs with nonequivalent groups. To begin with, one would expect a positive, *although by no means perfect*, correlation between a pretest and a posttest. In other words, the correlation is expected to be a positive fraction. Assuming now that the standard deviation of the pretest and the posttest are equal, it follows from (13.1) that the correlation between X and $Y - X$ will be negative. Note that, in order for this correlation to be positive, the standard deviation of the posttest would have to be larger than that of the pretest—large enough so that $\rho_{XY}\sigma_Y > \sigma_X$.

The smaller the correlation between the pretest and the posttest, the larger the standard deviation of the posttest would have to be in order to tip the scales in the direction of a positive correlation between initial status and gains. There is no reason to expect the standard deviation of the posttest to be larger than that of the pretest. If anything, the converse would be expected as a result of an intervention. Generally, therefore, one would expect the correlation between initial status and gains to be negative. What this means is that subjects scoring high on the pretest tend to exhibit smaller gain scores, whereas subjects low on the pretest tend to exhibit larger gain scores.

The preceding may have far-reaching implications for designs with nonequivalent groups. Assuming that the correlation between pretest and gain scores is negative, the group scoring lower on the pretest will tend to show greater gains than the comparison (control) group.

---

[12]As an exercise, you may wish to apply (13.1) and also calculate the correlation between X and $Y - X$, using a formula for the Pearson correlation coefficient—for example, see (17.8) in Chapter 17.

When the lower scoring group on the pretest is the one administered the treatment, gains attributed to the treatment may be due partly or solely to the negative correlation between the pretest and the gain scores. The converse may be true when the treatment is administered to the higher scoring group on the pretest. That is, a treatment may be declared ineffective because of little gains shown by the treatment group when this may be a consequence of the negative correlation between the pretest and gain scores. Notwithstanding the specific circumstances, the main point is that the correlation between the pretest and gain scores may lead to serious biases in the estimation of treatment effects.

ALTERNATIVES TO RAW DIFFERENCES

Now, because of the very serious interpretive and analytic problems inherent in raw difference scores, most authors are agreed that they should not be used. Several alternatives to raw difference scores have been proposed. Notable among these are standardized gain scores and residualized gains. We do not intend to review these approaches. Instead, we will comment on them briefly and give references where they are discussed in detail.

The use of standardized gain scores was proposed by Kenny (1979, Chapter 11) for a special type of growth model, referred to as the fan-spread pattern.[13] In essence, the approach involves transformations of the pretest and the posttest scores to standard scores. Discussions of this approach and/or illustrative analyses will be found in Huitema (1980, Chapter 15), Judd and Kenny (1981, Chapter 6), Linn (1981), Linn and Slinde (1977), and Reichardt (1979, pp. 184–185).

To cope with the problem of the correlation between initial status and gain scores (see above), various forms of residualized gains have been proposed (e.g., DuBois, 1957; Tucker, Damarin, & Messick, 1966). Essentially, a predicted posttest score is obtained on the basis of the pretest and is subtracted from the posttest, thereby leading to a residual score that is not correlated with the pretest. However, as pointed out by Cronbach and Furby (1970):

One cannot argue that the residualized score is a "corrected" measure of gain, since in most studies the portion discarded includes some genuine and important change in the person. The residualized score is primarily a way of singling out individuals who change more (or less) than expected. (p. 74)

Discussions of residualized scores will be found in the references given above in connection with standardized gain scores. Rogosa (1980b) offered a very good discussion of standardized and residual gains, and demonstrated the relation of the latter with the regression adjustment in the nonequivalent-control-group design.

REGRESSION ADJUSTMENT OR DIFFERENCE SCORES?

In view of the various difficulties associated with the two approaches to analysis in the nonequivalent-control-group design, it is fair to assume that you are wondering whether one of them is to be preferred. We believe that most authors seem to favor a regression adjustment with some correction for fallibility of the pretest scores (see Chapter 21, ANCOVA section). Some authors, notably Judd and Kenny (1981, Chapter 6), disagreed and argued that the choice

---

[13]For detailed discussions of different growth models in the nonequivalent-control-group design and suggested analytic approaches, see Bryk and Weisberg (1977).

between regression adjustment and some form of difference score is predicated on the kind of causal model that appears tenable in a given study. They further discussed the restrictive assumptions on which each of the approaches is based. Not surprisingly, Judd and Kenny (1981) concluded: "Assessing treatment effects in the nonequivalent group design is an extremely difficult process. Straightforward solutions to the problems posed in the analysis are frequently not possible" (p. 131).

Selectivity Bias

We opened this chapter by pointing out that what distinguishes the experiment from the quasi-experiment is the absence of randomization in the latter. Generally, formation of groups in quasi-experiments is almost always a result of self-selection (e.g., subjects choose to avail themselves of a treatment) and/or researchers' decisions dictated by practical considerations or constraints (e.g., the order in which subjects become available, convenience, economy, administrative constraints).[14] The specific nonrandom process notwithstanding, when groups are thus formed, there is almost always bound to be a correlation between group membership (e.g., treatment versus control) and omitted relevant variables, leading to bias in the estimation of treatment effects.

The type of bias in parameter estimation with which we are concerned here—labeled selectivity bias—is an instance of biased parameter estimation that is a consequence of model misspecification. As we have stated repeatedly, analytic techniques, no matter how fancy they may be, cannot salvage a misspecified model. It is for this reason that various authors have argued that statistical adjustments of the kind presented in the preceding sections are of no avail in quasi-experimental designs. Notable among such authors is Lord (1967, 1969), who, in a couple of statements that are models of brevity (each less than two pages), has stimulated a good deal of discussion among authors addressing the question of statistical adjustment (e.g., Bock, 1975, pp. 490–496; Holland & Rubin, 1983; Novick, 1983; Weisberg, 1979). Concluding one of his statements, Lord (1967) said:

With the data usually available for such studies, there is simply no logical or statistical procedure that can be counted on to make proper allowances for uncontrolled preexisting differences between groups. The researcher wants to know how the groups would have compared if there had been no preexisting uncontrolled differences. The usual research study of this type is attempting to answer a question that simply cannot be answered in any rigorous way on the basis of available data. (p. 305)

In a good discussion of the futility of controls in the face of selectivity, Lieberson (1985) argued that "the reason for taking into account the differences found between the populations is also the very same reason for doubting whether such efforts can be successful very often" (p. 19). This, because the groups being compared are formed by nonrandom processes that are generally unknown and cannot, therefore, be taken into account in the statistical adjustment.

Using Coleman et al.'s (1982) study of public versus private schools as an example, Lieberson pointed out that a statistical adjustment for initial differences in socioeconomic background of students in the two types of schools is based on the untenable assumption that enrollment in one type of school or the other is determined randomly within the different socioeconomic strata. It is safe to assume that the converse is true, namely that within any

---

[14]For a notable exception in which the researcher forms the groups according to a specific scheme, thereby avoiding bias in estimation of treatment effects in the absence of randomization, see Regression Discontinuity below.

given socioeconomic stratum, parents' decisions regarding the type of school in which to enroll their children is *not* random but rather determined by a variety of factors (e.g., aspirations, racial attitudes, safety, perceptions of the child's ability and motivation, perceptions of the school's educational policies and programs). Because of these and other factors, some parents are even willing to make extreme sacrifices in order to enroll their child in the school of their choice. Harris (1981) quoted the principal of a private high school in Los Angeles, composed of about 35% black and about 20% Oriental and Hispanic students, as saying: "We're a black-flight school" (p. 96). According to Harris, many of the parents in this school "struggle to scrape up the tuition, which averages $1,000; a few endorse welfare checks to pay part of the fees" (p. 96).

What all the preceding amounts to is that, after adjusting for some observed variables (socioeconomic status, in the public versus public schools study), the groups still differ on relevant omitted variables. Not surprisingly, Lieberson argued that "under some conditions, the application of controls generates results that are actually farther removed from the truth than would occur if no controls were applied whatsoever" (p. 22).

In recent years, methodologists have come to recognize that only by attempting to model the selection process may one hope to make the necessary adjustment for initial differences between groups. Work on the development of selection models was done primarily by econometricians. For a good, informal introduction and references for further study, see Rindskopf (1986). A good, formal introduction is given by Barnow, Cain, and Goldberger, (1980). See also Muthén and Jöreskog (1983).

As Stromsdorfer and Farkas (1980) pointed out, current selection models "are in their infancy" (p. 40), and are based on very restrictive assumptions whose violations may lead to serious bias in parameter estimation. Illustrating the precarious nature of the application of currently available selection models is a paper by Murnane, Newstead, and Olsen (1985) in which they discussed a "significant puzzle" (p. 23) posed by conflicting findings regarding the effectiveness of public versus Catholic high schools, despite the fact that they "were based on the same data and both used variants of the new techniques for controlling selectivity bias" (p. 23). Murnane et al. showed, among other things, that the two analyses in question were based on different assumptions.

2. Regression Discontinuity

Although it has a "very limited range of possible applications" (Campbell & Stanley, 1963, p. 231), and is "rarely used" (Mark & Cook, 1984, p. 108), the regression-discontinuity design (RDD) serves as an example of an approach that is based not on "approximations" to randomization but rather on utilization of a special selection model. The relatively few studies in which RDD was utilized deal almost exclusively with the effects of compensatory education programs (Trochim, 1984, p. 68; for an example of its use in the evaluation of a crime-control program, see Berk & Rauma, 1983).

Despite its limited use, we discuss this design for two reasons. One, RDD serves to illustrate a design in which the selection model is nonrandom but clearly specified by the researcher. As a result, the estimate of treatment effects is not biased. Two, the design is probably "underutilized" (Judd & Kenny, 1981, p. 101). It can prove useful in diverse research areas (e.g., education, medicine, criminal justice, therapy) when random assignment to groups is precluded because of ethical, political, or administrative considerations, to name but some.

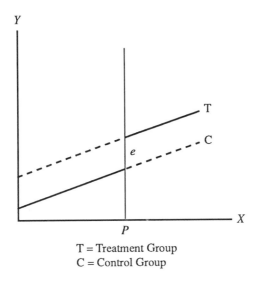

T = Treatment Group
C = Control Group

Figure 13.4

Initially, RDD was proposed by Thistlethwaite and Campbell (1960) from an analytic perspective as an alternative to the conventional approach of the matching of subjects in quasi-experimental designs. The RDD was subsequently accorded the status of a design, and a book devoted entirely to it was recently published (Trochim, 1984). (In a foreword to this book, Campbell traced the development of ideas regarding applications and analyses of the RDD.)

Essentially, RDD is predicated on the assignment of subjects to treatment and control groups strictly on the basis of a cutting point on a premeasure. Subjects above the cutting point are assigned to one group, whereas those below the cutting point are assigned to another. Depending on the aims of the study, the treatment is assigned to either the group scoring above the cutting point on the premeasure (e.g., selection on the basis of merit) or the one scoring below the cutting point (e.g., selection on the basis of need). The premeasure may be a pretest (i.e., a measure of the same variable as the dependent variable) or any variable deemed relevant for the study under consideration. The RDD is depicted in Figure 13.4 where, for illustrative purposes, subjects above the cutting point (P) on the premeasure (X) are assigned to the treatment, and those below P are assigned to the control group. An example of such a study would be admission of students scoring above a cutting score on a scholastic aptitude test, say, to an educational enrichment program (i.e., the treatment).

If the treatment has no effect, and if it is assumed that the regression of the dependent variable (Y) on the premeasure (X) is linear (this assumption is discussed below), then a single regression line would be expected to serve as a best fit for the scores of both groups. In other words, subjects' scores on the dependent variable would be best predicted, probabilistically, from a single regression equation regardless of whether or not they participated in the program. Referring to Figure 13.4, it would be expected under such circumstances that the regression line for the control group (the solid part of line C) would be extended to describe also the regression line for the treatment group (indicated by the dashed part). If, on the other hand, the treatment is effective in increasing performance on the dependent variable, then the regression line for the treatment group would be expected to be displaced above that of the control group (as illustrated by the solid part of line *T*). Under such circumstances, the difference between the two lines at the cutting score (the segment labeled *e*) would be taken as the effect of the treatment.

In our brief discussion of selection models (see above), we drew attention to their potentially crucial role in avoiding bias in the estimation of treatment effects. Cain (1975), who discussed this topic in connection with applications of regression analysis in quasi-experiments, distinguished between two types of subject selection processes: "those that are known and those that are unknown to the investigator" (p. 304). He went on to point out that "the critical difference for avoiding bias is not whether the assignments are random or nonrandom, but whether the investigator has *knowledge of and can model* this selection process" (p. 304).

The RDD, therefore, is an example of the type of design in which bias in the estimation of treatment effects may be avoided, not because of random assignment of subjects, but because the researcher has knowledge of the selection process. This, however, is not to be understood as implying that the RDD is free of problems and difficulties. On the contrary, it has more than it share of these. But, because they can be best understood in the context of analytic approaches to RDD, they are discussed in the next section.

ANALYSIS

The analysis of the RDD is aimed at comparing regression equations across groups (e.g., treatment versus control). This type of analysis is also applied in connection with several other designs (e.g., ATI and ANCOVA in Chapter 12; Regression Adjustment in the present chapter). As in the case of the earlier presentations, we do not go into the specifics of the analytic approach, which are dealt with and illustrated in Chapter 21.

Turning to some specific aspects of the application of this type of analysis in the RDD, it will be pointed out first that, because the assignment to the groups is based on the observed scores on the premeasure, errors of measurement do not lead to bias in the estimation of treatment effects. Therefore, no correction for measurement errors in the premeasure is called for (see, for example, Overall & Woodward, 1977a, 1977b; Rubin, 1974, 1977). In contrast, it will be recalled that errors of measurement of the premeasure may lead to serious bias in the estimation of treatment effects in the regression adjustment approach (see also Chapter 21, the section on ANCOVA, especially the discussion in connection with Figure 21.3).

Earlier in this chapter, hazards of extrapolating regression lines were discussed and illustrated (see the discussion in connection with Figure 13.2). The analytic approach for the RDD is actually based on extrapolations of the regression lines for the two groups (indicated by the dashed lines in Figure 13.4). Because the groups do not overlap on the premeasure, hazards due to extrapolation are very serious indeed.

For illustrative purposes, in Figure 13.5 are shown but two of various patterns in the data that may be overlooked when linearity is assumed, and extrapolations of the kind depicted in Figure 13.4 are made. In (*a*) of Figure 13.5, we illustrate how a nonlinear regression (the dashed line) may be erroneously interpreted as indicating a treatment effect (i.e., a pseudoeffect), by fitting linear regressions (the solid lines).

In (*b*) of Figure 13.5, we depict another example of an invalid conclusion that results from fitting linear regression when a nonlinear regression is more appropriate. An interpretation of the results on the basis of linear regression (the solid lines) would lead to the conclusion that there is an interaction between the treatment and the premeasure (see Chapter 21 about the

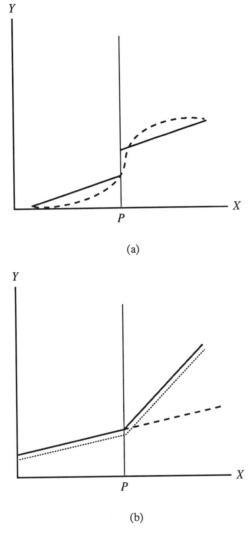

(a)

(b)

Figure 13.5

meaning of the test of the difference between the b's). This conclusion is based on the assumption that, had there been no treatment (i.e., no intervention), the regression line would have been the same for both groups (as is indicated by the extension of the bottom solid line). It is, however, possible that the treatment had no effect but that the regression is curvilinear (as indicated by the dotted line).

The two examples given in Figure 13.5 should suffice to underscore the importance of *not* relegating the question of linearity to the status of an assumption. A linear regression analysis should be performed only after it has been established that the trend is linear. But, even when a curvilinear regression analysis is performed,[15] it is still necessary to decide whether one is dealing with a curvilinear trend that indicates no treatment effect or with a linear trend that

[15]Curvilinear regression analysis is discussed in Chapter 18.

indicates a treatment effect. Stated differently, a choice has to be made between, for example, the two solid lines or the dashed line in (a) of Figure 13.5. Without additional information and a theoretical rationale, it is not possible to make a meaningful decision. For example, information about the trend of the data in a control group for which the scores on the premeasure cover the full range, that is, including also scores above the cutting point, would be useful in making this decision.

Because Campbell and his associates were the most influential authors in advancing and discussing the RDD, it will be instructive to show that even they were not immune to difficulties in arriving at valid conclusions regarding the trend in the data. Cook and Campbell (1976) warned that "the major threat to regression-discontinuity designs" (p. 271) comes from inferring treatment effects in situations where a nonlinear relation would have emerged in the absence of a treatment. It is noteworthy that this warning was made in the same section in which they offered results from a study by Seaver and Quarton (1976) as an example of a RDD in which being on the Dean's List had an effect on subsequent achievement. However, as Campbell (1984b, p. 20) himself pointed out, by the time he and Cook wrote their book (Cook & Campbell 1979, pp. 139–141), "Seaver and Quarton's data had been reanalyzed by Sween allowing for a curvilinear fit, totally removing all indications of any effect"[!] (Campbell, 1984b, pp. 20–21).

In addition to the difficulties discussed thus far, the RDD suffers from the fact that one of the groups generally is relatively small. Although this is not inherent in the design, it tends to occur in practice, as researchers assign to the treatment group individuals who score exceptionally high or low on the premeasure. Under such circumstances, the data lack stability, adversely affecting such aspects as generalizability, tests of statistical significance, and determinations of trends in the data (e.g., whether the trend is linear or curvilinear). Regarding statistical tests of significance, Goldberger (1972) showed that, for the RDD to have the same statistical power as a comparable randomized experiment, it would have to have almost three times the number of subjects than the one required for the randomized experiment.[16]

Our discussion of RDD was limited to situations in which assignment of subjects on the basis of a cutting score is strictly adhered to. Situations where deviations from a strict assignment rule take place because of political, administrative, and other considerations come easily to mind (see Trochim, 1984, for detailed examples). Needless to say, complications and difficulties discussed above become much more severe when one deviates from a strict assignment rule. For a detailed discussion of attempts to deal with deviations from a strict assignment rule, see Trochim (1984).

Our aim was to introduce basic ideas of RDD; thus, we do not address variations on and extensions of it (e.g., multiple cutting points, multiple variables). For a discussion of these topics, see Judd and Kenny (1981, Chapter 5), and Trochim (1984).

In sum, therefore, although the RDD may be useful for specific problems, it is also generally fraught with difficulties and potential sources of bias. Trochim (1984) discussed various limitations of the RDD. His statement regarding analytic problems may well serve as a summary for what we have been saying and a call for caution that should be borne in mind when using the RDD.

The statistical analysis of the regression-discontinuity design is not trivial. In typical circumstances, a good deal of judgment is required to accomplish the statistical modeling. The nature of the design makes it particularly susceptible to the influences of outliers, floor and ceiling effects, test "chance" levels, and similar factors that may be less salient in other strategies. In the end, one must rely heavily

---

[16]Power of statistical tests of significance is discussed in Chapter 15.

on assumptions of the statistical model used and on the ability to discern visually whether a program effect is plausible. (pp. 46–47)

3. Interrupted Time Series

A time series refers to a series of observations taken chronologically on a given variable. Time-series data are particularly abundant in such areas as business, economics, agriculture, and meteorology, as is exemplified by the prevalence of records of closing stock market prices, gross national product, and temperature. Time-series data are collected and analyzed for two main purposes: (a) to develop models to explain patterns that occur over time (e.g., trends, cycles, seasonal variations), and (b) to use the models for forecasting.

Interrupted time series is, as the name implies, a series that has been interrupted by some discrete event or intervention (e.g., a change in the driving speed limit, an oil embargo, the outbreak of war, the introduction of a law, a vaccine, an educational program). The purpose of studying an interrupted time series is to asses the effect of the intervention, or the treatment, by attempting to infer if and in what way it has changed the time-series data.

The literature on time-series designs and analysis is extensive; some of it quite technical. It is *not* our intention to present even a rudimentary treatment of this topic. Instead, we wish to make you aware of the existence of this promising approach. Accordingly, all we will do is offer some references to general introductory treatments of this topic, followed by references written from the perspective of sociobehavioral sciences, with a special emphasis on interrupted time series. A schematization of two elementary quasi-experimental interrupted time-series designs is then presented.

General introductions to time-series designs and analysis, along with illustrations of their applications, will be found in Bowerman and O'Connell (1979), Cryer (1986), Nelson (1973), O'Donavan (1983), and Pankratz (1983). Among books, chapters, and papers addressed to time-series designs from a sociobehavioral perspective are Algina and Olejnik (1982), Campbell (1969b), Cook and Campbell (1979, Chapter 5), Cook, Dintzer, and Mark (1980), Gottman (1981), Harrop and Velicer (1985), Judd and Kenny (1981, Chapter 7), Lewis-Beck (1986), McCleary and Hay (1980), McDowall, McCleary, Meidinger, and Hay (1980), and Swaminathan and Algina (1977).

SIMPLE INTERRUPTED TIME SERIES

Following is a schematization of a simple interrupted time-series design, where O stands for observations, and X for an intervention, a treatment.

$$O_1\ O_2\ O_3\ O_4\ X\ O_5\ O_6\ O_7\ O_8$$

For illustrative purposes, we use four observations prior to the intervention and four following it. Although, in general, time-series data consist of a larger number of observations, the number varies, depending on the specifics of the design as well as the substantive issue being studied. Thus, for example, a larger number of observations is required when this design is applied to a single case as contrasted with a group. Numerous examples of and references to applications of this design to group data will be found in the literature cited previously. For applications in single-case research, see Barlow and Hersen (1984), Kazdin (1982), and Kratochwill (1978).

Without going into the various threats to the internal validity of this design (for a detailed discussion, see Cook & Campbell, 1979, pp. 209–214), we trust that, on the basis of our discussion of such threats (Chapter 10), you recognize that the major threat in the design under consideration is that of history. We turn to the second design, in which attempts are made to control for this and other threats to internal validity.

INTERRUPTED TIME SERIES WITH NONEQUIVALENT CONTROL GROUP

Following is a schematization of this design using, again for illustrative purposes, four observations (O) prior to an intervention (X) and four after it.

$$O_1 \; O_2 \; O_3 \; O_4 \; X \; O_5 \; O_6 \; O_7 \; O_8$$

$$O_1 \; O_2 \; O_3 \; O_4 \quad O_5 \; O_6 \; O_7 \; O_8$$

Whereas the first group is administered a treatment after the fourth observation, the second group is meant to serve as a control and is not administered any treatment. Clearly, the degree to which threats to internal validity are controlled depends on the comparability of the two nonequivalent groups.

The present design may be conceived of as a generalization of the nonequivalent-control-group design, discussed in detail in earlier sections of this chapter. We believe it is not necessary to comment on the general advantages of having multiple observations prior to and after an intervention. The specific utilization of multiple observations is an integral aspect of the analysis of interrupted time-series data and is discussed and illustrated in the references given above. These references also include variations on the present design as well as more complex ones.

To reiterate: Our aim in this section was only to inform you of the availability of time-series designs for quasi-experiments and to provide you with some relevant references. Needless to say, time series can also be very useful in experimental research.

CONCLUDING REMARKS

We trust that it is clear from the presentation in this chapter that quasi-experimental research is an attempt to emulate experimental research. According to Cook and Campbell (1986), "the origins of quasi-experimentation lay in the desire to escape from the laboratory as well as in the desire to examine the causal consequences of phenomena for which random assignment was not considered possible" (p. 149).

The debate concerning the pros and cons of laboratory versus field research were reviewed in Chapter 12 and will, therefore, not be commented on here. As to causality, it was pointed out several times earlier that this complex and controversial topic is discussed in Chapter 24. Nevertheless, Cook and Campbell's statement may serve as a good starting point for our concluding remarks.

First and foremost, a causal statement implies a theory about the process that brought about or is affecting the phenomenon under study. Accordingly, quasi-experimentation should not be confused with post hoc searches for plausible theoretical explanations.

Second, as was discussed in detail in Chapters 9 and 10, even when guided by theory, validity of conclusions from any study depends on the soundness of the ruling out of alternative explanations. That doing this is generally easier and less tentative in experiments than in quasi-experiments should, we hope, be clear from the presentations in this and the preceding chapter. Indeed, "true experiments are less equivocal than quasi-experiments, and . . . permit fewer excuses for unwanted results" (Campbell & Boruch, 1975, p. 208).

Third, it goes without saying that even the best laid plans for an experiment may go awry. In the process of execution, many experiments are transformed into quasi-experiments and should be treated as such. Suffice it to point out that nonrandom subject attrition from groups that were equated by virtue of randomization leads to a study with nonequivalent groups fraught with all the difficulties and ambiguities that have occupied us in the present chapter.

Chapter 14
Nonexperimental Designs

In preceding chapters, attention was drawn to the lack of agreement regarding classification of research designs as well as the lack of consensus about terminology used to refer to what are essentially the same types of designs. It will be recalled that we expressed a preference for three broad classes of designs: experimental, quasi-experimental, and nonexperimental. Chapters 12 and 13 respectively dealt with experimental and quasi-experimental designs. The present chapter is addressed to nonexperimental designs.

Admittedly, the designation "nonexperimental" is almost all inclusive, excluding only experimental designs. In the hope of avoiding ambiguity, it will be pointed out that what serves to distinguish among the three classes of designs is the presence or absence of (a) manipulation of independent variables, and (b) randomization. In an experiment, both manipulation and randomization are present; in a quasi-experiment, manipulation is present, but randomization is absent; in a nonexperiment, both manipulation and randomization are absent. Lest we create a false impression of utter clarity, we remind you of the discussion in Chapter 13 regarding ambiguities as to what constitute treatments in quasi-experimental designs.

What about some of the terms used in lieu of nonexperimental? Until recently, the predominant term has probably been "correlational research." However, as was pointed out by various authors (e.g., Cook & Campbell, 1979, p. 295), this designation is a misnomer, because it refers to analytic rather than design characteristics.

Another term frequently used is "survey research." But its meaning varies widely. Thus, Hyman (1973), for example, viewed the survey as being "in sharp contrast to the experiment carried out in the artificial setting of the laboratory" (p. 324), and saw it as belonging to "the larger class of field methods" (p. 324). Statisticians, on the other hand, tend to use the term more restrictively as referring to "a method of gathering information from a number of individuals, a 'sample,' in order to learn something about the larger population from which the sample has been drawn" (Ferber, Sheatsley, Turner, & Waksberg, 1980, p. 3).

Yet another designation in common use is "observational research." However, as was pointed out in Chapter 13, some authors, particularly statisticians, use it to refer also to quasi-experimental designs. This is what prompted Cook and Campbell (1979) to propose the label "passive-observational studies" (p. 296). In Chapter 6, we expressed reservations about the use of the term "observational research" on the grounds that it is more appropriate as a characterization of data-collection procedures. We have similar reservations with respect to Cook and Campbell's designation.

To reiterate: There is no consensus regarding the term used to refer to designs presented in this chapter. Nor are any of the terms, including the one we use, free of ambiguity. We turn now to a consideration of major aspects of nonexperimental research, following which we present some simple designs.

PREDICTIVE VERSUS EXPLANATORY RESEARCH

The distinction between predictive and explanatory research was introduced in Chapter 3, where attention was also drawn to the lack of agreement among philosophers of science regarding the logical status of prediction and explanation.[1] It will be recalled that predictive research is aimed at the development of systems to predict criteria of interest by utilizing information from one or more predictors. Explanatory research is aimed at the testing of hypotheses formulated to explain phenomena of interest.

As was stated in Chapter 3, these two perspectives are not mutually exclusive. Nevertheless, the distinction between them is imperative, as it has far reaching implications for data collection, choice and application of analytic approaches, and interpretation of the results, to name but some major aspects. In a predictive study, it is conceivable, although not advisable, for theory to play no role in decisions regarding the kinds of data to be collected and how they are to be analyzed. Variables may be selected, retained, or dropped solely on the basis of practical considerations. Further, the designation of which variables are to serve as criteria and which are to serve as predictors is arbitrary; therefore, such choices can be decided in accordance with specific practical purposes and circumstances. Finally, the very serious threats to validity attendant with model misspecification in explanatory research do not arise in predictive research.

We reminded you of the distinction between the two perspectives, because the risk of confusing them is particularly great in nonexperimental research. Issues concerning predictive research were dealt with in Chapter 3 under the general heading of criterion-related validation. The present chapter is addressed solely to explanatory research.

FORMULATION AND TESTING OF MODELS

The point of departure in explanatory research and one that transcends all else is theory. In light of earlier discussions of the role of theory (see, in particular, Chapter 9), it should be clear that, in the absence of a theoretical framework, there is no way of telling which variables are relevant and which are not relevant for a given study. Nor is it possible to determine the role of variables included in a study (e.g., independent, dependent, control).

Chief among the implications of the difference between experimental and quasi-experimental designs, on one hand, and nonexperimental designs, on the other hand, is the direction in which inferences are made. In experimental and quasi-experimental research, inferences are made from the independent variables (the putative causes) to the dependent

---

[1]See comments and references in Chapter 3. See also Chapter 8, Research Design Perspective.

variable (the effect; the phenomenon to be explained). In nonexperimental research, inferences are generally made in the opposite direction. That is, beginning with a dependent variable, attempts are made to detect, to uncover, the independent variables.

We would like very much to avoid creating the *false* impression that what we said in the preceding paragraph is neither ambiguous nor controversial. As to ambiguity, it will suffice to remind you of our discussion of circumstances in which it is difficult to tell what the treatment is (e.g., when studying the effects of some global program; see Chapter 13). As to being controversial, it will suffice to mention the controversy surrounding the notion of causation (see Chapter 24).

Ambiguities and controversies aside, the propensity of confusing independent and dependent variables, of engaging in post hoc theorizing (see Chapter 9), is generally far greater in nonexperimental than in experimental or quasi-experimental research. When the researcher manipulates a variable(s) (e.g., administers different treatments), it stands to reason for him or her to have some expectations regarding its effects on the dependent variable and for these expectations to be expressed in the form of hypotheses to be tested. In nonexperimental research, on the other hand, researchers may even be inclined to refrain from formulating hypotheses, in the mistaken belief that they are thereby being "neutral," and are "letting the data speak for themselves."

Related to the foregoing, is the logic of the comparisons being made in the different designs. In experimental designs, comparisons are made among groups that, because of randomization (see Chapters 10 and 12), are equal (probabilistically) in all respects except for the independent variable (e.g., exposure to different treatments, to varying degrees of the same treatment). Assuming, for the sake of the present discussion, that various threats to internal validity may be reasonably ruled out (see Chapters 10, 11, and 12), observed differences among the groups on the dependent variable may be attributed to the independent variable.

As was discussed in detail in Chapter 13, the absence of randomization in quasi-experimental designs raises a host of very difficult, some maintain insurmountable, problems regarding the validity of comparisons among the groups. Ignoring, for the sake of the present discussion, these problems and complications that may arise in the execution of the research, the comparisons being made in quasi-experiments are still among groups exposed to different treatments (or to treatments and controls).

In nonexperimental designs, groups are very frequently formed on the basis of the dependent variable. Among examples that come readily to mind are groups formed on the basis of criminality, recidivism, aggression, motivation, mental or physical illness. The researcher then tries to uncover what it is that has led to (might have caused) the observed differences among the groups. The thing to note, in the context of the present discussion, is that, when groups are formed on the basis of their status on a dependent variable and differences among them are attributed to some cause (e.g., child abuse, type of diet, smoking, alcohol consumption), the possibility that people from the different groups have been exposed to the same "treatment" cannot be ruled out. The crux of the difficulties, under such circumstances, then, is that, in addition to numerous other problems (see below), statements to the effect that the groups being compared have been exposed to different treatments may not be tenable.

Dorn (1953), who provided a very good discussion of the contrast between experimental and nonexperimental designs in medical research, offered interesting illustrations of the kind of difficulties to which we have alluded. Thus, after discussing obstacles to the conduct of an experiment, or even a quasi-experiment, on the effects of smoking on lung cancer, Dorn pointed out that when researchers attempt to study the problem nonexperimentally they tend to compare groups formed on the basis of the dependent variable. That is, people are classified on the basis of whether or not they suffer from lung cancer. The comparison that is then made "is between the proportion of smokers among persons with and without lung cancer; whereas the appropriate comparison to test the hypothesis in question is the proportion of persons with cancer of the lung among smokers and nonsmokers" (p. 679).

SAMPLING

Generally speaking, the internal validity of an *experiment* is not jeopardized when the subjects do not comprise a probability sample of some defined population. Assuming that other threats to internal validity can be ruled out, valid statements may be made about, say, effects of different treatments, because the subjects were randomly assigned to them. Obviously, the study may have no external validity.[2]

Excluding from consideration statements limited to descriptions of aggregates of people one happens to be studying, probability sampling is a *sine qua non* for validity of nonexperimental studies. Unfortunately, in various areas of sociobehavioral research, it is customary to present findings about comparisons among all sorts of groups (e.g., males and females; blacks, whites, and Hispanics; smokers and nonsmokers; voters and nonvoters) on assortments of variables (e.g., motivation, mental ability, income, attitudes) without the slightest concern about sampling and representativeness. Similarly, correlations among assorted variables, regression equations, and causal models are calculated and tested, and advanced as supporting or failing to support given explanations, despite the fact that data were obtained from aggregates of people who, for a variety of reasons (e.g., interest in the research topic, curiosity, coercion, remuneration), became subjects in the study. Whatever the reasons for participation, it is important to bear in mind that statistics (e.g., means, standard deviations, correlations, regression equations) based on nonprobability samples may have no resemblance to those that would be obtained from probability samples from populations of interest.

A prevalent mistaken notion is that difficulties arising when nonprobability samples are used can be alleviated, if not overcome altogether, by offering descriptions of the people studied. It should be stressed that even when the variables used in the description of nonprobability samples are relevant (in many reports, they are clearly not relevant), such descriptions are based on the untenable assumption that the people described are representative of the target population. In most instances, there is not even an allusion to a target population.

CONTROL

The major threat to validity in nonexperimental research emanates from uncontrolled confounding variables. Attempting to study patterns of causation (see below) among a relatively small number of variables, the researcher is faced with the impossible task of identifying and controlling myriad potentially confounding variables. Even when the goal of identifying the variables to be controlled is reasonably met, it is frequently very difficult to tell whether and how they may be controlled. The two major approaches to control in nonexperimental research are through subject selection and statistical adjustments. The crucial role of sampling in subject selection was discussed in the preceding section. Below, we comment on ambiguities attendant with the selection of subjects from broad classifications.

---

[2]For experimental designs, see Chapter 12. For internal and external validity, see Chapter 10.

This is not the place to go into the various approaches to statistical adjustment. They are presented and discussed in various chapters in the context of specific designs and the analytic approaches applicable to them. For present purposes, it will suffice to point out that our comments about the very difficult logical and analytic problems attendant with attempts to exercise statistical controls (see Chapters 10 and 13, comments on ANCOVA and partial correlation) are equally applicable to nonexperimental research.

Finally, it should be borne in mind that the exercise of controls in nonexperimental research may aggravate the situation by distorting relations among variables of interest, even altering the nature of the dependent variable. As always, the major safeguards against overlooking such occurrences are theory and common sense.

We turn now to a presentation of some elementary nonexperimental designs. As in preceding chapters, the aim here is an overview. When we deal with analytic approaches, we do so on an intuitive level and make reference to relevant chapters in this book and/or other sources for detailed treatments of such topics.

CATEGORICAL INDEPENDENT VARIABLES

Faced with potential or actual classifications of people on myriad variables (e.g., sex, race, marital status, religion, ethnicity), it is not surprising that laypersons and researchers alike form opinions as to how and why classes of people differ on almost every variable imaginable. Thus, it seems natural to inquire about relations between, say, sex and aggression, marital status and stress, place of residence and attitudes, race and temperament, socioeconomic status and mental health, and so forth.

The meaning and role of classification in measurement and research were discussed in various chapters (see especially Chapter 2 under Nominal Scale). For present purposes, therefore, we will only indicate that, by designs with categorical independent variables, we mean designs in which one or more broad classifications of people are used to explain the status of subjects on some phenomenon of interest (i.e., presumed dependent variable). Excluded from consideration is the highly questionable approach of categorizing a continuous independent variable (e.g., mental ability, anxiety, motivation) for the purpose of classifying people into distinct groups (e.g., high, average, low). Also excluded from consideration here are sophisticated and complex classifications and typologies arrived at on the basis of theoretical considerations and/or applications of the wide range of techniques referred to as cluster analysis.[3]

Now, no difficulties arise when the research is limited to *descriptions* of differences among groups on some dependent variable. Complexities and ambiguities are likely to abound when the categorical variable(s) is offered as an *explanation* for observed differences on the dependent variable. For example, observing differences between males and females on mechanical aptitude, it is easy to fall prey to an "explanation" that the differences are due to sex. However, in most instances, such explanations are actually pseudo explanations, or, as Baumeister (1988) put it, "a sex difference finding is a question, not an answer" (p. 1093). What is important, and left unanswered when differences are attributed to sex, is the question

---

[3]For some introductions to and/or reviews of cluster analysis and its use for classification, see Aldenderfer and Blashfield (1978, 1984), Blashfield (1980), Blashfield and Aldenderfer (1978), Everitt (1980), Hartigan (1975), Hudson et al. (1982), Lorr (1983), Meehl and Golden (1982), Mezzich and Solomon (1980), Romesburg (1984), and Sokal (1974).

what it is about males and females (i.e., the specific variables) that make them differ on the phenomena being studied.[4] The same may be said about differences among other kinds of groupings (e.g., religious, ethnic, racial).

Regardless of the difficulties outlined above, the design under consideration essentially entails comparisons among the broad categories or groupings on the dependent variable of interest. Accordingly, probability sampling is a necessary, although not sufficient, condition for valid inferences. Such samples are obtained from within each grouping, or class, as each is treated as a separate population for the purpose of group comparisons. Sample sizes *need not* reflect the relative frequencies of the groups in what may be conceived of as an overall population. Because of consideration of statistical analyses, one may be well advised to obtain samples of equal size for all the groups being compared.

ONE INDEPENDENT VARIABLE

As in the case of the designs presented in preceding chapters, we assume that the dependent variable is continuous. Under such circumstances, group comparisons are generally focused on mean differences. These include estimation and interpretation of such aspects as magnitudes of effects (i.e., effect size; see Chapters 9 and 15) as well as tests of statistical significance.

ANALYSIS

When the independent variable is comprised of two categories only (e.g., males and females), a *t* test would be used for testing the difference between two means. For variables comprised of more than two categories (e.g., Catholics, Jews, Moslems, and Protestants), a one-way (simple) analysis of variance (ANOVA) would be applied.

We mentioned the *t* test and ANOVA, because these are the only kinds of analytic approaches that students trained in certain disciplines are exposed to. As is shown in Chapter 19, the same results may be obtained through the application of multiple regression analysis in which the categorical independent variable (group membership, in the present context) is represented by a set of coded vectors. For now, we would only like to point out that the multiple regression approach is preferable, because it is more general in that it can accommodate categorical, continuous, and combinations of the two types of independent variables in the same analysis.

Doing an ANOVA, or a multiple regression analysis with coded vectors, yields a global answer as to whether there are statistically significant differences among the means of the groups studied. However, the interest, in most instances, is in differences between means of specific groups or combinations of groups. Thus, in a study of, say, the effects of ethnicity on income, one may wish, for example, to study differences in income between specific ethnic groups as well as between combinations of ethnic groups (e.g., European versus Asian extraction). This is accomplished by what are referred to as multiple comparisons—a topic also presented in Chapter 19.

---

[4]In view of concerns regarding sexism in research, it is not surprising that the question of whether or not sex differences should be studied and routinely reported has attained the level of ideological and political debates (for some recent exchanges, see Baumeister, 1988; Eagly, 1987; McHugh, Koeske, & Frieze, 1986; Rothblum, 1988. For a suggested model for the study of gender-related behavior, see Deaux & Major, 1987).

MULTIPLE INDEPENDENT VARIABLES

Researchers are frequently interested in comparing groups that have been classified on more than one variable. For example, a researcher may wish to study differences in mean income for groups that have been classified on race *and* religion, ethnicity *and* political party affiliation. Needless to say, cross classifications may be created on more than two variables.

Because such designs *seem* similar to factorial designs in experimental research (see Chapter 12), some researchers treat them as such. Thus, they speak of the main effects and interactions among the categorical variables used in the cross classifications. Referring to one of the examples given above, they would speak of the main effects of race, religion, and of the interaction between race and religion on income.

The resemblance between the design under consideration and factorial designs in experimental research is only superficial. We cannot go into the detailed explanation of the differences between the two designs. Nor can we go into the differences in analytic approaches that would generally be taken in the two designs (we do this in Chapter 20). All we will do here is hint at the major difficulty. Overlooking issues concerning model specification in nonexperimental research, especially omission of relevant variables, when the design under consideration is treated as if it were a factorial design in experimental research, it is assumed, wittingly or unwittingly, that the variables are independent of each other. Clearly, this is not the case in nonexperimental research, where the variables may not only be correlated, but where the correlation may even be a consequence of one of the "independent" variables affecting the other.

Our comment was, of necessity, brief. We return to this topic in Chapter 20 (see Categorical Independent Variables in Nonexperimental Research).

CONTINUOUS INDEPENDENT VARIABLES

We begin with a brief comment about designs with a single independent variable and then turn to ones with multiple independent variables. We would again like to stress that our aim is limited to an intuitive introduction. Our plea for patience and tolerance for ambiguity made in connection with designs presented in Chapters 12 and 13 is even more pertinent in connection with the designs to be presented here. Depending on your background, you may even find the presentation confusing and frustrating. All we can do is assure you that, in Part 3, we explain and illustrate how models presented schematically here are analyzed and interpreted. You may find it useful to skim relevant sections of Chapters 17 and 18 when reading the presentation that follows.

ONE INDEPENDENT VARIABLE

Several times earlier (see, for example, Chapter 13, the discussion in connection with Figure 13.1), it was pointed out that the omission of relevant variables that are correlated with the independent variables constitutes a specification error that leads to biased estimates of the effects of the independent variables in the model. That such errors are unavoidable in nonexperimental research should be obvious. All one can do is attempt to minimize them by including in the design major relevant variables. In any event, it is fairly certain that a design with a single independent variable in nonexperimental research is bound to be grossly misspecified in virtually any instance that comes to mind. Therefore, we would like it understood that we mention this kind of design for purely didactic purposes. All that will be pointed out is that, when such a design is used, it is generally analyzed through simple regression analysis, where the dependent variable is regressed on the independent variable. This type of analysis is presented in Chapter 17, where the assumptions underlying it (e.g., linearity) are also discussed.

MULTIPLE INDEPENDENT VARIABLES

Obviously, a correct model specification cannot be attempted without advancing a theory of the phenomenon under investigation, including formulations regarding the nature of the relations among the independent variables. We cannot even begin doing this here without going far afield. Instead, we limit ourselves to synthetic models aimed at introducing some terminology and demonstrating how different theoretical formulations lead to different conceptions about the roles of the same variables and, in turn, to different approaches to the analysis.

SINGLE-STAGE MODELS

A single-stage model refers to a model in which a dependent variable is said to be affected by a set of intercorrelated independent variables. An example of such a model, consisting of three independent variables and a dependent variable, is depicted in Figure 14.1. To use a substantive example, we will assume that the independent variables are Socioeconomic Status (*SES*), Mental Ability (*MA*), and Motivation (*MOT*). The dependent variable is Academic Achievement (*AA*). Several points will be made about this model.

The independent variables are treated as being on the same level of discourse. That is, none of them is said to affect (or to be affected by) any of the other variables. All that is indicated by the curved, bidirectional arrows connecting the variables is that they are correlated. Such variables are often referred to as exogenous variables.

An *exogenous* variable is a variable whose variability is assumed to be determined by causes outside the model under consideration. Stated differently, no attempt is made to explain the variability of an exogenous variable or its relations with other exogenous variables. (Pedhazur, 1982, p. 178)

In contrast, "an *endogenous* variable is one whose variation is to be explained by exogenous and other endogenous variables in the causal model" (Pedhazur, 1982, p. 178).

In the model depicted in Figure 14.1, then, *SES*, *MA*, and *MOT* are treated as correlated exogenous variables. What this means is that the correlations among these variables are treated as given, not subject to explication. Thus, for example, the possibility that *SES* and *MOT* are correlated, because the former affects the latter, cannot be entertained in such a model. It may be that the researcher using such a model is unwilling or unable to offer a theoretical rationale for the correlations among these variables. Whatever the reasons, it should be noted that, according to the model, these variables have only direct effects on the dependent variable, as is indicated by the arrows emanating from them. Situations in which the effect of a given variable may be, in part or totally, indirect, through the mediation of other variables, are precluded in single-stage models.

Other variables affecting *AA*, subsumed under *e*, are assumed to be *not* correlated with the

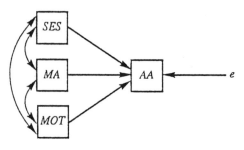

Figure 14.1

independent variables in the model. As was pointed out above, violation of this assumption constitutes a specification error.

In sum, therefore, a single-stage model, also referred to as a single-equation model, is one in which the dependent variable is expressed as a function of correlated independent variables and omitted variables that are *not* correlated with the independent variables.

ANALYSIS

Assuming that the model is correctly specified and that other assumptions are also met, multiple regression analysis would be the method of choice for single-stage designs of the kind depicted in Figure 14.1. This approach is discussed in detail in Chapter 18, where it is pointed out that regression coefficients are interpreted as the effects of the independent variables on the dependent variables. Among other things, the choice between unstandardized regression coefficients (i.e., *b*'s) and standardized regression coefficients (i.e., β's) is considered.

Instead of interpreting regression coefficients, researchers frequently take another approach, one that can be broadly characterized as variance partitioning. Essentially, the aim is to partition the variance of the dependent variable and attribute different portions of it to the various independent variables. Examples of variance partitioning are hierarchical regression analysis and commonality analysis. In Chapter 18, we discuss why variance partitioning has little to recommend itself. For now, it will only be pointed out that, depending on the specific approach used, variance partitioning is either inappropriate or uninformative when applied in single-stage models.

MULTISTAGE MODELS

Multistage models consist of one or more exogenous variables and two or more endogenous variables. The stages refer to the number of endogenous variables, each of which is designated, in turn, as a dependent variable. To clarify our meaning, two models in which the same substantive variables that were used in the single-stage model are presented in Figure 14.2. In (*a*), *MOT* (Motivation) is depicted as being affected by *SES* (Socioeconomic Status) and *MA* (Mental Ability), whereas *AA* (Academic Achievement) is depicted as being affected by the three aforementioned variables. Hence, (*a*) is a two-stage model. It can be seen that

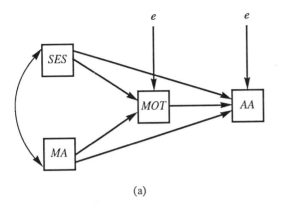

(a)

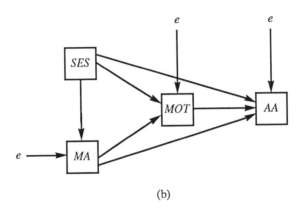

(b)

Figure 14.2

(b) is a three-stage model.[5] To reiterate: *We cannot be concerned here with the overriding questions of theory and correct model specification. Our sole purpose in using these models is illustrative.*

Now, according to Model (a), SES and MA are taken as correlated and are shown to have direct as well as indirect effects (through MOT) on AA. Using the same variables, alternative models are conceivable. For example, it may be hypothesized that SES has only an indirect effect on AA. Accordingly, the arrow from SES to AA would be deleted.

Turning to Model (b) of Figure 14.2, it will be noted that (a) SES is said to affect MA, (b) SES and MA are said to affect MOT, and (c) SES, MA, and MOT are said to affect AA. As in (a), other models may be formulated. For example, one may hypothesize that the correlation between MA and MOT is due solely to their common cause, SES. What this means is that it is hypothesized that MA does *not* affect MOT. To reflect such an hypothesis, the arrow from MA to MOT would be deleted.

The models depicted in Figure 14.2 may also be referred to as multiequation models in which each of the endogenous (dependent) variables is expressed as a function of the

---

[5]In both models, the dependent variables are also affected by variables not in the model and subsumed under the various *e*'s in the figure.

variables said to affect it and an error term under which variables not included in the equation are subsumed. Thus, two equations are required for Model (*a*)—one for *MOT* and one for *AA*. Three equations (one for each endogenous variable) are required for Model (*b*).

ANALYSIS

The type of models we have presented, and the terminology we have used, are generally discussed under the heading of *Path Analysis*. We discuss and illustrate analyses of such models in Chapter 24. For now, only some general comments relevant to the topic under consideration will be made.

Given certain assumptions, notably that the relations among the variables are linear and that error terms (*e*'s) are not correlated with variables preceding them in the model (see Pedhazur, 1982, p. 582, for a discussion of these and other assumptions), estimates of effects of variables in models such as those depicted in Figure 14.2 can be obtained through the application of multiple regression analysis. Specifically, each endogenous variable is re-gressed on the variables said to affect it, and the *b*'s (unstandardized coefficients) or β's (standardized coefficients) are taken as indicating the effects of the variables with which they are associated. Thus, two multiple regression analyses would be performed for (*a*): (a) regressing *MOT* on *SES* and *MA*, and (b) regressing *AA* on *SES*, *MA*, and *MOT*. For (*b*), three regression analyses would be performed. Note that the single-stage model, presented in Figure 14.1, can be conceived of as a special case. In other words, using a single-equation model, one is in effect using a single-stage path analysis model.

To give you an idea of the implications of the different models we have presented, we will focus on the role of *SES*. Assume, for the sake of the present discussion, that *SES does not* affect *AA* directly but that it *does* affect it indirectly through the mediation of other variables. Given this assumption and using the model depicted in Figure 14.1, the inevitable conclusion would be that *SES* is irrelevant, so far as *AA* is concerned. This, because, as was pointed out earlier, in a single-stage model only direct effects are estimable.

Assume now that Model (*a*) of Figure 14.2 is formulated. In addition to the estimate of the direct effect of *SES* on *AA*, which will be the same as that obtained for the model in Figure 14.1, an estimate of its indirect effect, through *MOT*, will also be obtained. If Model (*b*) were advanced instead, *SES* would be shown to have the following three indirect effects:

(1) $SES \rightarrow MA \rightarrow AA$

(2) $SES \rightarrow MOT \rightarrow AA$

(3) $SES \rightarrow MA \rightarrow MOT \rightarrow AA$

In sum, then, depending on the model used, one will arrive at different conclusions regarding the effect of *SES* on *AA*. The thing to remember, however, is that an analysis is carried out to ascertain the viability of the model, *not* to generate such a model.

CATEGORICAL AND CONTINUOUS INDEPENDENT VARIABLES

As in experimental and quasi-experimental designs (see Chapters 12 and 13), the design may be comprised of both categorical and continuous independent variables. In the simplest case, a design may consist of one categorical and one continuous independent variable. Some examples would be studies of the effects of years of experience and sex on salary, locus of control and race on stress, and religiosity and marital status on attitudes towards abortions.

ANALYSIS

Analyses of designs with categorical and continuous independent variables proceed as in analogous experimental and quasi-experimental designs. Broadly speaking, the analysis consists of comparisons of the regression of the dependent variable on the continuous independent variable(s) across the categories of the categorical variable. This analytic approach is presented in Chapter 21. Here, we will attempt to clarify our meaning by considering the first example given above, namely the effect of years of experience and sex on salary. When years of experience is conceived of as a control variable, that is, when it is desired to see whether males and females are paid differently after "adjusting" for years of experience, the analysis proceeds as in an experimental design consisting of a treatment and a concomitant variable (see Chapter 12, Design 4). When, however, years of experience is conceived as interacting with sex in their effects on salary, the analysis proceeds as in an attribute–treatments–interaction (ATI; see Chapter 12, Design 7).

Two things will be noted. One, as was pointed out in Chapter 12, we may conceive of a design as comprised of a treatment and a concomitant variable but upon analysis discover that the two variables interact, requiring that it be treated as an ATI design. The converse is also possible. That is, when in an ATI design it is concluded that the treatments and the attribute do not interact, the design is treated as one with treatments and a concomitant variable. Two, it should be clear that, whereas the analysis proceeds in the same way regardless of whether the design is experimental, quasi-experimental, or nonexperimental, interpretation of the results depends very much on the type of design.

LONGITUDINAL RESEARCH: A COMMENT

It is with some hesitancy that we decided to comment on longitudinal research. We are concerned lest we give the impression that we are "dealing" with this important and complex topic when all we have in mind is to acquaint you with some ideas and references related to it. We hope that you will view our effort in this light.

To begin with, the placement of the comment in the present chapter should not be taken to mean that longitudinal research is necessarily nonexperimental. In principle, it may be carried out in experimental, quasi-experimental, or nonexperimental designs, although it has "been recognized as the *sine qua non* of good evaluation in nonexperimental settings" (Marco, 1974, p. 225). We are inclined to say that most longitudinal research is carried out in nonexperimental designs except that the validity of such a statement would depend on the definition of longitudinal research one adopts.

In their review of the history of and rationale for longitudinal research, Baltes and Nesselroade (1979) drew attention to the diversity of its definitions and cited Zazzo's remark that "*longitudinal* is a blanket term and describes not a method but a wide variety of methods" (p. 4). They noted, however, that "the one sine qua non of longitudinal research is that *the entity under investigation is observed repeatedly as it exists and evolves over time*" (p. 4). A critical aspect of the preceding is that such studies are concerned with persistence or change of the entity with the passage of time, as is stressed in Baltes and Nesselroade's (1979) "working definition":

Longitudinal methodology involves repeated time-ordered observation of an individual or individuals with the goal of identifying processes and causes of intraindividual change and of interindividual patterns of intraindividual change in behavioral development. (p. 7)

The unique characteristics of longitudinal research can be seen when it is contrasted with cross-sectional research. Being based on an observation at a single point in time, cross-sectional research may be likened to a snapshot of the phenomenon of interest. Accordingly, it is incapable of providing answers to questions concerning persistence, change, growth, or developmental processes—the very problems that constitute the focus of longitudinal research.

It is, therefore, not surprising that McCall (1977) stated: "The longitudinal method is the lifeblood of developmental psychology" (p. 341), or when other authors and researchers stress the importance of longitudinal research when the goal is the study of causation. Some authors even contend that, in the absence of experimentation, only longitudinal research lends itself to the study of causation in general and reciprocal causation in particular. Lieberson (1985), who maintained that *"longitudinal data provide the only fully appropriate 'test' of a causal proposition's validity"* (p. 180), said that it is incumbent on researchers who use cross-sectional data for causal analysis to do more than acknowledge problems with such use. In the absence of good reasons, Lieberson argued, "it is best to forget the problem as a doable problem at the present time" (p. 182).

The foregoing should not be taken to imply that cross-sectional research has not been used in attempts to address issues of change, developmental processes, or causation. Quite the contrary, because of the much greater demands and complexities of longitudinal research (see below), most attempts to address such questions have relied on cross-sectional research, as is exemplified by comparisons among age groups at a given point in time or in the study of relations among variables measured simultaneously in one or more groups (e.g., most applications of causal modeling).[6]

In fact, longitudinal research in sociobehavioral sciences is the exception. For example, in a chapter on design and analysis in developmental research, Appelbaum and McCall (1983) stated: "Unfortunately, the number of longitudinal studies conducted is woefully small" (p. 418). Visser (1982) similarly pointed out: "Of the 1160 references in a textbook on developmental psychology . . . only about 2% refer to longitudinal research" (p. 14). Yet, referring to his book on longitudinal data analysis, Visser (1982) made a most telling remark: "If this study had a message, it would be: *'don't do longitudinal research if you can avoid it'* [italics added]" (p. 16). The great disparity between the claimed superiority of longitudinal research and its infrequent use can be traced to several factors, notable among which are the following.

Longitudinal research is costly and fraught with great difficulties and pitfalls as a result of the relatively long periods of time it takes to carry out. The most obvious difficulty arises from the high percentage of subject attrition that in many instances may nullify any of the potential benefits of longitudinal research. According to Visser (1982): "In longer psychological studies, 30 to 50% drop out is normal, higher percentages are not unusual" (p. 28; see also, Schaie & Hertzog, 1982). Add to this the almost unavoidable difficulties arising as a result of repeated measurement (e.g., sensitization, practice), potential changes in the mean-

---

[6]Again, we use the term "relations" in a broad sense to include effects.

ing of measures across time, changes in personnel, effects of history, information diffusion, to name but some, and problems of internal and external validity become overwhelming.

Generally requiring very long periods of time, longitudinal research cannot provide answers to pressing questions. Moreover, considering the volatility of theories and research in sociobehavioral sciences (see Chapters 7 and 9), it is likely that, by the time an answer becomes available from a longitudinal study, for the interest in the question to have diminished, if not dissipated altogether, or for the question to have been reconceptualized so that the answer appears irrelevant.

The prevailing attitude of funding agencies coupled with the pressing need for frequent publications for professional advancement are, to say the least, not conducive for the strong and ongoing commitment that longitudinal research requires.

As if the preceding were not problems enough, it will be noted that longitudinal data are generally more complex than cross-sectional data. Rogosa (1980b), who discussed difficulties arising from the complexities of longitudinal data and outlined analytic approaches, stated that longitudinal data "are not a panacea for all research problems and their relative advantages over cross-sectional data are sometimes overestimated" (p. 136).

General discussion of longitudinal research, data analysis, and/or illustrative applications will be found in the following: Appelbaum and McCall (1983); Goldstein (1979); *Journal of Economics and Business*, 1980, *32*, 89–181; Kessler and Greenberg (1981); Mason and Fienberg (1985); Mednick, Harway, and Finello (1984); Nesselroade and Baltes (1979); Plewis (1985); Rogosa (1979, 1980b, 1980c); Schaie (1983); Schaie and Hertzog (1982); Visser (1982). Also, analytic approaches for time-series analysis (for references, see Chapter 13) are frequently applied in longitudinal data analysis.

In addition to the preceding, it will be pointed out that analytic approaches developed in the context of Structural Equation Modeling (*SEM*; see Chapters 23 and 24) have proven very useful for longitudinal data analysis. Following are some references where you will find general discussions and/or applications of *SEM* in longitudinal research: Crano and Mendoza (1987), Ecob (1987), Hertzog and Nesselroade (1987), Gollob and Reichardt (1987), Huba and Bentler (1982a), Huba and Harlow (1986, 1987), Jöreskog and Sörbom (1977, 1985, 1989), Kohn and Schooler (1983), McArdle (1986), McArdle and Epstein (1987), Mortimer, Finch, and Kumka (1982), Newcomb and Bentler (1988), and Sörbom (1975).

CONCLUDING REMARKS

We hope that even the few simple designs presented in this chapter have given you an idea of the complexity attendant with nonexperimental research. In order not to complicate matters at this stage, we made no distinction between variables and their indicators, despite the fact that unobserved variables were involved (e.g., mental ability, motivation). In Chapter 24, we contrast analyses of designs with single and multiple indicators.

Chapter 15
Introduction to Sampling

Sampling permeates nearly every facet of our lives, because "in science and human affairs alike we lack the resources to study more than a fragment of the phenomena that might advance our knowledge" (Cochran, 1977, p. 1). It is a truism that decisions, impressions, opinions, beliefs, and the like are based on partial information. Informally, oftentimes unconsciously, we are constantly engaged in some sort of sampling activity. Thus, we do not usually reserve judgment about the food we eat until we have finished consuming it. As Samuel Johnson (quoted by Coser, 1975) put it: "You don't have to eat the whole ox to know that the meat is tough" (p. 698). Similarly, limited observations, bits and pieces of information, are generally resorted to when forming impressions and drawing conclusions about people, groups, objects, events, and other aspects of our environment.

That partial information upon which we act in our daily lives may be nonrepresentative is an all too familiar experience. Whether it be the purchase of a box of strawberries on the basis of the appearance of the top layer or the formation of an impression about a new acquaintance on the basis of very limited information, additional information may prove one wrong. The reason, of course, is that the portion sampled informally is very often *not* representative of the whole.

More formal instances of sampling affecting us directly or indirectly abound. Thus, sampling is regularly resorted to in business and manufacturing in accounting, auditing, and quality control. Government statistics (e.g., employment, energy consumption) are almost always based on samples. Items comprising a measure (e.g., of achievement, interests) may be thought of as a sample of all possible items. So are various samples taken for the purpose of health care (e.g., blood, urine). And hardly a day goes by without the media reporting on some poll, survey, or research study that relied on sampling. Add to this the countless consumer research studies taking place (e.g., ratings of television programs, new product assessments), and it is highly likely for most people to have partaken in one sampling scheme or another.

Formal sampling is a process aimed at obtaining a representative portion of some whole, thereby affording valid inferences and generalizations to it. In the present chapter, we introduce several sampling schemes and then turn to some general considerations in the

318

determination of sample size. The role of sampling as an integral step in the research design process is stressed. In view of the wide scope of sampling theory and techniques, our presentation is necessarily limited to an overview of some of their aspects. For detailed presentations of sampling theory and designs, see, for example, Cochran (1977), Hansen, Hurwitz, and Madow (1953), Jaeger (1984), Kalton (1983), Kish (1965), McCarthy (1951), Moser and Kalton (1972), Sudman (1976), Williams (1978), and Yates (1960).

Some Definitions

Compared with its usage in lay terminology, where it loosely refers to all the inhabitants of a particular region or land, the term *population* has a much more circumscribed meaning in the context of sampling. Specifically, it refers to "the aggregate of all of the cases that conform to some designated set of specifications" (Chein, 1981, p. 419). Cases, also referred to as *elements* or basic units of the population, need not be individuals. They may, for example, be classes, schools, counties, states, events, occasions, and so forth.

The aggregate is the target population to which one wishes to generalize. In evaluating the effects of a preschool program, for example, one may wish to generalize to all preschoolers in the United States, in a given state, a given city, a given district, a given school. The definition of the target population should be as explicit as possible with respect to content, units, extent, and time so as to avoid ambiguity regarding which elements belong to it and which do not belong to it.

A *sampling frame* is a list that identifies the individual elements of the population. In principle, the sampling frame should contain all the elements in the population. In practice, however, omissions and/or duplications of elements commonly occur (for discussions of sampling frame problems and recommendations for dealing with them, see, for example, Cochran, 1977; Kalton, 1983; Kish, 1965; Moser & Kalton, 1972; Yates, 1960).

A *sample* consists of a subset of elements from the population selected according to a sample design, which specifies the rules and operations by which the sample is to be chosen from the population. Usually, a statistic, some value based on the sample (e.g., mean, proportion, variance), is calculated and is used to make an inference to the corresponding parameter or value based on the population.

PURPOSES AND ADVANTAGES OF SAMPLING

Most people probably view sampling as a compromise to be avoided whenever possible. Yet, examining a sample rather than a population is usually preferable because of its greater feasibility, economy, and accuracy.

FEASIBILITY AND ECONOMY

Studying the population of interest is frequently not a viable option. For example, although public opinion polls have become routine vehicles for assessing attitudes and beliefs about a wide variety of issues and concerns, it is hardly possible to canvass reactions of all Americans. Total coverage may be financially very costly, even prohibitive, producing a voluminous amount of data to be handled and analyzed, not to mention inefficient utilization of human resources. Even if coverage of all Americans were attempted, it is clear that the scope of information sought would necessarily be very limited.[1]

In addition, conditions relevant to the issues under investigation may change during the time it takes to study the population. Under such circumstances, responses of people contacted at early stages of the study may be substantially different from those provided by people approached at later stages. In light of the volatility of current events, it is even likely for data to be irrelevant by the time they were collected and analyzed.

Lack of knowledge of the consequences of a study is another reason why samples are used. In medicine, for instance, it would hardly be prudent to administer a new drug to everyone prior to ascertaining its effects, both beneficial and deleterious. It would similarly be unwise to expose all school children to a new curriculum or teaching method before determining whether or not it is more efficient, produces greater gains, and the like than the one in current use.

Finally, sampling is mandatory in situations where the elements are destroyed or rendered useless in the process of obtaining the information sought. How many light bulbs would there be left to sell, if every one that was manufactured had to be tested to determine whether it met a minimum burning time standard?

ACCURACY

A benefit of sampling that is perhaps least understood is the potential for increased accuracy. To appreciate why this is so, it is necessary to bear in mind that sampling errors are but one of many sources of error in a study. Suffice it to mention errors of measurement, nonresponse, recording, and coding to recognize that such errors may be more detrimental to the validity of the study than sampling errors. Not surprisingly, "the larger the data set is the larger the *percentage* of nonsampling errors will be" (Williams, 1978, p. 46).

In general, limiting the investigation to a sample affords improved management and control in such areas as the training and supervision of interviewers and testers, obtaining responses, and amassing and analyzing the data. In addition, sampling affords the opportunity of allocating a greater share of available resources toward such important aspects as instrument development or refinement.

PROBABILITY VERSUS NONPROBABILITY SAMPLING

Although the question "Is the sample representative of the population?" comes readily to mind, it is unanswerable, because information about the population is generally unavailable. This is why sampling is resorted to in the first place. However, even when certain information about a population is available (e.g., ethnicity, gender, race), and even if it were demonstrated that a particular sample is similar to the population with respect to it, there would still be no way of telling whether the similarity holds with respect to other variables including the ones under study. In short,

---

[1]Even in the national census conducted every 10 years, only very general information is collected from all respondents. For more detailed information, a small sample is used.

there is no such thing as a "representative," "unbiased," "fair," or otherwise "acceptable" sample: such adjectives are strictly applicable to the sampling process that produces the sample, and their application to the sample itself is at best a piece of verbal shorthand and at worst a sign of muddled thinking. *A sample can be judged only in relation to the process that produced it* [italics added]. (Stuart, 1968, p. 613)

Broadly speaking, there are two processes by which a sample may be obtained: probability or nonprobability sampling. We begin with the latter.

NONPROBABILITY SAMPLING

Nonprobability sampling is a catch-all term referring both to samples of convenience (also termed accidental, accessible, haphazard, expedient, volunteer), where the allusion to "sample selection" is but a euphemism, as well as to more purposive methods of selection (e.g., judgment sampling, quota sampling) where the researcher generally delineates criteria and procedures for obtaining the sample. The specific label notwithstanding, what such samples share is that a decision is made as to what target populations they represent. The more purposive methods start out with some assumptions regarding the population, which serve as criteria in search of a "representative" sample, whereas the more haphazard methods generally begin with "sample selection."

Arguments in favor of nonprobability sampling typically are based on considerations of feasibility and economic constraints. Whatever the specific reasons, nonprobability sampling in sociobehavioral research is so prevalent that it is not uncommon for researchers to refer to this fact as justification for their own use of such sampling. But the incontrovertible fact is that, in nonprobability sampling, it is not possible to estimate sampling errors. Therefore, validity of inferences to a population cannot be ascertained.

PROBABILITY SAMPLING

Although the selection of samples can be traced back to ancient times (e.g., Duncan, 1984, 1988; Fienberg, 1971; Hasofer, 1967; Kruskal & Mosteller, 1980), formal utilization of probability sampling has a relatively short history, dating to the early 20th century. Prior to that, sample surveys were distrusted by both nonstatisticians and statisticians (Dalenius, 1957), who preferred to rely on more or less complete coverage of the population in question.

Although they differ in the specifics of their sample designs, the various probability sampling methods are alike in that every element of the population of interest has a known nonzero probability of being selected into the sample, and random selection is used at some point or another in the sampling process.

It is the reliance on random methods of sample selection that provides protection against selection bias and that enables one to calculate a probability of selection for each element in the population. Stated differently, with probability sampling, the various sample outcomes occur with known probabilities. Hence, the validity of using sample statistics as estimates of population parameters.

The remainder of this chapter is devoted to probability sampling. After an explication of the underlying principles, some of the more commonly used sampling designs are presented.

SAMPLING DISTRIBUTIONS

The validity of sample statistics as estimates of population parameters is predicated on the relation between the properties of a population and those of samples drawn from it. It is this relation, encapsulated in the notion of *sampling distribution*, that makes it possible to attach probabilities to inferences made from statistics to parameters. Although the particulars of a sampling distribution may differ from statistic to statistic (e.g., mean, proportion, total), and from one sample design to another, the underlying concepts remain the same. Therefore, using simple random sampling, the sampling distribution of the mean will be developed so as to elaborate on these concepts.

Let us assume that we are interested in assessing the performance of a particular population of individuals on some scale. A summary index that probably comes first to mind is the mean performance, which for a population is symbolized by the Greek letter μ (mu). However, being a measure of central tendency, the mean tells only part of the story. In addition, a measure of variability of the scores about the mean is necessary. One of the most useful measures of variability is the variance (see Chapter 17, for a review), which for a population is calculated as follows:

$$\sigma_x^2 = \frac{\Sigma(X - \bar{X})^2}{N} = \frac{\Sigma x^2}{N} \tag{15.1}$$

where σ_x^2 = population variance of X (σ is the Greek letter sigma); Σx^2 = sum of squared deviations of X from the mean of X. Recall that capital letters are generally used to depict raw scores, whereas lower case letters are used to depict deviation scores. Thus, $x = X - \bar{X}$. The deviation sum of squares may be obtained from the raw scores (see Chapter 17):

$$\Sigma x^2 = \Sigma X^2 - \frac{(\Sigma X)^2}{N} \tag{15.2}$$

In most sampling presentations, the population variance is expressed in an alternate form as

$$S_x^2 = \frac{\Sigma(X - \bar{X})^2}{N - 1} = \frac{\Sigma x^2}{N - 1} \tag{15.3}$$

Notice that the only difference between (15.1) and (15.3) is that, in the former, the denominator is N, whereas in the latter, it is $N - 1$. For large populations, the difference between the two approaches zero because $S^2 = [N/(N - 1)]\sigma^2$, and as N increases, $N/(N - 1)$ approaches 1. S^2 has the advantage of simplifying the various sampling formulas. The standard deviation is the square root of the variance (σ or S respectively).

A NUMERICAL EXAMPLE

For illustrative purposes, scores on a variable X (e.g., age in months, math achievement, attitude toward abortion) for a miniature population consisting of 8 individuals are presented in Table 15.1.

Table 15.1
Population Values for N = 8

Individual #	X	X²
1	26	676
2	22	484
3	36	1296
4	28	784
5	28	784
6	20	400
7	40	1600
8	32	1024
Σ	232	7048

Now, the mean (μ) for this population is 29 (i.e., 232/8). Using the summary information from the last line of Table 15.1 and applying (15.2), the deviation sum of squares is:

$$\Sigma x^2 = 7048 - \frac{(232)^2}{8} = 320$$

With this value as the numerator of (15.3), the variance is:

$$S_x^2 = \frac{320}{7} = 45.71$$

SIMPLE RANDOM SAMPLING

Suppose now that we wanted to use sampling to estimate the mean of the population under consideration. The most basic approach to probability sampling is simple random sampling. For a population of size N, there are $N!/[(N - n)!n!]$ distinct samples of size n (sample size). Recalling that the population we are using consists of 8 subjects and assuming an n of 2,

$$\frac{8!}{(8 - 2)!2!} = \frac{8!}{6!2!} = \frac{(8)(7)}{(2)(1)} = \frac{56}{2} = 28$$

Thus, 28 nonoverlapping samples of $n = 2$ may be obtained from a population of 8 subjects. For $n = 3$, 56 nonoverlapping samples may be obtained, and so forth. In simple random sampling, the n elements are drawn in such a way as to ensure that each of the distinct samples has an equal chance of being selected.

Ideas concerning tables of random numbers and their use were introduced in Chapter 10 (see Randomization), where a computer-generated table consisting of 300 random digits was also presented. This table will now be used to select a random sample of 2 individuals from those listed in Table 15.1. As the population under consideration consists of 8 subjects, single digits will be used. Assuming we use the table of random numbers given in Chapter 10 (under MINITAB output) and enter at row 4 and column 13, the first individual to be selected is #4 ($X = 28$). Moving down the column, the next is #8 ($X = 32$).

The mean for this particular sample of 2 individuals is 30. The aim is to make an inference about the population mean on the basis of this sample mean. One way of doing this is to test the hypothesis that the sample mean does not differ significantly from the population mean. Alternatively, a confidence interval around the sample mean could be constructed. Before illustrating the latter approach, some additional concepts will be introduced.

Table 15.2

28 Samples of Size n = 2 From Population of Size N = 8

Sample Number	Sample Elements	Sample Values	Sample Mean
1	1, 2	26, 22	24
2	1, 3	26, 36	31
3	1, 4	26, 28	27
4	1, 5	26, 28	27
5	1, 6	26, 20	23
6	1, 7	26, 40	33
7	1, 8	26, 32	29
8	2, 3	22, 36	29
9	2, 4	22, 28	25
10	2, 5	22, 28	25
11	2, 6	22, 20	21
12	2, 7	22, 40	31
13	2, 8	22, 32	27
14	3, 4	36, 28	32
15	3, 5	36, 28	32
16	3, 6	36, 20	28
17	3, 7	36, 40	38
18	3, 8	36, 32	34
19	4, 5	28, 28	28
20	4, 6	28, 20	24
21	4, 7	28, 40	34
22	4, 8	28, 32	30
23	5, 6	28, 20	24
24	5, 7	28, 40	34
25	5, 8	28, 32	30
26	6, 7	20, 40	30
27	6, 8	20, 32	26
28	7, 8	40, 32	36

SAMPLING DISTRIBUTION OF THE MEAN

For any given population, the sample space, that is, all possible nonoverlapping samples of a given size that may be drawn from it, can, in principle, be constructed. Above, it was pointed out that there are 28 distinct samples of size $n = 2$ for a population consisting of 8 elements. These are listed in an arbitrary fashion in Table 15.2. The mean of each sample is given in the last column. The mean of all the sample means is equal to the population mean (i.e., 29). As would be expected, sample means vary about the population mean. It is the distribution of means for all possible sample means (of a given size) that constitutes the *sampling distribution* of the mean.

Using the 28 means listed in the last column of Table 15.2, the variance of the mean can be calculated by applying (15.1):

$$\sigma_{\bar{x}}^2 = \frac{480}{28} = 17.14$$

(480 is the deviation sum of squares, which you may wish to verify by applying (15.2).) $\sigma_{\bar{x}}^2 =$ the variance of the mean. The square root ($\sigma_{\bar{x}}$), called the standard error of the mean, is equal

to 4.14 for the present example. It is knowledge of the variability of the sampling distribution (whether expressed as a variance or as a standard error) that enables us to make inferences to the population parameter with more or less precision as the case may be.

We have gone through the process of generating the sampling distribution and the calculation of the standard error of the mean in the hope of thereby giving you a better feel for these concepts. Clearly, if it were always necessary to generate the sampling distribution, the very purpose of sampling would be negated. Fortunately, the standard error of the mean can be estimated on the basis of a single sample, which for the case of a known population standard deviation is equal to:

$$\sigma_{\bar{x}} = \frac{S_x}{\sqrt{n}} \tag{15.4}$$

where $\sigma_{\bar{x}}$ = standard error of the mean; S_x = population standard deviation based on the square root of (15.3); n = sample size.

An expanded version of (15.4), which includes a finite population correction factor, *fpc* (i.e., $1 - n/N$), is given as:

$$\sigma_{\bar{x}} = \sqrt{(1 - \frac{n}{N})} \frac{S_x^2}{n} \tag{15.5}$$

The inclusion of *fpc* is to correct for the constraint of sampling without replacement. In sampling without replacement, also referred to as simple random sampling, once an element has been selected into the sample, it cannot be selected again on subsequent draws. Consequently, at any draw, elements not previously chosen have an equal probability of selection. In sampling with replacement, also called unrestricted sampling, elements are put back and may, therefore, be selected again. Under such circumstances, the probability of selection is the same for all elements at *every* stage of the drawing. For obvious reasons, sampling without replacement is used most often in sociobehavioral sciences.

Note that n/N of (15.5) refers to the sampling fraction (also called *f*), that is, the ratio of the sample size to the population size. As the population size increases relative to the sample size, n/N approaches zero, hence *fpc* approaches 1, and the difference between sampling with and without replacement is negligible for all practical purposes. Generally speaking, in sociobehavioral research, populations are large relative to samples and, therefore, *fpc* may be omitted in most instances.[2]

In our example, the sampling fraction is large ($^2/_8$ or 25%). Therefore, we will use (15.5) to calculate the standard error:

$$\sigma_{\bar{x}} = \sqrt{(1 - \frac{2}{8})} \frac{45.71}{2} = 4.14$$

Squaring this result yields a variance of 17.14. Note that these are the same results that were obtained when the standard error (and variance) were computed directly from the deviations of the 28 sample means around the population mean.

Examine (15.4) and notice that it is based solely on the population standard deviation and the sample size. Accordingly, the variability of the sampling distribution is directly related to the variability in the population of the characteristic under study and inversely related to the sample size. Holding the sample size constant, the standard error in a homogeneous popula-

---

[2]As a rule of thumb, *fpc* is usually omitted when the sampling fraction is less than 5%.

tion (i.e., relatively small standard deviation) would be smaller than in a more heterogeneous one. For example, given that the variability in population A is $S = 5$, whereas in population B it is $S = 25$, samples of size 25 drawn from the two populations would yield standard errors (using 15.4) of 1 and 5 respectively.

An increase in sample size (assuming no change in population standard deviation) results in a decrease of the standard error, thereby affording a more precise estimate. Thus, selecting a sample of 100 from population A (see above) would yield a standard error of .5.

Notice that it is the size of the sample, rather than the size of the population, that plays the vital role. This is why a random sample of 500 can be just as reliable for making inferences about a population of, say, 100,000 as about one consisting of 10,000. Failure to appreciate this fact is what leads many to place undue emphasis on the sampling fraction. This has led to the commonly held belief that larger sampling fractions are better. In fact, it is only when the sampling fraction is large that the population size needs to be taken into account through the inclusion of *fpc* in (15.5).

CENTRAL LIMIT THEOREM

The central limit theorem summarizes some of the concepts introduced in preceding sections. This important theorem states that, as the sample size increases, the sampling distribution of the mean tends to approximate a normal distribution even when the population distribution is not normal.

When the distribution of the population is normal, the sampling distribution of the mean is normally distributed for any sample size. For nonnormal population distributions, good approximations are achieved with sample sizes of 30 or more. Moreover, the shape of the original distribution notwithstanding, the mean of the sampling distribution will be equal to the mean of the population (μ), and the standard deviation of the sampling distribution (i.e., the standard error) will be equal to $S/\sqrt{n}$.

CONFIDENCE INTERVALS

Earlier, the mean of a sample of 2 drawn from the hypothetical population of 8 subjects was found to be 30. As the sample mean is an unbiased estimator of the population mean,[3] 30 could be used as an estimate of the population mean. It is, however, necessary to take sampling fluctuations into account. One way to accomplish this is to construct a confidence interval around the sample mean. For good reviews of confidence intervals see, for example, Hays (1988), Li (1964), Snedecor and Cochran (1980), and Wallis and Roberts (1956). Succinctly, the aim is to set up "*an estimated range of values with a given high probability of covering the true population value*" (Hays, 1988, p. 206). The width of this interval is based on both the degree of confidence one wishes to have in the inference as well as the ever-present sampling error. The magnitude of the sampling error can be described by the standard error of the mean, which in the present example was calculated as 4.14.

The confidence interval of $\bar{X}$ can be expressed as:

$$\bar{X} \pm z_{\alpha/2}\sigma_{\bar{x}} \tag{15.6}$$

where $z_{\alpha/2}$ is the tabled z value at $\alpha/2$ (see tables of the normal distribution in statistics books).

---

[3]Properties of estimators are discussed below.

For the 95% confidence interval ($\alpha = .05$), $z = 1.96$.[4] Therefore, the upper limit is:

$$30 + (1.96)(4.14) = 38.11$$

and the lower limit is:

$$30 - (1.96)(4.14) = 21.89$$

Alternatively, this can be expressed as:

$$21.89 \leq \mu \leq 38.11$$

It is *not* appropriate to conclude that the population mean lies between these two limits. Rather, what is implied by the construction of confidence intervals is that, if many such intervals were to be constructed in like fashion, 95% of them would contain the population mean. Obviously, the hope is that the single interval just constructed is one of those 95%.

Needless to say, one would usually not draw a sample of size 2 from a population of size 8, as we have done for illustrative purposes only. Also, it is obvious that the scores in our population are not normally distributed. Therefore, the use of the standard normal curve to construct confidence intervals is, strictly speaking, not appropriate. Nevertheless, the approximation is remarkably close. When confidence intervals were constructed for all of the 28 sample means from the sampling distribution (see Table 15.1), 96% of them actually contained the known population mean.

ESTIMATING THE POPULATION STANDARD DEVIATION

Thus far, we have assumed knowledge of the population standard deviation. Obviously, for our illustrative population of size $N = 8$, it was a simple matter to calculate the standard deviation. When the standard deviation of the population (S) is not known, which is almost always the case, the sample standard deviation (s) is used as its estimate and is then used in the calculation of the standard error of the mean ($s_{\bar{x}}$).[5]

We reiterate: Because our aim was to introduce basic concepts of sampling and statistical inference, we limited our presentation to the estimation formulas for the mean. Clearly, the parameter of interest need not be a mean. It could, for example, be a correlation or a regression coefficient. For each parameter of interest, corresponding estimation formulas are available.

PROPERTIES OF ESTIMATORS

Estimation formulas are referred to as *estimators*, whereas the particular values obtained as a result of applying the formulas to sample data are referred to as *estimates*. In the present section, we consider two desirable properties of estimators.[6] Being idealizations, desirable properties are not always realized. Moreover, under certain circumstances, one may prefer to use estimators lacking some desirable characteristic (e.g., when a biased estimator is pre-

---

[4]For the 99% confidence interval, $z = 2.58$. Consult tables of the normal distribution for other values.

[5]In the construction of confidence intervals, the 1.96 (in the case of 95% confidence intervals) would be replaced with the appropriate tabled t value with $n - 1$ df.

[6]Other desirable properties include efficiency (yielding small standard errors for a given sample size) and sufficiency (the estimator contains all of the information available in the data about the parameter; see, for example, Hays, 1988).

ferred over an unbiased one; see below). Properties of estimators are affected by the specifics of the sampling scheme used. Nevertheless, because our presentation is meant to be introductory, this aspect will be overlooked.

ESTIMATOR UNBIASEDNESS

An estimator is unbiased, if the expected value of the statistic equals the population value. The notion of expectation was introduced in the context of the presentation of reliability (Chapter 5), where it was defined as the average in the long run of an indefinite number of repeated random samples. In other words, in the long run, if we were to calculate the average of all possible values of a statistic (e.g., mean, proportion, total), we would "expect" it to equal the parameter.

The mean of a random sample is an example of an unbiased estimator. That is, $E(\bar{X}) = \mu$. On the other hand, the sample standard error is a biased estimator of the population standard error, although the bias is small in most instances.

Generally speaking, unbiased estimators are more desirable than biased estimators. An estimator is biased if the average of all sample estimates of a given sample size is *not* equal to the parameter. Bias may arise for a variety of reasons. For example, selection biases may occur if the sampling is nonrandom. Even if the sampling is random, biases may result from inadequate sampling frames or a variety of nonresponse patterns. Systematic measurement error (see Chapters 4 and 5) also contributes to bias. In addition, the particular formula used may lead to bias.

Although the term bias has negative connotations, under certain conditions, biased estimators may be more desirable than unbiased ones. In particular, this would be the case when the bias is relatively small and when the variance of a biased estimator is much smaller than that of a corresponding unbiased estimator. When the variance is large, the fact the there is no bias present provides little comfort. Kendall (1959) expressed this notion in an amusing poem about the "mighty hunter" Hiawatha who kept missing the target but, quoting statistical principles, attempted to convince the tribesmen that his performance was statistically not different from theirs. Nevertheless, the tribesmen concluded that, although a brilliant statistician, Hiawatha was a "useless bowman," and took away his bow and arrows. The poem concludes:

> In the corner of the forest
> Dwells alone my Hiawatha
> Permanently cogitating
> On the normal law of error
> Wondering in idle moments
> Whether an increased precision
> Might perhaps be rather better
> Even at the risk of bias
> If thereby one, now and then, could
> Register upon the target. (p. 24)

Mean Square Error (MSE) is the average of all of the squared deviations of the estimates from the true population value and can be expressed as sum of two components:

$$MSE = \text{variance} + \text{bias}^2$$

Bias is defined as the deviation of the average of all estimates from the true population value. Variance refers to the average of the squared deviations of the estimates from the expected value of the estimates. Recall that for unbiased estimators, the expected value is equal to the population value. It is clear from this that with unbiased estimators, the *MSE* is equal to the variance.

ESTIMATOR CONSISTENCY

Another desirable property of estimators is consistency. A consistent estimator is one that yields sample estimates with a higher probability of approaching the population value as sample size increases. An unbiased estimator (e.g., the mean) is also a consistent estimator. This is because increases in sample size lead to a reduction in variance thereby producing a distribution of estimates that is more concentrated around the population parameter. A biased estimator is consistent if, in addition to the reduction in variance, bias approaches zero with increasing sample sizes.

Simple Random Sampling: Constraints

In spite of its appeal and seeming simplicity, simple random sampling is not used often in research. From a practical point of view, the task of selecting a random sample from a list can be extremely tedious and time consuming. More often than not, lists (let alone numbered lists) of elements of relatively large populations are difficult, if not impossible, to come by. Additional constraints arise when the population of interest resides in geographically wide areas. For example, a simple random sample of the population of the United States would probably yield a sample so dispersed as to make it an economic and physical nightmare. Problems attendant with widely dispersed samples are especially acute when the research requires some sort of personal interaction with subjects (e.g., interviews).

Practical considerations aside, the multifaceted objectives of many investigations further reduce the usefulness of simple random sampling. For example, an investigator may be interested not only in estimating a population parameter but also in studying specific subgroups of the population. Even when the interest is limited to the population parameter, the minimum sample size required may be effectively reduced by utilizing strategies that introduce known characteristics of the population and/or its subgroups into the sampling process. To address these and other issues, modifications and restrictions of simple random sampling have been advanced.

SELECTED SAMPLING STRATEGIES

We limit our review to three major sampling strategies—systematic, stratified, and cluster[7]—offering descriptions, uses, advantages, disadvantages as well as some comparisons among them. For more detailed formal presentations of these as well as other strategies, see the references cited throughout this chapter.

---

[7]It should be noted that, even within these approaches, variations and extensions exist.

SYSTEMATIC SAMPLING

Systematic sampling refers to a process of sampling in which, following a random start, every kth element is selected into the sample. Dividing the population size by the sample size yields k (i.e., $k = N/n$). Although various solutions have been proposed for situations where the division does not yield an integer, given relatively large population sizes, it would suffice to round k to the nearest integer and proceed with the sampling as planned. A random number between 1 and k is selected for the starting point of the sampling. From there on, every kth element is chosen until the desired sample size is reached.[8]

The primary reasons for using systematic rather than simple random sampling are the convenience and simplicity with which it can be applied. When the elements of the population are ordered or listed in some fashion (e.g., on paper, on magnetic tape, on disk, on individual cards), it is quite simple to use a constant selection interval for sampling. Consider a sampling frame composed of a large number of cards. Applying simple random sampling in this situation may be arduous and time consuming, as it entails the selection of n random elements. In systematic sampling, on the other hand, once k and a random start have been determined, it is quite easy to use the constant interval k to select every kth card.

Note that, once k and the random start are selected, the entire sample is determined. This is quite unlike the situation in simple random sampling where the composition of the sample is not known until the final element is randomly drawn. In addition, whereas in simple random sampling any combination of elements is possible, in systematic sampling some combinations of elements can not occur. For example, elements that are closer to each other in the list than the interval k would not be selected into the same sample.

In addition to convenience and simplicity, systematic sampling has, under certain conditions, the advantage of yielding estimates that are more precise than those produced by simple random sampling or even stratified sampling (see below). Unfortunately, the converse is also true (see, for example, Cochran, 1977; Jaeger, 1984; Kish, 1965).

ESTIMATING VARIANCES

As is the case with many sampling situations, typically, only one systematic sample is drawn. Although an estimate of the mean in a single systematic sample is straightforward, estimating the variance is a "formidable problem" theoretically (Kish, 1965, p. 117). In fact, a minimum of two samples, hence two random starts, is required for a valid estimate of the variance. Because in most instances only one random start is made, there is, technically speaking, no valid way to calculate the variance.

Nevertheless, given the reasonableness of certain assumptions concerning the distribution of the population in the list, an estimate of the variance on the basis of a single random start is viable. For example, if it can be assumed that the elements of the population are randomly distributed in the list, then the variance estimation formulas for simple random sampling may be used. Various other assumptions and solutions have been proposed; the bias in some of them being quite high (for a review of some of these, see, for example, Cochran, 1977; Kish, 1965).

---

[8]Variations on the described strategy include using more than one random start, treating the list as circular in nature, and sampling both forward and backward from a random start (see, for example, Jaeger, 1984, Chapter 6).

ORDER CONCERNS

Systematic sampling is particularly dependent on the ordering and structuring of the lists used. For random orderings, systematic sampling functions like simple random sampling and would be used primarily for convenience. Serious problems arise for the case of periodic or cyclic orderings, particularly when the cycles correspond to the sampling interval. Under such circumstances, the resulting samples may be very homogeneous, limiting their usefulness in estimating the population parameter. In the extreme case, when the sampling interval corresponds exactly to the cycle, one may end up with a sample of identical elements. Kruskal and Mosteller (1979, p. 114) gave a real-life example of just such an occurrence. A systematic sample of soldiers was drawn from lists that were arranged according to rank by bunkhouse. Selecting every 32nd soldier on the list resulted in a sample consisting of soldiers of the same rank (i.e., sergeant).

STRATIFIED SAMPLING

In stratified sampling, the population of interest is first divided into nonoverlapping subdivisions, called strata, on the basis of one or more classification variables.[9] For purposes of sample selection and initial parameter estimation, each stratum is treated independently. That is, within each stratum, elements are randomly selected and individual estimates (e.g., mean, proportion) are obtained. These separate estimates are then weighted in order to arrive at an estimate for the population.

As an example, suppose one wanted to use sampling in order to estimate what percent of the student body at a given university own a personal computer. This may be done by resorting to simple random sampling from the entire student population. Alternatively, stratified sampling could be used by dividing the student population into a number of mutually exclusive and exhaustive strata on the basis of schools or colleges (e.g., liberal arts, business, education), type of degree program (e.g., undergraduate or graduate), or some other classification. Random samples would be drawn from the strata and the separate stratum estimates would then be weighted to get an overall estimate.

Generally speaking, the intent in stratified sampling is to reduce sampling variability by creating relatively homogeneous strata with respect to the dependent variable of interest. This is accomplished by selecting a stratification variable that is correlated with the dependent variable, much like creating blocks in randomized blocks designs (see, for example, Edwards, 1985, Chapter 15; Kirk, 1982, Chapter 6).

POTENTIAL BENEFITS OF STRATIFIED SAMPLING

An advantage of stratified sampling is that it affords, in addition to a population estimate, parameter estimates for subgroups of the population. Referring to the example given above, one may want to estimate the percent of student computer ownership in the various disciplines. Using stratified sampling, it is possible to ensure that sufficient numbers of students within the strata are sampled so as to permit separate subgroup estimation.

A second advantage of stratified sampling, already alluded to, is the *possibility* of in-

---

[9]For convenience, we will speak of the stratifying variable in the singular. Keep in mind, however, that multiple stratifying variables may be used.

creased statistical efficiency of the estimates. We emphasize possibility as, oftentimes, the increase in precision is minimal at best. As Kish (1965) pointed out, "the usual modest gains from proportionate sampling sharply contrast with the exaggerated notions prevalent about this method" (p. 89). This is due largely to the fact that stratification variables are typically selected on the basis of ready availability (e.g., sex, race) rather than on the basis of relevance. Nevertheless, stratified sampling continues to appeal to researchers, because, with proportionate allocation (see below), statistical efficiency can be no worse than with simple random sampling, and, under the right circumstances, it can be better.

A third advantage of stratified sampling is its greater convenience and the potentially greater diversity in procedures and data collection methods that it affords as compared with simple random sampling. Thus, sampling frames organized according to some well defined and naturally occurring strata may be readily available rather than for the population at large. For example, student lists may be available by schools and colleges rather than university-wide.

Each stratum is treated independently; therefore, different strategies for sample selection could be utilized within the different strata. Thus, simple random sampling may be conveniently carried out in some strata, whereas systematic sampling may be applied in other strata. In addition, the geographic location of certain elements of the population may necessitate different modes of data collection; a mail-survey may be carried out in one stratum, whereas face-to-face interviews may be conducted in another.

POTENTIAL DISADVANTAGES OF STRATIFIED SAMPLING

Offsetting potential benefits of stratified sampling are some potential disadvantages, chief among them being greater cost and complexity during both the selection (e.g., questions of allocation and stratum boundary definitions) and estimation (e.g., more complex estimators) phases as compared with simple random sampling.

When the interest is in estimating parameters of more than one variable, it may turn out that a given stratifying variable is relevant for some of them and not for others. For instance, suppose it was desired to estimate average height as well as average body temperature for adults. Stratifying the population by sex may yield more precise estimates of height than of body temperature.

Further, although, generally speaking, the sample size required for stratified sampling is the same or smaller than that for simple random sampling, it may turn out to be larger in certain designs. Dramatic increases in the required sample size would occur in designs consisting of a relatively large number of stratifying variables and when a minimum sample size is needed for every combination.

SOME CONSIDERATIONS IN SAMPLE SELECTION

The range of possible stratifying variables is virtually endless. Some (e.g., sex, race, socioeconomic status, political party affiliation) seem obvious, almost forcing themselves on the researcher. Others (e.g., diagnostic groups, size of company, type of employees) may be less obvious. In either case, difficulties may arise in connection with definitions of strata and/or efforts required to obtain the necessary information for the purpose of classification.

The overriding consideration in the selection of a stratifying variable is its relation with the dependent variable in question. Clearly, using a stratifying variable that is not related to the dependent variable will not lead to any gains, as within-strata variability would not be expected to be smaller than for a simple random sample. Stratifying voters, for example, on the basis of height or weight would probably not lead to any benefits, as the variability in voting within and between strata would be expected to be about the same.

When the use of more than one stratifying variable is contemplated, an additional consideration in the choice of variables is that they be as unrelated among themselves as possible while at the same time being related to the dependent variable. For example, stratifying by both socioeconomic status and education, rather than using either variable by itself, would probably not appreciably improve the efficiency of the estimates, because the two variables are correlated.

Once the choice of stratifying variables is made, the number of strata to be formed needs to be addressed. Categorical variables typically used for stratification purposes (e.g., sex, race, religion, party affiliation) often are comprised of a rather delimited number of fairly distinct categories, rendering the choice of number of strata not problematic.

When the stratifying variable is continuous (e.g., income), the question of the number of strata is more involved, focusing also on boundary demarcations among them. Suggested strategies to deal with continuous stratifying variables will be found in Cochran (1977), Dalenius (1957), Dalenius and Hodges (1959), and Jaeger (1984).

Having decided on the number of strata, it is necessary to decide how to allocate the total sample size among them. Broadly speaking, proportionate or disproportionate allocation may be used.

PROPORTIONATE ALLOCATION

In proportionate allocation, strata sample sizes are kept proportional to the strata population sizes. This method of selection "is what people generally and vaguely mean by talking of 'representative sampling,' of samples which are 'miniatures of the population,' and by the notion that the 'different parts of the population should be approximately represented in the sample'" (Kish, 1965, p. 82).

Proportionate allocation is accomplished by using a uniform sampling fraction in each stratum. For example, assume that a population of 15,000 elements is divided into 4 strata consisting of 6,000, 4,200, 3,300, and 1,500 elements. Further, assume that it is decided to sample 750 elements in total. The population sampling fraction ($f = n/N$) is equal to 750/15000 or .05. Sample sizes within strata are obtained by multiplying the size of each by the sampling fraction, yielding sample sizes of 300, 210, 165, and 75 for stratum 1 through 4 respectively.

When the sampling fraction is the same within each of the strata, the estimation formulas are simpler, because they are based on samples that are self-weighting. That is, it is not necessary to first calculate the separate stratum estimates and then to weight these in order to get an overall estimate. Instead, the entire stratified sample can be used directly to calculate the estimate. In addition, proportionate stratification yields estimates that are at least as efficient as those of a simple random sampling of the same size.

DISPROPORTIONATE ALLOCATION

As the term implies, disproportionate allocation does not produce strata sample sizes proportional to strata population sizes. Instead of relying on a uniform sampling fraction for each stratum, variable sampling fractions are utilized.

The most prevalent way of accomplishing this is through the use of optimum allocation that strives to minimize the overall sampling variance by striking a balance between the differences in variability within individual strata and the differing costs of sampling. In order to get a more precise estimate of the overall sampling variance, a larger sampling fraction is used for more heterogeneous strata. Further, because the costs of sampling elements may differ from stratum to stratum, it may prove to be more cost effective to use higher rates for strata that are less costly to sample.

Under favorable circumstances, the gains in precision through the use of optimum allocation as opposed to proportionate allocation may be considerable. However, unlike proportionate allocation, whose efficiency can never be worse than simple random sampling, optimum allocation may produce estimates that are less precise than those produced by a simple random sampling of the same sample size. Accordingly, optimum allocation is best reserved for situations where there is great disparity in the within-strata variances and diversity in the within-strata sampling costs.

Recall that one potential benefit of stratified sampling is that strata can be studied and compared in their own right. When this is the purpose, another form of disproportionate allocation frequently used is equal allocation. Obviously, when strata are of equal size, equal allocation is also proportionate allocation. However, strata are often of unequal size. Consequently, selecting the same sample size from each stratum means that a different sampling fraction is used in each of them. Although equal allocation may be preferable for estimating differences among strata, it may not yield the best results if the overall population parameter is of interest as well, particularly if strata differ widely in size and variability.

POSTSTRATIFICATION

In contrast to the foregoing, poststratification refers to the practice of introducing stratification at the estimation rather than the sampling phase. This is usually done in an attempt to adjust for what is deemed a relevant stratifying variable. As was noted previously, the use of an ancillary variable to create strata prior to sampling is akin to blocking in a randomized block design. In contrast, poststratification is analogous to the use of analysis of covariance (see Chapter 21) for the purpose of adjustment for initial group differences. As with any post hoc approach, poststratification is susceptible to abuse and misinterpretation.

Poststratification may, however, be validly resorted to when information necessary to create the strata is not readily available for all elements of the population prior to the sampling. Under such circumstances, simple random sampling is used to select the sample. Once the sample elements are identified, it may be possible to stratify them according to some auxiliary variable. If, in addition, the proportion of the population contained in the various strata is known, then poststratification can be used to introduce appropriate weighting so as to potentially improve the precision of the estimates.

CLUSTER SAMPLING

In the sampling strategies reviewed thus far, it was not necessary to distinguish between the elements of the population and the sampling units, as they are generally the same. There are, however, sampling strategies where sampling units are comprised of more than one element. Thus, instead of sampling individual elements of the population, aggregates or clusters of elements are randomly selected, hence the name cluster sampling.[10]

---

[10]Although we focus on simple random sampling of clusters, other probability strategies could be used (e.g., systematic sampling).

STRATEGIES OF SAMPLE SELECTION

In its simplest form, cluster sampling consists of sampling clusters only once and treating all elements of the selected clusters as comprising the sample. For obvious reasons, this is referred to as single-stage sampling. In contrast, in multistage sampling, selection proceeds in stages, each of which requires a different type of sampling frame from which appropriate clusters are to be drawn.

As an example of single-stage clustering, suppose a sample of 2,000 was sought to estimate the average achievement in science of fifth graders in a city's public schools. Because students are clustered into separate schools, using schools as the sampling units comes readily to mind. If the average fifth grade enrollment in the city's elementary schools is, for argument's sake, 100 students, then 20 schools could be randomly selected and, within each of these schools, all fifth graders would be tested. In contrast, simple random sampling would generally result in a considerably larger number of schools that would have to be visited.

Turning to an example of multistage cluster sampling, assume that a researcher is to conduct face-to-face interviews with a sample of residents of a particular state. Drawing a simple random sample would not only necessitate a listing of every resident of the state, it would also likely yield a sample too dispersed for practical purposes. Instead, with cluster sampling, the following procedure could be used to secure the sample: (a) A random sample of counties is drawn; (b) within the counties selected, districts are randomly drawn; (c) within each district, blocks are randomly sampled; (d) within the blocks selected, buildings are randomly drawn; and (e) all residents within the buildings selected comprise the sample. Alternatively, people may be randomly selected within buildings.[11]

SOME ADVANTAGES OF CLUSTER SAMPLING

From the preceding, it should be clear that advantages of cluster sampling center on practical concerns, which include the convenience and ease with which it can be applied, as well as its economic benefits. In the first place, how detailed the sampling frame needs to be depends on the nature of the clustering. During the early stages of the sampling, clusters can be comprised of predefined groupings and categories for which lists are easy to obtain (e.g., states, counties, school districts). Listings of the individual elements of the population are not required. It is only for clusters selected at the final stage that listings of the elements are required.

An additional important benefit of cluster sampling is the geographic proximity of sampled elements that helps reduce administrative problems and financial costs, especially in situations requiring face-to-face contact (e.g., interviews).

SOME DISADVANTAGES OF CLUSTER SAMPLING

To the extent that cluster sampling relies on some sort of categorization scheme to create the clusters, it resembles stratified sampling where an auxiliary variable is used to create the strata. The similarities end there, however. Recall that in stratified sampling the strata are formed so that sampling can be performed within each stratum. Consequently, the final

---

[11]When maps, rather than lists are available, a form of cluster sampling, called area sampling, can be used to select the clusters.

sample contains, to a greater or lesser extent depending on the allocation used, elements from *all* strata. In contrast, in cluster sampling only a sample of the clusters is selected. The precision of estimates based on cluster sampling is, therefore, dependent on the particular clusters chosen. In contrast to stratified sampling, where the intent is to have strata that are as homogeneous as possible, in cluster sampling, the aim is to form clusters that are as heterogeneous as possible. This is similar to the case of systematic sampling.

Cluster sampling is generally less efficient than a simple random sampling of the same sample size. This is compounded by the relative complexity of the various estimation formulas, particularly those involving the estimation of variances. Therefore, the judicious use of cluster sampling rests on balancing the loss in precision with the increase in convenience and economy.

SAMPLE SIZE

Our concern thus far has been with "representativeness" of samples. Of equal importance is precision of estimates. As explained in earlier sections (e.g., Sampling Distribution of the Mean), precision is largely affected by sample size. Issues concerning sample size are germane to both random selection and random assignment (i.e., randomization; see Chapter 10). It is for this reason that we have stressed the importance of using a "sufficient" number of replications so as to give randomization a chance to work. Satirizing research based on small samples, E. B. Wilson (quoted in Strauss, 1968) stated: "The investigator reported that one-third of the rats were improved on the experimental medication, one-third remained the same and the other third couldn't be reported on because *that* rat got away" (p. 569).

Allusions to sample size have been made repeatedly throughout this chapter as well as in earlier ones. In Chapter 9, it was pointed out that the decision regarding sample size is a complex one, subject to a host of concerns. These include, in addition to those discussed in preceding sections (e.g., sampling strategy, type of estimators, practical and economic considerations),[12] effect size (ES), Type I and Type II errors. It is for this reason that we found it necessary to introduce these concepts in our discussion of the logic of tests of significance (see Chapter 9). Among other things, we described the complex relations among the aforementioned elements and sample size.

Without repeating the presentation of Chapter 9, we remind you that Type I error—designated as α—refers to the probability of rejecting the null hypothesis when it should not be rejected. Type II error—designated as β—refers to the probability of failing to reject the null hypothesis when it should be rejected. Furthermore, $1 - \beta$ is the power of the statistical test.

The notion of ES was introduced in Chapter 9 on an intuitive level. In the next section, this topic is discussed somewhat more formally. We then turn to some general considerations regarding determination of sample size and power analysis.

EFFECT SIZE

We would like to begin by reminding you of the ambiguity surrounding the meaning of ES, because it is used interchangeably to refer to magnitude of effects, their importance, or their

---

[12]For the sake of simplicity, we focus on simple random sampling. Discussions of sample size determination for other sampling strategies will be found in some of the specialized sampling references mentioned throughout this chapter.

meaningfulness. Because of difficulties in defining importance or meaningfulness (see Chapter 9), it is not surprising that attempts to define ES operationally are couched in terms of magnitude, strength, and the like.

The concern with magnitude of effects is not new; it is based on concepts developed by Pearson and Neyman, Harris, Kelley, and Fisher (Keren & Lewis, 1979; Matthews & Brewer, 1977). Contemporary proddings to include measures of strength of association in addition to (or in some cases instead of) tests of significance can loosely be traced to three orientations, although demarcations among them often blur.

The first orientation has to do with statistical power analysis, of which ES estimation is an integral component (e.g., Brewer, 1972; Cohen, 1962, 1965, 1973a, 1988; Kraemer, 1985; Kraemer & Thiemann, 1987; Miller & Knapp, 1971; Overall & Dalal, 1965; Tversky & Kahneman, 1971).

The origin of the second orientation can be traced to Hays's (1963) formulation of ω^2 (omega squared) and his recommendation that it be used as an aid in assessing and interpreting research results. Estimation procedures for a variety of analysis of variance designs were subsequently presented and compared (e.g., Carroll & Nordholm, 1975; Cohen, 1973b; Glass & Hakstian, 1969; Halderson & Glasnapp, 1972; Keren & Lewis, 1979; Keselman, 1975; Maxwell, Camp, & Arvey, 1981; Vaughan & Corballis, 1969). Extensions to multivariate analysis were also proposed (e.g., Cramer & Nicewander, 1979; Huberty, 1972, 1982; Sachdeva, 1973; Shaffer & Gillo, 1974; Smith, 1972; Stevens, 1972; Tatsuoka, 1970).

The third orientation in which ES estimation has gained considerable prominence has been variously called meta-analysis, research integration, quantitative synthesis, quantitative review, quantitative assessment of research domains. Allusion to these approaches was made in Chapter 9 (see Past Research and Literature Review), where some major references were also given. For present purposes, it will only be pointed out that the aggregation of ES's is one of two primary approaches used in meta-analyses (the other being the aggregation of p values).

As our concern here is with ES from the perspective of statistical power analysis, it is fitting that we turn to one of the most prominent and influential contributors in this area for a definition. According to Cohen (1988), ES refers to " 'the *degree* to which the phenomenon is present in the population,' or 'the degree to which the null hypothesis is false' " (pp. 9–10).

But how does one define degree? Or, what is a large ES? It should be clear that, because of the nature of the units of most measures used in sociobehavioral research, there cannot be a simple or agreed upon answer to such questions.

Is, for example, a difference of 10 points between two means large, medium, or small? In the absence of additional information about the nature of the units of the measure being used, not to mention other factors (e.g., cost of the study), such a question would be viewed as fatuous by most people. Even when more is known about the units of the measure used, assessment of the magnitude of a difference (the "degree" of an effect) is by no means simple. Not surprisingly, one suggested solution is to translate the difference into some standard score. Thus, for example, the above mentioned difference of 10 points between the means would be translated into a standardized difference by dividing it by a "relevant" standard deviation.

Relevant was inserted in quotation marks, because it is not always clear which standard deviation to use. Of course, no problem arises when the standard deviations in the two groups are the same. Assuming, for the sake of simplicity, that the standard deviation in each group is 20, then a 10-point difference between the means would be translated into a standardized difference of .5. When the group standard deviations do not differ much from each other, an average of the two may be used. When, however, it is concluded that the difference between the standard deviations is marked, then the use of the root mean square of the population variance is recommended (see Cohen, 1988, p. 44).

Our intention in the preceding paragraph was *not* to present approaches to the standardization of differences between two means but to indicate that decisions have to be made about the relevant standard deviation to be used. To further underscore this, it will be pointed out that Glass et al. (1981) argued that when the mean of an experimental group is compared to that of a control group the standard deviation of the latter be used in the calculation of a standardized difference.

The standardized difference between means is but one of various indices proposed for the purpose of assessing ES. Another set of indices has to do with the proportion of variance of the dependent variable accounted for by the independent variable(s) or the proportion of variance shared by the variables under consideration. Among such indices are r^2, R^2, η^2 (eta squared), ϵ^2 (epsilon squared), and ω^2 (omega squared). It will be noted in passing that limitations and interpretational problems in the use of proportions of variance as indices of ES are discussed in some subsequent chapters (see especially, Chapters 17 and 18; see also, Haase, Ellis, & Ladany, 1989; Murray & Dosser, 1987; O'Grady, 1982; Sechrest & Yeaton, 1981a, 1981b, 1982; Smith, 1982; Strube, 1988).

All we have attempted to do in the foregoing paragraphs is give a flavor of some approaches to the estimation of ES. For comprehensive general presentations, see Cohen (1988) or Kraemer and Thiemann (1987). Presentations addressed to specific designs are also available. Among these are various univariate analysis of variance designs (e.g., Barcikowski, 1981; Hopkins, Coulter, & Hopkins, 1981; Koele, 1982; Levin, 1975; Rotton & Schonemann, 1978; Tiku, 1967), multivariate analysis of variance (e.g., Stevens, 1980), multiple regression (e.g., Milton, 1986), and chi square (e.g., Overall, 1980).

The importance of assessing ES from a substantive perspective was discussed in some detail in Chapter 9. It was, however, pointed out that, because this is, generally speaking, a demanding and complex task, researchers who consider ES altogether (many do not) tend to do so in terms of conventional guidelines. Probably the most frequently used guidelines are ones proposed by Cohen (1988). Using the kind of findings generally observed in sociobehavioral research as his frame of reference, Cohen proposed criteria for small, medium, and large effects. Thus, for example, he proposed that a difference between means of .2 of a standard deviation be deemed as small, .5 as medium, and .8 as large. When expressed as correlation coefficients, the preceding are equivalent to .1 for a small effect, .3 for a medium effect, and .5 for a large one.

At the risk of being repetitive, it will be pointed out that what the foregoing presentation boils down to is that, if sample size is to be determined rationally in light of considerations of Type I and Type II errors (hence the power of the statistical test), then the size of the effect to be detected must be decided upon. Accordingly, for all its shortcomings, the use of conventional guidelines for ES is preferable to the common practice of ignoring this matter altogether.

That this is so is evident when conventional guidelines for ES are used to assess the power of statistical tests in published research. In a pioneering review of articles published in the *Journal of Abnormal and Social Psychology*, Cohen (1962) showed that the median power was .17, .46, and .89 to detect small, medium, and large effects respectively (bear in mind that power of .5 means a 50–50 chance of correctly rejecting the null hypothesis). It has since become almost a pastime to demonstrate that similar conditions prevail in other research areas. Among areas reviewed are education (Brewer, 1972), counseling (Haase, Waechter, & Solomon, 1982), marketing (Sawyer & Ball, 1981), social psychology (Cooper & Findley, 1982), medicine (Freiman, Chambers, Smith, & Kuebler, 1978), and psychotherapy (Kazdin & Bass, 1989). The general findings in these and other reviews is that only when it is assumed that large effects are of interest (needless to say, ES is not alluded to by the authors of the papers being reviewed) is it found that power is adequate. It should be noted, however, that large effects sizes are not generally encountered in sociobehavioral research (Feldt, 1973).

It has been our experience when discussing these topics in our classes for students invariably to raise questions to the effect: If all this is so important, how come we have not seen it mentioned in the research literature we have been reading? Indeed, despite frequent exhortations by methodologists and authors of textbooks, issues concerning the determination of sample size and its effect on the power of statistical tests are not addressed in the broad spectrum of sociobehavioral research. In the vast majority of studies, sample size is determined through anything but a rational decision process. Cohen's (1965) characterization of how sample size is generally arrived at is as apt as any one might come across.

As far as I can tell, decisions about *n* in much psychological research are generally arrived at by such considerations as local tradition ("At Old Siwash U., 30 cases are enough for a dissertation"); subject-matter precedent ("I'll use samples of 20 cases, since that's how many Hook and Crook used when they studied conditioning under anxiety"); data availability ("I can't study more *idiots savants* than we have in the clinic, can I?"); intuition or one of its more presumptuous variants, "experience"; and negotiation ("If I give them the semantic differential, too, then it's only fair that I cut my sample to 40"). (p. 98)

We turn to a presentation of power analysis in the context of which we first discuss determination of sample size and then determination of power.

Power Analysis

When we speak of performing a power analysis, we are referring to any strategy that studies the relations among the four elements that are involved in statistical tests of significance (i.e., ES, α, β, and N). As was explained in Chapter 9, fixing any three of the four elements determines the fourth. Accordingly, four types of power analyses can be performed. However, as was also pointed out in this chapter and in Chapter 9, the most rational approach is to determine the sample size necessary to detect a given ES at prespecified α and β (hence, power). It is for this reason that we focus primarily on this type of power analysis. We then turn to the determination of the power of the statistical test for a given ES, α, and N. We do not address the remaining two approaches to power analysis (for a description, see Cohen, 1988). In addition, we do not address the issue of the reliability (see Chapter 5) of the measures used. There has been some controversy as to the effects of reliability on power (e.g., Cleary & Linn, 1969; Cleary, Linn, & Walster, 1970; Cohen, 1988; Fleiss, 1976; Nicewander & Price, 1978, 1983; Overall & Woodward, 1975, 1976; Sutcliffe, 1958, 1980). Noting that different authors had focused on different aspects of the problem, Zimmerman and Williams (1986) concluded that, in general, power increases with increased reliability.

DETERMINATION OF SAMPLE SIZE

Approaches to the determination of sample size include formulas, both general and specific to given research or sampling designs (e.g., Cochran, 1977; Hays, 1988; Jaeger, 1984; Kirk, 1982; Kish, 1965; Winer, 1971), tables (e.g., Rotton & Schonemann, 1978; Tiku, 1967), and power function charts (e.g., Pearson & Hartley, 1951). A more comprehensive treatment will be found in Cohen (1988).[13] This well-established reference book (the first edition

---

[13]See also Kraemer and Thiemann (1987).

appeared in 1969) provides a detailed presentation of the elements of power analysis and illustrative applications in diverse research contexts. The bulk of the book is devoted to two types of tables that are presented for various statistics (e.g., t test, correlation, analysis of variance, multiple regression): (a) *sample size tables* as a function of α, β, and ES; and (b) *power tables* as a function of α, ES, and N (see below).

In order to determine the appropriate sample size to be used in a study, one would need to first postulate the ES of interest, α, and β (or alternatively power). Using the tables provided by Cohen (1988), one would enter the selected α table, locate the row corresponding to the desired power, and read off the minimum sample size required per group under the estimated ES column.

As an example, assume that a researcher is interested in comparing the effects of two different methods of teaching reading. The researcher stipulates that, in order to be considered meaningful, differences between means need to be on the order of at least .4 of a standard deviation (i.e., somewhere between a small, .2, and a medium, .5, effect, by Cohen's criteria). Assume, further, that $\alpha = .05$, and power $= .80$. Entering the $a_2 = .05$ section (for a two-tailed test at $\alpha = .05$) of Table 2.4.1 (p. 55) in the power $= .80$ row, and reading off under the .40 column (for $d = .40$), it is determined that a minimum sample size of 99 per group is required.

For comparative purposes, keeping α and power as in the preceding example (i.e., $\alpha = .05$, and power $= .80$), the required sample size for $d = .2$ is 393 per group, whereas for $d = 1$ (i.e., the groups differ by one standard deviation), 17 individuals per group are necessary. If it were desired to keep Type II error as small as Type I (i.e., $\beta = .05$ and power $= .95$), then the corresponding sample size per group for $d = .4$ is 163.

Our examples were limited to the simplest case of a difference between two means, as we felt this would suffice to illustrate how sample size is affected as a result of varying one or more of the other three elements (ES, α, and β). In more complex designs, decisions, especially regarding ES, become more complicated. For example, when the design consists of more than two means (i.e., a categorical variable with more than two categories, or simple ANOVA; see Chapter 19), various patterns of differences among the means may be expected. For the purpose of determining sample size, it is necessary to translate the expected pattern into an index of ES. As another example, in factorial designs (i.e., designs with two or more categorical independent variables; see Chapter 20), one may choose different levels of power for different components of the design. For example, one may prefer to have higher power for an interaction term. These and other considerations in more complex designs are discussed in the references given earlier. (See especially Cohen, 1988, for thorough discussions and illustrations.)

Computer Programs.   In recent years, computer programs for power analysis have been appearing. For a review of some such programs, see Goldstein (1989).

DETERMINATION OF POWER

Undoubtedly, the most important role of power analysis is at the design stage for the purpose of determining sample size. It could, however, also be invaluable after the fact as a means of assessing results. Although failure to reject the null hypothesis may be due to many diverse reasons (e.g., the null is in fact true, the theory is faulty, the validity of measures used is dubious), given the generally low power of sociobehavioral research (see discussion above), it is entirely possible that one tenable explanation is that the research was not designed with sufficient power to reject the null hypothesis for a given ES at a given α (usually because the sample size was too small). Therefore, performing a power analysis on data that have been analyzed and/or published may be illuminating, especially if the ES is considered meaningful. Thus, given the ES detected, the α, and the sample size used, power can be ascertained. If the power of the test is found to be low, then judgment may be suspended until the research can be repeated under more favorable conditions.

The various formulas, tables, books, and computer programs referred to above can also be used to ascertain the power, given the ES, α and N.[14]

CONCLUDING REMARKS

This chapter was meant to provide an overview of sampling in sociobehavioral research. General sampling concepts were presented and typical sampling strategies were introduced. In addition, the very important topics of sample size and statistical power were commented upon.

This chapter concludes Part 2, which was devoted to broad aspects of scientific inquiry and research design. In the remaining chapters, which constitute Part 3, we present analytic approaches alluded to repeatedly in Parts 1 and 2.

---

[14]Power calculation can also be requested on the MANOVA procedure of SPSS–X by specifying the keyword POWER. See Chapter 16, for an introduction to computer programs in general and SPSS in particular.

PART 3
ANALYSIS

Chapter 16
Computers and Computer Programs

Computers permeate virtually every facet of our lives. Indeed, the time is rapidly approaching when "the computer illiterate will be cut off from most sources of information. The human brain unaided by computers will appear feebleminded" (Kemeny, 1983, p. 216). The ubiquity of computers and the diverse functions they perform belie the prediction made about 40 years ago by the RAND Corporation "that because computers were so large and expensive, no more than 12 corporations in the United States would ever need or be able to afford one" (Brzezinski, 1984, p. 7). The enormity of the evolution and the speed with which it has occurred can be appreciated by the oft-cited analogy (e.g., Rochester & Gantz, 1983) that, had the auto industry developed in a similar fashion, it would be possible nowadays to buy for $2.50 a Rolls Royce that would get 2 million miles to the gallon.

Within sociobehavioral sciences, the use of computers for data management and analysis come most readily to mind. As is well known, however, the diverse uses to which computers can be put in research, academic, and clinical endeavors are virtually limitless, including such activities as information retrieval and exchange, presentation of stimuli in research settings, simulations, artificial intelligence, authoring systems, computer assisted instruction, computerized testing, and counseling applications.

As you have surely gathered, we focus on the utilization of computers for data analysis. The present chapter is meant to serve several purposes. First, we give an overview of the use of statistical software packages, highlighting their strengths, weaknesses, potential abuses, and the like. Second, we review programs we have chosen to use in this book. Third, we describe our practice in reporting input, output, and commentaries. Fourth, we share with you some of what we found useful in our work in the hope that you may find it helpful both in the learning process and in subsequent applications.

ADVANTAGES OF COMPUTER DATA ANALYSIS

With the exception of the very simplest of statistics (e.g., mean, frequencies), most data analytic procedures require many computations. Hence, even with small data sets, hand calculations are often rather involved and tedious. More important, hand calculations are

342

highly susceptible to all sorts of errors, including inversion of numbers, misplacement of decimal points, reversal of signs, and omission of portions of formulas. Relegating the drudgery of data analysis to the computer diminishes the likelihood of such errors, not to mention the more efficient utilization of time and personnel.

The great benefit of computer analysis when samples are large is obvious. In "olden days," it was generally simpler to collect data than to analyze them. The reverse is probably true today. Due to technological advances, it has become easy to analyze extremely large data sets. The widespread availability of computers has also made applications of highly sophisticated analytic procedures almost routine. Although many of the methods currently in use were available for some time, they were rarely used, because they involved many complex computations. If you were to scan statistics books published in the 1940's and the 1950's, you would find that large portions of them are taken up by all sorts of schemes and work sheets designed to assist the reader in carrying out and keeping track of calculations involved in, say, multiple regression analysis or factor analysis.

Incidentally, it was not long ago that even mainframe computers could not handle relatively large numbers of variables in, say, a factor analysis. Approximations of overall solutions were arrived at on the basis of analyses of segments of data the computer could handle. Even then, the "turn around time"—a term from those "olden days" referring to the time one had to wait for the results—was at least 24 hours. Indeed, we have come a long way in a very short time!

MAINFRAME AND PERSONAL COMPUTERS

It is useful to distinguish in a very broad sense between a mainframe computer and a micro or personal computer (PC). We say "in a very broad sense," because no hard and fast distinctions among the various types of computers are possible. Over the years definitions of what constitutes a mainframe computer versus a mini or a micro have constantly been changing, with the focus shifting to various aspects of the machines (e.g., amount of storage, speed, number of users). The distinctions often blur, especially as technology advances. Thus, what is considered a mainframe at one time is considered a mini at another time. Some of today's micros are more powerful than even the most powerful mainframe computers of the near past. Even in terms of the number of users served, the current growth in networking will probably contribute to a further obscuring of distinctions among various types of computers. When we speak of a mainframe machine, we mean a centralized computer installation at a large institution, such as a university, research center, government agency, that serves many users. By a PC, we mean a self-contained desk-top system, typically used by one individual at a time.

MISCONCEPTIONS ABOUT AND MISUSES OF COMPUTERS

The widespread availability of user-friendly software has brought the most complex statistical analyses within easy reach of just about anyone. Not unexpectedly, this has been accompanied by misconceptions and misuses, some of which will be reviewed.

BELIEF IN THE INFALLIBILITY OF COMPUTERS
AND COMPUTER PROGRAMS

Often likened to black boxes, the inner workings of which are obscured from vision, hence, from comprehension, computers and their programs are invested with magical qualities and infallibility. Faced with neatly printed output, it appears almost inconceivable to entertain the notion that it may contain errors. Complicating matters is the increasing use of computers to solve problems the answers to which cannot possibly be checked by humans. The philosophical dilemma faced when this occurs was aptly captured in the title of a story about the solution of a very complex mathematical problem by a supercomputer: "Is a Math Proof a Proof If No One Can Check It?" (Browne, 1988). In an interesting discussion of "inscrutable computers," Sechrest (1985) drew attention to the same problem and cited Tymoczko as having suggested that "it appears that a new standard of proof has been admitted into mathematics." This being "in effect, 'the computer told me so'" (p. 84).

The profound dilemma of not being able to check answers to extremely complex problems obtained by computers aside, it is necessary to recognize that the mistaken notion that results displayed by the computer are error-free actually exists on several levels. In the first place, there is a lack of appreciation of errors that may arise at the data entry stage. What we have in mind are essentially clerical errors such as numbers entered incorrectly, data omitted, and the like. As an example, in what amounted to "a statistical detective story" (Coale & Stephan, 1962, p. 338), it was found that, due to punching errors of the 1950 census data—whereby data on a few of the cards were punched in the wrong position—frequencies of certain categories (e.g., teen-age widows) were highly exaggerated.[1] It is imperative, therefore, that the data be checked prior to any analyses and that any suspicious finding be investigated thoroughly. We return to this topic in a subsequent section.

Coupled with errors introduced during data entry are errors emanating from inappropriate use of software for statistical analysis. Although the naive user seems to believe otherwise, it is not the function of the computer to check whether the model specifications are correct and whether the underlying assumptions have been met. Even "if the model is not the correct model (variables omitted, or inserted in reversed sequence) parameter estimates will be returned, *no* red lights will flash, *no* alarm bells ring" (Macdonald, 1977, p. 84). Or, as Cliff (1987) put it: "No one has yet built into a computer program a feature that checks the values of a variable and prints out 'Shame! Shame! Shame!'" (p. 285) when a model has been misspecified or an assumption has been violated.

Another type of error in computer analysis—one that most users find difficult to entertain—stems from what are referred to as "bugs" in the software.[2] Some bugs are easier to detect than others. Perhaps easiest to detect are those that cause the program to run not as intended, either aborting and printing an error message or producing results that are so outlandish that it is obvious that an error has occurred.

Contrary to what is probably a common belief among users, even well-established programs are not bug-free. One instance when bugs are prone to creep in is when such programs are revised and updated. Thus, routines that operated properly in earlier releases may not do so in later ones. For example, in Chapter 19, we give a sample run of the ONEWAY procedure of SPSS, where we also use the CONTRAST subcommand. When the problem

---

[1]See Kruskal (1981) for other examples of similar errors.

[2]For the origin of the terms "bugs" and "debugging" of computer programs, see, for example, Rochester and Gantz (1983, pp. 83–84). Although far less common than software errors, the possibility that hardware-related errors have occurred cannot be totally overlooked (see, for example, Ziegler & Lanford, 1979).

was run on SPSS–X Release 2.0, the program functioned properly. When, however, the identical input was used in Release 3.0, the request for contrasts resulted in an error message to the effect that the number of contrasts requested exceeded the limit permissible for the given problem. Incidentally, *the same error message was given even when only one contrast was specified.* (The error has been fixed in Release 3.1.) We can envision the befuddlement of a novice attempting to replicate the results of the above noted analysis should he or she be using Release 3.0. We believe that not many novices would attribute the errors to the program. Furthermore, not many would pay attention to the release number. It is our guess that most would first blame themselves and search for some input errors. Failing to find any, they would probably put the blame on us.

"The most dangerous errors, however, give results that appear to be correct with no indication that something might have gone wrong—as occurs when improper computational formulas or reference distributions are used" (Dallal, 1988, p. 212). This type of error derives not so much from specific programming errors as from reliance on inappropriate solutions and algorithms.

SOFTWARE-DRIVEN THINKING

Procedures included in popular software packages exert undue (we are tempted to say almost total) influence on the kind of analyses that are being carried out. Users, even the more sophisticated ones, tend to limit their thinking about choices of analytic techniques in terms of software availability. This is attested to, among other things, by sudden spurts in the use of specific types of analyses following their incorporation in some statistical package.

On a more specific level, naive users tend to use defaults of available procedures (see below) and reproduce output indiscriminately. No wonder, many are the instances when output that has no bearing on the problem being investigated is reported and "interpreted."

PROLIFERATION OF ANALYSES

One deleterious consequence of the ready availability of statistical software packages and the increased ease with which they can be used is the proliferation of analyses performed in any one study. Faced with the ready availability of a large array of analytic approaches, researchers seem unable to resist the temptation of "seeing what will happen," if they "used" them on their data. It has almost become the norm to analyze data every which way, mining it, bombarding it with every available analysis, regardless of whether or not it is appropriate and/or relevant. As we keep stressing in various places, data analysis is not to be conducted in a vacuum but rather should be determined and delimited by the specifics of the study (e.g., theory, definitions, problems, hypotheses).

STATISTICAL BACKGROUND

We trust that, in view of our almost exclusive reliance on computer analysis in this book, you will not construe the foregoing discussion as an attempt to discourage you from using computers. Because of prevalent misconceptions, we felt it necessary to stress that, although the computer is a very powerful tool, it is a tool nevertheless and should be treated accordingly. It is our hope that this book will contribute to your intelligent utilization of computers.

Obviously, the best safeguard against improper and erroneous applications is knowledge of the analytic approaches used. It is this that we are attempting to impart in our commentaries on computer inputs and outputs we present.

As stated in several places, we use small numerical examples in the hope of encouraging you to replicate with the aid of a calculator some or all the calculations whenever feasible. Going through the calculations not only helps illuminate the concepts involved but also helps develop a feel for what might be wrong results. Once the concepts are thoroughly understood, remaining analyses can be relegated to the computer.[3] In the chapters that follow, we start out whenever possible by presenting an example in which all of the hand calculations are shown. Following that, we rely on computer analyses to illustrate our presentation.

With the foregoing in mind, we turn now to a discussion of statistical software in general and three packages in particular. You would do well to begin using statistical software early on in your learning by replicating the examples provided in this text, by running variations on them (e.g., changing some data points, testing different models, selecting different options), and by running additional examples (e.g., from other texts, journal articles, ones that you make up).

STATISTICAL SOFTWARE

The present section begins with some observations about major components of statistical software. We then comment on the evaluation of such software and delineate our criteria for the selection of programs to be used in this book. This is followed by some general considerations in the use of computer programs. The section concludes with a description of conventions we follow in presenting input, output, and commentaries on both.

COMPONENTS OF STATISTICAL SOFTWARE

Most statistical software programs share, in varying degrees, several major components:

1. Data Description, under which are subsumed strategies for identifying and naming variables, defining the format of the data, designating an external data file to be used when necessary, providing extended labels for variables and/or values, and indicating missing values.

2. Data Transformations and Manipulations, which include means for sorting data according to some desired criterion, recoding or transforming data, creating new variables, and merging two or more data files.

3. General Purpose Utilities for managing output: its destination, display format, and optional comments and titles.

4. Data Analysis. At the core of the programs are assorted procedures for descriptive and inferential statistics.

As might be expected, programs vary with respect to procedures included, their precision, scope, complexity, defaults, and options, to name but some major aspects. Programs may also differ with respect to various other features, among which are editing capabilities, file manipulations, facilities for generating reports, user-friendliness, detail and quality of manuals and instructions, and hardware requirements.

---

[3]However, see comments below about the importance of checking and rechecking to ascertain that the computer programs you are using are functioning properly.

EVALUATING STATISTICAL SOFTWARE

Even a casual perusal of computer oriented publications that cater to the public at large (e.g., *PC Magazine*, *PC Week*, *Infoworld*, *Byte*), not to mention professional journals and books devoted to scientific research, would reveal a bewildering array of statistical software. Most potential users do not have the means, not to mention expertise and stamina, required to wade through and test even a small fraction of the programs available. As with the purchase of other products, decisions are frequently made on the basis of price, advertisement, hearsay, availability, and the like.

In the absence of expert advice (e.g., an instructor, a statistical consultant), one would be well advised to peruse reviews of statistical software. It should, however, be noted that such reviews vary greatly in quality, some being little more than excerpts of advertisements and/or press releases by product manufacturers or vendors. This is particularly true of reviews in computer magazines where "statisticians are . . . in a minority among reviewers" (Berk, 1987, p. 227). Not only do many reviews contain errors and misguided recommendations (e.g., Greitzer, 1985; Petzold, 1985; Sandberg-Diment, 1986; Stoll, 1986), some even tend to deem it an asset when the running of a program requires little or no knowledge of statistics.

Within the scientific literature, there is no lack of discerning reviews and descriptions of both integrated and special-purpose statistical software. These appear with varying regularity in such publications as *Educational and Psychological Measurement*; *Multivariate Behavioral Research*; *American Statistician*; *Journal of the American Statistical Association*; *American Journal of Epidemiology*; *Journal of Marketing Research*; *Behavior Research Methods, Instruments and Computers*; and *Educational Statistician*. When consulting reviews, keep in mind that many are outdated by the time they are published. It is not uncommon for newer versions of programs—with enhancements and corrections—to be available long before the older versions are reviewed in print. Wainer and Thissen's statement in 1986 holds even more forcefully today: "Nowadays trying to get an up-to-date review of software or hardware is like trying to shovel the walk while it is still snowing" (p. 12).

Obviously, it is outside the scope of this presentation to provide a review of statistical software packages, be they for the mainframe or for the PC. Instead, we make some general comments about programs we have selected for inclusion in this text. As you read our criteria for software selection and our descriptions of the specific software chosen, we would like you to bear several things in mind.

Our remarks about and illustrations of programs are meant to serve as an introduction. In no way should our presentation be taken as a review of the programs in question. *Nor should it be deemed a substitute for acquaintance with the respective manuals* (see below). Moreover, we only address selected features of the programs as we highlight various aspects related to the topics covered in this book. Consequently, we do not mention other issues that might be considered important in a comprehensive review of a program (e.g., file transfer capabilities, specific hardware requirements, cost, documentation, customer services).

When we started working on this book, PC-based statistical software was in its infancy and few of the available programs at the time could be considered as serious alternatives to the software available on the mainframe.[4] Over the last few years, many new programs and updates of existing ones were introduced. We found it necessary to update our sample runs several times as new versions (both mainframe and PC) of the programs we discuss became available. It is a safe bet that, by the time the book appears in print, not only will more

---

[4]This was due in large part to limitations of the then available PC hardware.

programs be available, but also newer versions of the ones we discuss will have been released. Accordingly, although we expect our overall approach to be relevant for newer versions, you are urged to carefully study the documentation for the version you are using and make whatever changes and adjustments necessary when trying to replicate our analyses or relate our commentaries to the input and/or output.

CRITERIA FOR SOFTWARE SELECTION

As with any type of software (e.g., word processors, spreadsheets), the various statistical packages each have their own claque of fans[5] as well as detractors. Although using one program only would have made our task considerably simpler and easier (probably yours too), it would have been shortsighted and unwise for the following reasons:

1. The presentation of more than one program increases the likelihood of your having access to at least one of them.
2. Even if they contain the same so-called routines, programs do not necessarily provide the same information.
3. Seeing comparable results displayed differently by the various programs is bound to deepen your understanding and reinforce your learning.
4. Exposure to several programs enhances flexibility needed especially when moving from one environment to another (e.g., from a mainframe to a PC, from one institution to another).

We limited our choices to programs available for both the PC and the mainframe, thereby providing for the greatest degree of flexibility. Except for some differences to which we draw attention when the need arises, the examples we include can be analyzed with a given program on both the PC and the mainframe with little or no modification.

The programs we have selected are among the most comprehensive, offering a wide variety of analytic procedures and options. Further, they are well established and undergo periodic revisions, updates, and expansions. However, as indicated earlier, even such programs are not immune to errors. Therefore, vigilance and routine checking by the user are imperative (see discussion below).

SPECIFIC SOFTWARE SELECTED

Only the general purpose programs that are used throughout the text are introduced in this chapter. Special purpose programs (e.g., LISREL, EQS) are presented where appropriate in selected chapters. Below, we identify the versions of the PC and mainframe programs used, along with the relevant documentation. In subsequent sections, we elaborate on some differences that may exist between PC and mainframe versions of the same program. Thereafter, *except in cases where ambiguity may arise, we will refer to the programs by their generic name instead of indicating a version type. Thus, for example, we refer to SPSS instead of SPSS–X Release 3.1 or SPSS/PC+ V3.1.* In the same vein, unless we feel it necessary for clarity, we will refrain from specifying which version the selected output came from.

---

[5]Some even approach the topic with fervor, proclaiming with pride that they only use SAS, or SPSS, or what have you.

SPSS[6]

1. Mainframe version: SPSS–X, Release 3.1. Documentation: *SPSS–X user's guide*, 3rd Edition, (SPSS Inc., 1988).

2. PC version: SPSS/PC+ V3.1; SPSS/PC+ Advanced Statistics V3.1. Documentation: *SPSS/PC+ update for V3.0 and V3.1* (SPSS Inc., 1989); *SPSS/PC+ V2.0 base manual* (Norusis & SPSS Inc., 1988c); *SPSS/PC+ advanced statistics V2.0* (Norusis & SPSS Inc., 1988a).[7]

SAS[8]

1. Mainframe version: SAS Release 5.16. Documentation: *SAS user's guide: Basics, version 5 edition* (SAS Institute Inc., 1985b); *SAS user's guide: Statistics, version 5 edition* (SAS Institute Inc., 1985c).

2. PC version: SAS Release 6.03. Documentation: *SAS introductory guide for personal computers, version 6 edition* (SAS Institute Inc., 1985a); *SAS/STAT guide for personal computers, version 6 edition* (SAS Institute Inc., 1987).

MINITAB[9]

1. Mainframe version: Minitab Release 6.1.1. Documentation: *Minitab statistical software, reference manual, release 6.1* (Minitab Inc., 1988); *Minitab handbook* (Ryan, Joiner, & Ryan, 1985).

2. PC version: Minitab Release 6.1.1—Standard Version.[10] Documentation: Same as for mainframe version. See also, *Minitab user's guide: Microcomputer version, release 6* (Minitab Inc., 1987).

COMPUTER TERMINOLOGY AND HARDWARE CONCERNS

We assume some basic familiarity with computer terminology, such as hard and floppy disks, RAM, directories and subdirectories, megabyte (MB), DOS, text editor, and the like. In addition, we do not go into details of the hardware requirements nor the limits of the programs (e.g., number of cases, number of variables), because these vary, depending on the particular machine and program version.

Mainframe. The three packages are available on a variety of mainframe machines. For the most part, commands internal to the programs are the same, whereas commands that depend to some extent on the particular operating system may differ. You will need to check at your particular installation about such matters as the text editor(s) available, default operation, relevant system commands for accessing software, printing output.

---

[6]SPSS is a registered trademark of SPSS Inc.

[7]Also available from SPSS is SPSS/PC+ Studentware (Norusis & SPSS Inc., 1988b). This scaled-down program is limited to 20 variables and does not contain all of the procedures included in the larger PC version. Of the SPSS procedures we illustrate, ONEWAY and REGRESSION could also be run on SPSS/PC+ Studentware, provided the input is not in matrix format.

[8]SAS is a registered trademark of SAS Institute, Inc.

[9]Minitab is a registered trademark of Minitab, Inc.

[10]We would like to thank Minitab Inc. for furnishing us with a review copy of the Minitab PC version.

PC. The programs we include are available for the IBM PC[11] and compatibles. Although differences exist in minimum hardware requirements, both among the programs as well as within the programs for specific procedures, on the whole, the following are required or highly recommended: 640K RAM, hard disk, and math coprocessor. The amount of hard disk storage space required depends, of course, on the specific program and on whether or not it is installed in its entirety. For example, MINITAB takes up approximately 1.6 MB of hard disk space, whereas the SPSS Base and Advanced Systems use about 8 MB of space.

SOME GENERAL CONSIDERATIONS

The following concerns and issues apply to some extent or another to all the programs discussed.

MANUALS

When referring to a manual, we mean the appropriate manual for the version of the program we are using. Although variations in depth and breadth of coverage certainly exist, manuals—in particular the ones for the programs we include—typically contain instructions and information regarding (a) general use of the program (e.g., data description specifications, transformations, use of external files), (b) available procedures, (c) differences among the various methods of analysis, and (d) default options. In addition, illustrative applications and explanations of both input and output files are included.

The sheer size of some manuals can be overwhelming. For example, the *SAS user's guide: Basics, version 5 edition* is 1290 pages long, and the corresponding *SAS user's guide: Statistics, version 5 edition* contains 956 pages. Keep in mind, however, that a manual is a reference guide and should be approached as such. You should learn the basics, usually contained in the first few chapters, and then refer to the specific procedure of interest for details concerning its particulars.

The manual, no matter how good it is, should not serve as a substitute for data analysis textbooks and other methodological writings. Failure to consult the manual breeds ignorance, but so does reliance on the manual as the sole or primary source of information about the analysis in question.

BATCH VERSUS INTERACTIVE PROCESSING

Two basic modes of execution are available for most statistical software. In batch mode, a command file (consisting of all of the commands of interest) is created with a text editor (see below) and is then submitted in its entirety for processing. In interactive mode, commands are entered and processed one at a time.[12] The results of either processing mode are directed to the default or specified device (e.g., screen, printer, disk file).

---

[11]When we use the term IBM PC, we also mean IBM PC/XT, IBM PC/AT, and PS/2. IBM, IBM PC, IBM PC/XT, IBM PC/AT, and PS/2 are registered trademarks of International Business Machines Corporation.

[12]We are making a broad distinction between batch and interactive processing. Within the latter, various possibilities exist (see, for example, SAS Institute Inc., 1985b, p. 5).

Many programs, in particular those for the PC, stress their interactive mode. Deemed more user-friendly, it enables one to observe intermediate results, which may then be taken into account when deciding on subsequent steps. Although situations certainly exist when results of earlier stages of an analysis are useful for decisions regarding what is to be done in subsequent stages, we believe that interactive processing promotes, to some degree, a "let's see what happens if . . . " attitude. As we stated earlier, it is this attitude that is partly responsible for the proliferation of data-driven analyses.

Furthermore, interactive processing is inefficient under many, if not most, conditions. Commands are executed as they are entered and are, for the most part, lost following their entry. Therefore, in many situations, commands may have to be reentered (e.g., when they are applicable for several analyses or when reanalyses are necessary because of errors in the commands and/or data).

In batch mode an input file is created and saved; therefore, it can be easily retrieved and edited. In addition, a file prepared for one software package can be amended so as to make it suitable for use in another package. In any case, *all of the examples in this book are set up for batch processing*. Differences between the command structure for batch and interactive processing are generally negligible.

CREATING AND EDITING INPUT FILES

Except when one is working totally interactively (see above), a text editor is used to create, edit, and store the files that include the commands and/or the data. If you are working on a mainframe, you will have to become familiar with the particular editor(s) at your installation (e.g., IBM System Product editor, also referred to as XEDIT). On a PC, several options are available, including (a) the text editor supplied with a given software package (e.g., Review for SPSS), (b) stand alone text editors, such as KEDIT[13] or TED[14], and (c) any word processor that can read and write files in ASCII format. We discuss our own strategy in a later section.

DEFAULTS

Many of the commands and specifications in statistical software have preassigned values— defaults—that the computer assumes are operative unless otherwise specified. These defaults affect virtually every aspect of the analysis, including specifications related to the format of the data, handling of missing data, layout of the results, output device, and specific method of analysis. As defaults serve different functions, their impact on the outcomes of analyses vary; some are fairly innocuous, whereas others have serious consequences.

Some defaults, especially those governing data description, are assigned values that would be appropriate for basic types of analyses and relatively simple data sets. For example, SPSS assumes by default that the data are in fixed format (see below). Other defaults, although they may appear to be cosmetic, serve more practical purposes. Thus, in the absence of a title specification, the program may assign its own default title. Likewise, when no specific names are assigned to the variables, programs will supply their own default

---

[13]KEDIT, a product of the Mansfield Software Group, is a very powerful and versatile editor similar in its look and commands to the mainframe IBM editor XEDIT.

[14]TED is "a tiny, full-screen editor intended for line-oriented files up to 64K in size (Kihlken, 1988). For a description of the program, a listing of the program code, and instructions for downloading it, see *PC Magazine*, November 15, 1988.

names (e.g., VAR 1, VAR 2 . . .). Overriding such defaults is generally to be preferred, as it helps customize the output to best suit one's needs. We strongly suggest that you get into the habit of using titles, variable names, labels, and comments with sufficient detail so that the output will be informative even with the passage of time. Thus, if you are analyzing an example from this book, indicate—in the title or in a comment—the chapter, page number, and type of analysis performed. This is particularly important when you are doing several different analyses of the same data.

We turn now to defaults that may appreciably affect results of a given analysis. One set of such defaults has to do with the definition of the data, for example, how the program handles missing values (e.g., blanks read as missing). If the nature of your data does not conform to the program defaults (e.g., you have coded all missing data as "0" or "9"), omitting the missing value command may have serious consequences. A related concern with missing data is how they are handled by the particular procedure requested (e.g., is there a listwise or pairwise deletion of missing data by default).

Another set of defaults has to do with methods of analysis. For example, when doing a factor analysis (see Chapter 22), many issues need to be addressed (e.g., number of factors to extract, type of rotation). In the absence of specifications, some programs (e.g., SPSS) make *all* the decisions by default. Frequently, the programmed defaults are not the "best" or most appropriate ones (Wainer & Thissen, 1986). Clearly, it is imperative that you know the defaults of programs you are using so that you may override them when necessary.

We have dealt with potential problems arising from the use of defaults, because we believe they are all too often overlooked. In our overview of the statistical programs later in this chapter, as well as in the examples throughout Part 3, we mention some common defaults as they impact on the commands in question.

IMPORTANCE OF CHECKING PROGRAMS

Given that not all computer programs are created equal and that errors exist even in the more established ones, it is imperative that they be routinely checked and evaluated. It is not sufficient to run the manual examples, because they generally do not utilize all features of a given procedure. In addition, manual examples may themselves contain errors. Model data (e.g., a familiar data set that has been worked out by hand, textbook examples), should be subjected to extensive testing. This enables one to, among other things, become familiar with the peculiarities of a program, its output format and nomenclature, as well as to check on accuracy of results and compare the output with that of other programs.

The importance of testing software does not diminish once one has checked for accuracy and has attained a comfort level with a program. As new versions are released, errors in established routines do creep in (see example of SPSS ONEWAY given earlier), default options change, output may be modified both in what is generated and how it is displayed and labeled. Even if no new releases have been issued, it is a good idea to periodically test a program, especially on the mainframe, as it may be altered without notifying users. In sum, when using model problems, *test new or updated programs as well as existing ones that you have not run for some time.*

ERROR AND OTHER MESSAGES

Programs typically issue several types of error messages or warnings as they encounter inconsistencies or problems in the commands and/or the data. Some messages are strictly informational. Others may indicate that an adjustment was made prior to the analysis (e.g., data that do not conform to specifications are treated as missing).

Errors in the commands and/or their specifications will generally be indicated on the output or in a special log file (see comments on SAS, below). Whether or not processing ceases for the command in question as well as for subsequent ones will depend on the nature of the error and on the program being used. An error specific to one particular command may only affect that command. Alternatively, errors may affect several or all subsequent commands.

Different programs may treat the same error differently. For example, if, through an error of typing, a nonsymmetric correlation matrix is used as input for factor analysis (see Chapter 22), SPSS will issue the following message:

>THE CORRELATION MATRIX IS NOT SYMMETRIC. THIS ANALYSIS WILL BE TERMINATED.

SAS, on the other hand, issues the following:

WARNING: CORRELATION MATRIX READ FROM INPUT DATA SET IS NOT SYMMETRIC.

(Some versions contain the additional statement: Values in the lower triangle are used). Whatever the message, *the program then proceeds with the analysis*. If the error is in the upper triangle, the user will get the correct results. If, on the other hand, the error is in the lower triangle, the results will be in error.

We believe the practice followed by SPSS in this case to be preferable. It is anyone's guess how many users pay attention to a message such as the above when results of the analysis are given. It should also be noted that in some versions of SAS, the LOG (where the messages are given; see introduction to SAS, below) is part of the output file, whereas in others a separate log file is generated. The likelihood of users calling for the log file when results are provided is, in our opinion, extremely small. We hope that this example has convinced you of the importance of *always* examining the log when using SAS.

Deciphering error messages is not always an easy task. The extent and clarity of error messages vary across and within programs. Some errors are clearly identified as soon as they are encountered; others produce cryptic messages that do not seem to apply to the commands at hand. In addition, there are times when in actuality there is only one error; its appearance early on in the input file, however, may generate a slew of error messages. Users attempting to correct "all" the errors instead of only the culprit may actually introduce new errors that will affect a reanalysis.

It is also important to be alert to peculiarities of programs, as when no error message is given, but neither is the desired output produced. For example, failure to correctly specify subcommands in MINITAB will not necessarily cause a message to be printed. However, neither will the options requested by the subcommand be printed.

Conventions Followed in this Book

We remind you that our examples are meant to be illustrative. By no stretch of the imagination is our discussion exhaustive of the various commands and options that are available. In addition, there are usually several commands and specifications that may accomplish similar goals. Our choice of one command over another is not meant to imply that it is the only command available nor that it is necessarily the preferable route to take under all circumstances. Sometimes we alternate between various specifications in order to foster flexibility and comparisons.

INPUT FILES

Except when otherwise noted, input files are in accordance with specifications for batch processing using the PC version of the respective program. In the case of MINITAB and SAS, very little, if any, modifications would be required in order to run the files on mainframe computers. Greater differences exist between the PC and mainframe versions of SPSS, in particular with regards to matrix data. We refer to these as is necessary.

If you are working on a PC, we assume that you have a hard disk that is organized in directories according to functions and programs. Program files, be they for your word processor, data base manager, spreadsheet, or statistical package, are typically installed in separate directories. In general, one would want to be able to access these types of programs from any directory; therefore, a DOS PATH command specifying their location needs to issued.[15] A typical PATH command may look something like:

PATH C:\;C:\DOS;C:\WP;C:\SPSS;C:\UTIL;

Work files (e.g., data, input and output files, letters, manuscripts, spreadsheet files) are stored in directories (or subdirectories) according to some function. In organizing your own work, you may choose to place all of your input files in one directory called \DATA. Alternatively, you may decide to organize your work in several directories. Whatever you do, we strongly recommend that your work files *not* reside in the same directory with your program files. Working in directories other than the program directories is important for a variety of reasons. In the first place, the likelihood of accidentally deleting program files is greatly diminished. In addition, it is more efficient to be working in directories that are organized according to some function (e.g., the same data file can be used as input for several different programs).

The directory that you are working in is called the current or default directory. We recommend that you create and store input files in the current directory (e.g., \DATA) and execute the program from it. As a result, output files will be written to this directory.

We indicated earlier that a text editor is required for creating and editing input files and that several options are available to the user. An editor is included as part of most software packages. Such editors tend to be rather limited. In any case, a user who wishes to use several packages may find it necessary to learn to use several editors. It is because we want the versatility and power of a good ASCII editor, and because we do not wish to spend time and effort learning editing commands specific to packages we use, that *we use KEDIT to create and edit all input files.*[16]

---

[15]Typically, the path statement would be included in the AUTOEXEC.BAT file that is automatically executed whenever DOS is started or restarted.

[16]If you are using a word processor or text editor rather than the editor that came with the statistical program, you should make sure that your cursor is advanced to the line immediately following your last line of text. Some word processors and text editors do not automatically issue a carriage return, line-feed sequence at the end of the last line. Consequently, the end of file character that appears at the end of the line would cause an error when the file is processed.

Inline Data.   There are three basic ways in which to store the data set to be analyzed: (a) It can be included with the commands in the command file (i.e., inline data, also called infile or in-stream), (b) it can reside in an external file, or (c) it can be saved as a special system file specific to the program used. All the data sets in our illustrative examples are very small; thus, we include them inline in the interest of simplifying the input commands.

OUTPUT FILE

Default batch processing (on the PC) operates somewhat differently for the programs we are illustrating. Output files are automatically generated for SPSS and SAS, although the default name for the SPSS output file is not very helpful (see discussion under SPSS section, below). Output files need to be specified for MINITAB.

We generate output files for all analyses, which we then edit, omitting irrelevant or superfluous material, adding comments and other text, and customizing the output according to our needs. We find it most efficient to use KEDIT to do the preliminary editing, such as omitting large blocks of text or moving blocks and columns. Subsequently, we import the file into a word processor (e.g., WordPerfect[17]) to tailor the layout to our needs. *As a result of our editing, the format of the output may differ slightly from that generated by the programs.* We suggest that you run our examples so that you may compare our presentation with the actual output.

USE OF COMMENTS

All of the programs permit the embedding of comments and notes in the input file (e.g., COMMENT, *, /*). These comments are then printed on the output file, in the order that they are encountered, enabling the user to document and detail the output.

For the sake of uniformity and ease of presentation, we do *not* use the comment commands available in the various programs. Instead, we use two kinds of comments:

1. Brief comments, annotating specific commands in the input file. These are placed on the command line to which they refer, and are printed in italics and placed in brackets (e.g., *[This is a comment]*) to distinguish them from the commands and to indicate that they are not part of the input file.

2. Extensive comments on both the input and the output. These comments, placed in special sections under the heading "Commentary," are interspersed throughout the analysis chapters.

We use the format of the commentaries to introduce and discuss analytic and substantive issues. Therefore, even if you are familiar with a program we are using, we urge you not to skip the commentaries. At the very least, scan them and read those sections in which new subject matter is presented and discussed.

INTRODUCTION TO SELECTED PROGRAMS

In this section, we present an overview of the general purpose statistical software packages we use in this text and elaborate further on conventions we follow in using them.

---

[17]WordPerfect is a registered trademark of WordPerfect Corporation.

SPSS

The SPSS system is made up of command keywords and their specifications. The former consist of operation commands (e.g., SET, SHOW), data definition and manipulation commands (e.g., DATA LIST, RECODE), and procedure commands (e.g., ANOVA, REGRESSION). The specifications consist of subcommands and additional keywords (e.g., STATISTICS=ALL), arithmetic and other types of operators and functions (e.g., $+$, $-$, SQRT), delimiters (e.g., /), as well as user-supplied details (e.g., variable names). Specifications for subcommands are separated from the subcommand keyword by either an equals sign ($=$) or a blank (e.g., STATISTICS=ALL is equivalent to STATISTICS ALL).

Commands typically begin in the first column and are separated from subcommands by a slash (/). Their order is relatively flexible, although logic does dictate that certain commands precede others. On the PC version, commands and subcommands can be abbreviated to their first three letters. The same is generally true for the mainframe version, except when the truncation creates ambiguity, in which case four-letter abbreviations may be used.

Executing an SPSS command file generally results in the generation of an output file that by default includes not only the results but also all of the commands, general information, messages, warnings, and errors. The PC version also generates a LOG file that displays the commands as well as error messages.

CONVENTIONS FOLLOWED IN THIS TEXT

One of the differences between the mainframe and PC versions of SPSS is in their use of command terminators and continuation lines. On the PC, all commands, be they in batch or interactive mode, and regardless of how many lines they occupy, are ended with a command terminator—by default either with a period or a blank line. On the mainframe, interactive commands require a command terminator whereas commands used in batch processing do not.[18] In batch mode on the mainframe, continuation lines have to be indented at least one column.[19] For consistency, we terminate all commands with a period and indent continuation lines. Although it is not necessary to indent on the PC, we do so for two reasons: (a) Files created for the PC can be run on the mainframe without having first to modify continuation lines, and (b) it is helpful to offset the commands so that they are easily distinguishable from specifications.

Whenever possible, we request STATISTICS=ALL rather than specifying selected statistics, as this does not appreciably increase the amount of output for the small data sets we are using. From a pedagogical perspective, it is useful to examine as much information as is available and to compare it to any calculations done by hand. In addition, differences exist between the PC and mainframe versions in the specification of this subcommand for certain procedures. Whereas on the mainframe version additional statistics are requested by name only, on the PC version they have to be specified either by name or by number, depending on the procedure used. Specifying STATISTICS=ALL obviates the need on our part to indicate the specific version the subcommand applies to. We would like to stress, however, that, with sizable data sets, this specification may produce voluminous output, much of which you may not need or want. Therefore, *use the specification ALL judiciously.*

---

[18]Prior to Release 3, only batch mode processing was available on the mainframe; command terminators were treated as errors. In Release 3, they are ignored.

[19]Note that the requirement that continuation lines be indented applies only to commands and not to the data.

TYPICAL COMMAND STRUCTURE

Batch execution of an input file in SPSS can be accomplished in two ways:

1. At the same time that SPSS is invoked at the DOS prompt, the name of the input file can be specified. Thus, if your input file is named T171 (for Table 17.1), at the DOS prompt you would issue the following:
SPSSPC T171
2. Alternatively, at the SPSS prompt (i.e., SPSS/PC:), you can retrieve the file by issuing the INCLUDE command:
INCLUDE T171.

The SPSS examples that we include generally consist of the following.[20]

OUTPUT FILE SPECIFICATION

By default, every time the PC version of SPSS is executed anew, it generates an output file (also called a listing file) with the name SPSS.LIS. Consequently, if you reenter SPSS prior to renaming a previously generated output file, that file will be overwritten by the new output file. To guard against this, we recommend that you instruct SPSS to override this default by placing the following SET[21] command at the beginning of your command file, using as the 'filename' the same name you used for the input file:

SET LISTING = 'filename.LIS'.

This line should not be included when running on the mainframe. Depending on the particulars at your installation, you will either have to specify the name of the output file at the time of execution, or one will be generated by default.

TITLE

We recommended earlier that you get in the habit of using the TITLE command, despite the fact that it is optional. The titles we use generally indicate the source of the data and/or the type of analysis performed, as in the following:

TITLE TABLE 17.1 REGRESSION OF Y ON X.

DATA DEFINITION

At the very least, a DATA LIST command is required in order to provide information about the variable names and their format. In addition, it can be used to specify the location of variables; whether they are numeric (the default) or alphanumeric (i.e., string variables); the

---

[20]To automatically exit SPSS when the processing of the batch file is concluded, include as the last line of your file the command FINISH.

[21]An initialization file (called SPSSPROF.INI) can be created containing SET commands that are issued on a regular basis. For example, our initialization file turns off the menus and the automatic loading of REVIEW, suppresses pauses, and resets the output page length and width.

number of records (lines) per case; as well as an external data file to be used, if the data are not inline. We focus below on the identification of variables and their format.[22]

Variable identification follows a slash (/) on the DATA LIST command. The order of the named variables determines their order in the active file. Variable names can be from one to eight characters long and consist primarily of a combination of letters and numbers. They must begin with a letter and contain no embedded spaces. When many similar variables need to be identified, such as individual test items, it is often useful to employ the TO convention (e.g., ITEM1 TO ITEM25) rather than specifying each individual variable.[23]

The DATA LIST command also contains information concerning the format of the data. Two basic formats are available:

1. Fixed format, the default, assumes that the variables occupy the same column(s) for every case in the file. Accordingly, the location of a variable follows its name (e.g., SEX 4, MOT 15–17). Blank fields are treated as missing by default. Further, it is assumed that any decimal points will be coded in the data. It is possible to indicate implied (i.e., not actually recorded in the data) decimal points by specifying the number of decimals in parentheses immediately following the column location [e.g., GPA 8–9 (1). Thus, if the number 35 appeared in columns 8 and 9, it would be read as 3.5].[24] An abbreviated format is available for variables that have the same width and format and that occupy adjacent columns. The names of all such variables are listed, followed by the beginning column for the first variable and the ending column for the last variable (e.g., Y X T 1–6; two columns are allotted for each of the three variables). Following is an example incorporating some of the variations available with fixed format:

DATA LIST/SEX 1 AGE 3–4 GPA 5–6 (1) Y X1 TO X5 20–31.

2. Free format implies that the variables appear in the same order, but not necessarily in the same columns, for all cases in the data file. The only requirement is that variables be separated by at least one blank or a comma. Although we begin each case on a new line, cases may be entered consecutively on the same line.[25] On the DATA LIST command, all that is necessary is that FREE format be indicated and the names of the variables be provided, as in the following:

DATA LIST FREE/SEX AGE GPA Y X1 TO X5.

In our examples, we alternate in our use of free and fixed formats. We would like to alert you, however, to a potential disadvantage of free format, particularly when data sets are long and complex. The data are read and assigned in order of the named variables; therefore, omissions and errors in data entry (either accidentally or intentionally, because data are missing) could result in the wrong assignment of data to variables. For this reason, *it is recommended that, except for small and complete data sets (as in our illustrative examples), fixed format be used.*

---

[22]All of our examples use only one record per case (the default). Data sets with more than one record per case are defined differently on the DATA LIST command, depending on whether the mainframe or PC version is used. There are several ways to specify external data files (e.g., FILE HANDLE command; FILE='specification' on the DATA LIST command), in part dependent on the particular installation. In situations where a system file has been generated, a GET command, accessing the previously defined system file, is used rather than a DATA LIST command.

[23]Another use of the TO convention is when reference has to be made to a contiguous list of variables that have previously been defined. For example, consider the following:

DATA LIST FREE/SEX AGE ACH MA SES MOT.

Subsequent reference to this variable list in assorted procedures could be:

VARIABLES=SEX TO MOT.

[24]Explicitly coded decimal points take precedence over implied ones.

[25]On the mainframe, there is also a more restricted freefield data format, called LIST, where the data for each case must begin on a new line (record) and must occupy only one line.

OPTIONAL DATA DEFINITION

Optional data definition commands can be used to provide descriptive labels to variables (i.e., VARIABLE LABELS) and to specific values of categorical variables (i.e., VALUE LABELS; see Chapter 21). In addition, if your data do not conform to the default assumption where blank fields are treated as missing (in fixed format only), you may find it necessary to include a MISSING VALUES command and/or to recode blanks via a SET command.

MATRIX DATA

Instead of, or in addition to, raw data input, SPSS can handle matrix input entered by the user or generated by other SPSS procedures. The ability to analyze matrix input and its specific contents is partially dependent on the particular procedure used. *Matrix input is handled differently by the PC and mainframe versions* (see Chapter 22, where we present an example of matrix input with the appropriate commands for both versions).

DATA

With inline data, the following command structure is required:[26]

BEGIN DATA.
lines of data
END DATA.

Whenever the raw data are used (as opposed to matrix data), we include a LIST command that in its default specification generates a list in the output file of all of the variables for all the cases.[27] In addition to producing a permanent record of the data in the output, this enables one to check the results of coding, formatting, transformations, and the like.

PROCEDURES

SPSS has many procedures for data analysis and reporting. We have included examples of the following: RELIABILITY (Chapter 5), REGRESSION (Chapters 17, 18, 19, 20, 21, and 24), ONEWAY (Chapter 19), MANOVA (Chapter 20), PLOT (Chapter 21), and FACTOR (Chapter 22).

SAS

A SAS program is made up of a series of SAS statements whose function is to provide information and to request that an analysis or operation be performed. These statements,

---

[26]When processing in batch mode with inline data on the *mainframe*, the first procedure can be placed immediately before the BEGIN DATA, data set, END DATA sequence. On the *PC*, however, the first procedure must follow the reading of the data. For the sake of consistency, we always place the first procedure after END DATA in our examples.

[27]Of course, doing this for large data sets would generally be inadvisable. Instead, selected variables and/or cases could be listed through appropriate specifications on the LIST command.

which must end in a semicolon, consist of SAS keywords and names as well as special characters and operators.

SAS keywords (e.g., DATA, CARDS, FORMAT) are special reserved words that function in much the same fashion as do commands, subcommands, and operators within the SPSS system. SAS names are given to variables, data sets, files, and the like. Their maximum length is eight characters consisting of letters, numbers, and underscores (i.e., _). They must begin with either a letter or underscore and contain no embedded blanks.

The various SAS statements can be classified as follows:

1. DATA step statements whose primary purpose is to create and tailor SAS data sets. It is in this step that variables are defined and named, their format specified, manipulations and transformations requested, file management handled, and so forth.

2. PROC step statements request that particular procedures and their associated specifications be performed.

3. Selected SAS statements that can be used anywhere (e.g., TITLE, COMMENT).

There are very few rules governing spacing and placement of SAS statements. Statements can begin in any column, can extend to several lines without indentation, and several statements can appear on the same line. Additionally, several DATA and/or PROC steps can be used in the same SAS program.

When a SAS program is executed, both a LOG file and an output file are typically generated. The LOG file consists of general information, a listing of the statements processed, information about the data set(s) created, and messages about errors encountered. The output file contains the results generated by the various PROC statements. You are urged to always examine the LOG (see earlier comments on this topic).

CONVENTIONS FOLLOWED IN THIS TEXT

Although not required, to enhance the visual display, we indent statements belonging to the same step. Also, to facilitate editing, we place separate statements on separate lines.

TYPICAL COMMAND STRUCTURE

When executing in batch mode, SAS typically generates a LOG file and an output file that have the same file name as the input file but are given different file type extensions (e.g., SASLOG, LISTING on some mainframes; .LOG, .LST on the PC). Assuming that the input file name is T171, executing SAS would entail issuing the following command at the DOS prompt:

SAS T171

SAS examples that we include generally consist of the following.

TITLE

A TITLE statement can appear anywhere in a SAS program. By placing it at the beginning of the program and not overriding it with another TITLE statement subsequently, we associate the title with the entire run. It is also possible to designate titles within PROC statements, each time tailoring them to the specific analysis requested. Titles must be enclosed in apostrophes. For example:

TITLE 'DATA FROM TABLE 17.1. FIRST X = 4 CHANGED TO 10';

DATA STEP

For our purposes, the DATA step consists of statements that create and name a SAS data set by indicating the variables to be used and their format, and by specifying any necessary transformations and/or manipulations. There are many additional statements that can potentially be included at this step; their functions being to identify existing data sets, manage files (e.g., merge two files), tailor reports, and the like.

DATA STATEMENT

The DATA statement begins the DATA step, instructing SAS to build a data set.[28] If no name is provided, SAS assigns the name DATA1 to the first data set, DATA2 to the second, and so forth. An example of a statement naming a data set is:

DATA T171;

The DATA statement contains options for elaborating on the specifics of the data set. These options are placed in parentheses immediately following the data set to which they apply. One particular option concerns the type of data set. By default, SAS assumes that TYPE=DATA. Other types of data include COV (covariance), SSCP (sums of squares, cross products), and CORR (correlation) matrices. These matrices can be produced by SAS procedures or entered by the user. In Chapter 18, for example, the following DATA statement is used to indicate that the data set, named T181, is a correlation matrix:

DATA T181 (TYPE=CORR);

INPUT STATEMENT

The purpose of the INPUT statement is to identify the variables by naming them and indicating their format. Of several different input styles, which may be mixed within the same INPUT statement, we present two:

1. Column input is appropriate for fixed format data. In its simplest form, the variable is named followed by the column(s) it occupies. By default, numeric variables are assumed; a character variable is identified with a $ immediately after it is named. Implied decimals are signified with a period followed by the number of decimal digits (e.g., .2 indicates two digits after the decimal point). Explicit decimals override any implied ones. Blank fields, or ones that contain a period, are treated as missing data by default. An example of an INPUT statement is:

INPUT SUBJNAME $ 1–10 SEX 11 GPA 14–15 .1 GREV 17–20;

2. List input is appropriate for data that are in free format. That is, data values are separated by at least one blank (missing values are indicated with a single period). Under such circumstances, all that is

---

[28]Alternatively, an existing data set can be accessed. Furthermore, more than one data set can be created or accessed.

required is that variable names be given. Example:
INPUT X Y;

CARDS STATEMENT

CARDS is the last statement in the DATA step when the data are included within the SAS program. Its format is:

CARDS;

The data lines follow the CARDS statement. It is not necessary to indicate the end of the data lines, if the line immediately following the data contains a semicolon. This is the typical case, because a PROC statement is usually placed there. If for some reason a semicolon does not appear on the line following the data, as when a PROC statement is continued to the next line, it is necessary to include a null line (containing only a semicolon) immediately following the data.

PROC STEP

Various PROC statements, governing all sorts of analyses and operations, are available. Certain statements are common to several SAS procedures, whereas others are unique to a given procedure. Examples of shared statements are BY (see Chapter 19), CLASS (see Chapter 19), and MODEL (see Chapters 17, 18, and 19).

We generally include a PROC PRINT that lists the input data on the output file. Other procedures illustrated are PROC REG (Chapters 17, 18), PROC MEANS (Chapter 19), PROC GLM (Chapter 19), and PROC FACTOR (Chapter 22).

MINITAB

MINITAB is a general purpose program organized around a worksheet consisting of rows and columns. The data are stored in the worksheet in columns C# (e.g., C1, C5, C100). Constants are stored as K# (e.g., K1, K2, K15). Matrices are stored as M# (e.g., M1, M3, M4). The size of the worksheet depends on the version of MINITAB and the storage capabilities of the computer used.

MINITAB commands begin with a keyword (e.g., READ, REGRESS). These keywords, which can be abbreviated to their first four letters, are followed by specifications, called arguments, which indicate such things as where to read the variables, which variables to plot, and what are the names of variables. Each command must start on a new line; continuation lines are indicated by placing an ampersand (&) at the end of the line to be continued. Commands can occur any number of times and with little restriction as to their order so long as it is logical.

Although the minimum specification of a command and its associated arguments is sufficient, an appealing feature of MINITAB is that the user may insert additional text in order to make the commands more readable and understandable. The additional text has *no* effect on the execution of the program. Thus, assume, for example, that one wanted to enter two variables into the first two columns of the worksheet. The required command is:

READ C1 C2

In order to make it more readable, the command could be:

READ the first variable into C1 and the second into C2

For the sake of clarity, we have used upper and lower case letters. Either one or both types may be used.

Some commands have special options in the form of subcommands. To use a subcommand, a semicolon is placed at the end of the main command. Each subcommand begins on a new line and is itself ended with a semicolon. The last subcommand is ended with a period.

CONVENTIONS FOLLOWED IN THIS TEXT

As is our practice with the other programs, we indent subcommand lines to distinguish them from their main commands.

TYPICAL COMMAND STRUCTURE

MINITAB expects, by default, that the command file be given the extension MTB (e.g., T174.MTB),[29] signifying an executable file. Files are executed by first entering MINITAB and issuing the following command at the MINITAB prompt (i.e., MTB):

EXEC 'filename'

For the example above, this would be:

EXEC 'T174'

It is not necessary to provide the extension, because it conforms to the default file type. If a different file extension is given (e.g., T174.INP), then the complete file name would have to be entered (e.g., EXEC 'T174.INP').[30]

Unlike the other programs used in this text, MINITAB does not provide for the inclusion of a title. This can, however, be accomplished by inserting a MINITAB comment in the form of a NOTE, which is listed as part of the output file. Our MINITAB examples generally consist of the following.

OUTPUT FILE SPECIFICATION

By default, MINITAB's output scrolls on the screen and no output file is generated. Consequently, we include two commands at the beginning of the command file that together will route the output to a file and control the maximum page size.

OH refers to the output height. In interactive mode, it controls the maximum number of lines sent to the screen at any one time (default=24), before MINITAB pauses and asks if you want to continue. In batch mode, OH also controls the maximum page size routed to an output file. Setting OH=0 will suppress all pauses and paging.

---

[29]This is the format appropriate for the PC version. Naming conventions for file extensions may differ from one mainframe installation to another.

[30]To exit automatically from Minitab when execution of the batch file is concluded, include the command STOP as the last line of the command file.

OUTFILE.   The OUTFILE command directs the output to a specified file. The name of the file is placed in apostrophes. It is not necessary to specify an extension; MINITAB automatically appends the extension .LIS. Thus, the following will generate an output file called T174.LIS:

OUTFILE 'T174'

The output will continue to scroll on your screen at the same time that it is sent to the file unless you include a NOTERM subcommand as part of the OUTFILE command.

ENTERING THE DATA

READ.   When the data are contained within the command program, they are entered into the columns of the worksheet by issuing the READ command, which stipulates the columns into which the data that follow are to be read.[31] Thus, the command:

READ C2 C10

would place the first variable into C2 and the second into C10. If consecutive columns are to be used, the column specification can name the first column followed by a dash and then the last column, as in READ C1–C5. The data lines themselves immediately follow this command. By default, it is assumed that they are in free format with explicit decimal points, if necessary. At least one blank and/or comma separates the values of the variables; the missing data code is an asterisk (*) for numeric data. If alphanumeric variables are included, or if the data structure needs to be defined more specifically, a FORMAT subcommand may be issued.

MISCELLANEOUS COMMANDS

There are many commands that can be used to tailor either the entire output or specific parts of it. Following are some that we use in subsequent chapters.

NAME.   Once the data have been defined, names may be assigned to the columns. Names are enclosed in apostrophes and consist of up to eight characters, with the stipulation that they *not* begin or end with a blank nor contain some special characters. To give C1 and C2 the names PRE and POST respectively, the following command would be used:

NAME C1 'PRE' C2 'POST'

Subsequent to its being named, a column may be referred to in the command file by either its name or by its column number. Names and column numbers may be intermixed, as in:

PRINT C1 'POST'

PRINT.   An example of the PRINT command, used to list the data on the output, is:

PRINT C1-C4 M1 M2 K5

BRIEF.   For several procedures (e.g., REGRESS), the amount of output can be controlled through the BRIEF subcommand.

---

[31]The READ command is also used to read from an external file that is in ASCII format. A file saved in MINITAB format, by issuing the SAVE command, can be placed in the worksheet with the RETRIEVE command.

ANALYSIS COMMANDS

Of the various analysis commands, we include CORREL (Chapters 18 and 19), HISTO-GRAM (Chapter 10), PLOT (Chapter 17 and 18), RANDOM (Chapter 10), REGRESS (Chapters 17, 18, and 19), and SAMPLE (Chapter 10).

CONCLUDING REMARKS

This chapter was intended as an overview of the role of computers and statistical software packages in general, as well as an introduction to the specific packages used in this text. The remaining chapters in Part 3 deal with specific analyses that have been referred to in both Part 1 (Measurement) and Part 2 (Design). In addition, each of these chapters (see also Chapters 5 and 10) contains examples of computer analyses accompanied by extensive commentaries. While studying subsequent chapters, you may find it useful or necessary to refer to the present chapter for general comments on a statistical package being used and/or on our practice in reporting input and output files.

Chapter 17
Simple Regression Analysis

Concepts of regression were mentioned and commented upon in diverse contexts such as criterion-related validation and differential prediction (Chapter 3), formulation of problems and hypotheses (Chapter 9), and different types of research designs (Chapters 12–14). However, we refrained from dealing with the mechanics of the analysis, focusing instead on meaning, on the role played by the method in the design of the study and in the interpretation of the results. The focus in this and subsequent chapters is on analytic aspects. Just as we have suggested that you read or skim relevant chapters of Part 3 when studying measurement and design issues, we recommend that you read or skim relevant chapters in Parts 1 and 2 when studying the chapters comprising Part 3.

The concepts of variance and covariance are central not only to regression analysis but to scientific inquiry in general; therefore, we begin this chapter with a brief review of them. We then turn to a detailed presentation of simple regression analysis.

Variance

Variability (e.g., among people, objects, organizations, nationalities) is what arouses a scientist's curiosity and impels him or her to search for its causes. No wonder that Galton (1889), whose work has served as the major impetus for the study of individual differences, expressed his astonishment at statisticians' failure to study variability:

It is difficult to understand why statisticians commonly limit their inquiries to Averages, and do not revel in more comprehensive views. Their souls seem as dull to the charm of variety as that of the native of our flat English counties, whose retrospect of Switzerland was that, if its mountains could be thrown into its lakes, two nuisances would be got rid of at once. (p. 62)

Even if your statistical background is rudimentary, you are probably familiar with the basic notions of indices of central tendency (e.g., mean, median) and variability (e.g., range, variance). You probably also know that both kinds of indices are necessary for a meaningful description of a set of data.

One of the most useful indices of variability is the variance. When based on a sample, the estimate of the variance of a set of X scores is:

$$s_x^2 = \frac{\Sigma(X - \bar{X})^2}{N - 1} = \frac{\Sigma x^2}{N - 1} \qquad (17.1)$$

where s_x^2 = sample variance of X; Σx^2 = sum of squared deviations of X from the mean of X; N = sample size. The standard deviation, s, is, of course, the square root of the variance.

Recall that capital letters are generally used to depict raw scores, whereas lower case letters are used to depict deviation scores. Note that the numerator of (17.1) calls for the sum of squared deviation scores. Hereafter, when we say "sum of squares" we mean "sum of squared deviation scores." An algebraic identity of the numerator of (17.1), particularly useful when calculating by hand or with the aid of a calculator, is:

$$\Sigma x^2 = \Sigma X^2 - \frac{(\Sigma X)^2}{N} \qquad (17.2)$$

Note that only raw scores are utilized in (17.2). The first term on the right refers to the *sum of the squared* raw scores, whereas the numerator of the second term refers to the *square of the sum* of the raw scores.

A NUMERICAL EXAMPLE

In Table 17.1, illustrative data for two variables, Y and X, are reported. We begin by using these data for the calculation of variances. Subsequently, they are used for the calculation of covariance and for regression analysis, where some substantive examples of what the two variables might be are also given.

The information necessary for the calculation of the variances of Y and X is given at the bottom of Table 17.1, as are results of intermediate calculations and the answers. We begin by calculating the sum of squares. Using ΣY and ΣY^2 from Table 17.1, and applying (17.2):

$$\Sigma y^2 = 903 - \frac{(129)^2}{20} = 70.95$$

Applying now (17.1),

$$s_y^2 = \frac{70.95}{19} = 3.73$$

Calculate the variance of X and check your answer with the one given at the bottom of Table 17.1.

Table 17.1

Illustrative Data for Y and X

Y	Y²	X	X²	XY
5	25	1	1	5
5	25	1	1	5
4	16	1	1	4
4	16	1	1	4
3	9	1	1	3
8	64	2	4	16
7	49	2	4	14
6	36	2	4	12
6	36	2	4	12
5	25	2	4	10
10	100	3	9	30
8	64	3	9	24
8	64	3	9	24
6	36	3	9	18
5	25	3	9	15
10	100	4	16	40
8	64	4	16	32
8	64	4	16	32
7	49	4	16	28
6	36	4	16	24
Σ: 129	903	50	150	352
M: 6.45		2.50		
ss:	70.95		25	29.50
s²:	3.73		1.32	1.55
s:	1.93		1.15	

Note. M = Mean; ss = deviation sum of squares, or sum of products (i.e., Σy^2, Σx^2, Σxy); s^2 = variance, or covariance (i.e., s_y^2, s_x^2, s_{yx}); s = standard deviation (i.e., s_y, s_x). See text for explanation.

Covariance

In their attempts to explain or predict status of people (objects, institutions, and the like) on a given variable, researchers resort, among other things, to studying how it is related to, how it covaries with, other variables. The sample covariance is defined as

$$s_{yx} = \frac{\Sigma(Y - \bar{Y})(X - \bar{X})}{N - 1} = \frac{\Sigma yx}{N - 1} \tag{17.3}$$

where s_{yx} = covariance of Y with X; Σyx = sum of the cross product deviations of pairs of Y and X scores from their respective means. As in the case of sum of squares, when we say "sum of products," we mean deviations sum of products. Note that the covariance is a symmetric index (i.e., $s_{yx} = s_{xy}$) and that the variance of a variable may be conceived of as its covariance with itself.

Using raw scores to calculate the sum of products:

$$\Sigma yx = \Sigma YX - \frac{(\Sigma Y)(\Sigma X)}{N} \tag{17.4}$$

For the data of Table 17.1:

$$\Sigma yx = 352 - \frac{(129)(50)}{20} = 29.5$$

And

$$s_{yx} = \frac{29.5}{19} = 1.55$$

Being a function of the properties of the units of the measures of the two variables, the covariance is generally not interpretable substantively. A change in the units of measurement will result in a change in the magnitude of the covariance. Assume, for the sake of a simple illustration, that for the data reported in Table 17.1 Y is length, expressed in feet, and X is weight, expressed in pounds. Transforming length into inches, the covariance between Y and X would be 18.63, which is, within rounding error, 12 times larger (i.e., feet into inches) than the covariance reported above. The important thing is that this value, and a host of others that would result from similar transformations, expresses the same covariability between length and weight for the objects under consideration. This has to do with the concept of invariance under transformation discussed in Chapter 2 (see Scales of Measurement)—a topic pertinent to standardization, to which we now turn.

STANDARDIZATION

You are probably familiar with the concept of standard scores. Recall that:

$$z_y = \frac{Y - \bar{Y}}{s} = \frac{y}{s} \tag{17.5}$$

where z = standard score; Y = raw score; $\bar{Y}$ = mean; s = standard deviation.

Converting a set of raw scores into z scores constitutes a special kind of transformation—one that results in a set of standard scores (i.e., the z's) whose mean is 0 and whose standard deviation is 1, regardless of the magnitudes of the mean and standard deviation of the raw scores. Consequently, it would appear that problems attendant with the interpretation of the magnitude of the covariance (see above) may be overcome by standardizing the variables (i.e., transforming them into z scores). As it turns out, the covariance of two variables expressed in z scores is the Pearson correlation coefficient:

$$r_{yx} = \frac{s_{yx}}{s_y s_x} \tag{17.6}$$

where r = sample correlation coefficient between Y and X; s_{yx} = sample covariance; s_y, s_x = sample standard deviations of Y and X respectively.

You are probably more familiar with other expressions of r. We purposely used the one given above, because it demonstrates that, in the calculation of r, the covariance—the numerator of (17.6)—is standardized by dividing it by the product of the standard deviations (the denominator). Stated differently, r is a standardized covariance. As another way of seeing this, assume that (17.6) is applied to z scores. Because the standard deviation of such scores is 1, the denominator of (17.6) would be equal to 1, showing clearly that r is the covariance of the z scores.

Following are a couple of other expressions of r:

$$r_{yx} = \frac{\Sigma yx}{\sqrt{\Sigma y^2 \Sigma x^2}} \tag{17.7}$$

And

$$r_{yx} = \frac{N\Sigma YX - (\Sigma Y)(\Sigma X)}{\sqrt{N\Sigma Y^2 - (\Sigma Y)^2} \sqrt{N\Sigma X^2 - (\Sigma X)^2}} \tag{17.8}$$

Note that deviation scores are used in (17.7), whereas raw scores are used in (17.8). There are various other algebraically identical expressions of r. Regardless of the formula used, and regardless of whether it is manifest from its format, the raw scores are standardized in the process of the calculation of r.

Using summary data from the bottom of Table 17.1, we illustrate the calculation of r by applying (17.6) through (17.8).

Using (17.6)

$$r_{yx} = \frac{1.55}{(1.93)(1.15)} = .70$$

Using (17.7)

$$r_{yx} = \frac{29.50}{\sqrt{(70.95)(25)}} = .70$$

Using (17.8)

$$r_{yx} = \frac{(20)(352) - (129)(50)}{\sqrt{(20)(903) - (129)^2} \sqrt{(20)(150) - (50)^2}} = .70$$

As an exercise, we suggest that you transform Y and/or X (e.g., multiply by a constant, add a constant), calculate r, and convince yourself that, although the covariance changes, r remains the same.

Most measures used in sociobehavioral research have units that are, to say the least, difficult to interpret (see Chapters 2 through 4). Because r is independent of the units of measures of the variables being correlated, it is extremely appealing to sociobehavioral researchers. Contributing to the immense popularity of r is its deceptively simple interpretation. As a consequence of the standardization of the raw scores, the maximum value of r is $|1.00|$; $r = +1.00$ means a perfect positive correlation; $r = -1.00$ means a perfect negative correlation; and $r = .00$ means no linear relation. These properties of r lend it an aura of simplicity incarnate in the eyes of many. It would seem that one need not worry about the what and the how of the measures one uses, as it is "perfectly clear" that the closer r is to 1, the stronger the relation between the variables under consideration.

What is, however, overlooked by many is that problems and difficulties attendant with the interpretation of the units of measures used are *not* solved by the application of r, rather they are *evaded*. Difficulties in applying and interpreting r were discussed and illustrated in connection with differential prediction (see Chapter 3). Later in this chapter, we address some misconceptions and misapplications of r.

SIMPLE LINEAR REGRESSION

Broadly speaking, regression analysis is a method of analyzing variability of a dependent variable, or a criterion, by resorting to information on one or more independent variables, or predictors. In various chapters (see especially Chapters 3, 8, and 14), we drew attention to the important distinction between predictive and explanatory research, and suggested that the terms predictors and criteria be used to refer to variables in the former, whereas the terms independent and dependent variables be used in the latter. Although the mechanics of regression analysis are the same in both research contexts, the interpretation of the results, particularly specific elements (e.g., regression coefficients), is predicated on the research context in which they were obtained. Moreover, certain applications of regression analysis (e.g., variable selection procedures; see Chapter 18) may be meaningful or useful in one context and not in the other.

Compared with explanatory research, applications and interpretations of regression analysis in predictive research are relatively uncomplicated. Although we will occasionally comment on the use of regression analysis in predictive research, mostly by way of contrast with explanatory research, our concern will be almost exclusively with the latter.[1] Specifically, then, we will discuss the application and interpretation of regression analysis in the context of attempts to use independent variables to explain dependent variables.

The present chapter is devoted to simple linear regression, namely regression analysis with one independent variable. "Linear" means that a unit change in the independent variable is associated with an expected constant change in the dependent variable (see below). Subsequent chapters deal with extensions to multiple regression analysis.

We follow the convention of using Y and X to signify the dependent and independent variables respectively. Although it will be convenient to speak of individuals' scores, the presentation is, generally speaking, also applicable to situations in which the unit of analysis is not the individual (e.g., groups, institutions), and when the values are not scores, in the strict sense of this term (e.g., values on a manipulated variable: hours of practice, frequency of exposure, and the like).

Now, a person's score on the dependent variable may be expressed as follows:

$$Y_i = \alpha + \beta X_i + \epsilon_i \qquad (17.9)$$

where Y_i is the score of individual i on the dependent variable; X_i is the score of individual i on the independent variable; α (alpha) and β (beta) are constants; ϵ_i (epsilon) is random error for individual i. Equation (17.9) refers to a population. The corresponding equation for a sample is:

$$Y = a + bX + e \qquad (17.10)$$

where a, b, and e are estimators of their corresponding parameters in (17.9). Hereafter, we omit subscripts—see (17.10)—whenever there is no danger of ambiguity.

THE REGRESSION EQUATION

Essentially, the aim of regression analysis is to find a solution for b of (17.10) such that, when it is applied to the scores on the independent variable, X, explanation or prediction of

---

[1]For a presentation in which the focus is on predictive research, see Chapter 3.

the dependent variable, Y, will be maximized. Stated differently, the solution being sought is one that will minimize errors of explanation or prediction. More specifically, the aim is to minimize the sum of the squared errors (Σe^2); hence the name "least squares" given to this type of solution.

The least squares equation, or the *regression equation*, is

$$Y' = a + bX \qquad (17.11)$$

where Y' = predicted score on the dependent variable; a = intercept—the value of Y at which the regression line intercepts the Y axis, or the value of Y' when X is zero; b = regression coefficient, or the slope of the regression line (see Figure 17.1, below, for a depiction of the regression line). As is explained below, b indicates the expected change in Y associated with a unit change in X. Note that $Y - Y'$ (observed minus predicted score), referred to as residual, is the error—e of (17.10). It is that part of the Y score that is left unexplained, or not predictable, on the basis of the regression equation, and it is the $\Sigma(Y - Y')^2$, that is, the sum of the squared residuals (see below), that is minimized by the solution for the constants of the regression equation.

Of several equivalent formulas for the calculation of b, we begin by using the following one:

$$b = \frac{\Sigma yx}{\Sigma x^2} \qquad (17.12)$$

The formula for a is

$$a = \bar{Y} - b\bar{X} \qquad (17.13)$$

A NUMERICAL EXAMPLE

The data of Table 17.1 are used to illustrate the calculation of the regression equation as well as to elaborate on its meaning in the context of some substantive examples. Beginning with the calculations and using relevant values from the bottom of Table 17.1

$$b = \frac{29.50}{25.00} = 1.18$$

$$a = 6.45 - (1.18)(2.5) = 3.50$$

The regression equation for the data of Table 17.1 is:

$$Y' = 3.50 + 1.18X$$

Thus, to obtain an individual's predicted score, his or her X score is multiplied by 1.18 (b), to which 3.50 (a) is added. It was stated above that b indicates the expected change in the dependent variable, Y, associated with a unit change in the independent variable, X. For the data under consideration, then, for an increment of one unit in X, the expected increment in Y is 1.18.

Regression analysis can be applied in different research designs (e.g., experimental, nonexperimental). Although the mechanics of the analysis are the same, regardless of the design, the validity of the interpretation of the results is predicated on its specific properties. Thus, what was said in Chapters 10 through 14 about the different designs (e.g., internal and external validity, randomization, manipulation and manipulation checks) has direct bearing on the interpretation of the results. Some *sketches* of substantive examples[2] will be offered in the hope of clarifying these points.

Beginning with some examples of experimental designs in which simple regression analysis may be applicable, and referring to the illustrative data of Table 17.1, consider the following: (a) X may be number of exposures (i.e., 1, 2, 3, or 4) to a list of words and Y may be the number of words remembered; (b) X may be a dosage of some drug (e.g., a stimulant) and Y a rating of subject's agitation or irritability; and (c) X may be number of months in some program (e.g., Head Start, training, therapy) and Y may be academic achievement, social adjustment, mental health, and the like.

What the preceding examples have in common is that the independent variable is manipulated, that it is, loosely speaking, continuous as contrasted with categorical (i.e., it is composed of levels that differ in degree rather than in kind)[3] and that subjects are randomly assigned to the different levels.

Turning now to the regression equation, b (the regression coefficient) is interpreted as the effect of the independent variable on the dependent variable. Referring to the first example given above, it would be concluded that, for each additional exposure to the list of words, subjects are expected to remember 1.18 words more. Or, referring to the second example, for each unit of increase in the drug, an increment of 1.18 in the rating of agitation is expected.

It was said above that a (the intercept) indicates the expected value of Y when X is zero. Whether or not a is substantively meaningful depends accordingly on whether or not it is meaningful to speak of zero treatment level (i.e., no treatment) within a given research context. Referring again to the first two examples given above, it makes no sense to determine how many words subjects *not* exposed to the list remember. In contrast, it is meaningful to determine the level of agitation of subjects who have not been administered the drug. In given contexts, the researcher may deem it imperative to determine performance under conditions of no treatment, as a form of control, a base line, for the interpretation of the effect of the treatment. Because a is not substantively meaningful in much of sociobehavioral research, we deal mostly with regression coefficients.

Instead of experimental research, the illustrative studies given above could be conducted as quasi-experiments. It will be recalled that what differentiates the two designs is *not* variable manipulation (i.e., administration of treatments) but rather whether or not subjects were randomly assigned to the levels (or categories) of a variable.[4] The consequences of the difference between the two designs are far reaching, particularly with respect to specification errors. We return to this very important topic later in this chapter, in connection with regression assumptions.

We turn now to some examples of nonexperimental research: (a) X may be grade in school and Y may be academic achievement, moral development, motivation, and the like. For the data of Table 17.1, then, this would mean that samples of children from grades 1 through 4 served as subjects. (b) X may be socioeconomic status and Y political involvement, persuasibility, locus of control, and the like. (c) X may be hours of TV watching per day and Y aggression, lethargy, or what have you.

As was discussed in detail in Part 2 (especially Chapter 14), the interpretation of results is generally much more complex and precarious in nonexperimental research. Some authors

---

[2]In view of the comments that follow, we are tempted to say caricatures of substantive examples.

[3]See Chapter 2, Scales of Measurement, and Chapter 8, Measurement Perspective.

[4]For a discussion of randomization and its role in research, see Chapter 10. For detailed discussions and contrasts between experimental and quasi-experimental designs, see Chapters 12 and 13.

even refrain from using terms such as independent and dependent variables when the re-search is nonexperimental, let alone making statements regarding the *effects* of the former on the latter. Such authors would, therefore, *not* interpret regression coefficients (b's) obtained in nonexperimental research as indices of the effects of the variables with which they are associated on the dependent variable.[5]

For present purposes, it would suffice to remind you of our discussions of hazards of misinterpretation in connection with the use of proxy variables, relations of independent variables among themselves and/or with omitted variables (see, for example, Chapters 13 and 14). Referring to examples given above, it would not require much thought or effort to come up with convincing arguments that grade level may be a proxy for age or that hours of TV watching may be a proxy for home environment. It would be equally easy to come up with explanations according to which part or all of the effects of the aforementioned variables may be due to their relations with variables omitted from the equation (i.e., due to specifica-tion errors; see below).

REGRESSION EQUATION FOR STANDARD SCORES

When the independent and dependent variables are standardized, the regression equation is

$$z_y' = \beta z_x \tag{17.14}$$

where z_y' = predicted standard score of Y; β = standardized regression coefficient; z_x = standard score on X. A comment about notation is in order. There is no consensus about symbols used in regression analysis. Although some authors adhere strictly to the practice of using Greek letters to represent parameters and Roman letters for their corresponding statis-tics, others do not. In (17.9) and (17.10), we followed this practice. However, along with many authors, *we will, henceforth, use* β *as a symbol for the standardized regression coefficient*. Unfortunately, lack of consistency in notation is part of the statistical scene. You may recall, for example, that β is also used to depict Type II error (see Chapters 9 and 15). The important thing is to avoid ambiguity about notation in a given context. Accordingly, we make specific mention of our usage whenever we feel that ambiguity may arise.

Unstandardized (b) and standardized (β) coefficients are related as follows:

$$\beta = b\frac{s_x}{s_y}$$

or   (17.15)

$$b = \beta\frac{s_y}{s_x}$$

where s_x and s_y are the standard deviations of X and Y respectively.

Note that, unlike the regression equation for raw scores, the regression equation for standard scores has no intercept (a). Stated differently, when z scores are used, $a = 0$. The reason for this can be seen readily by inspecting (17.13) and recalling that the mean of z scores is zero.

As with the unstandardized regression coefficient, the standardized coefficient is inter-preted as indicating the expected change in the dependent variable associated with a unit

---

[5]We return to this topic in the context of multiple regression analysis (Chapter 18).

change in the independent variable. However, because the standard deviation of z scores is 1 (see above), this is tantamount to a statement about a one standard deviation change in the independent variable.

Earlier, $b = 1.18$ was obtained. Taking the standard deviations from the bottom of Table 17.1 and applying (17.15)

$$\beta = 1.18\frac{1.15}{1.93} = .70$$

The regression equation is:

$$z_y' = .70z_x$$

Accordingly, a change of one unit (i.e., one standard deviation) in the independent variable, when expressed as z scores, is expected to result in a change of .70 standard deviations in the dependent variable.

For simple regression, $\beta = r$ (the correlation between the independent and dependent variables). Earlier, $r = .70$ was calculated for the data of Table 17.1; this is equal to the value of the beta weight. From the foregoing discussion, it is clear that the maximum value of β in simple regression is $|1.00|$.[6] In view of our brief overview of r (see above), it should come as no surprise when we say that the interpretation of the standardized regression coefficient is deceptively simple. Researchers are inclined to interpret β instead of b when they are unable to attach substantive meaning to a unit change on the independent variable. But, as was noted in connection with r, the use of β evades rather than solves the problem.

REGRESSION EQUATION FOR DEVIATION SCORES

To enhance understanding of the regression equation and as a prelude to the next topic, another format—one that is applicable when subjects' status on the independent variable is expressed in deviation scores—will be presented. Recall that the regression equation for raw scores is

$$Y' = a + bX$$

Substituting (17.13) for a,

$$Y' = (\bar{Y} - b\bar{X}) + bX$$
$$= \bar{Y} + b(X - \bar{X})$$
$$Y' = \bar{Y} + bx \tag{17.16}$$

From (17.16), it can be seen that the predicted score is composed of two parts: (a) the mean of the dependent variable, and (b) the product of the individual's deviation from the mean of the independent variable (x) and the regression coefficient (b). To appreciate the meaning of (17.16), it will be discussed in the context of an experiment, although it applies equally to regression analysis in other types of explanatory research. In an experimental design, the researcher determines the levels of the independent variable to which subjects are then randomly assigned. Under such circumstances, x is the deviation of a given level of the

---

[6]Contrary to what you might read in some sources, this is not necessarily the case in multiple regression analysis when the independent variables are correlated (see Chapter 18).

independent variable from the overall mean, that is, from the mean of all the levels. Further-more, all subjects assigned to a given level have the same deviation score on X. It should be clear that individuals receiving the same treatment level have identical predicted scores composed of the overall mean of the dependent variable and a part due to having been exposed to a specific level of the independent variable.

When the independent variable has *no* effect on the dependent variable, the regression coefficient (b) would equal zero. Another way of stating this is that the independent and dependent variables are not related,[7] or that information regarding individuals' status on the independent variable is irrelevant to their status on the dependent variable.

Although the same predicted scores will be obtained regardless of the specific formula used, it is particularly clear from (17.16) that, when b is zero, the predicted score for all subjects is equal to the mean of the dependent variable. Thus, when information about the independent variable is irrelevant, the best prediction, in the least squares sense, is the mean of the dependent variable. What this means is that the sum of squared errors, or residuals, will be minimized. This can be seen when it is recognized that in the situation we are describing,

$$Y - Y' = Y - \bar{Y}$$

As you probably know, the sum of the squared deviations from the mean (Σy^2) is the smallest as compared with the sum of squared deviations from any other constant.

When $b \neq 0$, when the independent variable *does* affect the dependent variable, the sum of squared errors of prediction, or residuals, will be smaller than Σy^2. Much of regression analysis revolves around the idea of partitioning the Σy^2 into two components: one that is attributed to regression and one that is viewed as error. It is to this topic that we now turn.

PARTITIONING OF SUM OF SQUARES

Consider the following identity:

$$Y = \bar{Y} + (Y' - \bar{Y}) + (Y - Y') \tag{17.17}$$

Each person's score on the dependent variable is expressed as composed of the following three elements:

1. The mean of the dependent variable, which is, of course, the same for all subjects.
2. The deviation of the predicted score from the mean of the dependent variable, referred to as the deviation due to regression. As was explained in the preceding section, subjects exposed to the same level of the independent variable have the same predicted score. Hence, the deviation due to regression is also the same for these subjects.[8]
3. The deviation of the observed score from the predicted score, that is, error or residual.

It will be instructive to show these elements and their role in regression analysis using, for illustrative purposes, the data of Table 17.1. The regression equation for these data is

$$Y' = 3.50 + 1.18X$$

---

[7]Note from (17.15) that b is zero when β (i.e., r_{yx}) = .00.
[8]As is shown in Chapter 19, this holds true also when the independent variable is categorical, that is, when subjects are exposed to different treatments, as contrasted with different levels of the same treatment. In such designs, the deviation due to regression is the same for subjects exposed to a given treatment.

Calculating Y' for individuals whose $X = 1$, that is, those exposed to level 1 of the X

$$3.50 + (1.18)(1) = 4.68$$

Now, Y for the first individual in Table 17.1 is 5. Expressing this score as composed of the elements indicated in (17.17)

$$5 = 6.45 + (4.68 - 6.45) + (5 - 4.68)$$
$$5 = 6.45 + (-1.77) + (.32)$$

Similar calculations for all the subjects are reported in Table 17.2. As can be seen from Column 3, predicted scores for individuals exposed to the same level of the independent variable are the same, as are the deviations due to regression reported in Column 5. The residuals are reported in Column 7. The values in Columns 4, 5, and 7 correspond to the three elements of (17.17), which when added will yield each individual's score on Y.

We recommend that you study Table 17.2 carefully and, if necessary, recalculate its elements. At the bottom of the table, are reported the sums of the columns, from which some of the consequences of the least squares solution will be noted: (a) $\Sigma Y = \Sigma Y'$ (accordingly, the mean of predicted scores equals the mean of observed scores); and (b) the sum of the deviations due to regression equals zero, as is the sum of the residuals.

REGRESSION AND RESIDUAL SUMS OF SQUARES

Subtracting $\bar{Y}$ from each side of (17.17) the deviation of a score on the dependent variable from the mean is expressed thus:

$$(Y - \bar{Y}) = (Y' - \bar{Y}) + (Y - Y') \tag{17.18}$$

It can be shown that:

$$\Sigma(Y - \bar{Y})^2 = \Sigma(Y' - \bar{Y})^2 + \Sigma(Y - Y')^2$$

or

$$\Sigma y^2 = ss_{reg} + ss_{res} \tag{17.19}$$

where ss_{reg} = sum of squares regression; ss_{res} = sum of squares residuals.

When analyzing variability of the dependent variable by resorting to information on one or more independent variables, it is more convenient to work with its sum of squares, Σy^2, instead of its variance.[9] This is how (17.19) is expressed: *The sum of squares of the dependent variable is partitioned into two components—one due to regression and one due to residuals.*

Recall that, when the independent variable has *no* effect on the dependent variable, $b = 0$, and $ss_{res} = \Sigma y^2$. From (17.19), it is clear that, under such circumstances, $ss_{reg} = 0$, as all of the variability of the dependent variable is attributed to error. The converse is, of course, true when $ss_{reg} = \Sigma y^2$. Under such circumstances, $ss_{res} = 0$, as all of the variability of the dependent variable is attributed to the effect(s) of the independent variable(s). Needless to say, neither of the preceding extreme cases is encountered in empirical research. Much of the effort in the design and execution of research is directed toward maximizing the part of the sum of squares that is attributed to regression.

---

[9]As was shown earlier in this chapter, the variance is obtained by dividing the sum of squares by $N - 1$.

Table 17.2

Elements of Y Scores

(1) X	(2) Y	(3) Y'	(4) Ȳ	(5) Y' − Ȳ	(6) (Y' − Ȳ)²	(7) Y − Y'	(8) (Y − Y')²
1	5	4.68	6.45	−1.77	3.1329	.32	.1024
1	5	4.68	6.45	−1.77	3.1329	.32	.1024
1	4	4.68	6.45	−1.77	3.1329	−.68	.4624
1	4	4.68	6.45	−1.77	3.1329	−.68	.4624
1	3	4.68	6.45	−1.77	3.1329	−1.68	2.8224
2	8	5.86	6.45	−.59	.3481	2.14	4.5796
2	7	5.86	6.45	−.59	.3481	1.14	1.2996
2	6	5.86	6.45	−.59	.3481	.14	.0196
2	6	5.86	6.45	−.59	.3481	.14	.0196
2	5	5.86	6.45	−.59	.3481	−.86	.7396
3	10	7.04	6.45	.59	.3481	2.96	8.7616
3	8	7.04	6.45	.59	.3481	.96	.9216
3	8	7.04	6.45	.59	.3481	.96	.9216
3	6	7.04	6.45	.59	.3481	−1.04	1.0816
3	5	7.04	6.45	.59	.3481	−2.04	4.1616
4	10	8.22	6.45	1.77	3.1329	1.78	3.1684
4	8	8.22	6.45	1.77	3.1329	−.22	.0484
4	8	8.22	6.45	1.77	3.1329	−.22	.0484
4	7	8.22	6.45	1.77	3.1329	−1.22	1.4884
4	6	8.22	6.45	1.77	3.1329	−2.22	4.9284
Σ: 50	129	129.00	129.00	0.00	34.8100	0.00	36.1400

In column 6 of Table 17.2, the deviations due to regression are squared and added to yield $ss_{reg} = 34.81$. Similarly, in column 8, the residuals are squared and added to yield $ss_{res} = 36.14$. Note that the two components sum to 70.95, which is the sum of squares of Y, calculated earlier in Table 17.1. In regression analysis, as in the analysis of variance, the sum of squares of Y is often referred to as the total sum of squares. Hereafter, we will follow this usage.

The detailed calculations of the various sums of squares in Table 17.2 were shown in order to enhance your understanding. There are, however, much simpler ways to arrive at the same results. Following are three equivalent expressions of the regression sum of squares, along with their applications to the data of Table 17.1 ($b = 1.18$ was calculated above). Other values are taken from the bottom of Table 17.1.

$$ss_{reg} = \frac{(\Sigma xy)^2}{\Sigma x^2} \tag{17.20}$$

$$= \frac{(29.50)^2}{25} = 34.81$$

$$ss_{reg} = b\Sigma xy \tag{17.21}$$

$$= (1.18)(29.5) = 34.81$$

$$ss_{reg} = b^2\Sigma x^2 \tag{17.22}$$

$$= (1.18)^2(25) = 34.81$$

An easy way to calculate the residual sum of squares is

$$SS_{res} = \Sigma y^2 - SS_{reg} \qquad (17.23)$$

For the data of Table 17.1

$$SS_{res} = 70.95 - 34.81 = 36.14$$

PARTITIONING INTO PROPORTIONS

The regression and residual components can be expressed as proportions of the total sum of squares

$$\frac{\Sigma y^2}{\Sigma y^2} = \frac{SS_{reg}}{\Sigma y^2} + \frac{SS_{res}}{\Sigma y^2}$$

$$1 = \frac{SS_{reg}}{\Sigma y^2} + \frac{SS_{res}}{\Sigma y^2} \qquad (17.24)$$

where the first term on the right indicates the proportion of the total sum of squares due to regression, and the second term indicates the proportion of the total sum of squares that is due to residuals or error.

For the data under consideration

$$\frac{34.81}{70.95} + \frac{36.14}{70.95} = .49 + .51 = 1$$

Thus, .49 (or 49%) of the total sum of squares (or the variance) is due to regression, whereas .51 (or 51%) is due to residuals or error.

It will be instructive to express the preceding indices in another format. Dividing (17.20)—one of the expressions of regression sum of squares—by the total sum of squares

$$\frac{(\Sigma xy)^2}{\Sigma x^2} \div \Sigma y^2 = \frac{(\Sigma xy)^2}{\Sigma x^2 \Sigma y^2} = r_{xy}^2 \qquad (17.25)$$

As is indicated in (17.25), the proportion of sum of squares due to regression is equal to the squared correlation coefficient between the independent and the dependent variable.[10] Earlier, we calculated $r = .70$. $(.70)^2 = .49$, which is the value obtained above for the proportion of the sum of squares due to regression.

From (17.24) and (17.25), it follows that the proportion of the sum of squares due to residuals is equal to $1 - r_{xy}^2$. For the data of Table 17.1, $1 - .49 = .51$, which is the proportion of the total sum of squares due to residuals obtained above.

Having calculated the squared correlation between the independent and the dependent variables, the regression and residual sums of squares can easily be obtained as follows:

$$SS_{reg} = r^2 \Sigma y^2 \qquad (17.26)$$

and

$$SS_{res} = (1 - r^2)\Sigma y^2 \qquad (17.27)$$

---

[10](17.25) is the square of (17.7).

In view of the equivalence of expressions of regression and residual components as sums of squares, variances, or proportions, results may be reported in any of these formats. Many researchers prefer to report and interpret proportions or percentages of variance because of their independence of the properties of the scales used to measure the dependent variable.[11] Following are some of the more frequent expressions researchers use when interpreting r^2: It is the proportion of variance (a) "due to regression"; (b) "predictable by the predictor"; (c) "accounted for by, or due to, the independent variable"; and (d) "explained by the independent variable."

Needless to say, the choice from among expressions such as the preceding when interpreting r^2 is not at all arbitrary. Rather, it is predicated, among other things, on the research context, the design, and the theoretical formulation. It will suffice to contrast the interpretation of r^2 as the proportion of variance predictable with the one according to which it is the proportion of variance explained. Speaking of predictable variance is relatively uncomplicated and is appropriate in predictive research. As we have pointed out in various places, a variable may be useful for predictive purposes even when, for example, its relation with the criterion is spurious. Speaking of variance explained, on the other hand, implies an explanatory perspective with all that it entails. Under such circumstances, skepticism regarding the validity of the measures, the design, the theoretical rationale, to name some major aspects, may invalidate, to a greater or lesser extent, claims regarding explained variance.

The foregoing issues aside, the interpretation of r^2 is not as simple and straightforward as many practitioners seem to believe. What we have in mind is the penchant to interpret the magnitude of r^2 as an index of the effect of the independent variable on the dependent variable (i.e., effect size; see Chapters 9 and 15). The prevailing view seems to be: The larger the proportion of variance a variable accounts for, the better, the more important, it is. "Happiness is variance explained," Lieberson (1985, p. 91) declared in a cogent critique of researchers' "obsession" (p. 91) with the notion of explained variance.

In subsequent chapters (e.g., Chapter 18), we will have occasion to comment in greater detail on misconceptions regarding the meaning of proportion of variance accounted for, particularly in connection with the widespread practice of partitioning it among several independent variables for the purpose of determining their relative importance. For now, because we are dealing with one independent variable, we comment briefly on potential misconceptions in the interpretation of r^2.

The allure that r^2 holds for many researchers stems from the fact that it is a standardized index, not dependent on the properties of the measures used. But, as we have already pointed out in connection with r, standardization of measures does not come to grips with the issue of interpreting the units of measures.

When the interest is in studying the effect of the independent variable(s) on the dependent variable, it is the unstandardized regression coefficient(s) that holds the greater promise for a more meaningful interpretation. Assuming that doubt is not cast about the validity of the research (e.g., with respect to design, measures, analysis), b provides the answer to what is probably the overriding question in the mind of most researchers: What is the expected change in Y associated with a unit change in X?

The foregoing remarks should not be construed that r^2 has no meaning or that it plays no role in regression analysis. As is shown below, it reflects the spread of the points about the regression line. The wider the spread, the lower r^2 is. Because $1 - r^2$ is the proportion of variance attributed to error, it should come as no surprise that r^2 plays an important role in tests of statistical significance (see Influence Analysis, below).

---

[11]We comment on this practice below.

GRAPHS

Visual displays of data are invaluable both for enhancing one's understanding of the patterns in them as well as for detecting patterns, anomalies, and departures from assumptions that may go unnoticed when one relies solely on calculations. For example, our calculations and interpretations of the results in connection with the illustrative data of Table 17.1 were based on the assumption that the regression of Y on X is *linear*. One way to check whether there are serious departures from linearity is to study a plot of the data.

The data of Table 17.1 are plotted in Figure 17.1. Also included in the figure is the regression line and several other dashed lines whose meanings are explained below. Conventionally, the horizontal axis (abscissa) is used for X, and the vertical axis (ordinate) is used for Y. Such plots are also referred to as scatterplots or scattergrams (see Cleveland & McGill, 1984, for a discussion of "The many faces of a scatterplot").

We begin by noting that the regression line is a graphic depiction of the regression equation, where a (the intercept) is the point on the Y axis intercepted by the regression line. The regression coefficient, b, indicates the slope of the regression line. Instead of using the regression equation, one can accordingly use the regression line to obtain predicted scores. To predict Y for a given X, draw a vertical line originating from the latter and extend it until it intersects the regression line, at which point draw a horizontal line to the Y axis. The value of Y where the horizontal line intersects the Y axis is Y'. This approach is illustrated in Figure 17.1 for the case of X being equal to the mean of X. Note the dashed vertical line originating from the mean of X and the horizontal line that intersects the Y axis at 6.45. The identical value is obtained through the application of the regression equation.

We purposely chose a value of X equal to the mean of X. Note that, when $X = \bar{X}$, $Y' = \bar{Y}$. That this is so can be seen clearly from (17.16), which is repeated here for convenience

$$Y' = \bar{Y} + bx$$

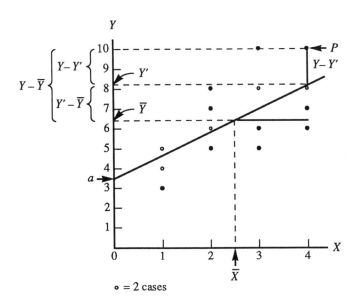

$\circ$ = 2 cases

Figure 17.1

When $X = \bar{X}$, $x = 0$. Consequently, $Y' = \bar{Y}$ regardless of the magnitude of b. Thus, lines originating from the means of X and Y, and paralleling the axes, always intersect on the regression line.

We now repeat (17.13)

$$a = \bar{Y} - b\bar{X}$$

It can be seen that, when $b = 0$, the intercept (a) is equal to the mean of Y. Thus, when the independent variable does not affect the dependent variable (or is not related to it), the regression line is horizontal and originates from the mean of the dependent variable. Assuming, for the sake of illustration, that $b = 0$ for the data of Table 17.1, the regression line would have been the dashed line in Figure 17.1, which we have extended by a solid line. Under such circumstances, drawing vertical lines from any of the X's would lead to the same prediction, namely the mean of Y. This is consistent with our earlier discussion that when X and Y are not related, the best prediction, in the least-squares sense, is the mean of Y.

DRAWING THE REGRESSION LINE

As with any straight line, two points are necessary for drawing the regression line. Of various approaches to the choice of such points, the simplest one is to choose the intercept (a) for the first point. To obtain the second point, draw lines originating from the means of X and Y, and paralleling the axes. The intersection of the two lines provides the second point.

REGRESSION AND RESIDUAL SEGMENTS

Earlier—see (17.18)—it was shown how the deviation of each score on the dependent variable from the mean of the dependent variable is partitioned into two parts: one attributed to regression and one to residual (see also columns 5 and 7 of Table 17.2). One of the scores from our illustrative data will now be used in order to depict the aforementioned elements as segments of a line comprising the deviation of the score on Y from the mean of Y. Specifically, the score for the first person in the group administered level 4 of the independent variable will be used. This person, whose $Y = 10$, is identified in Figure 17.1 by the letter P.

Now, for individuals whose score on X is 4, the predicted score, Y', is 8.22 (see column 3 of Table 17.2). This value is indicated in Figure 17.1 at the point at which the dashed line originating from the regression line intersects with the Y axis. For each of the subjects in this group, therefore, the deviation due to regression is 1.77 (i.e., $8.22 - 6.45$), which is the distance between Y' and the mean of Y indicated in Figure 17.1.

The deviation of P's Y score from Y' (i.e., the residual) is 1.78 (i.e., $10 - 8.22$). This is the vertical distance from the observed Y to the regression line, indicated in Figure 17.1 by the solid line from P to the regression line. This segment is also indicated on the Y axis. Note that the two line segments (i.e., deviation due to regression and the residual) comprise the line depicting the deviation of P's Y score from the mean of Y. In sum, the deviation of P's Y score from the mean of Y, 3.45, is equal to the length of the two adjacent line segments (1.77 + 1.78).

COMPUTER GRAPHICS

Not much effort is required to plot a small data set by hand. But the plotting of a relatively large data set by hand can become a chore. With the aid of a computer, personal or mainframe, data plotting can be accomplished with relative ease.

Numerous computer programs are available for generating graphics of varying degrees of complexity and quality. Some such programs are dedicated to graphics only, whereas others are part of statistical packages. Computer programs in general, and those we are using in various chapters, are discussed in Chapter 16. All the packages mentioned in Chapter 16 have facilities to generate graphics either as part of some general analytic procedures or through a separate procedure(s) dedicated to plotting. For illustrative purposes, the data of Table 17.1 will be plotted using MINITAB.

MINITAB

Input

```
OH=0
OUTFILE 'T171'
READ C1-C2
5   1        [data for first subject]
.   .
6   4        [data for last subject]
NAME C1 'Y' C2 'X'
PLOT 'Y' 'X';
   YSTART 0 12;        [subcommands specifying start and end values]
   XSTART 0 5.
```

Commentary

We named our input file T171.MTB. To run, we typed at the MTB prompt: EXEC 'T171'. Note that it is not necessary to include the extension (see Chapter 16).

Output

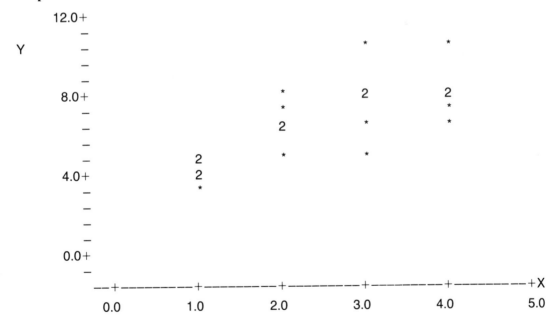

Commentary

MINITAB also has the facility for printing high resolution graphs. These, however, cannot be sent to an output file. Instead, they are generated on the screen using the commands given above, except that, instead of PLOT, the command GPLOT is used. Having generated the plot on the screen, it can be printed by striking the letter *P* (see *Minitab user's guide: Microcomputer version*, p. 15).

PROGRAMS FOR THE PERSONAL COMPUTER

There are many graphics programs for the PC. Of the midrange-priced graphic programs that we had an opportunity to review, we found *Harvard Graphics* (1988)[12] and *Microsoft Chart* (1987)[13] the most versatile. Incidentally, both may be interfaced with SPSS/PC.

TESTS OF SIGNIFICANCE

The logic and role of statistical tests of significance were discussed in Chapter 9 (see also Chapter 15). Among topics presented were (a) the distinction between statistical significance and substantive meaningfulness, (b) the null hypothesis, (c) effect size, (d) Type I (α) and Type II (β) errors, and (e) power of the statistical test of significance. If necessary, review these topics in the aforementioned chapters.

Although there are specialized formulas for tests of significance in simple regression analysis, we present instead a general approach and formulas applicable to any number of independent variables. It is this general approach that will also be used in subsequent chapters, not only in designs in which the independent variables are continuous but also in ones where they are categorical or a combination of both types of variables.

TESTING THE REGRESSION SUM OF SQUARES

Earlier, it was shown how the total sum of squares is partitioned into the following two parts: (a) regression sum of squares, attributed to the effect of the independent variable; and (b) residual sum of squares, or error. It stands to reason, therefore, that a test of statistical significance be addressed to whether the sum of squares attributed to regression is significant at a prespecified α level. This is accomplished as follows:

$$F = \frac{ss_{reg}/df_1}{ss_{res}/df_2} = \frac{ss_{reg}/k}{ss_{res}/(N-k-1)} \tag{17.28}$$

where df = degrees of freedom; k = number of independent variables; N = sample size. Each sum of squares is divided by its df to yield a mean square (*MS*). The df for the regression sum of squares (df_1) equal the number of independent variables (k), which for simple regression is 1. The df for the residual sum of squares (df_2) equal $N - k - 1$, which for simple regression are $N - 2$ (i.e., $N - 1 - 1$).

The mean square regression is divided by the mean square residuals to yield an F ratio with df for its numerator and denominator equal to the df for the mean square regression and the mean square residuals respectively. It is with these df that one enters the table for the

---

[12]Harvard Graphics is a registered trademark of Software Publishing Corporation.
[13]Microsoft Chart is a registered trademark of Microsoft Corporation.

distribution of F (see Appendix). An F ratio larger than the critical value at the prespecified α level leads to the rejection of the null hypothesis.[14] In the present case, this is tantamount to the rejection of the hypothesis that the regression sum of squares does not differ significantly from zero.

We now apply (17.28) to the data of Table 17.1. Earlier we calculated: $ss_{reg} = 34.81$ and $ss_{res} = 36.14$. $N = 20$. Therefore,

$$F = \frac{34.81/1}{36.14/18} = 17.34$$

with 1 and 18 df. For illustrative purposes, we select $\alpha = .01$. The tabled value of F (see Appendix) with 1 and 18 df is 8.28. Accordingly, the null hypothesis is rejected. One format used in reporting results such as these is: $F(1, 18) = 17.34$, $p < .01$. The values in the parentheses are the df, and $p < .01$ means probability less than .01.

REPORTING THE RESULTS

The guiding principle in reporting summaries of analyses should be that the information suffice for a meaningful interpretation of the results. Thus, for example, a meaningful interpretation is precluded when indices of central tendency are not accompanied by indices of variability (see beginning of this chapter). Ideally, the information reported should also suffice for the replication of the analysis or for the calculation of an alternative one, should an interested reader wish to do this (e.g., because of a suspicion that an error has been committed or because of the belief that an alternative analysis is more appropriate).[15]

At a minimum, descriptive statistics (e.g., means, standard deviations), the regression equation, and a summary of the tests of significance should be reported. What else is reported depends on the specifics of the study. For example, in nonexperimental designs with more than one independent variable, it is essential that correlations among the independent variables be reported.

TABULAR SUMMARY

Formats of reports, tables, figures, and what is to be included in them depend on editorial policies and standards established by specific journals, professional associations, universities, and funding agencies. Nevertheless, we believe it will be helpful to give an example of a general format for a tabular summary of the analysis, which you can then adapt for your specific needs and requirements. For general discussions of the construction of tables and their relations to the text, along with illustrations, see Ehrenberg (1977, 1981).

For illustrative purposes, the results of the analysis of the data of Table 17.1 are reported in Table 17.3.

The title should be brief, yet convey the gist of what the table is about. As our data are illustrative, we included an example of how a title might look.

---

[14]The null hypothesis is rejected, if the F ratio is equal to or larger than the critical value. For convenience, we will speak of an F ratio being larger than or exceeding the critical value.

[15]As is shown in Chapter 18, having the means, standard deviations, and the correlations among all the variables, the regression analysis can be replicated. Variants of the original regression analysis, or other analyses, may also be carried out.

Table 17.3

Summary of Analysis of Reading Achievement

Source	SS	df	MS	F
Regression	34.81	1	34.810	17.34*
Residual	36.14	18	2.008	
Total	70.95	19		

*p < .01

Under source, we used the generic terms regression and residual. It is preferable to refer to the variable(s) to which the regression sum of squares is attributed. Instead of Regression, then, we might have said, for example: Frequency of Exposure; Time in Program; Grade; SES; Teaching Styles.

Proportions of variance due to regression and residual (see below) could have been included instead of, or in addition to, the *ss*. But, as we said, standards and requirements for reporting vary. For example, among other instructions about the preparation of tables, the *Publication manual of the American Psychological Association* (1983) states: "Do not include columns of data that can be calculated easily from other columns" (p. 90). Following these instructions, one would *not* include both *ss* and *MS* in the summary table, let alone both *ss* and proportions of variance. Having the *df* and *ss*, *MS* can be easily calculated (*MS* = *ss/df*). Conversely, having *df* and *MS*, *ss* can be easily calculated (*ss* = *MS* x *df*). American Psychological Association journals follow the practice of reporting only *df* and *MS*.

VARIANCE AND STANDARD ERROR OF ESTIMATE

A formula for the calculation of the *F* ratio was given as (17.28). We focus now on the denominator of this formula as we will use it, or its square root, frequently in this and in subsequent chapters. The denominator of (17.28) is actually the variance of the residuals, which was referred to above as the Mean Square Residuals (*MSR*). Another term used to refer to *MSR* is the variance of estimate, symbolized as $s_{y.x}^2$. The subscripts are meant to indicate that it is the regression of *Y* on *X* that is being analyzed, to distinguish it from the regression of *X* on *Y* (see below). Formally

$$s_{y.x}^2 = MSR = \frac{ss_{res}}{N - k - 1} \tag{17.29}$$

The variance of estimate, or *MSR*, for the data of Table 17.1 is 36.14/18 = 2.01. The standard deviation of the residuals, referred to as the standard error of estimate, is the square root of the *MSR*, which for our illustrative data is $\sqrt{2.01} = 1.42$. As will become evident from subsequent presentations, in some analyses, we will use the variance of estimate, whereas in others we will use the standard error of estimate.

TESTING PROPORTION OF VARIANCE DUE TO REGRESSION

Earlier, we showed the equivalence of expressing the regression and residual components as sums of squares, variances, or proportions. We also commented on researchers' preference to report and interpret their results in proportions (or percentages) of total variance (or sum of squares) due to regression and to error. Using proportions in tests of significance yields results identical to those obtained previously.

The simplest way to see that this is so is to recall that $ss_{reg} = r^2 \Sigma y^2$—see (17.26)—and $ss_{res} = (1 - r^2) \Sigma y^2$—see (17.27). Substituting these alternative expressions of the sums of squares in (17.28)

$$F = \frac{r^2 \Sigma y^2 / k}{(1 - r^2) \Sigma y^2 / (N - k - 1)} \tag{17.30}$$

Canceling Σy^2 from the numerator and the denominator

$$F = \frac{r^2 / k}{(1 - r^2) / (N - k - 1)} \tag{17.31}$$

Clearly, it makes no difference whether the test is applied to the sum of squares or to the proportion of the total sum of squares or of the variance. We will use the two approaches interchangeably.

We now apply (17.31) to the data of Table 17.1. Earlier we calculated $r^2 = .49$. Therefore,

$$F = \frac{.49 / 1}{(1 - .49) / (20 - 1 - 1)} = 17.29$$

with 1 and 18 df. The slight discrepancy between the two F's is due to the rounding of r^2.

STING THE REGRESSION COEFFICIENT

It was pointed out earlier that it is more meaningful to interpret the regression coefficient, b, than the r^2.[16] A test of the b is carried out by dividing it by its standard error

$$t = \frac{b}{s_b} \tag{17.32}$$

where $t = t$ ratio; $s_b = $ standard error of b, calculated as follows:

$$s_b = \sqrt{\frac{s_{y.x}^2}{\Sigma x^2}} = \frac{s_{y.x}}{\sqrt{\Sigma x^2}} \tag{17.33}$$

where $s_{y.x}^2$ and $s_{y.x}$ are respectively the variance of estimate and the standard error of estimate—see (17.29); Σx^2 is the sum of squares for the independent variable, X.

In Table 17.1, we calculated $\Sigma x^2 = 25$; $s_{y.x} = 1.42$ (see calculation above). For the data under consideration

$$s_b = \frac{1.42}{\sqrt{25}} = .28$$

For the present data, $b = 1.18$ (see calculations in earlier section). Therefore,

$$t = \frac{1.18}{.28} = 4.21$$

---

[16]We have, however, also drawn attention to difficulties in the interpretation of b—difficulties that stem primarily from problems in interpreting the units of the measures used. You may wish to read the discussion of b and β in connection with this presentation.

The *df* for the *t* ratio equal the *df* associated with the *MSR*, or the variance of estimate (18 for the data being analyzed). When the *F* ratio has 1 *df* for the numerator, $t = \sqrt{F}$ with *df* equal to the denominator *df* of *F*. Earlier, we calculated $F = 17.34$, which is, within rounding error, equal to the square of the *t* calculated above.

CONFIDENCE INTERVALS

Stated more formally, the *t* test for a regression coefficient is

$$t = \frac{b - \beta}{s_b} \qquad (17.34)$$

where β is the hypothesized regression coefficient. Note that β here refers to the parameter, *not* the standardized coefficient (see comment on notation under Regression Equation for Standard Scores). When the null hypothesis tested is that $\beta = 0$, (17.34) is reduced to (17.32). But from (17.34), it can be seen that other hypotheses about the magnitude of β can be tested.

A statistically significant *t*, at a prespecified α level, leads to the rejection of the null hypothesis. As has been pointed out by many authors, particularly by those critical of tests of the null hypothesis, rejection of the null hypothesis that $\beta = 0$ is generally not very enlightening. Suffice it to point out that, whereas the null hypothesis is almost always false, its rejection is largely dependent on the power of the statistical test (see Chapters 9 and 15). Furthermore, the rejection of the null hypothesis provides no information about the precision with which *b* is estimated.

Because of these and other considerations, many authors appropriately recommend that confidence intervals be used instead. The notion of confidence interval was introduced in Chapter 15 in connection with the confidence interval of the mean. For the case of the regression coefficient, the confidence interval is calculated as follows:

$$b \pm t(\alpha/2, df)s_b$$

where *t* is the tabled *t* ratio at $\alpha/2$ with *df* associated with the *MSR*, and s_b is the standard error of *b*. For illustrative purposes, the 95% confidence interval will be calculated. The tabled *t* at .05/2 (i.e., .025) with 18 *df* is 2.101. Alternatively, this value may be obtained by taking the $\sqrt{F}$ with 1 and 18 *df* (i.e., 4.41). Recalling that, for the data analyzed above, $b = 1.18$, and $s_b = .28$, the 95% confidence interval is

$$1.18 \pm (2.101)(.28) = .59 \text{ and } 1.77$$

As explained in Chapter 15, it is *not* appropriate to conclude that β is within this range. Rather, if many such intervals were to be constructed in like fashion, β would be contained in 95% of them. Obviously, the hope is that the single interval just constructed is one of those 95%. For the example under consideration

$$.59 \le \beta \le 1.77$$

Obviously, the narrower the range, the more precise the estimation. Further, when setting a confidence interval, the test of the null hypothesis that, say, $\beta = 0$, becomes a special case. Thus, in the present example, 0 is not included in the range, and the hypothesis that $\beta = 0$ is, therefore, rejected at $\alpha = .05$. But so are other hypotheses within range of the confidence interval.

CONCLUDING REMARK

The several ways for carrying out tests of significance presented in this section are equivalent when applied in simple regression analysis. Specifically, tests of the sum of squares due to regression, the r^2 and the b are equivalent. As is shown in subsequent chapters, the same does not hold true in multiple regression analysis.

ASSUMPTIONS

We postponed a discussion of assumptions underlying regression analysis until now, because we felt that you will be in a better position to appreciate their role after having grasped the general ideas of this analytic approach. In this section, we give an overview of the assumptions underlying regression analysis, with special emphasis on those whose violation may lead to serious biases and distortions. Steering clear of such violations and distortions may indeed be likened to walking through a "minefield" (Bibby, 1977, p. 35). The subsequent section is devoted to some major diagnostics aimed at detecting departures from assumptions.

MODEL SPECIFICATION

By far the most important assumption is that the model being tested has been correctly specified. That is, it is assumed that the regression equation reflects faithfully the theoretical formulation regarding the effect(s) of the independent variable(s) on the dependent variable. To the extent that the model itself is dubious, or that serious doubt is cast about the regression equation meant to reflect it, nothing else matters.

The term "specification errors" is generally used to refer to errors regarding the specification of the theoretical model (see, for example, Duncan, 1975, Chapter 8; Hanushek & Jackson, 1977, pp. 79–86; Kmenta, 1971, pp. 391–405; Pedhazur, 1982, pp. 35–36 and 225–230). "It is quite a useful euphemism for what in blunter language would be called 'using the wrong model'" (Duncan, 1975, p. 101). Because specification errors may render a research effort meaningless, not to mention misleading and even harmful, we found it necessary to draw attention to them in various chapters (e.g., Chapters 3, 13, and 14).

Below, we discuss several assumptions about the error term in the regression equation—ϵ of (17.9). For now, we will note that one of these assumptions is that the errors are not correlated with the independent variable(s). Violation of this assumption may lead to serious biases in the estimation of the regression coefficients and thereby to erroneous conclusions regarding the effects of the variables with which they are associated.

Now, because variables affecting the dependent variable and *not* included in the model are of necessity relegated to the error term, it follows that the omission of relevant variables that are correlated with the independent variable(s) may result in serious bias. This is, potentially, the most damaging of the specification errors, as it poses the most serious threat to valid interpretation of regression results.

It is, of course, never possible to tell whether all relevant variables correlated with the independent variable(s) were included in the model or whether the model has been correctly specified. However, it stands to reason that, because the regression equation is meant to reflect the theoretical model, the most important safeguard against flagrant omissions of important relevant variables that are correlated with the independent variables is the sound-ness of the theoretical formulation. Regrettably, in many research reports, important omitted variables that are correlated with the independent variables almost force themselves on the reader, casting grave doubts as to whether the authors of such reports have made any attempt to arrive at a reasonably specified model.

The research design is the second most important aspect to have bearing on the potential for biased parameter estimation due to the omission of relevant variables. To recognize that this is so, it would suffice to recall the discussions of the role of control and randomization (see Chapter 10). The assumption that relevant omitted variables are not correlated with the variables in the model is most plausible when randomization has been resorted to. This is the great strength of the experiment versus the quasi-experiment so far as internal validity is concerned (see Chapter 13, especially Experiment Versus Quasi-Experiment).

Thus, even when only one of many important variables known to affect a dependent variable is used in experimental research, it is plausible, because of randomization, to assume that the omitted important variables are not correlated with the one whose effect is studied. Consequently, the estimate of the effect of the variable in question (i.e., b) is not biased. The situation is radically different when attempts are made to study the effect of a single variable in quasi-experimental or nonexperimental research, because it is highly likely for the variable used in the study to be correlated with a host of relevant variables not included in the equation.[17]

Another form specification errors may take is the wrong specification of the manner in which the variables in the model, singly or in combination, affect the dependent variable. Examples of such errors are specifications that (a) the regression is linear, when curvilinear regression more appropriately reflects the process under investigation (see Diagnostics, below); and (b) the variables have only main effects, when interaction effects are called for (see Chapter 12). In subsequent chapters, we return to these topics in connection with the presentation of analytic approaches associated with them.

Finally, although much less damaging than omission of relevant variables, inclusion of irrelevant variables also constitutes a form of specification errors. The inclusion of an irrelevant variable does not lead to bias in the estimation of the regression coefficient(s) for the relevant variable(s) in the equation, but it may adversely affect the test of significance of the coefficient(s) for the relevant variable(s). The moral is that it is unwise to include variables just because of a desire to play it safe or in order to "see what will happen" when variables that play no part in one's theory were to be included.

MEASUREMENT

It is assumed that the independent variables are measured without error. Random measure-ment errors in the independent variable(s) lead to biased estimation of regression coeffi-cients. In the case of simple regression, measurement errors lead to the underestimation, or attenuation, of the regression coefficient. In Chapter 5 (see Adverse Effects of Unreliability), we commented on this topic and indicated some suggested corrective measures. We return to this topic in Chapter 21 in connection with comparisons of regression coefficients across groups (see the discussion related to Figure 21.3).

The consequences of random measurement errors in multiple regression analysis are much

---

[17]See the comments on the application of regression analysis in experimental and nonexperimental research in connection with the substantive examples given earlier in this chapter for the data of Table 17.1.

more complex (for detailed discussions, see Blalock, Wells, & Carter, 1970; Bohrnstedt & Carter, 1971; Cochran, 1968, 1970; Linn & Werts, 1982). Unlike simple regression analysis, random measurement errors in multiple regression may lead to either overestimation or underestimation of regression coefficients. Further, the biasing effects of measurement errors are not limited to the estimation of the regression coefficient for the variable being measured but affect also estimates of regression coefficients for other variables correlated with the variable in question. Thus, estimates of regression coefficients for variables measured with high reliability may be biased as a result of their correlations with variables measured with low reliability.

Generally speaking, the lower the reliabilities of the measures used and the higher the intercorrelations among the variables, the more adverse the biasing effects of measurement errors. Under such circumstances, regression coefficients should be interpreted with great circumspection. Caution is particularly called for when attempting to interpret magnitudes of standardized regression coefficients as indicating the relative importance of the variables with which they are associated. It would be wiser to refrain from such attempts altogether when measurement errors are prevalent.

Thus far, we have *not* dealt with the effects of errors in the measurement of the dependent variable. Such errors do not lead to bias in the estimation of the unstandardized regression coefficient (b). They do, however, lead to the attenuation of the correlation between the independent and the dependent variable, hence, to the attenuation of the standardized regression coefficient (β).[18] Because $1 - r^2$ (or $1 - R^2$ in multiple regression analysis) is part of the error term, it can be seen that measurement errors in the dependent variable reduce the sensitivity of the statistical analysis.

Of various approaches and remedies for managing the magnitude of the errors and of taking account of their impact on the estimation of model parameters, probably the most promising are those incorporated in structural equation modeling (*SEM*). Chapters 23 and 24 are devoted to analytic approaches for such models, where it is also shown how measurement errors are taken into account when estimating the parameters of the model.

Although approaches to managing measurement errors are useful, greater benefits would be reaped if researchers were to pay more attention to the validity and reliability of measures; if they directed their efforts towards optimizing them instead of attempting to counteract adverse effects of poorly conceived and poorly constructed measures.

FIXED AND RANDOM VARIABLES

Originally, the regression model was developed for the case of fixed independent variables, that is, for situations in which the researcher fixes the values of the independent variable and limits generalizations to these values. Clearly, fixing the values of the independent variable implies that it is under the researcher's control—a goal achieved most often in experimental research.

In contrast to a fixed variable, a random variable is one that may take alternative values according to chance. More formally, "a random variable has the property that it assumes different values, each with a probability less than or equal to 1" (Pindyck & Rubinfeld, 1981, p. 19; see also Edwards, 1964, Chapter 4; Fox, 1984, pp. 396–399; Keppel, 1982, pp. 519–520).

Random variables in regression analysis are most often encountered in situations where

---

[18]Earlier in this chapter, it was pointed out that, in simple regression, $r = \beta$.

the researcher is either unable or unwilling to manipulate the independent variable(s). Instead, a sample is obtained from some defined population, and the effect(s) of the independent variable(s) on the dependent variable are studied.

Issues concerning contrasts between experimental and nonexperimental research aside (see, in particular, Chapters 12 and 14), it has been shown (see, for example, Kmenta, 1971, pp. 297–304) that when other regression assumptions, especially ones concerning model specification (see above), are reasonably met, regression results hold equally for random independent variables.

RESIDUALS

Assumptions about the residuals are as follows:

1. They are not correlated with the independent variables. Because of the important implications of this assumption for specification errors, it was discussed above.

2. The expected value of ϵ_i, that is, the mean over many replications, is zero. Violation of this assumption leads to bias in the estimation of the intercept but not of the regression coefficients. It, therefore, is of concern only in the rare situations when attempts are made to interpret the intercept substantively.

3. The variance of the residuals is constant for all levels of the independent variable. That is, variance of residuals at all levels of X is the same. This condition is referred to as *homoscedasticity*, and departures from it as *heteroscedasticity*. Heteroscedasticity does not lead to bias in parameter estimation, but it has an adverse effect on the error term and thereby on statistical tests of significance. Generally, heteroscedasticity leads to lower standard errors of parameter estimates, hence, to the potential of declaring the estimates statistically significant at a given level, when in the presence of homoscedasticity, they might have been declared nonsignificant.

4. Errors are independent of one another. That is, errors associated with one observation are not correlated with errors associated with any other observation. Violation of this assumption, often referred to as autocorrelation, affects the validity of tests of significance. Autocorrelation is particularly prone to arise when subjects are measured repeatedly, as in time-series or longitudinal designs.

The foregoing assumptions are required in order to obtain Best Linear Unbiased Estimates (BLUE) of parameters (for discussions of BLUE, see, for example, Hanushek & Jackson, 1977, pp. 46–56; Pindyck & Rubinfeld, 1981, pp. 51–55).

For the purpose of tests of significance it is, additionally, assumed that:

5. The residuals are normally distributed.

Detection of departures from assumptions is dealt with in the next section, where suggested measures to deal with such departures are also indicated. For now, we would like to reiterate that the most important assumptions, hence, the ones requiring the greatest attention, are those related to model specification and to measurement. Departures from assumptions 2 through 5 about the residuals are generally less damaging, particularly when the sample is relatively large.

DIAGNOSTICS

In this section, we review some of the methods available for determining the appropriateness of the least-squares solution. It should be noted that it is in the context of multiple regression analysis that the diagnostics to be presented have their greatest utility. In simple regression analysis, problems may even be detected through rudimentary approaches (e.g., data plots).

Moreover, some diagnostics are applicable only when more than one independent variable is used. Nevertheless, we felt it best to introduce some basic ideas and approaches in the context of simple regression analysis, as it is in this context that they are easiest to present and follow. Among other things, indices that can be expressed in simple algebra when one independent variable is used require matrix algebra for multiple independent variables.

DATA PLOTS

Earlier in this chapter (see Graphs), we commented on the usefulness of plotting data for the purpose of detecting patterns in them and/or departures from regression assumptions. In an excellent paper on the importance of plotting data, Anscombe (1973) constructed four small data sets that, when subjected to a simple regression analysis, yield identical results (e.g., r^2's, regression equations, df, regression and residual sums of squares). On the basis of the analysis, then, one would be led to believe that the least-squares solutions are equally good and appropriate for the four data sets. However, upon plotting the data, it becomes evident that the application of linear regression analysis is inappropriate or questionable for three of the four data sets (e.g., the regression is curvilinear).

We strongly recommend that you study Anscombe's illuminating paper in which he purposely constructed rather extreme cases. For illustrative purposes, we will construct a less extreme example. To this end, we will make a change in the data of Table 17.1. Specifically, we will interchange the scores on Y for subjects whose X scores are 2 and 4. The results of this change are reported in Table 17.4.

Earlier, we used MINITAB to plot the data of Table 17.1. For comparative purposes, the same program will be used to plot the data of Table 17.4 and to calculate the regression of Y on X.

Table 17.4
Data from Table 17.1.
Y's For X = 2 and X = 4 interchanged[a]

Y	X
5	1
5	1
4	1
4	1
3	1
10	2
8	2
8	2
7	2
6	2
10	3
8	3
8	3
6	3
5	3
8	4
7	4
6	4
6	4
5	4

[a]See text for explanation.

MINITAB

Input

```
OH=0
OUTFILE 'T174'
NOTE DATA FROM TABLE 17.4
READ C1-C2
5  1          [data for first subject]
.   .
5  4          [data for last subject]
NAME C1 'Y' C2 'X'
PLOT 'Y' 'X';
   YSTART 0 12;        [subcommands specifying start and end values]
   XSTART 0 5.
REGRESS 'Y' 1 'X'   [regress Y on one variable, namely X]
```

Commentary

We named our input file T174.MTB. To run, at the MTB prompt, we typed: EXEC 'T174'.

Output

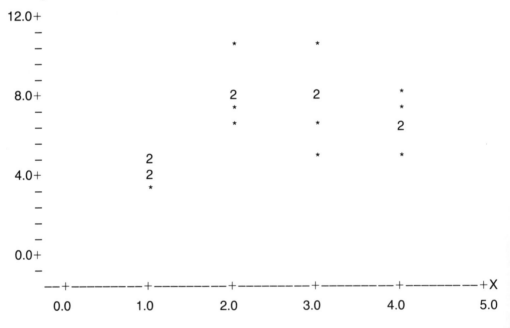

Commentary

Contrast this plot with the one obtained earlier for the original data of Table 17.1 and note that in the earlier graph the trend appeared linear, whereas in the present one it appears to follow a curve. When we discuss curvilinear regression analysis in Chapter 18, we use the data of Table 17.4 and show that a quadratic curve fits them well. For present purposes, it will be instructive to consider the results from a linear regression analysis of these data and the conclusion one would reach, if one did not attempt to determine whether the linearity assumption is tenable.[19]

Output

The regression equation is
Y = 4.90 + 0.620 X

Predictor	Coef	Stdev	t-ratio	p
Constant	4.900	1.011	4.85	0.000
X	0.6200	0.3692	1.68	0.110

s = 1.846   R-sq = 13.5%   R-sq(adj) = 8.7%

Analysis of Variance

SOURCE	DF	SS	MS	F	p
Regression	1	9.610	9.610	2.82	0.110
Error	18	61.340	3.408		
Total	19	70.950			

Commentary

The preceding was obtained as a result of the REGRESSION statement given as the last line of the input above.

As you can see, under coef(ficient), the first value (Constant) is the intercept, a, and the second is the regression coefficient, b.

Stdev is the standard error. Thus, the second term, .3692, refers to the standard error of the b (see 17.33).

The t-ratio is obtained by dividing the coefficient by its standard error (see 17.32). The t ratio for the b, therefore, is 1.68 with 18 df (i.e., df associated the residual, $N - k - 1$; see Analysis of Variance table).

The F ratio is obtained by dividing the MS Regression by the MS Error: 9.610/3.408 = 2.82, with 1 and 18 df. Recall that the $\sqrt{F} = t$. Thus, $\sqrt{2.820} = 1.68$.

R–sq(uared) = 13.5%, is, in the present case, the Pearson correlation squared, multiplied by 100. Note that $r^2 = ss_{reg}/ss_{tot} = 9.61/70.95 = .135$.

Assuming that $\alpha = .05$ was selected, the tabled t ratio with 18 $df = 2.101$. Equivalently, the tabled value for F with 1 and 18 $df = 4.41$. On the basis of either ratio, it would be concluded that the null hypothesis that $\beta = 0$ cannot be rejected. Stated differently, it would be concluded that the effect of X on Y, or the proportion of variance due to regression, is statistically not significantly different from zero. The preceding is also evident from the p value reported in the output.

As was noted previously, a quadratic regression fits the data well. This is an example of the penalty for applying and interpreting linear regression analysis without determining first whether the linearity assumption is tenable. In many, if not most, reports of research in which regression analysis is applied, there is not even a hint that the linearity assumption was addressed. Our guess is that the proportion of studies in which failure to reject the null hypothesis was due to the application of linear regression when the pattern of the data did not warrant it is rather large.

---

[19]We strongly suggest that you replicate the analysis by hand or with the aid of a calculator, following our approach in the analysis of the data of Table 17.1.

It is important to not be oblivious to other departures from assumptions or to peculiarities in the data. We said earlier that data plots can be very useful in detecting not only departures from linearity but also data anomalies. It is, however, residual analysis—a topic to which we now turn—that is particularly powerful for such purposes.

RESIDUAL ANALYSIS

Residual analysis is an indispensable complement to regression analysis, as it focuses on what may have been overlooked by the latter: data anomalies and departures from assumptions. In what follows, we review some major approaches to the analysis of residuals. For more detailed treatments of this topic, see Anscombe (1960), Anscombe and Tukey (1963), Belsley, Kuh, and Welsch (1980), Cook and Weisberg (1982b), and Draper and Smith (1981).

COMPUTER ANALYSIS

Ideas and methods of residual analysis will be presented as part of commentaries on relevant computer output. Although most computer programs for regression analysis offer some facility for residual analysis, they vary greatly in scope as well as in the ease with which such an analysis can be accomplished. Generally speaking, however, the large packages (e.g., SAS and SPSS) offer the most extensive facilities for residual analysis. For illustrative purposes, we use output from SPSS.

SPSS

The data of Table 17.1 was input as follows:

Input

```
SET LISTING='T171.LIS'.
TITLE TABLE 17.1, REGRESSION OF Y ON X.
DATA LIST FREE/Y,X.
BEGIN DATA.
5  1          [data for first subject]
.  .
6  4          [data for last subject]
END DATA.
LIST.
REGRESSION VAR Y,X/DES/STAT ALL/DEP Y/ENTER/
   RESIDUALS=ID(X)/CASEWISE DEFAULTS ALL ZRESID SRESID/
   SCATTERPLOT=(*RESID,*PRE)(*RESID,X).
```

Commentary

We remind you that, in Chapter 16, we offered general introductions to computer programs, including SPSS, and pointed out that our runs were done on the PC—hence, the period for command terminators.

As indicated on the DATA LIST statement, a free format is used for the input. The command LIST at the end of the data instructs the program to list the data.

DES on the regression command asks for the default statistics (i.e., Means, Standard Deviations, and Correlations among the variables).

Finally, DEP Y specifies that the dependent variable is Y. When ENTER is specified without any variable names, all the independent variables are entered in a single step. Alternatively, only selected variables may be entered, or other variable selection methods (e.g., forward, stepwise) may be used. The preceding comments apply, of course, to designs with more than one independent variable. For our example, only ENTER (or, equivalently, ENTER X) is applicable.

Although we report only excerpts pertinent to the topic being discussed, we suggest that you replicate our run and compare the output from the regression analysis with the calculations done by hand earlier in this chapter.

The rest of the subcommands are commented upon below in connection with the output relevant to them.

Output

Casewise Plot of Standardized Residual

Case #	X	-3.0 0.0 3.0 0: . . . . . : . . . . . :0	Y	*PRED	*RESID	*ZRESID	*SRESID
1	1.00	. . * .	5.00	4.6800	.3200	.2258	.2435
2	1.00	. . * .	5.00	4.6800	.3200	.2258	.2435
3	1.00	. * . .	4.00	4.6800	-.6800	-.4799	-.5175
4	1.00	. * . .	4.00	4.6800	-.6800	-.4799	-.5175
5	1.00	. * . .	3.00	4.6800	-1.6800	-1.1856	-1.2785
6	2.00	. . * .	8.00	5.8600	2.1400	1.5103	1.5577
7	2.00	. . * .	7.00	5.8600	1.1400	.8045	.8298
8	2.00	. * .	6.00	5.8600	.1400	.0988	.1019
9	2.00	. * .	6.00	5.8600	.1400	.0988	.1019
10	2.00	. * . .	5.00	5.8600	-.8600	-.6069	-.6260
11	3.00	. . * .	10.00	7.0400	2.9600	2.0890	2.1546
12	3.00	. . * .	8.00	7.0400	.9600	.6775	.6988
13	3.00	. . * .	8.00	7.0400	.9600	.6775	.6988
14	3.00	. * . .	6.00	7.0400	-1.0400	-.7340	-.7570
15	3.00	. * . .	5.00	7.0400	-2.0400	-1.4397	-1.4849
16	4.00	. . * .	10.00	8.2200	1.7800	1.2562	1.3546
17	4.00	. * .	8.00	8.2200	-.2200	-.1553	-.1674
18	4.00	. * .	8.00	8.2200	-.2200	-.1553	-.1674
19	4.00	. * . .	7.00	8.2200	-1.2200	-.8610	-.9284
20	4.00	. * . .	6.00	8.2200	-2.2200	-1.5667	-1.6895
Case #	X	0: . . . . . : . . . . . :0 -3.0 0.0 3.0	Y	*PRED	*RESID	*ZRESID	*SRESID

Commentary

On the residuals subcommand, ID(X) was specified as a case identifier (see column labeled X to the left of the plot). In addition to the defaults (Y, *PRED, *RESID), we called for the temporary variables (identified by an *) *ZRESID and *SRESID. Finally, we indicated that ALL the cases be listed.[20]

---

[20]Because of our small data set, we called for all the cases in the casewise plot of the residuals. With large data sets, casewise plots are used primarily for the detection of outliers (see below). When "all" is *not* requested on the casewise subcommand, standardized residuals $\geq |3|$ are plotted by default.

*PRED and *RESID are predicted scores and raw residuals respectively (compare with columns 3 and 7 of Table 17.2). *ZRESID are standardized residuals. Because the mean of residuals is zero, all that is necessary to obtain standardized residuals is to divide each raw residual by its standard deviation. Earlier, it was shown how the standard deviation of the residuals is calculated—see (17.29); for the data under consideration it is 1.42. Dividing each element in the *RESID column by this standard error yields the standardized residuals (i.e., *ZRESID column).

By default, it is the *ZRESID's that are plotted in the casewise plot; other variables can be plotted instead. One of the major purposes of calculating and plotting standardized residuals is to detect outliers.

OUTLIERS

As the name implies, an outlier is an unusual, atypical, data point—one that stands out from the rest of the data. Outliers may lead to serious distortions of results. However, they may also provide insights about unexpected processes in the phenomenon being studied. In a discussion of miracles and statistics, Kruskal (1988) suggested "that miracles are the extreme outliers of nonscientific life" (p. 929). He went on to say: "It is widely argued of outliers that investigation of the mechanism for outlying may be far more important than the original study that led to the outlier" (p. 929).

Whatever their origins, it is important to identify outliers and then take "appropriate" action. We placed appropriate in quotation marks, because action would, in the first place, depend on one's speculation about the origin of a given outlier. In addition, as is discussed below, it is not always clear what should be done about an outlier.

In regression analysis, an outlier is defined as a data point having a large residual. Because the magnitudes of raw residuals are affected by the units of the measures used, it is easier to determine what constitutes large residuals after they have been standardized. These are the *ZRESID's reported and plotted above.

Having standardized the residuals, a criterion is still necessary to determine when a residual is an outlier. As a rule of thumb, some authors recommend that standardized residuals greater than 2 be considered large. For the present data, one case (11) has a standardized residual slightly larger than 2.

When calculating standardized residuals, it is assumed that the residuals have equal variances. Because this is generally not the case, it has been recommended (e.g., Belsley et al., 1980; Cook & Weisberg, 1982b; Stevens, 1984; Weisberg, 1980) that studentized residuals be calculated instead. In the output given above, these residuals are labeled *SRESID.

A *Studentized Residual* is obtained by dividing the residual by its estimated standard deviation, which for simple regression analysis is defined as follows:

$$s_{e_i} = s_{y.x} \sqrt{1 - \left[\frac{1}{N} + \frac{(X_i - \bar{X})^2}{\Sigma x^2} \right]} \qquad (17.35)$$

Notice that the first term on the right (the standard error of estimate) was used above in the calculation of standardized residuals. The second term varies for different values of X_i. For illustrative purposes, we will calculate the standard deviation for the residuals when $X = 1$. Recalling that $s_{y.x} = 1.42$; $N = 20$; the mean of $X = 2.5$; and $\Sigma x^2 = 25$ (see Table 17.1)

$$s_{e_1} = 1.42 \sqrt{1 - \left[\frac{1}{20} + \frac{(1 - 2.5)^2}{25} \right]} = 1.317$$

Dividing a residual by its standard error, we obtain a t ratio with df equal to those associated with the MSR ($N - k - 1$). Using, for illustrative purposes, the first residual given above, namely .32

$$t = \frac{.32}{1.317} = .243$$

This value, within rounding error, is reported above under *SRESID. The standard error we have calculated (i.e., 1.317) is used as the denominator for all the residuals associated with $X = 1$. As an exercise, you may wish to calculate the studentized residuals for other values of X and check your answers with the values given in the SPSS output.

When the assumptions of the model are reasonably met, studentized residuals have a t–distribution with $N - k - 1$ df (for the present example, $df = 18$). These t values can be used to test the statistical significance of any studentized residual.

The studentized residuals we have been describing are referred to as "internal" studentized residuals, to distinguish them from a related entity referred to as "external" studentized residuals (for discussions of this distinction, see Cook & Weisberg 1982b; Hoaglin & Welsch, 1978; Velleman & Welsch, 1981). External studentized residuals (not reported here) are labeled *SDRESID (Studentized Deleted Residuals) in SPSS. As different programs may use different labels, it is important that you check the manual for the program you are using. For example, in SAS (REG), external studentized residuals are labeled RSTUDENT.

RESIDUAL PLOTS

Residual plots are invaluable for detecting departures from assumptions underlying regression analysis (e.g., linearity, normality, homoscedasticity). We present and comment on two of the most basic ones: (a) residuals against predicted scores (Y'), and (b) residuals against the independent variable (X). It is useful, although not necessary, to use standardized values in such plots. The two plots were generated by SPSS from the following subcommand in the regression procedure:

SCATTERPLOT=(*RESID,*PRE)(*RESID,X).[21]

---

[21]The entire input file used with SPSS was given earlier in this Chapter.

Output

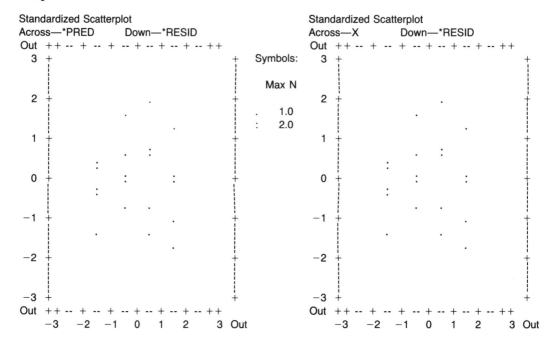

Commentary

Look first at the labels of the plots and note that standardized values (the default) are used. Also, by default, the size of such plots is small. In both plots, the ordinate represents the residuals (see Down − *RESID). In the plot on the left, the abscissa represents the predicted values (see Across − *PRED), whereas in the plot on the right, it represents the independent variable (see Across − X). Look now at the "symbols" between the plots and note the explanation: In the present example, a single dot represents one case and two adjacent dots represent two cases.

The 0 point on the ordinate represents the mean of the residuals. For the purpose of examining the plot, it is helpful to draw a horizontal line originating from this point. Two additional horizontal lines, originating from the +2 and −2 points on the ordinate (i.e., 2 standard deviations above and below the mean) may also be drawn. For the regression assumptions to be considered tenable, the points should appear to be randomly dispersed, with most of them within the range of ±2 standard deviations from the mean. Discernable trends in the points and/or extreme values (i.e., outliers, see above) would raise doubts about such assumptions. In the present example, these assumptions appear plausible.

Although the departure from linearity of the data of Table 17.4 was clear from the data plot (see Data Plots), we recommend that, for comparative purposes, you analyze these data using as a guide our analysis of the data of Table 17.1. Among other things, study the casewise as well as the residual plots and compare them with the analogous plots given earlier for the data of Table 17.1.

HOMOSCEDASTICITY

Residual plots such as the ones given above are also very useful for checking on the homoscedasticity assumption (i.e., constant variance for the residuals; see section on As-

$Y - Y'$

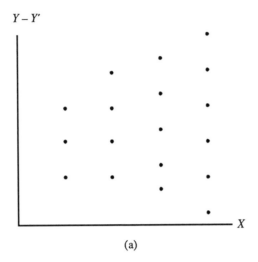

(a)

$Y - Y'$

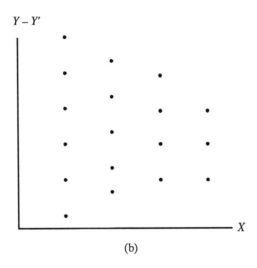

(b)

Figure 17.2

sumptions). In Figure 17.2, we give two artificial examples of how heteroscedasticity might look like in residual plots. In (a), the variance of the residuals increases with increments in X, whereas in (b), the converse is true.

Among suggested remedies for heteroscedasticity are various data transformations and weighted least-squares solutions (see, for example, Fox, 1984, pp. 180–184; Weisberg, 1980, pp. 122–125). The suggested approaches are designed to counteract adverse effects of heteroscedasticity on regression estimates. As with outliers, however, heteroscedasticity may provide important insights into the phenomenon under study (for a discussion of this point, see Downs & Rocke, 1979).

OTHER PLOTS

In conclusion, we would like to point out that various other plots may be used to check on the plausibility of regression assumptions. Among these are histograms of residuals and normal probability plots, both of which are aimed at checking on the normality assumption. For discussions of a variety of plots along with illustrations using BMDP and SAS, see du Toit, Steyn, and Stumpf (1986, Chapter 7). For examples of input, output, and commentaries using SAS, see Freund and Littell (1986).

INFLUENCE ANALYSIS

Although it has been recognized for some time that certain observations may have greater influence than others on regression results, it is only in recent years that influential observations have become the focus of formal study and that approaches aimed at detecting them have been developed. In their comprehensive treatment of influence analysis, Belsley et al. (1980) defined an influential observation thus:

An influential observation is one which, either individually or together with several other observations, has a demonstrably larger impact on the calculated values of various estimates (coefficients, standard errors, t–values, etc.) than is the case for most of the other observations. (p. 11)

"A bewilderingly large number" (Chatterjee & Hadi, 1986, p. 379) of approaches to influence analysis have been proposed. Lack of agreement on a method of choice is, in part, due to the different answers authors have in mind when they think of the question "Influence on what?"

In what follows, we introduce, by way of numerical examples, only two indices: leverage and Cook's D (distance) statistic. As with residual analysis, one of the reasons we present ideas of influence analysis in the context of simple regression analysis is that this can be done using simple algebra. The meaning of such indices can, thus, be readily grasped.

Again, as with residual analysis, inspection of data scatterplots in simple regression analysis may frequently suffice to detect influential observations. The situation is much more complex in multiple regression analysis, where the full richness and utility of influence analysis may be particularly appreciated. However, what we say here about this topic is generalizable to such designs.

LEVERAGE

As the name implies, leverage refers to action akin to a lever whose distance from the fulcrum leads to increased power to move or lift an object. For simple regression analysis, leverage can be calculated as follows:

$$h_i = \frac{1}{N} + \frac{(X - \bar{X})^2}{\Sigma x^2} \tag{17.36}$$

where h_i = leverage for ith observation; N = number of observations; Σx^2 = sum of squares of the independent variable.

When matrix algebra is used, leverages are obtained from the diagonal of what has been labeled the Hat Matrix: hence, "h" (see Hoaglin & Welsch, 1978; Velleman & Welsch, 1981).

Note from the numerator of the second term that leverage is at a minimum (i.e., $1/N$) when X is equal to the mean of X. Further, the more X deviates from the mean, the larger the leverage.

A NUMERICAL EXAMPLE

For the purpose of this numerical example, we changed *one* X value in the data of Table 17.1—specifically, the first observation in the group whose $X = 4$ was changed to 10. All other values remained the same. Assume, for now, that the preceding change is a result of incorrect input. The value of Y for the observation under consideration is 10 and, by mistake, 10 was also entered for X.

SAS

For the present analysis, the REG(ression) procedure from SAS was used. For an overview of SAS, see Chapter 16.

Input

```
TITLE 'DATA FROM TABLE 17.1. FIRST X = 4 CHANGED TO 10';
DATA T171;
   INPUT Y X;   [free format]
   CARDS;
   5  1  [data for first subject]

   .   .
   10 10  [data for first subject in level X = 4. See text.]

   .   .
   6  4  [data for last subject]
PROC PRINT;   [calls for printing of the input]
PROC REG;    [calls for the REG procedure]
   MODEL Y=X/P R INFLUENCE;   [see commentary, below]
```

Output

R-Square .4711 *[for simple regression, $R^2 = r_{yx}^2$]*

Parameter Estimates

Variable	DF	Parameter Estimate	Standard Error	T for H0: Parameter=0	Prob > |T|
INTERCEP	1	4.607513	0.56207095	8.197	0.0001
X	1	0.658031	0.16432294	4.004	0.0008

Commentary

Under PARAMETER ESTIMATE are reported the INTERCEP(t) ($a = 4.61$) and the regression coefficient ($b = .66$). The corresponding values for the original data were 3.5 for a and 1.18 for b. Thus, a change in one X value resulted in marked changes in the regression equation. As is shown below, the observation that was changed has high leverage. It should, however, be borne in mind that we are using a small data set. In large data sets, a change in a single observation will, generally speaking, not have as strong an effect. Assuming now that $\alpha = .01$ was selected by the researcher, the conclusion that would be reached is that the b for X is statistically significant. Substantively, the interpretation would be that the expected change in Y associated with a unit change in X is .66. Equivalently, it would be concluded that the proportion of variance accounted for (.4711) is statistically significant (see Tests of Significance earlier in this chapter).

Output

Obs	Dep Var Y	Predict Value	Residual	Student Residual	Hat Diag H	Cook's D
1	5.0000	5.2655	−0.2655	−0.193	0.0920	0.002
2	5.0000	5.2655	−0.2655	−0.193	0.0920	0.002
3	4.0000	5.2655	−1.2655	−0.920	0.0920	0.043
4	4.0000	5.2655	−1.2655	−0.920	0.0920	0.043
5	3.0000	5.2655	−2.2655	−1.647	0.0920	0.137
6	8.0000	5.9236	2.0764	1.482	0.0583	0.068
7	7.0000	5.9236	1.0764	0.768	0.0583	0.018
8	6.0000	5.9236	0.0764	0.055	0.0583	0.000
9	6.0000	5.9236	0.0764	0.055	0.0583	0.000
10	5.0000	5.9236	−0.9236	−0.659	0.0583	0.013
11	10.0000	6.5816	3.4184	2.430	0.0505	0.157
12	8.0000	6.5816	1.4184	1.008	0.0505	0.027
13	8.0000	6.5816	1.4184	1.008	0.0505	0.027
14	6.0000	6.5816	−0.5816	−0.413	0.0505	0.005
15	5.0000	6.5816	−1.5816	−1.124	0.0505	0.034
16	10.0000	11.1878	−1.1878	−1.559	0.7215	3.148
17	8.0000	7.2396	0.7604	0.546	0.0687	0.011
18	8.0000	7.2396	0.7604	0.546	0.0687	0.011
19	7.0000	7.2396	−0.2396	−0.172	0.0687	0.001
20	6.0000	7.2396	−1.2396	−0.890	0.0687	0.029

Commentary

The preceding is some of the output obtained as a result of specifying the options P (predicted), R (residual analysis), and INFLUENCE on the MODEL statement (see Input above).

Student Residual are *studentized* residuals, referred to earlier as internal studentized residuals and labeled as *SRESID in the SPSS output.

Hat Diag H is leverage. The label refers to the diagonal elements of the Hat Matrix from which they are obtained (see above). In various other programs, the label "lever" is used instead.

For present purposes, we focus on the contrast between the 16th observation (the one we have changed) and all the rest (we inserted the lines around the 16th observation in order to highlight it).

Look first at the Student Residual column and note that, on the basis of the studentized residual, one would not be led to suspect that there is anything unusual about the 16th observation. In other words, had we relied solely on residual analysis, as described in the preceding section, we would have concluded that the data are "well behaved."

Turning now to the Hat Diag H, it will be noted that the leverage for the 16th observation is much larger than for any of the other observations. As a rule of thumb, it has been suggested (e.g., Belsley et al., 1980, p. 17; Hoaglin & Welsch, 1978, p. 18) that $h_i > 2(k + 1)/N$ be considered high and deserving of attention. As earlier, k is the number of independent variables, and N is the number of observations. For the present data, this criterion is $2(1 + 1)/20 = .20$. Accordingly, all observations, except for the 16th, have small leverage. The same is true for Cook's D, which is discussed below.

In sum, therefore, on the basis of the leverage, it is clear that observation number 16 is an influential one. It was pointed out earlier that, in simple regression analysis, this would frequently also be evident from a data plot. We suggest that you plot the data and note how the 16th observation is clearly detached from the rest of the data. Below we comment on what to do about influential observations. At this stage, we only point out that, had the leverage of the 16th observation been due to an input error, it would have been detected even in a data plot.

Before discussing Cook's D, a different change will be made in the 16th observation of the data of Table 17.1. Instead of changing X, Y is changed. Specifically, $Y = 10$ is changed to $Y = 1$. The value of X for this observation was restored to what it was in the original data, that is, to 4. The input file for SAS REG is identical to the one given above.

Output

DATA FROM TABLE 17.1. Y = 10 CHANGED TO 1 IN X = 4

R-Square .1219

Parameter Estimates

Variable	DF	Parameter Estimate	Standard Error	T for H0: Parameter=0	Prob > |T|
INTERCEP	1	4.40000000	1.10875305	3.968	0.0009
X	1	0.64000000	0.40485937	1.581	0.1313

Commentary

In this particular example, the regression equation turns out to be similar to the one obtained previously when X was changed. Note, in particular, that, in the preceding analysis, b was .66, whereas in the present one it is .64. However, note also that the standard error for the b in the present analysis is about 2.5 times larger than the one for the b in the preceding analysis. Consequently, although in the preceding analysis b was found to be statistically significant, in the present analysis, the b is statistically not significant, at a conventional α level of, say, .05.

Recall that r^2 reflects the dispersion of the data points about the regression line; the closer the data points are to the regression line, the larger is the r^2. In the extreme case, when all the points are on the regression line, r^2 is, of course, at its maximum: 1.00. From the foregoing, it should be clear that it is possible for two identical regression equations to be associated with different r^2, depending on the dispersion of the points about the two lines. Further, that two different regression equations may be associated with identical r^2's. Now, r^2 is the proportion of variance accounted for; $1 - r^2$ is the proportion of variance *not* accounted for, or error. The larger the residuals, the larger is the $1 - r^2$. It is this element that enters in the calculation of standard errors—for example, standard error of estimate, see (17.29)—and affects the magnitude of the standard error of the b. In the present example, the proportion of variance attributed to error (i.e., $1 - r^2$) is .8781, as contrasted with .5289 in the preceding example.

As is shown below, the change we have introduced in the 16th observation has led to an extremely large residual for this observation which, in turn, is the primary reason for the reduction in r^2. Reiterating what was said earlier in this chapter, although it is the b that should be the focus of interpretation, the role played by r^2 in tests of significance should not be overlooked.

Output

Obs	Dep Var Y	Predict Value	Residual	Student Residual	Hat Diag H	Cook's D
1	5.0000	5.0400	−0.0400	−0.021	0.1400	0.000
2	5.0000	5.0400	−0.0400	−0.021	0.1400	0.000
3	4.0000	5.0400	−1.0400	−0.554	0.1400	0.025
4	4.0000	5.0400	−1.0400	−0.554	0.1400	0.025
5	3.0000	5.0400	−2.0400	−1.087	0.1400	0.096
6	8.0000	5.6800	2.3200	1.182	0.0600	0.045
7	7.0000	5.6800	1.3200	0.673	0.0600	0.014
8	6.0000	5.6800	0.3200	0.163	0.0600	0.001
9	6.0000	5.6800	0.3200	0.163	0.0600	0.001
10	5.0000	5.6800	−0.6800	−0.346	0.0600	0.004
11	10.0000	6.3200	3.6800	1.875	0.0600	0.112
12	8.0000	6.3200	1.6800	0.856	0.0600	0.023
13	8.0000	6.3200	1.6800	0.856	0.0600	0.023
14	6.0000	6.3200	−0.3200	−0.163	0.0600	0.001
15	5.0000	6.3200	−1.3200	−0.673	0.0600	0.014
16	1.0000	6.9600	−5.9600	−3.175	0.1400	0.820
17	8.0000	6.9600	1.0400	0.554	0.1400	0.025
18	8.0000	6.9600	1.0400	0.554	0.1400	0.025
19	7.0000	6.9600	0.0400	0.021	0.1400	0.000
20	6.0000	6.9600	−0.9600	−0.511	0.1400	0.021

Commentary

Focusing again on the 16th observation, note that the studentized residual is $> |3|$. Note also that most of the other residuals are very small, only three of them being $> |1|$. For illustrative purposes, assume it was discovered that the score of the 16th observation was not recorded correctly and, therefore, it was decided to delete this observation and reanalyze the data. We suggest that, as an exercise, you run the analysis after deleting the 16th observation. If you did this, you would find, among other differences, that $r^2 = .4374$ as contrasted with .1219 obtained before the deletion of the 16th observation (see above). We remind you, however, of our comment about sample size in relation to the effect a single observation may have on regression results.

Turning now to leverage, note that the leverage for the 16th observation is not only small but also no different from the leverage for the other observations in the same group. This is to be expected, as they all have the same X—see (17.36) for the calculation of leverage. Here, then, is an example of why it is important to do *both* residual analysis and influence analysis.

Examine now COOK'S D for the 16th observation and notice that although it is not as large as the one obtained in the preceding analysis (i.e., 3.148 in the preceding analysis, as compared with .820 in the present one), it is considerably larger than for the rest of the observations. This is because, as is shown in the next section, Cook's D is affected by large residuals and/or large leverage.

COOK'S D

Cook (1977, 1979) proposed his D (distance) index for the detection of influential observations, which may be calculated as follows:

$$D_i = \left[\frac{r_i^2}{k + 1} \right] \left[\frac{h_i}{1 - h_i} \right] \tag{17.37}$$

where D_i = Cook's D for the ith observation; r_i = studentized residual for the ith observation; h_i = leverage for the ith observation. From (17.37), it is clear that an observation may have a large Cook's D because it has a large studentized residual, a large leverage, or both.

For illustrative purposes, we apply (17.37) to the 16th observation.

$$D_{16} = \left[\frac{-3.175^2}{1 + 1} \right] \left[\frac{.14}{1 - .14} \right] = .820$$

For approximate tests of significance of Cook's D, see Cook (1977, 1979) and Weisberg (1980, pp. 108–109). For diagnostic purposes, it would suffice to scrutinize the observations with largest values of Cook's D. In the present artificial example, it is clear that attention needs to be directed to the 16th observation only.

Before commenting on remedies, we would like to remind you that we have limited our attention to two aspects of influence analysis. Discussions of other indices, particularly useful in multiple regression analysis, will be found in the references given earlier (see also Bollen & Jackman, 1985; Cook & Weisberg, 1982a; Stevens, 1984). To our knowledge, SAS REG offers the most extensive facilities for influence analysis.

REMEDIES

What to do about outliers and/or influential observations depends on what one knows or surmises about their origin. Broadly speaking, they may be a result of some error (e.g., scoring, equipment failure) or because the observations with which they are associated represent something substantively different from the rest of the data.

The treatment of outliers and influential observations that can be traced to a specific error is fairly straightforward. When the error is correctable (e.g., scoring), the remedy is obvious: Rerun the analysis after having made the necessary corrections. When the error is not correctable (e.g., as a result of equipment failure), delete the observation(s) in question and rerun the analysis. It is important, however, to note any such deletions when reporting on the study.

Clearly, the situation is much more complex when the researcher suspects that an outlier or an influential observation is due to some substantive cause, as what to do about it depends on the validity of one's speculations. Upon the inspection of an outlier, a researcher may, for example, speculate that it has arisen because it represents an individual with some unique combination of attributes. Similarly, an influential observation may lead the researcher to question the validity of a theoretical formulation or its applicability beyond certain values of the independent variable. Under either of the preceding circumstances, the researcher may decide to rerun the analysis after deleting the observation in question. It is, however, important to recognize that the researcher may be, wittingly or not, explaining away a bothersome outlier or an influential observation so as to justify its rejection.

The situation is further complicated, as the deletion of problematic observations and rerunning the analysis may lead to new problems (e.g., new outliers). The researcher may then decide to try some other remedy or return to the original analysis. It should be clear, however, that trying out all sorts of remedies and settling for the one that is most appealing opens the door to hazards of post hoc theorizing—a topic discussed in various places (see, for example, Chapter 9).

With the aid of computer programs, it has become relatively easy to identify outliers and influential observations. However, this has also led to the misconception that appropriate remedial action is equally easy. In most instances, this takes the form of outright rejection of such observations with very little concern about their possible meaning. Referring to techniques for detecting outliers, Johnson (1985) decried their use as a "technological fix":

> The existence of such procedures has prompted many investigators (and perhaps some statisticians) to believe that statistical procedures will sort a data set into the "good guys" and the "bad guys" and to believe further that one can simply discard the "bad guys" and proceed to a full dress probability analysis on the "good guys" with the same assurance as though the initial data set had been well behaved. (p. 958)

The onus of interpreting what the outliers and/or influential observations mean in a given set of data and the decision about what to do is, needless to say, on the researcher. As with all aspects of research, the most important guide is theory.[22] Whatever the reasons for the rejection of observations, the researcher owes the reader a complete reporting of criteria used for the designation of outliers and influential observations, what has been done about them, and why. In addition, generally speaking, major aspects of results of analyses with and without the outliers and/or the influential observations should be reported. Finally, and most important as well as promising from a substantive perspective, is the design of new research to put to the test theoretical speculations that have led to the rejection of the observations in question.

THE CORRELATION MODEL: A COMMENT

When we introduced the Pearson correlation coefficient, r, in the beginning of this chapter, we pointed out that we were doing this in order to show its relations to some of the elements of the regression model. In the course of the presentation, we discussed r in connection with standardized and unstandardized regression coefficients. Also, we showed that r^2 is the proportion of variance attributed to the independent variable.

Although we will not go into the details, we cannot leave the topic of regression analysis without alerting you to the very important point that it is distinct from the correlation model.

---

[22]For illustrative applications of influence analysis within the context of some substantive examples, see Bollen and Jackman (1985), Belsley et al. (1980, pp. 39–63), Cook and Weisberg (1982b), and Williams (1982). For detailed discussions of rejection of outliers, see Anscombe (1960) and Anscombe and Tukey (1963).

In the bivariate correlation model, both variables are random and assumed to follow a bivariate normal distribution. Further, in contrast to the regression model, no distinction is made between an independent and a dependent variable. Instead, the interest is in the relation between the two variables.[23]

In addition to other serious difficulties concerning the interpretation of r, one of its most serious shortcomings is that it is population specific. As was pointed out in Chapter 3, the magnitude of the correlation coefficient is affected by the variability of the population from which the sample was drawn. It will be recalled that, other things equal, the more homogeneous the population, the lower the correlation coefficient. Tukey (1954), who confessed to being a member of the "informal society for the suppression of the correlation coefficient—whose guiding principle is that most correlation coefficients should never be calculated" (p. 38), branded r as "the enemy of generalization, a focuser on the 'here and now' to the exclusion of the 'there and then'" (Tukey, 1969, p. 89).

The deficiencies of r aside and regardless of whether or not one agrees with authors who counsel avoiding its use, it is of utmost importance to recognize that, *unless it is used for descriptive purposes in the group being studied*, r must be calculated on the basis of data obtained from a probability sample. It seems superfluous to state that, when calculated on the basis of some haphazard group of people or what has been euphemistically termed "convenience sampling," r has little meaning. Yet, it is necessary to state the obvious because most correlational studies (including factor analyses of correlation matrices) reported in the literature are *not* based on probability samples.

One final word of caution. Computer programs for regression analysis routinely report correlation results as well. It is very important that you learn what is and what is not relevant output for the specific study under consideration. For example, when, as in the illustrations we have given in this chapter, the independent variable is fixed, it makes no sense whatsoever to interpret the correlation between it and the dependent variable. In fact, through the selection of values for the independent variable, the magnitude of r may be determined at will. Do not be misled by the fact that r^2 is still interpretable under such circumstances. As was shown in this chapter, r^2 indicates the proportion of variance, or sum of squares, attributed to the independent variable. In contrast, r is meant to indicate the *linear* relation between two random variables.

Fisher's (1958) succinct statement aptly summarizes the issues reviewed briefly in this section: "The regression coefficients are of interest and scientific importance in many classes of data where the correlation coefficient, if used at all, is an artificial concept of no real utility" (p. 129).

CONCLUDING REMARKS

The aim of this chapter was to introduce the basic elements of regression analysis. Because the presentation was limited to simple regression analysis (i.e., one independent variable), calculation and interpretation of results were fairly easy and straightforward. However, with the exception of experimental research, simple regression analysis is almost always woefully inadequate. It is only a naive researcher who would trust simple regression analysis in quasi-

---

[23]For discussions of the distinction between the regression and correlation models, see Binder (1959), Ezekiel and Fox (1959, pp. 279–280), Fox (1968, pp. 167–190, 211–223), Kendall (1951), Thorndike (1978, Chapter 2), and Warren (1971).

experimental or nonexperimental designs. For such designs, multiple regression analysis is particularly useful. Multiple regression analysis is introduced in the next chapter; its application to various designs are elaborated and illustrated in the next four chapters.

STUDY SUGGESTIONS

1. In a study of the effects of TV watching on aggression, average number of hours watched per day and ratings of aggressive behavior were obtained for a group of 20 children. Following are the data (fictitious), where Y = aggression (the higher the score, the more aggressive the perceived behavior); X = hours of TV watching. The second, third, and fourth pairs of columns are continuations of the first pair of columns.

Y	X	Y	X	Y	X	Y	X
3	1	4	4	8	4	9	5
5	2	6	4	8	5	10	6
6	3	8	4	7	5	9	6
4	3	5	4	9	5	8	6
5	3	7	4	8	5	7	6

What is (are) the:
(a) means; sums of squares; variances and standard deviations of Y and X; sum of cross products and covariance of Y with X?
(b) regression equation for Y on X for raw scores?
(c) regression equation for Y on X for standard scores?
(d) regression sum of squares?
(e) residual sum of squares?
(f) ratio of the regression sum of squares to the total sum of squares? What does this ratio represent?
(g) F ratio for the test of significance of the regression sum of squares?
(h) t ratio for the test of significance of the regression coefficient? What should the square of this t ratio be equal to?
  Plot the data and interpret the results.

2. Following are summary data:
$N = 300$; $\bar{X} = 45.00$; $\bar{Y} = 70.00$; $s_x = 4.32$; $s_y = 6.63$; $r_{xy} = .60$
What is (are) the:
(a) standardized regression coefficient (β)?
(b) regression equation for Y on X for raw scores?
(c) regression equation for Y on X for deviation scores?
(d) predicted score (Y') for a person whose X score is 42?
(e) Assume that the person whose predicted score was calculated under (d) has an observed score of 62 (i.e., $Y = 62$). Express this person's Y score as composed of the following three components: grand mean, due to regression, residual.
(f) Under what conditions will the unstandardized regression coefficient (b) be equal to standardized coefficient (β)?

3. Given that: $N = 100$; $\Sigma y^2 = 456.38$; $r_{xy} = .68$
   What is the:
   (a) regression sum of squares?
   (b) residual sum of squares?
   (c) F ratio for the test of significance of the regression of Y on X?

4. Use the data given under study suggestion 1. *Change the Y value for the first subject from 3 to 8.* Using a computer program and/or hand calculations, regress Y on X.
   What is (are) the:
   (a) r^2?
   (b) regression equation?
   (c) regression sum of squares?
   (d) residual sum of squares?
   (e) F ratio for the test of significance of the regression of Y on X?
   (f) residuals, standardized and studentized residuals, leverage, Cook's D?
   Plot: (1) the data, (2) residuals against X, and (3) residuals against Y'.
   Compare and study these results with those obtained under study suggestion 1, paying special attention to the regression equation, outliers, and influential observations.

Answers

1. (a) $\bar{Y} = 6.80$; $\bar{X} = 4.25$; $\Sigma y^2 = 73.20$; $\Sigma x^2 = 35.75$; $s_y^2 = 3.85$; $s_x^2 = 1.88$; $s_y = 1.96$; $s_x = 1.37$; $\Sigma xy = 41.00$; $s_{xy} = 2.16$
   (b) $Y' = 1.93 + 1.15X$—see (17.12) and (17.13)
   (c) $z_y' = .80z_x$
   (d) $ss_{reg} = 47.02098$—see, e.g., (17.22)
   (e) $ss_{res} = 26.17902$—see (17.27)
   (f) .64; r^2 or the proportion of variance of Y accounted for by X.
   (g) $F = 32.33$ with 1 and 18 df—see (17.28)
   (h) $t = 5.686$ with 18 df—see (17.32); $t^2 = F$ (i.e., $5.686^2 = 32.33$)
2. (a) .60 ($\beta = r$)
   (b) $Y' = 28.60 + .92X$
   (c) $Y' = 70.00 + .92x$—see (17.16)
   (d) 67.24
   (e) $62 = 70.00 + (67.24 - 70.00) + (62 - 67.24)$—see (17.17)
      $= 70.00 + \quad (-2.76) \quad + \quad (-5.24)$
   (f) when $s_y = s_x$—see (17.15)
3. (a) 211.03
   (b) 245.35
   (c) $F = 84.29$ with 1 and 98 df
4. (a) .29
   (b) $Y' = 4.10769 + .69231X$
   (c) $ss_{reg} = 17.13462$
   (d) $ss_{res} = 41.81538$
   (e) $F = 7.38$ with 1 and 18 df

(f)

	RESIDUAL	STANDARDIZED RESIDUAL	STUDENTIZED RESIDUAL	LEVERAGE	COOK'S D
First Subject:	3.2000	2.0995	2.5951	.3455	1.7771
Last Subject:	−1.2615	−.8277	−.8903	.1357	.0622

Chapter 18
Multiple Regression Analysis

Simple regression analysis (i.e., regression analysis with one independent variable) was the subject of the preceding chapter. The present chapter is devoted to multiple regression analysis (i.e., regression analysis with multiple independent variables). The presentation is necessarily limited, its main objective being an introduction of some major concepts, with an emphasis on application and interpretation.

The basic ideas of multiple regression analysis can be presented with relative ease for the special case of two independent variables. This is fortunate, as simple algebra can be used and the calculations can be carried out by hand with relative ease. Generalizations to designs with more than two independent variables are conceptually straightforward, although formulas become unwieldy, making it essential to use matrix algebra. Because we *do not* assume that you are conversant with matrix algebra, we do not resort to it. Instead, we rely on computer analysis for extensions to designs with more than two independent variables.

The foregoing should not be construed as implying that knowledge of matrix algebra is neither important nor useful. Although one can do without matrix algebra by relying on computer analysis, an understanding of basic concepts of matrix algebra is essential for a thorough understanding of multiple regression analysis and extensions to multivariate analysis. Accordingly, we strongly recommend that you acquire a working knowledge of matrix algebra so that you may benefit from its great conceptual power, not to mention being able to follow presentations that rely exclusively on it. You will find introductory presentations of matrix algebra in Dorf (1969), Green (1976), Mason (1984; included in this book are programs written in BASIC that can be run on personal computers), Namboodiri (1984), and Searle (1966). For an introduction to multiple regression analysis using matrix notation, see Pedhazur (1982, Chapter 4).

THE RESEARCH CONTEXT

In earlier chapters (e.g., Chapters 8 and 14), we commented on the distinction between explanatory and predictive research. Multiple regression analysis may be applied in both types of research. However, not only does the interpretation of the results depend on the type of research to which it is applied, certain applications of multiple regression analysis are meaningful in only one type or the other. A notable case in point are procedures for variable selection (e.g., forward, stepwise), which may be useful in predictive research but *should not* be applied in explanatory research, as they are, at best, atheoretical. Our concern in this and subsequent chapters is with explanation; therefore, we will not present approaches applicable exclusively to prediction (for such applications, see Pedhazur, 1982, Chapter 6).

As discussed in Part 2, different types of designs (e.g., experimental, nonexperimental) may be used in explanatory research. In the present chapter, we focus on the application of multiple regression analysis in nonexperimental designs, because it is in this context that most of the complexities and difficulties in interpreting results arise. Applications of multiple regression analysis to experimental and quasi-experimental designs are presented in subsequent chapters.

TWO INDEPENDENT VARIABLES

As indicated above, multiple regression analysis with two independent variables will be presented in simple algebra, and all calculations will be done by hand.

SQUARED MULTIPLE CORRELATION: R^2

We begin by examining one of the formulas for the calculation of the squared multiple correlation, symbolized as R^2, which for the case of two independent variables, X_1 and X_2, is

$$R_{y.12}^2 = \frac{r_{y1}^2 + r_{y2}^2 - 2r_{y1}r_{y2}r_{12}}{1 - r_{12}^2} \tag{18.1}$$

where $R_{y.12}^2$ = squared multiple correlation of the dependent variable, Y, with the two independent variables, X_1 and X_2. Note that the dependent variable appears as the first subscript and is separated from the independent variables by a period. For convenience, we use numbers to designate the independent variables. Other subscripts, including abbreviated variable names, can be used. When we believe that there is no ambiguity, we use Y to designate the dependent variable and numbers to refer to the independent variables.

Notice that, to apply (18.1), the three correlations for the variables under consideration are required. Such correlations are frequently referred to as *zero-order correlations*, to distinguish them from ones in which more than two variables are involved (e.g., semipartial correlations, discussed below).

Let us start our examination of (18.1) by assuming that the correlation between the independent variables is zero (i.e., $r_{12} = 0$). Under such circumstances, (18.1) reduces to

$$R_{y.12}^2 = r_{y1}^2 + r_{y2}^2$$

This makes sense, as the lack of correlation between the independent variables means that they do not share anything. Thus, whatever information each variable provides with respect to the dependent variable is unique to it. Clearly, under such circumstances, the proportion of variance attributed to each of the independent variables is equal to the square of its correlation with the dependent variable. Further, the sum of the proportions of variance accounted for by the independent variables is equal to R^2.

The preceding holds true for any number of independent variables so long as *the correlations among them are zero*. This is not as rare an occurrence as you may think. In fact, it is characteristic of well designed and well executed experiments, making it possible to identify unambiguously not only the proportion of variance accounted by each of the independent variables but also by their interactions (see Chapter 20).

As was stated previously, in the present chapter, we concentrate on the more complex situation—one in which the independent variables are correlated. Let us examine what takes place when this is the case. Let us assume that the three zero-order correlations are of the same sign, say, all positive. Under such circumstances, the numerator of (18.1) will be *smaller* than the sum of the squared zero-order correlations of the dependent variable with each of the independent variables. How much smaller will depend on the magnitudes of the correlations involved. The magnitude of R^2 is affected also by the magnitude of the denominator of (18.1)—a fraction that is a function of the squared correlation between the independent variables. Without going into the details, it will be noted that although R^2 will be smaller than the sum of the squared zero-order correlations of the dependent variable with the independent variables, it will be at least as large as the larger of the two.

It is, however, possible for R^2 to be larger than the sum of the squared zero-order correlations of the dependent variable with each of the independent variables. For illustrative purposes, assume that the sign of the correlation between the independent variables is negative, whereas the signs of the correlations of each of them with the dependent variable are positive. Under such circumstances, the third term in the numerator of (18.1) would be added to the first two, resulting in a value *larger* than the sum of the squared zero-order correlations of the independent variables with the dependent variable. Whatever the specific value added, the resulting R^2 would be still larger, because the numerator would be divided by a fraction.

As a less intuitive example of how R^2 is affected by the pattern of the interrelations among the variables, assume that the correlation between the dependent variable, Y, and one of the independent variables, say X_2, is zero but that the other two correlations are *not* equal to zero. Judging by zero-order correlations only, one may be inclined to reject X_2 as being useless. But think now what happens when (18.1) is applied. The numerator reduces to the first term only (i.e., r_{y1}^2). However, the denominator is a fraction (because $r_{12} \neq 0$). Consequently, R^2 will be larger than r_{y1}^2. In this example, X_2 is an instance of what has been referred to as a *suppressor variable* (see Pedhazur, 1982, pp. 104–105, and the references given therein).

We urge you not to worry about the subtleties of the examples we have presented, particularly the last one. All we wish to do at this stage is help you get a feel for (18.1). We believe it important to show from the very beginning that, when the independent variables are correlated, the situation may become complex, even in the simple case of two independent variables. You may well imagine how much more complex the situation may become in designs with more than two independent variables that are intercorrelated. A major lesson to be learned from the examples presented is that exclusive reliance on and interpretation of zero-order correlations when the independent variables are correlated is, to say the least, imprudent.

A NUMERICAL EXAMPLE

Before dealing with other aspects of multiple regression analysis, we will apply (18.1) to some data. In Table 18.1, illustrative data are given for four variables and 30 subjects. In the present section, we use part of the data of Table 18.1 to illustrate calculations of multiple

Table 18.1
Illustrative Data for Four Variables

AA	MA	SES	MOT
57	90	2	12
77	90	3	10
64	91	2	14
78	94	4	12
64	97	5	18
80	93	5	23
92	100	6	20
70	103	4	10
97	105	3	19
82	115	3	12
88	120	3	14
98	112	6	20
75	96	5	13
45	86	4	9
70	84	5	16
76	91	5	16
74	93	4	13
77	99	3	9
55	89	4	10
85	94	5	15
65	96	4	7
89	102	6	20
70	100	4	11
98	103	7	21
85	110	5	22
80	109	6	13
95	104	7	18
43	87	3	9
86	92	2	16
51	94	2	14

Note. AA = Academic Achievement, *MA* = Mental Ability, *SES* = Socioeconomic Status, *MOT* = Motivation.

regression analysis with two independent variables. Subsequently, when we discuss multiple regression with more than two independent variables, we use all the data of Table 18.1.

When we discussed Single-Stage and Multistage Models in Chapter 14 (see especially the discussion in connection with Figures 14.1 and 14.2), we said that we will illustrate analyses of such models in Chapter 18. This is why we are using here the same variables and some of the models presented in Chapter 14. We suggest that you read relevant sections of Chapter 14 in conjunction with the present discussion. We reiterate what we said in Chapter 14: The models are used for illustrative purposes only. We cannot go into discussion of their validity from a substantive perspective. Furthermore, although issues of validity and reliability of the measures used are of utmost importance, we will not be concerned with them here.[1]

For the analyses in this section, we assume that Socioeconomic Status (*SES*) and Mental Ability (*MA*) are the independent variables and that Motivation (*MOT*) is the dependent variable. For convenience, as well as for relating the presentation to the notation in (18.1),

---

[1]Validity and reliability were treated in detail in Part 1 of this book. For some comments on the effects of measurement errors on regression statistics, see Chapter 17, under Assumptions.

SES will be designated as variable 1, *MA* as variable 2, and *MOT* as *Y*. Following are the zero-order correlations among these variables:

$$r_{y1} = .536 \quad r_{y2} = .313 \quad r_{12} = .256$$

We suggest that, as an exercise, you use the data given in Table 18.1 and one of the formulas given in Chapter 17, or any alternative formula you prefer, to calculate these correlations. Applying (18.1):

$$R^2_{y.12} = \frac{(.536)^2 + (.313)^2 - 2(.536)(.313)(.256)}{1 - (.256)^2} = .320$$

Thus, about 32% percent of the variance in *MOT* (.320 x 100) is accounted for by both *SES* and *MA*.

THE REGRESSION EQUATION

For two independent variables, the regression equation is

$$Y' = a + b_{y1.2}X_1 + b_{y2.1}X_2 \tag{18.2}$$

where Y' = predicted score; a = intercept; the two b's are referred to as partial regression coefficients. Loosely speaking, this means that, when a regression coefficient is calculated for a given independent variable, an adjustment is made for the correlation of the variable in question with the other independent variable. Stated differently, the other variable is partialed out. For each coefficient, the variable that is partialed out is indicated after the period in the subscript. Thus, X_2 is partialed out when the b for X_1 is calculated and conversely for the b associated with X_2 (the calculations are shown below).

The present example consists of two independent variables. Consequently, there is only one variable to be partialed out when each of the b's is calculated. Such b's are referred to as first-order partial regression coefficients, the order indicating the number of partialed variables. With more than two independent variables, higher-order partial regression coefficients are calculated. In general, the order of the b's in a given equation is equal to the number of independent variables, k, minus one (i.e., $k - 1$). In a design with, say, five independent variables, the b's are of the fourth order, because four independent variables are partialed out when each of them is calculated. Thus, when the b for variable 1 is calculated, variables 2, 3, 4, and 5 are partialed out. When the b for variable 2 is calculated, variables 1, 3, 4, and 5 are partialed out, and so forth for the other b's.

In sum, whatever the number of independent variables, the solution is aimed at arriving at a set of differential weights (i.e., the b's) such that when they are applied to scores on the independent variables to obtain predicted scores (Y'), the correlation between these scores and the dependent variable is maximized. It can be shown (see Pedhazur, 1982, pp. 55–56) that the squared multiple correlation between a dependent variable and a set of independent variables is equal to the squared zero-order correlation between the dependent variable and the predicted scores (i.e., between Y and Y'). This results in the minimization of the squared residuals, which is what the least squares approach is about.

Because analyses are sometimes carried out in stages, entering independent variables sequentially, a mistaken notion has taken hold, even in some textbooks, that the magnitudes of the b's for a given set of variables are affected by the order in which they were entered into the analysis. We hope that, in light of what we said above, you recognize that this idea is utterly wrong. It is true, that when the independent variables are correlated, the magnitudes and even the signs of b's change as additional variables are brought into the equation. However, *when all the variables are in the equation, the b's will be the same, regardless of the order in which they were entered into the analysis.*

We stressed the invariance of the b's not only because of mistaken notions surrounding them, but also because this idea is directly related to model specification and specification errors (see, for example, Chapter 17). A sure sign that a model is misspecified is that inclusion of an additional(s) variable(s) in the equation leads to changes in the magnitudes and/or signs of the b's for variables already in the equation. This, of course, means that the assumption regarding the errors not being correlated with the independent variables is violated (see Chapter 17).

There is one other reason for our stressing the idea of the invariance of the b's. Later in this chapter, we discuss the idea of variance partitioning and show that, contrary to the b's, the determination of proportions of variance attributed to each of the independent variables is predicated on the order in which the variables are entered into the analysis.

Returning now to (18.2), it will be noted that the cumbersome subscript notation used in it can be greatly simplified, because in any given equation, it is clear which is the dependent variable and also which independent variables are partialed out in the calculation of the b for any given independent variable. Using a simplified notation, (18.2) can be restated as

$$Y' = a + b_1 X_1 + b_2 X_2 \tag{18.3}$$

It is this notation that we will use, with the understanding that the b's are partial regression coefficients whose order always equals $k - 1$ (where k is the number of independent variables).

Using the simplified notation, the two first-order b's are calculated as follows:

$$b_1 = \frac{r_{y1} - r_{y2}r_{12}}{1 - r_{12}^2} \cdot \frac{s_y}{s_1} \qquad b_2 = \frac{r_{y2} - r_{y1}r_{12}}{1 - r_{12}^2} \cdot \frac{s_y}{s_2} \tag{18.4}$$

where $s =$ standard deviation.

The intercept is calculated as follows:

$$a = \bar{Y} - b_1 \bar{X}_1 - b_2 \bar{X}_2 \tag{18.5}$$

where the b's are the partial regression coefficients, and the other terms are the means of the variables involved.

We will now take a close look at (18.4), beginning with the assumption that the correlation between the independent variables is zero (i.e., $r_{12} = 0$). Under such circumstances, the formula for each b is reduced to the correlation of the dependent variable with the variable in question, multiplied by the ratio of the standard deviation of the former by the latter. For example, $b_1 = r_{y1}(s_y/s_1)$, which is one of the formulas for the calculation of b in simple regression analysis—compare with (17.15), where β is used instead of r. In sum, when the independent variables are not correlated, the partialing process has no effect, as it is not necessary.

As was said earlier, in connection with (18.1), the independent variables are not correlated in well designed experiments. It is safe to say that in nonexperimental research, the independent variables are always correlated, to a greater or lesser extent, and, therefore, partial regression coefficients have to be calculated.

Look now at the numerator of the first term in (18.4) and note that the sign of the b for a given variable would not necessarily be the same as the sign of the zero-order correlation of the variable in question with the dependent variable. Further, depending on the pattern and magnitude of the correlations among the three variables, b for a given variable may be equal to zero, although the zero-order correlation of the dependent variable with the variable in question is *not* zero. The converse is also true: Whereas the zero-order correlation of a variable with the dependent variable may be equal to zero, the b associated with it may be *not* equal to zero.

The preceding are but some examples of the consequences of the partialing, or adjustment, process, underscoring the hazards of interpreting zero-order statistics when the independent variables are correlated.

Before dealing with the interpretation of partial regression coefficients, we will calculate the regression equation for the three-variable problem we have used above in the calculation of R^2. Recall that using data from Table 18.1, we treated *MOT* as the dependent variable, Y, and *SES* and *MA* as independent variables 1 and 2 respectively. The zero-order correlations for these data were reported earlier as

$$r_{y1} = .536 \quad r_{y2} = .313 \quad r_{12} = .256$$

In order to apply (18.4), we also need the standard deviations of the three variables. They are[2]

$$s_y(MOT) = 4.392 \quad s_1(SES) = 1.455 \quad s_2(MA) = 8.915$$

Applying (18.4),

$$b_1 = \frac{.536 - (.313)(.256)}{1 - (.256)^2} \cdot \frac{4.392}{1.455} = 1.472$$

$$b_2 = \frac{.313 - (.536)(.256)}{1 - (.256)^2} \cdot \frac{4.392}{8.915} = .093$$

The means for the variables in question are

$$MOT = 14.533 \quad SES = 4.233 \quad MA = 97.967$$

Applying (18.5),

$$a = 14.533 - (1.472)(4.233) - (.093)(97.967) = -.809$$

Using the variable names given in Table 18.1, the regression equation is

$$MOT' = -.809 + 1.472(SES) + .093(MA)$$

This, then, is the equation that would be used when seeking to predict individuals' scores on *MOT* on the basis of their status on *SES* and *MA*. We turn now to the interpretation of the b's.

Each b is interpreted as indicating the expected change in the dependent variable associated with a unit change in the variable in question while partialing out the other independent variable. Another way this is often stated is that the b indicates the expected change in the dependent variable associated with a unit change in the variable in question while controlling for, or holding constant, the other variable.

For the example under discussion, the expected change in *MOT* associated with a unit change in *SES* while controlling for *MA* is 1.472, and the expected change in *MOT* associated

---

[2]As an exercise, we suggest that you calculate the standard deviations using the formula given in Chapter 17 or an alternative one that you may prefer.

with a unit change in *MA* while controlling for *SES* is .093. When viewed from a purely statistical frame of reference, such interpretations seem uncomplicated. However, from a substantive frame of reference, they may be neither meaningful nor feasible. Consider the present equation. Even if it were assumed that the model it reflects is not seriously mis-specified (a clearly untenable assumption), statements about the effect of *MA* while holding *SES* constant, or of the effect of *SES* while holding *MA* constant, "tend to have an air of fantasy about them" (Pedhazur, 1982, p. 225).

The difficulty is not inherent in the analytic method (i.e., regression analysis) but in the context in which it is applied. The primary problem has to do with the type of design used. In nonexperimental designs, it is necessary to consider whether a variable whose *b* one wishes to interpret as an effect is susceptible to manipulation. But, even if one were to conclude that this is so, the notion of manipulating the variable in question while holding constant other variables with which it is correlated, or of which it may even be a cause, may be fanciful. No amount of speculation can tell what effect a variable manipulated in a well designed experi-ment will have. As Box (1966) so aptly put it: "To find out what happens to a system when you interfere with it you have to interfere with it (not just passively observe it)" (p. 629).

Is one, therefore, to conclude, as some authors do, that *b*'s obtained in nonexperimental research should not be interpreted as indices of effects? We think this to be too extreme a posture. However, we do believe that circumspection is called for when making such an interpretation. The question of correct model specification is crucial. Regrettably, all too often, one encounters interpretations of *b*'s as indices of the effects of the variables with which they are associated, despite the fact that the model used, wittingly or unwittingly, is flagrantly misspecified, even ludicrous. It is against the gross and glib misinterpretations of *b*'s that we felt it important to caution you. We turn now to less complex issues concerning the interpretation of *b*'s.

In Chapter 17, a distinction was made between unstandardized (*b*) and standardized (β) regression coefficients. Recall that the former are used with raw scores, whereas the latter are used with standard scores (i.e., *z* scores). The regression coefficients we have calculated are unstandardized. Look again at (18.4) and note that the magnitude of the *b* is largely deter-mined by the ratio of the standard deviation of the dependent variable to the standard deviation of the independent variable in question. The magnitudes of standard deviations are, in turn, affected by the units of the measures used. This has important implications for the substantive interpretation of *b*'s as well as for comparisons among them.

A very small (large) *b* may be deemed substantively important (unimportant), depending on the units and variability of the specific measures used. Moreover, a very small *b* may be statistically significant, whereas a very large one may be statistically *not* significant. From the preceding, it also follows that *b*'s in a given regression equation are generally not comparable. In the example under consideration, the *b* for *SES* is much larger than that for *MA*. But what meaning, if any, is there in comparing a unit change in *SES* with a unit change in *MA*? In view of the unique types of scales used in most of sociobehavioral research, even comparisons of units on two measures of the "same" variable (e.g., units on two different measures of *SES*) are generally inappropriate.[3] Note, in addition, that for the measures supposedly used in the example under consideration the standard deviation of *MA* is much larger than that of *SES*.[4] Needless to say, the converse may be true for two other measures of these variables or as a result of transformation of one or both of the measures used in the present example.

---

[3]For a discussion of this topic in the broader context of measurement, see Chapters 2 and 4.

[4]Recall that no measures were used at all. We made up the data for illustrative purposes.

It is because of the lack of comparability of b's that researchers turn to β's when they attempt to speak of the relative importance of variables. We comment on this approach in the next section, after we show how standardized coefficients are calculated.

STANDARDIZED REGRESSION COEFFICIENTS

Recall that the standard deviation of standard scores is 1.00. Look now at (18.4) and note that, when the scores are standardized, the right hand terms (i.e., the ratios of the two standard deviations) reduce to 1. Consequently, with two independent variables, the standardized coefficients are calculated as follows:

$$\beta_1 = \frac{r_{y1} - r_{y2}r_{12}}{1 - r_{12}^2} \qquad \beta_2 = \frac{r_{y2} - r_{y1}r_{12}}{1 - r_{12}^2} \qquad (18.6)$$

Assume that the independent variables are not correlated (i.e., $r_{12} = 0$). It follows that each β is equal to the zero-order correlation of the dependent variable with the independent variable in question. This principle was explained earlier in connection with unstandardized coefficients, where it was pointed out that, when the independent variables are not correlated, a partialing process is not necessary. Thus, $\beta_1 = r_{y1}$, and $\beta_2 = r_{y2}$. This generalizes to any number of independent variables, so long as they are not correlated.

When the independent variables are correlated, as they almost always are in nonexperimental research, the magnitudes and signs of the β's are affected by the patterns and magnitudes of the correlations among all the variables (i.e., the independent variables and the dependent variable). The signs of the β's are the same as the signs of the b's corresponding to them. Therefore, as explained in connection with the latter, the sign and/or the magnitude of a β may differ from the sign and/or magnitude of the zero-order correlation of the dependent variable with the independent variable in question. Also, it is possible for β to exceed 1.00. It will be recalled that this is not the case in simple regression analysis, where $\beta = r$ (see Chapter 17).

An expression of R^2 involving β's and r's is

$$R_{y.12}^2 = \beta_1 r_{y1} + \beta_2 r_{y2} \qquad (18.7)$$

As was pointed out above, when the independent variables are not correlated, each β is equal to its corresponding r. Under such circumstances, the squared multiple correlation is equal to the sum of the squared β's, which is equivalent to the sum of the squared zero-order correlations of each of the independent variables with the dependent variable. It will be noted in passing that (18.7) is generalizable to any number of independent variables.

Applying (18.6) and (18.7) to the data under consideration,

$$\beta_1 = \frac{.536 - (.313)(.256)}{1 - (.256)^2} = .488$$

$$\beta_2 = \frac{.313 - (.536)(.256)}{1 - (.256)^2} = .188$$

$$R_{y.12}^2 = (.488)(.536) + (.188)(.313) = .320$$

The same R^2 was obtained when (18.1) was applied.

Recall that when z scores are used, $a = 0$. The regression equation for the data under consideration is

$$z'_{MOT} = .488z_{SES} + .188z_{MA}$$

Before commenting on this equation, we show how b's and β's are related.

$$b_j = \beta_j \frac{s_y}{s_j} \tag{18.8}$$

and

$$\beta_j = b_j \frac{s_j}{s_y} \tag{18.9}$$

where s = standard deviation; y = dependent variable; j = the jth independent variable. Formulas (18.8) and (18.9) are applicable to designs with any number of independent variables. Thus, having calculated b's, β's are easily obtainable and vice versa. For illustrative purposes, we apply (18.8) for the calculation of b for SES. The β for this variable is .488. Earlier, we reported

$$s_y(MOT) = 4.392 \quad s_1(SES) = 1.455$$

Therefore,

$$b_{SES} = .488 \frac{4.392}{1.455} = 1.473$$

which is, within rounding, the same value obtained earlier.

As was already pointed out, because the b's are not comparable, researchers are inclined to compare β's instead. A researcher using this approach would conclude, on the basis of the β's in the present example, that the effect of SES on MOT is about 2.5 times larger than the effect of MA.

This interpretation appears simple and almost automatic. However, as was pointed out in Chapter 17, when one is unable to attach substantive meaning to a unit change on some measure in its original form, nothing is gained by standardizing the scores, except for the false comfort of not having to face the problem. The biggest drawback in relying on the interpretation of β's is that the potential for self-delusion is greatly increased. One is much more prone to overlook one's lack of understanding of the meaning of the effects of the variables one is studying, not to mention their differential effects, and speak glibly of expected changes in the dependent variable associated with standard deviation changes in the independent variables.

In addition, it will be noted that the β's are population specific. What this means is that, although the effects of the independent variables on the dependent variable, as reflected by the b's, may be relatively stable across populations and settings, the β's may vary greatly, because they are sensitive to fluctuations in variances and covariances across populations. Consequently, as is discussed and illustrated in Chapter 21, comparisons across groups and settings should be based on b's, *not* β's. Detailed treatments of the contrast between the use of b's and β's will be found in Alwin (1988), Blalock (1964, 1968), Hargens (1976), Kim and Ferree (1981), Kim and Mueller (1976), Pedhazur (1982, pp. 247–251), Richards (1982), Schoenberg (1972), and Tukey (1954).

VARIANCE PARTITIONING

Prompted, at least in part, by difficulties in interpreting regression equations (see preceding section), researchers have sought alternative approaches. Probably the most popular ones are those aimed at partitioning the variance accounted for (i.e., R^2) into components attributed to the different independent variables. We would like to state at the outset that, in our opinion, the various methods that may be subsumed under the general heading of variance partitioning are of little merit. Moreover, no orientation has led to greater confusion and misinterpretation of regression results than variance partitioning. Had it not been for our wish to give you an idea of the pitfalls of this orientation, so that you may be in a better position to evaluate research in which it has been employed, we would have refrained from presenting it altogether.

INCREMENTAL VARIANCE PARTITIONING

Our presentation is limited to a brief overview of one method that may be labeled incremental, or hierarchical, variance partitioning. For more detailed discussions of this method as well as others (e.g., commonality analysis), along with critiques of influential studies in which they were applied, see Pedhazur (1982, Chapter 7).

The idea behind incremental partitioning of variance, so far as the mechanics of the analysis go, is simple. As the name implies, R^2 is partitioned incrementally. This is accomplished by entering the independent variables into the analysis in a sequence, one variable at a time,[5] and noting at each stage the increment in R^2 due to the variable being entered.

On the basis of the discussion in the beginning of this chapter, it should be clear that only when the independent variables are not correlated will increments in proportions of variance accounted for by each of the independent variables remain the same, regardless of the order in which the variables are entered into the analysis. When the independent variables are correlated, the proportion of variance attributed to a given variable may vary, to a greater or lesser extent, depending on the stage at which it is entered into the analysis and on its relations with the variables that have already been taken into account. This is in contrast to the b's, whose magnitudes for a given set of variables are not affected by the order in which they are entered into the analysis (see discussion above).

The overall R^2 for a given set of variables (i.e., R^2 for the dependent variable with all the independent variables under consideration) is *not* affected by the order in which the variables are entered. What is affected is how the R^2 pie, so to speak, is sliced among the different independent variables. The obvious question, then, is: How does one decide on the order of entry of the variables? Before addressing this critical question, calculation of variance partitioning will be illustrated, using the data of the three-variable problem presented in preceding sections. In the course of doing this, the concept of semipartial correlation will be introduced.

---

[5]Instead of entering single variables, blocks of variables may be entered and the increment in R^2 due to each block noted. See Pedhazur (1982, Chapter 7).

A NUMERICAL EXAMPLE

Data for three variables taken from Table 18.1 were used earlier to illustrate the calculation of R^2 and the regression equation. The dependent variable was Motivation (*MOT*), and the two independent variables were Socioeconomic Status (*SES*), designated as variable number 1, and Mental Ability (*MA*), designated as variable number 2. We repeat here some of the results obtained earlier.

$$r_{y1} = .536 \quad r_{y2} = .313 \quad r_{12} = .256$$

$$R^2_{y.12} = .320$$

An incremental partitioning of variance will now be carried out by entering *SES* (i.e., variable 1) first. In the presentation that follows, we use the more general notation of multiple regression analysis even when dealing with zero-order correlations. Thus, we use $R^2_{y.1}$ to stand for r^2_{y1}—similarly for other zero-order correlations. Now, when variable 1 is entered first into the analysis, it accounts for .287 ($R^2_{y.1} = r^2_{y1}$) of the variance in the dependent variable. As both variables account for .320 (i.e., $R^2_{y.12}$), it follows that the increment in the proportion of variance accounted for by variable 2 is equal to the difference between the two R^2's

$$R^2_{y.12} - R^2_{y.1} = .320 - .287 = .033$$

For the present example, it is concluded that, when *SES* is entered first, it accounts for .287 of the variance of *MOT* and that *MA* then adds .033 to the variance accounted for. Or, equivalently, *SES* accounts for about 29% of the variance and the increment due to *MA* is about 3%.

Let us see now what happens when the order of entry of the variables is reversed. Entering *MA* first, it accounts for .098 ($R^2_{y.2}$), or about 10%, of the variance of *MOT*. The increment due to *SES* is

$$R^2_{y.12} - R^2_{y.2} = .320 - .098 = .222$$

or 22%.

Increments in the proportion of variance accounted for of the kind we have been describing are also referred to as "squared semipartial correlations."

SEMIPARTIAL CORRELATION

For the present discussion, it will be assumed that three variables—designated as 1, 2, and 3—are used. Furthermore, 1 is the dependent variable, and 2 and 3 are correlated independent variables. We begin by focusing on the relation between variables 1 and 2. It is possible, of course, to calculate r_{12}. But because 2 and 3 are correlated, a researcher may wish to study the relation between 1 and 2, after having taken out, or partialed, from the latter whatever it shares with variable 3. This, in essence, is the idea of a semipartial correlation, which, for the situation we have been describing, is symbolized as follows: $r_{1(2.3)}$.

Note the pattern of the subscript notation. The variable outside the parentheses is the dependent variable. The variable to the left of the period is the one whose relation with the dependent variable is calculated after having partialed out, or controlled for, the variable to the right of the period. In other words, it is the correlation between variable 1 and variable 2 after having partialed variable 3 from variable 2. Equivalently, it is the semipartial correlation between 1 and 2, partialing 3 from 2. Semipartial correlations are also referred to as part correlations.

The formula for the semipartial correlation we have been describing is

$$r_{1(2.3)} = \frac{r_{12} - r_{13}r_{23}}{\sqrt{1 - r_{23}^2}} \tag{18.10}$$

Several things will be noted about (18.10). First, it is composed of the three zero-order correlations for the variables under consideration. Second, the first term of the numerator is the zero-order correlation of the variables whose semipartial correlation is sought. Third, when the correlation between the two independent variables is zero (i.e., when $r_{23} = 0$), the semipartial correlation between 1 and 2, partialing 3 from 2, is equal to the zero-order correlation between 1 and 2. This makes sense, as one is partialing a variable (3) from another variable (2) when the two variables have nothing in common. Fourth, the magnitude and the sign of the semipartial correlation are determined by the pattern and magnitudes of the three zero-order correlations. Of various possibilities, some will be noted for illustrative purposes. It is possible, for example, for r_{12} and $r_{1(2.3)}$ to be of different signs. The two may be of the same sign, but differ in magnitude. One of them may be equal to zero, and the other may be not equal to zero.

Applying (18.10) to the numerical example used above, the semipartial correlation between MOT and SES, after partialing MA from the latter, will be calculated. Recalling that MOT was designated as Y, and that SES and MA were designated as 1 and 2 respectively, and using the zero-order correlations given above

$$r_{y(1.2)} = \frac{r_{y1} - r_{y2}r_{12}}{\sqrt{1 - r_{12}^2}} = \frac{.536 - (.313)(.256)}{\sqrt{1 - (.256)^2}} = .472$$

The square of this semipartial correlation, .22, is the same as the proportion of variance incremented by variable 1 when it is entered after variable 2 (see above).

For completeness of presentation, the semipartial correlation of Y with variable 2, after partialing 1 from the latter, is calculated.

$$r_{y(2.1)} = \frac{r_{y2} - r_{y1}r_{12}}{\sqrt{1 - r_{12}^2}} = \frac{.313 - (.536)(.256)}{\sqrt{1 - (.256)^2}} = .182$$

Again, the square of this semipartial correlation, .033, is equal to the increment in the proportion of variance due to variable 2 when it is entered after variable 1 (see above).

In sum, the squared multiple correlation of Y with 1 and 2 can be partitioned in two different ways, each of which can be expressed in two equivalent forms.

$$R_{y.12}^2 = R_{y.1}^2 + (R_{y.12}^2 - R_{y.1}^2) = r_{y1}^2 + r_{y(2.1)}^2$$

$$R_{y.12}^2 = R_{y.2}^2 + (R_{y.12}^2 - R_{y.2}^2) = r_{y2}^2 + r_{y(1.2)}^2$$

Clearly, either approach may be used for the calculations. However, because formulas for higher-order semipartial correlations, necessary for designs with more than two independent variables (see below), become quite cumbersome, it is simpler to carry out the calculations using differences between R^2's.

The semipartial correlations dealt with thus far are referred to as first-order semipartial correlations, as only one variable is being partialed out. With more than two independent variables, higher-order semipartial correlations are necessary. Earlier, it was pointed out that, in any given regression equation, partial regression coefficients are all of the same order. In contrast, semipartial correlations for a given set of independent variables are *not* of the same order. As each variable is added to the analysis, the order of the semipartial correlation is incremented by one. When the first variable is entered, a zero-order correlation between it and the dependent variable is calculated, as there are not yet any variables that have to be controlled. When the second variable is entered, it is necessary to control for, or partial out, whatever it shares with the first variable. Hence, a first-order semipartial correlation is calculated. When the third variable is entered, a second-order semipartial correlation has to be calculated, partialing out the first two from the third. When a fourth variable is entered, a third-order semipartial correlation is calculated, and so forth.

INTERPRETATION

As always, the calculations are the easy part, particularly because they can be carried out with the aid of computer programs. It is the interpretation that matters. In the case of variance partitioning, the interpretation is particularly difficult, as the situation is inherently ambiguous.

For illustrative purposes only, it will be useful to assume that the correlations among the variables under consideration are all positive. Under such circumstances, the later the point of entry of a given variable, the smaller the proportion of variance it will be shown to increment.[6] The actual amount will depend on the correlation of the variable in question with all the variables that have already been taken into account. In nonexperimental research, it is not uncommon for a variable entered first to account for what might be viewed as a reasonable proportion of the variance, but when entered at a later stage, say, at the third or the fourth step, to add very little, even nothing.

Clearly, then, variables entered at earlier stages in the analysis are given the edge. Again, we face the critical question as to how one decides about the order in which the variables are to be entered. In explanatory research, the decision about the order of entry of variables must be made on the basis of one's theory regarding the process by which the variables under consideration affect the dependent variables. We elaborate on this statement by way of very simple alternative models in which the three variables of the numerical example given above—*MOT*, *SES*, and *MA*—are involved. In Figure 18.1 are depicted three models in each of which *MOT* is treated as the dependent variable. As with other examples, we are *not* concerned with the validity of these models. They are used for purely illustrative purposes.

Before discussing the three models, it will be pointed out that, in Chapter 14, a distinction was introduced between exogenous and endogenous variables. This was done in the context of illustrative models in which the variables used in Figure 18.1 were treated as exogenous or endogenous (see Figures 14.1 and 14.2 and the discussion related to them). For present purposes, it will suffice to point out that, when two or more variables are treated as exogenous, correlations among them are treated as given, hence, not the subject of study.

With the preceding in mind, we turn first to model (*a*) of Figure 18.1, where the curved line connecting *SES* and *MA* is meant to indicate that these variables are correlated. The arrows emanating from *SES* and *MA* are meant to indicate that both affect *MOT*. In this

---

[6]When the correlations differ in sign, it is possible for a variable entered at a later step to lead to a greater increment in R^2 than when entered at an earlier step.

model, therefore, *SES* and *MA* are treated as exogenous variables. What this means is that the researcher is unable or unwilling to state why these variables are correlated. Under such circumstances, there is no meaningful way to carry out a variance partitioning. All one can do is state the proportion of variance accounted for by both variables taken together, that is, the squared multiple correlation of *MOT* with *SES* and *MA*.

In model (*b*), on the other hand, *SES* is treated as exogenous, whereas both *MA* and *MOT* are treated as endogenous. For a model of this kind, one may do an incremental partitioning of variance, beginning with *SES* and then entering *MA*. If model (*c*) were advanced instead, the incremental partitioning of variance would proceed by entering *MA* first and then *SES*. In the preceding section, both approaches were illustrated in connection with the numerical example.

From the foregoing, it should be clear that, unless the researcher is willing to advance a causal model delineating the process by which the independent variables affect the dependent variable, there is no way of telling whether and in what manner the proportion of variance may be meaningfully partitioned. Bear in mind that, even with three variables, additional models to those depicted in Figure 18.1 are possible. You may well imagine how complex the situation would become in designs with more than three variables.

Complexity and validity of the causal models advanced aside, the most important point to note with respect to variance partitioning is that the components thus obtained represent different *types* of effects. Without going into the details, (see Pedhazur, 1982, Chapter 7, for

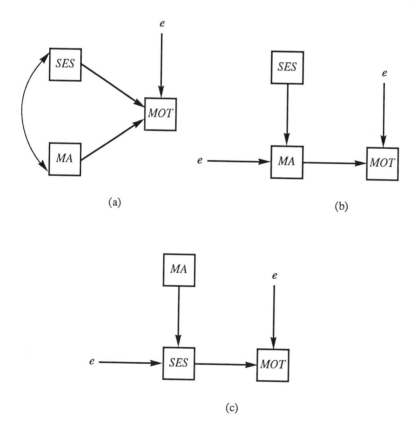

(a)

(b)

(c)

Figure 18.1

a detailed discussion, along with numerical examples), it will only be pointed out that various components obtained as a result of variance partitioning represent squared semipartial correlations of different orders. It is, therefore, not meaningful to compare such components for the purpose of determining the relative importance of the variables with which they are associated. This is ironic, as most applications of variance partitioning are, in our estimation, motivated by this very goal.

TESTS OF SIGNIFICANCE

Several kinds of tests of significance, each addressed to a different question, may be applied in multiple regression analysis. In the present section, we discuss and illustrate two such tests: (a) a test of R^2, and (b) tests of partial regression coefficients (b's).

TEST OF R^2

The test of R^2 is accomplished as follows:

$$F = \frac{R^2/k}{(1 - R^2)/(N - k - 1)} \qquad (18.11)$$

where R^2 = squared multiple correlation of the dependent variable with all the independent variables; k = number of independent variables; N = sample size. Note that (18.11) is a generalization of the test of r^2 presented in Chapter 17—see (17.31) and the discussion related to it. The numerator consists of the proportion of variance accounted for by the independent variables divided by its df. The denominator consists of the proportion of variance *not* accounted for $(1 - R^2)$, that is, the error term, divided by its df. The F ratio has k and $N - k - 1$ df for the numerator and the denominator respectively.

The application of (18.11) constitutes an omnibus test, namely whether the proportion of variance accounted for by all the independent variables, taken simultaneously, is statistically significant. Equivalently, it is a test of whether one or more of the regression coefficients is significantly different from zero, the alternative hypothesis being that all the regression coefficients are equal to zero.

We now apply (18.11) to the numerical example analyzed earlier in this chapter. For this example, we calculated $R^2_{y.12} = .32$; $N = 30$. Therefore,

$$F = \frac{.32/2}{(1 - .32)/(30 - 2 - 1)} = 6.35$$

with 2 and 27 df. Assuming that $\alpha = .01$ was selected by the researcher, the tabled value for .01 with 2 and 27 df is 5.49 (see Appendix). It would, therefore, be concluded that R^2 is statistically significant at the .01 level of significance.

As was explained in Chapter 17—see (17.28) and the discussion related to it—instead of testing R^2, one can test the regression sum of squares. Having calculated R^2, the regression and residual sums of squares can be readily obtained and vice versa. For the data being analyzed, the total sum of squares (i.e., Σy^2) is 559.47 (as an exercise, you may wish to calculate this value). Therefore, the regression sum of squares is $R^2 \Sigma y^2 = (.32)(559.47) =$

179.03. One way the residual sum of squares can be obtained is by subtraction: $\Sigma y^2 - ss_{reg}$.
For the numerical example under consideration

$$ss_{res} = 559.47 - 179.03 = 380.44$$

We repeat (17.28) with a new number.

$$F = \frac{ss_{reg}/df_1}{ss_{res}/df_2} = \frac{ss_{reg}/k}{ss_{res}/(N - k - 1)} \tag{18.12}$$

where df = degrees of freedom; k = number of independent variables; N = sample size.
Each sum of squares is divided by its df to yield a mean square. The df for the regression sum
of squares (df_1) equal the number of independent variables (k), which, for the present
example, is 2. The df for the residual sum of squares (df_2) equal $N - k - 1$, which, for the ·
present example, is 27 (i.e., $30 - 2 - 1$).

Applying (18.12) to the numerical example analyzed above,

$$F = \frac{179.03/2}{380.44/27} = 6.35$$

As expected, this F ratio is the same as the one obtained above for the test of R^2. We
repeat: Testing R^2 or the regression sum of squares amounts to the same thing.

TESTS OF b's

A conclusion that one or more of the b's is statistically significant, arrived at on the basis of a
significant R^2 (see preceding section), is generally not very enlightening. It goes without
saying that it is more informative to know which of the b's is statistically significant. This is
accomplished by testing each of the b's. The concept of testing a b was introduced and
illustrated in Chapter 17 in the context of simple regression analysis. It was shown that,
dividing the b by its standard error, a t ratio with df equal to those associated with the Mean
Square Residuals (MSR) is obtained—see (17.32) and the discussion related to it. The same
approach is taken in multiple regression analysis, except that, when calculating the standard
error of a b for a given independent variable, the correlations of the variable in question with
the rest of the independent variables are taken into account.

We begin by showing the formula for the standard error of a b of any order, that is, in an
equation with any number of independent variables. This is followed by the format such
standard errors take for first-order b's, that is, b's in equations with two independent variables. The standard errors of first-order b's are then calculated for the numerical example
under consideration, and the two b's are tested.

The standard error for b_1, for example, in an equation with k independent variables is

$$s_{b_{y1.2...k}} = \sqrt{\frac{s^2_{y.12...k}}{\Sigma x_1^2 (1 - R^2_{1.2...k})}} \tag{18.13}$$

where $s_{b_{y1.2...k}}$ = standard error of b_1; $s^2_{y.12...k}$ = variance of estimate, or the MSR[7]; $R^2_{1.2...k}$ =
squared multiple correlation of *independent variable* 1 (the variable for whose b the standard

---

[7] The concept of variance of estimate was introduced in Chapter 17. See (17.29) and the discussion related to it.

error is being calculated) *treated as a dependent variable*, with the rest of the independent variables—similarly for the other b's.

Note that, when the independent variables are not correlated, as is generally the case in experimental designs, the denominator of (18.13) reduces to Σx^2 for the variable in question, which is the same as for the test of the b in simple regression analysis—see (17.33). The squared multiple correlation of the independent variable in question with the rest of the independent variables indicates how much the former shares with the latter. The larger this R^2, the larger the standard error of the b. Clearly, this is an undesirable situation.[8]

For the special case of two independent variables that we have been considering in this section, (18.13) takes the following form:

$$s_{by1.2} = \sqrt{\frac{s^2_{y.12}}{\Sigma x_1^2(1 - r_{12}^2)}} \qquad s_{by2.1} = \sqrt{\frac{s^2_{y.12}}{\Sigma x_2^2(1 - r_{12}^2)}} \qquad (18.14)$$

Note, again, that the higher the correlation between the two independent variables, the larger the standard error of each of the b's.

The residual sum of squares (ss_{res}) for the numerical example under consideration is 380.44 (see calculation above). The df associated with ss_{res} are 27 ($N - k - 1$). Consequently, the variance of estimate, or the MSR, for the present example is $380.44/27 = 14.09$. Note that this is the numerator in (18.14) for the standard error for each of the b's. Earlier we reported $r_{12} = .256$. All we need now to calculate the two standard errors are the sums of squares for the two independent variables. They are[9]

$$\Sigma x_{1(SES)}^2 = 61.39 \quad \Sigma x_{2(MA)}^2 = 2304.84$$

Applying now (18.14), the standard errors of the b's are

$$s_{b_1} = \sqrt{\frac{14.09}{(61.39)(1 - .256^2)}} = .496$$

$$s_{b_2} = \sqrt{\frac{14.09}{(2304.84)(1 - .256^2)}} = .081$$

The b's for the present example are

$$b_{1(SES)} = 1.472 \qquad b_{2(MA)} = .093$$

Dividing each b by its standard error produces the following:

$$t_{b_1} = \frac{1.472}{.496} = 2.97 \qquad t_{b_2} = \frac{.093}{.081} = 1.15$$

The df for each of these t ratios are 27 (df associated with MSR, i.e., $N - k - 1$). Assuming that $\alpha = .01$ was preselected, one would check a table of t with 27 df at the .01 level. Alternatively, one may obtain the tabled value of t by taking the square root of F with 1 and 27 df, which is 2.77 (see Appendix). Accordingly, it is concluded that the regression coeffi-

---

[8]Later in this chapter, we comment on problems that arise when the independent variables are highly correlated—a condition referred to as "high multicollinearity." In that context, we make reference to the concept of tolerance of a variable, which is the term $1 - R^2$ of the denominator of (18.13).

[9]You may wish to calculate these sums of squares. The data are given in Table 18.1.

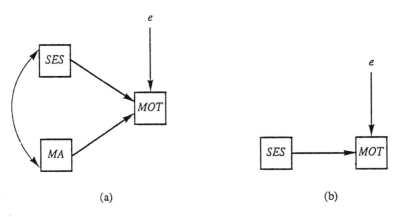

Figure 18.2

cient for *SES* (i.e., b_1) is statistically significant, whereas the regression coefficient for *MA* (i.e., b_2) is statistically not significant.

DEL REVISION

In view of the fact that the *b* for *MA* is statistically not significant, the original model is "revised." We placed revised in quotation marks, because model revision is not as simple as it may appear to be from what we will do here. Before we elaborate further, we would like to stress that we are overlooking here the very important distinction between statistical significance and substantive importance—a distinction discussed in detail in earlier chapters (see especially Chapters 9 and 15). After all, we made up the data for illustrative purposes. Moreover, because of our relatively small "sample" size (i.e., 30), the power of the statistical tests we are using may be low.

Returning to the issue of model revision, it will be noted first that this is done post hoc—a strategy that is seriously flawed (see Chapter 9). Second, tests of separate *b*'s do not constitute a test of the model as a whole. We return to this topic in Chapter 24. A third point, related to the preceding one, is that when, unlike the present example, a model consists of more than two independent variables, and when more than one of the *b*'s is found to be statistically not significant, deletion of one variable whose *b* is statistically not significant may lead to radical changes in other *b*'s and their related tests of significance. We return to these points later on in this chapter and in greater detail in subsequent chapters. All we want to do at this stage is to forewarn you that model revision is not as simple as it might appear from the present example.

With the preceding remarks in mind, we will show what is entailed in the revision of the model for the present example. In earlier chapters (e.g., Chapter 14, Figure 14.1 and the discussion related to it), it was noted that, when a dependent variable is regressed on two or more independent variables and each of the *b*'s is interpreted as indicating the effect of the variable with which it is associated while controlling for the rest of the independent variables, a single-stage model in which all the independent variables are treated as exogenous is used wittingly or unwittingly. For the present example, this takes the form of model (*a*) of Figure 18.2, where the unanalyzed relation between the two independent variables is depicted by the curved line connecting them. The arrows emanating from the independent variables to the dependent variable indicate that both are hypothesized to affect it.[10]

Now, because the b for MA was shown to be statistically not significant, MA is deleted from the model. Consequently, the regression equation in which MA is *not* included has to be calculated. In the present case, this means the calculation of a simple regression equation where MOT is the dependent variable and SES is the independent variable. The results of this analysis will be reported without showing the calculations. (We suggest that you do them as an exercise. If necessary, see Chapter 17, where a similar analysis was carried out.)

The equation for the regression of MOT on SES, using the data of Table 18.1 is

$$MOT' = 7.686 + 1.618SES$$

This revised model is depicted in (b) of Figure 18.2.

The proportion of variance accounted for is, of course, equal to the squared zero-order correlation between MOT and SES, that is, $(.536)^2 = .287$ (see calculation earlier in this chapter). If you were to test this proportion of variance for significance (we suggest you do), you would find that $F(1, 28) = 11.27$. Equivalently, if you were to test the b for SES, you would find that $t(28) = 3.36$, which is equal to the square root of the F.

TESTS OF RELATED STATISTICS

A test of significance of a b in a multiple regression equation is equivalent to a test of (a) the standardized coefficient (β) corresponding to it; (b) the proportion of variance accounted for by the variable whose b is being tested, when the variable is entered last into the analysis; and (c) the partial correlation coefficient corresponding to it. Because we have not discussed the partial correlation coefficient, we will comment on the first two points only (for a presentation of partial correlation coefficient and its relation to the semipartial correlation coefficient, see Pedhazur, 1982, Chapter 5).

Earlier in this chapter, we showed the relation between b's and β's, and we calculated the latter for the numerical example under consideration: $\beta_1 = .488$, and $\beta_2 = .188$. Although standard errors for β's can be calculated, it is not necessary to do this when the b's have been tested, as the test of each of the latter is equivalent to the test of each of the former.

Turning now to the second point made above, it will be noted that the proportion of variance incremented by a variable when it enters last into the analysis is a squared semipartial correlation of the highest order possible for a given set of independent variables. When the concept of the squared semipartial correlation was presented earlier in this chapter, it was shown that one way of expressing it is as a change in R^2 or as a difference between two R^2's. The test of a difference between two such R^2's is tantamount to a test of the squared semipartial correlation.

A test of the difference between two R^2's takes the following form:

$$F = \frac{(R^2_{y.12...k_1} - R^2_{y.12...k_2})/(k_1 - k_2)}{(1 - R^2_{y.12...k_1})/(N - k_1 - 1)} \tag{18.15}$$

where $R^2_{y.12...k_1}$ = squared multiple correlation for Y with k_1 independent variables (the larger R^2, that is, the one for the full model); $R^2_{y.12...k_2}$ = squared multiple correlation for Y with k_2

---

[10]Model (a) of Figure 18.2 is a repetition of Model (a) of Figure 18.1.

variables, where k_2 is a subset of k_1 (the smaller R^2, that is, the restricted model). The F ratio has $k_1 - k_2$ df for the numerator, and $N - k_1 - 1$ df for the denominator.

In the present situation, we are concerned with a special case of (18.15), one in which k_1 is the number of all the independent variables, and k_2 is the number of these variables minus one (i.e., $k_1 - 1$)—the omitted variable being the one that is entered last into the analysis. Under such circumstances, the df for the numerator of the F ratio is 1. Using the numerical example analyzed above, F ratios will be calculated and will be shown to equal the squares of the t ratios for their corresponding b's.

We begin by testing the squared semipartial correlation of Y with 2, partialing out 1 from 2, that is $r^2_{y(2.1)} = .033$ calculated above. Using results reported earlier,

$$F = \frac{(R^2_{y.12} - R^2_{y.1})/(k_1 - k_2)}{(1 - R^2_{y.12})/(N - k_1 - 1)} = \frac{(.320 - .287)/(2 - 1)}{(1 - .320)/(30 - 2 - 1)} = 1.31$$

which is, within rounding, equal to the square of the t ratio for b_2 (1.15) calculated above. Note that the difference between the two R^2's in the numerator is the squared semipartial correlation being tested.

Carrying out the test for $r^2_{y(1.2)}$,

$$F = \frac{(R^2_{y.12} - R^2_{y.2})/(k_1 - k_2)}{(1 - R^2_{y.12})/(N - k_1 - 1)} = \frac{(.320 - .098)/(2 - 1)}{(1 - .320)/(30 - 2 - 1)} = 8.81$$

which is, within rounding, equal to the square of the t ratio for b_1 (2.97). Again, the difference between the two R^2's in the numerator is the squared semipartial correlation being tested.

In some methods of variance partitioning, notably commonality analysis (see Pedhazur, 1982, pp. 199–211), the increment in the proportion of variance accounted for (i.e., increment in R^2) by a variable when it is entered last into the analysis is referred to as its uniqueness. From (18.15) and the illustrations that followed it, it can be seen that tests of b's in a given regression equation are equivalent to tests of uniqueness of the variables with which they are associated. Stated differently, a test of a b, regardless of its place in the regression equation, is equivalent to a test of the proportion of variance incremented by the variable with which it is associated when the variable is entered last in an incremental partitioning of variance (see earlier section for a discussion of incremental partitioning of variance).

We are making this point *not* because we recommend the use and substantive interpretation of uniqueness, but because there is widespread misunderstanding surrounding various elements that may be identified in a multiple regression analysis and the meaning of tests of significance that may be applied to them.

THREE INDEPENDENT VARIABLES

For convenience, we present an example with three independent variables. Concepts presented in connection with this example are applicable to designs with any number of independent variables.

A NUMERICAL EXAMPLE

The illustrative data to be used are reported in Table 18.1. Academic Achievement (*AA*) will be treated as the dependent variable, and the other three variables—*MA* (Mental Ability), *SES* (Socioeconomic Status), and *MOT* (Motivation)—as the independent variables. It will be recalled that, in the preceding section, *MOT* was treated as the dependent variable, and *SES* and *MA* were treated as the independent variables. This analysis will be replicated so that we may use it to explain some aspects of the output as well as to shed light on tests of different models.

For illustrative purposes, regression procedures from two computer packages—SPSS and SAS—will be used. For the SPSS run, with which we begin, the raw data of Table 18.1 will be used as input. For the SAS run, summary data (i.e., means, standard deviations, and correlations) will be used as input.

SPSS

Input

```
SET LISTING='T181.LIS'.
TITLE TABLE 18.1.
DATA LIST/AA 1–2 MA 3–5 SES 7 MOT 9–10. [fixed format input]
BEGIN DATA.
57 90 2 12      [data for first subject]
  .   .   .
51 94 2 14      [data for last subject]
END DATA.
LIST.
REGRESSION VAR ALL/DES/STAT=ALL/DEP MOT/ENTER SES/ENTER MA/
   DEP AA/ENTER SES/ENTER MA/ENTER MOT.
```

Commentary

The basic layout of SPSS input was explained in connection with its use in Chapter 17 (see also Chapter 16). Here we comment only on specific aspects of the REGRESSION runs we are calling for. We remind you, however, that the comments in the brackets are *not* part of the input file.

As you can see, we call for two analyses, or two equations. In Equation Number 1, the DEPendent variable is *MOT*, and the independent variables are *SES* and *MA*. The independent variables are entered in two steps, beginning with *SES*. Consequently, a simple regression analysis will be carried out first, regressing *MOT* on *SES*. Subsequently, a multiple regression analysis in which *MOT* is regressed on both *SES* and *MA* will be carried out. These analyses were done by hand in the preceding section.

In Equation Number 2, *AA* is the DEPendent variable. The three independent variables, *SES*, *MA*, and *MOT*, are entered sequentially in three steps. Consequently, in the first step, a simple regression analysis will be done. This will be followed by a multiple regression analysis with two independent variables. In the final step, a multiple regression analysis with three independent variables will be done.

It is, of course, not necessary to enter independent variables in separate steps. We do this, because we intend to use some of the intermediate analyses thereby obtained in the course of explaining the results (see commentaries on output, below).

Output

	Mean	Std Dev
AA	75.533	15.163
MA	97.967	8.915
SES	4.233	1.455
MOT	14.533	4.392

N of Cases = 30

Correlation:

	AA	MA	SES	MOT
AA	1.000	.637	.505	.653
MA	.637	1.000	.256	.313
SES	.505	.256	1.000	.536
MOT	.653	.313	.536	1.000

Commentary

This output should require no explanation. We include it for quick reference to the zero-order correlations, and because we will use these summary data as input for the SAS run (see below).

tput

ation Number 1   Dependent Variable..   MOT
inning Block Number 1. Method: Enter   SES

tiple R	.53574			Analysis of Variance				
quare	.28701	R Square Change	.28701			DF	Sum of Squares	Mean Square
isted R Square	.26155	F Change	11.27135	Regression		1	160.57367	160.57367
ndard Error	3.77441	Signif F Change	.0023	Residual		28	398.89299	14.24618

F = 11.27135   Signif F = .0023

--- Variables in the Equation ---

riable	B	SE B	95% Confdnce Intrvl B		Beta	Part Cor	Tolerance	T	Sig T
S	1.61760	.48182	.63064	2.60456	.53574	.53574	1.00000	3.357	.0023
onstant)	7.68550	2.15296	3.27536	12.09563					

Commentary

This excerpt is for the simple regression of *MOT* on *SES*. If necessary, study it in conjunction with relevant segments of preceding sections where these results were calculated by hand and discussed. Our comments here are limited to some aspects of the output with which you may be less familiar.

Various terms included in the output and discussed below (e.g., R Square Change, Confidence Interval, Tolerance, Summary Table) were obtained as a result of our choice of STAT=ALL (see input above).

As only one independent variable is used, Multiple R = .53574 is the zero-order correlation between *SES* and *MOT* (see correlation matrix above).

R Square Change refers to the increment in R^2 that is due to a variable(s) entered at this step, and F Change refers to the test of this increment. However, as this is the first step in the analysis, R Square Change and its test are the same as the R Square and its test.

Adjusted R Square has to do with the shrinkage of R^2—a topic discussed later in this chapter.

95% Confdnce Intrvl = 95% confidence interval for each of the b's in the regression equation. Confidence intervals were discussed in Chapter 17.

When the semipartial correlation was introduced earlier in this chapter, it was pointed out that it is also referred to as Part Correlation. This is how it is labeled in SPSS output (i.e., Part Cor). At this stage, there are no independent variables to partial out. Hence, Part Cor is the same as the zero-order correlation.

Tolerance is equal to $1 - R_i^2$, where i is an independent variable for which tolerance is calculated. In words, tolerance for a given independent variable is equal to one minus its squared multiple correlation with the rest of the independent variables. Thus, tolerance refers to what a given independent variable does *not* share with the other independent variables. The dependent variable plays *no* role in the calculation of tolerance.

Clearly, when variable i is not correlated with the other independent variables, taken simultaneously, $R_i^2 = 0$, and tolerance is 1.00. The higher the correlation of variable i with the rest of the independent variables (an undesirable condition, discussed below under Multicollinearity), the closer to 0 is the tolerance.

As only one independent variable was entered at this stage, Tolerance is necessarily 1.00. In the commentary on the next step, calculation of Tolerance is illustrated.

Output

Beginning Block Number 2. Method: Enter   MA

Variable(s) Entered on Step Number 2.. MA

Multiple R	.56583				Analysis of Variance		
R Square	.32016	R Square Change	.03315			DF	Sum of Squares	Mean Squ.
Adjusted R Square	.26980	F Change	1.31645	Regression	2	179.11848	89.559
Standard Error	3.75326	Signif F Change	.2613	Residual	27	380.34818	14.086

F = 6.35759   Signif F = .0055

-------------- Variables in the Equation --------------

Variable	B	SE B	95% Confdnce Intrvl B		Beta	Part Cor	Tolerance	T	Sig T
SES	1.47209	.49562	.45517	2.48902	.48755	.47131	.93453	2.970	.0062
MA	.09279	.08087	−.07314	.25871	.18833	.18206	.93453	1.147	.2613
(Constant)	−.78847	7.68962	−16.56627	14.98932					

Commentary

This is the second (also the last) step in the analysis in which *MOT* is treated as the dependent variable. You should have no difficulty in interpreting this output, particularly if you study it in conjunction with the discussions of the same results given earlier in this chapter.

Note that the 95% interval of the b for *MA* includes 0, thus, indicating that it is statistically not significant at the .05 level. This is, of course, also evident from the t ratio (1.147) and its associated probability (.2613). Had both variables been entered in a single step and had it been decided to delete *MA*, it would have been necessary to rerun the analysis, using *SES* only (we did this in the hand calculations earlier in this chapter). In the present run, however, all that is necessary is to use the results obtained at the first step where only *SES* was entered.

The R Square Change (.03315) is the difference between R^2 at this step and the one obtained at the preceding step (i.e., $.32016 - .28701$). The difference, or increment, under consideration was earlier labeled squared semipartial, or part, correlation. Look now under Part Cor and note that $r_{MOT(MA.SES)} = .18206$, the square of which is, of course, equal to the value of the R Square Change.

Similarly, the square of the Part Cor for SES (.222) is what the R Square Change would be, if SES were to be entered second, instead of first, into the analysis. Stated differently, it is the increment in R^2 due to SES when it is entered last. See discussions, along with calculations using these data, in the section entitled Semipartial Correlation.

The F Change is the test of the increment in R^2 due to the variable(s) entered in the current step. Thus, in the step being considered, the F Change $= 1.31645$ with 1 and 27 *df* is a test of the increment in proportion of variance (.03315) due to MA, or the squared semipartial correlation of MOT with MA, partialing out SES. Note that $\sqrt{1.31645} = 1.147$, which is equal to the *t* ratio for the *b* associated with MA (see section entitled Tests of Related Statistics in which the equivalence of these tests is discussed and illustrated).

Finally, the F Change discussed here is a special case of the test of the difference between two R^2's discussed earlier—see (18.15) and the discussion related to it.

Turning to tolerance, it will be noted that it is the same for both variables (.93453). In line with the explanation of tolerance above, it can be seen that, in the special case of only two independent variables, tolerance is $1 - r^2$ (where *r* is the correlation between the two independent variables). The correlation between SES and MA is .256 (see output above). Accordingly, the tolerance for either of these variables is $1 - (.256)^2 = .9345$.

Output

Summary table

Step	Variable	Rsq	F(Eqn)	SigF	RsqCh	FCh	SigCh
1	In: SES	.2870	11.271	.002	.2870	11.271	.002
2	In: MA	.3202	6.358	.005	.0331	1.316	.261

Commentary

The summary table is very useful, as it enables one to see, at a glance, major aspects of the analysis. The information included here is only part of the SPSS output for such tables. Also, we changed the placement of the column labeled Variable.

Under Variable is indicated the variable entered (In) at each step. Although in the present example only one variable was entered at each step, more than one variable may be entered at any given step.

Rsq is the squared multiple correlation of the dependent variable with all the independent variables that have been entered up to and including a given step. Thus, for Step 1, it is the squared correlation between MOT (the dependent variable) and SES, whereas in Step 2, it is the squared multiple correlation of MOT with SES and MA.

F(Eqn) is the *F* ratio for the equation at a given step, that is, for all the independent variables that have been entered up to and including a given step. Equivalently, it is the test of Rsq at the given step. Thus, the F(Eqn) at Step 1 is for the equation that consists of only SES as the independent variable (or of $R^2 = .2870$), whereas the F(Eqn) at Step 2 is for the equation that consists of SES and MA as the independent variables (or of $R^2 = .3202$). In short, these are the *F* ratios (*not* F Change) reported in the output for each of the steps (see above).

RsqCh is the change, or increment, in R^2 due to the variable(s) entered at a given step. When only one independent variable is entered, RsqCh is the squared semipartial correlation of the dependent variable with the variable being entered, partialing out from it all the variables entered in the preceding steps. FCh is the F ratio for the change in R^2 at the given step. Compare these results with those given earlier at each step.

This concludes the presentation and commentaries on the output for Equation Number 1 in which *MOT* was treated as the dependent variable. *We turn now to output for Equation Number 2 in which AA* was treated as the dependent variable.

Output

Equation Number 2   Dependent Variable..   AA

Variable(s) Entered on Step Number   1..   SES

Multiple R	.50538			Analysis of Variance			
R Square	.25540	R Square Change	.25540		DF	Sum of Squares	Mean Square
Adjusted R Square	.22881	F Change	9.60431	Regression	1	1702.90067	1702.9006
Standard Error	13.31563	Signif F Change	.0044	Residual	28	4964.56600	177.3059

$F = 9.60431$ Signif $F = .0044$

-- Variables in the Equation --

Variable	B	SE B	95% Confdnce Intrvl B		Beta	Part Cor	Tolerance	T	Sig T
SES	5.26779	1.69979	1.78593	8.74965	.50538	.50538	1.00000	3.099	.0044
(Constant)	53.23303	7.59536	37.67464	68.79141					

Beginning Block Number 2. Method: Enter   MA

Variable(s) Entered on Step Number 2..   MA

Multiple R	.72890			Analysis of Variance			
R Square	.53130	R Square Change	.27590		DF	Sum of Squares	Mean Square
Adjusted R Square	.49658	F Change	15.89350	Regression	2	3542.44114	1771.2205
Standard Error	10.75833	Signif F Change	.0005	Residual	27	3125.02553	115.7416

$F = 15.30322$ Signif $F = .0000$

-- Variables in the Equation --

Variable	B	SE B	95% Confdnce Intrvl B		Beta	Part Cor	Tolerance	T	Sig T
SES	3.81862	1.42063	.90372	6.73352	.36635	.35415	.93453	2.688	.0122
MA	.92412	.23180	.44850	1.39973	.54335	.52526	.93453	3.987	.0005
(Constant)	-31.16465	22.04148	-76.39004	14.06074					

Beginning Block Number 3. Method: Enter   MOT

Variable(s) Entered on Step Number 3..   MOT

Multiple R	.80736			Analysis of Variance			
R Square	.65183	R Square Change	.12052		DF	Sum of Squares	Mean Square
Adjusted R Square	.61165	F Change	9.00020	Regression	3	4346.03240	1448.6774
Standard Error	9.44912	Signif F Change	.0059	Residual	26	2321.43427	89.2859

$F = 16.22515$ Signif $F = .0000$

-- Variables in the Equation --

Variable	B	SE B	95% Confdnce Intrvl B		Beta	Part Cor	Tolerance	T	Sig T
SES	1.67887	1.43722	-1.27538	4.63312	.16107	.13518	.70437	1.168	.2534
MA	.78925	.20850	.36067	1.21782	.46405	.43805	.89108	3.785	.0008
MOT	1.45354	.48451	.45762	2.44946	.42105	.34717	.67984	3.000	.0059
(Constant)	-30.01857	19.36297	-69.81973	9.78259					

Step	Variable	Rsq	F(Eqn)	SigF	RsqCh	FCh	SigCh
1	In: SES	.2554	9.604	.004	.2554	9.604	.004
2	In: MA	.5313	15.303	.000	.2759	15.893	.000
3	In: MOT	.6518	16.225	.000	.1205	9.000	.006

Commentary

The above are excerpts from the three steps for Equation Number 2 (see Input). See commentaries on Equation Number 1, for explanation of elements of such output. Here we comment on issues concerning substantive interpretation, specifically those of model specification. We plan to focus on the role of *SES*; therefore, we will first summarize the results for this variable at the successive steps, assuming that $\alpha = .05$ was selected a priori for tests of significance.

When *SES* is entered as the first and only variable, the *b* associated with it is 5.26779, with $t(28) = 3.099, p < .05$. Also, *SES* accounts for about 26% (R Square $= .2554$) of the variance of *AA*. Had the analysis stopped here, then, it would have been concluded that the effect of *SES* on *AA* is 5.27 or that the expected change in *AA* associated with a unit change in *SES* is 5.27.

Looking now at the results of the second step, it is noted that, whereas the effect of *SES* is still statistically significant—$t(27) = 2.688, p < .05$, its effect on *AA* (i.e., its *b*) is now shown as 3.81862. Before elaborating on the reason for the change in the *b*, we examine what happens to it when the third variable (*MOT*) is entered. Look at the results of step 3 and note that not only is the *b* for *SES* still smaller (1.67887) but also that it is statistically not significant—$t(26) = 1.168, p > .05$.

The reason the magnitude of the *b* for *SES* changes at each step is because *SES* is correlated with the variables entered in Steps 2 and 3. Although, in the present example, the effect of the addition of variables correlated with *SES* has led to decreases in the magnitude of the *b* for *SES*, the effect may be in the opposite direction. Depending on the pattern and magnitudes of the correlations among the variables under consideration, addition of variables correlated with a variable already in the equation may lead to an increase or a decrease in its *b* and/or a change in its sign.

Now, recall that the test of a *b* is equivalent to the test of the proportion of variance that the variable with which it is associated would account for if it were entered last in the analysis. Look now at Step 1 and note that *SES* accounts for about 26% of the variance in *AA*. When *MA* is added (Step 2), the Part Cor of *AA* with *SES*, partialing *MA* from the latter (i.e., a first-order semipartial correlation), is .35415. Therefore, if *SES* were to be entered after *MA*, it would be shown to add about .13 (i.e., $.35415^2$) to the proportion of variance accounted for (i.e., increment in R^2), or about 13% of the variance. Further, if *SES* were to be entered after *MA* and *MOT*, it would be shown to increment R^2 by only about .018, or add about 2% to the variance accounted for ($.13518^2$ x 100; see Part Cor at Step 3, which at this step are second-order semipartial correlations).

Several comments will now be made about this analysis, beginning with the most important issue, that of model specification. As we have said so often, the regression equation is meant to reflect the model under consideration. Now, when specification errors were discussed (e.g., in Chapter 17), it was pointed out that probably the gravest of such errors is the omission of relevant variables that are correlated with the variables in the equation. Stated differently, this is tantamount to estimating and testing a misspecified model. It is from this perspective that the results of the analysis reported here have to be viewed.

Needless to say, the three different models reflected in the three steps reported above cannot all be valid. In fact, in light of the results of Step 3, the validity of the models reflected in Steps 1 and 2 has to be questioned. But this is only part of the story. Remember that the analysis was carried out in steps in order to show and comment on some of the intermediate results, as was just done in connection with *SES*. Assume now that the researcher has acted as he or she should have and formulated the model a priori on the basis of theory, *not* post hoc on the basis of examining the results. Assume further that a single-stage model was formulated, according to which *SES*, *MA*, and *MOT* affect *AA*. This model is displayed as (*a*) of Figure 18.3, where the three independent variables are depicted as correlated exogenous variables (see above), as indicated by the curved lines connecting them.

On the basis of the analysis (i.e., Step 3), it would be concluded that the effect of *SES* on *AA* is statistically not significant. The same conclusion would, of course, be reached when a researcher uses a default model by regressing *AA* on the three independent variables. Be that as it may, the researcher would probably conclude that *SES* is not a relevant variable, so far as Academic Achievement is concerned, and would probably revise the model by deleting *SES*.[11] Because *SES* is correlated with *MA* and *MOT*, its deletion would affect the magnitudes of the *b*'s for the remaining variables. Consequently, a new analysis would have to be done—one in which *AA* is regressed on *MA* and *MOT* only. For completeness, we report some results of such an analysis.

The regression equation for the "revised" model is

$$AA' = -29.61592 + .81602MA + 1.73441MOT$$

Compare these *b*'s with those obtained for the same variables before the deletion of *SES* (i.e., Step 3, above). R^2 for this analysis is .63355, as compared with R^2 of .65183 obtained in the analysis in which *SES* was also included (i.e., Step 3). The difference between these R^2's (.01828) was shown above to be the increment in the proportion of variance that is due to *SES* when it is entered last in the analysis.

Because the revised model involves only two independent variables, you may find it useful to calculate these and other results (e.g., tests of *b*'s) by hand, following the example given in the beginning of this chapter. You will find summary information you will need (i.e., correlations, means, and standard deviations) in the beginning of the output given above.

Suppose now that a single-stage model is not tenable from a theoretical perspective. Assume, for example, that the researcher reasons that *SES* does not have a direct effect on *AA* but that it does affect it indirectly through *MOT*. Stated differently, the researcher hypothesizes that the effect of *SES* on *AA* is mediated by *MOT*. Note that the status of *MA* in the model has also to be specified. For illustrative purposes, we will show two alternative models.

In (*b*) of Figure 18.3, *SES* and *MA* are treated as correlated exogenous variables, both affecting *MOT*, and the three affecting *AA*. However, it was already shown that the direct effect of *SES* on *AA* is statistically not significant. In addition, it was shown in the earlier analysis (i.e., Equation Number 1) that the direct effect of *MA* on *MOT* is statistically not significant. The model may then be revised to reflect these findings (but see our earlier comments about model revision and model testing).

But what if model (*c*) of Figure 18.3 was formulated by the researcher? According to this model, only *SES* is treated as an exogenous variable whose effect on *AA* is mediated by both

---

[11]As was pointed out earlier, we are overlooking here the important distinction between substantive importance and statistical significance.

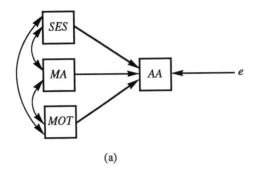

(a)

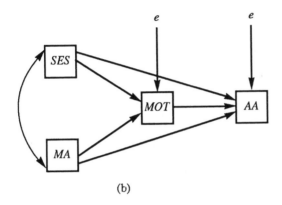

(b)

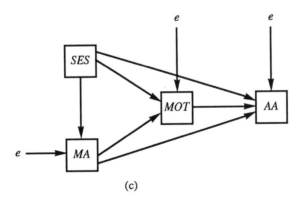

(c)

Figure 18.3

MA and *MOT*. In this model, the effects of *SES* on *AA* and that of *MA* on *MOT* are the same as in the preceding models. Accordingly, the researcher may decide to revise the model.

We urge you *not* to worry about the details of the alternative models, about the methods one would use in analyzing them, or about issues concerning model revision. All we want to do at this stage is impress upon you that everything hinges on the model the researcher uses wittingly or unwittingly. A researcher who advances model (*a*) would have to conclude, on the basis of the illustrative data, that *SES* is not a relevant variable. However, a researcher who advances model (*b*) or (*c*) might conclude that, although *SES* does not affect *AA* directly, it is an important variable, as it affects *AA* indirectly via *MOT* in model (*b*) and via *MOT* and *MA* in model (*c*). Parameter estimation and the testing of models such as those depicted in (*b*) and (*c*) are illustrated in Chapter 24.

For illustrative purposes, we focused on the status of *SES*. Needless to say, the roles of all the variables are specified by the given model, and their effects also have to be examined.

SAS

It was said above that, instead of using raw data, summary data will be used for the SAS run. We do this in order to demonstrate that, having the necessary summary data, most of the regression results can be obtained. This is particularly useful when working with a large data set or when replicating other researchers' analyses. We believe you will benefit greatly from practicing reanalysis, as well as analyses of alternative models, of summary data from published reports (e.g., journal articles). Not only will this enhance your understanding of the analytic method used, but it will also lead to a better understanding of what a given author has done and how he or she has interpreted the results.

Various computer packages (e.g., SAS, SPSS) have options for using summary data as input. Raw data were used as input for the analysis with SPSS (see above); therefore, we thought it would be useful to illustrate the analysis of summary data using another package, namely SAS. The summary data necessary are means, standard deviations, correlation matrix, and number of subjects. Instead of standard deviations and the correlation matrix, a variance-covariance matrix (often referred to as a covariance matrix) among the variables can be used, because the two are equivalent.

Having this information, analyses proceed in the same manner as when raw data are used as input. The results are the same, regardless of the type of input used. Obviously, analyses dealing with scores of individual subjects or that require such scores (e.g., predicted scores, residual analysis) cannot be applied when the input is in the form of summary data.

The reporting of summary statistics of the kind mentioned above is essential for an understanding of the results, not just because someone may wish to reanalyze the data. Therefore, chances are that, when you wish to reanalyze data from a published report, you will have the summary data necessary to do this. Unfortunately, this is not always the case. For example, some researchers report the correlation matrix but *not* the standard deviations. Under such circumstances, only regression equations with standardized coefficients can be calculated. We reiterate: Failure to report standard deviations constitutes poor reporting regardless of whether or not a reanalysis of the data is contemplated.

In view of our detailed analyses and commentaries on the results in connection with the SPSS output, we limit our illustration of the use of summary data as input to a regression analysis in which *AA* is regressed on *SES*, *MA*, and *MOT*. This same analysis was done above at Step 3 of the SPSS run. The summary data we use as input were obtained from the SPSS run (see beginning of the output in the preceding section).

Input

```
TITLE 'TABLE 18.1';
DATA T181 (TYPE=CORR);
```

```
INPUT _TYPE_ $ 1–4 _NAME_ $ 5–8 AA MA SES MOT;
CARDS;
MEAN        75.533 97.967 4.233 14.533
STD         15.163  8.915 1.455  4.392
N           30     30     30     30
CORR AA  1.000   .637   .505   .653
CORR MA   .637 1.000   .256   .313
CORR SES .505   .256 1.000   .536
CORR MOT .653   .313   .536 1.000
PROC PRINT;
PROC REG DATA=T181;
   MODEL AA=SES MA MOT/ALL;
```

Commentary

TYPE=CORR on the DATA statement signifies that a correlation matrix will be read in.

On the INPUT statement, TYPE, which is indicated to occupy the first four columns of the input lines (i.e., $ 1–4), is used to identify the specific information read in. Thus, TYPE for the first line of data is MEAN (i.e., means of the variables named on the INPUT statement; see above). For the second line of the data, TYPE identifies the information as the STD (standard deviation). For the third line, TYPE is N (number of subjects). For the remaining lines, TYPE indicates CORRelation coefficients. Each line represents one line of the correlation matrix for the four variables under consideration.

NAME, which occupies the next four columns (i.e., $ 5–8) on the INPUT statement, is used for variable names. Note that these four columns are left blank for the other TYPEs read in before the correlation matrix.

PROC PRINT asks for the printing of the input.

PROC REG is the procedure used here to do the regression analysis. Other SAS procedures can also be used for regression analysis—see Chapter 1 in *SAS/STAT guide for personal computers* (SAS Institute Inc., 1987) or in *SAS user's guide: Statistics* (SAS Institute Inc., 1985c, for mainframe). Note that the data set to be used is identified on the PROC statement.

On the MODEL statement, the variable to the left of the equal sign is the dependent variable (i.e., *AA*). To the right of the equal sign are the independent variables. ALL refers to the printing of all the available statistics.

More than one model statement may be used. Thus, three model statements would be required, if one wanted to obtain some of the results obtained earlier from SPSS when these data were entered in three separate steps. One MODEL statement would specify only *SES* as the independent variable. Another would specify *SES* and *MA* as the independent variables, and yet another would specify *SES*, *MA*, and *MOT* as the independent variables. *It is the last MODEL that is used here.*

Output

Dependent Variable: AA

Analysis of Variance

Source	DF	Sum of Squares	Mean Square	F Value	Prob>F
Model	3	4346.72825	1448.90942	16.232	0.0001
Error	26	2320.85225	89.26355		
C Total	29	6667.58050			

Root MSE	9.44794	R-square	0.6519	
Dep Mean	75.53300	Adj R-sq	0.6118	

Parameter Estimates

Variable	DF	Parameter Estimate	Standard Error	T for H0: Parameter=0	Prob > |T|	Type I SS	Standardized Estimate	Squared Semi-Partial Corr Type I	Toleran
INTERCEP	1	-30.005521	19.36101598	-1.550	0.1333	171157	0		
SES	1	1.667771	1.43703071	1.161	0.2564	1700.399717	0.16003474	0.25502500	0.704073
MA	1	0.789093	0.20847384	3.785	0.0008	1839.307051	0.46394283	0.27585824	0.891107
MOT	1	1.456944	0.48454852	3.007	0.0058	807.021482	0.42200728	0.12103663	0.679636

Commentary

The preceding consists of results of the overall analysis followed by the regression equation and associated statistics. Note that some of the labels used are different from those used in SPSS. For example, what is referred to as Model in SAS is referred to as Regression in SPSS; what SAS labels Error, SPSS labels Residual; Parameter Estimate in SAS is B in SPSS. Nevertheless, you should encounter no difficulties in discerning what most of the terms refer to, especially if you compare the outputs from the two programs. Incidentally, the small discrepancies between results of the two programs are primarily due to our input of summary statistics to three decimal places.

There are, however, a couple of terms that may baffle you, because they are qualified by the designation Type I. Thus, although you will probably figure out that SS stands for Sum of Squares, it is safe to assume that you will be wondering what a Type I SS means. Further, assuming that your knowledge of semipartial correlation is based on the presentation in this chapter or on similar presentations in other sources, you will surely wonder about the meaning of a Squared Semi-Partial Corr Type I, as we have made no mention of different types of such correlations. Before explaining the meaning of these terms, it will be pointed out that SAS identifies them as Type I to distinguish them from what are labeled as Type II in SAS PROC REG. The latter were *not* included in the output given above.

It goes without saying that it is always important to study the manual for the computer program one is using in order to become familiar with what the program does, how it does it, and what output it provides. However, manuals often provide insufficient information. Moreover, because presentations in such manuals tend to be technical, they probably seem cryptic to many a person not familiar with the specific analytic technique being presented. As a case in point, here is what the *SAS/STAT guide for personal computers* (SAS Institute Inc., 1987) says about the two aforementioned terms:

SS1 prints the sequential sum of squares (Type I SS) along with the parameter estimates for each term in the model. See Chapter 9, "The Four Types of Estimable Functions," for more information on the different types of sums of squares. (p. 789)

SSCOR1 prints the squared semi-partial correlation coefficients using Type I sums of squares. This is calculated as SS/SST, where SST is the corrected total SS. If NOINT is used, the uncorrected total SS is used in the denominator. (p. 788)

We believe that many a user will be at a loss when attempting to decipher the preceding. It can be argued that it is not the function of manuals to teach the novice but rather to provide succinct information to the knowledgeable user. One may even be inclined to agree with such assertions, when faced with the ever-expanding sizes and numbers of manuals, threatening to overwhelm even seasoned users. SAS, for example, publishes a number of manuals. The one from which we have just quoted is 1028 pages long.

Be that as it may, we remind you of our exhortations to become fully familiar with the program you are using. To demonstrate how important this is, it will be noted that, although the output from the mainframe version of the same program is identical to that given above, the *squared* semipartial correlations are *mislabeled* as "*SEMI-PARTIAL CORR.*" The problem is exacerbated as the error is repeated in the manual: "SCORR1 prints the semi-partial [sic] correlation coefficients using Type I sum of squares" (*SAS user's guide: Statistics, version 5 edition*, SAS Institute Inc., 1985c, p. 660). Incidentally, this is *all* that the manual for the mainframe states. Compare with the statement in the manual for the PC version (see above) and notice that the additional explanations given in it may help a new user discern the meaning of the term. We assume that the additional explanations will be incorporated in the manual for Version 6 of the mainframe.

As you may recall, we have suggested that you run an example(s) with which you are thoroughly familiar when you are trying to learn about a given computer program. We have also suggested that you compare the output of such a program with output from one or more other programs. It is this latter route we will take to illustrate what might occur to you, if you tried to discern the meaning of the terms under consideration by comparing the SAS output with that of SPSS, given earlier.

Beginning with the Squared Semi-Partial Corr Type I, we will assume that you are at a loss about its meaning and that you are perusing the SPSS output in search of results equal to the ones reported here. For the sake of simplicity, we will also assume that the SPSS analysis was carried out in the three steps as we reported them above. If you now inspect the SPSS output, you will notice that each of the three terms listed in SAS under Squared Semi-Partial Corr Type I is reported separately, in the same sequence, at each of the SPSS steps, under R Square Change. Because a Summary Table was also included, this can also be seen at a glance in the column labeled RsqCh (R Squared Change).

Regardless of where you look, we believe that finding these values in the SPSS output, or for that matter in output from some other program, you may still be confused. The reason we say this is that the values reported in SAS refer to different orders of correlations. Thus, the first value is a squared zero-order correlation; the second is a squared first-order semipartial correlation; the third is a squared second-order semipartial correlation. Had the problem consisted of more than three variables, then a fourth term would have been a squared third-order semipartial correlation, and so forth.

We would like to emphasize that the values reported in SAS under the heading of Squared Semi-Partial Corr Type I are *not* wrong. But they may, in our opinion, confuse inexperienced users. What the column consists of is an incremental partitioning of R^2.

Having grasped what is meant by Type I semipartial correlations in SAS, it is rather straightforward to see that SS Type I is sum of squares corresponding to the given proportion of variance a variable is said to increment. In other words, it is an incremental partitioning of the sum of squares. Earlier, it was shown how regression and residual sums of squares can be obtained from proportions of variance accounted for and vice versa. The same principle applies to incremental partitioning of variance and sum of squares. Specifically, multiplying the proportion of variance a given variable increments by the total sum of squares, Σy^2, yields the sum of squares incremented by the variable in question. This, then, is Type I SS in SAS.

For the present example, $\Sigma y^2 = 6667.58050$ (see output, above). Thus, multiplying the first Type I Squared Semi-Partial Corr by this value yields 1700.39972, which is the first value reported under Type I SS—similarly for the remaining terms, which you may wish to recalculate. This is why SAS refers to this Type I as the sequential sum of squares (see quotation, above).

One final comment about the comparison of the two outputs. Overlooking slight discrepancies between the results in the two outputs mentioned earlier, you can see the sequential sum of squares in SPSS by inspecting the regression sum of squares in each of the three steps. The regression sum of squares at Step 1 is what *SES* increments. As the regression sum of squares at Step 2 is for *SES and MA*, it follows that the difference between the two regression sums of squares is due to what *MA* increments—similarly, for variables entered in subsequent steps. The identical approach is used to obtain the proportion of variance incremented by each variable as it enters into the analysis.

SHRINKAGE

It will be recalled that the least squares solution is aimed at arriving at a set of weights (the *b*'s) that when applied to the independent variables will maximize the correlation between them and the dependent variable.[12] Now, although it stands to reason that sample data used for parameter estimates contain sampling errors, these are not taken into account when the least squares solution is applied. Thus, for example, when the squared multiple correlation is calculated, the zero-order correlations among the variables are taken at face value, even though they are expected to vary, to a greater or lesser extent, from one sample to another. In short, the correlations are treated as being error-free, despite the fact that this is probably never true.

What the preceding amounts to is that there is a certain degree of capitalization on chance when sample data are used for the estimation of the population squared multiple correlation, which tends to lead to inflated, or positively biased, estimates. Consequently, attempts have been directed toward estimating the degree of bias by calculating what has come to be called the shrunken, or adjusted, squared multiple correlation.

Various formulas were proposed to estimate the amount of shrinkage of the squared multiple correlation (for reviews, see Carter, 1979; Cotter & Raju, 1982). Following is one of the more frequently used "shrinkage" formulas:

$$\hat{R}^2 = 1 - (1 - R^2)\frac{N - 1}{N - k - 1} \tag{18.16}$$

where $\hat{R}^2$ = shrunken, or adjusted, squared multiple correlation; R^2 = squared multiple correlation calculated for the given sample; N = sample size; k = number of independent variables, or predictors. Formula (18.16) is used in most computer programs for regression analysis (e.g., SAS, SPSS), and the results are generally labeled Adjusted R Square.

The application of (18.16) will be illustrated for $R^2 = .65183$, which was obtained above for the regression of *AA* on *SES*, *MA*, and *MOT* (see SPSS output for Step 3 or SAS output). In this example, $N = 30$, and $k = 3$. Therefore,

$$\hat{R}^2 = 1 - (1 - .65183)\frac{30 - 1}{30 - 3 - 1} = .61165$$

Compare with the output given previously.

For the present example, therefore, the estimated shrinkage of R^2 is about .04. Examination of (18.16) will reveal that the estimated shrinkage is affected by the magnitude of R^2 and by the ratio of the number of independent variables to sample size. Other things equal, the larger the R^2, the smaller the amount of estimated shrinkage. Assume, for example, that R^2

---

[12]See The Regression Equation, earlier in this chapter.

= .30, but that N and k are the same as above. Applying (18.16), it is found that the adjusted $R^2 = .219$. The estimated shrinkage is now .081, as compared to .04, obtained above.

The larger the ratio of the number of independent variables to sample size, the larger the estimated shrinkage. Using again the numerical example analyzed above, let us assume that the same R^2 was obtained but that the number of independent variables was 6 instead of 3. Applying (18.16), it is found that the adjusted $R^2 = .561$. Thus, for the R^2 under consideration, a 1/5 ratio of independent variables to subjects yields an estimated shrinkage of .09, as compared with .04 obtained previously, where the ratio was 1/10.

To underscore the importance of the ratio of the number of independent variables to sample size being small, it will be pointed out that in the extreme case when the number of independent variables is equal to the number of subjects minus one, the multiple correlation will be perfect, regardless of the variables used, and regardless of what their relations with the dependent variable are in the population. This can be easily illustrated when considering a zero-order correlation. When only two subjects are used, the correlation is necessarily perfect (1.0 or -1.0), as a straight line may be drawn between the two points representing the two subjects. This will be so no matter what the variables are (e.g., shoe size and social security number; telephone number and age), so long as the two subjects differ on them. The same principle holds for multiple independent variables.

Although the extreme situation described in the preceding paragraph may be rare, many studies come dangerously close to it; yielding extremely unstable, hence, untrustworthy, results. The importance of being sensitive to such occurrences is well illustrated by the following episode related by Lauter (1984):

Professor Goetz cites as an example a major recent civil case in which a jury awarded hundreds of thousands of dollars in damages based on a statistical model presented by an economist testifying as an expert witness. The record of the case shows, he says, that the economist's model was extrapolated on the basis of *only six observations* [italics added]. (p. 10)

According to Goetz, the model was never challenged by the defense attorney, because "the poor guy didn't know what to ask" (p. 10).

Shrinkage can be minimized by increasing the size of the sample in relation to the number of independent variables. As a rule of thumb, a ratio of 1/30 (i.e., 30 subjects per independent variable) has been suggested. For our numerical example, this would mean 90 subjects instead of the 30 we have used. Assuming that 90 subjects were used, and the same R^2 was obtained, applying (18.16), the adjusted $R^2 = .63968$. The estimated shrinkage would be .012, as compared with .04 obtained above.

Although rules of thumb of the kind given above are useful as safeguards against flagrant overestimation of R^2, it should be clear from our discussions in Chapters 9 and 15 that sample size should be determined more rationally, in light of decisions regarding effect size, significance level (α), and power of the statistical test ($1 - \beta$). In the aforementioned chapters, it was pointed out that the most complex decision has to do with effect size. This decision becomes especially complex in designs of the kind considered here, as different aspects of the model may be tested. It will suffice to remind you of the distinction made earlier between a test of R^2 and tests of individual regression coefficients (b's). Obviously, decisions regarding effect size cannot be made without deciding first which of the preceding will be tested.

We will not go into the details involved in such decisions nor into procedures used to arrive at sample size after having made them. (For a good discussion, along with tables, see Cohen & Cohen, 1983, pp. 116–119; Cohen, 1988, Chapter 9; see also Milton, 1986.) We do, however, wish to caution you against facile solutions. For example, it is rather tempting to select some R^2, perhaps following some convention, as an effect size and, using the number of independent variables, the level of significance, and power, look up the sample size required in tables such as those provided by Cohen and Cohen (1983). It is, however, very important not to lose sight of the fact that not only is the use of proportion of variance accounted for as an effect size of dubious value but also that R^2 is population specific. Making matters even worse is the fact that R^2 provides no information about what is probably of greatest interest, namely the effects of specific variables.

Two final comments will be made. One, our presentation was limited to formula-based estimates of shrinkage. An alternative approach that many authors deem preferable is cross validation (for a description and relevant references, see Pedhazur, 1982, pp. 149–150).

Two, all we said about shrinkage is predicated on the use of *probability samples*. It should be clear that, when "samples of convenience" are used, there is no way of telling what might happen. But when nonprobability samples are utilized, the problem of shrinkage pales in comparison to very serious problems that arise concerning the validity of the research endeavor altogether.

MULTICOLLINEARITY

Issues concerning adverse effects of intercorrelations among independent variables are generally discussed under the heading of multicollinearity. There is no consensus about the meaning of this term.

Some use it to refer to the existence of any correlations among the independent variables, whereas others reserve the term to describe a situation in which the independent variables are highly correlated, although there is, understandably, no agreement what "high" means. Still others speak of different degrees of multicollinearity. (Pedhazur, 1982, p. 233)

In what follows, we comment briefly on approaches to the detection of multicollinearity, some of its adverse effects, and proposed remedies.[13]

DETECTION

Multicollinearity refers to correlations among the independent variables only. Therefore, in designs with only two independent variables, it is sufficient to inspect the zero-order correlation between them. In designs with more than two independent variables, this is no longer the case, as it is possible, for example, for the zero-order correlations between independent variables to be relatively low and for the squared multiple correlation of an independent variable with the rest of the independent variables to be high. After all, this is why one resorts to multiple regression analysis in the first place.

Various approaches to the detection of multicollinearity are based on analyses of properties of the correlation matrix among the independent variables (e.g., the determinants of such matrices; see Pedhazur, 1982, pp. 233–235). Such approaches will not be presented here (see Belsley et al., 1980, Chapter 3, for a detailed presentation; see also Mansfield & Helms,

---

[13]For a more detailed discussion, including sources of ambiguity in the use of the term multicollinearity, numerical examples, and relevant references, see Pedhazur (1982, pp. 232–247).

1982). Instead, the concept of tolerance, which was explained earlier in connection with the SPSS output, will be considered.

The idea behind tolerance, it will be recalled, is to determine the proportion of variance that is unique to a given independent variable. Inspection of the tolerance for each variable, therefore, can be useful in pinpointing variables for which multicollinearity is high. Various computer programs include an option for printing tolerance as part of the output.[14] Examples of such output were given earlier for SPSS and SAS.[15] In the event you are using a program that does not include tolerance as part of its output, you can calculate it readily by applying the following formula:

$$\text{Tol}_i = \frac{(1 - R^2)F_i}{(N - k - 1)\beta_i^2} \tag{18.17}$$

where Tol_i = tolerance for the ith independent variable; R^2 = squared multiple correlation of the *dependent* variable with all the independent variables; F_i = the F ratio for the testing of the regression coefficient for the ith variable; β_i = standardized coefficient for the ith variable. Note that the terms in (18.17) are reported routinely by almost any program for multiple regression analysis.

For illustrative purposes, (18.17) will be used to calculate tolerance for *SES* in the numerical example analyzed earlier in this chapter. For this example, $N = 30$, and $k = 3$. From the SPSS output given earlier, $R^2 = .65183$; $\beta = .16107$; $T = 1.168$. Recall that $F = t^2$. Therefore, in the application of (18.17) the preceding t is squared.

$$\text{Tol}_{SES} = \frac{(1 - .65183)(1.168)^2}{(30 - 3 - 1)(.16107)^2} = .70416$$

The same value, within rounding, is reported in the outputs for SPSS and SAS, given earlier in this chapter. As an exercise, you may wish to calculate the tolerance for the other two independent variables and compare your results with the outputs.

ADVERSE EFFECTS

Multicollinearity has adverse effects on regression analysis and may even render the results uninterpretable. To begin with, it will be recalled that, in the calculation of the regression coefficient for each variable, the other variables are partialed out, or controlled for. It, therefore, stands to reason that the magnitudes of the b's are affected by high multicollinearity. Although generally speaking, high multicollinearity leads to a reduction in the magnitudes of b's, the nature of the specific effects of multicollinearity are complex, as they depend on the pattern and magnitudes of intercorrelations among all the variables, including the dependent variable. For a detailed discussion, including research examples, see Pedhazur (1982, pp. 237–245, 254–258).

---

[14]Some computer programs provide other relevant information, or warn the user of the presence of high multicollinearity. MINITAB uses the latter approach.

[15]Computer programs offer various other options for detection of multicollinearity. Of the programs reviewed in Chapter 16, SAS offers the most detailed ones.

Multicollinearity may occur as a result of, among other things, poor model specification and measurement related issues. A prime example of the latter is the use of multiple indicators of the same variable (e.g., several measures of mental ability, job satisfaction) in a regression analysis. When this is done, the indicators are necessarily treated as distinct variables. Partialing such "variables" in the process of calculating partial regression coefficients is tantamount to partialing a variable from itself. Surely, this is not the researcher's intention when he or she attempts to determine the effect of the variable. However, this is what takes place anyway. We do not think it necessary to elaborate on the strange conclusions that may be reached because of the use of multiple indicators in regression analysis. Unfortunately, the research literature is replete with them (for examples, see Pedhazur, 1982, e.g., pp. 254–258).

We hope that you will not construe the preceding comments as an argument against the use of multiple indicators. As you may recall, we stressed the very important role of multiple indicators in various places (e.g., Chapter 4). The correct conclusion to be reached from the foregoing comments is that multiple indicators have no place in a regression analysis, as they may wreak havoc in the results.

The inclusion of multiple indicators in a regression analysis can be viewed, in a broader sense, as an instance of model misspecification, as distinct variables and indicators of the same variable are treated on the same level of discourse; that is, they are all treated as distinct, albeit correlated, variables. Multiple indicators are integral to structural equation modeling (*SEM*) in which the measurement model is distinguished from the structural model (see Chapters 23 and 24).

High multicollinearity also has an adverse effect on the stability of regression coefficients. This can be clearly seen upon examination of the formula for the standard error of such coefficients. Examine (18.13) and notice that tolerance is part of the denominator. The lower the tolerance, the larger the standard error of the b. As the test of the b consists of dividing it by its standard error, thereby obtaining a t ratio (see earlier discussion and illustrations), it follows that, other things being equal, the higher the multicollinearity, the smaller the t ratios for tests of the b's and the wider are the confidence intervals for the b's.

In the face of high multicollinearity, it may turn out that most, even all, of the b's are statistically not significant, despite the fact that R^2 may be relatively high and statistically significant. Although this may appear puzzling, even contradictory, it really is not. R^2 indicates the proportion of variance accounted for by the independent variables taken simultaneously, whereas a test of a b is addressed to the proportion of variance added uniquely by the variable in question.[16]

REMEDIES

Concluding their thorough review of multicollinearity, Farrar and Glauber (1967) stated: "It would be pleasant to conclude on a note of triumph that the problem has been solved . . . Such a feeling, clearly, would be misleading. Diagnosis, although a necessary first step, does

---

[16]In the next section, dealing with curvilinear regression, we return to some of the points made here about the effects of multicollinearity on the magnitudes and tests of significance of the b's as well as on squared semipartial correlations.

For an excellent discussion of seemingly contradictory results of different tests of significance in multiple regression analysis, see Cramer (1972).

not insure cure" (p. 107). The difficulties stem from issues concerning theoretical formulation regarding the phenomena under study and research design. As Pedhazur (1982) put it: "High multicollinearity is symptomatic of insufficient, or deficient, information, which no amount of data manipulation can rectify" (p. 247).

Remedies that come most readily to mind are probably the least appropriate. For example, in the face of high multicollinearity, it is tempting to delete some of the variables that appear to cause the problem and then to reanalyze the data. It should, however, be recognized that steps toward detection of multicollinearity are taken in what is presumably a correctly specified model. Deletion of variables, under such circumstances, would constitute introduction of specification errors.

Probably one of the most detailed discussions of various approaches to deal with, or offset, the effects of multicollinearity will be found in Belsley et al. (1980, Chapter 4; see also Chatterjee & Price, 1977, Chapter 7). Among proposed remedies is the grouping of highly intercorrelated variables in blocks, either on the basis of judgment or as a result of the application of principal components or factor analysis. However, the most important question of why variables placed in a given block are highly correlated still has to be faced and answered. Are, for example, variables treated as a block highly correlated because they are actually multiple indicators of the same variable (see above), or are some of the variables in the given block causes of other variables in the same block? If the latter answer is plausible, then the analysis and testing of a single-stage model is inappropriate. In short, the most important question, that of model specification, still has to be faced.

CURVILINEAR REGRESSION ANALYSIS

Several times earlier, we drew attention to the potential deleterious consequences of not verifying whether the regression is indeed linear. Linearity, and departure from it, were discussed in Chapter 17 in connection with assumptions underlying regression analysis. Among other things, it was shown, through a numerical example, that, when the assumption of linearity is violated, application of linear regression leads to erroneous conclusions regarding the effect of the independent variable on the dependent variable (see Table 17.4 and the analysis related to it).

For some research problems, the objective is *not* to apply linear regression in the first place but to study nonlinear relations among variables. Thus, on the basis of theoretical considerations, it may be expected that the effect of the independent variable, X, on the dependent variable, Y, is *not* constant, as in linear regression, but that it varies for different values of X. Examples of such expectations abound in broad areas of the study of growth, learning, attitude formation and change, to name but a few (for a hypothetical example, see Chapter 3, Figure 3.1, and the discussion related to it).

The topic of nonlinear relations is quite complex. In the present section, we introduce only some elementary ideas about polynomial regression, which is probably the simplest approach to the study of curvilinear relations within the context of ordinary least-squares solutions. More advanced presentations, including analytic approaches for models for which ordinary least-squares solutions are inappropriate, will be found in, among other sources, Draper and Smith (1981), Kmenta (1971), Pindyck and Rubinfeld (1981), and Williams (1959).

THE POLYNOMIAL EQUATION

For the simplest case of one independent variable, to which this presentation is limited, the polynomial equation is one in which the independent variable is raised to a certain power. The degree of the polynomial is indicated by the highest power to which the independent variable is raised. Thus, when the independent variable, X, is raised to the second power, the equation, a second-degree polynomial, also referred to as a quadratic equation, is

$$Y' = a + b_1X + b_2X^2$$

A third-degree polynomial or a cubic equation is one in which X is raised to the third power

$$Y' = a + b_1X + b_2X^2 + b_3X^3$$

The highest degree polynomial possible for a given set of data is equal to the number of distinct values of the independent variable minus one. Thus, when X consists of only two distinct values, the equation is necessarily linear; when it consists of three distinct values, a quadratic equation may be fit, and so forth. It is, of course, not necessary to fit the highest degree polynomial equation to a set of data. For example, although, in a given set of data, it may be possible to raise X to the 5th power (i.e., X consists of 6 distinct values), theoretical considerations may lead one to hypothesize that the regression is quadratic (i.e., X is to be raised to the second power only). In sociobehavioral research, studies of trends beyond the cubic (i.e., raising X to the third power) are very rare, regardless of the number of distinct values of X.

Unlike linear regression analysis, polynomial regression analysis is carried out *hierarchically*, beginning with X, followed by X^2, then X^3, and so forth. The objective is to determine whether the powered vector of X, entered at a given step, adds meaningfully and significantly to the explanation of Y. Accordingly, some aspects of interpretations and tests of significance applied in linear regression analysis are not applicable in polynomial regression analysis. A notable case in point is the interpretation and the testing of b's.

Assuming, for the sake of discussion, that the polynomial equation consists of one independent variable, then it makes no sense to interpret a b as indicating the effect of the variable with which it is associated, while holding the other "variables" constant. Clearly, the b's are associated *not* with different variables but with the *same* variable raised to different powers. From what was said above about the analysis of polynomial regression being carried out hierarchically, and from what was said earlier about tests of significance of b's, it should also be clear that the only b that can be meaningfully tested is the one associated with the highest powered vector in the given equation. Tests of other b's in the same equation are *not* meaningful and should *not* be carried out. We elaborate on these points by way of a numerical example to which we now turn.

A NUMERICAL EXAMPLE

For the present example, we return to data given in Chapter 17, Table 17.4, which we repeat for convenience as the first two columns of Table 18.2. It will be recalled that these data were used in Chapter 17 as an example for which linear regression analysis is inappropriate. This was done by plotting the data. In addition, it was shown that the overlooking of departures from linearity resulted in the erroneous conclusion that X has a statistically nonsignificant

Table 18.2
Data for Curvilinear Regression

Y	X	X²	X³
5	1	1	1
5	1	1	1
4	1	1	1
4	1	1	1
3	1	1	1
10	2	4	8
8	2	4	8
8	2	4	8
7	2	4	8
6	2	4	8
10	3	9	27
8	3	9	27
8	3	9	27
6	3	9	27
5	3	9	27
8	4	16	64
7	4	16	64
6	4	16	64
6	4	16	64
5	4	16	64

Note. The data for Y and X were taken from Table 17.4.

effect on Y. The same data will now be subjected to a polynomial regression analysis using SPSS. Subsequently, input statements for MINITAB and SAS will be given.

SPSS

Input

```
SET LISTING='T182.LIS'.
TITLE TABLE 18.2.      POLYNOMIAL REGRESSION.
DATA LIST FREE/Y,X.    [free format input]
COMPUTE X2=X**2.       [raise X to second power]
COMPUTE X3=X**3.       [raise X to third power]
BEGIN DATA.
5   1                  [data for first subject]
.   .
5   4                  [data for last subject]
END DATA.
LIST.
REGRESSION DES/VAR Y,X,X2,X3/CRIT TOL(.00001)/STAT=ALL/
   DEP Y/ENTER X/ENTER X2/ENTER X3/
   DEP Y/ENTER X X2/SCATTERPLOT=(*PRE,X).
```

Commentary

We assume that by now you are familiar with the SPSS layout. Our comments are limited to aspects unique to this run.

CRIT refers to several Criteria that may be selected to control such aspects as variable inclusion in, or removal from, the regression equation. For illustrative purposes, we selected a criterion of very low TOLerance so that the cubic term be entered into the equation. Had the default criterion $(.01)$[17] been used, the cubic term would not have been included in the equation, despite the specification that it be entered (see ENTER X3 on regression command).

Note that, in order to do a polynomial regression analysis using the REGRESSION procedure of SPSS, the terms have to be entered in separate steps (three for the present analysis). In effect, three separate regression analyses are requested—linear in the first step, quadratic in the second, and cubic in the third.

Differences between results of successive steps provide information necessary for the decision regarding the degree of polynomial that best fits the data. For example, the difference between the R^2's obtained in the first and second steps indicates the proportion of variance incremented by the quadratic term. Similarly, the difference between the regression sums of squares for these steps indicates the regression sum of squares incremented by the quadratic term. Accordingly, when doing polynomial regression analysis, it is useful to call for a Summary Table, as much of the necessary information is included in it. Because we specified STAT=ALL, the Summary Table would be included in the output. (See SPSS manual for Summary Table option when STAT=ALL is not specified.)

We asked for a second equation in which only X and X2 are entered, for the sole purpose of illustrating a plot of predicted scores against X (see output, below).

Output

WARNING 10555, Text: .00001
TOO LOW TOLERANCE ON REGRESSION CRITERIA SUBCOMMAND—When a variable with very low tolerance is entered into a regression equation, computational problems can arise and numerical results can be inaccurate.

Correlation:

	Y	X	X2	X3
Y	1.000	.368	.255	.168
X	.368	1.000	.984	.951
X2	.255	.984	1.000	.991
X3	.168	.951	.991	1.000

Commentary

In general, it is useful to study the correlation matrix. In the present case, we included it in order to draw attention to the fact that, when a variable is raised to successive powers, high intercorrelations are bound to result. Note that, excluding the dependent variable from consideration, the lowest zero-order correlation is .951 (i.e., between X and X^3). Here is a special case of high multicollinearity (see above) that is a consequence of data transformation.[18] The implications of high multicollinearity in polynomial regression are discussed below. For now, note the warning about the very low tolerance and the potential adverse effects this may have on the results.

---

[17]Recall that we are using the PC version. The default in version 3 for the mainframe is .0001.

[18]In the discussion of multicollinearity (see above) it was pointed out that the use of zero-order correlations is inadequate for the purpose of detecting it. Yet, in cases such as the present one, even the zero-order correlations suffice to make the point.

Output

```
---------------------------------- Variables in the Equation ----------------------------------
```

Variable	B	SE B	Beta	Tolerance	T	Sig T
X	.62000	.36920	.36803	1.00000	1.679	.1104
(Const)	4.90000	1.01111			4.846	.0001

```
---------------------------------- Variables in the Equation ----------------------------------
```

Variable	B	SE B	Beta	Tolerance	T	Sig T
X	6.37000	1.62712	3.78123	.03101	3.915	.0011
X2	-1.15000	.32034	-3.46738	.03101	-3.590	.0023
(Const)	-.85000	1.78358			-.477	.6397

```
---------------------------------- Variables in Equation ----------------------------------
```

Variable	B	SE B	Beta	Tolerance	T	Sig T
X	15.83333	8.03465	9.39866	1.2392E-03	1.971	.0663
X2	-5.40000	3.54965	-16.28161	2.4609E-04	-1.521	.1477
X3	.56667	.47140	7.35420	7.5314E-04	1.202	.2468
(Const)	-6.80000	5.25357			-1.294	.2139

Commentary

The preceding are excerpts from the three steps in which the terms were entered. Examine first the b's for the linear term (X) in the three separate equations and note the large fluctuations in their magnitudes (.62, 6.37, and 15.833), which are a consequence of high multicollinearity (discussed earlier in this chapter). Examine now the columns labeled Tolerance in the three steps and note the very low values in the second and third steps, which are indicative of very high multicollinearity in the data.

Because each of the b's is a partial coefficient, it stands to reason that the size of a b for a given vector will vary greatly when vectors highly correlated with the vector in question are omitted or added to an equation. We focused on the b's for X for illustrative purposes only. The same holds true for b's of other terms of the polynomial equation.

Although the example under consideration consists of the *same* variable raised to different powers, it also serves to illustrate the general phenomenon of drastic fluctuations of b's as a consequence of high multicollinearity. Thus, whereas the specific results will vary depending, among other things, on the standard deviations of the independent variables under consideration and on the correlations of the independent variables with the dependent variable,[19] something similar to what has occurred here with respect to the b's will occur when two or more indicators of the same variable are used in a regression equation. Similar effects will also occur when variables that are highly correlated are omitted from, or added to, an equation—a topic discussed, under specification errors, in several chapters.

Examine now the Betas (i.e., standardized coefficients). As you may recall, we drew attention to the misconception that the upper limit of β is 1.00. Although the present example is admittedly extreme, because of the very high multicollinearity, we included the β's to help dispel the aforementioned misconception.

We now direct your attention to the tests of the b's in the last stage, where all the terms

---

[19]This point was discussed earlier under Adverse Effects of multicollinearity.

have been entered. Note that, assuming $\alpha = .05$ had been selected, none of the b's is statistically significant (check t table with 26 df, or take $\sqrt{F}$ from F table with 1 and 26 df). Here is an example of what we said earlier regarding adverse effects of high multicollinearity on the b's and their standard errors. It is, however, important to note that we are using this for illustrative purposes, as *only the test of the b for X3 is relevant here*. Remember that the b is a partial regression coefficient associated with a given variable, while partialing out, controlling for, the other variables. Further, the test of the b is equivalent to the test of the increment in R^2 due the variable in question when it is entered last in the analysis. But, as was pointed out above, in the present case, all the b's refer to the *same* variable raised to successive powers. Consequently, although it makes sense to test the b for X3, thereby determining whether the increment due to the cubic component is statistically significant, *over and above the linear and the quadratic components*, it makes no sense to test the other b's. For example, the test of the b for X is, in effect, addressed to the question whether the linear component is statistically significant after taking into account the quadratic and cubic components. This is not a meaningful question,[20] and this is why it was said earlier that, in polynomial regression, the analysis proceeds hierarchically.

In sum, on the basis of the test of the b for X2 in the second step, it is concluded that the quadratic term is statistically significant. On the basis of the test of the b for X3 in the third step, it is concluded that the cubic term is statistically not significant. We return to these points below.

Output

Summary table

Step	Variable	Rsq	RsqCh	FCh	SigCh
1	In: X	.1354	.1354	2.820	.110
2	In: X2	.5082	.3728	12.888	.002
3	In: X3	.5490	.0407	1.445	.247

Commentary

As indicated above, because polynomial regression proceeds hierarchically, the summary table is particularly useful. Given here are relevant excerpts of the table, from which it may be noted that .1354 of the variance of the dependent variable is due to the linear component; .3728 is due to what the quadratic adds over the linear (see RsqCh at Step 2); and .0407 is due to what the cubic adds over the linear and the quadratic (see RsqCh at Step 3). The sum of the three elements is R^2 (.5490; see Rsq at Step 3).

FCh refers to the F ratios for tests of RsqCh and are carried out by applying (18.15), which we suggest you examine now. Note that, because single terms are entered at each step, df for the numerator of the F ratio at each step equal 1 (i.e., $k_1 - k_2 = 1$). From (18.15), the denominator df equal $N - k_1 - 1$, where k_1 is the number of independent variables associated with the larger R^2. In the present case, k_1 refers to the number of terms in the larger R^2. Therefore, denominator df are 18 (20 − 1 − 1) at Step 1, 17 (20 − 2 − 1) at Step 2, and 16 (20 − 3 − 1) at Step 3.

---

[20]Incidentally, because of high multicollinearity (see above), the answer to this question is bound to be, in most instances, negative.

The F ratio at Step 1 is for the test of the linear component and is equal to the square of the t ratio for the b in the equation given at the first step (i.e., when only X is entered). The same results were reported in Chapter 17 (see the analysis of the data of Table 17.4). In Chapter 17, it was assumed that the regression is linear and, therefore, whatever the linear component did not explain was relegated to the error term. In contrast, in the present analysis, proportions of variance incremented by the quadratic and the cubic terms are identified, thereby reducing successively the error term as well as the df associated with it.

Look now at the F ratio for the quadratic term and note that the increment associated with it is statistically significant. Furthermore, the F ratio associated with this increment is equal to the squared t ratio associated with X2 at the second step when X and X2 were entered. Finally, the F ratio associated with the increment due to the cubic term is equal to the square of the t ratio for the test of the b for X3.

What it all amounts to is that, as was said repeatedly, polynomial regression analysis proceeds hierarchically. Sequential proportions of variance accounted for, or regression sums of squares (see below), are inspected and tested, and a decision when to stop is made on the basis of the criterion selected (i.e., meaningfulness and/or statistical significance).

As you may have surmised, on the basis of earlier presentations regarding the relation between regression sums of squares and proportions of variance accounted for, all that needs be done to transform sequential proportions of variance accounted for into regression sums of squares is to multiply the former by the total sum of squares (Σy^2), which, for the present example, is 70.950. Accordingly, the regression sum of squares due to each degrees of the polynomial, entered sequentially, are

$$\text{Linear: } (.1354) (70.950) = 9.61$$

$$\text{Quadratic: } (.3728) (70.950) = 26.45$$

$$\text{Cubic: } (.0407) (70.950) = 2.89$$

These terms can be easily obtained from the SPSS output (not reported here) by calculating the difference between the regression sum of squares at two adjacent steps. For example, the regression sum of squares due to the quadratic term would be obtained by subtracting the regression sum of squares for linear from the sum of squares for linear *and* quadratic terms.

A QUADRATIC EQUATION

It was shown above that the proportion of variance incremented by the cubic term (.04) is statistically not significant at the .05 level of significance. Assuming, for present purposes, that statistical significance is the sole criterion for the decision regarding the degree of polynomial that best fits the data, it would be concluded that a second-degree polynomial equation is required.

Before proceeding, we would like to stress that the foregoing should *not* be construed as a recommendation that statistical significance be used as the sole criterion. We hope that, on the basis of what we said in earlier chapters, it is clear that we believe the criterion of meaningfulness to be much more important. However, in view of our discussions of the distinction between statistical significance and substantive meaningfulness, and the complexity attendant with attempts to decide what is a substantively important effect (see Chapters 9 and 15), it should also be clear that we cannot address this question here without giving a detailed substantive example and without repeating much of our earlier comments on this complex topic. Barring the use of arbitrary guidelines for what is to be considered meaningful—a practice of which we were skeptical in earlier chapters—there is no way that we can address, for example, the question of whether the 4% of the variance that is said to be due to the cubic term is important or meaningful, statistical significance notwithstanding.

In sum, because of conventions in sociobehavioral research, it is very easy to select some level of significance, carry out the analysis, write up the results, and even have them published. The hard part is to decide what it all means, and that is, in part, what a decision about effect size entails.

Returning now to the analysis and using statistical significance as the criterion, it is decided to drop the cubic term. This necessitates a reanalysis of the data, fitting a second-degree polynomial. The quadratic equation is given at the second step of the analysis above

$$Y' = -0.85 + 6.37X - 1.15X2$$

Output

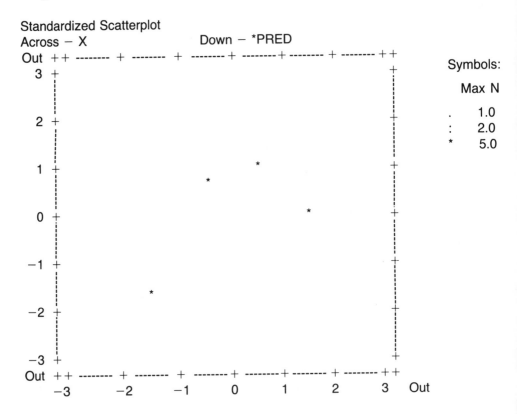

Commentary

It is always instructive to plot and study the curve for a given polynomial equation. In anticipation of a quadratic equation for the data under consideration, we called for a regression of Y on X and X2 only so that we might generate this scatterplot. Note that the ordinate consist of predicted scores and the abscissa of X. Further, each "*" stands for five points (see under Symbols).

In SPSS, such plots are reported for standardized scores. The same type of plot can be generated using raw scores. To plot the curve, use the regression equation to obtain predicted scores for the different values of the independent variable and then connect the points thus obtained. As there are four levels of X in the present data, four predicted values are obtained. They are, for $X = 1$ through 4 respectively, 4.37, 7.29, 7.91, and 6.23. Various procedures are available to plot such data (e.g., PLOT in SPSS).

OTHER COMPUTER PROGRAMS AND PROCEDURES

From the illustrative analyses given above it should be clear that any computer program for multiple regression analysis may be used to do polynomial regression analysis. The ease with which this can be accomplished, and the degree of detail in the output obtained, will vary. Some statistical packages include more than one program or procedure that may be used for polynomial regression analysis. Given below are input statements for SAS and MINITAB. In the interest of space, we do not comment on the input, nor do we provide any output. As we have stated several times earlier, one of the best ways to become familiar with a given program is to compare its capabilities and output with those of other programs used to carry out the same analysis. If you have access to these programs, we suggest you run them and compare your output with that given above. We believe that, with the aid of the output and the commentaries given above, you will be able to figure out the output from the other programs.

SAS

Input

```
TITLE 'TABLE 18.2.   POLYNOMIAL REGRESSION';
DATA T182;
    INPUT Y X;      [free format input]
    XSQ=X**2;       [raise X to second power]
    XCUB=X**3;      [raise X to third power]
    CARDS;
5   1               [data for first subject]
.   .
5   4               [data for last subject]
PROC REG;
    MODEL Y=X XSQ XCUB/ALL
```

MINITAB

Input

```
OH=0
OUTFILE 'T182'
NOTE CURVILINEAR REGRESSION.   DATA FROM TABLE 18.2
READ C1–C2
    5   1               [data for first subject]
    .   .
    5   4               [data for last subject]
LET C3=C2**2            [raise C2 to the second power. Put in C3]
LET C4=C2**3            [raise C2 to the third power. Put in C4]
```

```
NAME C1 'Y' C2 'X' C3 'X2' C4 'X3'
CORRELATION C1–C4          [generate a correlation matrix]
BRIEF 3                    [calling for "full" output]
REGRESS C1 3 C2–C4         [regress Y on X, X2, and X3]
```

CONCLUDING REMARKS

Continuous independent variables were used in this and the preceding chapter. A regression approach for the analysis of data from a design in which the independent variable is categorical is presented in the next chapter. An extension of this approach to designs consisting of multiple categorical independent variables is given in Chapter 20. Designs consisting of both categorical and continuous variables are dealt with in Chapter 21.

STUDY SUGGESTIONS

1. Given that

$$r_{y1} = .45 \quad r_{y2} = .50 \quad r_{12} = .00$$

What is $R^2_{y.12}$?

2. Following are data for 20 subjects on three variables. The data for Y and X were taken from study suggestion 1 of Chapter 17, where it was suggested that you think of the former as aggression and of the latter as hours of TV watching. If you are inclined to continue with the same substantive example, think of E as a rating of parents' education.

Y	X	E		Y	X	E		Y	X	E		Y	X	E
3	1	5		4	4	4		8	4	4		9	5	3
5	2	6		6	4	5		8	5	3		10	6	3
6	3	5		8	4	3		7	5	4		9	6	4
4	3	4		5	4	2		9	5	4		8	6	3
5	3	3		7	4	4		8	5	3		7	6	2

We recommend that you do all the necessary calculations by hand or with the aid of a calculator. If you have access to a computer and appropriate software, carry out the same analysis by computer, and compare the output with results you obtain through hand calculations.

What is (are) the
(a) Pearson correlations for all variable pairs?
(b) $R^2_{y.x,e}$?
(c) F ratio for the test of significance of $R^2_{y.x,e}$?
(d) regression sum of squares?
(e) residual sum of squares?
(f) regression equation for Y on X and E for standard scores?

(g) regression equation for Y on X and E for raw scores?

(h) t ratios for the test of the b's? Assuming you have selected $\alpha = .05$, what would you conclude on the basis of these results?

(i) proportion of variance of Y accounted for by E after X has been taken into account? What is the t ratio for the test of this increment?

3. Given that

$$r_{y1} = .5 \quad r_{y2} = .0 \quad r_{12} = .3$$

What is $r_{y(2.1)}$ equal to?

4. Given that

$$N = 150 \quad R^2_{y.1234} = .63 \quad R^2_{y.13} = .29$$

What is the

(a) proportion of variance of Y incremented by variables 2 and 4 after variables 1 and 3 have been taken into account?

(b) F ratio for the test of this increment?

(c) estimate of the shrunken (adjusted) $R^2_{y.1234}$?

5. Express $r^2_{y(2.134)}$ as a difference between two squared multiple correlations.

6. Following are: (a) a correlation matrix, (b) means (M), and (c) standard deviations (s) based on responses of 185 subjects to measures of a dependent variable, Y, and four independent variables, X_1, X_2, X_3, and X_4.

	Y	X_1	X_2	X_3	X_4
Y	1.00	.35	.42	.29	.38
X_1	.35	1.00	.23	.31	.12
X_2	.42	.23	1.00	.27	.30
X_3	.29	.31	.27	1.00	.43
X_4	.38	.12	.30	.43	1.00
M:	64.52	36.78	41.22	9.65	53.12
s:	12.62	6.06	7.17	1.89	10.17

Assuming you have access to a computer and software with the option for entry of summary data (e.g., SAS, SPSS), regress Y on the four independent variables. What is (are) the

(a) $R^2_{y.1234}$ and its associated F ratio?

(b) regression and residual sums of squares?

(c) regression equation?

(d) t ratios for the tests of the b's. Assuming you have selected $\alpha = .05$, what would you conclude on the basis of these results?

(e) proportion of variance of Y incremented by X_3 when it is entered last in the analysis? What is the t ratio for the test of this increment?

7. There is research evidence that the regression of foreign students' attitudes toward the host country on time in the country is of the form of a U-shaped curve (see Jacobson, Kumata, & Gullahorn, 1960, pp. 215–216, and references given therein). For illustrative purposes, use the following fictitious data for 35 students on attitudes toward a host country (Y; the higher the score, the more positive the attitude) and number of months in

the country (X) to carry out an analysis to test the hypothesis that the regression of Y on X is quadratic.

Y	X	Y	X	Y	X	Y	X	Y	X	Y	X	Y	X
7	2	5	6	3	12	2	18	3	24	5	30	7	36
7	2	5	6	3	12	2	18	3	24	5	30	7	36
6	2	4	6	3	12	1	18	3	24	4	30	6	36
5	2	4	6	2	12	1	18	2	24	4	30	6	36
5	2	4	6	2	12	1	18	2	24	3	30	6	36

What is (are) the
(a) proportion of variance accounted for by the linear component and the F ratio associated with it?
(b) proportion of variance due to the quadratic component and the F ratio associated with it?
(c) proportion of variance due to the cubic component and the F ratio associated with it?
(d) quadratic regression equation?
Plot the data and interpret the results along the lines indicated above (remember, however, that these data are fictitious).

Answers

1. .4525—see (18.1)
2. (a) $r_{yx} = .801$; $r_{ye} = -.369$; $r_{xe} = -.614$
   (b) $R^2_{y.xe} = .66658$—see (18.1)
   (c) $F = 16.99$ with 2 and 17 df—see (18.11)
   (d) $ss_{reg} = 48.79358$
   (e) $ss_{res} = 24.40642$
   (f) $z'_y = .92253z_x + .19715z_e$—see (18.6)
   (g) $Y' = -.19893 + 1.32007X + .37531E$—see (18.4) and (18.5)
   (h) t: 5.20   1.11   —see (18.14)
       df: 17   17
       sig. t: .0001   .2820

   The effect of parents' education (E) is statistically nonsignificant. Accordingly, one would delete it from the equation. The results where only X is used are given in study suggestion 1 of Chapter 17. (Recall, however, that we are using a small N. Moreover, we are ignoring substantive meaningfulness.)
   (i) .02422; $t = 1.11$ with 17 df (equivalent to the test of the corresponding b)
3. $-.16$—see (18.10)
4. (a) .34
   (b) $F = 66.62$ with 2 and 145 df—see (18.15)
   (c) .62—see (18.16)
5. $R^2_{y.1234} - R^2_{y.134}$
6. (a) $R^2_{y.1234} = .30849$; $F = 20.08$ with 4 and 180 df

(b) $ss_{reg} = 9040.24668$; $ss_{res} = 20264.40292$
(c) $Y' = 6.77180 + .51290X_1 + .49156X_2 + .19317X_3 + .31547X_4$
(d)

t:	3.72	4.18	.40	3.61
df:	180	180	180	180
sig. t:	.0003	.0000	.6889	.0004

Conclude to remove X_3
(e) .00062; $t = .40$ with 180 df (equivalent to the test of the corresponding b) or $F = t^2$
$= .16$ with 1 and 180 df

7. (a) .00365; $F = .12$ with 1 and 33 df
   (b) .86698; $F = 214.44$ with 1 and 32 df
   (c) .00271; $F = .66$ with 1 and 31 df
   (d) $Y' = 7.10479 - .56449X + .01528X^2$

Chapter 19
A Categorical Independent Variable

In Chapters 17 and 18, regression analysis was presented for designs with continuous independent variables. The present chapter is devoted to the application of regression analysis in designs with a categorical independent variable. Recall that a categorical variable consists of two or more mutually exclusive and exhaustive categories (e.g., treatments, marital status; see, for example, Chapters 2 and 8). Application of regression analysis in designs with more than one categorical variable is presented in the next chapter. At the conclusion of this and the next chapter, we comment on the equivalence between the approach we are presenting and the analysis of variance (ANOVA).

CODING CATEGORICAL VARIABLES

Broadly speaking, application of regression analysis in designs with categorical independent variables is similar to that in designs with continuous independent variables. In both, the objective is to use information contained in the independent variables in an attempt to determine whether, and to what extent, they affect the dependent variable or help explain it. The nature of the information is, of course, different and has to do with the distinction between continuous and categorical variables.

When the independent variable is categorical, the question addressed boils down to whether, and to what extent, being in the different groups, or categories, makes a difference so far as the dependent variable is concerned. Although the mechanics of the analytic approach to be presented are the same, regardless of how the categories were formed and regardless of substantive considerations, interpretation of the results is very much predicated on such matters. Suffice it to point out that a categorical independent variable may be used in different designs (e.g., experimental, nonexperimental) to realize why this is so.

In order to utilize information about category or group membership, it is necessary to render it in a format susceptible to analysis. In the context of regression analysis, this is accomplished by a coding process. In what follows, three coding schemes—Dummy, Effect, and Orthogonal—are presented. As is shown, *the three coding schemes yield identical results, so far as the overall analysis is concerned*, although unique characteristics make one or another more useful for some specific purpose.

Dummy Coding

Dummy coding consists of 1's and 0's, with 1 signifying membership in a category under consideration and 0 signifying *no* membership in that category. This coding scheme is also referred to as binary coding, or indicator variables. Consider, for example, a categorical variable consisting of two categories (e.g., male and female, treatment and control, black and white); 1's may be assigned to members of one of the categories (e.g., treatment) and 0's to those who are *not* in this category (e.g., control). Obviously, the codes can be reversed. We return to this point later on.

For the sake of generality and ease of reference, consecutive capital letters will be used to refer to different categories of a variable. Thus, for a variable consisting of three categories, the letters A, B, and C will be used to refer to the three categories, regardless of what they may represent (e.g., three different treatments, two treatments and a control group, three ethnic groups, three religious denominations).

Assume now that the objective is to apply dummy coding to a categorical variable consisting of three categories. This can be accomplished by creating three coded columns or vectors in each of which subjects belonging to one of the categories are identified by assigning them 1's, whereas subjects in the other categories are assigned 0's. Thus, in column 1, subjects in A are assigned 1's, whereas subjects *not* in A (i.e., those in B and C) are assigned 0's. In column 2, 1's are assigned to subjects in B and 0's to those *not* in B. In column 3, 1's are assigned to subjects in C and 0's to those *not* in C. Schematically, this looks as follows:

Category	Column 1	Column 2	Column 3
A	1	0	0
B	0	1	0
C	0	0	1

If, for example, the number of subjects in each of the categories were 100, then each of the columns would consist of 100 1's and 200 0's. Several points will be made about this coding scheme.

One, in any given column, only subjects in the category assigned 1 are uniquely identified. All others are lumped together by virtue of being assigned 0, regardless of the category to which they belong.

Two, subjects in any given category are assigned 1's in one column only. Their codes in the rest of the columns are 0's. Consequently, it is convenient to speak of a given category being identified in the column in which its subjects are assigned 1's. Thus, in the example under consideration, category A is identified in Column 1, B in Column 2, and C in Column 3.

Three, any two of the three columns are necessary and sufficient to identify the three categories. Consider Columns 1 and 2. Category A is identified in Column 1, and B is identified in Column 2. What about C? It is identified by virtue of having 0's in both columns. Thus, a category that has 0's in all the columns is also uniquely identified. As another example, consider Columns 2 and 3. A is identified by virtue of having 0's in both columns. B and C are identified respectively by virtue of having a 1 in Columns 2 and 3.

To code a categorical variable, therefore, *generate a number of vectors equal to the number of categories minus one*. In each vector, assign 1's to subjects in one of the categories and 0's to all others. Thus, a variable with four categories requires three coded vectors; one with five categories, four coded vectors; and so forth. As is noted below, the number of coded vectors necessary is equal to the number of *df* (degrees of freedom) associated with differences among categories.

A question that comes readily to mind is whether it matters which of the categories is assigned 0's in all the vectors. The answer is no, so far as the overall analysis is concerned. However, as is shown below, in a design in which one of the groups serves as a control, it is advantageous to assign 0's in all vectors to subjects belonging to it.

A NUMERICAL EXAMPLE

In Table 19.1, illustrative data are presented for 6 subjects in each of four categories, *A*, *B*, *C*, and *D* of a categorical independent variable. The column labeled *T* (treatment) consists of sequential identification numbers for the four categories. We use the label *T* for convenience, *not* to imply that the approach is limited to variables in which the categories represent treatments. Of course, any label will do, although labels that convey the nature of the variable in question are preferable (e.g., religion or *R*). The column labeled *Y* consists of the scores on the dependent variable. It is these scores that we wish to analyze in order to determine whether there are statistically significant differences among the means of the four categories.

As the numbers in *T* are used for category identification, it makes no sense to regress *Y* on *T* or to calculate the correlation between these two vectors. Recall that categories of a categorical variable differ in kind, not in degree (see Chapter 2). Therefore, not only can the assignment of the numerals be changed at will, but any set of four unique numerals will do.

In view of the preceding, you may well wonder why two identification schemes (i.e., letters and numbers) were included in Table 19.1, but the necessary coded vectors were not included. Obviously, either letters or numerals would have sufficed for identification purposes. The two were included for different purposes. Letters were included for convenience of reference to the different categories in the presentation that follows. Numerals were included so that they may be used variously in analyses by computer. To clarify the latter, we outline how a vector consisting of group identification numbers, such as *T* of Table 19.1, may be used in computer analysis.

As was noted and illustrated in connection with analyses in Chapter 18, virtually all computer programs for statistical analysis include facilities for data manipulation. Consequently, as is shown below, a computer program can be employed to generate the required coded vectors by using information contained in the column consisting of category identification. For several reasons, this approach is preferable to one in which the coded vectors are actually entered as input.

One, regardless of the number of categories, a single identification vector is sufficient. When, in contrast, coded vectors are used as input, the number of vectors required is equal to the number of categories minus one. This can become particularly laborious when the number of categories is relatively large.

Two, with a small data set, it makes little difference whether the coded vectors are entered as input or generated by computer. This is not the case with large data sets. For example, assume that instead of 6 subjects in each category, as in our example, the number was 600. Not only would the use of a single vector for category identification constitute a considerable saving in labor, it would also be less susceptible to errors of input.

Table 19.1
Illustrative data for Four Categories

Category	T	Y
	1	8
	1	8
A	1	12
	1	12
	1	10
	1	10
	2	7
	2	8
B	2	8
	2	10
	2	11
	2	10
	3	10
	3	11
C	3	14
	3	13
	3	12
	3	12
	4	12
	4	13
D	4	13
	4	15
	4	15
	4	16

Three, as is shown below, the use of a category identification column provides the greatest flexibility to generate any coding scheme one may wish.

Finally, as is also shown below, some procedures in computer programs (e.g., ANOVA in SPSS, GLM in SAS) do *not* require coded vectors, but they do require a category identification column.

In sum, including a category identification vector affords the greatest flexibility for analyzing the data by different computer programs, using different coding schemes, or different procedures.

For illustrative purposes, several computer programs will be used to analyze the data of Table 19.1. As has been our practice, excerpts of input and output, along with commentaries, will be given.

MINITAB

Input

```
OH=0
OUTFILE 'T191'
NOTE DUMMY CODING.   DATA FROM TABLE 19.1
READ C1-C2
1  8   [first subject in T 1]
.  .
1 10   [last subject in T 1]
2  7   [first subject in T 2]
.  .
2 10   [last subject in T 2]
3 10   [first subject in T 3]
```

.   .

3 12   *[last subject in T 3]*
4 12   *[first subject in T 4]*

.   .

4 16   *[last subject in T 4]*
INDICATOR C1 C3-C6
NAME C1 'T' C2 'Y' C3 'D1' C4 'D2' C5 'D3' C6 'D4'
PRINT C1-C6
REGRESS C2 3 C3-C5

Commentary

For a general description of running MINITAB in batch mode, and for an explanation of our practice in naming input and output files, see Chapter 16.

Using READ, the data of Table 19.1 are read into columns 1 and 2.

INDICATOR is used to generate a set of dummy coded vectors corresponding to the categories indicated in the column specified (C1, in the present case). MINITAB requires that the categories be identified by a set of consecutive integers (see Manual, p. 169) as exemplified by T of Table 19.1. MINITAB generates a number of coded vectors equal to the number of categories; thus, four columns (C3-C6) are required for their storage (see output, below).

As discussed above, only three dummy vectors are necessary for the present analysis. Having all four available, however, affords the flexibility of not only selecting any three that are deemed most useful for a given design but also to operate on these vectors for the purpose of generating other coding schemes (see Effect Coding, below).

NAME is used to name Column 1 as T, Column 2 as Y, and Column 3 through Column 6 as D(ummy)1—the vector in which category 1 (i.e., A) is identified; D(ummy)2—the vector in which category 2 (B) is identified; and so forth. We follow a similar practice in naming coded vectors with the other coding schemes presented later on.

PRINT calls for the printing of Columns 1 through 6.

REGRESS calls for a regression analysis (see Manual, p. 104). Note that we called for the regression of Y (C2) on C3, C4, and C5. Other combinations of three dummy vectors could be used. We comment on this point later on.

Output

Row	T	Y	D1	D2	D3	D4	
1	1	8	1	0	0	0	
2	1	8	1	0	0	0	*[first two subjects in T 1]*
.	.	.	.	.	.	.	
7	2	7	0	1	0	0	
8	2	8	0	1	0	0	*[first two subjects in T 2]*
.	.	.	.	.	.	.	
13	3	10	0	0	1	0	
14	3	11	0	0	1	0	*[first two subjects in T 3]*
.	.	.	.	.	.	.	
19	4	12	0	0	0	1	
20	4	13	0	0	0	1	*[first two subjects in T 4]*
.	.	.	.	.	.	.	

Commentary

In the interest of space, only excerpts of the listing are included. As you can see, the columns labeled T and Y comprise the data of Table 19.1, which were read as input. The next four columns are the dummy vectors generated by the INDICATOR command (see Input).

Output

s = 1.581   R-sq = 63.9%   R-sq(adj) = 58.5%

Analysis of Variance

SOURCE	DF	SS	MS	F	p
Regression	3	88.500	29.500	11.80	0.000
Error	20	50.000	2.500		
Total	23	138.500			

Commentary

These results will be identical, regardless of which coding scheme is used or which three of the four dummy vectors are used. Notice that $R^2 = .639$, indicating that about 64% of the variance in Y is due to the differences among the four categories of the independent variable; s = the standard error of estimate, or the square root of the MS Error (i.e., $\sqrt{2.500}$).

Notice also that the format of the analysis of variance table is very much like the one used in Chapter 17 (Table 17.3) to illustrate how results of regression analysis might be reported. The df for Regression (3) are equal to the number of coded vectors, which is the number of categories, or groups, minus one. The df for Error (residual) are, as before, $N - k - 1$ (24 − 3 − 1). However, whereas, in designs with continuous independent variables, k referred to the number of independent variables, in designs with categorical variables, it refers to the number of coded vectors used to represent the categorical variables. In the present example, there is only one independent variable, but k is 3, because three coded vectors are required to represent it. *Coded vectors representing a given independent variable should be treated as a set.* In the present example, any three of the four dummy vectors that were generated (see output above) represent the *same* variable. Moreover, as is shown below, other coding schemes could be used to achieve the same end.

Lest you be inclined to think that we are belaboring the obvious, it will be pointed out that we have encountered not only studies in which coded vectors were treated as if each represented a separate independent variable but also ones in which coded vectors representing *different* independent variables[1] were subjected to stepwise regression analysis. Not surprisingly, such analyses resulted in the retention of fractions of variables (for a discussion and research examples, see Pedhazur, 1982, pp. 391–392).

Needless to say, a computer program cannot distinguish between columns constituting distinct independent variables and coded vectors that represent the same independent variable. It is the researcher who must keep this distinction in mind and interpret the results accordingly.

Returning to the output given above, dividing a sum of squares by the df associated with it yields a mean square (MS). Dividing the Regression MS (29.5) by the Error MS (2.5) yields

---

[1] In Chapter 20, we show how coded vectors are used to represent more than one categorical independent variable.

$F(3, 20) = 11.8$. Assuming that $\alpha = .05$ was selected, it would be concluded that R^2 is statistically significant. Equivalently, this would lead to the rejection of the null hypothesis that the four category means are equal to each other.

Output

The regression equation is
Y = 14.0 − 4.00 D1 − 5.00 D2 − 2.00 D3

Predictor	Coef	Stdev	t-ratio
Constant	14.0000	0.6455	21.69
D1	−4.0000	0.9129	−4.38
D2	−5.0000	0.9129	−5.48
D3	−2.0000	0.9129	−2.19

Commentary

In the course of explaining the regression equation, it will be necessary to refer to the category means. They are

$$A = 10 \quad B = 9 \quad C = 12 \quad D = 14$$

To understand the meaning of the elements of the regression equation, bear in mind that, when it is applied to obtain predicted scores on the dependent variable (Y'), the codes in the coded vectors are used as scores. Let us then apply the regression equation to the first individual in category A. This individual's "scores" are: 1 on D1, and 0 on all the other vectors. Therefore,

$$Y' = 14 - 4(1) - 5(0) - 2(0) = 10$$

Several things will be noted.

One, the predicted score is equal to the mean of the group to which an individual belongs. This holds true regardless of the coding scheme, as group means are the best estimates, in the least squares sense. That is, the residual sum of squares is at a minimum when predicted scores are equal to the group means.

Two, individuals in any given group or category have the same scores on the vectors representing the independent variable. Therefore, their predicted scores are also the same: their group mean.

Three, for any category identified in a given vector, only two terms of the regression equation are pertinent: the b associated with the vector in which the category is identified, and a (the intercept). The b's for the other vectors are irrelevant, as the scores on them are 0's. For the present example, then, predicted scores for categories identified in the three dummy vectors are

$$\text{For } A: 14 - 4(1) = 10$$
$$\text{For } B: 14 - 5(1) = 9$$
$$\text{For } C: 14 - 2(1) = 12$$

In line with what was said above, these are the dependent variable means for the three categories. Incidentally, in the preceding calculations, we could have omitted the 1's, as in the present coding scheme the score in the relevant vector is always 1.

Four, the only term of the regression equation relevant for the prediction of scores for individuals in the category assigned 0's in all the vectors (D, in the present example), is a (the intercept). Note that $a = 14$, which is equal to the mean of D.

Five, from preceding points three and four, it follows that each b is equal to the deviation of the mean for the group identified in the vector with which it is associated from the mean of the group assigned 0's in all the vectors (D, in the present case). Thus, the mean of category A is 10, and its deviation from the mean of D (14) is -4, which is the reported value of b for D1. The deviation of the mean of B from the mean of D is -5 ($9 - 14$), which is the value of b for D2. The deviation of the mean of C from the mean of D is -2 ($12 - 14$), which is the value of b for D3.

In sum, the b's reflect contrasts between each category mean and the mean of the group assigned 0's in all the vectors. It follows that a test of a b amounts to a test of the difference between the mean of the group identified in the vector with which the b is associated and the mean of the group assigned 0's throughout.

Tests of this kind are of interest when it is desired to contrast each category with some comparison group. In experimental research, this is exemplified by designs consisting of several treatments and a control group. Referring to the present example, A, B, and C may be three different treatments, and D the control group.

In nonexperimental research also, it may be of interest to contrast each of several groups with some comparison group. For the example under consideration, A, B, and C may be three minority groups, and D may be the majority. The interest may be to contrast the mean dependent variable (e.g., income, attitudes) of each minority group with that of the majority.

Following Dunnett (1955), such contrasts are carried out, pursuant to an overall ANOVA (see below), by doing t tests between the mean of each treatment and the mean of the control group (see, for example, Edwards, 1985, pp. 148–150; Pedhazur, 1982, pp. 287–289; Winer, 1971, pp. 201–204). The same t ratios are obtained when the b's of the regression equation with dummy coding are tested. Thus, the t ratios given above for the b's associated with D1, D2, and D3 are identical to those obtained by calculating, pursuant to an ANOVA, three t tests between the mean of each of the categories and the mean of D. Clearly, when the design consists of several treatments and a control, it is advantageous to assign the 0's in all the vectors to the latter, thereby obviating the need to calculate the t ratios pursuant to the overall analysis.

As always, the df (degrees of freedom) associated with a t ratio for the test of a b equal those associated with the residual sum of squares (i.e., $N - k - 1$). When the t ratios are used for comparisons between each of several treatments and a control group, or between each of several groups and a comparison group, a special table prepared by Dunnett (1955) has to be consulted to check which of them is statistically significant at a given α. This table is also reproduced in various statistics books (e.g., Edwards, 1985; Kirk, 1982; Winer 1971).

For the present example, the t ratios for the comparisons between D, and A, B, C respectively are -4.38, -5.48, and -2.19 (see Output, above). The tabled values in a Dunnett table for 3 treatments and 20 df are (a) for a one-tailed test: 2.19 (.05 level), 2.97 (.01 level); and (b) for a two-tailed test: 2.54 (.05 level), 3.29 (.01 level). Assuming that a one-tailed test at the .01 level was selected a priori, it would be concluded that the difference between the means of A and D, and that between B and D, are statistically significant, whereas the difference between C and D is statistically not significant.[2]

It was indicated above that any combination of three of the four dummy vectors generated through the use of INDICATOR (see Input and Output, above) will lead to the same overall

---

[2]The topic of one- versus two-tailed tests of significance is controversial. For some discussions, see Burke (1953), Cohen (1965), and Kaiser (1960a).

results. The regression equation will, however, reflect the specific vectors used. For the example under consideration, the following three additional combinations of three dummy vectors are possible: (a) D1, D2, D4; (b) D1, D3, D4; and (c) D2, D3, D4. As an exercise, we suggest that you run these three combinations of dummy vectors. If you are using MINITAB, you can do this in the same run by adding the following three statements to the input given above:

REGRESS C2 3 C3 C4 C6
REGRESS C2 3 C3 C5 C6
REGRESS C2 3 C4 C5 C6

Study the regression equations to verify that they have the properties described above.

Dummy coding is not limited to designs consisting of several treatments and a control group. It may be used for any design in which the independent variable(s) is categorical. Under such circumstances, it makes no difference which of the categories is assigned 0's in all the coded vectors, as the tests of the b's are irrelevant. Instead, the results of the overall analysis are interpreted and may be followed by multiple comparisons among means—a topic discussed later in this chapter.

CORRELATION AMONG DUMMY VECTORS

For completeness of presentation, we describe briefly the properties of correlations among dummy coded vectors.

Input

CORRELATION C2-C5

Commentary

Although not shown earlier, this statement in which we call for the correlations among Column 2 through Column 5 was part of the input file for the analysis of data of Table 19.1.

Output

	Y	D1	D2	D3
D1	−0.300			
D2	−0.541	−0.333		
D3	0.180	−0.333	−0.333	
D4	0.661	−0.333	−0.333	−0.333

Commentary

Before commenting on these correlations, we take this opportunity to acquaint you with some terminology. Although the preceding are Pearson correlations, they are sometimes referred to by different names because of the properties of the variables being correlated. Specifically, when two dichotomous or binary variables are correlated (in our example, any two dummy vectors), it is sometimes referred to as a phi correlation coefficient. When a dichotomous variable and a continuous variable are correlated (in our example, the correlation between any dummy vector and the dependent variable), it is sometimes referred to as a point-biserial correlation coefficient. These coefficients have special properties. For example, the maximum value of a point-biserial correlation is *not* 1.00 (for a discussion of these coefficients and their properties, see Nunnally, 1978, pp. 131–134, 143–146).

Turning now to the correlations among dummy vectors, it will be noted that such vectors are always negatively correlated. The magnitudes of the correlations can be easily calculated through the following formula (see Cohen, 1968, p. 429):

$$r_{ij} = -\sqrt{\frac{n_i n_j}{(n - n_i)(n - n_j)}} \tag{19.1}$$

where n_i = sample size in category or group i; n_j = sample size in category j; n = total sample size in g categories or groups. When the sample sizes in the different categories are equal, (19.1) reduces to

$$r_{ij} = -\frac{1}{g - 1} \tag{19.2}$$

where g = number of groups or categories of the independent variable. As there is an equal number of subjects in the categories for the data of Table 19.1, the correlation between any two dummy vectors is

$$r_{ij} = -\frac{1}{4 - 1} = -.333$$

which is the same as the values reported above.

UNEQUAL SAMPLE SIZES

The example we have analyzed consisted of equal numbers of subjects in all categories. It is recommended that equal n's be used, because they lead to greater sensitivity of tests of significance and because potential distortions due to departures from assumptions underlying such tests are thereby minimized (see Li, 1964, pp. 147–148, 197–198).

The foregoing recommendation notwithstanding, a researcher may, on the basis of other considerations, decide to use unequal n's. For example, in an experimental design, subjects in unequal numbers may be randomly assigned to different treatments on the basis of the costs involved in the administration of each treatment. Similarly, in nonexperimental research, it may be decided to obtain unequal sample sizes from different populations. As long as appropriate randomization and/or sampling procedures are followed, unequal n's do not pose threats to the validity of a study.

The situation is radically different when the unequal n's are a consequence of subject attrition or nonresponse, because randomization and/or sampling is thereby abrogated. In earlier chapters (Chapters 10 and 12, and 13), we commented on the threats to validity posed by subject attrition or nonresponse. We remind you of these earlier discussions, because our comments here are limited to the very narrow aspect of the mechanics of the analysis with unequal n's. Needless to say, the most important considerations are those of validity of the research design.

With the preceding remarks in mind, it will be pointed out that, from *a strictly analytic perspective*, the use of unequal n's with dummy coding for a single independent variable poses no difficulties. The coding and the analysis proceed in exactly the same manner as with equal n's. The properties of the regression equation, including tests of significance of the b's, have the same meaning as in designs with equal n's. A numerical example of an analysis with unequal n's, using dummy coding, will be found in Pedhazur (1982, pp. 318–320).

Effect Coding

Effect coding is very similar to dummy coding. In fact, the only difference between the two schemes is that, whereas in dummy coding, one of the categories is assigned 0's in all the coded vectors, in effect coding, one of the categories is assigned -1's in all the vectors. As it makes no difference which of the categories is assigned the -1's, it is convenient to do this for either the first or the last category of the independent variable. We will use the last category. As in dummy coding, the number of coded vectors necessary is equal to the number of categories of the independent variable minus one. In each vector, one of the categories is identified by assigning 1's to its members, 0's to members of all other categories, except for members of the last category who are assigned -1's. The reason why this is called effect coding we explain later, in connection with the interpretation of the regression equation.

A NUMERICAL EXAMPLE

For comparative purposes, we will use the data analyzed in the preceding section with dummy coding (i.e., the data of Table 19.1). As with dummy coding, the coded vectors will not be entered as input. Instead, they will be generated by the computer programs we will be using. The data will be analyzed first through MINITAB and then through SPSS.

MINITAB

Input

```
OH=0
OUTFILE 'T191'
NOTE EFFECT CODING.   DATA FROM TABLE 19.1
READ C1-C2
        [data of Table 19.1 are placed here. See Input to previous
        MINITAB run, earlier in this chapter]
INDICATOR C1 C3-C6
LET C7=C3-C6    [subtract C6 from C3.   Put in C7]
LET C8=C4-C6    [subtract C6 from C4.   Put in C8]
LET C9=C5-C6    [subtract C6 from C5.   Put in C9]
NAME C2 'Y' C7 'E1' C8 'E2' C9 'E3'
PRINT C1-C9
REGRESS C2 3 C7-C9
```

Commentary

Earlier in this chapter, when these data were analyzed with dummy coding through MINI-TAB, it was pointed out that INDICATOR is used to generate four dummy-coded vectors, which are placed in Columns 3 through 6. Recall that Columns 3 through 6 identify, in succession, categories *A*, *B*, *C*, and *D* of the independent variable by assigning 1's to the category being identified and 0's to all others (if necessary, refer to Commentary on the Input for the previous MINITAB run).

Of the various ways in which a computer program may be used to generate effect coding, we have chosen to show how this may be accomplished by operating on the dummy-coded vectors generated by the INDICATOR statement. Examine now the three LET statements and notice that C(olumn)6 is subtracted in turn from each of the other columns. C6 consists of 0's for the first three categories and 1's for the last category; therefore, the subtractions result in three new vectors that differ from C3–C5 only with respect to the codes used for the last category (*D*). Whereas in C3–C5, *D* was assigned 0, in the new vectors, it is assigned −1 (see output, below). As you can see from the LET statements, the new vectors are stored in Columns 7 through 9, which are then named E(ffect)1, E(ffect)2, and E(ffect)3.

We call for the regression of the dependent variable, *Y*, which is stored in C2, on the 3 effect-coded vectors stored in C7–C9.

Output

Row	C1	Y	C3	C4	C5	C6	E1	E2	E3	
1	1	8	1	0	0	0	1	0	0	
2	1	8	1	0	0	0	1	0	0	*[first two subjects in T 1]*
.	.	.	.	.	.	.	.	.	.	
7	2	7	0	1	0	0	0	1	0	
8	2	8	0	1	0	0	0	1	0	*[first two subjects in T 2]*
.	.	.	.	.	.	.	.	.	.	
13	3	10	0	0	1	0	0	0	1	
14	3	11	0	0	1	0	0	0	1	*[first two subjects in T 3]*
.	.	.	.	.	.	.	.	.	.	
19	4	12	0	0	0	1	−1	−1	−1	
20	4	13	0	0	0	1	−1	−1	−1	*[first two subjects in T 4]*
.	.	.	.	.	.	.	.	.	.	

Commentary

Instead of storing the effect-coded vectors in C7–C9, we could have stored them in C3–C5, thereby overwriting the indicator vectors that were stored in these columns. We did not do so for three reasons. One, we wanted to print all the columns, as above, so that you can see what takes place when the LET statements are executed. Two, it is useful to retain the original indicator vectors so that they may be used to generate vectors for other coding schemes (e.g., orthogonal coding; see below). Three, by retaining both sets of vectors, the analysis done earlier with dummy coding and the one presented here could be accomplished in a single run. This is what we did, although we present the results as if they were obtained in two separate runs.

Output

s = 1.581   R-sq = 63.9%   R-sq(adj) = 58.5%

Analysis of Variance

SOURCE	DF	SS	MS	F	p
Regression	3	88.500	29.500	11.80	0.000
Error	20	50.000	2.500		
Total	23	138.500			

Commentary

These results are identical to those obtained with dummy coding (see preceding section), demonstrating what was said earlier, namely that the overall results are the same regardless of the coding scheme used. For commentaries on the overall results, see preceding section. The different coding schemes lead to different regression equations. The properties of the regression equation for dummy coding were described in the preceding section. Here we explain the properties of the regression equation obtained when effect coding is used.

THE REGRESSION EQUATION

In order to explain the meaning of the terms of the regression equation with effect coding, it is necessary to define an effect. The effect of a given category (e.g., treatment, group) is defined as the deviation of its mean from the average of all the category means. When the categories consist of equal n's, the average of the category means is equal to the mean of all the scores on the dependent variable, that is, the grand mean.[3] Thus, when the grand mean is calculated, all subjects are treated as if they belonged to a sample from the same population. The same holds true for other statistics (e.g., total sum of squares, variance).

In Chapter 17—see (17.17) and the related discussion—it was shown how each individual's score on the dependent variable can be expressed as a composite of the grand mean of the dependent variable, an element due to regression, and a residual. For the case of one categorical independent variable, and expressed in parameter estimates, this takes the following form.

$$Y_{ij} = \bar{Y} + b_j + e_{ij} \tag{19.3}$$

where Y_{ij} = score on the dependent variable for individual i in category j; $\bar{Y}$ = grand mean of dependent variable; b_j = effect of treatment j; e_{ij} = error, or residual, associated with individual i in category j.

Such a decomposition for the case of a continuous independent variable was shown in Chapter 17, Table 17.2, where the components were used to calculate the regression and residual sums of squares. A similar table may be constructed for the design used here. We suggest you do this as an exercise. Pattern the table after Table 17.2 and check your calculations by comparing the regression and residual sums of squares with those given in the output above.

For the present data, the four category means are

$$A = 10 \quad B = 9 \quad C = 12 \quad D = 14$$

Therefore, the grand mean is 11.25, and the effects for the four categories are

$$A = 10 - 11.25 = -1.25$$

$$B = 9 - 11.25 = -2.25$$

$$C = 12 - 11.25 = .75$$

$$D = 14 - 11.25 = 2.75$$

Because effects are defined as deviation scores, they sum to zero.

Output

The regression equation is
Y = 11.25 − 1.25 E1 − 2.25 E2 + 0.750 E3

---

[3] The case of unequal n's is discussed later.

Commentary

Notice first that $a = 11.25$, which is equal to the grand mean of the dependent variable. Examine now the b's for the three coded vectors and notice that each reflects the effect of the treatment identified in the vector with which it is associated. Thus, A is identified in E1,[4] and its effect was shown above to be -1.25; B is identified in E2, and its effect was shown to be -2.25; C is identified in E3, and its effect was shown to be .75—hence, the name effect coding for this scheme.

As there is no single vector for the identification of D (analogous to dummy coding, D is identified as a result of having -1's in all the vectors), there is no b corresponding to it. However, because the sum of all the effects is equal to zero (see above), the effect for D has to be equal to the sum of the effects for the other treatments, after the sign has been reversed. The sum of the effects (i.e., the b's) for the present example is

$$(-1.25) + (-2.25) + (.75) = -2.75$$

Reversing the sign of this sum, the effect for D is 2.75. Compare with the result obtained above.

The meaning of the b's and the reason for the reversal of their signs for the case of the category assigned -1's in all the vectors will be further clarified through the use of the regression equation to predict scores for individuals in the different categories. As in the case of dummy coding (see preceding section), only two terms of the regression equation are relevant for each of the categories identified in one of the coded vectors. They are the intercept (a) and the regression coefficient (b) associated with the vector in which the category is identified. Recall that, with effect coding, these are respectively the grand mean and the effect of the treatment in question.

Using the relevant terms of the regression equation given above, predicted scores for individuals in categories A, B, and C are obtained as follows:

$$\text{For } A: 11.25 - 1.25(1) = 10$$

$$\text{For } B: 11.25 - 2.25(1) = 9$$

$$\text{For } C: 11.25 + .75(1) = 12$$

The preceding are, of course, the means of the three categories. As was pointed out in connection with the application of the equation for dummy coding, the 1's could have been omitted, as the score on the relevant vector is always 1. In essence, therefore, the application of the regression equation amounts to adding the grand mean and the effect of the category or treatment in question.

Turning now to category D, it will be noted that all the terms of the regression equation are relevant to the prediction of scores for members of this category, because, unlike the other categories that have scores of 0 in all the vectors but one, D has scores (i.e., -1's) in all the vectors.

Applying the regression equation to scores of individuals in D yields

$$Y' = 11.25 - 1.25(-1) - 2.25(-1) + .75(-1) = 14$$

which is, of course, the mean for category D. Note that the multiplications of the b's by the -1 scores results in the reversal of their signs, which is in effect what was done above when the effects were summed and the sign reversed to obtain the effect for this category.

---

[4]As explained in the section on Dummy Coding, by identified, we mean the group assigned 1 in the vector.

We did not include the tests of the b's in the above output, because they are generally not of interest in the context of effect coding, as they are addressed to the question whether the mean of the category associated with the b being tested is different from the grand mean. This is in contrast to tests of b's when dummy coding is used (see preceding section), demonstrating once more that the user has to know which aspects of the output are relevant in the specific analysis carried out.

In sum, when effect coding is used, it is the test of the R^2, or the regression sum of squares, when all the coded vectors are taken simultaneously that is relevant. A statistically significant R^2 leads to the rejection of the null hypothesis that the category means are equal to each other. However, as was noted in connection with dummy coding, such global tests are generally followed by multiple comparisons between specific category means. Before turning to this topic, we show how SPSS may be used to carry out the same analysis as the one obtained through MINITAB.

SPSS

Input

```
SET LISTING='T191.LIS'.
TITLE TABLE 19.1.  A CATEGORICAL INDEPENDENT VARIABLE.
DATA LIST FREE/T Y.
IF (T EQ 1) E1 =    1.   [1]   [numbers in brackets
IF (T NE 1) E1 =    0.   [2]   are not part of input]
IF (T EQ 2) E2 =    1.   [3]
IF (T NE 2) E2 =    0.   [4]
IF (T EQ 3) E3 =    1.   [5]
IF (T NE 3) E3 =    0.   [6]
IF (T EQ 4) E1 =  -1.   [7]
IF (T EQ 4) E2 =  -1.   [8]
IF (T EQ 4) E3 =  -1.   [9]
BEGIN DATA.
     [Data for T and Y from Table 19.1 go here]
END DATA.
LIST.
REGRESSION VAR Y TO E3/DES/STAT=ALL/DEP Y/ENTER.
```

Commentary

As with MINITAB, we do not read in the coded vectors but are instead generating them by operating on the category identification vector, T. Of various ways that this could be done, we illustrate the use of IF statements, where EQ means *equal to*, and NE means *not equal to*.[5] Thus, for example, when [1] is executed, subjects whose T score is equal to 1 (i.e., subjects identified as belonging to category 1, or A of Table 19.1) are assigned 1 in a new vector labeled E1 (for Effect coding, category 1). When [2] is executed, 0 is assigned in E1 for subjects whose T is not equal to 1, that is, to all other subjects.

At this stage, E1 is a dummy vector, consisting of 1's for subjects in A and 0's for all

---

[5]Other IF statements can be used to accomplish the same end. You may wish to experiment with different IF statements. Examples of different IF statements are given below under Orthogonal Coding. For a general discussion of IF statements, see SPSS Manual.

others. Similarly, [3] and [4] result in a dummy vector in which category 2 (i.e., *B* of Table 19.1) is identified. Further, [5] and [6] generate a dummy vector in which category 3 (i.e., *C*) is identified.[6] Instead of using [7] through [9], on which we comment in the next paragraph, we could have used two additional IF statements to generate a dummy vector in which category 4 (i.e., *D*) would have been identified. Having four dummy vectors, we could have then operated on them, using COMPUTE statements (see SPSS Manual) to generate effect-coded vectors in exactly the same way as the LET statements were used to operate on the INDICATOR vectors in MINITAB (see above).

We used [7] through [9] to insert −1's in vectors E1 through E3 for subjects in category 4 (i.e., *D*), thereby ending up with three effect-coded vectors. It is important to bear in mind that IF statements are executed sequentially. Thus, when [7] through [9] are executed, whatever is in E1 through E3 for subjects whose T is equal to 4 is overwritten (in the present example, 0's were inserted because of the preceding IF statements).

Output

T	Y	E1	E2	E3	
1.00	8.00	1.00	0.0	0.0	
1.00	8.00	1.00	0.0	0.0	*[first two subjects in T 1]*
.	.	.	.	.	
2.00	7.00	0.0	1.00	0.0	
2.00	8.00	0.0	1.00	0.0	*[first two subjects in T 2]*
.	.	.	.	.	
3.00	10.00	0.0	0.0	1.00	
3.00	11.00	0.0	0.0	1.00	*[first two subjects in T 3]*
.	.	.	.	.	
4.00	12.00	−1.00	−1.00	−1.00	
4.00	13.00	−1.00	−1.00	−1.00	*[first two subjects in T 4]*
.	.	.	.	.	

Commentary

We listed the data, using LIST (see Input) so that you may see that the IF statements have generated effect-coded vectors. It is good practice to list data whenever transformations are carried out, thereby being in a position to check whether the vectors generated are in fact the intended ones.

Output

	Mean	Std Dev
Y	11.250	2.454
E1	0.0	.722
E2	0.0	.722
E3	0.0	.722

N of Cases = 24

---

[6]It should be clear, we hope, that had the aim been to carry out an analysis with dummy coding, the three vectors generated thus far would have sufficed. Under such circumstances, it would have been preferable to label the columns accordingly (i.e., D1, D2, and D3).

Commentary

Each vector is treated as if it were a distinct variable;[7] thus, these statistics are based on $N = 24$. That is, means and standard deviations are calculated across all subjects, ignoring category memberships. Thus, the mean of Y is the grand mean discussed above (see commentaries on MINITAB output). *Category means on the dependent variable have to be calculated separately.* Alternatively, they can be obtained by using the regression equation, as was shown above. *Category Std Dev (Standard Deviations) also have to be calculated separately.*

Examine now the means for the coded vectors and notice that they are all equal to 0. This will always be the case with effect coding, regardless of the number of categories, so long as the n's in all the categories are equal. Under such circumstances, each coded vector consists of an equal number of 1's and -1's, the former identifying a given category, the latter associated with the category assigned -1's in all the vectors (all other categories are assigned 0's). Consequently, the sum of the scores is zero, and the mean is zero. It is useful to inspect the means as a quick check on whether errors of input have been committed. Means that are not equal to 0 indicate such errors.

With unequal n's, the coded vector means will not be equal to zero. Using the number of cases in the category identified in a given vector and in the one assigned -1, it is easy to calculate its mean and see whether it is equal to the one reported in the output.

In the interest of space, we do not report the correlation matrix. It will be noted, however, that, with equal n's, the correlation between any two effect-coded vectors, regardless of the number of categories, is .50. This can serve as another quick check on whether errors of input have occurred.

Output

Equation Number 1   Dependent Variable..   Y

Beginning Block Number   1.   Method: Enter

Variable(s) Entered on Step Number   1..   E3
                                      2..   E2
                                      3..   E1

				Analysis of Variance			
Multiple R	.79937						
R Square	.63899	R Square Change	.63899		DF	Sum of Squares	Mean Squa
Adjusted R Square	.58484	F Change	11.80000	Regression	3	88.50000	29.500(
Standard Error	1.58114	Signif F Change	.0001	Residual	20	50.00000	2.500(

Variable	B
E3	.75000
E2	−2.25000
E1	−1.25000
(Constant)	11.25000

Commentary

These excerpts from the output are included so that you may compare them with that obtained earlier through MINITAB. Because we commented on the MINITAB output, we do not comment on the one given here. When in doubt, refer to the comments on the MINITAB output.

---

[7]See comment on this point in connection with the MINITAB output earlier in this chapter.

MULTIPLE COMPARISONS AMONG MEANS

Several times earlier, it was stated that, for the case of an independent categorical variable, a test of R^2, or of the regression sum of squares, is addressed to the global question of whether the category means are equal to each other. Of greater interest are more focused questions regarding differences between means of specific categories or combinations of categories. Answers to such questions are obtained through multiple comparisons.

Various approaches to multiple comparisons among means have been proposed, and the literature dealing with this topic is extensive. Our presentation is limited to an introduction of some basic approaches. For more detailed discussions and other approaches, see Edwards (1985), Games (1971), Keppel (1982), Kirk (1982), and Winer (1971).

A *comparison*, or a *contrast*, is a linear combination, L, of the following form:

$$L = c_1\bar{Y}_1 + c_2\bar{Y}_2 + \ldots + c_j\bar{Y}_j \tag{19.4}$$

where c = coefficient by which a given mean, $\bar{Y}$, is multiplied; j = number of means being compared. For any given comparison, it is required that the sum of the coefficients be equal to zero.

Using the four categories of the numerical example analyzed above, and letting the letters stand for category means, following are some illustrative comparisons.

	A	B	C	D
(1)	1	-1	0	0
(2)	$-1/2$	$-1/2$	0	1
(3)	$-1/3$	$-1/3$	1	$-1/3$
(4)	-1	-1	0	2
(5)	-1	-1	3	-1

Notice that, as required, the sum of the coefficients in each of the five comparisons is zero. Later we use the numerical example analyzed above to illustrate the calculation and testing of such comparisons. For now, we comment in a general sense on what is accomplished by each of these comparisons.

In (1), the mean of A is multiplied by 1 and the mean of B by -1. Accordingly, the mean of B is subtracted from the mean of A. If instead it were desired to subtract the mean of A from the mean of B, then the coefficients -1 and 1 would be applied to A and B respectively. The 0 coefficients for C and D indicate that these means are not involved in this comparison.

In (2), the average of the means of A and B is subtracted from the mean of D.

In (3), the average of the means of A, B, and D is subtracted from the mean of C.

It is more convenient to work with integers than with fractions, as in (2) and (3). This is particularly so when the coefficients are to be entered as input in a multiple regression computer program. Conversion to integers is easily accomplished through multiplication by a constant. Thus, multiplying the coefficients in comparison (2) by 2 yields comparison (4). Comparisons (2) and (4) are equivalent; coefficients from either of them may be used to test the contrast between the average of A and B, and the mean of D. Similarly, comparisons (3) and (5) are equivalent, as the latter was obtained by multiplying each of the coefficients in the former by 3. In what follows, we will use integers for the comparisons of interest.

A distinction is made between what are labeled, planned, and post hoc comparisons. As the name implies, *planned comparisons* are ones hypothesized in advance of the analysis.

They are, therefore, also referred to as a priori comparisons. In contrast, *post hoc*, or a posteriori, comparisons are ones carried out in light of results of the overall analysis. Each of these approaches will be explained and illustrated, beginning with planned comparisons.

Planned Comparisons

On the basis of theoretical considerations, the researcher may hypothesize that certain treatments are more effective than others or that the performance of certain groups is better than that of other groups. Under such circumstances, an omnibus test of the null hypothesis that the treatment means are equal to each other is of little interest. Instead, it is the hypothesized differences, that is, the planned comparisons, that are tested. There are two types of planned comparisons: orthogonal and nonorthogonal. We begin with the former.

ORTHOGONAL COMPARISONS

Orthogonal means at right angles (90°). When two vectors, or variables, are orthogonal, the correlation between them is zero. Two comparisons are orthogonal when the sum of the products of the coefficients for their respective elements is zero. Referring again to the four categories of the numerical example analyzed above, consider the following comparisons.

	A	B	C	D
(1)	1	−1	0	0
(2)	1	1	−2	0
(3)	0	0	1	−1
(4)	1	1	−1	−1
(5)	1	1	1	−3
(6)	1	0	−1	0

Notice, first, that the requirement that the sum of the coefficients for each comparison be zero is satisfied in all of them. Let us check some of the comparisons to see whether or not they are orthogonal, beginning with (1) and (2). To see whether these comparisons are orthogonal, their respective coefficients are multiplied, and the products then added:

(1):	1	−1	0	0
(2):	1	1	−2	0
(1)(2):	1	−1	0	0

The sum of the products of the coefficients is zero. Hence, (1) and (2) are orthogonal. What about comparisons (2) and (3)?

(2):	1	1	−2	0
(3):	0	0	1	−1
(2)(3):	0	0	−2	0

The sum of the products of the coefficients is *not* zero. Hence, (2) and (3) are *not* orthogonal.

What about (2) and (5)?

(2):	1	1	-2	0
(5):	1	1	1	-3
(2)(5):	1	1	-2	0

The sum of the products of the coefficients is zero. Hence, (2) and (5) are orthogonal.

We suggest that you carry out similar calculations to check on other comparisons. You will find, for example, that (1) and (4) are orthogonal, as are (1) and (5). However, (4) and (5) are *not* orthogonal (the sum of the products of their coefficients is 4).

When all the comparisons within a given set are orthogonal, it is said that they are mutually orthogonal. Thus, for example, (1), (4), and (5) are *not* mutually orthogonal (see preceding paragraph). Henceforth, when we say that a set of comparisons is orthogonal, we mean mutually orthogonal. The number of orthogonal comparisons possible for a given number of categories is equal to the number of categories minus one. Recall that this is also the number of coded vectors necessary to represent a categorical variable and that it corresponds to the *df* associated with the among category differences.

For the four categories given above, then, three orthogonal comparisons are possible. There is, however, more than one set that satisfies this condition. Referring to the comparisons given above, (1), (3), and (4) are orthogonal, as are (1), (2), and (5). The preceding are but two of various sets of orthogonal comparisons possible for a four-category variable. Which specific set is used depends, of course, on one's theory. This, after all, is how one arrives at a priori comparisons. Assume, for example, that the four categories of the independent variable in the above comparisons are different therapies, or different teaching styles, but that A and B are more "directive," whereas C and D are more "nondirective." Alternatively, the research may be nonexperimental, where A and B may be samples from two Eastern States, and C and D samples from two Western States. For either of the preceding, it is conceivable for a researcher to advance three hypotheses, reflected by comparisons (1), (3), and (4), according to which A is superior to B; C is superior to D; and the average of A and B is superior to the average of C and D.

It is not difficult to envision other kinds of substantive concerns that would be reflected instead by comparisons (1), (2), and (5), according to which A is superior to B; the average of A and B is superior to C; and the average of A, B, and C is superior to D. We repeat: The specific comparisons reflect one's theory regarding the differences between treatments or combinations of treatments.

It is not required that the number of hypotheses be equal to the number of orthogonal comparisons possible in a given design. Thus, referring to the above comparisons, a researcher may formulate only two hypotheses, say, those reflected by (1) and (2). This does not preclude doing also post hoc (see below) comparisons between other means or combinations of means.

TEST OF A COMPARISON

Any comparison can be tested as follows:

$$F = \frac{[c_1\bar{Y}_1 + c_2\bar{Y}_2 + \ldots + c_j\bar{Y}_j]^2}{MSR\left[\sum \dfrac{(c_j)^2}{n_j}\right]} \tag{19.5}$$

where the numerator is the square of the comparison, as defined by (19.4). MSR = Mean Square Residuals from the overall analysis; n_j = number of subjects in category j. The df for the numerator of this F is 1. This is why some authors refer to it as a single, or individual, df F. The denominator df are equal to the df associated with the MSR (i.e., $N - k - 1$), where N = total number of subjects; k = number of coded vectors, or df for the among categories differences.

Two things will be noted about this F ratio. One, because the df for its numerator is 1, a t ratio may be obtained by taking the $\sqrt{F}$. The df for the t ratio are equal to the df for the denominator of the F (i.e., those for the MSR). Two, as is shown below, (19.5) is also used for tests of planned nonorthogonal and post hoc comparisons, except that probability levels are adjusted accordingly.

A NUMERICAL EXAMPLE

The testing of comparisons (1), (3), and (4) will be illustrated for the numerical example analyzed earlier. In a subsequent section (see Orthogonal Coding), it is shown how these tests are obtained from the output of a multiple regression analysis through the use of orthogonal coding. Results obtained earlier and necessary for the testing of the aforementioned comparisons are repeated.

$$\text{Means: } A = 10 \quad B = 9 \quad C = 12 \quad D = 14$$

$$MSR = 2.5, \text{ with 20 } df$$

$$n = 6 \text{ in each category}$$

We apply (19.5) to the comparisons under consideration. Between A and B (1):

$$F = \frac{[(1)(10) + (-1)(9)]^2}{2.5\left[\dfrac{(1)^2}{6} + \dfrac{(-1)^2}{6}\right]} = \frac{1}{.83} = 1.20$$

Between C and D (2);

$$F = \frac{[(1)(12) + (-1)(14)]^2}{2.5\left[\dfrac{(1)^2}{6} + \dfrac{(-1)^2}{6}\right]} = \frac{4}{.83} = 4.82$$

Between the averages of A and B, and of C and D (3);

$$F = \frac{[(1)(10) + (1)(9) + (-1)(12) + (-1)(14)]^2}{2.5\left[\dfrac{(1)^2}{6} + \dfrac{(1)^2}{6} + \dfrac{(-1)^2}{6} + \dfrac{(-1)^2}{6}\right]} = \frac{49}{1.67} = 29.34$$

The df for each of the above F ratios are 1 and 20, for the numerator and denominator respectively. Assuming that $\alpha = .05$ was selected, the tabled value for $F(1, 20) = 4.35$. Accordingly, it is concluded that comparison (1) is statistically not significant, whereas (2) and (3) are statistically significant.

When orthogonal comparisons are hypothesized, the omnibus test of the null hypothesis that all category means are equal to each other is not relevant. It may be shown that the overall F ratio, that is, the F ratio for the test of the R^2, or the regression sum of squares, is equal to the average of the F ratios for a set of orthogonal comparisons. For the numerical example analyzed here, it was found earlier that the overall $F(3, 20) = 11.80$, which is, within rounding, equal to the average of the three F ratios for the above orthogonal comparisons: $(1.20 + 4.82 + 29.34)/3 = 11.79$.

From the preceding, it follows that it is possible for an overall F ratio to be statistically not significant and for F ratios for specific orthogonal comparisons to be statistically significant. However, as was said above, the overall F ratio is irrelevant when orthogonal comparisons are hypothesized. This is in contrast to post hoc comparisons (see below) that are carried out only when the overall F ratio is statistically significant.

NONORTHOGONAL COMPARISONS

As was stated above, planned comparisons may be nonorthogonal. Under such circumstances, an approach that has been referred to as *Bonferroni t statistics* (Miller, 1966) or the Dunn (1961) procedure is used. In this approach, F ratios are calculated in exactly the same way as was done above for the case of orthogonal comparisons, that is, by applying (19.5), except that the overall α level is adjusted for the number of comparisons done.

For a given α and a given number of nonorthogonal comparisons, i, an F or t ratio for a comparison has to exceed α/i in order to be declared statistically significant. Assume that $\alpha = .05$ and that two nonorthogonal comparisons are tested. For a comparison to be declared statistically significant, its F or t ratio has to exceed the critical value of $.05/2 = .025$. If five such comparisons were hypothesized, and assuming an overall $\alpha = .05$, then the critical value of $.05/5 = .01$ would be used.

Tables for what are either referred to as Bonferroni test statistics or Dunn Multiple Comparison Test are reproduced in various statistics books (e.g., Edwards, 1985; Kirk, 1982; Myers, 1979). Such tables are entered with the number of comparisons, i, and df for error, or the MSR (i.e., $N - k - 1$). For example, assume that 6 nonorthogonal comparisons were hypothesized, that the df for MSR are 60, and that overall $\alpha = .05$. Entering a table for Bonferroni t statistics for 6 comparisons with 60 df for error, the critical value is 2.73. Thus, the t ratio for a comparison would have to exceed 2.73 (or equivalently an F ratio of 7.45), for the comparison to be declared statistically significant.[8]

Referring again to the comparisons given above, it will be assumed that the researcher formulated the two hypotheses reflected by comparisons (2) and (6). These comparisons are not orthogonal, as the sum of the products of their coefficients is *not* zero (verify that it is 3). Using the results obtained earlier, we apply (19.5) to these comparison. Between the average of A and B, and the mean of C (2):

$$F = \frac{[(1)(10) + (1)(9) + (-2)(12)]^2}{2.5\left[\frac{(1)^2}{6} + \frac{(1)^2}{6} + \frac{(-2)^2}{6}\right]} = \frac{25}{2.5} = 10.0$$

Between A and C (6):

$$F = \frac{[(1)(10) + (-1)(12)]^2}{2.5\left[\frac{(1)^2}{6} + \frac{(-1)^2}{6}\right]} = \frac{4}{.83} = 4.82$$

---

[8]For different applications of the Bonferroni t statistics and for some modifications, see Keppel (1982, p. 147–149).

Entering an F table for $\alpha = .025$ (see, for example, Edwards, 1985), the critical value for 1 and 20 df is 5.87. It is, therefore, concluded that the first comparison is statistically significant but that the second is not. Alternatively, t ratios can be obtained: $\sqrt{10.0} = 3.16$; $\sqrt{4.82} = 2.20$. Entering a Bonferroni t statistics table for $\alpha = .05$, with 20 df, for two comparisons, the critical value is 2.42. The same conclusions are, of course, reached.

Recall that the b's in the regression equation with effect coding reflect category effects. Hence, multiple comparisons can be obtained and tested by using the b's instead of the category means. For a detailed discussion and illustrations of the equivalence of the two approaches, see Pedhazur (1982, pp. 299–304).

UNEQUAL SAMPLE SIZES

As in the case of dummy coding, we comment here only on the mechanics of the analysis with unequal sample sizes. We remind you, however, that, in the section on dummy coding, we made some general remarks about threats to the validity of a study when unequal n's are due to attrition or nonresponse.

As far as the mechanics of the analysis are concerned, effect coding with unequal n's proceeds in exactly the same manner as with equal n's. The interpretation of the regression equation is also the same in both cases except that, with unequal n's, the intercept (a) is equal to the unweighted average of the category means. What this means is that the average of the category means is calculated without taking into account the number of subjects on which the means are based. As with equal n's, each b indicates the effect of the category identified in the vector with which it is associated except that such effects are deviations of category means from the *unweighted* average of the category means.

Multiple comparisons among means based on equal and unequal n's proceed in the same manner, as are tests of such comparisons using (19.5). However, when comparisons are made between combinations of means for the case of unequal n's, it is unweighted combinations that are used. That this is so can be seen from the numerator of (19.5), where the linear combination is arrived at without taking into account the number of subjects each mean is based on. Sample sizes are, however, taken into account in the calculation of the error term, that is, in the denominator of (19.5). For more details about the use of effect coding with unequal n's, including a numerical example with multiple comparisons among means, see Pedhazur (1982, pp. 320–323).

ORTHOGONAL CODING

When orthogonal comparisons are hypothesized, their coefficients can be used in the coded vectors representing the independent variable in a multiple regression analysis. When this is done, results of the overall analysis are the same as for any other coding scheme, but some intermediate results have interesting properties, which will be commented upon in connection with SPSS output for a reanalysis of the data of Table 19.1.

SPSS

Input

SET LISTING='T191ORT.LIS'.
TITLE TABLE 19.1.   ANALYSIS WITH ORTHOGONAL CODING.

DATA LIST FREE/T Y.
IF (T EQ 1) O1 = 1.   [EQ = equal]
IF (T EQ 2) O1 = −1.
IF (T GT 2) O1 = 0.   [GT = greater than]
IF (T LT 3) O2 = 0.   [LT = less than]
IF (T EQ 3) O2 = 1.
IF (T EQ 4) O2 = −1.
IF (T LT 3) O3 = 1.
IF (T GT 2) O3 = −1.
BEGIN DATA.
        [data of Table 19.1 go here]
END DATA.
LIST.
REGRESSION VAR Y TO O3/DES/STAT=ALL/DEP Y/ENTER.

Commentary

As in earlier analyses, we do not enter the coded vectors as input. Instead, we use a category identification vector, T, and IF statements to generate the necessary vectors. Following the practice adopted for dummy and effect coding, the coded vectors are named O(rthogonal)1, O2, and so forth. However, unlike the other coding schemes, these vectors do *not* refer to categories being identified but to given comparisons, or contrasts. Thus, O1 refers to the first comparison, that is, the one between *A* and *B*—similarly, for the other vectors (see listing of data and commentaries, below).

Because we commented on the REGRESSION statement in earlier analyses, we will not comment on it here except to point out that the analyses with the three coding schemes (i.e., dummy, effect, and orthogonal) could have been done in a single run. To this end, the REGRESSION procedure would include three subcommands. Using the same dependent variable in each of the subcommands, a different set of coded vectors, corresponding to one of the three coding schemes, would be entered.

Output

T	Y	O1	O2	O3	
1.00	8.00	1.00	0.0	1.00	
1.00	8.00	1.00	0.0	1.00	*[first two subjects in T 1]*
.	.	.	.	.	
2.00	7.00	−1.00	0.0	1.00	
2.00	8.00	−1.00	0.0	1.00	*[first two subjects in T 2]*
.	.	.	.	.	
3.00	10.00	0.0	1.00	−1.00	
3.00	11.00	0.0	1.00	−1.00	*[first two subjects in T 3]*
.	.	.	.	.	
4.00	12.00	0.0	−1.00	−1.00	
4.00	13.00	0.0	−1.00	−1.00	*[first two subjects in T 4]*
.	.	.	.	.	

Commentary

These excerpts are included so that you may see the orthogonal coding generated by the IF statements. Notice that the codes in each of the vectors correspond to the coefficients for the comparison of interest. Look back at the six comparisons listed earlier in connection with the explanation of the meaning of orthogonal comparisons and notice that in O1 the coefficients of comparison (1) in which A is contrasted with B are used as codes. In O2, the coefficients of comparison (3) in which C is contrasted with D are used as codes. Finally, the codes in O3 are the coefficients of comparison (4) in which the average of A and B is contrasted with the average of C and D. In short, whatever the coefficients for a given set of orthogonal comparisons, they are used as the codes for orthogonal coding.

Output

	Mean	Std Dev
Y	11.250	2.454
O1	0.0	.722
O2	0.0	.722
O3	0.0	1.022

N of Cases = 24

Correlation:

	Y	O1	O2	O3
Y	1.000	.147	−.294	−.728
O1	.147	1.000	.000	.000
O2	−.294	.000	1.000	.000
O3	−.728	.000	.000	1.000

Commentary

As with effect coding, the means of orthogonally coded vectors are zero. Unlike effect and dummy coding, however, the coded vectors are *not* correlated when orthogonal coding is used. This, of course, is consistent with the definition of orthogonality given earlier.

The absence of correlations among the coded vectors has interesting implications for the analysis and for the interpretation of the results. Although, in the case under consideration, we are dealing *not* with three independent variables but with *one* independent categorical variable that is represented by three coded vectors, the present analysis will also be used in a broader sense to serve as an illustration of what would take place in analyses of designs in which each vector represents a distinct independent variable, as long as there are no correlations among the vectors. This would probably never happen in nonexperimental research. However, it is what would take place in well designed and well executed experiments with multiple independent variables.

To begin with, unlike the other coding schemes, in orthogonal coding, the proportion of variance accounted for (i.e., R^2) and, hence, the regression sum of squares, can be partitioned unambiguously among the specific comparisons involved. The same holds true for designs with multiple independent variables that are not correlated.

When the concept of R^2 was introduced in the beginning of Chapter 18, it was pointed out that, when the independent variables are not correlated, R^2 is equal to the sum of the squared zero-order correlations of the dependent variable with each of the independent variables. This is now illustrated using the zero-order correlations between the dependent variable and the coded vectors (see the column or row labeled Y in the above output):

$$R^2_{y.123} = (.147)^2 + (-.294)^2 + (-.728)^2$$

$$.638 = .022 + .086 + .530$$

It will be noted that the same R^2, within rounding errors, was obtained in the analyses of these data with dummy and effect coding (see earlier sections). However, whereas, in analyses with dummy or effect coding, the variance accounted for should *not* be partitioned, in the case of orthogonal coding, variance partitioning may be carried out. For the example under consideration, it can be stated that, of the variance of the dependent variable, about 2% is accounted for by the first contrast, about 9% by the second contrast, and about 53% by the third contrast. Similar statements can be made when the vectors represent distinct independent variables that are not correlated.

Output

Variable	B	SE B	Beta	Correl	Tolerance	T	Sig T
O3	−1.75000	.32275	−.72848	−.72848	1.00000	−5.422	.0000
O2	−1.00000	.45644	−.29435	−.29435	1.00000	−2.191	.0405
O1	.50000	.45644	.14718	.14718	1.00000	1.095	.2863
(Constant)	11.25000	.32275					

Commentary

The results of the overall analysis are the same as those obtained with dummy and effect coding and are, therefore, not reproduced here.

Several interesting aspects of this excerpt of the output will be commented upon. Look at the columns labeled Beta and Correl(ation) and notice that they are, as expected, identical. In Chapter 18, it was shown that, when the independent variables are not correlated, the β (standardized regression coefficient) for each variable is equal to the zero-order correlation of the dependent variable with the variable in question—see comments on (18.6). The same holds true for orthogonally coded vectors.

In Chapter 18, it was shown that Tolerance is 1.0 when the independent variables are not correlated. This is also true for orthogonally coded vectors.

We turn now to the regression equation with the unstandardized coefficients—the column labeled B. As may be noted, a (Constant) is equal to the grand mean of the dependent variable (11.25).

The test of a given b is, in effect, a test of the comparison reflected in the vector with which it is associated. Because of the way SPSS REGRESSION is programmed, the comparisons may be listed in an order different from the one in which they were labeled, as is exemplified in the present analysis. However, this has no bearing on the interpretation and the testing of b's, even when the independent variables (or coded vectors) are correlated (see Chapter 18, for discussions of the meaning of b's and their tests).

The t ratios for the three b's are listed in the column labeled T. Assuming $\alpha = .05$ was selected, and using the probability levels associated with the t's, it is concluded that the comparison between the averages of A and B and that of C and D (i.e., O3) is statistically significant, as is the comparison between C and D (O2). The comparison between A and B (O1) is statistically not significant.

Recall that $t^2 = F$ with 1 df for the numerator (the df for the denominator of F are the same as those associated with the t). Squaring the three t ratios given in the output, the following F

ratios are obtained: 29.398, 4.800, and 1.199. As expected, these are, within rounding, the same values obtained earlier when (19.5) was used to test the three orthogonal comparisons under consideration.

From the preceding, it should be clear that, when orthogonal comparisons are hypothesized, it is useful to employ their coefficients in orthogonal coding, thereby obtaining the tests of the comparisons in the form of tests of the b's associated with the vectors in which the comparisons are reflected. However, as was demonstrated earlier, regardless of the coding method, orthogonal comparisons may be carried out through the application of (19.5).

The magnitudes of the b's are affected by the specific coefficients used for the comparisons (e.g., fractions or integers; see above). That this is so can be seen from the relation between β's and b's (i.e., standardized and unstandardized coefficients). In Chapter 18—see (18.8)—it was shown that b is equal to the β corresponding to it multiplied by the ratio of the standard deviation of the dependent variable to the standard deviation of the independent variable in question. Clearly, the only terms affected by the choice of different codes for the orthogonal comparisons are the standard deviations of the coded vectors. Accordingly, β's are not affected by the choice of specific coefficients used in the comparisons, whereas b's are affected. The important thing to note, however, is that the tests of the b's and, hence, tests of comparisons reflected by them, will be the same, regardless of the choice of specific codes, as long as the comparisons are orthogonal. Furthermore, predicted values using the regression equation will be the same (i.e., category means) regardless of the specific codes used. For a more detailed discussion of these points as well as numerical illustrations, see Pedhazur (1982, pp. 309–311).

UNEQUAL SAMPLE SIZES

It is possible to carry out orthogonal comparisons among means or use their coefficients in orthogonal coding when n's are unequal. For a discussion, along with a numerical illustration, see Pedhazur (1982, pp. 325–328).

Post Hoc Comparisons

Post hoc comparisons may be carried out only when the overall F ratio is statistically significant. As the name implies, such comparisons are carried out not for the purpose of testing hypotheses formulated on the basis of theoretical considerations, but rather in an attempt to see what is going on in the data.

All the cautions sounded in connection with post hoc theorizing (see especially Chapter 9) apply, of course, to the present situation, which has been aptly characterized as "data snooping." Therefore, although post hoc comparisons may be useful for following up on one's hunches, it is important not to forget that one came by them in the course of a "fishing expedition."

Approaches to post hoc comparisons vary in scope, from ones limited to pairwise comparisons between means based on equal n's to ones applicable to comparisons of combinations of means based on equal or unequal n's. The approaches vary also with respect to what might be termed statistical permissiveness. That is, some are more permissive in that they are based on relatively lenient criteria, whereas others are more conservative in that they are based on more stringent criteria. Consequently, a given comparison may be declared statistically significant by one approach and statistically not significant by another. Detailed discussions, as well as examples of such occurrences, will be found in the references given in the beginning of this section. Our presentation is limited to an approach developed by Scheffé (1959), because it is the most versatile and the most conservative. In other words, the Scheffé, or S, method is applicable to comparisons of any combinations of means, as well as for equal and unequal n's, and is less likely than other approaches to indicate that a given comparison is statistically significant.

Although specialized formulas and notation were developed in connection with the Scheffé approach, they will not be presented here (see, for example, Pedhazur, 1982, pp. 297–298). Instead, we use an alternative procedure that entails the application of (19.5), as was done earlier for planned comparisons. However, when used for Scheffé multiple comparisons, the F ratio obtained from the application of (19.5) has to exceed $kF_\alpha;k, N - k - 1$, where k is the number of coded vectors representing the independent variable, or the number of categories minus one, $F_\alpha;k, N- k - 1$ is the tabled value of F with k and $N - k - 1$ df at the prespecified α level.

We hope that the procedure will become clearer when its application to some comparisons among means of the numerical example of Table 19.1 is illustrated. For present purposes, the following results, obtained earlier, are necessary.

$$\text{Means: } A = 10 \quad B = 9 \quad C = 12 \quad D = 14$$

$$MSR = 2.5, \text{ with } 20 \text{ } df$$

$$n = 6 \text{ in each category}$$

For illustrative purposes, it will be assumed that the only hypothesis formulated by the researcher was that the category means differ from each other. This is, of course, the crudest hypothesis possible for the situation under consideration. Needless to say, more focused hypotheses of the kind illustrated in the section dealing with planned comparisons are preferable. A researcher who limits himself or herself to the kind of global hypothesis presented here betrays little knowledge and understanding of the phenomenon he or she is studying and, assuming that the categories represent treatments, what he or she is doing. Be that as it may, it will be recalled that, for the data under consideration, the null hypothesis that the category means are equal to each other was rejected: $F(3, 20) = 11.80, p < .01$. Accordingly, the researcher may now proceed with post hoc multiple comparisons. Assume that, for reasons that we will not go into, he or she decides to apply the Scheffé procedure to the following comparisons:

	A	B	C	D
(1)	0	−1	1	0
(2)	0	−2	1	1

Apply (19.5) to each of these comparisons.

Between B and C (1):

$$F = \frac{[(-1)(9) + (1)(12)]^2}{2.5\left[\frac{(-1)^2}{6} + \frac{(1)^2}{6}\right]} = \frac{9}{.83} = 10.84$$

Between B, and the average of C and D (2):

$$F = \frac{[(-2)(9) + (1)(12) + (1)(14)]^2}{2.5 \left[\frac{(-2)^2}{6} + \frac{(1)^2}{6} + \frac{(1)^2}{6} \right]} = \frac{64}{2.5} = 25.60$$

Thus far, the calculations are identical to those carried out earlier for planned comparisons. In fact, had the preceding been planned comparisons, these two F ratios, each with 1 and 20 df, would have been taken as the tests of the comparisons. As the comparisons are not orthogonal (the sum of the products of their coefficients is 3), a Bonferroni test (see Nonorthogonal Comparisons, above) would have been applied. Checking a table for Bonferroni test statistics for two comparisons at the .01 level, 20 df for error, it is found that $t = 3.16$. The corresponding F is, therefore, 9.99 (3.16^2). It would have been concluded that both comparisons are statistically significant.

However, as explained above, when comparisons are post hoc and the Scheffé method is used, the F ratio for the test of a comparison has to exceed a tabled F value multiplied by k (number of coded vectors, or df for the among category differences) in order for the comparison to be declared statistically significant. For $\alpha = .01$, the tabled value of $F(3, 20) = 4.94$. Therefore, to be declared significant by the Scheffé method, an F ratio for a comparison has to exceed $(3)(4.94) = 14.82$. For the above comparisons, therefore, it is concluded that (1) is statistically not significant, whereas (2) is statistically significant.

MULTIPLE REGRESSION AND ANALYSIS OF VARIANCE: MECHANICS AND TERMINOLOGY

If you are familiar with the analysis of variance (ANOVA), you have probably realized that the analyses in this chapter could have been carried out via ANOVA. You may have even wondered whether it was worth your while to make the effort to learn a new approach and new terminology when the same results could be obtained through the application of an approach with which you are already familiar. Even if your background in statistics is meager, you have surely come across terminologies of MR and ANOVA while reading textbooks or the research literature. You may have even pondered what, if any, are the differences between the two approaches.

The purpose of this section is to answer such questions on the level of the mechanics of the analysis and the terminology used. The more important question of whether or not there are advantages in using one approach over the other is not addressed in the present section (we do this in the next chapter, after discussing factorial designs).

Another aim of this section is to acquaint you with the general layout and terminology of ANOVA, and with computer programs for such analyses, so that you may be in a better position to follow research literature in which ANOVA is reported and to run ANOVA programs when you so desire.

We begin with some general observations about data displays and terminology. This is followed by the application of ONEWAY of SPSS to the analysis of the data of Table 19.1. The same data are then analyzed by the GLM procedure of SAS.

DATA DISPLAYS AND TERMINOLOGY

The erroneous impression that MR and ANOVA are two distinct analytic approaches is reinforced by the different formats generally used in each to display the same data and the

Table 19.2
Data From Table 19.1 Displayed for ANOVA

A	B	C	D
8	7	10	12
8	8	11	13
12	8	14	13
12	10	13	15
10	11	12	15
10	10	12	16

different terminologies used to present what are essentially the same results. For illustrative purposes, we present in Table 19.2 the data of Table 19.1 in a format generally used in the context of ANOVA.

For present purposes, it will be assumed that the coded vectors (e.g., dummy coding) for the analysis of the data of Table 19.1 were *not* generated by computer, as was done earlier, but are used as input, as they appear in the data listings given as part of the output for each of the preceding analyses. Faced with the two rather different looking formats, people not versed in statistics are prone to form the impression that MR and ANOVA are two distinct analytic systems.

If you were to peruse textbooks devoted exclusively to ANOVA, you would generally find the data displayed as in Table 19.2. In order to analyze such data by MR, you would have to place all the scores on the dependent variable in a single vector and then use some coding scheme to represent the independent variable. As is shown in the next chapter, this approach generalizes to more than one independent variable and to interactions between them.

In the context of ANOVA, then, data are generally presented under separate headings of groups or treatments. Accordingly, the analysis is conceived of as the partitioning of the total sum of squares into between groups or treatments sum of squares, and within groups or treatments sum of squares. In MR, on the other hand, there appear to be no group distinctions in the data presentation. The dependent variable is contained in a single vector, which is regressed on the independent variable(s). Accordingly, the analysis is conceived of as the partitioning of the total sum of squares into regression and residual components. However, as was shown in this chapter, in MR, information about group membership or treatments is contained in coded vectors. The terminology of the two approaches notwithstanding, it is shown below that, when applied to the same design and data, they yield identical results.

With the preceding remarks in mind, it is shown now how the data of Table 19.2 are analyzed through ONEWAY of SPSS. In the context of the commentaries, attention is also drawn to similarities of results obtained here and those obtained earlier through the applications of MR as well as to the different terminologies used in the two analytic approaches.

SPSS

Input

```
SET LISTING='T192.LIS'.
TITLE TABLE 19.2. ONE-WAY ANOVA.
DATA LIST FREE/T Y.
BEGIN DATA.
        [data as displayed in Table 19.1 go here]
END DATA.
LIST.
ONEWAY Y BY T(1,4)/STAT=ALL/
   CONTRAST = 1 −1 0 0/
```

CONTRAST = 0 0 1 −1/
CONTRAST = 1 1 −1 −1/
CONTRAST = 0 −1 1 0/
CONTRAST = 0 −2 1 1.

Commentary

In the context of ANOVA, a design with one independent categorical variable is referred to as a one-way, or simple, ANOVA. Hence, the name of this procedure, which distinguishes it from designs with multiple independent categorical variables, generally referred to as factorial designs (see Chapter 20). SPSS has another procedure, called ANOVA, that may be used for the analysis of one-way as well as factorial designs. We are using ONEWAY, because we wish to illustrate tests of contrasts (see below), not available in the ANOVA procedure. *In the discussion that follows, we use ANOVA to refer to the analysis of variance, not to the procedure thus named in SPSS.*

Notice that the data are read in as displayed in Table 19.1 (i.e., a category identification vector, T, and the dependent variable, Y). This is identical to what we did when these data were analyzed by MR programs. However, T is used differently in the two analytic procedures. When MR was applied to these data, T was used to generate coded vectors (e.g., dummy, effect) necessary for the analysis instead of reading them in as input. Accordingly, T was used only at the data transformation stage (e.g., with INDICATOR in MINITAB; with IF statements in SPSS). No mention of T was made at the analysis stage.

In ANOVA procedures, on the other hand, a category identification, as in T, is required. In ONEWAY of SPSS, the dependent variable, Y, is declared first. This is followed by the keyword BY, the identification vector, and its lowest and highest values, which in the present example are (1,4). As is shown in the next chapter, the same approach generalizes to more than one independent categorical variable.

Parenthetically, other programs for ANOVA may use different formats, but the overall approach is the same. For example, in ANOVA or GLM procedures of SAS (see below) the category identification vector is identified as a CLASS variable, which may be stated in either numeric format, as in T in the present example, or in character format (e.g., A, B, C; Treat1, Treat2, Control).

When we said earlier that using a category identification vector as input affords the greatest flexibility to carry out different types of analyses, or the same type of analysis with different procedures, we had in mind its use for the generation of different coding schemes for MR, as was demonstrated in preceding sections, and its use in ANOVA, as is demonstrated in the present section. Incidentally, the two analyses (i.e., MR and ONEWAY) could be carried out in a single run.

In addition to the command for the overall analysis, contrast subcommands were included to test specific comparisons. These are explained later in connection with the relevant output.

Output

OBS	T	Y	
1	1	8	
2	1	8	*[first two subjects in T 1]*
.	.	.	
7	2	7	
8	2	8	*[first two subjects in T 2]*
.	.	.	

13	3	10	
14	3	11	[first two subjects in T 3]
.	.	.	
19	4	12	
20	4	13	[first two subjects in T 4]
.	.	.	

--- O N E   W A Y ---

Variable Y
By Variable T

Analysis of Variance

Source	DF	Sum of Squares	Mean Squares	F Ratio	F Prob.
Between Groups	3	88.5000	29.5000	11.8000	.0001
Within Groups	20	50.0000	2.5000		
Total	23	138.5000			

Group	Count	Mean	Standard Deviation	Minimum	Maximum
Grp 1	6	10.0000	1.7889	8.0000	12.0000
Grp 2	6	9.0000	1.5492	7.0000	11.0000
Grp 3	6	12.0000	1.4142	10.0000	14.0000
Grp 4	6	14.0000	1.5492	12.0000	16.0000
Total	24	11.2500	2.4539	7.0000	16.0000

Commentary

From the excerpts of the data listing, you can see the format on which the program operates.

Turning first to the Analysis of Variance, it will be noted that, except for differences in labels, the results are identical to those obtained earlier when these data were analyzed by MR. What are labeled here Between Groups and Within Groups were labeled Regression and Residual respectively in the MR analyses.

We comment now on some differences in intermediate results obtained from the application of the two approaches. To begin with, in ANOVA procedures, statistics for groups (e.g., means, standard deviations) are generally obtained as part of the output. In MR, on the other hand, such statistics may be obtained for the vectors (e.g., dependent variable mean and standard deviation for all subjects, without distinction of group membership). Group statistics have to be calculated separately. In preceding sections, it was shown how the regression equation may be used to obtain category means.

In MR, the proportion of variance accounted for is obtained routinely in the form of R^2. Some ANOVA procedures also report R^2 (e.g., ANOVA of SAS). When using a procedure that does not report this information, as is the case for the procedure used here, it can be obtained by calculating what, in the context of ANOVA, is referred to as η^2 (eta squared; see Hays, 1988, p. 369; Kerlinger, 1986, pp. 216–217):

$$\eta^2 = \frac{ss_b}{ss_t} \qquad\qquad (19.6)$$

where ss_b = Between Groups Sum of Squares; ss_t = Total Sum of Squares. For the present analysis

$$\eta^2 = \frac{88.5}{138.5} = .63899$$

The equivalence of the Between Groups and the Regression Sums of Squares was noted above. Therefore, dividing either of them by the Total Sum of Squares amounts to the same thing. Hence, $\eta^2 = R^2$ for the same data. Here, then, is another example of different terms used to refer to the same entity.

Output

Contrast Coefficient Matrix

	Grp 1	Grp 2	Grp 3	Grp 4
Contrast 1	1.0	−1.0	.0	.0
Contrast 2	.0	.0	1.0	−1.0
Contrast 3	1.0	1.0	−1.0	−1.0
Contrast 4	.0	−1.0	1.0	.0
Contrast 5	.0	−2.0	1.0	1.0

	Value	S. Error	T Value	D.F.	T Prob.
Contrast 1	1.0000	.9129	1.095	20.0	.286
Contrast 2	−2.0000	.9129	−2.191	20.0	.040
Contrast 3	−7.0000	1.2910	−5.422	20.0	.000
Contrast 4	3.0000	.9129	3.286	20.0	.004
Contrast 5	8.0000	1.5811	5.060	20.0	.000

Commentary

As was shown in preceding sections, advantage may be taken of specific coding schemes to obtain intermediate results of interest. For example, it was shown that, when using dummy coding in a design consisting of several treatments and a control group, tests of differences between the mean of each treatment and the mean of the control group are obtained in the form of tests of regression coefficients. Depending on the computer program used for ANOVA, such tests may be obtained by specifying the desired contrasts, as in ONEWAY, or they may have to be calculated after the overall results have been obtained.

The preceding excerpt of the output was obtained as a result of the CONTRAST subcommands (see Input). As you can see, the requested contrasts are listed, followed by tests of each. For comparative purposes, we specified contrasts tested earlier in the context of the MR analyses. The first three contrasts were used earlier in the analysis of these data with orthogonal coding, whereas Contrasts 4 and 5 were used earlier to illustrate the application of the Scheffé method for post hoc multiple comparisons.

Notice that, in the results reported above, t tests are used. When the same comparisons were tested earlier by applying (19.5), F tests with 1 df for the numerator were used. If you squared the values given here or, equivalently, took the square roots of the F's for the same contrasts tested earlier, you would see that the results are identical.

From the preceding, it follows that desired results may be obtained in a variety of ways, with varying degrees of ease, depending on the specific features of the computer program and on how they are utilized.

We now illustrate the use of several SAS procedures for the analysis of the data of Table 19.2. We do this not only for comparative purposes with the previous analyses of these data but also because we wish to acquaint you with the GLM procedure.

SAS

Input

```
TITLE 'TABLE 19.1. A CATEGORICAL INDEPENDENT VARIABLE';
DATA T191;
  INPUT T Y;
  CARDS;
      [data as displayed in Table 19.1 go here]
PROC PRINT;
PROC MEANS;
  BY T;
PROC GLM;
  CLASS T;
  MODEL Y = T/SOLUTION;
  CONTRAST 'T1 VS T2' T 1 −1 0 0;
  CONTRAST 'T3 VS T4' T 0 0 1 −1;
  CONTRAST 'T1+T2 VS T3+T4' T 1 1 −1 −1;
  CONTRAST 'T2 VS T3' T 0 −1 1 0;
  CONTRAST 'T2 VS T3+T4' T 0 −2 1 1;
```

Commentary

For general explanations about SAS input and output files, see Chapter 16.

PROC PRINT calls for the printing of the data. We do not report output generated by it, as it looks very much like the listing of the data given for the analysis through ONEWAY (see preceding section).

PROC MEANS calls for descriptive statistics (e.g., means and standard deviations). BY T calls for the reporting of these statistics for each of the categories of the independent variable. We do not reproduce the results of this PROCedure, as they are similar to those given for ONEWAY (above).

SAS has several procedures that could be used for the analysis of the data of Table 19.2. Probably the most obvious choice would be PROC ANOVA. Alternatively, coded vectors could be entered as input or generated by operating on the category identification vector, T, and then applying PROC REG in a manner very similar to the one used earlier with MINI-TAB or REGRESSION of SPSS. (Examples of the use of PROC REG with continuous independent variables are given in Chapters 17 and 18.)

We decided to use GLM, because it is an extremely versatile and powerful procedure for the analysis of data within the context of the General Linear Model. Consequently, it can be used, among other things, for analyses in which the independent variables are categorical (as in ANOVA procedures), continuous, and/or both (as in regression procedures). We elaborate on this point after commenting on the remaining input statements.

PROC GLM invokes this procedure. CLASS T declares the category identification vector as a classificatory, or grouping, variable (e.g., treatments, groups). The MODEL statement identifies the dependent variable as Y and the independent variable as T. SOLUTION requests parameter estimates in the form of a regression equation (see output).

This general setup is very similar to the ONEWAY of SPSS, where the keyword BY is used to accomplish the same purpose (see preceding section). As was pointed out earlier, SAS accepts numbers or names for category identification, whereas SPSS requires numbers.

The CONTRASTS called for are the same ones used in ONEWAY above. Notice that contrast labels are inserted in single quotes.

Before proceeding with the output and commentaries, the generality of GLM will be illustrated by commenting on how it could be used to analyze these data in a manner done through MR programs in earlier sections of this chapter. Instead of the above setup, we could have read in coded vectors according to any scheme we wished to use (e.g., dummy, effect), or we could have generated such vectors by operating on the T vector (e.g., by using IF statements; see SAS manual). For the sake of illustration, assume that three effect-coded vectors were generated and labeled E1, E2, and E3. Under such circumstances, the following statements would be used:

PROC GLM;
    MODEL Y=E1 E2 E3;

This would yield results of a MR analysis in which Y is regressed on the three coded vectors. Notice that neither CLASS nor the CONTRAST statements would be used in conjunction with this model statement. You may wish to run the data of Table 19.1 in this manner and compare the results with those obtained here as well as with those obtained in the application of MINITAB and SPSS REGRESSION to the analysis of the same data.

This, then, is but one instance of GLM's great versatility. As is evident from the preceding, the model statement can contain categorical variables, continuous variables, or both kinds of variables.

Output

General Linear Models Procedure
Class Level Information

Class	Levels	Values
T	4	1 2 3 4

Number of observations in data set = 24

Dependent Variable: Y

Source	DF	Sum of Squares	Mean Square	F Value	Pr> F
Model	3	88.50000000	29.50000000	11.80	0.0001
Error	20	50.00000000	2.50000000		
Corrected Total	23	138.50000000			

R-Square	Root MSE	Y Mean
0.638989	1.581139	11.2500000

Parameter		Estimate	T for H0: Parameter=0	Pr > |T|	Std Error of Estimate
INTERCEPT		14.00000000	21.69	0.0001	0.64549722
T	1	−4.00000000	−4.38	0.0003	0.91287093
	2	−5.00000000	−5.48	0.0001	0.91287093
	3	−2.00000000	−2.19	0.0405	0.91287093

Commentary

Note, first, that the results of the overall analysis are identical to those obtained several times earlier. Furthermore, R^2 is reported as part of the output (see comments about the calculation of η^2 in the preceding section).

When, as in the present analysis, a CLASS statement is used, an equation such as the above (under Estimate) can be obtained by specifying SOLUTION as an option on the MODEL statement (see Input). This type of output is generated routinely when CLASS is *not* used, that is, when vectors specified in the MODEL (be they variables or coded vectors representing categorical variables) are used as in a MR program (see the MODEL statement with E1, E2, and E3, above).

Inspect now the parameter estimates and their tests and note that they are identical to those obtained when the dependent variable was regressed on dummy vectors, and the last category of the T vector was treated as a control group (i.e., the category assigned 0's in all the coded vectors). Our comments about the properties of the regression equation with dummy coding (earlier in this chapter) are equally applicable to results reported here and will, therefore, not be repeated.

Output

Contrast	DF	Contrast SS	Mean Square	F Value	Pr > F
T1 VS T2	1	3.00000000	3.00000000	1.20	0.2863
T3 VS T4	1	12.00000000	12.00000000	4.80	0.0405
T1+T2 VS T3+T4	1	73.50000000	73.50000000	29.40	0.0001
T2 VS T3	1	27.00000000	27.00000000	10.80	0.0037
T2 VS T3+T4	1	64.00000000	64.00000000	25.60	0.0001

Commentary

As the same contrasts were calculated and commented upon several times earlier (e.g., ONEWAY output, above), you should encounter no difficulties in interpreting these results. It will only be pointed out that, in ONEWAY t ratios are reported, whereas here F ratios are reported. Note, however, that the Mean Square for each contrast has 1 df (hence, $t^2 = F$). Dividing each Mean Square by the $MSR = 2.5$ (see output above) the F Values are obtained.

CONCLUDING REMARKS

Quite a bit of ground has been covered in the course of presenting analyses for a design with an independent categorical variable. Depending on your background and/or on the rate with which you have been reading the preceding sections, you may be at a loss, suffering from information overload. It may, therefore, be helpful to offer, in retrospect, an explanation of what we had hoped to achieve, a synopsis of the major points covered, and some general suggestions about making use of the materials we presented.

Our main aim was to show how information about a categorical variable may be coded, thereby rendering it in a format suitable for use as an independent variable in a regression analysis. We meant our detailed discussions of a design with a single independent categorical variable to serve as a foundation to an approach that is generalizable to designs with more than one categorical independent variable (see Chapter 20) and to ones consisting of categorical as well as continuous independent variables (see Chapter 21).

We have gone through different coding schemes for two reasons. One, to show that some coding schemes are more useful for certain kinds of designs than others (e.g., dummy coding for a design with several treatments and a control group). Two, in order to demonstrate that the overall results are the same, regardless of the coding scheme used. We suggest that you do not worry about memorizing the features of each coding scheme. You can always check on what they are when you plan to use them. As you keep using them, you will also come to know their properties.

What was said about the coding schemes applies even with greater force to our use of different computer programs or procedures and our discussions of various aspects of the input and the output. Needless to say, all of this was not meant to be memorized. We had two purposes in mind. First, we wanted to acquaint you with a variety of computer packages and procedures within such packages in the hope of thereby preventing the formation of the wrong impression that unless you have access to a specific program we, or someone else, may have used you cannot carry out the kind of analyses presented.

Second, and related to the first point, we felt that, by following our discussions of various programs, you will learn to use computer programs intelligently and judiciously. Towards this end, we felt it important to show you that certain aspects of output may be irrelevant in a given analysis (e.g., tests of b's when effect coding is used).

In the beginning of the present section, we explained our aims in comparing MR and ANOVA, and for including examples of the application of ANOVA procedures. Because the multiple regression approach is more comprehensive (see MR and ANOVA: Similarities and Contrasts, in Chapter 20), we recommend that it be generally used. This is why we stress the use of MR programs, or procedures such as GLM of SAS, in the hope that our detailed explanations of input and output of such programs will help you develop the skills to use them and to interpret their output.

Nevertheless, we thought it important to illustrate that there is nothing sacred about using MR programs. This is why we showed that, for the design under consideration, ANOVA programs could be used as an alternative. An analysis is not endowed with validity by virtue of the computer program used to carry it out. Any program may be used well or abused. For certain purposes, an ANOVA-like procedure may be preferable to a MR procedure (for an example, see Simple Main Effects, in Chapter 20). All this may appear trite to you. However, as we suggested in Chapter 16, applications of inappropriate analyses and misinterpretations of results are in large measure due to faith in the magical powers of computers and computer programs.

Our presentation of the computer programs we have used was by no means exhaustive. We have not even hinted at some of the options available in them. It will suffice to cite but one example. Programs such as ONEWAY in SPSS, and ANOVA and GLM in SAS, have options for a variety of multiple comparisons. We felt it more useful to concentrate on the most general approach, that is, through the use of contrast statements. We recommend that you try some of the options and that you run some variations on the analyses we have presented.

In sum, the materials we have presented are not meant to be read through and absorbed in the process. Rather they are meant to serve as guides while you learn progressively how to apply MR to different designs and how to make the best use of computer programs to which you have access. The approach introduced in this chapter is extended to multiple categorical independent variables in the next chapter.

STUDY SUGGESTIONS

1. One hundred subjects were randomly assigned in equal numbers to five treatments (A_1, A_2, A_3, A_4, and A_5). Dummy coding was used, where treatment A_1 was identified in D1, A_2 in D2, A_3 in D3, A_4 in D4, and A_5 was assigned 0's in all the vectors. The total sum of squares for the dependent variable (Σy^2) was 135.63. The dependent variable was regressed on the coded vectors. R^2 was found to be .32. The regression equation was

$$Y' = 25.60 + 13.24D1 + 9.10D2 - 11.00D3 + 6.31D4$$

   What is (are) the
   (a) correlation between any two of the coded vectors?
   (b) F ratio for the test of R^2?
   (c) regression and residual sums of squares?
   (d) means for the five groups?

2. Assume that for the problem given under study suggestion 1, effect coding was used instead. That is, A_1 was identified in E1, A_2 in E2, A_3 in E3, A_4 in E4, and A_5 was assigned -1 in all the vectors.
   (a) Use the means you have calculated on the basis of the information given in study suggestion 1 and indicate what the regression equation for effect coding would be.
   (b) Do you expect any of the answers you have given in (a) through (c) of study suggestion 1 to be different because of the use of a different coding scheme? If yes, spell out what the difference(s) would be.

3. According to the text "it is not meaningful to do incremental partitioning of the regression sum of squares or of the proportion of variance" when using coded vectors to represent a categorical variable. Explain why.

4. In a design consisting of four treatments (A_1, A_2, A_3, and A_4) effect coding was used such that A_1 was identified in E1, A_2 in E2, A_3 in E3, and A_4 was assigned -1 in all the vectors. The following regression equation was obtained:

$$Y' = 35.68 + 6.78E1 - 3.45E2 + 1.27E3$$

   What are the four treatment effects?

5. Fifteen subjects were randomly assigned in equal numbers to two treatments (A and B) and a control group (C). Following are their scores on a measure of the dependent variable:

A	B	C
5	8	3
6	6	4
5	7	4
7	8	5
7	9	5

   Use dummy coding to analyze these data. We recommend that you do all the calculations by hand or with the aid of a calculator. You may find it useful to also analyze the data by computer and to compare your hand calculations with the computer output.
   What is (are) the
   (a) means and standard deviations for the three groups?
   (b) proportion of variance of the dependent variable accounted for by the independent variable?

(c) F ratio for the test of this proportion?

(d) regression and residual sums of squares?

(e) regression equation and the t ratios for the test of the b's. What is the meaning of these tests?

6. Analyze the data given under study suggestion 5 using effect coding, assigning the -1's to C in all the vectors.

(a) What is the regression equation?

Assume that you have hypothesized that treatment B is more effective than A, and that treatment A is more effective than C.

(b) Test these comparisons. What kind of comparisons are they?

Assume now that you have hypothesized that B is more effective than A, and that the average of A and B is greater than C.

(c) Test these comparisons. What kind of comparisons are they?

7. Using the data given under study suggestion 5, assume that you have hypothesized the following orthogonal comparisons:

$$A > C; B > (A + C)/2$$

(a) Indicate the coding scheme you would use to carry out the analysis through multiple regression.

Regress the dependent variable on the coding scheme indicated under (a).

(b) What are the t ratios for the tests of the b's? What do these tests represent?

(c) What proportion of variance of the dependent variable is accounted for by the comparison between A and C?

(d) What proportion of variance is accounted for by the comparison of $(A + C)/2$ and B?

(e) What should the sum of the two proportions obtained under (c) and (d) be equal to?

Answers

1. (a) $-.25$—see (19.2)

   (b) $F = 11.18$ with 4 and 95 df

   (c) $ss_{reg} = 43.4016$; $ss_{res} = 92.2284$

   (d) Means: $A_1 = 38.84$; $A_2 = 34.70$; $A_3 = 14.60$; $A_4 = 31.91$; $A_5 = 25.60$

2. (a) Using the means arrived at under (d) of study suggestion 1, the regression equation for effect coding would be:

   $$Y' = 29.13 + 9.71E1 + 5.57E2 - 14.53E3 + 2.78E4$$

   (b) Only the correlation between the coded vectors would differ. Instead of $-.25$ it would be .50

3. The coded vectors represent a single variable. Hence, they have to be treated as a set (see text for a detailed explanation).

4. $A_1 = 6.78$; $A_2 = -3.45$; $A_3 = 1.27$; $A_4 = -4.60$

5. (a)

	A	B	C
M:	6.00	7.60	4.20
s:	1.00	1.14	.84

   (b) $R^2 = .7068$

   (c) $F = 14.47$ with 2 and 12 df

(d) $ss_{reg} = 28.9333$; $ss_{res} = 12.0000$

(e) $Y' = 4.2 \quad + 1.8D1 + 3.4D2$

t:	2.846	5.376
df:	12	12

where A was identified in D1 and B was identified in D2. Each t constitutes a test of the difference between the mean of the treatment identified in the vector in question and the mean of the control group. These t ratios have to be checked against values in Dunnett tables for 12 df and a prespecified α level (see text for explanation).

6. (a) $Y' = 5.93 + .07E1 + 1.67E2$

   (b) $B > A$: $F = 6.40$ with 1 and 12 df—see (19.5)

   $A > C$: $F = 8.10$ with 1 and 12 df.

   These comparisons are planned nonorthogonal.

   (c) $B > A$: see (b).

   $(A + B)/2 > C$: $F = 22.53$ with 1 and 12 df.

   These comparisons are planned orthogonal.

7. (a) O1: 1 for A, 0 for B, and -1 for C;

   O2: -1 for A and C, 2 for B.

   (b) For b_{O1}: $t = 2.846$ with 12 df;

   for b_{O2}: $t = 4.564$ with 12 df.

   Each t is a test of the comparison reflected in the vector with which the b in question is associated.

   (c) .198

   (d) .508

   (e) R^2

Chapter 20
Multiple Categorical Independent Variables: Factorial Designs

No aphorism is more frequently repeated in connection with field trials, than that we must ask Nature few questions, or, ideally, one question at a time. The writer is convinced that this view is wholly mistaken. Nature, he suggests, will best respond to a logical and carefully thought out questionnaire; indeed, if we ask her a single question, she will often refuse to answer until some other topic has been discussed. (Fisher, 1926, p. 511)

The anthropomorphic tenor of Fisher's statement aside, it captures the spirit of his revolutionary ideas and contributions to the design and analysis of experiments. Fisher was not only instrumental in dispelling the naive notion that the ideal experiment is one in which a single variable is manipulated while controlling for all other variables, but he also developed the conceptual and methodological tools for the design, execution, and analysis of experiments with multiple independent variables.

Although developed in the context of agricultural research, Fisher's ideas, methods, and even terminology (e.g., plots, blocks) were enthusiastically adopted by sociobehavioral scientists. His ANOVA methods became the primary, if not the sole, analytic approach in human and animal research. Incidentally, F tests and tables of distribution of F were so named in honor of Fisher.

The beneficial effects of Fisher's orientation and methodology on sociobehavioral research are undeniable.[1] Yet their unqualified adoption even in settings for which they were not suited, notably nonexperimental research, has led to grievous errors and misinterpretations. Some of these are discussed later in this chapter.

The most important advantage of experiments with multiple independent variables is that they make it possible to determine whether and how independent variables interact in their effects on the dependent variable. We introduced the concept of interaction in different contexts (e.g., control and external validity, in Chapter 10; design and analysis, in Chapters 12 and 14), where it was pointed out that it refers to the joint effect of two or more independent variables. Interactions may take different forms. Variables may, for example,

---

[1]Another of Fisher's major contributions to research design, that of randomization, was discussed in earlier chapters (e.g., Chapters 10 and 12).

reinforce the effects of each other, resulting in a combined effect that is larger than the sum of their separate effects. Conversely, variables may operate at cross purposes, counteracting the effects of each other, resulting in a combined effect that is smaller than the sum of their separate effects.

Examples of interactions abound, as is reflected even in everyday expressions regarding beneficial or detrimental effects of combinations of conditions, exemplified by references to the deadly combination of alcohol and drugs, detrimental effects of smoking and consumption of large quantities of alcohol or coffee. Harmful, even deadly, interaction effects of medicines with types of diets or with physical conditions (e.g., allergies) are well known. In fact, in order to avoid harmful interactions, some pharmacists have begun using computers to cross check customers' profiles and medicines they take (Belkin, 1984). Medical research has also been directed towards detection of beneficial interactions. For example, on the basis of their review and reanalysis of data from 30 studies, Laska et al. (1984; see also Beaver, 1984) concluded that caffeine increases the effectiveness of pain relievers such as aspirin. Examples of interactions in sociobehavioral research were given in the chapters mentioned above (see also numerical example, below).

In the context of ANOVA, independent variables are generally referred to as factors, hence, the term factorial designs.[2] Each factor may consist of two or more levels or categories. Factorial designs are generally described with reference to the number of categories for each factor. For example, a 2 x 2 (2 by 2) design refers to a factorial design consisting of two factors, each with two levels or categories. Such designs were introduced and commented on in Chapter 12 (see Figures 12.2 and 12.3 and the discussions related to them). A 3 x 5 is also a two-factor design except that one of the factors consists of 3 categories and the other of 5 categories.

Factorial designs can consist of more than two factors, each comprised of any number of categories. For example, a 2 x 3 x 6 is a three-factor design: one factor with 2 categories, one with 3 categories, and one with 6 categories. In the bulk of the presentation that follows, we concentrate on a two-factor design. Pursuant to the discussion and illustrative analyses of such a design, we comment on designs consisting of more than two factors.

A NUMERICAL EXAMPLE

In Table 20.1, a numerical example for a 2 x 3 design is presented. The crossing of the two factors yields six combinations, referred to as cells. Each cell is identified by the letters representing the variables and appropriate subscripts. Thus, A_1B_1 refers to the cell whose subjects were administered the combination of the first category of the two independent variables. A_2B_3 refers to the combination of the second category of A with the third category of B—similarly for other combinations. This notation generalizes to designs with more than two factors. Notice that there are four subjects in each cell. Further, the scores on the dependent variable are the same as those used in the one-way ANOVA in Chapter 19 (i.e., data of Table 19.1), except that we split them up so that they appear as if they were obtained in a 2 x 3 design. The statistics included in the table are discussed below.

We will assume that the data of Table 20.1 were obtained in an experiment. Only later in this chapter do we comment on issues concerning the application of factorial ANOVA to

---

[2]Because of similarity of terms, factorial analysis of variance is sometimes erroneously referred to as factor analysis of variance. Factor analysis is presented in Chapter 22.

Table 20.1

Illustrative Data for a 2 × 3 Design

		B_1	B_2	B_3		
A_1		10 11 14 13	10 10 7 8	8 10 11 10		*Eff*
	M:	12.00	8.75	9.75	$\bar{A}_1 = 10.17$	−1.08
	Int:	2.08	−.67	−1.41		
A_2		8 8 12 12	12 12 12 13	13 15 15 16		
	M:	10.00	12.25	14.75	$\bar{A}_2 = 12.33$	1.08
	Int:	−2.08	.67	1.41		

$$\bar{B}_1 = 11.00 \qquad \bar{B}_2 = 10.50 \qquad \bar{B}_3 = 12.25 \qquad \bar{Y} = 11.25$$
$$\textit{Eff:} \quad -.25 \qquad\qquad\qquad -.75 \qquad\qquad\qquad 1.00$$

Note. M = Mean; *Eff* = Effect; *Int* = Interaction. See text for explanation.

nonexperimental designs. Being an experiment, at least one of the variables has to be manipulated, and subjects have to be randomly assigned (see Chapter 12).

The design under consideration may be one in which both independent variables are manipulated. Alternatively, it may consist of a manipulated and a classificatory, or grouping, variable. A couple of examples of each will be given.

Turning first to examples where both variables are manipulated, *B* may be type of crime (e.g., murder, burglary, arson), and *A* may be the race of the perpetrator (e.g., black, white). The dependent variable may be perceived severity of crime. We cannot go into details of the specific manner in which the variables are manipulated, the setting, execution, type of subjects, sample size, the measurement of the dependent variable, to name but some of the issues a researcher doing such a study would have to consider. Solely for illustrative purposes, assume that subjects are randomly assigned to watch a videotape, or read a description, of the commission of one of three crimes by either a black or a white person and are then asked to rate the severity of the crime. As is shown below, three effects may be identified: type of crime, race of the perpetrator, and interaction between the two variables.

Now, depending on the theoretical rationale, which we also cannot go into here, a researcher may hypothesize one or two main effects but no interaction. A main effect of crime would mean that there are differences in perceived severity of types of crimes, regardless of the race of the perpetrator. A main effect for race of perpetrator would mean that perceived severity of crime is affected by the race of the perpetrator, regardless of specific crime committed.

Alternatively, the researcher may hypothesize that there is an interaction between the two variables. For example, the researcher may expect murder to be rated as more severe when it is committed by a black than by a white. In contrast, the researcher may expect burglary to be rated as more severe when committed by a white than by a black.

To reiterate: We cannot go into theoretical formulations concerning our illustrations. Moreover, there are various aspects of the design that we cannot address, some of which we would like at least to mention. It is likely for the researcher to have different expectations about perception of crime severity, depending on whether the subjects (i.e., the perceivers) are males or females, blacks or whites, urbanites or suburbanites, or what have you. Under such circumstances, the type of subject may be held constant (e.g., using only white males) or built in as a factor in the design.[3]

Assuming the researcher wishes to introduce subjects' sex as a factor, then the design under consideration would become a 2 x 2 x 3 (subject's sex, perpetrator's race, and type of crime). To complicate matters a little more, it is possible for the researcher to also have different expectations about perception of crime severity, depending on whether the perpetrator is male or female. This would then become a 2 x 2 x 2 x 3 (subject's sex, perpetrator's sex, perpetrator's race, and type of crime). As was stated above, we will comment on designs with more than two independent variables later on. Here we just wanted to draw attention to some of the important decisions that have to be made and that we are not addressing.

Following are some other substantive examples in connection with the 2 x 3 design under consideration. B may be teaching methods, A sex (race) of the teacher, and Y academic achievement; B may be work settings, A managerial styles, and Y job satisfaction; B may be different kinds of drugs, A different diets, and Y blood pressure. You can no doubt come up with numerous other examples from your field of interest.

Turning now to examples of a 2 x 3 design in which one of the variables is manipulated and the other is classificatory, A may be two types of communication, or two types of therapy; B may be different diagnostic groupings, or marital status, or religious affiliation; and Y may be attitudes, or adjustment, or what have you. Here too the researcher may hypothesize only main effects (e.g., different effects of therapies, regardless of diagnostic groupings; differences among the diagnostic groupings, regardless of type of therapy). Alternatively, an interaction may be hypothesized, according to which certain types of diagnostic groupings are expected to benefit more from a certain type of therapy. Whatever the specifics, in a design where a classificatory variable is used, stratified randomization is carried out. That is, subjects from each strata (e.g., manic-depressives) are randomly assigned to the different treatments (e.g., therapies).

THE MODEL

In Chapter 19, a model for the case of one independent variable was introduced—see (19.3) and the discussion related to it. For two independent categorical variables, the model, expressed in the form of parameter estimates, is

$$Y_{ijk} = \bar{Y} + a_i + b_j + (ab)_{ij} + e_{ijk} \tag{20.1}$$

where Y_{ijk} = score for subject k in cell ij, or treatment combination a_i and b_j; $\bar{Y}$ = grand mean of the dependent variable; a_i = effect of treatment i; b_j = effect of treatment j; $(ab)_{ij}$ = effect of treatment combination ij, or interaction; e_{ijk} = error or residual for individual k in cell ij. We will elaborate on the meaning of the preceding terms by referring to Table 20.1.

---

[3]See discussion of Forms of Control in Chapter 10. See also Factorial Designs in Chapter 12.

MAIN EFFECTS

Examine Table 20.1 and notice that we have calculated cell means as well as means of each column and row of the table. The latter—referred to as marginal means—are calculated for each factor as if it were the only one in the design. Thus, column means are calculated as if there were no rows, and row means are calculated as if there were no columns. For example, marginal mean A_1, 10.17, is the mean for the 12 subjects administered A_1, ignoring the fact that they belong to different categories of B. When n's in the cells are equal, this is the same as calculating the average of the cell means for row A_1.[4] Similarly, the marginal mean of B_1, 11.00, is equal to the mean of the 8 subjects administered this treatment or the average of the two cell means under B_1.

As in the case of a one-way design (see Chapter 19), an effect is defined as the deviation of a category mean from the grand mean. When dealing with more than one independent variable, effects for each independent variable, referred to as main effects, are calculated using marginal means. That is, main effects for each independent variable are calculated as if there were no other independent variables. This is how the effects reported in Table 20.1 were calculated (see *Eff* for columns and rows). For example, the effect of A_1, -1.08, is equal to the deviation of mean A_1 from the grand mean ($10.17 - 11.25$)—similarly for the other effects. Recall that, because effects are calculated as deviations from the grand mean, their sum for any factor is equal to zero.

INTERACTION

The interaction term for any given cell is defined as follows:

$$(AB)_{ij} = (\bar{Y}_{ij} - \bar{Y}) - (\bar{Y}_{A_i} - \bar{Y}) - (\bar{Y}_{B_j} - \bar{Y}) \tag{20.2}$$

Examine the three terms on the right of the equal sign and notice that the first term is equal to deviation of the mean of cell ij from the grand mean; the second term is the effect of category i of factor A (see above); and the third term is the effect of category j of factor B (see above). From (20.2), it can be seen that the interaction term for a given cell is zero when the deviation of the cell mean from the grand mean is equal to the sum of the effects of the categories corresponding to the cell under consideration. What the preceding boils down to is that it is sufficient to resort to the grand mean and the main effects in order to predict the mean of the cell under consideration. If, on the other hand, the deviation of a cell mean from the grand mean is *not* equal to the sum of the effects of the categories corresponding to it, then it is necessary to resort to the concept of an interaction between the variables.

Using (20.2), interaction terms for the cells of Table 20.1 were calculated (see *Int* in cells). Notice that the interaction terms for each row and each column sum to zero. Accordingly, in the design under consideration, the terms for two cells only (any two will do) have to be calculated through the application of (20.2). Terms for the remaining cells may then be obtained to satisfy the restriction that their sum for columns and rows be zero. The number of terms for the interaction that have to be calculated in any design by using (20.2) is equal to the number of df for interaction. As is shown below, $df = 2$ for the interaction in the present example.

---

[4]Our discussions and illustrations are limited to the case of equal cell frequencies. Later in this chapter, we comment on the case of unequal cell frequencies.

In the foregoing, reference was made to interaction terms for each cell. However, the interaction between two variables refers simultaneously to the terms in all the cells. That is, a conclusion that there is no interaction between the two variables is valid only when the interaction terms in *all* the cells are zero. Small departures from zero may occur because of sampling fluctuations. This, of course, is what is meant when it is concluded that an interaction is statistically not significant (tests of significance are presented below).

Table 20.1 will now be examined in yet another way to get an additional perspective on the meaning of the interaction. Look at the pairs of cell means for each of the columns (i.e., for different *B* treatments) and notice that, in each case, they are associated with the same *A* treatments; that is, one of the cells is associated with treatment A_1 and the other with A_2. Now, if the effects of *A* are independent of the effects of *B*, that is, if there is no interaction, it follows that the differences between cell means for each of the pairs should be equal to each other. Moreover, the difference should equal the difference between the effects of A_1 and A_2. This can be expressed as follows:

$$A_1B_1 - A_2B_1 = A_1B_2 - A_2B_2 = A_1B_3 - A_2B_3 = A_1 - A_2$$

where the first six terms refer to cell means, and the last two terms refer to the row effects.

For the data of Table 20.1, this is clearly not the case. The differences between the cell means are 2.00 under B_1, -3.50 under B_2, and -5.00 under B_3. However, the difference between the row effects is -2.16. What all this boils down to is that there is an interaction between *A* and *B*: The effects of the *A* treatments vary, depending on the levels of *B*'s with which they are combined. Assume, for the sake of illustration, that the higher the score, the "better" (e.g., better adjustment, higher achievement, more positive attitude). It is clear that, under B_1, A_1 is superior to A_2 but that the reverse is true under B_2 and B_3. Moreover, although A_2 is superior to A_1 under both B_2 and B_3, the magnitude of the difference between the two *A* treatments is greater under the latter.

In the preceding discussion, no mention was made of tests of significance. Below, we show how the interaction is tested. Later in this chapter, it is shown that, when an interaction is statistically significant, tests of simple main effects are carried out. On the basis of such tests, it may, for example, turn out that the difference between A_1 and A_2 under B_1 is statistically not significant but that the differences between these treatments under B_2 and B_3 are statistically significant.

Statistical significance aside, we cannot comment on the specific decisions a researcher might make on the basis of the illustrative results, as these would have to be based, among other things, on the meaningfulness of the differences between the *A* treatments, the costs involved in their administration as well as the administration of the treatments with which they are to be combined (i.e., the *B*'s).

What was said about differences between cell means of rows across columns applies also to differences between cell means of columns across rows. That is, in the absence of an interaction, differences between cell means for any two columns would be expected to be equal to each other and to the difference between the effects of the columns under consideration. It is not necessary to inspect differences between cell means for both columns and rows, as the presence of an interaction refers to the joint effect of the factors represented by both. As an exercise, you may wish to make the relevant comparisons of cell means for the columns and note that an interaction is indicated (a more detailed explanation of comparisons of cell means of the kind described here will be found in Pedhazur, 1982, pp. 349–353).

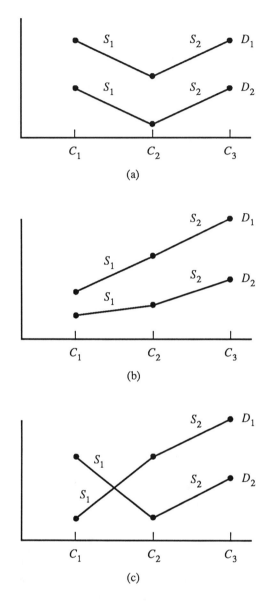

Figure 20.1

GRAPHING THE MEANS

Graphs of means are very useful for ascertaining whether there is an interaction. To graph the means, assign one of the factors to the abscissa and plot its cell means across the levels of the other factor. Connect the plotted means for any given level by straight lines. Before plotting the means for the data of Table 20.1, we will use the three graphs given in Figure 20.1 to explain what one is looking for in such graphs.

For convenience, we use the same type of design as the one we have been analyzing but with different factor names, C and D, so as to make it clear that these plots *do not* refer to the means of Table 20.1. Notice that factor C is assigned to the abscissa. Means for the different categories of C at each of the D levels are indicated by dots, and are connected by lines labeled S with appropriate subscripts for convenience of reference.

What one is looking for in graphs such as those depicted in Figure 20.1 is whether or not all sets of corresponding line segments are parallel. By a set of corresponding line segments, we mean lines connecting respective cell means at the levels of one of the factors. In Figure 20.1, there are two such sets, distinguished by different subscripts. Thus, for example, S_1 refers to the set of lines connecting the means of C_1 and C_2 at the different levels of D. When there is no interaction, all corresponding line segments are parallel. When at least one set of line segments is not parallel, an interaction is indicated.

Look now at (a) of Figure 20.1 and notice that both sets of line segments are parallel. As can be seen, cell means at the two levels of D are equidistant for all the categories of C. That is, for all the C categories, the mean for D_1 is larger than the mean for D_2 by the same amount. This, then, indicates that the effects of D do not vary across the levels of C, which is what the absence of an interaction means.

Examine now (b) of Figure 20.1 and notice that both sets of line segments are not parallel, indicating that C and D interact. Assuming, as before, that higher means indicate superior performance, it is evident that D_1 is superior to D_2 at all levels of C but not by the same amount. When, as in the present example, the rank order of the treatment effects does not change (i.e., D_1 is always superior to D_2, although not by the same amount), the interaction is referred to as an *ordinal interaction*.

Assuming, for the sake of illustration, that D_1 is a much costlier treatment than D_2, it is possible that a researcher may conclude on the basis of results such as those depicted in (b) that an investment in D_1 is warranted only when it is combined with treatment C_3. It is conceivable for such a decision to be arrived at even when it is concluded, on the basis of tests of simple main effects (see below), that the differences between D_1 and D_2 are statistically significant at each of the C levels. This, of course, has to do with the distinction between statistical significance and substantive importance discussed in earlier chapters (e.g., Chapters 9 and 15).

Another type of interaction is depicted in (c) of Figure 20.1. Two things will be noted. First, one set of line segments, S_2, is parallel. This illustrates what was said above, namely that only when all sets (two, in the present case) are parallel is it concluded that there is no interaction.

Second, under C_1, D_2 is superior to D_1, but the converse is true for the other C levels. This is an example of a *disordinal interaction*, that is, the rank order of the effectiveness of treatments changes.[5]

The cell means for the data of Table 20.1 are plotted in Figure 20.2, from which it is evident that A and B interact. As this interaction was discussed earlier, we will not comment on it here. Instead, we will use this opportunity to caution you against interpreting plots such as in Figure 20.1 and 20.2 as indicating trends in the sense that such terms are used in the context of regression or correlation analysis. Figure 20.2 will be used to explain what we have in mind. On the basis of this figure, one might be tempted to conclude that the regression of the dependent variable, Y, on B appears linear and positive under A_2 but curvilinear under A_1. *Interpretations of this kind are wrong.* The reason is that B is a categorical variable, and, therefore, the placement of the categories on the abscissa is arbitrary. Suffice it to point out that, if the order of the B's were reversed, that is, beginning

---

[5]Concepts of ordinal and disordinal interactions were discussed and illustrated in Chapter 3 (see Figure 3.5, and the discussion related to it; see also, Chapter 21).

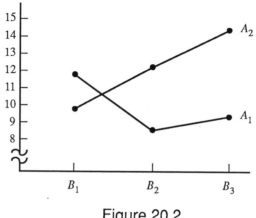

Figure 20.2

with B_3 and ending with B_1, then this time it would be *erroneously* concluded that the regression is negative under A_2. A different erroneous conclusion about presumed trends would be reached with yet another ordering of the B's. In sum, the plots are useful only for the kind of comparisons of line segments discussed above, *not for the study of trends.*

SCORES AS COMPONENTS OF THE MODEL

Having calculated the various components of the model for the design of Table 20.1, it will be instructive to express each subject's score in terms of these components, that is, as expressed in (20.1). These are reported in Table 20.2, and labeled accordingly in Columns 2–5 and 7. The values for Columns 1–6 were taken from Table 20.1. For example, in Column 3, the effects of A, as reported in Table 20.1, were inserted.

It will be noted that values in Columns 3–5 are identical for individuals within any given cell, as they reflect main effects and interaction terms corresponding to it. Adding these values and the value in Column 2 (i.e., grand mean) for each individual yields the values of Column 6, which are the cell means (cell means were inserted in Column 6, despite the fact that, because of rounding, summations for two of the cells are slightly discrepant from the mean). As discussed below, the values in Column 6 are also the predicted scores (Y') that would be obtained as a result of applying the regression equation obtained from regressing Y on the coded vectors representing the main effects and interaction. That is, these are the best estimates in a least-squares sense.

From the preceding, it also follows that Column 7 could be labeled residual (i.e., $Y - Y'$). The residual for the first subject, for example, is $10 - 12 = -2.00$. Because the residuals in each cell are deviations from the cell mean, they sum to zero. In ANOVA terminology, these are referred to as within cell deviations; the sum of their squares, across all subjects, is termed as within cells, or error, sum of squares.

Look now at the last row of Table 20.2, labeled *ss*. The values reported in this row are obtained by squaring and summing the elements in the Columns indicated. Before commenting on the separate *ss*, they will be added:

$$27.99 + 13.00 + 54.11 + 43.00 = 138.10$$

As it turns out, this is the total sum of squares, which you may wish to calculate as an exercise. The calculations that yielded the *ss* of Table 20.2 are actually one way of partition-

Table 20.2
Data of Table 20.1 Expressed as Components of the Model

Cell	(1) Y	(2) $\bar{Y}$	(3) a_i	(4) b_j	(5) ab_{ij}	(6) $\bar{Y}_{ij}$	(7) e_{ijk}
	10	11.25	−1.08	−.25	2.08	12.00	−2.00
A_1B_1	11	11.25	−1.08	−.25	2.08	12.00	−1.00
	14	11.25	−1.08	−.25	2.08	12.00	2.00
	13	11.25	−1.08	−.25	2.08	12.00	1.00
	10	11.25	−1.08	−.75	−.67	8.75	1.25
A_1B_2	10	11.25	−1.08	−.75	−.67	8.75	1.25
	7	11.25	−1.08	−.75	−.67	8.75	−1.75
	8	11.25	−1.08	−.75	−.67	8.75	−.75
	8	11.25	−1.08	1.00	−1.41	9.75	−1.75
A_1B_3	10	11.25	−1.08	1.00	−1.41	9.75	.25
	11	11.25	−1.08	1.00	−1.41	9.75	1.25
	10	11.25	−1.08	1.00	−1.41	9.75	.25
	8	11.25	1.08	−.25	−2.08	10.00	−2.00
A_2B_1	8	11.25	1.08	−.25	−2.08	10.00	−2.00
	12	11.25	1.08	−.25	−2.08	10.00	2.00
	12	11.25	1.08	−.25	−2.08	10.00	2.00
	12	11.25	1.08	−.75	.67	12.25	−.25
A_2B_2	12	11.25	1.08	−.75	.67	12.25	−.25
	12	11.25	1.08	−.75	.67	12.25	−.25
	13	11.25	1.08	−.75	.67	12.25	.75
	13	11.25	1.08	1.00	1.41	14.75	−1.75
A_2B_3	15	11.25	1.08	1.00	1.41	14.75	.25
	15	11.25	1.08	1.00	1.41	14.75	.25
	16	11.25	1.08	1.00	1.41	14.75	1.25
ss:			27.99	13.00	54.11		43.00

Note. ss = sum of squared values in the given column. See text, for explanation of table.

ing the total sum of squares into sums of squares due to the separate components of the model under consideration, that is, due to A, B, A x B (interaction), and residual (error). There are much simpler ways for obtaining these results. Below, we show how this is done through the use of coding and the application of multiple regression analysis. The virtue of the presentation of Table 20.2 is that it shows clearly the anatomy of each score and of each sum of squares. We strongly suggest that you study Table 20.2 and compare it with results obtained later through computer analysis of these data.

TESTS OF SIGNIFICANCE

In order to test terms of the two-factor model analyzed above, it is necessary to determine the *df* for each of the terms and for error. The *df* associated with each factor, or main effect, equal the number of its categories minus one. Therefore, *df* for $A = i − 1$; *df* for $B = j − 1$, where i and j are number of categories in A and B respectively.

The *df* for interaction, A x B, equal the product of *df* for the main effects, that is, $(i − 1)(j − 1)$.

The *df* for the residual, or error, equal

$$N − (i − 1) − (j − 1) − (i − 1)(j − 1) − 1$$

Table 20.3

Summary of Analysis of Factorial Design, for data of Table 20.1

Source	SS	df	MS	F
A	27.99	1	27.99	11.71*
B	13.00	2	6.50	2.72
A × B	54.11	2	27.06	11.32*
Residual	43.00	18	2.39	
Total	138.10	23		

*$p < .05$

where N is the number of subjects and the other terms are as defined above. In words, the *df* for the residual equal the number of subjects minus the *df* for the terms in the model, minus one. For the numerical example of Table 20.1, *df* are 1 for A $(2 - 1)$, 2 for B $(3 - 1)$, 2 for A x B (1×2), and 18 for residual $(24 - 1 - 2 - 2 - 1)$. We are ready now to test the terms of this design.

Dividing each *ss* by its *df* yields a Mean Square (*MS*). An *F* ratio for each term of the model is obtained by dividing its *MS* by the Mean Square Residual (*MSR*). The *df* for the numerator of each *F* ratio are those associated with the term tested. The *df* for the denominator of all the *F* ratios equal those associated with the residual. These tests are summarized in Table 20.3.

Assuming that $\alpha = .05$ was selected, it can be seen from Table 20.3 that the effects of A and A x B are statistically significant. Interpretations of main effects are meaningful when, unlike the results for the present analysis, the interaction is statistically not significant. Under such circumstances, it makes sense to speak of effects of levels of one factor across those of another factor. Thus, assuming that, in the present analysis, A and B but not the interaction were found to be statistically significant, it would have then made sense to speak of effects of A ignoring B, and of the effects of B ignoring A. Moreover, because B consists of 3 categories, it would have also been meaningful and appropriate to do multiple comparisons among its levels. The specific type of comparisons (i.e., planned orthogonal, planned non-orthogonal, post hoc) would have, of course, been determined by the hypotheses formulated. Multiple comparisons among levels of main effects are carried out in a manner similar to comparisons among means in a one-way design shown in Chapter 19.

When, as in the present example, the interaction is statistically significant, it is generally not meaningful, although *not* wrong, to interpret results of tests of main effects. After all, the motivation for studying interactions is to ascertain whether the effects of a given factor vary depending on the levels of the other factor with which they are combined. Having found this to be the case (i.e., that the interaction is statistically significant), it makes little sense to act as if it is not so, which is what interpretation of main effects amounts to. Instead, differential effects of the various treatment combinations should be studied. As is shown below, this is accomplished by doing what are referred to as tests of simple main effects.

Before turning to a regression analysis of the data analyzed above, the proportion of variance accounted for by each of the terms will be calculated. We do this here so that we may compare the results with those obtained below in the regression analysis. In Chapter 19, it was shown that, in the context of a one-way ANOVA, the proportion of variance accounted for by between treatments, or groups, is obtained by calculating η^2—see (19.6) and the discussion related to it. This approach generalizes to factorial designs. Specifically, to obtain the proportion of variance accounted for by each of the terms of the model, divide the *ss* associated with it by the total ss. Using the results reported in Table 20.3, proportions of variance accounted for by the terms of the design are

$$A: 27.99/138.10 = .20$$

$$B: 13.00/138.10 = .09$$

$$A \times B: 54.11/138.10 = .39$$

We comment on these results when we show them to be identical to those obtained in a regression analysis with coded vectors.

REGRESSION ANALYSIS OF FACTORIAL DESIGNS

Factorial designs may be analyzed through regression analysis by regressing the dependent variable on a set of coded vectors representing the main effects and interactions. Although any of the coding schemes presented in Chapter 19 may be used, it is generally preferable to use effect coding, as the regression equation thus obtained reflects the effects of the factors and their interaction as defined earlier. Accordingly, we will use effect coding.

It will be noted in passing that dummy coding in factorial designs has properties that make it susceptible to misinterpretation by a novice. Therefore, we recommend that it *not* be used in such designs. For a discussion and illustrations of potential problems with the interpretation of results with dummy coding, see O'Grady and Medoff (1988). For a discussion and numerical examples of applications of dummy and orthogonal coding in factorial designs, see Pedhazur (1982, pp. 365–370).

In a factorial design, each factor, or independent variable, is coded as shown in Chapter 19 for the case of a design with one independent variable. When any of the factors is coded, all other factors are ignored. Interactions are then obtained by multiplying in turn each of the coded vectors of one factor by each of the coded vectors of the other factor. Recall that the number of coded vectors necessary to represent a factor is equal to the number of its categories minus one, or the number of df associated with it. Therefore, for the numerical example of Table 20.1, it is necessary to generate one vector for A and two vectors for B. Multiplication of the vector for A by each of the vectors for B will yield two coded vectors for the interaction, corresponding to the df associated with it (see Table 20.3).

Because we are planning to generate the coded vectors by a computer program, we will show schematically what it is that we are after. We hope that doing this will also clarify the preceding description of coding in factorial designs. The coding scheme for Table 20.1 is presented in Table 20.4, where the columns were numbered for ease of reference. Note that Column 1 is used to code A. Examine this column along with the cell identifications and note that, regardless of the B's, cells in A_1 are assigned 1, whereas those in A_2 are assigned -1. Consistent with our practice of referring to the category assigned 1 in a given vector as the category identified in that vector, Column 1 is labeled A_1. Inspect now Column 2, and notice that cells in B_1 are assigned 1, those in B_2 are assigned 0, and those in B_3 are assigned -1. Column 2 is, therefore, labeled B_1. Furthermore, as you can see, B_2 is identified in Column 3. We repeat: When A is coded, B is ignored and vice versa. The first three columns represent the main effects. As indicated in the table, the interaction vectors are obtained by multiplying in turn the vector representing the main effects of A (1) by each of the vectors representing the main effects of B (2 and 3).

Whether the codes are read as input or generated by computer (as we do below), each

Table 20.4
Effect Coding for a 2 × 3 Design

Cell	(1) A_1	(2) B_1	(3) B_2	(4) 1 × 2 A_1B_1	(5) 1 × 3 A_1B_2
A_1B_1	1	1	0	1	0
A_1B_2	1	0	1	0	1
A_1B_3	1	-1	-1	-1	-1
A_2B_1	-1	1	0	-1	0
A_2B_2	-1	0	1	0	-1
A_2B_3	-1	-1	-1	1	1

subject is assigned the 5 codes that identify uniquely the cell to which he or she belongs. Thus, for example, all subjects belonging to A_1 and B_1 are assigned the 5 codes indicated in the first row of Table 20.4 (1 1 0 1 0). Subjects belonging to A_2 and B_3 are assigned the 5 codes in the last row of Table 20.4 (−1 −1 −1 1 1)—similarly for the other category combinations or cells. A multiple regression analysis is then carried out in which the dependent variable is regressed on the coded vectors.

From the above description of the coding, it should be clear that it is generalizable to designs with any number of categories for each factor. For example, for a 3 x 5 design, 2 and 4 coded vectors to represent the main effects of the first and second factors respectively would be generated in the manner described above. Each vector from the first set (2) would then be multiplied by each of the vectors from the second set (4), thus yielding 8 vectors to represent the interaction. As discussed later, the approach described here is also generalizable to designs consisting of more than two factors. We turn now to an analysis of the data of Table 20.1, using SPSS.

SPSS

Input

```
SET LISTING='T201REG.LIS'.
TITLE FACTORIAL DESIGN.   DATA FROM TABLE 20.1.
DATA LIST/A 1 B 2 Y 4-5.      [fixed format input]
IF (A EQ 1) A1 = 1.
IF (A EQ 2) A1 = -1.
IF (B EQ 1) B1 = 1.
IF (B EQ 2) B1 = 0.
IF (B EQ 3) B1 = -1.
IF (B EQ 1) B2 = 0.
IF (B EQ 2) B2 = 1.
IF (B EQ 3) B2 = -1.
COMPUTE A1B1=A1*B1.
COMPUTE A1B2=A1*B2.
BEGIN DATA.
11 10
11 11
11 14
11 13
12 10
```

```
12 10
12  7
12  8
13  8
13 10
13 11
13 10
21  8
21  8
21 12
21 12
22 12
22 12
22 12
22 13
23 13
23 15
23 15
23 16
END DATA.
LIST.
REGRESSION VAR Y TO A1B2/DES/STAT ALL/DEP=Y/
   ENTER A1/ ENTER B1 B2/ENTER A1B1 A1B2/DEP=Y/
   TEST (A1)(B1 B2)(A1B1 A1B2).
```

Commentary

The first vector (Column 1) identifies categories of A, the second vector (Column 2) identifies categories of B. Y is read in from Columns 4 and 5. Study this input in conjunction with Table 20.1 and/or Table 20.2.

As in Chapter 19, IF statements are used to generate the coded vectors representing the main effects of A and B. Two COMPUTE statements are then used to multiply the A vector by each of the B vectors, thereby generating the interaction vectors.

The general format of the REGRESSION command was commented upon in Chapters 18 and 19. Notice that the vectors representing the different terms of the model are entered in three steps. We explain why we do this in the commentary on the output.

TEST—a keyword in METHOD subcommand—enables one to specify subsets of variables, in the parentheses, to be tested separately. We are using this device to test sets of coded vectors associated with the different terms of the design. This approach, which can be extended to designs with more than two factors, is explained in commentary on the relevant excerpt of the output.

Output

Correlation:	Y	A1	B1	B2	A1B1	A1B1
Y	1.000	−.451	−.212	−.297	.595	.127
A1	−.451	1.000	−.000	.000	.000	.000
B1	−.212	−.000	1.000	.500	−.000	−.000
B2	−.297	.000	.500	1.000	−.000	−.000
A1B1	.595	.000	−.000	−.000	1.000	.500
A1B2	.127	.000	−.000	−.000	.500	1.000

Commentary

In the interest of space, we do not reproduce the listing of the data (called for by LIST) nor the means and the standard deviations. It will only be pointed out that, as was explained in Chapter 19, means of effect coded vectors with equal n's equal zero.

Examine now the correlations among the coded vectors and notice that vectors representing a given term (e.g., Factor B) are correlated, but that *vectors representing different terms are not correlated*. This will always be the case, regardless of the number of factors and the number of categories within factors, as long as the design consists of equal cell frequencies. Stated differently, in designs with equal cell frequencies, coded vectors representing different terms are mutually orthogonal. In such designs, referred to as orthogonal designs, the regression sum of squares, or the proportion of variance accounted for, can be partitioned unambiguously among the different terms.[6]

In view of the preceding, the order in which the sets of coded vectors representing different terms are entered into the analysis is immaterial. Moreover, the same results would be obtained, if *all* the coded vectors were entered simultaneously. Entering coded vectors representing each term in successive steps is done for convenience. We did this also, because we wish to explain some of the terms of the output.

Output

Equation Number 1   Dependent Variable..   Y

Beginning Block Number   1.   Method: Enter   A1

					Analysis of Variance			
Multiple R	.45097							
R Square	.20337	R Square Change	.20337			DF	Sum of Squares	Mean Squar
Adjusted R Square	.16716	F Change	5.61631	Regression		1	28.16667	28.1666
Standard Error	2.23945	Signif F Change	.0270	Residual		22	110.33333	5.0151

$$F = 5.61631 \qquad \text{Signif } F = .0270$$

Commentary

Here, Multiple R is equal to the zero-order correlation of the dependent variable with the vector representing Factor A (see correlation matrix above). Accordingly, the square of this correlation (.20337) indicates the proportion of variance accounted for by A. Further, multiplying R Square by the total sum of squares (138.50) yields the regression sum of squares (28.16667). Both these values are, within rounding, the same as those obtained earlier (see Table 20.3 and the text following it).

Compare now the F ratio given here (5.61631) with the one obtained in Table 20.3 for the test of A (11.79). Not only are the two F ratios different, but the df for their denominators are also different (22 here, and 18 in the earlier analysis). These differences have to do with the differences in the residuals or errors in the two analyses. At this stage in the present analysis, the design is treated as if it consisted of one factor, namely A. Therefore, anything that is *not* due to A is treated as error. Thus, the regression sums of squares due to B (13.00) and to A x B (54.11) are here part of the error term as are the df associated with these two terms. Subtracting these sum of squares from the residual sum of squares reported above yields

$$110.33 - 13.00 - 54.11 = 43.22$$

which is, within rounding, the same as the residual obtained in Table 20.3—similarly for the df. Subtracting the df for B and A x B from the Residual df reported above yields $22 - 2 - 2 = 18$, which are the df associated with the Residual in Table 20.3.

---

[6]Later in this chapter, we comment on nonorthogonal designs.

What all the preceding amounts to is that, so far as the analysis of the factorial design is concerned, only some of the information reported in the above output is relevant. Specifically, R Square is relevant as is the Regression Sum of Squares and its df, hence, also the Mean Square Regression. In contrast, information concerning the Residual is *not* relevant, and, therefore, neither is the F ratio.

Why, then, carry out the analysis in successive steps? As we said above, it is done for convenience only. In the present step, we obtain directly the regression sum of squares, and the proportion of variance, due to A. Had all the vectors been entered in a single step, additional calculations would have been required to obtain this information.[7] In the steps that follow, we show that the type of output reported above is used somewhat differently.

Another reason we entered the sets of vectors in separate steps is to use the opportunity to do what we just did, namely explain which parts of the output are relevant in analyses of this kind.

Output

Variables in the Equation

Variable	B
A1	-1.08333
(Constant)	11.25000

Commentary

The intercept (Constant) is equal to the mean of the dependent variable, Y. This is always the case with effect coding for orthogonal designs (i.e., designs with equal cell frequencies) with any number of factors consisting of any number of categories.

The regression coefficient (B) for A1 is equal to the effect of treatment, or category, A_1 (compare with Table 20.1). As explained in Chapter 19 in connection with effect coding, the effect of A_2 (1.0833) is obtained by reversing the sign of the effect of A_1.

Because the vectors representing the other terms are *not* correlated with the vector representing A, the b for A1 will *not* change when any, or all, of the other terms are entered into the analysis (see output for the next two steps, below). The test of the b will, however, change, as its standard error is affected by the Residual, which changes from one step to another (see explanation above). In any case, because tests of b's are not of interest when using effect coding (see Chapter 19), we do not reproduce them here.

Output

Beginning Block Number   2. Method: Enter   B1   B2

Variable(s) Entered on Step Number   2..   B2
                                     3..   B1

				Analysis of Variance			
Multiple R	.54519				DF	Sum of Squares	Mean Square
R Square	.29723	R Square Change	.09386				
Adjusted R Square	.19182	F Change	1.33562	Regression	3	21.16667	13.72222
Standard Error	2.20605	Signif F Change	.2855	Residual	20	97.33333	4.86667

F = 2.81963   Signif F = .0651

Commentary

Recall that SPSS output at each step refers to all the "variables" (coded vectors, in the present example) up to and including the step under consideration. Thus, the above output refers to the regression of Y on the variable(s) entered at the preceding step(s), A, *and* those entered at

---

[7]But see the output generated by the keyword TEST, given below.

this step, B. This is why regression $df = 3$ (1 for A, entered in preceding step, plus 2 for B, entered at this step). R Square (.29723), therefore, refers to the proportion of variance accounted for by *both* A and B. In order to determine the proportion of variance due to B, subtract R Square of the preceding step from R Square of the current step

$$.29723 - .20337 = .09386$$

Similarly, this holds for the regression sum of squares

$$41.16667 - 28.16667 = 13.00000$$

with $2\ df\ (3 - 1)$. Compare these results with those obtained earlier in Tables 20.2 and 20.3.

Two points will be made. One, having output such as given above, it is not necessary to carry out the subtraction between the R Squares, as this information is provided by R Square Change (see above). We explained how this information is obtained so that you may obtain it when using a program that does not report R Square Change or one that does not enable the user to enter variables in successive steps.[8]

Two, R Square Change is, of course, the proportion of variance incremented by the variables entered at this step. We discussed such increments in detail in Chapters 18 (see Variance Partitioning). When the independent variables are not correlated, R Square Change due to a given variable must equal its squared correlation with the dependent variable.[9] The same holds true when coded vectors are used to represent variables in factorial designs except that it applies to *sets* of vectors representing the different terms of the design. Thus, in a factorial design consisting of factors A and B, the proportion of variance *accounted for or incremented* by each of the terms of the design is

$$A:\ R^2_{Y.A}$$

$$B:\ R^2_{Y.B}$$

$$A \times B:\ R^2_{Y.AB}$$

In the preceding, the subscripts refer to the terms of the design regardless of the number of coded vectors necessary to represent them. In other words, it applies to any design consisting of two factors, regardless of the number of categories in each factor. Referring to the above output,

$$R^2_{Y.A,B} - R^2_{Y.A} = .09386 = R^2_{Y.B} = R^2_{Y.B1,B2}$$

where the first two terms represent R Square Change. Obviously, had the vector representing A been correlated with the vectors representing B, the R Square Change would *not* have been equal to $R^2_{Y.B1,B2}$.

The residual or the error term required is one that indicates the proportion of variance (or sum of squares) *not* accounted for by all the terms of the design. That is,

$$1 - R^2_{Y.A,B,AB} = 1 - (R^2_{Y.A} + R^2_{Y.B} + R^2_{Y.AB})$$

In order, then, to obtain the relevant residual information (i.e., ss, df, and the associated MSR), an additional analysis in which all the coded vectors are included would have to be run (see commentary on last step in the SPSS analysis, below).

------

[8]Later in this section, we comment on the use of such programs to carry out the analysis under consideration.
[9]You may find it helpful to review materials presented in the beginning of Chapter 18, especially the discussion in connection with (18.1).

Output

Variables in the Equation

Variable	B
A1	−1.08333
B2	−.75000
B1	−.25000
(Constant)	11.25000

Commentary

As expected, the Constant and the *b* for A1 are the same as in the preceding step. The *b*'s for B1 and B2 are the effects of these two categories (compare with Table 20.1). As explained earlier, to obtain the effect for category B3, sum the effects for B1 and B2 and reverse the sign

$$(-.75) + (-.25) = -1.00$$

The effect of B3 is 1.00 (compare with Table 20.1).

Output

Beginning Block Number 3. Method: Enter   A1B1   A1B2

Variable(s) Entered on Step Number 4.. A1B2
5.. A1B1

					Analysis of Variance			
Multiple R	.83038							
R Square	.68953	R Square Change	.39230			DF	Sum of Squares	Mean Square
Adjusted R Square	.60329	F Change	11.37209	Regression		5	95.50000	19.10000
Standard Error	1.54560	Signif F Change	.0006	Residual		18	43.00000	2.38889

F = 7.99535   Signif F = .0004

Commentary

The proportion of variance due to the interaction is .39230 (i.e., R Square Change). The regression sum of squares for interaction is

$$95.50000 - 41.16667 = 54.33333$$

with 2 *df*. As this is the last step in the analysis, having thus included all the terms of the model, the Residual information is relevant, as it refers to the portion *not* explained by the model.

With output such as the above, therefore, the simplest way to go about testing the terms of the model is to obtain, by subtraction, at each step the sum of squares regression due to a given term, and then divide each term by its *df* to obtain a *MS*. The *F* ratios can then be calculated by dividing each *MS* by the *MSR* (Mean Square Residual) of the last step, which, for the present data, is 2.38889 with 18 *df*. These calculations are the same as those carried out in Table 20.3. We suggest that you carry them out and compare your results with those of Table 20.3.

Output

Variables in the Equation

Variable	B
A1	−1.08333

B2	−.75000
B1	−.25000
A1B2	−.66667
A1B1	2.08333
(Constant)	11.25000

Commentary

The b's for A and B are the same as in the preceding step. Therefore, we comment only on the b's for the interaction vectors. The b for any product vector indicates the interaction term for the cell corresponding to the categories identified in the coded vectors used to generate it. This can be best understood by referring to the two product vectors under consideration. Look back at Table 20.4 (if you ran this example, examine also the data listing you have obtained through LIST) and note that category A_1 was identified in vector A1, and category B_1 was identified in vector B1. Therefore, the b for A1B1 (2.08333) is the interaction term for cell A_1B_1 (compare with Table 20.1). Similarly, b for A1B2 (−.66667) is the interaction term for cell A_1B_2 (compare with Table 20.1). In view of the constraint that the sum of interaction terms for rows and columns is zero, the interaction terms for the remaining cells can be readily obtained (see explanation in connection with Table 20.1).

The above constitutes the final regression equation, which may also be used to obtain predicted scores on the dependent variable. Recall that, for this purpose, the codes are treated as scores on independent variables. For illustrative purposes, we will predict the dependent variable score for the first individual in the present example, using the scores (i.e., codes) on the independent variables (i.e., coded vectors), as given in the first line of Table 20.4.

$$Y' = 11.25 - 1.08(1) - .25(1) - .75(0) + 2.08(1) - .67(0) = 12.00$$

As expected, this is the mean of the cell to which this individual belongs. As all individuals in this cell have the same scores on the independent variables, their predicted scores are also the same. We suggest that you use the regression equation and relevant scores on the independent variables to predict dependent variable scores for individuals in the other cells. Compare your results with the cell means reported in Table 20.1.

Output

Equation Number   2   Dependent Variable..   Y

Beginning Block Number   1.   Method: Test   A1   B1   B2   A1B1   A1B2

Hypothesis Tests

DF	Sum of Squares	Rsq Chg	F	Sig F	Source	
1	28.16667	.20337	11.79070	.0030	A1	
2	13.00000	.09386	2.72093	.0928	B1	B2
2	54.33333	.39230	11.37209	.0006	A1B1	A1B2
5	95.50000		7.99535	.0004	Regression	
18	43.00000				Residual	
23	138.50000				Total	

Commentary

This output was generated by the TEST keyword (see last line of Input). As you can see, it provides a succinct summary of the contributions of each of the terms of the design, as well as tests of significance, much like Table 20.3, with which we suggest that you compare this output. When doing the analysis with SPSS REGRESSION, therefore, using TEST obviates the need to carry out the analysis in successive steps and the calculation based on them, as we have done above. Including DEP=Y before the TEST keyword will yield a regression equation in addition to the above output.

In presenting the analysis through a set of successive steps, we had two things in mind. One, we wanted to use the opportunity to explain various aspects of the analysis; we did this in the commentaries. Two, we wanted to show what kind of information one needs so that any program for multiple regression analysis may be used to generate it. Thus, assuming a program is available that does not enable one to enter variables in successive steps, it should be clear from our presentation that the program may be used to emulate our three successive steps by carrying out three separate regression analyses, regressing Y on (a) A, (b) on A and B, and (c) on A, B, and $A \times B$. This, in effect, is what was done in the three steps above.

In the present analysis, it was found that not only is the interaction statistically significant but also that it accounts for the largest proportion of the variance (.39). Accordingly, as was stated earlier, it is not meaningful to interpret main effects. Instead, one proceeds to calculate, test, and interpret simple main effects, a topic to which we now turn.

SIMPLE MAIN EFFECTS

To understand the ideas behind the calculations, tests, and interpretations of simple main effects, it is helpful to view the factorial design analyzed above as a juxtaposition of two sets of one-way designs. To show this clearly, we constructed Table 20.5 in which summary data of Table 20.1 are displayed twice.

Look first at Part I of the table and notice that we have sliced Table 20.1 by rows, thereby depicting it as constituting two one-way designs in which the same three levels of B are used, but with different A's. For the sake of illustration, assume that A is sex. Then this is tantamount to conducting two separate studies in which the effects of the three levels of B are studied. However, whereas subjects in one of the studies are males, those in the other study are females. Stated differently, by thus slicing up the design, sex is no longer treated as a variable, as each one-way design consists of either males or females. What was said about sex applies equally to designs in which A is a manipulated variable, as each one-way design would consist of only one of the A treatments.

Look now at Part II of Table 20.5 and notice that this time we sliced Table 20.1 by columns, depicting the same summary data as if they were obtained from three one-way designs. This time, B is no longer a variable. It is as if three separate studies were conducted to study the same A treatments. For example, A may be two types of reinforcement. B may be three teaching methods. As displayed in Part II, the difference between the same two types of reinforcements is studied separately under each of the teaching methods. Therefore, B is constant in each of the studies.

In a design such as that depicted in Table 20.5, one may study the simple main effects of B (i.e., effects of B at A_1 and at A_2), simple main effects of A (i.e., effects of A at B_1, at B_2, and at B_3), or both.

Regression sums of squares for simple main effects are calculated as in designs with one independent variable (i.e., as in one-way designs). Referring to the design of Table 20.1, to calculate regression sums of squares for simple main effects for B, two analyses are required: (a) using the 12 subjects at A_1, and (b) using the 12 subjects at A_2. To calculate simple main

Table 20.5

Effects Displayed for Calculation of Simple Main Effects. Data of Table 20.1

I.		B_1	B_2	B_3	$\bar{Y}$
A_1	$\bar{Y}$:	12.00	8.75	9.75	10.17
	Int:	2.08	−.67	−1.41	
	Eff:	−.25	−.75	1.00	
A_2	$\bar{Y}$:	10.00	12.25	14.75	12.33
	Int:	−2.08	.67	1.41	
	Eff:	−.25	−.75	1.00	

II.		B_1	B_2	B_3	Eff
A_1	$\bar{Y}$:	12.00	8.75	9.75	−1.08
	Int:	2.08	−.67	−1.41	
A_2	$\bar{Y}$:	10.00	12.25	14.75	1.08
	Int:	−2.08	.67	1.41	
	$\bar{Y}$:	11.00	10.50	12.25	

Note. $n = 4$ in each cell. *Int* = Interaction; *Eff* = Main Effect. Means, Main Effects, and Interaction terms were taken from Table 20.1.

effects for A, three analyses are required: (a) using the 8 subjects at B_1, (b) using the 8 subjects at B_2, and (c) using the 8 subjects at B_3. We could proceed now in this manner and calculate the regression sums of squares for simple main effects for the data of Table 20.1 but will not do this (you may wish to do it as an exercise). Instead, we show how the same can be accomplished using the main effect and interaction terms obtained earlier. Subsequently, we show how tests of simple main effects may be easily obtained through computer analysis.

SUMS OF SQUARES FOR SIMPLE MAIN EFFECTS

The information needed for the calculation of simple main effects for the data of Table 20.1 is given in Table 20.5. As indicated in the note to Table 20.5, all the information was obtained from Table 20.1. However, as was demonstrated in the preceding section, this information is also obtainable from the regression equation with effect coding.

It will now be shown how the sum of squares for simple main effects may be obtained, using the information of Table 20.5. In the preceding section, it was shown how individuals' scores in Table 20.1 can be expressed as components of the model and how such components can be used to calculate the sums of squares for the different terms of the design (see Table 20.2 and the discussion related to it). We use the same ideas to calculate simple main effects, beginning with those for B.

Look at the three columns of B of Table 20.5, Part I, at A_1. It is clear that all the subjects at this level (12, for our numerical example) are given the same A treatment. Notice that the marginal mean for A_1 (i.e., the average of the three cell means) is 10.17. Consistent with the definition of a treatment effect (see Chapter 19), the effect of each B at A_1 is equal to the deviation of its mean from 10.17. Thus, the effect of B_1 is

$$12.00 - 10.17 = 1.83$$

Note, however, that this is also the sum of the main effect and interaction term associated with this cell:

$$(-.25) + (2.08) = 1.83$$

Similarly, this holds for the effects of the other two B's

For B_2: $8.75 - 10.17 = -1.42$

Sum of Effects for B_2: $(-.67) + (-.75) = -1.42$

For B_3: $9.75 - 10.17 = -.42$

Sum of Effects for B_3: $(-1.41) + (1.00) = -.41$

The discrepancy between the last two terms is due to rounding errors.

What the preceding amounts to is that each person's score at A_1 can be expressed as composed of three components: (a) the mean of the three B's (10.17); (b) the effect of the treatment the individual is administered, which is equal to the sum of the effects of the cell to which the individual belongs; and (c) a residual.

Analogous to calculations of regression sum of squares in Table 20.2, the regression, or among treatments, sum of squares for B at A_1 can be obtained by squaring the treatment effect for each individual and summing. A treatment effect is, of course, the same for all individuals who are administered it. Therefore, instead of squaring the effect for each individual and summing, the same may be accomplished by squaring each effect, multiplying by the number of people who were administered the given treatment and then summing. However, because in the present analysis 4 people were administered each treatment, the regression sum of squares may also be obtained as follows:

$$ss_{reg} \text{ for } B \text{ at } A_1: 4[(1.83)^2 + (-1.42)^2 + (-.41)^2] = 22.13$$

Using relevant corresponding terms, the effects for B at A_2 are

For B_1: $(-2.08) + (-.25) = -2.33$

For B_2: $(.67) + (-.75) = -.08$

For B_3: $(1.41) + (1.00) = 2.41$

Therefore, ss_{reg} for B at A_2 is $4[(-2.33)^2 + (-.08)^2 + (2.41)^2] = 44.97$

The sum of the regression sums of squares for the two levels of A is

$$22.13 + 44.97 = 67.10$$

In view of the method used for the calculation of these sums of squares, it should come as no surprise that their sum equals the regression sum of squares for B plus the regression sum of squares for the interaction. From Table 20.3, $ss_B = 13.00$, and $ss_{AB} = 54.11$, and their sum is equal, within rounding, to the sum of regression sums of squares for the simple main effects of B. As is shown below, the same principle holds true for the sum of the regression sums of squares for the simple main effects for A. This, therefore, can serve as a check on the calculations.

Using the same method as above, the regression sums of squares for the simple main effects of A are calculated. This time the calculations are done to correspond to one-way analyses as displayed in Part II of Table 20.5. Notice that, in this part of the table, B for each analysis is a constant, and the effects for A_1 and A_2 respectively are -1.08 and 1.08. Therefore, the effects at B_1 are

$$\text{For } A_1\text{: } (-1.08) + (2.08) \quad = 1.00$$

$$\text{For } A_2\text{: } (1.08) \quad + (-2.08) = -1.00$$

As would be expected, the difference between these two effects is equal to the difference between the two means under B_1 (i.e., $12.00 - 10.00$; see Table 20.5).

Recalling that $n = 4$ in each cell, the regression sum of squares for the simple main effects for A at B_1 is

$$4[(1.00)^2 + (-1.00)^2)] = 8.00$$

The effects at B_2 are

$$\text{For } A_1\text{: } (-1.08) + (-.67) = -1.75$$

$$\text{For } A_2\text{: } (1.08) \quad + (.67) \quad = 1.75$$

The difference between the two effects (-3.50) is equal to the difference between the two respective means (i.e., $8.75 - 12.25$; see Table 20.5). The regression sum of squares for the simple main effects for A at B_2 is

$$4[(-1.75)^2 + (1.75)^2] = 24.5$$

The effects at B_3 are

$$\text{For } A_1\text{: } (-1.08) + (-1.41) = -2.49$$

$$\text{For } A_2\text{: } (1.08) \quad + (1.41) \quad = 2.49$$

The difference between these effects (-4.98) is equal, within rounding, to the difference between the two respective means (i.e., $9.75 - 14.75$; see Table 20.5). The regression sum of squares for the simple main effects for A at B_3 is

$$4[(-2.49)^2 + (2.49)^2] = 49.60$$

As a check on the calculations, the sums of squares for the simple main effects of A are added:

$$8.00 + 24.50 + 49.60 = 82.10$$

This sum is equal to the sum of ss_A (27.99) and ss_{AB} (54.11) (these values were obtained from Table 20.3).

TESTS OF SIMPLE MAIN EFFECTS

To test the regression sum of squares for a simple main effect, it is divided by its df to obtain a MS (Mean Square), which is then divided by the MSR (Mean Square Residual), yielding an F ratio. For tests of simple main effects, the MSR used is the one obtained from the analysis of the factorial design.

Using the regression sums of squares for the simple main effects calculated above, and the MSR from Table 20.3 (2.39 with 18 df), the tests of significance are summarized in Table 20.6.

Table 20.6

Summary of Tests of Simple Main Effects for data of Table 20.1

Source	SS	df	MS	F
B at A_1	22.13	2	11.06	4.63
B at A_2	44.97	2	22.48	9.41
A at B_1	8.00	1	8.00	3.35
A at B_2	24.50	1	24.50	10.25
A at B_3	49.60	1	49.60	20.75
Residual	43.00	18	2.39	
Total	138.10	23		

Note. The Residual values were obtained from Table 20.3.

Notice that, for tests of simple main effects of B, the *df* for the F ratios are 2 and 18 for the numerator and the denominator respectively. The *df* for the F ratios for the tests of simple main effects of A are 1 and 18 for the numerator and denominator respectively. It is recommended that, for tests of simple main effects, the prespecified α be divided by the number of simple main effects tested for a given factor. Assume, for example, that $\alpha = .05$ was selected by the researcher. As two tests are done for simple main effects of B, the obtained F has to exceed 4.56, which is the critical value of F for $\alpha/2 = .05/2 = .025$, with 2 and 18 *df* (see, for example, Table IX in Edwards, 1985, p. 530). Accordingly, it is concluded that both tests of simple main effects are statistically significant. As each of these tests involves a comparison among three means, multiple comparisons may be carried out in a manner described in Chapter 19. The specific type of comparison (i.e., planned or post hoc) will depend on the kind of hypotheses advanced by the researcher.

Because three tests were carried out for simple main effects for A, the obtained F has to exceed a critical value of F for $\alpha/3 = .05/3 = .017$, with 1 and 18 *df*. Tables generally available in statistics books do not provide values for this probability level. For present purposes, it would suffice to point out that the tabled values for F with 1 and 18 *df* for .05 and .01, respectively, are 4.41 and 8.28. Thus, it is clear that the difference between A_1 and A_2 is statistically not significant at B_1 but is statistically significant at B_2 and at B_3. When using a computer program for the analysis, the probability levels for the obtained F's are generally reported (see below). Therefore, it is not necessary to resort to the kind of crude approximation we used.

For completeness of presentation, we carried out tests of simple main effects for both A and B. Depending on substantive considerations, the researcher may be interested in testing simple main effects of only one factor or even of only some simple main effects of one factor. In short, what is being tested depends on the researcher's hypotheses. Later on, we comment generally on formulation of hypotheses for factorial designs.

COMPUTER ANALYSIS

Of various computer programs that may be used for the analysis of factorial designs, we decided to illustrate the use of MANOVA (Multivariate Analysis of Variance) of SPSS, because one of its subcommands lends itself to facile specifications for tests of simple main effects. We comment on the MANOVA procedure below.

SPSS

Input

SET LISTING='T201MAN.LIS'.
TITLE TABLE 20.1, 2 BY 3.   TESTS OF SIMPLE MAIN EFFECTS.
DATA LIST/A 1 B 2 Y 4–5.
BEGIN DATA.
    [data to be read are identical to those given
    earlier, under REGRESSION analysis]
END DATA.
LIST.
MANOVA Y BY A(1,2) B(1,3)/PRINT=CELLINFO(MEANS)/
    DESIGN=A,B,A BY B/DESIGN=A B WITHIN A(1), B WITHIN A(2)/
    DESIGN=B A WITHIN B(1), A WITHIN B(2), A WITHIN B(3).

Commentary

MANOVA (Multivariate Analysis of Variance) is one of the most versatile and powerful procedures of any of the popular statistical packages. Multivariate means that the design consists of more than one dependent variable (for an introduction to multivariate analysis, including relevant references, see Pedhazur, 1982, Chapters 17 and 18). MANOVA can also be used for univariate analysis, that is, analysis with one dependent variable, which is what we are doing here.

For the overall factorial analysis of variance, we could have used ANOVA of SPSS. However, as was stated above, we use MANOVA, because its DESIGN subcommand lends itself to easy specifications of tests of simple main effects.

As explained in Chapter 19 (see the application of ONEWAY of SPSS), the numbers in the parentheses following each factor indicate its lowest and highest levels.

Three design subcommands were included. Their meaning is explained in the commentaries on the output generated by them.

Output

Cell Means and Standard Deviations
    Variable.. Y

FACTOR	CODE	Mean	Std. Dev.	N
A	1			
B	1	12.000	1.826	4
B	2	8.750	1.500	4
B	3	9.750	1.258	4
A	2			
B	1	10.000	2.309	4
B	2	12.250	.500	4
B	3	14.750	1.258	4
For entire sample		11.250	2.454	24

Commentary

This part of the output was generated by the PRINT subcommand. Various other options may be specified in this subcommand.

Output

* * * * * ANALYSIS OF VARIANCE—DESIGN 1 * * * * *

Source of Variation	SS	DF	MS	F	Sig of F
WITHIN CELLS	43.00	18	2.39		
A	28.17	1	28.17	11.79	.003
B	13.00	2	6.50	2.72	.093
A BY B	54.33	2	27.17	11.37	.001

Commentary

As indicated in the title, these results were generated by the first DESIGN subcommand. Examine this subcommand in the Input and notice that it calls for A, B, and A BY B. We did this for comparative purposes with earlier analyses of the same data. Compare these results with those given in Table 20.3 or in the REGRESSION output and notice that they are identical. What is labeled here WITHIN CELLS was labeled in the earlier analyses RE-SIDUAL. We commented on the earlier results; therefore, we will not comment on the ones given here. If necessary, see the comments given in earlier sections.

Output

* * * * * ANALYSIS OF VARIANCE—DESIGN 2 * * * * *

Source of Variation	SS	DF	MS	F	Sig of F
WITHIN CELLS	43.00	18	2.39		
A	28.17	1	28.17	11.79	.003
B WITHIN A(1)	22.17	2	11.08	4.64	.024
B WITHIN A(2)	45.17	2	22.58	9.45	.002

Commentary

In the second DESIGN subcommand, we called for A and for *B within A_1* and *A_2*. The same results, within rounding, were obtained earlier and reported in Table 20.6. It will be noted that the probability of F for B within A_1 is .024. Assume, as in the earlier analysis, that $\alpha =$ .05 was selected by the researcher. The probability reported here is $<.025$ (i.e., .05/2; see Tests of Simple Main Effects, above). It is, therefore, concluded that this simple main effect is statistically significant. From the probability of the F for the test of B within A_2, it is clear that this simple main effect is also statistically significant.

Output

* * * * * ANALYSIS OF VARIANCE—DESIGN 3 * * * * *

Source of Variation	SS	DF	MS	F	Sig of F
WITHIN CELLS	43.00	18	2.39		
B	13.00	2	6.50	2.72	.093
A WITHIN B(1)	8.00	1	8.00	3.35	.084
A WITHIN B(2)	24.50	1	24.50	10.26	.005
A WITHIN B(3)	50.00	1	50.00	20.93	.000

Commentary

In this DESIGN subcommand, we called for analyses of A *within* the B's. Compare these results with those reported in Table 20.6. Recall that, for $\alpha = .05$, the probability for each of these tests of simple main effects is $.05/3$. Therefore, as noted in the earlier analysis, the difference between A_1 and A_2 at B_1 is statistically not significant, whereas the differences between these treatments at the other two levels of B are statistically significant.

Two final comments will be made. One, either the REGRESSION analysis or the MANOVA would have sufficed. We used both to illustrate their equivalence as well as to acquaint you with some features unique to each. Two, both analyses can be performed in a single run. Actually, this is what we did, although we reported the results as if they were obtained in separate runs.

HYPOTHESIS FORMULATION

A general discussion of hypotheses, their format, and implications for, among other things, data analysis was given in Chapter 9. In the present section, we comment briefly on hypothesis formulation in connection with factorial designs.

In line with the earlier discussion that it is generally not meaningful to interpret main effects in the presence of an interaction, we comment first on hypotheses about main effects and then about hypotheses concerning interaction. We cannot go into theoretical considerations that have led to specific hypotheses without going far afield; therefore, we confine our comments to hypotheses about effects of A, B, and their interaction on the dependent variable, Y, whatever the variables and regardless of the number of categories of each of the independent variables. In short, our comments are applicable to any experimental design consisting of two factors.[10]

We remind you that in an experimental design both independent variables may be manipulated, or one may be a manipulated variable and the other a classificatory, or grouping, variable. Furthermore, our comments are limited to a design consisting of two factors, because this is the only design with which we have been dealing. What we say here applies, in a general sense, to designs with more than two factors, except that the situation is more complex because of higher-order interactions that may be obtained in such designs (see below). You may find it useful to substitute for A and B variables from your field of interest.

Hypotheses about main effects of one or both factors are meaningful when, on the basis of theoretical considerations, an interaction is *not* expected. Under such circumstances, it makes sense to formulate hypotheses about the effects of one factor without reference to the other, which is what the absence of an interaction means.

Accordingly, hypotheses about each factor are formulated as if the design consisted of one factor, that is, as if it were a one-way design. We will use Factor A to illustrate the kind of hypotheses that may be advanced. Note carefully that we are *not* concerned here with the specifics of the wording that will depend in part on characteristics of the variables used, but rather with the gist of the hypotheses.

To begin with, it may be hypothesized that people exposed to different levels of A will differ in their performance on Y. Note, however, that this is the crudest of hypotheses about main effects. Generally speaking, it betrays little knowledge of the phenomenon being

---

[10]Nonexperimental designs are commented upon later on.

studied and the nature of the manipulations used. Be that as it may, when A is found to be statistically significant, post hoc multiple comparisons among levels of A may be carried out.[11]

A more focused hypothesis about main effects would refer to differences between the effects of specific levels or combinations of levels. It may, for example, be hypothesized that people exposed to A_1 will manifest better performance on Y than those exposed to A_2, that those exposed to A_3 will do better than those exposed to A_4, and that those exposed to A_1 and A_2 will do better than those exposed to A_3 and A_4. As you have probably discerned, the preceding correspond to three orthogonal comparisons among the A levels. Alternatively, hypotheses could refer to planned nonorthogonal comparisons among the A levels. What was said about hypotheses of main effects of A applies equally to hypotheses about main effects of B. We turn now to hypotheses about interaction.

When an interaction between A and B is expected, it stands to reason that the researcher has some idea about the specific form it might take. Accordingly, it is suggested that a general statement about the presence of an interaction be followed by specific expectations regarding simple main effects. The hypothesis, stated along general lines, might be as follows: There is an interaction between A and B in their effects on Y. Specifically, under condition B_1 (or for individuals administered B_1), people exposed to A_1 will exhibit better performance on Y than those exposed to A_2. The converse is true under condition B_2; that is, individuals exposed to A_2 will do better than those exposed to A_1. Hypotheses about other simple main effects may be stated along similar lines.

In the preceding hypotheses, the interaction was expected to be disordinal. Needless to say, one might expect the interaction to be ordinal (see earlier section about ordinal and disordinal interactions). Under such circumstances, one possibility would be to begin the hypothesis by a statement to the effect that there is an ordinal interaction between A and B in their effects on Y. This would then be followed with a statement along these lines: Although A_1 is superior to A_2 across all the levels of B, the difference between A_1 and A_2 is greatest under B_2, and smallest under B_3. Whatever the hypotheses about the form of the interaction, tests of simple main effects would be carried out to test them.

In conclusion, we would like to reiterate that our examples were *not* meant to indicate specific wordings of hypotheses but rather the gist of hypotheses that may be formulated, either about main effects or about interactions.

HIGHER-ORDER DESIGNS

Our presentation was limited to designs consisting of two factors. Designs consisting of more than two factors are referred to as higher-order designs. It is *not* our objective to give a detailed presentation of such designs but rather to offer some general comments about their elements and how they are analyzed. You will find detailed discussions and numerical examples of higher-order designs in, among other sources, Box, Hunter, and Hunter (1978), Edwards (1985), Keppel (1982), Kirk (1982), Myers (1979), and Winer (1971). We suggest that you use examples from these or other sources and that you practice analyzing them using either the ANOVA approach as given in these books and/or the regression approach outlined at the end of this section.

As in the case of a two-factor design, in higher-order designs, main effects are obtained

---

[11]See Chapter 19, for discussions of planned and post hoc multiple comparisons among means.

for each factor. In addition, interaction terms are obtained for all combinations of two factors, three factors, and so on. An interaction between two factors, or variables, regardless of the number of categories of each, is referred to as a first-order interaction. It is this type of interaction with which we dealt in the preceding sections. An interaction between three factors is referred to as a second-order interaction, between four factors as a third-order interaction, and so forth.

We will use a couple of examples to illustrate what is meant by the preceding statements. Consider, first, a design consisting of three factors A, B, and C. In such a design, three main effects are obtained, one for each of the factors. As three combinations of two factors are possible, three first-order interactions are obtained: $A \times B$, $A \times C$, and $B \times C$. Finally, one second-order interaction is obtained: $A \times B \times C$.

In a design consisting of four factors A, B, C, and D, the following terms are obtained. Four main effects:

$$A, B, C, D$$

Six first-order interactions:

$$A \times B$$

$$A \times C$$

$$A \times D$$

$$B \times C$$

$$B \times D$$

$$C \times D$$

Four second-order interactions:

$$A \times B \times C$$

$$A \times B \times D$$

$$A \times C \times D$$

$$B \times C \times D$$

One third-order interaction:

$$A \times B \times C \times D$$

As you can see, the number of elements with which one has to contend grows by leaps and bounds with each additional factor. We use the term contend advisedly, as higher-order interactions very often elude interpretation. Although the widespread availability of computer programs makes analysis of factorial designs with multiple factors routine, the interpretation of results, especially in the presence of higher-order interactions, is anything but routine.

Before offering some examples, we will outline the general analytic approach. Terms obtained in factorial designs are examined in a descending order, beginning with the highest-order interaction. We use the term examine in a broad sense, to refer to examination with respect to both substantive meaningfulness and statistical significance. Nevertheless, in what follows, it will be convenient to speak of statistical significance only, particularly because the comments are made in the abstract. We urge you, however, to always bear in mind that the most important consideration is that of substantive meaningfulness.[12]

---

[12]The distinction between statistical significance and substantive meaningfulness was discussed in several earlier chapters. See especially Chapters 9 and 15.

Action taken at a given step depends on the conclusions reached in preceding ones. Thus, in a two-factor design, for example, one first examines the interaction. If the interaction is statistically *not* significant, one proceeds with the examination of main effects. If, on the other hand, the interaction is statistically significant, one proceeds with tests of simple main effects, as illustrated in the preceding section.

To convey a flavor of the complexities that arise with higher-order designs, it would suffice to comment briefly on the examination process for a three-factor design. As before, we use the letters A, B, and C to stand for the three factors. The first term to be examined is the second-order interaction: $A \times B \times C$. We consider, in turn, action taken when this interaction is, and when it is not, statistically significant, beginning with the latter.

When the second-order interaction is statistically *not* significant, the three first-order interactions are examined, and action is taken accordingly. Essentially, the design is treated as composed of three two-factor designs. That is, for each first-order interaction, the effects of two factors and their interaction are studied across the third factor. For example, $A \times B$ is studied across the levels of C. When first-order interactions are statistically significant, simple main effects are examined in a manner shown earlier. When they are statistically not significant, main effects are examined.

When the second-order interaction is statistically significant, one examines what are referred to as simple interaction effects. What this means is interactions between two factors within each level of the third factor. For illustrative purposes, we will assume that the design under consideration is the simplest possible, that is, a $2 \times 2 \times 2$, also referred to as 2^3, as depicted in Figure 20.3.

To obtain simple interactions between, say, B and C, one would calculate the interaction between B and C separately under A_1 and under A_2. Look at Figure 20.3 and notice that it is as if the three-factor design was sliced up into two two-factor designs, one under A_1 and one under A_2—similarly, for simple interactions between other factors.

When a simple interaction is statistically significant, one examines what are referred to as simple-simple main effects. Assume that the simple interaction between B and C under A_1 is

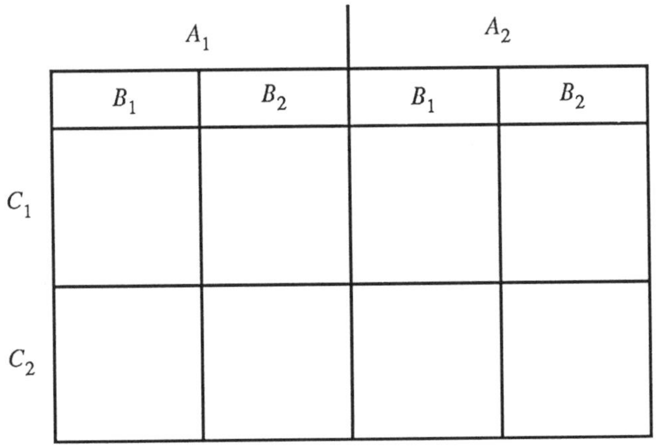

Figure 20.3

statistically significant. Examples of simple-simple main effects would then be differences between C_1 and C_2 separately at A_1B_1 and at A_1B_2, that is, going down the two columns under A_1. Instead of or in addition to the preceding, one could study differences between B_1 and B_2 at A_1C_1 and at A_1C_2, that is, going across the rows under A_1.

As you can see, even with three factors, each at two levels only, matters can become quite complicated, not so much from the analytic perspective but rather from the interpretive one. You may well envision how more complicated matters may become when the factors consist of more than two levels. Results in designs consisting of more than three factors may be extremely difficult to interpret. No wonder that, as lore has it, many researchers pray that their higher-order interactions be statistically *not* significant.

A RESEARCH EXAMPLE

We believe that a brief description of a study may be helpful at this point. Dutton and Lake (1973) conducted a study aimed at testing

the notion that "reverse discrimination," defined as more favorable behavior by whites toward minority group members than toward other whites, may result from whites' observations of "threatening cues of prejudice in their own behavior." (p. 94)

We will not describe the study in detail but only such aspects of it that help illustrate some of the ideas about factorial designs, discussed above.

Dutton and Lake randomly assigned white males and females to two conditions: High Threat and Low Threat. Under High Threat, subjects were given cues designed to lead them to believe that they are prejudiced toward minority group members. Under Low Threat, no such cues were given. After the administration of these treatments, subjects were informed that the study was over, and they were instructed to go to another building where they would be paid the promised amount for participation in the study.

Subjects were paid the same amount in change. Upon leaving the building, each subject was approached, according to a random scheme, by either a black or a white panhandler, who asked whether he or she could spare some change for food. The dependent variable was the amount of donation in cents.

Dutton and Lake's study is the same type of design described above, and depicted in Figure 20.3. Anticipating our review of their study, we used Dutton and Lake's letter designations for the factors. Thus, referring to Figure 20.3 and to Dutton and Lakes's study, A = Race of Panhandler, B = Threat Conditions, and C = Sex of Subject.

Following is a description of some aspects of the results. The second-order interaction was not statistically significant. Consequently, as indicated above, the three first-order interactions are examined. Of these, only Race of Panhandler (A) by Threat Condition (B) was statistically significant. Dutton and Lake, therefore, proceeded to examine simple main effects and found, as hypothesized, that donations to a black panhandler were larger under the High Threat than the Low Threat Condition (recall that those under High Threat were led to believe that they are prejudiced toward minority group members). In contrast, and again as hypothesized, donations to a white panhandler under the two threat conditions were about the same.

Several times earlier, it was pointed out that, in the presence of an interaction, it is generally not meaningful to interpret main effects. Dutton and Lake's results are a case in point. The only main effect found to be statistically significant was for Threat Condition (B). Interpreting this result at face value (Dutton & Lake did not), one would be led to believe that donations are larger under High Threat than Low Threat, regardless of the Race of Panhandler (A). However, in view of the interaction between A and B, and simple main effects described in the preceding paragraph, it is clear that this conclusion would be inappropriate and misleading.

Continuous Independent Variables

Our presentation of factorial designs was limited to categorical independent variables. Such designs may also consist of continuous independent variables, in addition to, or in lieu of, categorical independent variables. As an example, consider a two-factor design in which one of the factors is categorical (e.g., reward, no reward; male, female) and the other continuous (e.g., hours of study; dosage of a drug). In such designs, one would study the trend for the regression of the dependent variable on the continuous variable, using polynomial regression in a manner similar to that shown in Chapter 18 (see Curvilinear Regression). In addition, one would study the effect of the categorical variable, and the interaction between the continuous and the categorical independent variables.

Examples of factorial designs with continuous independent variables may be found in, among other sources, Kirk (1982, pp. 379–387), Myers (1979, pp. 445–456), and Winer (1971, pp. 388–391 and 478–484). The presentation and analyses of numerical examples in these books is that of the ANOVA approach. We believe you will benefit from reanalyzing some of the examples in these books, or others, using the REGRESSION approach and comparing your results with those obtained through the ANOVA approach.

COMPUTER ANALYSIS

We conclude this section with some general remarks about the use of computer programs for the analysis of higher-order factorial designs. As in the case of two-factor designs, programs employing either ANOVA or REGRESSION approaches may be used. Among programs employing the ANOVA approach, MANOVA is particularly useful, as its DESIGN subcommand lends itself to specifications of tests of simple interactions, simple-simple main effects, and the like, much like our earlier illustration of the use of this program for the analysis of simple main effects.

Any multiple regression program can, of course, be used to carry out the analysis according to the REGRESSION approach. For such an analysis, each factor is coded as if it were the only one in the design. The coded vectors may be entered as input or generated by the computer (for example, by the use of category identification vectors and IF statements, along the lines of our analysis of the two-factor design earlier in this chapter). Cross-product vectors are generated to represent the relevant interaction terms. The dependent variable, Y, is then regressed on the coded vectors.

As was suggested earlier, taking numerical examples depicted and analyzed as ANOVA (some references to books where such examples may be found were given earlier), casting them in a REGRESSION format, and replicating the analysis through application of a multiple regression program, will enhance your understanding of both approaches to the analysis of factorial designs.

NONORTHOGONAL DESIGNS

In Chapter 19, we commented on designs with unequal n's and pointed out that they may arise by intention or because of subject attrition. The same is true for the case of factorial designs. The analysis and interpretation of factorial designs with unequal n's—variously referred to as nonorthogonal, unbalanced, designs with unequal cell frequencies—has generated a great deal of controversy, even confusion, among statisticians and researchers. Appelbaum and Cramer's (1974) portrayal of the state of knowledge in this area probably applies with equal force today: "The nonorthogonal multifactor analysis of variance is perhaps the most misunderstood analytic technique available to the behavioral scientist, save factor analysis" (p. 335).

It is not our intention to present here suggested solutions to problems arising from unequal cell frequencies in factorial designs but rather to comment briefly on this issue as viewed from an analytic and a research perspective.

From an analytic perspective, ambiguities arise in a factorial design with unequal cell frequencies, because main effects and interactions tend to be correlated to a greater or lesser degree (hence, the designation nonorthogonal given such designs). Consequently, in nonorthogonal designs, it is not possible to partition unambiguously the proportion of variance accounted for, or the regression sum of squares, into components attributable to each of the terms of the design. The various suggested solutions, most of which apply some variant of multiple regression analysis, have to do with how to deal with this analytic problem (see Pedhazur, 1982, pp. 371–382, for a presentation of one such solution, along with a numerical example and relevant references).

The problem of unequal cell frequencies is considerably more complex from a design perspective. Except for the special case of proportional cell frequencies (see Pedhazur, 1982, pp. 372–373), it is highly unlikely for unequal cell frequencies to be used by design. In most, if not all, instances, unequal cell frequencies arise because of what is broadly referred to as subject attrition, subject mortality, missing data. Under such circumstances, the overriding consideration—one that goes to the heart of the internal validity of the study—is what has led to subject attrition. When subject attrition is related in some systematic manner to treatments or treatment combinations, it follows that groups, created initially by a process of randomization, may no longer be comparable. Consequently, observed differences between treatments or treatment combinations may be due, in part or solely, to differences among unequal groups.

Needless to say, in most instances, it is virtually impossible to ascertain the whys of subject attrition. It is because of our inability to think of and take into account myriad variables affecting a given phenomenon that we resort to randomization.[13] Clearly, systematic subject attrition may void the randomization process, thereby casting doubt about the validity of the comparisons made. The crux of the difficulty is that it is probably never possible to tell whether or not the randomization process has been compromised by subject attrition, as this is tantamount to being able to specify what its consequences should look like. However, to repeat, it is because of our inability to do this that we resort to randomization in the first place.

It is of utmost importance to recognize that, specifics notwithstanding, all analytic solutions to the problem of unequal cell frequencies are based on the assumption that subject attrition is random. Considering broad areas of sociobehavioral research and the type of variables involved, it is our belief that, in most instances, subject attrition is anything but

---

[13]See Chapter 10, for a discussion of Randomization and its crucial role in the research design.

random. But because a solution is impossible without the assumption of random attrition, "there would seem to be no remedy short of pretending that the missing observations are random" (Appelbaum & Cramer, 1974, p. 336).

This is, admittedly, not a happy state of affairs. It is our conviction that the availability of various analytic approaches to "deal with" unequal cell frequencies has served to deflect attention from the more important question of the why of subject attrition and from the implications answers to this question might have for the validity of the study. Instead of resorting to what appear to be facile solutions, particularly when carried out by computer programs, researchers should direct greater efforts toward uncovering and understanding reasons for subject attrition as they relate to the phenomenon studied, the setting, the treatments, the subjects, and the like. It is such an orientation that holds promise for a better understanding of the phenomenon and the people studied.

Categorical Independent Variables in Nonexperimental Research

Our presentation thus far has dealt exclusively with factorial designs in experimental research. We turn now to designs with multiple categorical independent variables in nonexperimental research. Note that we *intentionally* refrain from referring to them as factorial designs. This will probably strike certain people, mainly those trained in the ANOVA tradition, as nitpicking. However, as we will attempt to show in this section, much of the confusion surrounding the use, analysis, and interpretation of such designs stems from the lack of a clear distinction between them and factorial designs in experimental research.

Perhaps the best place to begin is to note that, in the rush to take advantage of Fisher's momentous contributions to the design and analysis of experiments (see beginning of this chapter), his conceptions, terminology, and analytic approaches were transplanted and applied uncritically, even mindlessly, to nonexperimental designs with categorical independent variables. Because of their superficial resemblance to factorial designs in experimental research, they came to be treated, rather mistreated, as if they were experiments.

An admittedly simple example, which we borrow from Pedhazur (1982, p. 383), will suffice to make our case, as more sophisticated ones would only serve to strengthen it. Assume that, in a study of educational attitudes of school personnel, the following two independent variables are used: (a) Status (administrator or teacher), and (b) Sex. Researchers trained to think in terms of ANOVA would almost automatically conceive of this as a 2 × 2 factorial design and would, therefore, attempt to estimate main effects of Status, Sex, and the interaction between them. We said attempt, because complications almost always arise in such designs as a result of unequal cell frequencies—a topic we address later on.

As is true of regression analysis, the application of ANOVA implies a theoretical model of the process by which the independent variables affect the dependent variable. Regrettably, however, many people using ANOVA appear to be oblivious of this. As Draper and Smith (1981) pointed out: "The question 'What model are you considering?' is often met with 'I am not considering one—I am using analysis of variance'" (p. 423).

What, therefore, are the implications of treating the example given above as a factorial design, and estimating and testing terms such as main effects and interaction? In a skeletal form, they are that Status and Sex are independent of each other, that each may affect educational attitudes, that they may also have a joint effect (i.e., interaction) on educational attitudes, and that relevant omitted variables (i.e., variables that affect educational attitudes and are not included in the model) are not correlated with Status and Sex.

As will be recalled, a state of affairs of the kind we have been describing can be attained only in experimental research, when at least one of the variables is manipulated and when randomization is resorted to. Probably the greatest threat to valid analysis and interpretation of results when a nonexperimental design with categorical independent variables is cast in the form of factorial ANOVA, and interpreted accordingly, is the delusion that the study has thereby been transformed into one that satisfies the requirements of experimental research. Indeed, the use of ANOVA in nonexperimental research, "not infrequently produces in both the investigator and his audience the illusion that he has experimental control over the independent variables. Nothing could be more wrong" (Humphreys & Fleishman, 1974, p. 468).

Pedhazur (1982) pointed out the following in connection with the example given above:

It is well known that these variables [Status and Sex] are correlated: most school administrators are males, whereas the majority of teachers are females. Is, then, an observed difference in educational attitudes between administrators and teachers due to status or due to sex? Conversely, does a difference between males and females reflect a difference due to sex or due to status? And what, if any, is the meaning of an interaction between status and sex? (p. 383)

Complicating matters further are other extremely important issues, such as omitted relevant variables correlated with the independent variables and the likelihood that one or both of the latter are proxies.[14]

Probably the best way to summarize the discussion thus far is to note that, on a conceptual level, the study described above is no different from studies with continuous independent variables in nonexperimental research, discussed in earlier chapters (see especially Chapters 14 and 18). What was said about model specification (e.g., single-stage and multistage models, correlations among the independent variables, specification errors) in nonexperimental research for designs consisting of continuous independent variables applies also to designs in which the independent variables are categorical. In sum, then, whether the variables are continuous or categorical, the objective, on the conceptual level, is the same, namely to discern the effects of correlated independent variables on the dependent variable.

There are, however, differences in the way the analysis proceeds and the type of indices obtained, depending on whether the design consists of continuous or categorical independent variables. The differences stem from the fact that, except for the special case of categorical variables consisting of two categories, such variables are represented by more than one coded vector. Early on in Chapter 19, we cautioned against treating each of a set of coded vectors representing a categorical variable as if it were a distinct variable. It should also be clear that, when categorical variables are represented by multiple coded vectors, the analysis *does not* yield a single index of the effect of each variable, analogous to a regression coefficient associated with each continuous independent variable. Because it is not possible to address here the analytic issues in the detail they deserve, we refer you to Pedhazur (1982, pp. 371–392) for such a discussion, some numerical illustrations, as well as relevant references.

Categorizing Continuous Independent Variables

The impact of attempts to apply ANOVA concepts and methods in nonexperimental research is nowhere more evident than in the practice of categorizing continuous variables. In order to fit their data into the Procrustean bed of ANOVA, researchers categorize continuous variables

---

[14]See Chapter 13, for a discussion of proxy variables.

they are using. Thus, scores, for example, on mental ability, motivation, anxiety, locus of control, are used to construct categories of high and low; high, average, and low; internals and externals; introverts and extraverts; or whatever other categories strike one's fancy so that the data may be cast in an ANOVA format.

It should be noted that, although our comments about categorizing continuous variables are made in the context of nonexperimental research, they apply equally to experimental research. Thus, it would be equally imprudent to treat a manipulated continuous variable (e.g., hours of study, number of reinforcements, dosages of a drug) as if it were a categorical variable. We focus on nonexperimental designs, because, in such designs, the likelihood is greater for the researcher to categorize continuous variables and to proceed as if they were categorical. We believe that, in experimental designs, researchers who are trained in the ANOVA tradition are less likely to categorize a manipulated continuous variable, as methods for studying trends (e.g., by using orthogonal polynomials) are an integral part of such training and of textbooks devoted to ANOVA.

But, to repeat, the consequences of categorizing a continuous variable in experimental research are equally harmful. For an example of an experimental design with a continuous independent variable that is analyzed both ways (i.e., as continuous and as categorical), leading to different conclusions, see Pedhazur (1982, pp. 397–399).

As has been pointed by various authors (e.g., J. Cohen, 1983), categorizing continuous variables leads to serious losses of information. Important as this issue is (for a discussion and a numerical example, see Pedhazur, 1982, pp. 450–454), categorization of continuous variables has even more harmful effects.

First, the nature of the variable changes, as it is generally treated as if it were a categorical variable, *not* as a continuous variable that has been categorized. We will not go into a discussion of the meaning of such a change, as contrasts between continuous and categorical variables were discussed in Chapters 3 and 8. In the present context, it will suffice to note that, as a result of the change in the nature of the variable, the very idea of trends (e.g., linear, quadratic) in the data is precluded.

Second, categorizing continuous variables in nonexperimental research and casting the design in an ANOVA format tends to create the false impression that a nonexperimental design has thereby been transformed into an experimental design or, at the very least, into something closely approximating it. In other words, casting the design in an ANOVA format, researchers are, in our opinion, more inclined to analyze their data and interpret the results as if they were obtained in experimental research.

In fairness, it should be noted that, because of training and the prevailing climate of research, there was a time when most researchers resorted to categorization of variables almost automatically. This was the time when ANOVA reigned supreme and when most if not all the training in design and analysis was limited to it. On a personal note, the first author would like to point out that, during his graduate training, he was exposed exclusively to ANOVA designs. When time came to work on his dissertation, he "naturally" cast his problem in the form of a factorial design and proceeded to categorize continuous variables he used without giving it a second thought. Frankly, he did not know any better. This only serves to illustrate what we said in various chapters (e.g., Chapter 9) of the effects of training and specialization on the manner in which research problems are conceptualized, the research designed and executed, the data analyzed, and the results interpreted.

In recent years, researchers and students have not only come to recognize the equivalence of ANOVA and MR with coded vectors, but, more importantly, they have generally been exposed to the broader conception of the linear model, under which the two analytic approaches are subsumed. One beneficial consequence of this is that researchers have come to recognize that it is not necessary to categorize continuous variables in order to fit them into a factorial ANOVA format, not to mention the deleterious consequences of then treating the design as if it were experimental. This is not to say that the ANOVA tradition has been universally abandoned. Current research in this tradition is too numerous to cite. Attesting to the enduring popularity of categorizing continuous variables and casting the research in the form of a factorial ANOVA is the frequent response to critics that everyone is doing it. For example, Das and Kirby (1978) gave the following response to Humphreys' (1978) criticism of their splitting measures at their medians (referred to as median splits):

Das and Kirby (1977) did not introduce median splits into the research literature in psychology. In fact, single median splits have been done routinely by psychologists. We divide people on the basis of age, intelligence, and high and low verbal ability. Double median splits such as the one we used in our 1977 article can be easily found in personality research. (p. 878)

Unfortunately, categorization of continuous variables persists in some research areas, as if no arguments were ever advanced against this strategy. For example, using Rotter's (1966) measure of Locus of Control, researchers have been applying median splits for the purpose of identifying what have come to be known as "externals" and "internals"—this despite Rotter's (1975) assertion that "there is absolutely no justification for thinking in terms of a typology" (p. 62).[15]

An example of an area in which categorization is practiced with a vengeance is sex-role research. You have probably come across some of the numerous studies in which scores on some measure of masculinity and femininity are used to create such categories as masculine, feminine, and androgynous. These are then used in the form of factorial designs, to estimate and test, for example, main effects of masculinity, femininity, and the interaction between them. A veritable minor industry dealing with interactions has evolved in this area. It consists of all sorts of strange suggestions and approaches that, we regret to say, are by and large of little merit. Some are downright wrong (for some examples of the suggested approaches and the debate surrounding them, see Lubinski, 1983; Lubinski, Tellegen, & Butcher, 1981, 1983; Spence, 1983; Stokes, 1983; Stokes, Childs, & Fuehrer, 1981; Tellegen & Lubinski, 1983).

ANOVA AND REGRESSION: SIMILARITIES AND CONTRASTS

In Chapter 19, we discussed ANOVA and REGRESSION approaches from the perspectives of the mechanics of the analysis and of terminology. We conclude the present chapter with some general remarks about similarities and contrasts between the two approaches from design and analytic perspectives.

From the presentation in the preceding chapter, it should be clear, we hope, that either ANOVA or REGRESSION with coded vectors may be used for the analysis of data from experimental as well as nonexperimental research with one categorical independent variable. It should be equally clear, from the presentation in the present chapter, that both approaches can be used for the analysis of orthogonal factorial designs. The same holds true for designs consisting also of manipulated continuous variables, which in the context of ANOVA can be handled through the use of orthogonal polynomials (see, for example, Edwards, 1985;

---

[15]In Chapter 21, we comment briefly on Locus of Control in connection with an ATI numerical example in which we use this construct. See Table 21.1 and the discussion related to it.

Keppel, 1982; Kirk, 1982; Myers, 1979; Winer, 1971). For such designs, therefore, the choice between the two approaches may be determined by training, the availability of or preference for specific computer programs, and even taste.

Although there is a good deal of controversy regarding the analysis of nonorthogonal factorial designs, most suggested approaches aimed at adjusting for the correlations among the terms of the design are based on applications of multiple regression analysis. Even computer programs for ANOVA (e.g., SPSS) incorporate options for such approaches for the case of nonorthogonal designs. We believe that using the REGRESSION approach for nonorthogonal factorial designs is preferable, as the decision regarding the nature of the adjustment has to be made explicitly. Carrying out the analysis by selecting an option in programs such as ANOVA of SPSS is, in our opinion, more prone to lead to inappropriate choices and/or misinterpretations of results.

Had the preceding been the only difference between the two approaches, it would have understandably not sufficed to lead to a clear preference for the REGRESSION approach. The most compelling reason for a preference of the REGRESSION over the ANOVA approach is that it is more comprehensive from conceptual, design, and analytic perspectives. Conceptually, all variables, be they categorical or continuous, are viewed alike, in the sense of providing information to be used in attempts to explain or predict the dependent variable.

From design and analysis perspectives, REGRESSION is superior to ANOVA, because, unlike the latter, it is equally applicable to experimental and nonexperimental designs when the independent variables are continuous and/or categorical. The contrast between the two approaches is perhaps clearest for the case of continuous independent variables in nonexperimental designs. It will be recalled that, under such circumstances, a researcher has to resort to arbitrary categorization of continuous variables in order to fit them in an ANOVA straightjacket. Doing this is inadvisable, it was pointed out earlier, not only because it results in loss of information, but primarily because it generally leads to a change in conception regarding the nature of the variables and the design. Researchers are generally prone to treat continuous variables that were categorized as if they were categorical variables. Further, applying ANOVA, they are also more prone to *erroneously* treat the design as if it were experimental, as exemplified by routine attempts to estimate and interpret main effects and interactions.

The foregoing is not meant to imply that researchers using the REGRESSION approach do not run risks of misapplications and misinterpretations. We believe, however, that a researcher using multiple regression analysis in a nonexperimental design with continuous variables is more likely to be sensitized to the correlations among the independent variables, as they are part and parcel of the analytic approach. Moreover, the likelihood of routinely creating product vectors to represent interactions is much smaller. Even when some such terms are created, researchers have to contend with the controversy surrounding their use and interpretation (see Pedhazur, 1982, pp. 385–387, for a discussion and relevant references). In contrast, when doing ANOVA, all of this is done naturally, albeit erroneously.

The generality and elegance of the REGRESSION approach will, we hope, become even more evident in Chapter 21, where we show its application to designs with continuous and categorical variables. As is pointed out in Chapter 21, when researchers apply, for example, analysis of covariance (ANCOVA), they are using a REGRESSION approach, although they may not know this.

STUDY SUGGESTIONS

1. Consider the following hypothetical study. Subjects were randomly assigned to read a statement advocating reform of Medicare programs. The presumed source of the statement was manipulated as follows: (1) Profession (A): A_1 = Physician, A_2 = Social Worker; and (2) Sex (B): B_1 = Male, B_2 = Female. Subjects were asked to rate the statement on a 7-point scale, ranging from 1 = disagree very strongly to 7 = agree very strongly. Following are illustrative data:

	Male	Female
	B_1	B_2
A_1: Physician	4	2
	4	2
	3	3
	4	3
A_2: Social Worker	3	6
	4	6
	4	7
	6	7

Using effect coding, regress the dependent variable on the coded vectors representing the main effects and the interaction. We recommend that you do all the necessary calculations by hand as well as by computer, using more than one program (e.g., SPSS REGRESSION and MANOVA; SAS REG and GLM). Compare the results of the various analyses. What is (are) the
   (a) cell means and standard deviations?
   (b) regression equation.
      What does each term of the equation represent?
      What would a predicted score be equal to when this equation is applied to the scores (codes) of an individual on the coded vectors?
   (c) sum of squares due to A and the associated F ratio?
   (d) sum of squares due to B and the associated F ratio?
   (e) sum of squares due to A by B and the associated F ratio?
   (f) mean square residual?
   (g) proportion of variance accounted for by each factor and by the interaction between them?
   (h) sums of squares for simple main effects of A within B and their associated F ratios? What should the sum of these sums of squares be equal to?
   (i) sums of squares for simple main effects of B within A and their associated F ratios? What should the sum of these sums of squares be equal to?
   (j) Express each person's score as composed of the following components: grand mean, effects of A, B, $A \times B$, and residual.
   Plot the cell means and interpret the results.
2. Consider a factorial design in which 10 subjects were randomly assigned to each treatment combination (i.e., each cell). The means of each cell are as follows:

	B_1	B_2	B_3
A_1	10	8	6
A_2	8	12	10

Assume that effect coding was used and that identification of various categories was as follows: A_1 in Vector 1; B_1 in Vector 2; B_2 in Vector 3. Vector 4 was obtained as a result of multiplying Vector 1 by Vector 2; Vector 5 was obtained as a result of multiplying Vector 1 by Vector 3. What is (are) the

(a) correlation between Vectors 1 and 3?

(b) df for the F ratio associated with the interaction (i.e., $A \times B$)?

(c) regression equation that would be obtained from the regression of Y on all the coded vectors?

(d) effects of treatments B_1 and B_2?

(e) interaction term for each cell?

(f) sum of squares due to A?

(g) sum of squares due to B?

(h) sum of squares due to $A \times B$?

(i) sum of squares for the simple main effect of B at A_1?

Assume that the residual sum of squares is 162.

(j) What is the F ratio for the main effect of B?

3. In an A by B by C design, A is comprised of 3 categories, B of 3 categories, and C of 4 categories. Ten subjects were randomly assigned to each cell. Assuming you were to use effect coding in a multiple regression to analyze the data, what is (are) the:

(a) number of independent variables?

(b) number of coded vectors you would generate for each main effect and interaction term?

(c) df associated with each main effect and interaction term?

(d) df associated with the overall error term (i.e., MSR)?

(e) correlations between vectors representing any one term of the design (i.e., main effects or interaction) and vectors representing any other term?

Answers

1. (a)

		B_1	B_2
A_1	M:	3.75	2.50
	s:	.50	.58
A_2	M:	4.25	6.50
	s:	1.26	.58

(b) $Y' = 4.250 - 1.125A1 - .250B1 + .875A1B1$

where A_1 was identified in vector A1, B_1 in vector B1.

$a = 4.25 = \bar{Y}$ (i.e., grand mean of dependent variable);

$b_{A1} = -1.125 =$ effect of treatment A_1 (i.e., $\bar{Y}_{A1} - \bar{Y}$);

$b_{B1} = -.250 =$ effect of treatment B_1 (i.e., $\bar{Y}_{B1} - \bar{Y}$);

$b_{A1B1} = .875 =$ interaction term for cell A_1B_1.

The predicted score will equal the mean of the cell to which the individual in question belongs.

(c) ss_{reg} due to A: 20.25; $F = 32.40$ with 1 and 12 df

(d) ss_{reg} due to B: 1.00; $F = 1.60$ with 1 and 12 df

(e) ss_{reg} due to $A \times B$: 12.25; $F = 19.60$ with 1 and 12 df

(f) $MSR = .625$

(g) proportion of variance accounted for by:
$A = .49390; B = .02439; A \times B = .29878$

(h) ss for A within $B_1 = .50; F = .80$ with 1 and 12 df;
ss for A within $B_2 = 32.00; F = 51.20$ with 1 and 12 df;
$.50 + 32.00 = 32.50 = ss_A + ss_{AB} = 20.25 + 12.25$

(i) ss for B within $A_1 = 3.12; F = 5.00$ with 1 and 12 df;
ss for B within $A_2 = 10.13; F = 16.20$ with 1 and 12 df;
$3.12 + 10.13 = 13.25 = ss_B + ss_{AB} = 1.00 + 12.25$

(j) first person in A_1B_1:
$4 = 4.25 - 1.125 - .25 + .875 + .25$
last person in A_2B_2:
$7 = 4.25 + 1.125 + .25 + .875 + .50$
(see Table 20.2 and text for explanation)

2. (a) .00

(b) 2 and 54

(c) $Y' = 9 - 1V1 + 0V2 + 1V3 + 2V4 - 1V5$

(d) $B_1 = 0; B_2 = 1$

(e)

	B_1	B_2	B_3
A_1	2	-1	-1
A_2	-2	1	1

(f) 60

(g) 40

(h) 120

(i) 80

(j) $F = 6.67$ with 2 and 54 df

3. (a) 3

(b) 2 for A; 2 for B; 3 for C; 4 for $A \times B$; 6 for $A \times C$; 6 for $B \times C$; 12 for $A \times B \times C$

(c) the df for each term equal the number of coded vectors used to code the given term
(e.g., for $A = 2; A \times C = 6$)

(d) 324

(e) .00

Chapter 21
Attribute–Treatments–Interactions;
Analysis of Covariance

As has been amply demonstrated in many research areas, individual differences account for the bulk of the variance of phenomena studied. Depending on the researcher's theoretical orientation and training, variance due to individual differences is either treated as error or serves as the focus of study. Probably no other author has discussed this issue with greater insight and clarity than Cronbach (1957) in his classic paper on the two disciplines of scientific psychology. Because Cronbach addressed broad differences between two approaches to research, we believe you will benefit from reading his statement even if your field of study is not psychology. Briefly, Cronbach distinguished between experimentalists and correlationists.

Individual differences have been an annoyance rather than a challenge to the experimenter. His goal is to control behavior, and variation within treatments is proof that he has not succeeded. Individual variation is cast into that outer darkness known as "error variance."

The correlational psychologist is in love with just those variables the experimenter left home to forget. He regards individual and group variations as important effects of biological and social causes. All organisms adapt to their environments, but not equally well. His question is: what present characteristics of the organism determine its mode and degree of adaptation? (p. 674)

As Cronbach pointed out:

It is not enough for each discipline to borrow from the other. Correlational psychology studies only variance among organisms; experimental psychology studies only variance among treatments. A united discipline will study both of these, but it will also be concerned with the otherwise neglected interactions between organismic and treatment variables. (p. 681)

The foregoing statements serve to underscore one of the main themes of our book, namely that measurement, design, and analysis are interrelated and feed into one another in the overall research enterprise. As is well known, people trained in experimental research are usually taught to apply, almost exclusively, the analysis of variance, whereas those trained in what Cronbach referred to as correlational psychology are taught to apply, almost exclusively, correlation and regression analysis. Consequently, the very nature of the problems researchers within each camp address is molded and constrained by the methods with which

545

they are familiar. Many researchers from both camps seem unaware of the existence and promise of analytic approaches that afford one to study group differences while taking individual differences into account.

Contrary to the impression one may get from listening to either camp, researchers are not faced with an either/or predicament. Procedures are available for taking individual differences into account without having to give up the notion of differences among groups, settings, treatments. In fact, failure to study interactions between subjects' attributes and treatments may, and often does, lead to the conclusion that "nothing" is taking place in a study.

ATTRIBUTE–TREATMENTS–INTERACTION (ATI) ANALYSIS: SYNOPSIS

Basic ideas and terminology of ATI designs were presented in Chapter 12 (see Design 7). Here, we begin with a synopsis of the analysis of an ATI design, followed by a numerical example. We then show that the same analytic approach is applicable in Analysis of Covariance (ANCOVA) designs. For the sake of simplicity, we present the most rudimentary design possible. Generalizations to more complex designs are commented upon later.

Assume that a researcher is interested in studying the effects of two treatments (e.g., teaching methods, drugs, communications) on some dependent variable (e.g., academic achievement, aggression, conformity). Assume further that he or she expects the treatments to have differential effects on subjects, depending on some attribute of theirs (e.g., mental ability, anxiety, persuasibility). In other words, the researcher expects an interaction between the treatments and some attribute of the subjects. Under such circumstances, subjects would be randomly assigned to the treatments, and the attribute of interest would be measured *prior* to the administration of the treatments. Following the administration of the treatments, a measure of the dependent variable would be obtained.

For the sake of generality, we will use X to stand for an attribute, Y for a dependent variable, and A and B for two treatments. An ATI analysis involves comparisons of regression equations for Y on X obtained under A and B. Because each regression equation is comprised of an intercept (a) and a regression coefficient (b), regression equations may differ on either of the parameter estimates, on both, or on neither of them.[1] Therefore, the analysis proceeds in a sequence of tests, the results of each determining the one to follow. The first test is addressed to the question whether there is a statistically significant difference between the b's. A difference between the b's that is statistically not significant leads to the conclusion that the effect of X on Y is the same under both treatments. Graphically, this takes the form of parallel regression lines, as exemplified in (1) and (2) of Figure 21.1.

Assuming that higher scores signify better performance, it is clear that, in both (1) and (2), subjects administered treatment A performed better than those administered treatment B, regardless of their score on the attribute, X. Moreover, in both (1) and (2), there is a constant difference between the effects of treatments A and B, this being equal to the difference between the two intercepts. Note the analogy between the preceding statement and that about main effects in a factorial design (see Chapter 20). In both cases, a statement is made about

---

[1]If necessary, review the presentation of simple regression analysis in Chapter 17.

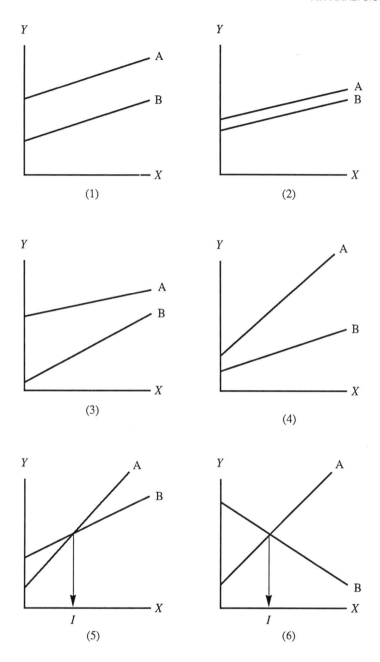

Figure 21.1

the effect of one variable without having to qualify it by making reference to levels of the other variable. In short, *a conclusion that there is no significant difference between the b's is tantamount to a statement that there is no interaction between the treatments and the attribute.*

When it is concluded that the difference between the b's is statistically not significant, the next step is to test the difference between the a's. A statistically significant difference between the a's indicates that the two treatments (or treatment and control) differ from each other by a constant (the difference between the a's) along the continuum of the attribute. Referring to Figure 21.1, it may be found, for example, that there is a statistically significant difference between the a's in (1) but not in (2).

A conclusion that the difference between the a's is not statistically significant (after having concluded that there is no interaction between the treatments and the attribute) is tantamount to a statement that a single regression equation would suffice to fit the data of both groups. If, on the other hand, the difference between the a's is statistically significant, it means that two equations consisting of the same b (referred to below as a common b) but of two different a's are required to fit the data of the two groups. Referring to (1) and (2) of Figure 21.1, it would appear that the former would require two regression equations with a common b but different a's, whereas a single regression equation would suffice for the latter.

ORDINAL AND DISORDINAL INTERACTIONS

As was stated above, a statistically significant difference between the b's means that there is an interaction between the treatments and the attribute. The interaction can take various forms, four of which are depicted in (3), (4), (5), and (6) of Figure 21.1.

A distinction between *ordinal* and *disordinal* interactions was introduced in Chapter 3 (see Figure 3.5 and the discussion related to it), and was also referred to in other chapters (e.g., Chapters 12 and 20). In the present context, an *ordinal interaction* means that the rank order of the effects of the treatments does not change along the continuum of the attribute. Examples of ordinal interactions are given in (3) and (4) of Figure 21.1, where A is superior to B, although not by the same amount, along the continuum of X. Note that the differential effectiveness of A over B varies, depending on the specific nature of the interaction and the specific level of X. Thus, in (3), the difference between A and B is relatively large for lower levels of X and becomes increasingly smaller with increments in the size of X. The converse is true in (4).

A *disordinal interaction* means that the rank order of the effects of the treatments changes within the range of interest of the attribute. Another way of stating this is that the regression lines intersect within the range of interest of the attribute. Note that both characterizations of a disordinal interaction include a qualifying statement regarding the range of interest of the attribute. To clarify this, it would suffice to contrast (3) and (4) with (5) and (6). Clearly, had the regression lines in (3) and (4) been extended, they too would have intersected. However, their intersection would occur at points along the continuum of the attribute that are either not within the range of interest in the given study or at values of the attribute that do not even exist.[2]

Look first at (4) and assume that the point of origin on the scale for the measurement of X is zero. Extending the regression lines would lead to their intersection at some negative value of X, which is clearly not in the range of interest on the attribute variable. Consider now the situation depicted in (3). Assume that X is Mental Ability and that the researcher's interest is in the effects of A and B on Y for people whose scores on Mental Ability are within the range of 90 to 120. Extending the regression lines may show that they intersect at a score that is well outside this range, say, 160. Consequently, so far as the researcher is concerned, the interaction is ordinal.

---

[2]Extensions of regression lines constitute extrapolations—a practice against which we cautioned several times earlier (see, for example, Chapter 13).

Other examples come readily to mind, but the preceding would suffice to serve as a contrast with the cases where the regression lines intersect within the range of interest, as depicted in (5) and (6). Turning to these cases, it will be noted that, in both of them, A is superior to B for subjects whose scores on X are above I—the point of intersection. In contrast, B is superior to A for subjects whose scores on X are below I.

But notice that the disordinal interactions depicted in (5) and (6) are very different from each other. In (5), the regression of Y on X is positive under both treatments, whereas in (6) it is positive under A but negative under B. To clarify this, we will offer an example of each. Think of X in (5) as Mental Ability, of Y as Academic Achievement, and of the two treatments as two teaching methods. Broadly speaking, assume that A is a method that emphasizes problem solving, whereas B emphasizes drill. Accordingly, it appears that B is superior to A for students whose scores on Mental Ability are relatively low, whereas the converse is true for students whose scores on Mental Ability are relatively high. Turning to (6), think of X as some personality variable, say, Locus of Control, of A and B as two Leadership Styles, and of Y as Productivity. From (6), it appears that the regression of Productivity on Locus of Control is positive under Leadership Style A and negative under Leadership Style B. Employees whose scores are below I on Locus of Control are more productive under Leadership Style B, whereas the converse is true for employees whose scores are above I.

REGIONS OF SIGNIFICANCE

As explained in the preceding section, an interaction between treatments and an attribute means that the difference between the treatments is not the same along the continuum of the attribute. It is possible for differences between treatments at certain points on the attribute continuum to be so small as to be deemed substantively not meaningful. Thus, for example, assuming that A is a costlier treatment than B, a researcher obtaining results such as those depicted in (4) of Figure 21.1 may conclude that, although A appears superior to B along the continuum of the attribute, its use is warranted only for subjects whose scores on the attribute are above a certain point, where differences between the treatments are deemed meaningful.

Look now at (5) and (6) and notice that, for subjects whose scores on X are at the point of intersection (I), predicted scores on Y are identical regardless of which treatment they were administered. Although predicted scores for subjects who are close to I differ, some of these differences may be deemed too small to be substantively meaningful.

The foregoing remarks involved decisions regarding effect size—a complex topic dealt with in earlier chapters (e.g., Chapters 9 and 15). A simpler, *although certainly not preferable*, approach is to rely solely on statistical tests of significance. In view of the fact that our examples are presented in a substantive and practical vacuum, so to speak, we are unable to address issues of effect size; instead, we resort to statistical tests of significance.

In the presence of an interaction in an ATI design, regions of significance and nonsignificance may be established using the Johnson-Neyman technique (how this is done is illustrated below in connection with the numerical example). For example, in (5) and (6) of Figure 21.1, a range of scores on the attribute close to I may be identified as a region of nonsignificance, meaning that, for scores on X within this range, there are no statistically significant differences between the effects of the two treatments on Y. Two regions of significance are defined—one below and one above the region of nonsignificance—where the effects of the treatments on Y are statistically significant.

Note that the setting up of regions of significance is analogous to tests of simple main effects in the presence of an interaction in a factorial design (see Chapter 20). Recall that we argued that it generally does not make sense to carry out and interpret tests of main effects in the presence of an interaction. The same holds true in ATI designs. As an example of the dubious meaning of a test of the difference between intercepts in the presence of an interaction, contrast (3) and (4) of Figure 21.1. It may turn out that the difference between the a's in (3) is statistically significant, whereas that in (4) is not. However, in either case, what is of interest is the nature of the interaction as well as the regions of significance. Tests of differences between a's when the interaction is disordinal—for example, (5) and (6) of Figure 21.1—are even more questionable.

We hope that our brief discussion and illustrations of attribute-treatments-interactions have served to convince you of the great virtue of the ATI design in taking individual differences into consideration. To underscore this point, we will conclude by using an admittedly extreme example of what might happen when individual differences are over-looked. Look at (6) of Figure 21.1 and notice that, because of the nature of the interaction depicted, differences between the Y means for the two treatments would be very small. In fact, depending on the scatter of the data points about the regression lines, the Y means may even be identical. Under such circumstances, failure to take the relevant attribute, X, into consideration would lead to the conclusion that there is no difference between the effects of A and B. Inclusion of X would lead to an utterly different conclusion.

A NUMERICAL EXAMPLE

For our numerical example, we use the illustrative data given in Table 21.1. Included in the table are descriptive statistics and the regression equations of Y on X for each of the treatments. In the course of the computer analysis that follows, we make reference to these statistics. As a review, you may find it useful to replicate our calculations, using the presentation in Chapter 17 as a guide.

To give the example some substantive meaning, assume that Y is Academic Achievement and that X is Locus of Control (LOC). Without going far afield, it will be noted that Rotter (1966) proposed the construct LOC to refer to beliefs regarding control of reinforcement following behavior. Briefly, internal control refers to the perception that one's actions and their consequences are primarily due to one's personal traits and behavior. External control, on the other hand, refers to the perception that one's actions and their consequences are determined primarily by forces outside oneself (e.g., luck, chance, fate).

Assume now that students' LOC was measured and that they were then randomly assigned to one of two teaching styles: Directive or Nondirective. The researcher expects a disordinal interaction between LOC (the attribute) and the teaching styles (the treatments) in their effects on achievement. Specifically, students who tend to be externally controlled are ex-pected to achieve more when exposed to a Directive than a Nondirective teaching style, whereas those who tend to be internally controlled are expected to achieve more when exposed to a Nondirective than a Directive style.

We remind you, again, that we cannot go into details of theoretical formulations, defini-tions (e.g., of Directive and Nondirective), and measurement (e.g., of LOC). We hope it is clear from earlier chapters that these are but some of the important issues a researcher must address when planning and executing a study. It will, however, be instructive to comment briefly on measurement and analysis as they relate to our example. A good deal of research has been directed to the study of LOC and its relations with other variables. In much, if not most, of this research, Rotter's I-E scale was used.

In Chapter 20, it was pointed out that Rotter (1975) was critical of the common practice of using some cutting point (e.g., median splits) to classify people into internals and externals.

Table 21.1
Illustrative Data for an ATI Analysis

	Teaching style		
Directive		Nondirective	
Y	X	Y	X
3	1	13	1
3	2	17	2
5	2	16	2
6	2	9	2
6	4	15	2
7	4	14	4
8	2	13	4
9	5	7	4
10	3	11	5
11	6	6	6
12	3	6	6
13	7	5	6
14	3	11	7
16	4	6	7
16	7	5	7
17	8	8	8
19	6	6	9
19	8	4	9
22	6	3	11
22	9	4	11
M:	11.90	4.60	8.95	5.65
ss:	697.80	108.80	372.95	174.55
sp:	222.20		−206.35	
s:	6.06	2.39	4.43	3.03
r:	.806		−.809	
	$Y' = 2.51 + 2.04X$		$Y' = 15.63 - 1.18X$	

Note. M = Mean; ss = Sum of Squares; sp = Sum of Products; s = Standard Deviation. r = correlation. Y = Academic Achievement. X = Locus of Control, scored in Externality direction.

In view of our earlier discussions (e.g., Chapter 20), you probably recognize that the reason researchers have used Rotter's scale in a manner that he claimed to be inappropriate was because they wanted to fit it in an ANOVA mold. Using an ATI design and the kind of analysis presented here obviates the questionable practice of categorizing continuous variables (LOC, in our example).

Depending on your background and substantive interests, you may prefer to think of other variables in connection with our numerical example. Thus, for example, instead of LOC, you may wish to think of the attribute as Introversion-Extraversion. Instead of Academic Achievement and Teaching Styles, you may prefer to think of Adjustment and types of Therapy respectively. Alternatively, the attribute may be employees' Authoritarianism, the treatments two Management Styles, and the dependent variable Productivity, Job Satisfaction, or what have you. Other examples come readily to mind.

SPSS

For the analysis, which we will carry out using SPSS, we will need a coded vector to represent membership in the two treatments, as well as the product of the attribute, X, by the coded vector to represent the attribute-treatments-interaction. As in the analyses done in earlier chapters (e.g., Chapter 19), we will read in a T(reatment) vector in which the group exposed to the Directive teaching style will be assigned 1, and the group exposed to the Nondirective style will be assigned 2. Effect coding for the treatments will then be generated by IF statements, and the product vector will be generated by a COMPUTE statement.

Input

```
SET LISTING='T211SPS.LIS'.
TITLE TABLE 21.1. ATI DESIGN.
DATA LIST/ Y,X,T 1–6.   [fixed format; 2 columns for each variable]
VALUE LABELS T 1 'DIRECTIVE' 2 'NONDIRECTIVE'.  [assign labels]
IF (T EQ 1) E=1.      [generate an effect coded vector to
IF (T EQ 2) E=–1.   represent the treatments]
COMPUTE XE=X*E.  [product vector representing interaction term]
BEGIN DATA.
 3 1 1
 3 2 1    [data for the first two subjects in T 1]
 .   . .
13 1 2
17 2 2    [data for the first two subjects in T 2]
 .   . .
END DATA.
LIST.
PLOT HSIZE = 40/VSIZE = 20/
   VERTICAL=MIN(0)/HORIZONTAL=MIN(0)/
   PLOT=Y WITH X BY T.
PROCESS IF (T EQ 1).     [analyze data of T 1 only]
REGRESSION VAR Y, X/DES/STAT ALL/DEP Y/ENTER.
PROCESS IF (T EQ 2).     [analyze data of T 2 only]
REGRESSION VAR Y, X/DES/STAT ALL/DEP Y/ENTER.
REGRESSION VAR=Y TO XE/DES/STAT=ALL/
   DEP=Y/ENTER X/ENTER E/ENTER XE/
   DEP=Y/ENTER E.
```

Commentary

See Chapter 16, for a general description of SPSS and our practice in presenting input, output, and commentaries.

Because general comments about the REGRESSION procedure were made in preceding chapters, we comment here only on aspects directly pertinent to this run.

PLOT procedure is used to plot Y with X by T(reatments). Because of the labels assigned above, subjects will be identified by the first letter of their group label (i.e., D or N). HSIZE and VSIZE are subcommands enabling one to control the sizes of the horizontal and vertical axes, which we set to 40 columns and 20 rows. VERTICAL and HORIZONTAL are subcommands enabling one to assign labels to the two axes and/or control their scaling. We used them to specify that the MINimum value be 0.

"PROCESS IF is a temporary transformation and is executed when the data are read for the next procedure" (*SPSS/PC+ V2.0: Base manual*, Norusis & SPSS Inc., 1988c, p. C122). We use it to do two separate regression analyses of Y on X: one for the group assigned 1 in the T vector (i.e., Directive), the other for the group assigned 2 (i.e., Nondirective). PROCESS

IF *is available only on the PC version*. On the mainframe version, the same can be accomplished by the SPLIT FILE command, which is *not* available on the PC.

In addition to the regression analyses in the separate groups (see above), the REGRESSION procedure is used to analyze the data for both groups simultaneously. Two analyses are specified. In the first analysis—the one central to the topic under consideration—Y is regressed on X, E, and XE, entered in separate steps in the order listed. In the second analysis, Y is regressed on the coded vector, E. We explain why we do the second analysis when we comment on the output generated by it.

Output

Y	X	T	E	XE	
3	1	1	1.00	1.00	
3	2	1	1.00	2.00	*[data for first two subjects in T 1]*
.	.	.	.	.	
13	1	2	−1.00	−1.00	
17	2	2	−1.00	−2.00	*[data for first two subjects in T 2]*
.	.	.	.	.	

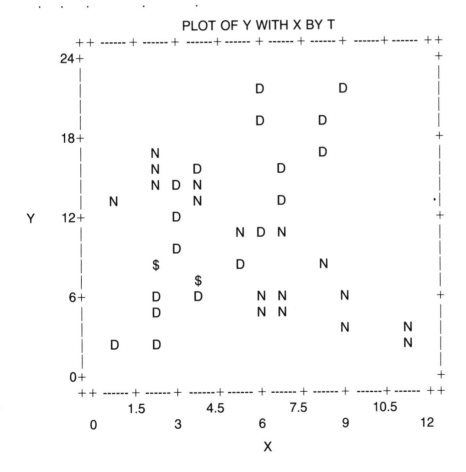

PLOT OF Y WITH X BY T

40 cases plotted.
D:DIRECTIV N:NONDIREC $:Multiple occurrence

Commentary

As with the input, we list the data for only the first two subjects in each of the groups. Examine the column labeled E (generated by the IF statements) and the column XE (generated by the COMPUTE statement).

Because the analysis consists of comparisons of regression equations, it is essential to verify that there are no departures from linearity. Accordingly, it is useful to plot the data. Inspect the plot and notice that the regression of Y on X in each of the groups appears linear. (For comments regarding analysis when the regression is not linear, see Extensions and Generalizations, later in this chapter.) It is clear, however, that the regression of Y on X is positive for "Directive" and negative for "Nondirective." You may wish to draw the two regression lines, using the Y and X means and a of the regression equation for the group in question (reported in Table 21.1 and in the output below). For an explanation, see Chapter 17, Drawing the Regression Line.

Output

[Directive]

	Mean	Std Dev
Y	11.900	6.060
X	4.600	2.393

N of Cases = 20

Correlation:

	Y	X
Y	1.000	.806
X	.806	1.000

Equation Number 1   Dependent Variable..   Y

Variable(s) Entered on Step Number 1..   X

------------------------------------ Variables in the Equation ------------------------------------

Variable	B	SE B	Beta	T	Sig T
X	2.04228	.35298	.80643	5.786	.0000
(Constant)	2.50551	1.82050		1.376	.1856

[Nondirective]

	Mean	Std Dev
Y	8.950	4.430
X	5.650	3.031

N of Cases = 20

Correlation:

	Y	X
Y	1.000	−.809
X	−.809	1.000

Equation Number 1   Dependent Variable..   Y

Variable(s) Entered on Step Number 1..   X

------------------------------------- Variables in the Equation -------------------------------------

Variable	B	SE B	Beta	T	Sig T
X	−1.18218	.20263	−.80876	−5.834	.0000
(Constant)	15.62933	1.29193		12.098	.0000

Commentary

Examine first the correlations between X and Y under the two treatments and notice that they are almost identical but with opposite signs (.806 and −.809, for Directive and Nondirective respectively). Recall that, when there is only one independent variable, the standardized regression coefficient (β) is equal to the zero-order correlation (see Chapter 17). Look now at the Betas reported under Variables in the Equation and notice that they are equal to their respective zero-order correlations. Thus, using β's as indices of effects, one would be led to conclude that the magnitude of the effect of X on Y is almost identical under the two treatments except that it is positive under one of them and negative under the other.

For convenience of comparison, we report the regression equations obtained in the above analyses (see Variables in the Equation output):

$$Y'_D = 2.50551 + 2.04228X$$

$$Y'_N = 15.62933 - 1.18218X$$

where D = Directive, and N = Nondirective (compare with results reported in Table 21.1).

The b's have, of course, the same signs as the β's. However, note that had the b's been used as indices of the effects of X on Y, the conclusion would have been that they differ in magnitude *as well as* in sign. As was discussed in various places (e.g., Chapter 3, Differential Validity), *it is comparisons of b's that are of interest* when dealing with more than one treatment or group.

Referring to our substantive example, we will assume that LOC is scored in the direction of Externality. That is, higher scores indicate Externality, whereas lower scores indicate Internality. Clearly, students whose scores are closer to the Externality end of the continuum tend to do better under the Directive teaching style, whereas those whose scores are closer to the Internality end of the continuum tend to do better under the Nondirective teaching style.

Assuming that α = .05 were selected, it will be noted that both b's are statistically significant (see the T ratios for the b's in the outputs for Variables in the Equation). Referring again to our substantive example, one would conclude that the expected change in Academic Achievement associated with a unit change in LOC is 2.04 units under Directive teaching style and −1.18 under Nondirective teaching style.

Output

[both groups]

Equation Number 1   Dependent Variable..   Y

Variable(s) Entered on Step Number 1..   X

-------------------------------- Variables in the Equation ------------------------------------

Variable	B	SE B	Beta	T	Sig T
X	−.05138	.32161	−.02591	−.160	.8739
(Constant)	10.68832	1.86490		5.731	.0000

Commentary

When a design consists of more than one group, statistics can be calculated on the basis of all subjects combined (i.e., ignoring group membership) or separately within each of the groups. The term "total statistics" is used to refer to estimates based on all subjects combined. The term "within-groups statistics" is used to refer to estimates based on subjects within each group. Thus, within-groups statistics were given in the earlier segments of the output, whereas total statistics are given in this segment. To conserve space, we did not reproduce the descriptive statistics (e.g., means, correlations). For present purposes, it is of interest to point out that the total correlation between X and Y is −.026 (this is also evident from the Beta reported above). Contrast this with the two within-groups correlations obtained earlier (.806 for Directive and −.809 for Nondirective). Contrast also the regression equation reported here with the two within-groups regression equations obtained earlier.

As you can see, total and within-groups statistics may differ in magnitude and/or sign. Also, it is, of course, possible, as illustrated here, for the within-groups statistics to differ from each other in magnitude and/or sign.

The distinctions introduced here have implications that go far beyond the topic under consideration. Suffice it to point out that they play a central role in issues concerning the unit of analysis (see, Pedhazur, 1982, pp. 526–547, where between-groups statistics are also discussed). Without going far afield, it will be pointed out that, had a researcher using the present data been oblivious to the question of the unit of analysis (regrettably many are) and had only total statistics been used (as in the present step), it would have been concluded that there is virtually no relation between X and Y, or that X has no effect on Y. But from the within-groups analysis given earlier, we know that such a conclusion would be *erroneous*.

In what follows, we comment on the different types of statistics only in so far that it is necessary to indicate the specific type appropriate for a given analysis. Thus, in an ATI design, it would be appropriate to use a total regression equation only after it has been determined that there are no significant differences between the within-groups regression equations. An example of how such results might look like was given in (2) of Figure 21.1.

On the basis of the information available at this step, it is not possible to tell whether or not the total regression equation reported here is appropriate. In saying this, we are ignoring the fact that, from the within-groups analyses, we know that the two regression equations are radically different from each other.

Output

Beginning Block Number   2. Method: Enter   E

Variable(s) Entered on Step Number 2..   E

Multiple R	.27556		Analysis of Variance			
R Square	.07593	R Square Change	.07526		DF	Sum of Squares	Mean Squa
Adjusted R Square	.02598	F Change	3.01345	Regression	2	87.91162	43.9556
Standard Error	5.37729	Signif F Change	.0909	Residual	37	1069.86338	28.9152

F =   1.52016   Signif F = .2320

----------------------------------- Variables in the Equation -----------------------------------

Variable	B	SE B	T	Sig T
X	.05594	.31945	.175	.8620
E	1.50437	.86661	1.736	.0909
(Constant)	10.13832	1.84478	5.496	.0000

Commentary

At this step, the effect-coded vector representing the two treatments was entered. Parenthetically, the increase in R^2 due to the addition of E (.07526) is not statistically significant at the .05 level (see F Change above). What concerns us here, however, is the meaning of the regression equation obtained at this stage. To this end, it is necessary to describe yet another type of regression coefficient—referred to as a common regression coefficient, b_c.

COMMON REGRESSION COEFFICIENT

A common regression coefficient based on k groups may be calculated as follows:

$$b_c = \frac{\Sigma xy_1 + \Sigma xy_2 + \ldots + \Sigma xy_k}{\Sigma x_1^2 + \Sigma x_2^2 + \ldots + \Sigma x_k^2} \tag{21.1}$$

where Σxy_1 = sum of the products in group 1; Σx_1^2 = sum of the squares in group 1— similarly for the other terms. Note that the common b is calculated by pooling the sums of products and the sums of squares within the groups. This is why it is also referred to as a pooled within-groups regression coefficient.

Obtaining the relevant values from Table 21.1

$$b_c = \frac{222.20 + (-206.35)}{108.80 + 174.55} = .05594$$

which is the same as the value reported in the above output.

From (21.1) and from the numerical example, it should be clear why it was stated earlier, in connection with Figure 21.1, that the use of a common b is appropriate only after it has been established that there is no significant difference between the b's of the separate regression equations, that is, when it is concluded that the regression lines are parallel, as in (1) of Figure 21.1.

Although we have not yet tested the differences between the b's for the present data (we do this in the next step), it is clear from the plot given earlier as well as from the two b's of the separate regression equations reported above that a common b is inappropriate for the present data. Consequently, *for the present data*, the output reported in this step *is irrelevant*. As is discussed below, the output from this step *is relevant* when it is concluded that the difference between the b's is statistically not significant.

This demonstrates, once more, the importance of knowing what piece of computer output is or is not relevant for a given design and analysis. Further, it demonstrates that, when the analysis is carried out without product terms to represent the interaction (the XE vector in our example; see next step), one is using wittingly or unwittingly a common b without establishing its appropriateness.

The potential deleterious consequences of failing to establish the validity of using a common b are clearly illustrated in the present numerical example. On the basis of the within-groups b's (see separate analyses above), one would conclude that X affects Y but differently under each treatment. In contrast, on the basis of the total b (the first step in the combined analysis) or the common b (the present step), it would be concluded that X does *not* affect Y.[3]

Output

Beginning Block Number   3. Method: Enter   XE

Variable(s) Entered on Step Number 3..   XE

Multiple R	.82330			Analysis of Variance			
R Square	.67782	R Square Change	.60189		DF	Sum of Squares	Mean Squ
Adjusted R Square	.65097	F Change	67.25424	Regression	3	784.76290	261.58
Standard Error	3.21892	Signif F Change	.0000	Residual	36	373.01210	10.36

$$F = \quad 25.24624 \quad \text{Signif } F = .0000$$

Commentary

Note, first, the considerable increment in R^2 (.60189) as a result of adding the product vector, XE, indicating clearly that there is a strong interaction between the X and the treatments in their effects on Y. To test whether this increment is statistically significant, one would apply the general formula for the test of an increment in R^2, given in Chapter 18—see (18.15) and the discussions and illustrations related to it. As was shown in Chapter 18, this is what is reported as the F Change in the type of output and analysis given here. For the increment due to XE, then, $F(1, 36) = 67.25$, $p < .05$.

As is shown below, when the ATI design consists of two groups only (e.g., two treatments, a treatment and a control group), the same test is available as a test of the b for the product vector (XE). When, on the other hand, the design consists of more than two groups, the increment in R^2 or in the regression sum of squares due to the interaction vectors has to be tested as above.

A conclusion that the interaction is not statistically significant or, equivalently, that the b's do not differ from each other is based on the failure to reject the null hypothesis. Thus, a conclusion that there is no interaction is tantamount to accepting the null hypothesis with all the logical and statistical problems attendant in doing this (see Chapters 9 and 15). In order to minimize Type II error (i.e., failure to reject the null hypothesis when it should have been rejected; see Chapters 9 and 15), it is suggested that a relatively large α (e.g., .10; even .25) be used for tests of interactions.

In the beginning of this chapter (see ATI Analysis: Synopsis), it was stated that the first thing to do is to determine whether there is an interaction between the attribute and the treatments. Accordingly, *it is the last step in the analysis* (i.e., the current step) *that is inspected first*. We proceeded in the opposite direction, because we wanted to acquaint you with the properties of the indices obtained at each step, and because we wanted to illustrate misleading conclusions that might be reached when only certain steps are carried out (e.g., when a product vector is not used at all).

---

[3]Ignoring, for the sake of discussion, the fact that, in the present example, neither the total nor the common b is statistically significant, it will be noted that they are almost identical in magnitude but that they differ in sign ($-.05138$ and $.05594$ respectively). It is possible for the two types of b's to differ in magnitude and/or sign. For a discussion of the relations among different types of correlations and regression coefficients, see Pedhazur (1982, pp. 536–540, and references given therein).

When, as in the present case, it is concluded that there is a statistically significant interaction, one proceeds to develop separate regression equations and to establish regions of significance. It is to these topics we turn, beginning with the former. At the conclusion of this section, we offer a summary of the steps and comment on the ones taken when it is concluded that there is no interaction between the attribute and the treatments.

Separate Equations from an Overall Analysis

Using the data of Table 21.1, we began by doing regression analyses of Y on X for each of the treatments (Directive and Nondirective), obtaining, among other things, two separate regression equations. In the present section, we show how the separate regression equations can be obtained from an analysis in which the groups are combined. Henceforth, we will use the term *overall analysis* to refer to an analysis based on combined groups.

An overall analysis may include some or all of the terms of a given design. In the computer analysis of Table 21.1 above, we did three overall analyses: (a) including only X, (b) including X and E, and (c) including X, E, and XE. It was shown that properties of the same term differ in the three analyses. For example, when only X is included in an overall analysis, b is the total regression coefficient. When both X and E are entered, b for X is the common regression coefficient.

Unless otherwise stated, we use the term *overall regression equation* to refer to the equation obtained from an overall analysis in which *all the terms of the design have been included*, that is, the attribute(s), the coded vector(s) representing treatments (groups), and the product vector(s) representing the interaction.

Output referred to in the preceding section as constituting the last step of the analysis of the data of Table 21.1 (i.e., Step Number 3) is one from an overall analysis that includes all the terms of the design. The overall regression equation from this analysis is

Output

------------------------------------- Variables in the Equation -------------------------------------

Variable	B	SE B	T	Sig T
X	.43005	.19659	2.188	.0353
E	-6.56191	1.11201	-5.901	.0000
XE	1.61223	.19659	8.201	.0000
(Constant)	9.06742	1.11201	8.154	.0000

Commentary

For convenience, we repeat the separate regression equations obtained earlier

$$Y'_D = 2.50551 + 2.04228X$$

$$Y'_N = 15.62933 - 1.18218X$$

Recall that effect coding was used in the E vector. Accordingly, the properties of the overall regression equation are analogous to those of the regression equation with effect coding in designs with categorical variables (see Chapters 19 and 20)[4] except that different terms are used to obtain the intercepts (a's) and regression coefficients (b's) of the separate regression equations. Specifically, a and the b associated with the coded vector, E, are used to obtain the a's of the separate equations. The b's for X and for the product vector, XE, are used to obtain the b's of the separate equations.

Turning first to a of the overall regression equation, it will be pointed out that it is equal to the average of the a's for the separate regression equations. For the present example

$$9.06742 = (2.50551 + 15.62933)/2$$

The b for E in the overall regression equation is equal to the deviation of the a for the treatment identified in E (i.e., the group assigned 1) from the average of the a's of the separate equations (i.e., the overall a). For our example

$$b_E = -6.56191 = 2.50551 - 9.06742$$

Therefore, to obtain the a for the group identified in the coded vector, add the overall a and the b for the coded vector

$$9.06742 + (-6.56191) = 2.50551$$

Analogous to effect coding in designs with categorical variables, to obtain the a for the treatment assigned -1 in the coded vector, reverse the sign of the b for this vector and add the overall a. For the present example

$$9.06742 + 6.56191 = 15.62933$$

The b's for X and for the product vector, XE, have properties analogous to those discussed in preceding paragraphs in connection with the a's except that they refer to b's for the continuous variable (attributes in ATI designs). Specifically, the b for X in the overall regression equation is equal to the average of the b's of the separate equations. For the present example

$$.43005 = [(2.04228) + (-1.18218)]/2$$

Note carefully that the average of the b's is not the same as the common b discussed earlier. Earlier, it was shown that the common b can be calculated by applying (21.1) or by doing an overall regression analysis in which the product of the attribute and the coded vector (XE, in the present example) is *not* included (see Step Number 2, above). For the numerical example being analyzed, the common b was found to be .05594 (see Step Number 2), whereas the average of the b's is .43005. The average of the within-groups b's is equal to the common b when the within-groups sums of the squares for X are equal to each other (for a numerical example where this is the case, see the analysis of the data of Table 21.2, under ANCOVA, later in this chapter).

Returning to the procedure for obtaining the separate b's from the overall regression equation, it will be noted that the b for XE is equal to the deviation of the b of the regression equation for the group identified in E (i.e., the group assigned 1) from the average of the b's. For the present example

$$b_{XE} = 1.61223 = 2.04228 - .43005$$

---

[4]Other coding schemes (e.g., dummy) can be used. The properties of the overall regression equation with dummy coding are analogous to the properties of the regression equation with dummy coding in designs with categorical variables. As an exercise, we suggest that you reanalyze the numerical example using dummy coding. If necessary, refer to Pedhazur (1982, pp. 464–468) for guidance.

Therefore, to obtain the b for the group identified in E (Directive, in our example), add the b's for X and XE in the overall regression equation.

$$b_D = .43005 + 1.61223 = 2.04228$$

To obtain the b for the group assigned -1 in E (Nondirective, in our example), reverse the sign of the b for XE and add the b for X. For the present example

$$b_N = .43005 + (-1.61223) = -1.18218$$

Compare these values with those reported above in the separate regression equations.

Let us take a closer look at the b for the product vector, XE. From what was said above, it can be seen that, with effect coding for the case of two groups, b_{XE} is equal to half the difference between the two separate b's. Clearly, the closer the separate b's are to each other, the smaller b_{XE} is. In the extreme case, when the separate b's are equal to each other, b_{XE} is necessarily zero. From the preceding, it follows that a test of b_{XE} is tantamount to a test of the difference between the two b's. Furthermore, as will be recalled, a test of the difference between the separate b's is tantamount to a test of the interaction between the attribute and the treatments.

Look at the output for the overall regression equation given above, and note that the t ratio for the test of b_{XE} is 8.201, with 36 df (i.e., df associated with the MSR from the overall analysis; see Step 3, above). Now, the square of this t is 67.26, which is, within rounding, the same value as the F Change obtained earlier for the test of the interaction. The equivalence of the two tests should come as no surprise when it is recalled (see, for example, Chapter 18) that the test of a b is equivalent to the test of the proportion of variance incremented when the variable with which the b is associated is entered last into the analysis. Although, in the present case, we are concerned with a product vector (*not* a variable), the test of its b amounts to the same thing. In sum, in *ATI designs consisting of two groups*, all that is necessary to determine whether an attribute-treatments interaction is statistically significant is to examine the t ratio for b_{XE} in the overall regression equation.

Summary of Analytic Steps

Although earlier we gave a synopsis of the steps in the analysis of an ATI design, we believe it will be helpful to offer here a brief summary of the steps, as they relate to computer analysis. It is useful, although not essential, to enter the terms (X, E, and XE) in separate steps, as was done above, having thereby whatever output is deemed relevant in a given analysis. When, instead, all the terms are entered in a single step, additional runs may be required in the event it is concluded that there is no attribute-treatments interaction.

As in the output given above, we will refer to the steps by number: Step 1, consisting of X; Step 2, consisting of X and E; Step 3, consisting of X, E, and XE. One begins by inspecting the output of Step 3 in order to determine whether or not there is an attribute-treatments interaction. In the special case of two groups, the t ratio for the b associated with the product of the attribute and the coded vectors (XE, in our example) constitutes a test of the interaction.[5]

What is done next depends on what is concluded regarding the interaction. When, as in

---

[5]We comment on designs with more than two treatments later on in this chapter.

our numerical example, it is concluded that there is a statistically significant interaction, separate regression equations are derived from the overall regression equation, given in Step 3. It is, of course, possible to obtain the separate equations by doing two separate analyses, as we have done earlier (see output generated by the PROCESS IF commands). Regardless of how one calculates the separate regression equations, this is followed by the calculation of regions of significance—a topic presented in the next section.

When, on the other hand, it is concluded that there is no attribute-treatments interaction, one does an analysis in which separate equations for the treatments (groups) are developed such that they have a common b for the attribute, X, but separate a's. This is accomplished by doing an analysis in which only X and E are included, as in Step 2 above. One then tests whether there is a statistically significant difference between the a's. In the special case of two groups, a test of b_E in the equation obtained in this step is tantamount to a test of the difference between the two a's, as this is equivalent to the test of the proportion of variance incremented by the coded vector, E, over and above what is accounted for by the attribute, X.

Assuming it is concluded that there is a statistically significant difference between the a's, then one tests the common b (i.e., the b for the attribute; X, in our example). If it is concluded that the b is statistically significant, then two equations with separate a's, but with a common b for X, are reported and interpreted. We show how this is done later in this chapter, in the section on ANCOVA. When the common b is not statistically significant, the design reduces to one consisting of a categorical variable only (i.e., the treatments) and is dealt with accordingly (see below).

When, after having concluded that there is no interaction, it is also concluded that there is no statistically significant difference between the a's of the separate regression equations, a single regression equation for both groups is indicated. Such an equation is obtained by entering only X in an overall analysis (i.e., Step 1). The regression equation thus obtained is treated as if it was derived in a single group. That is, one tests the b for X (what was earlier labeled the total b), and proceeds to interpret the results.

Lest you think that we have been unduly repetitive in describing the sequence of steps to be taken in the analysis of an ATI design, we would like to point out that we did this because of the potential for errors in this type of analysis, as is evidenced in the research literature.

We turn now to the last piece of output from the present run, the one generated by: DEP=Y/ENTER E (see Input, above).

Output

Equation Number 2   Dependent Variable..   Y

Variable(s) Entered on Step Number 1..   E

				Analysis of Variance			
Multiple R	.27416						
R Square	.07517	R Square Change	.07517		DF	Sum of Squares	Mean Squa▶
Adjusted R Square	.05083	F Change	3.08844	Regression	1	87.02500	87.0250
Standard Error	5.30826	Signif F Change	.0869	Residual	38	1070.75000	28.1776

$$F = \quad 3.08844 \quad \text{Signif } F = .0869$$

-- Variables in the Equation --

Variable	B	SE B	95% Confdnce Intrvl B		T	Sig
E	1.47500	.83931	−.22409	3.17409	1.757	.086
(Constant)	10.42500	.83931	8.72591	12.12409	12.421	.000

Commentary

We hope you recognize that, in regressing Y on only the coded vector, E, we are carrying out the kind of analysis introduced in Chapter 19. Referring to the substantive example we have been using in connection with these data, we are testing here the difference between the means on Academic Achievement for students who were exposed to either Directive or Nondirective teaching styles. Our aim in doing this is to show what might take place when subjects' relevant attributes (Locus of Control, in our example) are not taken into account.

Following the approach explained in Chapter 19, we use the regression equation to calculate the Y means for the two treatment groups

$$\bar{Y}_D = 10.425 + 1.475 = 11.90$$

$$\bar{Y}_N = 10.425 + (-1.475) = 8.95$$

where D = Directive, and N = Nondirective. Compare with the means reported in Table 21.1. Look now at the test of the R^2 and notice that $F(1, 38) = 3.08844$, $p > .05$. This, of course, is also a test of the difference between the above two means. Assuming that $\alpha = .05$ was selected, then it would be concluded that the difference between the means of groups exposed to different teaching styles is statistically not significant. But, as we know from the earlier analysis, a radically different picture emerges when Locus of Control is taken into account. Although our data are fictitious, they serve to illustrate what probably happens in many studies of treatment effects when relevant attributes of the subjects are not taken into account.

Regions of Significance

Earlier, it was pointed out that a finding of an attribute-treatments interaction is followed by the calculation of regions of significance. Relevant to such regions is the point of intersection of the regression lines. Recall that an interaction is deemed ordinal when the point of intersection is outside the range of the research interest; it is deemed disordinal when the point of intersection is within the range of interest.

The point of intersection, $X_{int.}$, is calculated as follows:

$$X_{int.} = \frac{a_1 - a_2}{b_2 - b_1} \tag{21.2}$$

where the a's and the b's are respectively the intercepts and the regression coefficients of the separate regression equations.

The separate regression equations for the data of Table 21.1, analyzed above, are repeated.

$$Y'_D = 2.50551 + 2.04228X$$

$$Y'_N = 15.62933 - 1.18218X$$

Applying (21.2)

$$X_{int.} = \frac{(2.50551) - (15.62933)}{(-1.18218) - (2.04228)} = 4.07$$

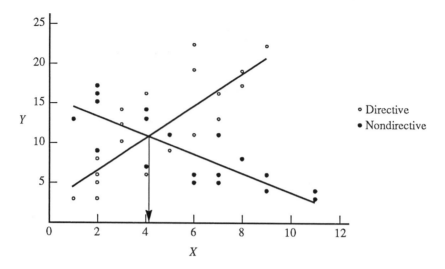

Figure 21.2

The X value at which the two regression lines intersect is 4.07. The two regression lines are depicted in Figure 21.2. Note that the perpendicular line drawn from the point where the regression lines intersect meets the abscissa at an X score of about 4.07.

As is evident from Figure 21.2, the closer the X values are to the point of intersection, the smaller the differences between subjects' predicted scores, as obtained from the separate equations. Further, at the point of intersection, predicted scores are identical.

$$Y'_D = 2.50551 + (2.04228)(4.07) = 10.82$$

$$Y'_N = 15.62933 - (1.18218)(4.07) = 10.82$$

In view of the preceding, it is of interest to determine at which values of the attribute are the differences between the two treatments statistically significant and at which values are the differences statistically not significant. The Johnson-Neyman technique and its extensions were designed to help accomplish this.

JOHNSON–NEYMAN TECHNIQUE

The technique developed originally by Johnson and Neyman (1936) was designed to determine regions of significance for the difference between the effects of the two treatments at a given value of the attribute. Potthoff (1964), who argued that such nonsimultaneous regions are appropriate only when testing the difference at a single value of the attribute, extended the Johnson–Neyman technique to apply to the determination of simultaneous regions of significance along the continuum of the attribute. For good discussions of nonsimultaneous and simultaneous regions of significance, see Rogosa (1980a, 1981).

In what follows, we give formulas for the calculation of simultaneous regions of significance and illustrate their application to the data of Table 21.1. Subsequently, we comment on the calculation of nonsimultaneous regions of significance.

The regions of significance are obtained by solving for the two X values in the following formula:

$$X = \frac{-B \pm \sqrt{B^2 - AC}}{A} \tag{21.3}$$

where the terms of (21.3) are defined as follows:

$$A = \frac{-2F_\alpha}{N-4}(ss_{res})\left[\frac{1}{\Sigma x_1^2} + \frac{1}{\Sigma x_2^2}\right] + (b_1 - b_2)^2 \tag{21.4}$$

$$B = \frac{2F_\alpha}{N-4}(ss_{res})\left[\frac{\bar{X}_1}{\Sigma x_1^2} + \frac{\bar{X}_2}{\Sigma x_2^2}\right] + (a_1 - a_2)(b_1 - b_2) \tag{21.5}$$

$$C = \frac{-2F_\alpha}{N-4}(ss_{res})\left[\frac{N}{n_1 n_2} + \frac{\bar{X}_1^2}{\Sigma x_1^2} + \frac{\bar{X}_2^2}{\Sigma x_2^2}\right] + (a_1 - a_2)^2 \tag{21.6}$$

where F_α = tabled value of F with 2 and $N - 4$ df at a preselected α level; N = total number of subjects; n_1, n_2 = number of subjects in groups 1 and 2 respectively; ss_{res} = residual sum of squares from the overall analysis when all the terms of the design are included— equivalently, it is the sum of residual sums of squares from the regression of Y on X in the separate groups; Σx_1^2, Σx_2^2 = sum of squares of the attribute, X, for groups 1 and 2 respectively; $\bar{X}_1$, $\bar{X}_2$ = attribute means for groups 1 and 2 respectively; b_1, b_2 = regression coefficients for groups 1 and 2 respectively; a_1, a_2 = intercepts for groups 1 and 2 respectively.

Simultaneous regions of significance will now be calculated for the data of Table 21.1. Following is the information necessary for the calculations:

$$\Sigma x_1^2 = 108.80 \qquad \Sigma x_2^2 = 174.55$$
$$\bar{X}_1 = 4.60 \qquad \bar{X}_2 = 5.65$$
$$a_1 = 2.51 \qquad a_2 = 15.63$$
$$b_1 = 2.04 \qquad b_2 = -1.18$$
$$ss_{res} = 373.01$$

Except for the ss_{res}, all the values were taken from the bottom of Table 21.1. The ss_{res} was taken from the output for the overall analysis in which all the terms of the design were included (see Step 3 of the output in earlier sections). As was noted above, the same value may be obtained by summing the residual sums of squares obtained in the separate analyses (see output for the separate analyses, where the residual sums of squares for groups 1 and 2 respectively are 244.01 and 129.01).

Using $\alpha = .05$ and recalling that $N = 40$, the tabled F with 2 and 36 df is 3.26. We are ready now to apply (21.3) through (21.6).

$$A = \frac{-2(3.26)}{36}(373.01)\left[\frac{1}{108.80} + \frac{1}{174.55}\right] + [(2.04) - (-1.18)]^2 = 9.36$$

$$B = \frac{2(3.26)}{36}(373.01)\left[\frac{4.60}{108.80} + \frac{5.65}{174.55}\right] + (2.51 - 15.63)(2.04 + 1.18) = -37.20$$

$$C = \frac{-2(3.26)}{36}(373.01)\left[\frac{40}{400} + \frac{4.60^2}{108.80} + \frac{5.65^2}{174.55}\right] + (2.51 - 15.63)^2 = 139.89$$

$$X = \frac{37.20 \pm \sqrt{(-37.20)^2 - (9.36)(139.89)}}{9.36}$$

$$X_1 = 3.05 \qquad X_2 = 4.90$$

These two X values are used to establish a region of nonsignificance. Differences in Y scores for subjects whose X scores are within the range of 3.05 and 4.90 are statistically not significant. There are two regions of significance: one for X scores above 4.90 and one for X scores below 3.05.

Referring to the substantive example we have been using, it would be concluded that there are statistically no significant differences in Academic Achievement for students exposed to either a Directive or a Nondirective teaching style, whose scores on Locus of Control range between about 3 and 5. Academic Achievement of students whose scores on Locus of Control are above 5 is statistically significantly higher for those exposed to a Directive than a Nondirective teaching style. Conversely, Academic Achievement of students whose scores on Locus of Control are below 3 is statistically significantly higher for those exposed to a Nondirective than a Directive teaching style. At the risk of being repetitive, we remind you that, although we are limiting our comments to statistical significance, what is more important is substantive meaningfulness of differences.

Our illustration of the calculation of regions of significance was done for the case of a disordinal interaction. The same approach is taken when the interaction is ordinal except that one of the regions of significance is not applicable, as it is outside the range of the research interest. Referring to Figure 21.1, it may, for example, turn out that, for an ordinal interaction such as depicted in (3), there is a region of significance for relatively low scores of X, whereas the converse is true for an ordinal interaction such as that depicted in (4).

The approach to the determination of nonsimultaneous regions of significance is the same as for simultaneous regions of significance except that the tabled value of F used in the numerator of (21.4) through (21.6) is for 1 and $N - 4$ df, and the F is *not* multiplied by 2 (see Pedhazur, 1982, p. 470). Examples of calculations of nonsimultaneous regions of significance will be found in Johnson and Jackson (1959, pp. 432–438) and Walker and Lev (1953, pp. 398–404). Examples of calculations of both simultaneous and nonsimultaneous regions of significance will be found in Huitema (1980, Chapter 13) and Rogosa (1980a).

Our presentation was limited to the case of two groups and one attribute. Extensions to multiple groups and/or multiple attributes will be found in the references given in the preceding paragraph and in Johnson and Fay (1950), Potthoff (1964), and Rogosa (1981).

Finally, Borich, Godbout, and Wunderlich (1976) developed computer programs for the analysis of ATI designs, which include nonsimultaneous regions of significance as part of the output. Alternatively, a statistical package may be adapted to yield regions of significance. (For examples using SPSS and SAS, see Karpman, 1986. We caution you, however, to check his program statements carefully before using them, as they contain a couple of typographical errors.)

ANALYSIS OF COVARIANCE

Ideas of Analysis of Covariance (ANCOVA) were introduced in Chapters 12 and 13, where it was pointed out that it is employed for two radically different purposes: (a) to control for individual differences, and (b) to adjust for differences among nonequivalent groups. Each of these purposes is considered in turn.

ANCOVA for Control

As was pointed out in earlier chapters (e.g., Chapters 10 and 12), identification of dependent variance due to individual differences has the potential of reducing the error term, thereby increasing the sensitivity of the analysis. A design aimed at accomplishing this consists of treatments and concomitant variables—generally subjects' attributes—to be controlled for (see Chapter 12, Design 4). Because concomitant variables are often referred to as covariates, the analysis applied in such designs is referred to as ANCOVA.

From design and analytic perspectives, ATI and ANCOVA are alike. Both are comprised of a manipulated categorical variable (e.g., different treatments) and a nonmanipulated continuous variable (usually an attribute).[6] As was pointed out in Chapter 12 (see Design 7), the distinction between them has to do with the reasons for the inclusion of the attribute. In an ATI design, the attribute is generally included because it is expected to interact with the treatments. In contrast, when regarded as a concomitant variable, the attribute is included to enhance control.

From the foregoing, it follows that, in both designs, the analysis begins with an examination of the differences among the b's of the separate regression equations but with differing expectations. In the ATI design, the b's are expected to be heterogeneous, as this is what constitutes an attribute–treatments interaction (see earlier sections of this chapter). In the design with a concomitant variable, on the other hand, the b's are expected to be homogeneous. In presentations of ANCOVA (e.g., Cochran, 1957; Elashoff, 1969), this is referred to as homogeneity of regression coefficients—a major condition for the valid application of ANCOVA (see below).

Obviously, results of a study may go counter to expectations. When, in an ATI design, it turns out that there is no attribute-treatments interaction (i.e., the b's are homogeneous), main effects are interpreted. In effect, the design is treated as one with a concomitant variable. Further, when, in a design with a concomitant variable, it turns out that the b's are heterogeneous, the focus of the study shifts from a concern with main effects to one addressed to the interaction between the concomitant variable and the treatments. In other words, the design is treated as an ATI.

A NUMERICAL EXAMPLE

For illustrative purposes, assume that subjects were randomly assigned to either a treatment or a control group and that a relevant attribute, X, was measured *prior* to the administration

---

[6]For convenience, we are speaking of the simplest of such designs, but what we say applies equally to designs with multiple categorical independent variables (i.e., factorial designs) and/or multiple attributes, which, in ANCOVA nomenclature, are referred to as multiple covariates.

Table 21.2

ANCOVA for Control. Illustrative Data

	Control		Experimental	
	Y	X	Y	X
	4	1	4	1
	3	1	5	1
	4	2	7	2
	6	2	8	2
	6	2	8	2
	5	3	6	3
	7	3	7	3
	5	4	9	4
	7	4	8	4
	9	5	9	5
M:	5.60	2.70	7.10	2.70
ss:	28.40	16.10	24.90	16.10
sp:	16.80		15.30	
s:	1.78	1.34	1.66	1.34
r:	.786		.764	
	$Y' = 2.78 + 1.04X$		$Y' = 4.53 + .95X$	

Note. M = Mean; ss = Sum of Squares; sp = Sum of Products; s = Standard Deviation. r = correlation. Y = Dependent Variable. X = Covariate.

of the treatment. At the conclusion of the study, a measure of the dependent variable, Y, was obtained. The aim is to study the difference between the treatment and the control group after having controlled for the attribute. Illustrative data for such a study are given in Table 21.2. Also included in the table are descriptive statistics and the separate regression equations. Similar calculations were carried out in Table 21.1.

Although most computer packages for statistical analysis include one or more procedures for ANCOVA, we will not use any of them, because they are susceptible to misapplications and misinterpretations. The reason is that, in such programs, it is generally difficult to tell how the analysis was carried out and what some terms in the output represent. Searle and Hudson (1982), who reviewed ANCOVA output of programs from popular statistical packages (e.g., BMDP, SAS, SPSS), reported that "no two of these 10 computing packages are exactly the same" (pp. 740–741). They concluded their review, saying: "Computer output for the analysis of covariance is not all that it is made out to be by its labeling. Values with labels that appear to be the same can be quite different because they do in fact represent different calculations" (p. 744). Incidentally, in light of the content of their paper and the journal in which it was published, it is clear that Searle and Hudson were addressing knowledgeable readers with experience in using ANCOVA programs. It goes without saying that novice users of such programs are even less in a position to tell what results they are getting.

Fisher (1958), who developed ANCOVA, stated "that it combines the advantages and reconciles the requirements of the two very widely applicable procedures known as regression and analysis of variance" (p. 281). Not surprisingly, ANCOVA has been referred to as "regression control" (Fleiss, 1986, p. 186). As is demonstrated below, doing ANCOVA through a multiple regression program not only enables one to see clearly what is taking place but also affords the control necessary to carry out the analysis in the required sequence. For comparative purposes with the ATI analysis in preceding sections, we use REGRESSION of SPSS.

SPSS

Input

```
SET LISTING='T212SPS.LIS'.
TITLE TABLE 21.2.   ANCOVA FOR CONTROL.
DATA LIST/ Y,X,T 1-6.
IF (T EQ 1) E=1.
IF (T EQ 2) E=-1.
COMPUTE XE=X*E.
BEGIN DATA.
   4 1 1
   3 1 1   [data for the first two subjects in T 1]
   . . .
   4 1 2
   5 1 2   [data for the first two subjects in T 2]
   . . .
END DATA.
LIST.
REGRESSION VAR=Y TO XE/DES/STAT=ALL/
   DEP=Y/ENTER X/ENTER E/ENTER XE/
   DEP=Y/ENTER E.
```

Commentary

As indicated above, the analytic approach is identical to the one done for the ATI design (i.e., Table 21.1). Therefore, the present analysis, output, and commentaries are not as detailed as the ones given earlier for the ATI design.

As in the ATI design, we do two regression analyses: (a) regressing Y on X, E, and XE; and (b) regressing Y on E. In line with our suggestion in connection with the earlier analysis, the terms of the first equation are entered in three steps, so as to obviate the need for additional runs, depending on the conclusion reached on the basis of an examination of the results.

Output

Summary table

Step	Variable	Rsq	RsqCh	Fch	SigCh
1	In: X	.4957	.4957	17.696	.001
2	In: E	.6700	.1743	8.979	.008
3	In: XE	.6711	.0011	.053	.821

Commentary

In the analysis of the ATI design (see earlier sections of this chapter), we presented output for each step, because we wanted to explain the meaning of terms obtained at each of them. Normally, however, it is more efficient to begin by examining the summary table, excerpts of which are given above. One begins with the last step—the one in which the product vector was entered. From the column labeled RsqCh (R Square Change), it is clear that the proportion of variance incremented by XE is trivial (.0011). Accordingly, it is concluded that there is *no* interaction between the covariate and the treatments. Recall that this is equivalent to a conclusion that the b's are homogeneous and that the use of the common b is, therefore, valid.

From the output at Step 3 (not reported here), the overall regression equation is

$$Y' = 3.65839 + .99689X - .87578E + .04658XE$$

Use this equation to calculate the separate regression equations, following the procedure described in connection with the analysis of the ATI design. Compare your results with the regression equations reported in Table 21.2. Note that the two b's are very similar to each other, as would be expected in light of what was said above about the absence of an interaction.

Turning to Step 2 of the summary table, it will be noted that the increment in the proportion of variance due to the coded vector, E, is .1743. This would almost certainly be deemed an important increment in most research settings. However, as explained earlier, we rely solely on statistical tests of significance. Accordingly, it will be noted that $F(1,17) = 8.979$. Assuming that $\alpha = .01$ was selected, it is clear (see SigCh) that the increment is statistically significant. Therefore, results reported at this step of the analysis are retained and interpreted.

Before reporting output from Step 2, it will be pointed out that, had it been concluded that RsqCh due to the coded vector, E, is neither substantively meaningful nor statistically significant, the results of Step 1 would have been examined and action deemed appropriate on the basis of them taken.[7] This is what we had in mind when we said above that entering the terms in separate steps obviates the need for additional runs.

Output

Variable	B	SE B	T	Sig T
X	.99689	.19726	5.054	.0001
E	−.75000	.25029	2.996	.0081
(Constant)	3.65839	.58848	6.217	.0000

Commentary

To begin with, it will be noted that the B for the covariate, X, is a common b—see (21.1) and the discussion related to it. In the present example, the common b is equal to the average of the within-groups b's. In other words, the b for X in the overall regression equation (see above) is equal to the common b. As explained earlier (see Separate Equations from Overall Analysis), this occurs when the within-groups sums of squares for X are equal to each other, which is the case for the data analyzed here—see Table 21.2, where the sum of squares for X is 16.10 in each of the groups.

Having concluded, on the basis of Step 3, that the b's are homogeneous, a common b may be validly used. The test of this b, $t(17) = 5.054$, $p < .01$, leads to the conclusion that the contribution of the covariate, or its effect on Y, is statistically significant. Had the common b been statistically not significant, it would have been concluded that control for the attribute, X, does not add significantly to the analysis or that the covariate is irrelevant.

The test of the b associated with E is a test of the difference between the intercepts (a's) of the equations for the experimental and the control groups in which a common b is used for the covariate. Recall that the test of a b is equivalent to the test of the proportion of variance

---

[7]For a numerical example of such an occurrence, see ANCOVA for Adjustment in the next section.

incremented by the variable with which it is associated when the variable is entered last in the analysis (see Chapter 18). Accordingly, in the present case, the t ratio for the test of the difference between the intercepts is equal to $\sqrt{FChg}$ for Step 2 in the Summary table (see above).

On the basis of the preceding, it is concluded that two separate equations with a common b fit the data. Using the previous output, the intercepts of the regression equations for the control and experimental groups are calculated

$$a_C = 3.65839 + (-.75) = 2.90839$$

$$a_E = 3.65839 + (.75) \quad = 4.40839$$

The regression equations for the two groups are

$$Y'_C = 2.90839 + .99689X$$

$$Y'_E = 4.40839 + .99689X$$

In sum, it is concluded that, after controlling for the covariate, the difference between the experimental and the control group is statistically significant. Subjects in the experimental group are expected to do 1.5 units (the difference between the intercepts) better than subjects in the control group, along the continuum of the covariate.

utput

Equation Number 2   Dependent Variable..   Y

Beginning Block Number   1. Method: Enter   E

Multiple R	.41747		Analysis of Variance			
R Square	.17428	R Square Change	.17428		DF	Sum of Squares	Mean Square
Adjusted R Square	.12841	F Change	3.79925	Regression	1	11.25000	11.25000
Standard Error	1.72079	Signif F Change	.0670	Residual	18	53.30000	2.96111

$$F = \quad 3.79925 \quad \text{Signif } F = .0670$$

------------------------------------ Variables in the Equation ------------------------------------

Variable	B	SE B	T	Sig T
E	-.75000	.38478	-1.949	.0670
(Constant)	6.35000	.38478	16.503	.0000

Commentary

As indicated, this output is from the second equation, where Y was regressed on E—an effect coded vector, in which the control group was assigned 1 and the experimental group was assigned -1 (see IF statements in Input, in the beginning of the analysis of this example). The analysis reported here, is one in which only the independent categorical variable (experimental versus control) is used. Following procedures presented in Chapter 19, where this type of design was presented, we use the regression equation reported above to calculate the means of the two groups.

$$\bar{Y}_C = 6.35 + (-.75) = 5.60$$

$$\bar{Y}_E = 6.35 + (.75) \quad = 7.10$$

Compare with the means reported in Table 21.2.

In the present case, the difference between the means, 1.5, is the same as the difference between the intercepts, obtained above. This rarely happens. In the next section, dealing with adjusted means, we explain how it happens. For now, however, we wish to point out that the probability associated with the F ratio, or the t for b_E, is $> .05$. Therefore, assuming that $\alpha = .05$ was selected, it would be concluded that the difference between the means of the experimental and control groups is statistically not significant.

However, exactly the same difference was found to be statistically significant after controlling for a relevant covariate (see Step 2 of the first equation). Clearly, the difference between the two analyses stems from the reduction in the error term as a consequence of including a relevant covariate. Note that, although the b tested in both equations is of the same magnitude $(-.75)$, its standard error is smaller in the equation that also includes the covariate than in the present analysis $(.25029$ and $.38478$ respectively in the earlier and the present analysis). The reduction of the error term, it will be recalled, is the rationale for using ANCOVA.

It should be clear that, in view of the requirement of random assignment, when ANCOVA is used for the purpose of control, differences between the means on the covariate are expected to be generally small. Because we wanted to make the point in the strongest possible terms, we constructed data with identical covariate scores for the two groups—hence identical means (i.e., 2.70; see Table 21.2). We hope that, on the basis of our analysis, you recognize that what is relevant in ANCOVA is the regression of the dependent variable on the covariate in the groups being compared, *not* whether the groups differ on the covariate.

This should serve to dispel a mistaken notion regarding the use of ANCOVA. All too frequently one encounters comments to the effect that a covariate is not useful when the groups do not differ on it. Some researchers even inform readers that they contemplated doing ANCOVA, but upon discovering that their groups did not differ significantly on the covariate, they discarded the idea. The misconception probably stems from the widespread use (rather misuse) of ANCOVA to adjust for group differences on the covariate—a topic discussed below.

Adjusted Means

When groups differ on a relevant covariate, it stands to reason that they would also differ to a greater or lesser extent on the dependent variable. Accordingly, when ANCOVA is applied, dependent variable means are adjusted for whatever differences there are between the groups on the covariate. The formula for the calculation of adjusted means is

$$\bar{Y}_{j(adj)} = \bar{Y}_j - b(\bar{X}_j - \bar{X}) \tag{21.7}$$

where $\bar{Y}_{j(adj)}$ = adjusted mean for group j; $\bar{Y}_j$ = mean of group j before adjustment; b = common regression coefficient; $\bar{X}_j$ = mean of group j on the covariate; $\bar{X}$ = grand mean of the covariate. Several points will be made about (21.7).

One, from the term in the parenthesis, it can be seen that an adjustment is made when the mean of the group on the covariate deviates from the grand mean. Other things equal, the larger the deviation of the group mean from the grand mean, the greater the adjustment. As was discussed above, when ANCOVA is used for control (the purpose with which we are concerned in this section), subjects are randomly assigned to groups, and the expectation (in a probabilistic sense) is that the group means on the covariate will not differ from each other and, hence, will be equal to the grand mean of the covariate. Consequently, the term inside the parentheses is expected to be zero, leading to adjusted means that are equal to the unadjusted means. In the example analyzed above (i.e., data of Table 21.2), the two groups have the same mean on the covariate. Therefore, the adjusted means would be equal to the unadjusted means. Although the covariate means will, in general, not be identical, the difference between them will be relatively small due to randomization. Hence, mean adjustments will be negligible.

Two, when the b in (21.7) is zero, there will be no adjustment regardless of the initial differences of the groups on the covariate. Note carefully that it is a *common b* that is used in the calculation of adjusted means. The common b may equal zero because the covariate is irrelevant. This would happen when, within each of the groups, the covariate and the dependent variable are not correlated. But the common b may be zero, or close to it, even when the covariate is correlated with the dependent variable within each group. This would occur when the b's in the separate equations are heterogeneous, especially when they have opposite signs.[8] Of course, a common b should *not* be used under such circumstances. This demonstrates why homogeneity of regression coefficients is crucial for the valid application of ANCOVA. Regrettably, ANCOVA is frequently applied without bothering to investigate whether the b's are homogeneous.

Three, it can be shown (see Pedhazur, 1982, pp. 507–513) that the difference between the intercepts of the separate regression equations with a common b is equal to the difference between adjusted means. Therefore, testing the difference between the separate intercepts, as was done above, is tantamount to testing the difference between adjusted means.

Finally, it was pointed out above that, for our numerical example, the adjusted means are equal to the means of the dependent variables. This, therefore, is why, in our example, the difference between the intercepts is equal to the difference between the dependent variable means.

Difference Scores: A Comment

In many research areas (e.g., academic achievement, attitudes, productivity), a measure of the dependent variable is obtained prior to the administration of treatments. For obvious reasons, such designs are referred to as pretest–posttest designs (see, for example, Design 3 in Chapter 12). Issues concerning difference scores were discussed in Chapter 13. Our concern here is limited to the possible use of difference scores as an alternative to ANCOVA; that is, analyzing scores obtained by subtracting pretest scores from their corresponding posttest scores.

Without going into the details, it will be pointed out that, when difference scores are analyzed, a common b of 1.0 is used by default. Analysis of difference scores, then, is a special case of ANCOVA, except that the common b is not estimated. Moreover, this is done without determining whether the within-group b's are homogeneous. On these grounds, it should be clear why ANCOVA is also the preferred approach in pretest-posttest designs.

---

[8]An extreme example of this was given earlier in the analysis of the ATI design, where the common b was close to zero because the b's in the two groups were of opposite signs.

ANCOVA for Adjustment

Complex logical and design problems arising in quasi-experimental research were discussed in Chapter 13. It will be recalled that they stem from the fact that attempts to determine treatment effects, or differences among treatments, are based on comparisons among none-quivalent groups. The pivotal and highly controversial issue in designs of this kind is the validity of adjustments for initial differences among groups. ANCOVA is the approach most frequently used for this purpose. In fact, much of the controversy surrounding the validity of comparisons among nonequivalent groups revolves around the validity of using ANCOVA for the purpose of adjusting for initial differences among the groups.

It is not our intention to repeat what we said in Chapter 13 about potential biases when ANCOVA is used for equating nonequivalent groups. All we will do here is illustrate, by means of a numerical example, the application of ANCOVA for this purpose. We suggest that you refer to the discussions of ANCOVA in Chapter 13 when reading the present section. After the presentation of the numerical example, we discuss biasing effects of errors of measurement of the covariate.

A NUMERICAL EXAMPLE

As in the numerical example of the preceding section, we use an experimental and a control group, for which a covariate was obtained *prior* to the administration of the treatment. The illustrative data to be used are given in Table 21.3.

It will be noted that the data for the Control group are the same as those used in the numerical example of ANCOVA for Control in the preceding section (i.e., Table 21.2). The data for the Experimental group were generated by adding a constant of 5 to the Y and X scores of the Experimental group of Table 21.2.

Table 21.3
ANCOVA for Adjustment. Illustrative Data

	Control		Experimental	
	Y	X	Y	X
	4	1	9	6
	3	1	10	6
	4	2	12	7
	6	2	13	7
	6	2	13	7
	5	3	11	8
	7	3	12	8
	5	4	14	9
	7	4	13	9
	9	5	14	10
M:	5.60	2.70	12.10	7.70
ss:	28.40	16.10	24.90	16.10
sp:		16.80		15.30
s:	1.78	1.34	1.66	1.34
r:		.786		.764
	$Y' = 2.78 + 1.04X$		$Y' = 4.78 + .95X$	

Note. M = Mean; ss = Sum of Squares; sp = Sum of Products; s = Standard Deviation. r = correlation. Y = Dependent Variable. X = Covariate.

Substantive examples of studies of nonequivalent groups were given in Chapter 13. For present purposes, we offer a couple of examples, in the hope that they will be helpful when thinking about the analysis. Assume that it is desired to study the effects of an enrichment program on academic achievement. Because students selected into the program, or those who choose to participate in the program (see Selectivity Bias in Chapter 13), tend to be higher on relevant variables (e.g., prior academic achievement, ability, motivation) than those who are to serve as controls, it is decided to covary prior academic achievement (ability, motivation, or what have you). In short, ANCOVA with a relevant covariate is used to adjust for initial differences between the Experimental and the Control groups.

In the preceding example, the group scoring lower on the covariate served as the Control group. Examples of studies in which the Experimental group is lower on the covariate than the Control group are frequently encountered in remedial programs (e.g., remedial reading) or compensatory education programs (e.g., Head Start).

Although we are using a design with a treatment and a control group, the same analytic approach is applied when the aim is to compare the effects of different treatments administered to nonequivalent groups.

SPSS

Input

```
SET LISTING='T213SPS.LIS'.
TITLE TABLE 21.3. ANCOVA FOR ADJUSTMENT.
DATA LIST/ Y,X,T 1-6.
VALUE LABELS T 1 'CONTROL' 2 'EXPERIM'.
IF (T EQ 1) E=1.
IF (T EQ 2) E=-1.
COMPUTE XE=X*E.
BEGIN DATA.
 4 1 1
 3 1 1    [data for first two subjects in T 1]
 . . .
 9 6 2
10 6 2    [data for first two subjects in T 2]
 . . .
END DATA.
LIST.
PLOT HSIZE = 40/VSIZE = 20/
  VERTICAL=MIN(0)/HORIZONTAL=MIN(0)/
  PLOT=Y WITH X BY T.
REGRESSION VAR=Y TO XE/DES/STAT=ALL/DEP=Y/ENTER E/
  DEP=Y/ENTER X/ENTER E/ENTER XE.
```

Commentary

We commented on input identical to this one earlier in this chapter; therefore, we will not comment on the present input except to point out that we are doing two regression analyses. In the first, Y is regressed on the coded vector, E, only (Experimental versus Control). Recall that this is equivalent to an ANOVA (see Chapter 19). ANCOVA is carried out in the second analysis.

Output

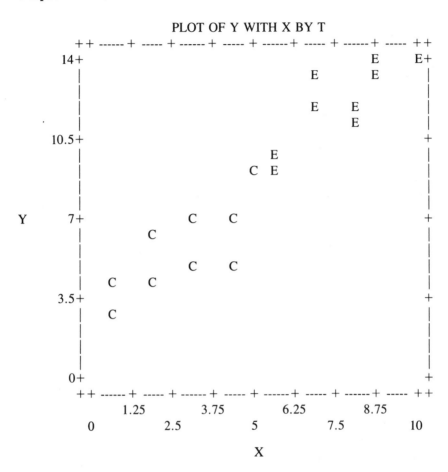

PLOT OF Y WITH X BY T

20 cases plotted.
C:CONTROL   E:EXPERIM $:Multiple occurrence

Commentary

Study the plot and notice that a single regression line would probably fit the data of both groups almost as well as two separate regression lines. However, notice also that such a conclusion is based on extrapolation, the hazards of which were discussed in Chapter 13 (see Figures 13.2, 13.4, 13.5, and the discussions related to them).

Output

Equation Number 1   Dependent Variable..   Y

Beginning Block Number   1. Method: Enter   E

Multiple R	.89360		Analysis of Variance			
R Square	.79853	R Square Change	.79853		DF	Sum of Squares	Mean Square
Adjusted R Square	.78733	F Change	71.34146	Regression	1	211.25000	211.25000
Standard Error	1.72079	Signif F Change	.0000	Residual	18	53.30000	2.96111

F =   71.34146   Signif F = .0000

```
------------------------------------ Variables in the Equation ------------------------------------
```

Variable	B	SE B	T	Sig T
E	−3.25000	.38478	−8.446	.0000
(Constant)	8.85000	.38478	23.000	.0000

Commentary

Using this regression equation and recalling that the Control and Experimental groups respectively were assigned 1 and −1 in the coded vector, E, the means for the two groups are

$$\text{Control: } 8.85 + (-3.25) = 5.60$$

$$\text{Experimental: } 8.85 + (3.25) \ \ = 12.10$$

Compare with the means reported in Table 21.3.

In view of the fact that no adjustment has been made for initial differences between the groups, it is not surprising that the difference between the two means (6.50) is statistically significant, $F(1, 18) = 71.34$, $p < .01$.

We turn now to output of the second analysis to see what happens when an adjustment is made for initial differences between the groups, that is, when these data are subjected to ANCOVA.

Output

Summary table

Step	Variable	Rsq	RsqCh	FCh	SigCh
1	In: X	.9106	.9106	183.332	.000
2	In: E	.9195	.0089	1.877	.188
3	In: XE	.9198	.0003	.053	.821

Commentary

As was pointed out in the preceding section, the most efficient place to begin is with the examination of the last step in the summary table. Clearly, there is no interaction between the covariate and the independent variable. In other words, the b's are homogeneous. We, therefore, turn to Step 2.

From Step 2 of the Summary table, it can be seen that the proportion of variance incremented by the use of separate intercepts for the two groups (.0089) is not statistically significant at, say, the .05 level. Incidentally, even if the proportion of variance incremented at this step were statistically significant, it is doubtful that it would be deemed substantively important in most research areas. On the basis of Step 2, therefore, it is concluded that, after adjusting for initial differences on the covariate (i.e., Step 1), there is no statistically significant difference between the Experimental and Control groups (adjusted means are calculated below).

Output

```
------------------------------------ Variables in the Equation ------------------------------------
```

Variable	B	SE B	T	Sig T
X	.99689	.19726	5.054	.0001
E	−.75776	.55303	1.370	.1884
(Constant)	3.66615	1.05584	3.472	.0029

Commentary

We are reporting this equation for two reasons: (a) so that we have the common b (.99689) for the calculation of adjusted means (see below); and (b) to demonstrate what was stated earlier, namely that the difference between adjusted means is equal to the difference between the intercepts of the separate equations in which a common b is used for the covariate. Using relevant terms from the regression equation given above, the intercepts of the equations for the Control and Experimental groups respectively are

$$a_c = 3.66615 + (-.75776) = 2.90839$$

$$a_e = 3.66615 + (.75776) \quad = 4.42391$$

The two regression equations are

$$Y'_C = 2.90839 + .99689X$$

$$Y'_E = 4.42391 + .99689X$$

Turning now to Step 1, it is clear that the proportion of variance accounted for by the covariate (.9106) is both substantively meaningful and statistically significant. Therefore, it is an equation in which only the covariate, X, is used that is retained and interpreted.

Output

Equation Number 2   Dependent Variable..   Y

Beginning Block Number   1. Method: Enter   X

		Analysis of Variance			
Multiple R	.95425		DF	Sum of Squares	Mean Squar
R Square	.91060 R Square Change	.91060			
Adjusted R Square	.90563 F Change	183.33151 Regression	1	240.89796	240.8979
Standard Error	1.14630 Signif F Change	.0000 Residual	18	23.65204	1.3140

$$F = \quad 183.33151 \quad \text{Signif F} = .0000$$

---------------------------------- Variables in the Equation ----------------------------------

Variable	B	SE B	T	Sig T
X	1.23791	.09143	13.540	.0000
(Constant)	2.41285	.54011	4.467	.0003

Commentary

Given in this part of the output are what we have earlier labeled total statistics. That is, all subjects are treated as if they belonged to a single group. Issues concerning the validity of ANCOVA adjustment aside (see Chapter 13, and Measurement Errors, below), total statistics were calculated, because it was concluded that neither the b's nor the a's of the separate regression equations are statistically significantly different from each other.

Note, however, that, because of their properties (see Pedhazur, 1982, pp. 530–540), total and within group statistics may differ very much from each other. For example, the within group correlations of X and Y for the Control and Experimental groups respectively are .786 and .764 (see Table 21.3), as compared with the total correlation of .954 given above.

ADJUSTED MEANS

Following is the information necessary for the calculation of the adjusted means. The means were taken from Table 21.3. The common b (b_c) was taken from Step 2 of the output given above.

	Control	*Experimental*
$\bar{Y}$:	5.60	12.10
$\bar{X}$:	2.70	7.70

$$b_c = .99689$$

The grand mean of the covariate is 5.20. Applying (21.7), the adjusted means for the Control and Experimental groups are

$$\bar{Y}_{C(adj)} = 5.60 - .99689(2.70 - 5.20) = 8.09223$$

$$\bar{Y}_{E(adj)} = 12.10 - .99689(7.70 - 5.20) = 9.60778$$

Notice that the dependent variable mean for the group whose covariate mean is lower (Control in the present case) is adjusted upwards (from 5.60 to 8.09), whereas that for the group whose covariate mean is higher (Experimental) is adjusted downwards (from 12.10 to 9.61). As a result, a difference of 6.5 between the *unadjusted* means is reduced to 1.52 between the *adjusted* means. The latter difference is equal to the difference between the intercepts of the separate equations with the common b (given above). We repeat: A test of the difference between intercepts of regression equations in which a common b is used for the covariate is the same as a test of the difference between adjusted means. As Pedhazur showed (1982, pp. 507–520), the former approach is much more efficient in designs with multiple groups and/or multiple covariates.

Recall that the difference between the unadjusted means is statistically significant, whereas the difference between the adjusted means is not. Thus, much as in competitive sports, the initially superior group is, in effect, handicapped when ANCOVA is applied. After adjusting for the superiority of this group, it is concluded, in the present case, that there is no statistically significant difference between the groups. In other words, the difference between the groups on the dependent variable is attributed to their initial differences, *not* to the fact that one has received a treatment and the other has served as a control group. Referring to one of the substantive examples given above, it would be concluded that, after adjusting for initial differences on a relevant covariate, the effect of the enrichment program on academic achievement is not statistically significant.

Although, in the present example, the difference between adjusted means is statistically not significant, it should be clear that, depending on specific patterns in the data as well as sample sizes, differences among adjusted means may be statistically significant.

Lest the preceding demonstration lull you into a sense of undeserved faith in the almost magical powers of ANCOVA to equate what was initially different, we remind you of earlier discussions, especially in Chapter 13, of serious difficulties and potential biases to the valid application of ANCOVA for adjustment (see also Measurement Errors, below). "It is even possible for the remaining bias after adjustment to be larger in absolute value than the initial bias without any adjustment" (Weisberg, 1979, p. 1149).

In essence, it all boils down to the validity of an answer to an intrinsically unanswerable question: What would have happened, if the groups were not different from each other? Or, as put by Anderson (1963): "One may well wonder what exactly it means to ask what the data would look like if they were not what they are" (p. 170).

Measurement Errors

General discussions of adverse effects of measurement errors on correlation and regression coefficients were given in Chapters 5 and 17. When the reliability of the measure of the covariate is not perfect (it probably never is), random measurement errors lead to an attenuation in the estimate of the regression coefficient.[9] That is, the estimated b is smaller than what it would have been had the measure of the covariate been not fallible.[10] Specifically

$$b = \beta r_{xx} \tag{21.10}$$

where b = estimated regression coefficient; β = true regression coefficient (*not* the standardized coefficient); r_{xx} = reliability of the covariate measure. Because r_{xx} is a fraction, except when the reliability is perfect, $b < \beta$. This type of error may lead to serious distortions when ANCOVA is used for adjustment for initial differences between groups.

Consider, for example, the following summary data for two groups, A and B, where the means on the covariate, X, and the dependent variable, Y, are

$$\bar{X} \qquad \bar{Y}$$

$$A: \quad 5.0 \quad 10.0$$

$$B: \quad 10.0 \quad 16.0$$

Assume that it is known that, when X is measured without error, a single regression equation fits the data for both groups, and that this equation is

$$Y' = 4.0 + 1.2X$$

Suppose now that a measure of X whose reliability is .7 in group A as well as in group B is used. Applying (21.10), the estimate of b is:

$$(1.2)(.7) = .84$$

Using this b to estimate the two intercepts

$$a_A = 10.0 - (.84)(5.0) \;\; = 5.8$$

$$a_B = 16.0 - (.84)(10.0) = 7.6$$

On the basis of these results, it would be concluded that the difference between A and B, after adjusting for the covariate, is -1.8. Thus, using a fallible covariate results in an underadjustment for the initial differences between the groups on the covariate and to the erroneous conclusion that the two equations have different intercepts. This situation is depicted in Figure 21.3, where the solid line is the common regression line for both groups, when a perfectly reliable covariate is used, whereas the dashed lines are the separate regression lines based on a fallible covariate. The dots on the regression lines represent the points of intersection of X and Y means for each of the groups.

In the context of the numerical example analyzed above, the erroneous interpretation amounts to saying that there is a difference between the treatment and the control groups,

---

[9]Recall that the covariate may be a pretest. Further, what we say here is applicable to other situations as well. For example, when a fallible predictor is used in a study of differential prediction or bias in selection (see Chapter 3; also, Cronbach, 1980; Hulin, Drasgow, & Parsons, 1983, Chapter 5; Linn, 1984; Linn & Werts, 1971).

[10]See Chapter 5, for discussions of different kinds of errors and different formulations regarding reliability of measures.

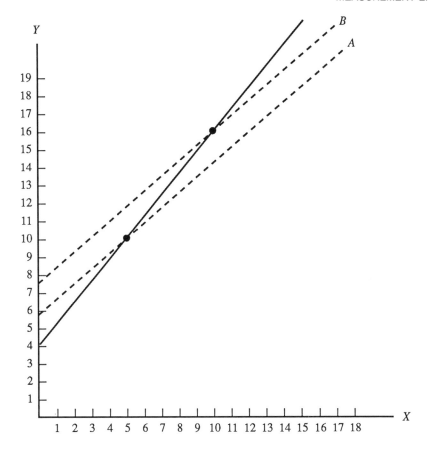

Figure 21.3

after equating them for the difference on the covariate. The specific consequences of the underadjustment will depend on which of the two groups is administered the treatment and which serves as the nonequivalent control group. If the group higher on the covariate (i.e., group *B*) is administered the treatment, it will be erroneously concluded that the treatment had an effect, after adjusting for initial differences on the covariate. If, on the other hand, the group lower on the covariate (i.e., *A*) is assigned to the treatment, it will be erroneously concluded that the treatment was ineffective, even harmful, as the group that did not receive it (i.e., *B*) performed better after the two groups have been equated. The latter situation is characteristic of social programs designed to help those most in need (e.g., compensatory education programs). Critics (e.g., Campbell & Boruch, 1975; Campbell & Erlebacher, 1970) have argued that the use of fallible covariates leads to underadjustment and to conclusions that such programs are ineffective or even harmful.[11]

---

[11]It is important to recognize that ANCOVA does not necessarily lead to underadjustment. The situation we have been describing is based on the simplest of models (some would say an unrealistic model) and on very restrictive assumptions. For discussions of conditions under which ANCOVA would lead to overadjustment or no bias in adjustment, see Bryk and Weisberg (1977) and Cronbach, Rogosa, Floden, and Price (1977).

Consistent with presentations in earlier sections of this chapter, it should be clear that what was said about differences between intercepts when a fallible covariate is used applies equally to differences between adjusted means. For completeness of presentation, however, this will now be demonstrated for the illustrative example used above. Applying (21.7) when the b estimated on the basis of a fallible covariate is used (.84), the adjusted means are

$$\bar{Y}_{A(adj)} = 10.0 - (.84)(5.0 - 7.5) = 12.1$$

$$\bar{Y}_{B(adj)} = 16.0 - (.84)(10.0 - 7.5) = 13.9$$

As expected, the difference between the two adjusted means, -1.8, is the same as the difference between the two intercepts obtained above.

Applying (21.7) again, this time using what we said above to be the true β (1.2)

$$\bar{Y}_{A(adj)} = 10.0 - (1.2)(5.0 - 7.5) = 13.0$$

$$\bar{Y}_{B(adj)} = 16.0 - (1.2)(10.0 - 7.5) = 13.0$$

Having used the regression coefficient that is presumably based on a perfectly reliable measure of the covariate, the adjusted means are shown to be identical.

Before turning to suggested remedies, we would like to stress that, when ANCOVA is applied for the purpose of control (see earlier section dealing with this topic), a fallible covariate does not lead to bias in estimates of adjusted means. The power of the statistical analysis is, however, adversely affected.

SUGGESTED REMEDIES AND ALTERNATIVES TO ANCOVA

Although there is general agreement that a fallible covariate leads to biased estimates of adjusted means, there is no agreement as to what to do about it. Various approaches have been proposed, all basically aimed at correcting for measurement errors (e.g., DeGracie & Fuller, 1972; Lord, 1960; Porter, 1967; Stroud, 1972). Huitema (1980, Chapter 13), who gave an overview of some of the approaches, illustrated the application of the one proposed by Porter (1967), according to which subjects' true scores on the covariate are estimated on the basis of their observed scores and are then used instead of the latter in the ANCOVA (estimation of true scores was discussed in Chapter 5).

Illustrating the lack of agreement regarding corrections for unreliability of the covariate measure is the lack of agreement concerning the kind of reliability estimate to be used for the purpose of estimating subjects' true scores (see, Huitema, 1980, p. 312, for alternative suggestions, along with relevant references).

Some authors find ANCOVA seriously deficient and particularly ill-suited to deal with dynamic models of change and growth. Notable among critics of ANCOVA are Bryk and Weisberg (1976, 1977; see also Bryk, Strenio, & Weisberg, 1980; Weisberg, 1979), who asserted that it is "chosen for mathematical convenience rather than as a serious attempt to model a real situation" (1976, p. 152). As an alternative, they offered what they labeled a value-added approach. A contrast between the application of the two approaches to data from a Head Start program is given in Bryk and Weisberg (1976). Another alternative to AN-COVA, taken from the frame of reference of structural equation modeling (see Chapter 24), was proposed by Sörbom (1978, 1982).

Regression Discontinuity: A Comment

The Regression Discontinuity Design (RDD) was presented in Chapter 13. To reiterate briefly, in this design, subjects are assigned to treatments (or treatment and control) on the basis of their scores on a premeasure, a covariate. Specifically, subjects above and below a cutting score on the premeasure are assigned to the different groups (see Figure 13.4).

It is not our intention to repeat here the advantages of this design nor the cautions called for in its application and the interpretation of the results. We mention this design here to reiterate two points made in connection with it in Chapter 13.

One, the analytic approach presented in this chapter is also applicable to the RDD. A test of the difference between the intercepts (after having established that the b's are homogeneous) is equivalent to a test of the difference between the two groups at the cutting point, P (see the segment labeled e in Figure 13.4). In fact, when we generated the data of Table 21.3 for the purpose of illustrating the application of ANCOVA for adjustment, we did so with the intention of using them also as illustrative of the RDD. Look back at Table 21.3 and note that subjects whose score on X is ≤ 5 are in the Control group, whereas those whose score on X is > 5 are in the Experimental group. This, then, could serve as an example of the assignment of subjects on the basis of a cutting score on the premeasure. For reasons of interpretability, some authors (e.g., Judd & Kenny, 1981, Chapter 5; Trochim, 1984, Chapter 5) recommend that the cutting score on the premeasure be subtracted from each of the original scores and that the resulting scores be used in the analysis instead of the original scores.

Two, as was pointed out in Chapter 13, because the assignment in RDD is on the basis of the premeasure, no correction for errors of measurement of the premeasure is called for (see, for example, Overall & Woodward, 1977a, 1977b; Rubin, 1974, 1977).

ANCOVA in Nonexperimental Research

Our discussion and illustrations of ANCOVA were addressed to its application in experimental (control purpose) and quasi-experimental (adjustment purpose) designs. The same analytic approach can, of course, be taken when it is desired to compare regression equations across groups in nonexperimental research. For example, it may be desired to determine whether the regression of salary on educational background (or achievement on achievement motivation; self-concept on anxiety) is the same or different for males and females (or blacks and whites). In fact, we discussed such applications in connection with differential prediction and selection bias in Chapter 3.

Obviously, interpretive problems inherent in nonexperimental research do not disappear just because ANCOVA is applied to the data. What was said about this topic in Chapter 14 (e.g., model specification; internal and external validity) applies, of course, to the situation considered here. We are making this point because of the tendency to overlook it when ANCOVA is applied in nonexperimental research. For a couple of comments on the misuse of ANCOVA in studies of communication in the families of schizophrenics, and of sex differentials in salaries, see respectively Woodward and Goldstein (1977) and Wolins (1978).

Finally, consistent with our recommendation that the term interaction be used only in designs in which at least one variable is manipulated (see Chapter 20, Nonexperimental Research), we recommend that it not be used when ANCOVA is applied in nonexperimental research. Thus, we recommend that, in such designs, results be interpreted and discussed with reference to differences or similarities of regression equations, *not* interactions and main effects. For example, we recommend that a difference between b's *not* be interpreted as an interaction between the specific continuous and categorical variables one is studying. We recognize that some would view our recommendation as quibbling about terminology. Nevertheless, we believe this distinction in terminology may help prevent some flagrant misinterpretations of ANCOVA when applied in nonexperimental research.

EXTENSIONS AND GENERALIZATIONS

Our presentation of the analysis of ATI designs and ANCOVA was limited to the simplest case: linear regression with one attribute and a categorical variable consisting of two categories. The same approach can, however, be extended and generalized to more variables and to more complex designs. In this section, we sketch the approach to some extensions and generalizations, along with relevant references.

Before doing this, we would like to stress that the issue of whether or not the regression of the dependent variable on the attribute is linear should not be relegated to the status of an assumption. Moreover, on the basis of theoretical formulations, the researcher may actually hypothesize that the regression in one or both groups is curvilinear (see Chapter 18). For a presentation of curvilinear regression analysis in an ATI design, and a numerical example in which the regression is linear in one group and quadratic in another, see Pedhazur (1982, pp. 477–487).

Two Groups, Multiple Attributes.[12]   The extension to designs with multiple attributes for the case of two groups is straightforward. As before, a coded vector (e.g., effect coding) is used to represent the categorical variable. Products of the coded vector with each of the attributes are then generated to represent the interaction. Because there are multiple product vectors, the interaction is tested by testing the increment in the proportion of variance accounted for by the product vectors when they are entered last into the analysis—for example, testing R Square Change due the product vectors, by applying (18.15). Using a program such as REGRESSION of SPSS and entering the product vectors as the last step, the F Change will constitute a test of the interaction.

Multiple Groups, One Attribute.   Following procedures presented in Chapter 19, coded vectors are generated to represent the categorical variable (i.e., number of coded vectors equal to the number of groups minus one). Each of the coded vectors is then multiplied by the attribute to represent the interaction. Again, because the interaction is represented by multiple vectors, it is tested by testing R Square Change due to them.

The same applies to tests among intercepts. Recall that, when it is concluded that there is no interaction, the product vector is dropped and one proceeds to test the difference between the intercepts. In the case of two groups, this can be done by either testing the b for the coded vector in an equation in which the product vector is *not* included or by testing the R Square Change due the coded vector (see numerical examples in preceding sections).

Because, in the case of multiple groups, there is more than one coded vector, the test of differences among intercepts is done by testing the proportion of variance incremented by the coded vectors over and above the attribute (i.e., R Square Change). Analogous to multiple

---

[12]It should be clear that what we say applies equally to ATI designs and to designs in which the attribute is used as a covariate (i.e., when ANCOVA is applied).

comparisons among means (see Chapter 19), a priori or post hoc comparisons among intercepts may also be carried out. For an analysis of a numerical example of four groups with one attribute, see Pedhazur (1982, pp. 498–513).

Multiple Groups, Multiple Attributes.   As you have probably surmised, the analytic approach in this design is the same as the one outlined in the preceding section except that the coded vectors are multiplied by each of the attributes to represent the interaction. An analysis of a numerical example for four groups and two attributes will be found in Pedhazur (1982, pp. 513–519).

Factorial Designs.   The examples presented thus far have consisted of one categorical variable. The same analytic approach can be generalized to multiple categorical variables (i.e., factorial designs) with one or multiple attributes. Following procedures presented in Chapter 20, one codes the terms of the design as if it consisted of categorical variables only. That is, coded vectors are used to represent main effects of each factor. Products of the main-effects vectors are generated to represent interactions.

The coded vectors (for main effects and interactions) are then multiplied by the attribute(s). A test of R Square Change due to the products of all the coded vectors with the attribute(s) constitutes a test of homogeneity of regression coefficients in the cells of the design. As in designs with a single categorical variable, the step taken next depends on whether it is concluded that the coefficients are homogenous or heterogeneous. If the former, a common *b* is used and the analysis proceeds as in a factorial design but with the added aspect that the terms (i.e., interaction, main effects) are tested after adjusting for the attribute(s). If the latter, separate regression equations for the regression of the dependent variable on the attribute(s) within the cells are studied.

We do not know of textbook examples of factorial ATI designs. Discussions and numerical examples of factorial ANCOVA are available in various textbooks (e.g., Johnson & Jackson, 1959; Namboodiri, Carter, & Blalock, 1975; Wildt & Ahtola, 1978; Winer, 1971). In most presentations, the conventional approach to the calculations is used. We suggest that you replicate such analyses, using the multiple regression approach sketched in the preceding paragraph. Doing this will, we believe, help you develop an understanding of the analysis of this type of design.

CONCLUDING REMARKS

With this chapter, we conclude the presentation of analytic approaches for the major research designs introduced in Part 2. The next two chapters are devoted to factor analysis, which, from the perspective of this book, is particularly pertinent to questions of construct validation. The last chapter is then devoted to Structural Equation Modeling.

STUDY SUGGESTIONS

1. Following are summary data for two groups:

	A	B
$\bar{X}$:	47.20	46.32
$\bar{Y}$:	60.17	68.11
Σx^2:	18.16	10.12
Σy^2:	31.09	26.13
Σxy:	17.11	13.40

For each group, calculate the
(a) regression equation for Y on X.
(b) regression sum of squares.
(c) residual sum of squares.
(d) proportion of variance of Y accounted for by X.
(e) standardized regression coefficient (β).

2. Using data from study suggestion 1, calculate the common regression coefficient (b_c).

3. In a study consisting of three groups (A, B, and C), scores on a measure of a dependent variable, Y, and of an attribute, X, were obtained. Effect coding was used to code group membership as follows: A was identified in E1, B in E2, and C was assigned -1 in both vectors. Product vectors XE1 and XE2 were generated. The overall regression equation was

$$Y' = 3.00 + 2.08X + .80E1 - .30E2 + .42XE1 - .08XE2$$

What are the separate regression equations for the three groups?

4. Sixty students were randomly assigned in equal numbers to one of two teaching methods: P (e.g., problem-solving orientation) and D (drill). The researcher hypothesized that there is an interaction between the teaching methods and an attribute, X (e.g., mental ability) in their effects on the dependent variable, Y (e.g., achievement). Following are illustrative data.

	P		D
Y	X	Y	X
5	5	15	5
15	5	19	5
7	6	13	5
17	6	15	6
14	5	17	6
14	7	22	7
12	8	17	7
19	8	20	8
15	10	24	10
20	10	19	10
24	10	22	9
14	11	18	10
23	11	23	11
16	13	23	12

26	13	22	13
17	14	19	12
27	14	20	14
33	15	25	14
22	16	27	15
23	15	22	15
27	17	25	16
25	18	25	18
27	20	19	18
34	20	25	19
28	23	22	19
36	23	29	21
38	27	24	21
30	29	30	25
39	29	32	29
35	31	29	31

What is (are) the

(a) means, standard deviations, Σx^2, and correlation between X and Y within each of the groups?

(b) proportion of variance due to the interaction between the treatments and the attribute, and the associated F ratio?

(c) overall regression equation (i.e., for the regression of Y on X, a vector representing treatments, and the interaction)?

(d) separate regression equations for the two groups?

(e) point of intersection of the two regression lines?

(f) the Johnson–Neyman regions of significance for $\alpha = .05$?

Plot the data and interpret the results.

5. Thirty subjects were randomly assigned in equal numbers to one of three treatments (A, B, and C). Scores on a pretest were obtained prior to the administration of the treatments. Following are illustrative data, where Y = dependent variable; X = pretest:

A		B		C	
Y	X	Y	X	Y	X
1	1	1	1	4	1
3	1	2	1	3	1
2	3	2	2	4	2
3	3	3	2	3	2
4	3	3	4	5	2
3	4	3	4	3	4
5	4	3	5	5	4
4	5	5	5	4	6
4	6	4	6	7	6
6	6	5	6	8	7

Using effect coding (identify A in E1, B in E2, and assign -1 to C in both vectors), carry out an analysis of covariance with X as the covariate.

What is (are) the

(a) means, standard deviations, and r_{xy} in each of the groups?

(b) total r_{xy} (i.e., across the three treatments)?

(c) overall regression equation?

(d) separate regression equations in each of the groups?

(e) proportion of variance due to the interaction between the treatments and the covariate, and the associated F ratio?

(f) common regression coefficient (b_c) and its associated t ratio?

(g) proportion of variance accounted for by the treatments after controlling for the covariate, and the associated F ratio?

(h) regression equations for the three groups, using a common b and separate a's?

(i) adjusted means for the three groups?

Plot the data and interpret the results.

6. Use only the Y scores of study suggestion 5 and carry out an analysis to determine whether there are statistically significant differences ($\alpha = .05$) among the three means.

(a) What is the proportion of variance accounted for by the three treatments, and the associated F ratio?

(b) Are the differences among the three treatments statistically significant?

Compare these results with those obtained in study suggestion 5.

Answers

		A	B
1. (a)	Y':	$15.80 + .94X$	$6.97 + 1.32X$
(b)	ss_{reg}:	16.08	17.69
(c)	ss_{res}:	15.01	8.44
(d)	r^2:	.52	.68
(e)	β:	.72	.82

(If necessary, see chapter 17)

2. $b_c = 1.08$—see (21.1)

3. $Y'_A = 3.80 + 2.50X$
   $Y'_B = 2.70 + 2.00X$
   $Y'_C = 2.50 + 1.74X$

4. (a)

	P		D	
	Y	X	Y	X
M:	22.733	14.633	22.067	13.700
s:	9.036	7.703	4.631	6.983
Σx^2:		1720.967		1414.300
r:		.864		.833
N:		30		30

(b) $.05501$; $F = 11.67937$ with 1 and 56 df

(c) $Y' = 11.19953 + .78303X - 3.29595E + .23039XE$

(d) $Y'_p = 7.90358 + 1.01342X$
    $Y'_D = 14.49549 + .55264X$

(e) 14.31—see (21.2)

(f) $A = .09706$ $B = -1.40991$ $C = 14.48112$
    see (21.4–21.6)
Left region: below 6.66
Right region: above 22.39
    see (21.3)

5. (a)

		A		B		C
	Y	X	Y	X	Y	X
M:	3.50	3.60	3.10	3.60	4.60	3.50
s:	1.43	1.78	1.29	1.96	1.71	2.22
r:		.74		.86		.70

(b) .68
(c) $Y' = 1.70907 + .56729X - .36400E1 - .63930E2 + .03130XE1 - .00334XE2$
(d) $Y'_A = 1.34507 + .59859X$
    $Y'_B = 1.06977 + .56395X$
    $Y'_C = 2.71236 + .53933X$
(e) .00085; $F = .03$ with 2 and 24 df
(f) $b_c = .56291$; $t = 5.853$ with 26 df
(g) .18167; $F = 6.58$ with 2 and 26 df
(h) $Y'_A = 1.47353 + .56291X$
    $Y'_B = 1.07353 + .56291X$
    $Y'_C = 2.62983 + .56291X$
(i) $M_{(adj.)}$: $A = 3.48124$; $B = 3.08124$; $C = 4.63753$
    (Note that the difference between any two intercepts is equal to the difference between the two corresponding adjusted means. E.g., $1.47353 - 1.07353 = 3.48124 - 3.08124 = .40$. For tests among adjusted means, see Pedhazur, 1982, pp. 505–512.)

6. (a) .16790; $F = 2.72$ with 2 and 27 df
(b) no

Chapter 22
Exploratory Factor Analysis

The literature on factor analysis (*FA*) is vast and generally complex. Perusing even small segments of this literature in an effort to understand what *FA* is, how it is applied, and how the results are interpreted is bound to bewilder and frustrate most readers. This is due to a wide variety of contrasting and contradictory views on almost every aspect of *FA*, serious misconceptions surrounding it, and lack of uniformity in terminology and notation.

Not surprisingly, Gould (1981) characterized *FA* as "a bitch" (p. 238), although we think a more apt description is that of a forest in which one can get lost in no time. This chapter is literally an *introduction* to *FA*. It is *not* simply space considerations that constrain us from attempting to do more than that. Rather a more thorough treatment is not possible without resorting to complex statistical theory and matrix algebra. In fact, some remarks about matrices and their properties will be necessary even for our rudimentary presentation.

We believe you will get the gist of the presentation, even if you have no background in matrix algebra, provided you are willing and able to tolerate some unavoidable ambiguities. Be that as it may, we strongly advise you to acquire some knowledge of matrix algebra so as to be in a position to follow more detailed presentations of *FA* as well as other multivariate analytic procedures. You will find introductions to matrix algebra in practically any book on multivariate analysis or on *FA* (see below; see also beginning of Chapter 18, for some references).

General and not too complex presentations of *FA* will be found, among other sources, in Bentler (1976), Comrey (1973), Cureton and D'Agostino (1983), Gorsuch (1983), Kim and Mueller (1978a, 1978b), Long (1983a), McDonald (1985), and Mulaik (1982). Among books on multivariate analysis that include presentations of *FA* are Cliff (1987), Cooley and Lohnes (1971), Green (1978), Overall and Klett (1972), and Stevens (1986). Presentations of *FA* from a measurement perspective were given by Guilford (1954), Magnusson (1967), and Nunnally (1978).

Our presentation is not a formal one. Rather we attempt by means of simple numerical examples to give a nontechnical exposition from a measurement perspective. Our emphasis is on the meaning of some basic factor analytic concepts and on the interpretation of results of *FA*.

COMPUTER PROGRAMS

Most statistical packages for mainframe and personal computers include some procedure(s) for exploratory *FA*. MacCallum (1983), who compared factor analytic procedures in BMDP, SAS, and SPSS, found "two fairly serious problems" (p. 230) in the three packages. The first problem is that decisions a user may leave to the computer program are "far too many to suit most factor analysts" (p. 230). The second problem "concerns the limited number of options available with respect to some important issues" (p. 230).

For our very limited purposes, any one of the aforementioned packages will do equally well. Our preferences aside, in this chapter, we use SPSS, because we are under the impression that it is the most widely used of them. At the conclusion of the SPSS run for the first example, we give input statements for SAS using the same data. If you are using SAS, or any other computer program, we suggest you replicate our analyses and compare your output with the SPSS output we report. Needless to say, you should also study the manual of the program you are using.

FACTOR ANALYSIS AND THEORY

In Chapter 4, we found it necessary to discuss the crucial role of *FA* in construct validation. In fact, it is concern with construct validation that impels us to offer a rudimentary presentation of *FA*. Accordingly, we believe you will benefit from reading relevant sections of Chapter 4 before turning to the current presentation. *In particular, we suggest you read the sections dealing with the distinction between exploratory and confirmatory factor analysis.*

Exploratory *FA* is *not*, or should not be, a blind process in which all manner of variables or items are thrown into a factor-analytic "grinder" in the expectation that something meaningful will emerge. The aphorism GIGO (Garbage In, Garbage Out) is probably nowhere more evident than in applications of *FA* aimed at seeing what will happen or what will emerge.

Further, contrary to widespread misconceptions, *FA* is *not* a method for uncovering real dimensions, or reality underlying a set of indicators. As will become evident, almost anything can be uncovered, if one tries hard and long enough (e.g., extracting different numbers of factors, using different methods of rotation of factors).

Viewed from the perspective of construct validation, it should be clear that meaningful application of *FA* is unthinkable without theory. As Thurstone (1948) put it: "Factorial methods will be fruitful in the advancement of psychology only in so far as we use these methods in close relation to psychological ideas" (p. 408). In sum, if there is anything we would like to impress upon you before plunging into the numbers it is that you should follow the rule: When you have no theoretical rationale for doing a *FA*, *DON'T*!

NUMERICAL EXAMPLES

We will introduce various concepts gradually, by means of two numerical examples. The first and simpler example of uncorrelated factors is presented and analyzed in the present section. The second example of correlated factors is presented and analyzed in a subsequent section.

UNCORRELATED FACTORS

Notions of latent variables and their indicators were introduced and discussed in Chapters 2 and 4. It is in attempts to assess the validity of indicators of constructs (latent variables) that we will be applying *FA*. In what follows, we use the example introduced in Chapter 4, namely the measurement of self-concept. For the sake of illustration, we assume that the researcher has formulated some theory regarding two aspects of self-concept, namely Academic Self-Concept and Social Self-Concept, and that he or she is using three indicators of each. Note that the preceding implies, among other things, a specification regarding the relation between the two dimensions of self-concept. We will assume that the researcher hypothesized that the two dimensions are moderately correlated.

In what follows, we introduce some rudimentary concepts of matrices we refer to in the course of the presentation.

Some Observations About Matrices

A *matrix* is a two-dimensional table of numbers or symbols. The dimensions of a matrix are indicated by the number of its rows and columns. Assume that the six indicators of self-concept under consideration were administered to a sample of 200 subjects and that scores on the six indicators for each subject were recorded in a separate row. This would result in a 200 (rows, for subjects) by 6 (columns, for indicators) data matrix.

It is convenient to place the correlations between all pairs of indicators (i.e., columns of the data matrix) in a matrix, referred to as a correlation matrix. An illustrative correlation matrix among six indicators is given in Table 22.1. It is this correlation matrix we will use in our first numerical example.[1] We inserted the lines in the body of the matrix to facilitate our discussion of it. Several points will now be made about the properties of a correlation matrix.

1. A correlation matrix consists of the same number of rows and columns. Such a matrix is referred to as a *square* matrix.

2. No matter how many subjects are used in the study, the dimensions of the correlation matrix equal the number of indicators (variables)—six in our example—as it is the correlations among the indicators (across subjects) that are calculated.

3. Matrices are indicated by bold capital letters. The correlation matrix is indicated by a bold capital R (i.e., **R**) often referred to as an R matrix.

4. The diagonal of a matrix going from its top left corner to its bottom right corner is referred to as the principal, or main, diagonal. Note that the principal diagonal of a correlation matrix consists of 1's, signifying the correlation of each indicator with itself.

5. A correlation matrix is *symmetric*, consisting of the same elements above and below the principal diagonal except that they are transposed. For example, look at the first column of Table 22.1 (labeled $Y1$) and notice that the same values are also reported as the first row ($Y1$). This is because the correlation is a symmetric index. Thus, the correlation between $Y2$ and $Y1$ (indicated at the intersection of the second row and the first column) is .502, as is the correlation between $Y1$ and $Y2$ (indicated at the intersection of the first row and the second column).

6. Because the correlation matrix is symmetric, it is frequently reported in the form of a *triangular* matrix. When the values above the principal diagonal are omitted, the matrix is referred to as *lower*

---

[1] As explained in Chapter 24, there is a decided advantage in analyzing covariances instead of correlations among the indicators. Nevertheless, we use correlations, because the presentation is thereby greatly simplified. Incidentally, correlations are used in most factor analytic applications.

Table 22.1

Illustrative Correlation Matrix for Six Indicators of Self-Concept. N = 200.

	Y1	Y2	Y3	X1	X2	X3
		I			II	
Y1	1.000	.502	.622	.008	.027	−.029
Y2	.502	1.000	.551	.072	.030	−.059
Y3	.622	.551	1.000	.028	−.049	.018
X1	.008	.072	.028	1.000	.442	.537
X2	.027	.030	−.049	.442	1.000	.413
X3	−.029	−.059	.018	.537	.413	1.000
		III			IV	

Note. Y's are indicators of Academic Self-Concept; X's are indicators of Social Self-Concept.

triangular. When the values below the principal diagonal are omitted, it is referred to as *upper triangular.* Many computer programs accept triangular matrices as input and report symmetric matrices in the form of lower triangular ones.

As we present different topics, it will become necessary to explain some additional aspects of matrices. We turn to an examination of the correlation matrix of Table 22.1. To facilitate this, we organized the matrix so that indicators of each of the dimensions of self-concept are grouped together. Also, to highlight the pattern of the correlations among the indicators, we inserted lines in the body of the matrix creating, in effect, four 3 by 3 submatrices, labeled I through IV. Notice that I consists of the correlations among the indicators of Academic Self-Concept (the *Y*'s), whereas IV consists of the correlations among the indicators of Social Self-Concept (the *X*'s). The two other submatrices (II and III) consist of the correlations among indicators of the different dimensions of self-concept.

Study submatrices I and IV and note that there are moderate positive correlations among the indicators of each of the dimensions of self-concept (for example, the correlations among indicators of Academic Self-Concept range from .502 to .622). In short, indicators within submatrices I and IV seem to be measuring the same thing to a moderate degree.

Examine now the submatrix of the correlations among indicators of different dimensions (either II or III) and note that the correlations are low, most close to zero. It appears, therefore, that whatever the *Y* indicators are tapping has little to do with whatever the *X* indicators are tapping.

The remarks in the preceding paragraphs amount to an "eye ball *FA*." They are tantamount to saying that two dimensions, or factors, underlie the correlation matrix. Further, and contrary to the researcher's expectation, these dimensions have little to do with each other.

If all correlation matrices were this small and the pattern of the correlations this clear, there would be no compelling need to resort to *FA*. We began with this type of correlation matrix to demonstrate intuitively what it is that one is after when subjecting a correlation matrix to *FA*.

The data of Table 22.1 will now be analyzed using the FACTOR procedure of SPSS. Note that, instead of using a correlation matrix as input, the raw data may be used. Obviously, raw data have to be used when a correlation matrix has not yet been generated. When raw data are used, it is useful to save the correlation matrix (see, e.g., SPSS manual) so that it may be used in the event it is decided to run some additional factor analyses. Doing this is advantageous, not only because it is convenient when the sample size and the number of indicators are relatively large, but also because it may result in substantial savings in computer time.

SPSS

Input

```
SET LISTING='T221SPS.LIS'.
TITLE TABLE 22.1. RUN ON PC VERSION.
DATA LIST MATRIX FREE/Y1 Y2 Y3 X1 X2 X3.
N 200.
BEGIN DATA.
1.0
.502 1.0
.622 .551 1.0
.008 .072 .028 1.0
.027 .030 −.049 .442 1.0
−.029 −.059 .018 .537 .413 1.0
END DATA.
FACTOR VARIABLES=Y1 TO X3/
    READ CORRELATION TRIANGLE/
    PRINT ALL/CRITERIA=FACTORS(2)/
    EXTRACTION=PAF/ROTATION=VARIMAX/
    PLOT=EIGEN ROTATION(1,2).
```

```
TITLE TABLE 22.1.  RUN ON MAINFRAME
MATRIX DATA VARIABLES=Y1 Y2 Y3 X1 X2 X3/
    FORMAT=NODIAGONAL/N=200
BEGIN DATA
.502
.622 .551
.008 .072 .028
.027 .030 −.049 .442
−.029 −.059 .018 .537 .413
END DATA
FACTOR MATRIX IN(COR=*)/
    PRINT ALL/CRI=FAC(2)/EXT=PAF/
    ROT=VAR/PLOT=EIG ROT(1,2)/
```

Commentary

We included input setups for both the PC and the mainframe, because they differ from each other. As you can see, the difference between the two versions has to do with the way correlation matrices are read in as input (see manuals for the PC and mainframe versions for conventions regarding matrix input). For both versions, we are reading in a lower triangular matrix. Note, however, that, for the mainframe version, we do this without the diagonal (see NODIAGONAL. This option is *not* available on the PC version.) Also, as a result of the differences in the matrix input for the two versions, specifications of the variables and matrices in the FACTOR procedure differ. The remaining subcommands and keywords are the same in both versions. For illustrative purposes, we use the truncated format in the mainframe version. The output of both versions is the same.

Of the various decisions that may be made or left to the program defaults, we comment briefly on the following two: the method of factor extraction and the number of factors to be extracted.

The default extraction method in SPSS is Principal Components analysis (*PCA*). In our commentary on the second excerpt of the output, we contrast *PCA* with *FA*. For now, it will only be stated: If you want a *FA*, *do not leave the method of extraction to the default*. As indicated in our input statements, we called for Principal Axis Factoring (PAF), the most widely used method of factor extraction.

The decision regarding the number of factors to be extracted is by no means simple, and criteria for arriving at it have been a source of heated debates in the factor analytic literature. Probably the most widely used statistical criterion is that factors whose eigenvalue (see below) is at least 1 be retained. This criterion, referred to as minimum eigenvalue of 1, or eigenvalue greater than unity, is the default value in SPSS. As many authors have pointed out, although such a criterion may be defensible, albeit not very useful, in the context of *PCA*, it is inappropriate for *FA*.

In sum, although statistical criteria for the number of factors to be extracted can be easily established and incorporated into computer programs, the important thing to note is that such criteria are not useful. Indeed, they are potentially harmful, because they appear to relieve the researcher of the responsibility of making what is in many instances a complex decision, which should be made primarily on the basis of substantive considerations. Consistent with the "theoretical formulation" regarding the two dimensions of self-concept (see above), we called for the extraction of two factors (see CRITERIA subcommand in the Input).

Output

Determinant of Correlation Matrix = .2078342
Bartlett Test of Sphericity = 308.18068, Significance = .00000

Commentary

Only excerpts of output relevant to our presentation are reported. We suggest that you run our examples so that you may be in a position to see not only what we have omitted but also our rearrangements of some aspects of the output.

THE DETERMINANT OF A MATRIX

Determinants of matrices play important roles in various statistical analyses (for details, see references to matrix algebra in Chapter 18). A determinant of a matrix is denoted by two vertical lines surrounding it. For example, the determinant of a correlation matrix is denoted as $|\mathbf{R}|$.

A determinant is a unique number associated with a square matrix (only square matrices have determinants). For the case of a correlation matrix, the determinant may vary between 0 and 1. When it is 0, there is at least one linear dependency in the matrix. What this means is that one or more columns in the data matrix can be derived by transforming other columns (e.g., multiplying a column by a constant) or by forming a linear combination of columns (e.g., addition, subtraction). An example of a data matrix containing a linear dependency is one consisting of two or more subtest scores as well as a total score, derived by, say, adding the subtest scores. Clearly, the information provided by the total score is completely redundant with that provided by the subtest scores. When the data contain a linear dependency, SPSS reports the following: Determinant of Correlation Matrix = .0000000.

Data matrices containing linear dependencies should *not* be used in *FA*. Attempts to factor analyze such matrices will be met with either failure or spurious results, depending on the computer program used. Either of the two major computer packages we have been using (SPSS and SAS) will terminate the analysis, indicating that the data are not appropriate for *FA*. Examples of error messages are: "CORRELATION MATRIX IS ILL-CONDITIONED FOR FACTOR PROCESSING" (SPSS); "ERROR: Communality greater than 1.0" (SAS). Some programs may exclude one or more vectors from the analysis, thereby arriving at a solution, but the likelihood for the results being artifactual is high.

When the determinant of a correlation matrix is 1, all the correlations in the matrix are equal to 0. Such a matrix, labeled an *identity* matrix, consists of 1's in the principal diagonal and 0's above and below it.

As is well known, one can test a correlation coefficient to ascertain whether it is statistically significant at a specified level of significance. It is common practice for researchers to report correlation matrices used in factor analyses, adorned with asterisks to indicate which of the correlations are significant and at what α level (e.g., one asterisk for the .05 level, two for the .01, and so forth). Suffice it to point out that, with the large number of tests generally carried out on correlation matrices used in *FA*, a certain number of correlations would be expected to be statistically significant by chance, even when all the correlations are zero in the population.

BARTLETT'S TEST OF SPHERICITY

What is of interest when contemplating the *FA* of a correlation matrix is to determine first whether the hypothesis that all the correlations, tested simultaneously, are not statistically different from 0 can be rejected. Stated differently, the null hypothesis is that the matrix is an identity matrix (see above). Such a test, referred to as Bartlett's test of sphericity (Bartlett, 1950; see also, Cooley & Lohnes, 1971, p. 103; Gorsuch, 1983, p. 149; Maxwell, 1977, p. 49) is reported above in the SPSS output.

We show how this test is calculated, because some computer programs do not report it. For this reason, we also show below (see commentary on the next excerpt of output) how to calculate the determinant, using output reported in virtually all computer programs for *FA*:

$$\chi^2 = - \left\{ [\dot{N} - 1] - \left[\frac{2k + 5}{6} \right] \right\} \text{Log}_e \ |\mathbf{R}| \tag{22.1}$$

where χ^2 = Chi-square; N = sample size; k = number of items (indicators, variables); Log_e = Natural log; $|\mathbf{R}|$ = determinant of the correlation matrix. The *df* associated with this χ^2 are $[k(k-1)]/2$ (i.e., the number of correlations above, or below, the principal diagonal of the correlation matrix). For the data of Table 22.1: $N = 200$, $k = 6$. From the SPSS output given above: $|\mathbf{R}| = .2078342$. $\text{Log}_e \ .2078342 = -1.57101$. Applying (22.1),

$$\chi^2 = - \left\{ [200 - 1] - \left[\frac{2(6) + 5}{6} \right] \right\} [-1.57101] = 308.180$$

which is, within rounding, the same as the value reported above. One would enter a χ^2 table (see Appendix) with $df = 15$, $[6(6 - 1)]/2$, at a selected α level to determine whether the null hypothesis can be rejected. Assuming, for example, that the .01 was selected, the tabled value is 30.578. Clearly, the hypothesis that the correlation matrix is an identity matrix can be rejected. Incidentally, SPSS reports the level of significance but not the *df* (see above).

McDonald (1985) presented an instructive example of what might happen when the researcher does not bother (many do not) to determine first whether the correlation matrix differs from an identity matrix. "Using random numbers from a population in which all correlations are zero" (p. 24), McDonald generated a 10 by 10 correlation matrix. He then demonstrated that the null hypothesis that the matrix is an identity matrix cannot be rejected. Subjecting the matrix to a *PCA* and using the criterion of eigenvalue larger than unity for the number of components to be retained (see above), five components were retained. Pointing out that his results are "plausible and very silly" (p. 24), McDonald aptly labeled them: "How to lie with factor analysis" (p. 78).[2]

As can be seen from (22.1), Bartlett's sphericity test is affected by sample size. When N is large, as it should be in factor analytic studies (we comment on sample size later on), the null hypothesis will almost always be rejected. This is why the application of Bartlett's test

---

[2]We suggest that you use McDonald's matrix (p. 25) and subject it to *FA*. If you are using SPSS, follow our input example but do *not* specify the number of factors to be retained. Using the default value, SPSS will extract five factors. These results too will appear "plausible" and just as "silly."

should be "used as a lower bound to the quality of the matrix" (Dziuban & Shirkey, 1974, p. 360). That is, when the hypothesis that the correlation matrix is an identity matrix cannot be rejected, the matrix should not be factor analyzed. However, rejection of the null hypothesis should not be construed as evidence that the correlation matrix is appropriate for *FA*. In sum, Bartlett's sphericity test should be used "as a general protection against foolish optimism when hunting for relations in a mass of data" (McDonald, 1985, p. 24).

Other approaches to the assessment of the appropriateness of a matrix for factor analysis are available (see, for example, Dziuban & Shirkey, 1974; Stewart, 1981) and are given as output in various computer programs, including SPSS. We turn now to another excerpt of the SPSS output.

Output

Initial Statistics:

Variable	Communality	*	Factor	Eigenvalue	Pct of Var	Cum Pct
Y1	.42842	*	1	2.12243	35.4	35.4
Y2	.36190	*	2	1.92911	32.2	67.5
Y3	.47586	*	3	.63290	10.5	78.1
X1	.35620	*	4	.54282	9.0	87.1
X2	.25300	*	5	.42551	7.1	94.2
X3	.34436	*	6	.34724	5.8	100.0

Commentary

The first two columns in this output refer to variables, whereas the remaining columns refer to components (see below). Some versions of SPSS (e.g., for the PC, IBM mainframe) include a column of asterisks, as above, to indicate that the output is composed of two sets of distinct elements. Yet this has not sufficed to avert confusion among users. It would have been better had SPSS organized the output differently. Below, we explain what each set means.

Regardless of the method of extraction the user calls for, and the column labeled "Factor" notwithstanding, the output given in this section *is from a PCA, not a FA*. Accordingly, we turn to a brief discussion of the distinction between *PCA* and *FA*.

PCA versus *FA*

It is perhaps best to begin by pointing out that, as with various other aspects, there is a good deal of disagreement regarding the status of *PCA* vis-a-vis *FA*. Cliff (1987), who attributed the disagreements to "a certain amount of ideology" (p. 349), portrayed the state of affairs thus:

Some authorities insist that component analysis is the only suitable approach, and that the common-factors methods just superimpose a lot of extraneous mumbo jumbo, dealing with fundamentally unmeasurable things, the common factors. Feelings are, if anything, even stronger on the other side. Militant common-factorists insist that components analysis is at best a common factor analysis with some error added and at worst an unrecognizable hodgepodge of things from which nothing can be determined. Some even insist that the term "factor analysis" must not be used when a components analysis is performed. (p. 349)

Then there are those who characterize the controversy as much ado about nothing, maintaining that results yielded by the two approaches tend to be very similar. Cautioning that such an assumption "can lead to serious error," Borgatta, Kercher, and Stull (1986) provided an example, based on hypothetical data, "to show how the results can be substantially different" (p. 160). Lending further support to Borgatta et al.'s claim are Hubbard and Allen's (1987) reanalyses of "seven well-known data sets" (p. 301).

We believe that focusing on the conditions under which results from *FA* and *PCA* may or may not be different deflects attention from the main issue, namely that they constitute distinct models with different goals (e.g., Bentler, 1976; Cattell, 1965; Harman, 1976; Jöreskog, 1979a; Kim & Mueller, 1978a; Maxwell, 1977; Wolins, 1982).

Succinctly, *PCA* is a data reduction method. The aim in applying it is to arrive at a relatively small number of components that will extract most of the variance of a relatively large set of indicators (variables, items). This is accomplished by linear transformations of the indicators, subject to two conditions. One, components extract variance in descending order. That is, the first component is designed to extract the maximum variance possible; the second component is designed to extract the maximum variance possible from what is left after the first has been extracted; the third is designed to extract the maximum variance possible from what is left after the first two have been extracted, and so forth. Two, the components are not correlated with each other.

Analogous to multiple regression analysis, components in a *PCA* may be conceived of as dependent variables whose values are obtained by differentially weighting the indicators, which are treated as the independent variables or as formative indicators (see Chapter 4). In contrast, in *FA*, the indicators are viewed as reflective of unobserved variables (i.e., the factors). In other words, the indicators are treated as dependent variables and the factors as the independent variables.

For both models, the off-diagonal elements of the matrix are the correlations among the indicators. The matrices differ with respect to the elements in the principal diagonal. In *PCA*, the principal diagonal consists of unities, that is, the variances of the indicators (recall that the variance of a standardized variable is 1.0).[3] In contrast, the principal diagonal of the matrix analyzed in *FA* consists of communality estimates, that is, estimates of the variance accounted for by the common factors (see below). Such a matrix is referred to as a reduced correlation matrix.

Thus, *FA* is aimed at explaining *common variance* (i.e., variance shared by the indicators, items, variables; see below), whereas *PCA* is designed to extract *total variance*. That is, in addition to common variance, principal components extract both variance that is unique to an indicator as well as error variance. This prompted Wolins (1982) to declare: "Its [*PCA*] erroneous use as a *FA* procedure implies that the variables analyzed are error free and no variable has specific variance" (p. 67). Even more emphatically, Cattell (1965) stated: "The trick of putting ones in the diagonals, though comforting in accounting fully for the variance of variables, perpetrates a hoax, for actually it really drags in all the specific and error variance . . . to inflate specious, incorrect common factors" (p. 201).

Two points that follow from the foregoing will be noted. One, unless the first few components extract a sizable percentage of the total variance, there is little to be gained from the application of a *PCA*. As a rule of thumb, one would want the first two or three

---

[3]As was noted earlier, our concern in this chapter is limited to analyses of correlation matrices.

components to extract over 50% of the variance. Two, it does not make sense to rotate components, nor to attach substantive meaning to them (rotation and interpretation of factors are discussed later on).

Look now at the first column of the output given above, labeled Communality, and note that it refers to the variables (indicators) and that it consists of fractions. Had this been a *PCA* (the default in SPSS), the Communality column would have consisted of 1's. We return to the concept of communality later.

Turning now to the output to the right of the asterisks, we remind you that it is from a *PCA*, regardless of the method of extraction specified. We, therefore, recommend that you substitute the label Component for that of Factor.

A thorough explanation of the meaning of an eigenvalue, denoted by λ (also referred to as characteristic root, latent root) without resorting to matrix theory is impossible. For our proposes, it will suffice to point out that an eigenvalue is equal to the sum of the squared loadings of the indicators (items, variables) on the component or the factor with which the eigenvalue is associated. Consistent with this meaning and with our description of the extraction of components, the λ's in the output given above are in descending order of magnitude.

Now, because the variance of each of the indicators is 1.0, the total variance is equal to k—the number of indicators. In our numerical example, therefore, the total variance is 6.0. Dividing an λ by k indicates the proportion of the total variance accounted for by the component with which the λ is associated. This is what is reported in the column labeled "Pct of Var." For the first λ, for example: $2.12243/6 = .35374$, or 35.4%.

Cumulative percentages of the total variance extracted by the components are reported in the column labeled "Cum Pct." For example, the first component extracts 35.4% and the second 32.2%. The "Cum Pct" is, therefore, within rounding, 67.5. Notice that, when the number of components extracted is equal to the number of the variables (6 in our example), "Cum Pct" is equal to 100.0. However, notice also that, after extracting the first two components, increments in proportion of variance extracted by remaining components are diminishingly small.

When the determinant of the correlation matrix is not 0 (see earlier discussion of this point), the number of nonzero λ's will be equal to the number of indicators. In line with what was said above about the aim of *PCA*, one would want λ's, from, say, the third or the fourth and beyond, to be relatively small.

CALCULATION OF |R|

When we said earlier that the determinant of a correlation matrix can be calculated by using output from virtually any computer program, we had in mind the λ's reported for a *PCA*. To obtain the determinant of the correlation matrix, calculate the product of all the λ's; that is,

$$\lambda_1\lambda_2 \ldots \lambda_k$$

For our numerical example,

$$(2.12243)(1.92911) \ldots (.34724) = .20784$$

Compare this result with the output given earlier.

COMMUNALITIES AND THEIR ESTIMATES

Communality is the squared multiple correlation of an indicator (item, variable), taken as the dependent variable, with the extracted factors treated as independent variables. Stated differently, it is the proportion of variance in the indicator that is accounted for by the extracted factors. Earlier, we said that the diagonal of the reduced correlation matrix that is subjected to *FA* consists of the communalities. We hope that you can see that this places the factor analyst in a bind—a sort of Catch–22. The communalities have to be inserted in the diagonal of the correlation matrix before it is factor analyzed. However, from the definition of communality, it is clear that it can be obtained only after the matrix has been factor analyzed and after the number of factors to be retained has been decided upon.

The way around the problem is to use estimates of the communalities. The literature of factor analysis is replete with presentations and discussions of the "best" communality estimate. With the advent of computer programs, the issue of what is the best communality estimate has become less critical, as most programs perform iterations designed to improve upon the initial estimates. The most widely used initial communality estimate is the squared multiple correlation (SMC) of each indicator treated as the dependent variable with the remaining indicators treated as the independent variables. SPSS uses SMC's as the default communality estimates and reports them in the Initial Statistics section given in the preceding section. Thus, for example, the communality for $Y1$, .42842, is the SMC of $Y1$ with the remaining five indicators treated as the independent variables. As is shown below, these initial estimates are changed as a result of iterations.

Output

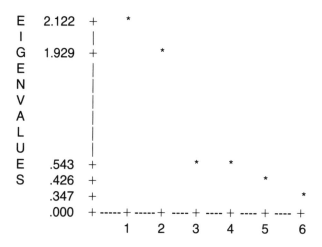

```
E   2.122  +      *
I          |
G   1.929  +          *
E          |
N          |
V          |
A          |
L          |
U          |
E   .543   +              *      *
S   .426   +                        *
    .347   +                              *
    .000   + ----- + ----- + ---- + ---- + ---- + ---- +
               1     2      3      4      5      6
```

Commentary

This plot of the λ's in descending order of magnitude—referred to as a scree plot (see below)—is obtained by specifying PLOT=EIGEN (see Input). Cattell (1966b) proposed it as an aid in determining the number of factors to be retained. He suggested that the plot of the λ's be examined to identify a clear break, akin to an elbow, between large λ's and small ones—the latter appearing to lie on a horizontal line. Considering factors with small λ's as trivial, or "rubbish," Cattell labeled this criterion for the number of factors to be retained as the *scree* test, after the geological term that refers to rubble at the foot of a steep slope. It should be noted that it is the λ's of the *PCA* that are used in the above scree plot.

In the above plot, there is a marked break after the first two λ's. Using the scree criterion, the conclusion would be to retain the first two factors. Incidentally, for the present example, the same conclusion would be reached using the criterion of eigenvalue larger than unity (see above). Later in this chapter, we return to the question of the number of factors to be retained.

Output

PAF Extracted 2 factors. 11 Iterations required.

Factor Matrix: Rotated Factor Matrix:

	FACTOR 1	FACTOR 2		FACTOR 1	FACTOR 2
Y1	.75124	−.04834	Y1	.75278	−.00526
Y2	.67114	−.02246	Y2	.67133	.01599
Y3	.82022	−.04990	Y3	.82173	−.00287
X1	.08708	.75555	X1	.04370	.75929
X2	.03195	.58223	X2	−.00142	.58310
X3	.01118	.70855	X3	−.02939	.70803

Final Statistics:

Variable	Communality	*	Factor	Eigenvalue	Pct of Var	Cum Pct
Y1	.56670	*	1	1.69629	28.3	28.3
Y2	.45094	*	2	1.41722	23.6	51.9
Y3	.67526	*				
X1	.57844	*				
X2	.34001	*				
X3	.50217	*				

Commentary

The first line in this excerpt of output indicates that two factors were extracted by the PAF method and that 11 iterations were required. Earlier, it was pointed out that, by default, SPSS uses the SMC as initial estimates of the communalities. The program then goes through a series of reestimations of the communalities, which is terminated either when the default number of iterations (25) has been reached or when the estimates converge on a default criterion (.001). Both default values can be changed on the CRITERIA subcommand. The communalities reported under the heading Final Statistics are the ones estimated after the 11 iterations (they are discussed below). Compare them with the initial estimates given earlier.

Factor Matrices

The columns to the left of the vertical line constitute the unrotated factor matrix. The rotated factor matrix (to the right of the vertical line) is reported later in the output. We moved it here for comparison purposes (see below). Furthermore, we inserted the boxes to highlight "high" loadings (see below). For this output, we concentrate on the unrotated factor matrix, after which we comment briefly on the rotated matrix.

Probably the best way to approach the meaning of the coefficients reported in an unrotated matrix is to view each of its rows as an equation, analogous to a multiple regression equation, in which the indicator, expressed in standard scores, is the dependent variable, and the factors (two in our example) are the independent variables. For example, the equation to predict $Y1$ is

$$z'_{Y1} = .75124F_1 - .04834F_2$$

Notice the analogy with the regression equation with standardized regression coefficients (β's) presented in Chapter 18. As was shown in Chapter 18—see (18.6) and the discussion related to it—when the independent variables are not correlated, each β is equal to the zero-order correlation between the independent variable with which it is associated and the dependent variable. Under such circumstances, squaring a β is tantamount to squaring a zero-order correlation, thereby obtaining the proportion of variance of the dependent variable that is accounted by the independent variable in question.[4]

The method of extracting the unrotated factors in PAF is the same as that described above in connection with the extraction of principal components except that it is carried out on the reduced correlation matrix (i.e., the matrix with estimated communalities in the diagonal). Consequently, unrotated factors are not correlated, and the coefficients associated with them can be interpreted in the same manner as that of the β's in the preceding paragraph. Specifically, the square of a coefficient in the factor matrix indicates the proportion of variance of a given indicator that is accounted for by the factor in question. Using $Y1$ again as an example, it can be seen that about .56 ($.75124^2$), or about 56%, of its variance, is accounted for by Factor 1, whereas .002 ($-.04834^2$), or about .2%, of its variance is accounted for by Factor 2.

The matrix we have been discussing is a *factor pattern matrix*, consisting of the coefficients (weights) for the regression of each indicator on the factors. A matrix consisting of correlations between indicators and factors is referred to as a *factor structure matrix*. From what was said in the preceding paragraphs regarding the properties of the factor pattern when the factors are uncorrelated, it follows that, under such circumstances, the factor pattern and the factor structure matrices are identical. In other words, the above Factor Matrix is the factor pattern matrix and is also the factor structure matrix.

The fact that the vast majority of applications of *FA* are limited to uncorrelated factors has probably contributed to a lack of a clear distinction between the properties of the aforementioned matrices and the lack of uniformity regarding the terms used to refer to the elements of each. Some authors use the term loadings (i.e., weights) to refer to elements of the factor pattern matrix and the term correlations to refer to elements of the factor structure matrix. Other authors use the term loadings to refer to elements of the factor structure matrix (i.e., correlations).

In the case of uncorrelated factors the loadings and the correlations are the same; thus, there seems to be no harm in doing this. However, as is shown below, the elements of the pattern and structure matrices are *not* the same when the factors are correlated. We follow the practice of using the term loadings to refer to elements of the factor pattern matrix and the term correlations to elements of the factor structure matrix.

When, as in the present example, factors are not correlated, there is no ambiguity with respect to the proportion of variance of the indicators that is attributed to each of them. In our artificial example, it is easy to see that, for the first three indicators (the Y's), the bulk of the variance accounted for is due to Factor 1, whereas the converse is true for the X's. In other

---

[4]If necessary, refer to the sections dealing with the meaning and interpretation of standardized regression coefficients (β's) in Chapters 17 and 18.

words, the Y's have high loadings on Factor 1 only, whereas the X's have high loadings on Factor 2 only.

Generally speaking, results of a *FA* are not as neat as in the present example. In most analyses of real data, all items tend to have high loadings on the first unrotated factor (see analysis of the next numerical example). Further, many of the items have relatively high loadings on additional unrotated factors. In an attempt to render results more interpretable, factors may be rotated. Rotation of factors is discussed in the context of the next numerical example. For completeness of presentation, we included the rotated factor matrix above. All we would like to do here is to point out that, in the present example, the rotated matrix is very similar to the unrotated one.

In the preceding paragraphs, reference was made to high loadings. Obviously, the criterion of what is a high loading is arbitrary. Many researchers prefer to speak of meaningful, instead of high, loadings. Further, because, in most instances, researchers report and interpret loadings for uncorrelated factors, they tend to use a cutoff of .3 (accounting for 9% of the variance) or .4 (accounting for 16% of the variance) for what they consider meaningful loadings.[5] Whatever the specific criterion, it is the high, or meaningful, loadings that play a crucial role in the interpretation and the naming of factors. These issues are discussed later on.

EIGENVALUES

Earlier, it was stated that an λ (eigenvalue) is equal to the sum of the squared loadings of the indicators on the factor with which the λ is associated. Referring to the loadings on Factor 1, given above,

$$\lambda_1 = (.75124)^2 + (.67114)^2 + \ldots + (.01118)^2 = 1.69628$$

Compare this with the first eigenvalue reported under Final Statistics. We suggest that you calculate the sum of the squared loadings for Factor 2 and compare with the second λ.

Note that the two λ's reported here are different from the first two reported earlier under Initial Statistics. The earlier λ's are from *PCA*, whereas the ones reported here are from *FA*.

The "Pct of Var" refers to the percent of the total variance attributed to a given factor and is calculated as shown earlier (i.e., λ/k).

COMMUNALITY AND UNIQUENESS

In line with what was said in Chapter 18, when the independent variables are not correlated, the squared multiple correlation is equal to the sum of the squared zero-order correlations of the independent variables with the dependent variable. Accordingly, the squared multiple correlation of $Y1$ with the two factors is .56670 [i.e., $(.75124)^2 + (-.04834)^2$]. Denoted as h^2, this, as was stated earlier, is the definition of the communality of an indicator. Look now at the communality column and note that the same value is reported for $Y1$.

Recalling that the variance of a standardized variable is 1.0, it follows that the proportion of variance of an indicator that is unique to it can be expressed as follows:

$$u^2 = 1.0 - h^2 \qquad (22.2)$$

---

[5]As was noted above, when the factors are not correlated, the loadings also equal the correlations of indicators with the factors.

where u^2 = uniqueness.

The u^2 of Y_1, for example, is

$$1.0 - .56670 = .43330$$

The uniqueness of an indicator is composed of two components: (a) variance specific to it (s^2), and (b) variance due to random errors (e^2). That is,

$$u^2 = s^2 + e^2 \qquad (22.3)$$

It follows that the variance of an indicator can be expressed as

$$1.0 = h^2 + s^2 + e^2 \qquad (22.4)$$

Results of *FA* do not afford the partitioning of u^2 into its components. Yet (22.4) provides an important link between *FA* and reliability theory. In Chapter 5, reliability (r_{tt}) was defined as 1.0 minus the proportion of variance due to random errors. From (22.4), it follows thus:

$$r_{tt} = 1.0 - e^2 = h^2 + s^2 \qquad (22.5)$$

In words, the reliability of an indicator is equal to its communality (the proportion of variance of the indicator accounted for by the common factors) plus its specificity (the proportion of variance accounted for by a factor specific to it). Accordingly, having a good estimate of r_{tt}, the specificity of an indicator may be estimated as follows:

$$s^2 = r_{tt} - h^2 \qquad (22.6)$$

We return to these issues in Chapter 23, in the context of confirmatory factor analysis.

Output

Reproduced Correlation Matrix:

	Y1	Y2	Y3	X1	X2	X3
Y1	.56670*	−.00328	.00340	−.02090	.03114	−.00315
Y2	.50528	.45094*	−.00061	.03053	.02163	−.05059
Y3	.61860	.55161	.67526*	−.00573	−.04616	.04419
X1	.02890	.04147	.03373	.57844*	−.00068	.00068
X2	−.00414	.00837	−.00284	.44268	.34001*	.00011
X3	−.02585	−.00841	−.02619	.53632	.41289	.50217*

The lower left triangle contains the reproduced correlation matrix; The diagonal, communalities; and the upper right triangle, residuals between the observed correlations and the reproduced correlations.

There are 1 (6.0%) residuals (above diagonal) that are > 0.05

Commentary

Earlier, we said that *FA* is aimed at explaining relations (e.g., correlations) among indicators. Consequently, a factor analytic solution may be assessed by how closely the original correlation matrix can be reproduced. As indicated in the explanation given in the SPSS output above, three different pieces of information are reported in a matrix format: (a) The diagonal consists of the communalities (compare with output given earlier); (b) below the diagonal are the reproduced correlations; and (c) above the diagonal are the residuals, or the deviations of the original correlations from the reproduced ones.

Figure 22.1 is used to demonstrate how the reproduced correlations are obtained. The

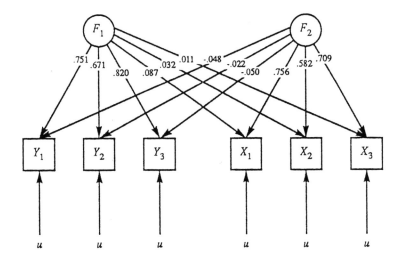

Figure 22.1

coefficients inserted on the arrows, rounded to three decimal places, were taken from the Factor Matrix given earlier. They are the effects of the two common factors (latent variables) on the indicators (observed variables). Each indicator is shown to be affected, in addition, by a unique term (u), which is composed of indicator specificity (s) and/or measurement errors (e).

Notice that the u's are shown to be not correlated among themselves nor with the factors (there are no arrows connecting them). From the model depicted in Figure 22.1, it can be seen that the correlation between any two indicators is viewed as being due to causes (i.e., factors) common to them. It is this notion that is used in the attempt to reproduce the correlations among the indicators. For the correlation between Y_1 and Y_2:

$$\hat{r}_{y1y2} = (.75124)(.67114) + (-.04834)(-.02246)$$
$$= \quad (.50419) \quad + \quad (.00109) \quad = .50528$$

where $\hat{r}$ refers to a reproduced correlation. Compare with the output given above (see intersection of row Y2 and column Y1).

To reproduce the correlation between two indicators, multiply their coefficients on the respective factors and sum the products. In exploratory *FA*, indicators have coefficients on all factors. However, as can be seen from the above example, factors differ in their contribution to the reproduction of the correlation between two given indicators. Thus, although Y_1 and Y_2 have coefficients on both factors, it is their relatively high coefficients on F_1 that matter. Stated differently, Y_1 and Y_2 are correlated, because they reflect the same factor (or unobserved variable). The same is true for all pairwise correlations among the Y's. Similarly, correlations among the X's are primarily due to their relatively high coefficients on F_2.

What about the correlation between any of the X's with any of the Y's? Clearly, it would be expected to be low, because they are shown to be caused primarily by (or to reflect) different factors. That is, they do not have high coefficients on the same factor. Thus, for the correlation between Y_1 and X_3,

$$\hat{r}_{y1x3} = (.75124)(.01118) + (-.04834)(.70855)$$
$$= \quad (.00840) \quad + \quad (-.03425) \quad = -.02585$$

To assess the fit of the model, residual correlations are obtained by subtracting the reproduced correlations from their respective observed correlations, much as residual scores are obtained by subtracting predicted scores from observed ones. For example, the reproduced correlation between Y_1 and Y_2 was shown to be .50528. The observed correlation between these variables is .502 (see Table 21.1). The residual is, therefore,

$$.502 - .50528 = -.00328$$

the value reported in the output given above, at the intersection of row Y1 and column Y2.

Now, a good fit of the model is indicated when all the residuals are very small, say, less than .05. By default, SPSS uses this criterion and reports the number and percent of residuals that exceed it. As indicated in the output given above, only one residual is $> .05$. On the basis of these results, one would be inclined to conclude that the model fits the data well. Assessment of model fit is not as simple and straightforward. We return to this topic in the context of confirmatory factor analysis.

Instead of using the Factor Matrix, the Rotated Factor Matrix may be used to obtain identical reproduced correlations. This is so *not* because the two matrices happen to be very similar in the present example. As is shown and explained in connection with the second numerical example, the same holds true even when there are considerable differences between the two matrices.

As indicated earlier, we give input statements for analyzing the same numerical example through SAS. However, because of space considerations, we do not comment on the input. For general comments on SAS, see Chapter 16. For comments on SAS matrix input, see Chapter 18. As was suggested earlier, if you run SAS, consult the manual. Compare your output with that we have reported.

SAS

Input

```
TITLE 'TABLE 22.1   PRINCIPAL AXES, ORTHOGONAL';
DATA CORREL (TYPE=CORR);
  INPUT _TYPE_ $ 1–4 _NAME_ $ 5–7 Y1 Y2 Y3 X1 X2 X3;
  CARDS;
N               200     200     200     200     200     200
CORR Y1    1.000    .502    .622    .008    .027  -.029
CORR Y2     .502   1.000    .551    .072    .030  -.059
CORR Y3     .622    .551   1.000    .028  -.049   .018
CORR X1     .008    .072    .028   1.000    .442   .537
CORR X2     .027    .030  -.049    .442   1.000   .413
CORR X3    -.029   -.059    .018    .537    .413  1.000
PROC FACTOR METHOD=PRINIT PRIORS=SMC N=2 ALL SCREE PLOT ROTATE=V;
```

CONCLUDING REMARKS

For the example analyzed in this section, it is clear that indicators presumed to tap a given dimension of self-concept (i.e., Academic or Social) have relatively high loadings on the same factor and relatively low loadings on the other, thereby lending a certain degree of support to their construct validity. It is, however, also clear that, had these results been based on real data, the researcher would have had to conclude that, contrary to the hypothesis (see

CORRELATED FACTORS **607**

introductory remarks to the numerical example), the two dimensions are relatively independent of each other.

In our discussion of the use of *FA* for construct validation (Chapter 4), we outlined alternative courses of action that may be taken when results go counter to one's expectations. In addition, we pointed out that *FA* is an example of internal structure analysis and that what is needed, also, for construct validation is an external structure analysis.

We turn now to the second numerical example.

CORRELATED FACTORS

Basic ideas and concepts of *FA* were introduced in the preceding section. Because we constructed a simple numerical example in which correlations among indicators of two aspects of self-concept (Academic and Social) were close to zero, the factor structure underlying the correlation matrix was transparent even by inspection. Recall that the unrotated factor matrix was clearly interpretable.

For the present numerical example, we again assume that six indicators presumed to tap two aspects of self-concept (Academic and Social) are used. The correlation matrix to be analyzed—reported in Table 22.2—was obtained by modifying the matrix of Table 22.1 so that correlations among indicators presumed to tap different aspects of self-concept are now moderate. Correlations among indicators presumed to tap the same aspect of self-concept were not altered. Thus, submatrices I and IV of the two tables are identical, whereas submatrices II and III differ. A glance at the correlation matrix of Table 22.2 should suffice to recognize that the situation is not as clear cut as the one dealt with in the preceding section.

SPSS

Input

```
SET LISTING='T222SPS.LIS'.
TITLE TABLE 22.2.   ORTHOGONAL AND OBLIQUE ROTATIONS.
DATA LIST MATRIX FREE/Y1 Y2 Y3 X1 X2 X3.
N 200.
BEGIN DATA.
1.0
.502 1.0
.622 .551 1.0
.228 .272 .188 1.0
```

Table 22.2
Illustrative Correlation Matrix for Six Indicators of Self-Concept. N = 200.

	Y1	Y2	Y3	X1	X2	X3
	I			II		
Y1	1.000	.502	.622	.228	.307	.198
Y2	.502	1.000	.551	.272	.230	.259
Y3	.622	.551	1.000	.188	.249	.223
X1	.228	.272	.188	1.000	.442	.537
X2	.307	.230	.249	.442	1.000	.413
X3	.198	.259	.223	.537	.413	1.000
	III			IV		

Note. Y's are indicators of Academic Self-Concept; X's are indicators of Social Self-Concept.

```
.307 .230 .249 .442 1.0
.198 .259 .223 .537 .413 1.0
END DATA.
FACTOR VARIABLES=Y1 TO X3/
   READ CORRELATION TRIANGLE/
   PRINT ALL/CRITERIA=FACTORS(2)/EXTRACTION=PAF/
   ROTATION=NOROTATE/PLOT=EIGEN ROTATION(1,2)/
   ROTATION=VARIMAX/ROTATION=OBLIMIN.
```

Commentary

The input given here is for the PC version. To run this example on the mainframe, see the previous analysis. *Our comments in the present section are, by and large, limited to aspects not discussed earlier. When in doubt about an aspect of input and/or output, refer to the comments on the analysis of the previous numerical example.*

We call first for ROTATION=NOROTATE in order to show the plot of the unrotated factor matrix, which is then contrasted with plots of rotated factor matrices. Two types of rotations (explained below) are then called for.

Output

Determinant of Correlation Matrix = .1838493
Bartlett Test of Sphericity = 332.23555, Significance = .00000

Commentary

On the basis of Bartlett's Test of Sphericity, the hypothesis that the input correlation matrix does not differ significantly from an identity matrix is rejected.

Output

Initial Statistics:

Variable	Communality	*	Factor	Eigenvalue	Pct of Var	Cum Pct
Y1	.44353	*	1	2.74665	45.8	45.8
Y2	.36927	*	2	1.31073	21.8	67.6
Y3	.46762	*	3	.64121	10.7	78.3
X1	.36014	*	4	.48246	8.0	86.4
X2	.27724	*	5	.46042	7.7	94.0
X3	.33908	*	6	.35854	6.0	100.0

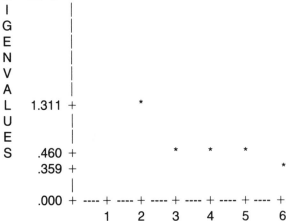

Commentary

The scree plot confirms our expectation that two factors underlie the correlation matrix of Table 22.2. Unlike the previous example, there is a sharp drop from the first λ (eigenvalue) to the second one; the former being about twice as large as the latter. *We remind you that these λ's are from a principal components analysis.* Some researchers may, on the basis of these results, conclude that the first "factor" is more important than the second one. We comment on this issue below.

Output

PAF Extracted   2 factors.   13 Iterations required.

Factor Matrix:

	FACTOR 1	FACTOR 2
Y1	.68041	−.33688
Y2	.62902	−.22569
Y3	.70963	−.42783
X1	.58283	.49822
X2	.52569	.27218
X3	.55192	.43724

Final Statistics:

Variable	Communality	*	Factor	Eigenvalue	Pct of Var	Cum Pct
Y1	.57644	*	1	2.28285	38.0	38.0
Y2	.44660	*	2	.86095	14.3	52.4
Y3	.68662	*				
X1	.58791	*				
X2	.35043	*				
X3	.49580	*				

Commentary

Recall that the sum of the squared loadings on a given factor is equal to the λ associated with it. Note that: (a) The difference between the λ's of the first two factors is even greater than that between the λ's associated with the first two components; (b) all the indicators have relatively high loadings on the first factor; and (c) on the second factor, indicators of Academic Self-Concept (*Y*'s) have negative loadings, whereas indicators of Social Self-Concept (*X*'s) have positive loadings.

Researchers interpreting these results would be inclined to arrive at the following conclusions. One, the first is a "strong" general factor (i.e., a factor that is reflected by all the indicators). Two, the second is a "weaker" bipolar factor, that is, a factor on which indicators have loadings at opposite ends of the continuum. Referring to our substantive example, one would be inclined to conclude that, contrary to expectations, there is a general self-concept factor and a second factor on which indicators of Academic Self-Concept and Social Self-Concept are at opposite ends.

Before accepting these conclusions, however, it is important to recognize that the factor matrix on which they are based is largely a consequence of the method of factor extraction (i.e., the first factor extracts the maximum variance possible; the second extracts the maximum variance of what is left; and so forth—see preceding section). In fact, results such as those obtained here are fairly typical for unrotated factor matrices. To clarify how they come about, we report and comment upon the plot of the unrotated factor matrix.

Output

Horizontal Factor 1   Vertical Factor 2

Symbol	Variable	Coordinates	
1	Y1	.680	−.337
2	Y2	.629	−.226
3	Y3	.710	−.428
4	X1	.583	.498
5	X2	.526	.272
6	X3	.552	.437

```
                                    |
                                    |
                                    |
                                    |
                                    |                    4
                                    |
                                    |                    6
                                    |
                                    |
                                    |                  5
                                    |
                                    |
                                    |
                                    |
--------------------------------------------------------------------------------
                                    |
                                    |
                                    |
                                    |
                                    |                 2
                                    |
                                    |                    1
                                    |
                                    |                    3
                                    |
                                    |
                                    |
                                    |
                                    |
```

Commentary

Examine the horizontal axis, Factor 1, and note that its placement is best in the sense of simultaneously maximizing the loadings of the indicators on it. Placing the axis in a different position may result in an increase in the loadings of some of the indicators but also in a decrease in the loadings of others. For example, it is possible to increase the loadings for indicators 1, 2 and 3 (the Y's) by placing the first axis closer to them, but this will also result in a reduction of the loadings for indicators 4, 5, and 6 (the X's).

Recall that one of the restrictions concerning the extraction of factors is that they be *not* correlated with each other. To satisfy this restriction, axes representing the different factors have to be placed at right angles to each other. Examine the placement of the vertical axis, Factor 2. Because of the configuration of the numbers representing the indicators, they are necessarily polarized on it: half the indicators having positive and the other half having negative loadings. Results such as these, which are due to the method of factor extraction, have led to proposals that the factors be rotated.

Rotation of Factors

An examination of the reproduced correlation matrix (not reported here) reveals that all the residuals are very small, indicating that two factors provide a good fit for the data. However, a good fitting solution is not necessarily susceptible to a meaningful interpretation. It is in attempts to improve interpretability of results that factors are rotated.

Factor rotations can probably be best understood when considered in connection with the plot of the two unrotated factors given above. The two axes serve as a grid on which the indicators are mapped. Visualize a rotation of the grid about the origin. Clearly, the configuration of the points representing the indicators will remain the same, regardless of the nature of the rotation. The mapping of the indicators on the rotated grid (i.e., the loadings) will, however, change. This is the idea behind rotation of factors. Although more appropriately referred to as transformations than rotations of factors, the latter terminology has taken hold as a result of the practice of graphic rotations that preceded current analytic approaches.

Because there is an infinite number of ways in which factors can be transformed or rotated, the question arises: Are some rotations better than others? Criteria for determining what are better rotations are not always clear or agreed upon. The reason is that rotations are resorted to for the purpose of improving interpretability of factor-analytic results, and interpretability is, by its very nature, inextricably intertwined with theory. What might be viewed as a meaningful rotation from one theoretical perspective may be considered not meaningful, even utterly inappropriate, from another.

To illustrate this, it would suffice to sketch how different conceptions of mental ability would probably lead to different ideas regarding the appropriateness of factor transformations. Recall that, in many, if not most, instances, the first factor in the unrotated factor matrix appears to be a general factor. It should, therefore, come as no surprise when researchers who conceive of mental ability as a general ability reject the notion of factor rotations. It should be equally not surprising when researchers who conceive of mental ability as a set of differentiated abilities insist that, to be interpretable, factors must be rotated. However, even such researchers may disagree strongly about the type of rotation they deem appropriate (e.g., orthogonal versus oblique; see below), depending, among other things, on their conceptions regarding relations among the various aspects of mental ability.[6] We return to these issues later on. For now, it will be pointed out that application of *FA* is conceived of as a blend of science and art.

Differences in orientations regarding the type of factor rotations aside, there remains a need for criteria for assessing rotated solutions. It was Thurstone's (1947) concept of simple structure that has had the greatest impact on the development of various rotational approaches aimed at improving interpretability. Much has been written about simple structure (see references given in the beginning of this chapter). Without going into the details of the various criteria, we will show how the ideal simple structure would look like in the context of our numerical example. Recalling that our example is concerned with the use of six indicators, three of which are presumed to measure Academic Self-Concept and three Social Self-Concept, the ideal simple structure resulting from a *FA* would look as follows:

	F_1	F_2
Indicator		
Y_1	*	0
Y_2	*	0
Y_3	*	0
X_1	0	*
X_2	0	*
X_3	0	*

where F_1 and F_2 refer to two factors; the Y's refer to indicators of Academic Self-Concept, and the X's to Social Self-Concept; an asterisk means that the indicator has a loading on the factor, whereas a 0 means that the indicator has no loading on the factor.

Being an ideal, this type of simple structure is one aspired to, rather than achieved, in actual applications. Rotation of factors is aimed at obtaining a structure that, broadly speaking, is characterized by: (a) each indicator having a high, or meaningful, loading on one factor only, and (b) each factor having high, or meaningful, loadings for only some of the indicators.[7] There are two broad classes of factor rotations: Orthogonal and Oblique. We begin with the former.

ORTHOGONAL ROTATIONS

The idea of orthogonality was introduced in Chapter 19 (see Orthogonal Comparisons), where it was pointed out that orthogonal means at right angles and that variables or vectors that are orthogonal are not correlated. To rotate factors orthogonally, means to rotate them so that they remain at right angles to each other. Referring to the plot of the unrotated factors given earlier, this means a rigid rotation of the axes about their origin.

Of various orthogonal rotations, we illustrate the application of Varimax, which is by far

---

[6]Our choice of illustration was by no means accidental. As we noted in Chapter 4, the impetus for the development of *FA* came from attempts to study the structure of mental ability. Much of the developments and controversies regarding methods of factor extractions and rotations emanate from different conceptions of mental ability by innovators such as Spearman, Thurstone, Cattell, and Guilford.

[7]See earlier comments on high and meaningful loadings.

the most widely used. Varimax is aimed at maximizing variances of the factors (see Gorsuch, 1983, for an excellent discussion of and comparisons among various rotational approaches). This is accomplished by a transformation resulting in high loadings for some of the indicators on any given factor and low loadings for all the others. Note, however, that "maximizing the varimax function means that any tendency toward a general factor in the solution is minimized. **Varimax is inappropriate if the theoretical expectation suggests a general factor may occur**" (Gorsuch, 1983, p. 185). Parenthetically, Quartimax—another rotational approach—"is probably the orthogonal rotation procedure of choice when a general factor is expected" (Stewart, 1981, p. 59).

Here, then, is an example of the relation between theory and the type of rotation. It also underscores our earlier admonition not to rely on computer program defaults (Varimax is the default in many programs, including SPSS) but to make choices consistent with one's theoretical formulation.

Output

Rotated Factor Matrix:

	FACTOR 1	FACTOR 2	Communality
Y1	.73794	.17857	.57644
Y2	.62715	.23083	.44660
Y3	.81874	.12761	.68662
X1	.12696	.75617	.58791
X2	.22828	.54619	.35044
X3	.14241	.68958	.49580
λ:	1.69672	1.44709	3.14381

Commentary

Only the Rotated Factor Matrix (without the boxes) is part of the output. We added the other terms that will be used to clarify the results obtained from the rotation.

Examine first the loadings and notice that, in contrast to the unrotated Factor Matrix (see above), there does not appear to be a general factor. Instead, only the Y's have relatively high loadings on Factor 1, and only the X's have relatively high loadings on Factor 2. Further, unlike the unrotated factor solution, the second factor is not bipolar (i.e., positive and negative loadings). Thus, the rotation resulted in a simpler structure than that of the unrotated Factor Matrix.

Look now at the last row. Recall that λ is equal to the sum of the squared loadings on a factor. Now, the sum of the two λ's is 3.14381. However, this is also, within rounding, the sum of the two λ's obtained earlier, that is, before the rotation (i.e., 2.28285 + .86095). What was accomplished by the rotation is a more even distribution of the λ's. In other words, the "Pct of Var" attributed to each of the factors is more evenly distributed as a result of the rotation.

This can also be seen from the communalities. The communality of an indicator (h^2) is the sum of its squared loadings on the factors (e.g., for $Y1$: $.73794^2 + .17857^2 = .57644$). The communalities calculated here are the same as those reported earlier. Thus, although the loadings change as a result of the rotation of factors, the proportion of variance the factors account for in each indicator (i.e., h^2) is unchanged. We reiterate: The rotation distributed the same variance more evenly between the two factors.

Referring to our substantive example, the Rotated Factor Matrix is consistent with the conception of two aspects of self-concept. Regardless of the researcher's conception about the relation between the two aspects (recall that, in our example, we assumed that the researcher expected them to be correlated), the orthogonal rotation forces them to be *not* correlated.

Output

```
Horizontal Factor 1     Vertical Factor 2
                        |
                        |
                        |
                        |
                        |
                        |
                        |         4
                        |
                        |         6
                        |
                        |         5
                        |
                        |
                        |
                        |
                        |
                        |
                        |
                        |                              2
                        |                                      1
                        |                                           3
                        |
                        |
--------------------------------------------------------------------------------
                        |
                        |
                        |
                        |
                        |
                        |         Symbol  Variable   Coordinates
                        |
                        |            1      Y1       .738    .179
                        |            2      Y2       .627    .231
                        |            3      Y3       .819    .128
                        |            4      X1       .127    .756
                        |            5      X2       .228    .546
                        |            6      X3       .142    .690
                        |
                        |
                        |
                        |
```

Commentary

A contrast between this plot and the one for the Unrotated Factor Matrix, given earlier, should help you see what has been accomplished by the rotation of the axes. Also, examine the configuration of the indicators in the present plot and try to visualize an even simpler structure that may be obtained by placing one axis in the center of the indicators represented by 1, 2, and 3, and another axis in the center of the indicators represented by 4, 5, and 6. Doing this, however, will result in the angle between the axes being oblique, not a right angle as required in orthogonal rotations.

OBLIQUE ROTATIONS

Orthogonal rotation of factors is employed, almost automatically, in the vast majority of applications of *FA*. Cattell (1978) maintained that, although some may do so because of "cheapness and convenience . . . , in half of these cases it is evidently done in ignorance of the issue rather than by deliberate intent" (p. 128). Thurstone (1947) attributed the widespread preference for uncorrelated factors to "statistical and mathematical convenience" and also to "our ignorance of the nature of the underlying structure of mental traits" (p. 139). He went on to say: "The reason for using uncorrelated reference traits can be understood, but it cannot be justified" (p. 139).

There is no denying that orthogonally rotated solutions have the advantage of simplicity. Along with the aforementioned authors and others, however, we believe that such solutions are, in most instances, naive, unrealistic, portrayals of sociobehavioral phenomena. We hasten to admit that what is viewed as naive or unrealistic is largely predicated on one's theoretical conceptions about the phenomena being studied.

Different postures regarding the "appropriate" method for rotating factors cannot be resolved by an appeal to some objective criterion of "correctness," as they reflect different frames of reference in viewing phenomena. A notable case in point is that historically "most of the British factorists and a few of the American factorists insisted on orthogonal rotations" (Spearritt, 1985, p. 1814). This division along, almost exclusively, national lines is not surprising in light of different conceptions in the two cultures regarding structure of mental ability, roles of heredity and environment in mental functioning, class structure, to name but some of the major issues.

From the perspective of construct validation, the decision whether to rotate factors orthogonally or obliquely reflects one's conception regarding the structure of the construct under consideration. It boils down to the question: Are aspects of a postulated multidimensional construct intercorrelated? The answer to this question is relegated to the status of an assumption when an orthogonal rotation is employed. This is grounds enough to question the wisdom of limiting oneself to orthogonal rotations, even when theoretical formulations lead one to expect factors to be not correlated. The preferred course of action is, in our opinion, to rotate both orthogonally and obliquely. When, on the basis of the latter, it is concluded that the correlations among the factors are negligible, the interpretation of the simpler orthogonal solution becomes tenable.

Our recommendation is by no means as simple as it may sound. The reason is that magnitudes of correlations among factors are affected by the method of oblique rotation and by criteria used within a given method.

Output

Oblimin   Rotation

Pattern Matrix:				Structure Matrix:		
	FACTOR 1	FACTOR 2			FACTOR 1	FACTOR 2
Y1	.75699	.00500		Y1	.75922	.34297
Y2	.62309	.09025		Y2	.66338	.36844
Y3	.85794	−.07115		Y3	.82617	.31189
X1	−.05561	.78997		X1	.29709	.76514
X2	.10840	.53557		X2	.34752	.58397
X3	−.02174	.71357		X3	.29685	.70386

Factor Correlation Matrix:

	FACTOR 1	FACTOR 2
FACTOR 1	1.00000	
FACTOR 2	.44647	1.00000

Commentary

Of various oblique rotation procedures, SPSS provides for Direct Oblimin, which is aimed at simplifying the Factor Pattern Matrix, while allowing for correlations among the factors. Magnitudes of correlations among factors are affected by the choice of a parameter δ (delta), whose default value is zero. Positive values of δ tend to increase correlations among factors, whereas negative values tend to decrease them. We return to this issue later on. For the present analysis, we used the default (see ROTATION=OBLIMIN in the Input given earlier).

For comparative purposes, we placed the Pattern and Structure matrices side by side. Their properties were explained earlier. To reiterate: The Pattern Matrix consists of loadings analogous to partial standardized regression coefficients (β's) in a multiple regression analysis (see Chapter 18), whereas the Structure Matrix consists of zero-order correlations between each indicator and the factors. When factors are not correlated (i.e., when orthogonal rotations are performed), the two matrices are identical. When factors are correlated as a result of oblique rotations, the two matrices differ.

Recall that, in the present context, each indicator is treated as a dependent variable, and the factors are treated as independent variables. Consistent with the interpretation of β's, each coefficient in the Pattern Matrix indicates the effect of a given factor on a given indicator, while partialing out or controlling for the other factor(s). For example, .75699 indicates the effect of Factor 1 on Y1, while controlling for Factor 2. Inspection of the Pattern Matrix reveals a clear distinction between the Y and X indicators, with the former affected primarily by Factor 1 and the latter affected primarily by Factor 2. The correlation between the factors is .45.

Taken together, these results lend support to the conception that the six indicators tap two correlated aspects of a construct (i.e., Academic and Social Self-Concept in the present example).

Obviously, these results are also consistent with other theoretical conceptions (e.g., that the indicators reflect other aspects of self-concept, two aspects of another construct, two correlated constructs). The choice among alternative explanations is in the realm of theoretical considerations, not as a result of data in search of a theory. We return to this issue later on, under Interpretation and Naming of Factors.

Examine now the Structure Matrix. The elements in this matrix are zero-order correlations of each indicator with each factor; thus, their interpretation is ambiguous when the factors are correlated. Depending on the correlation between the factors, the Pattern and Structure matrices may be radically different from each other. Recalling the properties of multiple regression with correlated independent variables (see Chapter 18), the following will be noted: (a) Whereas the elements in the Structure Matrix cannot exceed 1.0, this is not true for the elements of the Pattern Matrix; and (b) coefficients referring to the same indicator in the two matrices may be of opposite signs.

COMMUNALITIES

Earlier, the communality of an indicator was defined as its square multiple correlation with the factors. Recalling that the elements of the Pattern Matrix are analogous to β's and those of the Structure Matrix to r's, it is instructive to illustrate the calculation of communalities using a formula involving these terms. For convenience, we repeat (18.7):

$$R^2_{y.12} = \beta_1 r_{y1} + \beta_2 r_{y2} \tag{22.7}$$

For illustrative purposes, we apply (22.7) to the calculation of the communality for $Y1$. Using the coefficients reported above in the Pattern and Structure matrices:

$$h^2_{y1} = (.75699)(.75922) + (.00500)(.34297) = .57644$$

Compare with the communality for this indicator reported earlier (e.g., under Final Statistics).

Whether or not the factors are rotated and regardless of the type of rotation, the communalities are the same. Attempts to attribute portions of a communality to different factors are not unlike attempts to partition the variance in multiple regression (see Chapter 18). Briefly, when the factors are not correlated, there is no ambiguity with respect to the allocation of proportions of variance attributed to each factor, although the specific elements may differ, depending on the specific orthogonal rotation used. In contrast, when factors are correlated, the partitioning is no longer clear-cut. The higher the correlation between the factors, the more questionable and ambiguous are attempts to partition the communality.

REPRODUCING THE CORRELATION MATRIX

So far as the fit goes, a two-factor solution will be shown to yield the same fit, regardless of the rotation used. What changes, as a result of the specific rotation, is the nature of the explanation of why given indicators are correlated.

As was done earlier (see Figure 22.1), we explain these ideas with the aid of a figure. In Figure 22.2 are depicted results from the orthogonal (a) and oblique (b) solutions for the data of Table 22.2. The coefficients on the arrows, rounded to three decimal places, were taken from the Pattern matrices of the orthogonal and the oblique solutions. The value on the double-headed arrow in (b) is the correlation between the factors. The correlation between Y_1 and Y_2, for example, is reproduced as follows:

From the Orthogonal solution (a),

$$(.738)(.627) + (.179)(.231) = .504$$

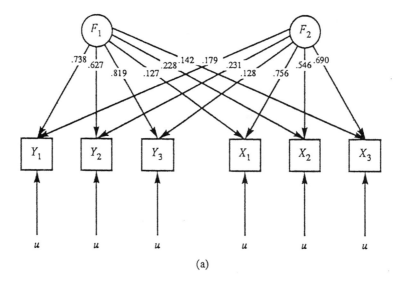

(a)

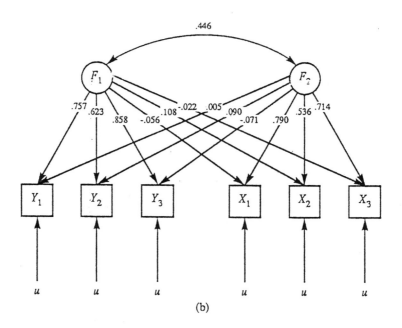

(b)

Figure 22.2

From the Oblique solution (b),

$$(.757)(.623) + (.005)(.090) + (.757)(.446)(.090) + (.005)(.446)(.623) = .504$$

Output

Horizontal Factor 1   Vertical Factor 2

Symbol	Variable	Coordinates	
1	Y1	.757	.005
2	Y2	.623	.090
3	Y3	.858	−.071
4	X1	−.056	.790
5	X2	.108	.536
6	X3	−.022	.714

Commentary

As compared with the plot for the orthogonal rotation, the present plot depicts a somewhat simpler structure.

VARYING DELTA

It was said above that positive values of δ tend to increase correlations among factors, whereas negative values tend to decrease them. For illustrative purposes, we comment on the results of two additional oblique rotations with δ's of .5 and .8. We suggest that you replicate these analyses by including the relevant δ in a subcommand. Thus, for δ = .5: CRITERIA=FACTORS(2) DELTA(.5)

For δ = .8, substitute .8 in the parentheses. *Except for the CRITERIA subcommand, the input statements are identical to those given for the preceding analysis.* If you ran the preceding, you would find that the correlation between the factors is .72 for δ = .5 and .88 for δ = .8. Recall that, for δ = 0, the correlation between the factors is .45.

One aspect of the controversy surrounding oblique rotations has to do with the magnitude of correlations among factors (Gorsuch, 1983, p. 200). Although most seem agreed that solutions in which the correlations among factors are high or low should be rejected, there is no agreement about the meaning of these terms. In this matter too, the best guide is one's theoretical formulation. As Taylor (1977) put it: "A statistical analysis cannot deduce a 'correct' positioning of the axes" (p. 101). In sum, "If the oblique solution . . . yields factor correlations that cannot be justified as reasonable, the investigator should be prepared to modify the solution" (Comrey, 1978, p. 655).

Not surprisingly, critics of *FA* view the wide latitude researchers have in choosing a factor-analytic solution as a prescription for unfettered subjectivity. For example, Reyment, Blackith, and Campbell (1984) challenged the usefulness of *FA* and suggested that it "has maintained its position for so long because, to a considerable extent, it allows the experimenter to impose his preconceived ideas on the raw data" (p. 102).

Such a posture is an instance of a more general orientation regarding the role of facts and data in the research process. We hazard a guess that Reyment et al. would endorse the slogan: "Let data speak for themselves!" However, as discussed in earlier chapters (see Chapters 7 and 9), we believe this to be an empty phrase, reflecting a simplistic view of the perceptual process in general and scientific inquiry in particular.

FA should be employed as an aid in attempts to assess the plausibility of a model of phenomena. This, of course, implies that the researcher has ideas about the nature and structure of the phenomena in question. Such ideas emanate explicitly or implicitly from a broader theoretical conception in which the construct under study is embedded. Viewed thus, *FA* can play a major role in the process of construct validation (see Chapter 4).

Recall that we assumed that the researcher is using six indicators to measure two correlated aspects of self-concept (Academic and Social). Even a superficial examination of the four solutions (one orthogonal, three oblique with varying deltas) should suffice to convince one that the solution with δ = 0 is very much consistent with this conception.

The use of *FA* for the purpose of assessing a model should not be limited to the correlations among the factors. The factor pattern matrix also deserves careful study. Accordingly, we suggest that you study the factor patterns obtained in the three oblique solutions and note that, whereas the one for δ = 0 was clearly consistent with the notion of two correlated facets of self-concept, this is not at all the case for the two other solutions. Because of space considerations, the factor patterns of the other two solutions are not reproduced. It will, however, be pointed out that, on the basis of the factor pattern for the rotation with δ = .8, for example, one would have to conclude that the six indicators reflect two highly correlated *bipolar* factors—a conception greatly at odds with the theoretical formulation of self-concept advanced in connection with the data of Table 22.2.

As a further indication of complexities attendant with oblique rotations, it will be pointed out that the correlation matrix among factors may be subjected to factor analysis, thereby obtaining higher-order factors (see, for example, Cattell, 1978; Gorsuch, 1983; Horn & Cattell, 1966).

Finally, recall that we recommended that both orthogonal and oblique rotations be applied and that the results from the former be retained and interpreted when correlations among factors are low. As an exercise, we suggest that you subject the data of Table 22.1 to a *FA* with oblique rotation, using the default delta. That is, run the data of Table 22.1 using the same input statements we used for the first analysis with oblique rotation for the data of Table 22.2. If you would do this, you would find that the correlation between the factors is .009. Study and compare the Pattern and Structure matrices of the oblique solution and note that they are very similar to each other and also to the Structure matrix of the orthogonal solution. On the basis of these results, it is tenable to retain and interpret the orthogonal solution. Importantly, this decision is arrived at on the basis of an examination of the two solutions, *not* because of an assumption of orthogonality of factors.

SELECTED ISSUES

In this section, we comment on selected issues concerning applications of *FA*. General discussions of these and related issues will be found in references given in the beginning of this chapter.

Interpretation and Naming of Factors

Knowledge in the substantive area investigated is a prerequisite for meaningful interpretation of results of factor analysis. However, even when approached with knowledge, the undertaking is generally not an easy one, which prompted McNemar (1951) to remark: "When interpreting factors all factorists struggle and struggle and struggle" (p. 357). This is due, among other things, to diverse and varying criteria regarding the number of factors to retain, the method of factor rotation, criterion for high loading.

In attempts to draw attention to abuses of *FA* and to warn against mindless applications, some authors (e.g., McNemar, 1951; Shulman, 1973) resorted to satire. Thus, Shulman (1973) advanced the thesis that "the naming of factors is *not* a rational act" but rather an "example *par excellence* of what Freud referred to as Primary Process Thinking, untainted by the reality principle" (p. 90). Among afflictions suffered by factor analysts, Shulman listed "*extraction trauma*," "*vector envy*," and "*rotation anxiety*," the major cause of which is "the *fear of losing a principal component!!!*" (pp. 91–92).

Confusion and artifice are almost inevitable byproducts of relinquishing one's responsibility to think and to decide, of relegating the necessary decisions to an analytic technique, be it *FA* or any other method. As we stressed throughout, there is little to be gained and much to be lost by applying *FA* in the absence of any notions regarding the structure of the phenomena studied. This is not to say that the notions are always clearly articulated, nor does it imply the shutting of one's eyes and mind to results that go counter to one's expectations or the spurning of hunches they may inspire. It does, however, mean that (a) variables are selected because they are deemed relevant in the context of the theoretical formulations regarding the phenomena, *not* because they happen to be available; and (b) hunches arrived at on the basis of *FA* are treated as such, *not* as hypotheses confirmed by the results from which they were garnered.

Our decision to present exploratory *FA* in the context of construct validity was meant to stress the role of theory in guiding its application, the determination of criteria, and the interpretation of results. Although admittedly the researcher has a great deal of latitude in making various key decisions (e.g., methods of factor extraction and rotation, number of factors to retain, magnitude of a loading considered high), the decisions are made within a theoretical context, not in the course of unleashing data in the pursuit of a theory.

Approaching the interpretation and naming of factors from the perspective of construct validation, one would examine factor loadings to ascertain whether they are consistent with one's theoretical definition of the construct[8]—specifically whether indicators presumed to reflect the same dimension of a construct have high loadings on the same factor and also whether indicators presumed to reflect different dimensions have high loadings on different factors. From the preceding, it follows that, to be consistent with a conception of a multi-dimensional construct, indicators should have relatively low loadings on factors they are not presumed to tap.

Although it is reasonable to scrutinize several solutions consisting of different numbers of factors and/or different rotations, such procedures should be recognized for what they are: *exploratory*. Hence, they may serve as a basis for the formulation of hypotheses to be tested in a newly designed study, preferably using confirmatory *FA* (see Chapter 23). Our analyses of Table 22.2, using four different factor rotations, exemplify such exploratory approaches. Recall that one of the solutions was clearly consistent with the enunciated theoretical formulation regarding the structure of self-concept. In Chapter 23, we show how the same problem is investigated through confirmatory *FA*.

From the perspective of theory in general, and construct validation in particular, a factor by any other name would *not* have the same meaning. Factor naming should not be done in a cavalier fashion. A pithy factor name captures and conveys the flavor of its meaning, as derived from the nomological network in which it is embedded (see Chapter 4). It stands to reason that, when *FA* is applied in the process of construct validation, factor naming is more or less a natural outgrowth of the theoretical considerations that have led to the definition of the construct, including its dimensions and the relations among them. Even when results of *FA* do not lend themselves to a facile interpretation and naming of factors, the fact that the analysis was motivated by a theoretical formulation reduces the likelihood of using unsuitable, misleading, or vacuous factor names.

Finally, important as *FA* is, it can shed light on only one aspect of the process of construct validation, namely internal structure analysis. Other aspects, especially external structure analysis, should also be studied (see Chapter 4).

Sampling and Sample Size

The role of sampling in research design in general, and in parameter estimation and hypothesis testing in particular, was discussed in various chapters (see especially Chapters 9 and 15). For present purposes, we comment on sampling (i.e., "representativeness") and sample size as they relate to *FA*.

---

[8]See Chapters 4 and 8, for discussions of definitions.

REPRESENTATIVENESS

It will be recalled that terms such as representative and representativeness are used as shorthand for samples obtained through probability sampling. Strictly speaking, probability sampling is required when, as is almost always the case, results of *FA* are to be generalized beyond the group from which the data were obtained. Nonetheless McNemar's (1951) charge that "factorists have developed an immunity to sampling problems" (p. 358) is as applicable today as it was when made four decades ago. This is largely due to difficulties in securing probability samples in most areas of sociobehavioral research.

It would be unrealistic and imprudent to reject out of hand factor analytic studies in which probability samples were not utilized. Having said that much, we wish to stress that it does *not* mean that anything goes. There is, we believe, a world of difference between situations which may be construed as appearing to be representative of a population one has in mind and situations where this is clearly not the case.

As *FA* is most often applied to a matrix of Pearson correlation coefficients, it follows that what was said in Chapters 3 and 17 about this type of correlation is applicable in the present context as well. In particular, we would like to remind you of the following: (a) The relation between the variables is assumed to be linear, and (b) changes in variability of the variables being correlated affect the magnitude of the correlation coefficient.

Flagrant distortions of correlations as a result of arbitrary changes in variability of the variables are, in our opinion, readily detectable. We have in mind situations in which the variances of the variables under study are wittingly or unwittingly increased or decreased arbitrarily. This happens most often when subjects from widely disparate groups are included in a single analysis, and/or when certain types of subjects are singled out for analysis.

Admonitions against inducing spurious correlations among variables by combining heterogeneous groups were sounded early on in the history of sociobehavioral research. Spearman (1904), for example, criticized researchers who "have purposely thrown together subjects of all sorts and ages, and thus have gone out of their way to invite fallacious elements into their work" (p. 223). Dealing with circumstances "when not to factor analyze," Guilford (1952) criticized studies in which "different populations are thrown together without questioning what effect this may have upon the intercorrelations" (p. 32).[9]

Of particular relevance to present considerations is the issue of the unit of analysis and the consequent distinctions among total, within-groups, and between-groups statistics (introduced in Chapter 21). Without going into the details (see Pedhazur, 1982, pp. 526–547, and the references given therein), it will be pointed out that, when more than one group is available (e.g., males and females; children, adolescents, adults; groups exposed to different treatments), it is possible to calculate within-groups, between-groups, and total statistics.

Whether one chooses to study statistics for within-groups, between-groups, or both depends on the specific questions addressed. Total statistics are, however, rarely of interest, as they are hybrids of within- and between-groups statistics (see Cronbach, 1976b). As a case in point, consider our analysis of the data of Table 21.1. Using two groups, we showed that whereas the total correlation between X and Y is $-.026$, the within-groups correlations are $.806$ and $-.809$.[10]

The preceding is but one example of the many ways in which total and within-groups

---

[9]Guilford's (1952) article warrants careful study, as it deals succinctly with a variety of faulty practices that are unfortunately also common in present-day applications of FA.

[10]We suggest that you review the discussion of this topic in connection with the analysis of the data of Table 21.1.

correlations may differ from each other. Even when within-groups correlations are similar to each other, total correlations may differ from them in magnitude and/or sign. This would happen when, for example, there are differences in group means on the variables (indicators) being correlated. In Chapter 24, we comment on comparisons of factor structures across samples from different populations.

In various substantive areas, it is almost obvious that factor structures for different groups (classified by sex, race, ethnicity, and the like) would differ. Nevertheless, many researchers appear oblivious to problems arising from combining heterogeneous groups. Notable examples of this may be found in the recent spate of factor analytic studies in the areas of sex-role research and of student ratings of instructors.

Turning to the second situation referred to above, namely the selection of certain types of subjects, it should be clear that correlations among indicators might be affected greatly by the specific type of subjects selected. For example, when the selection of subjects leads to severe restrictions of range, correlations among indicators may be very low, even approaching zero.[11] Clearly, *FA* of such correlations may lead to radically different results from those that would be obtained from correlations based on the continua of the variables in the populations from which the subset of subjects was selected.

SAMPLE SIZE

Although there is general agreement that large samples are imperative for stability of factor analytic results, there is no agreement as to what constitutes large. For example, Cattell (1978) referred to samples below 200 subjects as "smallish" (p. 492). Although recommending a sample size of "at least 200 subjects," Comrey (1978) added: "I have found continued reduction in the perturbation in factor analytic results up to samples of 2,000 cases before the factor structure stabilized" (p. 649).

Various authors have offered rules of thumb for the determination of sample size in relation to the number of indicators (variables). Nunnally (1978), for example, suggested that "a good rule is to have at least 10 times as many subjects as variables" (p. 421). Offering somewhat looser guidelines, Cliff (1987) stated: "With 40 or so variables, a group of 150 persons is about the minimum, although 500 is preferable" (p. 339).

Wolins (1982) correctly branded such rules of thumb as "incorrect" (p. 64) answers to the sample-size question, as it depends on the specific aims of the analysis and the properties of the data. As Wolins pointed out, the required sample size varies, depending, among other things, on the number of factors expected; whether or not it is "necessary to obtain good estimates of individual factor loadings" (p. 64); whether or not the variables are "well-behaved" (p. 64); and the magnitudes of the correlations among the variables.

As but one example of the foregoing considerations, it will be pointed out that, in general, larger samples are required when the data consist of single items as compared with data consisting of multi-item scales. Thorndike (1982), for example, asserted that, for data consisting of items, "samples of 500 or 1000 would seem none too large" (p. 91).

The situation is complex and cannot be resolved with some simple answers, let alone rules of thumb. Suffice it to remind you that issues concerning the determination of sample size are quite complex even in the much simpler designs dealt with in Chapters 9 and 15. As you may recall, we stressed the importance of distinguishing between statistical significance and substantive meaningfulness. Accordingly, we pointed out that, even when one's aim is

---

[11]See Chapter 3, for a discussion of the effect of restriction of range on the correlation coefficient.

relatively simple, as in the case of attempting to test the difference between two means, it is necessary to decide not only on Type I and Type II errors but also on the considerably more difficult issue of effect size. Surely, therefore, it is unrealistic to expect a simple answer to the sample-size question when dealing with much more complex designs, such as *FA*. In view of the fact that ours is but an introduction to *FA*, all we can do is reiterate the general recommendation that you should use large samples.[12]

Composite Scores

Having arrived at what is deemed a satisfactory factor-analytic solution, it is useful to combine scores on indicators said to reflect a given factor so as to arrive at a composite score for each individual on that factor. Broadly speaking, the following two approaches may be taken: (a) calculating factor scores, and (b) constructing factor-based scales.

FACTOR SCORES

The topic of factor scores is quite complicated, primarily because a unique solution is unobtainable. This predicament, referred to as indeterminacy, means that "more than one set of factor scores can be constructed that satisfy all the necessary characteristics to be legitimate factor scores for a given factor pattern" (Gorsuch, 1983, p. 258; for a good discussion of determinacy, see McDonald & Mulaik, 1979). Consequently, different estimation procedures, aimed at achieving some desired characteristics (e.g., maximizing reliabilities of composites, minimizing correlations among composites) have been proposed. Understandably, there is no agreement as to a preferred method of factor score estimation, nor is there even agreement regarding a choice between factor scores and factor-based scales (see below).

Discussions of factor scores will be found in practically any of the references given in the beginning of this chapter. Among papers devoted specifically to this topic are: Alwin (1973); Glass and Maguire (1966); Saris, de Pijper, and Mulder (1978); Smith (1974a, 1974b); and Susmilch and Johnson (1975).

FACTOR-BASED SCALES

Along with many authors, we believe factor scores to be of limited usefulness. Of greater potential is the application of *FA* for the purpose of constructing factor-based scales. *FA* can be invaluable for the construction of homogeneous scales aimed at measuring unidimensional constructs, or specific dimensions of multidimensional constructs. Much, if not most, applications as well as misapplications of *FA* are done with this aim in mind. Under such circumstances, *FA* is used primarily for identification and selection of indicators (items). The most common practice is to consider items having a loading above a cutoff (e.g., .4) on one factor only as candidates for inclusion in a given scale.

Scores on factor-based scales are obtained most often by summing the scores on the items comprising them. Regardless of their factor loadings, therefore, items included in a given

---

[12]We return to the question of sample size in Chapter 23, in the context of the distinction between the test of significance of a model and attempts to assess how well it fits the data.

scale are, in effect, assigned a weight of 1, whereas those not included in the scale are assigned a weight of 0. This practice seems justified, as reviews of the literature indicate that differential weighting, particularly when dealing with items (indicators), is not worth the trouble (see, for example, Nunnally, 1978, pp. 296–297; Stanley & Wang, 1970; Wang & Stanley, 1970).

The specific number of items included in a given scale depends, of course, on various considerations, the most important being adequate "coverage" or "sampling" of the domain, and reliability. In this matter too, rules of thumb have been proposed, with the suggested minimum number of items having meaningful loadings on a factor varying between three and five, for the factor to be deemed adequate for interpretation (see, for example, Bentler, 1976; Kim & Mueller, 1978a).

Misapplication or mindless application of *FA* is sadly the rule rather than the exception (e.g., Comrey, 1978; Korth, 1975; Nunnally, 1978; Stewart, 1981). Furthermore, frequently researchers pay no attention to results they themselves report. For example, it is quite common for researchers to provide evidence that a scale they have constructed or used is multifactorial and yet ignore this information when it comes to the selection and/or scoring of items. It is as if reporting results of *FA* is the thing to do but not the thing to be acted upon. Regardless of the factor structure and pattern, all the items are retained and scored as if they measured a unitary construct. Broadly speaking, this boils down to contradictory conceptions. On one hand it is claimed, or at least indicated by items having high loadings on different factors, that different aspects are being measured; on the other hand, when all the items are summed together, these same items are treated as if they had high loadings on one factor only.

Reporting Results of *FA*

Although adequate reporting of research results is always imperative, it is particularly so in the case of *FA*, because the results are greatly affected by various decisions the researcher makes in the process of obtaining them (e.g., method of factor extraction, how many factors to retain, method of factor rotation). It is, therefore, all the more surprising that reports of results of *FA* are by and large woefully inadequate. In many instances, reports are limited to some brief statement about the number of factors that have "emerged" or to an indication of factor loadings above some cutoff.

Various authors (e.g., Comrey, 1973, 1978; McDonald, 1985; Nunnally, 1978; Skinner, 1980; Weiss, 1971) commented on the poor reporting of factor-analytic studies and made recommendations about information essential to report. Because so much depends on the choice of method and on specific decisions in its application, the guiding principle in reporting results of *FA* should be that the information provided be relevant and adequate not only to understand what the researcher has done but also to enable a reader to do a reanalysis, using the same method with, perhaps, different decision rules and/or other methods. This implies that, among other things, the following be included in the report:

1. The theoretical rationale for the specific application of *FA*.

2. A detailed description of the subjects (the sample) and the items (indicators, variables), including means and standard deviations.

3. Methods used in the analysis, including communality estimates, factor extraction, and rotation.

4. Criteria employed, such as those for the number of factors retained, cutoff for meaningful loadings.

5. The correlation matrix.

6. The structure matrix for orthogonally rotated solutions. The structure and pattern matrices, as well as the correlations among the factors, for obliquely rotated solutions.

However, because of space considerations or constraints set by journal editors, it may not be possible to include all the relevant information. This is especially likely to occur when the number of indicators is relatively large and/or more than one solution has been explored. Under such circumstances, the author should inform readers of whatever additional information is available upon request.

CONCLUDING REMARKS

We remind you that our aim in this chapter has been to introduce and illustrate some basic ideas of exploratory *FA* from the frame of reference of construct validation. Guided by theory and applied intelligently, exploratory *FA* can prove useful in shedding light on properties of an existing measure or one being constructed. As was pointed out, however, this analytic approach is also susceptible to abuses and misinterpretations. Some of the problems and difficulties inherent in the exploratory approaches presented in the present chapter disappear or are alleviated in confirmatory *FA*, the topic of the next chapter.

STUDY SUGGESTIONS

1. Following is an illustrative correlation matrix for eight items (indicators). $N = 300$.
   Do a principal axes factor analysis. Extract two factors and call for orthogonal
   (varimax) and oblique ($\delta = 0$) rotations.

	X_1	X_2	X_3	X_4	X_5	X_6	X_7	X_8
X_1	1.00							
X_2	.33	1.00						
X_3	.44	.35	1.00					
X_4	.09	.14	.06	1.00				
X_5	.12	.08	.05	.06	1.00			
X_6	.18	.15	.18	.12	.08	1.00		
X_7	.15	.13	.17	.10	.11	.42	1.00	
X_8	.17	.14	.18	.13	.15	.38	.37	1.00

Following are excerpts of the output:

PAF Extracted   2 factors

Factor Matrix: Rotated Factor Matrix:

	FACTOR 1	FACTOR 2	FACTOR 1	FACTOR 2
X1	.53742	.37203	.15292	.63549
X2	.44136	.28348	.14028	.50545
X3	.54333	.37599	.15468	.64238
X4	.20391	−.02862	.17113	.11451
X5	.19065	−.03682	.16671	.09956

X6	.55287	−.32610	.62956	.12516
X7	.52999	−.34751	.62676	.09394
X8	.52418	−.29001	.58411	.13296

Reproduced Correlation Matrix:

	X1	X2	X3	X4	X5	X6	X7	X8
X1	.42723*	−.01266	.00812	−.00894	.03124	.00419	−.00554	−.00381
X2	.34266	.27516*	.00361	.05812	.00629	−.00158	−.00540	−.00914
X3	.43188	.34639	.43657*	−.04003	−.03974	.00222	.01271	.00424
X4	.09894	.08188	.10003	.04240*	.02007	−.00207	−.01802	.01481
X5	.08876	.07371	.08974	.03993	.03770*	−.03741	−.00384	.03939
X6	.17581	.15158	.17778	.12207	.11741	.41201*	.01366	−.00437
X7	.15554	.13540	.15729	.11802	.11384	.40634	.40165*	−.00859
X8	.17381	.14914	.17576	.11519	.11061	.38437	.37859	.35886*

The lower left triangle contains the reproduced correlation matrix; The diagonal, communalities; and the upper right triangle, residuals between the observed correlations and the reproduced correlations.

Oblimin   Rotation

Pattern Matrix:			Structure Matrix:	
	FACTOR 1	FACTOR 2	FACTOR 1	FACTOR 2
X1	−.00421	.65563	.30879	.65362
X2	.01726	.51610	.26365	.52434
X3	−.00414	.66271	.31223	.66073
X4	.15789	.07678	.19454	.15215
X5	.15707	.06159	.18648	.13658
X6	.66153	−.04355	.64074	.27227
X7	.66694	−.07711	.63013	.24129
X8	.60918	−.02187	.59874	.26896

Factor Correlation Matrix:

	FACTOR 1	FACTOR 2
FACTOR 1	1.00000	
FACTOR 2	.47740	1.00000

(a) Using relevant values from the unrotated and the orthogonally rotated factors, calculate the item communalities.

(b) Using relevant values from the unrotated and the orthogonally rotated factors, calculate the reproduced correlations between all item pairs.

(c) Calculate the residuals (i.e., observed correlations minus predicted ones).

(d) Examine the results of the oblique solution. What is the correlation between the two factors?

(e) Using relevant values from the oblique solution, calculate the item communalities.

(f) Using relevant values from the oblique solution, calculate the reproduced correlations among the items.

(g) Assuming you were to accept the oblique solution, what would you conclude about items X4 and X5?

2. Shaffer (1983) studied the dimensionality of congressional foreign policy attitudes using a principal components analysis. We suggest that you subject Shaffer's correlation matrix to a principal axis factor analysis, doing extractions and rotations paralleling those carried out by him. Study Shaffer's results and yours. Critically evaluate Shaffer's arguments in favor of principal components analysis and against rotations for the purpose of studying dimensionality of attitudes. Following are a couple of examples of assertions deserving special scrutiny:

(a) Unidimensionality of the attitudes is questionable, because "the intercorrelations [among the items] are far from perfect" (p. 433).

(b) "I pay careful attention to unrotated factor loadings, since rotated loadings may reflect an arbitrary decision to maximize some variables on a component, while dramatically reducing others" (p. 435).

3. You will find numerous examples of applications of factor analysis in books and articles referred to throughout the chapter as well as in various journals. In most instances, the correlation matrices are reported. We recommend that you reanalyze some examples, especially those you find substantively interesting. In addition to replicating the author(s) analyses, try some variations (e.g., calling for additional output, extracting a different number of factors, using different rotations). Evaluate the results and conclusions in light of your reanalyses.

Answers

1. (a) For X1:

$$.53742^2 + .37203^2 = .15292^2 + .63549^2 = .42723$$

—similarly for the other items. Compare your results with those reported on the diagonal of the reproduced correlation matrix.

(b) Between X2 and X3:

Unrotated: $(.44136)(.54333) + (.28348)(.37599) = .34639$
Rotated: $(.14028)(.15468) + (.50545)(.64238) = .34639$

—similarly for correlations between other items. Compare your results with those reported in the lower triangle of the reproduced correlation matrix.

(c) For the correlation between X1 and X2:
$.33 - .34266 = -.01266$—similarly for the other residuals. Compare your results with those reported in the upper triangle of the reproduced correlation matrix.

(d) .47740

(e) For X1:
$(-.00421)(.30879) + (.65563)(.65362) = .42723$—see (22.7)—similarly for the other items. Compare your results with those reported on the diagonal of the reproduced correlation matrix.

(f) Between X2 and X3:
$(.01726)(-.00414)+(.51610)(.66271)+(.01726)(.66271)(.47740)+(-.00414)$
$(.51610)(.47740) = .34639$—similarly for correlations between other items. Compare your results with those reported in the lower triangle of the reproduced correlation matrix.

(g) The statistics associated with X4 and X5 (e.g., communalities, loadings) are relatively small. Assuming one were to use the result to construct two measures of whatever the two factors are tapping, it would be advisable to exclude these items. In other words, one measure would be comprised of items X1–X3, the other of X6–X8.

2. (a) Unidimensionality does *not* imply perfect correlations among the items but rather that a single factor suffices to account for the correlations among the items. In his summary and conclusions, Shaffer (1983) stated that "a principal components analysis failed to reveal anything other than a general 'Foreign Policy Liberalism' factor" (p. 443). This could have been gleaned from the unrotated factor solution. Examine the eigenvalues and scree plot. Also examine the first two *unrotated factors* and note that all items have fairly high loadings on the first factor. Except for item 4, all items have low loadings on the second factor.

(b) See this chapter, for discussions of the role of rotations and our comments about the inadvisability of rotating principal components.

Chapter 23
Confirmatory Factor Analysis

Distinctions between Exploratory Factor Analysis (*EFA*) and Confirmatory Factor Analysis (*CFA*), and basic notions concerning their applications in the context of construct validation, were introduced in Chapter 4. Although there is no clear demarcation line between *EFA* and *CFA* (e.g., Cliff, 1987; Marradi, 1981; Nunnally, 1978), the two approaches differ in important ways.

Being aimed at the testing of a model and the assessment of its fit to data, it is obvious that the formulation of a model is a prerequisite for the application of *CFA*. Although this neither guarantees the formulation of a meaningful model nor insures the sagacious application of *CFA* to it, it does hold promise for decreasing the incidence of mindless applications of *FA*. Most important, *when applying CFA, the model is there for all to see—especially the person testing it*.

Even when guided by theory, as it always should be, *EFA* places greater constraints on the researcher as compared with *CFA*. Following are some contrasts between the two approaches.[1]

1. In *EFA*, all indicators have loadings (not necessarily meaningful ones) on all the factors, whereas a major feature of *CFA* is that the researcher can specify which indicators load on which factors. In addition, in *CFA*, it is possible to, among other things, fix the loadings for given indicators; set the loadings for two or more indicators equal to each other.

2. Whether or not factors are correlated is an all-or-nothing decision in *EFA*. In other words, in *EFA*, it is *not* possible to specify that only some of the factors are intercorrelated. In contrast, in *CFA*, it is possible to specify not only which factors are intercorrelated but also the magnitudes of the correlations and whether correlations between certain factors are equal to each other.

3. In *EFA*, it is assumed that errors in indicators are not correlated. In *CFA*, on the other hand, correlated errors may be treated as part of the model being tested.[2]

---

[1]When necessary, refer to Chapter 22 for a presentation of *EFA*.

[2]For a more detailed discussion of these and other contrasts between *EFA* and *CFA*, see Long (1983a).

SEM AND *CFA*

CFA can be viewed as a submodel of the more general Structural Equation Modeling (*SEM*) approach (see Chapter 24). Specifically, it is a measurement model of relations of indicators (manifest variables) to factors (latent variables) as well as relations among the latter. Accordingly, it is eminently suited for internal- and cross-structure analysis in the process of construct validation (see Chapter 4).

What follows is *not* a formal presentation of *CFA*, as this would require the use of matrix algebra and complex statistical theory. As with the presentation of *EFA* (Chapter 22), in this and the subsequent chapter, we give an informal introduction to very important recent developments in the conceptualization of research problems and their associated analytic approaches. In doing so, we have two aims in mind: (a) to enable you to follow reports in which these approaches have been used, and (b) to help you begin learning to apply them.

Journal editors too have come to recognize the urgent need for introductions to *SEM* to assist their readers as well as themselves. For example, in the foreword to a special issue on *SEM* in *Child Development* (1987, *58*, 1–175), Bronson candidly stated that neither the editors "nor (we expect) most of the readers of *Child Development* feel competent to arrive at an intelligent evaluation" (p. 1) of *SEM*.

Introductory presentations of *SEM* will be found in Bohrnstedt (1983); Bollen (1989); Cuttance and Ecob (1987); Hayduk (1987); Judd, Jessor, and Donovan (1986); and Long (1983a, 1983b, 1988).

ESTIMATION PROCEDURES AND COMPUTER PROGRAMS

Of various estimation procedures, a Maximum Likelihood (ML) solution is the most frequently used in *SEM*. ML is based on a complex statistical theory that we will not go into. Instead we offer this brief characterization of its objective: Given specific distributional assumptions, a ML solution is based on a search for estimates of parameters most likely to have generated the observed data. Mulaik (1972) offered the following explanation of ML estimation:

> The idea of a maximum-likelihood estimator is this: We assume that we know the *general form* of the population distribution from which a sample is drawn. For example, we might assume the population distribution is a multivariate normal distribution. But what we do not know are the population parameters which give this distribution a particular form among all possible multivariate normal distributions. . . . In the absence of such knowledge, however, we can take arbitrary values and treat them *as if* they were population parameters and then ask ourselves what is the *likelihood* . . . of observing certain values for the variables on a single observation drawn from such a population. If we have more than one observation, then we can ask what is the joint likelihood of obtaining such a sample of observation vectors?. . . . Finally, we can ask: What values for the population parameters make the sample observations have the greatest joint likelihood? When we answer this question, we will take such values to be *maximum-likelihood estimators* of the population parameters. (p. 162)

For more formal introductions to ML, with special reference to *SEM*, see Bollen (1989), Everitt (1984), Gorsuch (1983), Long (1983a, 1983b), and Mulaik (1972, 1975).

ML computations for *SEM* are extremely complex and laborious, practically impossible to carry out without the aid of a computer. In fact, the widespread use of ML solutions for *SEM* was launched when Jöreskog and his associates incorporated his pioneering work into various computer programs, the most popular of which is LISREL (LInear Structural RELations. Jöreskog & Sörbom, 1989).[3]

LISREL requires a basic understanding of matrices, as it is in this form that the model to be tested has to be specified. Although we do not assume knowledge of matrix algebra on your part, it will be necessary to present the matrices used in LISREL on an expository level to help you understand the input and output for this program.[4] Further, because LISREL uses Greek notation, you will have to become familiar with some letters of the Greek alphabet.

We will also use another computer program—EQS (Bentler, 1985),[5] which does not resort to matrix terminology nor to Greek notation for model specification. Although both programs have options for several estimation procedures, we limit our presentation to ML solutions. (For discussions of other estimation procedures, see the manuals for these programs and the references given therein. Also, see the references given above.) Other computer programs for *SEM* are available (see, for example, McDonald, 1985).

As was pointed out above, *CFA* is a submodel of *SEM*. Thus, the present chapter is addressed to one aspect of the full model presented in Chapter 24. We chose to begin with *CFA*, because it is important in its own right, and because it can facilitate your understanding of more complex models introduced in Chapter 24. Only matrices relevant to *CFA* are presented in this chapter. Additional matrices used in *SEM* are presented in Chapter 24.

Furthermore, basic ideas regarding model testing and fitting introduced in this chapter are expanded and expounded upon in the next one. We hope that such a gradual presentation will facilitate the learning of *SEM*. In sum, Chapters 23 and 24 should be viewed as parts of one unit.

Our approach to the presentation of *CFA* and *SEM* (Chapter 24) will be done exclusively through the analysis of numerical examples. After a brief orientation to each computer program, we use commentaries on the input and the output for the given program to explain the basic ideas and the interpretation of results.

In an effort to help you learn to use LISREL and EQS intelligently, we discuss input and output in some detail. Yet our coverage is far from exhaustive and is not meant to supplant the manuals for these programs. It is essential that you become familiar with the manual for the program you are using and that you refer to it for detailed instructions and explanations. The manuals also contain examples of analyses of various designs accompanied by valuable explanations.

LISREL: AN ORIENTATION

All analyses in this and the subsequent chapter were done with *PC–LISREL version 7.16*.[6] Although, at the time of this writing, LISREL 7 for the mainframe has not been released, it undoubtedly will be available when this book is published. Obviously, we have no way of knowing whether the mainframe and the PC versions will be identical. In view of the fact that

---

[3]LISREL is a registered trademark of Scientific Software, Inc. For information about LISREL and related programs, contact Scientific Software, Inc., P.O. Box 397, Fairplay, CO 80440.

[4]We remind you that, in Chapter 22, we introduced some basic ideas about matrices. Also we recommended that you learn matrix algebra and provided some references for introductory treatments of this important subject. See also, beginning of Chapter 18.

[5]EQS is a registered trademark of BMDP Statistical Software, Inc. For information about EQS, contact BMDP, 1440 Sepulveda Boulevard, Suite 316, Los Angeles, CA 90025.

[6]We would like to thank Scientific Software Inc. for furnishing us with a review copy of this program.

the same manual is meant to be applicable for both versions, it stands to reason that this will be the case. Yet although a single manual was available for the PC and mainframe versions of LISREL VI, they were not identical in all respects.

In any case, as is well known, computer programs frequently undergo corrections, updates, and revisions. It is, therefore, imperative that you check the characteristics and options for the specific version of the program you are using. For convenience, *we will refer to the program as LISREL* and to its guide (Jöreskog & Sörbom, 1989) as *the LISREL manual or just the* Manual. We turn now to an introduction to this program.

In order to acquaint you with the matrices used in the submodel under consideration, we will use an example of a design with six manifest variables (indicators) and three latent variables (factors). Latent exogenous variables are designated as ξ's (xi), referred to in LISREL as KSI.[7] Indicators (manifest variables) of KSI's are designated as X's. Coefficients signifying effects of KSI's on X's are designated as λ's (lambda). Errors in X's are designated as δ's (delta).

The λ's are incorporated in a matrix Λ_x (LAMBDA X),[8] specified as LX in the input. The number of rows in LX is equal to the number of indicators, specified as NX in the input. The number of columns in LX is equal to the number of KSI's—specified as NK in the input—said to affect the indicators. For our example, then, matrix LX (LAMBDA X) would look like this:

$$
\begin{array}{cccc}
& \xi_1 & \xi_2 & \xi_3 \\
& (\text{KSI 1}) & (\text{KSI 2}) & (\text{KSI 3}) \\
\begin{matrix} X_1 \\ X_2 \\ X_3 \\ X_4 \\ X_5 \\ X_6 \end{matrix} &
\left[\begin{matrix}
\lambda_{11} & \lambda_{12} & \lambda_{13} \\
\lambda_{21} & \lambda_{22} & \lambda_{23} \\
\lambda_{31} & \lambda_{32} & \lambda_{33} \\
\lambda_{41} & \lambda_{42} & \lambda_{43} \\
\lambda_{51} & \lambda_{52} & \lambda_{53} \\
\lambda_{61} & \lambda_{62} & \lambda_{63}
\end{matrix} \right]
\end{array}
$$

Several points will be made in connection with this and other matrices used in LISREL.

1. The matrix consists of the elements enclosed by the brackets. For expository purposes, we included row and column labels.

2. Elements of a matrix are identified by their coordinates, that is, by their row and column numbers. Therefore, the subscripts associated with the λ's are *not* necessary. We use them to clarify how individual elements are referred to. For example, λ_{41} is used to refer to the effect of factor 1 (ξ_1) on X_4.

3. In LISREL input, it is necessary to refer to elements of matrices in order to specify their status (e.g., whether they are free, fixed; see below). Several alternative formats may be used for this purpose. Using λ_{41} as an example, following are three equivalent formats that may be used to refer to it in LISREL input:

$$\text{LX(4,1)} \quad \text{LX(4 1)} \quad \text{LX 4 1}$$

Note the pattern: a two-letter identification of the matrix in question followed by the coordinates of the element in question. Such formats may be used to identify elements in any of the LISREL matrices.

An alternative format is one consisting of a two-letter identification of the matrix in question followed by a number indicating the position of a given element in it. Using this

---

[7]Notions of exogenous and endogenous variables were introduced in Chapter 14.

[8]As was pointed out in Chapter 22, matrices and vectors are depicted by bold letters.

format, elements are assigned numbers consecutively row-wise, beginning with the first element of the first row.

For the matrix given above, therefore, λ_{11} is assigned the number 1, λ_{12} the number 2, and so on up to 18 for λ_{63}. Thus, instead of referring to λ_{41} by its coordinates, as above, one may use the present format and refer to it as LX 10 (i.e., 10th element). As another example, following are some formats identifying λ_{52}:

$$LX(5\ 2)\quad LX\ 5\ 2\quad LX\ 5,2\quad LX\ 14$$

where coordinates are used in the first three, whereas the element number (14th) is used in the last.

For other formats for the identification of elements in LISREL matrices, see the Manual. We turn now to the two other matrices that comprise the submodel under consideration.

Φ (PHI) is a variance–covariance matrix of the latent exogenous variables (ξ's)—specified as PH in the input. That is, the principal diagonal of this matrix consists of variances of KSI's, whereas the off-diagonal elements consist of covariances between KSI's. As variance is a special case of covariance (i.e., the covariance of a variable with itself; see Chapter 17), it is convenient to refer to a variance–covariance matrix as a covariance matrix.

PHI is a square-symmetric covariance matrix whose dimension is equal to the number of KSI's. For the example given above, PHI is a 3 by 3 matrix (3 KSI's). Because PHI is symmetric, it is generally presented as a lower triangular matrix.[9] It is in this form that it is presented in LISREL.

As explained below (see commentary on Input), in the numerical examples used in the present chapter, the PHI's are correlation matrices. Recall that a correlation matrix is a special case of a covariance matrix, that is, when standard scores are used. Accordingly, the principal diagonal of such a matrix consists of 1's (variances of standard scores), whereas the off-diagonal elements are correlation coefficients (covariances of standard scores).[10] Following is PHI for the example introduced above (i.e., 3 KSI's):

$$
\begin{array}{c}
\begin{array}{ccc}
\text{KSI 1} & \text{KSI 2} & \text{KSI 3}
\end{array}\\
\begin{array}{c}
\text{KSI 1}\\ \text{KSI 2}\\ \text{KSI 3}
\end{array}
\left[
\begin{array}{ccc}
\phi_{11} & & \\
\phi_{21} & \phi_{22} & \\
\phi_{31} & \phi_{32} & \phi_{33}
\end{array}
\right]
\end{array}
$$

Using ϕ_{32} as an example, following are alternative formats that may be used to refer to it:

$$PH\ 3\ 2\quad PH(3\ 2)\quad PH\ 5$$

where coordinates are used in the first two formats; the element number (5th) is used in the last format. As explained above, elements are numbered row-wise, beginning with the first row. When the lower triangular format is used for symmetric matrices, elements above the principal diagonal are not counted.

The last matrix of the LISREL submodel with which we are concerned in this chapter is Θ_δ (THETA DELTA), specified as TD in the input. Above, it was pointed out that δ signifies errors in indicators (manifest variables). THETA DELTA is a covariance matrix of δ's. That is, elements of the principal diagonal of THETA DELTA are variances of errors of indicators whereas off-diagonal elements are covariances (or correlations) between errors of indicators.

As in the case of PHI, THETA DELTA is square-symmetric and is presented in the form

---

[9]See Some Observations about Matrices in Chapter 22, for explanations of matrix terminology used here.

[10]If necessary, review these topics in Chapters 17 and 22.

of a lower triangular matrix. In the above example, six indicators were used (6 X's). Consequently, THETA DELTA is a 6 by 6 matrix, as follows:

$$
\begin{bmatrix}
\theta_{11} \\
\theta_{21} & \theta_{22} \\
\theta_{31} & \theta_{32} & \theta_{33} \\
\theta_{41} & \theta_{42} & \theta_{43} & \theta_{44} \\
\theta_{51} & \theta_{52} & \theta_{53} & \theta_{54} & \theta_{55} \\
\theta_{61} & \theta_{62} & \theta_{63} & \theta_{64} & \theta_{65} & \theta_{66}
\end{bmatrix}
$$

Using formats explained above, the covariance of errors of indicators X_5 and X_6, say, may be referred to as

$$
\text{TD(6 5)} \quad \text{TD 6 5} \quad \text{TD 20}
$$

where TD refers to THETA DELTA. Coordinates are used in the first two formats; the element number (20th) is used in the last.

As a final example, some alternative formats referring to the variance of errors in X_4 are:

$$
\text{TD(4 4)} \quad \text{TD 4 4} \quad \text{TD 10}
$$

ESTIMATION

Elements in LISREL matrices may be of three kinds:
- *fixed parameters* that have been assigned specified values,
- *constrained parameters* that are unknown but equal to one or more other parameters, and
- *free parameters* that are unknown and not constrained to be equal to any other parameter. (Manual, p. 5)

Using the covariance (or correlation) matrix among the observed (manifest) variables, signified as **S** in LISREL, elements specified as free or constrained are estimated by ML (or by another procedure specified by the user). The estimated values are then used to reproduce the covariance (or correlation) matrix among the observed variables, signified as Σ in LISREL.

As was stated earlier, we use and interpret results obtained through ML estimation, although we do not discuss the method of estimation itself (for good introductions, see Bollen, 1989; Long 1983a, 1983b). It will only be pointed out that it is discrepancies between **S** and Σ that enter into the testing of the model and assessment of its fit. Clearly, the closer corresponding elements of the two matrices are to each other, the better the fit of the model to the data. We return to these topics in the context of commentaries on the analyses of numerical examples.

SPECIFYING A MODEL

Using the example of the six indicators given above, we will illustrate how a model is specified in LISREL. First, we depict the model in Figure 23.1.

Figures such as this one were used in various chapters, where it was pointed out that they

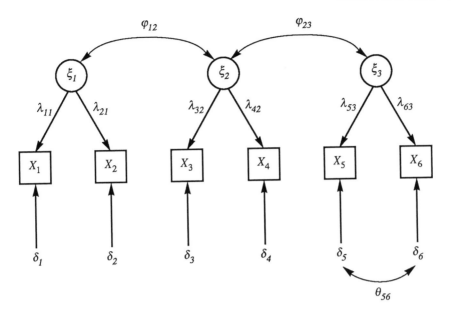

Figure 23.1

are very useful in bringing into the open, so to speak, the researcher's expectations and assumptions about the model being tested. As a result, researchers and readers are in a better position to comprehend the model and assess the validity of its assumptions and implications.

As in earlier chapters, latent variables are depicted by circles, whereas manifest variables are depicted by squares. Furthermore, unidirectional arrows indicate effects of a given variable on another, whereas curved bidirectional arrows indicate covariances (or correlations) between variables.

According to the model depicted in Figure 23.1, each latent variable is manifested by two indicators. Thus, X_1 and X_2 are indicators of ξ_1, and so forth. It is hypothesized that ξ_1 is correlated with ξ_2, and ξ_2 is correlated with ξ_3, but ξ_1 is *not* correlated with ξ_3 (there is no curved line connecting them). Finally, except for an hypothesized correlation between the errors of X_5 and X_6 (indicated by the curved line), all other errors are hypothesized to be *not* correlated. Note also that the absence of lines between errors in indicators and latent variables signifies that δ's are *not* correlated with the ξ's. This is one of the assumptions of *SEM* (see Manual, p. 4; also Long, 1983a, 1983b).

Here is the general equation expressing the measurement model:

$$\mathbf{x} = \mathbf{\Lambda}_x \mathbf{\xi} + \mathbf{\delta} \tag{23.1}$$

where $\mathbf{x}$ is a q by 1 (6 by 1, for our example) vector of indicators of the latent exogenous variables; $\mathbf{\Lambda}_x$ (LAMBDA X) is a q by n (6 by 3, for our example) matrix of coefficients, loadings, of $\mathbf{x}$ on the latent variables (ξ); $\mathbf{\delta}$ is a q by 1 (6 by 1, for our example) vector of errors in the measurement of $\mathbf{x}$.

Spelling out the matrices:

$$
\underset{\mathbf{x}}{\begin{bmatrix} x_1 \\ x_2 \\ x_3 \\ x_4 \\ x_5 \\ x_6 \end{bmatrix}} = \underset{\mathbf{\Lambda}}{\begin{bmatrix} \lambda_{11} & 0 & 0 \\ \lambda_{21} & 0 & 0 \\ 0 & \lambda_{32} & 0 \\ 0 & \lambda_{42} & 0 \\ 0 & 0 & \lambda_{53} \\ 0 & 0 & \lambda_{63} \end{bmatrix}} \underset{\mathbf{\xi}}{\begin{bmatrix} \xi_1 \\ \xi_2 \\ \xi_3 \end{bmatrix}} + \underset{\mathbf{\delta}}{\begin{bmatrix} \delta_1 \\ \delta_2 \\ \delta_3 \\ \delta_4 \\ \delta_5 \\ \delta_6 \end{bmatrix}}
$$

The covariance matrix of the ξ's is

$$
\begin{array}{cccc}
 & \text{KSI 1} & \text{KSI 2} & \text{KSI 3} \\
\begin{array}{c} \text{KSI 1} \\ \text{KSI 2} \\ \text{KSI 3} \end{array} & \begin{bmatrix} \phi_{11} & & \\ \phi_{21} & \phi_{22} & \\ 0 & \phi_{32} & \phi_{33} \end{bmatrix}
\end{array}
$$
$$\mathbf{\Phi}$$

The diagonal elements are variances of the ξ's, whereas the off-diagonal elements are covariances (correlations) between ξ's. Note the 0, signifying no correlation between ξ_1 and ξ_3.

The covariance matrix of the δ's is

$$
\begin{bmatrix}
\theta_{11} & & & & & \\
0 & \theta_{22} & & & & \\
0 & 0 & \theta_{33} & & & \\
0 & 0 & 0 & \theta_{44} & & \\
0 & 0 & 0 & 0 & \theta_{55} & \\
0 & 0 & 0 & 0 & \theta_{65} & \theta_{66}
\end{bmatrix}
$$
$$\mathbf{\Theta}_\delta$$

The diagonal consists of variances of errors. Except for the covariance between δ_5 and δ_6, the covariances between the δ's are indicated to be 0.

Before showing how the model depicted in Figure 23.1 is specified in LISREL, some general observations are in order. We used a simple model to illustrate some basic aspects of the specification process. According to our model, any given indicator is affected by only one latent variable. It is, however, possible to formulate and test models according to which an indicator is said to be affected by more than one factor (see Multitrait-Multimethod Matrix, later in this chapter). Furthermore, at this stage, we have refrained from using constraints (e.g., that effects of KSI on X_1 and X_2 are equal). Such constraints are discussed and illustrated later in this chapter, under Measurement Models). Finally, although the question of model identification is of utmost importance, we refrain from commenting on it in the present chapter. Instead, we address this very complex topic in Chapter 24.

Turning now to the matter of model specification, it will be pointed out that, in LISREL, this is done on a MOdel statement. Examples of MO statements are given and commented upon in connection with the numerical examples. For now, it will only be pointed out that it is necessary to specify the number of the X's (according to Figure 23.1, NX = 6), the number of the KSI's (for Figure 23.1, NK = 3), and the forms and modes of LX (LAMBDA X), PH (PHI), and TD (THETA DELTA) matrices. Form refers to the shape of the matrix (e.g., symmetric, full, identity). Mode refers to whether the matrix is FRee or FIxed (see above).

LISREL DEFAULTS

Default forms and modes are available for each of the matrices used in LISREL. Forms of matrices that are not the same as the defaults have to be specified on the MO statement. *It is important that you check the default forms for each of the matrices involved in a model you are testing and to specify on the MOdel statement the forms for matrices that differ from the defaults.* (For a summary of default forms and modes for the matrices used in LISREL, see Manual, p. 12, Table 1.3.)

To clarify the preceding, we will use the three matrices involved in *CFA*, with reference to the model depicted in Figure 23.1. We begin by addressing the form of the matrices. Their modes are addressed subsequently.

MATRIX FORM

The default form of PH (PHI) is SYmmetric, as depicted above. Several other forms for PH may be specified. For example, one may specify that it is DIagonal. What this means is that, according to the model, the covariances between the KSI's (latent variables) are equal to 0. According to the model of Figure 23.1, only the covariance between ξ_1 and ξ_3 is equal to 0. Consequently, PH is SYmmetric (default form and, therefore, not necessary to specify), although not all of its elements are FRee (see Matrix Mode, below).

The default form of LX (LAMBDA X) is FUll, as depicted above for the model of Figure 23.1. Instead, LX may, for example, be an identity matrix. That is, the principal diagonal consists of 1's—all off-diagonal elements equal 0 (see Chapter 22). Again, although LX for the model under consideration is the default (FUll, hence, not necessary to specify on the MOdel statement), it does not mean that all of its elements are free. In the model under consideration, they are not (see the 0's in the LAMBDA X matrix, above).

The default form for TD (THETA DELTA) is DIagonal. What this means is that, according to the model, the covariances between errors of indicators equal 0. Note that this form is *not* applicable for the model under consideration, because according to it, the covariance between δ_5 and δ_6 is *not* 0. Accordingly, it is necessary to specify on the MO statement that TD = SYmmetric.

MATRIX MODE

The default mode for PH is FRee. That is, all its elements are to be estimated. But, according to the model depicted in Figure 23.1, the covariance between KSI 1 and KSI 3 is 0. Therefore, it is necessary to specify that this value is fixed (i.e., set to 0). This is done by using a FIxed statement followed by the identification of the matrix and the element in question. Earlier, two formats for identifying elements in a given matrix were introduced and explained. Using these formats, following are alternative statements for fixing the element of PH corresponding to the covariance between KSI 1 and KSI 3:

FI PH(3 1)   PH 3 1   PH 4

See PH matrix above and note that we are concerned with the element in its third row and first column or with the 4th element.

Before turning to the next matrix, it will be pointed out that FIxed statements may consist of more than one element. Further, elements from different matrices may be included in the same FI statement. This is also true of FRee statements (see below).

The default mode for LX is FIxed. That is, all the elements are set to zero. Accordingly, it is necessary to FRee those elements that are to be estimated. How this is done will be illustrated for the model depicted in Figure 23.1:

$$FR \ LX(1 \ 1) \ LX(2 \ 1) \ LX(3 \ 2) \ LX(4 \ 2) \ LX(5 \ 3) \ LX(6 \ 3)$$

Alternatively, the preceding can be specified by using relevant numbered elements in LX as follows:

$$FR \ LX \ 1 \ LX \ 4 \ LX \ 8 \ LX \ 11 \ LX \ 15 \ LX \ 18$$

To clarify the latter format, following is a matrix corresponding to LX given above where its elements are numbered consecutively and those specified as FR circled.

$$\begin{bmatrix} \textcircled{1} & 2 & 3 \\ \textcircled{4} & 5 & 6 \\ 7 & \textcircled{8} & 9 \\ 10 & \textcircled{11} & 12 \\ 13 & 14 & \textcircled{15} \\ 16 & 17 & \textcircled{18} \end{bmatrix}$$

Instead of using the default LX mode on the MO statement, LX = FR may be specified. When this is done, the converse of the operation used above has to be carried out. That is, it is necessary to fix those elements of LX that are not to be estimated. The choice between the two approaches is a matter of convenience.

As was noted above, the default form of TD is diagonal. Its default mode is free. Specifying that TD = SY, however, means that the diagonal elements are still free but that the off-diagonal elements are *fixed*. Jöreskog and Sörbom decided to use this mixed mode, because, when the matrix is not diagonal, "usually only a few of the off-diagonal elements are free and these can be declared free by a FR line" (Manual, p. 14). In our example, only one of the off-diagonal elements is free. Therefore, specifying TD = SY on the MO statement would require a specification of FR (6 5) on the FRee line. When a relatively large number of the off-diagonal elements of TD are free, it is more convenient to specify TD = SY,FR on the MO statement, and then use the FIxed line to fix those elements that are not free.

If this is your first encounter with LISREL matrices and control statements, you are almost certainly overwhelmed. We would, therefore, like to stress that the presentation here was intended to give you only a general idea of the system. Rest assured that we will come back to most of the points made here by way of our numerical examples and/or our commentaries on them. To repeat, however, *it is imperative that you study the manual in order to develop a facility in using LISREL correctly and efficiently.*

NUMERICAL EXAMPLES

Several numerical examples, aimed at illustrating different aspects of the application of *CFA*, will be analyzed. For comparative purposes, we begin by analyzing the same numerical examples used to illustrate *EFA* in Chapter 22. In addition to differences between the two approaches discussed earlier, it will be seen that some difficulties or controversies arising in the application of *EFA* (e.g., estimates of communalities, factor rotations) do not arise in the context of *CFA*.

For illustrative purposes, two models will be fitted and tested for each of the numerical examples of Chapter 22: (a) uncorrelated factors and (b) correlated factors. This will enable us to illustrate and explain tests and fits of different models. For ease of comparison, input and output for the two models estimated from the same data set will be presented alongside each other.

After the analyses of the numerical examples of Chapter 22 through LISREL, an orientation to EQS will be presented. One of the numerical examples analyzed through LISREL will then be analyzed through EQS.

We turn next to applications of *CFA* to the analysis of Multitrait-Multimethod Matrices. This is followed by an illustrative application of *CFA* to some measurement models.

One of the best ways to learn to use LISREL and/or EQS and become familiar with the output is to replicate published analyses and to experiment with variations on the models presented. We strongly recommend that you begin by replicating our analyses, perhaps calling for more detailed output than that we are reporting. After having developed some facility in running a program of your choice, it would be a good idea for you to vary the models we are presenting, analyze them, and study the results. You can then reanalyze more complex models reported in the literature. Most reports using *SEM* provide the information necessary for a reanalysis. Again, we suggest that you not only replicate the analyses reported but also try some variations on the models presented.

UNCORRELATED FACTORS

The correlation matrix analyzed in this section is taken from Chapter 22, Table 22.1. It will be recalled that, for illustrative purposes, we assumed that we are using six indicators of two dimensions of self-concept: Academic and Social. The same substantive example will be used in the application of *CFA* to these data.

Following are input statements for *two* LISREL solutions, which have been placed alongside each other for ease of comparison.[11] In the context of commentaries on the input, we comment also on the two models. We remind you of our practice of inserting brief comments in brackets alongside some input statements. *These comments are not part of the input file.* (See Chapter 16, for an explanation of our practice and format in reporting input statements, displaying output, and commenting on input and/or output.)

LISREL

Input

```
TABLE 22.1, TWO UNCORRELATED FACTORS          TABLE 22.1, TWO CORRELATED FACTORS
DA NI=6 NO= 200                               DA NI=6 NO=200
LA                    [LAbels for indicators]  LA
X1 X2 X3 X4 X5 X6                             X1 X2 X3 X4 X5 X6
KM                    [Correlation matrix]     KM
1.0 .502 1.0 .622 .551 1.0 .008 .072 .028 1.0 .027   1.0 .502 1.0 .622 .551 1.0 .008 .072 .028 1.0 .027
.030 −.049 .442 1.0 −.029 −.059 .018 .537 .413        .030 −.049 .442 1.0 −.029 −.059 .018 .537 .413
1.0                                           1.0
MO NX=6 NK=2 PH=FI  [Model statement]          MO NX=6 NK=2 PH=ST
FR LX 1 LX 3 LX 5 LX 8 LX 10 LX 12            FR LX 1 LX 3 LX 5 LX 8 LX 10 LX 12
ST 1 PH 1 1 PH 2 2                            LK
LK                    [LAbels for KSI's]       ACADEMIC SOCIAL
ACADEMIC SOCIAL                               OU RS
OU RS
```

---

[11] Instead of running each problem separately, they may be stacked (see Manual, p. 74).

Commentary

Before commenting on specific input statements, some general observations will be made about LISREL input.

In LISREL, "The term 'line' is used . . . in the sense of an input record from a terminal or a punched card. On a terminal the end of a record is specified by a RETURN character" (Manual, p. 51). We will use the term control statement, or statement, and line interchangeably. Although several statements, separated by semicolons, may be placed on the same physical line, for the sake of clarity, we refrain from doing this.

Line names consist of two-letters (e.g., MO, OU) and may contain one or more parameters with certain keywords.

The following statements (lines) are required for any run: (a) DAta, (b) MOdel, and (c) OUtput. Additional lines may be necessary for the definition of the data and/or the model. We turn now to an explanation of the input statements given above.

Although not required, *a title line(s) is strongly recommended*. Only a title line(s) may precede the DA line. *Make sure that title lines do not begin with the letters DA*, as this would be interpreted as a DA line resulting in the termination of the run and error messages that you may find puzzling. Although we used brief titles to indicate the source of the data and the type of model tested, we remind you of our recommendation (Chapter 16) that you include clear and ample documentation of output. As you can see from the titles, the input on the left is for uncorrelated factors whereas that on the right is for correlated ones. We begin by commenting on the statements that are identical in the two inputs and then comment on statements for which the inputs differ.

DA = DAtaparameters statement; NI = Number of Input variables; NO = Number of Observations; other parameters may be included in the DA statement. For example, MA = type of matrix to be analyzed may be specified. By default, the covariance matrix (CM) is analyzed. Note that MA refers to the type of matrix to be analyzed, *not* to the type of matrix read in. Thus, for example, one may read in raw data, or a correlation matrix (KM) along with standard deviations (SD). However, when MA is not specified on DA (i.e., when the default is used), the covariance matrix will be analyzed (see Measurement Models, later in this chapter, for an example).

As we are reading in a correlation matrix only (see KM, below), it will be analyzed by default. Had we read in a correlation matrix *and* standard deviations, we would have had the choice of the following: (a) using the default (i.e., not specifying MA), thereby analyzing the covariance matrix; or (b) specifying MA = KM, in which case the correlation matrix would be analyzed.

LAbel statements are optional. We suggest that you label both the indicators and the latent variables (see LK, below), thereby facilitating your reading of the output. In Table 22.1, we used Y's for the first three indicators and X's for the last three. We could have, of course, used the same labels here. Instead, we chose to label all the indicators as X's so as to be consistent with LISREL's nomenclature according to which indicators of KSI's are referred to as X's (see NX on the MO statement, and LX on the FR statement).

KM = correlation matrix. Specifying KM only signifies that the correlation matrix that follows is in free format. Note that the lower triangle of the correlation matrix is read in with blanks separating the different elements. Other types of free and fixed formats are available. In the Manual (see p. 277), it is recommended that data *not* be included in the input file, that an external file be used instead, as this would facilitate the detection of certain kinds of input errors. We do not follow this practice, because our data sets are small.

MO refers to the MOdel statement. On it, we specify that the number of indicators is 6

(NX = 6), and the number of KSI's (latent variables) is 2 (NK = 2). Note that, because TD (THETA DELTA) is *not* specified, the default (DIagonal, FRee) will be used.

Thus far, the statements for both runs are identical. Note, however, that PH = FI in the input for the uncorrelated factors whereas PH = ST for the input for correlated factors. We comment on these differences later on.

As was pointed out earlier, LX (LAMBDA X) is fixed by default. It is, therefore, necessary to free the elements that are to be estimated. Earlier, we explained how this is done by using a FRee statement. LX in the present example consists of 6 rows (6 *X*'s) and two columns (2 KSI's). We suggest that you write out this matrix, numbering its elements in the manner shown earlier. Doing this will enable you to see that elements 1, 3, and 5 refer to coefficients for KSI 1, whereas 8, 10, and 12 refer to coefficients for KSI 2 (this matrix is also displayed below as part of the LISREL output).

In sum, in so using the FR statement, we specify that the first three *X*'s are reflective indicators of KSI 1, whereas the last three *X*'s are reflective indicators of KSI 2. This, it will be recalled, is in sharp contrast with *EFA*, where each indicator has loadings on all the factors.

LK is used to label the latent KSI variables, which we have labeled ACADEMIC and SOCIAL.

Earlier, it was pointed out that one of the issues that must be addressed before attempting to analyze the data is that of model identification. We comment on this topic in Chapter 24. For now, it will suffice to point out that:

A factor analytic model cannot be identified until a metric, or scale, of the common factors has been established. If the scale of a factor is not established, there exists an indeterminacy between the variance of a common factor and the loadings of observed variables on that factor. . . . [I]t is not possible to estimate both loadings on and the variances of common factors. (Long, 1983a, pp. 49–50)

Two approaches are most commonly used to resolve the indeterminacy alluded to above. In one approach, the metric (measurement units) of one of the indicators is selected to serve as the metric for a given KSI. This approach is explained and used in Chapter 24. In the second approach, used throughout this chapter, the variances of the KSI's are fixed to equal 1.0, thus, standardizing the latent variables. It is necessary to distinguish between standardization of observed variables and that of latent variables. When analyzing correlation matrices, as we are doing in the present examples, the observed variables (indicators) are standardized (see Chapter 17). If a covariance matrix were analyzed instead, the observed variables would, of course, not be standardized. But the latent variables could still be standardized (see Measurement Models, later in this chapter).

With the foregoing remarks in mind, we turn to the specification of PH on the MO statements in the two inputs, beginning with the one for uncorrelated factors. Earlier, it was pointed out that PH is the covariance matrix of the KSI's. Note that PH = FIxed was specified on the MO statement in the input for the uncorrelated factors. As a result, all elements, *including the variances of the KSI's*, are set to 0. To alter this, we use the STarting-values statement, one of the purposes of which is to "define non-zero values for fixed parameters" (Manual, p. 67).

Note that we have specified a starting value of 1 (ST 1) for PH 1 1 and PH 2 2. These are the elements of the diagonal of PH; thus, the variances of the two KSI's are fixed to equal 1.0. As no mention was made of the remaining element, PH 2 1, it is fixed at 0 (because of PH = FI on the MO statement). Accordingly, it is hypothesized that the covariance (i.e., the correlation in the present case) between KSI 1 and KSI 2 is zero, which is what we want for this model.

Various other approaches could be taken to accomplish the same end. For example, PH could be declared DIagonal and FIxed. We chose instead the above approach to show clearly the differences between the two analyses.

Turning now to the MO statement for the correlated factors, it will be noted that PH = ST. In this specification, ST *does not* refer to starting values (discussed above) but rather to "a symmetric matrix with fixed ones in the diagonal (a correlation matrix)" (Manual, p. 12). ST—one of the possible forms of PH (Manual, p. 12)—facilitates specification of PH when it is hypothesized that latent variables are correlated. As you can see, using PH = ST obviated the need for using ST 1 to fix the variances of the KSI's—the approach taken for the case of uncorrelated factors.

To enhance your understanding of the system, we will indicate how the same result could have been accomplished using a different approach. We could have used the same statements as for the uncorrelated factors (i.e., the same PH and the same STart values of 1). In addition, it would have been necessary to FRee PH 2 1. This could have been included in the statement in which the LX's were freed.

The present example consists of two KSI's only; therefore, it does not matter much which of these two approaches is taken. With larger numbers of KSI's, however, it is more convenient to use PH = ST, provided it is hypothesized that *all* the factors are intercorrelated. PH = ST should *not* be used when only some of the factors are hypothesized to be intercorrelated (see Manual, p. 14). Under such circumstances, relevant FIxed and/or FRee statements must be used.

OUtput must be the last input line for each LISREL problem. Specifying OU only, ML estimation is assumed and default output is printed. Specifying RS, residual statistics will be included in the output. (For various options for estimation procedures and additional output that may be specified on the OUtput line, see Manual pp. 71–73.)

This concludes our commentaries on the input. We turn now to a presentation of *excerpts* of output, along with commentaries. As in the case of the input, outputs for the two solutions are placed alongside each other.

Output

DOS—L I S R E L 7.16

BY

KARL G JORESKOG AND DAG SORBOM

TABLE 22.1

COVARIANCE MATRIX TO BE ANALYZED

	X1	X2	X3	X4	X5	X6
X1	1.000					
X2	.502	1.000				
X3	.622	.551	1.000			
X4	.008	.072	.028	1.000		
X5	.027	.030	−.049	.442	1.000	
X6	−.029	−.059	.018	.537	.413	1.000

Commentary

LISREL output begins with a listing of the input, thus, enabling the user to check on potential errors. The listings look exactly as the inputs given earlier; thus, they are not reproduced here.

The input listing is followed by a catalog of the numbers and types of variables the user has specified. This too is not reproduced here.

The next piece of output, the covariance matrix to be analyzed, is reproduced here for ease of reference. In the present example, this is also the correlation matrix which was read in. As was pointed out above, however, the type of matrix that is analyzed is determined by the specification of MA on the DA statement.

Output

TABLE 22.1, UNCORRELATED FACTORS PARAMETER SPECIFICATIONS	TABLE 22.1, CORRELATED FACTORS PARAMETER SPECIFICATIONS

LAMBDA X

	ACADEMIC	SOCIAL			ACADEMIC	SOCIAL
X1	1	0		X1	1	0
X2	2	0		X2	2	0
X3	3	0		X3	3	0
X4	0	4		X4	0	4
X5	0	5		X5	0	5
X6	0	6		X6	0	6

PHI

	ACADEMIC	SOCIAL			ACADEMIC	SOCIAL
ACADEMIC	0			ACADEMIC	0	
SOCIAL	0	0		SOCIAL	7	0

THETA DELTA

X1	X2	X3	X4	X5	X6		X1	X2	X3	X4	X5	X6
7	8	9	10	11	12		8	9	10	11	12	13

Commentary

As is indicated by the subtitle of this segment of output, specifications of the parameters of the model are displayed in these matrices. A zero means the parameter in question is fixed. For example, in the uncorrelated factor solution, all elements of PHI are fixed; in the correlated factor solution, only the diagonal elements of PHI are fixed (see discussion of PH in connection with the MO statement, above).

Fixed parameters (i.e., signified by 0's in these matrices) can be assigned start values. Referring again to the PHI matrix, it will be recalled that the diagonal elements (indicated here as fixed) were fixed to 1's using the ST 1 statement (see Input and commentaries).

As you can see, parameters to be estimated are numbered sequentially across matrices. This numbering scheme differs in the following two ways from the one introduced and used earlier for the purpose of identifying elements in a matrix:

1. According to the scheme used earlier, all elements of the matrix were numbered. Here, only elements that are to be estimated are numbered. In other words, fixed elements are not numbered. As a result, the same element may be assigned different numbers depending on the scheme used. For example, the indicators of KSI 1 (ACADEMIC) are numbered here as 1, 2, and 3, whereas, using the scheme presented earlier, the same elements were numbered 1, 3, and 5 on the FR card (see Input, above).

2. According to the scheme used earlier, elements of each matrix are numbered independently of the other matrices. According to the scheme used here, elements are numbered sequentially across matrices.

As you can see, the two numbering schemes serve different purposes. The present one shows that 12 parameters are to be estimated for the uncorrelated model, whereas 13 are to be estimated for the correlated model. The additional parameter to be estimated in the latter model is that of the correlation between the two latent variables—indicated by the number 7 in the PHI matrix. In fact, this is the only difference between the two models.

Output

TABLE 22.1, UNCORRELATED FACTORS
LISREL ESTIMATES (MAXIMUM LIKELIHOOD)
LAMBDA X

	ACADEMIC	SOCIAL
X1	.753	.000
X2	.667	.000
X3	.826	.000
X4	.000	.758
X5	.000	.583
X6	.000	.708

PHI

	ACADEMIC	SOCIAL
ACADEMIC	1.000	
SOCIAL	.000	1.000

THETA DELTA

X1	X2	X3	X4	X5	X6
.433	.555	.317	.425	.660	.498

SQUARED MULTIPLE CORRELATIONS FOR X – VARIABLES

X1	X2	X3	X4	X5	X6
.567	.445	.683	.575	.340	.502

TABLE 22.1, CORRELATED FACTORS
LISREL ESTIMATES (MAXIMUM LIKELIHOOD)
LAMBDA X

	ACADEMIC	SOCIAL
X1	.753	.000
X2	.667	.000
X3	.826	.000
X4	.000	.759
X5	.000	.583
X6	.000	.708

PHI

	ACADEMIC	SOCIAL
ACADEMIC	1.000	
SOCIAL	.013	1.000

THETA DELTA

X1	X2	X3	X4	X5	X6
.433	.555	.317	.424	.660	.499

SQUARED MULTIPLE CORRELATIONS FOR X – VARIABLES

X1	X2	X3	X4	X5	X6
.567	.445	.683	.576	.340	.501

Commentary

To better understand this segment of the output, it will be pointed out that each indicator can be depicted as being affected by one or more latent variables (ξ's) and an error term (δ). Using X_1 as an example, this takes the following form:

$$x_1 = \lambda_{11}\xi_1 + \lambda_{12}\xi_2 + \delta_1 \qquad (23.2)$$

where the λ's are the coefficients of the effects of the latent variables in question on X_1. Note the resemblance of (23.2) to equations presented in Chapters 17 and 18 in connection with regression analysis. Differences in notations aside, the equation presented here differs from those presented in Chapters 17 and 18 in that it does not include an intercept. This is because, in most applications of *CFA*, correlations or covariances are analyzed. In either case, the means equal zero, hence, the intercept also equals zero. This is why we used a lower case x in (23.2).

According to the models being tested, ξ_2 *does not* affect X_1. In other words, $\lambda_{12} = 0$. In fact, this coefficient was fixed to 0 (see the Input, the output PARAMETER SPECIFICA-TIONS, and the commentaries). Accordingly, (23.2) can be restated as

$$x_1 = \lambda_{11}\xi_1 + \delta_1 \qquad (23.3)$$

For the models tested here, each indicator is said to be affected by only one ξ; thus, the format of (23.3) can be used to express each of the remaining five indicators.

The preceding could be expressed much more succinctly, using matrix notation (see, for example, Long, 1983a, p. 27; Pedhazur, 1982, p. 641). In any case, the λ's are contained in the LAMBDA X matrix given above. Thus, for example, the estimated effect of KSI 2 (SOCIAL) on X_5 is .583—similarly for the other indicators.

Recalling the assumption that errors are *not* correlated with the latent variables, it can be shown (e.g., Long, 1983a, p. 48) that:

$$\sigma_{11} = \lambda_{11}^2 \phi_{11} + \theta_{11} \tag{23.4}$$

where σ_{11} = variance of X_1; λ_{11} = effect of ξ_1 on X_1; ϕ_{11} = variance of ξ_1, the first element of the diagonal of Φ (PHI; an example of such a matrix was given earlier, in connection with Figure 23.1); θ_{11} = variance of δ_1, the first element of the diagonal of Θ_δ (THETA DELTA; an example of such a matrix was given earlier, in connection with Figure 23.1). In the present analyses, however, THETA DELTA is DIagonal FRee. That is, the covariances among the errors are fixed to 0. Thus, only variances of errors are estimated (see commentary on Input). This is why, in the output given above, THETA DELTA is reported as a row vector rather than as a matrix. The first element of this row (.433) is the estimated error variance for the first indicator (X_1); the second element is the estimated error variance for X_2; and so forth.

In the analyses under consideration, the variances of the ξ's were fixed to equal 1.0 (see ST 1 of Input, and commentary). Accordingly, the variance of any of the indicators can be expressed as the square of the effect of the latent variable in question plus the variance of errors. For X_1, for example, this takes the following form:

$$\sigma_{11} = \lambda_{11}^2 + \theta_{11} \tag{23.5}$$

—similarly for the variances of the other indicators. Clearly, (23.5) is a special case of (23.4), when the variance of the latent variable equals 1.0.

The application of (23.5) will now be illustrated, using estimates reported in the above output. Recall that we are analyzing a correlation matrix. Hence, the variance of each of the indicators is 1.0. Taking, as a first example, the variance of X_1, it will be noted that λ_{11} = .753 (see LAMBDA X, above), and that θ_{11} = .433 (see THETA DELTA, above). Therefore,

$$(.753)^2 + .433 = .567 + .433 = 1.000$$

Accordingly, about 57% of the variance of X_1 is accounted for by KSI 1, whereas about 43% is due to error.[12]

Referring to the substantive example used in connection with these illustrative data, Academic Self-Concept accounts for about 57% of the variability of X_1, and about 43% of its variability is due to errors or unique to it.

As another example, consider X_6, whose coefficient (λ_{62}) is .708 (see LAMBDA X, above), and whose error variance (θ_{66}) is .498 (see THETA DELTA, above). Accordingly,

$$(.708)^2 + .498 = .501 + .498 = .999$$

Thus, Social Self-Concept (ξ_2) accounts for about 50% of the variance of X_6, and about 50% of its variance is due to errors or unique to it.

Before proceeding, we would like to stress that *the validity of interpretations of specific results of SEM is predicated on the soundness of the model and on whether it is deemed as providing a good fit to the data* (model fit is discussed below). Even if it is concluded that the model under consideration is tenable, the possibility of questioning it on substantive grounds is not thereby precluded. To give but two examples, it may be argued that the two latent variables constitute two dimensions of a different construct (e.g., two dimensions of ego strength are being tapped by the indicators in question) or that the two latent variables refer to two distinct constructs (e.g., one to self-concept and the other to ego strength).

---

[12]It should be noted that error variance is comprised of two components: (a) random errors, and (b) unique to the indicator in question. We return to this point later in this chapter (see Measurement Models).

We hope you recognize the issues we raise here as not unlike those we raised in connection with the naming of factors in the application of *EFA* (Chapter 22). The application of *EFA* or *CFA* is but one aspect of the ongoing complex process of construct validation, discussed in Chapter 4. In sum, we hope you will beware of being beguiled by fancy analyses. Theoretical considerations should be your point of departure and critical thinking your primary tool.

Returning to the excerpt of output under consideration, look at the segment labeled SQUARED MULTIPLE CORRELATIONS FOR X − VARIABLES. The definition of these squared multiple correlations (SMC) is

$$1 - \hat{\theta}_{ii}/\hat{\sigma}_{ii} \tag{23.6}$$

"where $\hat{\theta}_{ii}$ is the estimated error variance and $\hat{\sigma}_{ii}$ is the fitted variance of the i:th variable" (Manual, p. 42).

When, as in the kind of models under consideration, an indicator is said to reflect only one latent variable, SMC is the proportion of variance of the indicator accounted for by the latent variable in question. Accordingly, SMC can be taken as an estimated reliability of the indicator with which it is associated. Recall, however, that θ is comprised of both random errors and variance unique to the indicator (see footnote 12). In the presence of the latter, therefore, SMC would underestimate reliability. (For suggested interpretations of SMC when an indicator is said to be affected by more than one latent variable, see Bollen, 1989, pp. 220–221 and 288.)

Referring to results given above, and *assuming that the model fits the data* (see below), estimated reliabilities of X_1, X_2, and X_3 as indicators of Academic Self-Concept are respectively .567, .445, and .683. Those of X_4, X_5, and X_6 as indicators of Social Self-Concept are respectively .575, .340, and .502.

Finally, we draw your attention to the results reported for the analysis with correlated factors. Note that the estimated correlation between the two latent variables is practically 0 (.013; see PHI matrix). We discuss this correlation in the next section, in connection with tests of the models.

Output

MEASURES OF GOODNESS OF FIT FOR THE WHOLE MODEL :	MEASURES OF GOODNESS OF FIT FOR THE WHOLE MODEL :
CHI-SQUARE WITH 9 DEGREES OF FREEDOM = 9.11 (P = .427)	CHI-SQUARE WITH 8 DEGREES OF FREEDOM = 9.09 (P = .335)

Commentary

The output on the left is for the uncorrelated-factors solution, that on the right for the correlated-factors solution.

You are probably familiar with the χ^2 (chi-square) goodness-of-fit test of differences between observed and expected frequencies. The same general idea is behind the χ^2 used here, although the manner in which it is carried out is much more complex. Instead of a formal explanation, we explain the idea behind this test and how the results are interpreted. This is followed by a brief discussion of the assumptions underlying the test and some general suggestions for its use.

Earlier, it was pointed out that the estimated parameters of a model may be used to reproduce the covariance or correlation matrix. It is a function of discrepancies between the observed covariance matrix and the reproduced one (see FITTED RESIDUALS, below) that is involved in the χ^2 test reported above.

The degrees of freedom (df) associated with the χ^2 equal the number of observed variances and covariances minus the number of parameters estimated. The number of variances and covariances is equal to $k(k + 1)/2$, where k is the number of indicators (manifest variables). In the example under consideration, $k = 6$. Hence, the number of observed variances and covariances is 21. In the solution for uncorrelated factors, 12 parameters are estimated (see PARAMETER SPECIFICATIONS and commentaries, above). Hence, $df = 9$. Because an additional parameter is estimated in the solution for correlated factors (i.e., the correlation between the factors), $df = 8$.

The null hypothesis being tested is that the model provides a satisfactory fit for the observed data, that is, elements of the correlation or the covariance matrix reproduced by using parameter estimates of some model are statistically not significantly different from the observed correlation or covariance matrix. The probabilities associated with the χ^2's for the models of uncorrelated and correlated factors are respectively .427 and .335. Assuming, for the sake of illustration, that $\alpha = .05$ was selected for the analyses under consideration, it would be concluded that both models provide satisfactory fits to the data. Before addressing the question of how one would select between the two models, we comment on both the logic of the testing strategy and the assumptions underlying the χ^2 test.

LOGIC OF TESTING STRATEGY

The strategy for tests of statistical significance outlined above differs from the customary use of such tests, as explicated in Chapters 9 and 15. Without repeating the discussion in the aforementioned chapters, some of the ideas relevant for present purposes will be briefly reviewed.

In customary applications, the researcher wishes to reject the null hypothesis (e.g., that means do not differ from each other, that observed frequencies are not different from expected ones) so as to be in a position to assert that the alternative substantive hypothesis was supported. As you can see from the explanation given above, the converse approach is taken in the present context. The null hypothesis constitutes the substantive hypothesis that the researcher is generally interested in supporting. Thus, whereas, in customary applications of χ^2, the researcher wishes to obtain large values that would lead to the rejection of the null hypothesis, in applications of the kind discussed here, it appears that the smaller the χ^2, the better, as this would lead to failure to reject the null hypothesis.

Logical problems and difficulties attendant with attempts to support the null hypothesis were discussed in Chapter 9, where it was argued that a failure to reject the null hypothesis should not be construed as evidence supporting it. In addition, issues concerning Type I and Type II errors, power of the statistical test, and sample size were discussed in Chapters 9 and 15. For present purposes, it will only be recalled that the lower the power of the test, the greater the probability of *not* rejecting the null hypothesis. In the present context, then, it would appear that tests with low power are preferable.

Below, we comment on sample size and on indices of fit of a model. Recall, however, that, other things equal, the larger the sample size, the greater the power of the test and vice versa. Therefore, with small samples, the probability of supporting one's hypothesis—even when the model fit is very poor—is relatively high. In contrast, with large samples, the probability of supporting one's hypothesis—even when the model provides what is deemed a very good fit—is relatively low. We turn now to the major assumptions underlying the χ^2 test under consideration.

ASSUMPTIONS

1. *Multivariate Normality*. It is assumed that the observed variables follow a multivariate normal distribution. As you probably know, a bivariate normal distribution is a generalization of the concept of the normal distribution (the so-called bell-shaped curve) to the case of the joint distribution of two variables (see, for example, Hays, 1988, pp. 587–588, 879–881). The multivariate normal distribution is a generalization of this concept to the joint distribution of more than two variables. Discussions of the multivariate normal distribution will be found in books on multivariate analysis (e.g., Srivastava & Carter, 1983, Chapter 2; Stevens, 1986, pp. 205–212).

Although procedures for the evaluation of multivariate normality have been proposed, they are not easily implemented (for some suggestions and illustrations, see Stevens, 1986, pp. 207–212). It is, however, easier to check on conditions necessary for multivariate normality. For example, for multivariate normality to hold, it is necessary, *although not sufficient*, that each of the variables be normally distributed or that all bivariate distributions be normal. Such assumptions are more readily checked by available computer packages (see Stevens, 1986, pp. 212–215; see also, Bentler, 1985, pp. 53–54).

The "χ^2-measure is . . . very sensitive to departures from multivariate normality of observed variables" (Manual, p. 43). When the assumption of multivariate normality is not met, "the statistical basis of the method is lost and standard errors and chi square tests have little meaning" (Bentler, 1982a, p. 421). Probably because it is usually not met in practice, Bentler (1984) branded the assumption of multivariate normality as a "straightjacket" (p. 105) and, thus, advocated the use of estimation procedures that are not based on it (Bentler, 1985). Similar views were expressed by Jöreskog and Sörbom (Manual, p. 43), who, therefore, incorporated various other methods of estimation in LISREL. In addition, they developed PRELIS—a computer program designed for, among other things, data screening, transformations, calculations of measures of association among non-normally distributed variables, and ordinal variables.[13] (For a description of PRELIS, see LISREL manual, pp. 19–20.)

2. *Matrix Analyzed*. It is assumed that a *covariance* matrix is analyzed. Thus, χ^2 tests and standard errors (discussed later in this chapter) are not applicable to situations where a correlation matrix is analyzed. Nevertheless, correlation matrices are analyzed in many applications of *CFA* (this is true for all but one of the examples of the present chapter). The reason researchers frequently choose to analyze correlations instead of covariances is that they are unable to attach substantive meaning to the units of the measures they are using. This is not unlike the situation in regression analysis, where researchers choose to interpret standardized regression coefficients (β's) instead of unstandardized coefficients (b's; see Chapters 17 and 18). As we pointed out in the aforementioned chapters, reliance on standardized regression coefficients does not address problems and ambiguities attendant with the measures used but rather serves to evade them. The same holds true in the present context, once more highlighting the importance of developing meaningful measures.

3. *Sampling and Sample Size*. This topic was discussed in some detail in Chapter 22 in the context of *EFA*. As the issues raised are generally applicable to *CFA*, they are not repeated here. Instead, we focus on issues concerning sample size, as they relate to tests of significance in *CFA*.

For the χ^2 test to be valid, it is further assumed that "the sample size is sufficiently large" (Manual, p. 42). Understandably, there is no agreement about the meaning of "sufficiently large." Using Monte Carlo studies, various authors (e.g., Anderson & Gerbing, 1984; Boomsma, 1987) studied the effects of sample size on tests of significance, convergence, and the like. Some also proposed rules of thumb regarding sample size. Boomsma (1987), for

---

[13]PRELIS is a registered trademark of Scientific Software, Inc., P.O. Box 397, Fairplay, CO 80440. We would like to thank Scientific Software Inc., for furnishing us with a review copy of this program.

example, recommended that a sample size of at least 200 be used in factor analytic studies. For a recent review of issues concerning determination of sample size in *SEM*, see Tanaka (1987), who, among other things, pointed out that, unlike the situation in multiple regression analysis where rules of thumb about sample size are formulated with regard to the ratio of the number of subjects to the number of variables, in *SEM*, the ratio of concern is that of the number of subjects to the number of estimated parameters.[14] Interestingly, Tanaka (1987) stated: "Recent developments in latent-variable models that make fewer assumptions about the distribution of the data and allow for data nonnormality will require more subjects than more standard methods, such as ML and GLS" (p. 143).

We hope you appreciate the Catch–22 researchers face when having to decide on sample size. As was discussed above, the smaller the sample, the greater the probability of "support-ing" the null hypothesis, which is the hypothesis of interest. But the valid interpretation of the χ^2 test is predicated on sufficiently large samples. Using large samples, however, in-creases the probability of rejecting the model.

In view of the difficulties attendant with the use of the χ^2 statistics reviewed above, Jöreskog and Sörbom suggested that it not be used for hypothesis testing but rather as a "goodness (or badness)-of-fit measure in the sense that large χ^2-values correspond to bad fit and small χ^2-values to good fit. The degrees of freedom serve as a standard by which to judge whether χ^2 is large or small" (Manual, p. 43).

In a relatively early application of LISREL, Wheaton, Muthén, Alwin, and Summers (1977) proposed, "*somewhat in passing* [italics added]" (Wheaton, 1987, p. 127), a χ^2/df ratio of 5 or less as a rough indication of reasonable fit *for their models*. Referring to Wheaton et al.'s criterion, Carmines and McIver (1981) suggested instead, on the basis of their experience, a χ^2/df ratio of 2 or 3 as a criterion of fit. As often happens with rules-of-thumb, the χ^2/df ratio has become very popular and appears to have acquired surplus meaning. Deploring the popularity of the χ^2/df ratio, Wheaton (1987) argued against its use as an index of fit and pointed out, among other things, that it is affected by sample size—one of the very problems it was meant to overcome (see also, Hoelter, 1983a).

Various other indices of fit have been proposed. We introduce some of them in the commentary on the next excerpt of output and later on in connection with the output from EQS. We turn now to the use of the χ^2 for tests of nested models.

NESTED MODELS

When one or more free parameters of a model are constrained (e.g., constraining them to equal zero), the model thus obtained is said to be nested in the one from which it was derived. A nested model, therefore, is a "special case" (Long, 1983a, p. 65) or "a specialization" (Bentler & Bonett, 1980, p. 592) of a more comprehensive model. Referring to the numerical examples under consideration, the uncorrelated-factors model is nested in the correlated-factors model, as it is obtained by constraining the correlation between the factors to equal zero.

It stands to reason for a given model to fit the data better than one nested in it. A question that naturally arises is: "Does the improvement in fit provided by a more comprehensive model warrant preferring it to a more parsimonious model nested in it?" You will probably not be surprised to learn that an answer to this question may be attempted from statistical

---

[14]For a similar point in the context of *EFA*, see Chapter 22.

tests of significance or from substantive perspectives. The discussion here is limited to the former.

A test of significance in improvement of fit can be viewed as a test of the improvement that results from freeing one or more parameters of a model, thereby obtaining the more comprehensive model in which it is nested.

A large drop in χ^2, compared to the difference in degrees of freedom, indicates that the changes made in the model represent a real improvement. On the other hand, a drop in χ^2 close to the difference in the number of degrees of freedom indicates that the improvement in fit is obtained by "capitalizing on chance," and the added parameters may not have real significance and meaning. (Manual, p. 44)

The application of such a test will now be illustrated using the numerical examples analyzed above. From the output given earlier, we have: (a) CHI-SQUARE = 9.11, with 9 df, for uncorrelated factors; and (b) CHI-SQUARE = 9.09, with 8 df, for correlated factors. Accordingly, for a test of the difference between the two models, CHI-SQUARE = .02, with 1 df. Clearly, there is virtually no improvement in fit.

Because the difference between the two models under consideration concerns only one parameter (i.e., whether or not the factors are correlated), it follows that, in cases such as the present one, a test of the difference between the two models is tantamount to a test of the one parameter from the more restricted model that was freed.[15] Recalling that the estimated correlation between the factors is .013 (see output above), the results of the test of improvement of fit are to be expected. The present example should also serve to illustrate another point, namely that, even if the difference between the two chi-squares was statistically significant, it would have been imprudent, on substantive grounds, to take the correlation seriously.

In sum, on the basis of this analysis, one would be justified in retaining the more restricted model. Recall that, for illustrative purposes, we assumed that the six manifest variables analyzed above are indicators of two dimensions of self-concept. Assuming it were hypothesized that the two dimensions in question are correlated, the results of the test between the two models would lead to the rejection of this hypothesis.

Finally, suppose, for the sake of another illustration, that the indicators used above were said to be reflective of two constructs (e.g., motivation and anxiety) instead of two dimensions of a single construct. Suppose, further, that it was hypothesized that the two constructs in question are correlated. In light of the above results, this hypothesis would be rejected.[16]

Output

TABLE 22.1, TWO UNCORRELATED FACTORS
GOODNESS OF FIT INDEX = .985
ADJUSTED GOODNESS OF FIT INDEX = .965
ROOT MEAN SQUARE RESIDUAL = .026

FITTED RESIDUALS

	X1	X2	X3	X4	X5	X6
X1	.000					
X2	.000	.000				
X3	.000	.000	.000			
X4	.008	.072	.028	.000		
X5	.027	.030	−.049	.000	.000	
X6	−.029	−.059	.018	.000	.000	.000

TABLE 22.1, TWO CORRELATED FACTORS
GOODNESS OF FIT INDEX = .985
ADJUSTED GOODNESS OF FIT INDEX = .961
ROOT MEAN SQUARE RESIDUAL = .026

FITTED RESIDUALS

	X1	X2	X3	X4	X5	X6
X1	.000					
X2	.000	.000				
X3	.000	.000	.000			
X4	.000	.065	.020	.000		
X5	.021	.025	−.055	−.000	.000	
X6	−.036	−.065	.010	.000	.000	.000

[15]Tests of specific coefficients in a model are discussed in Chapter 24.

[16]The question of what would lead one to claim to be dealing with two dimensions of the same construct, as opposed to two constructs, was addressed in Chapter 4.

Commentary

The three indices of fit reported in the beginning of this excerpt of the output are related to the matrix that follows them; thus, we begin with some comments about the latter.

FITTED RESIDUALS are obtained by subtracting reproduced correlations (covariances) from their respective observed correlations (covariances). To clarify this, we illustrate how correlations between indicators are reproduced using relevant parameter estimates of the model in question. To this end, we present in Figure 23.2 the two models under considera-

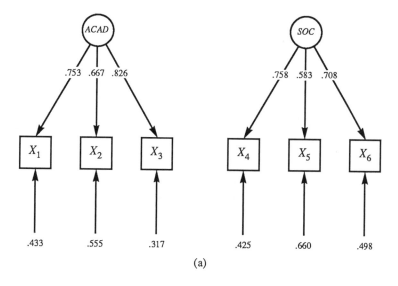

(a)

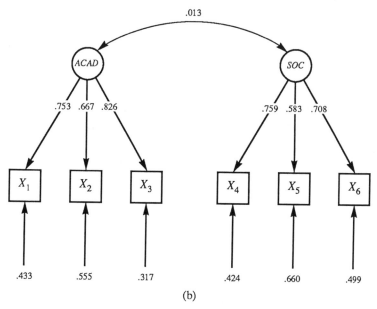

(b)

Figure 23.2

tion, along with their estimated parameters. Values reported on the arrows emanating from the factors or latent variables (ACADemic and SOCial Self-Concept) are estimates of their effects on the indicators (these were taken from LAMBDA X reported earlier). Values reported at the base of arrows referring to error terms are *variances* (obtained from THETA DELTA reported earlier).

Turning first to the uncorrelated-factor solution (*a*), we begin by showing how correlations between indicators of the same factor are reproduced. For illustrative purposes, we do this for the correlation between X1 and X2. Look at the arrows pointing to these two indicators. According to this model, both indicators reflect or are affected by the same latent variable (or factor), namely ACADemic Self-Concept. In addition, the errors of each are *not* correlated. Clearly, the correlation between these indicators is depicted as being due solely to the latent variable they reflect. Accordingly, their coefficients on ACAD are multiplied:

$$(.753)(.667) = .502$$

Incidentally, reproduced correlations (covariances) are reported in the FITTED COVARIANCE MATRIX in LISREL output (not given here). As the observed correlation between these two indicators is .502 (see beginning of this output or Table 22.1), the fitted residual is

$$.502 - .502 = .000$$

which is the value reported in the FITTED RESIDUALS matrix. If you used the relevant coefficients to reproduce the correlations between indicators of the same latent variable, you would find that they are all the same as their respective observed variables. Hence, the .000 in the FITTED RESIDUALS matrix for indicators of the same latent variable.

Turning now to indicators of different variables, it is clear that, according to model (*a*), they have nothing in common. Hence, correlations between such indicators are expected to be zero. Therefore, the FITTED RESIDUALS for such indicators are equal to their observed correlations (i.e., subtracting zero from each observed correlation). Compare these values with the input correlation matrix given in the beginning of this output or in Table 22.1.

Turning now to the correlated-factors model (*b*), it should be clear that the reproduced correlations for indicators of the same latent variable are obtained in the manner illustrated for model (*a*). Therefore, we show only how correlations between indicators of different latent variables are reproduced. For illustrative purposes, we do this for the correlation between X1 and X6. Examine (*b*) of Figure 23.2 and notice that, according to it, X1 and X6 are expected to be correlated, because they reflect correlated latent variables.

The magnitude of the reproduced correlation is affected by the coefficients affecting each of the indicators and by the correlation between the two factors. Because the latter is close to zero (i.e., .013), the reproduced correlation between X1 and X6 is expected to be very small. From Figure 23.2 (*b*), the effect of ACAD on X1 is .753; the effect of SOC on X6 is .708; the correlation between ACAD and SOC is .013. Using these values, the reproduced correlation between the two indicators is:

$$(.753)(.013)(.708) = .007$$

Now, the observed correlation between X1 and X6 is −.029 (see beginning of the output). The residual is, therefore,

$$(-.029) - (.007) = -.036$$

which is the same as the value reported in the FITTED RESIDUALS matrix.

From the foregoing explanation, it follows that, the better the fit of a model, the smaller the fitted residuals. In the extreme case of a prefect fit, all fitted residuals will equal zero.

Relatively large residuals may serve as clues to specification errors in the model being fitted. What is to be regarded a large residual is, of course, an arbitrary decision. Nevertheless, when, as in the present examples, a correlation matrix is analyzed, it is not difficult to decide on some reasonable cutoff, say .05, as in such situations, a fitted residual may range from 0 to $|1.0|$. In view of the fact that most of the fitted residuals in the above examples are $<|.05|$, it may be concluded that the models fit the data well.

When a covariance matrix is analyzed (see Chapter 24), the decision as to what is to be considered a large residual is more complicated, as under such circumstances, magnitudes of covariances and, hence, residuals are affected by the units of the scales used to measure the indicators in question.[17] It is for this reason that LISREL provides an additional matrix, that of standardized residuals (see Manual, pp. 31–32 for a description). "In principle, each standardized residual can be interpreted as a standard normal deviate and considered 'large' if it exceeds the value 2.58 in absolute value" (Manual, p. 32). In view of the small fitted residuals in our numerical examples (see above) it is not surprising that virtually all the standardized residuals (not reported here) are small. For the correlated-factors solution, only one value is slightly greater than 1; for the uncorrelated-factor solution, only two values are slightly greater than $|1.0|$.

Although fitted or standardized residuals are useful, there is understandably an interest in a single index of overall fit of the model to the data. The need for such an index of fit is especially urgent in view of the problems and difficulties attendant with the use of the χ^2 goodness-of-fit test (see above). In particular, indices of fit are intended to overcome problems arising from the effect of sample size on tests of significance. In a broader context, this has to do with the distinction between tests of significance and effect size, addressed in several places (e.g., Chapters 9 and 15).

Various authors (e.g., Bentler & Bonett, 1980; Hoelter, 1983a; Jöreskog & Sörbom, 1989) proposed different fit indices. (For a review, see Wheaton, 1987. For a review of the effect of sample size on various fit indices, see Marsh, Balla, & McDonald, 1988.) In various places in this chapter and the next one, we introduce and comment on some of the indices that have been proposed. In the present context, we address only overall indices of fit that are part of the LISREL output. Later, when we present output of EQS, we describe and comment on indices Bentler and Bonett proposed.

LISREL reports three indices of fit, shown in the beginning of the excerpt of output under consideration. The simplest to describe is the ROOT MEAN SQUARE RESIDUAL (RMR), which is a kind of an average of the fitted residuals. Specifically, it is the square root of the average of the squared fitted residuals. Accordingly, when a correlation matrix is analyzed, a decision about the magnitude of RMR will follow the same line of reasoning as that suggested earlier in connection with fitted residuals. For the analyses under consideration, the RMR's (.026) may be considered small.

The GOODNESS OF FIT INDEX (GFI) is based on properties of the observed and reproduced correlation (covariance) matrices (its definition, in matrix notation, is given in the Manual, p. 44). ADJUSTED GOODNESS OF FIT INDEX (AGFI) refers to an adjusted GFI for degrees of freedom in the model (see Manual, p. 44). Both indices "should be between zero and one, although it is theoretically possible for them to become negative" (Manual, p. 44).

---

[17]For an introduction to properties of covariances and correlations, see beginning of Chapter 17.

Jöreskog and Sörbom refrained from offering criteria for what is to be considered a "good" fit. Moreover, by and large, they appeared to have ignored their indices of fit in their illustrative examples. A notable case in point is their analysis of a model of Stability of Alienation (Manual, pp. 169–177).[18] Having analyzed a given model (Model B), Jöreskog and Sörbom reported a χ^2 of 71.47 with 6 df, and concluded: "This is not considered an acceptable fit" (Manual, p. 175). They, therefore, fitted a modified model (Model C), for which they found the χ^2 is 6.33 with 5 df. On the basis of the marked drop in the χ^2, associated with a single degree of freedom (see Nested Models, above), they concluded that the modified model "fits quite well" (Manual, p. 175).

We are *not* concerned here with the very important substantive issues of this model that constitutes part of a larger study by Wheaton et al. (1977), from which Jöreskog and Sörbom borrowed the data. Our *sole concern* is with the issue of the assessment of a model's fit.

It is notable that Jöreskog and Sörbom did not even report their indices of fit. If you were to reanalyze the data (we strongly suggest you do this as an exercise),[19] you would find that, for Model B, which Jöreskog and Sörbom rejected, GFI = .975, and AGFI = .913. Recalling that the maximum value for these indices is 1.0, one cannot but wonder what their magnitude would have to be to qualify as indicating a satisfactory fit.

If you were to adopt criteria suggested by some authors, you would conclude that the above indices did indicate a good fit. For example, Cole (1987) stated that values greater than .9 and .8 for GFI and AGFI respectively "usually indicate good fit" (p. 586).

Indicative of difficulties in determining what constitutes a good fit is the fact that other authors fitting the models advanced by Jöreskog and Sörbom to the same data arrived at different conclusions. Thus, on the basis of the analysis of the residuals for Model B (the one rejected by Jöreskog & Sörbom), Everitt (1984) concluded that "the model fits the data fairly well; this highlights, perhaps, the problem . . . of relying too heavily on the chi-square statistic as a measure of fit" (p. 60).

It is important to note that Everitt's conclusion was based on residuals obtained from an earlier version of LISREL. According to Jöreskog and Sörbom, standardized residuals reported in LISREL versions prior to Version 7 are *underestimated* (see Manual, pp. 31–32). Here is what they said about this topic in the section on LISREL 7 vs LISREL 6: "Standardized residuals (called normalized residuals in LISREL 6) *may differ considerably* [italics added] between LISREL 6 and LISREL 7. An oversimplified formula for the asymptotic variances of the residuals was used in LISREL 6" (Manual, p. v).

If you followed our recommendation and replicated the analyses of this example, we suggest that you compare the standardized residuals reported by Everitt (1984, p. 61) and those reported in LISREL 7 output. You would find that some of them do indeed differ considerably. It is probably safe to assume that, had the standardized residuals reported in LISREL 7 been available to him, Everitt would have reached a different conclusion about the fit of the model. Be that as it may, that this happens to an erudite author should give us cause to be extremely cautious when using computer programs whose results we cannot check.[20] According to the LISREL manual, "in LISREL 7, the correct formula [for the standard error of fitted residuals] is used" (p. 32). It should be noted, however, that even knowledgeable readers are not in a position to check on the correctness of the formula, as all that is stated is

---

[18]Although they are testing a structural model (see Chapter 24) rather than *CFA*, the broad issues of assessment of fit apply in both circumstances.

[19]On the examples diskette supplied with PC–LISREL, the files for this example are identified as EX64.

[20]For a more detailed discussion of this topic, see Chapter 16.

that it "is a very complicated function of the elements of **S**. This is derived in Volume II" (Manual, p. 31), which has not been published yet.

Also of special interest is the reanalysis of this example by Bentler and Bonett (1980; see also, Bentler, 1982b, 1985). We discuss Bentler–Bonett fit indices later on (see commentaries on EQS output). For now, it is of interest to note that they reported an index of fit of .967 for Model B and stated that "the remaining increment in fit that might be possible would be only .033 (= $1.0 - .967$)" (p. 602). Bentler and Bonett drew attention to the role played by the large sample size ($N = 932$) in obtaining the statistically significant chi-square (i.e., one that would lead to the rejection of the model; see earlier discussion of this point).

We realize that we have probably succeeded in confusing you, although this was not our intention. What we really wished to do was to alert you to the fact that the interpretation of indices of fit is by no means straightforward. Moreover, as illustrated in the present example, results may differ depending on the version of LISREL used. But, as Steiger (1988) pointed out, the fact that different versions of LISREL "might produce different results . . . does not occur to some authors" (p. 285).

Discrepancies in results of versions of the same program or of different programs aside, it should be noted that identical results may be interpreted quite differently, depending on the indices and criteria used, as well as on who is doing the interpretation. It is worth noting that the people we quoted are leaders in the field of *SEM*. The fact that they disagree about the interpretation of results from the same analysis should serve to underscore the complexities one may face when attempting to interpret results from the application of *SEM*.

So what is one to do? Although we return to the issue of indices of fit several times in this and the next chapter, we would like to stress that exclusive reliance on one kind of index is unwise. A conclusion should be arrived at on the basis of a careful scrutiny of all the results (see Manual, p. 45, for some observations on this topic).

In addition, attention has to be paid to the power of the test used in *SEM*. Pointing to a lack of concern with this issue among researchers applying *SEM*, Saris, Den Ronden, and Satorra (1987) stated: "In our view the procedures for testing structural equation models have not been sufficiently rigorous" (p. 216). Saris and his associates (Saris et al., 1987; Saris & Stronkhorst, 1984; Satorra & Saris, 1985) proposed an approach to the estimation of the power of the likelihood ratio test, illustrating its application to the evaluation of diverse studies in which *SEM* was used (see, especially, Saris et al., 1987). For power calculations using LISREL or a special program (LISPOWER)—part of a utilities diskette supplied with PC–LISREL—see LISREL manual, pp. 217–221.

Finally, it goes without saying that the accuracy of the calculations should be checked. The tendency not to doubt computer output, even when something appears blatantly amiss, is particularly great when dealing with complex analyses of the kind carried out by programs such as LISREL and EQS.

We believe it worthwhile to illustrate this by describing a textbook example of what might happen when output is accepted implicitly. Using LISREL V, Dillon and Goldstein (1984) presented a reanalysis of data from Bagozzi's (1980b) study. For present purposes, it will suffice to point out that they stated as follows: "The χ^2 for the test of the model has a probability level of 0.423, indicating a good fit. In addition, the residuals . . . are relatively small, which also indicates a good fit" (p. 473).[21]

---

[21]Incidentally Bagozzi's sample was relatively small (122). Also, a structural model (not *CFA*) is tested. See footnote 18.

Nevertheless, when they returned to this example in the context of their presentation of goodness-of-fit indices, Dillon and Goldstein (1984) stated:

We find that GFI = 0.225 and AGFI = −0.86, which indicate particularly poor fits. Note that this is in marked contrast to the conclusion based on the χ^2 of 15.40 with 15 df. As we indicated, different criteria will undoubtedly lead to different evaluations. (p. 485).

In light of our discussion above, it should be clear that we do not question the statement that different indices and criteria may lead to different conclusions regarding the results. As it happens, however, *the indices reported by Dillon and Goldstein are in error.* Evidently, LISREL V contained a programming error that led to the incorrect calculation of GFI. Using the FITTED MOMENTS matrix reported in LISREL V (in the present case, these are the reproduced correlations discussed earlier) and the observed correlation matrix,[22] and applying the formula for GFI given in the *LISREL V User's guide* (p. I.40), we obtained a GFI of .969!

We suggest that you use Bagozzi's (1980b) correlation matrix and analyze the model tested by Dillon and Goldstein using LISREL 7. You will find that all your results agree with those reported by Dillon and Goldstein *except for GFI and AGFI*, which are respectively .969 and .926. Another reason we recommend that you reanalyze Bagozzi's data is that it will afford you comparisons with analyses of the same data by Bentler (1985, pp. 100–104) and by Jöreskog and Sörbom (1982, 1989, pp. 151–156).

CORRELATED FACTORS

In this section, we apply *CFA* to the data of Table 22.2. Because the input statements are identical to those given for the analysis of Table 22.1, they are not given here. Commentaries on input and output will be kept to a minimum. When necessary, refer to the preceding section for explanations. As before, two analyses—one with uncorrelated factors and one with correlated factors—are reported alongside each other.

Output

TABLE 22.2
COVARIANCE MATRIX TO BE ANALYZED

	X1	X2	X3	X4	X5	X6
X1	1.000					
X2	.502	1.000				
X3	.622	.551	1.000			
X4	.228	.272	.188	1.000		
X5	.307	.230	.249	.442	1.000	
X6	.198	.259	.223	.537	.413	1.000

---

[22]Although Bagozzi also reports the standard deviations, Dillon and Goldstein (1984) analyzed the correlation matrix. To replicate their analysis, we too used the correlation matrix.

TABLE 22.2, UNCORRELATED FACTORS LISREL ESTIMATES (MAXIMUM LIKELIHOOD) LAMBDA X			TABLE 22.2, CORRELATED FACTORS LISREL ESTIMATES (MAXIMUM LIKELIHOOD) LAMBDA X		
	ACADEMIC	SOCIAL		ACADEMIC	SOCIAL
X1	.753	.000	X1	.761	.000
X2	.667	.000	X2	.681	.000
X3	.826	.000	X3	.807	.000
X4	.000	.758	X4	.000	.739
X5	.000	.583	X5	.000	.607
X6	.000	.708	X6	.000	.708

PHI

	ACADEMIC	SOCIAL		ACADEMIC	SOCIAL
ACADEMIC	1.000		ACADEMIC	1.000	
SOCIAL	.000	1.000	SOCIAL	.438	1.000

THETA DELTA

X1	X2	X3	X4	X5	X6	X1	X2	X3	X4	X5	X6
.433	.555	.317	.425	.660	.498	.421	.536	.350	.454	.632	.499

MEASURES OF GOODNESS OF FIT FOR THE WHOLE MODEL : CHI-SQUARE WITH 9 DEGREES OF FREEDOM = 33.51 (P = .000)

MEASURES OF GOODNESS OF FIT FOR THE WHOLE MODEL : CHI-SQUARE WITH 8 DEGREES OF FREEDOM = 10.06 (P = .261)

Commentary

As you can see, for the uncorrelated-factors model, the χ^2 is statistically significant by conventional α levels, whereas, for the correlated-factors model, it is not. Furthermore, the difference of 23.45 (33.51 − 10.06) with 1 df between the two χ^2's indicates a marked improvement in fit as a result of freeing the correlation between the two factors (see tests of nested models in the preceding section). Assuming that it was hypothesized that the six indicators reflect two correlated dimensions of self-concept (Academic and Social), it would be concluded on the basis of the results of these analyses that the hypothesis was supported.

An important aspect of measurement models of the kind presented here is that errors of measurement of indicators are taken into account when correlations among latent variables are estimated. For the example under consideration, errors of measurement in their indicators are taken into account when the correlation between Academic and Social Self-Concept is estimated as .438 (see PHI in the correlated-factors solution).

Output

TABLE 22.2, UNCORRELATED FACTORS						TABLE 22.2, CORRELATED FACTORS					
GOODNESS OF FIT INDEX = .950 ADJUSTED GOODNESS OF FIT INDEX = .883 ROOT MEAN SQUARE RESIDUAL = .158						GOODNESS OF FIT INDEX = .983 ADJUSTED GOODNESS OF FIT INDEX = .956 ROOT MEAN SQUARE RESIDUAL = .037					

FITTED RESIDUALS

	X1	X2	X3	X4	X5	X6
X1	.000					
X2	.000	.000				
X3	.000	.000	.000			
X4	.228	.272	.188	.000		
X5	.307	.230	.249	.000	.000	
X6	.198	.259	.223	.000	.000	.000

FITTED RESIDUALS

	X1	X2	X3	X4	X5	X6
X1	.000					
X2	−.017	.000				
X3	.008	.001	.000			
X4	−.018	.052	−.073	.000		
X5	.105	.049	.035	−.006	.000	
X6	−.038	.048	−.027	.014	−.016	.000

Commentary

Look first at the GFI and AGFI and notice that both of these indices are relatively high even for the uncorrelated-factors model. According to criteria for GFI and AGFI suggested by some authors (see preceding section), it would appear that, contrary to the conclusion reached above strictly on the basis of tests of significance, the uncorrelated-factors model also fits the data well.

Examine now the RMR's (loosely speaking, the average of the residuals; see preceding section) for the two models and note that they are appreciably different from each other (.158 versus .037 for the uncorrelated and correlated factors respectively). On the basis of the RMR's, therefore, one would be inclined to conclude that the uncorrelated-factors model does *not* fit the data well.

The difference in the fit of the two models becomes especially clear upon examination of the matrices of FITTED RESIDUALS. Examine first the matrix for the uncorrelated factors. As explained in the preceding section, FITTED RESIDUALS are differences between observed and reproduced correlations. In the uncorrelated-factors model, indicators reflecting different factors (e.g., X1 and X4) have nothing in common; thus, reproduced correlations between such indicators are all equal to zero. As a result, the FITTED RESIDUALS corresponding to these elements are equal to the observed correlations between the indicators in question (compare with correlations reported in the beginning of this output).

Look now at the FITTED RESIDUALS for the correlated factors and note that most of them are relatively small. This is because the reproduced correlations using the parameter estimates for this model approximate the observed correlations. In the preceding section, it was shown, with the aid of Figure 23.2, how correlations of indicators of correlated factors are reproduced. Therefore, only one example of how this is done will be given for the present data. Specifically, we illustrate how the correlation between X1 and X6 is reproduced. From the output given earlier (see LISREL ESTIMATES), the coefficient for X1 = .761 and for X6 = .708. The correlation between the two factors is .438. The reproduced correlation is, therefore,

$$(.761)(.438)(.708) = .236$$

The observed correlation between X1 and X6 is .198 (see beginning of the output). The fitted residual is, therefore,

$$.198 - .236 = -.038$$

which is the same as the value reported in the matrix of FITTED RESIDUALS.

As an exercise, we suggest that you calculate the remaining values and compare your results with those in the above output. In doing this, you may find it helpful to depict the results of this analysis in a figure like the one we used in connection with the results of the earlier analysis (i.e., Figure 23.2).

Taken as whole, the results reported above indicate that two correlated factors underlie the relations among the six indicators under consideration. We hope that the present analyses serve to illustrate what was said in the preceding section regarding difficulties in interpreting overall indices of fit and that they reinforce the recommendation not to rely exclusively on any one type of goodness-of-fit index.

EQS: AN ORIENTATION

Bentler (1987) asserted that *SEM* is not used extensively because of reliance on "unnecessarily complicated" (p. 65) matrix language. To make *SEM* more accessible to researchers, Bentler (1985) developed EQS (pronounced "X")—a computer program that uses the simpler equations language. In addition, it eschews Greek notation. The analyses to be presented in this and the next chapter were carried out with *Version 2.1*.

As was the case with LISREL, this orientation and our commentaries on input and output are meant to serve as an introduction to some basic concepts and properties of EQS. It goes without saying that careful study of the manual and relevant references are prerequisites for competent application of the program.

Four types of variables may be used in EQS. Following are their codes, names, and meanings as presented in the manual (Bentler, 1985, p. 65). Henceforth, we will refer to it as the *EQS manual* or just Manual.

Code	Name	Meaning
V	Variable	Measured variable
F	Factor	Latent variable
E	Error	Residual of measured variable
D	Disturbance	Residual of latent variable

The model is specified by a set of regression-like equations. Each equation consists of a dependent variable (variable on the left-hand side of the equation), and one or more independent variables (variables on the right-hand side of the equation).

It is possible for a dependent variable to also be a predictor of other variables in a model. However, this does not mean it is an independent variable in the sense used by EQS. If a variable is ever structurally regressed on any other variable in the model, i.e., if it appears at least once on the left-hand side of one equation . . . , then it is a dependent variable, regardless of its relationships to other variables in the system. (Manual, p. 65)

This distinction between independent and dependent variables in EQS is readily seen in path diagrams. Variables to which one or more unidirectional arrows point are considered dependent variables, whereas those to which no unidirectional arrows point are considered independent variables.

Using, as an example, Figure 23.2, given earlier, the six indicators (X1 through X6) would be considered dependent variables, whereas the factors (ACAD and SOC) and the residuals would be considered independent variables. If, for example, in model (*b*) of Figure 23.2, it were hypothesized that ACAD affects SOC, that is, if the bidirectional arrow connecting the two latent variables were replaced by a unidirectional arrow emanating from ACAD and pointing to SOC, then the former would be an independent variable and the latter a dependent variable.

It is not required that all four types of variables be used in any given model. A case in point are models analyzed in the present chapter, all of which do not include D type variables.

As in LISREL, parameters may be fixed, free, or constrained. In EQS, a free parameter is indicated by an asterisk (*) attached to it. Parameters without asterisks are fixed.

EQS numbers the input variables sequentially: V1, V2, V3, and so forth. When a model entails only a subset of the input variables, EQS selects the relevant variables on the basis of the model equations.[23]

Other aspects of EQS are discussed in the context of commentaries on the numerical examples to which we now turn.

NUMERICAL EXAMPLES

For comparative purposes, EQS will be used to perform *CFA* on the correlation matrix given in Table 22.2. It will be recalled that this matrix was analyzed through LISREL in the preceding section. As in the previous analyses, two models will be analyzed: (a) two uncorrelated factors, and (b) two correlated factors. Also, as was done earlier, the input and output for both analyses will be presented alongside each other. We suggest that you make frequent comparisons of results obtained here with those obtained through LISREL.

EQS

Input

```
/TITLE                                      │  /TIT
  TABLE 22.2, UNCORRELATED FACTORS.         │    TABLE 22.2, CORRELATED FACTORS.
/SPECIFICATIONS                             │  /SPE
  CAS=200; VAR=6;                           │    CAS=200; VAR=6;
/LABELS                                     │  /LAB
  V1 = X1; V2 = X2; V3 = X3;                │    V1 = X1; V2 = X2; V3 = X3;
  V4 = X4; V5 = X5; V6 = X6;                │    V4 = X4; V5 = X5; V6 = X6;
  F1 = ACADEMIC; F2 = SOCIAL;               │    F1 = ACADEMIC; F2 = SOCIAL;
/EQUATIONS                                  │  /EQU
  V1 = .7*F1       + E1;                    │    V1 = *F1          + E1;
  V2 = .7*F1       + E2;                    │    V2 = *F1          + E2;
  V3 = .7*F1       + E3;                    │    V3 = *F1          + E3;
  V4 =      .7*F2  + E4;                    │    V4 =        *F2   + E4;
  V5=       .7*F2  + E5;                    │    V5=         *F2   + E5;
  V6 =      .7*F2  + E6;                    │    V6 =        *F2   + E6;
/VARIANCES                                  │  /VAR
  F1 TO F2 = 1;                             │    F1 TO F2 = 1;
  E1 TO E6 = *;                             │    E1 TO E6 = *;
/MATRIX                                     │  /COV
1.000                                       │    F1,F2 = *;
 .502  1.000                                │  /MAT
 .622   .551  1.000                         │  1.000
 .228   .272   .188  1.000                  │   .502  1.000
 .307   .230   .249   .442  1.000           │   .622   .551  1.000
 .198   .259   .223   .537   .413  1.000    │   .228   .272   .188  1.000
/END                                        │   .307   .230   .249   .442  1.000
                                            │   .198   .259   .223   .537   .413  1.000
                                            │  /END
```

Commentary

We begin with some general remarks about the input setup. The control language of EQS is organized in sections or paragraphs, each containing one or more sentences. Each paragraph is signified by a keyword that is preceded by a slash (e.g., /TITLE). A keyword occupies a

---

[23]In contrast, in LISREL, it is necessary to use the SElection statement when a subset of the input variables is to be used in the analysis. The same holds true for the reordering of variables in LISREL (see Chapter 24).

separate line and may be abbreviated to the first three letters. For illustrative purposes, we use the abbreviated format in the input on the right.

Sentences within a paragraph are separated by semicolons and may be presented in any order. Blanks may be added to facilitate readability and inspection of input flow. You are urged to heed Bentler's advice and "develop a standard practice that makes it easy to review the program input, e.g., starting keywords in column 1, and beginning statements below the keyword, indented a few characters" (Manual, p. 57).

We turn now to the separate paragraphs. In most instances, the input for both models is identical. Where the two differ, we comment on the differences.

/TITLE. The title may consist of one or more lines. All lines are printed only once. The first line of the title is printed as a header on all output pages. Although the title is optional, you are urged to use it and to include in it information germane to the run (see Chapter 16).

/SPECIFICATION. In addition to the information we have specified (i.e., the number of CASes and the number of input VARiables), various other specifications, among which are the method of analysis and the type of input, may be included. The default method of estimation is Maximum Likelihood (ML), and the default input is a covariance (correlation) matrix. We are using these defaults; therefore, no additional specifications are given in our examples.

/LABELS. One to eight character labels may be assigned to F or V type variables only (see above for the four types of variables used in EQS).

/EQUATIONS. In this paragraph, the model is specified in the form of a set of equations. "One and only one equation is required for each dependent variable. The dependent variables may be either observed or latent, and parameters within the equations may be specified as either fixed or free" (Manual, p. 65).

We follow Bentler's suggestion and include additional blanks so that one may readily see which variables are said to be affected by which factors.

As was noted earlier, an asterisk is used to indicate that a parameter is free. Thus, in our input, the loadings of V1 through V3 on F1, and those of V4 through V6 on F2, are free. The values attached to these parameters (i.e., .7)—referred to as start values or initial estimates—are user-supplied guesses about the sign and magnitude of free parameters. The program uses these values to begin the iteration process. Start values depend on the specific model and the scales of the measures used; thus,

it is difficult to give rules about the relative size of the coefficients in equations. Actually, it is only necessary to have a reasonably good guess about the size and sign of a few key start values, since the relative size of others then tends not to matter much in the iterative calculations. Thus, a few key factor loadings should always be on the large size. What is "large," of course, depends on the scale of the variables, how unmeasured variables are identified, and on the true model. (Manual, p. 67)

The better the guess about start values, the faster iterative calculations converge. Occasionally, poor choices of start values may result in the iterative process failing to converge (an example of this is given in Chapter 24). When this happens, one or more additional runs with better start values, gleaned from earlier runs, will generally lead to convergence.

When a start value is not specified, a default value of 1.0 is used. Default start values will generally do when, as in our examples, a correlation matrix is analyzed or when the scales of the measures used are relatively small. For illustrative purposes, we do not use start values in the model on the right.[24]

---

[24]In LISREL too, start values may be used. For some designs, start values are desirable, even essential (see input for MTMM, later in this chapter).

Finally, note that the coefficients for the Errors are fixed (no asterisks). By implication, they are set equal to 1.0. Thus, for example, V1 = .7*F1 + E1 (the first equation in the input above) is equivalent to V1 = .7*F1 + 1.0E1.

/VARIANCES. Independent variables must have variances. Notice that we fixed the variances of F1 and F2 to equal 1.0 (no asterisks). We did the same in the analysis of these data through LISREL, where we pointed out that this approach is commonly used to resolve the indeterminacy between variances of factors and loadings of observed variables on the factors (see earlier discussion of this point). Although we specified that the variances of the errors (E1 to E6) are free, we did not use start values (asterisks only).

/COVariances. Independent variables may have covariances. We are using COV only in the model on the right (i.e., model with correlated factors). When COV is not specified, as in the model on the left, it is assumed to be fixed at zero. "If a variable is involved in a covariance, its variance must also be specified in /VAR. . . . *Dependent variables cannot have covariances*" (Manual, pp. 71–72).

/MATRIX. This signifies that a covariance or a correlation matrix is part of the input file. A correlation matrix may be followed by standard deviations, which the program uses to calculate the covariance matrix that will be analyzed.

Of various input formats (see Manual, pp. 79–81), we are using a free format, according to which the lower triangular matrix is read in by rows with the first row consisting of one element, the second of two, and so forth. A semicolon (;) is *not* used to indicate the end of matrix input. The same is true for standard deviation input. We turn now to excerpts of the output.

Output

```
EQS, A STRUCTURAL EQUATIONS PROGRAM
   BY P.M. BENTLER

BMDP STATISTICAL SOFTWARE, INC.
   VERSION 2.1   COPYRIGHT (C) 1985,1986
      [data from Table 22.2]

   MATRIX TO BE ANALYZED:   6 VARIABLES
   (SELECTED FROM   6 VARIABLES), BASED ON   200 CASES.
            X1       X2       X3       X4       X5       X6
            V 1      V 2      V 3      V 4      V 5      V 6

X1   V 1    1.000
X2   V 2    0.502    1.000
X3   V 3    0.622    0.551    1.000
X4   V 4    0.228    0.272    0.188    1.000
X5   V 5    0.307    0.230    0.249    0.442    1.000
X6   V 6    0.198    0.259    0.223    0.537    0.413    1.000

BENTLER-WEEKS STRUCTURAL REPRESENTATION:

   NUMBER OF DEPENDENT VARIABLES = 6
      DEPENDENT V'S :    1  2  3  4  5  6

   NUMBER OF INDEPENDENT VARIABLES = 8
      INDEPENDENT F'S :    1  2
      INDEPENDENT E'S :    1  2  3  4  5  6
```

Commentary

EQS begins by printing the input, which is the same as that given earlier. The above excerpts are identical for both analyses (i.e., for uncorrelated and correlated factors).

The matrix to be analyzed is the same as the one that was read in. Had a correlation matrix and standard deviations been read in, and had the default in the /SPE paragraph been used, the covariance matrix would have been reported as the matrix to be analyzed.

As indicated earlier, EQS numbers the variables sequentially. It then provides a summary of the number of independent and dependent variables as specified by the equations. In the present example, dependent variables are type V only, whereas the independent variables are type F and E (see above for the four types of variables that may be used in EQS).

Output

TITLE: TABLE 22.2, UNCORRELATED FACTORS.

MAXIMUM LIKELIHOOD SOLUTION (NORMAL DISTRIBUTION THEORY)

PARAMETER ESTIMATES APPEAR IN ORDER.
NO SPECIAL PROBLEMS WERE ENCOUNTERED DURING OPTIMIZATION.

RESIDUAL COVARIANCE MATRIX (S-SIGMA) :

		X1 V 1	X2 V 2	X3 V 3	X4 V 4	X5 V 5	X6 V 6
X1	V 1	0.000					
X2	V 2	0.000	0.000				
X3	V 3	0.000	0.000	0.000			
X4	V 4	0.228	0.272	0.188	0.000		
X5	V 5	0.307	0.230	0.249	0.000	0.000	
X6	V 6	0.198	0.259	0.223	0.000	0.000	0.000

AVERAGE ABSOLUTE COVARIANCE RESIDUALS = 0.1026
AVERAGE OFF-DIAGONAL ABSOLUTE COVARIANCE RESIDUALS = 0.1436

TITLE: TABLE 22.2, CORRELATED FACTORS.

MAXIMUM LIKELIHOOD SOLUTION (NORMAL DISTRIBUTION THEORY)

PARAMETER ESTIMATES APPEAR IN ORDER.
NO SPECIAL PROBLEMS WERE ENCOUNTERED DURING OPTIMIZATION.

RESIDUAL COVARIANCE MATRIX (S-SIGMA) :

		X1 V 1	X2 V 2	X3 V 3	X4 V 4	X5 V 5	X6 V 6
X1	V 1	0.000					
X2	V 2	-0.017	0.000				
X3	V 3	0.008	0.001	0.000			
X4	V 4	-0.018	0.052	-0.073	0.000		
X5	V 5	0.105	0.049	0.035	-0.006	0.000	
X6	V 6	-0.038	0.048	-0.027	0.014	-0.016	0.000

AVERAGE ABSOLUTE COVARIANCE RESIDUALS = 0.0241
AVERAGE OFF-DIAGONAL ABSOLUTE COVARIANCE RESIDUALS = 0.0338

Commentary

For these analyses, the program reports that no special problems were encountered during optimization. "*This is the ideal case, and this message should be searched for prior to evaluating the meaning of any results*" (Manual, p. 89; see pp. 89–91 for other types of messages and their meanings).

The RESIDUAL COVARIANCE MATRICES are the same as the FITTED RESIDUALS in LISREL and will, therefore, not be commented upon. Two averages of the absolute residuals (i.e., ignoring their signs) are reported: The first is based on all the elements; the second is based only on the off-diagonal elements. "Usually, the off-diagonal elements are more critical to the goodness-of-fit chi-square statistics" (Manual, p. 92). Although LISREL reports a somewhat different kind of index (see RMR), the comments we have made about it are broadly applicable here too.

Output

MAXIMUM LIKELIHOOD SOLUTION
    (NORMAL DISTRIBUTION THEORY)

GOODNESS OF FIT SUMMARY

INDEPENDENCE MODEL CHI-SQUARE = 337.034,
    BASED ON   15 DEGREES OF FREEDOM.

CHI-SQUARE = 33.512, BASED ON 9 DEGREES OF FREEDOM.
PROBABILILITY VALUE FOR THE CHI-SQUARE STATISTIC IS LESS THAN 0.001

BENTLER-BONETT NORMED   FIT INDEX=   0.901
BENTLER-BONETT NONNORMED FIT INDEX=   0.873

MAXIMUM LIKELIHOOD SOLUTION
    (NORMAL DISTRIBUTION THEORY)

GOODNESS OF FIT SUMMARY

INDEPENDENCE MODEL CHI-SQUARE = 337.034,
    BASED ON   15 DEGREES OF FREEDOM.

CHI-SQUARE = 10.058, BASED ON 8 DEGREES OF FREEDOM.
PROBABILILITY VALUE FOR THE CHI-SQUARE STATISTIC IS 0.26099

BENTLER-BONETT NORMED   FIT INDEX=   0.970
BENTLER-BONETT NONNORMED FIT INDEX=   0.988

Commentary

Of the two CHI-SQUARE statistics, the second is the same as that reported in LISREL. Hence, what we said about the Chi-squares for the two models analyzed earlier through LISREL applies equally to those reported here. The first CHI-SQUARE (i.e., INDEPENDENCE MODEL) is explained below.

Difficulties with the use of the CHI-SQUARE test were discussed in connection with applications of LISREL in earlier sections, where it was also pointed out that various indices of overall fit have been proposed. Two such indices—GFI and AGFI—reported in LISREL were presented and explained. Bentler and Bonett (1980) proposed the two indices reported above, both of which are based on the notion of improvement of fit provided by a given model as compared with some baseline model.

Normed Fit Index (NFI). This index may be calculated as follows:

$$\text{NFI} = \frac{\chi_n^2 - \chi_s^2}{\chi_n^2} \tag{23.7}$$

where n = null model; s = substantive model. The null model is, in the present case, "the most restrictive, theoretically defensible model" (Bentler & Bonett, 1980, p. 600), according to which the correlations (or covariances) among all the observed variables are zero. The first CHI-SQUARE reported above is associated with the null model.[25] The substantive model is the one advanced on the basis of theoretical considerations. Two models are fitted in the above analyses: (a) uncorrelated factors; and (b) correlated factors. Using the χ^2's reported above, the NFI for the uncorrelated and correlated factors respectively are

$$\frac{337.034 - 33.512}{337.034} = .901 \qquad \frac{337.034 - 10.058}{337.034} = .970$$

Compare with the values reported above. The NFI may range from 0 to 1. Before commenting on criteria for "good" fit, we describe the second index.

Nonnormed Fit Index (NNFI). This index is similar to the NFI except that it is adjusted for *df* (degrees of freedom). It is calculated as follows:

$$\text{NNFI} = \frac{(\chi_n^2/df_n) - (\chi_s^2/df_s)}{(\chi_n^2/df_n - 1)} \tag{23.8}$$

where the terms are as defined under (23.7).

Using the χ^2's reported above, the NNFI for the uncorrelated and correlated factors respectively are

$$\frac{(337.034/15) - (33.512/9)}{(337.034/15 - 1)} = .873$$

$$\frac{(337.034/15) - (10.058/8)}{(337.034/15 - 1)} = .988$$

Compare with the results reported above. Unlike the NFI, it is possible for the NNFI to have

---

[25]To obtain the χ^2 for the null model through LISREL, replace MOdel statement in the input given earlier with the following:

MO NX = 6 NK = 6 LX = ID PH = DI TD = ZE. Note the general pattern: The number of KSI variables is set equal to the number of X's, LX is declared an identity matrix, PH is declared DIagonal, and TD is declared ZEro.

a negative sign. Addressing the question of interpretation of these indices, Bentler and Bonett (1980) stated:

Since the scale of the fit indices is not necessarily easy to interpret (e.g., the indices are not squared multiple correlations), experience will be required to establish values of the indices that are associated with various degrees of meaningfulness of results. In our experience, models with overall fit indices of less than .9 can usually be improved substantially. (p. 600)

This statement was apparently taken by various authors to mean that Bentler and Bonett did "suggest .9 as a threshold" (Wheaton, 1987, p. 133; see also, Schmitt & Stults, 1986, p. 14). Judd, Jessor, and Donovan (1986) even referred to it as "the 'magic' .90 level" (p. 166). Be that as it may, assuming that .9 were to be used as a cutoff in the present analyses, then, on the basis of NFI, it would have been concluded that even the uncorrelated-factors model fits the data well. A mere glance at the residuals for this model should suffice to convince one of the dubiousness of such a conclusion. We remind you that we made the same point in connection with the overall indices of fit in LISREL.

Two final points will be made in connection with Bentler and Bonett's fit indices. One, the same approach may be taken to assess incremental fit when one or more parameters of a model are freed (for examples, see Bentler & Bonett, 1980). Two, routine use of the "nullest" of null models (i.e., that the correlations or covariances among all the observed variables are zero) for the assessment of incremental fit is prone to lead to abuses. Cautioning against such abuses, Fornell (1983a) stated:

Without the requirement of strong theoretical justification for the null model, the Bentler and Bonett test makes it even easier for any given model to pass the test: simply specify the "worst possible model" as the null hypothesis and then test your model against it. In most cases, your favorite model will stand up to the test. (p. 447)

Sobel and Bohrnstedt (1985) asserted that the baseline models used by Bentler and Bonett "are inappropriate in all but the purely exploratory case" (p. 153). They suggested instead that, in confirmatory studies, a baseline model derived on the basis of knowledge of the phenomenon studied as well as theoretical considerations be employed. Earlier, we pointed out that various authors, including Bentler and Bonett, have reanalyzed a model from Wheaton et al. (1977). Using a different baseline model that they believed to be "more defensible in the research context and relevant theoretical consideration," Sobel and Bohrnstedt reported results leading them to "a conclusion that is in sharp contrast to that of Bentler and Bonett (1980)" (p. 175).

Cautioning against undue reliance on and indiscriminate use of indices of fit, especially as a means for model revision, Matsueda and Bielby (1986) correctly observed that this is tantamount to "transforming a powerful modeling and testing method into the data-dredging, exploratory approach it was meant to supplant" (p. 155). For a critique of various goodness-of-fit indices, their limitations for the assessment of models, and a proposed new index, see Mulaik et al. (1989).

Output

ITERATIVE SUMMARY			ITERATIVE SUMMARY	
ITERATION	PARAMETER ABS CHANGE		ITERATION	PARAMETER ABS CHANGE
1	0.290643		1	0.367141
2	0.008449		2	0.036481
3	0.000055		3	0.008963
			4	0.001188
			5	0.000294

Commentary

The iterative summary should be scanned prior to evaluating the meaning of the results. In fully iterated estimation, the iterative process failed if the average of absolute values of elements of the parameter change vector is larger than about .001 (or other convergence criterion chosen). . . . Note that the program uses a default maximum of 30 iterations, so if this number is reached the program will likely not have converged. A message will be printed warning the user not to trust the output if convergence was not achieved. (Manual, p. 95).

When convergence has not occurred, it may be achieved by doing a reanalysis, using as start values (see above) estimates that were reported in the output for the solution that failed to converge. (For further details, see Manual, pp. 94–96.)

As you can see, convergence occurred at the third and fifth iterations respectively, for the uncorrelated and correlated factors models. Recall that we did not use start values for the latter solution.

Output

MEASUREMENT EQUATIONS *[uncorrelated factors]*	MEASUREMENT EQUATIONS *[correlated factors]*
X1 =V1= 0.753*F1+ 1.000 E1	X1 =V1= 0.761*F1+ 1.000 E1
X2 =V2= 0.667*F1+ 1.000 E2	X2 =V2= 0.681*F1+ 1.000 E2
X3 =V3= 0.826*F1+ 1.000 E3	X3 =V3= 0.807*F1+ 1.000 E3
X4 =V4= 0.758*F2+ 1.000 E4	X4 =V4= 0.739*F2+ 1.000 E4
X5 =V5= 0.583*F2+ 1.000 E5	X5 =V5= 0.607*F2+ 1.000 E5
X6 =V6= 0.708*F2+ 1.000 E6	X6 =V6= 0.708*F2+ 1.000 E6

Commentary

Models estimated in the present chapter consist of measurement equations only. When a model consists also of structural equations (see Chapter 24), the output will include a section pertaining to construct equations.

The estimated parameters reported here (i.e., values indicated by asterisks) are the same as those reported in LISREL (see LISREL ESTIMATES).

Output

VARIANCES OF INDEPENDENT VARIABLES *[uncorrelated factors]*	VARIANCES OF INDEPENDENT VARIABLES *[correlated factors]*	COVARIANCES AMONG INDEPENDENT VARIABLES *[correlated factors]*
E	E	
E1 −X1 .433*	E1 −X1 .421*	F1 −ACADEMIC .438*
E2 −X2 .555*	E2 −X2 .536*	F2 −SOCIAL
E3 −X3 .317*	E3 −X3 .350*	
E4 −X4 .425*	E4 −X4 .454*	
E5 −X5 .660*	E5 −X5 .632*	
E6 −X6 .498*	E6 −X6 .499*	

Commentary

This section consists of variances and covariances (for the correlated model only) for the independent variables. The same estimates are reported in LISREL (under THETA DELTA for variances of the E's, and under PHI for the covariance between the F's).

This concludes our introduction to LISREL and EQS. In subsequent sections and in the next chapter, we use these programs to analyze other types of models. In the context of these analyses, we make additional comments on either of these programs as the need arises.

MULTITRAIT-MULTIMETHOD MATRIX

Ideas concerning the Multitrait-Multimethod Matrix (MTMM) were introduced in Chapter 4, where it was pointed out that analyses of such matrices are especially valuable in the process of construct validation. We suggest that you review relevant sections in Chapter 4 and concentrate on the distinctions between (a) *convergent* and *discriminant* validity, and (b) *trait* and *method* factors.

Various approaches to the analysis of the MTMM have been proposed (for a review, see Schmitt & Stults, 1986). We describe only the *CFA* approach, because it is the most versatile and most useful. For recent summaries and references to earlier proposals and applications, see Schmitt and Stults (1986) and Widaman (1985).

A NUMERICAL EXAMPLE

We will explain the application of *CFA* to the MTMM in the course of analyzing the illustrative data of Table 23.1, consisting of three traits (A, B, and C) as measured by three methods (1, 2, and 3). A, B, and C may, for example, be three attitudes (e.g., toward blacks, Hispanics, and Mexican-Americans). Alternatively, A, B, and C may be three personality traits (e.g., assertiveness, anxiety, aggression). Method 1 may be a summated rating scale, Method 2 may be an interview, and Method 3 may be some projective technique. Thus, referring to the first example given above, A_1, A_2, and A_3 are attitudes toward blacks, as measured by methods 1, 2, and 3 respectively—similarly for the two other attitudes, or traits. The scores on the three traits measured by the three methods are intercorrelated, yielding a 9 by 9 correlation matrix among observed (manifest) variables, as reported in Table 23.1

The purpose of using *CFA* for the analysis of the correlation matrix reported in Table 23.1 is to test the fit of a hypothesized model and to interpret the parameter estimates when the fit of the model is deemed acceptable. Needless to say, the model reflects one's theoretical conceptions regarding the process (or processes) that has led to the observed pattern of relations among the variables under study. For example, one might conceivably hypothesize that a single latent variable underlies the relations among the nine manifest variables reported in Table 23.1. Referring to the first example given above, it might be hypothesized that attitudes toward blacks (A), Hispanics (B), and Mexican-Americans (C) are manifestations of a general attitude toward minorities. Contrast this with but one of various possible alternatives, namely that three correlated latent variables, each concerned with attitudes toward a given minority group, underlie the correlation matrix of Table 23.1.

Latent variables dealt with thus far have referred to what may be labeled, in the present

Table 23.1
Multitrait-Multimethod Matrix (N = 300)

		Method 1			Method 2			Method 3		
		A_1	B_1	C_1	A_2	B_2	C_2	A_3	B_3	C_3
Method 1	A_1									
	B_1	.400								
	C_1	.350	.300							
Method 2	A_2	.550	.220	.150						
	B_2	.200	.520	.170	.600					
	C_2	.140	.150	.550	.480	.500				
Method 3	A_3	.500	.200	.160	.640	.360	.280			
	B_3	.210	.500	.200	.370	.640	.270	.460		
	C_3	.150	.120	.540	.310	.300	.600	.450	.400	

context, trait factors. Because three methods of measurement were used, one may wish to test hypotheses regarding method factors. For example, it may be hypothesized that the correlations among the manifest variables reported in Table 23.1 are due to three uncorrelated method factors.[26] One can, of course, formulate models consisting of both trait and method factors.

The preceding remarks should suffice to indicate that a relatively large and potentially bewildering number of models may be formulated. As Widaman (1985), who proposed what is probably the most systematic strategy of the application of *CFA* to MTMM, pointed out, "the many previous articles on methods of analyzing multitrait-multimethod data point to one unmistakable fact: representing the trends present in such data is a complicated undertaking" (p. 24). Illustrating the complexities is the fact that different authors analyzing the same MTMM by *CFA* may arrive at different conclusions (for some examples, see Widaman, 1985).

Our presentation is, obviously, not exhaustive. Furthermore, because our data are illustrative and our designations of traits and methods generic, our analysis cannot be guided by the necessary theoretical considerations. Instead, we illustrate the application of some aspects of the strategy proposed by Widaman (1985). References for further reading and for examples of substantive applications are given in the Study Suggestions.

Of the various models that may be advanced regarding the relations among the manifest variables in Table 23.1, the following will be analyzed:

Model 1: Three correlated trait factors.

Model 2: Three correlated method factors.

Model 3: Three correlated trait factors and three correlated method factors. According to this model, trait factors are *not* correlated with method factors.

To reiterate: The preceding are but some of the models that may be formulated. For example, it may be argued that a more reasonable Model 3 would be one according to which there are correlations among the trait factors but *not* among the method factors.

To determine the plausibility of each of the three models, we will look at various aspects

---

[26]See Chapter 4, for a consideration of what might constitute different methods and of the notion of correlations among methods.

of the results (e.g., chi-square test, residuals, indices of fit). We will also study nested models[27] in order to determine improvement in fit as follows:

1a. Model 1 over a null model (see preceding sections about the use of null models).

1b. Model 3 (trait and method factors) over Model 2 (method factors only). Note that, in both instances, the question addressed is whether trait factors lead to substantial improvement over a null model (1a) and over a model consisting of method factors only (1b).

2a. Model 2 over a null model.

2b. Model 3 (trait and method factors) over Model 1 (trait factors only). The question addressed this time is whether method factors lead to substantial improvement over a null model (2a) and over a model consisting of trait factors only (2b).

Analyses in this section will be carried out through LISREL. Because explanations of LISREL input and output were given earlier, output will be kept to a minimum, and comments will be brief, except for issues most germane to the example under consideration.

MODEL 1

According to this model, three intercorrelated trait factors are hypothesized to underlie the correlation matrix of Table 23.1 Specifically, it is hypothesized that A_1, A_2, and A_3 are indicators of one latent variable (e.g., attitudes toward blacks). B_1, B_2, and B_3 are hypothesized to be indicators of another latent variable (e.g., attitudes toward Hispanics). C_1, C_2, and C_3 are hypothesized to be indicators of yet another latent variable (e.g., attitudes toward Mexican-Americans). Note that the question whether given indicators are correlated, to a greater or lesser extent, because they are measured by the same method, is not addressed in this model. In other words, the fact that three different measurement methods are used is not taken into account in this model. We return to this point in the context of commentaries on the output. Following is the LISREL input.

LISREL

Input

```
TABLE 23.1 MTMM.   THREE CORRELATED TRAITS (MODEL 1)
DA NI=9 NO=300
LA
A1 B1 C1 A2 B2 C2 A3 B3 C3
KM
1.0 .4 1.0 .35 .3 1.0 .55 .22 .15 1.0
.2 .52 .17 .6 1.0 .14 .15 .55 .48 .5 1.0
.5 .2 .16 .64 .36 .28 1.0 .21 .5 .2 .37 .64
.27 .46 1.0 .15 .12 .54 .31 .3 .6 .45 .4 1.0
MO NX=9 NK=3 PH=ST TD=SY
LK
'TRAIT A' 'TRAIT B' 'TRAIT C'
FR LX 1 1 LX 2 2 LX 3 3 LX 4 1 LX 5 2 LX 6 3 LX 7 1 LX 8 2 LX 9 3
OU RS MI
```

---

[27]Notions regarding nested models and their tests were introduced earlier in this chapter.

Commentary

As was stated above, commentaries will be limited to specific aspects of the analysis and/or to elements not used in earlier analyses.

On the MO statement, nine manifest variables (NX = 9) are said to reflect three latent variables (NK = 3). The specification of which manifest variables serve as reflective indicators of which latent variables is accomplished through the FRee statement (e.g., LX 1 1 means that the first indicator is a reflector of KSI 1; TRAIT A in the example under consideration).

PH = ST means that PHI is a symmetric matrix whose diagonal elements are fixed to 1.0, whereas its off-diagonal elements are free. In other words, PH is a 3 by 3 correlation matrix of the KSI's.

The specification TD = SY means that THETA DELTA is "symmetric with free diagonal elements and *fixed off-diagonal* elements" (Manual, p. 14). In effect, TD is diagonal free. We could have, therefore, used the default (i.e., TD = DI,FR), as in previous analyses, except that the present format is necessary in order to obtain Modification Indices for the off-diagonal elements of TD.

Modification Indices are explained in the context of commentaries on the output. For now, it will only be pointed out that they are called for by specifying MI on the OUtput statement.

Output

MEASURES OF GOODNESS OF FIT FOR THE WHOLE MODEL :
CHI-SQUARE WITH 24 DEGREES OF FREEDOM = 431.07 (P = .000)
GOODNESS OF FIT INDEX = .749
ADJUSTED GOODNESS OF FIT INDEX = .529
ROOT MEAN SQUARE RESIDUAL = .087

Commentary

That the model does not provide a good fit to the data is evident not only from the statistically significant chi-square but also from the relatively small indices of fit (see earlier discussion of these indices). On the basis of these results, it is rather easy to conclude that the model is misspecified. It is, however, extremely difficult, if not impossible, to tell the form of the misspecification. Excluding simulation studies from consideration, assertions of having correctly identified sources of model misspecification are tantamount to a contradiction in terms, as they imply that the correct model is known.

The decisive role of model specification in measurement, design, and analysis was discussed in various chapters (see, in particular, Chapters 3, 14, 17, and 18). Among other things, various forms of misspecification—notably omission of relevant variables, misspecification of the nature of relations among variables (e.g., linear instead of curvilinear)—were shown to lead to distortions and bias in parameter estimates.

A model constitutes a theory about the phenomenon under investigation. It, therefore, stands to reason that *attempts to detect sources of model misspecification should be guided, first and foremost, by theoretical considerations, not to mention clear thinking.* We remind you of this, because hazards of overlooking serious model misspecification, of even not thinking about the soundness of a model, have increased with the advent of what have come to be known as *specification searches* (Leamer, 1978; for a discussion of specification searches in the context of *SEM*, see MacCallum, 1986) and model respecification (e.g., Costner & Schoenberg, 1973; Herting & Costner, 1985). The complex analytic approach of

SEM, coupled with its various diagnostic indices (e.g., modification indices, discussed below) are particularly fertile grounds for thoughtless model respecifications.

In a timely excellent discussion, Cliff (1983) cautioned against abuses of methods for the analysis of *SEM*:

Initially, these methods seemed to be a great boon to social science research, but there is some danger that they may instead become a disaster, a disaster because they seem to encourage one to suspend his normal critical faculties. Somehow the use of one of these computer procedures lends an air of unchallengeable sanctity to conclusions that would otherwise be subjected to the most intense scrutiny. (p. 116)

When faced with a bewildering array of arrows leading to and from a multitude of variables and indicators, and accompanied by all sorts of "esoteric" statistical terms and symbols, some researchers seem to find refuge in mental stupor. We believe the same condition afflicts referees and journal editors who are not versed in the analytic approaches under consideration and who, as a result, appear unable to detect even blatant misapplications.

Judging by many published reports, researchers appear more inclined to engage in post hoc theorizing when applying *SEM*. It seems almost natural to revise a causal model in order to improve its fit to the data. This tendency has been reinforced by the availability of diagnostic indices, prime examples of which are Modification Indices to which we now turn.

Output

MAXIMUM MODIFICATION INDEX IS 90.52 FOR ELEMENT (5, 4) OF THETA DELTA

Commentary

When MI is specified on the OUtput statement (see Input), LISREL reports Modification Indices for fixed and constrained parameters. Because of space consideration, we reproduced only the statement about the largest modification index.

For each fixed and constrained parameter, the modification index is a measure of predicted decrease in χ^2 if a single constraint is relaxed and the model is reestimated. . . . [T]hese indices . . . may be judged by means of a χ^2 distribution with 1 degree of freedom. The fixed parameter corresponding to the largest such index is the one which, when relaxed, will improve fit maximally. The improvement in fit is measured by a reduction in χ^2 which is expected to be close to the modification index. This procedure seems to work well in practice, but *it is recommended to use it only when relaxing a parameter makes sense from a substantive point of view and when the estimated value of this parameter can be clearly interpreted* [italics added]. (Manual, p. 45)

The value of MI in helping detect sources of model misspecification is, to say the least, dubious. In view of frequent abuses, it is necessary to state the obvious, namely that it is ludicrous to expect a computer program to reformulate a model on substantive grounds. All it can be made to do is indicate what might occur when changes are made within the confines of the model being fit. Obviously, it cannot be made to tell the user that an additional latent variable(s), say, needs to be included in the model (e.g., method factors, in our example).

For the case of MI, all that LISREL is designed to indicate is the expected reduction in the χ^2 as a result of freeing a given parameter. This is why Jöreskog and Sörbom recommended that the decision to free a parameter be made on the basis of substantive meaningfulness and interpretability (see above). The preceding notwithstanding, it should be noted that an "automatic model modification" feature has been introduced in LISREL 7.

This option is available to let the program automatically modify the model sequentially, by freeing in each step that fixed parameter . . . which corresponds to the largest modification index and continuing to do so for as long as this index is statistically significant. (Manual, p. 70)

It is worthwhile to note that automatic model modification is not unlike variable-selection procedures (e.g., forward, stepwise) in multiple regression analysis aimed at determining which variables are to be included in a regression equation. As we mentioned in Chapter 18 (see also, Pedhazur, 1982, Chapter 6), such an approach may be useful in predictive, *not* in explanatory, research.

Despite the option for specifying parameters that should not be set free (NF, Manual, p. 70) and despite Jöreskog and Sörbom's exhortation that automatic model modification be used "with careful judgment" (Manual, p. 70), we question the wisdom of its inclusion altogether. We hazard a guess that automatically modified models will be published with fair regularity in the near future, with "due credit" given Jöreskog and Sörbom for providing such a "wonderful" feature.[28]

It is our impression that MI have most frequently been used in the process of indiscriminate, even thoughtless, "improvement" of models. The almost reflexive reaction to a large MI is the postulation of correlated measurement errors for the indicators in question (or correlated residuals for the latent variables). This practice, which is deceptively safe and simple, does not, in most instances, address the issue of model misspecification but rather covers it up, so to speak. What is attributed to correlated measurement errors, or correlated residuals, is most frequently left uninterpreted, as if no further explanation is required. In short, the postulation of correlated errors creates an illusion of an explanation (see Bagozzi, 1983; Gerbing & Anderson, 1984).

As a case in point, consider the example we are analyzing here. In the above output, LISREL's message is that the MAXIMUM MODIFICATION INDEX IS 90.52 FOR ELEMENT (5, 4) OF THETA DELTA. It is rather easy to postulate that errors of the indicators in question are correlated, revise the model, and reestimate its parameters. Such a revision would mean that the errors of Traits A and B, when measured by Method 2 are correlated. Recalling that $\chi^2 = 431.07$ (see output above), it is safe to assume that a researcher taking such a course of action would repeat this process (or use the automatic modification option to begin with; see above) until the fit is deemed satisfactory. Browne (1982) referred to such practices as attempts to "legitimatize an analysis" and branded parameters that are freed to merely improve the fit as "wastebasket parameters" (p. 101).

We would like it understood that we are neither arguing against reformulations of one's theory nor against the design and execution of new studies, in light of results that lead to the rejection of one's initial theoretical formulation. This is an integral part of scientific research, as was made clear, we hope, in our discussion of science and theories (e.g., Chapters 7 and 9). What we are arguing against is an approach whereby the very process of theory formulation and testing is subverted. This, we submit, takes place when models are revised exclusively on the basis of the MI.

Returning to the example we are analyzing, *we know* that we have used three methods of measurement. Faced with a poor fit, it is, therefore, more plausible to attribute it to the omission of methods factors rather than to correlated measurement errors. In fact, one of the

---

[28]EQS has an option—the Lagrange Multiplier test—(Bentler, 1986) that yields results analogous to MI, as well as some not provided in LISREL. Our reservations and cautions regarding the use of MI are by and large applicable to this test as well.

reasons we ran this analysis was to illustrate how misleading an automatic conclusion that the errors are correlated may be. The same is illustrated in our next analysis, when only method factors are hypothesized (see output for Model 2).

Finally, when models are revised on the basis of the observed results, and the *same* data are then used to test the revised models, what may have started out as a confirmatory process has been transformed into an exploratory one. "It is regrettable, and bodes ill for scientific progress in the behavioral sciences, that this elementary principle is often ignored by investigators of all degrees of renown" (Cliff, 1987, p. 370). Almost any causal model can be made to fit the data by continuously revising it on the basis of the observed results. "Massaging" the model is probably a more appropriate characterization of such an exercise. It has all been captured in Coase's incomparable aphorism: "If you torture the data long enough nature will confess" (quoted by Wallace, 1977, p. 431).

We hope that you have replicated our analysis. If so, we suggest that you examine the FITTED RESIDUALS (not reported here) and notice that many of them are relatively large. This is even easier to appreciate upon examining the STANDARDIZED RESIDUALS (not reported here). As in the case of MI, exclusive reliance on residuals as guides to model revision is to be avoided. Residuals too should be treated as hints. Indeed, they should be viewed not only in connection with other indices but primarily in light of theoretical and design considerations (for discussions and illustrations, see Costner & Schoenberg, 1973; Herting & Costner, 1985; Sörbom, 1975).

MODEL 2

According to this model, three intercorrelated method factors are hypothesized to underlie the correlation matrix of Table 23.1. Specifically, it is hypothesized that traits A, B, and C (e.g., assertiveness, anxiety, and aggression) are correlated when they are measured by the same method (e.g., the same projective technique). In short, it is hypothesized that A_1, B_1, and C_1 reflect Method 1 (e.g., summated rating scales); A_2, B_2, and C_2 reflect Method 2 (e.g., an interview); A_3, B_3, and C_3 reflect Method 3 (e.g., a projective technique).

Input

Except for the names of the latent variables and the parameter specifications for LAMBDA X, the input for this model is the same as for Model 1 (see above). Therefore, only statements necessary to make the changes are given here.

```
LK
'METHOD 1' 'METHOD 2' 'METHOD 3'
FR LX 1 1 LX 2 1 LX 3 1 LX 4 2 LX 5 2 LX 6 2 LX 7 3 LX 8 3 LX 9 3
```

Output

TABLE 23.1   MTMM.   THREE METHODS.
        MEASURES OF GOODNESS OF FIT FOR THE WHOLE MODEL :
        CHI-SQUARE WITH 24 DEGREES OF FREEDOM = 678.88 (P = .000)
                GOODNESS OF FIT INDEX = .666
            ADJUSTED GOODNESS OF FIT INDEX = .374
                ROOT MEAN SQUARE RESIDUAL = .127

Commentary

As you can see from this excerpt, the fit of this model is even worse than that of Model 1 (compare with output given earlier). The poor fit of the present model is also evident from the excessive number of large STANDARDIZED RESIDUALS (not reported here).

Output

TABLE 23.1   MTMM.   THREE METHODS.

MAXIMUM MODIFICATION INDEX IS 100.12 FOR ELEMENT (6, 3) OF THETA DELTA

Commentary

Serious reservations regarding the use of Modification Indices (MI) for model revision were expressed in the commentaries on the output for Model 1. Therefore, all that will be pointed out here is that, on the basis of this output, researchers using MI for model revision would be inclined to free the parameter corresponding to the correlation between measurement errors of C2 and C1, that is, between two different methods used to measure the same trait (C). We turn now to Model 3.

MODEL 3

According to this model, three correlated trait factors and three correlated method factors are hypothesized to underlie the relations among the manifest variables given in Table 23.1. Note that *no* correlations are hypothesized between trait and method factors. The issue of whether or not it is meaningful to speak of correlations among methods was addressed in Chapter 4 and will, therefore, not be gone into here.

LISREL

Input

```
TABLE 23.1   MTMM.   THREE TRAITS AND THREE METHODS (MODEL 3)
DA NI=9 NO=300
LA
A1 B1 C1 A2 B2 C2 A3 B3 C3
KM
1.0 .4 1.0 .35 .3 1.0 .55 .22 .15 1.0
.2 .52 .17 .6 1.0 .14 .15 .55 .48 .5 1.0
.5 .2 .16 .64 .36 .28 1.0 .21 .5 .2 .37 .64
.27 .46 1.0 .15 .12 .54 .31 .3 .6 .45 .4 1.0
MO NX=9 NK=6 PH=FI
LK
'TRAIT A' 'TRAIT B' 'TRAIT C' 'METHOD 1' 'METHOD 2' 'METHOD 3'
PA LX
1 0 0 1 0 0
0 1 0 1 0 0
0 0 1 1 0 0
1 0 0 0 1 0
0 1 0 0 1 0
```

```
0 0 1 0 1 0
1 0 0 0 0 1
0 1 0 0 0 1
0 0 1 0 0 1
MA LX
.7 0 0 .4 0 0
0 .8 0 .4 0 0
0 0 .7 .4 0 0
.6 0 0 0 .7 0
0 .6 0 0 .7 0
0 0 .6 0 .7 0
.6 0 0 0 0 .7
0 .6 0 0 0 .7
0 0 .5 0 0 .7
ST 1 PH 1 1 PH 2 2 PH 3 3 PH 4 4 PH 5 5 PH 6 6
FR PH 2 1 PH 3 1 PH 3 2 PH 5 4 PH 6 4 PH 6 5
OU SE TV RS
```

Commentary

On the MO statement, NK = 6 means 6 latent variables (three traits and three methods). Compare with Models 1 and 2, where NK = 3.

When, as in the present case, it is desired to free only some of the off-diagonal elements of PH, PH = ST should *not* be used (see Manual, p. 14). Instead, we specify PH = FI, which means that PHI (covariance matrix among the KSI's) is symmetric FIxed (comprised of zeros). The ST 1 statement is used to fix the diagonal of PHI to 1's, thereby standardizing the variances of the latent variables (for an explanation, see commentaries on the input for the analyses of data from Table 22.1, presented earlier in this chapter). The FR statement is used to free the elements of PHI corresponding to correlations among trait factors (e.g., PH 2 1) and among methods factors (e.g., PH 5 4). Other approaches can be used to accomplish the same end.

In earlier analyses, a FR statement was used to specify the parameters of LAMBDA X that are to be estimated. We thought it would be useful to illustrate how this may be done through the use of a pattern matrix (PA). PA LX means that a pattern matrix for Lambda X follows (see Manual, pp. 65–66). As you can see, a pattern matrix consists of 1's and 0's, where the former signify free parameters and latter signify fixed ones. Pattern matrices are convenient when a matrix contains "many fixed and free elements" (Manual, p. 65).

MA LX means that a matrix of starting values for LAMBDA X follows. Starting values were mentioned earlier in this chapter (see commentaries on EQS input), where it was pointed out that these are guesses about the signs and magnitudes of the parameters that the program uses to begin the iteration process. When starting values are not supplied, LISREL uses automatic starting values. "Good" starting values lead to faster convergence, hence, less running time, which is particularly useful for large problems. The absence of starting values or a poor choice of such values may result in failure to achieve convergence in large problems and/or when, as in the present example, manifest variables are said to load on more than one latent variable.

When we ran this example on a mainframe (using LISREL VI) without starting values, a large number of iterations was required to reach convergence. Using PC–LISREL 7 without starting values, the run was aborted giving the following messages:

W_A_R_N_I_N_G : PHI is not positive definite
F_A_T_A_L E_R_R_O_R : Admissibility test failed.

When we reran the example without starting values but with a larger value for the admissibility test (AD; see Manual, p. 278), a solution was obtained after a large number of iterations. The same solution was obtained with relatively few iterations when the input given above (i.e., including the starting values) was used.

As you can see from the OU statement, no AD is specified (the default is used). Further, this time we do not call for MI (Modification Indices), but we call for SE (Standard Errors) and TV (t–Values), on which we comment below.

Output

TABLE 23.1   MTMM.   THREE TRAITS AND THREE METHODS
LISREL ESTIMATES (MAXIMUM LIKELIHOOD)

LAMBDA X

	TRAIT A	TRAIT B	TRAIT C	METHOD 1	METHOD 2	METHOD 3
A1	.804	.000	.000	.472	.000	.000
B1	.000	.752	.000	.302	.000	.000
C1	.000	.000	.833	.287	.000	.000
A2	.748	.000	.000	.000	.586	.000
B2	.000	.732	.000	.000	.608	.000
C2	.000	.000	.702	.000	.549	.000
A3	.660	.000	.000	.000	.000	.538
B3	.000	.703	.000	.000	.000	.456
C3	.000	.000	.667	.000	.000	.551

PHI

	TRAIT A	TRAIT B	TRAIT C	METHOD 1	METHOD 2	METHOD 3
TRAIT A	1.000					
TRAIT B	.441	1.000				
TRAIT C	.318	.335	1.000			
METHOD 1	.000	.000	.000	1.000		
METHOD 2	.000	.000	.000	−.178	1.000	
METHOD 3	.000	.000	.000	−.142	.452	1.000

THETA DELTA

A1	B1	C1	A2	B2	C2	A3	B3	C3
.135	.347	.220	.098	.091	.216	.265	.302	.249

MEASURES OF GOODNESS OF FIT FOR THE WHOLE MODEL :
CHI-SQUARE WITH 12 DEGREES OF FREEDOM = 3.57 (P = .990)
GOODNESS OF FIT INDEX = .997
ADJUSTED GOODNESS OF FIT INDEX = .990
ROOT MEAN SQUARE RESIDUAL = .009

Commentary

As you can see from the goodness-of-fit indices, the model fits very well—perhaps too well—but remember that the data are fictitious.

Examine now the coefficients in the LAMBDA X matrix and note that they are relatively large for the three traits and somewhat smaller for the three methods, the smallest ones associated with Method 1. We return to this matrix later on.

Turning to the PHI matrix, it will be noted that the correlations among the traits are moderate. As to the correlations among the methods, the one between Methods 2 and 3 is moderate, whereas the other two (i.e., between Method 1 and Method 2, and between Method 1 and Method 3) are low. As shown below, the latter correlations are statistically not significant. The more important question of the substantive meaningfulness of the two low correlations would have to be addressed in the context of the specific theoretical framework and the specific characteristics of the design. Nevertheless, in view of the fact that, in the present case, they refer to correlations between methods, it is safe to assume that many researchers would consider them not meaningful, regardless of whether or not they are statistically significant.

Output

T-VALUES

PHI

	TRAIT A	TRAIT B	TRAIT C	METHOD 1	METHOD 2	METHOD 3
TRAIT A	.000					
TRAIT B	4.167	.000				
TRAIT C	2.591	2.996	.000			
METHOD 1	.000	.000	.000	.000		
METHOD 2	.000	.000	.000	−.342	.000	
METHOD 3	.000	.000	.000	−.266	2.885	.000

Commentary

LISREL reports STANDARD ERRORS of the estimated parameters (not reproduced here). Dividing a parameter by its standard error yields a critical ratio (labeled T–VALUE in LISREL) that in large samples has an approximate z distribution. A value of approximately ±2.0 can, therefore, be interpreted as indicating that the parameter with which it is associated is statistically significant at the .05 level.[29] Recall, however, that, in the present example, a correlation matrix was analyzed. As was pointed out earlier (see Matrix Analyzed, under Assumptions), standard errors, hence, the t–values based on them, are valid only when the covariance matrix is analyzed.

We comment on these statistics here to acquaint you with this aspect of the output and to introduce the concept of tests of parameters. We reproduced the T–VALUES for elements in the PHI matrix only so that we may draw your attention to the small values associated with the correlations between Methods 1 and 2, and between Methods 1 and 3.

Ignoring, for present purposes, the question of substantive meaningfulness, results of tests of significance such as the above may serve as clues for model revision. Two points should, however, be borne in mind. One, elements retained in the model may change drastically when another element(s) is fixed (i.e., set equal to zero). Therefore, the fixing of elements that are statistically not significant should be done one at a time so that the effects on elements retained in the model may be ascertained. Two, this process of model revision is exploratory, providing clues for the reformulation of a model to be tested with new data.

As our example is illustrative, we will not engage in model revision. You may wish to do

---

[29]The same test is included in the EQS output, alongside the parameter estimates.

this as an exercise. Following are some results against which you may check yours: (a) fixing PHI 5 4, $\chi^2(13) = 3.75$; (b) fixing PHI 6 4, $\chi^2(13) = 3.66$; (c) fixing both elements, $\chi^2(14) = 3.81$. Recalling that, for the original model, $\chi^2(12) = 3.57$, we obtain $\chi^2(2) = .24$ (i.e., $3.81 - 3.57$), for a test of the difference between the original model and one in which both elements are fixed. Not surprisingly, relaxing the constraints on the correlations between Method 1 and Method 2 as well as between Method 1 and Method 3 does not lead to a statistically significant improvement in fit. Furthermore, the GFI and AGFI are virtually unchanged. In sum, fixing the two statistically nonsignificant correlations between methods factors does not have a noticeable effect on the fit of the model. *We remind you that, before accepting the revised model, it would, at the very least, have to be shown to provide a good fit to new data.*

In the interest of space, we do not report the results of the residual analysis. As you might have surmised from the RMR of .009 (reported earlier), the residuals are small. Suffice it to point out that the largest standardized residual is $-.838$.

TABULAR SUMMARY OF TESTS OF SUBMODELS

Tests of the models under consideration, as well as model comparisons and incremental fit, are presented in Table 23.2. Following the format used by Bentler and Bonett (1980), the table is divided in two sections. In the left-hand section are tests of the three models analyzed above. In addition, results are given for the null model (M_n) used to calculate Bentler–Bonett (1980) indices of fit—see (23.7) and (23.8). As was pointed out earlier, to obtain the chi-square for the null model, an additional LISREL run is required (see footnote 25).

The right-hand section of Table 23.2 consists of model comparisons. Note that, in the first three rows, each of the three models is compared to the null model. The ρ and Δ (Bentler–Bonett Nonnormed and Normed fit indices respectively) for such comparisons are routinely reported in EQS. When using LISREL, these indices of fit are obtained by applying (23.7) and (23.8) using relevant values from the left-hand section of the table.[30]

When the analysis of this example was introduced, an outline of models to be compared was given. The right-hand section of Table 23.2 is addressed to the model comparisons outlined earlier. Thus, the results of row 1 of Table 23.2 refer to comparison (1a)—the fit of Model 1 (traits only) over a null model. As can be seen from the table, Model 1 provides a marked and statistically significant—$\chi^2(12) = 1005.05$—improvement in fit over the null model—similarly for the comparison (2a)—the fit of Model 2 (methods only) over a null model (row 2).

Rows 4 and 5 refer to comparisons (2b) and (1b) respectively. In (2b), row 4, the question addressed is whether a model consisting of traits and method factors (Model 3) provides a better fit than a model consisting of traits only (Model 1). Stated differently, is it necessary to include method factors in addition to trait factors? The answer is clearly yes, both on the grounds of a statistical test of significance—$\chi^2(12) = 427.50$—and the magnitude of incremental fit (e.g., $\Delta = .298$). The question addressed in (1b), row 5, is whether it is necessary to include trait factors, in addition to method factors. Again, the answer is clearly yes— $\chi^2(12) = 675.31$ and the magnitude of incremental fit (e.g., $\Delta = .470$).

---

[30]For the calculation of the indices of incremental fit for rows 4 and 5, the denominator is the same as for those calculated for rows 1–3. The numerators consist of the relevant values for the models being compared. Earlier we drew attention to Sobel and Bohrnstedt's (1985) discussion of user-selected baseline models to calculate fit indices.

Table 23.2

Tests of Submodels

Model Test*			Model Comparison*				
Model	χ^2	df	Comparison	χ^2	df	ρ	Δ
1) M_n	1436.12	36	$M_n - M_1$	1005.05	12	.564	.700
2) M_1	431.07	24	$M_n - M_2$	757.24	12	.298	.527
3) M_2	678.88	24	$M_n - M_3$	1432.55	24	1.018	.998
4) M_3	3.57	12	$M_1 - M_3$	427.50	12	.454	.298
5)			$M_2 - M_3$	675.31	12	.720	.470

*Except for M_3, $p < .001$ for all chi-square statistics.

Note. M_n = Null model
M_1 = three correlated traits
M_2 = three correlated methods
M_3 = three correlated traits and three correlated methods

The results for Model 3 are depicted in Figure 23.3. Values on the unidirectional arrows were taken from LAMBDA X (see output for Model 3, given earlier). In the present example, they are coefficients of effects of trait and method factors on their respective indicators. Values on the bidirectional arrows were taken from PHI. In the present example, they are correlations among the factors. The dashed lines connecting M_1 with M_2, and M_1 with M_3 are meant to indicate statistically nonsignificant correlations. Values reported at the base of the arrows referring to the error terms were taken from THETA DELTA (recall that these are *variances*).

Examine Figure 23.3 and note that indicators of the three traits (A, B, and C) have relatively large coefficients on their respective trait factors. This constitutes evidence of convergent validity in the sense that different methods measuring the same trait appear to converge.[31] However, note that effects within each of the traits vary to a greater or lesser extent. For instance, effects of Trait B (.752, .732, and .703) are more uniform than those of Trait A (.804, .748, and .660). It is possible to fit and test a model in which effects of a given factor are constrained to be equal to each other.[32] For trait factors, such constraints would constitute a test of whether the different methods are equally valid in measuring a given trait. For example, constraining the effects of TRAIT B (KSI 2) to be equal to each other would enable one to test whether Methods 1, 2, and 3 are equally valid as measures of trait B. Equality constraints can also be tested for method factors in order to determine whether a given method contributes equally to the measurement of all the traits in the model.

Discriminant validity is indicated when correlations among trait factors are not "too high."[33] It has been suggested (see Widaman, 1985) that the presence or absence of discriminant validity be determined by testing whether or not correlations among traits differ from unity. This may be accomplished by comparing two models: (a) a model in which the correlations among traits are free, as in our Model 3; and (b) a model in which the correlations among traits are fixed to 1.0. The difference between the χ^2's for the two models, along with the difference between their associated degrees of freedom, is a test of the hypothesis that correlations among traits equal unity. When the χ^2-difference test is statistically not significant, it is concluded that the traits lack discriminant validity. In contrast, a statistically significant χ^2-difference test is taken as evidence of discriminant validity.

[31]See Chapter 4, for discussions of convergent and discriminant validity.
[32]An example of equality constraints is given later, under Measurement Models.
[33]See Chapter 4, for a discussion and examples.

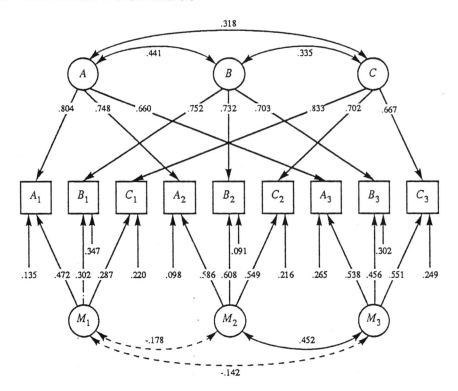

Figure 23.3

It is, however, essential not to overlook the very important distinction between statistical significance and substantive meaningfulness. Because relatively large samples are required for *CFA*, the likelihood is high for the χ^2-difference test to be statistically significant even when correlations among traits are very high, even close to 1.0. Thus, contradictory conclusions may be reached regarding discriminant validity, depending on whether a test of significance is used or magnitudes of the correlations are considered.

In view of the preceding, we recommend that magnitudes of correlations among traits, rather than a test of whether they differ statistically from unity, serve as the primary evidence regarding the presence or absence of discriminant validity. A stronger case may be made, we believe, for the use of the χ^2-difference test to determine whether correlations among traits differ significantly from zero, especially when the MTMM is used for external structure analysis in the process of construct validation.[34]

Our recommendations are, of course, a matter of judgment. Widaman (1985), for example, reasoned along opposite lines, asserting that "researchers employing multitrait-multimethod approaches typically have little interest in verifying that the trait construct intercorrelations depart significantly from zero" (p. 8). We hope that, regardless of whose recommendations you follow, you will not forget to assess correlations among traits on substantive grounds.

Finally, we remind you that, in our introduction to the analysis of MTMM, we pointed out that our model comparisons are by no means exhaustive. Other models may be of interest.

---

[34]The role of external structure analysis in the process of construct validation was discussed in Chapter 4.

For example, in our discussion of correlations among traits, we spoke as if we were dealing with a dichotomy: Traits are either correlated or they are not correlated. Clearly, one's expectations regarding correlations of specific traits may differ. On substantive grounds one may, for example, expect certain traits to be correlated and others to be not correlated. Such focused expectations can, of course, be tested, using the approach illustrated above. Thus, one may formulate and test a model according to which correlations among some traits are free and those among others fixed.

PARTITIONING THE VARIANCE

A useful approach to the interpretation of results of a *CFA* of a MTMM is to partition the variance of the indicators into three components: trait, method, and random errors. Our example consisted of standardized variables (i.e., we used a correlation matrix), and we have standardized the latent variables (see Input and Commentaries, in earlier sections); therefore, this partitioning is straightforward. The proportion of variance of a manifest variable accounted for by a trait or method factor is equal to the square of the coefficient for the given variable associated with a trait or method factor.

Partitioning of the variance will be illustrated for indicator A_1. Squaring the coefficients given in Figure 23.3, or in LAMBDA X of the output for Model 3, it can be seen that .65 of the variance of A_1 is accounted for by Trait A factor (i.e., $.804^2$), whereas about .22 of its variance is accounted for by Method 1 factor (i.e., $.472^2$). Incidentally, the sum of these two components is equal to the squared multiple correlation (SMC), indicating the proportion of systematic variance in a given indicator (see Manual, p. 42). The proportion of variance due to random errors, .13, is given in THETA DELTA or at the base of the arrow referring to errors in A_1. Recalling that standardized variables were used in the present example, it follows that the three components sum to 1.00, within rounding errors.

Using the approach outlined above, the variance of each of the nine indicators was partitioned and the results summarized in Table 23.3. Examination of Table 23.3 reveals that Method 1 is the most effective in measuring the three traits, whereas Method 3 is the least effective. Furthermore, more method variance is contributed by Methods 2 and 3 than by

Table 23.3

Variance Components due to Trait, Method,
and Error for Model 3. Data from Table 23.1

	Trait	Method	Error
Method 1			
A_1	.65	.22	.13
B_1	.57	.09	.35
C_1	.69	.08	.22
Method 2			
A_2	.56	.34	.10
B_2	.54	.37	.09
C_2	.49	.30	.22
Method 3			
A_3	.44	.29	.27
B_3	.49	.21	.30
C_3	.44	.30	.25

Note. See text for explanation.

Method 1. Finally, note the variability in the error variances, ranging from a low of .09 for B_2 (Trait B measured by Method 2) to a high of .35 for B_1 (Trait B measured by Method 1).

Taking a path-analytic approach (see Chapter 24), it is possible to use results of a *CFA* of a MTMM to decompose reproduced correlations between manifest variables. Accordingly, one can estimate how much of the correlation between two indicators is due to method and how much is due to trait effects. For examples of such analyses, see Schmitt and Stults (1986) and Schwarzer (1986).

MEASUREMENT MODELS

Classical test theory was presented in Chapter 5, where three measurement models were outlined: (a) Parallel, (b) Tau-equivalent, and (c) Congeneric. Briefly, measures are said to be *parallel* when their true scores are equal to each other and when their errors are equal to each other. Accordingly, variances of parallel measures are expected to be equal to each other, and their covariances are expected to be equal to each other. Measures are said to be *tau-equivalent* when only their true scores are equal to each other. Therefore, only covariances of such measures are expected to be equal to each other. Measures are said to be *congeneric* when their true scores are perfectly correlated. As a result, neither variances nor covariances for such measures are expected to be equal to each other.

Earlier, the notion of nested models was introduced. From the preceding description of the three models, it can be seen that the tau-equivalent model is nested in the congeneric model, and the parallel model is nested in the tau-equivalent model. These models can, therefore, be compared through confirmatory factor analysis (*CFA*). It stands to reason that the less restrictive the assumptions on which a model is based, the better its fit. Of the three models considered, thus, the parallel-measures model would, generally speaking, provide the least satisfactory fit, and the congeneric-measures model would provide the most satisfactory fit.

In the present section, we give a simple illustration of the application of *CFA* to comparisons among measurement models (for more detailed treatments, see Alwin & Jackson, 1979; Jöreskog, 1971a, 1974, 1978). Given in Table 23.4 is a correlation matrix and standard deviations for four indicators (e.g., items, rating scales) of some construct (e.g., job satisfaction, empathy). Using *CFA*, the three measurement models presented above will be compared hierarchically. To clarify the sequence of these comparisons, the models will be stated in the form of hypotheses with reference to Figure 23.4. As before, ξ (KSI) refers to a construct (latent variable); X_1 through X_4 to indicators; λ_1 (LAMBDA) through λ_4 to coefficients of the effect of ξ on the X's and δ_1 (DELTA) through δ_4 to error variances of the X's.

Parallel	H_1:	$\lambda_1 = \lambda_2 = \lambda_3 = \lambda_4$;	$\delta_1 = \delta_2 = \delta_3 = \delta_4$
		(constrained)	(constrained)
Tau-Equivalent	H_2:	$\lambda_1 = \lambda_2 = \lambda_3 = \lambda_4$;	$\delta_1, \delta_2, \delta_3, \delta_4$
		(constrained)	(unconstrained)
Congeneric	H_3:	$\lambda_1, \lambda_2, \lambda_3, \lambda_4$;	$\delta_1, \delta_2, \delta_3, \delta_4$
		(unconstrained)	(unconstrained)

Indicated in parentheses under each of the models are conditions describing whether or not given parameters have been constrained. Thus, for parallel measures, the λ's are constrained to be equal to each other, and the δ's are constrained to be equal to each other. For tau-

Table 23.4
Correlation Matrix and Standard Deviations
(s) for Four Indicators (N = 300)

	X_1	X_2	X_3	X_4
X_1	1.00	.42	.45	.51
X_2	.42	1.00	.46	.48
X_3	.45	.46	1.00	.55
X_4	.51	.48	.55	1.00
s:	1.04	1.19	1.32	1.25

equivalent measures, only the λ's are constrained to be equal to each other. This model, then, is obtained by relaxing the constraint regarding the δ's. The congeneric model is obtained by relaxing constraints on both the equality of the λ's and the equality of the δ's.

A comparison between H_1 and H_2 will indicate the improvement in fit provided by a model of tau-equivalent measures over one of parallel measures. A comparison between H_2 and H_3 will indicate the improvement in fit provided by a model of congeneric measures over one of tau-equivalent measures. Improvement in fit provided by a less restrictive model may be deemed not large substantively and/or may be statistically nonsignificant, thus, leading one to retain the more restrictive model.

The use of equality constraints will be illustrated through LISREL. To facilitate comparisons, input and output of the runs for the three models are presented alongside one another. We then give only input statements for EQS, along with some comment about the specification of constraints in this program.

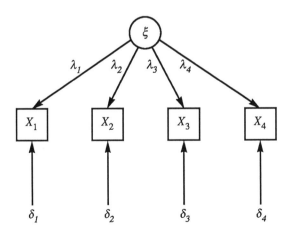

Figure 23.4

LISREL

Input

PARALLEL. TABLE 23.4	TAU-EQUIVALENT. TABLE 23.4	CONGENERIC. TABLE 23.4
DA NI=4 NO=300	DA NI=4 NO=300	DA NI=4 NO=300
LA	LA	LA
X1 X2 X3 X4	X1 X2 X3 X4	X1 X2 X3 X4
KM	KM	KM
1.0 .42 1.0 .45 .46 1.0	1.0 .42 1.0 .45 .46 1.0	1.0 .42 .45 .46 1.0
.51 .48 .55 1.0	.51 .48 .55 1.0	.51 .48 .55 1.0
SD	SD	SD
1.04 1.19 1.32 1.25	1.04 1.19 1.32 1.25	1.04 1.19 1.32 1.25
MO NX=4 NK=1 PH=ST	MO NX=4 NK=1 PH=ST	MO NX=4 NK=1 PH=ST LX=FR
FR LX 1	FR LX 1	OU RS
EQ LX 1 LX 2 LX 3 LX 4	EQ LX 1 LX 2 LX 3 LX 4	
EQ TD 1 TD 2 TD 3 TD 4	OU RS	
OU RS		

Commentary

Thus far, our LISREL input was limited to correlation matrices. In the present example, we are reading in a correlation matrix (KM) as well as standard deviations (SD). Using this information, the program will generate the covariance matrix, which will then be analyzed by default.[35]

The input up to the MOdel statement is identical for the three measurement models. Except for the addition of LX = FRee for the congeneric model, the MO statements are the same for the three models. On the MO statement, we specify that there are four *X*'s (manifest variables), one KSI (latent variable), and that PH = ST. As explained earlier, PH = ST means a correlation matrix among the latent variables. As there is only one latent variable in the present case, this statement is equivalent to a statement that fixes the variance of KSI to equal 1.0.[36]

As explained earlier (see also, Manual, p. 12), LAMBDA is fixed by default, whereas the default for THETA DELTA is diagonal free. Using LX = FR for the congeneric model calls for the estimation of the loadings of the four indicators on KSI. In contrast, for the other two models, only the first parameter is freed (see FR LX 1).

An EQuality constraint statement is used to specify which parameter estimates should be equal to each other (see Manual, p. 67). Thus, in the parallel and the tau-equivalent models, the four λ's (LX) are set equal to each other. In addition, in the parallel model, the four δ's (TD) are set equal to each other. Compare these model specifications with the three hypotheses given earlier.

Output

COVARIANCE MATRIX TO BE ANALYZED

	X1	X2	X3	X4
X1	1.082			
X2	.520	1.416		
X3	.618	.723	1.742	
X4	.663	.714	.908	1.563

---

[35]See commentaries on the DA statement in connection with the analysis of Uncorrelated Factors discussed earlier in this chapter.

[36]See commentaries on the analysis of Uncorrelated Factors earlier in this chapter, where it was pointed out that this is one method of establishing a metric for latent variables.

PARALLEL PARAMETER SPECIFICATIONS	TAU-EQUIVALENT PARAMETER SPECIFICATIONS	CONGENERIC PARAMETER SPECIFICATIONS
LAMBDA X	**LAMBDA X**	**LAMBDA X**

	KSI 1		KSI 1		KSI 1
X1	1	X1	1	VAR 1	1
X2	1	X2	1	VAR 2	2
X3	1	X3	1	VAR 3	3
X4	1	X4	1	VAR 4	4

PHI		PHI		PHI	
	KSI 1		KSI 1		KSI 1
KSI 1	0	KSI 1	0	KSI 1	0

THETA DELTA (PARALLEL)

X1	X2	X3	X4
2	2	2	2

THETA DELTA (TAU-EQUIVALENT)

X1	X2	X3	X4
2	3	4	5

THETA DELTA (CONGENERIC)

X1	X2	X3	X4
5	6	7	8

Commentary

Using the correlations and the standard deviations given as input, the covariance matrix to be analyzed was generated by the program. For example, the correlation between X_1 and X_2 is .42, and the standard deviations are 1.04 and 1.19 (see Table 23.4 or the Input). The covariance between X_1 and X_2 is, therefore,

$$(.42)(1.04)(1.19) = .520$$

Similarly this holds for the other terms.[37]

Of course, when a covariance matrix is available, it is simpler to use it as the input. However, when one has a correlation matrix and standard deviations, as we have here, it is more convenient to use them as the input and leave the generation of the covariance matrix to the program. As the covariance matrix is the same for the three models, we report it only once.

In the parameter specification matrices, parameters that are set equal to each other are assigned the same number. Thus, all elements in LX are assigned 1's in the parallel and tau-equivalent models, whereas, in the congeneric model, they are assigned the numbers 1 through 4 (see hypotheses and Input statements). Note also that, because only in the parallel model are the errors constrained to be equal to each other, the elements of TD are assigned the same number (2) in this model, whereas in the other two models they are numbered consecutively.

As indicated by the 0, the single value in the PHI matrix (i.e., the variance of the latent variable) is fixed. Because we specified PH = ST (see MO in the input), this value is set to 1.0 (see commentary on the MO statement).[38]

Output

PARALLEL. DATA FROM TABLE 23.4 LISREL ESTIMATES (MAXIMUM LIKELIHOOD)		TAU-EQUIVALENT DATA FROM TABLE 23.4 LISREL ESTIMATES (MAXIMUM LIKELIHOOD)		CONGENERIC DATA FROM TABLE 23.4 LISREL ESTIMATES (MAXIMUM LIKELIHOOD)	
LAMBDA X		**LAMBDA X**		**LAMBDA X**	
	KSI 1		KSI 1		KSI 1
X1	.831	X1	.816	VAR 1	.678
X2	.831	X2	.816	VAR 2	.756
X3	.831	X3	.816	VAR 3	.937
X4	.831	X4	.816	VAR 4	.965
PHI		PHI		PHI	
	KSI 1		KSI 1		KSI 1
KSI 1	1.000	KSI 1	1.000	KSI 1	1.000

---

[37]For a discussion of covariance and its relation to the correlation coefficient, see beginning of Chapter 17.

[38]The same could have been accomplished by fixing PH on the MO statement and then using a statement ST 1 PH 1. See example in the analysis of Uncorrelated Factors, earlier in this chapter.

Commentary

In the preceding, parameter estimates are given for the three models. As you can see, the same estimates are indicated for parameters that have been constrained to be equal to each other (i.e., LAMBDA X for the parallel and the tau-equivalent models; see Input and commentaries).

Output

MEASURES OF GOODNESS OF FIT FOR THE WHOLE MODEL :

CHI-SQUARE WITH 8 DEGREES OF FREEDOM = 28.61 (P = .000)	CHI-SQUARE WITH 5 DEGREES OF FREEDOM = 16.33 (P = .006)	CHI-SQUARE WITH 2 DEGREES OF FREEDOM = .49 (P = .783)
GOODNESS OF FIT INDEX = .956	GOODNESS OF FIT INDEX = .973	GOODNESS OF FIT INDEX = .999
ADJUSTED GOODNESS OF FIT INDEX = .945	ADJUSTED GOODNESS OF FIT INDEX = .945	ADJUSTED GOODNESS OF FIT INDEX = .996
ROOT MEAN SQUARE RESIDUAL = .179	ROOT MEAN SQUARE RESIDUAL = .122	ROOT MEAN SQUARE RESIDUAL = .009

STANDARDIZED RESIDUALS					STANDARDIZED RESIDUALS					STANDARDIZED RESIDUALS			
	X1	X2	X3	X4		X1	X2	X3	X4		X1	X2	X3	X4
X1	−3.933				X1	−2.098				X1	.000			
X2	−2.948	−.368			X2	−2.858	−.676			X2	.228	.000		
X3	−1.259	.548	3.109		X3	−.850	.846	1.234		X3	−.684	.465	.000	
X4	−.479	.400	3.736	1.192	X4	−.052	.812	3.727	1.702	X4	.465	−.684	.228	.000

Commentary

We begin with a consideration of each of the models separately. Assuming that $\alpha = .01$ was selected, then, on the grounds of tests of statistical significance, it would be concluded that both the parallel and the tau-equivalent models have to be rejected.

What about other indices of fit? Earlier, it was pointed out that there are no agreed-upon criteria for what would be considered a good fit solely on the basis of GFI and AGFI. Various authors have nevertheless suggested that values $> .90$ be taken as indicative of a satisfactory fit. Employing such a criterion alone, one would be inclined to conclude that even the parallel model provides a satisfactory fit. Inspection of the standardized residuals for the parallel model, however, reveals that four out of these ten residuals exceed the suggested criterion of an absolute value of 2.58 as being large (see Manual, p. 32), thus, casting doubt about the fit of this model. For the tau-equivalent model, two standardized residuals are large.

Using chi-squares and their associated *df* reported in the above output, model comparisons indicated earlier are now carried out.

1. Parallel model (H_1) versus Tau-equivalent model (H_2):

$$28.61 - 16.33 = 12.28$$

As *df* for the first and second chi-square statistics are, respectively 8 and 5, *df* = 3 for the test of the difference between the two models. Checking a table for the χ^2 distribution (see Appendix), it is concluded that this difference is statistically significant (i.e., $p < .01$).

2. Tau-equivalent model (H_2) versus Congeneric model (H_3):

$$16.33 - .49 = 15.84$$

with 3 *df* (i.e., 5−2 associated with the two models being compared), $p < .01$.

Thus, improvement in fit by a tau-equivalent model over a parallel model is statistically significant, as is improvement in fit by a congeneric model over a tau-equivalent model.

As we said and illustrated several times earlier, no single index would generally provide a clear cut answer to the question of model fit. For present purposes, we retain the congeneric model.

Output

THETA DELTA

X1	X2	X3	X4
.621	.845	.865	.632

SQUARED MULTIPLE CORRELATIONS
FOR X – VARIABLES

X1	X2	X3	X4
.426	.404	.503	.596

Commentary

Earlier, it was pointed out that, when an indicator is affected by a single latent variable, the SMC associated with it is an estimate of its reliability—see (23.6). Accordingly, the reliabilities of the indicators for the congeneric model are .426, .404, .503, .596, for indicators X_1 through X_4.

As discussed in Chapter 5—see also, Chapter 22, especially (22.3–22.6)—a distinction is made between nonsystematic variance (i.e., random measurement error) and systematic variance unique to a given indicator. Further, reliability as defined in the classical model refers to variance an indicator shares with other indicators *and* systematic variance unique to it. In the type of models analyzed here, no distinction is made between random errors and systematic variance unique to an indicator in question (i.e., THETA is comprised of both). To the extent that indicators include unique systematic variances, SMC or alternatives (see Manual, p. 79) would lead to underestimates of reliability (see Manual, p. 79). A strategy for separating nonsystematic from systematic variance unique to an indicator was suggested (and illustrated) by Alwin and Jackson (1979).

We turn now to the analysis of the same data using EQS.

EQS

Input

```
/TITLE
 PARALLEL.  TABLE 23.4
/SPECIFICATIONS
 CASES=300; VARIABLES=4;
/EQUATIONS
 V1=*F1 + E1;
 V2=*F1 + E2;
 V3=*F1 + E3;
 V4=*F1 + E4;
/VARIANCES
 E1=*;
 F1=1;
/CONSTRAINTS
 (E1,E1)=(E2,E2)=(E3,E3)=(E4,E4);
 (V1,F1)=(V2,F1)=(V3,F1)=(V4,F1);
/MATRIX
 1.0
 .42 1.0
 .45 .46 1.0
 .51 .48 .55 1.0
/STANDARD DEVIATIONS
 1.04 1.19 1.32 1.25
/END
```

```
/TITLE
 TAU-EQUIVALENT  TABLE 23.4
/SPECIFICATIONS
 CASES=300; VARIABLES=4;
/EQUATIONS
 V1=*F1 + E1;
 V2=*F1 + E2;
 V3=*F1 + E3;
 V4=*F1 + E4;
/VARIANCES
 E1 TO E4=*;
 F1=1;
/CONSTRAINTS
 (V1,F1)=(V2,F1)=(V3,F1)=(V4,F1);
/MATRIX
 1.0
 .42 1.0
 .45 .46 1.0
 .51 .48 .55 1.0
/STANDARD DEVIATIONS
 1.04 1.19 1.32 1.25
/END
```

```
/TITLE
 CONGENERIC.  TABLE 23.4
/SPECIFICATIONS
 CASES=300; VARIABLES=4;
/EQUATIONS
 V1=*F1 + E1;
 V2=*F1 + E2;
 V3=*F1 + E3;
 V4=*F1 + E4;
/VARIANCES
 E1 TO E4=*;
 F1=1;
/MATRIX
 1.0
 .42 1.0
 .45 .46 1.0
 .51 .48 .55 1.0
/STANDARD DEVIATIONS
 1.04 1.19 1.32 1.25
/END
```

Commentary

A general orientation to EQS was given earlier in this chapter (see also commentaries on input and output of earlier EQS runs). Accordingly, we limit our comments to aspects of the input not dealt with before.

To begin with, note that, as in LISREL, the input consists of a correlation matrix as well as a vector of standard deviations. As in LISREL, this information is used by the program to create the covariance matrix to be analyzed (see commentary on LISREL output for the analysis of these data).

Equality constraints are specified in the CONSTRAINTS paragraph. Elements being constrained are referred to by a "double label convention" (see EQS manual, pp. 74–75). For example, (E1,E1) refers to the variance of E1, whereas (V1,F1) refers to the loading of V1 on F1. Note that, in accordance with the assumptions of the measurement models under consideration, two constraints are specified for the parallel model, one for the tau-equivalent model, and none for the congeneric model. Compare these constraints with the constraints in the LISREL run above, and also with the three hypotheses stated earlier with reference to Figure 23.4.

As indicated earlier, we do not provide output for this run. If you are using EQS, compare your output with the one we have given above. We believe you will encounter no difficulties in interpreting the results.

CONCLUDING REMARKS

The models presented in this chapter are very useful for the analysis and evaluation of measurement models, especially in the context of construct validation. As was explained in the introduction to LISREL, such models comprise a submodel of structural equation modeling. This will become evident in the next chapter, where the full model is presented.

STUDY SUGGESTIONS

Note: To carry out analyses suggested below, you will need LISREL, EQS, or a comparable computer program.

1. Assume that, in a design with 5 indicators, it is hypothesized that the first three reflect one factor and the remaining two reflect another factor.
   (a) Using LISREL terminology, what are the dimensions of LAMBDA X and PHI for this model?
   (b) What do the elements of the diagonal of PHI in LISREL signify?
   (c) Assuming that the variances of the latent variables were fixed to 1.00, show how you would specify that the parameters associated with the indicators be estimated in LISREL and in EQS.
2. The following illustrative correlation matrix for eight items (indicators), $N = 300$, was used in Study Suggestion 1 of Chapter 22 to carry out exploratory factor analysis. Subject these data to two confirmatory factor analyses: (a) All the items reflect a single factor; and (b) the first 3 items reflect factor 1; the remaining 5 items reflect factor 2; the two factors are correlated.

	X_1	X_2	X_3	X_4	X_5	X_6	X_7	X_8
X_1	1.00							
X_2	.33	1.00						
X_3	.44	.35	1.00					
X_4	.09	.14	.06	1.00				
X_5	.12	.08	.05	.06	1.00			
X_6	.18	.15	.18	.12	.08	1.00		
X_7	.15	.13	.17	.10	.11	.42	1.00	
X_8	.17	.14	.18	.13	.15	.38	.37	1.00

Following are excerpts of LISREL output for both solutions:

[one factor]

MEASURES OF GOODNESS OF FIT FOR THE WHOLE MODEL :
CHI-SQUARE WITH 20 DEGREES OF FREEDOM = 81.25 (P = .000)
GOODNESS OF FIT INDEX = .924
ADJUSTED GOODNESS OF FIT INDEX = .863
ROOT MEAN SQUARE RESIDUAL = .073

[fifteen of the standardized residuals are > |2|]

[two correlated factors]

LISREL ESTIMATES (MAXIMUM LIKELIHOOD)
LAMBDA X

	KSI 1	KSI 2
X1	.646	.000
X2	.517	.000
X3	.677	.000
X4	.000	.198
X5	.000	.189
X6	.000	.646
X7	.000	.625
X8	.000	.599

PHI

	KSI 1	KSI 2
KSI 1	1.000	
KSI 2	.431	1.000

THETA DELTA

X1	X2	X3	X4	X5	X6	X7	X8
.582	.732	.542	.961	.964	.583	.610	.641

SQUARED MULTIPLE CORRELATIONS FOR X − VARIABLES

X1	X2	X3	X4	X5	X6	X7	X8
.418	.268	.458	.039	.036	.417	.390	.359

MEASURES OF GOODNESS OF FIT FOR THE WHOLE MODEL :
CHI-SQUARE WITH 19 DEGREES OF FREEDOM = 8.19 (P = .985)

GOODNESS OF FIT INDEX = .993
ADJUSTED GOODNESS OF FIT INDEX = .987
ROOT MEAN SQUARE RESIDUAL = .025
[only four standardized residuals are > |1|]

(a) On the basis of an examination of the goodness-of-fit indices and the standardized residuals, what would you conclude about the two solutions?

(b) What is the correlation between the two factors?

(c) What proportion of variance of each indicator is accounted for by the factor it reflects?

(d) On the basis of the results in (c), what would you be inclined to conclude about items 4 and 5?

3. Assume that, on the basis of results obtained in Study Suggestion 2, it was decided to delete items 4 and 5. Assume also that the following standard deviations are available for the original 8 items:

1.15 1.21 1.09 1.65 1.11 .98 1.12 1.17

Use these standard deviations along with the correlation matrix given in Study Suggestion 2 to test the following for $\alpha = .05$:

(a) A parallel model for two correlated factors fits the data (i.e., items 1, 2, and 3 are parallel for KSI 1; items 6, 7, and 8 are parallel for KSI 2).

(b) A tau-equivalent model for two correlated factors constitutes a statistically significant improvement in fit over the parallel model.

(c) A congeneric model for two correlated factors constitutes a statistically significant improvement in fit over the tau-equivalent model.

If you have used LISREL for the analysis of Study Suggestion 2, you can add the vector of standard deviations and use a SElect statement to select only the 6 items of interest for the present analysis.

If you have used EQS for the analysis of Study Suggestion 2, you can add the vector of the standard deviations. Specifying the variables of interest in the /EQUATIONS paragraph will select only them for the analysis. Following are excerpts of the LISREL output:

STUDY SUGGESTION 23.3　PARALLEL
LISREL ESTIMATES (MAXIMUM LIKELIHOOD)
LAMBDA X

	KSI 1	KSI 2
X1	.701	.000
X2	.701	.000
X3	.701	.000
X6	.000	.679
X7	.000	.679
X8	.000	.679

PHI

	KSI 1	KSI 2
KSI 1	1.000	
KSI 2	.422	1.000

THETA DELTA

X1	X2	X3	X6	X7	X8
.834	.834	.834	.734	.734	.734

MEASURES OF GOODNESS OF FIT
FOR THE WHOLE MODEL :
CHI-SQUARE WITH 16 DEGREES OF
FREEDOM = 23.63 (P = .098)
GOODNESS OF FIT INDEX = .976
ADJUSTED GOODNESS OF FIT INDEX = .968
ROOT MEAN SQUARE RESIDUAL = .081

STUDY SUGGESTION 23.3　TAU EQUIVALENT
LISREL ESTIMATES (MAXIMUM LIKELIHOOD)
LAMBDA X

	KSI 1	KSI 2
X1	.707	.000
X2	.707	.000
X3	.707	.000
X6	.000	.675
X7	.000	.675
X8	.000	.675

PHI

	KSI 1	KSI 2
KSI 1	1.000	
KSI 2	.419	1.000

THETA DELTA

X1	X2	X3	X6	X7	X8
.799	1.024	.668	.519	.781	.908

MEASURES OF GOODNESS OF FIT
FOR THE WHOLE MODEL :
CHI-SQUARE WITH 12 DEGREES OF
FREEDOM = 2.34 (P = .999)
GOODNESS OF FIT INDEX = .997
ADJUSTED GOODNESS OF FIT INDEX = .995
ROOT MEAN SQUARE RESIDUAL = .027

STUDY SUGGESTION 23.3　CONGENERIC
LISREL ESTIMATES (MAXIMUM LIKELIHOOD)
LAMBDA X

	KSI 1	KSI 2
X1	.740	.000
X2	.623	.000
X3	.743	.000
X6	.000	.645
X7	.000	.706
X8	.000	.686

PHI

	KSI 1	KSI 2
KSI 1	1.000	
KSI 2	.417	1.000

THETA DELTA

X1	X2	X3	X6	X7	X8
.775	1.076	.636	.544	.755	.898

MEASURES OF GOODNESS OF FIT
FOR THE WHOLE MODEL :
CHI-SQUARE WITH 8 DEGREES OF
FREEDOM = .48 (P = 1.00)
GOODNESS OF FIT INDEX = .999
ADJUSTED GOODNESS OF FIT INDEX = .999
ROOT MEAN SQUARE RESIDUAL = .010

4. Williams, Cote, and Buckley (1989) applied confirmatory factor analysis to 11 multitrait-multimethod matrices from published research. We recommend that you replicate some such analyses, using LISREL and/or EQS. Williams et al. provided partial results that you can use to check on your reanalyses.
5. As suggested in Chapter 1, we believe you will benefit from reading and even reanalyzing data from papers that have elicited criticisms. Following are some references to exchanges concerning specific applications of confirmatory factor analysis.
   (a) Bagozzi and Burnkrant (1979, 1985), Dillon and Kumar (1985).
   (b) Bollen (1980), Bollen and Grandjean (1981, 1983), Fornell (1983b).

Answers

1. (a) LAMBDA X is 5 by 2. PHI is 2 by 2.
   (b) Variances of latent exogenous variables.
   (c) In LISREL: FR LX 1 1 LX 2 1 LX 3 1 LX 4 2 LX 5 2
           Or: FR LX 1 LX 3 LX 5 LX 8 LX 10
   In EQS: /EQU
               V1 = *F1 + E1;
               V2 = *F1 + E2;
               V3 = *F1 + E3;
               V4 = *F2 + E4;
               V5 = *F2 + E5;
           /VAR
           E1 TO E5 = *;

2. (a) The single-factor model is rejected because of, among other things, the relatively large RMR and the relatively large number of standardized residuals $> |2|$. The two-factor model fits the data well. We suggest that you carry out one additional analysis identical to the two-factor model given above, except that the correlation between the factors is fixed equal 1.00 (do this by appropriate changes in connection with PHI). You will find the results identical to those given for the one-factor solution. The difference between the χ^2's for the two models (with 1 df) constitutes a test of the improvement resulting from freeing the correlation between the two factors, that is, hypothesizing that two correlated factors, rather than a single factor, underlie the relations among the indicators.
   (b) .431
   (c) When, as in the analysis under consideration, the variances of the latent variables are standardized, the proportion of variance of an indicator accounted for by the factor it reflects is equal to the square of its coefficient (i.e., λ). See (23.4)–(23.5) and the discussion related to them. For example, the proportion of variance of X1 accounted for by KSI 1 is $.646^2 = .417$
   The same results are reported under SQUARED MULTIPLE CORRELATIONS FOR X − VARIABLES (see discussion of this in commentaries on output in the chapter).
   (d) The variance accounted for in indicators 4 and 5 is very small. Assuming the analysis was carried out in the context of the validation of a two-dimensional construct, it would be advisable to delete these items. See Study Suggestion 3.

3. (a) As indicated in the above output, the probability for the χ^2 is $> .05$, lending support to the hypothesis that a parallel model fits the data.

(b) The χ^2 for the test of the difference between the two models is 21.29 (i.e., 23.63 − 2.34) with 4 *df*, $p < .5$, lending support to the hypothesis that a tau-equivalent model provides a better fit over a parallel model. Nevertheless, a decision to retain the parallel model is conceivable when considering other indices (e.g., fit indices, standardized residuals).

(c) The χ^2 for the test of the difference between the two models is 1.86 with 4 *df*, $p > .05$, leading to the rejection of the hypothesis that a congeneric model provides a better fit than a tau-equivalent model.

Chapter 24
Structural Equation Modeling

Before outlining the contents of this chapter, a comment about terminology is in order. There is no consensus about terms used to refer to the types of models to be presented in this chapter. Primarily for historical reasons, the term path analysis has been used to refer to the analysis of causal models when single indicators are employed for each of the variables in the model (see Pedhazur, 1982, Chapter 15, and references given therein). Because of the great popularity of the LISREL computer program (Jöreskog & Sörbom, 1989) for the analysis of causal models, some researchers and authors refer to them as LISREL, or LISREL-type, models. (Users of this program have even been referred to as LISRELites.) Among other terms used are causal modeling, analysis of covariance structures, latent variable models, structural modeling, and structural equation modeling (*SEM*). Along with various authors, we prefer the latter term.

We begin with some general observations on the notion of causation, because of its centrality in *SEM*. This is followed by an overview of structural models in LISREL. The topic of identification is then commented upon. Analyses of some simple models using LISREL are then presented. For two of the examples, EQS is also used. As in preceding chapters, various issues and ideas concerning applications and interpretations of *SEM* are introduced and discussed in the context of commentaries on input and/or output related to the examples we analyze. The chapter concludes with an overview of topics not presented.

CAUSATION

Causation is one of the most controversial topics in philosophy and science. Among other things, it has been characterized as "a notorious philosophical tar pit" (Davis, 1985, p. 8); "a logical labyrinth" (Hanson, 1969, p. 275). Addressing the question of what is a viable notion of causation, a leading statistician (Kempthorne, 1978) declared: "It may well be regarded as arrogant for me, a mere statistician, to raise this question. The history of the topic extends over centuries and even millennia" (p. 6).

Proponents of almost any position imaginable regarding causation in general, or in specific contexts (e.g., science, criminology, history), may be found among philosophers, scientists, logicians, statisticians, researchers, and practitioners.[1]

To give you a flavor of the diversity of positions, here is an almost random selection:

The concept of cause is generally considered to be the most important one for the development of science. (Hutten, 1962, p. 87)

The interesting fact remains that at present all branches of science that have reached a satisfactory state of precision espouse causality as a principle of their methodology. (Margenau, 1950, p. 412)

It would be very healthy if more researchers abandon thinking of and using terms such as *cause* and *effect*. (Muthén, 1987, p. 180)

The reason why physics has ceased to look for causes is that, in fact, there are no such things. The law of causality, I believe, . . . is a relic of a bygone age, surviving, like the monarchy, only because it is erroneously supposed to do no harm. (Russell, 1929, p. 180)

Cause is the most valuable concept in the methodology of the applied sciences. (Scriven, 1968, p. 79)

Let's drop that word *cause* and bring educational research out of the middle ages. (Travers, 1981, p. 32)

The notion of causation is so ingrained in our thoughts and conceptions that attempts to understand myriad phenomena or to communicate about them without resorting to it are practically inconceivable. Envision, if you can, attempts to understand change or to communicate about it without explicit or implicit reference to causation, or consider attempts to understand or communicate about, say, criminal behavior and the law, diagnosis and treatment of disease, death, origin of a fire, traffic accidents, personality and human behavior, morality, responsibility, or even economic trends, without the implication of causation.

Drawing attention to the pervasiveness of implicit or explicit allusions to causation in scientific discourse, Nagel (1965) concluded that "though the *term* may be absent, the *idea* for which it stands continues to have wide currency. . . . In short, the idea of cause is not as outmoded in modern science as is sometimes alleged" (p. 12).

This is to be expected, as an explicit or implicit notion of causation is indispensable for central concepts and principles of design, analysis, and interpretation of scientific research. Consider, for example, attempts to define control, spurious correlation, internal validity, change, without resorting to the notion of causation, or consider the causal allusions in euphemisms such as: independent and dependent variables; risk factor; effect; influence; impact; proportion of variance accounted by; inhibiting, precipitating or facilitating factors.

Decrying the reluctance among authors of texts in research to use the word "cause," Davis (1971) said: "This genuflection to the philosophy of science is pious cant since the only sensible reason to go through the agonies involved in research is the hope that you will find causes of things" (p. 6).

---

[1]Following is a selection of references exemplifying the diversity of positions on the issue of causation: Bagozzi (1980a), Blalock (1964, 1985a, 1985b), Bollen (1989), Braithwaite (1960), Brodbeck (1968), Bunge (1979), Cook and Campbell (1979), Hanson (1958, 1969, 1971), Harré and Madden (1975), Holland (1986), Hume (1960), Hutten (1962), Lerner (1965), Mackie (1965, 1974), Margenau (1950), Mulaik (1987), Scriven (1971, 1975), Simon (1957, 1968, 1979), Wallace (1972, 1974), and Wold (1956).

Symposia on causation have been appearing periodically in various journals. Following are some examples: *Issues in Criminology*, 1968, *3*, 129–194. *Journal of Educational Statistics*, 1987, *12*, 101–223. *The Journal of Philosophy*, 1967, *64*, 691–725. *Synthese*, 1986, *67*, 157–379; 1986, *68*, 1–180. See also, Glymour, Scheines, and Sprites (1988), Holland (1988), Marini and Singer (1988), and Leamer's (1988) discussion of the preceding chapters.

In sum, regardless of his or her philosophical stance about causation, the scientist *qua* scientist seems to find a causal framework indispensable when attempting to explain phenomena. This, of course, is not to say that support for causal claims is easy to come by, nor is it meant to underestimate hazards of making spurious causal claims. Of various aspects that have bearing on this endeavor, we comment on the following three: (a) the definition of causation, (b) the type of research design, and (c) the role of theory.

ON THE DEFINITION OF CAUSATION

In view of the great controversy surrounding the use of the term causation and in view of the fact that it is used in diverse contexts, it should be obvious that there is no consensus regarding its definition. Margenau (1950), who pointed out that "the words *cause* and *effect* are among the most loosely used in our language" (p. 389), asserted that science and scientists cannot be of much help in clarifying their meaning as they "are not primarily scientific terms" (p. 389). Some authors (e.g., Nagel, 1961) believe that it would be "an ungrateful and pointless task to canvass even partially the variety of senses that have been attached to the word 'cause'" (p. 73). Introducing his incisive discussion of causal inference in nonexperimental research, Blalock (1964) stated that he will not attempt a formal definition of causality and that "it indeed may turn out wise to treat the notion of causality as primitive or undefined" (p. 9). For a wide range of ideas on this issue as well as various attempts to define causation, see references given in footnote 1.

CAUSATION AND DESIGN TYPE

As was discussed in detail in Part 2, the design type has important implications for the validity of conclusions, inferences, and generalizations from research. Various authors have asserted that it is only through variable manipulation that one may hope to study causation. Thus, Holland (1986) reported: "Donald Rubin and I once made up the motto NO CAUSATION WITHOUT MANIPULATION to emphasize the importance of this restriction" (p. 959). And so strong were Kempthorne's (1978) feelings on this issue that he portrayed Bertrand Russell as being "very stupid" for not giving the "slightest recognition of the idea of experimentation" (p. 8) in connection with his discussion of causation. Further,

the incredible aspect of the whole business for me is that top minds of the world have written at length on causation and have written material which is useless, at best. It would seem that the notion of experimentally varying forces and observing the results, which is the basis of all good science, is given essentially no place. (p. 8)

Not surprisingly, Kempthorne (1978) decreed: "Behavioral science and sociobiology, to name two arenas, must move from observation to intervention or *we should ignore them* [italics added]. To say this is very hard to do is no answer" (p. 20).

Some authors (e.g., Holland, 1986; Kempthorne, 1978) rejected imputation of causation to any variable that is not manipulable, at least in principle. Thus, Kempthorne (1978) contended that "it is epistemological nonsense to talk about one trait of an individual *causing* or determining another trait of the individual" (p. 15). That variable manipulation holds the greatest promise for the study of causation is incontestable. Yet two things should be borne in mind. One, even in experimental designs, problems of internal validity loom large. Because we discussed artifacts and pitfalls in research in general in Chapter 11, and specific issues concerning experimental designs in Chapter 12, we will not repeat them here. Two, although manipulation is also an aspect of quasi-experimental designs (see Chapter 13), the absence of randomization in such designs leads to very difficult (insurmountable, according to some) obstacles to valid inferences.

Inability or unwillingness to manipulate variables[2] has led many to make causal inferences from nonexperimental research. This in turn has led to conferring the status of cause on variables that are not manipulable in principle (e.g., race, sex) or in practice (e.g., religious affiliation, marital status). Also, as was pointed out in Chapter 14, whereas, in experimental designs, one proceeds from the presumed cause to the presumed effect, the converse is true in nonexperimental designs.

THE ROLE OF THEORY

Hanson (1969), who has written most perceptively on causation, stated: "The language of causality is not *neutral*, it is impregnated with theories, *our* theories" (p. 292–293). Further,

causes certainly are connected with effects; but this is because our theories connect them, not because the world is held together by cosmic glue. The world *may* be glued together by imponderables, but that is irrelevant for understanding causal explanation. (Hanson, 1958, p. 64)

Clearly, then, the point of departure for *SEM* is a theoretical model inasmuch as it is the fit of a specific model to one's data that is being assessed. Although essential in any design aimed at studying causation, theory plays an especially crucial role in nonexperimental designs. Cochran (1965), who has written extensively on nonexperimental designs, related the following:

About 20 years ago, when asked in a meeting what can be done in observational studies to clarify the step from association to causation, Sir Ronald Fisher replied: "Make your theories elaborate". The reply puzzled me at first, since by Occam's razor the advice usually given is to make theories as simple as is consistent with the known data. What Sir Ronald meant, as the subsequent discussion showed, was that when constructing a causal hypothesis one should envisage as many *different* consequences of its truth as possible, and plan observational studies to discover whether each of these consequences is found to hold. (p. 252)

Judging by numerous misapplications of *SEM*, many researchers are evidently unconcerned about the requirement of a theoretical model. Some even seem to be operating on the misconception that *SEM* is a method for "uncovering" causal patterns in data. This is probably due to the allure of the powerful analytic techniques of *SEM*, the complexity of which tends "to overwhelm critical judgment" (Freedman, 1987a, p. 102; see also Cliff, 1983; Fornell, 1983a).

The temptation to apply sophisticated state-of-the-art methodology seems irresistible. Indeed, it is a rare and refreshing occurrence to encounter a statement by an author explaining why he or she has *not* applied *SEM*. It takes an erudite and discerning researcher to recognize when a given method is inapplicable and, thus, refrain from using it. This is exemplified by Schuessler who, among other things, wrote a textbook on the analysis of social data and edited three volumes of the *Sociological methodology* annual. In the preface to his book *Measuring social life feelings*, Schuessler (1982) reported that it has been suggested that he apply *SEM*. He then stated: "Although the suggestion is timely, it presup-

---

[2]See Part 2, especially Chapters 12–14, for controversies regarding the value of experiments in sociobehavioral research.

poses what is presently missing (at least in sociology)—namely, a theory about the relation between social life feelings and social background" (p. xii). Needless to say, Schuessler recognized that "it would be possible to write an arbitrary model and to quantify that, but *that would be more a statistical exercise than a serious sociological proposal*" [italics added] (pp. xii–xiii).

An additional factor contributing to indifference regarding the need for a sound causal model is the mistaken notion that all that is necessary to make claims about causation is to satisfy a set of rules. The primary ones being cited are the demonstration that the presumed cause and the presumed effect covary, that the former precedes the latter, and that covariation between the two is not spurious (see Baumrind, 1983, for a critique of research based on such notions). Great impetus for reliance on rules for the discovery and justification of causation John Stuart Mill (1852) gave in his canons, among which are the following methods: (a) agreement, (b) difference, (c) residue, and (d) concomitant variation. For example, according to the method of agreement:

If two or more instances of the phenomenon under investigation have only one circumstance in common, the circumstance in which alone all the instances agree, is the cause (or effect) of the given phenomenon. (p. 224)

A favorite example used by critics of Mill's method of agreement is the story of the person who, distressed by his habitual state of drunkenness, decided to determine its cause. On five consecutive nights he drank scotch and soda, bourbon and soda, brandy and soda, rum and soda, and gin and soda. Having determined that soda was the sole common element in all instances, he vowed never to touch soda again!

Regrettably, many of the causal models advanced in sociobehavioral sciences are on par with the preceding example. Not surprisingly, Guttman (1981) mocked the "flowering of 'causal' discoveries in sociology at a pace unheard of in the history of science" (p. 42). Voicing reservations about the state of causal models in the sociobehavioral sciences, Muthén (1987) asserted:

I find that it is absurd for a person to seriously formulate a path model or any other complex model of a phenomenon without years of prior analyses by him or her or others using more exploratory means. I often find that the number of equations a model has is inversely related to the quality and thoroughness of the model specification. (p. 180)

In sum, the formulation of a causal model is an arduous and long process entailing a great deal of critical thinking, creativity, insight, and erudition.

LISREL: ORIENTATION TO STRUCTURAL MODELS

LISREL is comprised of two main parts: measurement model and structural equation model. The measurement model was introduced and applied in Chapter 23. The present chapter is devoted to structural models. We begin with a brief orientation to the matrices and the notational system used in LISREL for estimation and testing of structural models. General issues concerning LISREL control statements and matrices (e.g., MOdel statement, identification of matrix elements, matrix form and mode) explained in Chapter 23 apply also to models and matrices to be presented here; thus, we will not explain them again. When in doubt, refer to Chapter 23. In addition, as we stressed in Chapter 23, it is very important that you study LISREL's guide (Jöreskog & Sörbom, 1989) and refer to it frequently.

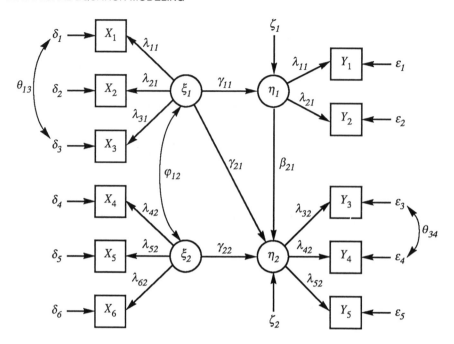

Figure 24.1

A Hypothetical Model

To facilitate understanding, matrices and notation used in LISREL will be explained with reference to the model depicted in Figure 24.1. To begin with, the notation used in the left-hand side of the figure should be familiar to you, as it was explained and used in Chapter 23. We recapitulate: ξ's refer to latent exogenous variables; X's refer to indicators of such variables; λ's refer to coefficients of effects of the latent variables on the indicators; δ's refer to errors in indicators. Furthermore, ϕ_{12} refers to the covariance between the two latent variables, whereas θ_{13} refers to the covariance between the errors of indicators X_1 and X_3.

Latent endogenous variables are designated as η's (eta), referred to in LISREL as ETA.[3] On the MOdel statement, NE is used to specify the number of ETA's. Indicators of ETA are designated as Y's. Effects of ETA's on Y's are designated as λ's (lambda) and are incorporated in a matrix Λ_y (LAMBDA Y), specified as LY in the input. Analogous to LAMBDA X (see Chapter 23), the number of rows in LY equals the number of indicators—Y's (five, in our example). The number of columns of LY equals the number of ETA's said to affect the indicators (two, in our example).

Errors in indicators of ETA's are designated as ϵ's (epsilon). Analogous to indicators of KSI, Θ_ϵ (THETA EPSILON) is a covariance matrix of ϵ's, specified as TE in the input. The principal diagonal of THETA EPSILON consists of variances of errors in indicators, whereas off-diagonal elements are covariances between errors in indicators. According to the model in Figure 24.1, there is a covariance between the errors of indicators Y_3 and Y_4.

---

[3]Notions of exogenous and endogenous variables were introduced in Chapter 14.

Effects of latent endogenous variables (ETA's) on latent endogenous variables, referred to as structural coefficients, are designated as β's. The β's are incorporated in a square matrix **B**—specified as BE in the input—whose dimension equals the number of latent endogenous variables (two, in our example). Note that, according to the model in Figure 24.1, η_1 is said to affect η_2.

Residuals or errors in equations are designated as ζ's (zeta). The variances and covariances of the residuals are incorporated in a matrix, designated as $\boldsymbol{\Psi}$ (psi)—specified as PS in the input—whose dimension equals the number of latent endogenous variables (two, in our example). The diagonal of $\boldsymbol{\Psi}$ consists of variances of residuals, whereas its off-diagonal elements refer to covariances of residuals. According to the model in Figure 24.1, the two ζ's are not related. Hence, PSI is diagonal.

Finally, effects of latent exogenous variables on latent endogenous variables, or structural coefficients, designated as γ's (gamma), are incorporated in $\boldsymbol{\Gamma}$ (uppercase gamma) and specified as GA in the input. The number of rows of $\boldsymbol{\Gamma}$ equals the number of latent endogenous variables (two, in our example), and the number of columns equals the number of latent exogenous variables (two, in our example). Note that, according to the model in Figure 24.1, ξ_1 is said to affect both η's, whereas ξ_2 is said to affect η_2 only.

THE MEASUREMENT MODEL

The following two equations express the measurement model:

$$\mathbf{y} = \boldsymbol{\Lambda}_y \boldsymbol{\eta} + \boldsymbol{\epsilon} \tag{24.1}$$

where **y** is a p by 1 (5 by 1, for our example) vector of indicators of the latent endogenous variables; $\boldsymbol{\Lambda}_y$ (LAMBDA Y) is a p by m (5 by 2, for our example) matrix of coefficients (loadings) of **y** on the latent variables (η); $\boldsymbol{\epsilon}$ (EPSILON) is a p by 1 (5 by 1, for our example) vector of errors of measurement of **y**. The variance–covariance matrix of such errors is designated as $\boldsymbol{\Theta}_\epsilon$.

$$\mathbf{x} = \boldsymbol{\Lambda}_x \boldsymbol{\xi} + \boldsymbol{\delta} \tag{24.2}$$

where **x** is a q by 1 (6 by 1, for our example) vector of indicators of the latent exogenous variables; $\boldsymbol{\Lambda}_x$ (LAMBDA X) is a q by n (6 by 2, for our example) matrix of coefficients (loadings) of **x** on the latent exogenous variables (ξ); $\boldsymbol{\delta}$ (DELTA) is a q by 1 (6 by 1, for our example) vector of errors of measurement of **x**. The variance-covariance matrix of such errors is designated as $\boldsymbol{\Theta}_\delta$.

Matrices involved in measurement models were discussed and illustrated in Chapter 23. Therefore, the matrices of the measurement model for Figure 24.1 will not be displayed here.

THE STRUCTURAL MODEL

The structural equation is

$$\boldsymbol{\eta} = \mathbf{B}\boldsymbol{\eta} + \boldsymbol{\Gamma}\boldsymbol{\xi} + \boldsymbol{\zeta} \tag{24.3}$$

where all terms and their associated matrices were defined above. The matrices and their elements for the structural model of Figure 24.1 are

$$\underbrace{\begin{bmatrix} \eta_1 \\ \eta_2 \end{bmatrix}}_{\boldsymbol{\eta}} = \underbrace{\begin{bmatrix} 0 & 0 \\ \beta_{21} & 0 \end{bmatrix}}_{\mathbf{B}} \underbrace{\begin{bmatrix} \eta_1 \\ \eta_2 \end{bmatrix}}_{\boldsymbol{\eta}} + \underbrace{\begin{bmatrix} \gamma_{11} & 0 \\ \gamma_{21} & \gamma_{22} \end{bmatrix}}_{\boldsymbol{\Gamma}} \underbrace{\begin{bmatrix} \xi_1 \\ \xi_2 \end{bmatrix}}_{\boldsymbol{\xi}} + \underbrace{\begin{bmatrix} \zeta_1 \\ \zeta_2 \end{bmatrix}}_{\boldsymbol{\zeta}}$$

Although we have said more than once that we do not assume that you are familiar with matrix algebra, we have recommended that you become familiar with its basic concepts and operations (see Chapter 22, for an introduction and references). It is toward this end that we show the results of carrying out the above matrix operations.

$$\eta_1 = \gamma_{11}\xi_1 + \zeta_1$$
$$\eta_2 = \beta_{21}\eta_1 + \gamma_{21}\xi_1 + \gamma_{22}\xi_2 + \zeta_2$$

If you are not familiar with matrix algebra, you are probably puzzled as to its value, considering that these equations, which seem simple enough, can be used instead of the matrix equation (24.3). The elegance and power of matrix algebra become evident when it is recognized that it can accommodate models of varying degrees of complexity, with any number of exogenous and endogenous variables. Bear in mind that ours is a very simple model consisting of only two exogenous and two endogenous variables. Hence, these two equations are relatively simple.

Whether or not you are familiar with matrix algebra, we suggest that you study the preceding two equations in conjunction with Figure 24.1, and note that they refer to the inner part of the figure depicting the structural model.

Following are the covariance matrices associated with the structural model under consideration.

$$\mathbf{\Phi} = \begin{bmatrix} \phi_{11} & \\ \phi_{21} & \phi_{22} \end{bmatrix} \qquad \mathbf{\Psi} = \begin{bmatrix} \psi_{11} & \\ 0 & \psi_{22} \end{bmatrix}$$

As indicated above, and as illustrated in Chapter 23, $\mathbf{\Phi}$ is the covariance matrix of the latent exogenous variables where the diagonal consists of variances, and the off-diagonal element is a covariance.

Furthermore, as indicated above, $\mathbf{\Psi}$ is the covariance matrix of the residuals (ζ's). Note that the off-diagonal element is 0, indicating that there is no relation between the residuals.

These matrices are symmetric; thus, they are presented in a lower triangle format. Study the matrices in conjunction with Figure 24.1

ASSUMPTIONS

The assumptions underlying the *SEM* models are

1. ζ is uncorrelated with ξ
2. ϵ is uncorrelated with η
3. δ is uncorrelated with ξ
4. ζ, ϵ, and δ are mutually uncorrelated
5. $\mathbf{I} - \mathbf{B}$ is non-singular. (Manual, p. 4)[4]

$\mathbf{I}$ is an identity matrix. All other terms were defined earlier.

This concludes our introduction to structural models. For a more detailed treatment, see the general references given in the beginning of Chapter 23. In the context of the numerical examples presented below, we comment further on *SEM* and show, among other things, that approaches such as regression and path analysis may be viewed as special cases of it.

---

[4]We remind you of our practice of referring to LISREL's guide as the Manual.

Identification

Before attempting to estimate and test individual model parameters as well as test the model as a whole, it is necessary to determine whether or not they are identified. The very complex topic of model identification has been treated extensively in econometric and *SEM* literature (e.g., Fox, 1968, Chapter 11; Frank, 1971, Chapter 12; Heise, 1975, Chapter 5; Koompmans, 1949; Wiley, 1973). Introductions to the identification problem will be found in Blalock (1969, Chapter 4), Bollen (1989, pp. 88–104), Duncan (1975, Chapters 5–7), Fox (1984, pp. 239–251, 289–293), Hayduk (1987, pp. 139–150), Long (1983a, pp. 34–55; 1983b, pp. 36–42), Saris and Stronkhorst (1984, Chapter 8).

"The identification problem is concerned with the question: Is there a unique set of parameter values consistent with this data?" (Manual, p. 16). What follows constitutes an attempt at an intuitive explanation of this statement. Essentially, identification has to do with the adequacy of information for parameter estimation. Probably the simplest way to see what is meant by this is to think of the use of equations for the estimation of parameters. When one equation is available for the estimation of one parameter, a single estimate may be obtained. The parameter thus estimated is said to be exactly (or just) identified. When more than one equation is available for the estimation of one parameter, more than one estimate may be obtained. When the estimates are consistent, the parameter is said to be overidentified. Finally, when a single equation is available for the estimation of more than one parameter, no unique solution can be obtained. In other words, different estimates of the parameters can be shown to have produced the same data (e.g., covariance matrix). Hence, the parameters are said to be underidentified or nonidentified.

In any given model, it is possible for some parameters to be identified and for others to be nonidentified. When all the parameters of a model are identified, the model as a whole is identified. A very important distinction is made between an exactly identified (just-identified or saturated) model and one that is overidentified. A just-identified model is one consisting of the exact amount of information necessary for estimating all of its parameters, as when having the exact number of equations required to solve for a number of unknowns. An overidentified model, on the other hand, consists of more information than is necessary for estimation of its parameters.

It is important to recognize that, regardless of its validity, a just-identified model always fits the data perfectly. Hence, *such a model is not testable* ($df = 0$). Only overidentified models are testable ($df > 0$), as only in regard to such models is it meaningful to both speak of and assess discrepancies between observed data and those reproduced by the model parameters (e.g., observed and reproduced covariance matrices; see explanations of fitted residuals in Chapter 23).

Underidentified models are, clearly, not testable. Not surprisingly, Namboodiri, Carter, and Blalock (1975) branded such models as "hopeless" (p. 503). An underidentified model may be rendered identified by imposing constraints on some of its elements (e.g., fixing coefficients to zero, one, or some other value; constraining two or more coefficients to be equal to each other). In Chapter 23, we alluded to the issue of underidentification in connection with the need to set a metric for latent variables. It will be recalled that we handled this by standardizing the variance of the latent variables. In the present chapter, we use instead reference indicators (i.e., fixing the coefficient of an indicator to equal 1.0; see below).

The main point to be borne in mind is that "underidentification is a theoretical rather than a statistical problem" (Heise, 1975, p. 152). Therefore, ploys to render the model identified will not do. A causal model reflects a theoretical formulation regarding the causal process in the phenomenon being investigated. The only logically defensible approach to the formulation of overidentified models is through theory.

Except for very simple models, determining whether or not a model is identified is by no means a simple task. Indeed, "proving that a model is identified presents one of the greatest practical difficulties in using the confirmatory factor model" (Long, 1983a, p. 36). It is not uncommon to encounter models claimed to be identified by their authors but shown to be nonidentified by others. For a discussion and examples of misconceptions regarding identification in confirmatory factor analysis, see Bollen and Jöreskog (1985).

In an effort to relieve somewhat the sense of frustration, if not helplessness, that our discussion has probably engendered, we would like to point out that computer programs for the analysis of *SEM* offer diagnostics that give helpful clues regarding the identifiability of a model being tested. LISREL, for example, not only gives a warning regarding the probability of a given parameter(s) being nonidentified, but it also checks whether certain conditions for identifiability are satisfied. (For a description of LISREL diagnostics and suggestions for checking on identifiability, see Manual, pp. 16–18. See also references given earlier for discussions of clues for problems concerning model identification—for example, negative variances or correlations exceeding 1.00.)

NUMERICAL EXAMPLES

Several numerical examples will be analyzed with the aim of explaining basic ideas of fitting and testing structural models. As in earlier chapters, our examples are *illustrative*. Accordingly, *we ignore the paramount question of their validity*. In fact, we even use the same data to fit and test models varying in complexity as well as in the number of posited latent variables and/or manifest variables just to draw attention to consequences and implications of specific changes in a given model.

A REGRESSION MODEL

We begin with a linear regression model, as it enables us to do the following: (a) show that it is a special case of structural modeling; (b) explain some aspects of LISREL input and output in relation to an analytic approach with which, we hope, you are fairly comfortable (to this end, we analyze the same example twice: first through a multiple regression program and then through LISREL); and (c) demonstrate that, in regression analysis, no distinction is made between latent variables and their presumed indicators.

The illustrative data we will be using for this and several subsequent analyses are given in Table 24.1. Note that the table consists of a correlation matrix and standard deviations for six

Table 24.1
Correlation Matrix and Standard Deviations (s) for Six Indicators (N = 200)

	Y_1	Y_2	Y_3	X_1	X_2	X_3
Y_1	1.00	.52	.45	.38	.42	.37
Y_2	.52	1.00	.58	.35	.44	.39
Y_3	.45	.58	1.00	.46	.48	.43
X_1	.38	.35	.46	1.00	.69	.77
X_2	.42	.44	.48	.69	1.00	.73
X_3	.37	.39	.43	.77	.73	1.00
s:	4.67	5.81	5.12	10.12	11.09	12.31

indicators: three Y's and three X's. Means are not included insofar as our concern in the analyses presented in this chapter is with covariance matrices. Accordingly, the intercept (a) in the regression analysis is equal to zero (see NOTE on CONSTANT in the output, below).

For the present analysis, we will assume that Y_1 is the dependent variable, and the three X's are the independent variables. Y_2 and Y_3, *used in subsequent analyses, are not dealt with in this example*. Following are the SPSS input statements.

SPSS

Input

```
SET LISTING='T241SPS.LIS'.
TITLE TABLE 24.1, USING Y1 AS THE DEPENDENT VARIABLE.
DATA LIST MATRIX FREE/Y1 Y2 Y3 X1 X2 X3.
BEGIN DATA
4.67 5.81 5.12 10.12 11.09 12.31
1.00  .52  .45   .38   .42    .37
 .52 1.00  .58   .35   .44    .39
 .45  .58 1.00   .46   .48    .43
 .38  .35  .46  1.00   .69    .77
 .42  .44  .48   .69  1.00    .73
 .37  .39  .43   .77   .73   1.00
200
END DATA
REGRESSION READ=STDDEV COR N/DES/VAR Y1 TO X3/STAT=ALL/
   DEP=Y1/ENTER X1 TO X3.
```

Commentary

Detailed explanations of SPSS input were given in earlier chapters (for commentaries on general regression input, see Chapter 18; for commentaries on matrix input, see Chapter 22). Therefore, only a couple of comments will be made here.

1. In Chapter 22, it was pointed out that matrix input is different for the PC and mainframe versions of SPSS, and examples of both were given. *The input listed here is for the PC version.*

2. As you can see from the last line of the input, Y_1 is designated as the dependent variable, and the three X's as the independent variables.

Output

NOTE   10597
VECTOR OF MEANS MISSING WITH MATRIX INPUT IN REGRESSION—If means are not supplied, SPSS/PC+ uses the default of 0.0. The constant term is also 0.0. If standard deviations are not supplied, SPSS/PC+ uses the default of 1.0.

Dependent Variable..   Y1

R Square   .19286

---------------------------------- Variables in the Equation ----------------------------------

Variable	B	SE B	Beta	T	Sig T
X3	.02007	.04227	.05291	.475	.6354
X2	.11839	.04136	.28114	2.862	.0047
X1	.06704	.04855	.14528	1.381	.1689
(Constant)	.00000				

Commentary

Detailed presentation of multiple regression analysis, including commentaries on output such as this one, were given in Chapter 18. Here, we address only issues and results relevant to the topic under consideration.

For illustrative purposes, it will be assumed that the dependent variable is Academic Achievement (*AA*) and that it is indicated by Y_1, say, Grade Point Average (*GPA*). Further, that the three *X*'s are indicators of Mental Ability (*MA*; e.g., Stanford–Binet), treated *erroneously* as three independent variables.

Examine the correlations among the *X*'s (see Input or Table 24.1) and notice that they are relatively high (ranging from .69 to .77), as would be expected for indicators of mental ability. Adverse effects of high correlations among independent variables were discussed in Chapter 18 under the heading of multicollinearity, where the special case of multiple indicators was also addressed. It was in this context that we pointed out that the application of regression analysis to the case of multiple indicators is inappropriate, because each indicator is of necessity treated as a distinct independent variable. For present purposes, it will be recalled that high multicollinearity adversely affects the magnitude and stability of the regression coefficients (*b*'s).

The results reported above illustrate these points. Notice that the correlations between the dependent variable and the three indicators are fairly similar, ranging from .37 to .42. However, because of high multicollinearity, the scale is tipped in favor of the indicator whose correlation with the dependent variable is the highest (X_2). To see clearly what is taking place, examine first the Betas (standardized coefficients) and observe that the one associated with X_2 is much larger than the other two—a result that would not be expected on the basis of the zero-order correlations between the indicators and the dependent variable.

Examine now the unstandardized coefficients and notice that, because the standard deviations for the three indicators are fairly similar, the pattern of the differences among the B's parallels that of the differences among the Betas. Finally, because the standard errors of the B's are similar, it turns out that only the B for X_2 is statistically significant at a conventional α level of, say, .05. Thus, using three indicators of the same construct in a regression analysis has led to the conclusion that the effect of only one of them is different from zero.

Depending on the pattern of relations among the indicators and their separate relations with the dependent variable as well, all sorts of puzzling results may be obtained. For example, the *b*'s may differ in their signs, or all the *b*'s may be statistically nonsignificant. The specific results notwithstanding, our aim was to demonstrate difficulties attendant with the use of multiple indicators in a regression analysis as a prelude to their appropriate use in *SEM*. Before showing how this is done, we analyze the regression model using LISREL.

LISREL

Input

TABLE 24.1, RUNNING AS MULTIPLE REGRESSION WITH Y1 AS DEPENDENT
DA NI=6 NO=200
LA
Y1 Y2 Y3 X1 X2 X3
KM
1.00
 .52 1.00
 .45 .58 1.00
 .38 .35 .46 1.00

.42   .44   .48   .69 1.00
.37   .39   .43   .77   .73 1.00
SD
4.67 5.81 5.12 10.12 11.09 12.31
SE
1 4 5 6/
MO NX=3 NY=1
OU SE TV SS

Commentary

For a general orientation to LISREL input, see Chapter 23. Here we focus on aspects not dealt with in Chapter 23 and on specific issues relevant to the topic under consideration. As explained in Chapter 23 (see Measurement Models), using the correlation matrix (KM) and standard deviations (SD), LISREL constructs a covariance matrix that is then analyzed by default.

SElect may be used to select a subset of variables for analysis and/or to reorder the variables. In LISREL, *it is expected that the endogenous variables or their indicators precede the exogenous ones*. When the input is differently organized, SE may be used to reorder the variables. Variables "should be listed either by numbers or by labels in the order one wants them in the model" (Manual, p. 62). For our example, it is not necessary to reorder the indicators. SE is used to select variables 1 (Y_1) and 4, 5, and 6 (the X's). The slash (/) at the end of the list of variables is required when a subset is selected; it is optional, when SE is used to reorder all the variables.

As you can see, the MOdel statement is very simple, consisting of only the numbers of Y's and X's. Under such circumstances, no distinction is made between latent and manifest variables. Thus, Y_1 is treated as η_1; X_1, X_2, and X_3 are treated respectively as ξ_1, ξ_2, and ξ_3. As a result, the following are set by the program:

$$\Lambda_y = I, \quad \Theta_\epsilon = 0, \quad \Lambda_x = I, \quad \Theta_\delta = 0, \quad \text{and } \Phi = S_{xx}$$

where I = identity matrix, Θ_ϵ and Θ_δ refer to measurement errors for Y's and X's respectively; and Φ is the covariance matrix of the exogenous variables. Notice that, in such a model, measurement errors are set equal to zero, and the observed covariance matrix of the X's (S_{xx}) is treated as the covariance matrix of the exogenous variables. Only parameters of B (effects of endogenous on endogenous variables); Γ (effects of exogenous on endogenous variables); and Ψ (residuals, or errors in equations) may be estimated in such models.[5] As there is only one endogenous variable in the present example, $B = 0$ (the default). For models consisting of more than one endogenous variable, *the properties of* B *have to be specified*. An example of how this is done is given in a subsequent analysis.

The model under consideration is depicted in Figure 24.2. The values indicated in the figure were taken from the LISREL output given below. For now, it will be pointed out that the values for the γ's (effects of ξ's on η) are equal to the their respective b's, obtained in the regression analysis (see above).

As you can see, *regression analysis is a special case of structural models where no distinction is made between latent and manifest variables and where it is assumed that the latter are measured without error*. Needless to say, this is extremely unrealistic. Admittedly, when discussing assumptions underlying the regression model, it is also pointed out that the independent variables are assumed to be measured without error. The problem, however, is

---

[5]See above and Chapter 23, for explanations of the preceding matrices.

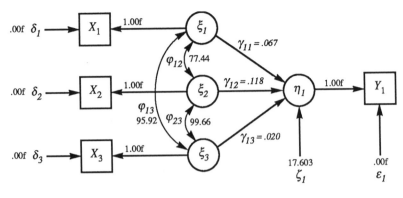

Figure 24.2

that, when regression analysis is applied, this assumption is hidden, so to speak. That is why even knowledgeable researchers tend to interpret results of regression analysis as if the measures of the independent variables were error free.

In contrast, specification of measurement errors (i.e., specification of parameters of matrices Θ_δ and Θ_ϵ) is an integral aspect of *SEM*. When single indicators are used, such matrices have to be fixed (usually to zero, as above) or else the model is not identified. Within the context of *SEM*, then, the unrealistic assumption of error-free measures hits one between the eyes, so to speak, whereas in regression it can be (most often is) ignored.

Finally, on the OUtput statement, we called for SE = Print standard errors, TV = Print *t*–values, and SS = Print standardized solution (see Manual, p. 72).

Output

TABLE 24.1, RUNNING AS MULTIPLE REGRESSION WITH Y1 AS DEPENDENT
COVARIANCE MATRIX TO BE ANALYZED

	Y1	X1	X2	X3
Y1	21.809			
X1	17.959	102.414		
X2	21.752	77.439	122.988	
X3	21.270	95.924	99.658	151.536

Commentary

As was pointed out above, LISREL uses the correlation matrix and the standard deviations to construct a covariance matrix that is then analyzed. The variances are, of course, the squared standard deviations. For example, $4.67^2 = 21.809$—the variance of Y_1. Covariances are obtained by multiplying the correlation between the variables under consideration by their respective standard deviations.[6] For example, the covariance between Y_1 and X_1 is

$$(.38)(4.67)(10.12) = 17.959$$

---

[6]See Chapter 17, for a discussion of covariance.

Output

PARAMETER SPECIFICATIONS
        GAMMA

	X1	X2	X3
Y1	1	2	3

        PSI

	Y1
Y1	4

Commentary

The default GAMMA is FUll FRee; PSI is SYmmetric FRee (see Manual, p. 12). In the present case, PSI is a scalar (for an explanation of matrix form and mode, see Chapter 23). As indicated in this excerpt of the output, four parameters are to be estimated. The three GAMMA's refer to the effects of the three KSI's on ETA, whereas PSI refers to the residual variance.

Output

LISREL ESTIMATES (MAXIMUM LIKELIHOOD)
        GAMMA

	X1	X2	X3
Y1	.067	.118	.020

        PSI

	Y1
Y1	17.603

SQUARED MULTIPLE CORRELATIONS FOR STRUCTURAL EQUATIONS

Y1
.193

MEASURES OF GOODNESS OF FIT FOR THE WHOLE MODEL :
CHI-SQUARE WITH 0 DEGREES OF FREEDOM = .00 (P = 1.000)
GOODNESS OF FIT INDEX = 1.000
ROOT MEAN SQUARE RESIDUAL =   .000

STANDARD ERRORS
        GAMMA

	X1	X2	X3
Y1	.049	.041	.042

T-VALUES
        GAMMA

	X1	X2	X3
Y1	1.381	2.862	.475

Commentary

Compare this output with that of SPSS given above and notice that, difference in terminology aside, the results of the two analyses are the same. Thus, the GAMMA's and their test statistics (i.e., standard errors and t values) are equal to their respective b's and their test statistics. The squared multiple correlation (.193) is also the same in both analyses.

Examine now the measures of goodness of fit and notice that the model fits the data perfectly. This is to be expected insofar as the model is exactly identified. As discussed earlier in this chapter, an exactly identified model, no matter how untenable it may be from a theoretical framework, will always fit the data perfectly. Such a model, it was pointed out, is not testable. Note that 0 df are associated with the chi-square.

Output

STANDARDIZED SOLUTION
     GAMMA

	X1	X2	X3
Y1	.145	.281	.053

PSI

	Y1
Y1	.807

Commentary

A standardized solution may be obtained by specifying SS on the OU statement (see last line of Input, above). As was pointed out in Chapters 17 and 18, researchers tend to resort to standardized solutions when they have difficulty interpreting raw coefficients. But, as was also pointed out, standardization does not address difficulties concerning interpretation of units on given measures.

When SS is specified on the OUt statement, only latent variables are standardized. A solution in which the observed variables are also standardized can be obtained by specifying SC (Standardize Completely) on the OUt statement (see Manual, pp. 38–40). In any case, specifying SC in the present analysis will yield the same results as above, because the latent and observed variables were equated (see earlier comments on the MOdel statement).

GAMMA consists of standardized effects of exogenous variables on endogenous variables. Note that the values reported are equal to the standardized regression coefficients (Betas) reported by SPSS for the analysis of these data (see above). Note also that PSI is equal to $1 - R^2$ (i.e., $1 - .193$).

To reiterate: We used a regression model to accomplish several things.

1. We wanted to show that such a model is a special case of a structural model—one in which no distinction is made between constructs and their indicators. Further, errors of measurement are not taken into account. It should be noted that an advantage of using LISREL for the analysis of models in which some or all the variables are measured with single indicators is that when reliability estimates of single indicators are available, they can be incorporated in the measurement model, thereby reducing or eliminating bias in parameter estimates due to measurement errors. For examples on how this is done, see Manual, pp. 136, 151–156; see also Acock and Scott (1980), and Hayduk (1987).

2. We wanted to demonstrate detrimental effects of treating multiple indicators of a construct as if they were distinct variables—a default strategy in applications of multiple regression analysis in such situations. As is shown in subsequent sections, the use of multiple indicators in measurement models is an integral part of programs for the analysis of *SEM* (e.g., LISREL, EQS).

3. We used LISREL to analyze a regression model as a means of introducing basic elements of the program as well as showing that the results parallel those obtained when a regression analysis program is applied. Moreover, although this may be obvious, we wanted to stress that the validity of a model is not enhanced, just because it is analyzed through a fancy program such as LISREL rather than through a run-of-the-mill regression program. We felt it particularly important to do this, in view of some of the examples given in the LISREL manual. It would suffice to single out an example of how LISREL may be used to carry out stepwise regression analysis (Manual, pp. 110–112). Several times earlier (e.g., Chapters 3 and 18), we pointed out that stepwise regression analysis may be useful in predictive research but that it is not only useless but potentially detrimental in explanatory research. Indeed, from the perspective of theory formulation and testing, "the most vulgar approach is built into stepwise regression procedures, which essentially automate mindless empiricism" (Berk, 1988, p. 164). No wonder, Leamer (1985, p. 312) branded it, "unwise regression" (p. 312).

The inclusion of an example of stepwise regression analysis in the manual, especially in the context of "a model building process" (Manual, p. 110), is unfortunate. Although users are cautioned that "personal judgment is necessary" (Manual, p. 111), we are afraid that those who need such caution most will be least prone to heed it or even notice it. Its inclusion in a manual focused on model testing, especially causal modeling, cannot but bestow an aura of respectability on stepwise regression analysis. We venture a guess that, in the not too distant future, researchers who apply, rather misapply, stepwise regression analysis in explanatory research will make reference to their use of LISREL or a LISREL-type analysis instead of some lowly regression program.

Parenthetically, when it comes to variable-selection procedures—of which stepwise regression analysis is but one example—conventional regression analysis programs are much more versatile and easier to use than LISREL.

EXOGENOUS VARIABLE WITH MULTIPLE INDICATORS; ENDOGENOUS VARIABLE WITH A SINGLE INDICATOR

For this example, we use the four indicators used in the regression model (preceding section), except that the three X's will be treated as indicators of a latent exogenous variable. We use only one indicator, Y_1, for the endogenous variable so that we may contrast specifications for a variable having multiple indicators (exogenous, in our example) with those for a variable with a single indicator (endogenous, in our example). In the subsequent example, we use multiple indicators for both variables. For illustrative purposes, it will be assumed again that the exogenous variable is mental ability (*MA*) and that the endogenous variable is academic achievement (*AA*). Thus, think of the three X's of Table 24.1 as indicators of *MA* (e.g., Stanford–Binet), and of Y_1 as an indicator of *AA* (e.g., *GPA*). The model is depicted in Figure 24.3, where the values indicated were taken from the LISREL output reported and commented upon below.

LISREL

Input

TABLE 24.1 DATA. EXOGENOUS VARIABLE WITH MULTIPLE INDICATORS. ENDOGENOUS VARIABLE WITH A SINGLE INDICATOR.

[input up to MO is identical with that of the preceding run]

MO NX=3 NK=1 NY=1 NE=1 TE=ZE

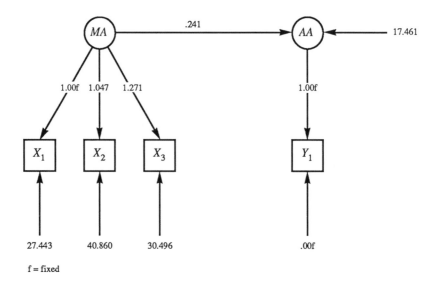

Figure 24.3

FR LX 2 LX 3
ST 1 LX 1 LY 1
LK
MA
LE
AA
OU RS SS

Commentary

As indicated above, except for the title, input up to the MOdel statement is identical to the one used in the analysis of the regression model in the preceding section. We, therefore, begin our comments with the MO statement.

We specified: (a) three indicators of an exogenous variable (NX = 3, NK = 1); and (b) one indicator of an endogenous variable (NY = 1, NE = 1). Recall that the covariance matrices of errors in indicators of exogenous and endogenous variables are respectively Θ_δ (THETA DELTA, or TD) and Θ_ϵ (THETA EPSILON, or TE). The default for these matrices is DIagonal, FRee (see Manual, p. 12). Because we are using the default TD, variances of errors in indicators of the exogenous variable but not covariances among them will be estimated. Because a single indicator is used for the endogenous variable, TE must be fixed for reasons of identification. This is most commonly done by setting it equal to 0 (i.e., TE = ZEro).[7]

GAMMA (effects of exogenous on endogenous variables) is FUll, FRee by default. In the present case, GAMMA is a scalar (i.e., a single value), indicating the effect of *MA* on *AA*. Compare this with the regression model (preceding section), where the three indicators were treated as distinct exogenous variables.

In Chapter 23, it was stated that, for the purpose of identification, units of measurement for latent variables must be established and that this can be done by either standardizing the

---

[7]TE may be fixed to an estimate of measurement error. For examples, see Manual, pp. 136, 151–156.

variances of the latent variables or setting the metric of each latent variable to be that of one of its indicators. The former approach was used throughout Chapter 23. The latter approach, which is used in the present chapter, consists of fixing the coefficient of one of the indicators to 1.00. Indicators thus used have been labeled reference indicators (Schoenberg, 1972, pp. 15–16).

So far as the mechanics are concerned, any indicator may be used as a reference indicator. The meaningful utilization of reference indicators is, however, predicated on the meaningfulness of their measurement units. Clearly, when indicators lack meaningful units—a rather common occurrence in sociobehavioral sciences—their use to set metrics for latent variables amounts to pretense that the metric problem has been properly addressed.

Faced with indicators whose units are uninterpretable, some researchers prefer to use standardized coefficients for the latent variables (see below). In view of our discussions of the shortcomings of standardized regression coefficients (see Chapters 17 and 18), we hope you recognize that similar difficulties arise when latent variables are standardized. Disheartening as these remarks may be, they had to be stated. LISREL is not a magic wand!

Other difficulties arising from the use of reference indicators, especially when comparing structural models across groups, have been identified (e.g., Blalock, 1982; Wilson 1981). For a recent exchange on this topic, see Bielby (1986a, 1986b), Henry (1986), Sobel and Arminger (1986), Williams and Thomson (1986a, 1986b).

Turning now to Λ_x (LX) and Λ_y (LY), it will be noted that, by default, they are FUll, FIxed. In the present example, the dimensions of LX are 3 by 1: a three-element column vector. Look at the FRee statement in the Input and notice that the second and third elements of LX are freed, thus, leaving the first one fixed to 0. Using a STarting-value of 1 for LX 1 (see Input), the first element is fixed to 1.00, thus, designating it as the reference indicator for the exogenous variable (MA). Notice that the only element of LY, LY 1, is also fixed to 1.00. Recalling that TE was set to zero (see above), these two specifications amount to equating the latent endogenous variable (AA) with the single indicator in question (Y_1).

It is good practice to use substantive labels for the latent variables. This can be accomplished by using LK for KSI variables and LE for ETA variables. As you can see, we labeled the former MA and the latter AA.

Finally, on the OU statement (last line of Input), we call for the residuals (RS) and for a standardized solution (SS).

Output

TABLE 24.1 DATA. EXOGENOUS VARIABLE WITH MULTIPLE INDICATORS.

PARAMETER SPECIFICATIONS

LAMBDA Y

	AA
Y1	0

LAMBDA X

	MA
X1	0
X2	1
X3	2

GAMMA

	MA
AA	3

```
PHI
            MA
         ----------
MA          4
   PSI
            AA
         ----------
AA          5
   THETA DELTA
            X1          X2          X3
         ----------  ----------  ----------
            6           7           8
```

Commentary

The covariance matrix to be analyzed is the same as the one given in the preceding section (regression model); thus, it was not repeated here.

We trust that, by now, you are comfortable with this kind of output. The 0's in LX and LY signify fixed indicators. Having set them to 1.00 (see ST 1 in Input), they were designated as reference indicators. Because a reference indicator is used for KSI, its variance is free (see 4 in PHI). Had we fixed PHI—a practice followed in Chapter 23—we would have also set the first element of LX to be free. Finally, because THETA EPSILON was set to zero (see TE = ZE in Input), it does not appear in the parameter specification.

Output

```
LISREL ESTIMATES (MAXIMUM LIKELIHOOD)
      LAMBDA Y
            AA
         ----------
Y1       1.000
      LAMBDA X
            MA
         ----------
X1       1.000
X2       1.047
X3       1.271
      GAMMA
            MA
         ----------
AA        .241
      PSI
            AA
         ----------
AA      17.461
      THETA DELTA
            X1          X2          X3
         ----------  ----------  ----------
          27.443      40.860      30.496
SQUARED MULTIPLE CORRELATIONS FOR X – VARIABLES
            X1          X2          X3
         ----------  ----------  ----------
            .732        .668        .799
```

MEASURES OF GOODNESS OF FIT FOR THE WHOLE MODEL :
CHI-SQUARE WITH 2 DEGREES OF FREEDOM = 3.63 (P = .163)
GOODNESS OF FIT INDEX =   .991
ADJUSTED GOODNESS OF FIT INDEX =   .955
ROOT MEAN SQUARE RESIDUAL = 1.116

Commentary

Examine first the section where measures of goodness of fit for the whole model are reported. Interpretation of such indices was discussed in detail in Chapter 23; therefore, only some brief comments will be made about them here.

Assuming that $\alpha = .05$ was selected, it would be concluded that the null hypothesis that the model fits the data cannot be rejected ($p > .05$ for the CHI-SQUARE). The GFI and the AGFI lend support to this claim.

As was pointed out in Chapter 23, when, as in the present case, a covariance matrix is analyzed, RMR is not readily interpretable, because its magnitude is affected by the units of the measures of the indicators. Under such circumstances, examination of the standardized residuals may be helpful. In the interest of space, we do not report the residuals. Instead, it will be pointed out that the standardized residuals are relatively small, the largest being 1.776.

Turning to the parameter estimates, bear in mind that LY 1 and LX 1 were set equal to 1.00 (see Input and commentaries). Following are brief comments on some of the estimates.

Of primary interest in the model under consideration is the estimate of the effect of *MA* on *AA*: .241 (see GAMMA). This brings us face to face with the difficult task of interpreting the effect substantively. Recall that the metrics of *MA* and *AA* were set to equal those of X_1 and Y_1 respectively. Now, it is rather easy to state that .241 is the expected change in *AA* associated with a unit change in *MA*. However, as discussed above, the meaningfulness of this statement is predicated on the meaningfulness of the measurement units of the indicators in question.

Instead of reproducing the standardized solution, which we called for (see OU statement), it will be pointed out that the standardized effect of *MA* on *AA* (the element in GAMMA) is .447. Thus, one may state that the expected change in *AA* associated with a unit change in *MA* is about one half of a standard deviation. We remind you, however, of our comment (see commentary on Input) about the interpretation of standardized coefficients.

The interpretation of the measurement model is less complicated. THETA DELTA indicates the error variance in each of the indicators. As explained in Chapter 23, SQUARED MULTIPLE CORRELATIONS (SMC) are reliability estimates of the indicators—see also (23.6) and the discussion related to it. Thus, the reliability estimates of X_1, X_2, and X_3 are respectively .732, .668 and .799.

In sum, we hope you see the advantage of the present approach in which indicators were distinguished from the latent exogenous variable they presumably reflect. In contrast, in a regression analysis, no such distinctions are made (see preceding section). Because a single indicator (Y_1) was used for the latent endogenous variable, it was necessary to fix its error variance (i.e., TE = ZE), thereby making the unrealistic assumption that the reliability of Y_1 is perfect (but see footnote 7). We turn now to an example in which multiple indicators are used for both KSI and ETA.

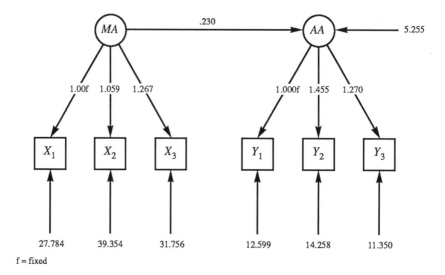

Figure 24.4

MULTIPLE INDICATORS FOR
EXOGENOUS AND ENDOGENOUS VARIABLES

We analyze here the same model as that analyzed in the preceding section. But, whereas in the preceding section multiple indicators were used for KSI only, here multiple indicators are used also for ETA. As in the preceding section, the three X's of Table 24.1 are taken as indicators of KSI (MA in our example). Whereas in the preceding section Y_1 was used as an indicator of ETA (AA in our example), here the three Y's of Table 24.1 are used as indicators of this variable. The model is depicted in Figure 24.4 with estimated values taken from the LISREL output reported and commented upon below.

LISREL

Input

TABLE 24.1. TWO LATENT VARIABLES WITH THREE INDICATORS FOR EACH

*[except for the omission of SElect statement (see commentary),
input up to MO is identical with that of earlier runs]*

```
MO NX=3 NK=1 NY=3 NE=1
FR LX 2 LX 3 LY 2 LY 3
ST 1 LX 1 LY 1
LK
MA
LE
AA
OU AL
```

Commentary

In the preceding runs, a SElect statement was necessary in order to choose the subset of indicators to be used in the analyses. Because all the indicators are used in the present run, and because it is not necessary to reorder them (as required, indicators of endogenous variables precede those for exogenous ones), no SElect statement is necessary.

Examine the MOdel statement and compare it with the one used in the preceding section. Notice that, in the preceding section, NY = 1, whereas here NY = 3. Furthermore, because, in the present example, multiple indicators are used for both latent variables, the default for both TD and TE may be used (i.e., DIagonal, FRee). Recall that, in the example of the preceding section, TE had to be fixed.

Examine now the FRee statement and notice that two elements are freed in each LAMBDA matrix. Look at the ST statement and notice that LX 1 is used as the reference indicator of *MA*, whereas LY 1 is used as the reference indicator of *AA*.

Finally, on the OU statement, we show how one may call for all the output. Doing this for small problems will not matter much as the output will be relatively small. For large problems, however, the output will be voluminous. Therefore, use this option with circumspection.

Output

TABLE 24.1.   TWO LATENT VARIABLES WITH THREE INDICATORS FOR EACH

LISREL ESTIMATES (MAXIMUM LIKELIHOOD)

LAMBDA Y

	AA
Y1	1.000
Y2	1.455
Y3	1.270

LAMBDA X

	MA
X1	1.000
X2	1.059
X3	1.267

GAMMA

	MA
AA	.230

PSI

	AA
AA	5.255

THETA EPS

Y1	Y2	Y3
12.599	14.258	11.350

THETA DELTA

X1	X2	X3
27.784	39.354	31.756

SQUARED MULTIPLE CORRELATIONS FOR Y – VARIABLES

Y1	Y2	Y3
.422	.578	.567

SQUARED MULTIPLE CORRELATIONS FOR X − VARIABLES

X1	X2	X3
.729	.680	.790

MEASURES OF GOODNESS OF FIT FOR THE WHOLE MODEL :
CHI-SQUARE WITH 8 DEGREES OF FREEDOM = 14.22(P = .076)
GOODNESS OF FIT INDEX =   .977
ADJUSTED GOODNESS OF FIT INDEX =   .941
ROOT MEAN SQUARE RESIDUAL =   1.933

Commentary

On the basis of the goodness-of-fit measures, one would be inclined to conclude that the model fits the data well. It will, however, be pointed out that of the standardized residuals (not reported here) four are $> |2|$. We comment on this point in connection with the standardized residuals given in EQS (see below).

Recalling that the SQUARED MULTIPLE CORRELATIONS are estimated reliabilities for the indicators, it can be seen that those for the Y's are fairly lower than those for the X's. Note especially the very low reliability estimate of Y_1 (.422), demonstrating how unrealistic it was to assume, as was done in the preceding section, that it is perfect.

We now show how the example under consideration is analyzed through EQS.

EQS

Input

```
/TITLE
TABLE 24.1.   TWO LATENT VARIABLES WITH THREE INDICATORS FOR
EACH
/SPECIFICATIONS
CASES=200; VARIABLES=6;
/LAB
V1=Y1; V2=Y2; V3=Y3; V4=X1; V5=X2; V6=X3;
F1=AA; F2=MA;
/EQUATIONS
V1=F1 + E1;
V2=*F1 + E2;
V3=*F1 + E3;
V4=          F2 + E4;
V5=         *F2 + E5;
V6=         *F2 + E6;
F1=*F2 + D1;
/VAR
E1 TO E6=*;
F2=*;
D1=*;
/MATRIX
1.00
 .52 1.00
 .45  .58 1.00
 .38  .35  .46 1.00
```

.42 .44 .48 .69 1.00
.37 .39 .43 .77 .73 1.00
/STANDARD DEVIATIONS
4.67 5.81 5.12 10.12 11.09 12.31
/END

Commentary

A general orientation to EQS was given in Chapter 23. The following will be recalled: (a) four types of variables are distinguished in EQS: V = Measured variable; F = Latent variable; E = Residual of measured variable; D = Residual of latent variable; (b) the model is specified through a set of regression-like equations—one for each of the dependent variables; and (c) an * indicates that the parameter(s) in question is to be estimated.

There are six indicators in the present example, and, thus, six V's and six E's. Analogous to the LISREL analysis of the same example, the first indicator in each set is used as a reference indicator for the latent variable it presumably reflects. Accordingly, no asterisks are included for F1 (*AA*) in the equation for V1 nor for F2 (*MA*) in the equation for V4.

Of the two latent variables, F1 is treated as a dependent variable and F2 as an independent variable. Notice that the E's and D are also treated as independent variables (for an explanation of how the terms independent variable and dependent variable are used in EQS, see Chapter 23).

Examine the VAR paragraph and notice that the variances to be estimated are analogous to those estimated in LISREL. Specifically, E1 to E6 (residuals of indicators) are analogous to THETA EPSILON and THETA DELTA; D1 (residual of F1) is analogous to PSI; and F2 (latent independent variable) is analogous to PHI.

Output

TABLE 24.1 TWO LATENT VARIABLES WITH THREE INDICATORS FOR EACH

BENTLER-WEEKS STRUCTURAL REPRESENTATION:

NUMBER OF DEPENDENT VARIABLES = 7
  DEPENDENT V'S : 1 2 3 4 5 6
  DEPENDENT F'S : 1

NUMBER OF INDEPENDENT VARIABLES = 8
  INDEPENDENT F'S : 2
  INDEPENDENT E'S : 1 2 3 4 5 6
  INDEPENDENT D'S : 1

PARAMETER ESTIMATES APPEAR IN ORDER.
  NO SPECIAL PROBLEMS WERE ENCOUNTERED DURING OPTIMIZATION.
            AVERAGE ABSOLUTE STANDARDIZED RESIDUALS = 0.0225
  AVERAGE OFF-DIAGONAL ABSOLUTE STANDARDIZED RESIDUALS = 0.0315

GOODNESS OF FIT SUMMARY

INDEPENDENCE MODEL CHI-SQUARE = 584.124,
BASED ON 15 DEGREES OF FREEDOM.

CHI-SQUARE = 14.217 ,BASED ON 8 DEGREES OF FREEDOM.
PROBABILITY VALUE FOR THE CHI-SQUARE STATISTIC IS 0.07629

BENTLER-BONETT NORMED   FIT INDEX= 0.976
BENTLER-BONETT NONNORMED FIT INDEX= 0.980

Commentary

We again call your attention to the general explanations of EQS output given in Chapter 23. Because of space consideration, we reproduced only excerpts that differ from those of LISREL. If you ran EQS and compared the output not reproduced here with that of LISREL, you would find that, differences in layout and labelling aside, the results are essentially the same. Therefore, we limit our comments to the differences between the two outputs.

The term standardized residuals is used differently in LISREL and in EQS. In the latter, it "can be interpreted in the metric of correlations among the input variables" (EQS manual, p. 92). Thus, relatively large standardized residuals are interpreted as indicative of poor fit. Assuming a cutoff of $|.05|$ were used, then four standardized residuals (not reproduced here) exceed it, two of which are the same as those $> |2|$ in LISREL.

It should be noted that the fitted residuals are identical in both programs. Differences between the two programs in what might be viewed as "large" residuals stem from differences in their definitions of standardized residuals. In any case, more will have to be known about the properties of standardized residuals in LISREL 7 before more firm guidelines for their interpretation may be advanced (see comment on this in Chapter 23).

Turning to the CHI-SQUARE's, the first is associated with the fit of the null or independence model. In Chapter 23, it was shown how this CHI-SQUARE is used in Bentler–Bonett fit indices. The second CHI-SQUARE is the same as that reported in LISREL.

Finally, recall that different indices of fit are given by the two programs (for explanations, see Chapter 23).

ONE EXOGENOUS AND TWO ENDOGENOUS VARIABLES: SINGLE INDICATORS

We turn now to a model consisting of one exogenous and two endogenous variables. Although the model we shall use is very simple, it will afford an opportunity to illustrate analyses of models in which a variable affects another variable directly, as well as indirectly through the mediation of other variables. We use the same model twice: first with single indicators and then with multiple indicators. A model with single indicators enables us to demonstrate once more that what are generally referred to as path-analytic models are special cases of *SEM*. Moreover, they are based on unrealistic assumptions insofar as the measurement aspects are concerned. As was done earlier, the model with single indicators will be analyzed first through a multiple regression program and then through LISREL. This will

Table 24.2

Correlation Matrix and Standard Deviations (s) for Nine Indicators (N = 200)

	Y_1	Y_2	Y_3	Z_1	Z_2	Z_3	X_1	X_2	X_3
Y_1	1.00	.52	.45	.29	.31	.27	.38	.42	.37
Y_2	.52	1.00	.58	.34	.30	.36	.35	.44	.39
Y_3	.45	.58	1.00	.23	.28	.35	.46	.48	.43
Z_1	.29	.34	.23	1.00	.53	.48	.41	.39	.38
Z_2	.31	.30	.28	.53	1.00	.45	.38	.31	.36
Z_3	.27	.36	.35	.48	.45	1.00	.42	.41	.40
X_1	.38	.35	.46	.41	.38	.42	1.00	.69	.77
X_2	.42	.44	.48	.39	.31	.41	.69	1.00	.73
X_3	.37	.39	.43	.38	.36	.40	.77	.73	1.00
s:	4.67	5.81	5.12	2.76	3.12	2.93	10.12	11.09	12.31

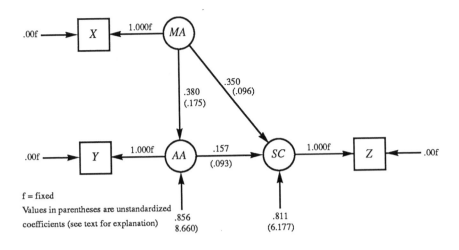

Figure 24.5

enable us to introduce some additional aspects of the latter in the context of regression results with which you are probably fairly comfortable. The same model with multiple indicators will then be analyzed.

Data to be used in both sections are reported in Table 24.2. Examine this table and notice that the data for the three Y's and the three X's are the same as those reported in Table 24.1 and used in the analyses of the preceding sections. What we have done, then, is add data for three Z's.

As in the preceding sections, we will assume that the Y's are indicators of Academic Achievement (AA) and that the X's are indicators of Mental Ability (MA). In addition, we will assume that the Z's are indicators of Self-Concept (SC). For illustrative purposes, it will be hypothesized that MA affects both AA and SC, whereas AA affects SC. This model, with the first indicator from each set of three, is depicted in Figure 24.5. The structural coefficients (that is, the coefficients for the effects of latent variables on latent variables) indicated in the figure have been obtained from the program outputs reported and commented upon below. The other coefficients are fixed (see below).

Notions of direct and indirect effects of variables were introduced in Chapter 14. To reiterate: The *direct effect* of a variable on another variable is that part of its effect that is not mediated, or transmitted, by other variables. A variable's *indirect effect* is that part of its effect that is mediated, or transmitted, by one or more variables. The *total effect* is the sum of the direct and indirect effect(s).[8] Thus, according to the model depicted in Figure 24.5, MA affects AA and SC directly (signified by the arrows emanating from it to the latter variables). In addition, MA affects SC indirectly, as mediated by AA. The total effect of MA on SC is the sum of its direct effect and its indirect effect, through AA. Notice that the latter has only a direct effect on SC. *We remind you that the models we are using are purely illustrative. We make no claims regarding their validity from a theoretical perspective.*

Because single indicators are used, it is necessary, for purposes of identification, to fix the coefficients of the effects of latent variables on their indicators, as well as the error of the

---

[8]For a detailed explanation of these and related concepts, see Pedhazur (1982, Chapter 15) and the references given therein; also, Bollen (1987, 1989), and Sobel (1987).

indicators. As can be seen from Figure 24.5, the former have been fixed to 1.00 and the latter to .00. Each latent variable has, thus, been equated with its indicator. As was pointed out in preceding sections, because these unrealistic assumptions are hidden in path-analytic applications, most researchers are probably not aware of them. It is for these reasons that we have decided to present and analyze this model first.

With the foregoing remarks in mind, we estimate the model parameters, using first the regression procedure of SPSS and then LISREL.

SPSS

Input

```
SET LISTING='T242SPS.LIS'.
TITLE TABLE 24.2  Y1, X1, AND Z1 INDICATORS OF THREE VARS.
DATA LIST MATRIX FREE/Y1 Y2 Y3 Z1 Z2 Z3 X1 X2 X3.
BEGIN DATA
4.67 5.81 5.12 2.76 3.12 2.93 10.12 11.09 12.31
1.00  .52  .45  .29  .31  .27  .38  .42  .37
 .52 1.00  .58  .34  .30  .36  .35  .44  .39
 .45  .58 1.00  .23  .28  .35  .46  .48  .43
 .29  .34  .23 1.00  .53  .48  .41  .39  .38
 .31  .30  .28  .53 1.00  .45  .38  .31  .36
 .27  .36  .35  .48  .45 1.00  .42  .41  .40
 .38  .35  .46  .41  .38  .42 1.00  .69  .77
 .42  .44  .48  .39  .31  .41  .69 1.00  .73
 .37  .39  .43  .38  .36  .40  .77  .73 1.00
200
END DATA
REGRESSION READ=STDDEV COR N/DES/VAR Y1 TO X3/
  DEP=Y1/ENTER X1/DEP=Z1/ENTER Y1 X1.
```

Commentary

For present purposes, it will only be pointed out that, when regression analysis is used for the analysis of path models, each dependent variable is in turn regressed on the variables affecting it. Accordingly, we called for two regression analyses: (a) Y_1 on X_1, and (b) Z_1 on Y_1 and X_1.

Output

```
Equation Number 1   Dependent Variable..   Y1
Variable(s) Entered on Step Number 1..   X1

R Square                          .14440
```

------------------------------------ Variables in the Equation ------------------------------------

Variable	B	SE B	Beta	T	Sig T
X1	.17536	.03033	.38000	5.781	.0000
(Constant)	.00000				

```
Equation Number 2   Dependent Variable..   Z1
Variable(s) Entered on Step Number 1..   X1
                                     2..   Y1
```

R Square	.18915				

------------------------------------- Variables in the Equation -------------------------------------

Variable	B	SE B	Beta	T	Sig T
X1	.09556	.01892	.35040	5.052	.0000
Y1	.09270	.04099	.15685	2.261	.0248
(Constant)	.00000				

Commentary

As always, one may choose standardized (β) or unstandardized (b) coefficients for the purpose of expressing effects of variables. In path-analytic applications, the former—referred to as path coefficients—are used most often. As indicated in earlier sections, the popularity of the β's stems from the seeming ease with which they can be interpreted. For completeness of presentation, both β's and b's (in parentheses) are reported in Figure 24.5. Examine the figure in conjunction with the above output and note, for example, that the path coefficients (i.e., β's) indicating the direct effects of MA and AA on SC are .35 and .157 respectively. Issues concerning the use of standardized coefficients aside, researchers using such coefficients would interpret these results as indicating that MA's direct effect on SC is more than twice as large as that of AA.

Look now at the same two direct effects expressed as path regression coefficients (i.e., b's) and note that, although they are very similar to each other, *they are not comparable*. This because they are based on different measurement units. Of course, a meaningful interpretation of the b's is predicated on the meaningfulness of the units of the measures used (see Chapters 17 and 18, and earlier in this chapter).

Now, the indirect effect of MA on SC is obtained by multiplying the effect of MA on AA by the effect of the latter on SC (for detailed explanations, see Pedhazur, 1982, Chapter 15). Using path coefficients, the indirect effect of MA on SC is

$$(.38)(.157) = .060$$

The total effect of MA on SC is, therefore,

$$.35 + .060 = .41$$

Using path regression coefficients instead, the indirect effect of MA on SC is

$$(.175)(.093) = .016$$

And the total effect is

$$(.096) + (.016) = .112$$

We turn now to an analysis of the same model using LISREL.

LISREL

Input

TABLE 24.2.   ONE EXOGENOUS AND TWO ENDOGENOUS.   SINGLE INDICATORS
DA NI=9 NO=200
LA
Y1 Y2 Y3 Z1 Z2 Z3 X1 X2 X3
KM
1.00

```
      .52 1.00
      .45  .58 1.00
      .29  .34  .23 1.00
      .31  .30  .28  .53 1.00
      .27  .36  .35  .48  .45 1.00
      .38  .35  .46  .41  .38  .42 1.00
      .42  .44  .48  .39  .31  .41  .69 1.00
      .37  .39  .43  .38  .36  .40  .77  .73 1.00
SD
4.67 5.81 5.12 2.76 3.12 2.93 10.12 11.09 12.31
SE
1 4 7/
MO NY=2 NX=1 BE=SD PS=DI
LK
MA
LE
AA SC
OU AL
```

Commentary

As explained earlier, SE may be used for selection and/or reordering of indicators. In the present example, SE is used to select indicators 1 (Y_1), 4 (Z_1), and 7 (X_1). Recall that, in LISREL, indicators of endogenous variables are expected to precede those of exogenous variables. As this is the case in our example, no reordering of indicators is necessary. The slash (/) is required when, as in the present example, a subset of indicators is selected.

Turning to the MO statement, note that no mention is made of KSI's and ETA's, thereby equating them with their respective indicators. Thus, NK = 1, NE = 2, and the following is set by the program:

$$\Lambda_y = \mathbf{I}, \quad \Theta_\epsilon = 0, \quad \Lambda_x = \mathbf{I}, \quad \Theta_\delta = 0, \quad \text{and } \Phi = \mathbf{S}_{xx}$$

(for an explanation, see examples in earlier sections).

PSi (residuals, or errors in equations) is SYmmetric FRee by default (see Manual, p. 12). We called for DIagonal, thus, specifying that there is no covariance between the two ZETA's (see earlier sections of the present chapter).

By default, GAMMA (effects of exogenous variables on endogenous variables) is FUll, FRee (see Manual, p. 12). We use the default, because we want the estimates of *MA* on both *AA* and *SC*. In the present case, then, GAMMA is a 2 by 1 vector of free parameters.

Earlier, it was pointed out that **B** is a matrix consisting of effects of latent variables (ETA's) on other latent variables, and that its default is FUll, FIxed. Because models analyzed thus far consisted of one ETA, it was appropriate to use the default **B**. The present model consists of two ETA's, and it is hypothesized that ETA 1 affects ETA 2. Therefore, it is necessary to specify **B** and free the relevant parameter.

As is the case with other matrices used in LISREL, parameter specifications of **B** may be accomplished in several ways. When each ETA is said to affect all the ETA's that follow it, the simplest way is to specify BE = SD, where SD is "a full square matrix with fixed zeros in and above the diagonal and all elements under the diagonal free (refers to **B** only)" (Manual, p. 12). *However, this assumes that the input variables are in the proper order*, as is the case in our example. An example of **B** for two ETA's was given earlier in connection with Figure 24.1. Examine that matrix and note that, except for the element below the diagonal, β_{21}, indicating the effect of ETA 1 on ETA 2, the remaining elements are 0's. Therefore, a specification of SD would suffice, *assuming that the variables are in the proper order*.

When the variables are not in the proper order, they can be reordered by using the SElect statement (see above). When one chooses not to reorder variables that require reordering, alternative approaches have to be employed for the purpose of specifying the free elements of **B** (i.e., elements to be estimated). Assuming that, in our example, Z_1 (indicator of *SC*) preceded Y_1 (indicator of *AA*), we could have reordered the variables using SE. Alternatively, we could have used the default BE (i.e., FU, FI) along with the following FRee statement:

FR BE 1 2

This instructs the program to free the second element of the first row of **B** and in so doing, to estimate the effect of ETA 2 on ETA 1. Note, however, that now ETA 2 is *AA* and ETA 1 is *SC*, and it is the estimate of this effect that we wish to obtain.

The remaining input statements will not be commented upon, as similar statements were used and commented upon in earlier examples.

Output

TABLE 24.2.   ONE EXOGENOUS AND TWO ENDOGENOUS.   SINGLE INDICATORS

LISREL ESTIMATES (MAXIMUM LIKELIHOOD)
       BETA

	AA	SC
AA	.000	.000
SC	.093	.000

       GAMMA

	MA
AA	.175
SC	.096

SQUARED MULTIPLE CORRELATIONS FOR STRUCTURAL EQUATIONS

AA	SC
.144	.189

Commentary

Compare these results with those given earlier in the analysis of the same example through SPSS REGRESSION. The covariance matrix is being analyzed here; thus, the effects reported are what were termed above path regression coefficients. Path coefficients are reported later (see STANDARDIZED SOLUTION). SQUARED MULTIPLE CORRELATIONS FOR STRUCTURAL EQUATIONS are equal to the respective R Squares reported in the regression analyses of these data (see above). Finally, we remind you that the estimated parameters in the present model are based on the very unrealistic assumption that the indicators are measured without error (see earlier discussion of this important point).

Output

MEASURES OF GOODNESS OF FIT FOR THE WHOLE MODEL :
CHI-SQUARE WITH 0 DEGREES OF FREEDOM = .00 (P = 1.000)
GOODNESS OF FIT INDEX = 1.000
ROOT MEAN SQUARE RESIDUAL = .000

Commentary

The model is exactly identified; thus, it fits the data perfectly. As an exercise, you may wish to reverse the directions of the arrows in Figure 24.5 (i.e., that *SC* affects *AA* and *MA*, and that *AA* affects *MA*) and reanalyze the data accordingly. You will find that this model too fits the data perfectly. We repeat: An exactly identified model, no matter how ill conceived it may be, fits the data perfectly.

Output

```
TOTAL AND INDIRECT EFFECTS
        TOTAL EFFECTS OF X ON Y
                MA
                ----------
    AA          .175
    SC          .112
        INDIRECT EFFECTS OF X ON Y
                MA
                ----------
    AA          .000
    SC          .016
        TOTAL EFFECTS OF Y ON Y
                AA          SC
                ----------  ----------
    AA          .000        .000
    SC          .093        .000
        INDIRECT EFFECTS OF Y ON Y
                AA          SC
                ----------  ----------
    AA          .000        .000
    SC          .000        .000
```

Commentary

Earlier, it was pointed out that a total effect of a variable is equal to its direct effect plus its indirect effect(s). When no variables are said to mediate the effect of a variable, its total effect is equal to its direct effect. In the present example, this is true for the effects of *MA* on *AA* (.175) and of *AA* on *SC* (.093; see LISREL ESTIMATES). The total effect of *MA* on *SC* (.112) is equal to its direct effect plus its indirect effect via *AA*. The same value was obtained above, when this model was analyzed through regression.

Output

```
STANDARDIZED SOLUTION
    BETA
                AA          SC
                ----------  ----------
    AA          .000        .000
    SC          .157        .000
        GAMMA
                MA
                ----------
    AA          .380
    SC          .350
```

PSI

AA	SC
.856	.811

Commentary

It was pointed out earlier that when SS (standardized solution) is specified on the OU statement only the latent variables are standardized. The values reported under BETA and GAMMA are equal to their respective β's obtained above in the regression analyses of the same data (see also, Figure 24.5). The values reported under PSI are equal to 1 minus their respective R^2's. For example, R^2 for AA was reported above as .144. PSI is, therefore, $1 - .144 = .856$.

ONE EXOGENOUS AND TWO ENDOGENOUS VARIABLES: MULTIPLE INDICATORS

The model to be analyzed in this section is depicted in Figure 24.6, where the values indicated were obtained from the output reported below. As you can see, the structural model is the same as that of the preceding section. However, whereas, in the preceding section, single indicators were used, multiple indicators are used in the present section.

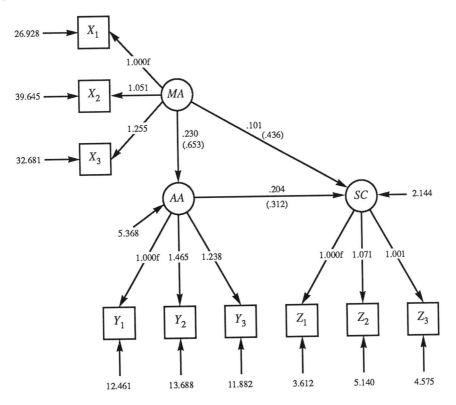

f = fixed

Values in parentheses are standardized coefficients

Figure 24.6

The illustrative data to be used are given in Table 24.2. Specifically the three *X*'s are taken as indicators of *MA* (Mental Ability), the three *Y*'s as indicators of *AA* (Academic Achievement), and the three *Z*'s as indicators of *SC* (Self-Concept). It will be recalled that the first indicator of each set was used in the analysis of this model in the preceding section.

LISREL

Input

TABLE 24.2. ONE EXOGENOUS AND TWO ENDOGENOUS VARIABLES: MULTIPLE INDICATORS

[except for the omission of SElect statement (see commentary),
input up to MO is identical with the run in preceding section]

```
MO NY=6 NE=2 NX=3 NK=1 BE=SD PS=DI
FR LX 2 LX 3 LY 3 LY 5 LY 10 LY 12
ST 1 LX 1 LY 1 LY 8
LK
MA
LE
AA SC
OU AL
```

Commentary

In the preceding run, a SElect statement was required in order to choose the subset of indicators to be used in the analysis. Such a statement is not required in the present analysis, because all the indicators are used, and because no reordering of variables is necessary.

The MO statement is similar in certain respects to that used in the analysis with single indicators (preceding section) and different in others. Beginning with the former, it will be pointed out that, because the structural model is the same in both, BE and PS are also the same. If necessary, refer to the preceding section for an explanation.

Unlike the preceding analysis, in the present one, it is necessary to specify the number of ETA's and KSI's, because multiple indicators are used. Furthermore, errors in indicators (TE and TD) were fixed to zero in the preceding analysis, whereas here the default (DI, FR) is used for these matrices.

Recall that the default for LY (LAMBDA Y) and LX (LAMBDA X) is FUll, FIxed. Therefore, it is necessary to specify the elements of these matrices that are to be estimated. This is accomplished through the FRee statement, where coefficients of two indicators for each latent variable are freed. In addition, the ST 1 designates the first indicator from each set as the reference indicator for the latent variable in question. We suggest that, as an exercise, you display LY and LX, number the elements in each,[9] and check against the FR and ST statements and also against the PARAMETER SPECIFICATIONS given below (hint: LX is a 3 by 1 column vector; LY is a 6 by 2 matrix).

The remaining statements are the same as those used in the preceding section.

---

[9]The use of consecutive numbers as one of the methods for identifying elements in matrices used in LISREL was explained in Chapter 23.

Output

PARAMETER SPECIFICATIONS
        LAMBDA Y

	AA	SC
Y1	0	0
Y2	1	0
Y3	2	0
Z1	0	0
Z2	0	3
Z3	0	4

        LAMBDA X

	MA
X1	0
X2	5
X3	6

        BETA

	AA	SC
AA	0	0
SC	7	0

        GAMMA

	MA
AA	8
SC	9

        PHI

	MA
MA	10

        PSI

AA	SC
11	12

        THETA EPS

Y1	Y2	Y3	Z1	Z2	Z3
13	14	15	16	17	18

        THETA DELTA

X1	X2	X3
19	20	21

Commentary

We believe you will have no difficulty in interpreting this output. If necessary, see explanations in Chapter 23 and earlier in the present chapter.

Output

LISREL ESTIMATES (MAXIMUM LIKELIHOOD)

LAMBDA Y

	AA	SC
Y1	1.000	.000
Y2	1.465	.000
Y3	1.238	.000
Z1	.000	1.000
Z2	.000	1.071
Z3	.000	1.001

LAMBDA X

	MA
X1	1.000
X2	1.051
X3	1.255

BETA

	AA	SC
AA	.000	.000
SC	.204	.000

GAMMA

	MA
AA	.230
SC	.101

PSI

AA	SC
5.368	2.144

THETA EPS

Y1	Y2	Y3	Z1	Z2	Z3
12.461	13.688	11.882	3.612	5.140	4.575

THETA DELTA

X1	X2	X3
26.928	39.645	32.681

SQUARED MULTIPLE CORRELATIONS FOR Y – VARIABLES

Y1	Y2	Y3	Z1	Z2	Z3
.429	.595	.547	.526	.472	.467

SQUARED MULTIPLE CORRELATIONS FOR X – VARIABLES

X1	X2	X3
.737	.678	.784

Commentary

Substantive interpretation of the results are, of course, precluded as the example is fictitious. All we can do is note that structural effects are contained in the GAMMA and BETA matrices. For example, the effect of *MA* on *AA* is .230; that of *AA* on *SC* is .204.

In the preceding analysis, latent variables were equated with single indicators purported to reflect them, thereby leading to estimated effects based on the unrealistic assumption of errorless measures. In contrast, in the present section, measurement errors are taken into account when arriving at estimates of the effects of latent variables

Examine the SQUARED MULTIPLE CORRELATIONS and notice that the estimated reliabilities of the X indicators are fairly larger than those of Y and Z indicators (for explanations, see Chapter 23 and earlier sections of the present chapter).

Output

MEASURES OF GOODNESS OF FIT FOR THE WHOLE MODEL :
CHI-SQUARE WITH 24 DEGREES OF FREEDOM = 29.82 (P = .191)
GOODNESS OF FIT INDEX = .969
ADJUSTED GOODNESS OF FIT INDEX = .942
ROOT MEAN SQUARE RESIDUAL = 1.509

Commentary

On the basis of the fit indices, it is plausible to conclude that the model fits the data rather well. Recall that, when the covariance matrix is analyzed, RMR and FITTED RESIDUALS (not reproduced here) are not readily interpretable. It will be noted that the bulk of the standardized residuals (not reproduced here) are relatively small, lending support to the assertion regarding the fit of the model.

Output

TOTAL AND INDIRECT EFFECTS
        TOTAL EFFECTS OF KSI ON ETA
                MA

    AA   .230
    SC   .147
        INDIRECT EFFECTS OF KSI ON ETA
                MA

    AA   .000
    SC   .047
        TOTAL EFFECTS OF ETA ON ETA
                AA   SC
                ---------- ----------
    AA   .000   .000
    SC   .204   .000

Commentary

In the preceding section, it was pointed out that a total effect of a variable is equal to its direct plus indirect effect(s)—also that, for the model under consideration, only *MA* has an indirect effect (on *SC*, through *AA*); the other total effects are comprised of direct effects only.

Output

```
STANDARDIZED SOLUTION
      BETA
                  AA          SC
               ----------  ----------
      AA          .000        .000
      SC          .312        .000
      GAMMA
                  MA
               ----------
      AA          .653
      SC          .436
```

Commentary

Issues concerning the choice and interpretation of standardized solutions were discussed in earlier sections and will, therefore, not be repeated here.

This concludes the LISREL analysis. We now give input statements for the analysis of the same model (i.e., the one depicted in Figure 24.6) through EQS. No output will be given, as we believe that in the event you are running EQS you will encounter no difficulties in interpreting the results, especially if you compare your output with the LISREL output given above.

EQS

Input

```
/TITLE
 TABLE 24.2.   ONE EXOGENOUS AND TWO ENDOGENOUS VARIABLES:
 MULTIPLE INDICATORS
/SPECIFICATIONS
 CASES=200; VARIABLES=9;
/LAB
 V1=Y1; V2=Y2; V3=Y3; V4=Z1; V5=Z2; V6=Z3; V7=X1; V8=X2; V9=X3;
 F1=AA; F2=SC; F3=MA;
/EQUATIONS
 V1=F1 + E1;
 V2=*F1 + E2;
 V3=*F1 + E3;
 V4=          F2 + E4;
 V5=         *F2 + E5;
 V6=         *F2 + E6;
 V7=               F3 + E7;
 V8=              *F3 + E8;
 V9=              *F3 + E9;
 F1=*F3 + D1;
 F2=*F1 + *F3 + D2;
/VAR
 E1 TO E9=*10;
 F3=*70;
 D1 TO D2=*4;
```

/MATRIX
1.00
.52 1.00
.45 .58 1.00
.29 .34 .23 1.00
.31 .30 .28 .53 1.00
.27 .36 .35 .48 .45 1.00
.38 .35 .46 .41 .38 .42 1.00
.42 .44 .48 .39 .31 .41 .69 1.00
.37 .39 .43 .38 .36 .40 .77 .73 1.00
/STANDARD DEVIATIONS
4.67 5.81 5.12 2.76 3.12 2.93 10.12 11.09 12.31
/END

Commentary

A general orientation to EQS and an explanation of its input conventions were given in Chapter 23. Therefore, only brief comments will be made here, focusing on the model under consideration.

Examine the EQUATIONS paragraph and notice that, analogous to the LISREL analysis, the first indicator of each latent variable is designated as a reference indicator (i.e., no asterisks attached to the F's in the equations for V1, V4, and V7).

Consistent with the EQS approach, the structural model is comprised of two equations. In the first equation, F1 (*AA*; see LABels paragraph) is designated as the dependent variable; in the second, F2 (*SC*) is designated as the dependent variable.

Finally, notice that we use default start values (i.e., no value attached to the asterisk), for the estimation of the various effects. For the variances, however, we do provide start values. As explained in Chapter 23, a poor choice of start values (the default of 1.00 would constitute a poor choice in the present case) can lead to difficulties in the obtained solution, especially with regards to convergence. In fact, this happened when we ran this example on the PC version of EQS, using default start values for the variances. On the mainframe version, however, we encountered no difficulties when the analysis was run with default start values for the variances.

SELECTED TOPICS

Our presentations of exploratory and confirmatory factor analysis (Chapter 22 and 23 respectively) and structural equation modeling (the present chapter) were clearly introductory. Consequently, various important topics and issues were not even alluded to. Our aim in this concluding section is to indicate some topics we did not address and to give selected references where you will find presentations and/or applications relevant to them.

The list of topics to be presented is by no means exhaustive. We remind you that, in earlier chapters (especially Chapter 9), we pointed out that analytic approaches with which one is familiar affect, among other things, the kind of research questions one entertains, the type of problems and hypotheses one formulates, and the kind of data one collects. It is considerations such as these that guided our selection of topics to be included. Our aim, therefore, is to apprise you of the much wider scope of applications of the analytic approaches under consideration than what you may have gathered from our presentation. Further, we believe the topics we have included will be of particular interest to you when you attempt to extend and deepen your knowledge of these important analytic approaches.

As may be expected, studies we refer to are not neatly classifiable under the categories we are using. Thus, a study used as an example of one of our categories (e.g., higher-order factors), may also serve as an example of one or more other categories we use (e.g., factorial invariance, models with structured means).

A word of caution is in order. Our selection of illustrative applications is not meant to imply that we have no reservations whatsoever about them. We cannot even begin to be concerned with the most important issue: namely the theoretical rationale underlying the models advanced in the studies to which we refer. In addition, to be intelligible, comments on certain aspects of the studies would require detailed discussions of complex issues that go far beyond the limited aims of our presentation.

Preceding matters aside, it is necessary to face the unfortunate fact that, as in other areas of sociobehavioral research, most researchers applying *SEM* appear unable to obtain probability samples. Difficulties arising from the use of samples of convenience, discussed in earlier chapters (e.g., Chapter 15), become even more pronounced when such samples are used for the purpose of comparing aspects such as factor structures and structural models. Finally, in some of the studies, sample sizes are relatively small.

In sum, although we attempted to select studies that do not contain blatant deficiencies, we do not wish to create the impression that they contain no flaws or weaknesses. The problem of greatest concern in most applications of *SEM*, including ones referred to below, is model specification. We urge you to read the studies illustrating topics which are of interest to you and critically evaluate them. Further, we believe you will benefit from reanalyzing some of the studies, perhaps even using modified models that you deem more plausible than those advanced by their authors.

Higher-Order Factors

The *idea* behind higher-order factors is rather straightforward: factor analysis applied to correlations or covariances among extracted factors. In exploratory factor analysis, a covariance or correlation matrix among factors (referred to as first-order or primary factors) is obtained by rotating the factors obliquely (see Chapter 22). In confirmatory factor analysis, this is accomplished by freeing off-diagonal elements of the factor covariance matrix (PHI in LISREL; see Chapter 23). The covariance or correlation matrix among the first-order factors can then be factor analyzed to yield second-order factors. In turn, a covariance matrix of second-order factors may be factor analyzed to yield third-order factors, and so forth. However, most applications stop at second-order factors. In the context of *SEM*, higher-order factors are exemplified as a hierarchy of latent variables affecting other latent variables.

Potential applications of higher-order factors come readily to mind, especially in the context of construct formulation and validation. Following are some examples, along with selected references: (a) mental ability conceived of as a set of primary abilities, which in turn reflect one or more higher-order factors (e.g., general intelligence; Gustafsson, 1984; Horn, 1988; Undheim & Gustafsson, 1987; Weeks, 1980); (b) first-order factors of social attitudes subsumed under two second-order factors: Liberalism and Conservatism (Kerlinger, 1984); (c) hierarchical structure of self-concept (Bynner, 1981; Marsh, 1987; Marsh & Shavelson, 1985); and (d) hierarchical structures of personality (Smith, 1988).

For general discussions of higher-order factors and illustrative applications, see Cattell (1988), Gorsuch (1983, Chapter 11), Mulaik (1988), and Rindskopf and Rose (1988).

Multisample Analysis

Our presentation of factor analysis and *SEM* was limited to analyses of data from a single sample. Frequently, interest centers on multisample analysis aimed at comparisons among them. Following are some situations in which multisample analyses are of special interest.

FACTORIAL INVARIANCE

When studying the factor structure of a construct(s), it is often of interest to determine whether or not the structure is invariant across different populations (e.g., racial, ethnic, gender). To this end, simultaneous factor analysis in two or more samples is carried out. By testing nested models sequentially, it is possible to determine if and in what particular aspects the samples differ (e.g., factor loadings, errors).

For a general discussion of simultaneous factor analysis and for illustrative applications, s_e Alwin and Jackson (1981), Jöreskog (1971a), LISREL 7 manual (Jöreskog & Sörbom ,989, Chapter 9). Following are some examples of simultaneous analyses: (a) adolescent self-concept across gender (Byrne & Shavelson, 1987); (b) self-esteem across race and sex (Hoelter, 1983b); (c) subjective mental health across gender (Bryant & Veroff, 1984); (d) symptoms of depression across gender (Newman, 1984); and (e) sex roles across gender (Marsh, 1985).

The analysis of multitrait-multimethod matrices for a single sample was presented in Chapter 23. An extension of this approach to comparisons across populations is given in Cole and Maxwell (1985).

PSYCHOMETRIC PROPERTIES OF MEASURES

Assessment of measurement models through *SEM* was presented and illustrated in Chapter 23. In many instances, it is of interest to determine whether a given measurement model is similar in two or more samples, or even on two or more occasions. A couple of instances in which such comparisons are of interest were mentioned in Chapter 13 in connection with applications of regression adjustment and difference scores in the nonequivalent-control-group design. By and large, however, comparisons have been made across gender, racial, ethnic, and socioeconomic groupings. Alwin and Jackson (1979) gave a good introduction to this topic along with illustrative applications. Following are selected references in which such comparisons are reported: (a) objective and subjective class status of whites and blacks (Kluegel, Singleton, & Starnes, 1977); (b) children's reports of parental socioeconomic status across several grades (Mare & Mason, 1980); (c) male and female responses to social desirability measures (O'Grady, 1988); (d) grades of whites and blacks in law school (Rock, Werts, & Flaugher, 1978); and (e) socioeconomic measures of whites and blacks (Wolfle & Robertshaw, 1983).

STRUCTURAL MODELS

Not surprisingly, researchers are frequently interested in determining whether or not a structural model is similar in different groups, under different conditions, or occasions. This is exemplified by the interest in comparing regression equations obtained from different groups, exposed to different treatments, and the like (e.g., Chapters 3 and 21). Comparisons of models with single indicators (path models) are discussed and illustrated, among others, by Schoenberg (1972), and Specht and Warren (1975). Following are examples of comparisons of structural models with multiple indicators, using LISREL: (a) mathematics achievement for men and women (Ethington & Wolfe, 1986); (b) family bias, schooling, and occupational status (Hauser, 1984); (c) vulnerability to stress among blacks and whites (Neff, 1985); (d) objective and subjective class status of blacks and whites (Jöreskog & Sörbom, 1989, pp. 242–244); and (e) postsecondary educational attainment among blacks and whites (Wolfle, 1985).

CAUSAL MODELS WITH STRUCTURED MEANS

In most instances, *SEM* has been applied to covariance matrices. Doing this ignores the means of the indicators, thereby precluding the possibility of estimating means for the latent variables. In other words, the means are set to equal zero. To give you a feel for what this means, consider an analogy with regression analysis applied to a covariance matrix whose elements have been obtained using correlations and standard deviations. Under such circumstances, the intercept would be zero.

Ignoring means, especially when the units of the measures used are not readily interpretable, may be a more tolerable way out in some circumstances than in others. Ignoring means is particularly troublesome when one is interested in determining effects of a treatment(s), or of a putative cause(s), after controlling for other variables.

Sörbom (1974, 1978, 1982) proposed an approach, referred to as an analysis with structured means, that affords both estimation of group means on latent variables and comparisons among them. Among other things, Sörbom proposed his approach as an alternative to the analysis of covariance. Following are references to discussions and/or applications of analyses with structured means: Cole and Maxwell (1985), Hayduk (1987, pp. 286–322), Jöreskog and Sörbom (1989, Chapter 10), Newcomb and Bentler (1987), and Schoenberg (1982).

Nonrecursive Models

In causal modeling, a distinction is made between recursive and nonrecursive models. A *recursive model* is one in which the causal flow is unidirectional. That is, there is no reciprocal causation between variables, either directly or through a loop. Our presentation was limited to recursive models.

A *nonrecursive model* is one in which there is reciprocal causation between endogenous variables, either directly of through a loop. For an introduction to nonrecursive models, see Berry (1984), and Duncan (1975, Chapter 7). Following are some examples of analyses of nonrecursive models: (a) health beliefs and preventive dental care (Chen & Land, 1986); (b) attitude similarity (Glass, Bengtson, & Dunham, 1986); (c) perceived job characteristics and job satisfaction (James & Jones, 1980); (d) peer influence and ambition (Jöreskog & Sörbom, 1989, pp. 145–151); (e) work, personality, and social stratification (Kohn & Schooler, 1983); and (f) stratification, work, and values (Slomczynski, Miller, & Kohn, 1981).

Formative Indicators

In Chapter 4, a distinction was made between reflective and formative indicators of latent variables. The models we have analyzed were all comprised of reflective indicators. Following are some examples of analyses of models in which some of the indicators are formative: (a) family background and achieved status (Alwin, 1988); (b) family origins and the schooling process (Alwin & Thornton, 1984); (c) educational attainment (Hauser, 1972); (d) effect of Head Start (Sörbom, 1982); and (e) objective and subjective class structure (Sörbom & Jöreskog, 1981).

Longitudinal Research

General merits of longitudinal research were discussed in Chapter 14. As you have probably surmised, longitudinal research is extremely useful in causal modeling, primarily because the time sequence in such studies affords more secure grounds for enunciating a pattern of causation. For general presentations of longitudinal research in the context of *SEM*, see Dwyer (1983, Chapter 11), Gollob and Reichardt (1987), Jöreskog (1979b), Jöreskog and Sörbom (1977), and Rogosa (1979).

Following is but a small selection of varied applications of *SEM* in longitudinal research: (a) age changes in factor structure of intellectual abilities (Cunningham, 1980); (b) mathematical ability—treatment comparisons with structured means (Hanna & Lei, 1985); (c) trait-state distinction (Hertzog & Nesselroade, 1987); (d) change in personality and intelligence factors (Lachman, 1983); (e) latent growth curves with WISC data (McArdle & Epstein, 1987); (f) persistence and change of self-concept (Mortimer, Finch, & Kumba (1982); (g) occupational experience and the self-concept (Mortimer & Lorence, 1979); (h) change and stability of self-esteem (O'Mally & Bachman, 1983); (i) sociogenesis of psychological disorder (Wheaton, 1978); and (j) assessing reliability and stability in panel models (Wheaton, Muthèn, Alwin, & Summers, 1977).

STUDY SUGGESTIONS

Note: To carry out analyses suggested below, you will need LISREL, EQS, or a comparable computer program.
1. What is the advantage in using multiple instead of single indicators of latent variables?
2. Following are an illustrative correlation matrix and standard deviations for 8 indicators of 4 variables (*N* = 250). SES is an indicator of Socioeconomic Status; MA1 and MA2 are indicators of Mental Ability; ASP1 and ASP2 are indicators of Aspirations; AA1, AA2, AA3 are indicators of Academic Achievement.

	SES	MA1	MA2	ASP1	ASP2	AA1	AA2	AA3
SES	1.00							
MA1	.32	1.00						
MA2	.30	.68	1.00					
ASP1	.32	.17	.12	1.00				
ASP2	.34	.20	.15	.47	1.00			
AA1	.29	.38	.30	.38	.32	1.00		
AA2	.33	.42	.35	.35	.21	.70	1.00	
AA3	.33	.34	.32	.34	.20	.60	.58	1.00

STANDARD DEVIATIONS:
1.09 60.12 58.63 5.62 10.36 7.84 6.59 7.18

Assume that SES and MA are exogenous variables; ASP and AA are endogenous variables. Also, the following is hypothesized: (a) SES affects ASP; (b) MA and ASP affect AA. Using LISREL and/or EQS, carry out two analyses to test the fit of this model. *In the first analysis, use single indicators only.* Specifically, use SES as an indicator of SES, MA1 as an indicator of MA, ASP1 as an indicator of ASP, AA1 as an indicator of AA. *In the second analysis, use all the indicators.* Following are some points to keep in mind when preparing these runs:

Use reference indicators for the analysis with multiple indicators.

In LISREL, use a SElect statement for the selection and/or reordering of variables (see LISREL manual, p. 62).

If you are using EQS, use reasonable start values; otherwise the program may fail to arrive at a solution.

Following are excerpts of LISREL output for both runs:

STUDY SUGGESTION 24.2.　SINGLE INDICATORS.

LISREL ESTIMATES (MAXIMUM LIKELIHOOD)

BETA

	ASP1	AA1
ASP1	.000	.000
AA1	.453	.000

GAMMA

	SES	MA1
ASP1	1.650	.000
AA1	.000	.042

MEASURES OF GOODNESS OF FIT FOR THE WHOLE MODEL :
CHI-SQUARE WITH 2 DEGREES OF FREEDOM = 4.13 (P = .127)
GOODNESS OF FIT INDEX = .992
ADJUSTED GOODNESS OF FIT INDEX = .959
ROOT MEAN SQUARE RESIDUAL = 7.943

STUDY SUGGESTION 24.2.　MULTIPLE INDICATORS

LISREL ESTIMATES (MAXIMUM LIKELIHOOD)

LAMBDA Y

	ASP	AA
ASP1	1.000	.000
ASP2	1.513	.000
AA1	.000	1.000
AA2	.000	.823
AA3	.000	.774

LAMBDA X

	SES	MA
SES	1.000	.000
MA1	.000	1.000
MA2	.000	.864

BETA

	ASP	AA
ASP	.000	.000
AA	.714	.000

GAMMA

	SES	MA
ASP	1.822	.000
AA	.000	.054

COVARIANCE MATRIX OF ETA AND KSI

	ASP	AA	SES	MA
ASP	17.977			
AA	14.930	42.829		
SES	2.164	2.699	1.188	
MA	39.065	177.110	21.444	2771.859

SQUARED MULTIPLE CORRELATIONS FOR Y – VARIABLES

ASP1	ASP2	AA1	AA2	AA3
.569	.384	.710	.681	.507

SQUARED MULTIPLE CORRELATIONS FOR X – VARIABLES

SES	MA1	MA2
1.000	.767	.602

MEASURES OF GOODNESS OF FIT FOR THE WHOLE MODEL :
CHI-SQUARE WITH 17 DEGREES OF FREEDOM = 22.87 (P = .153)
GOODNESS OF FIT INDEX =   .980
ADJUSTED GOODNESS OF FIT INDEX =   .957
ROOT MEAN SQUARE RESIDUAL = 14.346

The following questions refer to the *multiple-indicator solution.*

(a) What are the direct, indirect, and total effects of:

    (1) SES on ASP?

    (2) SES on AA?

    (3) MA on AA?

    (4) ASP on AA?

(b) Using relevant information from the output, indicate the estimated reliabilities of the 8 indicators.

(c) Why is the reported reliability of SES 1.00?

(d) What is the correlation between SES and MA?

3. Following are some references to exchanges concerning specific applications of structural equation modeling. We believe you will benefit not only from reading them but also from reanalyzing data contained in them along lines argued by participants. You may also find it useful to try other approaches to the analysis.

    (1) Alexander and Pallas (1983, 1986); Hauser and Sewell (1986).

    (2) Harry and Minor (1986); Menard and Morse (1984, 1986).

    (3) Hays, Widaman, DiMatteo, and Stacy (1987); Huba and Bentler (1982b); Huba, Wingard, and Bentler (1981); Martin (1982).

    (4) Jagodzinski and Kühnel (1987); Jagodzinski, Kühnel, and Schmidt (1987, 1988); Saris and Putte (1988).

    (5) Marsh (1988); Newman (1984).

Answers

1. Multiple indicators afford a distinction between measurement and structural models, hence, the study of properties of measures and the taking of them into account when studying relations among latent variables.

2. (a) (1) SES has *no* indirect effect on ASP. Its direct, hence, total, effect on ASP is 1.822.

    (2) SES has *no* direct effect on AA. Its indirect, hence, total, effect on AA is 1.30 (i.e., 1.822 x .714).

    (3) MA has *no* indirect effect on AA. Its direct, hence, total, effect on AA is .054.

    (4) ASP has *no* indirect effect on AA. Its direct, hence, total, effect on AA is .714.

Total and indirect effects may be obtained as part of the LISREL output by specifying EF on the OU statement (see LISREL manual, p. 72).

(b) The estimated reliabilities are indicated under SQUARED MULTIPLE CORRELA-TIONS FOR Y and X VARIABLES—see (23.6) and the discussion related to it. Thus, for example, the estimated reliability for ASP1 is .569 and that of ASP2 .384.

(c) Because a single indicator was used for SES, it was necessary to fix the error term to 0. The reliability is, therefore, necessarily 1.00. As was pointed out in the chapter, when reliability estimates for single indicators are available, it is possible to incorporate them in the measurement model instead of unrealistically fixing the error term to equal 0.

(d) The covariance between SES and MA is 21.444; the variances respectively of SES and MA are 1.188 and 2771.859. The correlation between SES and MA is, therefore, $21.444/\sqrt{(1.188)(2771.859)} = .374$. This value may be obtained by calling for the standardized solution.

References

Aaker, D. A., & Day, G. S. (1983). *Marketing research*. New York: Wiley.

Achen, C. H. (1986). *The statistical analysis of quasi-experiments*. Berkeley, CA: University of California Press.

Ackoff, R. L. (1953). *The design of social research*. Chicago: University of Chicago Press.

Acock, A. C., & Scott, W. J. (1980). A model for predicting behavior: The effect of attitude and social class on high and low visibility political participation. *Social Psychology Quarterly*, *43*, 59–72.

Adair, J. G. (1973). *The human subject: The social psychology of the psychological experiment*. Boston: Little, Brown.

Adair, J. G., & Fenton, D. P. (1971). Subject's attitudes toward psychology as a determinant of experimental results. *Canadian Journal of Behavioral Sciences*, *3*, 268–275.

Adams, R. McC., Smelser, N. J., & Treiman, D. J. (Eds.). (1982a). *Behavioral and social science research: A national resource. Part I*. Washington, DC: National Academy Press.

Adams, R. McC., Smelser, N. J., & Treiman, D. J. (Eds.). (1982b). *Behavioral and social science research: A national resource. Part II*. Washington, DC: National Academy Press.

Adler, F. (1947). Operational definitions in sociology. *American Journal of Sociology*, *52*, 438–444.

Adorno, T. W., Frenkel-Brunswik, E., Levinson, D. J., & Sanford, R. N. (1950). *The authoritarian personality*. New York: Harper & Row.

Aldenderfer, M. S., & Blashfield, R. K. (1978). Computer programs for performing hierarchical cluster analysis. *Applied Psychological Measurement*, *2*, 403–411.

Aldenderfer, M. S., & Blashfield, R. K. (1984). *Cluster analysis*. Newbury Park, CA: Sage.

Aldrich, J. H., & Nelson, F. D. (1984). *Linear probability, logit, and probit models*. Newbury Park, CA: Sage.

Aldrich, J. H., Niemi, R. G., Rabinowitz, G., & Rohde, D. W. (1982). The measurement of public opinion about public policy: A report on some new issue question formats. *American Journal of Political Science*, *26*, 391–414.

Alexander, K. L., & Pallas, A. M. (1983). Private schools and public policy: New evidence on cognitive achievement in public and private schools. *Sociology of Education*, *56*, 170–182.

Alexander, K. L., & Pallas, A. M. (1986). Reply to Hauser and Sewell. *Social Forces*, *65*, 250–257.

Algina, J., & Olejnik, S. F. (1982). Multiple time-series design: An analysis of data. *Evaluation Review*, *6*, 203–232.

Allen, M. J., & Yen, W. M. (1979). *Introduction to measurement theory*. Monterey, CA: Brooks/Cole.

Allport, F. H. (1955). *Theories of perception and*

the concept of structure. A review and critical analysis with an introduction to a dynamic-structural theory of behavior. New York: Wiley.

Allport, G. W. (1940). The psychologist's frame of reference. *Psychological Bulletin, 37*, 1–28.

Allport, G. W. (1961). *Pattern and growth in personality*. New York: Holt, Rinehart & Winston.

Allport, G. W. (1985). The historical background of social psychology. In G. Lindzey & E. Aronson (Eds.), *Handbook of social psychology* (Vol. 1, 3rd ed., pp. 1–46). New York: Random House.

Almond, G. A., & Genco, S. J. (1977). Clouds, clocks, and the study of politics. *World Politics, 29*, 489–522.

Althauser, R. P. (1974). Inferring validity from the multitrait-multimethod matrix: Another assessment. In H. L. Costner (Ed.), *Sociological methodology 1973–1974* (pp. 106–127). San Francisco: Jossey-Bass.

Althauser, R. P., & Heberlein, T. A. (1970). Validity and the multitrait-multimethod matrix. In E. F. Borgatta & G. W. Bohrnstedt (Eds.), *Sociological methodology 1970* (pp. 151–169). San Francisco: Jossey-Bass.

Altman, L. K. (1989, June 6). Errors prompt proposals to improve 'peer review' at science journals. *The New York Times*, p. C3.

Alwin, D. F. (1973). The use of factor analysis in the construction of linear composites in social research. *Sociological Methods & Research, 2*, 191–214.

Alwin, D. F. (1974). Approaches to the interpretation of relationships in the multitrait-multimethod matrix. In H. L. Costner (Ed.), *Sociological methodology 1973–1974* (pp. 79–105). San Francisco: Jossey-Bass.

Alwin, D. F. (1988). Measurement and the interpretation of effects in structural equation models. In J. S. Long (Ed.), *Common problems/proper solutions: Avoiding error in quantitative research* (pp. 15–45). Newbury Park, CA: Sage.

Alwin, D. F., & Jackson, D. J. (1979). Measurement models for response errors in surveys: Issues and applications. In K. F. Schuessler (Ed.), *Sociological methodology 1980* (pp. 68–119). San Francisco: Jossey-Bass.

Alwin, D. F., & Jackson, D. J. (1981). Applications of simultaneous factor analysis to issues of factorial invariance. In D. J. Jackson & E.

F. Borgatta (Eds.), *Factor analysis and measurement in sociological research: A multidimensional perspective* (pp. 242–279). Newbury Park, CA: Sage.

Alwin, D. F., & Thornton, A. (1984). Family origins and the schooling process: Early versus late influence of parental characteristics. *American Sociological Review, 49*, 784–802.

American Psychological Association. (1966). *Standards for educational and psychological tests and manuals*. Washington, DC: Author.

American Psychological Association. (1974). *Standards for educational & psychological tests*. Washington, DC: Author.

American Psychological Association. (1983). *Publication manual of the American Psychological Association* (3rd ed.). Washington, DC: Author.

American Psychological Association. (1985). *Standards for educational and psychological testing*. Washington, DC: Author.

Anderson, A. B., Basilevsky, A., & Hum, D. P. J. (1983). Measurement: Theory and techniques. In P. H. Rossi, J. D. Wright, & A. B. Anderson (Eds.), *Handbook of survey research* (pp. 231–287). New York: Academic Press.

Anderson, J. C., & Gerbing, D. W. (1984). The effect of sampling error on convergence, improper solutions, and goodness-of-fit indices for maximum likelihood confirmatory factor analysis. *Psychometrika, 49*, 155–173.

Anderson, N. H. (1963). Comparison of different populations: Resistance to extinction and transfer. *Psychological Review, 70*, 162–179.

Anderson, S., Auquier, A., Hauck, W. W., Oaks, D., Vandaele, W., & Weisberg, H. I. (1980). *Statistical methods for comparative studies. Techniques for bias reduction*. New York: Wiley.

Andreski, S. (1972). *Social sciences as sorcery*. London: Andre Deutsch.

Andrich, D. (1978). A binomial latent trait model for the study of Likert-style attitude questionnaires. *British Journal of Mathematical and Statistical Psychology, 31*, 84–98.

Andrich, D. (1988). *Rasch models for measurement*. Newbury Park, CA: Sage.

Anscombe, F. J. (1960). Rejection of outliers. *Technometrics, 2*, 123–147.

Anscombe, F. J. (1973). Graphs in statistical analysis. *The American Statistician, 27*(1), 17–21.

Anscombe, F. J., & Tukey, J. W. (1963). The

examination and analysis of residuals. *Technometrics*, *5*, 141–160.

Appelbaum, M. I., & Cramer, E. M. (1974). Some problems in the nonorthogonal analysis of variance. *Psychological Bulletin*, *81*, 335–343.

Appelbaum, M. I., & McCall, R. B. (1983). Design and analysis in developmental psychology. In P. H. Mussen (Ed.), *Handbook of child psychology* (Vol. 1, 4th ed., pp. 415–476). New York: Wiley.

Arbuthnot, J. (1972). Cautionary note on measurement of field independence. *Perceptual and Motor Skills*, *35*, 479–488.

Argyle, M. (1969). *Social interaction*. London: Tavistock.

Aristotle. (1962). *Aristotle on the art of fiction* (English translation of Aristotle's *Poetics*). (L. J. Potts, Trans.). New York: Cambridge University Press.

Armor, D. J. (1972). School and family effects on black and white achievement: A reexamination of the USOE data. In F. Mosteller & D. P. Moynihan (Eds.), *On equality of educational opportunity* (pp. 168–229). New York: Vintage Books.

Armstrong, J. S. (1985). *Long-range forecasting: From crystal ball to computer* (2nd ed.). New York: Wiley.

Aronson, E., Brewer, M., & Carlsmith, J. M. (1985). Experimentation in social psychology. In G. Lindzey & E. Aronson (Eds.), *Handbook of social psychology* (Vol. 1, 3rd ed., pp. 441–486). New York: Random House.

Arvey, R. D., & Faley, R. H. (1988). *Fairness in selecting employees* (2nd ed.). Reading, MA: Addison-Wesley.

Auden, W. H. (1950). *Nones*. New York: Random House.

Avison, W. R. (1978). Auxiliary theory and multitrait-multimethod validation: A review of two approaches. *Applied Psychological Measurement*, *2*, 431–449.

Bacon, F. (1870). *The new organon* (*The works of Francis Bacon*, Vol. 4). London: Longmans.

Bagozzi, R. P. (1980a). *Causal models in marketing*. New York: Wiley.

Bagozzi, R. P. (1980b). Performance and satisfaction in an industrial sales force: An examination of their antecedents and simultaneity. *Journal of Marketing*, *44*, 65–77.

Bagozzi, R. P. (1983). Issues in the application of covariance structure analysis: A further comment. *Journal of Consumer Research*, *9*, 449–450.

Bagozzi, R. P., & Burnkrant, R. E. (1979). Attitude organization and attitude–behavior relationship. *Journal of Personality and Social Psychology*, *37*, 913–929.

Bagozzi, R. P., & Burnkrant, R. E. (1985). Attitude organization and attitude–behavior relation: A reply to Dillon and Kumar. *Journal of Personality and Social Psychology*, *49*, 47–57.

Bagozzi, R. P., & Fornell, C. (1982). Theoretical concepts, measurement, and meaning. In C. Fornell (Ed.), *A second generation of multivariate analysis* (Vol. 2, pp. 24–38). New York: Praeger.

Bakan, D. (1966). The test of significance in psychological research. *Psychological Bulletin*, *66*, 423–437.

Baltes, P. B., & Nesselroade, J. R. (1979). History and rationale of longitudinal research. In J. R. Nesselroade & P. B. Baltes (Eds.), *Longitudinal research in the study of behavior and development* (pp. 1–39). New York: Academic Press.

Barber, B. (1961). Resistance by scientists to scientific discovery. *Science*, *134*, 596–602.

Barber, B. & Fox, R. C. (1958). The case of the floppy-eared rabbits: An instance of serendipity gained and serendipity lost. *American Journal of Sociology*, *64*, 128–136.

Barber, T. X. (1976). *Pitfalls in human research: Ten pivotal points*. New York: Pergamon Press.

Barber, T. X., & Silver, M. J. (1968a). Fact, fiction, and the experimenter bias effect. *Psychological Bulletin Monograph Supplement*, *70*(6, Pt. 2), 1–29.

Barber, T. X., & Silver, M. J. (1968b). Pitfalls in data analysis and interpretation: A reply to Rosenthal. *Psychological Bulletin Monograph Supplement*, *70*(6, Pt. 2), 48–62.

Barcikowski, R. S. (1981). Statistical power with group mean as the unit of analysis. *Journal of Educational Statistics*, *6*, 267–285.

Barlow, D. H., & Hersen, M. (1984). *Single case experimental designs: Strategies for studying behavior change* (2nd ed.). New York: Pergamon Press.

Barnow, B. S., Cain, G. G., & Goldberger, A. S. (1980). Issues in the analysis of selectivity bias. In E. W. Stromsdorfer & G. Farkas (Eds.), *Evaluation studies: Review annual* (Vol. 5, pp. 43–59). Newbury Park, CA: Sage.

Barrett, J. P. (1974). The coefficient of

determination—some limitations. *The American Statistician, 28*(1), 19–20.

Bartlett, M. S. (1950). Tests of significance in factor analysis. *British Journal of Psychology (Statistical Section), 3*, 77–85.

Basham, R. B. (1986). Scientific and practical advantages of comparative design in psychotherapy outcome research. *Journal of Consulting and Clinical Psychology, 54*, 88–94.

Bass, B. M. (1955). Authoritarianism or acquiescence? *Journal of Abnormal and Social Psychology, 51*, 616–623.

Bateson, N. (1984). *Data construction in social surveys.* London: Allen & Unwin.

Baumeister, R. F. (1988). Should we stop studying sex differences altogether? *American Psychologist, 43*, 1092–1095.

Baumrind, D. (1983). Specious causal attributions in the social sciences: The reformulated stepping-stone theory of heroin use as exemplar. *Journal of Personality and Social Psychology, 45*, 1289–1298.

Beauchamp, T. L., Faden, R. R., Wallace, R. J., & Walters, L. (Eds.). (1982). *Ethical issues in social science research.* Baltimore: Johns Hopkins University Press.

Beaver, W. T. (1984). Editorial: Caffeine revisited. *The Journal of the American Medical Association, 251*, 1732–1733.

Beere, C. A. (1983). Instruments and measures in a changing, diverse society. In B. L. Richardson & J. Wirtenberg (Eds.), *Sex role research: Measuring social change* (pp. 113–138). New York: Praeger.

Belkin, L. (1984, July 21). Computers cross-checking use of medicines. *The New York Times*, pp. A1, A52.

Bell, E. T. (1945). *The development of mathematics* (2nd ed.). New York: McGraw-Hill.

Belsley, D. A., Kuh, E., & Welsch, R. E. (1980). *Regression diagnostics: Identifying influential data and sources of collinearity.* New York: Wiley.

Bem, S. L. (1974). The measurement of psychological androgyny. *Journal of Consulting and Clinical Psychology, 42*, 155–162.

Bem, S. L. (1975). Sex role adaptability: One consequence of psychological androgyny. *Journal of Personality and Social Psychology, 31*, 634–643.

Bem, S. L., & Lenney, E. (1976). Sex typing and the avoidance of cross-sex behavior. *Journal of Personality and Social Psychology, 33*, 48–54.

Bentler, P. M. (1976). Factor analysis. In P. M. Bentler, D. J. Lettieri, & G. A. Austin (Eds.), *Data analysis strategies and designs for substance abuse research* (pp. 139–158). Washington, DC: U.S. Government Printing Office.

Bentler, P. M. (1982a). Confirmatory factor analysis via noniterative estimation: A fast, inexpensive method. *Journal of Marketing Research, 19*, 417–424.

Bentler, P. M. (1982b). Linear systems with multiple levels and types of latent variables. In K. G. Jöreskog & H. Wold (Eds.), *Systems under indirect observation: Causality, structure, prediction* (Part I, pp. 101–130). Amsterdam: North-Holland.

Bentler, P. M. (1984). Structural equation models in longitudinal research. In S. A. Mednick, M. Harway, & K. M. Finello (Eds.), *Handbook of longitudinal research* (Vol. 1, pp. 88–105). New York: Praeger.

Bentler, P. M. (1985). *Theory and implementation of EQS. A structural equations program.* Los Angeles: BMDP Statistical Software.

Bentler, P. M. (1986). *Lagrange Multiplier and Wald Tests for EQS and EQS/PC.* Los Angeles: BMDP Statistical Software.

Bentler, P. M. (1987). Drug use and personality in adolescence and young adulthood: Structural models with nonnormal variables. *Child Development, 58*, 65–79.

Bentler, P. M., & Bonett, D. G. (1980). Significance tests and goodness of fit in the analysis of covariance structures. *Psychological Bulletin, 88*, 588–606.

Berger, P. L., & Luckmann, T. (1967). *The social construction of reality: A treatise in the sociology of knowledge.* New York: Anchor Books.

Bergmann, G. (1954). Sense and nonsense in operationism. In P. G. Frank (Ed.), *The validation of scientific theories* (pp. 41–52). Boston: Beacon Press.

Berk, K. N. (1987). Effective microcomputer statistical software. *The American Statistician, 41*, 222–228.

Berk, R. A. (1979). Generalizability of behavioral observations: A clarification of interobserver agreement and interobserver reliability. *American Journal of Mental Deficiency, 83*, 460–472.

Berk, R. A. (Ed.). (1982). *Handbook of methods for detecting test bias.* Baltimore: Johns Hopkins University Press.

Berk, R. A. (1988). Causal inference for sociological data. In N. J. Smelser (Ed.), *Hand-*

book of sociology (pp. 155–172). Newbury Park, CA: Sage.

Berk, R. A., & Rauma, D. (1983). Capitalizing on nonrandom assignment to treatments: A regression-discontinuity evaluation of a crime-control program. *Journal of the American Statistical Association, 78,* 21–27.

Berkowitz, L. (1983). Preface. In L. Berkowitz (Ed.), *Advances in experimental social psychology* (Vol. 16, pp. ix-x). New York: Academic Press.

Berkowitz, L., & Donnerstein, E. (1982). External validity is more than skin deep: Some answers to criticisms of laboratory experiments. *American Psychologist, 37,* 245–257.

Berkson, J. (1947). "Cost-Utility" as a measure of the efficiency of a test. *Journal of the American Statistical Association, 42,* 246–255.

Berliner, D. C., & Cahen, L. S. (1973). Trait-treatment interaction and learning. In F. N. Kerlinger (Ed.), *Review of research in education 1* (pp. 58–94). Itasca, IL: Peacock.

Bernstein, I. N., Bohrnstedt, G. W., & Borgatta, E. F. (1975). External validity and evaluation research. A codification of problems. *Sociological Methods & Research, 4,* 101–128.

Berry, W. D. (1984). *Nonrecursive causal models.* Newbury Park, CA: Sage.

Berry, W. D., & Lewis-Beck, M. S. (Eds.). (1986). *New tools for social scientists: Advances and applications in research methods.* Newbury Park, CA: Sage.

Bersoff, D. N. (1981). Testing and the law. *American Psychologist, 36,* 1047–1056.

Beveridge, W. I. B. (1980). *Seeds of discovery.* New York: Norton.

Bhaskar, R. (1978). *A realist theory of science.* Atlantic Highlands, NJ: Humanities Press.

Bibby, J. (1977). The general linear model—A cautionary tale. In C. A. O'Muircheartaigh & C. Payne (Eds.), *The analysis of survey data* (Vol. 2, pp. 35–79). New York: Wiley.

Bickman, L. (1988). Some failures of basic social psychology. [Review of *Advances in applied social psychology* (Vol. 3)]. *Contemporary Psychology, 33,* 67–68.

Bickman, L., & Henchy, T. (Eds.). (1972). *Beyond the laboratory: Field research in social psychology.* New York: McGraw-Hill.

Bielby, W. T. (1986a). Arbitrary metrics in multiple-indicator models of latent variables. *Sociological Methods & Research, 15,* 3–23.

Bielby, W. T. (1986b). Arbitrary normalizations:

Comments on issues raised by Sobel, Arminger, and Henry. *Sociological Methods & Research, 15,* 62–63.

Binder, A. (1959). Considerations of the place of assumptions in correlational analysis. *American Psychologist, 14,* 504–510.

Bingham, W. V. D., & Moore, B. V. (1941). *How to interview.* New York: Harper & Brothers.

Bishop, G. F., Oldendick, R. W., Tuchfarber, A. J., & Bennett, S. E. (1980). Pseudo-opinions on public affairs. *Public Opinion Quarterly, 44,* 198–209.

Bishop, G. F., Tuchfarber, A. J., & Oldendick, R. W. (1986). Opinions on fictitious issues: The pressure to answer questions. *Public Opinion Quarterly, 50,* 240–250.

Blalock, H. M. (1964). *Causal inferences in non-experimental research.* Chapel Hill: University of North Carolina Press.

Blalock, H. M. (1968). Theory building and causal inference. In H. M. Blalock & A. B. Blalock (Eds.), *Methodology in social research* (pp. 155–198). New York: McGraw-Hill.

Blalock, H. M. (1969). Multiple indicators and the causal approach to measurement error. *American Journal of Sociology, 75,* 264–272.

Blalock, H. M. (1971). Causal models involving unmeasured variables in stimulus–response situations. In H. M. Blalock (Ed.), *Causal models in the social sciences* (pp. 335–347). Chicago: Aldine.

Blalock, H. M. (1982). *Conceptualization and measurement in the social sciences.* Newbury Park, CA: Sage.

Blalock, H. M. (Ed.). (1985a). *Causal models in panel and experimental designs.* New York: Aldine.

Blalock, H. M. (Ed.). (1985b). *Causal models in the social sciences* (2nd ed.). Chicago: Aldine.

Blalock, H. M., Wells, C. S., & Carter, L. F. (1970). Statistical estimation with measurement error. In E. F. Borgatta & G. W. Bohrnstedt (Eds.), *Sociological methodology 1970* (pp. 75–103). San Francisco: Jossey-Bass.

Blashfield, R. K. (1980). The growth of cluster analysis: Tryon, Ward, and Johnson. *Multivariate Behavioral Research, 15,* 439–458.

Blashfield, R. K., & Aldenderfer, M. S. (1978). The literature on cluster analysis. *Multivariate Behavioral Research, 13,* 271–295.

Bock, R. D. (1975). *Multivariate statistical meth-*

ods in behavioral research. New York: McGraw-Hill.

Bock, R. D., & Jones, L. V. (1968). *The measurement and prediction of judgment and choice*. San Francisco: Holden-Day.

Bodner, G. A. (1983, July 22). Should statistics alone be allowed to prove discrimination? *The Chronicle of Higher Education*, p. 56.

Bogdan, R., & Taylor, S. J. (1975). *Introduction to qualitative research methods: A phenomenological approach to the social sciences*. New York: Wiley.

Bohr, H. (1967). My father. In S. Rozental (Ed.), *Niels Bohr: His life and work as seen by his friends and colleagues* (pp. 325–339). New York: Wiley.

Bohrnstedt, G. W. (1969). Observations on the measurement of change. In E. F. Borgatta & G. W. Bohrnstedt (Eds.), *Sociological methodology 1969* (pp. 113–133). San Francisco: Jossey-Bass.

Bohrnstedt, G. W. (1983). Measurement. In P. H. Rossi, J. D. Wright, & A. B. Anderson (Eds.), *Handbook of survey research* (pp. 69–121). New York: Academic Press.

Bohrnstedt, G. W., & Borgatta, E. F. (1981). Foreward. In G. W. Bohrnstedt & E. F. Borgatta (Eds.), *Social measurement: Current issues* (pp. 9–20). Newbury Park, CA: Sage.

Bohrnstedt, G. W., & Carter, T. M. (1971). Robustness in regression analysis. In H. L. Costner (Ed.), *Sociological methodology 1971* (pp. 118–146). San Francisco: Jossey-Bass.

Bollen, K. A. (1980). Issues in the comparative measurement of political democracy. *American Sociological Review*, *45*, 370–390.

Bollen, K. A. (1987). Total, direct, and indirect effects in structural equation models. In C. C. Clogg (Ed.), *Sociological methodology 1987* (pp. 37–69). Washington, DC: American Sociological Association.

Bollen, K. A. (1989). *Structural equations with latent variables*. New York: Wiley.

Bollen, K. A., & Grandjean, B. D. (1981). The dimension(s) of democracy: Further issues in the measurement and effects of political democracy. *American Sociological Review*, *46*, 651–659.

Bollen, K. A., & Grandjean, B. D. (1983). Issues of theory, issues of fact. *American Sociological Review*, *48*, 138–140.

Bollen, K. A., & Jackman, R. W. (1985). Regression diagnostics: An expository treatment of outliers and influential cases. *Sociological Methods & Research*, *13*, 510–542.

Bollen, K. A., & Jöreskog, K. G. (1985). Uniqueness does not imply identification. A note on confirmatory factor analysis. *Sociological Methods & Research*, *14*, 155–163.

Boomsma, A. (1987). The robustness of maximum likelihood estimation in structural equation models. In P. Cuttance & R. Ecob (Eds.), *Structural modeling by example: Applications in educational, sociological, and behavioral research* (pp. 160–188). New York: Cambridge University Press.

Borgatta, E. F. (1968). My student, the purist: A lament. *Sociological Quarterly*, *8*, 29–34.

Borgatta, E. F., & Bohrnstedt, G. W. (1981). Levels of measurement. Once over again. In G. W. Bohrnstedt & E. F. Borgatta (Eds.), *Social measurement: Current issues* (pp. 23–37). Newbury Park, CA: Sage.

Borgatta, E. F., Kercher, K., & Stull, D. E. (1986). A cautionary note on the use of principal components analysis. *Sociological Methods & Research*, *15*, 160–168.

Borich, G. D., Godbout, R. C., & Wunderlich, K. W. (1976). *The analysis of aptitude–treatment interactions: Computer programs and calculations*. Chicago: International Educational Services.

Boring, E. G. (1954). The nature and history of experimental control. *American Journal of Psychology*, *67*, 573–589.

Boruch, R. F. (1975). On common contentions about randomized field experiments. In R. F. Boruch & H. W. Riecken (Eds.), *Experimental testing of public policy: The proceedings of the 1974 Social Science Research Council Conference on Social Experimentation* (pp. 107–142). Boulder, CO: Westview Press.

Bowerman, B. L., & O'Connell, R. T. (1979). *Time series and forecasting*. Boston, MA: Duxbury Press.

Bowers, K. S. (1973). Situationism is psychology: An analysis and a critique. *Psychological Review*, *80*, 307–336.

Box, G. E. P. (1966). Use and abuse of regression. *Technometrics*, *8*, 625–629.

Box, G. E. P. (1976). Science and statistics. *Journal of the American Statistical Association*, *71*, 791–799.

Box, G. E. P., Hunter, W. G., & Hunter, J. S. (1978). *Statistics for experimenters. An intro-*

duction to design, data analysis, and model building. New York: Wiley.

Bracht, G. H., & Glass, G. V. (1968). The external validity of experiments. *American Educational Research Journal, 5*, 437–474.

Bradburn, N. M. (1982). Discrepancies between concepts and their measurements: The urbanrural example. In W. H. Kruskal (Ed.), *The social sciences: Their nature and uses* (pp. 137–148). Chicago: University of Chicago Press.

Bradburn, N. M., Sudman, S., & associates. (1979). *Improving interview method and questionnaire design*. San Francisco: Jossey-Bass.

Braithwaite, R. B. (1960). *Scientific explanation: A study of the function of theory, probability and law in science*. New York: Harper Torchbooks.

Brandt, R. M. (1972). *Studying behavior in natural settings*. New York: Holt, Rinehart & Winston.

Braunwald, E. (1987). On analysing scientific fraud. *Nature, 325*, 215–216.

Brennan, R. L. (1983). *Elements of generalizability theory*. Iowa City, IA: American College Testing.

Brenner, M. (1978). Interviewing: The social phenomenology of a research instrument. In M. Brenner, P. Marsh, & M. Brenner (Eds.), *The social contexts of method* (pp. 122–139). New York: St. Martin's Press.

Brenner, M. (1981a). Patterns of social structure in the research interview. In M. Brenner (Ed.), *Social method and social life* (pp. 115–158). London: Academic Press.

Brenner, M. (Ed.). (1981b). *Social method and social life*. London: Academic Press.

Brenner, M. (1982). Response effects of "role-restricted" characteristics of the interviewer. In W. Dijkstra & J. van der Zouwen (Eds.), *Response behaviour in the survey-interview* (pp. 131–165). London: Academic Press.

Brenner, M., Marsh, P., & Brenner, M. (Eds.). (1978). *The social contexts of method*. New York: St. Martin's Press.

Brewer, J. K. (1972). On the power of statistical tests in the *American Educational Research Journal. American Educational Research Journal, 9*, 391–401.

Bridgman, P. W. (1927). *The logic of modern physics*. New York: Macmillan.

Bridgman, P. W. (1945). Some general principles of operational analysis. *Psychological Review, 52*, 246–249.

Bridgman, P. W. (1954). The present state of operationalism. In P. G. Frank (Ed.), *The validation of scientific theories* (pp. 74–79). Boston: Beacon Press.

Bridgman, P. W. (1959). *The way things are*. New York: Viking.

Bridgman, P. W. (1980). *Reflections of a physicist*. New York: Arno Press.

Briggs, S. R., & Cheek, J. M. (1986). The role of factor analysis in the development and evaluation of personality scales. *Journal of Personality, 54*, 106–148.

Britell, J. K. (1980, September 7). Hazards in social research. *The New York Times*, p. 18, Educ.

Brodbeck, M. (1959). Models, meaning, and theories. In L. Gross (Ed.), *Symposium on sociological theory* (pp. 373–403). New York: Harper & Row.

Brodbeck, M. (1963). Logic and scientific method in research on teaching. In N. L. Gage (Ed.), *Handbook of research on teaching* (pp. 44–93). Chicago: Rand McNally.

Brodbeck, M. (Ed.). (1968). *Readings in the philosophy of the social sciences*. New York: Macmillan.

Brody, J. E. (1983a, March 23). Influential theory on 'bonding' at birth is now questioned. *The New York Times*, pp. C1, C8.

Brody, J. E. (1983b, May 27). Masters and Johnson defend pioneer sex therapy research. *The New York Times*, p. 13.

Bronfenbrenner, U. (1974). Developmental research, public policy, and the ecology of childhood. *Child Development, 45*, 1–5.

Bronfenbrenner, U. (1979). *The ecology of human development: Experiments by nature and design*. Cambridge, MA: Harvard University Press.

Bronowski, J. (1965). *Science and human values* (rev. ed.). New York: Harper Torchbooks.

Bronowski, J. (1973). *The ascent of man*. Boston: Little, Brown.

Brown, R. (1965). *Social psychology*. New York: Free Press.

Browne, M. W. (1982). Covariance structures. In D. M. Hawkins (Ed.), *Topics in applied multivariate analysis* (pp. 72–141). Cambridge, UK: Cambridge University Press.

Browne, M. W. (1988, December 20). Is a math proof a proof if no one can check it? *The New York Times*, pp. C1, C17.

Bryant, F. B., & Veroff, J. (1984). Dimensions of subjective mental health in American men and women. *Journal of Health and Social Behavior*, *25*, 116–135.

Bryk, A. S., Strenio, J. F., & Weisberg, H. I. (1980). A method for estimating treatment effects when individuals are growing. *Journal of Educational Statistics*, *5*, 5–34.

Bryk, A. S., & Weisberg, H. I. (1976). Value-added analysis: A dynamic approach to the estimation of treatment effects. *Journal of Educational Statistics*, *1*, 127–155.

Bryk, A. S., & Weisberg, H. I. (1977). Use of the nonequivalent control group design when subjects are growing. *Psychological Bulletin*, *84*, 950–962.

Brzezinski, E. J. (1984). Microcomputers and testing: Where are we and how did we get there? *Educational Measurement: Issues and Practice*, *3*(2), 7–10.

Bugelski, B. R. (1981). Life and the laboratory. In I. Silverman (Ed.), *Generalizing from laboratory to life* (pp. 51–65). San Francisco: Jossey-Bass.

Bunge, M. (1979). *Causality and modern science* (3rd ed.). New York: Dover.

Burke, C. J. (1953). A brief note on one-tailed tests. *Psychological Bulletin*, *50*, 384–387.

Burke, C. J. (1963). Measurement scales and statistical models. In M. H. Marx (Ed.), *Theories in contemporary psychology* (pp. 147–159). New York: Collier-Macmillan.

Bynner, J. (1981). Use of LISREL in the solution to a higher-order factor problem in a study of adolescent self-images. *Quality and Quantity*, *15*, 523–540.

Bynner, J., & Coxhead, P. (1979). Some problems in the analysis of semantic differential data. *Human Relations*, *32*, 367–385.

Byrne, B. M., & Shavelson, R. J. (1987). Adolescent self-concept: Testing the assumption of equivalent structure across gender. *American Educational Research Journal*, *24*, 365–385.

Cain, G. G. (1975). Regression and selection models to improve nonexperimental comparisons. In C. A. Bennett & A. A. Lumsdaine (Eds.), *Evaluation and experiment: Some critical issues in assessing social programs* (pp. 297–317). New York: Academic Press.

Campbell, D. T. (1957). Factors relevant to the validity of experiments in social settings. *Psychological Bulletin*, *54*, 297–312.

Campbell, D. T. (1960). Recommendations for APA test standards regarding construct, trait, or discriminant validity. *American Psychologist*, *15*, 546–553.

Campbell, D. T. (1969a). Prospective: Artifact and control. In R. Rosenthal & R. L. Rosnow (Eds.), *Artifact in behavioral research* (pp. 351–382). New York: Academic Press.

Campbell, D. T. (1969b). Reforms as experiments. *American Psychologist*, *24*, 409–429.

Campbell, D. T. (1984a). Can we be scientific in applied social science? In R. F. Conner, D. G. Altman, & C. Jackson (Eds.), *Evaluation studies: Review annual* (Vol. 9, pp. 26–48). Newbury Park, CA: Sage.

Campbell, D. T. (1984b). Foreword. In W. M. K. Trochim, *Research design for program evaluation: The regression-discontinuity approach* (pp. 15–43). Newbury Park, CA: Sage.

Campbell, D. T., & Boruch, R. F. (1975). Making the case for randomized assignment to treatments by considering the alternatives: Six ways in which quasi-experimental evaluations in compensatory education tend to underestimate effects. In C. A. Bennett & A. A. Lumsdaine (Eds.), *Evaluation and experiment: Some critical issues in assessing social programs* (pp. 195–296). New York: Academic Press.

Campbell, D. T., & Erlebacher, A. (1970). How regression artifacts in quasi-experimental evaluations can mistakenly make compensatory education look harmful. In J. Hellmuth (Ed.), *Disadvantaged child. Compensatory education: A national debate* (Vol. 3, pp. 185–210). New York: Bruner/Mazel.

Campbell, D. T., & Fiske, D. W. (1959). Convergent and discriminant validation by the multitrait-multimethod matrix. *Psychological Bulletin*, *56*, 81–105.

Campbell, D. T., & Stanley, J. C. (1963). Experimental and quasi-experimental designs for research on teaching. In N. L. Gage (Ed.), *Handbook of research on teaching* (pp. 171–246). Chicago: Rand McNally.

Campbell, J. P. (1982). Editorial: Some remarks from the outgoing editor. *Journal of Applied Psychology*, *67*, 691–700.

Campbell, N. (1928). *An account of the principles of measurement and calculation*. London: Longmans, Green.

Campbell, N. (1952). *What is science?* New York: Dover.

Cannell, C. F. (1985a). Experiments in the improvement of response accuracy. In T. W. Beed & R. J. Stimson (Eds.), *Survey inter-*

viewing: Theory and techniques (pp. 24–62). Sydney: Allen & Unwin.

Cannell, C. F. (1985b). Interviewing in telephone surveys. In T. W. Beed & R. J. Stimson (Eds.), *Survey interviewing: Theory and techniques* (pp. 63–84). Sydney: Allen & Unwin.

Cannell, C. F., & Kahn, R. L. (1968). Interviewing. In G. Lindzey & E. Aronson (Eds.), *Handbook of social psychology* (Vol. 2, 2nd ed., pp. 526–595). Reading, MA: Addison-Wesley.

Cannell, C. F., Miller, P. V., & Oksenberg, L. (1981). Research on interviewing techniques. In S. Leinhardt (Ed.), *Sociological methodology 1981* (pp. 389–437). San Francisco: Jossey-Bass.

Cantril, H. (1944). *Gauging public opinion*. Princeton: Princeton University Press.

Caplan, R. D., Naidu, R. K., & Tripathi, R. C. (1984). Coping and defense: Constellations vs. components. *Journal of Health and Social Behavior, 25,* 303–320.

Carmines, E. G., & McIver, J. P. (1981). Analyzing models with unobserved variables: Analysis of covariance structures. In G. W. Bohrnstedt & E. F. Borgatta (Eds.), *Social measurement: Current issues* (pp. 65–115). Newbury Park, CA: Sage.

Carr, E. H. (1967). *What is history?* New York: Knopf.

Carroll, L. (1960). *Alice's adventures in wonderland & through the looking-glass*. New York: New American Library.

Carroll, R. M., & Nordholm, L. A. (1975). Sampling characteristics of Kelly's ϵ^2 and Hays' ω^2. *Educational and Psychological Measurement, 35,* 541–554.

Carter, D. S. (1979). Comparison of different shrinkage formulas in estimating population multiple correlation coefficients. *Educational and Psychological Measurement, 39,* 261–266.

Carter, L. F. (1971). Inadvertent sociological theory. *Social Forces, 50,* 12–25.

Carver, R. P. (1978). The case against statistical significance testing. *Harvard Educational Review, 48,* 378–399.

Cattell, R. B. (1944). Psychological measurement: Normative, ipsative, interactive. *Psychological Review, 51,* 292–303.

Cattell, R. B. (1965). Factor analysis: An introduction to essentials. I. The purpose and underlying models. *Biometrics, 21,* 190–215.

Cattell, R. B. (1966a). The principles of experimental design and analysis in relation to theory building. In R. B. Cattell (Ed.), *Handbook of multivariate experimental psychology* (pp. 19–66). Chicago: Rand McNally.

Cattell, R. B. (1966b). The scree test for the number of factors. *Sociological Methods & Research, 1,* 245–276.

Cattell, R. B. (1978). *The scientific use of factor analysis in behavioral and life sciences*. New York: Plenum.

Cattell, R. B. (1988). The meaning and strategic use of factor analysis. In J. R. Nesselroade & R. B. Cattell (Eds.), *Handbook of multivariate experimental psychology* (2nd ed., pp. 131–203). New York: Plenum.

Caws, P. (1959). Definition and measurement in physics. In C. W. Churchman & P. Ratoosh (Eds.), *Measurement: Definitions and theories* (pp. 3–17). New York: Wiley.

Chamberlin, T. C. (1965). The method of multiple working hypotheses. *Science, 148,* 754–759. (Original work published 1890)

Chapanis, N. P., & Chapanis, A. (1964). Cognitive dissonance: Five years later. *Psychological Bulletin, 61,* 1–22.

Chatterjee, S., & Hadi, A. S. (1986). Influential observations, high leverage points, and outliers in linear regression. *Statistical Science, 1,* 379–393.

Chatterjee, S., & Price, B. (1977). *Regression analysis by example*. New York: Wiley.

Chein, I. (1981). An introduction to sampling. In L. H. Kidder, *Selltiz, Wrightsman and Cook's research methods in social relations* (4th ed., pp. 419–444). New York: Holt, Rinehart & Winston.

Chen, M. S., & Land, K. C. (1986). Testing the health belief model: LISREL analysis of alternative models of causal relationships between health beliefs and preventive dental behavior. *Social Psychology Quarterly, 49,* 45–60.

Chernoff, P. R. (1978, December 27). For a Nobel math prize. *The New York Times,* p. A23.

Christensen, L. (1977). The negative subject: Myth, reality, or a prior experimental experience effect? *Journal of Personality and Social Psychology, 35,* 392–400.

Christie, R., & Garcia, J. (1951). Subcultural variation in authoritarian personality. *Journal of Abnormal and Social Psychology, 46,* 457–469.

Christie, R., Havel, J., & Seidenberg, B. (1958). Is the F scale irreversible? *Journal of Abnormal and Social Psychology, 56,* 143–159.

Christie, R., & Jahoda, M. (Eds.). (1954). *Stud-*

ies in the scope and method of "The authoritarian personality." Glencoe, IL: Free Press.

Churchman, C. W., & Ratoosh, P. (Eds.). (1959). *Measurement: Definitions and theories.* New York: Wiley.

Cleary, T. A. (1968). Test bias: Prediction of grades of Negro and white students in integrated colleges. *Journal of Educational Measurement, 5,* 115–124.

Cleary, T. A., & Linn, R. L. (1969). Error of measurement and the power of a statistical test. *British Journal of Mathematical and Statistical Psychology, 22,* 49–55.

Cleary, T. A., Linn, R. L., & Walster, G. W. (1970). Effect of reliability and validity on power of statistical tests. In E. F. Borgatta & G. W. Bohrnstedt (Eds.), *Sociological methodology 1970* (pp. 130–138). San Francisco: Jossey-Bass.

Cleveland, W. S., & McGill, R. (1984). The many faces of a scatterplot. *Journal of the American Statistical Association, 79,* 807–822.

Cliff, N. (1982). What is and isn't measurement. In G. Keren (Ed.), *Statistical and methodological issues in psychology and social sciences research* (pp. 3–38). Hillsdale, NJ: Erlbaum.

Cliff, N. (1983). Some cautions concerning the application of causal modeling methods. *Multivariate Behavioral Research, 18,* 115–126.

Cliff, N. (1987). *Analyzing multivariate data.* San Diego: Harcourt Brace Jovanovich.

Coale, A. J., & Stephan, F. F. (1962). The case of the indians and the teen-age widows. *Journal of the American Statistical Association, 57,* 338–347.

Cochran, W. G. (1957). Analysis of covariance: Its nature and uses. *Biometrics, 13,* 261–281.

Cochran, W. G. (1965). The planning of observational studies of human populations. *Journal of the Royal Statistical Society* (Series A), *128,* 234–255.

Cochran, W. G. (1968). Errors of measurement in statistics. *Technometrics, 10,* 637–666.

Cochran, W. G. (1970). Some effects of errors of measurement on multiple correlation. *Journal of the American Statistical Association, 65,* 22–34.

Cochran, W. G. (1977). *Sampling techniques* (3rd ed.). New York: Wiley.

Cochran, W. G. (1983). *Planning and analysis of observational studies.* New York: Wiley.

Cochran, W. G., & Cox, G. M. (1950). *Experimental designs.* New York: Wiley.

Cohen, J. (1962). The statistical power of abnormal-social psychological research. *Journal of Abnormal and Social Psychology, 65,* 145–153.

Cohen, J. (1965). Some statistical issues in psychological research. In B. B. Wolman (Ed.), *Handbook of clinical psychology* (pp. 95–121). New York: McGraw-Hill.

Cohen, J. (1968). Multiple regression as a general data-analytic system. *Psychological Bulletin, 70,* 426–443.

Cohen, J. (1973a). Eta-squared and partial eta-squared in fixed factor ANOVA designs. *Educational and Psychological Measurement, 33,* 107–112.

Cohen, J. (1973b). Statistical power analysis and research results. *American Educational Research Journal, 10,* 225–230.

Cohen, J. (1983). The cost of dichotomization. *Applied Psychological Measurement, 7,* 249–253.

Cohen, J. (1988). *Statistical power analysis for the behavioral sciences* (2nd ed.). Hillsdale, NJ: Erlbaum.

Cohen, J., & Cohen, P. (1983). *Applied multiple regression/correlation analysis for the behavioral sciences* (2nd ed.). Hillsdale, NJ: Erlbaum.

Cohen, M. R. (1953). *Reason and nature: An essay on the meaning of scientific method* (2nd ed.). Glencoe, IL: Free Press.

Cohen, M. R., & Nagel, E. (1934). *An introduction to logic and scientific method.* New York: Harcourt, Brace & World.

Cole, D. A. (1987). Utility of confirmatory factor analysis in test validation research. *Journal of Consulting and Clinical Psychology, 55,* 584–594.

Cole, D. A., & Maxwell, S. E. (1985). Multitrait-multimethod comparisons across populations: A confirmatory factor analytic approach. *Multivariate Behavioral Research, 20,* 389–417.

Cole, N. S. (1981). Bias in testing. *American Psychologist, 36,* 1067–1077.

Cole, N. S., & Moss, P. A. (1989). Bias in test use. In R. L. Linn (Ed.), *Educational measurement* (3rd ed., pp. 201–219). New York: Macmillan.

Coleman, J. S., Campbell, E. Q., Hobson, C. J., McPartland, J., Mood, A. M., Weinfeld, F.

D., & York, R. L. (1966). *Equality of educational opportunity*. Washington, DC: U.S. Government Printing Office.

Coleman, J. S., Hoffer, T., & Kilgore, S. (1982). *High school achievement: Public, Catholic, and private schools compared*. New York: Basic Books.

Comrey, A. L. (1973). *A first course in factor analysis*. New York: Academic Press.

Comrey, A. L. (1978). Common methodological problems in factor analytic studies. *Journal of Consulting and Clinical Psychology, 46,* 648–659.

Comrey, A. L., & Montag, I. (1982). Comparison of factor analytic results with two choice and seven choice personality item formats. *Applied Psychological Measurement, 6,* 285–289.

Constantinople, A. (1973). Masculinity-femininity: An exception to a famous dictum? *Psychological Bulletin, 80,* 389–407.

Converse, J. M. (1976). Predicting no opinion in the polls. *Public Opinion Quarterly, 40,* 515–530.

Converse, J. M., & Presser, S. (1986). *Survey questions: Handcrafting the standardized questionnaire*. Newbury Park, CA: Sage.

Converse, J. M., & Schuman, H. (1984). The manner of inquiry: An analysis of survey questions form across organizations and over time. In C. F. Turner & E. Martin (Eds.), *Surveying subjective phenomena* (Vol. 2, pp. 283–316). New York: Russell Sage Foundation.

Converse, P. E. (1970). Attitudes and nonattitudes: Continuation of a dialogue. In E. R. Tufte (Ed.), *The quantitative analysis of social problems* (pp. 168–189). Reading, MA: Addison-Wesley.

Cook, R. D. (1977). Detection of influential observation in linear regression. *Technometrics, 19,* 15–18.

Cook, R. D. (1979). Influential observations in linear regression. *Journal of the American Statistical Association, 74,* 169–174.

Cook, R. D., & Weisberg, S. (1982a). Criticism and influence analysis in regression. In S. Leinhardt (Ed.), *Sociological methodology 1982* (pp. 313–361). San Francisco: Jossey-Bass.

Cook, R. D., & Weisberg, S. (1982b). *Residuals and influence in regression*. New York: Chapman & Hall.

Cook, S. W., & Selltiz, C. (1964). A multiple-indicator approach to attitude measurement. *Psychological Bulletin, 62,* 36–55.

Cook, T. D. (1985). Postpositivist critical multiplism. In R. L. Shotland & M. M. Mark (Eds.), *Social science and social policy* (pp. 21–62). Newbury Park, CA: Sage.

Cook, T. D., & Campbell, D. T. (1976). The design and conduct of quasi-experiments and true experiments in field settings. In M. D. Dunnette (Ed.), *Handbook of industrial and organizational psychology* (pp. 223–325). Chicago: Rand McNally.

Cook, T. D., & Campbell, D. T. (1979). *Quasi-experimentation: Design & analysis issues for field settings*. Chicago: Rand McNally.

Cook, T. D., & Campbell, D. T. (1986). The causal assumptions of quasi-experimental practice. *Synthese, 68,* 141–180.

Cook, T. D., Dintzer, L., & Mark, M. M. (1980). The causal analysis of concomitant time series. In L. Bickman (Ed.), *Applied social psychology* (Vol. 1, pp. 93–135). Newbury Park, CA: Sage.

Cook, T. D., Gruder, C. L., Hennigan, K. M., & Flay, B. R. (1979). History of the sleeper effect: Some logical pitfalls in accepting the null hypothesis. *Psychological Bulletin, 86,* 662–679.

Cooley, W. W., & Lohnes, P. R. (1971). *Multivariate data analysis*. New York: Wiley.

Coombs, C. H. (1950). The concept of reliability and homogeneity. *Educational and Psychological Measurement, 10,* 43–56.

Coombs, C. H. (1953). Theory and methods of social measurement. In L. Festinger & D. Katz (Eds.), *Research methods in the behavioral sciences* (pp. 471–535). New York: Dryden.

Coombs, C. H. (1964). *A theory of data*. New York: Wiley.

Coombs, C. H., & Coombs, L. C. (1976). "Don't know": Item ambiguity or respondent uncertainty. *Public Opinion Quarterly, 40,* 497–514.

Cooper, H. M. (1984). *The integrative research review: A systematic approach*. Newbury Park, CA: Sage.

Cooper, H., & Findley, M. (1982). Expected effect sizes: Estimates for statistical power analysis in social psychology. *Personality and Social Psychology Bulletin, 8,* 168–173.

Copi, I. M. (1972). *Introduction to logic* (4th ed.). New York: Macmillan.

Cornfield, J. (1971). The university group diabetes program: A further statistical analysis of the mortality findings. *Journal of the American Medical Association, 217,* 1676–1687.

Corno, L., & Snow, R. E. (1986). Adapting teaching to individual differences among learners. In M. C. Wittrock (Ed.), *Handbook of research on teaching* (3rd ed., pp. 605–629). New York: Macmillan.

Coser, L. A. (1975). Presidential address: Two methods in search of a substance. *American Sociological Review, 40,* 691–700.

Costner, H. L. (1969). Theory, deduction, and rules of correspondence. *American Journal of Sociology, 75,* 245–263.

Costner, H. L. (1971). Utilizing causal models to discover flaws in experiments. *Sociometry, 34,* 398–410.

Costner, H. L., & Schoenberg, R. (1973). Diagnosing indicator ills in multiple indicator models. In A. S. Goldberger & O. D. Duncan (Eds.), *Structural equation models in the social sciences* (pp. 167–199). New York: Academic Press.

Cotter, K. L., & Raju, N. S. (1982). An evaluation of formula-based population squared cross-validity estimates and factor score estimates in prediction. *Educational and Psychological Measurement, 42,* 493–519.

Couch, A., & Keniston, K. (1960). Yeasayers and naysayers: Agreeing response set as a personality variable. *Journal of Abnormal and Social Psychology, 60,* 151–174.

Cowles, M., & Davis, C. (1982). On the origins of the .05 level of statistical significance. *American Psychologist, 37,* 553–558.

Cox, D. R. (1958). *Planning of experiments.* New York: Wiley.

Cox, E. P. III. (1980). The optimal number of response alternatives for a scale: A review. *Journal of Marketing Research, 17,* 407–422.

Coxhead, P., & Bynner, J. M. (1981). Factor analysis of semantic differential data. *Quality and Quantity, 15,* 553–567.

Coxon, A. P. M. (1982). *The user's guide to multidimensional scaling.* Exeter, NH: Heinemann Educational Books.

Cramer, E. M. (1972). Significance tests and tests of models in multiple regression. *The American Statistician, 26*(4), 26–30.

Cramer, E. M., & Nicewander, W. A. (1979). Some symmetric invariant measures of multivariate association. *Psychometrika, 44,* 43–54.

Crandall, R. (1973). The measurement of self-esteem and related constructs. In J. P. Robinson & P. R. Shaver (Eds.), *Measures of social psychological attitudes* (rev. ed., pp. 45–167). Ann Arbor, MI: Institute for Social Research.

Crano, W. D., & Mendoza, J. L. (1987). Maternal factors that influence children's positive behavior: Demonstration of a structural equation analysis of selected data from the Berkeley growth model. *Child Development, 58,* 38–48.

Crano, W. D., & Messé, L. A. (1985). Assessing and redressing comprehension artifacts in social intervention research. *Evaluation Review, 9,* 144–172.

Crocker, L., & Algina, J. (1986). *Introduction to classical and modern test theory.* New York: Holt, Rinehart & Winston.

Cronbach, L. J. (1946). Response set and test validity. *Educational and Psychological Measurement, 6,* 475–494.

Cronbach, L. J. (1951). Coefficient alpha and the internal structure of tests. *Psychometrika, 16,* 297–334.

Cronbach, L. J. (1957). The two disciplines of scientific psychology. *American Psychologist, 12,* 671–684.

Cronbach, L. J. (1970). *Essentials of psychological testing* (3rd ed.). New York: Harper & Row.

Cronbach, L. J. (1971). Test validation. In R. L. Thorndike (Ed.), *Educational measurement* (2nd ed., pp. 443–507). Washington, DC: American Council on Education.

Cronbach, L. J. (1976a). Five decades of public controversy over mental testing. In C. Frankel (Ed.), *Controversies and decisions: The social sciences and public policy* (pp. 123–147). New York: Russell Sage Foundation.

Cronbach, L. J. (1976b). *Research on classrooms and schools: Formulation of questions, design, and analysis* (Occasional paper). Stanford, CA: Stanford Evaluation Consortium, Stanford University.

Cronbach, L. J. (1980). Selection theory for a political world. *Public Personnel Management, 9,* 37–50.

Cronbach, L. J. (1982). Prudent aspirations for social inquiry. In W. H. Kruskal (Ed.), *The social sciences: Their nature and uses* (pp. 61–81). Chicago: University of Chicago Press.

Cronbach, L. J. (1986). Social inquiry by and for earthlings. In D. W. Fiske & R. A. Shweder

(Eds.), *Metatheory in social science: Pluralism and subjectivities* (pp. 83–107). Chicago: University of Chicago Press.

Cronbach, L. J., & Furby, L. (1970). How we should measure "change"—or should we? *Psychological Bulletin, 74,* 68–80.

Cronbach, L. J., & Gleser, G. C. (1965). *Psychological tests and personnel decisions* (2nd ed.). Urbana, IL: University of Illinois Press.

Cronbach, L. J., Gleser, G. C., Nanda, H., & Rajaratnam, N. (1972). *The dependability of behavioral measurements: Theory of generalizability for scores and profiles.* New York: Wiley.

Cronbach, L. J., & Meehl, P. E. (1955). Construct validity in psychological tests. *Psychological Bulletin, 52,* 281–302.

Cronbach, L. J., Rogosa, D. R., Floden, R. E., & Price, G. G. (1977). *Analysis of covariance in nonrandomized experiments: Parameters affecting bias* (Occasional paper). Stanford, CA: Stanford Evaluation Consortium, Stanford University.

Cronbach, L. J., & Snow, R. E. (1977). *Aptitudes and instructional methods: A handbook for research on interactions.* New York: Irvington.

Cryer, J. D. (1986). *Time series analysis.* Boston: Duxbury Press.

Cunningham, W. R. (1980). Age changes in the factor structure of intellectual abilities in adulthood and old age. *Educational and Psychological Measurement, 40,* 271–290.

Cureton, E. E. (1951). Validity. In E. F. Lindquist (Ed.), *Educational measurement* (pp. 621–692). Washington, DC: American Council on Education.

Cureton, E. E., & D'Agostino, R. B. (1983). *Factor analysis: An applied approach.* Hillsdale, NJ: Erlbaum.

Cuttance, P., & Ecob, R. (Eds.). (1987). *Structural modeling by example: Applications in educational, sociological, and behavioral research.* New York: Cambridge University Press.

Dalenius, T. (1957). *Sampling in Sweden: Contributions to the methods and theories of sample survey practice.* Stockholm: Almqvist & Wiksell.

Dalenius, T., & Hodges, J. (1959). Minimum variance stratification. *Journal of the American Statistical Association, 54,* 88–101.

Dallal, G. E. (1988). Statistical microcomputing—like it is. *The American Statistician, 42,* 212–216.

Das, J. P., & Kirby, J. R. (1978). The case of the wrong exemplar: A reply to Humphreys. *Journal of Educational Psychology, 70,* 877–879.

Davis, J. A. (1971). *Elementary survey analysis.* Englewood Cliffs, NJ: Prentice Hall.

Davis, J. A. (1985). *The logic of causal order.* Newbury Park, CA: Sage.

Dawes, R. M. (1972). *Fundamentals of attitude measurement.* New York: Wiley.

Dawes, R. M., & Smith, T. L. (1985). Attitude and opinion measurement. In G. Lindzey & E. Aronson (Eds.), *Handbook of social psychology* (Vol. 1, 3rd ed., pp. 509–566). New York: Random House.

Deaux, K., & Major, B. (1987). Putting gender into context: An interactive model of gender-related behavior. *Psychological Review, 94,* 369–389.

DeGracie, J. S., & Fuller, W. A. (1972). Estimation of the slope of covariance when the concomitant variable is measured with error. *Journal of the American Statistical Association, 67,* 930–937.

de Groot, A. D. (1969). *Methodology: Foundations of inference and research in the behavioral sciences.* The Hague: Mouton.

DeLamater, J. (1982). Response-effects of question content. In W. Dijkstra & J. van der Zouwen (Eds.), *Response behaviour in the survey-interview* (pp. 13–48). London: Academic Press.

Denzin, N. K. (1978). *The research act: A theoretical introduction to sociological methods* (2nd ed.). New York: McGraw-Hill.

de Unamuno, M. (1954). *Tragic sense of life* (J. E. Crawford Flitch, Trans.). New York: Dover.

Dewey, J. (1916). *Democracy and education: An introduction to the philosophy of education.* New York: Macmillan.

Dillon, W. R., & Goldstein, M. (1984). *Multivariate analysis: Methods and applications.* New York: Wiley.

Dillon, W. R., & Kumar, A. (1985). Attitude organization and the attitude-behavior relation: A critique of Bagozzi and Burnkrant's reanalysis of Fishbein and Ajzen. *Journal of Personality and Social Psychology, 49,* 33–46.

Dipboye, R. L., & Flanagan, M. F. (1979). Research settings in industrial and organizational psychology. Are findings in the field more generalizable than in the laboratory? *American Psychologist, 34,* 141–150.

Dipboye, R. L., & Flanagan, M. F. (1980). Reply

to Willems and Howard. *American Psychologist*, *35*, 388–390.

Dixon, P. N., Bobo, M., & Stevick, R. A. (1984). Response differences and preferences for all-category-defined and end-defined Likert formats. *Educational and Psychological Measurement*, *44*, 61–66.

Doby, J. T. (1967). Explanation and prediction. In J. T. Doby (Ed.), *An introduction to social research* (2nd ed., pp. 50–62). New York: Appleton-Century-Crofts.

Dorf, R. C. (1969). *Matrix algebra: A programmed introduction*. New York: Wiley.

Dorfman, D. D. (1978). The Cyril Burt question: New findings. *Science*, *201*, 1177–1186.

Dorn, H. F. (1953). Philosophy of inferences from retrospective studies. *American Journal of Public Health*, *43*, 677–683.

Downs, G. W., & Rocke, D. M. (1979). Interpreting heteroscedasticity. *American Journal of Political Science*, *23*, 816–828.

Draper, N., & Smith, H. (1981). *Applied regression analysis* (2nd ed.). New York: Wiley.

DuBois, P. H. (1957). *Multivariate correlational analysis*. New York: Harper & Brothers.

DuBois, P. H. (1970). *A history of psychological testing*. Boston: Allyn & Bacon.

Dudek, F. J. (1979). The continuing misinterpretation of the standard error of measurement. *Psychological Bulletin*, *86*, 335–337.

Duncan, O. D. (1975). *Introduction to structural equation models*. New York: Academic Press.

Duncan, O. D. (1978). Multiway contingency analysis. *Contemporary Sociology*, *7*, 403–405.

Duncan, O. D. (1984). *Notes on social measurement: Historical and critical*. New York: Russell Sage Foundation.

Duncan, O. D. (1988). Some ancient anticipations of probability. *Chance*, *1*(3), 16–24.

Duncan, S., Rosenberg, M. J., & Finkelstein, J. (1969). The paralanguage of experimenter bias. *Sociometry*, *32*, 207–219.

Dunn, O. J. (1961). Multiple comparisons among means. *Journal of the American Statistical Association*, *56*, 52–64.

Dunnett, C. W. (1955). A multiple comparison procedure for comparing several treatments with a control. *Journal of the American Statistical Association*, *50*, 1096–1121.

Dunnette, M. D., & Borman, W. C. (1979). Personnel selection and classification systems. *Annual Review of Psychology*, *30*, 477–525.

Dunn-Rankin, P. (1983). *Scaling methods*. Hillsdale, NJ: Erlbaum.

Durkheim, E. (1938). *The rules of sociological method* (8th ed.). (S. A. Solovay & J. H. Mueller, Trans.). Chicago: University of Chicago Press.

Dusek, J. B. (Ed.) (in conjunction with Hall, V. C., & Meyer, W. J.). (1985). *Teacher expectancies*. Hillsdale, NJ: Erlbaum.

du Toit, S. H. C., Steyn, A. G. W., & Stumpf, R. H. (1986). *Graphical exploratory data analysis*. New York: Springer-Verlag.

Dutton, D. G., & Lake, R. A. (1973). Threat of own prejudice and reverse discrimination in interracial situations. *Journal of Personality and Social Psychology*, *28*, 94–100.

Dwyer, J. H. (1983). *Statistical models for the social and behavioral sciences*. New York: Oxford University Press.

Dziuban, C. D., & Shirkey, E. C. (1974). When is a correlation matrix appropriate for factor analysis? Some decision rules. *Psychological Bulletin*, *81*, 358–361.

Eagly, A. H. (1987). Reporting sex differences. *American Psychologist*, *42*, 756–757.

Ecob, R. (1987). Applications of structural equation modeling to longitudinal educational data. In P. Cuttance & R. Ecob (Eds.), *Structural modeling by example: Applications in educational, sociological, and behavioral research* (pp. 138–159). New York: Cambridge University Press.

Edwards, A. L. (1957a). *The social desirability variable in personality assessment*. New York: Dryden.

Edwards, A. L. (1957b). *Techniques of attitude scale construction*. New York: Appleton-Century-Crofts.

Edwards, A. L. (1964). *Expected values of discrete random variables and elementary statistics*. New York: Wiley.

Edwards, A. L. (1967a). The social desirability variable: A broad statement. In I. A. Berg (Ed.), *Response set in personality assessment* (pp. 32–47). Chicago: Aldine.

Edwards, A. L. (1967b). The social desirability variable: A review of the evidence. In I. A. Berg (Ed.), *Response set in personality assessment* (pp. 48–70). Chicago: Aldine.

Edwards, A. L. (1985). *Experimental design in psychological research* (5th ed.). New York: Harper & Row.

Edwards, W. (1965). Tactical note on the relation

between scientific and statistical hypotheses. *Psychological Bulletin, 63,* 400–402.

Edwards, W., Lindman, H., & Savage, L. J. (1963). Bayesian statistical inference for psychological research. *Psychological Review, 70,* 193–242.

Ehrenberg, A. S. C. (1977). Rudiments of numeracy. *Journal of the Royal Statistical Society (Series A), 140,* 277–297.

Ehrenberg, A. S. C. (1981). The problem of numeracy. *The American Statistician, 35,* 67–71.

Ehrlich, H. J., & Rinehart, J. W. (1965). A brief report on the methodology of stereotype research. *Social Forces, 43,* 564–575.

Einhorn, H. J., & Bass, A. R. (1971). Methodological considerations relevant to discrimination in employment testing. *Psychological Bulletin, 75,* 261–269.

Einstein, A., & Infeld L. (1961). *The evolution of physics: The growth of ideas from early concepts to relativity and quanta* (2nd ed.). New York: Simon & Schuster.

Elashoff, J. D. (1969). Analysis of covariance: A delicate instrument. *American Educational Research Journal, 6,* 383–401.

Elashoff, J. D., & Snow, R. E. (1971). *Pygmalion reconsidered. A case study in statistical inference: Reconsideration of the Rosenthal–Jacobson data on teacher expectancy.* Worthington, OH: Charles A. Jones.

Elliott, W. J. (1983). Ear lobe crease and coronary artery disease: 1000 patients and review of the literature. *American Journal of Medicine, 75,* 1024–1032.

Ellis, R. J. (1988). Self-monitoring and leadership emergence in groups. *Personality and Social Psychology Bulletin, 14,* 681–693.

Ellmann, R. (1964). *The identity of Yeats.* New York: Oxford University Press.

Elmore, P. B., & LaPointe, K. A. (1975). Effect of teacher sex, student sex, and teacher warmth on the evaluation of college instructors. *Journal of Educational Psychology, 67,* 368–374.

Equal Employment Opportunity Commission, Civil Service Commission, Department of Labor, and Department of Justice. (1978). Uniform guidelines on employee selection procedures. *Federal Register, 43,* 38,290–38,315.

Erdos, P. L. (1970). *Professional mail surveys.* New York: McGraw-Hill.

Erickson, F. (1986). Qualitative methods in research on teaching. In M. C. Wittrock (Ed.), *Handbook of research on teaching* (3rd ed., pp. 119–161). New York: Macmillan.

Ethington, C. A., & Wolfle, L. M. (1986). A structural model of mathematics achievement for men and women. *American Educational Research Journal, 23,* 65–75.

Evans, P. (1976, December). The Burt affair. . . Sleuthing in science. *APA Monitor,* pp. 1, 4.

Evans, R. I., Rozelle, R. M., Lasater, T. M., Dembroski, T. M., & Allen, B. P. (1970). Fear arousal, persuasion, and actual versus implied behavioral change: New perspective utilizing a real-life dental hygiene program. *Journal of Personality and Social Psychology, 16,* 220–227.

Everitt, B. S. (1980). *Cluster analysis* (2nd ed.). New York: Halstead Press.

Everitt, B. S. (1984). *An introduction to latent variable models.* New York: Chapman & Hall.

Evertson, C. M., & Green, J. L. (1986). Observation as inquiry and method. In M. C. Wittrock (Ed.), *Handbook of research on teaching* (3rd ed., pp. 162–213). New York: Macmillan.

Ezekiel, M., & Fox, K. A. (1959). *Methods of correlation and regression analysis* (3rd ed.). New York: Wiley.

Ezrahi, Y. (1976). The Jensen controversy: A study in the ethics and politics of knowledge in democracy. In C. Frankel (Ed.), *Controversies and decisions: The social sciences and public policy* (pp. 149–170). New York: Russell Sage Foundation.

Farber, I. E. (1963). The things people say to themselves. *American Psychologist, 18,* 185–197.

Farrar, D. E., & Glauber, R. R. (1967). Multicollinearity in regression analysis: The problem revisited. *Review of Economics and Statistics, 49,* 92–107.

Fassnacht, G. (1982). *Theory and practice of observing behaviour* (C. Bryant, Trans.). New York: Academic Press.

Feigl, H., & Brodbeck, M. (Eds.). (1953). *Readings in the philosophy of science.* New York: Appleton-Century-Crofts.

Feldt, L. S. (1973). What size samples for methods/materials experiments? *Journal of Educational Measurement, 10,* 221–226.

Feldt, L. S., & Brennan, R. L. (1989). Reliability. In R. L. Linn (Ed.), *Educational measurement* (3rd ed., pp. 105–146). New York: Macmillan.

Ferber, R., Sheatsley, P., Turner, A., & Waksberg, J. (1980). *What is a survey?* Washington, DC: American Statistical Association.

Festinger, L. (1953). Laboratory experiments. In L. Festinger & D. Katz (Eds.), *Research methods in the behavioral sciences* (pp. 136–172). New York: Dryden Press.

Festinger, L. (1957). *A theory of cognitive dissonance.* Stanford, CA: Stanford University Press.

Festinger, L., & Carlsmith, J. M. (1959). Cognitive consequences of forced compliance. *Journal of Abnormal and Social Psychology, 58,* 203–210.

Feyerabend, P. (1978). *Against method: Outline of an anarchistic theory of knowledge.* London: Verso.

Fienberg, S. E. (1971). Randomization and social affairs: The 1970 draft lottery. *Science, 171,* 255–261.

Fienberg, S. E. (1980). *The analysis of cross-classified categorical data* (2nd ed.). Cambridge, MA: MIT Press.

Fillenbaum, S. (1966). Prior deception and subsequent experimental performance: The "faithful" subject. *Journal of Personality and Social Psychology, 4,* 532–537.

Fillenbaum, S., & Frey, R. (1970). More on the "faithful" behavior of suspicious subjects. *Journal of Personality, 38,* 43–51.

Fincher, C. (1975). Differential validity and test bias. *Personnel Psychology, 28,* 481–500.

Fishbein, M. (Ed.). (1967). *Readings in attitude theory and measurement.* New York: Wiley.

Fishbein, M., & Ajzen, I. (1972). Attitudes and opinions. *Annual Review of Psychology, 23,* 487–544.

Fishbein, M., & Ajzen, I. (1975). *Belief, attitude, intention, and behavior: An introduction to theory and research.* Reading, MA: Addison-Wesley.

Fisher, R. A. (1926). The arrangement of field experiments. *Journal of the Ministry of Agriculture of Great Britain, 33,* 503–513.

Fisher, R. A. (1958). *Statistical methods for research workers* (13th ed.). New York: Hafner.

Fisher, R. A. (1966). *The design of experiments* (8th ed.). New York: Hafner.

Fisher, R. A., & Yates, F. (1963). *Statistical tables for biological, agricultural and medical research* (6th ed.). New York: Hafner.

Fiske, D. W. (1949). Consistency of the factorial structures of personality ratings from different sources. *Journal of Abnormal and Social Psychology, 44,* 329–344.

Fiske, D. W., & Shweder, R. A. (1986a). Introduction: Uneasy social science. In D. W. Fiske & R. A. Shweder (Eds.), *Metatheory in social science: Pluralism and subjectivities* (pp. 1–18). Chicago: Chicago University Press.

Fiske, D. W., & Shweder, R. A. (Eds.). (1986b). *Metatheory in social science: Pluralism and subjectivities.* Chicago: Chicago University Press.

Fiske, E. B. (1980, January 8). Social scientists as policy-shapers. *The New York Times,* pp. C1, C4.

Fiske, E. B. (1981, April 26). School study said to fail to emphasize main point. *The New York Times,* p. 40.

Fitzpatrick, A. R. (1983). The meaning of content validity. *Applied Psychological Measurement, 7,* 3–13.

Flaugher, R. L. (1978). The many definitions of test bias. *American Psychologist, 33,* 671–679.

Fleishman, E. A., & Hempel, W. E. (1954). Changes in factor structure of a complex psychomotor test as a function of practice. *Psychometrika, 19,* 239–252.

Fleiss, J. L. (1976). Comment on Overall and Woodward's asserted paradox concerning the measurement of change. *Psychological Bulletin, 83,* 774–775.

Fleiss, J. L. (1986). *The design and analysis of clinical experiments.* New York: Wiley.

Fleiss, J. L., & Shrout, P. E. (1977). The effects of measurement errors on some multivariate procedures. *American Journal of Public Health, 67,* 1188–1191.

Fleming, D. (1967). Attitude: The history of a concept. *Perspectives in American History, 1,* 287–365.

Fornell, C. (1983a). Issues in the application of covariance structure analysis: A comment. *Journal of Consumer Research, 9,* 443–450.

Fornell, C. (1983b). Political democracy—how many dimensions? *American Sociological Review, 48,* 136–138.

Forthofer, R. N., & Lehnen, R. G. (1981). *Public program analysis: A new categorical data approach.* Belmont, CA: Lifetime Learning Publications.

Foster, S. L., & Cone, J. D. (1986). Design and use of direct observation procedures. In A. R. Ciminero, K. S. Calhoun, & H. E. Adams

(Eds.), *Handbook of behavioral assessment* (2nd ed., pp. 253–324). New York: Wiley.

Fowler, F. J. Jr., & Mangione, T. W. (1990). *Standardized survey interviewing: Minimizing interviewer-related error*. Newbury Park, CA: Sage.

Fox, J. (1984). *Linear statistical models and related methods: With applications to social research*. New York: Wiley.

Fox, K. A. (1968). *Intermediate economic statistics*. New York: Wiley.

Frank, C. R. (1971). *Statistics and econometrics*. New York: Holt, Rinehart & Winston.

Frankel, C. (1973). The nature and sources of irrationalism. *Science, 180*, 927–931.

Frankel, C. (Ed.). (1976). *Controversies and decisions: The social sciences and public policy*. New York: Russell Sage Foundation.

Franks, F. (1981). *Polywater*. Cambridge, MA: MIT Press.

Free, L. A., & Cantril, H. (1967). *The political beliefs of Americans: A study of public opinion*. New Brunswick, NJ: Rutgers University Press.

Freedman, D. A. (1987a). As others see us: A case study in path analysis. *Journal of Educational Statistics, 12*, 101–128.

Freedman, D. A. (1987b). A rejoinder on models, metaphors, and fables. *Journal of Educational Statistics, 12*, 206–223.

Freiman, J. A., Chambers, T. C., Smith, H., & Kuebler, R. R. (1978). The importance of beta, the Type II error and sample size in the design and interpretation of the randomized control trial. *New England Journal of Medicine, 299*, 690–694.

Freund, R. J., & Littell, R. C. (1986). *SAS system for regression*. Cary, NC: SAS Institute.

Frey, J. H. (1989). *Survey research by telephone* (2nd ed.). Newbury Park, CA: Sage.

Frick, R., & Semmel, M. I. (1978). Observer agreement and reliabilities of classroom observational measures. *Review of Educational Research, 48*, 157–184.

Friedlander, F. (1964). Type I and Type II bias. *American Psychologist, 19*, 198–199.

Friedman, N. (1967). *The social nature of psychological research: The psychological experiment as a social interaction*. New York: Basic Books.

Furby, L. (1973). Interpreting regression toward the mean in developmental research. *Developmental Psychology, 8*, 172–179.

Furedy, J. J. (1978). Negative results: Abolish the name but honour the same. In J. P. Sutcliffe (Ed.), *Conceptual analysis and methods in psychology: Essays in honor of W. A. O'Neil* (pp. 169–180). Sydney: Sydney University Press.

Furnham, A. (1984). Work values and beliefs in Britain. *Journal of Occupational Behaviour, 5*, 281–291.

Gable, R. K. (1986). *Instrument development in the affective domain*. Boston: Kluwer-Nijhoff.

Gage, N. L., Leavitt, G. S., & Stone, G. C. (1957). The psychological meaning of acquiescence set for authoritarianism. *Journal of Abnormal and Social Psychology, 55*, 98–103.

Gaito, J. (1980). Measurement scales and statistics: Resurgence of an old misconception. *Psychological Bulletin, 87*, 564–567.

Gale, G. (1984). Science and the philosophers. *Nature, 312*, 491–495.

Galle, O. R., Gove, W. R., & McPherson, J. M. (1972). Population density and pathology: What are the relations for man? *Science, 176*, 23–30.

Galton, F. (1889). *Natural inheritance*. London: Macmillan.

Games, P. A. (1971). Multiple comparisons of means. *American Educational Research Journal, 8*, 531–565.

Gardner, P. L. (1975). Scales and statistics. *Review of Educational Research, 45*, 43–57.

Garner, W. R. (1960). Rating scales, discriminability, and information transmission. *Psychological Review, 67*, 343–352.

Garner, W. R., Hake, H. W., & Erikson, C. W. (1956). Operationism and the concept of perception. *Psychological Review, 63*, 149–159.

Geertz, C. (1973). Thick description: Toward an interpretive theory of culture. In *The interpretation of cultures: Selected essays by Clifford Geertz* (pp. 3–30). New York: Basic Books.

Gerbing, D. W., & Anderson, J. C. (1984). On the meaning of within-factor correlated measurement errors. *Journal of Consumer Research, 11*, 572–580.

Gergen, K. J. (1973). Social psychology as history. *Journal of Personality and Social Psychology, 26*, 309–320.

Gergen, K. J. (1982). *Toward transformation in social knowledge*. New York: Springer-Verlag.

Gergen, K. J. (1986). Correspondence versus autonomy in the language of understanding human action. In D. W. Fiske & R. A. Shweder (Eds.), *Metatheory in social science: Plural-*

ism and subjectivities (pp. 136–162). Chicago: University of Chicago Press.

Gergen, K. J., & Gergen, M. M. (1981). *Social psychology*. San Diego: Harcourt Brace Jovanovich.

Ghiselli, E. E., Campbell, J. P., & Zedeck, S. (1981). *Measurement theory for the behavioral sciences*. San Francisco: Freeman.

Ghiselli, E. E., & Haire, M. (1960). The validation of selection tests in the light of the dynamic character of criteria. *Personnel Psychology*, *13*, 225–231.

Gibbons, J. D., & Pratt, J. W. (1975). P–values: Interpretation and methodology. *The American Statistician*, *29*(1), 20–25.

Gilbert, J. P., McPeek, B., & Mosteller, F. (1977). Statistics and ethics in surgery and anesthesia. *Science*, *198*, 684–689.

Glass, B. (1965). *Science and ethical values*. Chapel Hill, NC: University of North Carolina Press.

Glass, G. V. (1976). Primary, secondary, and meta-analysis of research. *Educational Researcher*, *5* (10), 3–8.

Glass, G. V., & Hakstian, A. R. (1969). Measures of association in comparative experiments: Their development and interpretation. *American Educational Research Journal*, *6*, 403–414.

Glass, G. V., & Maguire, T. O. (1966). Abuses of factor scores. *American Educational Research Journal*, *3*, 297–304.

Glass, G. V., McGaw, B., & Smith, M. L. (1981). *Meta-analysis in social research*. Newbury Park, CA: Sage.

Glass, J., Bengtson, V. L., & Dunham, C. C. (1986). Attitude similarity in three-generation families: socialization, status inheritance, or reciprocal influence? *American Sociological Review*, *51*, 685–698.

Gleick, J. (1988, April 19). The quest for true randomness finally appears successful. *The New York Times*, pp. C1, C8.

Glymour, C., Scheines, R., & Sprites, P. (1988). Exploring causal structure with the TETRAD program. In C. C. Clogg (Ed.), *Sociological methodology 1988* (pp. 411–448). Washington, DC: American Sociological Association.

Goldberg, P. A. (1965). Expectancy, choice, and the other person. *Journal of Personality and Social Psychology*, *2*, 895–897.

Goldberg, S. (1983). Parent–infant bonding: Another look. *Child Development*, *54*, 1355–1382.

Goldberger, A. S. (1972, June). *Selection bias in evaluating treatment effects: Some formal illustrations* (Discussion paper 123–72). Madison: University of Wisconsin, Institute for Research on Poverty.

Goldstein, H. (1979). *The design and analysis of longitudinal studies: Their role in measurement of change*. New York: Academic Press.

Goldstein, R. (1989). Power and sample size via MS/PC–DOS computers. *The American Statistician*, *43*, 253–260.

Goldstein, T. (1978, February 19). Measuring competence: Debating an indefinable. *The New York Times*, p. E7.

Gollob, H. F., & Reichardt, C. S. (1987). Taking account of time lags in causal models. *Child Development*, *58*, 80–92.

Goocher, B. E. (1965). Effects of attitude and experience on the selection of frequency of adverbs. *Journal of Verbal Learning and Verbal Behavior*, *4*, 193–195.

Goocher, B. E. (1969). More about often. *American Psychologist*, *24*, 608–609.

Gorden, R. L. (1975). *Interviewing: Strategy, techniques, and tactics* (rev. ed.). Homewood, IL: Dorsey Press.

Gorsuch, R. L. (1983). *Factor analysis* (2nd ed.). Hillsdale, NJ: Erlbaum.

Gottman, J. M. (1981). *Time-series analysis: A comprehensive introduction for social scientists*. New York: Cambridge University Press.

Gould, S. J. (1978). Morton's rankings of races by cranial capacity. *Science*, *200*, 503–509.

Gould, S. J. (1981). *The mismeasure of man*. New York: Norton.

Gouldner, A. W. (1962). Anti-Minotaur: The myth of value-free sociology. *Social Problems*, *9*, 199–213.

Gouldner, A. W. (1970). *The coming crisis of western sociology*. New York: Avon.

Green, B. F. (1981a). A primer of testing. *American Psychologist*, *36*, 1001–1011.

Green, B. F. (Ed.). (1981b). *Issues in testing: Coaching, disclosure, and ethnic bias*. San Francisco: Jossey-Bass.

Green, B. F., & Hall, J. A. (1984). Quantitative methods for literature reviews. *Annual Review of Psychology*, *35*, 37–53.

Green, P. E. (1976). *Mathematical tools for applied multivariate analysis*. New York: Academic Press.

Green, P. E. (1978). *Analyzing multivariate data.* Hinsdale, IL: Dryden Press.

Green, P. E., & Rao, V. R. (1970). Rating scales and information recovery—How many scales and response categories to use? *Journal of Marketing, 34,* 33–39.

Green, S. B., Lissitz, R. W., & Mulaik, S. A. (1977). Limitations of coefficient alpha as an index of test unidimensionality. *Educational and Psychological Measurement, 37,* 827–838.

Greenwald, A. G. (1968). On defining attitude and attitude theory. In A. G. Greenwald, T. C. Brock, & T. M. Ostrom (Eds.), *Psychological foundations of attitudes* (pp. 361–388). New York: Academic Press.

Greenwald, A. G. (1975). Consequences of prejudice against the null hypothesis. *Psychological Bulletin, 82,* 1–20.

Greenwald, A. G., Brock, T. C, & Ostrom, T. M. (Eds.). (1968). *Psychological foundations of attitudes.* New York: Academic Press.

Greitzer, J. (1985, November 5). The outlook is sunny for forecasting packages. *PC Week,* pp. 83–84, 86–88.

Groves, R. M., & Kahn, R. L. (1979). *Surveys by telephone: A national comparison with personal interviews.* New York: Academic Press.

Grünbaum, A. (1981). The placebo concept. *Behaviour Research and Therapy, 19,* 157–167.

Guilford, J. P. (1952). When not to factor analyze. *Psychological Bulletin, 49,* 26–37.

Guilford, J. P. (1954). *Psychometric methods* (2nd ed.). New York: McGraw-Hill.

Guilford, J. P. (1967). *The nature of human intelligence.* New York: McGraw-Hill.

Guion, R. M. (1977). Content validity—The source of my discontent. *Applied Psychological Measurement, 1,* 1–10.

Guion, R. M. (1978). "Content validity" in moderation. *Personnel Psychology, 31,* 205–213.

Guion, R. M. (1980). On trinitarian doctrines of validity. *Professional Psychology, 11,* 385–398.

Gulliksen, H. (1950). *Theory of mental tests.* New York: Wiley.

Gurel, L. (1968). Statistical sense and nonsense. *International Journal of Psychiatry, 6,* 127–131.

Gustafsson, J. E. (1984). A unifying model for the structure of intellectual abilities. *Intelligence, 8,* 179–203.

Guttman, L. (1981). What is not what in statistics. In I. Borg (Ed.), *Multidimensional data representations: When & why* (pp. 20–46). Ann Arbor, MI: Mathesis Press.

Guttman, L. (1985). The illogic of statistical inference for cumulative science. *Applied Stochastic Models and Data Analysis, 1,* 3–10.

Haase, R. F., Ellis, M. V., & Ladany, N. (1989). Multiple criteria for evaluating the magnitude of experimental effects. *Journal of Counseling Psychology, 36,* 511–516.

Haase, R. F., Waechter, D. M., & Solomon, G. S. (1982). How significant is a significant difference? Average effect size of research in counseling psychology. *Journal of Counseling Psychology, 29,* 58–65.

Hagenaars, J. A., & Heinen, T. G. (1982). Effects of role-independent interviewer characteristics on responses. In W. Dijkstra & J. van der Zouwen (Eds.), *Response behaviour in the survey-interview* (pp. 91–130). London: Academic Press.

Hakel, M. D. (1968). How often is often? *American Psychologist, 23,* 533–534.

Halderson, J. S., & Glasnapp, D. R. (1972). Generalized rules for calculating the magnitude of an effect in factorial and repeated measures ANOVA designs. *American Educational Research Journal, 9,* 301–310.

Hamblin, C. L. (1970). *Fallacies.* London: Methuen.

Hammond, K. R., & Adelman, L. (1976). Science, values, and human judgment. *Science, 194,* 389–396.

Hanna, G., & Lei, H. (1985). A longitudinal analysis using the LISREL-model with structured means. *Journal of Educational Statistics, 10,* 161–169.

Hansen, M. H., Hurwitz, W. N., & Madow, W. G. (1953). *Sample survey methods and theory: Volume I methods and applications.* New York: Wiley.

Hanson, N. R. (1958). *Patterns of discovery: An inquiry into the conceptual foundations of science.* New York: Cambridge University Press.

Hanson, N. R. (1969). *Perception and discovery: An introduction to scientific inquiry.* San Francisco: Freeman, Cooper & Company.

Hanson, N. R. (1971). *Observation and explanation: A guide to philosophy of science.* New York: Harper & Row.

Hanushek, E. A., & Jackson, J. E. (1977). *Statistical methods for social scientists.* New York: Academic Press.

Hargens, L. L. (1976). A note on standardized coefficients as structural parameters. *Sociological Methods & Research*, *5*, 247–256.

Harman, H. H. (1976). *Modern factor analysis* (3rd ed.). Chicago: University of Chicago Press.

Harnad, S. (Ed.). (1983). *Peer commentary on peer review: A case study in scientific quality control*. New York: Cambridge University Press.

Harré, R. (1972). *The philosophies of science: An introductory survey*. London: Oxford University Press.

Harré, R., & Madden, E. H. (1975). *Causal powers: A theory of natural necessity*. Totowa, NJ: Rowman & Littlefield.

Harris, C. W. (Ed.). (1963). *Problems in measuring change*. Madison, WI: University of Wisconsin Press.

Harris, M. (1981). Why private schools can pay off. *Money*, *10*(9), 92–98.

Harrop, J. W., & Velicer, W. F. (1985). A comparison of alternative approaches to the analysis of interrupted time-series. *Multivariate Behavioral Research*, *20*, 27–44.

Harry, J., & Minor, W. W. (1986). Intelligence and delinquency reconsidered: A comment on Menard and Morse. *American Journal of Sociology*, *91*, 956–962.

Hartigan, J. A. (1975). *Clustering algorithms*. New York: Wiley.

Hartley, E. L. (1967). Attitude research and the jangle fallacy. In C. W. Sherif & M. Sherif (Eds.), *Attitude, ego-involvement, and change* (pp. 88–104). New York: Wiley.

Harvard Graphics Version 2.12. (1988). Mountain View, CA: Software Publishing Corporation.

Hasofer, A. M. (1967). Random mechanisms in Talmudic literature. *Biometrika*, *54*, 316–321.

Hauser, R. M. (1972). Disaggregating a social-psychological model of educational attainment. *Social Science Research*, *1*, 159–188.

Hauser, R. M. (1984). Some cross-population comparisons of family bias in the effects of schooling on occupational status. *Social Science Research*, *13*, 159–187.

Hauser, R. M., & Goldberger, A. S. (1971). The treatment of unobservable variables in path analysis. In H. L. Costner (Ed.), *Sociological methodology 1971* (pp. 81–117). San Francisco: Jossey-Bass.

Hauser, R. M., & Sewell, W. H. (1986). A

child's garden of equations: Comment on Alexander and Pallas. *Social Forces*, *65*, 241–249.

Havighurst, R. J. (1970). Minority subcultures and the law of effect. *American Psychologist*, *25*, 313–322.

Hayduk, L. A. (1987). *Structural equation modeling with LISREL: Essentials and advances*. Baltimore: Johns Hopkins University Press.

Hayek, F. A. (1956). The dilemma of specialization. In L. D. White (Ed.), *The state of the social sciences* (pp. 462–473). Chicago: University of Chicago Press.

Hays, R. D., Widaman, K. F., DiMatteo, M. R., & Stacy, A. W. (1987). Structural-equation models of current drug use: Are appropriate models so simple(x)? *Journal of Personality and Social Psychology*, *52*, 134–144.

Hays, W. L. (1963). *Statistics for psychologists*. New York: Holt, Rinehart & Winston.

Hays, W. L. (1988). *Statistics* (4th ed.). New York: Holt, Rinehart & Winston.

Healey, T. (1976). Linguistic deterrent? *Science*, *193*, 98.

Hechinger, F. M. (1973, May 27). Home is crucial factor. *The New York Times*, p. E9.

Hechinger, F. M. (1981, May 11). Professor Coleman's troubles. *The New York Times*, p. A18.

Hedges, L. V., & Olkin, I. (1985). *Statistical methods for meta-analysis*. New York: Academic Press.

Hedges, L., & Olkin, I. (1986). Meta analysis: A review and a new view. *Educational Researcher*, *15*(8), 14–21.

Heise, D. R. (1969a). Separating reliability and stability in test–retest correlation. *American Sociological Review*, *34*, 93–101.

Heise, D. R. (1969b). Some methodological issues in semantic differential research. *Psychological Bulletin*, *72*, 406–422.

Heise, D. R. (1970). The semantic differential and attitude research. In G. F. Summers (Ed.), *Attitude measurement* (pp. 235–253). Chicago: Rand McNally.

Heise, D. R. (1974). Some issues in sociological measurement. In H. L. Costner (Ed.), *Sociological methodology 1973–1974* (pp. 1–16). San Francisco: Jossey-Bass.

Heise, D. R. (1975). *Causal analysis*. New York: Wiley.

Heisenberg, W. (1962). *Physics and philosophy: The revolution in modern science*. New York: Harper Torchbooks.

Hempel, C. G. (1965). *Aspects of scientific explanation and other essays in the philosophy of science*. New York: Free Press.

Henkel, R. E. (1976). *Tests of significance*. Newbury Park, CA: Sage.

Henry, N. W. (1986). On "Arbitrary Metrics" and "Normalization Issues". *Sociological Methods & Research, 15*, 59–61.

Henshel, R. L. (1980a). The purposes of laboratory experimentation and the virtues of deliberate artificiality. *Journal of Experimental Social Psychology, 16*, 466–478.

Henshel, R. L. (1980b). Seeking inoperative laws: Toward the deliberate use of unnatural experimentation. In L. Freese (Ed.), *Theoretical methods in sociology, seven essays* (pp. 175–199). Pittsburgh: University of Pittsburgh Press.

Herbert, J., & Attridge, C. (1975). A guide for developers and users of observation systems and manuals. *American Educational Research Journal, 12*, 1–20.

Herting, J. R., & Costner, H. L. (1985). Respecification in multiple indicator models. In H. M. Blalock (Ed.), *Causal models in the social sciences* (2nd ed., pp. 321–393). Chicago: Aldine.

Hertzog, C., & Nesselroade, J. R. (1987). Beyond autoregressive models: Some implications of the trait–state distinction for structural modeling of developmental change. *Child Development, 58*, 93–109.

Hesse, M. (1974). *The structure of scientific inference*. Berkeley, CA: University of California Press.

Hesse, M. (1978). Theory and value in the social sciences. In C. Hookway & P. Pettit (Eds.), *Action and interpretation: Studies in the philosophy of the social sciences* (pp. 1–16). Cambridge: Cambridge University Press.

Higbee, K. L. (1969). Fifteen years of fear arousal: Research on threat appeals: 1953–1968. *Psychological Bulletin, 72*, 426–444.

Hills, J. R. (1971). Use of measurement in selection and placement. In R. L. Thorndike (Ed.), *Educational measurement* (2nd ed., pp. 680–732). Washington, DC: American Council on Education.

Hoaglin, D. C., & Welsch, R. E. (1978). The hat matrix in regression and ANOVA. *The American Statistician, 32*, 17–22.

Hoelter, J. W. (1983a). The analysis of covariance structures: Goodness-of-fit indices. *Sociological Methods & Research, 11*, 325–344.

Hoelter, J. W. (1983b). Factorial invariance and self-esteem: Reassessing race and sex differences. *Social Forces, 61*, 834–846.

Hogarth, R. M. (Ed.). (1982). *Question framing and response frequency*. San Francisco: Jossey-Bass.

Holland, P. W. (1986). Statistics and causal inference. *Journal of the American Statistical Association, 81*, 945–960.

Holland, P. W. (1988). Causal inference, path analysis, and recursive structural equation models. In C. C. Clogg (Ed.), *Sociological methodology 1988* (pp. 449–484). Washington, DC: American Sociological Association.

Holland, P. W., & Rubin, D. B. (1983). On Lord's paradox. In H. Wainer & S. Messick (Eds.), *Principals [sic] of modern psychological measurement. A festschrift for Frederic M. Lord* (pp. 3–25). Hillsdale, NJ: Erlbaum.

Holmes, D. S., & Appelbaum, A. S. (1970). Nature of prior experimental experience as a determinant of performance in a subsequent experiment. *Journal of Personality and Social Psychology, 14*, 195–202.

Holton, G. (1972). Mach, Einstein, and the search for reality. In G. Holton (Ed.), *The twentieth-century sciences* (pp. 344–381). New York: Norton.

Homans, G. C. (1962). *Sentiments & activities: Essays in social science*. New York: Free Press.

Homans, G. C. (1978). What kind of a myth is the myth of a value-free social science? *Social Science Quarterly, 58*, 530–541.

Hooke, R. (1983). *How to tell the liars from the statisticians*. New York: Marcel Dekker.

Hopkins, K. D., Coulter, D. K., & Hopkins, B. R. (1981). Tables for quick power estimates when comparing means. *The Journal of Special Education, 15*, 389–394.

Horn, J. (1988). Thinking about human abilities. In J. R. Nesselroade & R. B. Cattell (Eds.), *Handbook of multivariate experimental psychology* (2nd ed., pp. 645–658). New York: Plenum.

Horn, J. L., & Cattell, R. B. (1966). Refinement and test of the theory of fluid and crystallized general intelligences. *Journal of Educational Psychology, 57*, 253–270.

Hovey, H. B. (1928). Effects of general distraction on the higher thought processes. *American Journal of Psychology*, *40*, 585–591.

Hovland, C. I. (1959). Reconciling conflicting results derived from experimental and survey studies of attitude change. *American Psychologist*, *14*, 8–17.

Howard, G. S. (1985). The role of values in the science of psychology. *American Psychologist*, *40*, 255–265.

Huba, G. J., & Bentler, P. M. (1982a). A developmental theory of drug use: Derivation and assessment of a causal modeling approach. In P. B. Baltes & O. G. Brim (Eds.), *Life-span development and behavior* (Vol. 4, pp. 147–203). New York: Academic Press.

Huba, G. J., & Bentler, P. M. (1982b). On the usefulness of latent variable causal modeling in testing theories of naturally occurring events (including adolescent drug use): A rejoinder to Martin. *Journal of Personality and Social Psychology*, *43*, 604–611.

Huba, G. J., & Harlow, L. L. (1986). Robust estimation for causal models: A comparison of methods in some developmental datasets. In P. B. Baltes, D. L. Featherman, & M. M. Lerner (Eds.), *Life-span development and behavior* (Vol. 7, pp. 69–111). Hillsdale, NJ: Erlbaum.

Huba, G. J., & Harlow, L. L. (1987). Robust structural equation models: Implications for developmental psychology. *Child Development*, *58*, 147–166.

Huba, G. J., Wingard, J. A., & Bentler, P. M. (1981). A comparison of two latent variable causal models for adolescent drug use. *Journal of Personality and Social Psychology*, *40*, 180–193.

Hubbard, R., & Allen, S. J. (1987). A cautionary note on the use of principal components analysis: Supportive empirical evidence. *Sociological Methods & Research*, *16*, 301–308.

Huberty, C. J. (1972). Multivariate indices of strength of association. *Multivariate Behavioral Research*, *7*, 523–528.

Huberty, C. J. (1982, March). *Some univariate–multivariate generalizations*. Paper presented at the annual meeting of the American Educational Research Association, New York City.

Huberty, C. J. (1987). On statistical testing. *Educational Researcher*, *16*(8), 4–9.

Hudson, H. C., et al. (1982). *Classifying social data: New applications of analytic methods for social science research*. San Francisco: Jossey-Bass.

Hudson, J. (1968). *A case of need*. New York: World Publishing.

Huff, D. (1954). *How to lie with statistics*. New York: Norton.

Huitema, B. E. (1980). *The analysis of covariance and alternatives*. New York: Wiley.

Hulin, C. L., Drasgow, F., & Parsons, C. K. (1983). *Item response theory: Applications to psychological measurement*. Homewood, IL: Dow Jones-Irwin.

Hume, D. (1960). *A treatise of human nature*. Oxford: Clarendon. (Original work published 1739)

Humphreys, L. G. (1978). Doing research the hard way: Substituting analysis of variance for a problem in correlational analysis. *Journal of Educational Psychology*, *70*, 873–876.

Humphreys, L. G., & Fleishman, A. (1974). Pseudo-orthogonal and other analysis of variance designs involving individual-differences variables. *Journal of Educational Psychology*, *66*, 464–472.

Hunter, J. E., & Schmidt, F. L. (1976). Critical analysis of the statistical and ethical implications of various definitions of *test bias*. *Psychological Bulletin*, *83*, 1053–1071.

Hunter, J. E., Schmidt, F. L., & Jackson, G. B. (1982). *Meta-analysis: Cumulative research findings across studies*. Newbury Park, CA: Sage.

Hunter, J. S. (1980). The national system of scientific measurement. *Science*, *210*, 869–874.

Hutten, E. H. (1962). *The origins of science: An inquiry into the foundations of western thought*. London: George Allen and Unwin.

Huxley, A. (1944). *Time must have a stop*. New York: Harper & Brothers.

Huxley, T. H. (n.d.). Biogenesis and abiogenesis. In *Discourses: Biological and geological essays* (pp. 232–274). New York: Appleton.

Huxley, T. H. (1895). On the educational value of the natural history sciences. In *Science and education: Essays* (pp. 38–65). New York: Appleton.

Hyman, H. H. (1973). Surveys in the study of political psychology. In J. N. Knutson (Ed.), *Handbook of political psychology* (pp. 322–355). San Francisco: Jossey-Bass.

Hyman, H. H., Cobb, W. J., Feldman, J. J., Hart, C. W., & Stember, C. H. (1954). *Interviewing in social research*. Chicago: University of Chicago Press.

Ingersoll, G. M. (1982). Experimental methods. In H. E. Mitzel (Ed.), *Encyclopedia of educational research* (5th ed., pp. 624–631). New York: Free Press.

Iverson, G. R. (1970). Statistics according to Bayes. In E. F. Borgatta & G. W. Bohrnstedt (Eds.), *Sociological methodology 1970* (pp. 185–199). San Francisco: Jossey-Bass.

Jackson, D. J. (1967). Acquiescence response styles: Problems of identification and control. In I. A. Berg (Ed.), *Response set in personality assessment* (pp. 71–114). Chicago: Aldine.

Jackson, D. N. (1969). Multimethod factor analysis in the evaluation of convergent and discriminant validity. *Psychological Bulletin, 72,* 30–49.

Jacobson, A. L. (1973). Some theoretical and methodological considerations for measuring intrasocietal conflict. *Sociological Methods & Research, 1,* 439–461.

Jacobson, E., Kumata, H., & Gullahorn, J. E. (1960). Cross-cultural contributions to attitude research. *Public Opinion Quarterly, 24,* 205–223.

Jacoby, J. (1978). Consumer research: How valid and useful are all our consumer behavior research findings? A state of the art review. *Journal of Marketing, 42,* 87–96.

Jacoby, J., & Matell, M. S. (1971). Three-point Likert scales are good enough. *Journal of Marketing Research, 8,* 495–500.

Jaeger, R. M. (1984). *Sampling in education and the social sciences.* New York: Longman.

Jagodzinski, W., & Kühnel, S. M. (1987). Estimation of reliability and stability in single-indicator multiple-wave models. *Sociological Methods & Research, 15,* 219–258.

Jagodzinski, W., Kühnel, S. M., & Schmidt, P. (1987). Is there a "Socratic effect" in nonexperimental panel studies? *Sociological Methods & Research, 15,* 259–302.

Jagodzinski, W., Kühnel, S. M., & Schmidt, P. (1988). Is the true score model or the factor model more appropriate? Response to Saris and Putte. *Sociological Methods & Research, 17,* 158–164.

James, L. R., & Jones, A. P. (1980). Perceived job characteristics and job satisfaction: An examination of reciprocal causation. *Personnel Psychology, 33,* 97–135.

Janis, I. L., & Feshbach, S. (1953). Effects of fear-arousing communications. *Journal of Abnormal and Social Psychology, 48,* 78–92.

Jenkins, J. G. (1946). Validity for what? *Journal of Consulting Psychology, 10,* 93–98.

Jensen, A. R. (1972). Sir Cyril Burt. *Psychometrika, 37,* 115–117.

Johnson, A. F. (1985). Beneath the technological fix: Outliers and probability statements. *Journal of Chronic Diseases, 38,* 957–961.

Johnson, H. G. (1950). Test reliability and correction for attenuation. *Psychometrika, 15,* 115–119.

Johnson, H. M. (1954). On verifying hypotheses by verifying their implications. *American Journal of Psychology, 67,* 723–727.

Johnson, M. L. (1953). Seeing's believing. *New Biology, 15,* 60–80.

Johnson, P. O., & Fay, L. C. (1950). The Johnson–Neyman technique, its theory and application. *Psychometrika, 15,* 349–367.

Johnson, P. O., & Jackson, R. W. B. (1959). *Modern statistical methods: Descriptive and inductive.* Chicago: Rand McNally.

Johnson, P. O., & Neyman, J. (1936). Tests of certain linear hypotheses and their applications to some educational problems. *Statistical Research Memoirs, 1,* 57–93.

Jones, C. O. (1974). Doing before knowing: Concept development in political research. *American Journal of Political Science, 18,* 215–228.

Jones, M. B., & Fennell, R. S. (1965). Runway performance in two strains of rats. *Quarterly Journal of the Florida Academy of Sciences, 28,* 289–296.

Jöreskog, K. G. (1971a). Simultaneous factor analysis in several populations. *Psychometrika, 36,* 409–426.

Jöreskog, K. G. (1971b). Statistical analysis of sets of congeneric tests. *Psychometrika, 36,* 109–133.

Jöreskog, K. G. (1974). Analyzing psychological data by structural analysis of covariance matrices. In D. H. Krantz, R. C. Atkinson, R. D. Luce, & P. Suppes (Eds.), *Contemporary developments in mathematical psychology* (Vol. 2, pp. 1–56). San Francisco: Freeman.

Jöreskog, K. G. (1978). Structural analysis of covariance and correlation matrices. *Psychometrika, 43,* 443–477.

Jöreskog, K. G. (1979a). Basic ideas of factor and component analysis. In J. Magidson (Ed.), *Advances in factor analysis and structural equation models* (pp. 5–20). Cambridge, MA: Abt Books.

Jöreskog, K. G. (1979b). Statistical estimation of structural models in longitudinal-developmental investigations. In J. R. Nesselroade & P. B. Baltes (Eds.), *Longitudinal research in the study of behavior and development* (pp. 303–351). New York: Academic Press.

Jöreskog, K. G., & Goldberger, A. S. (1975). Estimation of a model with multiple indicators and multiple causes of a single latent variable. *Journal of the American Statistical Association, 70,* 631–639.

Jöreskog, K. G., & Sörbom, D. (1977). Statistical models and methods for analysis of longitudinal data. In D. J. Aigner & A. S. Goldberger (Eds.), *Latent variables in socioeconomic models* (pp. 285–325). Amsterdam: North-Holland.

Jöreskog, K. G., & Sörbom, D. (1982). Recent developments in structural equation modeling. *Journal of Marketing Research, 19,* 404–416.

Jöreskog, K. G., & Sörbom, D. (1985). Simultaneous analysis of longitudinal data from several cohorts. In W. M. Mason & S. E. Fienberg (Eds.), *Cohort analysis in social research: Beyond the identification problem* (pp. 323–341). New York: Springer-Verlag.

Jöreskog, K. G., & Sörbom, D. (1989). *LISREL 7: A guide to the program and applications* (2nd ed.). Chicago: SPSS Inc.

Jourard, S. M. (1968). *Disclosing man to himself.* New York: Van Nostrand Reinhold.

Judd, C. M., Jessor, R., & Donovan, J. E. (1986). Structural equation models and personality research. *Journal of Personality, 54,* 149–198.

Judd, C. M., & Kenny, D. A. (1981). *Estimating the effects of social interventions.* New York: Cambridge University Press.

Julnes, G., & Mohr, L. B. (1989). Analysis of no-difference findings in evaluation research. *Evaluation Review, 13,* 628–655.

Kahan, B., Auerbach, R., Alter, B. J., & Bach, F. H. (1982). Histocompatibility and Isoenzyme differences in commercially supplied "BALB/c" mice. *Science, 217,* 379–381.

Kahane, H. (1973). *Logic and philosophy: A modern introduction* (2nd ed.). Belmont, CA: Wadsworth.

Kahn, R. L., & Cannell, C. F. (1957). *The dynamics of interviewing: Theory, technique, and cases.* New York: Wiley.

Kahneman, D. (1963). The semantic differential and the structure of inferences among attributes. *American Journal of Psychology, 76,* 554–567.

Kahneman, D., & Tversky, A. (1973). On the psychology of prediction. *Psychological Review, 80,* 237–251.

Kaiser, H. F. (1960a). Directional statistical decisions. *Psychological Review, 67,* 160–167.

Kaiser, H. F. (1960b). Review of *Measurement and statistics: A basic text emphasizing behavioral science applications. Psychometrika, 25,* 411–413.

Kalleberg, A. L., & Kluegel, J. R. (1975). Analysis of the multitrait-multimethod: Some limitations and alternatives. *Journal of Applied Psychology, 60,* 1–9.

Kalton, G. (1983). *Introduction to survey sampling.* Newbury Park, CA: Sage.

Kamin, L. (1974). *The science and politics of IQ.* Potomac, MD: Erlbaum.

Kaplan, A. (1946). Definition and specification of meaning. *Journal of Philosophy, 43,* 281–288.

Kaplan, A. (1964). *The conduct of inquiry: Methodology for behavioral science.* San Francisco: Chandler.

Karpman, M. B. (1986). Comparing two non-parallel regression lines with the parametric alternative to the analysis of covariance using SPSS-X or SAS—the Johnson–Neyman technique. *Educational and Psychological Measurement, 46,* 639–644.

Kavanagh, M. J., MacKinney, A. C., & Wolins, L. (1971). Issues in managerial performance: Multitrait-multimethod analyses of ratings. *Psychological Bulletin, 75,* 34–49.

Kazdin, A. E. (1977). Artifact, bias, and complexity of assessment: The ABCs of reliability. *Journal of Applied Behavior Analysis, 10,* 141–150.

Kazdin, A. E. (1982). *Single-case research designs: Methods for clinical and applied settings.* New York: Oxford University Press.

Kazdin, A. E., & Bass, D. (1989). Power to detect differences between alternative treatments in comparative psychotherapy outcome research. *Journal of Consulting and Clinical Psychology, 57,* 138–147.

Kelley, T. L. (1927). *Interpretation of educational measurements.* Yonkers-on-Hudson, NY: World Book.

Kelly, J. A., Caudill, M. S., Hathorn, S., & O'Brien, C. G. (1977). Socially undesirable sex-correlated characteristics: Implications for androgyny and adjustment. *Journal of Consulting and Clinical Psychology, 45,* 1185–1186.

Kemeny, J. G. (1959). *A philosopher looks at science.* Princeton, NJ: Van Nostrand.

Kemeny, J. G. (1983). The case for computer literacy. *Daedalus, 112,* 211–230.

Kempthorne, O. (1978). Logical, epistemological and statistical aspects of nature–nurture data interpretation. *Biometrics, 34,* 1–23.

Kempthorne, O. (1980). The teaching of statistics: Content versus form. *The American Statistician, 34*(1), 17–21.

Kendall, M. G. (1951). Regression, structure and functional relationship. *Biometrika, 38,* 11–25.

Kendall, M. G. (1959). Hiawatha designs an experiment. *The American Statistician, 13*(5), 23–24.

Kenny, D. A. (1979). *Correlation and causality.* New York: Wiley.

Keppel, G. (1982). *Design & analysis: A researcher's handbook* (2nd ed.). Englewood Cliffs, NJ: Prentice-Hall.

Keren, G., & Lewis, C. (1979). Partial omega squared for ANOVA designs. *Educational and Psychological Measurement, 39,* 119–128.

Kerlinger, F. N. (1984). *Liberalism and conservatism: The nature and structure of social attitudes.* Hillsdale, NJ: Erlbaum.

Kerlinger, F. N. (1986). *Foundations of behavioral research* (3rd ed.). New York: Holt, Rinehart & Winston.

Keselman, H. J. (1975). A monte carlo investigation of three estimates of treatment magnitude: Epsilon squared, eta squared, and omega squared. *Canadian Psychological Review, 16,* 44–48.

Kessler, R. C., & Greenberg, D. F. (1981). *Linear panel analysis: Models of quantitative change.* New York: Academic Press.

Kidd, R. F. (1976). Manipulation checks: Advantages or disadvantages? *Representative Research in Social Psychology 7,* 160–165.

Kidd, R. F. (1977). Manipulation checks: Some further considerations. *Representative Research in Social Psychology, 8,* 94–97.

Kiesler, C. A., Collins, B. E., & Miller, N. (1969). *Attitude change: A critical analysis of theoretical approaches.* New York: Wiley.

Kihlken, T. (1988, November 15). The tiniest editor you'll ever need. *PC Magazine,* pp. 281–

283, 289–290, 295, 297, 299, 303, 307, 311, 314, 318–319, 321–322.

Kim, J. O., & Ferree, G. D. (1981). Standardization in causal analysis. *Sociological Methods & Research, 10,* 187–210.

Kim, J. O., & Mueller, C. W. (1976). Standardized and unstandardized coefficients in causal analysis. *Sociological Methods & Research, 4,* 423–438.

Kim, J. O., & Mueller, C. W. (1978a). *Factor analysis: Statistical methods and practical issues.* Newbury Park, CA: Sage.

Kim, J. O., & Mueller, C. W. (1978b). *Introduction to factor analysis: What it is and how to do it.* Newbury Park, CA: Sage.

Kimble, G. A. (1978). *How to use (and misuse) statistics.* Englewood Cliffs, NJ: Prentice-Hall.

Kirk, R. E. (1982). *Experimental design: Procedures for the behavioral sciences* (2nd ed.). Belmont, CA: Brook/Cole.

Kirscht, J. P., & Dillehay, R. C. (1967). *Dimensions of authoritarianism: A review of research & theory.* Lexington, KY: University of Kentucky Press.

Kish, L. (1959). Some statistical problems in research design. *American Sociological Review, 24,* 328–338.

Kish, L. (1965). *Survey sampling.* New York: Wiley.

Kish, L. (1975). Representation, randomization, and control. In H. M. Blalock, A. Aganbegian, F. M Borodkin, R. Boudon, & V. Capecchi (Eds.), *Quantitative sociology. International perspectives on mathematical and statistical modeling* (pp. 261–284). New York: Academic Press.

Kitcher, P. (1985). *Vaulting ambition: Sociobiology and the quest for human nature.* Cambridge, MA: MIT Press.

Klopsteg, P. E. (1959). Support of basic research from GOVERNMENT. In D. Wolfle (Ed.), *Symposium on basic research* (pp. 185–201). Washington, DC: American Association for the Advancement of Science.

Kluegel, J. R., Singleton, R., & Starnes, C. E. (1977). Subjective class identification: A multiple indicator approach. *American Sociological Review, 42,* 599–611.

Kmenta, J. (1971). *Elements of econometrics.* New York: Macmillan.

Knorr, K. (1981). Social and scientific method or "What do we make of the distinction between the natural and the social sciences?" In M. Brenner (Ed.), *Social methods and social life* (pp. 27–52). New York: Academic Press.

Koele, P. (1982). Calculating power in analysis of variance. *Psychological Bulletin, 92,* 513–516.

Kohn, M. L., & Schooler, C. (1983). *Work and personality: An inquiry into the impact of social stratification.* Norwood, NJ: Ablex.

Komorita, S. S., & Graham, W. K. (1965). Number of scale points and the reliability of scales. *Educational and Psychological Measurement, 25,* 987–995.

Koompmans, T. C. (1949). Identification problems in economic model construction. *Econometrica, 17,* 125–143.

Korth, B. (1975). Exploratory factor analysis. In D. J. Amick & H. J. Walberg (Eds.), *Introductory multivariate analysis* (pp. 113–146). Berkeley, CA: McCutchan.

Kraemer, H. C. (1985). A strategy to teach the concept and application of power of statistical tests. *Journal of Educational Statistics, 10,* 173–195.

Kraemer, H. C., & Thiemann, S. (1987). *How many subjects? Statistical power analysis in research.* Newbury Park, CA: Sage.

Kratochwill, T. R. (Ed.). (1978). *Single subject research: Strategies for evaluating change.* New York: Academic Press.

Krebs, D. L., & Miller, D. T. (1985). Altruism and aggression. In G. Lindzey & E. Aronson (Eds.), *Handbook of social psychology* (Vol. 2, 3rd ed., pp. 1–71). New York: Random House.

Krimerman, L. I. (Ed.). (1969). *The nature and scope of social science: A critical anthology.* New York: Appleton-Century-Crofts.

Kruskal, J. B., & Wish, M. (1978). *Multidimensional scaling.* Newbury Park, CA: Sage.

Kruskal, W. (1981). Statistics in society: Problems unsolved and unformulated. *Journal of the American Statistical Association, 76,* 505–515.

Kruskal, W. (1988). Miracles and statistics: The casual assumption of independence. *Journal of the American Statistical Association, 83,* 929–940.

Kruskal, W., & Mosteller, F. (1979). Representative sampling, II: Scientific literature, excluding statistics. *International Statistical Review, 47,* 111–127.

Kruskal, W., & Mosteller, F. (1980). Representative sampling, IV: The history of the concept in statistics, 1895–1939. *International Statistical Review, 48,* 169–195.

Kubiniec, C. M., & Farr, S. D. (1971). Concept-scale and concept-component interaction in the semantic differential. *Psychological Reports, 28,* 531–541.

Kuder, G. F., & Richardson, M. W. (1937). The theory of the estimation of test reliability. *Psychometrika, 2,* 151–160.

Kuhn, T. S. (1970). *The structure of scientific revolutions* (2nd ed.). Chicago: University of Chicago Press.

Kupfersmid, J. (1988). Improving what is published: A model in search of an editor. *American Psychologist, 43,* 635–642.

Labovitz, S. (1967). Some observations on measurement and statistics. *Social Forces, 46,* 151–160.

Labovitz, S. (1968). Criteria for selecting a significance level: A note on the sacredness of the .05. *American Sociologist, 3,* 220–222.

Labovitz, S. (1970). The assignment of numbers to rank order categories. *American Sociological Review, 35,* 515–524.

Labovitz, S. (1972). Statistical usage in sociology: Sacred cows and ritual. *Sociological Methods & Research, 1,* 13–37.

Lachman, M. E. (1983). Perceptions of intellectual aging: Antecedent or consequence of intellectual functioning? *Developmental Psychology, 19,* 482–498.

Lakatos, I. (1978). *The methodology of scientific research programmes: Philosophical papers* (Vol. 1). (J. Worrall & G. Currie, Eds.). New York: Cambridge University Press.

Lana, R. E. (1969). Pretest sensitization. In R. Rosenthal & R. L. Rosnow (Eds.), *Artifact in behavioral research* (pp. 119–141). New York: Academic Press.

Landy, F. J., & Farr, J. L. (1980). Performance ratings. *Psychological Bulletin, 87,* 72–107.

Larsen, R. J., & Seidman, E. (1986). Gender schema theory and sex role inventories: Some conceptual and psychometric considerations. *Journal of Personality and Social Psychology, 50,* 205–211.

Laska, E. M., Sunshine, A., Mueller, F., Elvers, W. B., Siegel, C., & Rubin, A. (1984). Caffeine as an analgesic adjuvant. *The Journal of the American Medical Association, 251,* 1711–1718.

Lauter, D. (1984, December 10). Making a case

with statistics. *The National Law Journal*, pp. 1, 10.

Lavrakas, P. J. (1987). *Telephone survey methods: Sampling, selection, and supervision*. Newbury Park, CA: Sage.

Lawler, E. E. (1966). Ability as a moderator of the relationship between job attitudes and job performance. *Personnel Psychology, 19*, 153–164.

Lawler, E. E. (1967). The multitrait-multirater approach to measuring managerial job performance. *Journal of Applied Psychology, 51*, 369–381.

Leamer, E. E. (1978). *Specification searches: Ad hoc inferences in nonexperimental data*. New York: Wiley.

Leamer, E. E. (1983). Let's take the con out of econometrics. *The American Economic Review, 73*, 31–43.

Leamer, E. E. (1985). Sensitivity analyses would help. *The American Economic Review, 75*, 308–313.

Leamer, E. E. (1988). Discussion. In C. C. Clogg (Ed.), *Sociological methodology 1988* (pp. 485–493). Washington, DC: American Sociological Association.

Lehmann, E. L. (1968). Hypothesis testing. In D. L. Sills (Ed.), *International encyclopedia of the social sciences* (Vol. 7, pp. 40–47). New York: Macmillan.

Lemon, N. (1973). *Attitudes and their measurement*. New York: Wiley.

Lerner, D. (Ed.). (1965). *Cause and effect*. New York: Free Press.

Levin, H. M. (1970). A new model of school effectiveness. In *Do teachers make a difference? A report on recent research on pupil achievement* (pp. 55–78). Washington, DC: U.S. Office of Education.

Levin, J. R. (1975). Determining sample size for planned and post hoc analysis of variance comparisons. *Journal of Educational Measurement, 12*, 99–108.

Lewis-Beck, M. S. (1986). Interrupted time series. In W. D. Berry & M. S. Lewis-Beck (Eds.), *New tools for social scientists: Advances and applications in research methods* (pp. 209–240). Newbury Park, CA: Sage.

Lewontin, R. C., Rose, S., & Kamin, L. J. (1984). *Not in our genes. Biology, ideology, and human nature*. New York: Pantheon Books.

Li, J. C. R. (1964). *Statistical inference* (Vol. 1,

rev. ed.). Ann Arbor, MI: Edwards Brothers.

Lieberson, S. (1985). *Making it count: The improvement of social research and theory*. Berkeley, CA: University of California Press.

Light, R. J., & Pillemer, D. B. (1984). *Summing up: The science of reviewing research*. Cambridge, MA: Harvard University Press.

Likert, R. (1932). A technique for the measurement of attitudes. *Archives of Psychology, 140*, 44–53.

Lin, N. (1976). *Foundations of social research*. New York: McGraw-Hill.

Lindblom, C. E., & Cohen, D. K. (1979). *Usable knowledge: Social science and social problem solving*. New Haven: Yale University Press.

Lindsey, D. (1977). Participation and influence in publication review proceedings: A reply. *American Psychologist, 32*, 579–586.

Linn, R. L. (1968). Range of restriction problems in the use of self-selected groups for test validation. *Psychological Bulletin, 69*, 69–73.

Linn, R. L. (1981). Measuring pretest–posttest performance changes. In R. A. Berk (Ed.), *Educational evaluation methodology: The state of the art* (pp. 84–109). Baltimore: Johns Hopkins University Press.

Linn, R. L. (1983a). Person selection formulas: Implications for studies of predictive bias and estimates of educational effects in selected samples. *Journal of Educational Measurement, 20*, 1–15.

Linn, R. L. (1983b). Predictive bias as an artifact of selection procedures. In H. Wainer & S. Messick (Eds.), *Principals [sic] of modern psychological measurement. A festschrift for Frederic M. Lord* (pp. 27–40). Hillsdale, NJ: Erlbaum.

Linn, R. L. (1984). Selection bias: Multiple meanings. *Journal of Educational Measurement, 21*, 33–47.

Linn, R. L., & Dunbar, S. B. (1982). Predictive validity of admissions measures: Corrections for selection on several variables. *Journal of College Student Personnel, 23*, 222–226.

Linn, R. L., & Slinde, J. A. (1977). The determination of the significance of change between pre- and posttesting periods. *Review of Educational Research, 47*, 121–150.

Linn, R. L., & Werts, C. E. (1971). Considerations for studies of test bias. *Journal of Educational Measurement, 8*, 1–4.

Linn, R. L., & Werts, C. E. (1982). Measurement error in regression. In G. Keren (Ed.), *Statistical and methodological issues in psychology and social sciences research (pp. 131–154). Hillsdale, NJ: Erlbaum.

Lipset, S. M. (1983). On the limits of social science. In R. B. Smith (Ed.), An introduction to social research: A handbook of social science methods (Vol. 1, pp. 149–168). Cambridge, MA: Ballinger.

Lipton, J. P., & Hershaft, A. M. (1985). On the widespread acceptance of dubious medical findings. Journal of Health and Social Behavior, 26, 336–351.

Lissitz, R. W., & Green, S. B. (1975). Effect of the number of scale points on reliability: A monte carlo approach. Journal of Applied Psychology, 60, 10–13.

Lodge, M. (1981). Magnitude scaling: Quantitative measurement of opinions. Newbury Park, CA: Sage.

Loeber, R., & Dishion, T. (1983). Early predictors of male delinquency: A review. Psychological Bulletin, 94, 68–99.

Loevinger, J. (1948). The technic of homogeneous tests compared with some aspects of "scale analysis" and factor analysis. Psychological Bulletin, 45, 507–529.

Loevinger, J. (1957). Objective tests as instruments of psychological theory. Psychological Reports, 3, 635–694 (Monograph Supplement 9).

Lofland, J. (1971). Analyzing social settings: A guide to qualitative observation and analysis. Belmont, CA: Wadsworth.

Long, J. S. (1983a). Confirmatory factor analysis. Newbury Park, CA: Sage.

Long, J. S. (1983b). Covariance structure models. An introduction to LISREL. Newbury Park, CA: Sage.

Long, J. S. (Ed.). (1988). Common problems/proper solutions: Avoiding error in quantitative research. Newbury Park, CA: Sage.

Long, V. O. (1986). Relationship of masculinity to self-esteem and self-acceptance in female professionals, college students, clients, and victims of domestic violence. Journal of Consulting and Clinical Psychology, 54, 323–327.

Long, V. O. (1989). Relation of masculinity to self-esteem and self-acceptance in male professionals, college students, and clients. Journal of Counseling Psychology, 36, 84–87.

Lord, F. M. (1953). On the statistical treatment of football numbers. American Psychologist, 8, 750–751.

Lord, F. M. (1954). Further comment on "Football Numbers." American Psychologist, 9, 264–265.

Lord, F. M. (1960). Large-sample covariance analysis when the control variable is fallible. Journal of the American Statistical Association, 55, 307–321.

Lord, F. M. (1967). A paradox in the interpretation of group comparisons. Psychological Bulletin, 68, 304–305.

Lord, F. M. (1969). Statistical adjustments when comparing preexisting groups. Psychological Bulletin, 72, 336–337.

Lord, F. M., & Novick, M. R. (1968). Statistical theories of mental test scores. Reading, MA: Addison-Wesley.

Lorr, M. (1983). Cluster analysis for social scientists: Techniques for analyzing and simplifying complex blocks of data. San Francisco: Jossey-Bass.

Lubinski, D. (1983). The androgyny dimension: A comment on Stokes, Childs, and Fuehrer. Journal of Consulting and Clinical Psychology, 30, 130–133.

Lubinski, D., Tellegen, A., & Butcher, J. N. (1981). The relationship between androgyny and subjective indicators of emotional well-being. Journal of Personality and Social Psychology, 40, 722–730.

Lubinski, D., Tellegen, A., & Butcher, J. N. (1983). Masculinity, femininity, and androgyny viewed and assessed as distinct concepts. Journal of Personality and Social Psychology, 44, 428–439.

Lynd, R. S. (1939). Knowledge for what? The place of social science in American culture. Princeton, NJ: Princeton University Press.

Lyons, J. (1964). On the psychology of the psychological experiment. In C. Scheerer (Ed.), Cognition: Theory, research, promise (pp. 89–109). New York: Harper & Row.

MacCallum, R. (1983). A comparison of factor analysis programs in SPSS, BMDP, and SAS. Psychometrika, 48, 223–231.

MacCallum, R. (1986). Specification searches in covariance structure modeling. Psychological Bulletin, 100, 107–120.

Macdonald, K. I. (1977). Path analysis. In C. A. O'Muircheartaigh & C. Payne (Eds.), The analysis of survey data (Vol. 2, pp. 81–104). New York: Wiley.

MacIver, R. M. (1942). Social causation. Boston: Ginn.

Mackay, A. L. (1977). The harvest of a quiet eye:

A selection of scientific quotations. Bristol, UK: Institute of Physics.

Mackie, J. L. (1965). Causes and conditions. *American Philosophical Quarterly*, *2*, 245–264.

Mackie, J. L. (1974). *The cement of the universe: A study of causation.* London: Oxford University Press.

Magnusson, D. (1967). *Test theory.* Reading, MA: Addison-Wesley.

Maguire, T. O. (1973). Semantic differential methodology for the structuring of attitudes. *American Educational Research Journal*, *10*, 295–306.

Mahoney, M. J. (1976). *Scientist as subject: The psychological imperative.* Cambridge, MA: Ballinger.

Mahoney, M. J. (1977a). Editorial. *Cognitive Therapy and Research*, *1*, 1–3.

Mahoney, M. J. (1977b). The first year: Editorial report. *Cognitive Therapy and Research*, *1*, 363–365.

Mahoney, M. J. (1977c). Publication prejudices: An experimental study of confirmatory bias in the peer review system. *Cognitive Therapy and Research*, *1*, 161–175.

Manis, M. (1975). Comment on Gergen's "Social psychology as history." *Personality and Social Psychology Bulletin*, *1*, 450–455.

Mann, I. T., Phillips, J. L., & Thompson, E. G. (1979). An examination of methodological issues relevant to the use and interpretation of the semantic differential. *Applied Psychological Measurement*, *3*, 213–229.

Mansfield, E. R., & Helms, B. P. (1982). Detecting multicollinearity. *The American Statistician*, *36*, 158–160.

Maranell, G. M. (1974a). Introduction. In G. M. Maranell (Ed.), *Scaling: A sourcebook for behavioral scientists* (pp. xi–xix). Chicago: Aldine.

Maranell, G. M. (Ed.). (1974b). *Scaling: A sourcebook for behavioral scientists.* Chicago: Aldine.

Marco, G. L. (1974). A comparison of selected school effectiveness measures based on longitudinal data. *Journal of Educational Measurement*, *11*, 225–234.

Mare, R. D., & Mason, W. M. (1980). Children's reports of parental socioeconomic status: A multiple group measurement model. *Sociological Methods & Research*, *9*, 178–198.

Margenau, H. (1950). *The nature of physical reality: A philosophy of modern physics.* New York: McGraw-Hill.

Margenau, H. (1959). Philosophical problems concerning the meaning of measurement in physics. In C. W. Churchman & P. Ratoosh (Eds.), *Measurement: Definitions and theories* (pp. 163–176). New York: Wiley.

Marini, M. M., & Singer, B. (1988). Causality in the social sciences. In C. C. Clogg (Ed.), *Sociological methodology 1988* (pp. 347–409). Washington, DC: American Sociological Association.

Mark, M. M., & Cook, T. D. (1984). Design of randomized experiments and quasi-experiments. In L. Rutman (Ed.), *Evaluation research methods: A basic guide* (2nd ed., pp. 65–120). Newbury Park, CA: Sage.

Markus, H., & Zajonc, R. B. (1985). The cognitive perspective in social psychology. In G. Lindzey & E. Aronson (Eds.), *Handbook of social psychology* (Vol. 1, 3rd ed., pp. 137–230). New York: Random House.

Marradi, A. (1981). Factor analysis as an aid in the formulation and refinement of empirically useful concepts. In D. J. Jackson & E. F. Borgatta (Eds.), *Factor analysis and measurement in sociological research: A multidimensional perspective* (pp. 11–49). Newbury Park, CA: Sage.

Marsh, C. (1982). *The survey method: The contribution of surveys to sociological explanation.* London: Allen & Unwin.

Marsh, H. W. (1985). The structure of masculinity/femininity: An application of factor analysis to higher-order factor structures and factorial invariance. *Multivariate Behavioral Research*, *20*, 427–449.

Marsh, H. W. (1987). The hierarchical structure of self-concept and the application of hierarchical confirmatory factor analysis. *Journal of Educational Measurement*, *24*, 17–39.

Marsh, H. W. (1988). Causal effects of academic self-concept and academic achievement: A re-analysis of Newman (1984). *Journal of Experimental Education*, *56*, 100–103.

Marsh, H. W., Balla, J. R., & McDonald, R. P. (1988). Goodness-of-fit indexes in confirmatory factor analysis: The effect of sample size. *Psychological Bulletin*, *103*, 391–410.

Marsh, H. W., & Shavelson, R. (1985). Self-concept: Its multifaceted, hierarchical structure. *Educational Psychologist*, *20*, 107–123.

Martin, E. (1983). Surveys as social indicators: Problems in monitoring trends. In P. H. Rossi, J. D. Wright, & A. B. Anderson (Eds.), *Hand-

book of survey research (pp. 677–743). New York: Academic Press.

Martin, J. A. (1982). Application of structural modeling with latent variables to adolescent drug use: A reply to Huba, Wingard, and Bentler. *Journal of Personality and Social Psychology*, *43*, 598–603.

Masling, J. (1966). Role-related behavior of the subject and psychologist and its effects upon psychological data. In D. Levine (Ed.), *Nebraska Symposium on Motivation* (pp. 67–103). Lincoln, NE: University of Nebraska Press.

Mason, J. C. (1984). *BASIC matrix methods*. Boston: Butterworths.

Mason, W. M., & Fienberg, S. E. (Eds.). (1985). *Cohort analysis in social research: Beyond the identification problem*. New York: Springer-Verlag.

Matell, M. S., & Jacoby, J. (1971). Is there an optimal number of alternatives for Likert scale items? Study I: Reliability and validity. *Educational and Psychological Measurement*, *31*, 657–674.

Matell, M. S., & Jacoby, J. (1972). Is there an optimal number of alternatives for Likert-scale items? Effects of testing time and scale properties. *Journal of Applied Psychology*, *56*, 506–509.

Matsueda, R. L., & Bielby, W. T. (1986). Statistical power in covariance structure models. In N. B. Tuma (Ed.), *Sociological methodology, 1986* (pp. 120–158). Washington, DC: American Sociological Association.

Matthews, T. A., & Brewer, J. K. (1977, April). *Setting effect size and power in some typical behavioral research situations*. Paper presented at the annual meeting of the American Educational Research Association, New York City.

Maxwell, A. E. (1977). *Multivariate analysis in behavioral research*. London: Chapman & Hall.

Maxwell, S. E., Camp, C. J., & Arvey, R. D. (1981). Measures of strength of association: A comparative examination. *Journal of Applied Psychology*, *66*, 525–534.

Mayerberg, C. K., & Bean, A. G. (1978). Two types of factors in the analysis of semantic differential attitude data. *Applied Psychological Measurement*, *2*, 469–480.

McArdle, J. J. (1986). Latent variable growth within behavior genetic models. *Behavior Genetics*, *16*, 163–200.

McArdle, J. J., & Epstein, D. (1987). Latent growth curves within developmental structural equation models. *Child Development*, *58*, 110–133.

McCall, R. B. (1977). Challenges to a science of developmental psychology. *Child Development*, *48*, 333–344.

McCarthy, P. J. (1951). *Sampling: Elementary principles*. Ithica, NY: New York State School of Industrial and Labor Relations, Cornell University.

McCleary, R., & Hay, R. A. (1980). *Applied time series analysis for the social sciences*. Newbury Park, CA: Sage.

McDonald, R. P. (1985). *Factor analysis and related methods*. Hillsdale, NJ: Erlbaum.

McDonald, R. P., & Mulaik, S. A. (1979). Determinacy of common factors: A nontechnical review. *Psychological Bulletin*, *86*, 297–306.

McDowall, D., McCleary, R., Meidinger, E. E., & Hay, R. A. (1980). *Interrupted time series analysis*. Newbury Park, CA: Sage.

McGaw, B., Wardrop, J. L., & Bunda, M. A. (1972). Classroom observation schemes: Where are the errors? *American Educational Research Journal*, *9*, 13–27.

McGee, M. G., & Snyder, M. (1975). Attribution and behavior: Two field studies. *Journal of Personality and Social Psychology*, *32*, 185–190.

McGuire, W. J. (1969a). The nature of attitudes and attitude change. In G. Lindzey & E. Aronson (Eds.), *Handbook of social psychology* (Vol. 3, 2nd ed., pp. 136–314). Reading, MA: Addison-Wesley.

McGuire, W. J. (1969b). Theory-oriented research in natural settings: The best of both worlds for social psychology. In M. Sherif & C. W. Sherif (Eds.), *Interdisciplinary relationships in the social sciences* (pp. 21–51). Chicago: Aldine.

McGuire, W. J. (1973). The yin and yang of progress in social psychology: Seven Koan. *Journal of Personality and Social Psychology*, *26*, 446–456.

McGuire, W. J. (1983). A contextualist theory of knowledge: Its implications for innovation and reform in psychological research. In L. Berkowitz (Ed.), *Advances in experimental social psychology* (Vol. 16, pp. 1–47). New York: Academic Press.

McHugh, M. C., Koeske, R. D., & Frieze, I. H. (1986). Issues to consider in conducting nonsexist psychological research: A guide for researchers. *American Psychologist, 41*, 879–890.

McHugh, R. B. (1957). The interval estimation of a true score. *Psychological Bulletin, 54*, 73–74.

McIver, J. P., & Carmines, E. G. (1981). *Unidimensional scaling*. Newbury Park, CA: Sage.

McKelvie, S. G. (1978). Graphic rating scales: How many categories? *British Journal of Psychology, 69*, 185–202.

McNeil, B. J., Pauker, S. G., Sox, H. C., & Tversky, A. (1982). On the elicitation of preferences for alternative therapies. *The New England Journal of Medicine, 306*, 1259–1262.

McNemar, Q. (1951). The factors in factoring behavior. *Psychometrika, 16*, 353–359.

Medawar, P. (1967). *The art of the soluble*. London: Methuen.

Medawar, P. (1982). *Pluto's republic*. New York: Oxford University Press.

Medley, D. M. (1982). Systematic observation. In H. E. Mitzel (Ed.), *Encyclopedia of educational research* (5th ed., pp. 1841–1851). New York: Free Press.

Medley, D. M., & Mitzel, H. E. (1963). Measuring classroom behavior by systematic observation. In N. L. Gage (Ed.), *Handbook of research on teaching* (pp. 247–328). Chicago: Rand McNally.

Mednick, S. A., Harway, M., & Finello, K. M. (Eds.). (1984). *Handbook of longitudinal research* (Vols. 1–2). New York: Praeger.

Meehl, P. E. (1967). Theory-testing in psychology and physics: A methodological paradox. *Philosophy of Science, 34*, 103–115.

Meehl, P. E. (1970). Nuisance variables and the ex post facto design. In M. Radner & S. Winokur (Eds.), *Minnesota Studies in the Philosophy of Science* (Vol. 4, pp. 373–402). Minneapolis: University of Minnesota Press.

Meehl, P. E. (1971). High school yearbooks: A reply to Schwarz. *Journal of Abnormal and Social Psychology, 77*, 143–148.

Meehl, P. E. (1978). Theoretical risks and tabular asterisks: Sir Karl, Sir Ronald, and the slow progress of soft psychology. *Journal of Consulting and Clinical Psychology, 46*, 806–834.

Meehl, P. E., & Golden, R. R. (1982). Taxometric methods. In P. C. Kendall & J. N. Butcher (Eds.), *Handbook of research methods in clinical psychology* (pp. 127–181). New York: Wiley.

Meehl, P. E., & Rosen, A. (1955). Antecedent probability and the efficiency of psychometric signs, patterns, or cutting scores. *Psychological Bulletin, 52*, 194–216.

Menard, S., & Morse, B. J. (1984). A structuralist critique of the IQ–delinquency hypothesis: Theory and evidence. *American Journal of Sociology, 89*, 1347–1378.

Menard, S., & Morse, B. J. (1986). IQ and delinquency: A response to Harry and Minor. *American Journal of Sociology, 91*, 962–968.

Merton, R. K. (1948). The self-fulfilling prophecy. *Antioch Review, 8*, 193–200.

Merton, R. K. (1968). *Social theory and social structure* (enlarged ed.). New York: Free Press.

Merton, R. K. (1982). *Social research and the practicing professions* (A. Rosenblatt & T. F. Gieryn, Eds.). Cambridge, MA: Abt Books.

Messick, S. J. (1967). The psychology of acquiescence: An interpretation of research evidence. In I. A. Berg (Ed.), *Response set in personality assessment* (pp. 115–145). Chicago: Aldine.

Messick, S. (1975). The standard problem: Meaning and values in measurement and evaluation. *American Psychologist, 30*, 955–966.

Messick, S. (1980). Test validity and the ethics of assessment. *American Psychologist, 35*, 1012–1027.

Messick, S. (1981). Constructs and their vicissitudes in educational and psychological measurement. *Psychological Bulletin, 89*, 575–588.

Mezzich, J. E., & Solomon, H. (1980). *Taxonomy and behavioral science: Comparative performance of grouping methods*. New York: Academic Press.

Microsoft Chart. (1987). Redmond, WA: Microsoft Corporation.

Milavsky, J. R., Kessler, R. C., Stipp, H. H., & Rubens, W. S. (1982). *Television and aggression: A panel study*. New York: Academic Press.

Milavsky, J. R., Kessler, R. C., Stipp, H. H., & Rubens, W. S. (1984). *A comment* by J. Ronald Milavsky, Ronald C. Kessler, Horst H. Stipp, and William S. Rubens. *Journal of Communication, 34*, 182–187.

Mill, J. S. (1852). *A system of logic*. New York: Harper & Brothers.

Miller, D. C. (1983). *Handbook of research design and social measurement* (4th ed.). New York: Longman.

Miller, J. K., & Knapp, T. R. (1971). The importance of statistical power in educational research. *Occasional Paper 13*. Bloomington, IN: Phi Delta Kappa.

Miller, J., Slomczynski, K. M., & Schoenberg, R. J. (1981). Assessing comparability of measurement in cross-national research: Authoritarian–Conservatism in different sociocultural settings. *Social Psychology Quarterly, 44*, 178–191.

Miller, P. McC., & Wilson, M. J. (1983). *A dictionary of social science methods*. New York: Wiley.

Miller, P. V., & Cannell, C. F. (1988). Interviews in sample surveys. In J. P. Keeves (Ed.), *Educational research, methodology, and measurement: An international handbook* (pp. 457–465). New York: Pergamon.

Miller R. G. (1966). *Simultaneous statistical inference*. New York: McGraw-Hill.

Milton, S. (1986). A sample size formula for multiple regression studies. *Public Opinion Quarterly, 50*, 112–118.

Minitab Inc. (1987). *Minitab user's guide: Microcomputer version, release 6*. State College, PA: Author.

Minitab Inc. (1988). *Minitab statistical software, reference manual, release 6.1*. State College, PA: Author.

Miron, M. S. (1972). Universal semantic differential shell game. *Journal of Personality and Social Psychology, 24*, 313–320.

Miron, M. S., & Osgood, C. E. (1966). Language behavior: The multivariate structure of qualification. In R. B. Cattell (Ed.), *Handbook of multivariate experimental psychology* (pp. 790–819). Chicago: Rand McNally.

Mischel, W., Zeiss, R., & Zeiss, A. (1974). Internal–external control and persistence: Validation and implications of the Stanford preschool internal–external scale. *Journal of Personality and Social Psychology, 29*, 265–278.

Mishler, E. G. (1986). *Research interviewing: Context and narrative*. Cambridge, MA: Harvard University Press.

Mitchell, S. K. (1979). Interobserver agreement, reliability, and generalizability of data collected in observational studies. *Psychological Bulletin, 86*, 376–390.

Mohr, L. B. (1982). On rescuing the nonequivalent-control-group design. *Sociological Methods & Research, 11*, 53–80.

Molenaar, N. J. (1982). Response-effects of "formal" characteristics of questions. In W. Dijkstra & J. van der Zouwen (Eds.), *Response behaviour in the survey-interview* (pp. 49–89). London: Academic Press.

Montaigne. (1965). *The complete essays of Montaigne* (D. M. Frame, Trans.). Stanford: Stanford University Press.

Mook, D. G. (1983). In defense of external invalidity. *American Psychologist, 38*, 379–387.

Moore, D. S. (1979). *Statistics: Concepts and controversies*. San Francisco: Freeman.

Morgan, B. W. (1968). *An introduction to Bayesian statistical decision processes*. Englewood Cliffs, NJ: Prentice-Hall.

Morrison, D. E., & Henkel, R. E. (Eds.). (1970). *The significance test controversy*. Chicago: Aldine.

Mortimer, J. T., Finch, M. D., & Kumka, D. (1982). Persistence and change in development: The multidimensional self-concept. In P. B. Baltes & O. G. Brim (Eds.), *Life-span development and behavior* (Vol. 4, pp. 263–313). New York: Academic Press.

Mortimer, J. T., & Lorence, J. (1979). Occupational experience and the self-concept: A longitudinal study. *Social Psychology Quarterly, 42*, 307–323.

Moser, C. A., & Kalton, G. (1972). *Survey methods in social investigation*. New York: Basic Books.

Moses, L. E., & Oakford, R. V. (1963). *Tables of random permutations*. Stanford, CA: Stanford University Press.

Moss, L., & Goldstein, H. (Eds.). (1979). *The recall method in social surveys*. London: University of London Institute of Education.

Mosteller, F. (1981). Innovation and evaluation. *Science, 211*, 881–886.

Mulaik, S. A. (1972). *The foundations of factor analysis*. New York: McGraw-Hill.

Mulaik, S. A. (1975). Confirmatory factor analysis. In D. J. Amick & H. J. Walberg (Eds.), *Introductory multivariate analysis* (pp. 170–207). Berkeley, CA: McCutchan.

Mulaik, S. A. (1982). Factor analysis. In H. E. Mitzel (Ed.), *Encyclopedia of educational research* (5th ed., pp. 637–646). New York: Free Press.

Mulaik, S. A. (1987). Toward a conception of causality applicable to experimentation and causal modeling. *Child Development, 58*, 18–32.

Mulaik, S. A. (1988). Confirmatory factor analysis. In J. R. Nesselroade & R. B. Cattell (Eds.), *Handbook of multivariate experimental psychology* (2nd ed., pp. 259–288). New York: Plenum.

Mulaik, S. A., James, L. R., Van Alstine, J., Bennett, N., Lind, S., & Stilwell, C. D. (1989). Evaluation of goodness-of-fit indices for structural equation models. *Psychological Bulletin, 105*, 430–445.

Mullen, B., & Rosenthal, R. (1985). *BASIC Meta-analysis: Procedures and programs.* Hillsdale, NJ: Erlbaum.

Murnane, R. J. (1984). A review essay—comparisons of public and private schools: Lessons from the uproar. *Journal of Human Resources, 19*, 263–277.

Murnane, R. J., Newstead, S., & Olsen, R. J. (1985). Comparing public and private schools: The puzzling role of selectivity bias. *Journal of Business & Economic Statistics, 3*, 23–35.

Murphy, G. (1939). The research task of social psychology. *The Journal of Social Psychology, 10*, 107–120.

Murray, L. W., & Dosser, D. A. (1987). How significant is a significant difference? Problems with the measurement of the magnitude of effect. *Journal of Counseling Psychology, 34*, 68–72.

Muthén, B. O. (1987). Response to Freedman's critique of path analysis: Improve credibility by better methodological training. *Journal of Educational Statistics, 12*, 178–184.

Muthén, B., & Jöreskog, K. G. (1983). Selectivity problems in quasi-experimental studies. *Evaluation Review, 7*, 139–174.

Myers, J. L. (1979). *Fundamentals of experimental design* (3rd ed.). Boston: Allyn & Bacon.

Nagel, E. (1931). Measurement. *Erkenntnis, 2*, 313–333.

Nagel, E. (1961). *The structure of science: Problems in the logic of scientific explanation.* New York: Harcourt, Brace & World.

Nagel, E. (1965). Types of causal explanation in science. In D. Lerner (Ed.), *Cause and effect* (pp. 11–26). New York: Free Press.

Namboodiri, K. (1984). *Matrix algebra.* Newbury Park, CA: Sage.

Namboodiri, N. K. (1970). A statistical exposition of the "Before–After" and "After-Only" designs and their combinations. *American Journal of Sociology, 76*, 83–102.

Namboodiri, N. K., Carter, L. F., & Blalock, H. M. (1975). *Applied multivariate analysis and*

experimental designs. New York: McGraw-Hill.

Naylor, J. C., & Shine, L. C. (1965). A table for determining the increase in mean criterion score obtained by using a selection device. *Journal of Industrial Psychology, 3*, 33–42.

Neff, J. A. (1985). Race and vulnerability to stress: An examination of differential vulnerability. *Journal of Personality and Social Psychology, 49*, 481–491.

Nelson, C. R. (1973). *Applied time series analysis for managerial forecasting.* San Francisco: Holden-Day.

Nesselroade, J. R., & Baltes, P. B. (Eds.). (1979). *Longitudinal research in the study of behavior and development.* New York: Academic Press.

Newberry, B. H. (1973). Truth telling in subjects with information about experiments: Who is being deceived? *Journal of Personality and Social Psychology, 25*, 369–374.

Newcomb, M. D., & Bentler, P. M. (1987). Self-report methods of assessing health status and health service utilization: A hierarchical confirmatory factor analysis. *Multivariate Behavioral Research, 22*, 415–436.

Newcomb, M. D., & Bentler, P. M. (1988). *Consequences of adolescent drug use: Impact on the lives of young adults.* Newbury Park, CA: Sage.

Newman, R. S. (1984). Children's achievement and self-evaluations in mathematics: A longitudinal study. *Journal of Educational Psychology, 76*, 857–873.

Neyman, J. (1950). *First course in probability and statistics.* New York: Henry Holt.

Nicewander, W. A., & Price, J. M. (1978). Dependent variable reliability and the power of significance tests. *Psychological Bulletin, 85*, 405–409.

Nicewander, W. A., & Price, J. M. (1983). Reliability of measurement and the power of statistical tests: Some new results. *Psychological Bulletin, 94*, 524–533.

Nicholson, W., & Wright, S. R. (1977). Participants' understanding of the treatment in policy experimentation. *Evaluation Quarterly, 1*, 245–268.

Nietzsche, F. (1968). *The will to power* (W. Kaufmann & R. J. Hollingdale, Trans.). New York: Vintage.

Northrop, F. S. C. (1947). *The logic of the sci-*

ences and the humanities. New York: Macmillan.

Norusis, M. J., & SPSS Inc. (1988a). SPSS/PC+ advanced statistics V2.0. Chicago: SPSS Inc.

Norusis, M. J., & SPSS Inc. (1988b). SPSS/PC+ Studentware. Chicago: SPSS Inc.

Norusis, M. J., & SPSS Inc. (1988c). SPSS/PC+ V2.0 base manual. Chicago: SPSS Inc.

Novick, M. R. (1966). The axioms and principal results of classical test theory. Journal of Mathematical Psychology, 3, 1–18.

Novick, M. R. (1983). The centrality of Lord's paradox and exchangeability for all statistical inference. In H. Wainer & S. Messick (Eds.), Principals [sic] of modern psychological measurement. A festschrift for Frederic M. Lord (pp. 41–53). Hillsdale, NJ: Erlbaum.

Novick, M. R., & Jackson, P. H. (1974). Statistical methods for educational and psychological research. New York: McGraw-Hill.

Novick, M. R., & Lewis, C. (1967). Coefficient alpha and the reliability of composite measurements. Psychometrika, 32, 1–13.

Nunnally, J. (1960). The place of statistics in psychology. Educational and Psychological Measurement, 20, 641–650.

Nunnally, J. (1967). Psychometric theory. New York: McGraw-Hill.

Nunnally, J. (1978). Psychometric theory (2nd ed.). New York: McGraw-Hill.

Oaks, M. (1986). Statistical inference: A commentary for the social and behavioural sciences. Chichester, UK: Wiley.

O'Connor, E. F. (1972a). Extending classical test theory to the measurement of change. Review of Educational Research, 42, 73–97.

O'Connor, E. F. (1972b). Response to Cronbach and Furby's "How we should measure change—or should we?" Psychological Bulletin, 78, 159–160.

O'Donovan, T. M. (1983). Short term forecasting: An introduction to the Box–Jenkins approach. New York: Wiley.

O'Grady, K. E. (1982). Measures of explained variance: Cautions and limitations. Psychological Bulletin, 92, 766–777.

O'Grady, K. E. (1988). The Marlowe–Crowne and Edwards Social Desirability Scales: A psychometric perspective. Multivariate Behavioral Research, 23, 87–101.

O'Grady, K. E., & Medoff, D. R. (1988). Categorical variables in multiple regression: Some cautions. Multivariate Behavioral Research, 23, 243–260.

Olson, J. C., & Peter, J. P. (1984). External validity? In P. F. Anderson & M. J. Ryan (Eds.), 1984 AMA Winter Educators' Conference: Scientific method in marketing (pp. 81–84). Chicago: American Marketing Association.

O'Malley, P. M., & Bachman, J. G. (1983). Self-esteem: Change and stability between ages 13 and 23. Developmental Psychology, 19, 257–268.

O'Muircheartaigh, C. A. (1977). Response errors. In C. A. O'Muircheartaigh & C. Payne (Eds.), The analysis of survey data (Vol. 2, pp. 193–239). New York: Wiley.

Oppenheim, A. N. (1966). Questionnaire design and attitude measurement. New York: Basic Books.

Orne, M. T. (1962). On the social psychology of the psychological experiment: With particular reference to demand characteristics and their implications. American Psychologist, 17, 776–783.

Orne, M. T. (1969). Demand characteristics and the concept of quasi-controls. In R. Rosenthal & R. L. Rosnow (Eds.), Artifact in behavioral research (pp. 143–179). New York: Academic Press.

Ortega y Gasset, J. (1932). The revolt of the masses. New York: Norton.

Osgood, C. E. (1952). The nature and measurement of meaning. Psychological Bulletin, 49, 197–237.

Osgood, C. E., May, W. H., & Miron, M. S. (1975). Cross-cultural universals of affective meaning. Urbana, IL: University of Illinois.

Osgood, C. E., Suci, G. J., & Tennenbaum, P. H. (1957). The measurement of meaning. Urbana, IL: University of Illinois.

Ostrom, T. M. (1969). The relationship between the affective, behavioral, and cognitive components of attitude. Journal of Experimental Social Psychology, 5, 12–30.

Overall, J. E. (1980). Power of chi-square tests for 2 X 2 contingency tables with small expected frequencies. Psychological Bulletin, 87, 132–135.

Overall, J. E., & Dalal, S. N. (1965). Design of experiments to maximize power relative to cost. Psychological Bulletin, 64, 339–350.

Overall, J. E., & Klett, C. J. (1972). Applied

multivariate analysis. New York: McGraw-Hill.

Overall, J. E., & Woodward, J. A. (1975). Unreliability of difference scores: A paradox for measurement of change. *Psychological Bulletin, 82*, 85–86.

Overall, J. E., & Woodward, J. A. (1976). Reassertion of the paradoxical power of tests of significance based on unreliable difference scores. *Psychological Bulletin, 83*, 776–777.

Overall, J. E., & Woodward, J. A. (1977a). Common misconceptions concerning the analysis of covariance. *Multivariate Behavioral Research, 12*, 171–186.

Overall, J. E., & Woodward, J. A. (1977b). Nonrandom assignment and the analysis of covariance. *Psychological Bulletin, 84*, 588–594.

Page, M. M. (Ed.). (1980). *Beliefs, attitudes, and values: 1979 Nebraska Symposium on Motivation*. Lincoln, NE: University of Nebraska Press.

Palkovitz, R. (1985). Fathers' birth attendance, early contact, and extended contact with their newborns: A critical review. *Child Development, 56*, 392–406.

Pankratz, A. (1983). *Forecasting with univariate Box–Jenkins models: Concepts and cases*. New York: Wiley.

Pastore, N. (1950). A neglected factor in the frustration–aggression hypothesis: A comment. *The Journal of Psychology, 29*, 271–279.

Paul, D. E. (1985). Textbook treatments of genetics of intelligence. *The Quarterly Review of Biology, 60*, 317–326.

Paul, D. E. (1987). The nine lives of discredited data: Old textbooks never die–they just get paraphrased. *The Sciences, 27*(3), 26–30.

Paulhus, D. L., & Martin, C. L. (1988). Functional flexibility: A new conception of interpersonal flexibility. *Journal of Personality and Social Psychology, 55*, 88–101.

Pawson, R. (1989). *A measure for measures: A manifesto for empirical sociology*. London: Routledge.

Payne, S. L. (1951). *The art of asking questions*. Princeton: Princeton University Press.

Peaker, G. F. (1975). *An empirical study of education in twenty-one countries: A technical report*. New York: Wiley.

Pearson, E. S., & Hartley, H. O. (1951). Charts of the power function for analysis of variance tests, derived from the non-central F distribution. *Biometrika, 38*, 112–130.

Pearson, K. (1911). *The grammar of science* (3rd ed.). London: Adam & Charles Black.

Pedhazur, E. J. (1978). Wilson–Patterson Attitude Inventory. In O. K. Buros (Ed.), *The eighth mental measurements yearbook* (Vol. 1, pp. 1150–1152). Highland Park, NJ: Gryphon Press.

Pedhazur, E. J. (1982). *Multiple regression in behavioral research: Explanation and prediction* (2nd ed.). New York: Holt, Rinehart & Winston.

Pedhazur, E. J., & Tetenbaum, T. J. (1979). Bem sex role inventory: A theoretical and methodological critique. *Journal of Personality and Social Psychology, 37*, 996–1016.

Peirce, C. S. (1932). *Collected papers of Charles Sanders Peirce* (Vol. 2). (C. Hartshorne & P. Weiss, Eds.). Cambridge, MA: Harvard University Press.

Peirce, C. S. (1958). *Collected papers of Charles Sanders Peirce* (Vol. 7). (A. W. Burks, Ed.). Cambridge, MA: Harvard University Press.

Pencil, M. (1976). Salt passage research: The state of the art. *Journal of Communication, 26*(4), 31–36.

Peters, D. P., & Ceci, S. J. (1982). Peer-review practices of psychological journals: The fate of published articles, submitted again. *The Behavioral and Brain Sciences, 5*, 187–195.

Petersen, N. S. (1980). Bias in the selection rule—Bias in the test. In L. J. Th. van der Kemp, W. F. Langerak, & D. N. M. de Gruijter (Eds.), *Psychometrics for educational debates* (pp. 103–122). New York: Wiley.

Petersen, N. S., & Novick, M. R. (1976). An evaluation of some models of culture-fair selection. *Journal of Educational Measurement, 13*, 3–29.

Petzold, C. (1985, November 12). Turning data into information. *PC Magazine*, pp. 155–160.

Pezzullo, T. R., & Brittingham, B. E. (Eds.). (1979). *Salary equity: Detecting sex bias in salaries among college and university professors*. Lexington, MA: Heath.

Phillips, D. L. (1978). Hierarchies of interaction in sociological research. In M. Brenner, P. Marsh, & M. Brenner (Eds.), *The social contexts of method* (pp. 210–236). New York: St. Martin's Press.

Phillips, L. D. (1974). *Bayesian statistics for social scientists*. New York: Crowell.

Pindyck, R. S., & Rubinfeld, D. L. (1981). *Econometric models and economic forecasts* (2nd ed.). New York: McGraw-Hill.

Planck, M. (1968). A scientific autobiography. In M. Planck, *A scientific autobiography and other papers* (pp. 13–51). (F. Gaynor, Trans.). New York: Greenwood Press.

Platt, J. R. (1964). Strong inference. *Science*, *146*, 347–353.

Plewis, I. (1985). *Analysing change: Measurement and explanation using longitudinal data*. New York: Wiley.

Pocock, S. J., Hughes, M. D., & Lee, R. J. (1987). Statistical problems in the reporting of clinical trials. *The New England Journal of Medicine*, *317*, 426–432.

Polanyi, M. (1964). *Personal knowledge: Towards a post-critical philosophy*. New York: Harper Torchbooks.

Polanyi, M. (1968). Logic and psychology. *American Psychologist*, *23*, 27–43.

Popper, K. R. (1959). *The logic of scientific discovery*. New York: Basic Books.

Popper, K. R. (1968). *Conjectures and refutations: The growth of scientific knowledge*. New York: Harper Torchbooks.

Popper, K. R. (1972). *Objective knowledge: An evolutionary approach*. Oxford: Clarendon Press.

Porter, A. (1967). *The effects of using fallible variables in the analysis of covariance*. Unpublished doctoral dissertation, University of Wisconsin, Madison.

Porter, A. C., & Chibucos, T. R. (1975). Common problems for design and analysis in evaluative research. *Sociological Methods & Research*, *3*, 235–257.

Potthoff, R. F. (1964). On the Johnson–Neyman technique and some extensions thereof. *Psychometrika*, *29*, 241–256.

Prioleau, L., Murdock, M., & Brody, N. (1983). An analysis of psychotherapy versus placebo studies. *The Behavioral and Brain Sciences*, *6*, 275–285.

Proshansky, H. M. (1981). Uses and abuses of theory in applied research. In L. Bickman (Ed.), *Applied social psychology annual 2* (pp. 97–135). Newbury Park, CA: Sage.

Ralph, H. D. (1967). How to speak glibly about computers. *Oil and Gas Journal*, *65*(50), 61.

Ramsay, J. O. (1973). The effect of number of categories in rating scales on precision of estimation of scale values. *Psychometrika*, *38*, 513–532.

Rand Corporation. (1955). *A million random digits with 100,000 normal deviates*. New York: Free Press.

Rao, P., & Miller, R. L. (1971). *Applied econometrics*. Belmont, CA: Wadsworth.

Reagan, M. D. (1967). Basic and applied research: A meaningful distinction? *Science*, *155*, 1383–1386.

Reichardt, C. S. (1979). The statistical analysis of data from nonequivalent group designs. In T. D. Cook & D. T. Campbell (Eds.), *Quasi-experimentation: Design & analysis issues for field settings* (pp. 147–205). Chicago: Rand McNally.

Reichardt, C. S. (1985). Reinterpreting Seaver's (1973) study of teacher expectancies as a regression artifact. *Journal of Educational Psychology*, *77*, 231–236.

Reichardt, C. S., & Gollob, H. F. (1986). Satisfying the constraints of causal modeling. In W. M. K. Trochim (Ed.), *Advances in quasi-experimental design and analysis* (pp. 91–107). San Francisco: Jossey-Bass.

Reichenbach, H. (1938). *Experience and prediction*. Chicago: University of Chicago Press.

Reiser, M., Wallace, M., & Schuessler, K. (1986). Direction-of-wording effects in dichotomous social life feeling items. In N. B. Tuma (Ed.), *Sociological methodology 1986* (pp. 1–25). San Francisco: Jossey-Bass.

Reyment, R. A., Blackith, R. E., & Campbell, N. A. (1984). *Multivariate morphometrics* (2nd ed.). New York: Academic Press.

Reynolds, C. R. (1982). The problem of bias in psychological assessment. In C. R. Reynolds & T. B. Gutkin (Eds.), *The handbook of school psychology* (pp. 178–208). New York: Wiley.

Reynolds, C. R., & Brown, R. T. (Eds.). (1984). *Perspectives on bias in mental testing*. New York: Plenum.

Reynolds, H. T. (1977). *The analysis of cross-classification*. New York: Free Press.

Reynolds, P. D. (1979). *Ethical dilemmas and social science research*. San Francisco: Jossey-Bass.

Richards, I. A. (1926). *Principles of literary criticism* (2nd ed.). London: Routledge & Kegan Paul.

Richards, J. M. (1982). Standardized versus unstandardized regression weights. *Applied Psychological Measurement*, *6*, 201–212.

Riecken, H. W., & Boruch, R. F. (Eds.). (1974). *Social experimentation: A method for planning and evaluating social intervention.* New York: Academic Press.

Rindskopf, D. (1986). New developments in selection modeling for quasi-experimentation. In W. M. K. Trochim (Ed.), *Advances in quasi-experimental design and analysis* (pp. 79–89). San Francisco: Jossey-Bass.

Rindskopf, D., & Rose, T. (1988). Some theory and applications of confirmatory second-order factor analysis. *Multivariate Behavioral Research*, *23*, 51–67.

Rist, R. C. (1987). Do teachers count in the lives of children? A reply to Wineburg. *Educational Researcher*, *16*(9), 41–42.

Roberts, A. O. H. (1980). Regression toward the mean and the regression-effect bias. In G. Echternacht (Ed.), *Measurement aspects of Title I evaluations* (pp. 59–82). San Francisco: Jossey-Bass.

Robins, J. M., & Greenland, S. (1986). The role of model selection in causal inference from nonexperimental data. *American Journal of Epidemiology*, *123*, 392–402.

Robinson, W. S. (1957). The statistical measurement of agreement. *American Sociological Review*, *22*, 17–25.

Rochester, J. B., & Gantz, J. (1983). *The naked computer: A layperson's almanac of computer lore, wizardry, personalities, memorabilia, world records, mind blowers and tomfoolery.* New York: William Morrow.

Rock, D. A., Werts, C. E., & Flaugher, R. L. (1978). The use of analysis of covariance structures for comparing the psychometric properties of multiple variables across populations. *Multivariate Behavioral Research*, *13*, 403–418.

Rogers, R. W., & Mewborn, C. R. (1976). Fear appeals and attitude change: Effects of a threat's noxiousness, probability of occurrence, and the efficacy of coping responses. *Journal of Personality and Social Psychology*, *34*, 54–61.

Rogosa, D. (1979). Causal models in longitudinal research: Rationale, formulation, and interpretation. In J. R. Nesselroade & P. B. Baltes (Eds.), *Longitudinal research in the study of behavior and development* (pp. 263–302). New York: Academic Press.

Rogosa, D. (1980a). Comparing nonparallel regression lines. *Psychological Bulletin*, *88*, 307–321.

Rogosa, D. (1980b). Comparisons of some procedures for analyzing longitudinal panel data. *Journal of Economics and Business*, *32*, 136–151.

Rogosa, D. (1980c). Time and time again: Some analysis problems in longitudinal research. In C. E. Bidwell & D. M. Windham (Eds.), *The analysis of educational productivity* (Vol. 2, pp. 153–201). Cambridge, MA: Ballinger Press.

Rogosa, D. (1981). On the relationship between the Johnson–Neyman region of significance and statistical tests of parallel within-group regressions. *Educational and Psychological Measurement*, *41*, 73–84.

Rogosa, D., Brandt, D., & Zimowski, M. (1982). A growth curve approach to the measurement of change. *Psychological Bulletin*, *92*, 726–746.

Rogosa, D. R., & Willett, J. B. (1983). Demonstrating the reliability of the difference score in the measurement of change. *Journal of Educational Measurement*, *20*, 335–343.

Romesburg, H. C. (1984). *Cluster analysis for researchers.* Belmont, CA: Lifetime Learning Publications.

Rosenbaum, D. E. (1970, January 4). Statisticians charge draft lottery was not random. *The New York Times*, p. 66.

Rosenberg, M. (1979). Disposition concepts in behavioral science. In R. K. Merton, J. S. Coleman, & P. H. Rossi (Eds.), *Qualitative and quantitative social research* (pp. 245–260). New York: Free Press.

Rosenberg, M. J. (1965). When dissonance fails: On eliminating evaluation apprehension from attitude measurement. *Journal of Personality and Social Psychology*, *1*, 28–42.

Rosenberg, M. J. (1969). The conditions and consequences of evaluation apprehension. In R. Rosenthal & R. L. Rosnow (Eds.), *Artifact in behavioral research* (pp. 279–349). New York: Academic Press.

Rosenthal, R. (1963). On the social psychology of the psychological experiment: The experimenter's hypothesis as unintended determinant of experimental results. *American Scientist*, *51*, 268–283.

Rosenthal, R. (1966). *Experimenter effects in be-*

havioral research. New York: Appleton-Century-Crofts.

Rosenthal, R. (1968). Experimenter expectancy and the reassuring nature of the null hypothesis decision procedure. *Psychological Bulletin Monographs Supplement, 70*(6, Pt. 2), 30–47.

Rosenthal, R. (1969a). Empirical vs decreed validation of clocks and tests. *American Educational Research Journal, 6,* 689–691.

Rosenthal, R. (1969b). Interpersonal expectations: Effects of the experimenter's hypothesis. In R. Rosenthal & R. L. Rosnow (Eds.), *Artifact in behavioral research* (pp. 181–277). New York: Academic Press.

Rosenthal, R. (1984). *Meta-analytic procedures for social research.* Newbury Park, CA: Sage.

Rosenthal, R. (1987). Pygmalion Effects: Existence, magnitude, and social importance: A reply to Wineburg. *Educational Researcher, 16*(9), 37–41.

Rosenthal, R., & Jacobson, L. (1968). *Pygmalion in the classroom: Teacher expectation and pupils' intellectual development.* New York: Holt, Rinehart & Winston.

Rosenthal, R., & Rosnow, R. L. (Eds.). (1969a). *Artifact in behavioral research.* New York: Academic Press.

Rosenthal, R., & Rosnow, R. L. (1969b). The volunteer subject. In R. Rosenthal & R. L. Rosnow (Eds.), *Artifact in behavioral research* (pp. 59–118). New York: Academic Press.

Rosenthal, R., & Rubin, D. B. (1978). Interpersonal expectancy effects: the first 345 studies. *The Behavioral and Brain Sciences, 3,* 377–386, 410–415.

Rosenzweig, S. (1933). The experimental situation as a psychological problem. *Psychological Review, 40,* 337–354.

Rosnow, R. L., & Rosenthal, R. (1976). The volunteer subject revisited. *Australian Journal of Psychology, 28,* 97–108.

Ross, M., & Fletcher, G. J. O. (1985). Attribution and social perception. In G. Lindzey & E. Aronson (Eds.), *Handbook of social psychology* (Vol. 2, 3rd ed., pp. 73–122). New York: Random House.

Rossiter, C. (1968). Conservatism. In D. L. Sills (Ed.), *International encyclopedia of the social sciences* (Vol. 3, pp. 290–295). New York: Macmillan.

Roth, J. A. (1966). Hired hand research. *The American Sociologist, 1,* 190–196.

Rothblum, E. D. (1988). More on reporting sex differences. *American Psychologist, 43,* 1095.

Rotter, J. B. (1966). Generalized expectancies for internal versus external control of reinforcement. *Psychological Monographs, 80*(1, Whole No. 609).

Rotter, J. B. (1975). Some problems and misconceptions related to the construct of internal versus external control of reinforcement. *Journal of Consulting and Clinical Psychology, 43,* 56–67.

Rotton, J., & Schonemann, P. H. (1978). Power tables for analysis of variance. *Educational and Psychological Measurement, 38,* 213–229.

Rowley, G. L. (1976). The reliability of observational measures. *American Educational Research Journal, 13,* 51–59.

Rozeboom, W. W. (1960). The fallacy of the null-hypothesis significance test. *Psychological Bulletin, 57,* 416–428.

Rozeboom, W. W. (1961). Ontological induction and the logical typology of scientific variables. *Philosophy of Science, 28,* 337–377.

Rozeboom, W. W. (1966). *Foundations of the theory of prediction.* Homewood, IL: Dorsey Press.

Rubin, D. B. (1974). Estimating causal effects of treatments in randomized and nonrandomized studies. *Journal of Educational Psychology, 66,* 688–701.

Rubin, D. B. (1977). Assignment to treatment group on the basis of a covariate. *Journal of Educational Statistics, 2,* 1–26.

Rudner, R. (1953). The scientist *qua* scientist makes value judgments. *Philosophy of Science, 20,* 1–6.

Russell, B. (1929). *Mysticism and logic.* London: Allen & Unwin.

Rutstein, D. D. (1969). The ethical design of human experiments. *Daedalus, 98,* 523–541.

Ryan, B. F., Joiner, B. L., & Ryan, T. A., Jr. (1985). *Minitab handbook* (2nd ed.). Boston: Duxbury Press.

Saal, F. E., Downey, R. G., & Lahey, M. A. (1980). Rating the ratings: Assessing the psychometric quality of rating data. *Psychological Bulletin, 88,* 413–428.

Sachdeva, D. (1973). Estimating strength of relationship in multivariate analysis of variance. *Educational and Psychological Measurement, 33,* 627–631.

Sackett, G. P. (Ed.). (1978). *Observing behavior Volume II: Data collection and analysis methods.* Baltimore: University Park Press.

Sandberg-Diment, E. (1986, September 30). Powerful software deals with statistics. *The New York Times*, p. C3.

Sandelands, L. E., & Calder, B. J. (1984). Referencing and bias in social interaction. *Journal of Personality and Social Psychology*, *46*, 755–762.

Sanford, N. (1973). Authoritarian personality in contemporary perspective. In J. N. Knutson (Ed.), *Handbook of political psychology* (pp. 139–170). San Francisco: Jossey-Bass.

Saretsky, G. (1972). The OEO P.C. experiment and the John Henry effect. *Phi Delta Kappan*, *53*, 579–581.

Saris, W. E., Den Ronden, J., & Satorra, A. (1987). Testing structural equation models. In P. Cuttance & R. Ecob (Eds.), *Structural modeling by example: Applications in educational, sociological, and behavioral research* (pp. 202–220). New York: Cambridge University Press.

Saris, W. E., de Pijper, M., & Mulder J. (1978). Optimal procedures for estimation of factor scores. *Sociological Methods & Research*, *7*, 85–105.

Saris, W. E., & Putte, B. V. D. (1988). True score or factor models: A secondary analysis of the ALLBUS–test–retest data. *Sociological Methods & Research*, *17*, 123–157.

Saris, W. E., & Stronkhorst, L. H. (1984). *Causal modelling in nonexperimental research: An introduction to the LISREL approach*. Amsterdam, The Netherlands: Sociometric Research Foundation.

SAS Institute Inc. (1985a). *SAS introductory guide for personal computers, version 6 edition*. Cary, NC: SAS Institute Inc.

SAS Institute Inc. (1985b). *SAS user's guide: Basics, version 5 edition*. Cary, NC: SAS Institute Inc.

SAS Institute Inc. (1985c). *SAS user's guide: Statistics, version 5 edition*. Cary, NC: SAS Institute Inc.

SAS Institute Inc. (1987). *SAS/STAT guide for personal computers*. Cary, NC: SAS Institute Inc.

Satorra, A., & Saris, W. E. (1985). Power of the likelihood ratio test in covariance structure analysis. *Psychometrika*, *50*, 83–90.

Sawyer, A. G., & Ball, A. D. (1981). Statistical power and effect size in marketing research. *Journal of Marketing Research*, *18*, 275–290.

Schachter, S. (1959). *The psychology of affiliation: Experimental studies of the sources of gregariousness*. Stanford, CA: Stanford University Press.

Schaie, K. W. (Ed.). (1983). *Longitudinal studies of adult psychological development*. New York: Guilford Press.

Schaie, K. W., & Hertzog, C. (1982). Longitudinal methods. In B. B. Wolman (Ed.), *Handbook of developmental psychology* (pp. 91–115). Englewood Cliffs, NJ: Prentice-Hall.

Scheffé, H. (1959). *The analysis of variance*. New York: Wiley.

Schlenker, B. R. (1974). Social psychology and science. *Journal of Personality and Social Psychology*, *29*, 1–15.

Schmitt, N., Coyle, B. W., & Saari, B. B. (1977). A review and critique of analyses of multitrait-multimethod matrices. *Multivariate Behavioral Research*, *12*, 447–478.

Schmitt, N., & Stults, D. M. (1986). Methodology review: Analysis of multitrait-multimethod matrices. *Applied Psychological Measurement*, *10*, 1–22.

Schneider, B. (1970). Relationships between various criteria of leadership in small groups. *Journal of Social Psychology*, *82*, 253–261.

Schneider, D. J., Hastorf, A. H., & Ellsworth, P. C. (1979). *Person perception* (2nd ed.). Reading, MA: Addison-Wesley.

Schoenberg, R. (1972). Strategies for meaningful comparison. In H. L. Costner (Ed.), *Sociological methodology 1972* (pp. 1–35). San Francisco: Jossey-Bass.

Schoenberg, R. (1982). Multiple indicator models: Estimation of unconstrained construct means and their standard errors. *Sociological Methods & Research*, *10*, 421–433.

Schroeder, L. D., Sjoquist, D. L., & Stephan, P. E. (1986). *Understanding regression analysis: An introductory guide*. Newbury Park, CA: Sage.

Schuessler, K. F. (1982). *Measuring social life feelings*. San Francisco: Jossey-Bass.

Schultz, D. P. (1969). The human subject in psychological research. *Psychological Bulletin*, *72*, 214–228.

Schuman, H., & Kalton, G. (1985). Survey methods. In G. Lindzey & E. Aronson (Eds.), *Handbook of social psychology* (Vol. 1, 3rd ed., pp. 635–698). New York: Random House.

Schuman, H., & Presser, S. (1981). *Questions and answers in attitude surveys: Experiments* on question form, wording, and context. New York: Academic Press.

Schwarzer, R. (1986). Evaluation of convergent and discriminant validity by use of structural equations. In A. Angleitner & J. S. Wiggins (Eds.), *Personality assessment via questionnaires: Current issues in theory and measurement* (pp. 191–213). Berlin: Springer-Verlag.

Scott, W. A. (1960). Measures of test homogeneity. *Educational and Psychological Measurement, 20*, 751–757.

Scriven, M. (1959). Explanation and prediction in evolutionary theory. *Science, 130*, 447–482.

Scriven, M. (1968). In defense of all causes. *Issues in Criminology, 4*, 79–81.

Scriven, M. (1971). The logic of cause. *Theory and Decision, 2*, 49–66.

Scriven, M. (1975). Causation and explanation. *Nous, 9*, 3–16.

Scriven, M. (1983). The evaluation taboo. In E. R. House (Ed.), *Philosophy of evaluation* (pp. 75–82). San Francisco: Jossey-Bass.

Searle, S. R. (1966). *Matrix algebra for the biological sciences (including applications in statistics).* New York: Wiley.

Searle, S. R., & Hudson, G. F. S. (1982). Some distinctive features of output from statistical computing packages for analysis of covariance. *Biometrics, 38*, 737–745.

Seaver, W. B. (1973). Effects of naturally induced teacher expectancies. *Journal of Personality and Social Psychology, 28*, 333–342.

Seaver, W. B., & Quarton, R. J. (1976). Regression discontinuity analysis of dean's list effects. *Journal of Educational Psychology, 68*, 459–465.

Sechrest, L. (1963). Incremental validity: A recommendation. *Educational and Psychological Measurement, 23*, 153–158.

Sechrest, L. (1985). Social science and social policy: Will our numbers ever be good enough? In R. L. Shotland & M. M. Mark (Eds.), *Social science and social policy* (pp. 63–95). Newbury Park, CA: Sage.

Sechrest, L., & Yeaton, W. H. (1981a). Assessing the effectiveness of social programs: Methodological and conceptual issues. In S. Ball (Ed.), *Assessing and interpreting outcomes* (pp. 41–55). San Francisco: Jossey-Bass.

Sechrest, L., & Yeaton, W. H. (1981b). Empirical bases for estimating effect sizes. In R. F. Boruch, P. M. Wortman, & D. S. Cordray (Eds.), *Reanalyzing program evaluations.* San Francisco: Jossey-Bass.

Sechrest, L., & Yeaton, W. H. (1982). Magnitudes of experimental effects in social science research. *Evaluation Review, 6*, 579–600.

Secord, P. F. (1972). Foreword. In L. Bickman & T. Henchy (Eds.), *Beyond the laboratory: Field research in social psychology* (pp. xi–xii). New York: McGraw-Hill.

Secord, P. F. (1986). Explanation in the social sciences and in life situations. In D. W. Fiske & R. A. Shweder (Eds.), *Metatheory in social science: Pluralism and subjectivities* (pp. 197–221). Chicago: University of Chicago Press.

Shaffer, J. P., & Gillo, M. (1974). A multivariate extension of the correlation ratio. *Educational and Psychological Measurement, 34*, 521–524.

Shaffer, W. R. (1983). The dimensionality of congressional foreign policy attitudes. *Political Methodology, 9*, 433–446.

Shapiro, A. K. (1960). A contribution to a history of the placebo effect. *Behavioral Science, 5*, 109–135.

Shapiro, A. K. (1964). Factors contributing to the placebo effect: Their implications for psychotherapy. *American Journal of Psychotherapy, 18* (Supplement 1), 73–88.

Shavelson, R. J., & Bolus, R. (1982). Self-concept: The interplay of theory and methods. *Journal of Educational Psychology, 74*, 3–17.

Shavelson, R. J., Webb, N. M., & Burstein, L. (1986). Measurement of teaching. In M. C. Wittrock (Ed.), *Handbook of research on teaching* (3rd ed., pp. 50–91). New York: Macmillan.

Shaw, B. (1930). Preface on doctors. *Collected works: Plays* (Vol. 12, pp. 3–80). New York: Wise.

Sheatsley, P. B. (1951). The art of interviewing and a guide to interviewer selection and training. In M. Jahoda, M. Deutsch, & S. W. Cook (Eds.), *Research methods in social relations* (pp. 463–492). New York: Dryden.

Sheatsley, P. B. (1983). Questionnaire construction and item writing. In P. H. Rossi, J. D. Wright, & A. B. Anderson (Eds.), *Handbook of survey research* (pp. 195–230). New York: Academic.

Shindell, S. (1964). *Statistics, science, and sense.* Pittsburgh: University of Pittsburgh Press.

Shine, L. C. (1980). The fallacy of replacing an a priori significance level with an a posteriori significance level. *Educational and Psychological Measurement, 40*, 331–335.

Shorter, E. (1985). *Bedside manners: The troubled history of doctors and patients*. New York: Simon & Schuster.

Shotland, R. L., & Mark, M. M. (Eds.). (1985). *Social science and social policy*. Newbury Park, CA: Sage.

Shulman, L. S. (1973). On the application of primary process thinking to the naming of second-order factors. *Educational Psychologist, 10*, 90–92.

Silverman, I. (1977). *The human subject in the psychological laboratory*. New York: Pergamon Press.

Simon, H. A. (1957). *Models of man*. New York: Wiley.

Simon, H. A. (1968). Causation. In D. L. Sills (Ed.), *International encyclopedia of the social sciences* (Vol. 2, pp. 350–356). New York: Macmillan.

Simon, H. A. (1979). The meaning of causal ordering. In R. K. Merton, J. S. Coleman, & P. H. Rossi (Eds.), *Qualitative and quantitative social research: Papers in honor of Paul F. Lazarsfeld*. New York: Free Press.

Simpson, R. H. (1944). The specific meaning of certain terms indicating differing degrees of frequency. *The Quarterly Journal of Speech, 30*, 328–330.

Singh, B. R. (1985). A major shortcoming of professor Holmes' comparative methodology: The question of falsifiability. *Quality and Quantity, 19*, 155–165.

Skinner, H. A. (1980). Factor analysis and studies on alcohol. A methodological review. *Journal of Studies on Alcoholism, 41*, 1091–2001.

Slomczynski, K. M., Miller, J., & Kohn, M. L. (1981). Stratification, work, and values: A Polish–United States comparison. *American Sociological Review, 46*, 720–744.

Smelser, N. J. (1986). The Ogburn vision fifty years later. In N. J. Smelser & D. R. Gerstein (Eds.), *Behavioral and social science: Fifty years of discovery* (pp. 21–35). Washington, DC: National Academy Press.

Smelser, N. J., & Gerstein, D. R. (Eds.). (1986). *Behavioral and social science: Fifty years of discovery*. Washington, DC: National Academy Press.

Smith, B. D. (1988). Personality: Multivariate systems theory and research. J. R. Nesselroade & R. B. Cattell (Eds.), *Handbook of multivariate experimental psychology* (2nd ed., pp. 687–736). New York: Plenum.

Smith, I. L. (1972). The eta coefficient in MAN-OVA. *Multivariate Behavioral Research, 7*, 361–372.

Smith, K. W. (1974a). Forming composite scales and estimating their validity through factor analysis. *Social Forces, 53*, 168–180.

Smith, K. W. (1974b). On estimating the reliability of composite indexes through factor analysis. *Sociological Methods & Research, 2*, 485–510.

Smith, P. L. (1982). Measures of variance accounted for: Theory and practice. In G. Keren (Ed.), *Statistical and methodological issues in psychology and social science research* (pp. 101–129). Hillsdale, NJ: Erlbaum.

Smith, T. W. (1984). Nonattitudes: A review and evaluation. In C. F. Turner & E. Martin (Eds.), *Surveying subjective phenomena* (Vol. 2, pp. 215–255). New York: Russell Sage Foundation.

Snedecor, G. W., & Cochran, W. G. (1980). *Statistical methods* (7th ed.). Ames, IA: Iowa State University Press.

Snider, J. G., & Osgood, C. E. (Eds.). (1969). *Semantic differential technique*. Chicago: Aldine.

Snow, R. E. (1969). Unfinished Pygmalion [Review of *Pygmalion in the classroom: Teacher expectation and pupils' intellectual development*]. *Contemporary Psychology, 14*, 197–199.

Sobel, M. E. (1987). Direct and indirect effects in linear structural equation models. *Sociological Methods & Research, 16*, 155–176.

Sobel, M. E., & Arminger, G. (1986). Platonic and operational true scores in covariance structure analysis. *Sociological Methods & Research, 15*, 44–58.

Sobel, M. E., & Bohrnstedt, G. W. (1985). Use of null models in evaluating the fit of covariance structure models. In N. Tuma (Ed.), *Sociological Methodology 1985* (pp. 152–178). San Francisco: Jossey-Bass.

Sockloff, A. L. (Ed.) (n.d.). *Proceedings. The First Invitational Conference on Faculty Effectiveness as Evaluated by Students*. Philadelphia: Measurement and Research Center, Temple University.

Sokal, R. R. (1974). Classification: Purposes, principles, progress, prospects. *Science, 185*, 1115–1123.

Solomon, R. L. (1949). An extension of control group design. *Psychological Bulletin, 46*, 137–150.

Sörbom, D. (1974). A general method for studying differences in factor means and factor structure between groups. *British Journal of Mathematical and Statistical Psychology*, *27*, 229–239.

Sörbom, D. (1975). Detection of correlated errors in longitudinal data. *British Journal of Mathematical and Statistical Psychology*, *28*, 138–151.

Sörbom, D. (1978). An alternative to the methodology for analysis of covariance. *Psychometrika*, *43*, 381–396.

Sörbom, D. (1982). Structural equation models with structured means. In K. G. Jöreskog & H. Wold (Eds.), *Systems under indirect observation: Causality, structure, prediction* (Part I, pp. 183–195). Amsterdam: North-Holland.

Sörbom, D., & Jöreskog, K. G. (1981). The use of LISREL in sociological model building. In D. J. Jackson & E. F. Borgatta (Eds.), *Factor analysis and measurement in sociological research: A multi-dimensional perspective* (pp. 179–199). Newbury Park, CA: Sage.

Spearman, C. (1904). "General intelligence," objectively determined and measured. *American Journal of Psychology*, *15*, 201–293.

Spearritt, D. (1985). Factor analysis. In T. Husen & T. N. Postlethwaite (Eds.), *The international encyclopedia of education. Research and studies* (Vol. 4, pp. 1813–1824). New York: Pergamon Press.

Specht, D. A., & Warren, R. D. (1975). Comparing causal models. In D. R. Heise (Ed.), *Sociological methodology 1976* (pp. 46–82). San Francisco: Jossey-Bass.

Spence, J. T. (1983). Comment on Lubinski, Tellegen, and Butcher's "masculinity, femininity, and androgyny viewed and assessed as distinct concepts". *Journal of Personality and Social Psychology*, *44*, 440–446.

SPSS Inc. (1988). *SPSS-X user's guide* (3rd ed.). Chicago: SPSS Inc.

SPSS Inc. (1989). *SPSS/PC+ update for V3.0 and V3.1*. Chicago: SPSS Inc.

Srivastava, M. S., & Carter, E. M. (1983). *An introduction to applied multivariate statistics*. New York: North-Holland.

Srole, L. (1956). Social integration and certain corollaries: An exploratory study. *American Sociological Review*, *21*, 709–716.

Stallings, W. M. (1985). Mind your *p*'s and alphas. *Educational Researcher*, *14*(9), 19–20.

Stamp, J. (1929). *Some economic factors in modern life*. London: King.

Stamp, J. (1937). *The science of social adjustment*. London: Macmillan.

Stanley, J. C. (1966). A common class of pseudo-experiments. *American Educational Research Journal*, *3*, 79–87.

Stanley, J. C. (1971). Reliability. In R. L. Thorndike (Ed.), *Educational measurement* (2nd ed., pp. 356–442). Washington, DC: American Council on Education.

Stanley, J. C., & Wang, M. D. (1970). Weighting test items and test-item options, an overview of the analytical and empirical literature. *Educational and Psychological Measurement*, *30*, 21–35.

Steiger, J. H. (1988). Aspects of person–machine communication in structural modeling of correlations and covariances. *Multivariate Behavioral Research*, *23*, 281–290.

Stent, G. S. (1975). Limits to the scientific understanding of man. *Science*, *187*, 1052–1057.

Stevens, J. P. (1972). Global measures of association in multivariate analysis of variance. *Multivariate Behavioral Research*, *7*, 373–378.

Stevens, J. P. (1980). Power of the multivariate analysis of variance tests. *Psychological Bulletin*, *88*, 728–737.

Stevens, J. P. (1984). Outliers and influential data points in regression analysis. *Psychological Bulletin*, *95*, 334–344.

Stevens, J. (1986). *Applied multivariate statistics for the social sciences*. Hillsdale, NJ: Erlbaum.

Stevens, S. S. (1951). Mathematics, measurement, and psychophysics. In S. S. Stevens (Ed.), *Handbook of experimental psychology* (pp. 1–49). New York: Wiley.

Stevens, S. S. (1959). Measurement, psychophysics, and utility. In C. W. Churchman & P. Ratoosh (Eds.), *Measurement: Definitions and theories* (pp. 18–63). New York: Wiley.

Stevens, S. S. (1968). Measurement, statistics, and the schemapiric view. *Science*, *161*, 849–856.

Stewart, D. W. (1981). The application and misapplication of factor analysis in marketing research. *Journal of Marketing Research*, *18*, 51–62.

Stewart, W. W., & Feder, N. (1987). The integrity of the scientific literature. *Nature*, *325*, 207–214.

Stinchcombe, A. L. (1968). *Constructing social theories*. New York: Harcourt Brace & World.

Stine, W. W. (1989). Meaningful inference: The

role of measurement in statistics. *Psychological Bulletin, 105,* 147–155.

Stokes, J. (1983). Androgyny as an interactive concept: A reply to Lubinski. *Journal of Consulting and Clinical Psychology, 30,* 134–136.

Stokes, J., Childs, L., & Fuehrer, A. (1981). Gender and sex roles as predictors of self-disclosure. *Journal of Counseling Psychology, 28,* 510–514.

Stoll, M. (1986, September 23). Statistical software. *PC Week,* pp. 77–85, 92–94.

Storer, N. W. (1966). *The social system of science.* New York: Holt, Rinehart & Winston.

Stouffer, S. A. (1950). Some observations on study design. *American Journal of Sociology, 55,* 355–361.

Strauss, M. B. (Ed). (1968). *Familiar medical quotations.* Boston: Little, Brown & Company.

Stromsdorfer, E. W., & Farkas, G. (1980). Methodology. In E. W. Stromsdorfer & G. Farkas (Eds.), *Evaluation studies: Review annual* (Vol. 5, pp. 32–41). Newbury Park, CA: Sage.

Stroud, T. W. F. (1972). Comparing conditional means and variances in a regression model with measurement errors of known variances. *Journal of the American Statistical Association, 67,* 407–412.

Strube, M. J. (1988). Some comments on the use of magnitude-of-effect estimates. *Journal of Counseling Psychology, 35,* 342–345.

Stuart, A. (1968). Sample surveys: Non-probability sampling. In D. L. Sills (Ed.), *International encyclopedia of the social sciences* (Vol. 13, pp. 612–616). New York: Macmillan.

Sudman, S. (1976). *Applied sampling.* New York: Academic Press.

Sudman, S., & Bradburn, N. M. (1974). *Response effects in surveys: A review and synthesis.* Chicago: Aldine.

Sudman, S., & Bradburn, N. M. (1982). *Asking questions.* San Francisco: Jossey-Bass.

Suppe, F. (Ed.). (1977a). *The structure of scientific theories* (2nd ed.). Urbana, IL: University of Illinois Press.

Suppe, F. (1977b). The symposium: Main issues concerning the structure of theories—1969. In F. Suppe (Ed.), *The structure of scientific theories* (2nd ed., pp. 233–241). Urbana, IL: University of Illinois Press.

Susmilch, C. E., & Johnson, W. T. (1975). Factor scores for constructing linear composites. Do different techniques make a difference? *Sociological Methods & Research, 4,* 166–188.

Sutcliffe, J. P. (1958). Error of measurement and the sensitivity of a test of significance. *Psychometrika, 23,* 9–17.

Sutcliffe, J. P. (1980). On the relationship of reliability to statistical power. *Psychological Bulletin, 88,* 509–515.

Swaford, M. (1980). Three parametric techniques for contingency table analysis: A nontechnical commentary. *American Sociological Review, 45,* 664–690.

Swaminathan, H., & Algina, J. (1977). Analysis of quasi-experimental time-series designs. *Multivariate Behavioral Research, 12,* 111–131.

Tanaka, J. S. (1987). "How big is big enough?": Sample size and goodness of fit in structural equation models with latent variables. *Child Development, 58,* 134–146.

Tatsuoka, M. M. (1970). *Discriminant analysis: The study of group differences.* Champaign, IL: IPAT.

Tatsuoka, M. M. (1982). Statistical methods. In H. E. Mitzel (Ed.), *Encyclopedia of educational research* (5th ed., pp. 1780–1808). New York: Free Press.

Taylor, C. C. (1977). Principal component and factor analysis. In C. A. O'Muircheartaigh & C. Payne (Eds.), *The analysis of survey data* (Vol. 1, pp. 89–123). New York: Wiley.

Taylor, H. C., & Russell, J. T. (1939). The relationship of validity coefficients to the practical effectiveness of tests in selection: Discussion and tables. *Journal of Applied Psychology, 23,* 565–578.

Taylor, S. E., Lichtman, R. R., & Wood, J. V. (1984). Attributions, beliefs about control, and adjustment to breast cancer. *Journal of Personality and Social Psychology, 46,* 489–502.

Tedeschi, J. T. (1983). Social influence theory and aggression. In R. G. Geen & E. I. Donnerstein (Eds.), *Aggression: Theoretical and empirical reviews. Volume 1. Theoretical and methodological issues* (pp. 135–162). New York: Academic Press.

Tellegen, A., & Lubinski, D. (1983). Some methodological comments on labels, traits, interaction, and types in the study of "femininity" and "masculinity": Reply to Spence. *Journal of Personality and Social Psychology*, *44*, 447–455.

Tenopyr, M. L. (1977). Content—construct confusion. *Personnel Psychology*, *30*, 47–54.

Terwilliger, J. S., & Lele, K. (1979). Some relationships among internal consistency, reproducibility, and homogeneity. *Journal of Educational Measurement*, *16*, 101–108.

Tesser, A., & Krauss, H. (1976). On validating a relationship between constructs. *Educational and Psychological Measurement*, *36*, 111–121.

Theodorson, G. A., & Theodorson, A. G. (1969). *A modern dictionary of sociology*. New York: Crowell.

Thistlethwaite, D. L., & Campbell, D. T. (1960). Regression-discontinuity analysis: An alternative to the ex post facto experiment. *Journal of Educational Psychology*, *51*, 309–317.

Thomas, D. H. (1976). *Figuring anthropology: First principles of probability and statistics*. New York: Holt, Rinehart & Winston.

Thomson, W. (Lord Kelvin). (1891). *Popular lectures and addresses* (Vol. 1, 2nd ed.). London: Macmillan.

Thorndike, R. L. (1949). *Personnel selection: Test and measurement techniques*. New York: Wiley.

Thorndike, R. L. (1951). Reliability. In E. F. Lindquist (Ed.), *Educational measurement* (pp. 560–620). Washington, DC: American Council on Education.

Thorndike, R. L. (1968). [Review of *Pygmalion in the classroom*]. *American Educational Research Journal*, *5*, 708–711.

Thorndike, R. L. (1969). *But you have to know how to tell time. American Educational Research Journal*, *6*, 692.

Thorndike, R. L. (1982). *Applied psychometrics*. Boston: Houghton Mifflin.

Thorndike, R. L., & Hagen, E. P. (1977). *Measurement and evaluation in psychology and education* (4th ed.). New York: Wiley.

Thorndike, R. M. (1978). *Correlational procedures for research*. New York: Gardner Press.

Thorngate, W. (1975). Process invariance: Another red herring. *Personality and Social Psychology Bulletin*, *1*, 485–488.

Thurstone, L. L. (1937). Psychology as a quantitative rational science. *Science*, *85*, 227–232.

Thurstone, L. L. (1947). *Multiple-factor analysis*. Chicago: Chicago University Press.

Thurstone, L. L. (1948). Psychological implications of factor analysis. *American Psychologist*, *3*, 402–408.

Tiku, M. L. (1967). Tables of the power of the F-test. *Journal of the American Statistical Association*, *62*, 525–539.

Tinsley, H. E. A., & Weiss, D. J. (1975). Interrater reliability and agreement of subjective judgments. *Journal of Counseling Psychology*, *22*, 358–376.

Torgerson, W. S. (1958). *Theory and methods of scaling*. New York: Wiley.

Towstopiat, O. (1984). A review of reliability procedures for measuring observer agreement. *Contemporary Educational Psychology*, *9*, 333–352.

Travers, R. M. W. (1973). Preface. In R. M. W. Travers (Ed.), *Second handbook of research on teaching* (pp. v–viii). Chicago: Rand McNally.

Travers, R. M. W. (1981). Letter to the editor. *Educational Researcher*, *10*(6), 32.

Trochim, W. M. K. (1984). *Research design for program evaluation: The regression-discontinuity approach*. Newbury Park, CA: Sage.

Trochim, W. M. K. (1986). Editor's notes. In W. M. K. Trochim (Ed.), *Advances in quasi-experimental design and analysis* (pp. 1–7). San Francisco: Jossey-Bass.

Tryon, R. C. (1957). Reliability and behavior domain validity: Reformulation and historical critique. *Psychological Bulletin*, *54*, 229–249.

Tucker, L. R. (1966). Some mathematical notes on three-mode factor analysis. *Psychometrika*, *31*, 279–311.

Tucker, L. R., Damarin, F., & Messick, S. (1966). A base-free measure of change. *Psychometrika*, *31*, 457–473.

Tufte, E. R. (1974). *Data analysis for politics and policy*. Englewood Cliffs, NJ: Prentice-Hall.

Tukey, J. W. (1954). Causation, regression, and path analysis. In O. Kempthorne, T. A. Bancroft, J. W. Gowen, & J. D. Lush (Eds.), *Statistics and mathematics in biology* (pp. 35–66). Ames: Iowa State College Press.

Tukey, J. W. (1969). Analyzing data: Sanctification or detective work? *American Psychologist*, *24*, 83–91.

Turner, C. F., & Martin, E. (Eds.). (1984). *Surveying subjective phenomena* (Vols. 1–2). New York: Russell Sage Foundation.

Tversky, A., & Kahneman, D. (1971). Belief in the law of small numbers. *Psychological Bulletin*, *76*, 105–110.

Tversky, A., & Kahneman, D. (1974). Judgment under uncertainty: Heuristics and biases. *Science, 185,* 1124–1131.

Twain, M. (1935). *Mark Twain's notebook.* New York: Harper & Brothers.

Undheim, J. O., & Gustafsson, J. E. (1987). The hierarchical organization of cognitive abilities: Restoring general intelligence through the use of linear structural relations (LISREL). *Multivariate Behavioral Research, 22,* 149–171.

van der Ven, A. H. G. S. (1980). *Introduction to scaling.* New York: Wiley.

Vaughan, G. M., & Corballis, M. C. (1969). Beyond tests of significance: Estimating strength of effects in selected ANOVA designs. *Psychological Bulletin, 72,* 204–213.

Velleman, P. F., & Welsch, R. E. (1981). Efficient computing of regression diagnostics. *The American Statistician, 35,* 234–242.

Vernon, P. E. (1972). The distinctiveness of field independence. *Journal of Personality, 40,* 366–391.

Visser, R. A. (1982). *Analysis of longitudinal data in behavioral and social research: An exploratory survey.* Leiden, The Netherlands: DSWO Press.

Wade, N. (1976). IQ and heredity: Suspicion of fraud beclouds classic experiment. *Science, 194,* 916–919.

Wagner, R. F., Reinfeld, H. B., Wagner, K. D., Gambino, A. T., Falco, T. A., Sokol, J. A., Katz, S., & Zeldis, S. M. (1984). Ear-canal hair and the ear-lobe crease as predictors for coronary-artery disease. *The New England Journal of Medicine, 311,* 1317–1318.

Wainer, H. (1987). *The first four millennia of mental testing: From ancient China to the computer age.* Princeton, NJ: Educational Testing Service.

Wainer, H., & Braun, H. I. (Eds.). (1988). *Test validity.* Hillsdale, NJ: Erlbaum.

Wainer, H., & Thissen, D. (1986). *Plotting in the modern world.* Princeton, NJ: Educational Testing Service.

Walker, H. M., & Lev, J. (1953). *Statistical inference.* New York: Holt.

Wallace, S. R. (1965). Criteria for what? *American Psychologist, 20,* 411–417.

Wallace, T. D. (1977). Pretest estimation in regression: A survey. *American Journal of Agricultural Economics, 59,* 431–443.

Wallace, W. A. (1972, 1974). *Causality and scientific explanation* (2 Vols.). Ann Arbor: University of Michigan Press.

Wallis, W. A., & Roberts, H. V. (1956). *Statistics: A new approach.* New York: Free Press.

Walster, E., Cleary, T. A., & Clifford, M. M. (1970). Research note: The effect of race and sex on college admission. *Sociology of Education, 44,* 237–244.

Wang, M. D., & Stanley, J. C. (1970). Differential weighting: A review of methods and empirical studies. *Review of Educational Research, 40,* 663–705.

Wanous, J. P., & Lawler, E. E. (1972). Measurement and meaning of job satisfaction. *Journal of Applied Psychology, 56,* 95–105.

Warr, P. B., & Knapper, C. (1968). *The perception of people and events.* London: Wiley.

Warren, W. G. (1971). Correlation or regression: Bias or precision. *Applied Statistics, 20,* 148–164.

Waterman, A. T. (1959). Basic research in the United States. In D. Wolfle (Ed.), *Symposium on basic research* (pp. 17–40). Washington, DC: American Association for the Advancement of Science.

Weaver, W. (1961). The imperfections of science. *American Scientist, 49,* 99–113.

Webb, E. T., Campbell, D. T., Schwartz, R. D., Sechrest, L., & Grove, J. B. (1981). *Nonreactive measures in the social sciences* (2nd ed.). Boston: Houghton Mifflin.

Webb, N. M., Rowley, G. L., & Shavelson, R. J. (1988). Using generalizability theory in counseling and development. *Measurement and Evaluation in Counseling and Development, 21,* 81–90.

Webb, S., & Webb, B. (1968). *Methods of social study by Sidney and Beatrice Webb.* New York: Kelly.

Weber, S. J., & Cook, T. D. (1972). Subject effects in laboratory research: An examination of subject roles, demand characteristics, and valid inference. *Psychological Bulletin, 77,* 273–295.

Webster's third new international dictionary of the English language unabridged. (1981). Springfield, MA: Merriam Webster.

Weeks, D. G. (1980). A second-order longitudinal model of ability structure. *Multivariate Behavioral Research, 15,* 353–365.

Weick, K. E. (1967). Promise and limitations of laboratory experiments in the development of attitude change theory. In C. W. Sherif & M. Sherif (Eds.), *Attitude, ego-involvement, and change* (pp. 51–75). New York: Wiley.

Weick, K. E. (1968). Systematic observational

methods. In G. Lindzey & E. Aronson (Eds.), *Handbook of social psychology* (Vol. 2, 2nd ed., pp. 357–451). Reading, MA: Addison-Wesley.

Weick, K. E. (1985). Systematic observational methods. In G. Lindzey & E. Aronson (Eds.), *Handbook of social psychology* (Vol. 1, 3rd ed., pp. 567–634). New York: Random House.

Weimer, W. B. (1977). Science as a rhetorical transaction: Toward a nonjustificational conception. *Philosophy and Rhetoric, 10,* 1–29.

Weinberg, E. (1983). Data collection: Planning and management. In P. H. Rossi, J. D. Wright, & A. B. Anderson (Eds.), *Handbook of survey research* (pp. 329–358). New York: Academic.

Weisberg, H. I. (1979). Statistical adjustments and uncontrolled studies. *Psychological Bulletin, 86,* 1149–1164.

Weisberg, S. (1980). *Applied linear regression.* New York: Wiley.

Weiss, D. J. (1971). Further considerations in applications of factor analysis. *Journal of Counseling Psychology, 18,* 58–92.

Weiss, D. J., & Davison, M. L. (1981). Test theory and methods. *Annual Review of Psychology, 32,* 629–658.

Weisskopf, V. F. (1972). The significance of science. *Science, 176,* 138–146.

Werts, C. E., Breland, H. M., Grandy, J., & Rock, D. A. (1980). Using longitudinal data to estimate reliability in the presence of correlated measurement errors. *Educational and Psychological Measurement, 40,* 19–29.

Werts, C. E., Jöreskog, K. G., & Linn, R. L. (1971). Comment on 'The estimation of measurement error in panel data.' *American Sociological Review, 36,* 110–113.

Wetzel, C. G. (1977). Manipulation checks: A reply to Kidd. *Representative Research in Social Psychology, 8,* 88–93.

Wheaton, B. (1978). The sociogenesis of psychological disorder: Reexamining the causal issues with longitudinal data. *American Sociological Review, 43,* 383–403.

Wheaton, B. (1987). Assessment of fit in overidentified models with latent variables. *Sociological Methods & Research, 16,* 118–154.

Wheaton, B., Muthén, B., Alwin, D. F., & Summers, G. F. (1977). Assessing reliability and stability in panel models. In D. R. Heise (Ed.), *Sociological methodology 1977* (pp. 84–136). San Francisco: Jossey-Bass.

Whewell, W. (1847). *The philosophy of the inductive sciences: Founded upon their history* (Vols. 1–2, 2nd ed.). London: Parker. (Reprinted, 1966, by Johnson Reprint Corporation, New York)

White, L., Tursky, B., & Schwartz, G. E. (Eds.). (1985). *Placebo: Theory, research, and mechanisms.* New York: Guilford Press.

Whorf, B. L. (1956). *Language, thought, and reality.* New York: Wiley.

Widaman, K. F. (1985). Hierarchically nested covariance structure models for multitrait-multimethod data. *Applied Psychological Measurement, 9,* 1–26.

Wiggins, J. S. (1973). *Personality and prediction: Principles of personality assessment.* Reading, MA: Addison-Wesley.

Wildt, A. R., & Ahtola, O. T. (1978). *Analysis of covariance.* Newbury Park, CA: Sage.

Wiley, D. E. (1973). The identification problem for structural equation models with unmeasured variables. In A. S. Goldberger & O. D. Duncan (Eds.), *Structural equation models in the social sciences* (pp. 69–83). New York: Academic Press.

Wiley, D. E., & Wiley, J. A. (1970). The estimation of measurement error in panel data. *American Sociological Review, 35,* 112–117.

Willems, E. P., & Howard, G. S. (1980). The external validity of papers on external validity. *American Psychologist, 35,* 387–388.

Willett, J. B. (1988). Questions and answers in the measurement of change. In E. Z. Rothkopf (Ed.), *Review of research in education* (Vol. 15, pp. 345–422). Washington, DC: American Educational Research Association.

Williams, B. (1978). *A sampler on sampling.* New York: Wiley.

Williams, E. J. (1959). *Regression analysis.* New York: Wiley.

Williams, J. G. (1982). Internal exploration of regression data. *Political Methodology, 8,* 107–123.

Williams, L. J., Cote, J. A., & Buckley, M. R. (1989). Lack of method variance in self-reported affect and perceptions at work: Reality or artifact. *Journal of Applied Psychology, 74,* 462–468.

Williams, R., & Thomson, E. (1986a). Normalization issues in latent variable modeling. *Sociological Methods & Research, 15,* 24–43.

Williams, R., & Thomson, E. (1986b). Problems needing solutions or solutions needing problems? Final thoughts on the normalization controversy. *Sociological Methods & Research*, *15*, 64–68.

Wilson, G. D. (1975). *Manual for the Wilson–Patterson Attitude Inventory (WPAI)*. London: NFER.

Wilson, K. L. (1981). On population comparisons using factor indexes of latent variables. *Social Science Research*, *10*, 301–313.

Wilson, T. P. (1971). Critique of ordinal variables. *Social Forces*, *49*, 432–444.

Winch, P. (1958). *The idea of a social science*. London: Routledge & Kegan Paul.

Winch, R. F., & Campbell, D. T. (1969). Proof? No. Evidence? Yes. The significance of tests of significance. *American Sociologist*, *4*, 140–143.

Wineburg, S. S. (1987a). Does research count in the lives of behavioral scientists? A rejoinder. *Educational Researcher*, *16*(9), 42–44.

Wineburg, S. S. (1987b). The self-fulfillment of the self-fulfilling prophecy. A critical appraisal. *Educational Researcher*, *16*(9), 28–37.

Winer, B. J. (1971). *Statistical principles in experimental design* (2nd ed.). New York: McGraw-Hill.

Winkler, R. L. (1972). *An introduction to Bayesian inference and decision*. New York: Holt, Rinehart & Winston.

Winne, P. H., & Belfry, M. J. (1982). Interpretive problems when correcting for attenuation. *Journal of Educational Measurement*, *19*, 125–134.

Witkin, H. A., Dyk, R. B., Faterson, H. F., Goodenough, D. R., & Karp, S. A. (1962). *Psychological differentiation: Studies of development*. New York: Wiley.

Wold, H. (1956). Causal inference from observational data: A review of ends and means. *Journal of the Royal Statistical Society* (Series A), *119*, 28–61.

Wolf, F. M. (1986). *Meta-analysis: Quantitative methods for research synthesis*. Newbury Park, CA: Sage.

Wolfle, D. (1959). The support of basic research: Summary of the symposium. In D. Wolfle (Ed.), *Symposium on basic research* (pp. 249–280). Washington, DC: American Association for the Advancement of Science.

Wolfle, L. M. (1985). Postsecondary educational attainment among whites and blacks. *American Educational Research Journal*, *22*, 501–525.

Wolfle, L. M., & Robertshaw, D. (1983). Racial differences in measurement error in educational achievement models. *Journal of Educational Measurement*, *20*, 39–49.

Wolins, L. (1978). Sex differentials in salaries: Faults in analysis of covariance. *Science*, *200*, 723.

Wolins, L. (1982). *Research mistakes in the social and behavioral sciences*. Ames, IA: Iowa State University Press.

Wolinsky, J. (1983, July). Masters, Johnson respond to criticism. *APA Monitor*, p. 2.

Woodward, J. A., & Goldstein, M. J. (1977). Communication deviance in the families of schizophrenics: A comment on the misuse of analysis of covariance. *Science*, *197*, 1096–1097.

Wuebben, P. L. (1968). Experimental design, measurement, and human subjects: A neglected problem of control. *Sociometry*, *31*, 89–101.

Wuebben, P. L., Straits, B. C., & Schulman, G. I. (Eds.). (1974a). *The experiment as a social occasion*. Berkeley, CA: Glendessary Press.

Wuebben, P. L., Straits, B. C., & Schulman, G. I. (1974b). Traditional objections to experimentation. In P. L. Wuebben, B. C. Straits, & G. I. Schulman (Eds.), *The experiment as a social occasion* (pp. 15–19). Berkeley, CA: Glendessary Press.

Wylie, R. C. (1974). *The self-concept: A review of methodological considerations and measuring instruments* (Vol. 1, 2nd ed.). Lincoln, NE: University of Nebraska Press.

Yates, F. (1960). *Sampling methods for censuses and surveys*. London: Griffin.

Yeaton, W. H., & Sechrest, L. (1981). Critical dimensions in the choice and maintenance of successful treatments: Strength, integrity, and effectiveness. *Journal of Consulting and Clinical Psychology*, *49*, 156–167.

Yeaton, W. H., & Wortman, P. M. (Eds.). (1984). *Issues in data synthesis*. San Francisco: Jossey-Bass.

Zaltman, G., Lemasters, K., & Heffring, M. (1982). *Theory construction in marketing: Some thoughts on thinking*. New York: Wiley.

Zeaman, D. (1959). Skinner's theory of teaching machines. In E. Galanter (Ed.), *Automatic teaching: The state of the art* (pp. 167–175). New York: Wiley.

Zeisel, H. (1985). *Say it with figures* (6th ed.). New York: Harper & Row.

Zeller, R. A., & Carmines, E. G. (1980). *Measurement in the social sciences: The link be-*

tween theory and data. Cambridge: Cambridge University Press.

Ziegler, J. F., & Lanford, W. A. (1979). Effect of cosmic rays on computer memories. *Science, 206,* 776–788.

Ziman, J. (1968). *Public knowledge: The social dimension of science.* New York: Cambridge University Press.

Zimmerman, D. W., & Williams, R. H. (1986). Note on the reliability of experimental measures and the power of significance tests. *Psychological Bulletin, 100,* 123–124.

Zwier, G., & Vaughan, G. M. (1984). Three ideological orientations in school vandalism research. *Review of Educational Research, 54,* 263–292.

APPENDIX

Critical Values for F

df *error*	α	df *for Numerator*							
		1	*2*	*3*	*4*	*5*	*6*	*8*	*12*
1	.01	4052	4999	5403	5625	5764	5859	5981	6106
	.05	161.45	199.50	215.71	224.58	230.16	233.99	238.88	243.91
	.10	39.86	49.50	53.59	55.83	57.24	58.20	59.44	60.70
	.20	9.47	12.00	13.06	13.73	14.01	14.26	14.59	14.90
2	.01	98.49	99.00	99.17	99.25	99.30	99.33	99.36	99.42
	.05	18.51	19.00	19.16	19.25	19.30	19.33	19.37	19.41
	.10	8.53	9.00	9.16	9.24	9.29	9.33	9.37	9.41
	.20	3.56	4.00	4.16	4.24	4.28	4.32	4.36	4.40
3	.001	167.5	148.5	141.1	137.1	134.6	132.8	130.6	128.3
	.01	34.12	30.81	29.46	28.71	28.24	27.91	27.49	27.05
	.05	10.13	9.55	9.28	9.12	9.01	8.94	8.84	8.74
	.10	5.54	5.46	5.39	5.34	5.31	5.28	5.25	5.22
	.20	2.68	2.89	2.94	2.96	2.97	2.97	2.98	2.98
4	.001	74.14	61.25	56.18	53.44	51.71	50.53	49.00	47.41
	.01	21.20	18.00	16.69	15.98	15.52	15.21	14.80	14.37
	.05	7.71	6.94	6.59	6.39	6.26	6.16	6.04	5.91
	.10	4.54	4.32	4.19	4.11	4.05	4.01	3.95	3.90
	.20	2.35	2.47	2.48	2.48	2.48	2.47	2.47	2.46
5	.001	47.04	36.61	33.20	31.09	29.75	28.84	27.64	26.42
	.01	16.26	13.27	12.06	11.39	10.97	10.67	10.29	9.89
	.05	6.61	5.79	5.41	5.19	5.05	4.95	4.82	4.68
	.10	4.06	3.78	3.62	3.52	3.45	3.40	3.34	3.27
	.20	2.18	2.26	2.25	2.24	2.23	2.22	2.20	2.18
6	.001	35.51	27.00	23.70	21.90	20.81	20.03	19.03	17.99
	.01	13.74	10.92	9.78	9.15	8.75	8.47	8.10	7.72
	.05	5.99	5.14	4.76	4.53	4.39	4.28	4.15	4.00
	.10	3.78	3.46	3.29	3.18	3.11	3.05	2.98	2.90
	.20	2.07	2.13	2.11	2.09	2.08	2.06	2.04	2.02
7	.001	29.22	21.69	18.77	17.19	16.21	15.52	14.63	13.71
	.01	12.25	9.55	8.45	7.85	7.46	7.19	6.84	6.47
	.05	5.59	4.74	4.35	4.12	3.97	3.87	3.73	3.57
	.10	3.59	3.26	3.07	2.96	2.88	2.83	2.75	2.67
	.20	2.00	2.04	2.02	1.99	1.97	1.96	1.93	1.91
8	.001	25.42	18.49	15.83	14.39	13.49	12.86	12.04	11.19
	.01	11.26	8.65	7.59	7.01	6.63	6.37	6.03	5.67
	.05	5.32	4.46	4.07	3.84	3.69	3.58	3.44	3.28
	.10	3.46	3.11	2.92	2.81	2.73	2.67	2.59	2.50
	.20	1.95	1.98	1.95	1.92	1.90	1.88	1.86	1.83
9	.001	22.86	16.39	13.90	12.56	11.71	11.13	10.37	9.57
	.01	10.56	8.02	6.99	6.42	6.06	5.80	5.47	5.11
	.05	5.12	4.26	3.86	3.63	3.48	3.37	3.23	3.07
	.10	3.36	3.01	2.81	2.69	2.61	2.55	2.47	2.38
	.20	1.91	1.94	1.90	1.87	1.85	1.83	1.80	1.76

(*cont.*)

Critical Values for F

df *error*	α	df *for Numerator*							
		1	*2*	*3*	*4*	*5*	*6*	*8*	*12*
10	.001	21.04	14.91	12.55	11.28	10.48	9.92	9.20	8.45
	.01	10.04	7.56	6.55	5.99	5.64	5.39	5.06	4.71
	.05	4.96	4.10	3.71	3.48	3.33	3.22	3.07	2.91
	.10	3.28	2.92	2.73	2.61	2.52	2.46	2.38	2.28
	.20	1.88	1.90	1.86	1.83	1.80	1.78	1.75	1.72
11	.001	19.69	13.81	11.56	10.35	9.58	9.05	8.35	7.63
	.01	9.65	7.20	6.22	5.67	5.32	5.07	4.74	4.40
	.05	4.84	3.98	3.59	3.36	3.20	3.09	2.95	2.79
	.10	3.23	2.86	2.66	2.54	2.45	2.39	2.30	2.21
	.20	1.86	1.87	1.83	1.80	1.77	1.75	1.72	1.68
12	.001	18.64	12.97	10.80	9.63	8.89	8.38	7.71	7.00
	.01	9.33	6.93	5.95	5.41	5.06	4.82	4.50	4.16
	.05	4.75	3.88	3.49	3.26	3.11	3.00	2.85	2.69
	.10	3.18	2.81	2.61	2.48	2.39	2.33	2.24	2.15
	.20	1.84	1.85	1.80	1.77	1.74	1.72	1.69	1.65
13	.001	17.81	12.31	10.21	9.07	8.35	7.86	7.21	6.52
	.01	9.07	6.70	5.74	5.20	4.86	4.62	4.30	3.96
	.05	4.67	3.80	3.41	3.18	3.02	2.92	2.77	2.60
	.10	3.14	2.76	2.56	2.43	2.35	2.28	2.20	2.10
	.20	1.82	1.83	1.78	1.75	1.72	1.69	1.66	1.62
14	.001	17.14	11.78	9.73	8.62	7.92	7.43	6.80	6.13
	.01	8.86	6.51	5.56	5.03	4.69	4.46	4.14	3.80
	.05	4.60	3.74	3.34	3.11	2.96	2.85	2.70	2.53
	.10	3.10	2.73	2.52	2.39	2.31	2.24	2.15	2.05
	.20	1.81	1.81	1.76	1.73	1.70	1.67	1.64	1.60
15	.001	16.59	11.34	9.34	8.25	7.57	7.09	6.47	5.81
	.01	8.68	6.36	5.42	4.89	4.56	4.32	4.00	3.67
	.05	4.54	3.68	3.29	3.06	2.90	2.79	2.64	2.48
	.10	3.07	2.70	2.49	2.36	2.27	2.21	2.12	2.02
	.20	1.80	1.79	1.75	1.71	1.68	1.66	1.62	1.58
16	.001	16.12	10.97	9.00	7.94	7.27	6.81	6.19	5.55
	.01	8.53	6.23	5.29	4.77	4.44	4.20	3.89	3.55
	.05	4.49	3.63	3.24	3.01	2.85	2.74	2.59	2.42
	.10	3.05	2.67	2.46	2.33	2.24	2.18	2.09	1.99
	.20	1.79	1.78	1.74	1.70	1.67	1.64	1.61	1.56
17	.001	15.72	10.66	8.73	7.68	7.02	6.56	5.96	5.32
	.01	8.40	6.11	5.18	4.67	4.34	4.10	3.79	3.45
	.05	4.45	3.59	3.20	2.96	2.81	2.70	2.55	2.38
	.10	3.03	2.64	2.44	2.31	2.22	2.15	2.06	1.96
	.20	1.78	1.77	1.72	1.68	1.65	1.63	1.59	1.55
18	.001	15.38	10.39	8.49	7.46	6.81	6.35	5.76	5.13
	.01	8.28	6.01	5.09	4.58	4.25	4.01	3.71	3.37
	.05	4.41	3.55	3.16	2.93	2.77	2.66	2.51	2.34
	.10	3.01	2.62	2.42	2.29	2.20	2.13	2.04	1.93
	.20	1.77	1.76	1.71	1.67	1.64	1.62	1.58	1.53

(cont.)

Critical Values for F

		df *for Numerator*								
df *error*	α	*1*	*2*	*3*	*4*	*5*	*6*	*8*	*12*
19	.001	15.08	10.16	8.28	7.26	6.61	6.18	5.59	4.97
	.01	8.18	5.93	5.01	4.50	4.17	3.94	3.63	3.30
	.05	4.38	3.52	3.13	2.90	2.74	2.63	2.48	2.31
	.10	2.99	2.61	2.40	2.27	2.18	2.11	2.02	1.91
	.20	1.76	1.75	1.70	1.66	1.63	1.61	1.57	1.52
20	.001	14.82	9.95	8.10	7.10	6.46	6.02	5.44	4.82
	.01	8.10	5.85	4.94	4.43	4.10	3.87	3.56	3.23
	.05	4.35	3.49	3.10	2.87	2.71	2.60	2.45	2.28
	.10	2.97	2.59	2.38	2.25	2.16	2.09	2.00	1.89
	.20	1.76	1.75	1.70	1.65	1.62	1.60	1.56	1.51
21	.001	14.59	9.77	7.94	6.95	6.32	5.88	5.31	4.70
	.01	8.02	5.78	4.87	4.37	4.04	3.81	3.51	3.17
	.05	4.32	3.47	3.07	2.84	2.68	2.57	2.42	2.25
	.10	2.96	2.57	2.36	2.23	2.14	2.08	1.98	1.88
	.20	1.75	1.74	1.69	1.65	1.61	1.59	1.55	1.50
22	.001	14.38	9.61	7.80	6.81	6.19	5.76	5.19	4.58
	.01	7.94	5.72	4.82	4.31	3.99	3.76	3.45	3.12
	.05	4.30	3.44	3.05	2.82	2.66	2.55	2.40	2.23
	.10	2.95	2.56	2.35	2.22	2.13	2.06	1.97	1.86
	.20	1.75	1.73	1.68	1.64	1.61	1.58	1.54	1.49
23	.001	14.19	9.47	7.67	6.69	6.08	5.65	5.09	4.48
	.01	7.88	5.66	4.76	4.26	3.94	3.71	3.41	3.07
	.05	4.28	3.42	3.03	2.80	2.64	2.53	2.38	2.20
	.10	2.94	2.55	2.34	2.21	2.11	2.05	1.95	1.84
	.20	1.74	1.73	1.68	1.63	1.60	1.57	1.53	1.49
24	.001	14.03	9.34	7.55	6.59	5.98	5.55	4.99	4.39
	.01	7.82	5.61	4.72	4.22	3.90	3.67	3.36	3.03
	.05	4.26	3.40	3.01	2.78	2.62	2.51	2.36	2.18
	.10	2.93	2.54	2.33	2.19	2.10	2.04	1.94	1.83
	.20	1.74	1.72	1.67	1.63	1.59	1.57	1.53	1.48
25	.001	13.88	9.22	7.45	6.49	5.88	5.46	4.91	4.31
	.01	7.77	5.57	4.68	4.18	3.86	3.63	3.32	2.99
	.05	4.24	3.38	2.99	2.76	2.60	2.49	2.34	2.16
	.10	2.92	2.53	2.32	2.18	2.09	2.02	1.93	1.82
	.20	1.73	1.72	1.66	1.62	1.59	1.56	1.52	1.47
26	.001	13.74	9.12	7.36	6.41	5.80	5.38	4.83	4.24
	.01	7.72	5.53	4.64	4.14	3.82	3.59	3.29	2.96
	.05	4.22	3.37	2.98	2.74	2.59	2.47	2.32	2.15
	.10	2.91	2.52	2.31	2.17	2.08	2.01	1.92	1.81
	.20	1.73	1.71	1.66	1.62	1.58	1.56	1.52	1.47
27	.001	13.61	9.02	7.27	6.33	5.73	5.31	4.76	4.17
	.01	7.68	5.49	4.60	4.11	3.78	3.56	3.26	2.93
	.05	4.21	3.35	2.96	2.73	2.57	2.46	2.30	2.13
	.10	2.90	2.51	2.30	2.17	2.07	2.00	1.91	1.80
	.20	1.73	1.71	1.66	1.61	1.58	1.55	1.51	1.46

(*cont.*)

Critical Values for *F*

df *error*	α	df *for Numerator*							
		1	*2*	*3*	*4*	*5*	*6*	*8*	*12*
28	.001	13.50	8.93	7.19	6.25	5.66	5.24	4.69	4.11
	.01	7.64	5.45	4.57	4.07	3.75	3.53	3.23	2.90
	.05	4.20	3.34	2.95	2.71	2.56	2.44	2.29	2.12
	.10	2.89	2.50	2.29	2.16	2.06	2.00	1.90	1.79
	.20	1.72	1.71	1.65	1.61	1.57	1.55	1.51	1.46
29	.001	13.39	8.85	7.12	6.19	5.59	5.18	4.64	4.05
	.01	7.60	5.42	4.54	4.04	3.73	3.50	3.20	2.87
	.05	4.18	3.33	2.93	2.70	2.54	2.43	2.28	2.10
	.10	2.89	2.50	2.28	2.15	2.06	1.99	1.89	1.78
	.20	1.72	1.70	1.65	1.60	1.57	1.54	1.50	1.45
30	.001	13.29	8.77	7.05	6.12	5.53	5.12	4.58	4.00
	.01	7.56	5.39	4.51	4.02	3.70	3.47	3.17	2.84
	.05	4.17	3.32	2.92	2.69	2.53	2.42	2.27	2.09
	.10	2.88	2.49	2.28	2.14	2.05	1.98	1.88	1.77
	.20	1.72	1.70	1.64	1.60	1.57	1.54	1.50	1.45
40	.001	12.61	8.25	6.60	5.70	5.13	4.73	4.21	3.64
	.01	7.31	5.18	4.31	3.83	3.51	3.29	2.99	2.66
	.05	4.08	3.23	2.84	2.61	2.45	2.34	2.18	2.00
	.10	2.84	2.44	2.23	2.09	2.00	1.93	1.83	1.71
	.20	1.70	1.68	1.62	1.57	1.54	1.51	1.47	1.41
60	.001	11.97	7.76	6.17	5.31	4.76	4.37	3.87	3.31
	.01	7.08	4.98	4.13	3.65	3.34	3.12	2.82	2.50
	.05	4.00	3.15	2.76	2.52	2.37	2.25	2.10	1.92
	.10	2.79	2.39	2.18	2.04	1.95	1.87	1.77	1.66
	.20	1.68	1.65	1.59	1.55	1.51	1.48	1.44	1.38
120	.001	11.38	7.31	5.79	4.95	4.42	4.04	3.55	3.02
	.01	6.85	4.79	3.95	3.48	3.17	2.96	2.66	2.34
	.05	3.92	3.07	2.68	2.45	2.29	2.17	2.02	1.83
	.10	2.75	2.35	2.13	1.99	1.90	1.82	1.72	1.60
	.20	1.66	1.63	1.57	1.52	1.48	1.45	1.41	1.35
∞	.001	10.83	6.91	5.42	4.62	4.10	3.74	3.27	2.74
	.01	6.64	4.60	3.78	3.32	3.02	2.80	2.51	2.18
	.05	3.84	2.99	2.60	2.37	2.21	2.09	1.94	1.75
	.10	2.71	2.30	2.08	1.94	1.85	1.77	1.67	1.55
	.20	1.64	1.61	1.55	1.50	1.46	1.43	1.38	1.32

Source: Reproduced from E. F. Lindquist, *Design and Analysis of Experiments in Psychology and Education,* Houghton Mifflin, Boston, 1953, pp. 41–44, with the permission of the publisher.

Percentile Points for χ² Distribution

Probability

df	.99	.98	.95	.90	.80	.70	.50	.30	.20	.10	.05	.02	.01	.001
1	.03157	.03628	.00393	.0158	.0642	.148	.455	1.074	1.642	2.706	3.841	5.412	6.635	10.827
2	.0201	.0404	.103	.211	.446	.713	1.386	2.408	3.219	4.605	5.991	7.824	9.210	13.815
3	.115	.185	.352	.584	1.005	1.424	2.366	3.665	4.642	6.251	7.815	9.837	11.345	16.268
4	.297	.429	.711	1.064	1.649	2.195	3.357	4.878	5.989	7.779	9.488	11.668	13.277	18.465
5	.554	.752	1.145	1.610	2.343	3.000	4.351	6.064	7.289	9.236	11.070	13.388	15.086	20.517
6	.872	1.134	1.635	2.204	3.070	3.828	5.348	7.231	8.558	10.645	12.592	15.033	16.812	22.457
7	1.239	1.564	2.167	2.833	3.822	4.671	6.346	8.383	9.803	12.017	14.067	16.622	18.475	24.322
8	1.646	2.032	2.733	3.490	4.594	5.527	7.344	9.524	11.030	13.362	15.507	18.168	20.090	26.125
9	2.088	2.532	3.325	4.168	5.380	6.393	8.343	10.656	12.242	14.684	16.919	19.679	21.666	27.877
10	2.558	3.059	3.940	4.865	6.179	7.267	9.342	11.781	13.442	15.987	18.307	21.161	23.209	29.588
11	3.053	3.609	4.575	5.578	6.989	8.148	10.341	12.899	14.631	17.275	19.675	22.618	24.725	31.264
12	3.571	4.178	5.226	6.304	7.807	9.034	11.340	14.011	15.812	18.549	21.026	24.054	26.217	32.909
13	4.107	4.765	5.892	7.042	8.634	9.926	12.340	15.119	16.985	19.812	22.362	25.472	27.688	34.528
14	4.660	5.368	6.571	7.790	9.467	10.821	13.339	16.222	18.151	21.064	23.685	26.873	29.141	36.123
15	5.229	5.985	7.261	8.547	10.307	11.721	14.339	17.322	19.311	22.307	24.996	28.259	30.578	37.697
16	5.812	6.614	7.962	9.312	11.152	12.624	15.338	18.418	20.465	23.542	26.296	29.633	32.000	39.252
17	6.408	7.255	8.672	10.085	12.002	13.531	16.338	19.511	21.615	24.769	27.587	30.995	33.409	40.790
18	7.015	7.906	9.390	10.865	12.857	14.440	17.338	20.601	22.760	25.989	28.869	32.346	34.805	42.312
19	7.633	8.567	10.117	11.651	13.716	15.352	18.338	21.689	23.900	27.204	30.144	33.687	36.191	43.820
20	8.260	9.237	10.851	12.443	14.578	16.266	19.337	22.775	25.038	28.412	31.410	35.020	37.566	45.315

21	8.897	9.915	11.591	13.240	15.445	17.182	20.337	23.858	26.171	29.615	32.671	36.343	38.932	46.797
22	9.542	10.600	12.338	13.041	16.314	18.101	21.337	24.939	27.301	30.813	33.924	37.659	40.289	48.268
23	10.196	11.293	13.091	14.848	17.187	19.021	22.337	26.018	28.429	32.007	35.172	38.968	41.638	49.728
24	10.856	11.992	13.848	15.659	18.062	19.943	23.337	27.096	29.553	33.196	36.415	40.270	42.980	51.179
25	11.524	12.697	14.611	16.473	18.940	20.867	24.337	28.172	30.675	34.382	37.652	41.566	44.314	52.620
26	12.198	13.409	15.379	17.292	19.820	21.792	25.336	29.246	31.795	35.563	38.885	42.856	45.642	54.052
27	12.879	14.125	16.151	18.114	20.703	22.719	26.336	30.319	32.912	36.741	40.113	44.140	46.963	55.476
28	13.565	14.847	16.928	18.939	21.588	23.647	27.336	31.391	34.027	37.916	41.337	45.419	48.278	56.893
29	14.256	15.574	17.708	19.768	22.475	24.577	28.336	32.461	35.139	39.087	42.557	46.693	49.588	58.302
30	14.953	16.306	18.493	20.599	23.364	25.508	29.336	33.530	36.250	40.256	43.773	47.962	50.892	59.703

Note: For larger values of *df*, the expression $\sqrt{2\chi^2} - \sqrt{2df - 1}$ may be used as a normal deviate with unit variance, remembering that the probability for χ^2 corresponds with that of a single tail of the normal curve.

Source: Reproduced from E. F. Lindquist, *Design and Analysis of Experiments in Psychology and Education*, Houghton Mifflin, Boston, 1953, p. 29, with the permission of the publisher.

Author Index

Subject Index